PLUNKETT'S ENGINEERING & RESEARCH INDUSTRY ALMANAC 2018

The only comprehensive guide to the engineering & research industry

Jack W. Plunkett

Published by:
Plunkett Research®, Ltd., Houston, Texas
www.plunkettresearch.com

PLUNKETT'S ENGINEERING & RESEARCH INDUSTRY ALMANAC 2018

Editor and Publisher:
Jack W. Plunkett

Executive Editor and Database Manager:
Martha Burgher Plunkett

Senior Editor and Researchers:
Isaac Snider
Shuang Zhou

Editors, Researchers and Assistants:
Ashley Bass
John Brucato
Michael Cappelli
Gina Sprenkel

Information Technology Manager:
Seifelnaser Hamed

Special Thanks to:
Battelle
Pharmaceutical Research and Manufacturers of America (PhRMA)
U.S. Bureau of the Census
U.S. Bureau of Labor Statistics
U.S. Department of Energy, Office of Science
U.S. National Aeronautics & Space Administration (NASA)
U.S. National Nanotechnology Initiative
U.S. National Science Foundation
U.S. Patent and Trademark Office

Plunkett Research®, Ltd.
P. O. Drawer 541737, Houston, Texas 77254 USA
Phone: 713.932.0000   Fax: 713.932.7080
www.plunkettresearch.com

Copyright © 2018, Plunkett Research®, Ltd. All rights reserved. Except as provided for below, you may not copy, resell, reproduce, distribute, republish, download, display, post, or transmit any portion of this book in any form or by any means, including, but not limited to, electronic, mechanical, photocopying, recording, or otherwise, without the express prior written permission of Plunkett Research, Ltd. Additional copyrights are held by other content providers, including, in certain cases, Morningstar, Inc. The information contained herein is proprietary to its owners and it is not warranted to be accurate, complete or timely. Neither Plunkett Research, Ltd. nor its content providers are responsible for any damages or losses arising from any use of this information. Market and industry statistics, company revenues, profits and other details may be estimates. Financial information, company plans or status, and other data can change quickly and may vary from those stated here. **Past performance is no guarantee of future results.**

Plunkett Research®, Ltd.
P. O. Drawer 541737
Houston, Texas 77254-1737
Phone: 713.932.0000, Fax: 713.932.7080 www.plunkettresearch.com

ISBN13 # 978-1-62831-469-4 (eBook Edition # 978-1-62831-779-4)

Limited Warranty and Terms of Use:

Users' publications in static electronic format containing any portion of the content of this book (and/or the content of any related Plunkett Research, Ltd. online service to which you are granted access, hereinafter collectively referred to as the "Data") or Derived Data (that is, a set of data that is a derivation made by a User from the Data, resulting from the applications of formulas, analytics or any other method) may be resold by the User only for the purpose of providing third-party analysis within an established research platform under the following conditions: (However, Users may not extract or integrate any portion of the Data or Derived Data for any other purpose.)

- a) Users may utilize the Data only as described herein. b) User may not export more than an insubstantial portion of the Data or Derived Data, c) Any Data exported by the User may only be distributed if the following conditions are met:

    - i) Data must be incorporated in added-value reports or presentations, either of which are part of the regular services offered by the User and not as stand-alone products.
    - ii) Data may not be used as part of a general mailing or included in external websites or other mass communication vehicles or formats, including, but not limited to, advertisements.
    - iii) Except as provided herein, Data may not be resold by User.

"Insubstantial Portions" shall mean an amount of the Data that (1) has no independent commercial value, (2) could not be used by User, its clients, Authorized Users and/or its agents as a substitute for the Data or any part of it, (3) is not separately marketed by the User, an affiliate of the User or any third-party source (either alone or with other data), and (4) is not retrieved by User, its clients, Authorized Users and/or its Agents via regularly scheduled, systematic batch jobs.

LIMITED WARRANTY; DISCLAIMER OF LIABILITY: While Plunkett Research, Ltd. ("PRL") has made an effort to obtain the Data from sources deemed reliable, PRL makes no warranties, expressed or implied, regarding the Data contained herein. This book and its Data are provided to the End-User "AS IS" without warranty of any kind. No oral or written information or advice given by PRL, its employees, distributors or representatives will create a warranty or in any way increase the scope of this Limited Warranty, and the Customer or End-User may not rely on any such information or advice. Customer Remedies: PRL's entire liability and your exclusive remedy shall be, at PRL's sole discretion, either (a) return of the price paid, if any, or (b) repair or replacement of a book that does not meet PRL's Limited Warranty and that is returned to PRL with sufficient evidence of or receipt for your original purchase.

NO OTHER WARRANTIES: TO THE MAXIMUM EXTENT PERMITTED BY APPLICABLE LAW, PRL AND ITS DISTRIBUTORS DISCLAIM ALL OTHER WARRANTIES AND CONDITIONS, EITHER EXPRESSED OR IMPLIED, INCLUDING, BUT NOT LIMITED TO, IMPLIED WARRANTIES OR CONDITIONS OF MERCHANTABILITY, FITNESS FOR A PARTICULAR PURPOSE, TITLE AND NON-INFRINGEMENT WITH REGARD TO THE BOOK AND ITS DATA, AND THE PROVISION OF OR FAILURE TO PROVIDE SUPPORT SERVICES. LIMITATION OF LIABILITY: TO THE MAXIMUM EXTENT PERMITTED BY APPLICABLE LAW, IN NO EVENT SHALL PRL BE LIABLE FOR ANY SPECIAL, INCIDENTAL OR CONSEQUENTIAL DAMAGES WHATSOEVER (INCLUDING, WITHOUT LIMITATION, DAMAGES FOR LOSS OF BUSINESS PROFITS, BUSINESS INTERRUPTION, ABILITY TO OBTAIN OR RETAIN EMPLOYMENT OR REMUNERATION, ABILITY TO PROFITABLY MAKE AN INVESTMENT, OR ANY OTHER PECUNIARY LOSS) ARISING OUT OF THE USE OF, OR RELIANCE UPON, THE BOOK OR DATA, OR THE INABILITY TO USE THIS DATA OR THE FAILURE OF PRL TO PROVIDE SUPPORT SERVICES, EVEN IF PRL HAS BEEN ADVISED OF THE POSSIBILITY OF SUCH DAMAGES. IN ANY CASE, PRL'S ENTIRE LIABILITY SHALL BE LIMITED TO THE AMOUNT ACTUALLY PAID BY YOU FOR THE BOOK.

PLUNKETT'S ENGINEERING & RESEARCH INDUSTRY ALMANAC 2018

CONTENTS

Introduction   **1**
How to Use This Book   **3**
<u>Chapter 1:</u> **Major Trends Affecting the Engineering & Research Industry**   **7**
   1) Introduction to the Engineering & Research Industry   7
   2) A Short History of U.S. Industrial Research & Development   9
   3) R&D Expands in Chinese Research Parks/Patent Filings Soar   9
   4) Outsourcing and Offshoring of Research, Development and Engineering Grow Along With Globalization   10
   5) Original Design Manufacturing (ODM) Adds Value to Contract Electronics Manufacturing   11
   6) The State of the Biotechnology Industry Today   12
   7) From Korea to India to Singapore to China, Nations Compete Fiercely in Biotech Development   16
   8) Government Support for Stem Cell Research Evolves   17
   9) Nanotechnology Converges with Biotech   18
   10) Globalization and Worldwide Collaboration Fuel the Research Efforts of Major Corporations   19
   11) Number of Patent Applications Remains High/Patent Laws Change   20
   12) 3D Printing (Additive Manufacturing), Rapid Prototyping and Computer Aided Design   22
   13) Industrial Robots and Factory Automation   24
   14) Fuel Cell and Hydrogen Power Research Continues/Fuel Cell Cars Enter Market   25
   15) Electric Cars and Plug-in Hybrids (PHEVs) Enter Market in Low Numbers   28
   16) Major Research and Advancements in Lithium Batteries/Tesla and Panasonic Plan Gigafactory   30
   17) The Future: Pervasive Computing and Complete Mobility Will Be Standard   31
   18) Supercomputing Hits 93.01 Petaflops/IBM's Watson Expands Commercial Applications for Big Data   32
   19) Superconductivity Provides Advanced Electricity Distribution Technology   33
   20) Private Space Vehicles Begin to Fly, Including the SpaceShipTwo   34
   21) Technology Discussion—Synthetic Biology   35
   22) The Future of Transportation and Supply Chains: Massive Investments in Infrastructure, Growing Traffic and Adoption of Smarter Technologies   35
   23) HPTP Thermoplastics, Thermoset and Engineered Plastics Enable Advanced Products/Nanocomposites Offer the Ultimate in Advanced Materials   37
   24) Artificial Intelligence (AI), Deep Learning and Machine Learning Advance into Commercial Applications, Including Health Care and Robotics   39
<u>Chapter 2:</u> **Engineering & Research Industry Statistics**   **41**
  Engineering & Research Industry Statistics and Market Size Overview   42
  Quarterly Engineering & Research Industry Revenues, U.S.: 2017   43
  Engineering & Scientific Research & Development Services: Estimated Sources of Revenue, U.S.: 2011-2016   44

Continued on next page

Continued from previous page

Federal R&D Funding by Character of Work and Facilities and Equipment, U.S.: Fiscal Years 2017-2019	45
Federal R&D Budget & Distribution by Agency, U.S.: Fiscal Years 2017-2019	46
Federal R&D & R&D Plant Funding for National Defense, U.S.: Fiscal Years 2017-2019	47
Federal R&D & R&D Plant Funding for Health and Human Services, U.S.: Fiscal Years 2017-2019	48
Federal R&D & R&D Plant Funding for Space Flight, Research & Supporting Activities, U.S.: Fiscal Years 2017-2019	49
NASA Budget Appropriations & Projections: 2017-2023	50
Federal R&D & R&D Plant Funding for Basic Research, U.S.: Fiscal Years 2017-2019	51
Federal R&D & R&D Plant Funding for Agriculture, U.S.: Fiscal Years 2017-2019	52
Federal R&D & R&D Plant Funding for Transportation, U.S.: Fiscal Years 2017-2019	53
Federal R&D & R&D Plant Funding for Energy, U.S.: Fiscal Years 2017-2019	54
U.S. Department of Energy Funding for Science & Energy Programs: 2017-2019	55
U.S. National Nanotechnology Initiative (NNI) Budget: Fiscal Years 2016-2018	56
Research Funding for Biological Sciences, U.S. National Science Foundation: Fiscal Years 2017-2019	57
Research Funding for Engineering, U.S. National Science Foundation: Fiscal Years 2017-2019	58
Domestic U.S. Biopharmaceutical R&D & R&D Abroad, PhRMA Member Companies: 1980-2016	59
Top Foreign Countries by Number of Residents Receiving U.S. Patents: 2015	60
Top 30 U.S. Patent Recipient Organizations: 2016	61
Major Patenting U.S. Universities: 2016	62
The U.S. Drug Discovery & Approval Process	63
Employment in Engineering Occupations by Business Type, U.S.: 2014-February 2018	64
Employment in Life & Physical Science Occupations by Business Type, U.S.: May 2017	65
Chapter 3: Important Engineering & Research Industry Contacts	**67**
(Addresses, Phone Numbers and Internet Sites)	
Chapter 4: THE ENGINEERING & RESEARCH 500:	
Who They Are and How They Were Chosen	**105**
Index of Companies Within Industry Groups	106
Alphabetical Index	120
Index of Headquarters Location by U.S. State	124
Index of Non-U.S. Headquarters Location by Country	127
Individual Data Profiles on Each of THE ENGINEERING & RESEARCH 500	131
Additional Indexes	
Index of Hot Spots for Advancement for Women/Minorities	630
Index by Subsidiaries, Brand Names and Selected Affiliations	632
A Short Engineering & Research Industry Glossary	**651**

INTRODUCTION

PLUNKETT'S ENGINEERING & RESEARCH INDUSTRY ALMANAC is designed as a general source for researchers of all types.

The data and areas of interest covered are intentionally broad, ranging from the various aspects of the engineering and research industry, to emerging technology, to an in-depth look at the major firms (which we call "THE ENGINEERING & RESEARCH 500") within the many segments that make up the engineering and research industry.

This reference book is designed to be a general source for researchers. It is especially intended to assist with market research, strategic planning, employment searches, contact or prospect list creation and financial research, and as a data resource for executives and students of all types.

PLUNKETT'S ENGINEERING & RESEARCH INDUSTRY ALMANAC takes a rounded approach for the general reader. This book presents a complete overview of the engineering and research field (see "How To Use This Book"). For example, advances in design automation are discussed, as well as changes in research and development spending and patents.

THE ENGINEERING & RESEARCH 500 is our grouping of the biggest, most successful corporations in all segments of the engineering and research industry. Tens of thousands of pieces of information, gathered from a wide variety of sources, have been researched and are presented in a unique form that can be easily understood. This section includes thorough indexes to THE ENGINEERING & RESEARCH 500, by geography, industry, sales, brand names, subsidiary names and many other topics. (See Chapter 4.)

Especially helpful is the way in which PLUNKETT'S ENGINEERING & RESEARCH INDUSTRY ALMANAC enables readers who have no business or financial background to readily compare the strategies, financial records and growth plans of engineering and research companies and major industry groups. You'll see the mid-term financial record of each firm, along with the impact of earnings, sales and strategic plans on each company's potential to fuel growth and provide investment and employment opportunities.

No other source provides this book's easy-to-understand comparisons of growth, expenditures, technologies, corporations, research and many other items of great importance. The information within is crucial to people of all types who may be studying this, one of the most exciting industries in the world today.

By scanning the data groups and the unique indexes, you can find the best information to fit your personal research needs. The major companies are profiled and then ranked using several different groups of specific criteria. Which firms are the biggest employers? Which companies earn the most profits? These things and much more are easy to find.

In addition to individual company profiles, an analysis of engineering and research technologies and trends is provided. This book's job is to help you sort through clear summaries of today's technologies and trends in a quick and effective manner.

Whatever your purpose for researching the engineering and research field, you'll find this book to be a valuable guide. Nonetheless, as is true with all resources, this volume has limitations that the reader should be aware of:

- Financial data and other corporate information can change quickly. A book of this type can be no more current than the data that was available as of the time of editing. Consequently, the financial picture, management and ownership of the firm(s) you are studying may have changed since the date of this book. For example, this almanac includes the most up-to-date sales figures and profits available to the editors as of early 2018. That means that we have typically used corporate financial data as of late 2017.

- Corporate mergers, acquisitions and downsizing are occurring at a very rapid rate. Such events may have created significant change, subsequent to the publishing of this book, within a company you are studying.

- Some of the companies in THE ENGINEERING & RESEARCH 500 are so large in scope and in variety of business endeavors conducted within a parent organization, that we have been unable to completely list all subsidiaries, affiliations, divisions and activities within a firm's corporate structure.

- This volume is intended to be a general guide to a rapidly changing industry. That means that researchers should look to this book for an overview and, when conducting in-depth research, should contact the specific corporations or industry associations in question for the very latest changes and data. Where possible, we have listed contact names, toll-free telephone numbers and Internet site addresses for the companies, government agencies and industry associations involved so that the reader may get further details without unnecessary delay.

- Tables of industry data and statistics used in this book include the latest numbers available at the time of printing, generally through late 2017. In a few cases, the only complete data available was for earlier years.

- We have used exhaustive efforts to locate and fairly present accurate and complete data. However, when using this book or any other source for business and industry information, the reader should use caution and diligence by conducting further research where it seems appropriate. We wish you success in your endeavors, and we trust that your experience with this book will be both satisfactory and productive.

Jack W. Plunkett
Houston, Texas
May 2018

HOW TO USE THIS BOOK

The two primary sections of this book are devoted first to the engineering and research industry as a whole and then to the "Individual Data Listings" for THE ENGINEERING & RESEARCH 500. If time permits, you should begin your research in the front chapters of this book. Also, you will find lengthy indexes in Chapter 4 and in the back of the book.

> **Video Tip**
> For our brief video introduction to the engineering and research industry, see
> www.plunkettresearch.com/video/engineering.

THE ENGINEERING & RESEARCH INDUSTRY

Chapter 1: Major Trends Affecting the Engineering & Research Industry. This chapter presents an encapsulated view of the major trends that are creating rapid changes in the engineering industry today.

Chapter 2: Engineering & Research Industry Statistics. This chapter contains an extensive set of industry statistics.

Chapter 3: Important Engineering & Research Industry Contacts – Addresses, Telephone Numbers and Internet Sites. This chapter covers contacts for important government agencies and trade groups. Included are numerous important Internet sites.

THE ENGINEERING & RESEARCH 500

Chapter 4: THE ENGINEERING & RESEARCH 500: Who They Are and How They Were Chosen. The companies compared in this book were carefully selected from the engineering and research industry, largely in the United States. Many additional firms are based outside the U.S. For a complete description, see THE ENGINEERING & RESEARCH 500 indexes in this chapter.

Individual Data Listings:
Look at one of the companies in THE ENGINEERING & RESEARCH 500's Individual Data Listings. You'll find the following information fields:

Company Name:
The company profiles are in alphabetical order by company name. If you don't find the company you are seeking, it may be a subsidiary or division of one of the firms covered in this book. Try looking it up in

the Index by Subsidiaries, Brand Names and Selected Affiliations in the back of the book.

Industry Code:

Industry Group Code: An NAIC code used to group companies within like segments.

Types of Business:

A listing of the primary types of business specialties conducted by the firm.

Brands/Divisions/Affiliations:

Major brand names, operating divisions or subsidiaries of the firm, as well as major corporate affiliations—such as another firm that owns a significant portion of the company's stock. A complete Index by Subsidiaries, Brand Names and Selected Affiliations is in the back of the book.

Contacts:

The names and titles up to 27 top officers of the company are listed, including human resources contacts.

Growth Plans/ Special Features:

Listed here are observations regarding the firm's strategy, hiring plans, plans for growth and product development, along with general information regarding a company's business and prospects.

Financial Data:

Revenue (2017 or the latest fiscal year available to the editors, plus up to five previous years): This figure represents consolidated worldwide sales from all operations. These numbers may be estimates.

R&D Expense (2017 or the latest fiscal year available to the editors, plus up to five previous years): This figure represents expenses associated with the research and development of a company's goods or services. These numbers may be estimates.

Operating Income (2017 or the latest fiscal year available to the editors, plus up to five previous years): This figure represents the amount of profit realized from annual operations after deducting operating expenses including costs of goods sold, wages and depreciation. These numbers may be estimates.

Operating Margin % (2017 or the latest fiscal year available to the editors, plus up to five previous years): This figure is a ratio derived by dividing operating income by net revenues. It is a measurement of a firm's pricing strategy and operating efficiency. These numbers may be estimates.

SGA Expense (2017 or the latest fiscal year available to the editors, plus up to five previous years): This figure represents the sum of selling, general and administrative expenses of a company, including costs such as warranty, advertising, interest, personnel, utilities, office space rent, etc. These numbers may be estimates.

Net Income (2017 or the latest fiscal year available to the editors, plus up to five previous years): This figure represents consolidated, after-tax net profit from all operations. These numbers may be estimates.

Operating Cash Flow (2017 or the latest fiscal year available to the editors, plus up to five previous years): This figure is a measure of the amount of cash generated by a firm's normal business operations. It is calculated as net income before depreciation and after income taxes, adjusted for working capital. It is a prime indicator of a company's ability to generate enough cash to pay its bills. These numbers may be estimates.

Capital Expenditure (2017 or the latest fiscal year available to the editors, plus up to five previous years): This figure represents funds used for investment in or improvement of physical assets such as offices, equipment or factories and the purchase or creation of new facilities and/or equipment. These numbers may be estimates.

EBITDA (2017 or the latest fiscal year available to the editors, plus up to five previous years): This figure is an acronym for earnings before interest, taxes, depreciation and amortization. It represents a company's financial performance calculated as revenue minus expenses (excluding taxes, depreciation and interest), and is a prime indicator of profitability. These numbers may be estimates.

Return on Assets % (2017 or the latest fiscal year available to the editors, plus up to five previous years): This figure is an indicator of the profitability of a company relative to its total assets. It is calculated by dividing annual net earnings by total assets. These numbers may be estimates.

Return on Equity % (2017 or the latest fiscal year available to the editors, plus up to five previous years): This figure is a measurement of net income as a percentage of shareholders' equity. It is also called the rate of return on the ownership interest. It is a vital indicator of the quality of a company's operations. These numbers may be estimates.

Debt to Equity (2017 or the latest fiscal year available to the editors, plus up to five previous years): A ratio of the company's long-term debt to its shareholders' equity. This is an indicator of the overall financial leverage of the firm. These numbers may be estimates.

Address:
The firm's full headquarters address, the headquarters telephone, plus toll-free and fax numbers where available. Also provided is the internet site address.

Stock Ticker, Exchange: When available, the unique stock market symbol used to identify this firm's common stock for trading and tracking purposes is indicated. Where appropriate, this field may contain "private" or "subsidiary" rather than a ticker symbol. If the firm is a publicly-held company headquartered outside of the U.S., its international ticker and exchange are given.

Total Number of Employees: The approximate total number of employees, worldwide, as of the end of 2017 (or the latest data available to the editors).

Parent Company: If the firm is a subsidiary, its parent company is listed.

Salaries/Bonuses:
(The following descriptions generally apply to U.S. employers only.)

Highest Executive Salary: The highest executive salary paid, typically a 2017 amount (or the latest year available to the editors) and typically paid to the Chief Executive Officer.

Highest Executive Bonus: The apparent bonus, if any, paid to the above person.

Second Highest Executive Salary: The next-highest executive salary paid, typically a 2017 amount (or the latest year available to the editors) and typically paid to the President or Chief Operating Officer.

Second Highest Executive Bonus: The apparent bonus, if any, paid to the above person.

Other Thoughts:
Estimated Female Officers or Directors: It is difficult to obtain this information on an exact basis, and employers generally do not disclose the data in a public way. However, we have indicated what our best efforts reveal to be the apparent number of women who either are in the posts of corporate officers or sit on the board of directors. There is a wide variance from company to company.

Hot Spot for Advancement for Women/Minorities: A "Y" in appropriate fields indicates "Yes." These are firms that appear either to have posted a substantial number of women and/or minorities to high posts or that appear to have a good record of going out of their way to recruit, train, promote and retain women or minorities. (See the Index of Hot Spots For Women and Minorities in the back of the book.) This information may change frequently and can be difficult to obtain and verify. Consequently, the reader should use caution and conduct further investigation where appropriate.

Glossary: A short list of engineering and research industry terms.

Chapter 1

Major Trends Affecting the Engineering & Research Industry

Major Trends Affecting the Engineering & Research Industry:

1) Introduction to the Engineering & Research Industry
2) A Short History of U.S. Industrial Research & Development
3) R&D Expands in Chinese Research Parks/Patent Filings Soar
4) Outsourcing and Offshoring of Research, Development and Engineering Grow Along With Globalization
5) Original Design Manufacturing (ODM) Adds Value to Contract Electronics Manufacturing
6) The State of the Biotechnology Industry Today
7) From Korea to India to Singapore to China, Nations Compete Fiercely in Biotech Development
8) Government Support for Stem Cell Research Evolves
9) Nanotechnology Converges with Biotech
10) Globalization and Worldwide Collaboration Fuel the Research Efforts of Major Corporations
11) Number of Patent Applications Remains High/Patent Laws Change
12) 3D Printing (Additive Manufacturing), Rapid Prototyping and Computer Aided Design
13) Industrial Robots and Factory Automation
14) Fuel Cell and Hydrogen Power Research Continues/Fuel Cell Cars Enter Market
15) Electric Cars and Plug-in Hybrids (PHEVs) Enter Market in Low Numbers
16) Major Research and Advancements in Lithium Batteries/Tesla and Panasonic Plan Gigafactory
17) The Future: Pervasive Computing and Complete Mobility Will Be Standard
18) Supercomputing Hits 93.01 Petaflops/IBM's Watson Expands Commercial Applications for Big Data
19) Superconductivity Provides Advanced Electricity Distribution Technology
20) Private Space Vehicles Begin to Fly, Including the SpaceShipTwo
21) Technology Discussion—Synthetic Biology
22) The Future of Transportation and Supply Chains: Massive Investments in Infrastructure, Growing Traffic and Adoption of Smarter Technologies
23) HPTP Thermoplastics, Thermoset and Engineered Plastics Enable Advanced Products/Nanocomposites Offer the Ultimate in Advanced Materials
24) Artificial Intelligence (AI), Deep Learning and Machine Learning Advance into Commercial Applications, Including Health Care and Robotics

1) Introduction to the Engineering & Research Industry

📹 Video Tip
For our brief video introduction to the Engineering & Research industry, see www.plunkettresearch.com/video/engineering.

In industrialized nations, R&D investment has risen from an average of about 1.5% of Gross Domestic Product (GDP) in 1980 to about 2.0% today. Vast numbers of university students around the globe are enrolled in engineering and scientific disciplines—many of them dreaming about potential rewards if their future research efforts become commercialized. Global research collaboration (between companies and between companies and universities) is booming, as is patenting. In fact, it is difficult for patent authorities in the U.S. and elsewhere to keep up with demand. Globalization, immigration and cross-national collaboration have such a dramatic effect on research and design that nearly one-half of all patents granted in America list at least one non-U.S. citizen as a co-inventor. Major U.S. universities, like the University of Texas and the University of Wisconsin, as well as universities in such nations as China, Korea and Singapore, are eager to patent their inventions and reap the benefits of commercialized research. Top research universities earn millions of dollars each in yearly royalties on their patents.

The "2018 Global R&D Funding Forecast," published by the Industrial Research Institute and *R&D Magazine*, estimates global spending on research and development at $2.19 trillion for 2018, on a PPP or "purchasing power parity" basis. "PPP" means that the amounts are adjusted to account for the difference in the cost of living from nation to nation, relative to the United States. For example, PPP analysis finds that the cost of buying a given standard of living is considerably lower in China or India than it is in the U.S. Thus, $1 spent in China or India has more purchasing power than $1 spent in America.

The U.S. continues to lead the world in terms of total investment in research and development, at about $553 billion during 2018, up from $538 billion one year earlier. However, it ranks behind many other industrialized nations in terms of R&D as a percent of GDP, at 2.84%. For example, Japan's annual spending on R&D is estimated at 3.50% of GDP and South Korea's is 4.32%

Massive research outlays and grants are made by the U.S. federal government. The proposed federal research budget for fiscal 2019 was $118.1 billion (down from $119.0 proposed for the previous year). Substantial federal research dollars are flowing into such areas as advanced batteries, electronic patient health records, cancer research, nanotechnology, robotics, biotechnology, defense and renewable energy. Government research grants feed projects at universities throughout the U.S. and at many types of private corporations. The United States was expected to account for 25.25% of total global R&D in 2018, compared to 20.52% for Europe and 43.62% for Asia. Asia's share is up from 41.3% in 2015.

Many of the 50 U.S. states are also active in funding local research efforts. This generates significant competition between tech-savvy states for leading-edge research efforts, at both corporate and university facilities.

Meanwhile, U.S. corporations continue to fund massive engineering projects and research budgets of their own. Top research investors among U.S. companies include Amazon, Alphabet (Google), Merck & Co., Pfizer, Microsoft, IBM, Johnson & Johnson and Intel.

Engineering, science and research and development provide large numbers of well-paying jobs in America and around the world. Officially, the U.S. Bureau of Labor Statistics (BLS) estimates 1.44 million people working in architectural and engineering services as of February 2018. In addition, as of its mid-2017 survey, the same source counts 1.15 million in life, physical and social sciences. As of February 2018, BLS categorizes 665,300 Americans as employed in scientific research and development positions.

Corporations know that they must invest in R&D in order to stay competitive, but in many cases their R&D strategies are evolving. One change is the way in which funding is allocated. Strategies are shifting to include more alliances and joint ventures with other companies; more subsidiary spin-offs based on established technologies; more contracts and cooperative efforts with federal labs and agencies; and higher grants and projects of greater scope in partnership with universities. Companies are looking for ways to leverage their R&D investments in order to get more return on costs while gaining competitive advantage on a global scale.

Historically, corporate America's R&D dollars were spent at labs within the bounds of the U.S., but today, more and more projects are going to company-owned or outsourced labs overseas. Due to relatively low costs and large talent pools (including large numbers of new graduates with engineering and scientific degrees), the nations of Eastern Europe, China and India in particular have been attracting more of the total research dollars invested by major companies. Other hot beds of offshored research include Singapore, Taiwan and Korea.

China has the fastest-growing research budget in the world, and by 2020, the government's goal is to invest 2.5% of GDP annually in research.

According to the *2018 Global R&D Funding Forecast*, India's investment in R&D is an estimated 0.85% of GDP in R&D for 2018, or about $83.27 billion on a PPP basis, putting it in a league with the UK and France in total spending. Technical education is emphasized in India for a select group of students, particularly at its famous Indian Institute of Technology (IIT) campuses.

Certain countries have the lion's share of R&D activity. Corporations with the largest R&D budgets are nearly all headquartered in the U.S. and Canada in North America; in the UK, France, Germany, Switzerland, The Netherlands, Sweden and Italy in the European region; and in the Asia-Pacific nations of China, Taiwan, Japan, South Korea and Singapore. Korean government leaders are focused on increasing basic research capabilities and basic sciences, particularly at research-oriented universities.

Technology-oriented Israel invests very high amounts of GDP (3.00% or about $12.85 billion on a PPP basis in 2018) in research and development, and that nation has created one of the world's most successful high tech industries. Finland and Sweden also spend very high ratios of their domestic economies on R&D.

2) A Short History of U.S. Industrial Research & Development

Organized corporate research efforts began in the chemical dyes industry in Europe in the mid-1800s and soon were launched at a fairly rapid rate in America. In 1876, at the age of 29, Thomas Alva Edison opened a private laboratory in Menlo Park, New Jersey. Edison's efforts led to his record-setting 1,093 U.S. patents, including those for the phonograph and the incandescent light bulb. Edison's creativity and drive eventually enabled the birth of what would become the General Electric Company, still one of the world's premier research and manufacturing organizations. By 1900, about 40 corporate research facilities were operating in the U.S. Rapid acceleration was fostered by a growing middle class that created demand for new products, and was later fueled by the intense demands for leading-edge armaments, transport and other products created by World War II.

During the war, a man named Vannevar Bush was posted as the director of the Office of Scientific Research and Development within the U.S. Government. Bush's mandate was to spur intense innovation that would give America a technological edge in warfare. The results, over an astonishingly short period of time, ranged from advanced radar to the atomic bomb. Vannevar Bush argued persuasively for a long-term federal commitment to supporting industrial research. By 1962, the federal government was subsidizing nearly 60% of America's corporate research budget, for everything from medical breakthroughs to electronics to defense systems.

Thereafter, corporations rapidly increased their own investments in research and development efforts, resulting in a nationwide research base of unprecedented scope and cost. By 1992, however, corporate restructuring and cost cutting led to a brief period of retrenching and research budget slashing.

In the mid-1990s, companies creating or embracing new technologies were among the most exciting and successful firms in America. As corporations were striving to compete, the floodgates of research dollars were once again cranked open.

A final important thought about the development of industrial R&D: Depending on the nature of their industries, firms enter into research with widely varying expectations. For example, while aircraft maker Boeing invests billions of dollars in R&D yearly, that effort may yield a completely new aircraft model only once every eight or 10 years. In contrast, semiconductor maker Intel, which invests billions of dollars yearly, introduces breakthrough chip designs on a continual basis and invests only a tiny amount of its total budget in truly long-term research. Pharmaceutical makers are accustomed to a research-to-market cycle of as long as 10 years in order to discover, develop and commercially launch a new drug.

3) R&D Expands in Chinese Research Parks/Patent Filings Soar

There are three trends at work in the growth of R&D in China. The first is that R&D spending has been growing significantly since 2006. For 2017, gross expenditures on R&D in China were $279 billion (or 2.1% of GDP), which has risen 70.9% since 2012, according to the Ministry of Science and Technology of the People's Republic of China. China has R&D goals laid out in the *National Medium- and Long-Term Plan for the Development of Science and Technology*, which is updated on a regular basis. Of importance, the plan outlines ways to assimilate and then improve upon Western innovations. Methods include significant investment in domestic manufacturers along with patent laws that favor Chinese companies. The result is pressure on foreign firms to transfer technology into Chinese joint ventures in order to capture sales there.

Second, many Chinese companies are enjoying escalating success in the global marketplace. Telecommunications equipment makers such as Huawei Technologies, computer hardware makers such as Lenovo Group (which purchased the IBM laptop brand) and a host of growing companies like them are finding increased investments in research to be key to their continued growth. In the case of Huawei, the firm maintains 16 major research facilities around the world, including a $90 million facility in Helsinki. At the same time, Chinese firms are increasing their investments in product design and factory automation in order to create products in very high volume suitable for the rapidly growing number of middle-class Chinese consumers.

Next, hundreds of non-Chinese companies of many types have set up serious research labs in China. This includes leading companies such as Microsoft, Nokia, Nortel and Roche. GE alone has more than two dozen labs in China. Major computer research facilities include the IBM China Research Laboratory and the Intel China Research Center. Research in China is driven by multiple factors, including relatively low operating costs and salaries, the large base of engineers and scientists coming out of Chinese universities and the desire to have labs in close proximity to Chinese manufacturing centers and business markets.

There is no let-up in sight for this trend. Historically, the U.S. had more researchers at work than any other nation, at about 1.3 million. By 2012, China had caught up to and surpassed the U.S. in this regard, which earned China the right to claim the number-one rank among the world's research centers in terms of people involved. This trend is fed by the fact that China is cranking out engineers and PhD-level researchers from its universities at a rapid clip, while those degrees are often unpopular among American students. China produces hundreds of thousands of electrical engineering graduates on the bachelor's level yearly. Also, China is going out of its way to lure home thousands of Chinese-born scientists and engineers who have been working in the U.S. and elsewhere abroad.

The result is a growing perception of Chinese technical expertise as among the best in the world. While China grew in strength for many years as a low-end manufacturer of items like apparel and toys, it now attracts buyers both at home and in the West for its telecommunications equipment, mobile devices and online services. For example, Danish telecom carrier TDC A/S chose Huawei to provide telecom equipment to replace its old gear from Ericsson, not because Huawei prices were cheaper (they were actually more expensive), but because the firm's technical expertise was thought to be better suited for this job.

Meanwhile, patenting is rising in China. According to the Chinese State Intellectual Property Office (SIPO), 828,328 patent applications were received from Chinese applicants in 2008. In 2017, SIPO reported more than 3.70 million applications filed. Of those, more than 1.38 million were applications for invention patents, up 14.2% from 2016.

Chinese research facilities tend to be located in the same districts as the high-tech manufacturing centers that cater to foreign markets: the southern and eastern coastal regions. For example, on the eastern coast near Beijing, you'll find the Zhongguancun Science Park and the Tianjin High-Tech Industrial Park. Further down the coast, near Shanghai, you'll find the Caohejing and Zhangjiang High-Tech Parks. There are also major research parks near the nation's leading universities, such as the major science park next to the world-class Tsinghua University in Beijing.

Chinese technology sectors are quickly expanding well beyond consumer electronics and computer and telecom hardware where China has long had strength. For example, the automotive, transportation (particularly trains and airliners), biotechnology and nanotechnology industries are developing rapidly there.

4) Outsourcing and Offshoring of Research, Development and Engineering Grow Along with Globalization

China certainly isn't the only nation to watch for trends in research and innovation. Growing global demand for technology products and for many types of engineering, coupled with the communications capabilities of the internet, have launched an R&D boom in many other nations as well. As in China, some of this research is for locally owned manufacturers, but a great deal of it is conducted as offshoring for companies based in other nations. These nations with growing research and development bases have recently included Israel, Singapore, Taiwan and Korea.

For example, consider Taiwan, where total R&D spending grew more than fivefold between 1990 and 2007 to over $10 billion by government and industry combined. According to the Industrial Research Institute (IRI) and *Research Technology Management*

(RTM)/*R&D Magazine*, Taiwan's gross domestic expenditure on R&D in 2017 was forecasted to reach $27.66 billion, or 2.45% of GDP (the amount takes into account purchasing power parity (PPP), which is adjusted to account for the fact that wages and other operating costs may be lower in emerging nations than in mature economies like the U.S.). This is a significant amount for a relatively small nation. Taiwan is on the leading edge of technology-based manufacturing, and many of the world's top-ranked corporations by R&D budget are headquartered there. The country has great expertise, both in the laboratory and on the manufacturing floor, in such sectors as networking gear, semiconductors, computer memory and PC components. Taiwan's researchers are so prolific that they account for more than 5,000 U.S. patent filings yearly. Taiwan graduates about 49,000 scientists and engineers from its universities each year—an amazing number for a nation with a total population of a little more than 23 million. Taiwan operates three major science parks containing nearly 800 total manufacturers.

In India, the Industrial Research Institute (IRI) and *Research Technology Management* (RTM)/*R&D Magazine* forecasted 2017 PPP R&D expenditures at $77.46 billion, or 0.84% of GDP. Western drug discovery and manufacturing companies are forging partnerships with Indian firms at a great rate. For example, Eli Lilly, Amgen and Endo Pharmaceuticals have all entered into agreements with Bangalore-based Jubilant Biosys to develop potential candidates for the next blockbuster drugs. In a surprising shift from the Indian focus on developing low-cost generic versions of Western drugs, Indian firms are now working on developing new drugs with Western partners. At the same time, Western pharma firms are offering to share intellectual property rights on new drugs as well as a portion of the profits. GlaxoSmithKline was the first to begin this practice in its partnership with Ranbaxy Laboratories Limited. In addition to drug development, R&D in India is concerned with the InfoTech sector. Microsoft's research center in Bangalore has dozens of full time researchers on staff who are credited with the development of a valuable search tool used by Bing, Microsoft's search engine. India produces about 300,000 computer science graduates per year, and about 100 computer science PhDs.

South Korea's R&D spending was forecast to reach $83.91 billion, or 4.29% of GDP in 2017. Korean government leaders are focused on increasing basic research capabilities and basic sciences, particularly at research-oriented universities.

Since a great deal of research equipment and facilities are underused, a shared system that works along the same lines as Uber and Airbnb was created in 2011 called Science Exchange. Backed by silicon-valley investor Y Combinator, Science Exchange (www.scienceexchange.com) enables market-based collaboration between users and research facilities such as Harvard Medical School, Johns Hopkins University and the Mayo Clinic. The exchange provides ratings and reviews to help users find the best fit with regard to facilities and expertise, and also requires each party to sign an agreement outlining expectations, logistics and fees at the start. In early 2016, the exchange raised $25 million in Series B venture capital funding.

5) Original Design Manufacturing (ODM) Adds Value to Contract Electronics Manufacturing

One of the hottest growth areas in manufacturing over the past twenty years has been contract electronics manufacturing, that is, the manufacture by third-party firms of electronic goods ranging from smartphones to computer components to complete PCs and laptop computers. Some of the world's largest manufacturers are in this category, such as China's Hon Hai Precision Industry Co., Ltd. This industry is sometimes referred to as "Electronic Contract Manufacturing (ECM)" or "Electronics Manufacturing Services (EMS)". The popularity of consumer electronics and wireless devices worldwide fueled this growth.

This growth in contract manufacturing has been part of a steady, long-term evolution from traditional, in-house manufacturing. For many years, the world of manufacturing has been acquainted with the concept of original equipment manufacturers (OEMs). An OEM is a company that manufactures a component (or sometimes a completed product) for sale to a company that will integrate that component into a final product or assembly. For example, a personal computer made under a brand name by a given company may contain various components, such as hard drives, graphics cards, chips or speakers, manufactured by several different OEM "vendors," but the firm doing the final assembly/manufacturing process is the final manufacturer and the owner of the brand name.

Today, however, engineering and R&D also enter the picture, as many OEMs are evolving into "original design manufacturers" (ODMs): contract manufacturers that offer complete, end-to-end design, engineering and manufacturing services. ODMs, in close collaboration with their clients, design and build components or products, such as consumer electronics, that client companies can then brand and sell as their own. ODMs are the ultimate result of the convergence of several trends at once, including offshoring, globalization, value-added services, contract manufacturing, outsourcing and design collaboration via the internet.

Savvy managers began to see that they could differentiate themselves by becoming more than mere manufacturers. After all, manufacturing services alone can be commoditized—that is, they can become common services offered by a large number of firms at increasingly competitive prices. However, when manufacturers combine the ability to offer complete engineering, design and manufacturing in one turnkey deal, it's a new story. This collaboration with the client on the design and engineering of products also gives the contract manufacturer a chance to build a deeper relationship with the client. Thus, ODM was born.

ODM services can be particularly effective in nations that are noted for having an experienced technical talent pool. An example is Taiwan's expertise in personal computers, where such firms as Quanta Computer, Inc., Compal Electronics, Inc. and Inventec Corporation are known to be world-leading laptop designers and manufacturers for clients that sell under name brands. Other examples include India's expertise in chips and Israel's expertise in optical communications equipment.

ODM has also been highly effective in the automobile and passenger aircraft manufacturing industries. To a rapidly growing extent, carmakers are relying on their suppliers to perform the design, engineering and manufacturing of everything from transmissions to dashboard assemblies. The same holds true in the aircraft business. To a large degree, Boeing and Airbus are conducting final assembly of components manufactured (and in many cases designed and engineered) by their suppliers. The fact that components used in transportation equipment can be heavy and bulky doesn't mean that ODMs in these sectors have to be close to home. In fact, components for Boeing's new 787 are being made as far away as Japan, and automobile components are often manufactured in China for use in U.S. automotive plants.

(It is worth noting here that the phrase OEM has evolved to have a second meaning in addition to its traditional definition. A firm that buys a component and then incorporates it into a final product, or buys a completed product and then resells it under the firm's own brand name, is sometimes called an OEM. This confusing usage is most often found in the computer industry, where OEM is sometimes used as a verb. For example, a company executive describing his firm's strategy for the manufacture of a new tablet computer might say "we're going to OEM it.")

6) The State of the Biotechnology Industry Today

> **Video Tip**
> For our brief video introduction to the Biotech industry, see
> www.plunkettresearch.com/video/biotech.

Biotechnology can be defined as the use of living organisms (such as bacteria), biological processes or biological systems to create a desired end result or end product. Primary markets for biotechnology include: 1) Agriculture, where genetically-modified seeds are now in wide use in many nations. These seeds deliver plants that have much higher crop yields per acre, and often have qualities such as disease-resistance, resistance to herbicides and drought-resistance. 2) The manufacture of enzymes, including enzymes used in food processing (such as the making of certain dairy products) and in converting organic matter into ethanol for fuel. 3) Pharmaceuticals, where biotechnology creates such therapies as antibodies, interleukins and vaccines based on living organisms (as opposed to the chemical compounds that make up traditional drugs) that can target specific cellular conditions, often with dramatic results (such as the drug Keytruda that famously fought brain cancer for former U.S. President Jimmy Carter).

Biotechnology is a modern word that describes a very old science. For example, bio-enzymes have always been essential in the production of cheese. The modern difference is that much of the world's cheese production today utilizes a bio-engineered version of an enzyme called microbial chymosin. This chymosin is made by cloning natural genes into useful bacteria. Another example: For thousands of years, mankind has used naturally-occurring microbes to convert fruit juices into wine.

Analysts at global accounting firm E&Y estimate global biotech industry revenues for publicly-held companies at $139.4 billion in 2016 (latest data available), up from $130.3 billion in 2015 and $123.1 billion in 2014. The firm also estimates that revenues of publicly-held biotech companies in the U.S. alone were $112.2 billion in 2016, up from $107.4 billion in 2015 and $93.1 billion in 2014.

Genetically-engineered drugs, or "biotech" drugs, represent roughly 11% of the total global prescription drugs market. The U.S. Centers for Medicare & Medicaid Services (CMS) forecast called for prescription drug purchases in the U.S. to total about $360.1 billion during 2017, representing about $1,102 per capita. That projected total is up from only $200 billion in 2005 and a mere $40 billion in 1990.

Estimates of the size of the drugs market vary by source, but it is generally accepted that the global prescription drugs market was more than $1 trillion in 2016. By 2022, American drug purchases alone may top $495 billion, according to the CMS, thanks to a rapidly aging U.S. population, increased access to insurance and the continued introduction of expensive new drugs.

Advanced generations of drugs developed through biotechnology continually enter the marketplace. The results may be very promising for patients, as a technology-driven tipping point of medical care is approaching where drugs that target specific genes and proteins may eventually become widespread. However, it continues to be difficult and expensive to introduce a new drug in the U.S.

According to FDA figures, 46 new molecular entities (NMEs) and new biotech drugs (BLAs) were approved in the U.S. during 2017. These NMEs are novel, new active substances that are categorized differently from "NDAs" or New Drug Applications. NDAs may seek approval for drugs based on combinations of substances that have been approved in the past. Also, a large number of generic drug applications are being approved each year. That is, an application to manufacture a drug that was created as a brand name, and has now lost its patent so that competing firms may seek FDA approval to manufacture it.

New Drug Application Categories

Applications for drug approval by the FDA fall under the following categories:

BLA (Biologics License Application): An application for approval of a drug synthesized from living organisms. That is, they are drugs created using biotechnology. Such drugs are sometimes referred to as biopharmaceuticals.

NME (New Molecular Entity): A new chemical compound that has never before been approved for marketing in any form in the U.S.

NDA (New Drug Application): An application requesting FDA approval, after completion of the all-important Phase III Clinical Trials, to market a new drug for human use in the U.S. The drug may contain active ingredients that were previously approved by the FDA.

Biosimilars (generic biotech drugs): A term used to describe generic versions of drugs that have been created using biotechnology. Because biotech drugs ("biologics") are made from living cells, a generic version of a drug may not be biochemically identical to the original branded version of the drug. Consequently, they are described as "biosimilars" or "follow-on biologics" to set them apart.

In Europe, their manufacture and sale has been allowed for some time under special guidelines. In February 2012, the FDA created guidelines for biosimilars in the U.S. Manufacturers are now able to rely to a large extent on the clinical trials research previously conducted by the maker of the original version of the drug. In early 2015, a Sandoz International biosimilar (a generic version of Amgen's popular Neupogen) received approval from the FDA and was on track to become the first biosimilar to hit the U.S. market.

Priority Reviews: The FDA places some drug applications that appear to promise "significant improvements" over existing drugs for priority approval, with a goal of returning approval within six months.

Accelerated Approval: A process at the FDA for reducing the clinical trial length for drugs designed for certain serious or life-threatening diseases.

Fast Track Development: An enhanced process for rapid approval of drugs that treat certain life-threatening or extremely serious conditions. Fast Track is independent of Priority Review and Accelerated Approval.

Dozens of exciting new, biotech drugs that target specific genes are seeking regulatory approval. Many of these drugs are for the treatment of specific forms of cancer. In a few instances, doctors are making treatment decisions based on a patient's personal genetic makeup. (This strategy is often referred to as personalized medicine.) New breakthroughs in genetically targeted drugs occur regularly. An exciting drug for certain patients who suffer from the skin cancer known as melanoma is a good example. Zelboraf, developed by drug firms Roche Holding and Daiichi Sankyo, will dramatically aid melanoma patients who are shown through genetic tests to have a mutated gene called BRAF. In trials, about 50% of such patients saw their tumors shrink, compared to only 5.5% of patients who received traditional chemotherapy.

Stem cell research is also moving ahead briskly on a global basis. The Obama administration relaxed limitations on federal funding of stem cell research that were established by the preceding administration. In 2009, the National Institutes of Health set new guidelines for funding that will dramatically expand the number of stem cell lines that qualify for research funds from a previous 21 to as many as 700. However, research into certain extremely controversial stem cells, such as those developed via cloning, will not be funded with federal dollars. There is evidence of the potential for stem cells to treat many problems, from cardiovascular disease to neurological disorders.

Despite exponential advances in biopharmaceutical knowledge and technology, biotech companies enduring the task of getting new drugs to market continue to face long timeframes, daunting costs and immense risks. By one count, of every 1,000 experimental drug compounds in some form of pre-clinical testing, only one makes it to clinical trials. Then, only one in five of those drugs make it to market. Of the drugs that get to market, only one in three bring in enough revenue to recover their costs. Meanwhile, the patent expiration clock is ticking—soon enough, manufacturers of generic alternatives steal market share from the firms that invested all that time and money in the development of the original drug.

Global Factors Boosting Biotech Today:
1) A rapid aging of the population in nations including the EU, much of Asia and the U.S., such as more than 70 million surviving Baby Boomers in America who are entering senior years in rising numbers and require a growing level of health care. A significant portion of that care may be in the form of biotech drugs.
2) A renewed, global focus on producing and stockpiling effective vaccines.
3) Major pharmaceuticals firms paying top prices to acquire young biotech drug companies that own promising drugs.
4) A very significant market for genetically-engineered agricultural seeds ("Agribio"), with farmers in dozens of nations planting genetically modified seeds.
5) Aggressive investment in biotechnology research in Singapore, China and India, often with government sponsorship—for example, Singapore's massive Biopolis project.
6) Very promising research into synthetic biology.
7) Dramatic decreases in the cost of personal genetic studies, which can be a big boost to personalized medicine.
8) Highly advanced biotech technologies known as gene therapies are slowly beginning to prove their ability to cure patients.
9) Rapid growth in the overall prescription drug markets in developing nations.
10) An increased focus on the discovery and manufacture of new drugs ("orphan drugs") that impact rare diseases or relatively small portions of the population.
11) The advent of the genetic engineering process known as CRISPR, enabling scientists to repair defective cells.

Source: Plunkett Research, Ltd.

Internet Research Tip:
You can review current and historical drug approval reports at the following page at the FDA.
www.fda.gov/Drugs/InformationOnDrugs/default.htm

The FDA regulates biologic products for use in humans. It is a source of a broad variety of data on drugs, including vaccines, blood products, counterfeit drugs, exports, drug shortages, recalls and drug safety.
www.fda.gov/BiologicsBloodVaccines/default.htm

The FDA is attempting to help the drug industry bring the most vital drugs to market in shorter time with programs that include: Fast Track, Priority Review, Breakthrough Therapy Designation and Accelerated Approval. The benefits of Fast Track include scheduled meetings to seek FDA input into development as well as the option of submitting a New Drug Application in sections rather than submitting all components at once. The Fast Track designation is intended for drugs that address an unmet medical need, but is independent of Priority Review, Breakthrough Therapy Designation and Accelerated Approval. Priority drugs are those considered by the FDA to offer improvements over existing drugs or to offer high therapeutic value. The priority program, along with increased budget and staffing at the FDA, is having a positive effect on total approval times for new drugs. Breakthrough therapies show early clinical evidence of very important improvements over currently available drugs.

The FDA quickly approved Novartis' new drug Gleevec (a revolutionary and highly effective treatment for patients suffering from chronic myeloid leukemia). After priority review and Fast Track status, it required only two and one-half months in the approval process. This rapid approval, which enabled the drug to promptly begin saving lives, was possible because of two factors aside from the FDA's cooperation. First, Novartis mounted a targeted approach to this niche disease. Its research determined that a specific genetic malfunction causes the disease, and its drug specifically blocks the protein that causes the genetic malfunction. Next, thanks to its use of advanced genetic research techniques, Novartis was so convinced of the effectiveness of this drug that it invested heavily and quickly in its development.

Key Food & Drug Administration (FDA) terms relating to human clinical trials:

Phase I—Small-scale human trials to determine safety. Typically include 20 to 60 patients and are six months to one year in length.

Phase II—Preliminary trials on a drug's safety/efficacy. Typically include 100 to 500 patients and are one and a half to two years in length.

Phase III—Large-scale controlled trials for efficacy/safety; also the last stage before a request for approval for commercial distribution is made to the FDA. Typically include 1,000 to 7,500 patients and are three to five years in length.

Phase IV—Follow-up trials after a drug is released to the public.

Generally, Fast Track approval is reserved for diseases that are life-threatening and have no current therapies, such as rare forms of cancer. However, new policies are setting the stage for accelerated approval of drugs for less deadly but more pervasive conditions such as diabetes and obesity. Approval is also being made easier through the use of genetic testing to determine a drug's efficacy, as well as the practice of drug companies working closely with federal organizations. Examples of these new policies are exemplified in the approval of Iressa, which helps fight certain types of cancer in only a small percent of patients but is associated with a genetic marker that can help predict a patient's receptivity; and VELCADE, a cancer drug that received initial approval in only four months because the company that makes it worked closely with the National Cancer Institute to review trials.

Personal genetic codes are becoming less expensive and more widely attainable. Today, the cost of decoding the most important sections of the human genome for an individual patient has dropped dramatically.

Although total drug expenditures are currently small in developing nations such as India, China and Brazil, they have tremendous potential over the mid-term. This means that major international drug makers will be expanding their presence in these nations. However, it also means that local drug manufacturers have tremendous incentive to invest in domestic research and marketing.

The Coming BioIndustrial Era:

Some of the most exciting developments in the world of technology today are occurring in the biotech sector. These include advances in agricultural biotechnology, the convergence of nanotechnology and information technology with biotech and breakthroughs in synthetic biotechnology.

The rapidly growing worldwide base of biotechnology knowledge has the potential to create a new "bioindustrial era." For example, scientists' ability to capture refinable-oils from algae and other organisms (organisms that remove carbon from the atmosphere as they grow) may eventually create a new source of transportation fuel. Oil industry giant ExxonMobil has backed research in this regard at Synthetic Genomics, Inc. with hundreds of millions of dollars.

The use of enzymes in industrial processes may enable us to bio-engineer a long list of highly desirable substances at modest cost. The result could easily be a lower carbon footprint for many industrial processes, less industrial and residential waste to deal with and a significant increase in yields in chemicals, coatings, food and other vital sectors. DuPont's 2011 acquisition of global enzyme leader Danisco is a good indicator of the looming era of bioindustrial advancements, as DuPont made a $5.8 billion bet that it can help a vast variety of manufacturers to achieve significant product enhancements and efficiencies.

Source: Plunkett Research, Ltd.

Significant ethical issues face the biotech industry as it moves forward. They include, for example, the ability to determine an individual's likelihood to develop a disease in the future, based on his or her genetic makeup today; the potential to harvest replacement organs and tissues from animals or from cloned human genetic material; and the ability to genetically alter the basic foods that we eat. These are only a handful of the powers of biotechnology that must be dealt with by society. Watch for intense, impassioned discussion of such issues and a raft of governmental regulation as new technologies and therapies emerge.

The biggest single issue may be privacy. Who should have access to your personal genetic records? Where should they be stored? How should they be accessed? Can you be denied employment or insurance coverage due to your genetic makeup?

> *Internet Research Tip:*
> For the latest biotech developments check out www.biospace.com, a private sector portal for the biotech community, and www.bio.org, the web site of the highly regarded Biotechnology Industry Organization.

7) From Korea to India to Singapore to China, Nations Compete Fiercely in Biotech Development

Drug companies and government research agencies in many other countries are enhancing their positions on the biotech playing field, building their own educational and technological infrastructures, and in some case creating vast new biotech research districts or complexes. Not surprisingly, countries such as India, Singapore and China, which have already made deep inroads into other technology-based industries, are investing in major efforts in biotechnology, which is very much an information-based science. Firms that manufacture generics and provide contract research, development and clinical trials services are already common in such nations. In most cases, this was just a beginning, with original drug and technology development a rapidly evolving, symbiotic industry.

The government of Singapore, for example, has made biotechnology one of its top priorities for development, vowing to make it one of the staples of its economy. Its "Biopolis" research and development center opened in 2003. Biopolis is part of a master planned science and technology park called One-North. The complex is recognized as a center for stem cell and cell therapy research. It is a melting pot of scientists and corporations from all over the world, attracted to Singapore's central location, direct airline access to all of the world's major cities and status as a highly-respected health care center with a well-educated, largely English-speaking population. For example, the Novartis Institute for Tropical Diseases at Singapore has more than 100 researchers from 18 different nations. Biopolis was built in five phases at an estimated cost of $700 million. Phase I encompasses 1.99 million square feet and opened in 2003. Phase II added two seven-story buildings (398,268 square feet total) and opened in 2006. Phase III, completed in 2011, includes more than 400,000 square feet of laboratories, research facilities, office and retail space. Phases IV and V, adding additional space for research and clinical trials, were completed in 2013. (Another unit of the One-North development is called Fusionopolis, a 24-story building housing researchers, designers and entrepreneurs in media, software, communications and entertainment.)

Outsourcing and offshoring of biotech tasks to India has grown into a substantial industry. India's total pharmaceuticals industry revenue grew from $6 billion in 2005 to $36.7 billion in 2016, according to the India Brand Equity Foundation (IBEF), the latest data available. The Foundation expects revenues to reach $55 billion by 2020. More than 72% of prescriptions sold in India, by volume, are generics.

India already has hundreds of firms involved in biotechnology and related support services. In 2005, the nation tightened its intellectual property laws in order to provide stronger patent protection to the drug industry. As a result, drug development activity by pharma firms from around the world has increased in Indian locations in recent years, although at least one foreign firm was disappointed when it attempted to enforce its patents in India. The FDA has approved hundreds of industrial plants in India for drug manufacturing and raw material production for use in the U.S. (Many factories have also been approved within China.) Meanwhile, pharmaceutical firms have hired sales representatives within India in the thousands. McKinsey & Company forecasted that the number of pharmaceutical sales reps would triple between 2012 and 2022.

The costs of developing a new drug in India can be a small fraction of those in the U.S., although drugs developed in India still are required to go through the lengthy and expensive U.S. FDA approval process before they can be sold to American patients. India has its own robust biotech parks, including the well-established S. P. Biotech Park covering 300 acres in Hyderabad.

Stem cell (and cloning) research activity has been brisk in a number of nations outside the U.S. as well. To begin with, certain institutions around the world have stem cell lines in place, and some make them available for purchase. Groups that own existing lines include the National University of Singapore, Monash University in Australia and Hadassah Medical Centre in Israel. Sweden has also stepped onto the stage as a major player in stem cell research, with dozens of companies focused on the field, including firms such as Cellartis AB, which has one of the largest lines of stem cells in the world, and NeuroNova AB, which is focusing on regenerating nerve tissue.

More importantly, several Asian nations, including Singapore, South Korea, Japan and China, are investing intensely in biotech research centered on cloning and the development of stem cell therapies. The global lead in the development of stem cell therapies may eventually pass to China, where the Chinese Ministry of Science and Technology readily sees the commercial potential and is enthusiastically funding research. On top of funding from the Chinese government, investments in labs and research are being backed by Chinese universities, private companies, venture capitalists and Hong Kong-based investors.

China has made drug research a priority, and Chinese drug research spending has grown rapidly. The U.S. Department of Commerce estimated that China's market for drugs would rise from $108 billion in 2015 to about $167 billion by 2020. In addition, China is the world's largest producer of raw materials for drugs.

Meanwhile, leading biotech firms, including Roche, Pfizer and Eli Lilly, took advantage of China's high quality education systems and relatively low operating costs in order to establish R&D centers there. In this manner, offshore research can be complemented by offshore clinical trials. As of early 2017, China was the location of 11% of the world's clinical studies of biologic treatments, behind the U.S., which had 51%, according to the U.S. National Institutes of Health. Chinese firms with drugs in development include Hutchison China MediTech (Chi-Med), with eight drugs in development, and BeiGene Ltd. with four.

Many U.S. pharma companies have set up development centers in China. Merck opened such a center in Shanghai in 2015, while Johnson & Johnson did the same in 2014. Lilly, Merck, Tesaro, Inc. and Incyte Co. have multimillion dollar agreements to sell Chinese biotech drugs in foreign markets.

Taiwan has four biotech research parks. The Taiwanese government has a biotech development action plan which includes a $2 billion venture capital fund, a super-incubator and plans for expansion of the country's existing Development Center for Biotechnology. Meanwhile, Vietnam has plans to open six biotech research labs. Australia also has a rapidly developing biotechnology industry.

South Korea is a world leader in research and development in a wide variety of technical sectors, and it is pushing ahead boldly into biotechnology. Korean government leaders are focused on increasing research capabilities and basic sciences, particularly at research-oriented universities. The combination of government backing and extensive private capital in Korea could make this nation a biotech powerhouse. One area of emphasis there is stem cell research. (In Seoul, the government is also backing Digital Media City, a site that it hopes will become a world class hub of developers and entrepreneurs in electronic games, media content and communications technology. The project already houses tenants including LG Telecom, along with broadcasters, creative agencies and startups. The nation hopes that Digital Media City will eventually house 120,000 workers at 2,000 companies. In total, DMC is planned to contain 570,000 square meters of space.)

Another initiative is the Korea Research Institute of Bioscience and Biotechnology. In addition to fewer restrictions, many countries outside of the U.S. have lower labor costs, even for highly educated professionals such as doctors and scientists.

8) Government Support for Stem Cell Research Evolves

Shortly after taking office, U.S. President Barack Obama reversed an eight-year ban on the use of federal funding for embryonic stem cell research. Specifically, Obama issued Executive Order 13505, entitled "Removing Barriers to Responsible Scientific Research Involving Human Stem Cells." This executive order, dated March 9, 2009, charged the National Institutes of Health (NIH) with issuing new guidelines for stem cell research which became effective in July 2009. The order further authorized the NIH to "support and conduct responsible, scientifically worthy human stem cell research, including human embryonic stem cell research, to the extent permitted by law." The important words here are "human embryonic," since the harvesting of stem cells from discarded human embryos is what started the stem cell funding controversy in the first place. Further, this wording clearly eliminates the possibility of funding research projects involving stem cells that result from cloning. Under previous U.S. regulations, federal research funds were granted only for work with 21 specific lines of stem cells that existed in 2001. Harvesting and developing new embryonic lines did not qualify.

By mid-April 2009, the NIH had issued a new policy statement. The issue of funding remains politically charged. The NIH is taking a middle road. Its guidelines state that embryos donated for such research must be given voluntarily and without financial inducement. (Such embryos typically are donated by couples who have completed fertility treatments and have no need for remaining, redundant embryos. This is a common practice in seeking laboratory-aided pregnancies.)

Once a stem cell starts to replicate, a large colony, or line, of self-replenishing cells can theoretically continue to reproduce forever. Unfortunately, only about a dozen of the stem cell lines existing in 2001 were considered to be useful, and some scientists believe that these lines were getting tired.

The use of non-federal funding, however, was not restricted during the eight-year ban, although many groups did want to see further state or federal level restrictions on stem cell research or usage. A major confrontation continued between American groups that advocated the potential health benefits of stem cell therapies and groups that decried the use of stem cells on ethical or religious terms. Meanwhile, stem cell development forged ahead in other technologically advanced nations.

In November 2004, voters in California approved a unique measure that provides $3 billion in state funding for stem cell research. Connecticut, Massachusetts and New Jersey also passed legislation that permits embryonic stem cell research. California already has a massive biotech industry, spread about San Diego and San Francisco in particular. As approved, California's Proposition 71 created an oversight committee that determines how and where grants will be made, and an organization, the California Institute for Regenerative Medicine (CIRM, www.cirm.ca.gov), to issue bonds for funding and to manage the entire program. The money is being invested in research over 10 years.

As of early 2018, CIRM had made 973 grants totaling more than $2.53 billion. These grants are funding dedicated laboratory space for the culture of human embryonic stem cells (HESCs), particularly those that fall outside federal guidelines, in addition to underwriting staff positions, research models, training programs and more.

Corporate investment in stem cells has also been strong. AstraZeneca Pharmaceuticals invested $77 million in a startup firm in San Diego called BrainCells, Inc. to study how antidepressants might be used to spur brain cell growth. In late 2012, Osiris Therapeutics, Inc. received approval in Canada and New Zealand for the world's first stem cell drug Prochymal, which derives cells from the bone marrow of young adults to treat acute graft versus host disease (GvHD). Prochymal was in Phase III trials for treatment of Crohn's disease and acute graft versus host disease (GvHD), and Phase II trials for acute myocardial infarction in early 2016.

9) Nanotechnology Converges with Biotech

Because of their small size, nanoscale devices can readily interact with biomolecules on both the surface and the inside of cells. By gaining access to so many areas of the body, they have the potential to detect disease and deliver treatment in unique ways. Nanotechnology will help in the creation of "smart drugs" that are more targeted and have fewer side effects than traditional drugs.

Current applications of nanotechnology in health care include drug delivery (in immunosuppressants, hormone therapies, drugs for cholesterol control, and drugs for appetite enhancement) as well as advances in imaging, diagnostics and bone replacement. For example, the NanoCrystal technology developed by Elan, a major biotechnology company, enhances drug delivery in the form of tiny particles, typically less than 2,000 nanometers in diameter. The technology can be used to provide more effective delivery of drugs in tablet form, capsules, powders and liquid dispersions. Abbott Laboratories used Elan's technology to improve results in its cholesterol drug TriCor. Par Pharmaceutical Companies uses NanoCrystal in its Megace ES drug for the improvement of appetite in people with anorexia.

Since biological processes, including events that lead to cancer, occur at the nanoscale at and inside cells, nanotechnology offers a wealth of tools that are providing cancer researchers with new and innovative ways to diagnose and treat cancer. In America, the National Cancer Institute has established the Alliance for Nanotechnology in Cancer (http://nano.cancer.gov) in order to foster breakthrough research.

Nanoscale devices have the potential to radically change cancer therapy for the better and to dramatically increase the number of effective therapeutic agents. These devices can serve as customizable, targeted drug delivery vehicles capable of ferrying large doses of chemotherapeutic agents or therapeutic genes into malignant cells while sparing healthy cells, greatly reducing or eliminating the often unpalatable side effects that accompany many current cancer therapies.

At the University of Michigan at Ann Arbor, Dr. James Baker is working with molecules known as dendrimers to create new cancer diagnostics and therapies, thanks to grants from the National Institutes of Health and other funds. This is part of a major effort named the Michigan Nanotechnology Institute for Medicine and Biological Sciences. In 2014, Merck & Co. subsidiary NanoBio Corporation licensed the use of a nanoeumlsion adjuvant technology developed at the Institute.

A dendrimer is a spherical molecule of uniform size (five to 100 nanometers) and well-defined chemical structure. Dr. Baker's lab is able to build a nanodevice with four or five attached dendrimers. To deliver cancer-fighting drugs directly to cancer cells, Dr. Baker loads some dendrimers on the device with folic acid, while loading others with drugs that fight cancer. Since folic acid is a vitamin, many proteins in the body will bind with it, including proteins on cancer cells. When a cancer cell binds to and absorbs the folic acid on the nanodevice, it also absorbs the anticancer drug. For use in diagnostics, Dr. Baker is able to load a dendrimer with molecules that are visible to an MRI. When the dendrimer, due to its folic acid, binds with a cancer cell, the location of that cancer cell is shown on the MRI. Each of these nanodevices may be developed to the point that they are able to perform several advanced functions at once, including cancer cell recognition, drug delivery, diagnosis of the cause of a cancer cell, cancer cell location information and reporting of cancer cell death. Universities that are working on the leading edge of cancer drug delivery and diagnostics using nanotechnology include MIT and Harvard, as well as Rice University and the University of Michigan.

Meanwhile, at the University of Washington, a research group led by Babak A. Parviz has investigated manufacturing methods that resemble that of plants and other natural organisms by "self-assembly." If man-made machines could be designed to assemble themselves, it could revolutionize manufacturing, especially on the nanoscale level. Researchers are studying ways to program the assembly process by sparking chemical synthesis of nanoscale parts such as quantum dots or molecules which then bind to other parts through DNA hybridization or protein interactions. The group led by Professor Parviz is attempting to produce self-assembled high-performance silicon circuits on plastic. It is conceivable that integrated circuits, biomedical sensors or displays could be "grown" at rates exponentially faster than current processes.

10) Globalization and Worldwide Collaboration Fuel the Research Efforts of Major Corporations

Globalization is deeply affecting the corporate world at all levels. This can be seen in everything from the inexpensive consumer goods flooding into the U.S. from manufacturers in China to the growing business that American software makers have found overseas. The advent of extremely fast communication systems, such as the internet, global fiber-optic lines, e-mail and instant messaging, as well as overnight international courier services and well-established airline service to nearly anywhere in the world, helps to spur on globalization.

Meanwhile, there are legions of well-educated scientists and engineers in areas such as India, Eastern Europe and China who can be hired for salaries that are below those of their U.S.-based peers (although rising wages in China and India are diluting this effect). These factors all combine to make globalized research efforts attractive for many reasons. For example, a major automotive, pharmaceutical, software or hardware company in the U.S. can create a cost-effective, 24/7 research department by handing off research or design work from America to Ireland to Russia to India to Japan—it will always be daylight in some part of the world, and collaboration software makes it possible for employees to work together on the same project from anywhere on the planet.

One of the hottest spots for U.S. firms to open foreign research centers is the city of Bangalore in India. Initially a center for writing software code, Bangalore's supply of highly educated, English-speaking residents has enabled the city to evolve into a truly world-class research and development center. The labor pool is not only high-quality but also relatively low in cost.

Another concept with regard to collaboration is open innovation, in which ideas from a variety of sources including business partners, suppliers, employees, consumers and media are used by companies to develop new products outside of their normal internal R&D departments. First coined by Henry Chesbrough of the Center for Open Innovation at the Haas School of Business at the University of California, the approach affords greater speed and efficiency than traditional development process. FirstBuild, a subsidiary of Qingdao Haier Co., is using open innovation to develop new appliances that are being integrated into GE's product lines. Examples include a self-filling water pitcher for refrigerators, automatic oven racks that slide out when oven doors are opened and a countertop ice nugget maker called

Opal. FirstBuild test markets products before releasing them to GE. In the case of the Opal ice maker, it reached $2.7 million is sales on the Idiegogo crowd funding and marketing site in its first month.

> **SPOTLIGHT: InnoCentive**
>
> At www.innocentive.com, an entrepreneurial team has created a collaborative research portal. Companies needing answers to research problems can post details regarding their projects, along with a stated fee they are willing to pay for completion of research needs. Scientists and engineers from anywhere in the world can log in to select projects to work on. Fees offered run from a few thousand dollars to $1 million.
>
> Participants who log in may choose to view the site in English, Chinese, Japanese, Korean, German, Russian or Spanish. The site was launched in June 2001. By early 2017, InnoCentive boasted more than 380,000 scientists and scientific organizations in almost 200 countries offering to participate to work on research problems. Client companies include Avery Dennison, Eli Lilly and Company, Janssen, Proctor & Gamble and Solvay. The site has evolved to include social, health care, product design and market research problem challenges, along with its lists of technical and scientific challenges.

11) Number of Patent Applications Remains High/Patent Laws Change

In fiscal year 2016, the U.S. Patent & Trademark Office (PTO) received 605,571 patent applications, up from only 109,359 in 1970. To some extent, patents tend to reflect the health of R&D budgets. The greater the funding, the more patents are filed. At the same time, however, the rapid growth in the number of patent applications reflects today's increased focus on protection of intellectual property by corporations and universities along with the extremely high traffic from biotech firms attempting to patent gene expressions and other biological discoveries.

A patent application leads either to a patent grant or to a denial. The PTO granted 303,051 total patents during calendar year 2016 (which includes utility patents in addition to design, plant and reissue patents). In contrast, there were only 67,964 patents granted in 1970. A patent typically takes 18 to 24 months after application to receive a grant. The term of patent protection is currently defined as beginning on the date the patent is granted and ending 20 years from the earliest filing date of the application.

> **Patent Categories in the United States:**
>
> *Utility Patent*: may be granted to anyone who invents or discovers any new, useful and non-obvious process, machine, article of manufacture, or composition of matter, or any new and useful improvement thereof.
>
> *Design Patent*: may be granted to anyone who invents a new, original, and ornamental design for an article of manufacture.
>
> *Plant Patent*: may be granted to anyone who invents or discovers and asexually reproduces any distinct and new variety of plant.

> *Internet Research Tip:*
> For the latest official statistics from the U.S. Patent & Trademark Office, visit the web site of TAF, the patent office's Technology Assessment and Forecast branch.
> www.uspto.gov/web/offices/ac/ido/oeip/taf

Globally, there are 120 different national patent systems, and recent proposals to create a unified global patent system are creating buzz. "Harmonization" is the word used to describe the effort, and it will be difficult to bring about. According to the World Intellectual Property Organization (www.wipo.int), 90% of the approximately 7 million applications filed annually worldwide are filed in more than one country, which exponentially multiplies application fees, legal fees and hours spent (fees for multinational applications can surpass $75,000, and legal fees often reach $200,000 or more). IBM, which holds more patents than any other company in the world, spends more than $200 million annually on the protection of its intellectual property both at home and abroad. WIPO reported that 3.1 million patent applications were filed worldwide in 2016 (the latest data available).

An aborted 1989 attempt to establish an international system was bogged down when the U.S. could not agree with most other participating countries on a simple first-to-file regulation when awarding patents to filers with similar claims. In the U.S., the practice traditionally had been to award a patent to the filer who is proven to be the first to conceive an idea and develop it. Although fair, the system can prove costly as applicants spend time and money in the court systems to establish who was first with an idea.

An international patent system of a sort does exist in the form of the Patent Cooperation Treaty (PCT), overseen by WIPO and signed in 1970. A PCT application establishes a filing date in all contracting nations (of which there were 148 as of 2015). Filers must then proceed to file the necessary documents with the patent offices of separate contracting nations of the PCT, after an initial centralized processing and evaluation period (which usually is about 18 months). Filers thereby postpone examination and related expenses in national offices during that period. Top filing countries include the U.S., Japan, China and Germany.

Since patent applications have grown exponentially in recent years, examiners have less and less time to spend studying each application and researching past inventions. Some detractors claim that patents awarded in recent years may not have been for original ideas. One solution may be to use a wiki approach, in which scientists and inventors around the world could publish their opinions regarding a patent application in a central, online forum. New York Law School professor Beth Noveck, in concert with IBM and the U.S. Patent and Trademark Office, developed a system called Peer to Patent which scores wiki input so that patent examiners are given only the 10 highest-rating opinions, thereby safeguarding (to some extent) the veracity of the opinions entered.

Critics of the old U.S. patent system also cite unscrupulous patent-licensing companies called "trolls" that seek licensing fees by sending demand letters to presumed patent infringers, in many cases without basis of proof. Trolls also seek injunctions against large numbers of defendants, hoping to become enough of a nuisance that the supposed infringers will pay license fees just to make the problem go away. The U.S. Supreme Court made rulings in late 2006 and 2007 that limit injunctions, enable alleged infringers to file their own suits and/or make it easier for frivolous patents to be declared invalid. All three rulings were expected to curtail troll activity.

Another critical difference between the U.S. patent system and those elsewhere around the globe was the one-year waiting period, during which American filers may publish or speak at public forums about their ideas without jeopardizing their patent rights. Abroad, filers are required to keep their ideas top secret until a patent is awarded.

Yet another point of argument centers on patent subject matter. Traditionally, in the U.S., just about anything or any idea can be patented. Business practices, for example, are commonly patented, such as Amazon.com's "one-click" technology, as well as genetic discoveries and treatments. The latter is a particularly sticky point for developing nations such as those in Latin America and Africa.

However, a landmark case heard by the U.S. Court of Appeals for the Federal Circuit in 2008 may vastly change the nature of items that can be patented. The case, known as *In re Bilski*, created a new legal environment in which patents granted in the past for advances that would otherwise occur in the ordinary course of events without real innovation may be deemed invalid. This means, for example, that advances in business practices and software may have to be shown to be truly innovative in order to receive patent protection. This also may have a broad effect on organizations attempting to patent discoveries in the areas of biotechnology and genetics, such as proteins and genomes.

A 2012 ruling by the U.S. Supreme Court favored the Mayo Clinic when it challenged Nestlé subsidiary Prometheus over the latter's biotech test for a particular drug dosage. The Court ruled that the patent previously awarded Prometheus was invalid because it was based on a natural process, striking panic among a number of other biotechnology companies that combine science with natural processes and have or hope to receive patents.

In September 2011, the America Invents Act was signed into law by President Obama to further reform U.S. patent law. The act calls for a "first to file" system that awards patents based on the date the application is filed as opposed to the date the invention was made. It also creates new procedures, such as the ability to challenge a patent's validity directly with the Patent and Trademark Office (PTO) rather than going to court, to fight bad patents more efficiently. In addition, the act expands the ability of third parties to show prior art, meaning evidence of previous activity relating to the patent in question, to the PTO, thereby avoiding lengthy (and costly) court time. Detractors of the new law are concerned that a "first to file" system favors large, sophisticated filers who have knowledge of patent law over small entities or individuals. Another concern is that no additional funding was awarded to the PTO to handle the backlog of cases before it.

Further legislation was passed by the U.S. House of Representatives in 2013 due to a massive upswing in patent litigation since the passage of the America Invents Act. The Innovation Act is designed to neutralize patent trolls. It requires specificity in patent lawsuits, makes patent ownership more transparent, holds losing plaintiffs responsible for court costs and delays lengthy discovery phases (in which sometimes millions of internal documents such as emails and memos must be produced) to allow the courts to address the meaning of patent claims. The Innovation Act also protects end users such as small businesses by allowing technology vendors to fight lawsuits against trolls instead of their customers.

In addition, in 2014, the U.S. Supreme Court reviewed *Alice V CLS Bank*, a 2007 patent dispute regarding software that some found too abstract to be patented. The Court ruled that patents granted for the software were invalid due to the abstract nature of the software. While the ruling does not mark the end of patents for software, patents that are found to be valid in the future are likely to be for software that clearly improves the functions of computers or other technologies.

Meanwhile, the European Commission established a plan in 2007 for making it easier to apply for, obtain and defend patents across the nation members of the EU. Previously, patents were granted individually by each member nation, which created immense costs and delays. A similar effort failed in 2003 when members were unable to come to terms. Starting in 2011, a uniform application procedure applies for individual inventors and companies in up to 38 European countries. The process is overseen by the intergovernmental European Patent Organisation (www.epo.org).

Among competing tech companies, patents are something like badges of honor. Patents protect ideas and technologies as well as exclude competitors from making strides in particular areas of research. IBM leads the pack in the total number of utility patents awarded in the U.S. yearly. Patents are an immense asset to IBM, and it garners more than $1.5 billion in yearly licensing revenue from the patents it holds.

The firms on this list are consistently among the leaders, along with Fuji and GE. Not only do these extraordinary numbers of patents give these companies substantial bragging rights, the revenues generated can often make the difference between profits or losses in a difficult economy. As a result, watch for continued growth in the number of patent applications.

12) 3D Printing (Additive Manufacturing), Rapid Prototyping and Computer Aided Design

The news for automated design and engineering tools is excellent, and many firms that manufacture such tools are enjoying booming business. Advances in CAD (computer-aided design) and CAE (computer-aided engineering) hybrids are revolutionizing the way in which new designs are tested and enhanced. The combination of disciplines creates virtual prototypes on computers that make R&D faster and more efficient than ever before.

One of these automation tools, Finite Element Analysis (FEA), checks a computer-generated model for flaws. It analyzes how the model would react to extremes in heat, vibration and pressure by breaking it down into small pieces or cells in a three-dimensional grid. The computer applies simulated stimuli to one cell in the model and then tracks the response of that cell and those that surround it. The results often keep a flawed design from progressing to production and distribution.

The next big thing to define automated R&D was Design of Experiments (DOE). This statistical technology helps researchers program FEA to concentrate on particularly vulnerable areas, rather than running thousands of scans on all parts of a model, which may not be necessary.

Another stride in automation is behavioral modeling, a software application that forms the results found by the combination of FEA and DOE into family trees of cause-and-effect scenarios. Major variables such as model size and power are represented by large limbs, which branch out into scenarios showing how those variables react to different situations. The process allows researchers to isolate deal-breaking problems early on and pinpoint exact circumstances in which problems will likely occur. Industries adopting this new technology include automotive manufacturing, aerospace and shipyards.

Rapid prototyping via additive manufacturing (sometimes referred to as 3-D printing since the technology is somewhat like inkjet printing) is helping to boost the results of design engineers. There are numerous companies, both large and small, that offer additive manufacturing equipment and related services. For example, U.S. firm Stratasys (www.stratasys.com) offers industrial additive printers. Other major 3-D printer manufacturers include 3-D Systems Corp. (www.3dsystems.com), EOS GmbH (www.eos.info/en), Mcor Technologies Ltd. (mcortechnologies.com) and EnvisionTEC GmbH (envisiontec.com).

Gartner reported that global 3-D printer revenue reached $1.5 billion in 2015. By 2017, the firm expected revenue to rise to $3.97 billion.

The use of additive manufacturing technology is evolving. To begin with, a small number of manufacturers are now using additive printers (sometimes called "fabs") as small factories, churning out customized, finished products one at a time.

Today, these mini-manufacturing plants can create complicated parts or machinery one piece at a time, using this inkjet-like technology to fabricate on the fly. Also, the type of material utilized has improved. Today these systems use materials such as ceramic powders or metal powders as well as plastics in order to deposit exacting layers that create a final model or product. Eventually, nanotechnology may intersect with advanced additive printers for the manufacture of exacting components from nanocarbons. The better, industrial quality additive printers generally cost $10,000 and up, but the price of high quality models suitable for small businesses and hobbyists, such as MakerBot, had dropped to $1,300 by 2018.

Rolls-Royce completed a process that uses 3-D printing to build the front bearing housing of its Trent XWV-97 engines in 2015. The process uses a beam of electrons to melt layers of powdered alloy, which then solidifies to create the housings. Rolls-Royce's Trent XWB-97 engine, which is capable of 97,000 pounds of thrust, was successfully used to power an extra-wide-bodied A350 XWB. Similar technology was used by researchers at Monash University in Melbourne, Australia to build a small engine in its entirety using a laser instead of an electron beam.

GE is looking to additive manufacturing to produce more than 85,000 fuel nozzles for its Leap jet engines, a giant leap in capacity from current 3D printers. The company invested substantially in enhancements to its aerospace supply division, and had its nozzle production up and running by 2015. That was only the beginning for GE and its focus on 3-D printing. In September 2016, the company announced plans to acquire Arcam AB and SLM Solutions Group, two of the world's leading producers of 3-D printing machines. After the SLM offer was denied by shareholders, the company then acquired Germany's Concept Laser GmbH for $599 million. GE estimates that these acquisitions could save $3 billion to $5 billion in annual manufacturing costs, particularly in jet engine manufacturing. Additive designs helped GE eliminate 845 parts from its new turboprop engine (thereby significantly cutting the engine's weight) which is expected to launch in 2018. GE opened a $40 million, 125,000-square-foot Center for Additive Technology Enhancement near Pittsburgh, Pennsylvania in 2016, which uses 3-D printers extensively.

The big news in 3D printing is increased speed. Startup company Carbon3D, Inc. uses a technology in which printers project light continuously through a pool of resin. Objects gradually solidify onto an overhead platform that lifts them from the resin until fully formed. The results are similar to those made by conventional injection molds and take a fraction of the time used by other printing methods. Carbon3D's M1 printer is internet-connected and uses software and sensors to quickly form prototypes and production parts in low volumes. Meanwhile, HP, Inc. is working on two new 3-D printers that promise high-volume production at speeds up to 10 times faster than competing units.

Tens of thousands of free, downloadable product, toy and gadget designs that hobbyists can use to turn out items on their home 3D printers can be found on the internet. Leading firms in this sector include 3D Systems (formerly Z Corporation) in the U.S., Shapeways in The Netherlands and Germany's EOS, in addition to Stratasys (the owner of the Objet and Fortus brands).

One area with particularly exciting promise is the creation of custom medical devices, such as joint replacements, via additive printing. For example, Integra LifeSciences (www.integralife.com) uses additive technology to manufacture ceramic bone substitutes for use by orthopedic surgeons. In fact, medical applications are among the fastest growing use of this technology. Researchers at Princeton University used 3D printing to create a bionic ear, while University of Cambridge scientists printed retinal cells to create complex eye tissue. In dentistry, this includes dentures, dental bridges and dental crowns. Commercial applications have been designed that create these items using digital scans of a patient's mouth that is read by special 3D printers. Likewise, today's advanced hearing aids, so small that they fit within a patient's ear, must be manufactured on a personalized basis—a perfect market for 3D printing.

Additive printing is already appearing at bargain prices for use in the home by hobbyists, or for use in small engineering and design offices. 3D Systems (www.3dsystems.com) acquired Desktop Factory to offer printers at modest prices that are small enough to sit on a desktop. The machines can fabricate design models and custom prototypes. Meanwhile, NextEngine (www.nextengine.com) makes a 3-D desktop scanner that can perform a high definition scan of a three-dimensional object and then create a digital file of that scan. The file can then be used to generate a duplicate of the object in an additive printer.

For industrial purposes, additive manufacturing is truly a revolutionary technology, as engineers can quickly, and at low cost, hold a prototype in their hands that formerly would have been built slowly by hand or in a machine shop at high cost. More recently, the technology has evolved to the point that some types of final products, particularly those that formerly required complex machining, or those requiring customization or personalization, will soon commonly be manufactured with additive methods.

Additive manufacturing also has important implications for products and components that might best be manufactured on an as-needed ("just-in-time") basis in locations near the end-user. This could save valuable time and shipping costs, and avoid delays in final assembly of complex products. However, as additive manufacturing is a robotic, software-driven type of manufacturing, it is not likely to lead to a lot of new jobs on the factory floor.

Printer manufacturers such as EnvisionTEC (envisiontec.com) are working to develop 3D printed orthodontic aligners that can deliver proper biocompatibility, stability, flexion and strength. A commercial product is expected in 2018.

13) Industrial Robots and Factory Automation

The ISO 8373 defines industrial robots as being automatically controlled, reprogrammable, featuring a multipurpose manipulator capable of movement in three or more directions, including linear or rotational movement. It may be either fixed or mobile.

The type of joints used industrial robots indicate the classification and potential uses of a robot. The primary types of joints include:

Revolute joints—may include a hinge, a pin or an axle. They have one degree of freedom (DoF). That is, they can move in one direction or one manner.

Prismatic joints—also have one DoF. They move along a fixed axis. That is, they are pistons or similar sliding objects.

Spherical joints—with three DoFs. They can rotate or pivot around a round bearing. Ball joints used in automobiles are spherical joints.

Industrial robots are further classified by their mechanical organization:
- Articulated robots—feature an arm that can closely resemble the movement of a human arm. The arm may have several joints that are revolute joints.
- Cylindrical robots—feature an arm and design that do well in circular workspaces. They may include a combination of revolute and prismatic joints.
- Cartesian robots—feature an arm that has prismatic joints only and tend to be linear in action. This type of robot typically has great strength and lifting capacity. A gantry robot is a related type of cartesian robot.
- Parallel robots (also known as "parallel manipulators")—consist of three or more rotary or prismatic rotation points (axes). They can be used to manipulate large loads. A flight simulator (used to train pilots on the ground in a virtual environment) may be manipulated by a parallel robot.
- SCARA robots (Selective Compliance Arm for Robotic Assembly, or Selective Compliance Articulated Robot Arm)—a robot used to install components and move parts. It can mimic the motions of a human arm.

The International Federation of Robotics (IFR) estimated the total, worldwide base of operational industrial robots at the end of 2017 was 2.0 million. The IFR also estimates that this base will expand to approximately 3.0 million by the end of 2020. The global value of all robots sold during 2016 was placed by IFR at $40.0 billion. Industrial robots were selling at a rate of about 346,000 yearly during 2016.

The automotive and electronics industries have been prime drivers of robot sector growth in recent years. The largest markets for sales of robots are China, Korea, Japan, the U.S. and Germany. U.S. investment in factory automation and robotics is expected to be very substantial in coming years. China is investing very heavily in both factory robots and the development of its own robotic technologies.

China used its massive population base (1.4 billion), low wages and heavy investment of funds by both government agencies and corporations (domestic and foreign), to become a massive manufacturing engine over several decades. Today, however, China is at a dramatic point of change, with rapidly rising wages, an aging population, a shrinking workforce and very effective competition from lower-cost nations such as Vietnam. Consequently, China is seen as one of the highest growth markets in the world for factory automation. During 2016, Chinese manufacturers bought approximately 87,000 robots, and demand is expected to continue to soar.

Robotics companies plan significant investments in China-based factories and marketing efforts to capture their share of this market. For example, Yaskawa, a leading Japanese robotics firm, planned to boost output in its China plants to 12,000 units per year. Kuka, a Germany-based firm that is one of the world's leading makers of industrial robotics, opened a production plant in Shanghai that produces 3,000 robots each year.

China's latest Five Year Plan includes an initiative to make billions of yuan available for manufacturers to upgrade their facilities and technology with robots. The region of Guangdong pledged to invest $150 billion in industrial robotic equipment and the creation of two centers for advanced automation.

Robotics will not only help China with its workforce challenges while restraining total wage costs, it will also assist China in its vital effort to move its manufacturing upmarket into aerospace, medical technology and other sectors requiring very high levels of manufacturing precision and quality.

> **Pros and Cons-Are Robots Stealing Jobs?**
> In a 2017 paper, economists at MIT and Boston University found that up to 670,000 jobs in the U.S. were lost to robots in the manufacturing sector between 1990 and 2007. In an isolated area, each robot per thousand workers cut employment by 6.2 workers and wages by 0.7%. In Detroit, Michigan, an auto-making capital, the paper found a decrease in employment by three workers, and a decrease in wages of 0.25%. On a national scale, the effects were less, due to job creation in other sectors. However, on the positive side, as prices decrease due to robotics in sectors such as auto manufacturing, consumers may have more to spend which will create jobs in other sectors. Deloitte Consulting expects 2 million new positions in the manufacturing sector by 2025 through the development of new technologies. In order to fill those jobs, workers will require extensive training in advanced factory automation systems and computerized machine tools.
>
> Meanwhile, faster, cheaper robots are becoming available, making them affordable (as little as $25,000) for small to medium-sized factories. What remains to be seen is if the expected wave of new robotic technologies, such as drones and driverless cars, will spill over with further negative effects on employment and wages.

In the automotive sector, General Motors (GM) is working with Fanuc, a Japanese robotics manufacturer, Cisco Systems and Rockwell Automation to monitor robots and plant working conditions (such as temperature and humidity). Gathered data, stored in a cloud network, is analyzed and workers can service robots before they break or alter conditions to limit costly downtime when robots fail.

The future of the robotics and factory automation industry is extremely bright. China is a perfect example of the types of trends that will drive the industry forward: rising wages, a rapidly growing manufacturing sector, soaring global trade in manufactured goods and demographic challenges. Combined with today's very low penetration of robotics in most of the world's nations, dramatic increases in industrial robotics sales will occur for decades to come. Industries that will rely more and more on robotics and automation include food processing, pharmaceuticals, oil and gas, logistics and warehousing, automobile manufacturing, chemicals and textiles.

New cutting-edge robots allow humans to work alongside them. Thought to be too dangerous until recently, new models such as Baxter, made by Rethink Robotics, "learns" new tasks when a human moves the robot's arms through an operation. Baxter is in use on U.S. conveyor lines helping package items. Auto maker BMW uses heavy assembly robots made by Universal Robots to help humans complete final vehicle door assembly.

The transportation and logistics sector will be heavily influenced by robotics. For example, giant robots are in use at the Port of Los Angeles and the Port of Long Beach in the U.S. to unload container ships and move cargo containers on the docks. In early 2016, an automated terminal opened at the Port of Long Beach with a capacity of handling 3.3 million 20-foot container units yearly. Industry analysts estimate that robots can improve dock productivity by as much as 30%.

14) Fuel Cell and Hydrogen Power Research Continue/Fuel Cell Cars Enter Market

The fuel cell is nothing new, despite the excitement it is now generating. It has been around since 1839, when Welsh physics professor William Grove created an operating model based on platinum and zinc components. Much later, the U.S. Apollo space program used fuel cells for certain power needs in the Apollo space vehicles that traveled from the Earth to the Moon.

In basic terms, a fuel cell consists of quantities of hydrogen and oxygen separated by a catalyst. Inside the cell, a chemical reaction within the catalyst generates electricity. Byproducts of this reaction include heat and water. Several enhancements to basic fuel cell technology are under research and development at various firms worldwide. These include fuel cell membranes manufactured with advanced nanotechnologies and "solid oxide" technologies that could prove efficient enough to use on aircraft. Another option for fuel cell membranes are those made of hydrocarbon, which cost about one-half a much as membranes using fluorine compounds.

Fuel cells require a steady supply of hydrogen. Therein lies the biggest problem in promoting the widespread use of fuel cells: how to create, transport and store the hydrogen. At present, no one has been able to put a viable plan in place that would create a network of hydrogen fueling stations substantial enough to meet the needs of everyday motorists in the U.S. or anywhere else.

Many current fuel cells burn hydrogen extracted from such sources as gasoline, natural gas or methanol. Each source has its advantages and disadvantages. Unfortunately, burning a hydrocarbon such as oil, natural gas or coal to produce the energy necessary to create hydrogen results in unwanted emissions. Ideally, hydrogen would be created using renewable, non-polluting means, such as solar power or wind power. Also, nuclear or renewable sources could be used to generate electricity that would be used to extract hydrogen molecules from water.

The potential market for fuel cells encompasses diverse uses in fixed applications (such as providing an electric generating plant for a home or a neighborhood), portable systems (such as portable generators for construction sites) or completely mobile uses (powering anything from small hand-held devices to automobiles). The likely advantages of fuel cells as clean, efficient energy sources are enormous. The fuel cell itself is a proven technology—fuel cells are already in use, powering a U.S. Post Office in Alaska, for example. (This project, in Chugach, Alaska, is the result of a joint venture between the local electric association and the U.S. Postal Service to install a one-megawatt fuel cell facility.) Tiny fuel cells are also on the market for use in powering cellular phones and laptop computers.

FuelCell Energy of Danbury, Connecticut (www.fuelcellenergy.com), built a 59-megawatt fuel cell complex in Hwasung City, South Korea. The plant, which went online in 2014, is the world's largest to date. In 2017, the company announced a 20-megawatt fuel cell project with Korea Southern Power Company, with completion expected in 2018.

Shipments of fuel cell-equipped mobile devices may be very useful to certain types of customers as they can eliminate the need for frequent recharging of current battery-powered models. The Medis 24/7 Power Pack is a portable, disposable power source for small electronic devices such as cell phones and MP3 players. Manufactured by Medis Technologies, it is based on Direct Liquid Fuel cell technology, and may be of particular utility in military applications. Elsewhere, MeOH Power (formerly MTI MicroFuel Cells) manufactures a power pack for portable electronics that is based on direct methanol fuel cell technology.

In Bridgeport, Connecticut, a 14.9-megawatt fuel-cell complex generates enough electricity to power 15,000 homes (out of a total 51,000 in the city). In April 2015, a 1.4-megawatt cell went online at the University of Bridgeport.

Internet Research Tip: Micro Fuel Cells
For more information on research involving fuel cells for small applications, visit:
MeOH Power www.meohpower.com

Electric Vehicles vs. Fuel Cells
1) While the potential for fuel cell-powered vehicles seems promising, the majority of the automobile industry has focused instead on plug-in electric hybrids and all-electric vehicles as the alternative fuel base of choice for the near-term.
2) An important factor in that decision is the tremendous success and wide consumer acceptance of Toyota's Prius hybrid car. This success gave Toyota early dominance in the electric car field while other makers were still dreaming about fuel cells. A vital feature of the Prius is its very affordable price.
3) For fuel cells, the technical hurdles of distributing, storing and transporting hydrogen as a fuel are challenging. A massive investment in hydrogen filling stations would be required to make fuel cell vehicles practical for consumers.
4) Consumers, bureaucrats, investors and legislators already understand and trust the safety and ease of use of electricity, whether fixed or portable. This cannot be said for hydrogen.
5) Despite these obstacles, major automakers are continuing significant investments in fuel cell technology, with promising results. The costs of manufacturing fuel cells are dropping, to the point that they may eventually become affordable for passenger cars.

> 6) In the U.S., federal and state requirements for ever-higher average fuel efficiency ratings, and in some cases zero-emission vehicles, will encourage continued investment in fuel-cells. By 2016, limited numbers of fuel-cell powered vehicles were on the market in the U.S. and Japan.
> *Source: Plunkett Research, Ltd.*

GM invested $1 billion in fuel cell vehicle research. The company leased 199 fuel cell-equipped Equinox crossover vehicles to customers as a test called Project Driveway in three U.S. markets, starting in early 2008. Despite the setback of the financial problems of 2008-09 that led to bankruptcy and a government bailout, GM managed to keep Project Driveway going, in which more than 5,000 drivers provided feedback on Chevrolet Equinox FCV sedans. Some of those vehicles accumulated more than 120,000 miles each.

GM began a long-term collaboration with Honda in July 2013 to co-develop next generation fuel cells and hydrogen storage systems. Honda leased test models of its "FCX" fuel cell-powered car to small numbers of customers in the U.S. and Japan. In 2017, Honda launched a new generation of its fuel cell vehicle, to be called Clarity. (See http://automobiles.honda.com/fcx-clarity/.) GM is expected to follow with its own new FCV, per the companies' agreement. In January 2017, the two companies announced plans to invest a total of $85 million to form a joint venture called Fuel Cell System Manufacturing, where production is expected to begin as early 2020.

Honda is also promoting a concept called Home Energy Station that would convert natural gas into enough hydrogen to power fuel cells that could run a family's vehicle, as well as supply electricity and hot water for the family home. (See http://world.honda.com/FuelCell/HydrogenStation/HomeEnergyStationIV.) Meanwhile, Hyundai Motor Co. began limited sales of a hydrogen-powered SUV in California in mid-2014.

Toyota unveiled a fuel cell car at the Tokyo automobile show in November 2013. The vehicle, a $57,500 FVC sedan with a 312-mile range called the Mirai, launched in Japan and in California in the U.S. in 2015. The Japanese government has committed to creating a network of 100 hydrogen filling stations. In the U.S., as of early 2017, there were only 30 retail hydrogen fueling stations (and all were in the state of California), a serious stumbling block for Toyota, which was planning to build another 12 stations in the northeastern U.S. in conjunction with Air Liquide.

In a bid to boost sales, Toyota and Honda offer fuel cell customers credit cards for up to $15,000 in fuel over the first three years of ownership. They also provide a rental car for up to three weeks per year in case a customer needs a car for a long trip outside of the range of existing hydrogen fueling stations.

British startup manufacturer Riversimple, www.riversimple.com, hopes to launch a fuel cell-powered vehicle on a unique business model. Customers will pay one monthly fee to have access to the car, fuel, insurance and maintenance. The car is being designed by the same person who designed the Fiat 500. Though small, the vehicle is tough thanks to a body made of carbon composites. There is an electric motor for each of the car's wheels, and ultracapacitors capture and store energy when the brakes are engaged. As of early 2016, a prototype called the Rasa was on the road in the U.K. The company hopes to be in full production by late 2018.

Mercedes-Benz also has a fuel cell vehicle, the B-Class F-Cell. The B-Class F-Cell has a range of 249 miles and a top speed of 109 mph. As of 2015, prototypes of the vehicle were available to Americans only in Los Angeles and San Francisco, California. However, by 2017, the company reported that it was dropping fuel cell powered vehicles to instead focus on plug-in electric vehicles.

Another problem is that many people still have concerns about the safety of hydrogen. Naturally gaseous at room temperature, storing hydrogen involves using pressurized tanks that can leak and, if punctured, could cause explosions. It is also difficult to store enough hydrogen in a vehicle to take it the 300+ miles that drivers are used to getting on a tank of gasoline. To do so, hydrogen must be compressed to 10,000 pounds per square inch and stored on board in bulky pressure tanks.

In 2010, U.S. President Obama signed a Nationwide Hydrogen Highway Initiative hoping to provide subsidies for up to 200,000 hydrogen fueling stations not more than five miles apart. In June 2013, the California Energy Commission approved $18.7 million to expand its hydrogen fueling station program. As of early 2017, California had 30 operational stations for vehicles.

Meanwhile, governments are facing up to the economic and technical difficulties of boosting alternative fuels through loans and subsidies, and car makers have received no return on their massive investments in fuel cells. Nonetheless, a 2012 survey of automotive industry executives by global accounting firm KPMG found that 20% of respondents thought fuel cell vehicles could attract more consumer demand than electric vehicles by 2025. Fuel cells or hydrogen-powered engines may eventually gain traction, but the technological challenges and investment required remain daunting.

Ten states, led by California, have set serious goals for zero-emission vehicles within their borders. The end game is to have 15% of vehicles to be running on electric or hydrogen power sold within each state by 2025. The additional states (including New York, Massachusetts, Maine, New Jersey, Oregon, Vermont, Maryland, Connecticut and Rhode Island) hope to have tens of thousands of additional zero-emission vehicles on the roads by then. Combined, these states total about 23% of the U.S. car market. While these mandates will undoubtedly evolve to some extent, they put a serious burden on car makers. Using hydrogen as a fuel may become a prime method of fulfilling the mandates, especially if financial incentives and tax credits are substantial enough and a massive network of hydrogen fueling stations emerges. California's mandate begins with small numbers of vehicles in 2018, growing to 15.4% of total car sales by 2025. Car makers are fighting to have the mandate modified or overturned, as they are greatly alarmed over the potential development costs and deterred by the fact that consumers have responded poorly to-date to offerings of electric cars other than the Tesla.

15) Electric Cars and Plug-in Hybrids (PHEVs) Enter the Market in Low Numbers

Electric cars range from 100% electric power vehicles that have relatively short ranges and are plugged-in at home overnight to recharge—to cars like the Chevrolet Volt that will run primarily on an electric motor only, but include a small gasoline-powered generator engine that will recharge the batteries when needed and give an occasional boost to the drivetrain as well. The Volt is designed to go up to 53 miles without recharging, and has the ability to be recharged by plug-in at home, and has a range of 420 miles using gas and electric combined.

A little history is in order: An all-electric car has long sounded logical to many people. GM launched the EV1, an all-electric vehicle, in 1996. Unfortunately, the car was a complete flop, and the $1-billion project was abandoned in 1999. In 2002, Ford announced that it would give up on the Think, an electric car model in which it had invested $123 million. These efforts were an attempt to satisfy government demands, not an attempt to fill early consumer needs. Today, stringent U.S. government average fuel efficiency requirements continue to push manufacturers to offer electric vehicles, in order to bring down their brand's overall average mpg.

Plug-in hybrids (PHEVs) are similar to standard hybrids, but they enable the owner the option of plugging-in at home overnight to recharge the battery. This will eliminate the need to run the car's gasoline engine, using only battery power as long as the relatively short range isn't exceeded. (Standard hybrids recharge only by running the gasoline-powered side of the car, and by drawing on the drag produced by using the brakes.)

Initial PHEV sales have been low in number. For 2016, InsideEVs.com reported U.S. sales rose by 37% to 159,139 vehicles. Global sales were 777,497, a 41% increase. Sales will be helped by the nine U.S. states that have announced plans to require 15% of new car purchases to be made up of zero-emission vehicles by 2025.

Toyota previously decided to limit its production of electric vehicles to very small numbers for the near term. To explain these decisions, Vice Chairman Takeshi Uchiyamada stated, "The current capabilities of electric vehicles do not meet society's needs, whether it may be the distance the cars can run, or the costs, or how it takes a long time to charge." However, after sales of electric vehicles soared in China and in Europe in 2016, Toyota announced plans to create a unit dedicated to the production of a battery-powered car. The company expects to sell vehicles equipped with a new lithium-ion battery that could significantly cut charging time and double driving range based on patent filings made in 2017. By the early 2020s, Toyota plans to offer electric vehicles powered by solid-state batteries instead of lithium ion.

For now, large numbers of U.S. consumers remain skeptical about electric or hybrid cars in general. That may change, however, with the passages of laws such as California's Senate Bill 350, which calls for cutting greenhouse gas emissions to 40% below 1990 levels by 2030. Southern California Edison hopes to install 30,000 electric vehicle chargers in commercial buildings, parking lots and apartment complexes by 2019 (at a cost of $355 million).

Nine other states are following California's lead in requiring 15% of all cars sold to be either electric or hydrogen powered by 2025. However, many of these states, such as Vermont, are in locations that have much colder weather than that of California, and batteries based on current technology lose performance in colder temperatures. The vast majority of electric vehicles sold in the U.S. are sold in California and in the Southern states, where weather is comparatively warm.

Some states are voting to halt tax credits for electric vehicles, since the credit costs are high. Other states are imposing fees of up to $200 per year on electric car buyers since they do not pay gasoline taxes. (Gasoline taxes help state agencies to pay for road maintenance and other expenses, vital to drivers of gasoline and electric vehicles alike.) It is also possible that the Trump administration could roll back tax credits and electric or hydrogen requirements on a national level.

How electric vehicles might eventually gain significant market share:

1) Technical breakthroughs in batteries will eventually make all-electric vehicles more affordable while providing longer range. Nanotechnology may be the key. Government requirements for higher miles-per-gallon ratings on cars over the mid-term will force automakers to focus on electrics, in order to lower each maker's overall average. Similarly, several states have announced aggressive requirements that 15% of cars sold annually be zero-emission by the year 2025.
2) Electricity is user-friendly, easy to understand, and easy to obtain. Electric utility companies are generally in favor of the electric car trend. Governments have been extremely enthusiastic and supportive (including financial support for manufacturers and incentives for consumers).
3) Innovative entrepreneurs remain committed to electric vehicles.
4) Electric vehicle maker Tesla is setting the standard in electric vehicles, selling sizable quantities of its high-end cars, and boosting consumer acceptance of electric cars in general. The firm launched a new Model X crossover in late 2015, and offered a moderately-priced Model 3 sedan as of mid-2017, capable of traveling about 200 miles per charge. Tesla's long-term strategy includes as many as three additional $5 billion battery factories like the Gigafactory in Nevada which began production in early 2017.

Source: Plunkett Research, Ltd.

GM planned to launch a redesigned Volt with a 50-mile range and a sleeker design in late 2015 (after stopping production of the earlier version in June of that year to make way for the new model). GM offers the modestly priced Chevy Bolt, capable of driving 200+ miles between charges.

GM is collaborating with utility companies in nearly 40 states to work out issues relating to power grids and the added demand that electric vehicles pose. Nissan has similar alliances to promote plug-in stations (it also designated a supplier of home charging stations using a 220-volt plug similar to those used for clothes dryers that promised to recharge batteries in less than eight hours). GM and other manufacturers are working on computer chips and software to imbed in electric vehicles that will communicate with utility systems regarding the best times to recharge for the best prices. Recharging on a summer afternoon, for example, would put a strain on grids already powering air conditioners, while off-peak charging would not only be cheaper but more efficient since power plants typically have excess electrical capacity at night.

Tesla is the rock star of the electric car industry. Its sales have been impressive, despite the relatively high price of its initial models, and the company's own stock has soared, thrilling early investors. Tesla's introduced its latest Model S sedan (called the Model S 70D) in April 2015. It has a range of 240 miles per charge (a 15% improvement over the first Model S). In mid-2016, Tesla unveiled a cheaper version of the Model S with a range of only 200 miles per charge and a starting price of $66,000.

Tesla launched a new Model X crossover featuring gullwing doors in late 2015 at prices that can be as high as $130,000 for a fully equipped model. It also launched Model 3 sedan in 2017 with a base price of about $35,000, capable of traveling about 200 miles per charge. Tesla has taken a simple route to solve the problem of batteries: each car has thousands of small, lithium-ion batteries linked together, similar to the batteries found in consumer electronics. The firm also has a global system of convenient chargers in high traffic areas, called Tesla Superchargers, where Tesla owners can recharge at no cost.

For those with thinner wallets, the BMW i3 electric compact has a base price of about $42,400. The i3 is making headlines for its lightweight, two-module carbon fiber architecture. With a range of 186 miles, the i3 was released in Europe in late 2013 and in the U.S. in 2014.

A number of electric SUVs were in late stage development as of mid-2017. They include the Jaguar I-PACE, the Mercedes EQ, the Audi e-tron Quattro, an electric version of BMW's X3 and an all-electric Ford Explorer. Look for release of some models as early as 2018.

Volvo, which is owned by China's Geely Holding Group, made headlines in mid-2017 when it announced plans to switch its entire lineup of vehicles to hybrid electric-internal combustion engines, or to batteries only, by 2019. This is largely in response to China's increasingly strict mandate towards zero-emission vehicles due to a massive air pollution problem. China is a major Volvo market. Sales of electric vehicles within China surged by 70% in 2016. China hopes to have 5 million electric, hybrid and fuel-cell vehicles on the road by 2020, but this will be a difficult goal to meet.

> *Internet Research Tip: Electric Cars*
> For the latest on electric car manufacturers see:
> Electric Drive Transportation Association, www.electricdrive.org
> Global Electric Motorcars, www.gemcar.com
> Tesla Motors, www.teslamotors.com

16) Major Research and Advancements in Lithium Batteries/Tesla and Panasonic Open the Gigafactory

Although all-electric vehicles still make up only a fraction of the automotive market, the battery industry is expected by some analysts to boom. However, the extreme drop in gasoline prices that began in late 2014 and continued into 2017 is tempering near-term demand for hybrids and all-electric vehicles. Overall, today's batteries generally remain costly and inefficient compared to gasoline engines. Researchers at the University of Chicago and MIT contended that even if oil prices rebounded to $100 per barrel, battery prices would have to drop by a factor of three to be competitive, and be able to charge much faster than today. Current prices per kilowatt hour ran between $130 and $200 in mid-2017 (compared to $1,000 per kilowatt hour in 2010), and oil prices would have to inflate considerably for battery-powered vehicles to be cost competitive by 2020.

There remain many obstacles to all-electric vehicles: a shortage of battery charging stations available to the driving public, battery cost and driving range. Another challenge is the increasing demand for lithium, which has driven up prices by a factor of four since 2015. Cobalt is also used in lithium-ion batteries (its price has doubled since 2015). Nickel prices, another necessary component, are rising as well.

The biggest news in advanced batteries for automobiles is being made at Tesla, the U.S.-based maker of high end, all-electric vehicles. Tesla's automobiles are unique on several counts. To begin with, the firm has been very successful in attracting buyers for its Model S sedan and Model X crossover, as well as its Model 3, launched in 2017. Next, Tesla's unique technology ties together thousands of small lithium-ion batteries, similar to cellphone batteries, in each car, as opposed to the normal use of one or two giant batteries per vehicle. This has enabled Tesla's cars to have more power and a range in the neighborhood of 200 to 300 miles per charge. Tesla has also increased the power density of its batteries, meaning more storage per kilogram.

In 2014, Tesla broke ground on a massive battery factory, known as the Gigafactory, near Reno, Nevada. The long-term plan is for a 10 million square foot plant capable of manufacturing enough batteries to power 500,000 cars per year. It may employ as many as 6,500 people, and the total cost will be in the range of $5 billion. The factory had a soft opening in 2016, and began commercial production in early 2017. A facility known as Gigafactory 2 in the state of New York manufactures solar panels and solar roof tiles.

Tesla announced in February 2017 that it hoped to finalize locations for as many as three additional Gigafactories. As of 2018, Tesla was in discussion with the Chinese regarding a possible Gigafactory for the Shanghai region.

Why would Tesla make such massive investments? The cost per unit of battery power is the key to offering lower-priced car models in the near future. Tesla is banking on the launch of its new car, the Model 3, in the more-affordable $36,000 price range. Currently, Tesla buys most of its batteries from Panasonic. The company hopes to drop the battery cost per vehicle by at least 30% with the new factory. Panasonic is a major partner in the Gigafactory.

The company's next major project was the construction of the world's largest lithium-ion system in Australia. The 100-megawatt system will collect power from a wind farm built by Neoen that will be three times more powerful than any other battery system. CEO Elon Musk made headlines when announcing the project, promising to complete it within 100 days of signing an agreement or it would be paid for with $50 million of his own money. The battery bank was completed in November 2017, 40 days before deadline, and will, when fully operational, supply power to more than 30,000 homes. This was a significant proof-of-concept for large-scale energy storage systems.

A Chinese leader in advanced batteries is BYD Company Limited. BYD is already a global leader in contract manufacturing of batteries and handsets for mobile phones. For example, BYD manufactures batteries for iPhones and iPods.

However, another Chinese leader in battery manufacturing is CATL (Contemporary Amperex Technology Ltd). Its strategy includes a vast increase in production capacity through the opening of a new megafactory in southeast China, as early as 2020.

The holy grail of electric car research is the development of battery technology that will enable a car to go 400 to 500 miles between recharges, while maintaining a competitive retail price for the car. The expensive Tesla Roadster already claims a relatively long range of nearly 300 miles.

Wireless Battery Charging for Electric Buses

In the city of Gumi, South Korea, a small number of electric buses are utilizing exciting new technology that enables to them to recharge their batteries, while moving or parked, wirelessly—that is, without being plugged in. The technology is capable of focusing an electromagnetic field towards a specific direction (the bus). The field recharges the battery with little energy loss during transmission. While expensive (Gumi's small system cost nearly $5 million, including two advanced, carbon fiber buses), the technology is very promising as a means of promoting zero-emission public transit.

IBM is working on a radical new lithium battery that could be far lighter than current batteries and have a vehicle range of as much as 500 miles. The Battery 500 Project is researching a lithium-air battery that, instead of shuttling ions back and forth between two metal electrodes, moves them between one metal electrode and air. The concept is similar to zinc-air batteries used to power hearing aids. The problem is that zinc-air batteries are not rechargeable and limited to a very small size.

Lithium-ion batteries are also in use to store power electric utilities. In early 2017, AES Corp. began utilizing a bank of 400,000 batteries in Escondido, California built by Samsung SDI Co. for Sempra Energy.

Top Five Producers of Lithium-Ion Batteries:
Panasonic Corporation, www.panasonic.com
LG Chem. www.lgchem.com
Samsung SDI Co., www.samsungsdi.com
BYD, www.byd.com
CATL, www.catlbattery.com

---

17) The Future: Pervasive Computing and Complete Mobility Will Be Standard

The rapid adoption of tablet computers and the continued enhancement of smartphones have ushered in the decline of the importance of the desktop PC, while the reasonably portable laptop PC has been diminished in importance. Mobility, miniaturization, fast wireless connections, easy access to data, software as a service, and entertainment via apps and the cloud, as well as long-lasting batteries, reign supreme in this trend.

This relentless drive toward miniaturization will have a profound effect on the way we interact with computing devices over the mid-term. Rooms and automobiles that react to a person when he enters the car, home or office will become standard. Cars that use Bluetooth to connect automatically to a driver's smartphone are an important start in that direction. Wearable sensors and computers, such as the Google Glass, are quickly growing in sophistication. The so-called smart watch is evolving to the point that it is a convenient, always-with-you alternative to looking at a smartphone's screen for the latest news and emails.

There is much more to come in short order. In the U.S., MIT Project Oxygen (www.oxygen.lcs.mit.edu) began several years ago to define the nature of personal computing for the near future. It started in the Massachusetts Institute of Technology's Laboratory for Computer Science, and has long been a useful way to visualize computing of the near future. The intent of this initiative is to conceptualize new user interfaces that will create natural, constant utilization of information technology. The project states its goal as designing a new system that will be: pervasive—it must be everywhere; embedded—it must live in our world, sensing and affecting it; nomadic—users must be free to move around according to their needs; and always on—it must never shut down or reboot.

The Project Oxygen initiative is centered on harnessing speech recognition and video recognition technologies that will have developed to the point that computer data receptors can be embedded in the walls surrounding us, responding to our spoken commands and actions. (This theory is exemplified in Microsoft's Kinect add-on for its Xbox electronic game machine. Kinect responds to the user's hand or body gestures as commands, thanks to a sophisticated, built-in camera and related software.) As envisioned in Project Oxygen, a portable interface device would provide an ultimate array of personal functions. (This has come to life to a large extent in the form of the smartphone.) Meanwhile, stationary computers would manage communications with the user in a continuous, seamless fashion. Interfaces would include cameras and microphones embedded in "intelligent rooms" that would enable the user to communicate with this massive computing power via voice, motion or the handheld unit. The user's routine needs and tasks would be tended to automatically. (Apps are now taking care of many users' needs in this regard.) For example, the user would be recognized when entering a room, and the room's systems would be adjusted to suit the user's profile. Most of this system's functions would operate by downloading software from the internet on an as-needed basis. (As in today's software-as-a-service systems. The emphasis on cloud computing that is growing today is a boost to this vision.) While a few of the goals of Project Oxygen have yet to be realized in today's mobile computing devices, it's clear that technology trends are stampeding in the right direction for this always-on future.

Another major project, a joint effort of several institutions, is PlanetLab (www.planet-lab.org). Its purpose is to give the internet an upgrade, making it smarter, faster and safer. The project involves setting up numerous networked "nodes" that are connected to the existing internet. These nodes will perform several duties in overseeing the internet, including scanning and squashing viruses and worms before they have a chance to infect PCs; routing and rerouting bandwidth as necessary to get the maximum efficiency out of existing networks; and recognizing different users so anyone can set up their own preferences and software at any computer terminal instantly, as well as many other functions.

Other technologies that will advance dramatically and fuel immense leaps forward for computers over the mid-term will include artificial intelligence, virtual reality, nanotechnology, optics, speech recognition and sensors of all types.

The latest leap forward in the pervasive computing trend is the advance of digital personal assistants, such as Amazon's Echo and Google's Home. Amazon's Alexa web app is installed on a gadget called Amazon Echo that sits on a countertop, desk or shelf. Google offers a similar device called Google Home. All of these apps and platforms are voice-activated, and use connections to other apps and systems to find information such as directions, time, date, weather and trivia, or make purchases, which are reported audibly (users can choose their device's voice gender and language).

18) Supercomputing Hits 93.01 Petaflops/IBM's Watson Expands Commercial Applications for Big Data

The claim to the title of the world's fastest computer is a moving target. By late 2017, China was estimated by trackers of the "Top500" supercomputers list to have grown its base of such computers to 202 machines, up from only 37 in early 2015. This ranks China ahead of the U.S., as America has about 143 units, down considerably from 169 systems as of late 2016 and the lowest level since the Top 500's inception in 1992.

Hi-level IT teams understand the need to work on new, advanced systems in order to avoid falling behind in areas where strong computing matters most, such as simulating complex systems like weather, and biotechnology projects like protein folding. Simulation capability is vital for national security (for example, where simulations take the place of underground testing for weapons of mass destruction) and the advancement of basic science.

Speeds multiplied dramatically in 2011 through 2017, with the top system as of November 2017, the Sunway TaihuLight at the National Supercomputing Center in Wuxi, reaching 93.01 petaflops. It was followed by Tianhe-2 (MilkyWay-2) at the National Super Computer Center in Guangzhou, reaching 33.86 petaflops. Third on the list was the Piz Daint at the Swiss National Supercomputing Centre, reaching 19.59 petaflops, followed by the Gyoukou at the Japan Agency for Marine-Earth Science and Technology, reaching 19.14 petaflops. The Titan, a Cray XK7 supercomputer at the DOE/SC/Oak Ridge National Laboratory in the U.S., fell from third place to fifth, reaching 17.59 petaflops.

TaihuLight is especially noteworthy in that its components are all manufactured in China and its speed is about five times faster than the leading U.S. supercomputer. Meanwhile, Titan's processors are graphics processing units or GPUs, which are typically designed for use in video games (many supercomputers are built using at least some GPUs). These units use less electricity than ordinary CPUs, making them more efficient and cost effective.

As of early 2017, China was working on a new supercomputer prototype based on the Tianhe-2. The unit promises to perform calculations at exascale speeds, which are 1,000 times faster than petaflops. The first exascale machine was not expected to be in full operation until 2020 or later.

IBM, which developed a computer called "Watson" that achieved fame when it beat all human contestants on the *Jeopardy!* television game show, is also working to make complex computing services easily available. Watson quickly evolved to the point that it offers cloud-based computational services, such as image recognition, and text-to-speech generation, delivered over the internet. In the fall of 2015, IBM announced that it was supporting several advanced, Watson-based services available via its Watson business unit. These are essentially artificial intelligence (AI) software services that can be of vital assistance in projects involving big data/data mining, speech recognition, pattern recognition and "reasoning" in a vaguely human-like manner. The firm states that thousands of software developers worldwide are taking advantage of Watson's capabilities. Some efforts are as simple as e-commerce firms attempting to boost their sales. More advanced applications include medical research at MD Anderson Cancer Center and the Mayo Clinic, as well as investment and banking tools.

As of early 2018, the U.S. government announced was installing a new IBM supercomputing system called Summit at Oak Ridge National Laboratory. The new system promises speeds of up to 200 peak petaflops, and will be available to scientific users by early 2019.

Government and corporate customers alike will benefit from this race. While aerospace and biotech firms want supercomputing power for breakthrough research, government agencies benefit from supercomputers for a wide variety of needs. Additionally, major manufacturers in such areas as automobiles and health imaging equipment see supercomputers as a tool for improved product engineering and faster time-to-market.

19) Superconductivity Provides Advanced Electricity Distribution Technology

Superconductivity is based on the use of super-cooled cable to distribute electricity over distance, with little of the significant loss of electric power incurred during traditional transmission over copper wires. It is one of the most promising technologies for upgrading the ailing electricity grid.

Superconductivity dates back to 1911, when a Dutch physicist determined that the element mercury, when cooled to minus 452 degrees Fahrenheit, has virtually no electrical resistance. That is, it lost zero electric power when used as a means to distribute electricity from one spot to another. Two decades later, in 1933, a German physicist named Walther Meissner discovered that superconductors have no interior magnetic field. This property enabled superconductivity to be put to commercial use by 1984, when magnetic resonance imaging machines (MRIs) were commercialized for medical imaging.

In 1986, IBM researchers K. Alex Muller and Georg Bednorz paved the path to superconductivity at slightly higher temperatures using a ceramic alloy as a medium. Shortly thereafter, a team led by University of Houston physicist Paul Chu created a ceramic capable of superconductivity at temperatures high enough to encourage true commercialization.

In May 2001, the Danish city of Copenhagen established a first when it implemented a 30-meter-long "high temperature" superconductivity (HTS) cable in its own energy grids. Other small but successful implementations have occurred in the U.S.

Today, the Holy Grail for researchers is a quest for materials that will permit superconductivity at temperatures above the freezing point, even at room temperature. There are two types of super-conductivity: "low-temperature" superconductivity (LTS), which requires temperatures lower than minus 328 degrees Fahrenheit; and "high-temperature" superconductivity (HTS), which operates at any temperature higher than that. The former type requires the use of liquid helium to maintain these excessively cold temperatures, while the latter type can reach the required temperatures with much cheaper liquid nitrogen. Liquid nitrogen is pumped through HTS cable assemblies, chilling thin strands of ceramic material that can carry electricity with no loss of power as it travels through the super-cooled cable. HTS wires are capable of carrying more than 130 times the electrical current of conventional copper wire of the same dimension. Consequently, the weight of such cable assemblies can be one-tenth the weight of old-fashioned copper wire. HTS wiring is improving substantially thanks to the development of second-generation technologies.

While cable for superconductivity is both exotic and expensive, the cost is decreasing as production ramps up, and the advantages can be exceptional. Increasing production to commercial levels at an economic cost, as well as producing lengths suitable for transmission purposes remain among the largest hurdles for the superconductor industry. Applications that are currently being implemented include use in electric transmission bottlenecks and in expensive engine systems such as those found in submarines.

Another major player in HTS components is Sumitomo Electric Industries, the largest cable and wire manufacturer in Japan. The firm has begun commercial production of HTS wire at a facility in Osaka. In addition, Sumitomo has developed electric motors based on HTS coil. The superconducting motors are much smaller and lighter than conventional electric motors, at about 90% less volume and 80% less weight.

Another leading firm, AMSC, formerly American Superconductor, sells technology to wind turbine makers, enabling them to design full 10-megawatt class superconductor wind turbines that will operate with higher efficiency than traditional models. It is also participating in advanced-technology electric transmission projects.

Advanced-generation HTS cable has been developed at American Superconductor, utilizing multiple coatings on top of a 100-millimeter substrate, a significant improvement over its earlier 40-millimeter technology. The goal is to achieve the highest level of alignment of the atoms in the superconductor material resulting in higher electrical current transmission capacity. This will increase manufacturing output while increasing efficiency. This is a convergence of nanotechnology with superconductivity, since it deals with materials at the atomic level. The company is well set up to increase production as demand increases.

Leading Firms in Superconductivity Technology:
Sumitomo Electric Industries, http://global-sei.com
AMSC, www.amsc.com/about/index.html
Nexans, www.nexans.com
SuperPower, Inc., www.superpower-inc.com

20) Private, Reusable Rockets Launch Commercial Satellites, Lowering Costs

During 2017, 90 commercial satellites were launched, according to the Space Foundation, just short of 2014's record 92 launches. A big reason why satellite launches are proliferating is because satellites are becoming much smaller, lighter and cheaper to make, but also because the rockets that blast them into orbit are evolving as well.

There are a small number of companies involved in the development of reusable rockets, led by SpaceX, Boeing, Sierra Nevada Corp. and Blue Origin, among others. All are engaged in building spacecraft to deliver cargo and astronauts to platforms such as the International Space Station (ISS) as well as launch to satellites.

Blue Origin (www.blueorigin.com), which is backed by Amazon's Jeff Bezos, led the pack with its development of a reusable rocket, first achieved when its New Sheppard rocket completed a controlled, upright landing after a brief trip to space in November 2015. In December 2017, the company launched the first flight of its Crew Capsule 2.0 with a test dummy aboard.

Tesla Motors founder Elon Musk started SpaceX (www.spacex.com), which has its own reusable rocket called the Falcon, which has successfully delivered payloads and returned to Earth. The firm is also developing the "Falcon Heavy," intended to be the world's most powerful rocket. In addition, its Dragon free-flying spacecraft was the first commercial spacecraft to deliver cargo to the International Space Station and return cargo to Earth, in 2012. By early 2016, the company stated that it was profitable and had nearly 70 launches in its backlog of work, representing about $10 billion in contracts. The firm hopes to schedule launches as often as once per week by 2019.

Another company, Rocket Lab (www.rocketlab.com), promises to use its Electron rocket to deliver SmallSats to Low Earth Orbit (LEO) at an unprecedented frequency. The market for cost-effective, lightweight small satellites is growing rapidly.

Goldman Sachs estimated that improvements in rocket design and logistics have driven down launch costs by a factor of 10 between 2010 and 2017. Cost is measured by a cost-to-Low Earth Orbit (LEO) metric, or the price for one rocket to launch one kilogram of cargo into low Earth orbit. The Saturn V, a rocket used in the 1960s, had a cost-to-LEO of between $20,000 and $25,000, while the Falcon 9's ratio is between $4,000 and $5,000. Consider also the size differential between rockets. SpaceX's Falcon 9 has a payload of about 20 tons, which has to be filled in order to fly. Rocket Lab's much smaller 330.7 pound payload can more easily be filled, making it much faster and easier to schedule a flight, especially if multiple satellite firms can schedule loads on one flight.

New technology for constructing rockets calls for simplified engine design (using the same type of engine for both the first and second stages) and lightweight carbon composite materials to increase lift. Rocket Lab uses 3-D printing to produce rocket engines. Virgin Galactic's LauncherOne rocket is to be carried under the wing of a converted Boeing 747-400.

> **Rocket Companies to Watch:**
> ArianeSpace, (www.arianespace.com)
> Blue Origin (www.blueorigin.com)
> Firefly Aerospace (www.fireflyspace.com)
> Rocket Lab (www.rocketlabusa.com)
> SpaceX (www.spacex.com)
> Vector (vectorspacesystems.com)
> Virgin Galactic (www.virgingalactic.com)
>
> In addition, the governments of India, Russia, China and Japan are already operating, or working to develop, launch industries.

21) Technology Discussion—Synthetic Biology

Scientists have followed up on the task of mapping genomes by attempting to directly alter them. This effort has gone past the point of injecting a single gene into a plant cell in order to provide a single trait, as in many agricultural biotech efforts. There are now several projects underway to create entirely new versions of life forms, such as bacteria, with genetic material inserted in the desired combination in the laboratory.

Synthetic biology can be defined as the design and construction of new entities, including enzymes and cells, or the reformatting of existing biological systems. This science capitalizes on previous advances in molecular biology and systems biology, by applying a focus on the design and construction of unique core components that can be integrated into larger systems in order to solve specific problems.

In June 2004, the first international meeting on synthetic biology was held at MIT. Called Synthetic Biology 1.0, the conference brought together researchers who are working to design and build biological parts, devices and integrated biological systems; develop technologies that enable such work; and place this research within its current and future social context. The National Science Foundation provided a grant to fund a new Synthetic Biology Engineering Research Center ("SynBERC") at UC Berkeley.

Elsewhere, engineers and scientists from MIT, Harvard and other institutions are working on a concept called BioBricks, which are strands of DNA with connectors at each end. BioBricks comprise a standard for interchangeable parts. They were developed to speed the building of biological systems within living cells. There is now a Registry of Standard Biological Parts.

A leading proponent of synthetic biology is Dr. Craig Venter, well known for his efforts in sequencing the human genome. In 2010, the J. Craig Venter Institute announced a significant breakthrough in this field. Twenty-five researchers formed a team that deciphered the genetic instructions of a simple bacterium. In a demonstration project that cost $40 million, they built a computerized genetic code of the bacterium. They then manufactured a series of chemical DNA genetic sequences. Next, they housed these sequences in yeast and E. coli cells, and tied them together in a single, one million base-pair genome. Finally, they transplanted this genome into a host cell, transforming this essentially blank cell into a different species of bacteria.

A notable company in synthetic biology is Intrexon (www.dna.com), a biotech firm based in Blacksburg, Virginia and founded in 1998. Scientists at Intrexon have built a library of 70,000 standard DNA components that can be used to construct genes, thereby controlling gene expression. Uses for the technology include manufacturing proteins that might be used to create generic versions of patented biotech drugs, such as the growth hormone Epogen. The components also have potential in the agricultural and industrial sectors. Intrexon itself describes synthetic biology as "the engineering of biological systems to enable rational, design-based control of cellular function for a specific purpose." The firm's RheoSwitch Therapeutic System (RTS) enables *in vivo* transcriptional regulation of protein expression under control of an orally administered small-molecule ligand. It also allows for the reprogramming of living cell systems.

In 2012, researchers at Stanford University and the J. Craig Venter Institute developed the first software simulation of an entire 525-gene organism, a single-cell human bacterium found in genital and respiratory tracts. The breakthrough is a major step towards the development of computerized labs that could conduct thousands of experiments at accelerated rates.

In 2016, Venter and his team created a minimal genome for bacteria (less that the smallest-known naturally-occurring bacterial organism). It has the potential to enable scientists to conduct research into the basic genes that are necessary for life.

22) The Future of Transportation and Supply Chains: Massive Investments in Infrastructure, Mobility Services and Hyperloop

Rapidly advancing technologies will relieve some of the pressure and potential congestion caused by ever-growing automobile, truck, ship and airplane traffic. These technologies can be grouped in three broad areas: 1) self-driving cars and trucks, 2) improved traffic control in the skies and on the roads, and 3) improvements in freight handling and tracking technologies.

Self-driving (autonomous) automobiles and trucks will be of particular benefit on today's highly congested roads and highways. It is relatively easy for self-driving vehicles to understand and respond to road conditions on long stretches of divided highway, with prominent striping, little or no cross-traffic and fewer impediments like stop signs and sharp turns than found on city streets. These vehicles will be able to travel while closely spaced on highways, reducing the need for new highway construction. They will also travel together at consistent speeds, meaning less stop and go driving. Fully self-driving vehicles will become so advanced that they can provide passenger transportation on crowded city streets, with safety records that will far exceed those of human drivers. The term Mobility Services is widely used to describe car-sharing strategies like ZipCar, ride-hailing systems like Uber and other alternative personal transportation systems, including bicycle sharing.

Autonomous vehicles capable of driving themselves will have very profound effects on automobile manufacturing, usage, sales and ownership patterns. At least in dense urban environments, the result is very likely to be a large proportion of individuals who opt to use shared vehicles rather than user-owned cars. Automobile makers are keenly aware that individual car ownership may decline over the long term. These firms are positioning themselves to build and distribute cars best suited for the sharing economy and mobility services market.

While self-driving technology may enable cars to be spaced very close together on roadways, incredibly tight, bumper-to-bumper traffic already exists on busy streets in many of the world's largest cities. Variable pricing ("congestion pricing") for toll roads, toll bridges and tunnels may be one answer, by charging vehicles, self-driving or not, much higher tolls during times of highest congestion. This strategy gives drivers economic incentive to delay trips until hours with lighter traffic. Cities including London, Singapore and Stockholm have been testing variable toll systems in this regard. London instituted congestion pricing in 2003 and initially reduced traffic congestion by as much as 30%. New York City has been seriously considering the strategy, due to incredible gridlock on its streets. A panel created by the New York State government recommended, in 2018, fees of $2 to $5 on taxi or Uber-like trips, and over the long-term, fees of $11.52 for cars and $25.34 for trucks entering the busiest parts of New York City.

In addition to the traffic control advantages of self-driving car technology, other advanced technologies will improve traffic efficiency at airports and on congested city streets. Closely spaced traffic sensors in cities will alert ITS (intelligent transportation system) systems within cars and trucks in order to warn of congestion and suggest better routes. Advanced systems will also be able to control traffic lights for better demand-based timing.

At airports, highly advanced technologies will enable air traffic control to safely space aircraft closer together, reduce delays and route airlines so they can travel more directly to destinations with less circling and less fuel burned. Basic routing technologies such as these have already been applied to many railroad systems, greatly improving operating efficiencies.

Meanwhile, advancements in technology will improve the efficiencies of freight handling and tracking. RFID tags are already in widespread use, enabling freight systems to electronically receive vital details about freight containers, such as contents, shipper, date shipped and intended routing. Gathering big data from RFIDs and then analyzing that data with predictive software will enable more efficient warehousing and freight routing. An additional boost is now widely seen from warehouse robotics, efficiently moving the right pallet or parcel to the right place with greater speed and safety. Amazon.com, in its massive warehouses, is a world leader in this area. Automation is rapidly being adopted in ocean shipping ports as well.

While ride dispatch services like Uber and Lyft have dramatically changed the way that consumers get local transport on-demand, such technologies will soon revolutionize freight trucking as well, including the Uber Freight system. As the world speeds towards roughly 10 billion in global population by 2050, and the rapidly expanding global middle class buys more, consumes more, ships more and travels more, the opportunities for technology companies to fulfill these needs will spur innovation and investment on a very major scale worldwide.

A 2013 study published by the McKinsey Global Institute estimated that global investment needed for transportation infrastructure in roads, ports, airports and railways totaled $23.8 trillion through 2030. (The amount is expressed in 2010 dollars.) In addition, the report found the need for $33.5 trillion in investment in power generation, water systems and telecommunications over the same period. The total investment needed on average per year is $3.7 trillion, but actual amounts invested worldwide are running about $1 trillion short of that amount each year.

Technologies for high-speed long-distance trains as well as light rail will continue to advance. Ultra-fast Maglev trains may eventually be funded in select markets.

While various engineering associations and global think tanks have long pointed out this dire need for engineering and construction, one massive problem is constantly in the way of progress: funding. To begin with, governments are poor planners and savers. While voters are faced with crowded, out-of-date airports, potholes in roads and leaks in water mains, governments rarely have amassed reserves for replacement and expansion of infrastructure. This means that funding most often comes through borrowing via the issuance of bonds.

Another avenue for construction, ownership and funding of infrastructure is through private companies, such as Australia's massive Macquarie Infrastructure Company, which owns and operates such facilities as airport hangars and solar power generation plants. Elsewhere, private company Heathrow Airport Holdings owns and operates London's Heathrow Airport, as well as the airports at Glasgow, Aberdeen and Southampton.

Such projects are often funded through public-private partnerships. Since governments have generally failed to reserve sufficient funds for future infrastructure replacement and maintenance, and there is some practical limit to how much of future needs can be filled by private companies, such partnerships may be increasingly vital to the transportation and utilities sectors. Examples of such public-private partnerships include a deal between the Milwaukee Metropolitan Sewage District and United Water to improve the city's sewage system and multiple new toll roads in Texas, California and Virginia. However, government assistance is not necessarily a guarantee of financial success for private investors, and some joint projects have fallen into bankruptcy due to lower usage and toll revenue than originally forecasted.

SPOTLIGHT: Hyperloop

A futuristic alternative to high speed trains could be on the distant horizon thanks to a concept from Tesla Motors and SpaceX founder Elon Musk. His idea is to build a giant, above-ground tube atop pylons in which a 28-passenger pod would move at speeds up to 760 mph. The solar powered pod would travel through the tube, in which fans would remove sufficient air to eliminate most of the drag that naturally slows moving objects. Musk envisions a route between Los Angeles and San Francisco, which could take as little as 30 minutes to travel. The tube would be built along existing roads making construction and maintenance easier, and safety features would include pod wheels in case of system failure. Initially, Musk invited other companies to bid for building funding. By mid-2016, Hyperloop Technologies (hyperlooptech.com), Hyperloop One (hyperloop-one.com) and Hyperloop Transportation Technologies (www.hyperloop.global) had raised approximately $200 million collectively. Hyperloop One also built the first prototype, which completed a second phase of testing in the desert land in Nevada with a pod achieving a speed of 192 miles per hour and traveling 1,433 feet. However, in 2017, Musk indicated that he was interested in building a project himself, specifically a 29-minute route between New York City and Washington, D.C. Boring Co., a tunnel-carving firm owned by Musk, will likely help develop the plans.

23) HPTP Thermoplastics, Thermoset and Engineered Plastics Enable Advanced Products/Nanocomposites Offer the Ultimate in Advanced Materials

HPTPs: Engineered plastics are generating novel ways to reduce weight, reduce costs and increase performance of a wide variety of products. Sometimes referred to as HPTP for High Performance Thermoplastics, these advanced plastics generate performance enhancements that may include heat resistance, chemical resistance, compressive strength or stiffness. Such plastics can be very effective replacements for steel, titanium, ceramics or aluminum, particularly in applications like consumer electronics, aircraft, space vehicles or automobiles, where the reduction of overall product weight can be a vital concern. They have the added advantage of being corrosion resistant, which may eventually prove to be very important for new uses in ultradeep offshore oil wells.

Applications vary, and may include final plastics, or the use of thermoplastic resins as a compound in other materials. Today, high volume use of engineering thermoplastic (ETP) resins is found compounded into such basic plastic stocks as nylons, polyesters, polycarbonates (PC), polyphenylene ethers (PPE), polyacetals (POM) and polyphenylene sulfides (PPS).

Thermoplastics can also be compounded or combined with non-plastic materials to achieve even higher performance. Common composites of thermoplastics include high strength glass fibers. This can create a strong, lightweight material for uses such as aircraft seat frames or aircraft window bezels. Some composite manufacturers claim to achieve products that are 40% lighter than aluminum and much stiffer than steel or typical injection-molded plastics.

For example, Houston, Texas-based G.S.F. Plastics offers a wide variety of high performance thermoplastic compounds. Its GSF 1200 and GSF 2200 materials are available unfilled, or blended with fiberglass, carbon, graphite, and PTFE (Polytetrafluoroethylene). Each additive is used to enhance the exceptional properties of GSF's proprietary PEEK brand of plastics in a particular application. Glass fibers add rigidity. Carbon fibers or graphite allow for improved wear resistance. Also, the combination of PTFE, graphite and glass fibers give finished parts added lubricity, rigidity and enhanced wear.

Nanocomposites: The compounding of thermoplastics with nanoparticles has a great deal of potential for the future. Significant research is now going into thermoplastic nanocomposites. These composites will eventually be engineered to achieve a wide variety of desired levels of strength, smoothness or weight reduction. Additional properties that may be enhanced in this manner include optical, electrical, thermal or magnetic capabilities. Products using nanocomposites may enjoy better dimensional stability and flame retardance. For uses in such areas as automobile bodies or interiors, they may offer scratch resistance and reduced warping.

The carbon-based nano material known as graphene offers some of the greatest potential in such composites. Graphene, compared to more common carbon nanotubes, offers incredible strength, and it is the world's greatest conductor of electricity. Using graphene in a nanocomposite with thermoplastic has potential use as advanced smart materials in applications ranging from down-hole oil well testing and monitoring to advanced engine components. A great deal of basic research has been achieved in this area, and many nanocomposite patents will result, including patents on composites outside of plastics. In 2010, a patent was granted to Princeton University for a functional graphene-rubber nanocomposite. It appears to offer superb mechanical strength and thermal stability, as well as electrical conductivity. In 2011, a patent was granted for a composite of graphene and an elastomer for use in automobile tires. Graphene nanocomposites have the potential to save a great deal of weight over more conventional composites, due to its high strength-to-weight ratio.

NanoMaster is a government-sanctioned EU research project aimed at creating advanced uses for graphene-plastic nanocomposites. Several major EU-based chemicals firms have been active in this consortium. According to the NanoMaster group, the addition of 5% graphene doubles the mechanical properties of TPO (thermoplastic polyolefin) and PP (polypropylene), and a tensile strength increase of 80% was seen when compounding 1% (by weight) of graphene with PMMA (polymethylmethacrylate, a clear acrylic than can be used as a replacement for glass).

Elsewhere, Ovation Polymers of Medina, Ohio, is manufacturing graphene-thermoplastic compounds at commercial scale. Its Extima brand of graphene polymer utilizes a dispersion technology that the company states maximizes the effect of nano-materials for injection molding or extrusion, while retaining the physical, structural and thermal properties of the compound.

Thermoset plastics are different from thermoplastics. Thermosets contain polymers that cross-link together during the curing process. This reduces the risk that products will melt in the presence of heat. This makes thermosets particularly useful in appliances or in electronics that produce excess heat. However, they cannot easily be recycled. Thermoplastics, on the other hand, can be cured without creating any bonding. This means that they can be remolded or recycled readily.

Engineered thermoplastics are primarily processed into molded parts and objects. Usually, the polymers are compounded for injection-molding applications with the addition of fibers (for reinforcement), mineral fillers, or any of a variety of additives such as impact modifiers, lubricants, thermal and ultraviolet (UV) stabilizers, pigments, and other materials. The effect of incorporating additives can be pronounced. For example, a general-purpose PC (polycarbonate) that exhibits a tensile strength of 69 million pascals (MPa), when modified or reinforced with 30% glass fiber, will show a tensile strength of 145 MPa.

24) Artificial Intelligence (AI), Deep Learning and Machine Learning Advance into Commercial Applications, Including Health Care and Robotics

The concept of Artificial Intelligence (often referred to as "AI") continues to evolve, as scientists and software engineers gain a greater understanding of reasonably possible goals for this technology. In 1956, John McCarthy may have been the first to use the phrase, describing artificial intelligence as "the science and engineering of making intelligent machines." This was a pretty dramatic statement, considering the barely advanced state of computers and robotics at the time.

In 1950, computer pioneer Alan Turing proposed, in a paper titled *Computing Machinery and Intelligence*, a test that could determine whether or not a machine could "think." Essentially, he suggested that, in a situation where a person asked the same questions of both a machine and a human being, if he couldn't tell the difference between text answers coming from the machine and the human in blind results, then it might be reasonable to call the machine "intelligence." The Turing Test clearly avoids any discussion of what "consciousness" is.

Gary Marcus, a scientist at New York University, proposed another test, the Ikea Construction Challenge, to see whether or not a machine could assemble a piece of Ikea furniture when provided with a pile of parts and related instructions. Near the end of 2015, a group of well-known Silicon Valley investors, including Elon Musk and Peter Thiel, announced a long-term commitment to raise funds of as much a $1 billion for a new organization to be known as OpenAI, www.openai.com. OpenAI is a nonprofit group, dedicated to moving AI ahead to the point that it "will benefit humanity."

Another well-funded AI organization is the Allen Institute for Artificial Intelligence (AI2). Located in Seattle, the group was co-founded by Paul Allen, one of the co-founders of Microsoft, and scientist Oren Etzioni. AI2 has developed its own complex test for artificial intelligence called a GeoSolver.

While the practical definition and ultimate capabilities of AI are debated, industry has put AI to work and continues to invest very heavily in advanced development. Today, AI has synergies with many highly advanced technologies such as virtual reality, factory automation, robotics, self-driving cars, speech recognition and predictive analytics.

One of the more promising advancements is called "deep learning." In 2014, Google spent nearly $600 million to acquire UK-based DeepMind, an intensive learning research group. Deep learning is sometimes referred to in conjunction with phrases such as "machine learning" and "neural networking." The main point is that software can be trained by being constantly fed data, queried as to its meaning, and receiving feedback to its responses. It is essentially training a machine to respond correctly to data of a given nature or to data within a given set of circumstances.

The most compelling opportunities for the development and use of artificial intelligence software may be in engineering/research, investment analysis and, especially, health care. Simply put, health care is one of the world's largest and fastest-growing industries, and virtually all of the government and private health initiatives that pay for health care are desperately seeking ways to improve patient care outcomes, cut billing fraud, create operating efficiencies and generally slow the growth of costs overall.

IBM, clearly one of the world's top software engineering companies, is betting big on the massive, global opportunity in health care analytics via artificial intelligence. It has created a business unit called Watson Health, based on its advanced "Watson" supercomputing-artificial intelligence hardware/software technology, combined with massive health care database firms that it has aggressively acquired at a cost of several billion dollars. In early 2016, IBM announced the acquisition of Truven Health Analytics, Inc. for $2.6 billion, for the Watson Health unit. This acquisition helped Watson Health soar to a 5,000-employee juggernaut. Truven's databases and experience when combined with IBM's technologies will enable Watson Health to analyze and look for patterns or problems in billing, patient outcomes, insurance claims, drugs and drug usage, pricing and myriad other aspects of the health care system, from a data set covering about 300 million patients. One of Watson Health's competitors in this arena is Enlitic, Inc.

The trend toward "big data," that is, the building of massive databases such as the patient data referred to above, is giving a large boost to the potential of AI. In fact, the lines are blurring between AI and the analytics software used in big data projects.

Chapter 2

ENGINEERING & RESEARCH INDUSTRY STATISTICS

Contents:	
Engineering & Research Industry Statistics and Market Size Overview	**42**
Quarterly Engineering & Research Industry Revenues, U.S.: 2017	**43**
Engineering & Scientific Research & Development Services: Estimated Sources of Revenue, U.S.: 2011-2016	**44**
Federal R&D Funding by Character of Work and Facilities and Equipment, U.S.: Fiscal Years 2017-2019	**45**
Federal R&D Budget & Distribution by Agency, U.S.: Fiscal Years 2017-2019	**46**
Federal R&D & R&D Plant Funding for National Defense, U.S.: Fiscal Years 2017-2019	**47**
Federal R&D & R&D Plant Funding for Health and Human Services, U.S.: Fiscal Years 2017-2019	**48**
Federal R&D & R&D Plant Funding for Space Flight, Research & Supporting Activities, U.S.: Fiscal Years 2017-2019	**49**
NASA Budget Appropriations & Projections: 2017-2023	**50**
Federal R&D & R&D Plant Funding for Basic Research, U.S.: Fiscal Years 2017-2019	**51**
Federal R&D & R&D Plant Funding for Agriculture, U.S.: Fiscal Years 2017-2019	**52**
Federal R&D & R&D Plant Funding for Transportation, U.S.: Fiscal Years 2017-2019	**53**
Federal R&D & R&D Plant Funding for Energy, U.S.: Fiscal Years 2017-2019	**54**
U.S. Department of Energy Funding for Science & Energy Programs: 2017-2019	**55**
U.S. National Nanotechnology Initiative (NNI) Budget: Fiscal Years 2016-2018	**56**
Research Funding for Biological Sciences, U.S. National Science Foundation: Fiscal Years 2017-2019	**57**
Research Funding for Engineering, U.S. National Science Foundation: Fiscal Years 2017-2019	**58**
Domestic U.S. Biopharmaceutical R&D & R&D Abroad, PhRMA Member Companies: 1980-2016	**59**
Top Foreign Countries by Number of Residents Receiving U.S. Patents: 2015	**60**
Top 30 U.S. Patent Recipient Organizations: 2016	**61**
Major Patenting U.S. Universities: 2016	**62**
The U.S. Drug Discovery & Approval Process	**63**
Employment in Engineering Occupations by Business Type, U.S.: 2014-February 2018	**64**
Employment in Life & Physical Science Occupations by Business Type, U.S.: May 2017	**65**

Engineering & Research Industry Statistics and Market Size Overview

	Quantity	Unit	Year	Source
Total R&D Spending, Worldwide, PPP[1]	2,190	Bil. US$	2018	R&D
Total U.S. R&D Spending	553.0	Bil. US$	2018	R&D
Spending on R&D as a Percent of GDP:				
U.S.	2.8	%	2018	R&D
China	2.0	%	2018	R&D
Japan	3.5	%	2018	R&D
Germany	2.8	%	2018	R&D
Total Proposed U.S. Federal R&D Budget	118.1	Bil. US$	2019	OMB
Proposed R&D, National defense	57.2	Bil. US$	2019	OMB
Proposed R&D, Health and Human Services	24.7	Bil. US$	2019	OMB
Proposed R&D, Energy	12.7	Bil. US$	2019	OMB
Proposed R&D, NASA	10.7	Bil. US$	2019	OMB
Proposed R&D, National Science Foundation	4.2	Bil. US$	2019	OMB
Proposed R&D, Agriculture	1.9	Bil. US$	2019	OMB
Proposed R&D, Veterans Affairs	1.3	Bil. US$	2019	OMB
Proposed R&D, Commerce	1.4	Bil. US$	2019	OMB
Proposed R&D, Transportation	0.8	Bil. US$	2019	OMB
Proposed R&D, Interior	0.8	Bil. US$	2019	OMB
Proposed R&D, Patient-Centered Outcomes Research Trust Fund	0.6	Bil. US$	2019	OMB
Proposed R&D, Homeland Security	0.5	Bil. US$	2019	OMB
Proposed R&D, Smithsonian Institution	0.3	Bil. US$	2019	OMB
Proposed R&D, Environmental Protection Agency	0.3	Bil. US$	2019	OMB
Proposed R&D, Education	0.2	Bil. US$	2019	OMB
U.S. Employment in Architecture & Engineering Occupations	1.44	Million	Feb-18	BLS
U.S. Employment in Scientific R&D Occupations	665.3	Thous.	Feb-18	BLS
Actual Budget for Nanotechnology R&D, U.S. Government	1.56	Bil. US$	2017	NNI
Estimated Budget for Nanotechnology R&D, U.S. Government	1.47	Bil. US$	2017	NNI
Private & Public Investment in Nanotechnology, Worldwide	49.7	Bil. US$	2017	PRE
Biopharmaceutical R&D Spending, PhRMA Member Companies, U.S.	52.4	Bil. US$	2016	PhRMA
Biopharmaceutical R&D Spending, PhRMA Member Companies, Worldwide	65.5	Bil. US$	2016	PhRMA

U.S. Patents

Utility Patents Granted by Recipient, 2015:[2]	Number	%	Source
Total Patents Granted	298,407	100.0	USPTO
U.S. Corporation	133,434	44.72	USPTO
U.S. Government	991	0.33	USPTO
U.S. Individual	13,643	4.57	USPTO
Foreign Corporation	144,719	48.50	USPTO
Foreign Government	364	0.12	USPTO
Foreign Individual	5,256	1.76	USPTO
Top Patenting University, 2015	Univ. of California: 489 Patents		USPTO
Top Private Sector Patent Recipient, 2015	IBM: 7,309 Patents		USPTO
Top Foreign Country Receiving U.S. Patents, 2015	Japan: 54,422 Patents		USPTO

R&D = R&D Magazine
BLS = U.S. Bureau of Labor Statistics
PRE = Plunkett Research estimate.
PhRMA = Pharmaceutical Research and Manufacturers of America
OMB = Office of Management and Budget
NNI = U.S. National Nanotechnology Initiative
USPTO = U.S. Patent and Trademark Office

[1] PPP = Purchasing Power Parity Basis (an attempt to account for differences in local prices between one country and another, allowing the relative value of comparable goods or services to be compared across different economies).

[2] Utility Patents (representing 90% of total patents) are issued "for the invention of a new and useful process, machine, manufacture, or composition of matter, or a new and useful improvement thereof," according to USPTO definitions.

Source: Plunkett Research,® Ltd. Copyright © 2018, All Rights Reserved
www.plunkettresearch.com

Quarterly Engineering & Research Industry Revenues, U.S.: 2017

(In Millions of US$)

Kind of Business / Class of Customer	4Q^P	3Q	2Q	1Q	Prelim. Total
Engineering Services (NAICS 54133)	74,807	77,260	75,448	73,986	301,501
Government	21,329	21,522	20,562	19,538	82,951
Business	51,250	52,968	52,241	51,940	208,399
Household consumers & individual users	S	2,770	2,645	2,508	S
Scientific Research & Development Services (NAICS 5417)	35,666	33,376	33,159	32,408	134,609
Government	10,975	10,828	10,674	10,333	42,810
Business	23,328	21,317	21,515	21,089	87,249
Household consumers & individual users	1,363	1,231	970	S	S

Kind of Business / Class of Customer	4Q^P	3Q	2Q	1Q	Prelim. Avg.
Engineering Services (NAICS 54133)	100.0	100.0	100.0	100.0	100.0
Government	28.5	27.9	27.3	26.4	27.5
Business	68.5	68.6	69.2	70.2	69.1
Household consumers & individual users	S	S	S	S	S
Scientific Research & Development Services (NAICS 5417)	100.0	100.0	100.0	100.0	100.0
Government	30.8	32.4	32.2	31.9	31.8
Business	65.4	63.9	64.9	65.1	64.8
Household consumers & individual users	3.8	3.7	S	S	S

Note: Estimates have not been adjusted for seasonal variation or for price changes, and are based on data from the Quarterly Services Survey. Sector totals and subsector totals may include data for kinds of business not shown. Detail percents may not add to 100 percent due to rounding.

P = Preliminary estimate. S = Estimate has sampling variability higher than publication standard.

Source: U.S. Census Bureau
Plunkett Research, ® Ltd.
www.plunkettresearch.com

Engineering & Scientific Research & Development Services: Estimated Sources of Revenue, U.S.: 2011-2016

(In Millions of US$; Latest Year Available)

NAICS	Kind of business	2016	2015	2014	2013	2012	2011
Revenue for Taxable Firms							
54133	Engineering services	230,881	225,517	217,178	205,874	208,124	209,570
54138	Testing laboratories	17,203	17,190	16,257	16,146	15,324	15,431
54171	R&D in the physical, engineering and life sciences	99,665	92,803	86,013	80,564	77,059	76,589
Revenue for Tax-Exempt Firms							
54171	R&D in the physical, engineering and life sciences	32,190	34,017	34,541	34,561	33,662	32,587

Sources of Revenue	2016	2015	2014	2013
Total Revenue: Engineering Services (NAICS 54133)	**230,881**	**225,517**	**217,178**	**205,874**
Residential engineering projects (excludes apartment building projects)	8,117	7,162	NA	NA
Commercial, public, and institutional engineering projects (includes apartment building projects)	26,163	25,199	NA	NA
Industrial and manufacturing engineering projects	38,675	39,142	45,485	41,555
Transportation infrastructure engineering projects	25,200	23,435	20,382	18,148
Municipal utility engineering projects	8,310	7,896	S	S
Power generation and distribution engineering projects	15,342	12,046	23,010	25,465
Telecommunications and broadcasting engineering projects	3,093	3,500	3,261	3,137
Hazardous and industrial waste engineering projects	7,894	8,187	7,684	6,154
Other engineering projects	31,707	29,877	28,758	24,523
Construction services	20,983	21,171	19,530	19,536
Engineering advisory and drafting services	10,653	11,720	5,111	5,304
Surveying and mapping services	S	S	2,148	2,183
All other operating revenue	31,896	33,395	25,127	25,713
Total Revenue: Scientific R&D Svcs. (NAICS 5417), Taxable Employer Firms	**101,952**	**94,971**	**88,306**	**82,706**
Basic and applied research in natural and exact sciences, except biological sciences	9,965	9,059	7,412	7,682
Basic and applied research in engineering and technology	24,122	22,744	16,034	15,846
Basic and applied research in the biological and biomedical sciences	23,216	21,417	17,981	16,581
Basic and applied research in the social sciences and humanities	2,654	2,544	1,662	1,610
Production services for development	S	5,203	4,697	4,036
Licensing of right to use intellectual property	S	7,863	14,371	13,103
Original works of intellectual property	700	602	505	S
All other operating revenue	27,963	25,539	S	S
Total Revenue: Scientific R&D Svcs. (NAICS 5417), Tax-Exempt Employer Firms	**36,729**	**38,581**	**38,906**	**38,591**
Basic and applied research in natural and exact sciences, except biological sciences	1,813	1,782	2,539	2,236
Basic and applied research in engineering and technology	12,784	12,936	9,518	9,409
Basic and applied research in the biological and biomedical sciences	5,166	5,061	5,165	5,231
Basic and applied research in the social sciences and humanities	1,833	1,793	2,318	1,965
Production services for development	657	588	S	S
Licensing of right to use intellectual property	379	S	420	382
Original works of intellectual property	16	32	43	42
All other operating revenue	4,241	4,053	4,107	4,544
Contributions, gifts, and grants received	7,271	9,095	11,206	11,371
Investment and property income	1,862	2,051	2,660	2,601
All other non-operating revenue	707	774	609	767

NA = Not Available.
S = Estimate does not meet publication standards because of high sampling variability (coefficient of variation is greater than 30%) or poor response quality (total quantity response rate is less than 50%).

Source: U.S. Census Bureau
Plunkett Research® Ltd
www.plunkettresearch.com

Federal R&D Funding by Character of Work and Facilities and Equipment, U.S.: Fiscal Years 2017-2019

(In Millions of US$)

	2017 Actual	2018 Estimated[1]	2019 Proposed	Change, 2018-19 Dollar	Change, 2018-19 Percent
Basic Research	34,327	34,409	27,341	−7,068	−21%
Applied Research	38,148	37,559	31,648	−5,911	−16%
Experimental Development	80,057	79,481	95,417	15,936.0	20%
Facilities and Equipment	2,451	2,483	2,371	−112	−5%
Total	154,983	153,932	156,777	2,845.0	2.0%

Note: This table shows funding levels for Departments or Independent agencies with more than $200 million in R&D activities in 2019. Detail may not add to total because of rounding.

[1] Because an appropriation for FY 2018 was not passed by the time this chapter went to print, the chapter calculates FY 2018 estimates using an annualized version of the FY 2018 Continuing Resolution.

Source: EOP, OMB, Analytical Perspectives, Budget of the United States Government, Fiscal Year 2019
Plunkett Research, Ltd.
www.plunkettresearch.com

Federal R&D Budget & Distribution by Agency, U.S.: Fiscal Years 2017-2019

(In Millions of US$)

Funding Category	2017 Actual	2018 Estimated[1]	2019 Proposed	% of Total R&D ('19)
National defense[2]	49,197	43,616	57,156	48.41%
Nondefense Total	76,092	75,385	60,900	51.59%
Health and Human Services	34,222	33,772	24,742	20.96%
Energy	14,896	15,006	12,685	10.74%
NASA	10,704	10,243	10,651	9.02%
National Science Foundation	5,938	6,030	4,177	3.54%
Agriculture	2,585	2,487	1,914	1.62%
Veterans Affairs	1,346	1,338	1,345	1.14%
Commerce	1,794	1,833	1,361	1.15%
Transportation	904	929	826	0.70%
Interior	953	964	759	0.64%
Patient-Centered Outcomes Research Trust Fund	463	501	622	0.53%
Homeland Security	724	672	548	0.46%
Smithsonian Institution	251	242	271	0.23%
Environmental Protection Agency	497	496	269	0.23%
Education	254	243	240	0.20%
Other	561	629	490	0.42%
Total[3]	125,289	119,001	118,056	100.00%
Total (using the former definition of Development)	154,983	153,932	156,777	--

Notes: This table shows funding levels for Departments or Independent agencies with more than $200 million in R&D activities in 2019. Detail may not add to total because of rounding.

[1] Because an appropriation for FY 2018 was not passed by the time this chapter went to print, the chapter calculates FY 2018 estimates using an annualized version of the FY 2018 Continuing Resolution.

[2] The totals for Experimental Development spending in FY 2017-2019 do not include the DOD Budget Activity 07 (Operational System Development) due to changes in the definition of development. These funds are requested in the FY 2019 Budget request and support the development efforts to upgrade systems that have been fielded or have received approval for full rate production and anticipate production funding in the current or subsequent fiscal year.

[3] The total uses the new Experimental Development definition across the three fiscal years

Source: U.S. EOP, OMB, Analytical Perspectives, Budget of the United States Government, Fiscal Year 2019

Plunkett Research, Ltd.

www.plunkettresearch.com

Federal R&D & R&D Plant Funding for National Defense, U.S.: Fiscal Years 2017-2019

(In Millions of US$)

Funding Category and Agency	2017 Actual	2018 Estimated[1]	2019 Proposed	Change, 2018 - 19 Dollar	Change, 2018 - 19 Percent
Total[2]	49,197	43,616	57,156	13,540	31%
Military Construction	155	37	53	16	43%
Military Personnel	410	439	455	16	4%
Defense Health Program	1,452	336	362	26	8%
Research, Development, Test, and Evaluation	47,180	42,804	56,286	13,482	31%

Notes: This table shows funding levels for Departments or Independent agencies with more than $200 million in R&D activities in 2019. Detail may not add to total because of rounding.

[1]Because an appropriation for FY 2018 was not passed by the time this chapter went to print, the chapter calculates FY 2018 estimates using an annualized version of the FY 2018 Continuing Resolution.

[2]Unlike previous years, totals for Experimental Development spending in FY 2017-2019 do not include the DOD Budget Activity 07 (Operational System Development) due to changes in the definition of development. These funds are requested in the FY 2019 Budget request and support the development efforts to upgrade systems that have been fielded or have received approval for full rate production and anticipate production funding in the current or subsequent fiscal year.

Source: EOP, OMB, Analytical Perspectives, Budget of the United States Government, Fiscal Year 2019

Plunkett Research, Ltd.

www.plunkettresearch.com

Federal R&D & R&D Plant Funding for Health and Human Services, U.S.: Fiscal Years 2017-2019

(In Millions of US$; Latest Year Available)

	2017 Actual	2018 Estimated[1]	2019 Proposed	Change, 2018-19 Dollar	Change, 2018-19 Percent
Total	34,222	33,772	24,742	−9,030	−27%
Administration for Children and Families	16	5	89	84	1680%
Centers for Disease Control and Prevention	511	464	296	−168	−36%
Centers for Medicare and Medicaid Services	278	19	17	−2	−11%
Departmental Management	116	131	158	27	21%
Food and Drug Administration	390	410	410	0	0%
Health Resources and Services Administration	30	30	22	−8	−27%
National Institutes of Health[2]	32,881	32,713	23,750	−8,963	−27%

Notes: This table shows funding levels for Departments or Independent agencies with more than $200 million in R&D activities in 2019. Detail may not add to total because of rounding.

[1] Because an appropriation for FY 2018 was not passed by the time this chapter went to print, the chapter calculates FY 2018 estimates using an annualized version of the FY 2018 Continuing Resolution.

[2] The FY 2019 Budget proposes to consolidate the activities of the Agency for Healthcare Research and Quality (AHRQ) within NIH. The NIH total includes R&D funding that previously occurred in AHRQ.

Source: EOP, OMB, Analytical Perspectives, Budget of the United States Government, Fiscal Year 2019

Plunkett Research, Ltd.

www.plunkettresearch.com

Federal R&D & R&D Plant Funding for Space Flight, Research & Supporting Activities, U.S.: Fiscal Years 2017-2019

(In Millions of US$; Latest Year Available)

	2017 Actual	2018 Estimated[1]	2019 Proposed	Change, 2018-19 Dollar	Change, 2018-19 Percent
National Aeronautics and Space Administration	**10,704**	**10,243**	**10,651**	**408**	**4%**
Science	5,668	5,666	5,820	154	3%
Aeronautics	517	508	488	−20	−4%
Low Earth Orbit and Spaceflight Operations	2,542	2,166	1,727	−439	−20%
Safety, Security and Mission Services	269	262	257	−5	−2%
Deep Space Exploration Systems	976	937	1,392	455	49%
Construction and Environmental Compliance and Restoration	52	22	54	32	145%
Exploration Research and Technology	680	682	913	231	34%

Notes: This table shows funding levels for Departments or Independent agencies with more than $200 million in R&D activities in 2019. Detail may not add to total because of rounding.

[1] Because an appropriation for FY 2018 was not passed by the time this chapter went to print, the chapter calculates FY 2018 estimates using an annualized version of the FY 2018 Continuing Resolution.

Source: EOP, OMB, Analytical Perspectives, Budget of the United States Government, Fiscal Year 2019

Plunkett Research, Ltd.

www.plunkettresearch.com

NASA Budget Appropriations & Projections: 2017-2023

(In Millions of US$)

Budget Authority	FY 2017 Operating Plan	FY 2018 CR	FY 2019 PBR	FY 2020	FY 2021	FY 2022	FY 2023
NASA Total	**19,653.3**	**19,519.8**	**19,892.2**	**19,592.2**	**19,592.2**	**19,592.2**	**19,592.2**
Deep Space Exploration Systems	4,184.0	4,222.6	4,558.8	4,859.1	4,764.5	4,752.5	4,769.8
Exploration Systems Development	3,929.0	--	3,669.8	3,790.5	3,820.2	3,707.5	3,845.6
Advanced Exploration systems	97.8	--	889.0	1,068.6	944.3	1,045.0	924.1
Exploration Research and Development	157.2	--	--	--	--	--	--
Exploration Research and Technology	826.5	820.8	1,002.7	912.7	912.7	912.7	912.7
LEO and Spaceflight Operations	4,942.5	4,850.1	4,624.6	4,273.7	4,393.3	4,430.3	4,438.0
International Space Station	1,450.9	--	1,462.2	1,453.2	1,471.2	1,466.2	1,451.2
Space Transportation	2,589.0	--	2,108.7	1,829.1	1,858.9	1,829.2	1,807.3
Space and Flight Support(SFS)	902.6	--	903.7	841.4	888.2	934.9	954.6
Commercial LEO Development	--	--	150.0	150.0	175.0	200.0	225.0
Science	5,762.2	5,725.8	5,895.0	5,859.9	5,841.1	5,822.4	5,803.6
Earth Science	1,907.7	--	1,784.2	1,784.2	1,784.2	1,784.2	1,784.2
Planetary Science	1,827.5	--	2,234.7	2,199.6	2,180.8	2,162.1	2,143.3
Astrophysics	1,352.3	--	1,185.4	1,185.4	1,185.4	1,185.4	1,185.4
Heliophysics	674.7	--	690.7	690.7	690.7	690.7	690.7
Aeronautics	656.0	655.5	633.9	608.9	608.9	608.9	608.9
Education	100.0	99.3	--	--	--	--	--
Safety, Security, and Mission Services	2,768.6	2,749.8	2,749.7	2,744.8	2,738.6	2,732.3	2,726.1
Center Management and Operations	1,986.5	--	1,949.6	1,945.4	1,939.8	1,934.1	1,928.5
Agency Management and Operations	782.1	--	800.1	799.4	798.8	798.2	797.6
Construction and Environmental Compliance and Restoration	375.6	358.3	388.2	293.8	293.8	293.8	293.8
Construction of Facilities	305.4	--	305.3	210.9	210.9	210.9	210.9
Environmental Compliance and Restoration	70.2	--	82.9	82.9	82.9	82.9	82.9
Inspector General	37.9	37.6	39.3	39.3	39.3	39.3	39.3

Note: FY 2017 reflects funding amounts specified in Public Law 115-31, Consolidated Appropriations Act, 2017, as executed under the Agency's current FY 2017 Operating Plan. A full-year 2018 appropriation for this account was not enacted at the time the budget was prepared; therefore, the budget assumes this account is operating under the Continuing Appropriations Act, 2018. The amounts included for 2018 reflect the annualized level provided by the continuing resolution.

Source: U.S. National Aeronautics & Space Administration (NASA)
Plunkett Research, Ltd.
www.plunkettresearch.com

Federal R&D & R&D Plant Funding for Basic Research, U.S.: Fiscal Years 2017-2019

(In Millions of US$; Latest Year Available)

Funding Category and Agency	2017 Actual	2018 Estimated[1]	2019 Proposed	Change, 2018-19 Dollar	Change, 2018-19 Percent
Total	**34,327**	**34,409**	**27,341**	**−7,068**	**−21%**
Defense	16,701	16,859	12,114	−4,745	−28%
Health and Human Services	4,802	4,601	3,398	−1,203	−26%
Energy	3,607	3,713	4,150	437	12%
NASA	4,739	4,818	3,402	−1,416	−29%
National Science Foundation	1,119	1,038	921	−117	−11%
Agriculture	538	538	540	2	0%
Veterans Affairs	234	232	197	−35	−15%
Commerce	--	--	--	--	--
Transportation	54	54	40	−14	−26%
Interior	--	--	--	--	--
Patient-Centered Outcomes Research Trust Fund	49	53	31	−22	−42%
Homeland Security	224	220	225	5	2%
Smithsonian Institution	--	--	--	--	--
Environmental Protection Agency	34	28	28	0	0%
Education	11	11	11	0	0%
Other	2,215	2,244	2,284	40	2%

NOTES: This table shows funding levels for Departments or Independent agencies with more than $200 million in R&D activities in 2019. Detail may not add to total because of rounding.

[1] Because an appropriation for FY 2018 was not passed by the time this chapter went to print, the chapter calculates FY 2018 estimates using an annualized version of the FY 2018 Continuing Resolution.

Source: EOP, OMB, Analytical Perspectives, Budget of the United States Government, Fiscal Year 2019

Plunkett Research, Ltd.

www.plunkettresearch.com

Federal R&D & R&D Plant Funding for Agriculture, U.S.: Fiscal Years 2017-2019

(In Millions of US$; Latest Year Available)

Funding Category and Agency	2017 Actual	2018 Estimated[1]	2019 Proposed	Change, 2018-19 Dollar	Change, 2018-19 Percent
Total	2,585	2,487	1,914	−573	−23%
Agricultural Research Service	1,298	1,289	855	−434	−34%
Animal & Plant Health Inspection Service	40	39	34	−5	−13%
Economic Research Service	87	86	45	−41	−48%
Forest Service	282	281	235	−46	−16%
National Agricultural Statistics Service	9	9	9	0	0%
National Institute of Food and Agriculture	869	783	736	−47	−6%

Note: This table shows funding levels for Departments or Independent agencies with more than $200 million in R&D activities in 2019. Detail may not add to total because of rounding.

[1] Because an appropriation for FY 2018 was not passed by the time this chapter went to print, the chapter calculates FY 2018 estimates using an annualized version of the FY 2018 Continuing Resolution.

Source: EOP, OMB, Analytical Perspectives, Budget of the United States Government, Fiscal Year 2019

Plunkett Research, Ltd.

www.plunkettresearch.com

Federal R&D & R&D Plant Funding for Transportation, U.S.: Fiscal Years 2017-2019

(In Millions of US$; Latest Year Available)

Funding Category & Agency	2017 Actual	2018 Estimated[1]	2019 Proposed	Change, 2018-19 Dollar	Change, 2018-19 Percent
Total	904	929	826	−103	−11%
Federal Aviation Administration	433	439	351	−88	−20%
Federal Highway Administration	317	311	334	23	7%
Federal Motor Carrier Safety Administration	11	9	9	0	0%
Federal Railroad Adnimistration	43	43	24	−19	−44%
Federal Transit Administration	0	28	22	−6	−21%
Maritime Administration	0	1	0	−1	−100%
National Highway Traffic Safety administration	63	60	62	2	3%
Office of the Secretary	17	17	13	−4	−24%
Pipeline and Hazardous Materials Safety Administration	20	21	11	−10	−48%

Note: This table shows funding levels for Departments or Independent agencies with more than $200 million in R&D activities in 2019. Detail may not add to total because of rounding.

[1] Because an appropriation for FY 2018 was not passed by the time this chapter went to print, the chapter calculates FY 2018 estimates using an annualized version of the FY 2018 Continuing Resolution.

Source: EOP, OMB, Analytical Perspectives, Budget of the United States Government, Fiscal Year 2019

Plunkett Research, Ltd.
www.plunkettresearch.com

Federal R&D & R&D Plant Funding for Energy, U.S.: Fiscal Years 2017-2019

(In Millions of US$)

	2017 Actual	2018 Estimated[1]	2019 Proposed	Change, 2018-19 Dollar	Change, 2018-19 Percent
Total	14,896	15,006	12,685	−2,321	−15%
Fossil Energy Research and Development	399	419	292	−127	−30%
Science	5,438	5,307	4,127	−1,180	−22%
Electricity Delivery	144	144	46	−98	−68%
Nuclear Energy	764	955	754	−201	−21%
Energy Efficiency and Renewable Energy	1,445	1,492	524	−968	−65%
Advanced Research Projects Agency - Energy	306	295	0	−295	−100%
Cybersecurity, Energy Security, and Emergency Response	0	0	40	40	NA
Defense Environmental Cleanup	28	28	28	0	0%
National Nuclear Security Administration	6,357	6,351	6,859	508	8%
Power Marketing Administration	15	15	15	0	0%

Note: This table shows funding levels for Departments or Independent agencies with more than $200 million in R&D activities in 2019. Detail may not add to total because of rounding.

[1] Because an appropriation for FY 2018 was not passed by the time this chapter went to print, the chapter calculates FY 2018 estimates using an annualized version of the FY 2018 Continuing Resolution.

NA = Not Available

Source: EOP, OMB, Analytical Perspectives, Budget of the United States Government, Fiscal Year 2019

Plunkett Research, Ltd.

www.plunkettresearch.com

U.S. Department of Energy
Funding for Science & Energy Programs: 2017-2019

(In Thousands of US$)

Area of Scientific Research	FY 2017 Enacted	FY 2018 Annualized CR*	FY 2019 Congressional Request	FY 2019 Request vs FY 2017 Enacted Dollar	Percent
Energy Programs	**10,953,295**	**10,926,999**	**9,064,504**	**1,888,791**	**-17%**
Energy Efficiency and Renewable Energy	2,034,582	2,040,249	695,610	1,338,972	-66%
Sustainable transportation	612,959	608,797	163,500	-449,459	-73%
Vehicle technologies	306,959	304,874	68,500	-238,459	-78%
Bioenergy technologies	205,000	203,608	37,000	-168,000	-82%
Hydrogen and fuel cell technologies	101,000	100,315	58,000	-43,000	-43%
Renewable power	451,100	448,035	175,000	-276,100	-61%
Solar energy technologies	207,600	206,190	67,000	-140,600	-68%
Wind energy technologies	90,000	89,388	33,000	-57,000	-63%
Water power technologies	84,000	83,429	45,000	-39,000	-46%
Geothermal technologies	69,500	69,028	30,000	-39,500	-57%
Energy efficiency	761,641	756,469	142,000	-619,641	-81%
Advanced Manufacturing	257,500	255,751	75,000	-182,500	-71%
Federal energy management program	27,000	26,817	10,000	-17,000	-63%
Building Technologies	199,141	197,789	57,000	-142,141	-71%
Weatherization and intergovernmental programs	278,000	276,112	----	-278,000	-100%
Corporate support programs	264,500	262,704	215,110	-49,390	-19%
Rescission of prior year balances (Gen. Prov. EERE)	-55,618	-35,756	----	55,618	100%
Electricity Delivery and Energy Reliability	229,585	228,026	----	-229,585	-100%
Clean energy transmission and reliability	36,000	35,756	----	-36,000	-100%
Energy storage	31,000	30,790	----	-31,000	-100%
Transformer resilience and advanced components	6,000	5,959	----	-6,000	-100%
Infrastructure security and energy restoration	9,000	8,939	----	-9,000	-100%
Smart grid research and development	50,000	49,660	----	-50,000	-100%
Cybersecurity for energy delivery systems	62,000	61,579	----	-62,000	-100%
National electricity delivery	7,500	7,449	----	-7,500	-100%
Program direction	28,500	28,306	----	-28,500	-100%
Rescission of prior year balances (Gen. Prov.)	-415	-412	----	415	100%
Electricity Delivery	----	----	61,309	61,309	N/A
Cybersecurity, Energy Security, and Emergency Response	----	----	95,800	95,800	N/A
Nuclear Energy	1,015,821	1,008,922	757,090	-258,731	-26%
Fossil Energy Programs	662,261	667,882	697,175	34,914	5%
Uranium Enrichment D&D Fund	767,929	763,106	752,749	-15,180	-2%
Energy Information Administration	122,000	121,171	115,035	-6,965	-6%
Non-Defense Environmental Cleanup	246,762	245,324	218,400	-28,362	-12%
Science	5,390,972	5,354,362	5,390,972	----	N/A
Advanced Research Projects Agency - Energy.	305,245	303,172	----	-305,245	-100%
Nuclear Waste Disposal (+30M in DNWF 050)	----	----	90,000	90,000	N/A
Departmental Administration	120,692	120,009	139,534	18,842	16%
Inspector General	44,424	44,122	51,330	6,906	16%
Credit Programs	13,022	30,654	-500	-13,522	-104%

*A full-year 2018 appropriation for this account was not enacted at the time the budget was prepared; therefore, the budget assumes this account is operating under the Continuing Appropriations Act, 2018 (Division D of P.L. 115–56, as amended). The amounts included for 2018 reflect the annualized level provided by the continuing resolution.

Source: U.S. Department of Energy, Office of Science
Plunkett Research, Ltd.
www.plunkettresearch.com

U.S. National Nanotechnology Initiative (NNI) Budget: Fiscal Years 2016-2018

(In Millions of US$)

Government Agency	FY 2016 Actual	FY 2017 Estimated*	FY 2018 Proposed
Consumer Product Safety Commission (CPSC)	2.0	2.0	1.0
Department of Homeland Security (DHS)	1.0	0.8	0.7
Department of Commerce, National Institute of Standards and Technology (DOC/NIST)	82.5	82.4	65.3
Department of Defense (DOD)	149.3	144.5	139.9
Department of Energy (DOE)**	333.5	327.5	227.1
Department of the Interior, U.S. Geological Survey (DOI/USGS)	0.0	0.1	0.0
Department of Justice, National Institute of Justice (DOJ/NIJ)	1.3	1.4	1.4
Department of Transportation, Federal Highway Administration (DOT/FHWA)	1.5	0.5	1.5
Environmental Protection Agency (EPA)	13.9	10.0	4.5
Department of Health and Human Services (DHHS)	420.5	439.6	347.7
Food and Drug Administration (FDA)	11.7	11.0	10.9
National Institutes of Health (NIH)	397.7	417.5	325.7
National Institute for Occupational Safety and Health (NIOSH)	11.1	11.1	11.1
National Aeronautics & Space Administration (NASA)	13.4	12.0	6.1
National Science Foundation (NSF)	510.4	420.8	388.6
U.S. Department of Agriculture (USDA)	28.4	28.2	23.7
Agricultural Research Services (ARS)	3.0	3.0	3.0
Forest Services (FS)	6.4	7.2	3.7
National Institute of Food and Agriculture (NIFA)	19.0	18.0	17.0
Total Nanotechnology	**1,557.8**	**1,469.7**	**1,207.5**

Notes: totals may not add, due to rounding.

* 2017 numbers are based on 2017 enacted levels and may have changed under final operating plans.

** Funding levels for DOE include the combined budgets of the Office of Science, the Office of Energy Efficiency and Renewable Energy, the Office of Fossil Energy, the Office of Nuclear Energy, and the Advanced Research Projects Agency for Energy.

Source: U.S. National Nanotechnology Initiative (NNI)

Plunkett Research, ® Ltd.

www.plunkettresearch.com

Research Funding for Biological Sciences, U.S. National Science Foundation: Fiscal Years 2017-2019

(In Millions of US$)

Biological Sciences: Subactivity Area	FY 2017 Actual	FY 2018 TBD	FY 2019 Request	Change over 2017 Actual Amount	Change over 2017 Actual Percent
Molecular & Cellular Biosciences (MCB)	$137.02	--	$137.69	$0.67	0.5%
Integrative Organismal Systems (IOS)	215.63	--	184.97	-30.66	-14.2%
Environmental Biology (DEB)	145.42	--	146.16	0.74	0.5%
Biological Infrastructure (DBI)	130.35	--	175.14	44.79	34.4%
Emerging Frontiers (EF)	113.80	--	94.20	-19.60	-17.2%
Total Biological Sciences Activity	**$742.22**	--	**$738.16**	**-$4.06**	**-0.5%**

Note: Totals may not add due to rounding.

Source: U.S. National Science Foundation
Plunkett Research, Ltd.
www.plunkettresearch.com

Research Funding for Engineering, U.S. National Science Foundation: Fiscal Years 2017-2019

(In Millions of US$)

Engineering: Subactivity Area	FY 2017 Actual	FY 2018 (TBD)	FY 2019 Request	Change over 2017 Actual Amount	Change over 2017 Actual Percent
Chemical, Bioengineering, Environmental & Transport Systems (CBET)	183.54	0.00	180.00	-3.54	-1.9%
Civil, Mechanical & Manufacturing Innovation (CMMI)	221.05	0.00	216.90	-4.15	-1.9%
Electrical, Communications & Cyber Systems (ECCS)	113.78	0.00	111.60	-2.18	-1.9%
Engineering Education & Centers (EEC)	108.61	0.00	97.25	-11.36	-10.5%
Industrial Innovation & Partnerships (IIP)	250.26	0.00	248.42	-1.84	-0.7%
Emerging Frontiers and Multidisciplinary Activities (EFMA)	53.67	0.00	67.26	13.59	25.3%
Total, Engineering Activity	**930.92**	**0.00**	**921.43**	**-9.49**	**-1.0%**

Note: Totals may not add due to rounding.

Source: U.S. National Science Foundation
Plunkett Research, Ltd.
www.plunkettresearch.com

Domestic U.S. Biopharmaceutical R&D & R&D Abroad, PhRMA Member Companies: 1980-2016

(In Millions of US$; Latest Year Available)

Year	Domestic R&D	Annual % Chg.	R&D Abroad[1]	Annual % Chg.	Total R&D	Annual % Chg.
2016	52,418.2	9.0%	13,120.1	13.8%	65,538.3	9.9%
2015	48,110.5	18.1%	11,531.9	-7.9%	59,642.4	12.0%
2014	40,737.3	0.8%	12,515.9	11.6%	53,253.2	3.2%
2013	40,396.0	7.7%	11,217.6	-7.1%	51,613.6	4.1%
2012	37,510.2	3.1%	12,077.4	-1.6%	49,587.6	1.9%
2011	36,373.6	-10.6%	12,271.4	22.4%	48,645.0	-4.1%
2010	40,688.1	15.1%	10,021.7	-9.6%	50,709.8	9.2%
2009	35,356.0	-0.6%	11,085.6	-6.1%	46,441.6	-2.0%
2008	35,571.1	-2.8%	11,812.0	4.6%	47,383.1	-1.1%
2007	36,608.4	7.8%	11,294.8	25.4%	47,903.1	11.5%
2006	33,967.9	9.7%	9,005.6	1.3%	42,973.5	7.8%
2005	30,969.0	4.8%	8,888.9	19.1%	39,857.9	7.7%
2004	29,555.5	9.2%	7,462.6	1.0%	37,018.1	7.4%
2003	27,064.9	5.5%	7,388.4	37.9%	34,453.3	11.1%
2002	25,655.1	9.2%	5,357.2	-13.9%	31,012.2	4.2%
2001	23,502.0	10.0%	6,220.6	33.3%	29,772.7	14.4%
2000	21,363.7	15.7%	4,667.1	10.6%	26,030.8	14.7%
1999	18,471.1	7.4%	4,219.6	9.9%	22,690.7	8.2%
1998	17,127.9	11.0%	3,839.0	9.9%	20,966.9	10.8%
1997	15,466.0	13.9%	3,492.1	6.5%	18,958.1	12.4%
1996	13,627.1	14.8%	3,278.5	-1.6%	16,905.6	11.2%
1995	11,874.0	7.0%	3,333.5	*	15,207.4	*
1994	11,101.6	6.0%	2,347.8	3.8%	13,449.4	5.6%
1993	10,477.1	12.5%	2,262.9	5.0%	12,740.0	11.1%
1992	9,312.1	17.4%	2,155.8	21.3%	11,467.9	18.2%
1991	7,928.6	16.5%	1,776.8	9.9%	9,705.4	15.3%
1990	6,802.9	13.0%	1,617.4	23.6%	8,420.3	14.9%
1989	6,021.4	15.0%	1,308.6	0.4%	7,330.0	12.1%
1988	5,233.9	16.2%	1,303.6	30.6%	6,537.5	18.8%
1987	4,504.1	16.2%	998.1	15.4%	5,502.2	16.1%
1986	3,875.0	14.7%	865.1	23.8%	4,740.1	16.2%
1985	3,378.7	13.3%	698.9	17.2%	4,077.6	13.9%
1984	2,982.4	11.6%	596.4	9.2%	3,578.8	11.2%
1983	2,671.3	17.7%	546.3	8.2%	3,217.6	16.0%
1982	2,268.7	21.3%	505.0	7.7%	2,773.7	18.6%
1981	1,870.4	20.7%	469.1	9.7%	2,339.5	18.4%
1980	1,549.2	16.7%	427.5	42.8%	1,976.7	21.5%
Average		10.7%		10.7%		10.6%

Note: All figures include company-financed R&D only. Total values may be affected by rounding.

[1] R&D Abroad includes expenditures outside the United States by U.S.-owned PhRMA member companies, and R&D conducted abroad by the U.S. divisions of foreign-owned PhRMA member companies. R&D performed abroad by the foreign divisions of foreign-owned PhRMA member companies are excluded. Domestic R&D, however, includes R&D expenditures within the United States by all PhRMA member companies.

* R&D Abroad affected by merger and acquisition activity.

Source: Pharmaceutical Research and Manufacturers of America (PhRMA), *PhRMA Annual Membership Survey*, 2017
Plunkett Research, Ltd.
www.plunkettresearch.com

Top Foreign Countries by Number of Residents Receiving U.S. Patents: 2015

(By Utility Patents Granted; Latest Year Available)

Rank in 2015	Country*	Number of Patents in 2015	Share of All Patents in 2015 (%)
1	Japan	54,422	16.7
2	Korea, South	20,201	6.2
3	Germany	17,752	5.4
4	Taiwan	12,575	3.9
5	China	9,004	2.8
6	Canada	7,492	2.3
7	United Kingdom	7,167	2.2
8	France	7,026	2.2
9	Israel	3,804	1.2
10	India	3,415	1.0
11	Italy	3,090	0.9
12	Sweden	2,862	0.9
13	Switzerland	2,841	0.9
14	Netherlands	2,788	0.9
	United States Origin	155,982	47.9
	All Foreign Origin	169,997	52.1
	Total, U.S. and Foreign	325,979	100.0

* Notes: The country of origin is determined by the residence of the first-named inventor listed on a patent. Utility Patents (representing 90% of total U.S. patents) are issued "for the invention of a new and useful process, machine, manufacture, or composition of matter, or a new and useful improvement thereof," according to USPTO definitions. Additional categories include Design Patents (issued for a new original, and ornamental design for an article of manufacture); Plant Patents (for new or invented asexually reproduced plants and seedlings); and Reissue Patents (issued to correct errors in previously issued patents).

Source: U.S. Patent and Trademark Office (USPTO)

Plunkett Research, Ltd.

www.plunkettresearch.com

Top 30 U.S. Patent Recipient Organizations: 2016

(By Utility Patents Granted; Latest Year Available)

Rank	Patents	Organization
1	8,023	International Business Machines Corporation
2	5,504	Samsung Electronics Co., Ltd.
3	3,865	Canon Kabushiki Kaisha
4	3,414	Qualcomm, Inc.
5	3,267	Google, Inc.
6	3,118	Qualcomm, Inc.
7	2,566	General Electric Company
8	2,558	Microsoft Corporation
9	2,426	LG Electronics
10	2,261	Taiwan Semiconductor Manufacturing Co., Ltd.
11	2,168	Sony Corp.
12	2,101	Apple, Inc.
13	2,010	Samsung Display Co. Otd.
14	1,920	Toshiba Corp.
15	1,662	Amazon Technologies, Inc.
16	1,644	Seiko Epson Corporation
17	1,628	Dell Technologies
18	1,563	Fujitsu Limited
19	1,552	Telefonaktiebolaget L M Ericsson (Publ.)
20	1,540	Toyota Jidosha K.K.
21	1,530	Ford Global Technologies, L.L.C.
22	1,482	Siemens Aktiengesellschaft
23	1,441	Medtronic, Inc.
24	1,404	Ricoh Co., Ltd.
25	1,400	Panasonic Intellectual Property Management Co., Ltd.
26	1,360	Globalfoundries, Inc.
27	1,266	AT&T Corp.
28	1,198	Huawei Technologies Co., Ltd.
29	1,122	Robert Bosch GmbH
30	1,115	GM Global Technology Operations LLC

Note: Utility Patents (representing 90% of total U.S. patents) are issued "for the invention of a new and useful process, machine, manufacture, or composition of matter, or a new and useful improvement thereof," according to USPTO definitions. Additional categories include Design Patents (issued for a new original, and ornamental design for an article of manufacture); Plant Patents (for new or invented asexually reproduced plants and seedlings); and Reissue Patents (issued to correct errors in previously issued patents).

Source: U.S. Patent and Trademark Office (USPTO)

Plunkett Research, Ltd.

www.plunkettresearch.com

Major Patenting U.S. Universities: 2016
(By Utility Patents Granted During Calendar Year; Latest Year Available)

U.S. University	Patents
University of California, The Regents of	505
Massachusetts Institute of Technology	278
Stanford University	244
California Institute of Technology	201
Tsinghua University/Graduate School at Shenzhen	181
Wisconsin Alumni Research Foundation	168
Johns Hopkins University	167
University of Texas	162
University of Michigan	142
Columbia University	118
University of South Florida	114
Purdue Research Foundation	105
Cornell University/Cornell Research Foundation, Inc.	105
Harvard College, President and Fellows	104
Korea Institute of Science and Technology	100
New York University/Polytechnic Institute of New York University	93
University of Pennsylvania	92
University of Illinois	91
University of Florida Research Foundation, Inc.	91
King Fahd University of Petroleum and Minerals	90
Rutgers University	84
University of Washington	83
Northwestern University	81
University of Chicago/UChicago Argonne LLC	81
National Tsing Hua University	80
Korea Advanced Institute of Science and Technology	77
University of Maryland	72
University of Pittsburgh	72
National Taiwan University/National Taiwan University Hospital	65
Arizona State University	64
University of Utah Research Foundation/University of Utah	64
Georgia Tech Research Corp.	63
Duke University	60
Science & Technology Corp. at University of New Mexico	60
University of North Carolina	60
King Suad University	58
University of Massachusetts	58
Industry-Academic Cooperation at Yonsei University	57
Research Foundation of State University of New York	57

Notes: Only those universities with 40 or more patents are listed. Utility Patents (representing 90% of total U.S. patents) are issued "for the invention of a new and useful process, machine, manufacture, or composition of matter, or a new and useful improvement thereof," according to USPTO definitions. Additional categories include Design Patents (issued for a new original, and ornamental design for an article of manufacture); Plant Patents (for new or invented asexually reproduced plants and seedlings); and Reissue Patents (issued to correct errors in previously issued patents).

Source: U.S. Patent and Trademark Office (USPTO)
Plunkett Research, Ltd.
www.plunkettresearch.com

The U.S. Drug Discovery & Approval Process

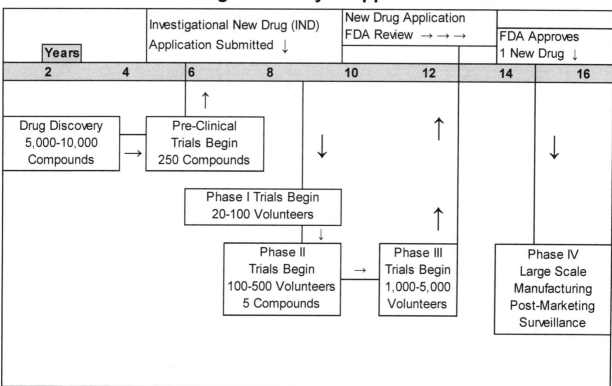

Note: The actual length of the development process varies. On average, it takes at least 10 years and an estimated $2.6 billion to create a successful new medicine (in 2013 dollars). Less than 12% of the candidate medicines that make it into phase I clinical trials will be approved by the FDA.

Source: Pharmaceutical Research and Manufacturers Association (PhRMA)
Plunkett Research, ® Ltd.
www.plunkettresearch.com

Employment in Engineering Occupations by Business Type, U.S.: 2014-February 2018

NAICS[1]	Industry Sector	2014	2015	2016	2017	Feb-18[P]
Number of Employed Workers *(Annual Estimates in Thousands of Employed Workers)*							
5413	Architectural and engineering services	1,375.2	1,400.6	1,403.7	1,435.2	1,443.7
54133,4	Engineering and drafting services	926.7	942.9	943.6	965.0	970.4
54138	Testing laboratories	165.8	163.5	164.1	166.0	165.1
5417	Scientific research and development services	636.0	659.1	667.9	659.8	665.3
54171	Physical, engineering and life sciences R&D	576.1	598.8	607.0	594.1	599.1
541713	Research and development in nanotechnology	22.2	23.1	23.0	21.6	22.5
541714	Research and development in biotechnology, except nanobiotechnology	140.2	150.1	164.7	176.8	180.2
541715	Research and development in the physical, engineering, and life sciences, except nanotechnology and biotechnology	413.7	425.5	419.2	395.7	396.4

Engineering Employment & Wage Estimates: May 2017 *(Wage & Salary in US$; Latest Year Available)*	Employment[2]	Median Hourly Wage	Mean Hourly Wage	Mean Annual Salary[3]	Mean Wage RSE[4] (%)
Aerospace Engineers	65,760	$54.34	$55.43	$115,300	0.7%
Agricultural Engineers	1,770	$35.95	$37.49	$77,970	1.2%
Biomedical Engineers	20,100	$42.33	$44.70	$92,970	1.0%
Chemical Engineers	33,500	$49.12	$54.05	$112,430	1.5%
Civil Engineers	298,910	$40.75	$44.13	$91,790	0.4%
Computer Hardware Engineers	66,770	$55.35	$57.52	$119,650	1.4%
Electrical Engineers	183,370	$45.70	$47.87	$99,580	0.4%
Electronics Engineers, Except Computer	134,930	$49.13	$51.33	$106,760	0.7%
Environmental Engineers	52,640	$41.73	$43.83	$91,180	0.7%
Health and Safety Engineers, Except Mining Safety Engineers and Inspectors	26,130	$42.55	$44.32	$92,190	0.6%
Industrial Engineers	265,520	$41.29	$43.43	$90,340	0.4%
Marine Engineers and Naval Architects	10,960	$43.74	$46.59	$96,910	1.5%
Materials Engineers	27,200	$45.48	$47.41	$98,610	1.3%
Mechanical Engineers	291,290	$41.29	$43.99	$91,500	0.4%
Mining and Geological Engineers, Including Mining Safety Engineers	6,150	$45.31	$49.86	$103,710	2.4%
Nuclear Engineers	16,700	$50.87	$52.36	$108,910	1.5%
Petroleum Engineers	32,010	$63.60	$74.41	$154,780	2.4%
Engineers, All Other	131,500	$46.75	$47.74	$99,310	0.4%
Architectural and Civil Drafters	95,960	$25.42	$26.50	$55,110	0.4%
Electrical and Electronics Drafters	26,060	$28.70	$30.64	$63,720	1.0%
Mechanical Drafters	58,190	$26.50	$27.96	$58,150	0.8%
Drafters, All Other	15,300	$24.18	$25.96	$53,990	1.3%
Aerospace Engineering and Operations Technicians	11,710	$32.33	$34.30	$71,340	3.8%
Civil Engineering Technicians	71,430	$24.82	$25.77	$53,600	0.5%
Electrical and Electronics Engineering Technicians	128,320	$30.60	$30.91	$64,290	0.4%
Electro-Mechanical Technicians	13,050	$27.28	$28.60	$59,490	1.0%
Environmental Engineering Technicians	17,590	$24.15	$25.77	$53,610	1.0%
Industrial Engineering Technicians	65,020	$26.10	$27.79	$57,810	0.9%
Mechanical Engineering Technicians	43,390	$26.62	$27.97	$58,180	0.8%
Engineering Technicians, Except Drafters, All Other	76,630	$29.92	$31.03	$64,550	0.8%
Surveying and Mapping Technicians	51,890	$20.84	$22.28	$46,350	0.6%

[1] For a full description of the NAICS codes used in this table, see www.census.gov/eos/www/naics/.
[2] Estimates for detailed occupations do not sum to the totals because the totals include occupations not shown separately. Estimates do not include self-employed workers.
[3] Annual wages have been calculated by multiplying the hourly mean wage by a "year-round, full-time" hours figure of 2,080 hours; for those occupations where there is not an hourly mean wage published, the annual wage has been directly calculated from the reported survey data.
[4] The relative standard error (RSE) is a measure of the reliability of a survey statistic. The smaller the relative standard error, the more precise the estimate.
P = Preliminary Estimate.

Source: U.S. Bureau of Labor Statistics
Plunkett Research, Ltd.
www.plunkettresearch.com

Employment in Life & Physical Science Occupations by Business Type, U.S.: May 2017

(Wage & Salary in US$; Latest Year Available)	Employment[1]	Median Hourly Wage	Mean Hourly Wage	Mean Annual Salary[2]	Mean Wage RSE[3] (%)
Life, Physical, and Social Science Occupations	1,148,300	$31.01	$35.76	$74,370	0.4%
Life Scientists	292,310	$35.43	$40.80	$84,860	0.9%
Agricultural and Food Scientists	31,750	$30.25	$33.88	$70,480	1.1%
Animal Scientists	2,550	$29.21	$33.10	$68,840	2.4%
Food Scientists and Technologists	15,020	$30.60	$34.61	$71,990	2.1%
Soil and Plant Scientists	14,180	$30.01	$33.26	$69,170	1.3%
Biological Scientists	104,550	$36.04	$40.41	$84,060	1.4%
Biochemists and Biophysicists	27,380	$43.84	$50.68	$105,410	3.8%
Microbiologists	21,870	$33.64	$37.69	$78,400	2.4%
Zoologists and Wildlife Biologists	17,710	$29.95	$31.85	$66,250	0.6%
Biological Scientists, All Other	37,590	$36.87	$38.56	$80,200	1.3%
Conservation Scientists	22,040	$29.56	$31.18	$64,850	0.8%
Foresters	8,300	$28.90	$29.67	$61,710	0.5%
Medical Scientists	118,560	$38.93	$45.64	$94,920	1.5%
Epidemiologists	6,870	$33.49	$36.65	$76,230	1.6%
Medical Scientists, Except Epidemiologists	111,690	$39.46	$46.19	$96,070	1.5%
Life Scientists, All Other	7,120	$35.84	$39.55	$82,270	2.1%
Physical Scientists	253,660	$37.88	$42.53	$88,470	0.6%
Astronomers	2,020	$48.36	$52.67	$109,560	3.0%
Physicists	16,710	$57.13	$59.17	$123,080	1.5%
Atmospheric and Space Scientists	8,940	$44.27	$45.05	$93,710	1.1%
Chemists	84,400	$35.94	$39.36	$81,870	0.9%
Materials Scientists	7,470	$47.85	$48.99	$101,910	1.5%
Environmental Scientists and Specialists, Including Health	81,920	$33.37	$36.64	$76,220	0.8%
Geoscientists, Except Hydrologists and Geographers	28,520	$43.20	$50.88	$105,830	1.5%
Hydrologists	6,350	$38.46	$40.53	$84,290	1.1%
Physical Scientists, All Other	17,320	$49.99	$51.53	$107,180	1.4%
Life, Physical, and Social Science Technicians	359,180	$22.01	$24.02	$49,970	0.4%
Agricultural and Food Science Technicians	21,120	$19.19	$20.63	$42,910	1.0%
Biological Technicians	74,980	$21.06	$22.79	$47,410	0.6%
Chemical Technicians	64,550	$22.73	$24.52	$51,010	0.9%
Geological and Petroleum Technicians	14,820	$26.05	$30.50	$63,450	2.8%
Nuclear Technicians	6,850	$38.64	$38.46	$80,000	1.6%
Miscellaneous Life, Physical, and Social Science Technicians	145,360	$21.97	$23.69	$49,270	0.5%
Environmental Science and Protection Technicians, Including Health	32,840	$21.87	$23.71	$49,310	0.8%
Forensic Science Technicians	15,070	$27.81	$29.43	$61,220	0.9%
Forest and Conservation Technicians	30,570	$17.37	$18.84	$39,180	0.3%
Life, Physical, and Social Science Technicians, All Other	66,890	$23.12	$24.60	$51,160	0.7%

[1] Estimates for detailed occupations do not sum to the totals because the totals include occupations not shown separately. Estimates do not include self-employed workers.
[2] Annual wages have been calculated by multiplying the hourly mean wage by a "year-round, full-time" hours figure of 2,080 hours; for those occupations where there is not an hourly mean wage published, the annual wage has been directly calculated from the reported survey data.
[3] The relative standard error (RSE) is a measure of the reliability of a survey statistic. The smaller the relative standard error, the more precise the estimate.

Source: U.S. Bureau of Labor Statistics
Plunkett Research, Ltd.
www.plunkettresearch.com

Chapter 3

IMPORTANT ENGINEERING & RESEARCH INDUSTRY CONTACTS

Addresses, Telephone Numbers and Internet Sites

Contents:

1) Aerospace & Defense Industry Associations
2) Aerospace Resources
3) Artificial Intelligence Associations
4) Automotive Industry Associations
5) Automotive Industry Resources
6) Automotive Parts, Repair & Supplies Associations
7) Automotive Safety
8) Biology-Synthetic
9) Biotechnology & Biological Industry Associations
10) Biotechnology Resources
11) Brazilian Government Agencies-Scientific
12) Business Model Resources
13) Canadian Government Agencies-Communications
14) Canadian Government Agencies-Defense
15) Canadian Government Agencies-General
16) Canadian Government Agencies-Scientific
17) Careers-Computers/Technology
18) Careers-First Time Jobs/New Grads
19) Careers-General Job Listings
20) Careers-Job Reference Tools
21) Careers-Science
22) Chemicals Industry Associations
23) Chinese Government Agencies-Science & Technology
24) Computer & Electronics Industry Associations
25) Computer & Electronics Industry Resources
26) Computer-Aided Engineering Resources
27) Construction Industry Resources & Associations
28) Corporate Information Resources
29) Design & Architectural Associations
30) Drone Associations
31) Economic Data & Research
32) Energy Associations-China, General
33) Energy Associations-Natural Gas
34) Energy Associations-Nuclear
35) Energy Associations-Oil Field Services/Drilling
36) Energy Associations-Petroleum, Exploration, Production, etc.
37) Engineering Indices
38) Engineering Industry Associations
39) Engineering Industry Resource
40) Engineering, Research & Scientific Associations
41) Environmental Organizations
42) Environmental Resources
43) Food Industry Associations, General
44) Geoengineering
45) Health Care Business & Professional Associations
46) Industry Research/Market Research
47) Internet Industry Associations
48) Internet Industry Resources
49) Manufacturing Associations-Machinery & Technology
50) Maritime Associations
51) Metals & Steel Industry Associations
52) Nanotechnology Associations
53) Nanotechnology Resources
54) Patent Organizations

55) Patent Resources
56) Plastics Industry Associations
57) Research & Development, Laboratories
58) RFID Industry Associations
59) Road & Highway Construction Industry Associations
60) Robotics & Automation Industry Associations
61) Satellite-Related Professional Organizations
62) Science & Technology Resources
63) Science Parks
64) Software Industry Associations
65) Software Industry Resources
66) Supercomputing
67) Sustainable Transportation
68) Technology Transfer Associations
69) Telecommunications Industry Associations
70) Telecommunications Resources
71) Temporary Staffing Firms
72) Trade Associations-General
73) Trade Associations-Global
74) Transportation Industry Resources
75) U.S. Government Agencies
76) Wireless & Cellular Industry Associations

1) **Aerospace & Defense Industry Associations**

Aerospace Industries Association
1000 Wilson Blvd., Ste. 1700
Arlington, VA 22209-3928 US
Phone: 703-358-1000
E-mail Address: *globalcustomerservice@ihs.com*
Web Address: www.aia-aerospace.org
The Aerospace Industries Association represents the nation's leading manufacturers and suppliers of civil, military, and business aircraft, helicopters, unmanned aerial vehicles, space systems, aircraft engines, missiles, materiel, and related components, equipment, services, and information technology.

Aerospace Industries Association of Canada (AIAC)
255 Albert St., Ste. 703
Ottawa, ON K1P 6A9 Canada
Phone: 613-232-4297
Web Address: www.aiac.ca
The Aerospace Industries Association of Canada (AIAC) is the national trade organization of Canada's aerospace manufacturing and service sector.

American Institute of Aeronautics and Astronautics (AIAA)
12700 Sunrise Valley Dr., Ste. 200
Reston, VA 20191-5807 USA
Phone: 703-264-7500
Fax: 703-264-7551
Toll Free: 800-639-2422
E-mail Address: custserv@aiaa.org
Web Address: www.aiaa.org
The American Institute of Aeronautics and Astronautics (AIAA) is a nonprofit society aimed at advancing the arts, sciences and technology of aeronautics and astronautics. The institute represents the U.S. in the International Astronautical Federation and the International Council on the Aeronautical Sciences.

China National Space Administration
8A Fuchenglu
Beijing, 100037 China
Phone: 86-10-88581377
Fax: 86-10-88581515
E-mail Address: webmaster@cnsa.gov.cn
Web Address: www.cnsa.gov.cn
The China National Space Administration is the governmental agency representing China in the space science, technology and the aerospace industry.

Council of Defense & Space Industry Associations (CODSIA)
1000 Wilson Blvd., Ste. 1800
Arlington, VA 22209 USA
Phone: 703-243-2020
Fax: 703-243-8539
E-mail Address: info@codsia.org
Web Address: www.codsia.org
The Council of Defense and Space Industry Associations (CODSIA) provides a central channel of communications for improving industry-wide consideration of the many policies, regulations, implementation problems, procedures and questions involved in federal procurement actions.

Defense MicroElectronics Activity (DMEA)
4234 54th St.
McClellan, CA 95652-2100 USA
Phone: 916-231-1555
Fax: 916-231-2855
Web Address: www.dmea.osd.mil
Defense MicroElectronics Activity (DMEA) was established by the Department of Defense to provide a broad spectrum of microelectronics services.

Federal Association of German Aerospace Industry (BDLI)
Bundesverband der Deutschen Luft- und Raumfahrtindustrie eV (BDLI)
ATRIUM Friedrichstrasse 60
Berlin, D-10117 Germany
Phone: 49-30-2061-40-0
Fax: 49-30-2061-40-90
E-mail Address: kontakt@bdli.de
Web Address: www.bdli.de
The German Aerospace Industries Association (BDLI) represents the German aviation and aerospace industry at the national and international levels.

Institute for Aerospace Research (IAR)
5145 Decelles Ave.
Montreal, QC H3T 2B2 Canada
Phone: 613-990-0765
Fax: 613-952-9907
E-mail Address: Matthew.Tobin@nrc-cnrc.gc.ca
Web Address: www.ic.gc.ca/eic/site/054.nsf/eng/00097.html
The Institute for Aerospace Research (IAR) is a branch of Canada's National Research Council that focuses its research and development activities on design, manufacture, performance, use and safety of air and space vehicles.

National Defense Industrial Association (NDIA)
2111 Wilson Blvd., Ste. 400
Arlington, VA 22201 USA
Phone: 703-522-1820
Fax: 703-522-1885
E-mail Address: trice@ndia.org
Web Address: www.ndia.org
The National Defense Industrial Association (NDIA), an association with more than 47,000 individuals as well as 1,375 corporate members, is dedicated to discussing defense industry concerns and promoting national security.

Washington Space Business Roundtable (WSBR)
1651 Old Meadow Rd., Ste. 500
c/o Sage Communications, LLC
McLean, VA 22102 USA
Phone: 703-584-5647
Fax: 703-564-5647
E-mail Address: info@wsbr.org
Web Address: www.wsbr.org
Washington Space Business Roundtable (WSBR) is a non-profit, membership-based group that acts as a leadership forum for the promotion of commercial space business and education in Washington D.C. and the surrounding area.

2) Aerospace Resources

Defense Science Technology Lab (DSTL)
Porton Down
Salisbury, Wiltshire SP4 0JQ UK
Phone: 44-1980-613000
Fax: 44-1980-613004
E-mail Address: centralenquiries@dstl.gov.uk
Web Address: www.dstl.gov.uk
Defense Science Technology Lab (DSTL) supplies scientific research and advice to the Ministry of Defense (MOD) and other government departments.

NASA Learning Technologies Project (LTP)
NASA Headquarters, Ste. 2R40
Washington, DC 20546 USA
Phone: 301-286-1112
E-mail Address: daniel.laughlin@gsfc.nasa.gov
Web Address: www.nasa.gov/offices/education/programs/national/ltp/home/index.html
The NASA Learning Technologies Project (LTP) is the space association's educational technology research and development division.

Space Foundation
4425 Arrowswest Dr.
Colorado Springs, CO 80907 USA
Phone: 719-576-8000
Toll Free: 800-691-4000
E-mail Address: Media@SpaceFoundation.org
Web Address: www.spacefoundation.org
Space Foundation represents the global space community. The Space Foundation is a nonprofit organization supporting space activities, professionals and education.

3) Artificial Intelligence Associations

Allen Institute for Artificial Intelligence (AI2)
2157 N. Northlake Way, Ste. 110
Seattle, WA 98103 USA
Phone: 206-548-5600
E-mail Address: ai2-info@allenai.org
Web Address: allenai.org
AI2 was founded in 2014 with the singular focus of conducting high-impact research and engineering in the field of artificial intelligence, all for the common good. AI2 is the creation of Paul Allen, Microsoft co-founder, and is led by Dr. Oren Etzioni, a world-renowned researcher and professor in the field of AI and computer science. Situated on the shores of Lake Union, AI2 employs over 40 of the world's best scientific talent in the field of AI, attracting individuals of varied interests and backgrounds from across the globe. AI2 prides itself on the diversity and collaboration of its team, and takes a results-oriented approach to complex challenges in AI.

Neural Information Processing System Foundation, Inc. (NIPS)
Web Address: https://nips.cc
NIPS is a leading organization gathering leaders from academia and the corporate world together for a highly regarded annual conference on artificial intelligence (AI), machine learning and related topics.

OpenAI
E-mail Address: info@openai.com
Web Address: www.openai.com
Near the end of 2015, a group of well-known Silicon Valley investors, including Elon Musk and Peter Thiel, announced a long term commitment to raise funds of as much a $1 billion for a new organization to be known as OpenAI, www.openai.com. OpenAI is a nonprofit group.

4) Automotive Industry Associations

Alliance of Automobile Manufacturers
803 7th St. NW, Ste. 300
Washington, DC 20001 USA
Phone: 202-326-5500
Fax: 202-326-5598
E-mail Address: info@autoalliance.org
Web Address: www.autoalliance.org
The Alliance of Automobile Manufacturers is a trade association composed of 9 car manufacturing companies including BMW Group, DaimlerChrysler, Ford Motor Company, General Motors, Mazda, Mitsubishi Motors, Porsche, Toyota and Volkswagen. Alliance members account for more than 90% of vehicles sold in the U.S.

Association of Global Automakers (Global Automakers)
1050 K St. NW, Ste. 650
Washington, DC 20001 USA
Phone: 202-650-5555
E-mail Address: info@globalautomakers.org
Web Address: www.globalautomakers.org
The Association of Global Automakers (Global Automakers), formerly the Association of International Automobile Manufacturers, Inc., is a trade association representing 14 international motor vehicle

manufacturers. Members concentrate on improving the safety and efficiency of vehicles, as well as investing in American communities.

Canadian Transportation Equipment Association (CTEA)
16 Barrie Blvd., Unit 3B
St. Thomas, ON N5P 4B9 Canada
Phone: 519-631-0414
Fax: 519-631-1333
E-mail Address: ccowell@atminc.on.ca
Web Address: www.ctea.ca
The Canadian Transportation Equipment Association (CTEA) standardizes the commercial vehicle equipment manufacturing industry in Canada.

Canadian Vehicle Manufacturers' Association (CVMA)
170 Attwell Dr., Ste. 400
Toronto, ON M9W 5Z5 Canada
Phone: 416-364-9333
Fax: 416-367-3221
Toll Free: 800-758-7122
E-mail Address: info@cvma.ca
Web Address: www.cvma.ca
The Canadian Vehicle Manufacturers' Association (CVMA) is the industry organization representing manufacturers of light and heavy duty motor vehicles in Canada. Association members collaborate to solve industry objectives in the way of consumer protection, the environment and vehicle safety.

United States Council for Automotive Research Inc. (USCAR)
1000 Town Center Dr., Ste. 300
Southfield, MI 48075 USA
Phone: 248-223-9000
E-mail Address: sbairley@uscar.org
Web Address: www.uscar.org
The United States Council for Automotive Research (USCAR) was founded in 1992. Its goal is to further strengthen the technology base of the U.S. auto industry through cooperative research and development. Its main focus is to create, support and direct U.S. cooperative research and development to advance automotive technologies. USCAR is composed of a number of specialized groups that focus on specific research areas. USCAR is governed by the three-member USCAR Council, whose membership includes the R&D vice presidents from each of the U.S. automakers.

5) Automotive Industry Resources

Automotive Center
1800 Crooks Rd.
Troy, MI 48084 USA
Phone: 248-244-8920
Web Address: www.plastics-car.com
The Automotive Center, sponsored by the American Chemistry Council's Plastics Division, strives to provide the automobile designer, stylist or engineer with up-to-the-minute research and information on plastics applications in cars.

6) Automotive Parts, Repair & Supplies Associations

Motor & Equipment Manufacturers Association (MEMA)
10 Laboratory Dr.
Research Triangle Park, NC 27709-3966 USA
Phone: 919-549-4800
Fax: 919-406-1465
E-mail Address: info@mema.org
Web Address: www.mema.org
The Motor & Equipment Manufacturers Association (MEMA) exclusively represents and serves manufacturers of motor vehicle components, tools and equipment, automotive chemicals and related products used in the production, repair and maintenance of all classes of motor vehicles.

Truck and Engine Manufacturers Association (EMA)
333 West Wacker Dr., Ste. 810
Chicago, IL 60606 USA
Phone: 312-929-1970
Fax: 312-929-1975
E-mail Address: ema@emamail.org
Web Address: www.truckandenginemanufacturers.org
The Truck and Engine Manufacturers Association (EMA) is the voice of the engine manufacturing and on-highway medium- and heavy-duty truck industries on domestic and international public policy, as well as regulatory and technical issues.

7) Automotive Safety

American Traffic Safety Services Institute (The) (ATSSA)
15 Riverside Pkwy., Ste. 100
Fredericksburg, VA 22406-1077 USA
Phone: 540-368-1701
Fax: 540-368-1717
Toll Free: 800-272-8772
E-mail Address: communications@atssa.com
Web Address: www.atssa.com
The American Traffic Safety Services Institute (ATSSA) is an international trade association whose members provide pavement markings, signage, work zone traffic control devices and other safety features on our nation's roadways.

8) Biology-Synthetic

SyntheticBiology.org
Web Address: syntheticbiology.org
Synthetic Biology is a consortium of individuals, labs and groups working together to advance the development of biological engineering. Its members include 37 labs from 22 different universities, including MIT, Cambridge and Harvard. Synthetic Biology does not maintain a headquarters, instead allowing members to update and edit the web site in order to disseminate knowledge.

9) Biotechnology & Biological Industry Associations

Biomedical Engineering Society (BMES)
8201 Corporate Dr., Ste. 1125
Landover, MD 20785-2224 USA
Phone: 301-459-1999
Fax: 301-459-2444
Toll Free: 877-871-2637
Web Address: www.bmes.org

The Biomedical Engineering Society (BMES) supports and advances the use of engineering and technology for human health and well being. It promotes the development of professionals in the biomedical engineering and bioengineering industry.

Biomedical Engineering Society of India
c/o Department of Biomedical Engineering
Manipal Insatiate of Technology
Manipal, Karnataka 576 104 India
Phone: 91-820-2924-214
Fax: 91-820-2571-071
E-mail Address: gm.bairy@manipal.edu
Web Address: www.bmesi.org.in
The Biomedical Engineering Society of India is an all India association which seeks to advance interdisciplinary cooperation among scientists, engineers, and medical doctors for the growth of teaching, research and practices of biomedical engineering.

Biotechnology Industry Organization (BIO)
1201 Maryland Ave. SW, Ste. 900
Washington, DC 20024 USA
Phone: 202-962-9200
Fax: 202-488-6301
E-mail Address: info@bio.org
Web Address: www.bio.org
The Biotechnology Industry Organization (BIO) represents members involved in the research and development of health care, agricultural, industrial and environmental biotechnology products. BIO has both small and large member organizations.

Society for Industrial Microbiology and Biotechnology (SIMB)
3929 Old Lee Hwy., Ste. 92A
Fairfax, VA 22030-2421 USA
Phone: 703-691-3357
Fax: 703-691-7991
Web Address: www.simhq.org
The Society for Industrial Microbiology and Biotechnology (SIMB) is a nonprofit professional association that works for the advancement of microbiological sciences as they apply to industrial products, biotechnology, materials and processes.

10) Biotechnology Resources

Bioengineering Industry Links
210 S. 33rd St., Rm. 240 Skirkanich Hall
UPenn, Dept. of Bioengineering, School of Eng. & Applied Science
Philadelphia, PA 19104-6321 USA
Phone: 215-898-8501
Fax: 215-573-2071
Web Address: www.seas.upenn.edu/be/misc/bmelink/cell.html
Bioengineering Industry Links is a web site provided by the University of Pennsylvania's Department of Bioengineering. This site features links to companies involved in cell and tissue engineering.

Centre for Cellular and Molecular Biology (CCMB)
Habsiguda, Uppal Rd.
Hyderabad, Telangana 500007 India
Phone: 91-40-2716-0222-31
Fax: 91-040-2716-0591
Web Address: www.ccmb.res.in
Centre for Cellular and Molecular Biology (CCMB) is one of the constituent Indian national laboratories of the Council of Scientific and Industrial Research (CSIR), a multidisciplinary research and development organization of the Government of India. CCMB's research is focused on seven areas: Biomedicine and Biotechnology; Genetics, Evolution and Genomics; Cell Biology and Development; Molecular and Structural Biology; Biochemistry and Biophysics; Infectious Diseases; and Computational Biology and Bioinformatics.

Institute for Cellular and Molecular Biology (ICMB)
Moffett Molecular Biology Bldg.
2500 Speedway, A4800
Austin, TX 78712 USA
Phone: 512-471-1156
Fax: 512-471-2149
E-mail Address: icmb@austin.utexas.edu
Web Address: www.icmb.utexas.edu
The Institute for Cellular and Molecular Biology (ICMB) web site offers a comprehensive dictionary of biotech terms, plus extensive research data regarding biotechnology. ICMB is located in The Louise and James Robert Moffett Molecular Biology Building at the University of Texas at Austin.

11) Brazilian Government Agencies-Scientific

National Council for Scientific & Technological Development
SHIS QI 1 Conjunto B - Blocos A, B, C & D
Edificio Santos Dumont
Brasilia, DF 71605-001 Brazil
Toll Free: 800-61-96-97
Web Address: www.cnpq.br
The National Council for Scientific & Technological Development (Conselho Nacional de Desenvolvimento Cientifico e Tecnologico, or CNPq) is a Brazilian government agency affiliated with the country's Ministry of Science and Technology. CNPq works to promote scientific and technological research in Brazil through grants and other support services. The organization also seeks to encourage the development of Brazilian scientists and researchers through the awarding of scholarships and fellowships to students in the sciences.

12) Business Model Resources

Fraunhofer Institute for Industrial Engineering & Organization
Nobelstrasse 12
Stuttgart, 70569 Germany
Phone: 49-711-970-01
Web Address: www.iao.fraunhofer.de/lang-en/
The Fraunhofer Institute for Industrial Engineering & Organization assists companies and institutions in introducing new business models and efficient processes in Germany. Clients range from major corporations and SMEs to public sector bodies and institutions.

13) Canadian Government Agencies-Communications

Canadian Radio-Television and Telecommunications Commission (CRTC)
Les Terrasses de la Chaudiere, Central Bldg.
1 Promenade du Portage
Gatineau, QC J8X 4B1 Canada
Phone: 819-997-0313
Fax: 819-994-0218
Toll Free: 877-249-2782
Web Address: www.crtc.gc.ca
The Canadian Radio-Television and Telecommunications Commission (CRTC) is the government agency responsible for the regulation of the Canadian broadcasting and telecommunications industries.

14) Canadian Government Agencies-Defense

Defense Research & Development Canada (DRDC)
101 Colonel By Dr., National Defense HQ.
Major-Gen. George R. Pearkes Bldg.
Ottawa, ON K1A 0K2 Canada
Phone: 613-995-2534
Toll Free: 888-995-2534
E-mail Address: information@forces.gc.ca
Web Address: www.drdc-rddc.gc.ca
The Defense Research & Development Canada (DRDC) is a branch of the Canadian Department of National Defense responsible for the technological and scientific R&D for the Canadian defense forces.

15) Canadian Government Agencies-General

Infrastructure Canada
180 Kent St., Ste. 1100
Ottawa, ON K1P 0B6 Canada
Phone: 613-948-1148
Toll Free: 877-250-7154
E-mail Address: info.infc.info@canada.ca
Web Address: www.infrastructure.gc.ca
Infrastructure Canada works with Transport Canada and sixteen crown corporations to coordinate federal projects that focus on cities and communities, as well as supports infrastructure improvement nationwide.

16) Canadian Government Agencies-Scientific

National Research Council of Canada's Herzberg Institute of Astronomy and Astrophysics (NRC-HIA)
5071 W. Saanich Rd.
Victoria, BC V9E 2E7 Canada
Phone: 250-363-0001
E-mail Address: Kevin.Farris@nrc-cnrc.gc.ca
Web Address: www.nrc-cnrc.gc.ca/eng/rd/nsi/
The National Research Council of Canada's Herzberg Institute of Astronomy and Astrophysic (NRC-Herzberg) operates Canada's national observatories, national astronomy data center and develops advanced astronomical instruments through industrial partnerships. In addition, it operates three research programs, Astronomy Technology Program (ATP), Optical Astronomy Program (OAP) and Radio Astronomy Program (RAP).

National Science Library
1200 Montreal Rd.
Ottawa, ON K1A 0R6 Canada
Phone: 613-998-8544
Fax: 613-998-2399
Toll Free: 800-668-1222
Web Address: http://nsl-bsn.nrc-cnrc.gc.ca/eng/home
The National Science Library, a division of National Research Council Canada is one of the largest information source service organizations in the world, with particular emphasis on the scientific and technical sectors.

17) Careers-Computers/Technology

ComputerJobs.com, Inc.
1995 N. Park Pl., Ste. 375
Atlanta, GA 30339 USA
Toll Free: 800-850-0045
Web Address: www.computerjobs.com
ComputerJobs.com, Inc. is an employment web site that offers users a links to computer-related job opportunities organized by skill and market.

Dice.com
12150 Meredith Dr.
Urbandale, IA 50323 USA
Phone: 515-280-1144
Fax: 515-280-1452
Toll Free: 888-321-3423
E-mail Address: techsupport@dice.com
Web Address: www.dice.com
Dice.com provides free employment services for IT jobs. The site includes advanced job searches by geographic location and category, availability announcements and resume postings, as well as employer profiles, a recruiter's page and career links. It is maintained by Dice Holdings, Inc., a publicly traded company.

Institute for Electrical and Electronics Engineers (IEEE) Job Site
445 Hoes Ln.
Piscataway, NJ 08855-1331 USA
Phone: 732-981-0060
Toll Free: 800-678-4333
E-mail Address: candidatejobsite@ieee.org
Web Address: careers.ieee.org
The Institute for Electrical and Electronics Engineers (IEEE) Job Site provides a host of employment services for technical professionals, employers and recruiters. The site offers job listings by geographic area, a resume bank and links to employment services.

Pencom Systems, Inc.
152 Remsen St.
Brooklyn, NY 11201 USA
Phone: 718-923-1111
Fax: 718-923-6065
E-mail Address: tom@pencom.com
Web Address: www.pencom.com
Pencom Systems, Inc., an open system recruiting company, hosts a career web site geared toward high-technology and scientific professionals, featuring an interactive

Plunkett Research, Ltd.

salary survey, career advisor, job listings and technology resources. Its focus is the financial services industry within the New York City area.

18) Careers-First Time Jobs/New Grads

Alumni-Network Recruitment Corporation
Alumni-Network Recruitment Corporation
Oakville, ON Canada
Phone: 905-465-2547
E-mail Address: karen@alumni-network.com
Web Address: www.alumni-network.com
Alumni-Network Recruitment Corporation is a professional search and recruiting firm, specializing in ERP, E-Commerce and Engineering.

CollegeGrad.com, Inc.
950 Tower Ln., Fl. 6
Foster City, CA 94404 USA
E-mail Address: info@quinstreet.com
Web Address: www.collegegrad.com
CollegeGrad.com, Inc. offers in-depth resources for college students and recent grads seeking entry-level jobs.

MonsterCollege
444 N. Michigan Ave., Ste. 600
Chicago, IL 60611 USA
E-mail Address: info@college.monster.com
Web Address: www.college.monster.com
MonsterCollege provides information about internships and entry-level jobs, as well as career advice and resume tips, to recent college graduates.

National Association of Colleges and Employers (NACE)
62 Highland Ave.
Bethlehem, PA 18017-9085 USA
Phone: 610-868-1421
E-mail Address: customer_service@naceweb.org
Web Address: www.naceweb.org
The National Association of Colleges and Employers (NACE) is a premier U.S. organization representing college placement offices and corporate recruiters who focus on hiring new grads.

19) Careers-General Job Listings

CareerBuilder, Inc.
200 N La Salle St., Ste. 1100
Chicago, IL 60601 USA
Phone: 773-527-3600
Fax: 773-353-2452
Toll Free: 800-891-8880
Web Address: www.careerbuilder.com
CareerBuilder, Inc. focuses on the needs of companies and also provides a database of job openings. The site has over 1 million jobs posted by 300,000 employers, and receives an average 23 million unique visitors monthly. The company also operates online career centers for 140 newspapers and 9,000 online partners. Resumes are sent directly to the company, and applicants can set up a special e-mail account for job-seeking purposes. CareerBuilder is primarily a joint venture between three newspaper giants: The McClatchy Company, Gannett Co., Inc. and Tribune Company.

CareerOneStop
Toll Free: 877-872-5627
E-mail Address: info@careeronestop.org
Web Address: www.careeronestop.org
CareerOneStop is operated by the employment commissions of various state agencies. It contains job listings in both the private and government sectors, as well as a wide variety of useful career resources and workforce information. CareerOneStop is sponsored by the U.S. Department of Labor.

LaborMarketInfo (LMI)
Employment Development Dept.
P.O. Box 826880, MIC 57
Sacramento, CA 94280-0001 USA
Phone: 916-262-2162
Fax: 916-262-2352
Web Address: www.labormarketinfo.edd.ca.gov
LaborMarketInfo (LMI) provides job seekers and employers a wide range of resources, namely the ability to find, access and use labor market information and services. It provides statistics for employment demographics on both a local and regional level, as well as career searching tools for California residents. The web site is sponsored by California's Employment Development Office.

Recruiters Online Network
E-mail Address: rossi.tony@comcast.net
Web Address: www.recruitersonline.com
The Recruiters Online Network provides job postings from thousands of recruiters, Careers Online Magazine, a resume database, as well as other career resources.

USAJOBS
USAJOBS Program Office
1900 E St. NW, Ste. 6500
Washington, DC 20415-0001 USA
Phone: 818-934-6600
Web Address: www.usajobs.gov
USAJOBS, a program of the U.S. Office of Personnel Management, is the official job site for the U.S. Federal Government. It provides a comprehensive list of U.S. government jobs, allowing users to search for employment by location; agency; type of work; or by senior executive positions. It also has special employment sections for individuals with disabilities, veterans and recent college graduates; an information center, offering resume and interview tips and other information; and allows users to create a profile and post a resume.

20) Careers-Job Reference Tools

Vault.com, Inc.
132 W. 31st St., Fl. 17
New York, NY 10001 USA
Fax: 212-366-6117
Toll Free: 800-535-2074
E-mail Address: customerservice@vault.com
Web Address: www.vault.com
Vault.com, Inc. is a comprehensive career web site for employers and employees, with job postings and valuable information on a wide variety of industries. Its features and

content are largely geared toward MBA degree holders.

21) Careers-Science

New Scientist Jobs
Quadrant House, Sutton
Surrey, SM2 5AS UK
Phone: 781-734-8770
E-mail Address: nssales@newscientist.com
Web Address: jobs.newscientist.com
New Scientist Jobs is a web site produced by the publishers of New Scientist Magazine that connects jobseekers and employers in the bioscience fields. The site includes a job search engine and a free-of-charge e-mail job alert service.

Science Careers
Phone: 202-312-6375
Web Address: jobs.sciencecareers.org
Science Careers is a web site that contains many useful categories of links, including employment newsgroups, scientific journals, hob postings and placement agencies. It also links to sites containing information regarding internship and fellowship opportunities for high school students, undergrads, graduates, doctoral and post-doctoral students.

22) Chemicals Industry Associations

American Chemical Society (ACS)
1155 16th St. NW
Washington, DC 20036 USA
Phone: 202-872-4600
Toll Free: 800-227-5558
E-mail Address: help@acs.org
Web Address: www.acs.org
The American Chemical Society (ACS) is a nonprofit organization aimed at promoting the understanding of chemistry and chemical sciences. It represents a wide range of disciplines including chemistry, chemical engineering and other technical fields.

Brazilian Chemical Industry Association
Av. Chedid Jafet, 222, Bloco C, Fl. 4
Vila Olimpia
Sao Paulo, SP 04551-065 Brazil
Phone: 55-11-2148-4700
Fax: 55-11-2148-4760
Web Address: www.abiquim.org.br
The Brazilian Chemical Industry Association (Associacao Brasileira da Industria Quimica, ABIQUIM) represents Brazilian manufacturers of chemical products and assists with a variety of issues related to the industry, including product quality; environmental and safety issues; human resource development; product advocacy; tariff negotiations; and trade agreements. ABIQUIM runs a 24-hour hotline for chemical transportation safety issues, and is also involved with plastics recycling efforts.

China Petroleum & Chemical Industry Federation (CPCIF)
Anhuili Asian Games Village Bldg. 16 siqu
Beijing, 100723 China
Phone: 86-10-8488-5415
Fax: 86-10-8488-5087
Web Address: www.cpcia.org.cn/English/
The China Petroleum & Chemical Industry Federation (CPCIF) is a non-government and nonprofit association composed of regional and local associations including the China Polyurethane Industry Association.

Council for Chemical Research (CCR)
1120 Route 73, Ste. 200
Mount Laurel, NJ 08054 USA
Phone: 856-439-0500
Fax: 856-439-0525
E-mail Address: info@ccrhq.org
Web Address: www.ccrhq.org
The Council for Chemical Research (CCR) represents industry, academia and government members involved in the chemical sciences and engineering.

23) Chinese Government Agencies-Science & Technology

China Ministry of Science and Technology (MOST)
15B Fuxing Rd.
Beijing, 100862 China
Web Address: www.most.gov.cn
The China Ministry of Science and Technology (MOST) is the PRC's official body for science and technology related activities. It drafts laws, policies and regulations regarding science and technology; oversees budgeting and accounting for funds; and supervises research institutes operating in China, among other duties.

24) Computer & Electronics Industry Associations

Business Technology Association (BTA)
12411 Wornall Rd., Ste. 200
Kansas City, MO 64145 USA
Phone: 816-941-3100
Fax: 816-941-4843
Toll Free: 800-826-6159
E-mail Address: brent@bta.org
Web Address: www.bta.org
The Business Technology Association (BTA) is an organization for resellers and dealers of business technology products. Its site offers buying groups, message boards, legal advice, news on industry trends and live chats.

Canadian Advanced Technology Alliances (CATAAlliance)
207 Bank St., Ste. 416
Ottawa, ON K2P 2N2 Canada
Phone: 613-236-6550
E-mail Address: info@cata.ca
Web Address: www.cata.ca
The Canadian Advanced Technology Alliances (CATAAlliance) is one of Canada's leading trade organizations for the research, development and technology sectors.

Computer & Communications Industry Association (CCIA)
900 17th St. NW, Ste. 1100
Washington, DC 20006 USA
Phone: 202-783-0070
Fax: 202-783-0534
Web Address: www.ccianet.org
The Computer & Communications Industry Association (CCIA) is a non-profit membership organization for companies and senior executives representing the computer, Internet, information technology (IT) and telecommunications industries.

Electronics Technicians Association international (ETA International)
5 Depot St.
Greencastle, IN 46135 USA
Phone: 765-653-8262
Fax: 765-653-4287
Toll Free: 800-288-3824
E-mail Address: eta@eta-i.org
Web Address: www.eta-i.org
The Electronics Technicians Association International (ETA International) is a nonprofit professional association for electronics technicians worldwide. The organization provides recognized professional credentials for electronics technicians.

Global Semiconductor Alliance (GSA)
12400 Coit Rd., Churchill Tower
Ste. 650
Dallas, TX 75251 USA
Phone: 972-866-7579
Fax: 972-239-2292
Toll Free: 888-322-5195
Web Address: www.gsaglobal.org
The Global Semiconductor Alliance (GSA) serves the entire supply chain of the global semiconductor industry, including intellectual property (IP), electronic design automation (EDA)/design, wafer manufacturing, test and packaging activities.

Indian Electrical & Electronics Manufacturers Association (IEEMA)
501 Kakad Chambers
132 Dr. Annie Besant Rd., Worli
Mumbai, 400018 India
Phone: 91-22-2493-0532
Fax: 91-22-2493-2705
E-mail Address: mumbai@ieema.org
Web Address: www.ieema.org
The Indian Electrical & Electronics Manufacturers Association (IEEMA) represents all sectors of the electrical and allied products businesses of the Indian electrical industry.

Institute for Interconnecting and Packaging Electronic Circuits (IPC)
3000 Lakeside Dr., Ste. 105 N
Bannockburn, IL 60015 USA
Phone: 847-615-7100
Fax: 847-615-7105
E-mail Address: answers@ipc.org
Web Address: www.ipc.org
The Institute for Interconnecting and Packaging Electronic Circuits (IPC) is a trade association for companies in the global printed circuit board and electronics manufacturing services industries.

International Disk Drive Equipment and Materials Association (IDEMA)
1226 Lincoln Ave., Ste. 100
San Jose, CA 95125 USA
Phone: 408-294-0082
Fax: 408-294-0087
E-mail Address: info@idema.org
Web Address: www.idema.org
The International Disk Drive Equipment and Materials Association (IDEMA) is a not-for-profit trade association that represents its members on issues concerning the hard drive industry worldwide.

International Microelectronics Assembly and Packaging Society (IMAPS)
P. O. Box 110127
Research Triangle Park, NC 27709-5127 USA
Phone: 919-293-5000
Fax: 919-287-2339
E-mail Address: modonoghue@imaps.org
Web Address: www.imaps.org
The International Microelectronics Assembly and Packaging Society (IMAPS) is dedicated to the advancement and growth of the use of microelectronics and electronic packaging through professional education, workshops and conferences.

Korea Association of Information and Telecommunications (KAIT)
NO. 1678-2, 2nd Fl. Dong-Ah Villat 2 Town
Seocho-dong, Seocho-gu
Seoul, 137-070 Korea
Phone: 82-2-580-0582
E-mail Address: webmaster@kait.or.kr
Web Address: www.kait.or.kr/eng
The Korea Association of Information and Telecommunications (KAIT) was created to develop and promote the InfoTech, computer, consumer electronics, wireless, software and telecommunications sectors in Korea.

Korea Electronics Association (KEA)
World Cup buk-ro 54-gil, Mapo-gu
Fl. 11
Seoul, 03924 Korea
Phone: 82-2-6388-6172
Web Address: www.gokea.org
The Korea Electronics Association (KEA) was established by Korea's Ministry of Commerce to promote the growth and development of the nation's electronics industry.

Korea Semiconductor Industry Association (KSIA)
182, Pangyoyeok-ro, Bundang-gu, Seongnam-si
Fl. 9-12, KSIA Bldg.
Gyeonggi-do, Korea
Phone: 82-2-570-5232
Fax: 82-2-577-1719
Web Address: www.ksia.or.kr
The Korean Semiconductor Industry Association (KSIA) represents the interests of Korean semiconductor manufacturers.

North America Chinese Clean-tech & Semiconductor Association (NACSA)
809-B Cuesta Dr., Ste. 208
Mountain View, CA 94040 USA
Web Address: www.nacsa.com
The North America Chinese Clean-tech & Semiconductor Association (NACSA), founded in Silicon Valley in 1996, is dedicated to the advancement of Chinese professionals in high-tech and related industries, including chip design, chip manufacture, system manufacture, equipment manufacture and software.

SEMATECH
257 Fuller Rd.
Albany, NY 12203 USA
Phone: 518-649-1000
E-mail Address: media.relations@sematech.org
Web Address: www.sunycnse.com/LeadingEdgeResearchandDevelopment/ResearchCentersPrograms/SEMATECH.aspx

SUNY Poly SEMATECH, formerly SEAMTECH is an international 12-member consortium of semiconductor manufacturing companies. The organization researches advanced technology and manufacturing effectiveness in the semiconductor industry, working to decrease time between innovation and manufacturing.

Semiconductor Equipment and Materials International (SEMI)
3081 Zanker Rd.
San Jose, CA 95134 USA
Phone: 408-943-6900
Fax: 408-428-9600
E-mail Address: semihq@semi.org
Web Address: www.semi.org
Semiconductor Equipment and Materials International (SEMI) is a trade association serving the global semiconductor equipment, materials and flat-panel display industries.

Semiconductor Industry Association (SIA)
1101 K St. NW, Ste. 450
Washington, DC 20005 USA
Phone: 202-446-1700
Fax: 202-216-9745
Toll Free: 866-756-0715
Web Address: www.semiconductors.org
The Semiconductor Industry Association (SIA) is a trade association representing the semiconductor industry in the U.S. Through its coalition of more than 60 companies, SIA members represent roughly 80% of semiconductor production in the U.S. The coalition aims to advance the competitiveness of the chip industry and shape public policy on issues particular to the industry.

Storage Network Industry Association (SNIA)
425 Market St., Ste. 1020
San Francisco, CA 94105 USA
Phone: 415-402-0006
Fax: 415-402-0009
E-mail Address: leo.leger@snia.org
Web Address: www.snia.org
The Storage Network Industry Association (SNIA) is a trade associated dedicated to viability of storage networks within the IT industry. SNIA sponsors technical work groups, produces the Storage Networking Conference series and maintains a Technology Center in Colorado Springs, Colorado.

Surface Mount Technology Association (SMTA)
6600 City West Pkwy., Ste. 300
Eden Prairie, MN 55424 USA
Phone: 952-920-7682
Fax: 952-926-1819
E-mail Address: ryan@smta.org
Web Address: www.smta.org
The Surface Mount Technology Association (SMTA) is an international network of professionals whose careers encompass electronic assembly technologies, microsystems, emerging technologies and associated business operations.

25) Computer & Electronics Industry Resources

Cisco Cloud Index
170 W. Tasman Dr.
San Jose, CA 95134 USA
Toll Free: 800-553-6387
Web Address: www.cisco.com/go/cloudindex
The Cisco Cloud Index covers three areas focused on data center and cloud traffic trends and next-generation service or application adoption. They include: Data center and cloud traffic forecast; Workload transition, which provides projections for workloads moving from traditional IT to cloud-based architectures; and Cloud readiness, which provides regional statistics on broadband adoption as a precursor for cloud services.

EETimes
Web Address: www.eetimes.com
The EETimes is an online magazine devoted to electronic engineers in the semiconductor, systems and software design fields.

Information Technology and Innovation Foundation (ITIF)
1101 K St. NW, Ste. 610
Washington, DC 20005 USA
Phone: 202-449-1351
E-mail Address: mail@itif.org
Web Address: www.itif.org
Information Technology and Innovation Foundation (ITIF) is a non-partisan research and educational institute (a think tank) with a mission to formulate and promote public policies to advance technological innovation and productivity internationally, in Washington, and in the States. Recognizing the vital role of technology in ensuring American prosperity, ITIF focuses on innovation, productivity, and digital economy issues.

26) Computer-Aided Engineering Resources

Center for Design Research (CDR) at Stanford University
Center for Design Research
Bldg. 560, 424 Panama Mall
Stanford, CA 94305-2232 USA
Phone: 650-723-9233
Fax: 650-725-8475
E-mail Address: tunison@stanford.edu
Web Address: www-cdr.stanford.edu
The web site of the Center for Design Research (CDR) at Stanford University provides information on the center's staff, laboratories and projects on design process and design tool development for engineering.

27) Construction Industry Resources & Associations

Precast/Prestressed Concrete Institute
200 W. Adams St., Ste. 2100
Chicago, IL 60606-6938 USA
Phone: 312-786-0300
Web Address: www.pci.org
The Precast/Prestressed Concrete Institute (PCI) is an organization dedicated to the precast and prestressed concrete industry and includes a staff of technical and marketing specialists.

28) Corporate Information Resources

bizjournals.com
120 W. Morehead St., Ste. 400
Charlotte, NC 28202 USA
Toll Free: 866-853-3661
E-mail Address:
gmurchison@bizjournals.com
Web Address: www.bizjournals.com
Bizjournals.com is the online media division of American City Business Journals, the publisher of dozens of leading city business journals nationwide. It provides access to research into the latest news regarding companies both small and large. The organization maintains 42 websites and 64 print publications and sponsors over 700 annual industry events.

Business Wire
101 California St., Fl. 20
San Francisco, CA 94111 USA
Phone: 415-986-4422
Fax: 415-788-5335
Toll Free: 800-227-0845
E-mail Address:
info@businesswire.com
Web Address:
www.businesswire.com
Business Wire offers news releases, industry- and company-specific news, top headlines, conference calls, IPOs on the Internet, media services and access to tradeshownews.com and BW Connect On-line through its informative and continuously updated web site.

Edgar Online, Inc.
11200 Rockville Pike, Ste. 310
Rockville, MD 20852 USA
Phone: 301-287-0300
Fax: 301-287-0390
Toll Free: 888-870-2316
Web Address: www.edgar-online.com
Edgar Online, Inc. is a gateway and search tool for viewing corporate documents, such as annual reports on Form 10-K, filed with the U.S. Securities and Exchange Commission.

PR Newswire Association LLC
350 Hudson St., Ste. 300
New York, NY 10014-4504 USA
Fax: 800-793-9313
Toll Free: 800-776-8090
E-mail Address:
MediaInquiries@prnewswire.com
Web Address: www.prnewswire.com
PR Newswire Association LLC provides comprehensive communications services for public relations and investor relations professionals, ranging from information distribution and market intelligence to the creation of online multimedia content and investor relations web sites. Users can also view recent corporate press releases from companies across the globe. The Association is owned by United Business Media plc.

Silicon Investor
E-mail Address:
si.admin@siliconinvestor.com
Web Address:
www.siliconinvestor.com
Silicon Investor is focused on providing information about technology companies. Its web site serves as a financial discussion forum and offers quotes, profiles and charts.

29) Design & Architectural Associations

Center for Universal Design (The) (CUD)
College of Design, North Carolina State University
Campus Box 8613
Raleigh, NC 27695-8613 USA
Phone: 919-515-3082
Fax: 919-515-8951
E-mail Address: cud@ncsu.edu
Web Address:
www.ncsu.edu/ncsu/design/cud/
The Center for Universal Design (CUD) is a national information, technical assistance and research center that evaluates, develops and promotes products and environments so that they can be used by all people, regardless of physical or mental limitations.

30) Drone Associations

Unmanned Systems Technology (UST)
E-mail Address:
info@unmannedsystemstechnology.com
Web Address:
www.unmannedsystemstechnology.com
Unmanned Systems Technology (UST) is a dedicated directory of component, service and platform suppliers within the unmanned systems industry. All categories of unmanned systems are included: Air vehicles (UAV/UAS/RPAS), Ground Vehicles and Robotic Systems (UGVs), Surface and Subsea vehicles (USV, UUV) and Space vehicles.

31) Economic Data & Research

Centre for European Economic Research (The, ZEW)
L 7, 1
Mannheim, 68161 Germany
Phone: 49-621-1235-01
Fax: 49-621-1235-224
E-mail Address: empfang@zew.de
Web Address: www.zew.de/en
Zentrum fur Europaische Wirtschaftsforschung, The Centre for European Economic Research (ZEW), distinguishes itself in the analysis of internationally comparative data in a European context and in the creation of databases that serve as a basis for scientific research. The institute maintains a special library relevant to economic research and provides external parties with selected data for the purpose of scientific research. ZEW also offers public events and seminars concentrating on banking, business and other economic-political topics.

Economic and Social Research Council (ESRC)
Polaris House
North Star Ave.
Swindon, SN2 1UJ UK
Phone: 44-01793 413000
E-mail Address:
esrcenquiries@esrc.ac.uk

Web Address: www.esrc.ac.uk
The Economic and Social Research Council (ESRC) funds research and training in social and economic issues. It is an independent organization, established by Royal Charter. Current research areas include the global economy; social diversity; environment and energy; human behavior; and health and well-being.

Eurostat
5 Rue Alphonse Weicker
Joseph Bech Bldg.
Luxembourg, L-2721 Luxembourg
Phone: 352-4301-1
E-mail Address: eurostat-pressoffice@ec.europa.eu
Web Address: ec.europa.eu/eurostat
Eurostat is the European Union's service that publishes a wide variety of comprehensive statistics on European industries, populations, trade, agriculture, technology, environment and other matters.

Federal Statistical Office of Germany
Gustav-Stresemann-Ring 11
Wiesbaden, D-65189 Germany
Phone: 49-611-75-2405
Fax: 49-611-72-4000
Web Address: www.destatis.de
Federal Statistical Office of Germany publishes a wide variety of nation and regional economic data of interest to anyone who is studying Germany, one of the world's leading economies. Data available includes population, consumer prices, labor markets, health care, industries and output.

India Brand Equity Foundation (IBEF)
Fl. 20, Jawahar Vyapar Bhawan
Tolstoy Marg
New Deli, 110001 India
Phone: 91-11-43845500
Fax: 91-11-23701235
E-mail Address: info.brandindia@ibef.org
Web Address: www.ibef.org
India Brand Equity Foundation (IBEF) is a public-private partnership between the Ministry of Commerce and Industry, the Government of India and the Confederation of Indian Industry. The foundation's primary objective is to build positive economic perceptions of India globally. It aims to effectively present the India business perspective and leverage business partnerships in a globalizing marketplace.

National Bureau of Statistics (China)
57, Yuetan Nanjie, Sanlihe
Xicheng District
Beijing, 100826 China
Fax: 86-10-6878-2000
E-mail Address: info@gj.stats.cn
Web Address: www.stats.gov.cn/english
The National Bureau of Statistics (China) provides statistics and economic data regarding China's economy and society.

Organization for Economic Co-operation and Development (OECD)
2 rue Andre Pascal, Cedex 16
Paris, 75775 France
Phone: 33-1-45-24-82-00
Fax: 33-1-45-24-85-00
E-mail Address: webmaster@oecd.org
Web Address: www.oecd.org
The Organization for Economic Co-operation and Development (OECD) publishes detailed economic, government, population, social and trade statistics on a country-by-country basis for over 30 nations representing the world's largest economies. Sectors covered range from industry, labor, technology and patents, to health care, environment and globalization.

Statistics Bureau, Director-General for Policy Planning (Japan)
19-1 Wakamatsu-cho
Shinjuku-ku
Tokyo, 162-8668 Japan
Phone: 81-3-5273-2020
E-mail Address: toukeisoudan@soumu.go.jp
Web Address: www.stat.go.jp/english
The Statistics Bureau, Director-General for Policy Planning (Japan) and Statistical Research and Training Institute, a part of the Japanese Ministry of Internal Affairs and Communications, plays the central role of producing and disseminating basic official statistics and coordinating statistical work under the Statistics Act and other legislation.

Statistics Canada
150 Tunney's Pasture Driveway
Ottawa, ON K1A 0T6 Canada
Phone: 514-283-8300
Fax: 514-283-9350
Toll Free: 800-263-1136
E-mail Address: STATCAN.infostats-infostats.STATCAN@canada.ca
Web Address: www.statcan.gc.ca
Statistics Canada provides a complete portal to Canadian economic data and statistics. Its conducts Canada's official census every five years, as well as hundreds of surveys covering numerous aspects of Canadian life.

32) Energy Associations- China, General

China Energy Association (CEA)
7 Nanlishi Road, Toutiao
Xicheng District
Beijing, 100045 China
Phone: 86-010-68051807
Fax: 86-010-68051799
E-mail Address: hzt1008@hotmail.com
Web Address: www.zhnx.org.cn
The China Energy Association (CEA) is a membership organization that represents the energy sources sector and energy industry. The organization publishes the Energy Resource World magazine.

33) Energy Associations- Natural Gas

Gas Technology Institute (GTI)
1700 S. Mount Prospect Rd.
Des Plaines, IL 60018-1804 USA
Phone: 847-768-0500
Fax: 847-768-0501
E-mail Address: publicrelations@gastechnology.org
Web Address: www.gastechnology.org
The Gas Technology Institute (GTI) is a not-for-profit research and development organization, and works

to develop and deploy technologies related to affordable energy production, sustainable energy development and the efficient use of energy resources. Its network of partners, investors and clients includes state and federal government agencies; natural gas utilities and pipeline companies; industrial companies; electric utilities; independent power producers; technology developers; and national laboratories. In addition to its Illinois headquarters (which houses 28 specialized laboratories working on various advanced energy technologies), GTI also maintains smaller offices and facilities in locations including Houston, Texas; Sacramento, California; and Washington D.C.

34) Energy Associations-Nuclear

China Atomic Energy Authority
China Atomic Energy Authority
Beijing, 100037 China
Web Address: www.caea.gov.cn
The China Atomic Energy Authority is involved in developing policies and regulations and the development programming, planning and industrial standards for peaceful uses of nuclear energy.

35) Energy Associations-Oil Field Services/Drilling

International Association of Geophysical Contractors (IAGC)
1225 N. Loop W., Ste. 220
Houston, TX 77008 USA
Phone: 713-957-8080
Fax: 713-957-0008
Toll Free: 866-558-1756
E-mail Address: iagc@iagc.org
Web Address: www.iagc.org
The International Association of Geophysical Contractors (IAGC) is the international trade association representing the industry that provides geophysical services to the oil and gas industry.

Petroleum Equipment Suppliers Association (PESA)
2500 Citywest Blvd., Ste. 1110
Houston, TX 77042 USA
Phone: 713-932-0168
E-mail Address: info@pesa.org
Web Address: www.pesa.org
The Petroleum Equipment Suppliers Association (PESA) is an organization of equipment manufacturers, well site service providers and supply companies serving the drilling and production segments of the petroleum industry.

36) Energy Associations-Petroleum, Exploration, Production, etc.

International Association of Drilling Contractors (IADC)
10370 Richmond Ave., Ste. 760
Houston, TX 77042 USA
Phone: 713-292-1945
Fax: 713-292-1946
E-mail Address: info@iadc.org
Web Address: www.iadc.org
The International Association of Drilling Contractors (IADC) represents the worldwide oil and gas drilling industry and promotes commitment to safety, preservation of the environment and advances in drilling technology.

Oil and Gas UK
Portland House, Fl.6 E.
Bressenden Place
London, SW1E 5BH UK
Phone: 44-020-7802-2400
E-mail Address: info@oilandgasuk.co.uk
Web Address: www.oilandgas.org.uk
The United Kingdom Offshore Operators Association (UKOOA) is the representative organization for the U.K. offshore oil and gas industry.

37) Engineering Indices

Cornell Engineering Library (The)
Engineering Library Cornell University
Carpenter Hall, Fl. 1
Ithaca, NY 14853 USA
Phone: 607-254-6261
E-mail Address: engrref@cornell.edu
Web Address: engineering.library.cornell.edu
Cornell University's Engineering Library web site has a number of resources concerning engineering research, as well as links to other engineering industry information sources.

38) Engineering Industry Associations

American Society of Heating, Refrigerating and Air-Conditioning Engineers
1791 Tullie Cir., N.E.
Atlanta, GA 30329 USA
Phone: 404-636-8400
Fax: 404-321-5478
E-mail Address: ashrae@ashrae.org
Web Address: www.ashrae.org
ASHRAE is a global society advancing human well-being through sustainable technology for the built environment. The Society and its members focus on building systems, energy efficiency, indoor air quality, refrigeration and sustainability within the industry. Through research, standards writing, publishing and continuing education, ASHRAE shapes tomorrow's built environment today

National Society of Professional Engineers (NSPE)
1420 King St.
Alexandria, VA 22314-2794 USA
Fax: 703-836-4875
Toll Free: 888-285-6773
Web Address: www.nspe.org
The National Society of Professional Engineers (NSPE) represents individual engineering professionals and licensed engineers across all disciplines. NSPE serves approximately 45,000 members and has more than 500 chapters.

39) Engineering Industry Resource

Engineering News-Record
2 Penn Plaza, Fl. 10
New York, NY 10121 USA
Phone: 212-904-3507
Fax: 212-904-2820

E-mail Address: support@construction.com
Web Address: enr.construction.com
(ENR)
Engineering News-Record (ENR) provides the news, analysis, commentary and data that engineering and construction industry professionals need to do their jobs more effectively. ENR publishes a weekly magazine with more than 70,000 paid subscribers, a website with over 90,000 unique visitors a month and a series of in-person events. Those who read ENR include contractors, project owners, engineers, architects, government regulators and industry suppliers. As such, the engineering information portal connects these diverse sectors of the industry with coverage about issues such as business management, design, construction methods, technology, safety, law, legislation, environment and labor.

40) Engineering, Research & Scientific Associations

Agency For Science, Technology And Research (A*STAR)
1 Fusionopolis Way
20-10 Connexis N. Twr.
Singapore, 138632 Singapore
Phone: 65-6826-6111
Fax: 65-6777-1711
E-mail Address: contact@a-star.edu.sg
Web Address: www.a-star.edu.sg
The Agency For Science, Technology And Research (A*STAR) of Singapore comprises the Biomedical Research Council (BMRC), the Science and Engineering Research Council (SERC), A*STAR Joint Council (A*JC), the A*STAR Graduate Academy (A*GA) and the Corporate Group. Both Councils fund the A*STAR public research institutes which conducts research in specific niche areas in science, engineering and biomedical science.

Alfred P. Sloan Foundation
630 Fifth Ave., Ste. 2550
New York, NY 10111 USA
Phone: 212-649-1649
Fax: 212-757-5117
E-mail Address: myerson@sloan.org
Web Address: www.sloan.org
The Alfred P. Sloan Foundation funds science and technology, economic performance, education, national issues and civics programs through research fellowships and grants.

American Association for the Advancement of Science (AAAS)
1200 New York Ave. NW
Washington, DC 20005 USA
Phone: 202-326-6400
Web Address: www.aaas.org
The American Association for the Advancement of Science (AAAS) is the world's largest scientific society and the publisher of Science magazine. It is an international nonprofit organization dedicated to advancing science around the globe.

American Association of Petroleum Geologists (AAPG)
1444 S. Boulder Ave.
Tulsa, OK 74119 USA
Phone: 918-584-2555
Fax: 918-560-2665
Toll Free: 800-364-2274
Web Address: www.aapg.org
The American Association of Petroleum Geologists (AAPG) is an international geological organization that supports educational and scientific programs and projects related to geosciences.

American Institute of Chemical Engineers (AIChE)
120 Wall St., Fl. 23
New York, NY 10005-4020 USA
Phone: 203-702-7660
Fax: 203-775-5177
Toll Free: 800-242-4363
Web Address: www.aiche.org
The American Institute of Chemical Engineers (AIChE) provides leadership in advancing the chemical engineering profession. The organization, which is comprised of more than 50,000 members from over 100 countries, provides informational resources to chemical engineers.

American Institute of Mining, Metallurgical and Petroleum Engineers (AIME)
12999 E. Adam Aircraft Cir.
Englewood, CO 80112 USA
Phone: 303-325-5185
Fax: 888-702-0049
E-mail Address: aime@aimehq.org
Web Address: www.aimehq.org
The American Institute of Mining, Metallurgical and Petroleum Engineers (AIME) is a trade association devoted to the science of the production and use of minerals, metals, energy sources and materials.

American Institute of Physics (AIP)
1 Physics Ellipse
College Park, MD 20740-3843 USA
Phone: 301-209-3100
E-mail Address: rgwbrown@aip.org
Web Address: www.aip.org
The American Institute of Physics (AIP) is a nonprofit organization aimed at the advancement and diffusion of knowledge of the science of physics and its application to human welfare. It serves individual scientists, students and the general public alike. Besides its Maryland headquarters, the AIP maintains a publishing center in New York and an international office in Beijing.

American National Standards Institute (ANSI)
1899 L St. NW, Fl. 11
Washington, DC 20036 USA
Phone: 202-293-8020
Fax: 202-293-9287
E-mail Address: info@ansi.org
Web Address: www.ansi.org
The American National Standards Institute (ANSI) is a private, nonprofit organization that administers and coordinates the U.S. voluntary standardization and conformity assessment system. Its mission is to enhance both the global competitiveness of U.S. business and the quality of life by promoting and facilitating voluntary consensus standards and conformity assessment systems and safeguarding their integrity.

American Nuclear Society (ANS)
555 N. Kensington Ave.
La Grange Park, IL 60526 USA
Phone: 708-352-6611
Fax: 708-352-0499
Toll Free: 800-323-3044

Web Address: www.ans.org
The American Nuclear Society (ANS) is a nonprofit organization unifying professional activities within the nuclear science and technology fields. ANS seeks to promote the awareness and understanding of the application of nuclear science and technology.

American Physical Society (APS)
One Physics Ellipse
College Park, MD 20740-3844 USA
Phone: 301-209-3200
Web Address: www.aps.org
The American Physical Society (APS) develops and implements effective programs in physics education and outreach. APS publishes a number of research journals dedicated to physics research, including Physical Review, Physical Review Letters and Reviews of Modern Physics.

American Society for Engineering Education (ASEE)
1818 North St. NW, Ste. 600
Washington, DC 20036-2479 USA
Phone: 202-331-3500
Fax: 202-265-8504
E-mail Address: board@asee.org
Web Address: www.asee.org
The American Society for Engineering Education (ASEE) is nonprofit organization dedicated to promoting and improving engineering and technology education.

American Society for Healthcare Engineering (ASHE)
155 N. Wacker Dr., Ste. 400
Chicago, IL 60606 USA
Phone: 312-422-3800
Fax: 312-422-4571
E-mail Address: ashe@aha.org
Web Address: www.ashe.org
The American Society for Healthcare Engineering (ASHE) is the advocate and resource for continuous improvement in the health care engineering and facilities management professions. It is devoted to professionals who design, build, maintain and operate hospitals and other healthcare facilities.

American Society for Nondestructive Testing (ASNT)
1711 Arlingate Ln.
P.O. Box 28518
Columbus, OH 43228-0518 USA
Phone: 614-274-6003
Fax: 614-274-6899
Toll Free: 800-222-2768
E-mail Address: mmonta@asnt.org
Web Address: www.asnt.org
The American Society for Nondestructive Testing (ASNT) is the world's largest technical society for nondestructive testing professionals. It promotes the discipline of nondestructive testing as a profession and facilitates nondestructive testing research and technology applications.

American Society of Agricultural and Biological Engineers (ASABE)
2950 Niles Rd.
St. Joseph, MI 49085 USA
Phone: 269-429-0300
Fax: 269-429-3852
Toll Free: 800-371-2723
E-mail Address: hq@asabe.org
Web Address: www.asabe.org
The American Society of Agricultural and Biological Engineers (ASABE) is a nonprofit professional and technical organization interested in engineering knowledge and technology for food and agriculture and associated industries.

American Society of Civil Engineers (ASCE)
1801 Alexander Bell Dr.
Reston, VA 20191-4400 USA
Phone: 703-295-6300
Toll Free: 800-548-2723
Web Address: www.asce.org
The American Society of Civil Engineers (ASCE) is a leading professional organization serving civil engineers. It ensures safer buildings, water systems and other civil engineering works by developing technical codes and standards.

American Society of Mechanical Engineers (ASME)
Two Park Ave.
New York, NY 10016-5990 USA
Phone: 973-882-1170
Fax: 973-882-1717
Toll Free: 800-843-2763
E-mail Address: CustomerCare@asme.org
Web Address: www.asme.org
The American Society of Mechanical Engineers (ASME) offers quality programs and activities in mechanical engineering. It also facilitates the development and application of technology in areas of interest to the mechanical engineering profession.

American Society of Mechanical Engineers (ASME), Textile Engineering Division
Two Park Ave.
New York, NY 10016-5990 USA
Phone: 973-882-1170
Toll Free: 800-843-2763
E-mail Address: CustomerCare@asme.org
Web Address: www.asme.org
The textile engineering division of the American Society of Mechanical Engineers (ASME) promotes product and process technology improvement in the retail fiber industry.

American Society of Naval Engineers (ASNE)
1452 Duke St.
Alexandria, VA 22314-3458 USA
Phone: 703-836-6727
Fax: 703-836-7491
E-mail Address: asnehq@navalengineers.org
Web Address: www.navalengineers.org
The American Society of Naval Engineers (ASNE) is a nonprofit professional organization dedicated to advancing the knowledge and practice of naval engineering in public and private operations.

American Society of Safety Engineers (ASSE)
520 N. Northwest Hwy
Park Ridge, IL 60068 USA
Phone: 847-699-2929
E-mail Address: customerservice@asse.org
Web Address: www.asse.org
The American Society of Safety Engineers (ASSE) is the world's oldest and largest professional safety organization. It manages, supervises and consults on safety, health and

environmental issues in industry, insurance, government and education.

American Vacuum Society (AVS)
125 Maiden Ln., Fl. 15
New York, NY 10038 USA
Phone: 212-248-0200
Fax: 212-248-0245
E-mail Address: ricky@avs.org
Web Address: www.avs.org
The American Vacuum Society (AVS) is a nonprofit organization that promotes communication, dissemination of knowledge, recommended practices, research and education in the use of vacuum and other controlled environments to develop new materials, process technology and devices. AVS facilitates communication between academia, government laboratories and industry.

ASM International
9639 Kinsman Rd.
Materials Park, OH 44073-0002 USA
Phone: 440-338-5151
Toll Free: 800-336-5152
E-mail Address: memberservicecenter@asminternational.org
Web Address: www.asminternational.org
ASM International is a worldwide network of materials engineers, aimed at advancing industry, technology and applications of metals and materials. It provides materials information, education and training, as well as networking opportunities for professionals within the materials industry.

Association for Consultancy and Engineering (ACE)
Alliance House
12 Caxton St.
London, SW1H 0QL UK
Phone: 44-20-7222-6557
Fax: 44-20-7990-9202
E-mail Address: consult@acenet.co.uk
Web Address: www.acenet.co.uk
The Association for Consultancy and Engineering (ACE) represents the business interests of the consultancy and engineering industry in the U.K.

Association for Electrical, Electronic & Information Technologies (VDE)
Stresemannallee 15
Frankfurt, 60596 Germany
Phone: 49-69-6308-284
Fax: 49-69-6308-9830
E-mail Address: presse@vde.com
Web Address: www.vde.com
The Association for Electrical, Electronic & Information Technologies (VDE) is a German organization with roughly 36,000 members, representing one of the largest technical associations in Europe.

Association for Facilities Engineering (AFE)
8200 Greensboro Dr., Ste. 400
McLean, VA 22102 USA
Phone: 571-395-8777
Fax: 571-766-2142
Web Address: www.afe.org
The Association for Facilities Engineering (AFE) provides education, certification, technical information and other relevant resources for plant and facility engineering, operations and maintenance professionals worldwide.

Association of Consulting Chemists and Chemical Engineers (ACC&CE)
P.O. Box 902
Murray Hill, NJ 07974-0902 USA
Phone: 908-464-3182
Fax: 908-464-3182
E-mail Address: info@chemconsult.org
Web Address: www.chemconsult.org
The Association of Consulting Chemists and Chemical Engineers (ACC&CE) was established to advance the practices of consulting chemists and chemical engineers.

Association of Consulting Engineers of Hong Kong
109-111 Gloucester Rd.
20/F Tung Wai Commercial Bldg.
Wanchai, Hong Kong Hong Kong
Phone: 852-3922-9845
Fax: 852-2691-2649
E-mail Address: info@acehk.org.hk
Web Address: www.acehk.org.hk
The Association of Consulting Engineers of Hong Kong promotes the professional consulting engineers, their business interests and rights, as well as sets standards of professional conduct and ethics for the consulting engineering profession.

Association of Consulting Engineers Singapore (ACES)
Thomson Rd. Post Office
P.O. Box 034
Singapore, 915702 Singapore
Phone: 65-63242682
Fax: 65-63242581
E-mail Address: secretariat@aces.org.sg
Web Address: www.aces.org.sg
The Association of Consulting Engineers Singapore (ACES) is a nonprofit association representing the independent consulting engineering profession in Singapore.

Association of Federal Communications Consulting Engineers (AFCCE)
P.O. Box 19333
Washington, DC 20036 USA
Web Address: www.afcce.org
The Association of Federal Communications Consulting Engineers (AFCCE) is a professional organization of individuals who regularly assist clients on technical issues before the Federal Communications Commission (FCC).

Association of German Engineers (The, VDI)
VDI e.V.
VDI-Platz 1
Dusseldorf, 40468 Germany
Phone: 49-(0)-211-6214-0
Fax: 49 (0) 211-6214-575
Web Address: www.vdi.de
The Association of German Engineers (VDI) promotes innovation and technology in Germany and represents one of the largest technical-scientific associations in Europe.

Association of German Machinery and Equipment Engineering (VDMA)
Friedrichstrasse 95
Berlin, 10117 Germany

Phone: 49-30-30-69-46-0
Fax: 49-30-30-69-46-20
E-mail Address: berlin@vdma.org
Web Address: www.vdma.org
The Association of German Machinery and Equipment Engineering (VDMA) represents the machinery and plant manufacturing industry and the associated information technology and system engineering sector. The website includes product database, and member company lists as well as publications and links.

Association of Official Analytical Chemists (AOAC)
2275 Research Blvd., Ste. 300
Rockville, MD 20850-3250 USA
Phone: 301-924-7077
Fax: 301-924-7089
Toll Free: 800-379-2622
E-mail Address: AOAC@aoac.org
Web Address: www.aoac.org
The Association of Official Analytical Chemists (AOAC) is a nonprofit scientific association committed to worldwide standards in analytical results. It develops analytical methods with focus on public health and safety in areas, including fertilizers, veterinary drugs, feeds, foods and beverages, soil and water, infant formula, pharmaceuticals and dietary supplements.

Association of Professional Engineers of Nova Scotia (APENS)
1355 Barrington St.
Halifax, Nova Scotia B3J 1Y9 Canada
Phone: 902-429-2250
Fax: 902-423-9769
Toll Free: 888-802-7367
E-mail Address: info@engineersnovascotia.ca
Web Address: http://secure.engineersnovascotia.ca/
The Association of Professional Engineers of Nova Scotia (APENS) is the licensing and regulatory body for the more than 5,000 professional engineers and engineers-in-training practicing in Nova Scotia.

ASTM International
100 Barr Harbor Dr.
P.O. Box C700
West Conshohocken, PA 19428-2959 USA
Phone: 610-832-9585
Toll Free: 877-909-2786
Web Address: www.astm.org
ASTM International, formerly the American Society for Testing & Materials, provides and develops voluntary consensus standards and related technical information that promote public health and safety. It also contributes to the reliability of materials for industries worldwide.

Audio Engineering Society, Inc. (AES)
551 Fifth Ave., Ste. 1225
New York, NY 10176 USA
Phone: 212-661-8528
Web Address: www.aes.org
The Audio Engineering Society (AES) provides information on educational and career opportunities in audio technology and engineering.

Brazilian Association of Chemical Engineering (ABEQ)
R. Libero Badaro, 152, Fl. 11
Sao Paulo, SP 01008-903 Brazil
Phone: 55-11-3107-8747
Fax: 55-11-3104-4649
E-mail Address: abeq@abeq.org.br
Web Address: www.abeq.org.br
The Brazilian Association of Chemical Engineering is a non-profit organization that works to promote the development of chemical engineering throughout the country. Among other activities, it sponsors a variety of industry networking meetings and publishes a quarterly scientific journal and a technical magazine, as well as distributing annual scholarships to undergraduate and graduate students in the sciences.

Brazilian Association of Mechanical Sciences and Engineering
Av. Rio Branco, 124, Fl. 14
Rio de Janeiro, RJ 20040-001 Brazil
Phone: 55-21-2221-0438
Fax: 55-21-2509-7128
E-mail Address: abcm@abcm.org.br
Web Address: www.abcm.org.br
The Brazilian Association of Mechanical Sciences and Engineering (Associacao Brasileira de Engenharia e Ciencias Mecanicas, or ABCM), founded in 1975, is a non-profit group that links engineers, universities, scientific institutions and businesses to develop the field of mechanical engineering in Brazil. ABCM publishes several technical journals and also sponsors a number of regular conferences for both students and professionals.

Broadcast Engineering Society (India)
912 Surya Kiran Bldg.
19, K.G. Marg
New Delhi, Delhi 110 001 India
Phone: 91-11-23316709
Fax: 91-11-23316710
E-mail Address: rksi2906@gmail.com
Web Address: www.besindia.com
The Broadcast Engineering Society (India) aims to promote the interests of the broadcast engineering profession at the national and international levels.

Canadian Council of Professional Engineers (CCPE)
180 Elgin St., Ste. 1100
Ottawa, Ontario K2P 2K3 Canada
Phone: 613-232-2474
Fax: 613-230-5759
Toll Free: 877-408-9273
E-mail Address: info@engineerscanada.ca
Web Address: www.engineerscanada.ca
The Canadian Council of Professional Engineers (CCPE), operating as Engineers Canada, is a national organization in Canada consisting of 12 provincial and territorial associations and organizations that license more than 160,000 professional engineers.

Center for Innovative Technology (CIT)
2214 Rock Hill Rd., Ste. 600
Herndon, VA 20170-4228 USA
Phone: 703-689-3000
Fax: 703-689-3041
Web Address: www.cit.org
The Center for Innovative Technology is a nonprofit organization designed to enhance the research and development capabilities

by creating partnerships between innovative technology start-up companies and advanced technology consumers.

Chemical Industry and Engineering Society of China (CIESC)
Fl. 7, Block B, No. 33
Beijing Anding Rd., Chaoyang District
Beijing, 100029 China
Phone: 86-10-6444-1885
E-mail Address: yyangyh@ciesc.cn
Web Address: www.ciesc.cn
The Chemical Industry and Engineering Society of China (CIESC) aims to advance chemical engineering professionals and the chemical industry through academic and educational development. CIESC is affiliated with the China Association for Science and Technology.

China Academy of Building Research (CABR)
30, Bei San Huan Dong Lu
Beijing, 100013 China
Phone: 010-84272233
Fax: 010-84281369
E-mail Address: office@cabr.com.cn
Web Address: www.cabr.cn
CABR is responsible for the development and management of the major engineering construction and product standards of China and is also the largest comprehensive research and development institute in the building industry in China. Some related institutes include Institute of Earthquake Engineering, Institute of Building Fire Research, Institute of Building Environment and Energy Efficiency (Building Physics), Institute of Foundation Engineering as well as many others.

China Association for Science and Technology (CAST)
3 Fuxing Rd.
Beijing, 100863 China
Phone: 8610-6857-1898
Fax: 8610-6857-1897
E-mail Address: cast-liasion@cast.org.cn
Web Address: english.cast.org.cn
The China Association for Science and Technology (CAST) is the largest national non-governmental organization of scientific and technological workers in China. The association has nearly 207 member organizations in the fields of engineering, science and technology.

China Engineering Cost Association (CECA)
No. 22 No.22 Baiwanzhuang St.
Bldg. 2 Fl. 7
Beijing, 100037 China
Phone: 86-10-68331163
Fax: 86-10-68331104
E-mail Address: ceca@ceca.org.cn
Web Address: www.ceca.org.cn
The China Engineering Cost Association aims to improve and promote the profession of engineering cost engineers and engineering project managers. The association provides examinations for engineering cost engineers, establishes standards in the industry and collects price information on materials and equipment. The association intercommunicates with many engineering cost organizations and specialists from Great Britain, Hong Kong, Korea, Japan, New Zealand, and Australia.

Chinese Academy of Sciences (CAS)
52 Sanlihe Rd.
Beijing, 100864 China
Phone: 86-10-6859-7521
Fax: 86-10-6851-1095
E-mail Address: cas_en@cas.cn
Web Address: english.cas.ac.cn
The Chinese Academy of Sciences (CAS) is an academic institution and research center active within the fields of natural and technological sciences. It brings together the operations of 124 science institutions, including five universities and supporting entities and over 104 research institutes throughout China.

Chinese Ceramic Society (CCS)
11 Sanlihe Rd.
Haidian District
Beijing, 100831 China
Phone: 86-10-57811248
Fax: 86-10-57811249
E-mail Address: zggsyxh@sina.com
Web Address: www.ceramsoc.com
The Chinese Ceramic Society (CCS) is an academic, nonprofit organization for professionals engaged in the science and technology of inorganic nonmetallic materials.

Chinese Hydraulic Engineering Society (CHES)
2-2 BaiGuang Rd.
Beijing, 100053 China
Phone: 86-1063202163
Fax: 86-1063202154
E-mail Address: Ches@mwr.gov.cn
Web Address: www.ches.org.cn
The Chinese Hydraulic Engineering Society (CHES) aims to promote hydraulic engineering professionals and the water resources sciences and technologies. CHES has 31 regional societies in China.

CIEMAT
Avenida Complutense 40
Madrid, 28040 Spain
Phone: 91-346-60-00
Fax: 91-346-64-80
E-mail Address: contacto@ciemat.es
Web Address: www.ciemat.es
The CIEMAT, a unit of Spain's Ministry of Education and Science, is a public research agency. Its areas of focus include solar energy, biomass energy, wind energy, environment, basic research, fusion by magnetic confinement, nuclear safety, and technology transfer. Primary operations include PSA, the Solar Platform of Almeria, where concentrating solar power (CSP) is researched; CEDER, the Centre for the Development of Renewable Energy Sources; and CETA-CIEMAT, a center for information technology research.

Community Research and Development Information Service (CORDIS)
Office for Official Publications of the European Union Communities
2 rue Mercier
Luxembourg, L-2985 Luxembourg
Phone: 352-2929-42210
E-mail Address: cordis-helpdesk@publications.europa.eu
Web Address: cordis.europa.eu

The Community Research and Development Information Service (CORDIS) provides information about research and development sponsored and supported by the European Union. It is managed by the Office for Official Publications of the European Union Communities (Publications Office).

DECHEMA (Society for Chemical Engineering and Biotechnology)
Theodor-Heuss-Allee 25
Frankfurt am Main, 60486 Germany
Phone: 49-69-75-64-0
Fax: 49-69-75-64-201
Web Address: dechema.de
The DECHEMA (Society for Chemical Engineering and Biotechnology) is a nonprofit scientific and technical society based in Germany. It was founded in 1926 to promote research and technical advances in the areas of chemical engineering, biotechnology and environmental protection.

Earthquake Engineering Research Institute (EERI)
499 14th St., Ste. 220
Oakland, CA 94612-1934 USA
Phone: 510-451-0905
Fax: 510-451-5411
E-mail Address: eeri@eeri.org
Web Address: www.eeri.org
The Earthquake Engineering Research Institute (EERI) is a national nonprofit technical organization of engineers, geoscientists, architects, planners, public officials and social scientists aimed at reducing earthquake risk by advancing the science and practice of earthquake engineering.

Energy Sources and Processing Segment ASME Group
11757 Katy Fwy., Ste. 380
Houston, TX 77079 USA
Phone: 281-493-3491
Fax: 281-493-3493
E-mail Address: HoustonASMEoffice@asme.org
Web Address: https://community.asme.org/energy_sources_and_processing_segment/groupleadership.aspx#_ga=1.249558919.1090361535.1445625241
Energy Sources and Processing Segment, formerly known as The International Petroleum Technology Institute (IPTI), is the division of ASME (the American Society of Mechanical Engineers) Group concerned with the special engineering needs of the petroleum industry.

Engineer's Club (The) (TEC)
1737 Silverwood Dr.
San Jose, CA 95124 USA
Phone: 408-316-0488
E-mail Address: INFO@engineers.com
Web Address: www.engineers.com
The Engineer's Club (TEC) provides a variety of resources for engineers and technical professionals.

European Association of Geoscientists & Engineers (EAGE)
De Molen 42
Db Houten, 3994 The Netherlands
Phone: 31-88-995-5055
Fax: 31-30-6343524
E-mail Address: eage@eage.org
Web Address: www.eage.org
EAGE is a professional association for geoscientists and engineers. It is a European-based organization with a worldwide membership providing a global network of commercial and academic professionals to all members. The association is truly multi-disciplinary and international in form and pursuits.

European Industrial Research Management Association
rue de al Loi, 81 A
Brussels, 1040 Belgium
Phone: 33-2-233-11-80
Web Address: www.eirma.org
EIRMA is not-for-profit organization which focuses on the effective global management and organization of business R&D and innovation within a European perspective. EIRMA engages over 100 major companies which are based in over 20 countries and operate in a wide range of sectors.

Federal Ministry of Education and Research - Germany
Heinemannstr. 2
Bonn, 53175 Germany
Phone: 49(0)-228-9957-0
Fax: 49(0)-228-9957-83601
E-mail Address: bmbf@bmbf.bund.de
Web Address: www.bmbf.de/en/nanotechnologie.php
The German Federal Ministry of Education and Research, Bundesministerium fur Bildung und Forschung (BMBF), is funding research and development in the field of future-oriented new technologies in Germany. The BMBF focuses its research efforts on high technology, life sciences and nanotechnologies, among other fields.

Federation of Technology Industries (FHI)
Leusderend 12
Leusden, 3832 RC The Netherlands
Phone: 31-33-465-7507
Fax: 31-33-461-6638
E-mail Address: info@fhi.nl
Web Address: federatie.fhi.nl
The Federation of Technology Industries (FHI) is the Dutch trade organization representing the industrial electronics, automation, laboratory technology and medical technology sectors in the Netherlands.

German Association of High-Tech Industries (SPECTARIS)
Werderscher Markt 15
Berlin, 10117 Germany
Phone: 49-30-4140-210
Fax: 49-30-4140-2133
E-mail Address: info@spectaris.de
Web Address: www.spectaris.de
The German Association of High-Tech Industries (SPECTARIS) is the trade association for technology and research in the consumer optics, photonics, biotech, laboratory technology and medical technology sectors.

Hong Kong Institution of Engineers (HKIE)
9/F Island Beverley
No. 1 Great George St.
Causeway Bay Hong, Hong Kong Hong Kong
Phone: 852-2895-4446
Fax: 852-2577-7791

E-mail Address: hkie-sec@hkie.org.hk
Web Address: www.hkie.org.hk
The Hong Kong Institution of Engineers (HKIE) promotes engineering professionals and maintains the standards of the profession.

IEEE Broadcast Technological Society (IEEE BTS)
445 Hoes Ln.
Piscataway, NJ 08854 USA
Phone: 732-562-5407
Fax: 732-981-1769
E-mail Address: a.temple@ieee.org
Web Address: bts.ieee.org
The IEEE Broadcast Technological Society (IEEE BTS) is the arm of the Institute of Electrical & Electronics Engineers (IEEE) devoted to devices, equipment, techniques and systems related to broadcast technology.

IEEE Communications Society (ComSoc)
3 Park Ave., Fl. 17
New York, NY 10016 USA
Phone: 212-705-8900
Fax: 212-705-8999
Web Address: www.comsoc.org
The IEEE Communications Society (ComSoc) is composed of industry professionals with a common interest in advancing communications technologies.

IEEE Oceanic Engineering Society (OES)
26 Rue De Keraveloc
Tregana
Locmaria-Plouzane, 29280 France
Phone: 332-98001371
Fax: 332-98001098
E-mail Address: rene.garello@telecom-bretagne.eu
Web Address: www.oceanicengineering.org
The IEEE Oceanic Engineering Society (OES) is the division of the IEEE that deals with electrical engineering at sea, including unmanned submarines and offshore oil platforms.

Illuminating Engineering Society (IES)
120 Wall St., Fl. 17
New York, NY 10005-4001 USA
Phone: 212-248-5000
Fax: 212-248-5017
E-mail Address: ies@ies.org
Web Address: www.ies.org
A recognized authority on lighting in North America, the Illuminating Engineering Society (IES) establishes scientific lighting recommendations. Members include engineers, architects, designers, educators, students, manufacturers and scientists.

Indian Institute of Technology - Roorkee
Indian Institute of Technology Roorkee
Roorkee, Uttarakhand 247 667 India
Phone: 91-1332-285311
E-mail Address: regis@iitr.ernet.in
Web Address: www.iitr.ac.in
Indian Institute of Technology - Roorkee is among the foremost institutes in higher technological education and engineering in India for basic and applied research.

Industrial Research Institute (IRI)
2300 Clarendon Blvd., Ste. 400
Arlington, VA 22201 USA
Phone: 703-647-2580
Fax: 703-647-2581
E-mail Address: information@iriweb.org
Web Address: www.iriweb.org
The Industrial Research Institute (IRI) is a nonprofit organization of over 200 leading industrial companies, representing industries such as aerospace, automotive, chemical, computers and electronics, which carry out industrial research efforts in the U.S. manufacturing sector. IRI helps members improve research and development capabilities.

Institute of Bioengineering and Nanotechnology, Singapore
31 Biopolis Way
The Nanos 04-01
Singapore, 138669 Singapore
Phone: 65-6824-7000
Fax: 65-6478-9080
E-mail Address: enquiry@ibn.a-star.edu.sg
Web Address: www.ibn.a-star.edu.sg
As a scientific research institute, Institute of Bioengineering and Nanotechnology (IBN) focuses its activities on the following key areas; developing a critical knowledge base in bioengineering and nanotechnology; generating new biomaterials, devices and processes; and producing and publishing high-quality scientific research.

Institute of Biological Engineering (IBE)
446 East High St., Ste. 10
Lexington, KY 40507 USA
Phone: 859-977-7450
Fax: 859-271-0607
E-mail Address: info@ibe.org
Web Address: www.ibe.org
The Institute of Biological Engineering (IBE) is a professional organization encouraging inquiry and interest in biological engineering and professional development for its members.

Institute of Electrical and Electronics Engineers (IEEE)
3 Park Ave., Fl. 17
New York, NY 10016-5997 USA
Phone: 212-419-7900
Fax: 212-752-4929
Toll Free: 800-678-4333
E-mail Address: society-info@ieee.org
Web Address: www.ieee.org
The Institute of Electrical and Electronics Engineers (IEEE) is a nonprofit, technical professional association of more than 430,000 individual members in approximately 160 countries. The IEEE sets global technical standards and acts as an authority in technical areas ranging from computer engineering, biomedical technology and telecommunications, to electric power, aerospace and consumer electronics.

Institute of Industrial Engineers (IIE)
3577 Parkway Ln., Ste. 200
Norcross, GA 30092 USA
Phone: 770-449-0460
Fax: 770-441-3295
Toll Free: 800-494-0460
E-mail Address: cs@iienet.org
Web Address: www.iienet2.org

The Institute of Industrial Engineers (IIE) is an international, non-profit association dedicated to the education, development, training and research in the field of industrial engineering.

Institute of Marine Engineering, Science and Technology (IMarEST)
1 Birdcage Walk
London, SW1H 9JJ UK
Phone: 44-20-7382-2600
E-mail Address: info@imarest.org
Web Address: www.imarest.org
The Institute of Marine Engineering, Science and Technology (IMarEST) works to promote the development of marine engineering, science and technology.

Institute of Physics and Engineering in Medicine (IPEM)
230 Tadcaster Rd.
Fairmount House
York, YO24 1ES UK
Phone: 44-1904-610-821
Fax: 44-1904-612-279
E-mail Address: office@ipem.ac.uk
Web Address: www.ipem.ac.uk
The Institute of Physics and Engineering in Medicine (IPEM) is an organization of scientists applying physics and engineering in medical and biological applications.

Institute of Structural Engineers (IStructE)
International HQ
47-58 Bastwick St.
London, EC1V 3PS UK
Phone: 44-20-7235-4535
Fax: 44-20-7235-4294
E-mail Address: pr@istructe.org
Web Address: www.istructe.org.uk
The Institute of Structural Engineers (IStructE) is a professional organization, headquartered in the U.K., that sets and maintains standards for professional structural engineers. It has 27,000 members in 105 countries worldwide.

Institution of Engineering and Technology (The) (IET)
Michael Faraday House
Six Hills Way
Stevenage, Herts SG1 2AY UK
Phone: 44-1438-313-311
Fax: 44-1438-765-526
E-mail Address: postmaster@theiet.org
Web Address: www.theiet.org
The Institution of Engineering and Technology (IET) is an innovative international organization for electronics, electrical, manufacturing and IT professionals.

Institution of Engineers, Singapore
70 Bukit Tinggi Rd.
Singapore, 289758 Singapore
Phone: 65-6469-5000
Fax: 65-6467-1108
Web Address: www.ies.org.sg
The Institution of Engineers, Singapore is the national society of engineers and its mission is the advancement of engineering in Singapore, and to advance and to promote the science, art and the profession of engineering.

Institution of Engineers, The (India)
8 Gokhale Rd.
Kolkata, 700 020 India
Phone: 91-33-2223-8335
E-mail Address: da@ieindia.org
Web Address: www.ieindia.org
The Institution of Engineers (India) is one of the largest multi-disciplinary engineering professional societies in India and was established to promote and advance the science, practice and business of engineering.

Institution of Mechanical Engineers-UK
1 Birdcage Walk
Westminster
London, SW1H 9JJ UK
Phone: 44-20-7222-7899
E-mail Address: enquiries@imeche.org
Web Address: www.imeche.org
Institution of Mechanical Engineers represents the mechanical engineering profession in UK. The UK has the sixth largest manufacturing industry in the world and this association recognizes engineering professionals in this field. In addition, its other major themes are the energy, environment and transport industries as well as hosting educational opportunities for engineers.

International Commission of Agricultural and Biosystems Engineering (CIGR)
100-73 Kitanokuchi Mozumecho Mukoshi
Kyoto, 617 0001 Japan
Phone: 81-90-9888-4050
Fax: 81-75-922-3683
Web Address: www.cigr.org
International Commission of Agricultural and Biosystems Engineering (CIGR) encourages and facilitates interregional exchange and the development of sciences and technologies in the field of agricultural engineering.

International Electrotechnical Commission (IEC)
3, rue de Varembe
P.O. Box 131
Geneva 20, CH-1211 Switzerland
Phone: 41-22-919-02-11
Fax: 41-22-919-03-00
E-mail Address: info@iec.ch
Web Address: www.iec.ch
The International Electrotechnical Commission (IEC), based in Switzerland, promotes international cooperation on all questions of standardization and related matters in electrical and electronic engineering.

International Federation of Automotive Engineering Societies (FISITA)
29 M11 Business Link
Stansted, CM24 8GF UK
Phone: 44-0-1279-833-470
E-mail Address: info@fisita.com
Web Address: www.fisita.com
The Federation Internationale des Societes d'Ingenieurs des Techniques de l'Automobile (FISITA) was founded in Paris in 1948 with the purpose of bringing engineers from around the world together in a spirit of cooperation to share ideas and advance the technological development of the automobile. FISITA is the umbrella organization for the national automotive societies in 37 countries around the world. Its network of member societies represents more than 200,000 automotive engineers around the globe.

International Federation of Consulting Engineers (FIDIC)
World Trade Center II, Geneva Airport Box 311
29 Route de Pre-Bois, Cointrin
Geneva 15, CH-1215 Switzerland
Phone: 41-22-799-49-00
Fax: 41-22-799-49-01
E-mail Address: fidic@fidic.org
Web Address: fidic.org
The International Federation of Consulting Engineers (FIDIC) represents globally its national member associations and the consulting engineering industry and profession. Its web site also promotes best practices in areas such as international contracts, risk management, and sustainable development.

International Society of Automation (ISA), The
67 T.W. Alexander Dr.
P.O. Box 12277
Research Triangle Park,
NC 27709 USA
Phone: 919-549-8411
Fax: 919-549-8288
E-mail Address: info@isa.org
Web Address: www.isa.org
The International Society of Automation (ISA), formerly known as the International Society for Measurement and Control is a nonprofit organization that serves the professional development and credential needs of control system engineers, instrument technicians and others within the field of automation and control.

International Society of Pharmaceutical Engineers (ISPE)
600 N. Westshore Blvd., Ste. 900
Tampa, FL 33609 USA
Phone: 813-960-2105
Fax: 813-264-2816
E-mail Address: ASK@ispe.org
Web Address: www.ispe.org
The International Society of Pharmaceutical Engineers (ISPE) is a worldwide nonprofit society dedicated to educating and advancing pharmaceutical manufacturing professionals and the biopharmaceutical industry.

International Standards Organization (ISO)
Chemin de Blandonnet 8
1214 Vernier
Geneva, CP 401 Switzerland
Phone: 41-22-749-01-11
Fax: 41-22-733-34-30
E-mail Address: central@iso.org
Web Address: www.iso.org
The International Standards Organization (ISO) is a global consortium of national standards institutes from 162 countries. The established International Standards are designed to make products and services more efficient, safe and clean.

International Union of Pure and Applied Physics (IUPAP)
Institute of Advanced Studies,
Nanyang Executive Centre #02-18
Nanyang Technological University,
60 Nanyang View
Singapore, 639673 Singapore
Phone: 65 9322-1289
Fax: 65-6794-4941
E-mail Address: IUPAP.Admin@ntu.edu.sg
Web Address: www.iupap.org
The International Union of Pure and Applied Physics (IUPAP) was established in 1922 as a global group. The aims of the Union are to stimulate and promote international cooperation in physics; sponsor international meetings; publish papers; and foster research and education.

Japan Science and Technology Agency (JST)
Kawaguchi Ctr. Bldg.
4-1-8 Honcho, Kawaguchi-shi
Saitama, 332-0012 Japan
Phone: 81-48-226-5601
Fax: 81-48-226-5651
Web Address: www.jst.go.jp/EN
The Japan Science and Technology Agency (JST) acts as a core organization for implementation of the nation's science and technology policies by conducting research and development, with particular emphasis on new technological needs.

Marine Technology Society (MTS)
1100 H St. NW, Ste. LL-100
Washington, DC 20005 USA
Phone: 202-717-8705
Fax: 202-347-4302
E-mail Address: membership@mtsociety.org
Web Address: www.mtsociety.org
The Marine Technology Society (MTS) is an organization devoted to the advancement, information exchange and application of marine technology.

Materials Research Society (MRS)
506 Keystone Dr.
Warrendale, PA 15086-7573 USA
Phone: 724-779-3003
Fax: 724-779-8313
E-mail Address: info@mrs.org
Web Address: www.mrs.org
The Materials Research Society (MRS) is dedicated to basic and applied research on materials of technological importance. MRS emphasizes an interdisciplinary approach to materials science and engineering. It is responsible for the publication of the Journal of Materials Science, a peer-reviewed journal focused on printing advanced research in materials science.

Minerals, Metals & Materials Society (The) (TMS)
184 Thorn Hill Rd.
Warrendale, PA 15086-7514 USA
Phone: 724-776-9000
Fax: 724-776-3770
Toll Free: 800-759-4867
E-mail Address: webmaster@tms.org
Web Address: www.tms.org
The Minerals Metals & Materials Society (TMS) is an organization of professionals and students involved in metallurgy and material engineering, promoting the exchange of information, education and technology.

National Academy of Engineering (NAE)
500 5th St. NW
Washington, DC 20001 USA
Phone: 202-334-3200
E-mail Address: dmote@nae.edu
Web Address: www.nae.edu
The National Academy of Engineering (NAE) is a nonprofit institution that conducts independent

studies to examine important topics in engineering and technology. It is the portal for all engineering activities at the National Academies, which include the National Academy of Sciences, the Institute of Medicine and the National Research Council.

National Academy of Science (NAS)
500 5th St. NW
Washington, DC 20001 USA
Phone: 202-334-2000
E-mail Address: worldwidefeedback@nas.edu
Web Address: www.nationalacademies.org
The National Academy of Science (NAS) is a private, nonprofit, self-perpetuating society of scholars engaged in scientific and engineering research. Three organizations comprise the NAS: The National Academy of Engineering, the National Academy of Sciences and the National Academy of Medicine.

National Research Council
500 Fifth St. NW
Washington, DC 20001 USA
Phone: 202-334-2000
Toll Free: 800-624-6242
E-mail Address: worldwidewebfeedback@nas.edu
Web Address: www.nationalacademies.org/nrc/
The National Academies of Sciences, Engineering and Medicine are private, nonprofit institutions that provide science, technology and health policy advice under a congressional charter. Its membership consists of world's most distinguished scientists, physicians and researchers; and activities include consensus studies, journals and periodicals, education and outreach and acknowledging exemplary professional achievement.

Netherlands Organization for Applied Scientific Research (TNO)
Anna van Buerenplein 1
The Hague, NL-2595 DA The Netherlands
Phone: 31-88-866-0000
E-mail Address: wegwijzer@tno.nl
Web Address: www.tno.nl
The Netherlands Organization for Applied Scientific Research (TNO) is a contract research organization that provides a link between fundamental research and practical application.

Optical Society of America (OSA)
2010 Massachusetts Ave. NW
Washington, DC 20036-1023 USA
Phone: 202-223-8130
Fax: 202-223-1096
E-mail Address: info@osa.org
Web Address: www.osa.org
The Optical Society of America (OSA) is an interdisciplinary society offering synergy between all components of the optics industry, from basic research to commercial applications such as fiber-optic networks. It has a membership group of over 16,000 individuals from over 100 countries. Members include scientists, engineers, educators, technicians and business leaders.

Professional Engineers Board Singapore (PEB)
52 Jurong Gateway Rd.
Singapore, 608550 Singapore
Phone: 65-6334-2310
Fax: 65-6334-2347
E-mail Address: registrar@peb.gov.sg
Web Address: www.peb.gov.sg
The Professional Engineers Board Singapore (PEB) is a statutory board in the Ministry of National Development. PEB was established since 1971 under the Professional Engineers Act in order to keep and maintain a register of professional engineers, a register of practitioners and a register of licensed corporations.

Royal Society (The)
6-9 Carlton House Ter.
London, SW1Y 5AG UK
Phone: 44-20-7451-2500
E-mail Address: science.policy@royalsociety.org
Web Address: royalsociety.org
The Royal Society, originally founded in 1660, is the UK's leading scientific organization and the oldest scientific community in continuous existence. It operates as a national academy of science, supporting scientists, engineers, technologists and researchers. Its web site contains a wealth of data about the research and development initiatives of its fellows and foreign members.

Royal Society of Chemistry (RSC)
Burlington House, Piccadilly
London, W1J 0BA UK
Phone: 44-20-7437-8656
Web Address: www.rsc.org
The Royal Society of Chemistry (RSC) is U.K.'s professional body for advancing the chemical sciences. The organization has 50,000 members.

Society of Automotive Engineers (SAE)
755 W. Big Beaver, Ste. 1600
Troy, MA 48084 USA
Phone: 248-273-2455
Fax: 248-273-2494
Toll Free: 877-606-7323
E-mail Address: automotive_hq@sae.org
Web Address: www.sae.org
The Society of Automotive Engineers (SAE) is a resource for technical information and expertise used in designing, building, maintaining and operating self-propelled vehicles for use on land, sea, air or space.

Society of Broadcast Engineers, Inc. (SBE)
9102 N. Meridian St., Ste. 150
Indianapolis, IN 46260 USA
Phone: 317-846-9000
E-mail Address: jporay@sbe.org
Web Address: www.sbe.org
The Society of Broadcast Engineers (SBE) exists to increase knowledge of broadcast engineering and promote its interests, as well as to continue the education of professionals in the industry.

Society of Cable Telecommunications Engineers (SCTE)
140 Philips Rd.
Exton, PA 19341-1318 USA
Fax: 610-884-7237
Toll Free: 800-542-5040
E-mail Address: scte@scte.org
Web Address: www.scte.org
The Society of Cable Telecommunications Engineers (SCTE) is a nonprofit professional association dedicated to advancing

the careers and serving the industry of telecommunications professionals by providing technical training, certification and information resources.

Society of Consulting Marine Engineers and Ship Surveyors (SCMS)
Unit 5, Prospect House
7 Ocean Way
Southampton, SO14 3TJ UK
Phone: 44-23-8001-6494
E-mail Address: sec@scmshq.org
Web Address: www.scmshq.org
The Society of Consulting Marine Engineers and Ship Surveyors (SCMS) is a professional organization for marine engineers in the U.K.

Society of Exploration Geophysicists (SEG)
8801 S. Yale, Ste. 500
Tulsa, OK 74137-3575 USA
Phone: 918-497-5500
Fax: 918-497-5557
Toll Free: 877-778-5463
Web Address: www.seg.org
The Society of Exploration Geophysicists (SEG) promotes the science of geophysics. The website provides access to their foundation, online publications and employment and education services.

Society of Hispanic Professional Engineers (SHPE)
13181 Crossroads Pkwy. N.
Ste. 450
City of Industry, CA 91746 USA
Phone: 323-725-3970
Fax: 323-725-0316
E-mail Address: shpenational@shpe.org
Web Address: oneshpe.shpe.org
The Society of Hispanic Professional Engineers (SHPE) is a national nonprofit organization that promotes Hispanics in science, engineering and math.

Society of Manufacturing Engineers (SME)
One SME Dr.
Dearborn, MI 48121 USA
Phone: 313-425-3000
Fax: 313-425-3400
Toll Free: 800-733-4763
E-mail Address: communications@sme.org
Web Address: www.sme.org
The Society of Manufacturing Engineers (SME) is a leading professional organization serving engineers in the manufacturing industries.

Society of Motion Picture and Television Engineers (SMPTE)
3 Barker Ave., Fl. 5
White Plains, NY 10601 USA
Phone: 914-761-1100
Fax: 914-761-3115
E-mail Address: marketing@smpte.org
Web Address: www.smpte.org
The Society of Motion Picture and Television Engineers (SMPTE) is the leading technical society for the motion imaging industry. The firm publishes recommended practice and engineering guidelines, as well the SMPTE Journal.

Society of Naval Architects and Marine Engineers (SNAME)
99 Canal Ctr. Plz., Ste. 310
Alexandria, VA 22314 USA
Phone: 703-997-6701
Fax: 703-997-6702
E-mail Address: cherzog@sname.org
Web Address: www.sname.org
The Society of Naval Architects and Marine Engineers (SNAME) is an internationally recognized nonprofit, professional society of members serving the maritime and offshore industries and their suppliers.

Society of Petroleum Engineers (SPE)
222 Palisades Creek Dr.
Richardson, TX 75080 USA
Phone: 972-952-9393
Fax: 972-952-9435
Toll Free: 800-456-6863
E-mail Address: spedal@spe.org
Web Address: www.spe.org
The Society of Petroleum Engineers (SPE) helps connect engineers in the oil and gas industry with ideas, answers, resources and technological information.

Society of Plastics Engineers (SPE)
6 Berkshire Blvd., Ste. 306
Bethel, CT 06081 USA
Phone: 203-775-0471
Fax: 203-775-8490
Web Address: www.4spe.org
The Society of Plastics Engineers (SPE) is a recognized medium of communication among scientists and engineers engaged in the development, conversion and applications of plastics.

Society of Women Engineers (SWE)
230 N La Salle St., Ste. 1675
Chicago, IL 60601 USA
Toll Free: 877-793-4636
E-mail Address: hq@swe.org
Web Address: societyofwomenengineers.swe.org
The Society of Women Engineers (SWE) is a nonprofit educational and service organization of female engineers.

SPIE
1000 20th St.
Bellingham, WA 98225-6705 USA
Phone: 360-676-3290
Fax: 360-647-1445
Toll Free: 888-504-8171
E-mail Address: customerservice@spie.org
Web Address: www.spie.org
SPIE is a nonprofit technical society aimed at the advancement and dissemination of knowledge in optics, photonics and imaging.

United Engineering Foundation (UEF)
c/o Glenmede
1650 Market St. Ste. 1200
Philadelphia, PA 19103 USA
E-mail Address: engfnd@aol.comdirector@unitedengineeringfnd.org
Web Address: www.uefoundation.org
The United Engineering Foundation (UEF) is a nonprofit organization chartered for the advancement of engineering arts and sciences in all branches.

World Federation of Engineering Organizations
Maison de l'UNESCO
1, rue Miollis
Paris, 75015 France

Phone: 33-1-45-68-48-46
Fax: 33-1-45-68-48-65
E-mail Address: info@wfeo.net
Web Address: www.wfeo.org
World Federation of Engineering Organizations (WFEO) is an international non-governmental organization that represents major engineering professional societies in over 90 nations. It has several standing committees including engineering and the environment, technology, communications, capacity building, education, energy and women in engineering.

41) Environmental Organizations

Center for Environmental Systems Research (CESR)
University of Kassel
Wilhelmshoher Allee 47, Raum 1130
Kassel, 34109 Germany
Phone: 0561-804-6110
Fax: 0561-804-6112
E-mail Address: info@cesr.de
Web Address: www.usf.uni-kassel.de/cesr/
The Center for Environmental Systems Research (CESR) is part of the University of Kassel. It operates four research groups: Global and Regional Dynamics, covering water and land use changes; Socio-Environmental Systems; Integrated Water Management; and Sustainable Energy and Material Flow Management. The CESR publishes many important papers and boosts education and research.

42) Environmental Resources

Environment Canada
10 Wellington, Fl. 23
Gatineau, QC K1A 0H3 Canada
Phone: 819-997-2800
Fax: 819-994-1412
Toll Free: 800 668-6767
E-mail Address: enviroinfo@ec.gc.ca
Web Address: www.ec.gc.ca
Environment Canada is the Canadian government's natural environment preservation department.

43) Food Industry Associations, General

Institute of Food Technologies (IFT)
525 W. Van Buren, Ste. 1000
Chicago, IL 60607 USA
Phone: 312-782-8424
Fax: 312-782-8348
Toll Free: 800-438-3663
E-mail Address: info@ift.org
Web Address: www.ift.org
The Institute of Food Technologies (IFT) is devoted to the advancement of the science and technology of food through the exchange of knowledge. The site also provides information and resources for job seekers in the food industry. Members work in food science, food technology and related professions in industry, academia and government.

44) Geoengineering

International Society for Soil Mechanics and Geotechnical Engineering (ISSMGE)
Geotechnical Engineering Research Ctr.
City University, Northampton Square
London, EC1V 0HB UK
Phone: 44-20-7040-8154
E-mail Address: secretariat@issmge.org
Web Address: www.issmge.org
The International Society for Soil Mechanics and Geotechnical Engineering (ISSMGE) is a professional body representing the interests and activities of engineers, academics and contractors all over the world that actively participate in geotechnical engineering. Its activities include conferences and publications.

45) Health Care Business & Professional Associations

Advanced Medical Technology Association (AdvaMed)
701 Pennsylvania Ave. NW, Ste. 800
Washington, DC 20004-2654 USA
Phone: 202-783-8700
Fax: 202-783-8750
E-mail Address: info@advamed.org
Web Address: www.advamed.org
The Advanced Medical Technology Association (AdvaMed) strives to be the advocate for a legal, regulatory and economic climate that advances global health care by assuring worldwide access to the benefits of medical technology.

Cryogenic Society of America, Inc. (CSA)
218 Lake St.
Oak Park, IL 60302-2609 USA
Phone: 708-383-6220
Fax: 708-383-9337
E-mail Address: csa@cryogenicsociety.org
Web Address: www.cryogenicsociety.org
The Cryogenic Society of America, Inc. (CSA) is a nonprofit organization that brings together those in all disciplines concerned with the applications of cryogenics, which refers to the art and science of achieving extremely low-temperatures. With membership spanning over 47 countries, the organization works to promote information sharing, increase awareness and conduct research in low temperature processes and techniques.

46) Industry Research/Market Research

Forrester Research
60 Acorn Park Dr.
Cambridge, MA 02140 USA
Phone: 617-613-5730
Toll Free: 866-367-7378
E-mail Address: press@forrester.com
Web Address: www.forrester.com
Forrester Research is a publicly traded company that identifies and analyzes emerging trends in technology and their impact on business. Among the firm's specialties are the financial services, retail, health care, entertainment, automotive and information technology industries.

Gartner, Inc.
56 Top Gallant Rd.
Stamford, CT 06902 USA

Phone: 203-964-0096
E-mail Address: info@gartner.com
Web Address: www.gartner.com
Gartner, Inc. is a publicly traded IT company that provides competitive intelligence and strategic consulting and advisory services to numerous clients worldwide.

MarketResearch.com
11200 Rockville Pike, Ste. 504
Rockville, MD 20852 USA
Phone: 240-747-3093
Fax: 240-747-3004
Toll Free: 800-298-5699
E-mail Address: customerservice@marketresearch.com
Web Address: www.marketresearch.com
MarketResearch.com is a leading broker for professional market research and industry analysis. Users are able to search the company's database of research publications including data on global industries, companies, products and trends.

Plunkett Research, Ltd.
P.O. Drawer 541737
Houston, TX 77254-1737 USA
Phone: 713-932-0000
Fax: 713-932-7080
E-mail Address: customersupport@plunkettresearch.com
Web Address: www.plunkettresearch.com
Plunkett Research, Ltd. is a leading provider of market research, industry trends analysis and business statistics. Since 1985, it has served clients worldwide, including corporations, universities, libraries, consultants and government agencies. At the firm's web site, visitors can view product information and pricing and access a large amount of basic market information on industries such as financial services, InfoTech, e-commerce, health care and biotech.

47) Internet Industry Associations

Cooperative Association for Internet Data Analysis (CAIDA)
9500 Gilman Dr.
Mail Stop 0505
La Jolla, CA 92093-0505 USA
Phone: 858-534-5000
E-mail Address: info@caida.org
Web Address: www.caida.org
The Cooperative Association for Internet Data Analysis (CAIDA), representing organizations from the government, commercial and research sectors, works to promote an atmosphere of greater cohesion in the engineering and maintenance of the Internet. CAIDA is located at the San Diego Supercomputer Center (SDSC) on the campus of the University of California, San Diego (UCSD).

Internet Society (ISOC)
1775 Wiehle Ave., Ste. 201
Reston, VA 20190-5108 USA
Phone: 703-439-2120
Fax: 703-326-9881
E-mail Address: isoc@isoc.org
Web Address: www.isoc.org
The Internet Society (ISOC) is a nonprofit organization that provides leadership in public policy issues that influence the future of the Internet. The organization is the home of groups that maintain infrastructure standards for the Internet, such as the Internet Engineering Task Force (IETF) and the Internet Architecture Board (IAB).

Internet Systems Consortium, Inc. (ISC)
950 Charter St.
Redwood City, CA 94063 USA
Phone: 650-423-1300
Fax: 650-423-1355
E-mail Address: info@isc.org
Web Address: www.isc.org
The Internet Systems Consortium, Inc. (ISC) is a nonprofit organization with extensive expertise in the development, management, maintenance and implementation of Internet technologies.

World Wide Web Consortium (W3C)
32 Vassar St., Bldg. 32-G515
Cambridge, MA 02139 USA
Phone: 617-253-2613
Fax: 617-258-5999
E-mail Address: susan@w3.org
Web Address: www.w3.org
The World Wide Web Consortium (W3C) develops technologies and standards to enhance the performance and utility of the World Wide Web. The W3C is hosted by three different organizations: the European Research Consortium for Informatics and Mathematics (ERICM) handles inquiries about the W3C in the EMEA region; Keio University handles W3C's Japanese and Korean correspondence; and the Computer Science & Artificial Intelligence Lab (CSAIL) at MIT handles all other countries, include Australia and the U.S.

48) Internet Industry Resources

American Registry for Internet Numbers (ARIN)
3635 Concorde Pkwy., Ste. 200
Chantilly, VA 20151-1125 USA
Phone: 703-227-9840
Fax: 703-263-0417
E-mail Address: info@arin.net
Web Address: www.arin.net
The American Registry for Internet Numbers (ARIN) is a nonprofit organization that administers and registers Internet protocol (IP) numbers. The organization also develops policies and offers educational outreach services.

Berkman Center for Internet & Society
23 Everett St., Fl. 2
Cambridge, MA 02138 USA
Phone: 617-495-7547
Fax: 617-495-7641
E-mail Address: cyber@law.harvard.edu
Web Address: cyber.law.harvard.edu
The Berkman Center for Internet & Society, housed at Harvard University's law school, focuses on the exploration of the development and inner-workings of laws pertaining to the Internet. The center offers Internet courses, conferences, advising and advocacy.

Congressional Internet Caucus Advisory Committee (ICAC)
1401 K St. NW, Ste. 200
Washington, DC 20008 USA

Phone: 202-638-4370
E-mail Address:
tlordan@netcaucus.org
Web Address: www.netcaucus.org
The Congressional Internet Caucus Advisory Committee (ICAC) works to educate the public, as well as a bipartisan group from the U.S. House and Senate about Internet-related policy issues.

Internet Assigned Numbers Authority (IANA)
12025 Waterfront Dr., Ste. 300
Los Angeles, CA 90094 USA
Phone: 310-301-5800
Fax: 310-823-8649
E-mail Address: iana@iana.org
Web Address: www.iana.org
The Internet Assigned Numbers Authority (IANA) serves as the central coordinator for the assignment of parameter values for Internet protocols. IANA is operated by the Internet Corporation for Assigned Names and Numbers (ICANN).

49) Manufacturing Associations-Machinery & Technology

Association for Manufacturing Technology (AMT)
7901 Westpark Dr.
McLean, VA 22102-4206 USA
Phone: 703-893-2900
Fax: 703-893-1151
Toll Free: 800-524-0475
E-mail Address: amt@amtonline.org
Web Address: www.amtonline.org
The Association for Manufacturing Technology (AMT) actively supports and promotes American manufacturers of machine tools and manufacturing technology.

German Machine Tool Builders' Association (VDW)
Verein Deutscher Werkzeugmaschinenfabriken e.V.
Corneliusstrasse 4
Frankfurt am Main, 60325 Germany
Phone: 49 69 75608 10
Fax: 49 69 756081 11
E-mail Address: vdw@vdw.de
Web Address: www.vdw.de
German Machine Tool Builders' Association (VDW) represents the industry nationally and internationally. The organization offers information, news and updates from fields, such as economics and statistics, technology, research, law and taxation to its members.

Indian Machine Tool Manufacturers Association (IMTMA)
Tumkur Rd., Madavara Post, 10th Mile
Bangalore Int'l Exhibition Ctr.
Bangalore, 562123 India
Phone: 91-80-6624-6600
Fax: 91-80-6624-6661
E-mail Address: imtma@imtma.in
Web Address: www.imtma.in
Indian Machine Tool Manufacturers Association (IMTMA) has a membership of over 492 organizations of all sizes spread across the country. Membership of IMTMA specializes in the complete range of metalworking machine tools and manufacturing solutions, accessories for machines, as well as the varied range of cutting tools and tooling systems.

National Center for Manufacturing Sciences (NCMS)
3025 Boardwalk Dr.
Ann Arbor, MI 48108-3230 USA
Fax: 734-995-0380
Toll Free: 800-222-6267
E-mail Address: info@ncms.org
Web Address: www.ncms.org
The National Center for Manufacturing Sciences (NCMS) is a non-profit membership organization dedicated to advancing the global competitiveness of North American manufacturing industry.

National Tooling and Machining Association (NTMA)
1357 Rockside Rd.
Cleveland, OH 44134 USA
Fax: 216-264-2840
Toll Free: 800-248-6862
E-mail Address: info@ntma.org
Web Address: www.ntma.org
The National Tooling and Machining Association (NTMA) helps members of the U.S. precision custom manufacturing industries achieve business success in a global economy through advocacy, advice, networking, information, programs and services.

Singapore Institute of Manufacturing Technology (SIMTech)
73 Nanyang Dr.
Singapore, 637662 Singapore
Phone: 65-6793-8383
E-mail Address: ido@SIMTech.a-star.edu.sg
Web Address: www.a-star.edu.sg/simtech
The Singapore Institute of Manufacturing Technology (SIMTech) has completed more than 880 projects with more than 410 companies, big and small, in the electronics, semiconductor, precision engineering, aerospace, automotive, marine, logistics and other sectors.

50) Maritime Associations

German Shipbuilding and Ocean Industries Association
Verband fur Schiffbau und Meerestechnik e.V.
Steinhoft 11 (Slomanhaus)
Hamburg, 20459 Germany
Phone: 49-040-2801-52-0
Fax: 49-040-2801-52-30
E-mail Address: info@vsm.de
Web Address: www.vsm.de
The VSM represents the political and commercial interests of the German maritime industry; shipyards building; oceangoing and inland waterway vessels; and marine equipment suppliers.

51) Metals & Steel Industry Associations

Chinese Society for Metals
Phone: 86-10-65270210
Fax: 86-10-65124122
E-mail Address:
csmoffice@csm.org.cn
Web Address: www.csm.org.cn
The Chinese Society for Metals is a non-profit organization that focuses on advancing science and technology in the metallurgical industry, materials science and engineering and the professionals in these fields.

Society for Mining, Metallurgy and Exploration (SME)
12999 E. Adam Aircraft Cir.
Englewood, CO 80112 USA
Phone: 303-948-4200
Fax: 303-973-3845
Toll Free: 800-763-3132
E-mail Address: cs@smenet.org
Web Address: www.smenet.org
The Society for Mining, Metallurgy and Exploration (SME) advances the worldwide mining and minerals community through information exchange and professional development.

52) Nanotechnology Associations

International Association of Nanotechnology (IANT)
NASA Ames Research Center
P.O. Box 151
Moffett Field, CA 94035 USA
Phone: 408-280-6222
Fax: 877-636-6266
E-mail Address: info@ianano.org
Web Address: www.ianano.org
The International Association of Nanotechnology is a non-profit organization that promotes research collaboration in nanoscience worldwide for the benefit of society. The IANT sponsors panel discussions, regional meetings and an international congress to discuss the development of nanotechnology.

53) Nanotechnology Resources

Center for Directed Assembly of Nanostructures
110 8th St., 1st Fl. MRC
Rensselaer Polytechnic Institute
Troy, NY 12180-3590 USA
Phone: 518-276-8846
Fax: 518-276-6540
E-mail Address: nanocenter@rpi.edu
Web Address: www.rpi.edu/dept/nsec
The Center for Directed Assembly of Nanostructures focuses on learning to produce nanomaterials in controlled ways, incorporating them into polymer and ceramic composites and assembling them into complex structures. It is part of the Rensselaer Polytechnic Institute, and was one of the first six National Science Foundation Nanoscale Science and Engineering Centers (NSF NSEC) established in 2001.

Centre for Large Space Structures and Systems (CLS3)
1425 Rene Levesque Blvd., W-700
Montreal, QC H3G-1T7 Canada
Phone: 514-499-3959
Fax: 514-499-8927
Toll Free: 877-533-2573
E-mail Address: info@cl3.ca
Web Address: www.cls3.ca
The Centre for Large Space Structures and Systems (CLS3) is a research center for large space systems and related systems technology. It is a recognized pioneer in Micro-Nano-Technologies (MNT) for aerospace and defense applications.

National Institute of Advanced Industrial Science and Technology-Nanomaterials Research Institute
1-1-1 Higashi
AIST Tusukubs Central 5
Tsukuba, Ibaraki 305-8565 Japan
E-mail Address: nmri-info-ml@aist.go.jp
Web Address: https://unit.aist.go.jp/nmri/index_en.html
The National Institute of Advanced Industrial Science and Technology-Nanomaterials Research Institute is Japan's foremost nanomaterials research institute.

National Nanotechnology Initiative (NNI)
4201 Wilson Blvd.
Stafford II, Rm. 405
Arlington, VA 22230 USA
Phone: 703-292-8626
Fax: 703-292-9312
E-mail Address: info@nnco.nano.gov
Web Address: www.nano.gov
The National Nanotechnology Initiative (NNI) is a federal R&D program established to coordinate the multiagency efforts in nanoscale science, engineering and technology. 20 department and independent agencies participate in the NNI. Other federal organizations contribute with studies, applications of the results from those agencies performing R&D and other collaborations. The NNI is part of the National Nanotechnology Coordination Office within the Nanoscale Science Engineering and Technology (NSET) subcommittee of the National Science and Technology Council (NSTC).

54) Patent Organizations

European Patent Office
Bob-van-Benthem-Platz 1
Munich, 80469 Germany
Phone: 49 89 2399-0
E-mail Address: press@epo.org
Web Address: www.epo.org
The European Patent Office (EPO) provides a uniform application procedure for individual inventors and companies seeking patent protection in up to 38 European countries. It is the executive arm of the European Patent Organization and is supervised by the Administrative Council.

World Intellectual Property Organization (WIPO)
34 chemin des Colombettes
Geneva, CH-1211 Switzerland
Phone: 41-22-338-9111
Fax: 41-22-733-5428
Web Address: www.wipo.int
The World Intellectual Property Organization (WIPO) has a United Nations mandate to assist organizations and companies in filing patents and other intellectual property data on a global basis. At its web site, users can download free copies of its WIPO magazine and search its international patent applications.

55) Patent Resources

Patent Board (The)
Web Address: www.patentboard.com
The Patent Board is an online platform, which offers tools and metrics for patent analysis and intellectual property investing. Its services include technology landscape analysis, portfolio assessment and merger and acquisition due diligence. The Patent Board platform is owned by Global Ventures, LLC.

56) Plastics Industry Associations

China Plastics Processing Industry Association (CPPIA)
6 E. Chang'an Ave.
Beijing, 100740 China
Phone: 86-10-6559-2882
Fax: 86-10-6527-8590
E-mail Address: ccpia@ccpia.com.cn
Web Address: www.cppia.com.cn
The China Plastics Processing Industry Association (CPPIA) promotes the industry which includes plastic pipe, injection molded products and other engineering plastics.

57) Research & Development, Laboratories

Advanced Technology Laboratory (ARL)
10000 Burnet Rd.
University of Texas at Austin
Austin, TX 78758 USA
Phone: 512-835-3200
Fax: 512-835-3259
Web Address: www.arlut.utexas.edu
Advanced Technology Laboratory (ARL) at the University of Texas at Austin provides research programs dedicated to improving the military capability of the United States in applications of acoustics, electromagnetic and information technology.

Argonne National Laboratory, Nuclear Engineering Division (ANL)
9700 S. Cass Ave.
Argonne, IL 60439-4814 USA
E-mail Address: neinfo@anl.gov
Web Address: www.ne.anl.gov
The Argonne National Laboratory-Nuclear Engineering Division (ANL) is engaged in research and development in the area of applied nuclear technologies such as nonproliferation, environmental remediation, fusion power and new initiatives.

Battelle Memorial Institute
505 King Ave.
Columbus, OH 43201-2693 USA
Phone: 614-424-6424
Toll Free: 800-201-2011
E-mail Address: solutions@battelle.org
Web Address: www.battelle.org
Battelle Memorial Institute serves commercial and governmental customers in developing new technologies and products. The institute adds technology to systems and processes for manufacturers; pharmaceutical and agrochemical industries; trade associations; and government agencies supporting energy, the environment, health, national security and transportation.

Brookhaven National Laboratory (BNL)
P.O. Box 5000
Upton, NY 11973-5000 USA
Phone: 631-344-8000
Web Address: www.bnl.gov
Brookhaven National Laboratory (BNL) is a research facility funded by the Office of Science within the Department of Energy. BNL conducts research in the physical, biomedical and environmental sciences, as well as in energy technologies and national security.

CERN (European Organization for Nuclear Research, LHC)
CERN
Geneva 23, CH-1211 Switzerland
Phone: 41-22-76-784-84
E-mail Address: cern.reception@cern.ch
Web Address: home.web.cern.ch
CERN, the European Organization for Nuclear Research, is one of the world's largest centers for scientific research. Its business is fundamental physics, finding out what the universe is made of and how it works. CERN is the operator of the Large Hadron Collider (LHC), a particle accelerator used by physicists to study the smallest known particles.

Commonwealth Scientific and Industrial Research Organization (CSRIO)
CSIRO Enquiries
Private Bag 10
Clayton South,
Victoria 3169 Australia
Phone: 61-3-9545-2176
Toll Free: 1300-363-400
Web Address: www.csiro.au
The Commonwealth Scientific and Industrial Research Organization (CSRIO) is Australia's national science agency and a leading international research agency. CSRIO performs research in Australia over a broad range of areas including agriculture, minerals and energy, manufacturing, communications, construction, health and the environment.

Computational Neurobiology Laboratory
CNL-S c/o The Salk Institute
10010 N. Torrey Pines Rd.
La Jolla, CA 92037 USA
Phone: 858-453-4100
Fax: 858-587-0417
Web Address: www.cnl.salk.edu
The Computational Neurobiology Laboratory at The Salk Institute strives to understand the computational resources of the brain from the biophysical to the systems levels.

Council of Scientific & Industrial Research (CSIR)
2 Rafi Marg
Anusandhan Bhawan
New Delhi, 110 001 India
Phone: 91-11-2373-7889
Fax: 91-11-2371-0618
E-mail Address: itweb@csir.res.in
Web Address: www.csir.res.in
The Council of Scientific & Industrial Research (CSIR) is a government-funded organization that promotes research and development initiatives in India. It operates in the fields of energy, biotechnology, space, science and technology.

Daresbury Laboratory
Sci Tech Daresbury
Keckwick Ln.
Warrington, Cheshire WA4 4AD UK
Phone: 44-1925-603000
Fax: 44-1925-603100
E-mail Address: enquiries@stfc.ac.uk
Web Address: http://www.stfc.ac.uk/1903.aspx
Daresbury Laboratory, operated by the Science & Technology Facilities

Council (STFC), is a strong resource in computational science and engineering. The STFC was formed in April 2007 from the merger of the Council for the Central Laboratory of the Research Councils (CCLRC) and the Particle Physics and Astronomy Council (PPARRC).

Electronics and Telecommunications Research Institute (ETRI)
218 Gajeongno
Yuseong-gu
Daejeon, 34129 Korea
Phone: 82-42-860-6114
E-mail Address: k21human@etri.re.kr
Web Address: www.etri.re.kr
Established in 1976, the Electronics and Telecommunications Research Institute (ETRI) is a nonprofit government-funded research organization that promotes technological excellence. The research institute has successfully developed information technologies such as TDX-Exchange, High Density Semiconductor Microchips, Mini-Super Computer (TiCOM), and Digital Mobile Telecommunication System (CDMA). ETRI's focus is on information technologies, robotics, telecommunications, digital broadcasting and future technology strategies.

Fraunhofer-Gesellschaft (FhG) (The)
Fraunhofer-Gesellschaft zur Forderung der angewandten Forschung e.V.
Postfach 20 07 33
Munich, 80007 Germany
Phone: 49-89-1205-0
Fax: 49-89-1205-7531
Web Address: www.fraunhofer.de
The Fraunhofer-Gesellschaft (FhG) institute focuses on research in health, security, energy, communication, the environment and mobility. FhG includes over 80 research units in Germany. Over 70% of its projects are derived from industry contracts.

Hanford Nuclear Site
825 Jadwin Ave., Ste. 1
Richland, WA 99352 USA
Phone: 509-376-7411
E-mail Address: Webmaster@rl.gov
Web Address: www.hanford.gov
The Hanford Nuclear Site is designed to solve critical problems related to the environment, energy production and use, U.S. economic competitiveness and national security.

Helmholtz Association
Anna-Louisa-Karsch-Strasse 2
Berlin, 10178 Germany
Phone: 49-30-206329-0
E-mail Address: info@helmholtz.de
Web Address: www.helmholtz.de/en
The Helmholtz Association is a community of 18 scientific-technical and biological-medical research centers. Helmholtz Centers perform top-class research in strategic programs in several core fields: energy, earth and environment, health, key technologies, structure of matter, aeronautics, space and transport.

Idaho National Laboratory (INL)
2525 Fremont Ave.
Idaho Falls, ID 83415 USA
Toll Free: 866-495-7440
Web Address: inlportal.inl.gov/portal/server.pt/community/home/255
Idaho National Laboratory (INL) is a multidisciplinary, multiprogram laboratory that specializes in developing nuclear energy with research concerning the environment, energy, science and national defense.

Industrial Technology Research Institute (ITRI)
195 Chung Hsing Rd.
Sec. 4 Chu Tung
Hsin Chu, 31040 Taiwan
Phone: 886-3-582-0100
Fax: 886-3-582-0045
Web Address: www.itri.org.tw
The Industrial Technology Research Institute (ITRI) is a nonprofit R&D organization founded in 1973 by the Ministry of Economic Affairs (MOEA) of Taiwan. It engages in applied research and technical service for Taiwan's industrial development. ITRI focuses on six areas of development: Information and Communications; Electronics and Optoelectronics; Material, Chemical and Nanotechnology; Medical devices and biomedical; Mechanical Systems; and Green Energy and Environment.

Institute for Telecommunication Sciences (ITS)
325 Broadway
Boulder, CO 80305-3337 USA
Phone: 303-497-3571
E-mail Address: info@its.bldrdoc.gov
Web Address: www.its.bldrdoc.gov
The Institute for Telecommunication Sciences (ITS) is the research and engineering branch of the National Telecommunications and Information Administration (NTIA), a division of the U.S. Department of Commerce (DOC). Its research activities are focused on advanced telecommunications and information infrastructure development.

Leibniz Association of German Research Institutes (WGL)
Chaussee Strasse 111
Berlin, D-10115 Germany
Phone: 49-030/20-60-49-0
Fax: 49-030/20-60-49-55
E-mail Address: info@leibniz-gemeinschaft.de
Web Address: www.leibniz-gemeinschaft.de
The Leibniz Association of German Research Institutes (WGL) is a research organization that comprises over 89 institutes. WGL works on international interdisciplinary research and acts as a bridge between traditional research and customer oriented applications. The association focuses on scientific excellence and social relevance.

Los Alamos National Laboratory (LANL)
P.O. Box 1663
Los Alamos, NM 87545 USA
Phone: 505-667-5061
E-mail Address: community@lanl.gov
Web Address: www.lanl.gov
The Los Alamos National Laboratory (LANL), a national energy lab in New Mexico, was originally built as a work site for the team that designed the first atomic bomb during World War II. Currently, it provides a

continual stream of research in physics and energy matters. Much of that research is put to use in the commercial sector.

MITRE Corporation
202 Burlington Rd.
Bedford, MA 01730-1420 USA
Phone: 781-271-2000
E-mail Address: media@mitre.org
Web Address: www.mitre.org
MITRE Corporation is a nonprofit engineering institution offering expertise in communications, information, space, environmental and aviation systems. It operates three federally funded research and development centers for the U.S. government.

National Renewable Energy Laboratory (NREL)
15013 Denver W. Parkway
Golden, CO 80401 USA
Phone: 303-275-3000
Web Address: www.nrel.gov
The National Renewable Energy Laboratory (NREL) reduces nuclear danger, transfers applied environmental technology to government and non-government entities and forms economic and industrial alliances.

National Research Council Canada (NRC)
1200 Montreal Rd., Bldg. M-58
Ottawa, ON K1A 0R6 Canada
Phone: 613-993-9101
Fax: 613-952-9907
Toll Free: 877-672-2672
E-mail Address: info@nrc-cnrc.gc.ca
Web Address: www.nrc-cnrc.gc.ca
National Research Council Canada (NRC) is comprised of 12 government organization, research institutes and programs that carry out multidisciplinary research. It maintains partnerships with industries and sectors key to Canada's economic development.

Oak Ridge National Laboratory (ORNL)
1 Bethel Valley Rd.
P.O. Box 2008
Oak Ridge, TN 37831 USA
Phone: 865-576-7658
Web Address: www.ornl.gov
The Oak Ridge National Laboratory (ORNL) is a multi-program science and technology laboratory managed for the U.S. Department of Energy by U.T.-Battelle, LLC. It conducts basic and applied research and development to create scientific knowledge and technological solutions.

Pacific Northwest National Laboratory (PNNL)
902 Battelle Blvd.
Richland, WA 99352 USA
Phone: 509-375-2121
Toll Free: 888-375-7665
E-mail Address: inquiry@pnl.gov
Web Address: www.pnnl.gov
The Pacific Northwest National Laboratory (PNNL) is a Department of Energy facility that conducts research in 10 areas of focus: Chemical and Molecular Sciences; Biological Systems Science; Climate Change Science; Subsurface Science; Chemical Engineering; Applied Materials Science and Engineering; Applied Nuclear Science and Technology; Advanced Computer Science, Visualization and Data; Systems Engineering and Integration; and Large-Scale User Facilities and Advanced Instrumentation.

Program on Vehicle and Mobility Innovation (PVMI)
1050 Steinberg Hall-Dietrich Hall
3620 Locust Walk
Philadelphia, PA 19104-6371 USA
Phone: 215-746-4831
E-mail Address: mackinstitute@wharton.upenn.edu
Web Address: pvmi.wharton.upenn.edu
The Program on Vehicle and Mobility Innovation (PVMI), formerly the International Motor Vehicle Program (IMVP), is a research project, funded by leading global car makers as well as government agencies, focused on enhancing automotive design and manufacturing methods. In 2013, the IMVP changed its name to the PVMI and was integrated into the Mack Institute for Innovation Management at the Wharton School, University Pennsylvania.

Sandia National Laboratories
1515 Eubank SE
Albuquerque, NM 87123 USA
Phone: 505-844-8066
Web Address: www.sandia.gov
Sandia National Laboratories is a national security laboratory operated for the U.S. Department of Energy by the Sandia Corporation. It designs all nuclear components for the nation's nuclear weapons and performs a wide variety of energy research and development projects.

Savannah River Site (SRS)
U.S. Dept. of Energy, P.O. Box A
Savannah River Operations Office
Aiken, SC 29802 USA
Phone: 803-952-7697
E-mail Address: will.callicott@srs.gov
Web Address: www.srs.gov
The Savannah River Site (SRS) is a nuclear fuel storage and production site that works to protect the people and the environment of the U.S. through safe, secure, cost-effective management of the country's nuclear weapons stockpile and nuclear materials. While the site is owned by the U.S. Department of Energy, it is operated by the subsidiaries of Washington Savannah River Company, LLC (WSRC), itself a wholly-owned subsidiary of Washington Group International.

Sloan Automotive Laboratory
60 Vassar St., Bldg. 31-153
Cambridge, MA 02139-4307 USA
Phone: 617-253-4529
Fax: 617-253-9453
Web Address: web.mit.edu/sloan-auto-lab
The Sloan Automotive Laboratory at MIT was founded in 1929 by Professor C.F. Taylor, with a grant from Alfred P. Sloan, Jr., CEO of General Motors, as a major laboratory for automotive research in the US and the world. The goals of the Laboratory are to provide the fundamental knowledge base for automotive engineering and to educate students to become technological leaders in the automotive industry.

SRI International
333 Ravenswood Ave.
Menlo Park, CA 94025-3493 USA
Phone: 650-859-2000
Web Address: www.sri.com
SRI International is a nonprofit research organization that offers contract research services to government agencies, as well as commercial enterprises and other private sector institutions. It is organized around broad divisions including biosciences, global partnerships, education, products and solutions division, advanced technology and systems and information and computing sciences division.

58) RFID Industry Associations

EPCglobal Inc.
1009 Lenox Dr., Ste. 202
Lawrenceville, NJ 08648 USA
Phone: 609-620-0200
E-mail Address: info@gs1us.org
Web Address: www.gs1.org/epcglobal
EPCglobal Inc. is a global standards organization for the Electronic Product Code (EPC), which supports the use of RFID. It was initially developed by the Auto-ID Center, an academic research project at the Massachusetts Institute of Technology (MIT). Today, offices and affiliates of EPCglobal are based in nearly every nation of the world. The nonprofit organization is a joint venture between GS1, formerly known as EAN International, and GS1 US, formerly known as the Uniform Code Council.

59) Road & Highway Construction Industry Associations

American Road & Transportation Builders Association (ARTBA)
1219 28th St. NW
Washington, DC 20007-3389 USA
Phone: 202-289-4434
E-mail Address: info@artba.org
Web Address: www.artba.org
ARTBA is a leading association that represents the interests of firms involved in designing, building and maintaining American roads and highways. Its membership totals about 6,500 firms and organizations. It publishes a significant amount of economic research and market intelligence regarding this industry.

60) Robotics & Automation Industry Associations

Industrial Wireless at Work (WINA)
1500 Sunday Dr., Ste. 102
Raleigh, NC 27607 USA
Phone: 919-314-6560
Fax: 919-314-6561
E-mail Address: info@wina.org
Web Address: www.wina.org
WINA's mission is to provide unbiased information and education about industrial wireless technologies and applications to accelerate the widespread deployment of wireless in the industrial market.

International Federation of Robotics (IFR)
Lyoner St. 18
Frankfurt am Main, 60528 Germany
Phone: 49-69-6603-1502
Fax: 49-69-6603-2502
E-mail Address: gl@ifr.org
Web Address: www.ifr.org
The International Federation of Robotics (IFR) promotes the robotics industry worldwide, including the fields of industrial robots for manufacturing and other purposes, service robots and robotics research. Among other things, it is focused on research, development, use and international co-operation in the entire field of robotics, and it seeks to act as a focal point for organizations and governmental representatives in activities related to robotics.

Laboratory Robotics Interest Group (LRIG)
E-mail Address: andy.zaayenga@lab-robotics.org
Web Address: www.lrig.org
Laboratory Robotics Interest Group (LRIG) is a membership group focused on the application of robotics in the laboratory. The organization currently has over 12,000 members, with individual chapters across the U.S. and in Europe.

Singapore Industrial Automation Association (SIAA)
1010 Dover Rd., Ste. 03-10
Singapore, 139658 Singapore
Phone: 65-6749-1822
Fax: 65-6841-3986
E-mail Address: secretariat@siaa.org
Web Address: www.siaa.org
The Singapore Industrial Automation Association (SIAA) is a non-profit organization which promotes the application of industrial automation with reference to business, technology & information services.

61) Satellite-Related Professional Organizations

Geospatial Information and Technology Association (GITA)
1360 University Ave. W., Ste. 455
St. Paul, MN 55104 USA
Phone: 844-447-4482
Fax: 844-223-8218
E-mail Address: president@gita.org
Web Address: www.gita.org
The Geospatial Information and Technology Association (GITA) is an educational association for geospatial information and technology professionals.

Society of Satellite Professionals International (SSPI)
250 Park Ave., Fl. 7
The New York Information Technology Ctr.
New York, NY 10177 USA
Phone: 212-809-5199
Fax: 212-825-0075
E-mail Address: rbell@sspi.org
Web Address: www.sspi.org
The Society of Satellite Professionals International (SSPI) is a nonprofit member-benefit society that serves satellite professionals worldwide.

62) Science & Technology Resources

Technology Review
1 Main St., Fl. 13
Cambridge, MA 02142 USA
Phone: 617-475-8000
Fax: 617-475-8000
Web Address: www.technologyreview.com
Technology Review, an MIT enterprise, publishes tech industry news, covers innovation and writes in-depth articles about research, development and cutting-edge technologies.

63) Science Parks

International Association of Science Parks (IASP)
Calle Maria Curie 35, Campanillas
Malaga, 29590 Spain
Phone: 34-95-202-83-03
Fax: 34-95-202-04-64
E-mail Address: iasp@iasp.ws
Web Address: www.iasp.ws
The International Association of Science Parks (IASP) is a worldwide network of science and technology parks. It enjoys Special Consultative status with the Economic and Social Council of the United Nations. Its 394 members represent science parks in 75 nations. It is also a founding member of the World Alliance for Innovation (WAINOVA). Its world headquarters are located in Spain, with an additional office in the Tsinghua University Science Park, Beijing, China.

64) Software Industry Associations

National Association of Software and Service Companies of India (NASSCOM)
International Youth Ctr.
Teen Murti Marg, Chanakyapuri
New Delhi, 110 021 India
Phone: 91-11-4767-0100
Fax: 91-11-2301-5452
E-mail Address: info@nasscom.in
Web Address: www.nasscom.org
The National Association of Software and Service Companies (NASSCOM) is the trade body and chamber of commerce for the IT and business process outsourcing (BPO) industry in India. The association's 1,400 members consist of corporations located around the world involved in software development, software services, software products, IT-enabled/BPO services and e-commerce.

65) Software Industry Resources

Software Engineering Institute (SEI)-Carnegie Mellon
4500 5th Ave.
Pittsburgh, PA 15213-2612 USA
Phone: 412-268-5800
Fax: 412-268-5758
Toll Free: 888-201-4479
E-mail Address: info@sei.cmu.edu
Web Address: www.sei.cmu.edu
The Software Engineering Institute (SEI) is a federally funded research and development center at Carnegie Mellon University, sponsored by the U.S. Department of Defense through the Office of the Under Secretary of Defense for Acquisition, Technology, and Logistics [OUSD (AT&L)]. The SEI's core purpose is to help users make measured improvements in their software engineering capabilities.

66) Supercomputing

Top 500 Supercomputer Sites
Prometeus GmbH
Fliederstr. 2
Waibstadt-Daisbach, D-74915 Germany
Phone: 49-7261-913-160
E-mail Address: info@prometeus.de
Web Address: www.top500.org
The Top 500 project was started in 1993 to provide a reliable basis for tracking and detecting trends in high-performance computing. Twice a year, a list of the sites operating the 500 most powerful computer systems is assembled and released. The Linpack benchmark is used as a performance measure for ranking the computer systems. The list contains a variety of information including system specifications and major application areas. The Top 500 web site is promoted by Prometeus GmbH.

67) Sustainable Transportation

Transportation Sustainability Research Center (TSRC)
University of California Richmond Field Station
1301 S. 46th St., Building 190
Richmond, CA 94804 USA
E-mail Address: sshaheen@berkeley.edu
Web Address: tsrc.berkeley.edu/
The Transportation Sustainability Research Center (TSRC) was formed in 2006 to combine the research forces of six campus groups at UC Berkeley: the University of California Transportation Center, the University of California Energy Institute, the Institute of Transportation Studies, the Energy and Resources Group, the Center for Global Metropolitan Studies, and the Berkeley Institute of the Environment. Research efforts are primarily concentrated in six main areas: advanced vehicles and fuels; energy and infrastructure; goods movement; innovative mobility; Mobility for special populations; and transportation and energy systems analysis.

68) Technology Transfer Associations

Association of University Technology Managers (AUTM)
One Parkview Plaza, Ste. 880
Oakbrook Terrace, IL 60015 USA
Phone: 847-686-2244
Fax: 847-686-2253
E-mail Address: info@autm.net
Web Address: www.autm.net
The Association of University Technology Managers (AUTM) is a nonprofit professional association whose members belong to over 300 research institutions, universities, teaching hospitals, government agencies and corporations. The association's mission is to advance the field of technology transfer and enhance members' ability to bring

academic and nonprofit research to people around the world.

Federal Laboratory Consortium for Technology Transfer
950 N. Kings Hwy., Ste. 105
Cherry Hill, NJ 08304 USA
Phone: 856-667-7727
E-mail Address: support@federallabs.org
Web Address: www.federallabs.org
In keeping with the aims of the Federal Technology Transfer Act of 1986 and other related legislation, the Federal Laboratory Consortium (FLC) works to facilitate the sharing of research results and technology developments between federal laboratories and the mainstream U.S. economy. FLC affiliates include federal laboratories, large and small businesses, academic and research institutions, state and local governments and various federal agencies. The group has regional support offices and local contacts throughout the U.S.

Licensing Executives Society (USA and Canada), Inc.
11130 Sunrise Valley Dr., Ste. 350
Reston, VA 20191 USA
Phone: 703-234-4058
Fax: 703-435-4390
E-mail Address: info@les.org
Web Address: www.lesusacanada.org
Licensing Executives Society (USA and Canada), Inc., established in 1965, is a professional association composed of about 3,000 members who work in fields related to the development, use, transfer, manufacture and marketing of intellectual property. Members include executives, lawyers, licensing consultants, engineers, academic researchers, scientists and government officials. The society is part of the larger Licensing Executives Society International, Inc. (same headquarters address), with a worldwide membership of some 12,000 members from approximately 80 countries.

State Science and Technology Institute (SSTI)
5015 Pine Creek Dr.
Westerville, OH 43081 USA
Phone: 614-901-1690
E-mail Address: contactus@ssti.org
Web Address: www.ssti.org
The State Science and Technology Institute (SSTI) is a national nonprofit group that serves as a resource for technology-based economic development. In addition to the information on its web site, the Institute publishes a free weekly digest of news and issues related to technology-based economic development efforts, as well as a members-only publication listing application information, eligibility criteria and submission deadlines for a variety of funding opportunities, federal and otherwise.

69) Telecommunications Industry Associations

Alliance for Telecommunications Industry Solutions (ATIS)
1200 G St. NW, Ste. 500
Washington, DC 20005 USA
Phone: 202-628-6380
E-mail Address: moran@atis.org
Web Address: www.atis.org
The Alliance for Telecommunications Industry Solutions (ATIS) is a U.S.-based body committed to rapidly developing and promoting technical and operations standards for the communications and related information technologies industry worldwide.

China Communications Standards Association (CCSA)
52 Garden Rd., Haidian District
Beijing, 100083 China
Phone: 86-10-6230-2730
Fax: 86-10-6230-1849
Web Address: www.ccsa.org.cn/english
The China Communications Standards Association (CCSA) is a nonprofit organization that works to standardize the field of communications technology across China. Its membership includes operators, telecom equipment manufacturers and universities and academies from across China.

European Telecommunications Standards Institute (ETSI)
ETSI Secretariat
650, route des Lucioles
Sophia-Antipolis Cedex, 06921 France
Phone: 33-4-92-94-42-00
Fax: 33-4-93-65-47-16
E-mail Address: info@etsi.org
Web Address: www.etsi.org
The European Telecommunications Standards Institute (ETSI) is a non-profit organization whose mission is to produce the telecommunications standards to be implemented throughout Europe.

International Telecommunications Union (ITU)
Place des Nations
Geneva 20, 1211 Switzerland
Phone: 41-22-730-5111
Fax: 41-22-733-7256
E-mail Address: itumail@itu.int
Web Address: www.itu.int
The International Telecommunications Union (ITU) is an international organization for the standardization of the radio and telecommunications industry. It is an agency of the United Nations (UN).

70) Telecommunications Resources

Infocomm Development Authority of Singapore (IDA)
10 Pasir Panjang Rd.
#10-01 Mapletree Business City
Singapore, 117438 Singapore
Phone: 65-6211-0888
Fax: 65-6211-2222
E-mail Address: info@ida.gov.sg
Web Address: www.ida.gov.sg
The goal of the Infocomm Development Authority of Singapore (IDA) is to actively seek opportunities to grow infocomm industry in both the domestic and international markets.

International Communications Project (The)
Unit 2, Marine Action
Birdhill Industrial Estate
Birdhill, Co Tipperary Ireland
Phone: 353-86-108-3932
Fax: 353-61-749-801

E-mail Address: robert.alcock@intercomms.net
Web Address: www.intercomms.net
The International Communications Project (InterComms) is an authoritative policy, strategy and reference publication for the international telecommunications industry.

71) Temporary Staffing Firms

Allegis Group
7301 Parkway Dr.
Hanover, MD 21076 USA
Toll Free: 800-927-8090
Web Address: www.allegisgroup.com
The Allegis Group provides technical, professional and industrial recruiting and staffing services. Allegis specializes in information technology staffing services. The firm operates in the United Kingdom, Germany and The Netherlands as Aerotek and TEKsystems, and in India as Allegis Group India. Aerotek provides staffing solutions for aviation, engineering, automotive and scientific personnel markets.

CDI Corporation
1717 Arch St., Fl. 35
Philadelphia, PA 19103-2768 USA
Phone: 215-636-1240
E-mail Address: vince.webb@cdicorp.com
Web Address: www.cdicorp.com
CDI Corporation specializes in engineering and information technology staffing services. Company segments include CDI IT Solutions, specializing in information technology; CDI Engineering Solutions, specializing in engineering outsourcing services; AndersElite Limited, operating in the United Kingdom and Australia; and MRINetwork, specializing in executive recruitment.

72) Trade Associations-General

Associated Chambers of Commerce and Industry of India (ASSOCHAM)
5, Sardar Patel Marg
Chanakyapuri
New Delhi, 110 021 India
Phone: 91-11-4655-0555
Fax: 91-11-2301-7008
E-mail Address: assocham@nic.in
Web Address: www.assocham.org
The Associated Chambers of Commerce and Industry of India (ASSOCHAM) has a membership of more than 300 chambers and trade associations and serves members from all over India. It works with domestic and international government agencies to advocate for India's industry and trade activities.

Brazilian Trade & Investment Promotion Agency (Apex-Brasil)
SBN, Quadra 02, Lote 11
Edificio Apex-Brasil
Brasilia, DF 70040-020 Brazil
Phone: 55-61-3426-0200
Web Address: www.apexbrasil.com.br
Apex-Brasil works to promote exports of Brazilian products and services, supporting some 70 industry sectors such as agribusiness, technology, civil engineering, entertainment, apparel and industrial equipment.

BUSINESSEUROPE
168 Ave. de Cortenbergh 168
Brussels, 1000 Belgium
Phone: 32-2-237-65-11
Fax: 32-2-231-14-45
E-mail Address: main@businesseurope.eu
Web Address: www.businesseurope.eu
BUSINESSEUROPE is a major European trade federation that operates in a manner similar to a chamber of commerce. Its members are the central national business federations of the 34 countries throughout Europe from which they come. Companies cannot become direct members of BUSINESSEUROPE, though there is a support group which offers the opportunity for firms to encourage BUSINESSEUROPE objectives in various ways.

Coalition of Service Industries (CSI)
1707 L St. NW, Ste. 1000
Washington, DC 20036 USA
Phone: 202-289-7460
E-mail Address: burzynska@uscsi.org
Web Address: servicescoalition.org
The Coalition of Service Industries (CSI) is a business organization dedicated to the reduction of barriers to U.S. service exports and to the development of constructive domestic service policies. It also publishes statistical information relating to the service industry on both state and national levels.

United States Council for International Business (USCIB)
1212 Ave. of the Americas
New York, NY 10036 USA
Phone: 212-354-4480
Fax: 212-575-0327
E-mail Address: azhang@uscib.org
Web Address: www.uscib.org
The United States Council for International Business (USCIB) promotes an open system of world trade and investment through its global network. Standard USCIB members include corporations, law firms, consulting firms and industry associations. Limited membership options are available for chambers of commerce and sole legal practitioners.

73) Trade Associations-Global

World Trade Organization (WTO)
Centre William Rappard
Rue de Lausanne 154
Geneva 21, CH-1211 Switzerland
Phone: 41-22-739-51-11
Fax: 41-22-731-42-06
E-mail Address: enquiries@wto.og
Web Address: www.wto.org
The World Trade Organization (WTO) is a global organization dealing with the rules of trade between nations. To become a

member, nations must agree to abide by certain guidelines. Membership increases a nation's ability to import and export efficiently.

74) Transportation Industry Resources

Institute of Transportation Studies
University of California
109 McLaughlin Hall, MC1720
Berkeley, CA 94720 USA
Phone: 510-642-3585
E-mail Address: its@its.berkeley.edu
Web Address: its.berkeley.edu/
The UC Berkeley Institute of Transportation Studies is one of the world's leading centers for transportation research, education, and scholarship. Areas of research focus include: transportation planning, logistics, infrastructure management, safety, transportation economics and public transportation.

75) U.S. Government Agencies

Bureau of Economic Analysis (BEA)
4600 Silver Hill Rd.
Washington, DC 20233 USA
Phone: 301-278-9004
E-mail Address: customerservice@bea.gov
Web Address: www.bea.gov
The Bureau of Economic Analysis (BEA), an agency of the U.S. Department of Commerce, is the nation's economic accountant, preparing estimates that illuminate key national, international and regional aspects of the U.S. economy.

Bureau of Labor Statistics (BLS)
2 Massachusetts Ave. NE
Washington, DC 20212-0001 USA
Phone: 202-691-5200
Fax: 202-691-7890
Toll Free: 800-877-8339
E-mail Address: blsdata_staff@bls.gov
Web Address: stats.bls.gov
The Bureau of Labor Statistics (BLS) is the principal fact-finding agency for the Federal Government in the field of labor economics and statistics. It is an independent national statistical agency that collects, processes, analyzes and disseminates statistical data to the American public, U.S. Congress, other federal agencies, state and local governments, business and labor. The BLS also serves as a statistical resource to the Department of Labor.

Federal Communications Commission (FCC)
445 12th St. SW
Washington, DC 20554 USA
Fax: 866-418-0232
Toll Free: 888-225-5322
E-mail Address: PRA@fcc.gov
Web Address: www.fcc.gov
The Federal Communications Commission (FCC) is an independent U.S. government agency established by the Communications Act of 1934 responsible for regulating interstate and international communications by radio, television, wire, satellite and cable.

Federal Communications Commission (FCC)-Wireless Telecommunications Bureau
445 12th St. SW
Washington, DC 20554 USA
Phone: 202-418-0600
Fax: 202-418-0787
Toll Free: 888-225-5322
E-mail Address: PRA@fcc.gov
Web Address: www.fcc.gov/wireless-telecommunications#block-menu-block-4
The Federal Communications Commission (FCC)-Wireless Telecommunications Bureau handles nearly all FCC domestic wireless telecommunications programs and policies, including cellular and PCS phones, pagers and two-way radios. The bureau also regulates the use of radio spectrum for businesses, aircraft/ship operators and individuals.

National Aeronautics and Space Administration (NASA)
NASA Headquarters
Ste. 2R40
Washington, DC 20546 USA
Phone: 202-358-0001
Fax: 202-358-4338
E-mail Address: public-inquiries@hq.nasa.gov
Web Address: www.nasa.gov
The National Aeronautics and Space Administration (NASA) is the U.S. space agency, handling all space-related research and development. The agency's work is organized into four principal areas: Aeronautics, Exploration Systems, Science and Space Operations.

National Institute of Standards and Technology (NIST)
100 Bureau Dr.
Stop 1070
Gaithersburg, MD 20899-1070 USA
Phone: 301-975-6478
Toll Free: 800-877-8339
E-mail Address: inquiries@nist.gov
Web Address: www.nist.gov
The National Institute of Standards and Technology (NIST) is an agency of the U.S. Department of Commerce that works with various industries to develop and apply technology, measurements and standards.

National Science Foundation (NSF)
4201 Wilson Blvd.
Arlington, VA 22230 USA
Phone: 703-292-5111
Toll Free: 800-877-8339
E-mail Address: info@nsf.gov
Web Address: www.nsf.gov
The National Science Foundation (NSF) is an independent U.S. government agency responsible for promoting science and engineering. The foundation provides colleges and universities with grants and funding for research into numerous scientific fields.

U.S. Census Bureau
4600 Silver Hill Rd.
Washington, DC 20233-8800 USA
Phone: 301-763-4636
Toll Free: 800-923-8282
E-mail Address: pio@census.gov
Web Address: www.census.gov
The U.S. Census Bureau is the official collector of data about the people and economy of the U.S. Founded in 1790, it provides official social, demographic and economic information. In addition to the Population & Housing Census, which

it conducts every 10 years, the U.S. Census Bureau numerous other surveys annually.

U.S. Department of Commerce (DOC)
1401 Constitution Ave. NW
Washington, DC 20230 USA
Phone: 202-482-2000
E-mail Address: TheSec@doc.gov
Web Address: www.commerce.gov
The U.S. Department of Commerce (DOC) regulates trade and provides valuable economic analysis of the economy.

U.S. Department of Labor (DOL)
200 Constitution Ave. NW
Washington, DC 20210 USA
Phone: 202-693-4676
Toll Free: 866-487-2365
Web Address: www.dol.gov
The U.S. Department of Labor (DOL) is the government agency responsible for labor regulations.

U.S. Nuclear Regulatory Commission (NRC)
11555 Rockville Pike
Rockville, MD 20852 USA
Phone: 301-415-7000
Fax: 301-415-3716
Toll Free: 800-368-5642
E-mail Address: OPA.Resource@nrc.gov
Web Address: www.nrc.gov
The U.S. Nuclear Regulatory Commission (NRC) is an independent agency established by Congress to ensure adequate protection of public health and safety, common defense and security and the environment in use of nuclear materials in the United States.

U.S. Patent and Trademark Office (PTO)
600 Dulany St.
Madison Bldg.
Alexandria, VA 22314 USA
Phone: 571-272-1000
Toll Free: 800-786-9199
E-mail Address: usptoinfo@uspto.gov
Web Address: www.uspto.gov
The U.S. Patent and Trademark Office (PTO) administers patent and trademark laws for the U.S. and enables registration of patents and trademarks.

U.S. Securities and Exchange Commission (SEC)
100 F St. NE
Washington, DC 20549 USA
Phone: 202-942-8088
Toll Free: 800-732-0330
E-mail Address: help@sec.gov
Web Address: www.sec.gov
The U.S. Securities and Exchange Commission (SEC) is a nonpartisan, quasi-judicial regulatory agency responsible for administering federal securities laws. These laws are designed to protect investors in securities markets and ensure that they have access to disclosure of all material information concerning publicly traded securities. Visitors to the web site can access the EDGAR database of corporate financial and business information.

76) Wireless & Cellular Industry Associations

Bluetooth Special Interest Group (SIG)
5209 Lake Washington Blvd. NE
Ste. 350
Kirkland, WA 98033 USA
Phone: 425-691-3535
Fax: 425-691-3524
Web Address: www.bluetooth.com
The Bluetooth Special Interest Group (SIG) is a trade association comprised of leaders in the telecommunications, computing, automotive, industrial automation and network industries that is driving the development of Bluetooth wireless technology, a low cost short-range wireless specification for connecting mobile devices and bringing them to market.

CDMA Development Group (CDG)
575 Anton Blvd., Ste. 440
Costa Mesa, CA 92626 USA
Phone: 714-545-5211
Fax: 714-545-4601
Toll Free: 888-800-2362
E-mail Address: cdg@cdg.org
Web Address: www.cdg.org
The CDMA Development Group (CDG) is composed of the world's leading code division multiple access (CDMA) service providers and manufacturers that have joined together to lead the adoption and evolution of CDMA wireless systems around the world.

Global System for Mobile Communication Association (GSMA)
The Wallbrook Bldg.
Fl. 2, 25 Wallbrook
London, EC4N 8AF UK
Phone: 44-207-356-0600
Fax: 44-20-7356-0601
E-mail Address: info@gsma.com
Web Address: www.gsmworld.com
The Global System for Mobile Communications Association (GSMA) is a global trade association representing nearly 800 GSM mobile phone operators from 219 countries.

Small Cell Forum
P.O. Box 23
Dursley, Gloucestershire GL11 5WA UK
E-mail Address: info@smallcellforum.org
Web Address: www.smallcellforum.org
The Small Cell Forum, formerly the Femto Forum is a not-for-profit membership organization founded in 2007 to promote femtocell deployment worldwide. Comprised of mobile operators, telecoms hardware and software vendors, content providers and innovative start-ups, the group's mission is to advance the development and adoption of femtocell products and services as the optimum technology for the provision of high-quality 2G/3G/4G coverage and premium services within the residential and small to medium business markets.

Wireless Communications Association International (WCAI)
1333 H St. NW, Ste. 700 W
Washington, DC 20005-4754 USA
Phone: 202-452-7823
Web Address: www.wcai.com
The Wireless Communications Association International (WCAI) is the principal nonprofit trade association representing the wireless broadband industry.

Chapter 4

THE ENGINEERING & RESEARCH 500: WHO THEY ARE AND HOW THEY WERE CHOSEN

Includes Indexes by Company Name, Industry & Location

The companies chosen to be listed in PLUNKETT'S ENGINEERING & RESEARCH INDUSTRY ALMANAC comprise a unique list. THE ENGINEERING & RESEARCH 500 were chosen specifically for their dominance in the many facets of the engineering and research industry in which they operate. Complete information about each firm can be found in the "Individual Profiles," beginning at the end of this chapter. These profiles are in alphabetical order by company name.

THE ENGINEERING & RESEARCH 500 companies are from all parts of the United States, Asia, Canada, Europe and beyond. Essentially, THE ENGINEERING & RESEARCH 500 includes companies that are deeply involved in the technologies, services and trends that keep the entire industry forging ahead.

Simply stated, THE ENGINEERING & RESEARCH 500 contains the largest, most successful, fastest growing firms in engineering, research and related industries in the world. To be included in our list, the firms had to meet the following criteria:

1) Generally, these are corporations based in the U.S., however, many firms are located in other nations.
2) Prominence, or a significant presence, in engineering, research, engineering services, equipment and supporting fields. (See the following Industry Codes section for a complete list of types of businesses that are covered).
3) The companies in THE ENGINEERING & RESEARCH 500 do not have to be exclusively in the engineering and research field.
4) Financial data and vital statistics must have been available to the editors of this book, either directly from the company being written about or from outside sources deemed reliable and accurate by the editors. A small number of companies that we would like to have included are not listed because of a lack of sufficient, objective data.

INDEXES TO THE ENGINEERING & RESEARCH 500, AS FOUND IN THIS CHAPTER AND IN THE BACK OF THE BOOK:	
Index of Rankings Within Industry Groups	p. 106
Alphabetical Index	p. 120
Index of U.S. Headquarters Location by State	p. 124
Index of Non-U.S. Headquarters Location by Country	p. 127
Index of Firms Noted as "Hot Spots for Advancement" for Women/Minorities	p. 630
Index by Subsidiaries, Brand Names and Selected Affiliations	p. 632

INDEX OF COMPANIES WITHIN INDUSTRY GROUPS

The industry codes shown below are based on the 2012 NAIC code system (NAIC is used by many analysts as a replacement for older SIC codes because NAIC is more specific to today's industry sectors, see www.census.gov/NAICS). Companies are given a primary NAIC code, reflecting the main line of business of each firm.

Industry Group/Company	Industry Code	2017 Sales	2017 Profits
Agricultural Equipment or Machinery (Farm Implement) Manufacturing			
Deere & Company (John Deere)	333111	27,006,199,808	2,159,099,904
Agricultural Seeds, Pesticides, Herbicides and Other Agricultural Chemical Manufacturing			
Monsanto Company	325320	14,640,000,000	2,260,000,000
Syngenta AG	325320	12,649,000,000	1,130,000,000
Aircraft Components, Parts, Assemblies, Interiors and Systems Manufacturing (Aerospace)			
Spirit AeroSystems Holdings Inc	336413	6,983,000,064	354,900,000
Aircraft Engine and Engine Parts Manufacturing			
GE Aviation	336412	27,375,000,000	6,642,000,000
Honeywell International Inc	336412	40,533,999,616	1,655,000,064
Rolls-Royce plc	336412	23,226,036,224	5,992,024,064
Safran SA	336412	21,000,000,000	
United Technologies Corporation	336412	59,837,001,728	4,552,000,000
Aircraft Manufacturing (Aerospace), including Passenger Airliners and Military Aircraft,			
Airbus SE	336411	82,450,792,448	3,547,877,120
Boeing Company (The)	336411	93,392,003,072	8,197,000,192
Bombardier Inc	336411	16,218,000,384	-516,000,000
Dassault Aviation SA	336411		
Embraer SA	336411	5,839,300,096	246,800,000
General Dynamics Corporation	336411	30,972,999,680	2,912,000,000
Gulfstream Aerospace Corporation	336411	8,550,000,000	1,600,000,000
Lockheed Martin Corporation	336411	51,048,001,536	2,002,000,000
Northrop Grumman Corporation	336411	25,802,999,808	2,015,000,064
Saab AB	336411	3,400,000,000	
Singapore Technologies Engineering Limited	336411	5,047,651,840	390,332,416
Textron Inc	336411	14,129,000,448	307,000,000
Aircraft, Missile and Space Vehicle (including Rockets), Drones, Satellites Manufacturing			
BAE Systems plc	336410	26,095,996,928	1,216,350,976
Airport Related Services, Baggage Handling			
Ferrovial SA	488119	15,075,699,712	560,646,144
ATV, Snowmobile, Golf Cart, Gocart and Race Car Equipment Manufacturing			
Kawasaki Heavy Industries Ltd	336999	14,149,711,872	244,121,504
Automobile (Car) and Truck Parts, Components and Systems Manufacturing, Including Gasoline Engines, Interiors and Electronics,			
Aisin Seiki Co Ltd	336300	30,240,219,136	934,712,192
Autoliv Inc	336300	10,382,600,192	427,100,000
Calsonic Kansei Corporation	336300	10,000,000,000	
Cummins Inc	336300	20,427,999,232	999,000,000

Industry Group/Company	Industry Code	2017 Sales	2017 Profits
Dana Incorporated	336300	7,208,999,936	111,000,000
Denso Corporation	336300	42,175,782,912	2,400,028,160
Eaton Corporation plc	336300	20,404,000,768	2,984,999,936
Faurecia SA	336300	24,922,449,920	753,537,984
Federal-Mogul LLC	336300	7,500,000,000	
Georg Fischer Ltd	336300	4,250,570,000	258,107,000
GKN plc	336300	13,774,391,296	716,422,144
Lear Corporation	336300	20,466,999,296	1,313,400,064
Magna International Inc	336300	38,946,000,896	2,206,000,128
Magneti Marelli SpA	336300	8,400,000,000	
Meritor Inc	336300	3,347,000,064	324,000,000
Rheinmetall AG	336300	7,000,000,000	
Robert Bosch GmbH	336300	93,512,400,000	3,921,810,000
Tenneco Inc	336300	9,274,000,384	207,000,000
Toyoda Gosei Co Ltd	336300	7,039,323,648	151,229,744
Valeo SA	336300	21,000,000,000	
Visteon Corporation	336300	3,145,999,872	176,000,000
Wanxiang Group Corporation	336300	20,000,000,000	
Automobile (Car) and Truck Transmission and Power Train Parts Manufacturing			
ZF Friedrichshafen AG (ZF)	336350	43,654,900,000	1,397,910,000
Automobile (Car) Manufacturing			
Audi AG	336111	74,252,271,616	4,390,081,536
BMW (Bayerische Motoren Werke AG)	336111	121,857,785,856	10,644,867,072
BYD Company Limited	336111	16,881,797,120	648,157,952
Daihatsu Motor Co Ltd	336111	16,750,000,000	
Daimler AG	336111	202,931,666,944	12,997,357,568
Dongfeng Motor Corporation	336111	18,444,100,000	2,074,800,000
FAW Group Corporation (First Automotive Works)	336111	68,174,700,000	
FCA US LLC	336111	11,750,000,000	
Ford Motor Co	336111	156,776,005,632	7,601,999,872
General Motors Company (GM)	336111	145,587,994,624	-3,864,000,000
GM Korea	336111	12,500,000,000	
Honda Motor Co Ltd	336111	130,419,228,672	5,744,074,752
Hyundai Motor Company	336111	89,000,000,000	
Isuzu Motors Limited	336111	18,196,256,768	874,399,104
Jaguar Land Rover Limited	336111	32,783,700,000	2,158,600,000
Kia Motors Corporation	336111	50,009,976,832	904,267,136
Mazda Motor Corporation	336111	29,945,622,528	873,672,512
Mitsubishi Motors Corp	336111	17,762,549,760	-1,849,487,616
Nissan Motor Co Ltd	336111	109,186,154,496	6,181,283,840
Peugeot SA (Groupe PSA)	336111	80,528,048,128	2,382,128,384
Porsche Automobil Holding SE	336111		
Renault SA	336111	72,575,270,912	6,315,295,744
SAIC Motor Corporation Limited	336111	132,474,000,000	5,283,550,000
Subaru Corporation	336111	30,985,580,544	2,630,464,000
Suzuki Motor Corporation	336111	29,528,061,952	1,490,180,736
Tata Motors Limited	336111	40,746,541,056	938,874,688
Tesla Inc	336111	11,758,750,720	-1,961,400,064

Industry Group/Company	Industry Code	2017 Sales	2017 Profits
Toyota Motor Corporation	336111	257,100,742,656	17,058,963,456
Volkswagen AG (VW)	336111	284,869,984,256	14,021,093,376
Volvo Car Corporation	336111	25,664,200,000	1,244,200,000
Basic Inorganic Chemicals Manufacturing, Including Acids, Carbides and Alkalies,			
Arkema	325180	10,281,805,824	711,304,320
Solvay SA	325180	13,449,331,712	1,310,232,448
Boilers and Condensers (Including Nuclear Reactors) and Heat Exchangers Manufacturing			
Areva SA	332410		
Babcock & Wilcox Enterprises Inc	332410	1,557,735,040	-379,824,000
Westinghouse Electric Company LLC	332410	4,150,000,000	
Commercial and Institutional Building Construction			
Kumho Industrial Co Ltd	236220	1,215,410,000	89,219,200
Communications Equipment Manufacturing			
L3 Technologies Inc	334200	9,573,000,192	677,000,000
Computer and Data Systems Design, Consulting and Integration Services			
Accenture plc	541512	36,765,478,912	3,445,148,928
CGI Group Inc	541512	8,596,961,280	820,606,400
NTT DATA Corporation	541512	16,140,051,456	611,943,360
Science Applications International Corporation (SAIC)	541512	4,449,999,872	148,000,000
Unisys Corp	541512	2,741,799,936	-65,300,000
Wipro Limited	541512	8,442,317,824	1,302,158,336
Computer Disks (Discs) and Drives, including Magnetic and Optical Storage Media Manufacturing			
Dell EMC	334112	27,500,000,000	
HGST Inc	334112	3,300,000,000	
NetApp Inc	334112	5,519,000,064	509,000,000
Nidec Corporation	334112	11,173,011,456	1,040,814,272
SanDisk Corporation	334112	5,500,000,000	
Seagate Technology plc	334112	10,771,000,320	772,000,000
Western Digital Corporation	334112	19,093,000,192	397,000,000
Computer Manufacturing, Including PCs, Laptops, Mainframes and Tablets			
Acer Inc	334111	8,095,631,872	96,065,608
ASUSTeK Computer Inc	334111	14,806,603,776	530,379,872
Casio Computer Co Ltd	334111	2,992,482,048	171,511,104
Cray Inc	334111	392,508,992	-133,829,000
Dell Technologies Inc	334111	61,642,000,000	492,000,000
Fujitsu Limited	334111	42,013,175,808	824,380,544
Fujitsu Technology Solutions (Holding) BV	334111	18,000,000,000	
Hewlett Packard Enterprise Company	334111	28,475,000,832	344,000,000
Hitachi Limited	334111	85,357,412,352	2,154,471,936
Lenovo Group Limited	334111	43,034,730,496	535,084,000
NEC Corporation	334111	24,827,977,728	254,425,200
Nintendo Co Ltd	334111	4,556,503,040	955,599,040
QuTech	334111		

Industry Group/Company	Industry Code	2017 Sales	2017 Profits
Computer Networking & Related Equipment Manufacturing			
Cisco Systems Inc	334210A	48,005,001,216	9,608,999,936
Juniper Networks Inc	334210A	5,027,200,000	306,200,000
Computer Peripherals and Accessories, including Printers, Monitors and Terminals Manufacturing			
Diebold Nixdorf Inc	334118	4,609,299,968	-233,100,000
NCR Corporation	334118	6,515,999,744	232,000,000
Seiko Epson Corporation	334118	9,547,755,520	450,158,400
TPV Technology Limited	334118	9,600,000,000	
Xerox Corporation	334118	9,971,000,320	195,000,000
Computer Software (Business and Consumer), Packaged Software and Software as a Service (Saas) Industry			
Waymo LLC	511210		
Computer Software, Accounting, Banking & Financial			
Intuit Inc	511210Q	5,176,999,936	971,000,000
Computer Software, Business Management & ERP			
BMC Software Inc	511210H	2,500,000,000	
CA Inc (CA Technologies)	511210H	4,036,000,000	775,000,000
Citrix Systems Inc	511210H	2,824,686,080	-20,719,000
SAP SE	511210H	28,970,831,872	4,961,841,664
SAS Institute Inc	511210H	3,240,000,000	
Computer Software, Data Base & File Management			
Oracle Corporation	511210J	37,728,002,048	9,335,000,064
Computer Software, Electronic Games, Apps & Entertainment			
Activision Blizzard Inc	511210G	7,016,999,936	273,000,000
Electronic Arts Inc (EA)	511210G	4,845,000,192	967,000,000
Konami Holdings Corporation	511210G	2,141,997,440	241,764,512
Take-Two Interactive Software Inc	511210G	1,779,747,968	67,303,000
Computer Software, Multimedia, Graphics & Publishing			
Adobe Systems Inc	511210F	7,301,505,024	1,693,954,048
Computer Software, Operating Systems, Languages & Development Tools			
Microsoft Corporation	511210I	89,950,003,200	21,204,000,768
Computer Software, Product Lifecycle, Engineering, Design & CAD			
Autodesk Inc	511210N	2,031,000,064	-582,099,968
Cadence Design Systems Inc	511210N	1,943,032,064	204,100,992
Dassault Systemes SA	511210N		
Mentor Graphics Inc	511210N	1,200,000,000	
PTC Inc	511210N	1,164,039,040	6,239,000
Synopsys Inc	511210N	2,724,879,872	136,563,008
Computer Software, Sales & Customer Relationship Management			
Amdocs Limited	511210K	3,867,154,944	436,825,984
Computer Software, Security & Anti-Virus			
McAfee Inc	511210E	2,681,000,000	
Symantec Corporation	511210E	4,019,000,064	-106,000,000

Industry Group/Company	Industry Code	2017 Sales	2017 Profits
VeriSign Inc	511210E	1,165,095,040	457,248,000
Connectors for Electronics Manufacturing			
Belden Inc	334417	2,388,643,072	93,210,000
Molex LLC	334417	4,100,000,000	
Construction Equipment and Machinery Manufacturing			
Caterpillar Inc	333120	45,461,999,616	754,000,000
Terex Corporation	333120	4,363,400,192	128,700,000
Construction of Railways, Marine Facilities and Subways			
Balfour Beatty plc	237990	9,850,447,872	239,282,160
China Railway Construction Corporation Limited (CRCC)	237990	108,541,911,040	2,559,370,752
Construction of Telecommunications Lines and Systems & Electric Power Lines and Systems			
Abengoa SA	237130		
Bouygues SA	237130	39,414,500,000	1,299,680,000
Doosan Heavy Industries & Construction Co Ltd	237130	13,567,075,328	-272,805,280
Construction of Water & Sewer Lines and Systems			
Layne Christensen Company	237110	601,971,968	-52,236,000
MWH Global Inc	237110	1,950,000,000	
Consulting Services: Process, Physical Distribution and Logistics			
WSP Global Inc	541614	5,503,131,136	169,084,416
Consumer Electronics Manufacturing, Including Audio and Video Equipment, Stereos, TVs and Radios			
Koninklijke Philips NV (Royal Philips)	334310	21,956,581,376	2,046,234,752
Panasonic Corporation	334310	68,415,385,600	1,391,466,496
Pioneer Corporation	334310	3,602,403,840	-47,084,036
Samsung Electronics Co Ltd	334310	188,000,000,000	
Sharp Corporation	334310	19,104,147,456	-231,758,912
Sony Corporation	334310	70,833,332,224	682,774,400
Contract Electronics Manufacturing Services (CEM) and Printed Circuits Assembly			
Benchmark Electronics Inc	334418	2,466,810,880	-31,965,000
Celestica Inc	334418	6,110,499,840	105,000,000
Compal Electronics Inc	334418	30,286,153,728	196,169,264
Flex Ltd	334418	23,862,933,504	319,564,000
Gemalto NV	334418	3,669,783,296	-523,484,192
Hon Hai Precision Industry Company Ltd	334418	160,590,135,296	4,733,508,608
HTC Corporation	334418	2,119,479,040	-576,809,600
Jabil Inc	334418	19,063,121,920	129,090,000
Plexus Corp	334418	2,528,051,968	112,062,000
Rohm Co Ltd	334418	3,279,392,768	246,245,584
Sanmina Corporation	334418	6,868,618,752	138,832,992
Electric Signal, Electricity, and Semiconductor Test and Measuring Equipment Manufacturing			
Agilent Technologies Inc	334515	4,472,000,000	684,000,000
Electrical Appliance Manufacturing, Small			
Dyson Limited	335210	4,358,690,000	

Industry Group/Company	Industry Code	2017 Sales	2017 Profits
Electricity Control Panels, Circuit Breakers and Power Switches Equipment (Switchgear) Manufacturing			
ABB Ltd	335313	34,311,999,488	2,212,999,936
Alps Electric Co Ltd	335313	7,017,533,440	325,321,440
Lite-On Technology Corporation	335313	7,320,765,440	89,710,800
Energy Conservation, Industrial Safety, Economics, Energy Efficiency and Technical Consulting			
Intertek Group plc	541690	3,944,025,088	409,343,392
Engineering Services, Including Civil, Mechanical, Electronic, Computer and Environmental Engineering			
AF AB	541330	1,540,250,000	90,531,400
Ambitech Engineering Corporation	541330		
Amey plc	541330	3,300,000,000	
Arcadis NV	541330	3,975,016,704	88,748,800
Artelia	541330	575,000,000	
ARUP Group Limited	541330	1,880,460,000	59,402,700
Associated Consulting Engineers	541330		
Aurecon Group Brand (Pte) Ltd	541330	1,200,000,000	
Beca Group Limited	541330		
Bilfinger Tebodin BV	541330		
BIOS-BIOENERGYSYSTEME GmbH	541330	5,700,000	
Black & Veatch Holding Company	541330	3,400,000,000	
Burns & McDonnell Inc	541330	2,450,000,000	
BuroHappold Ltd	541330	231,914,000	
CannonDesign	541330		
Cardno Limited	541330	913,414,336	6,663,301
CH2M HILL Inc	541330	5,200,000,000	
CHA Consulting Inc	541330	290,000,000	
China Chengda Engineering Co Ltd	541330		
China Energy Engineering Corporation Limited	541330	34,577,700,000	776,258,000
China HuanQiu Contracting & Engineering Corporation	541330		
China National Machinery Industry Corporation	541330		
China National Materials Co Ltd	541330	9,083,646,976	279,275,520
China Petroleum Engineering & Construction Corporation	541330		
China Petroleum Pipeline Engineering Co Ltd	541330		
China Power Engineering Consulting Group Corporation	541330		
Chiyoda Corporation	541330	5,624,604,672	-383,044,544
COWI A/S	541330	989,391,000	23,162,500
CRB	541330		
Dar Al-Handasah Consultants (Shair and Partners)	541330		
DLZ Corporation	541330	100,000,000	
DNV GL Group AS	541330	2,369,300,000	7,421,170
Dorsch Gruppe	541330		
Downer EDI Limited	541330	5,626,796,032	140,970,864
ECC	541330		
Engility Holdings Inc	541330	1,931,886,976	-35,191,000
ENGlobal Corporation	541330	55,765,000	-16,258,000
Eptisa	541330	110,000,000	
Gannett Fleming Inc	541330	395,000,000	

Industry Group/Company	Industry Code	2017 Sales	2017 Profits
Geosyntec Consultants Inc	541330		
Ghafari Associates LLC	541330		
GHD	541330	1,326,830,000	
Golder Associates Corporation	541330	1,000,000,000	
Gulf Interstate Engineering Company	541330		
Harsco Corporation	541330	1,607,062,016	7,822,000
Hatch Group	541330		
HDR Inc	541330	1,930,000,000	
HKS Inc	541330	380,000,000	
HNTB Corporation	541330		
HOK	541330	440,000,000	
IDOM	541330	383,316,000	
ILF Consulting Engineers Austria GmbH	541330		
Ingenium Group Inc	541330		
Integral Group Inc	541330		
IPS - Integrated Project Service LLC	541330		
JGC Corporation	541330	6,457,537,024	-205,487,264
KEO International Consultants WLL	541330		
KEPCO Engineering & Construction Company Inc	541330	459,021,000	19,872,500
Khatib & Alami	541330		
Kimley-Horn and Associates Inc	541330	722,298,000	
Kleinfelder Group Inc (The)	541330		
Lahmeyer International GmbH	541330		
Langan Engineering and Environmental Services Inc	541330		
Lauren Engineers & Constructors Inc	541330		
Leo A Daly Company	541330	160,000,000	
Louis Berger Group Inc (The)	541330	1,250,000,000	
Mason & Hanger	541330		
McDermott International Inc	541330	2,984,768,000	178,546,000
Michael Baker International LLC	541330	670,000,000	
Middough Inc	541330		
Mott MacDonald Limited	541330	850,000,000	
Nippon Koei Group	541330	901,983,000	29,274,500
NV5 Global Inc	541330	333,033,984	24,006,000
Oriental Consultants Global Co Ltd	541330		
Page Southerland Page Inc	541330	147,000,000	
Parsons Corporation	541330	3,016,000,000	156,000,000
Paul C Rizzo Associates Inc	541330		
Pininfarina SpA	541330	954,010,200	1,571,600
PM Group	541330	360,000,000	
Power Construction Corporation of China (PowerChina)	541330	49,000,000,000	
POWER Engineers Inc	541330		
Poyry PLC	541330	625,644,000	6,708,040
Ramboll Environ Inc	541330	415,071,000	
Ramboll Group A/S	541330	1,727,580,000	23,500,200
Ricardo plc	541330	501,495,520	35,322,604
Royal HaskoningDHV	541330	700,664,000	15,389,000
Sargent & Lundy LLC	541330		
Sembcorp Marine Ltd	541330	1,820,462,080	10,733,566

Industry Group/Company	Industry Code	2017 Sales	2017 Profits
Sener Ingenieria y Sistemas SA	541330	1,100,000,000	
SEPCO Electric Power Construction Corporation	541330		
Shanghai Construction Group Co Ltd	541330	21,634,900,000	396,765,000
Sheladia Associates Inc	541330		
SK Engineering & Construction Co Ltd	541330	6,029,540,000	81,842,200
Skidmore Owings & Merrill LLP	541330	345,000,000	
SMEC Holdings Limited	541330	450,000,000	
SNC-Lavalin Group Inc	541330	7,399,697,408	302,841,856
SSOE Group	541330		
Stanley Consultants Inc	541330		
Stellar Group Inc (The)	541330	575,000,000	
STV Group Incorporated	541330	525,000,000	
Taisei Corporation	541330	13,855,524,864	843,730,240
Tecnica y Proyectos SA (TYPSA)	541330	250,000,000	
Thornton Tomasetti Inc	541330		
TRC Companies Inc	541330		
Trevi-Finanziaria Industriale SpA (Trevi Group)	541330		
UniversalPegasus International Inc	541330		
VEPICA Grupo Internacional SL	541330		
VSE Corporation	541330	760,113,024	39,096,000
Waldemar S Nelson and Company Inc	541330		
WL Meinhardt Group Pty Ltd	541330		
WS Atkins plc	541330	2,400,000,000	
WSP Opus	541330		
Facilities Support Services			
Abertis Infraestructuras SA	561210	7,202,191,872	1,108,218,240
Factory Automation, Robots (Robotics) Industrial Process, Thermostat, Flow Meter and Environmental Quality Monitoring and Control Manufacturing			
Emerson Electric Co	334513	15,264,000,000	1,518,000,000
Rockwell Automation Inc	334513	6,311,300,096	825,699,968
Siemens AG	334513	102,557,483,008	7,466,225,664
Fibers, Artificial and Synthetic and Filaments Manufacturing			
Eastman Chemical Company	325220	9,548,999,680	1,384,000,000
Fluid Power Pump and Motor Manufacturing			
IMI plc	333996	2,493,946,880	230,878,784
Fossil Fuel Electric Power Generation			
Sembcorp Industries Ltd	221112	6,363,889,664	175,973,760
Fuel Cells Manufacturing			
FuelCell Energy Inc	335999A	95,666,000	-53,903,000
Generators, and Wind, Steam and Gas Turbine Equipment Manufacturing			
Alstom SA	333611	9,022,203,904	356,887,072
ENERCON GmbH	333611	5,000,000,000	
Siemens Gamesa Renewable Energy SA	333611	6,000,000,000	
Vestas Wind Systems A/S	333611	12,290,993,152	1,104,003,584

Industry Group/Company	Industry Code	2017 Sales	2017 Profits
Heavy Construction, Including Civil Engineering-Construction, Major Construction Projects, Land Subdivision, Infrastructure, Utilities, Highways and Bridges			
Baran Group Ltd	237000		
Bechtel Group Inc	237000	33,100,000,000	
Bilfinger SE	237000	4,994,195,968	-109,288,944
CDM Smith Inc	237000	1,330,000,000	
Chicago Bridge & Iron Company NV (CB&I)	237000	6,673,330,176	-1,458,193,024
Daelim Industrial Co Ltd	237000	1,155,110,000	459,302,000
Fluor Corporation	237000	19,520,970,752	191,376,992
Fomento de Construcciones y Contratas SA (FCC)	237000	7,164,948,992	145,769,232
GS Engineering & Construction Corporation	237000	10,936,700,000	-159,228,000
HOCHTIEF AG	237000	25,000,000,000	
Hyundai Engineering & Construction Company Ltd	237000	15,813,200,000	188,871,000
Jacobs Engineering Group Inc	237000	10,022,788,096	293,727,008
KBR Inc	237000	4,171,000,064	434,000,000
Larsen & Toubro Limited (L&T)	237000	16,763,789,312	926,631,552
PCL Construction Group Inc	237000	8,250,000,000	
Salini Impregilo SpA	237000	7,500,000,000	
Heavy Duty Truck (including Buses) Manufacturing			
AB Volvo	336120	38,000,000,000	
Daimler Trucks North America LLC	336120	36,712,725,000	
PACCAR Inc	336120	19,456,399,360	1,675,200,000
Highway, Street, Tunnel & Bridge Construction (Infrastructure)			
ACC Companies (The)	237310		
Acciona SA	237310	8,957,957,120	271,840,512
ACS Actividades de Construccion y Servicios SA	237310	38,000,000,000	
AECOM	237310	18,203,402,240	339,390,016
Aecon Group Inc	237310	2,224,120,576	22,335,314
Empresas ICA SAB de CV	237310		
Granite Construction Incorporated	237310	2,989,712,896	69,098,000
Kiewit Corporation	237310	8,700,000,000	
Sino-Thai Engineering & Construction PCL	237310	645,473,216	-19,640,086
Tutor Perini Corporation	237310	4,757,208,064	148,382,000
VINCI SA	237310	50,726,121,472	3,392,279,552
Household Laundry Equipment Manufacturing			
Whirlpool Corporation	335224	21,252,999,168	350,000,000
HVAC (Cooling, Heating, Ventilation and Air Conditioning) and Refrigeration Equipment Manufacturing			
Ingersoll-Rand plc	333400	14,197,600,256	1,302,599,936
Industrial Gas (i.e. Helium, Nitrogen, Oxygen, Neon) Manufacturing			
Air Products and Chemicals Inc	325120	8,187,599,872	3,000,399,872
Linde AG	325120	21,132,900,352	1,770,851,328
Industrial Machinery Manufacturing, Other			
Illinois Tool Works Inc	333249	14,314,000,384	1,687,000,064

Industry Group/Company	Industry Code	2017 Sales	2017 Profits
Internet Search Engines, Online Publishing, Sharing, Gig and Consumer Services, Online Radio, TV and Entertainment Sites and Social Media			
Alphabet Inc	519130	110,854,995,968	12,661,999,616
LCD (Liquid-Crystal Display), Radio Frequency (RF, RFID) and Microwave Equipment Manufacturing			
AU Optronics Corp	334419	11,635,615,744	1,453,802,496
Innolux Corporation	334419	11,078,100,000	1,246,190,000
LG Display Co Ltd	334419	25,000,000,000	
Machine Tool and Laser Manufacturing (for Bending, Buffing, Boring, Pressing, Grinding or Forming)			
ATS Automation Tooling Systems Inc	333517	801,350,784	27,739,992
Machinery and Engines Manufacturing, Including Construction, Agricultural, Mining, Industrial, Commercial and HVAC			
General Electric Company (GE)	333000	122,092,003,328	-5,785,999,872
Mitsubishi Corporation	333000	59,863,621,632	4,101,854,208
Medical Equipment and Supplies Manufacturing			
3M Company	339100	31,657,000,960	4,857,999,872
Bausch & Lomb Inc	339100	4,871,000,000	1,440,000,000
Baxter International Inc	339100	10,561,000,448	717,000,000
Becton Dickinson & Company	339100	12,092,999,680	1,100,000,000
Boston Scientific Corporation	339100	9,048,000,512	104,000,000
Essilor International SA	339100	9,249,425,408	974,338,752
GE Healthcare	339100	19,116,000,000	3,448,000,000
Hill-Rom Holdings Inc	339100	2,743,699,968	133,600,000
Siemens Healthineers	339100	13,800,000,000	2,500,000,000
Smiths Group plc	339100	4,671,698,944	803,304,384
Stryker Corporation	339100	12,444,000,256	1,020,000,000
Medical Imaging and Electromedical (Medical Devices) Equipment, including MRI, Ultrasound, Pacemakers, EKG and CAT			
Beckman Coulter Inc	334510	5,100,000,000	
Medtronic plc	334510	29,710,000,128	4,028,000,000
William Demant Holding Group	334510	2,183,934,720	290,440,640
Mining Machinery and Equipment Manufacturing			
ITT Inc	333131	2,585,299,968	113,500,000
Missile (Aerospace Defense) and Space Vehicle Manufacturing			
Raytheon Company	336414	25,347,999,744	2,024,000,000
SpaceX (Space Exploration Technologies Corporation)	336414	1,500,000,000	
Oil and Gas Exploration & Production			
BP plc	211111	241,417,994,240	3,388,999,936
Chevron Corporation	211111	134,673,997,824	9,194,999,808
ConocoPhillips Company	211111	29,105,999,872	-855,000,000
Eni SpA	211111	82,638,495,744	4,166,564,096
Exxon Mobil Corporation (ExxonMobil)	211111	237,162,004,480	19,709,999,104
Marathon Oil Corporation	211111	4,373,000,192	-5,722,999,808
OAO Lukoil	211111	84,000,000,000	
Petrobras (Petroleo Brasileiro SA)	211111	80,000,000,000	

Industry Group/Company	Industry Code	2017 Sales	2017 Profits
PetroChina Company Limited	211111	250,000,000,000	
Petroleos Mexicanos (Pemex)	211111	70,604,000,000	-14,194,000,000
Royal Dutch Shell plc	211111	305,179,000,832	12,977,000,448
Saudi Aramco (Saudi Arabian Oil Co)	211111	300,000,000,000	
Statoil ASA	211111	60,999,000,064	4,590,000,128
Total SA	211111	149,099,003,904	8,631,000,064
Oil and Gas Field Machinery and Equipment Manufacturing			
TechnipFMC plc	333132	15,056,900,096	113,300,000
Oil and Gas Field Services			
Baker Huges, A GE Company	213112	17,258,999,808	-73,000,000
Halliburton Company	213112	20,619,999,232	-463,000,000
Schlumberger Limited	213112	30,439,999,488	-1,504,999,936
Outsourced Computer Facilities Management and Operations Services			
IBM Global Business Services	541513	16,348,000,000	1,401,000,000
International Business Machines Corporation (IBM)	541513	79,138,996,224	5,752,999,936
Paints and Coatings Manufacturing			
Akzo Nobel NV	325510	11,869,891,584	1,027,439,552
Altana AG	325510	2,691,550,000	281,095,000
Clariant International Ltd	325510	6,100,000,000	
Paper Bag and Coated and Treated Paper Manufacturing			
Nitto Denko Corporation	322220	7,152,133,632	591,140,352
Petrochemicals Manufacturing			
ALFA SAB de CV	325110	17,616,193,536	-113,752,336
Evonik Industries AG	325110	17,806,071,808	885,425,664
ExxonMobil Chemical Company Inc	325110		4,518,000,000
LyondellBasell Industries NV	325110	34,483,998,720	4,879,000,064
Mitsui Chemicals Inc	325110	11,293,852,672	604,052,544
Sasol Limited	325110	14,282,388,480	1,687,804,928
Showa Denko KK	325110	7,270,235,136	311,812,928
Sumitomo Chemical Co Ltd	325110	18,206,476,288	796,366,720
Pharmaceuticals, Biopharmaceuticals, Generics and Drug Manufacturing			
Abbott Laboratories	325412	27,389,999,104	477,000,000
Alcon Inc	325412	13,000,000,000	
Allergan plc	325412	15,940,700,160	-4,125,499,904
Amgen Inc	325412	22,848,999,424	1,979,000,064
Astellas Pharma Inc	325412	12,219,722,752	2,037,460,608
AstraZeneca plc	325412	22,464,999,424	2,868,000,000
Bayer AG	325412	43,240,140,800	9,059,251,200
Bayer Corporation	325412	6,350,000,000	
Bayer HealthCare Pharmaceuticals Inc	325412	14,500,000,000	
Biogen Inc	325412	12,273,899,520	2,539,099,904
Bristol-Myers Squibb Co	325412	20,775,999,488	1,007,000,000
Eisai Co Ltd	325412	5,022,331,392	366,666,688
Eli Lilly and Company	325412	22,871,300,096	-204,100,000
Genentech Inc	325412	19,000,000,000	

Industry Group/Company	Industry Code	2017 Sales	2017 Profits
Gilead Sciences Inc	325412	26,107,000,832	4,627,999,744
GlaxoSmithKline plc	325412	42,993,876,992	2,182,025,216
Johnson & Johnson	325412	76,449,996,800	1,300,000,000
Merck & Co Inc	325412	40,121,999,360	2,393,999,872
Merck KGaA	325412	18,150,960,000	3,084,780,000
Merck Serono SA	325412	7,000,000,000	
Novartis AG	325412	50,134,999,040	7,703,000,064
Novo-Nordisk AS	325412	18,495,471,616	6,313,854,976
Pfizer Inc	325412	52,545,998,848	21,308,000,256
Roche Holding AG	325412	55,419,920,384	8,976,532,480
Sanofi Genzyme	325412	4,200,000,000	
Sanofi SA	325412	44,708,438,016	10,415,174,656
Takeda Pharmaceutical Company Limited	325412	16,136,119,296	1,070,803,136
UCB SA	325412	5,594,112,000	929,882,240
Photographic and Photocopying Equipment Manufacturing			
Agfa-Gevaert NV	333316	3,200,000,000	
Canon Inc	333316	38,010,204,160	2,253,801,216
FUJIFILM Holdings Corporation	333316	21,633,716,224	1,225,135,232
Nikon Corporation	333316	6,980,371,456	36,957,336
Ricoh Company Ltd	333316	18,901,612,544	32,504,194
Plastics Material and Resin Manufacturing			
Celanese Corporation	325211	6,140,000,256	843,000,000
Huntsman Corporation	325211	8,358,000,128	636,000,000
Kaneka Corporation	325211	5,107,341,312	190,832,880
Lanxess AG	325211	11,934,105,600	107,436,592
Shin-Etsu Chemical Co Ltd	325211	11,527,902,208	1,638,829,952
Union Carbide Corporation	325211	5,165,000,000	205,000,000
Power, Distribution and Specialty Transformer Manufacturing			
Mitsubishi Electric Corporation	335311	39,488,225,280	1,960,993,152
Schneider Electric SE	335311	30,500,000,000	
Power-Driven Handtool Manufacturing			
Stanley Black & Decker Inc	333991	12,747,200,512	1,226,000,000
Pressed and Blown Glass and Glassware (except Glass Packaging Containers) Manufacturing			
Corning Inc	327212	10,115,999,744	-497,000,000
Printing Ink Manufacturing			
DIC Corporation	325910	7,354,453,504	359,632,992
Radar, Navigation, Sonar, Space Vehicle Guidance, Flight Systems and Marine Instrument Manufacturing			
FLIR Systems Inc	334511	1,800,434,048	107,223,000
Teledyne Technologies Inc	334511	2,603,800,064	227,200,000
Real Estate Rental, Leasing, Development and Management, including REITs			
China State Construction Engineering Corp (CSCEC)	531100	6,100,000,000	
Road Transportation, Support Activities for			
Globalvia Inversiones SAU	488490	305,000,000	

Industry Group/Company	Industry Code	2017 Sales	2017 Profits
Scientific Research and Development (R&D) in Life Sciences, Medical Devices, Biotechnology and Pharmaceuticals (Drugs)			
Albany Molecular Research Inc	541711	600,000,000	
IQVIA Holdings Inc	541711	9,738,999,808	1,308,999,936
PAREXEL International Corporation	541711	2,500,000,000	
Pharmaceutical Product Development LLC	541711	1,350,000,000	
Scientific Research and Development (R&D) in Physics, Engineering, Telecommunications and Computers			
Amazon Lab126 Inc	541712		
BASF New Business GmbH	541712		
Fujitsu Laboratories Ltd	541712		
GE Global Research	541712		
Hewlett Packard Laboratories (HP Labs)	541712		
Hitachi High Technologies America Inc	541712	5,500,000,000	
IBM Research	541712		
Intellectual Ventures Management LLC	541712		
NEC Laboratories America Inc	541712		
Nokia Bell Labs	541712		
Palo Alto Research Center Incorporated (PARC)	541712		
Siemens Corporate Technology	541712		
Toshiba Corporate R&D Center	541712		
X Development LLC	541712		
Security Guard, Security Patrol, Armored Car, Security System, Locksmith and Other Security Services			
Johnson Controls International plc	561600	30,172,000,000	1,853,000,000
Semiconductor and Solar Cell Manufacturing, Including Chips, Memory, LEDs, Transistors and Integrated Circuits			
Advanced Micro Devices Inc (AMD)	334413	5,328,999,936	43,000,000
Advanced Semiconductor Engineering Inc	334413	9,909,624,832	835,820,352
Analog Devices Inc	334413	5,107,503,104	727,259,008
Atmel Corporation	334413	1,200,000,000	
Hoya Corporation	334413	4,562,260,480	808,086,528
Infineon Technologies AG	334413	8,722,122,752	975,573,632
Intel Corporation	334413	62,761,000,960	9,601,000,448
Maxim Integrated Products Inc	334413	2,295,614,976	571,612,992
Micron Technology Inc	334413	20,322,000,896	5,088,999,936
NVIDIA Corporation	334413	6,910,000,128	1,666,000,000
Qualcomm Incorporated	334413	22,290,999,296	2,465,999,872
STMicroelectronics NV	334413	8,346,999,808	802,000,000
Taiwan Semiconductor Manufacturing Co Ltd (TSMC)	334413	35,000,000,000	
Texas Instruments Inc (TI)	334413	14,961,000,448	3,681,999,872
Toshiba Corporation	334413	45,377,056,768	-8,996,301,824
United Microelectronics Corp	334413	5,016,540,000	
Semiconductor Manufacturing Equipment and Systems (Including Etching, Wafer Processing & Surface Mount) Manufacturing			
Applied Materials Inc	333242	14,536,999,936	3,433,999,872

Industry Group/Company	Industry Code	2017 Sales	2017 Profits
Ship Building and Repairing			
Daewoo Shipbuilding & Marine Engineering Co Ltd	336611	9,000,000,000	
Specialty Chemicals Manufacturing, Including Frangrances, Silicones, Biodiesel and Enzymes,			
BASF SE	325199	79,620,390,912	7,505,742,848
DowDupont Inc	325199	62,484,000,768	1,460,000,000
Spices, Flavors and Fragrances			
Tate & Lyle plc	311942	3,921,093,632	364,620,416
Surgical Appliance and Supplies (Medical Devices) Manufacturing			
Smith & Nephew plc	339113	4,765,000,192	767,000,000
Telecommunications, Telephone and Network Equipment Manufacturing, including PBX, Routers, Switches and Handsets Manufacturing			
ARRIS Group Inc	334210	6,614,391,808	92,027,000
Avaya Holdings Corp	334210	3,272,000,000	-182,000,000
Huawei Technologies Co Ltd	334210	92,080,000,000	
Tellabs Inc	334210	1,391,000,000	
UTStarcom Inc	334210		
VTech Holdings Limited	334210	2,079,299,968	179,000,000
ZTE Corporation	334210	17,344,118,784	728,123,200
Utilities Construction, including Pipelines, Water & Sewer Systems, Telecommunications Lines and Systems and Electric Power Lines and Systems			
Matrix Service Company	237100	1,197,508,992	-183,000
Vaccines, Skin Replacement Products and Biologicals Manufacturing			
CSL Limited	325414	6,680,297,984	1,350,438,400
Novozymes	325414	2,406,153,216	516,467,712
Wireless Communications and Radio and TV Broadcasting Equipment Manufacturing, including Cellphones (Handsets)			
Apple Inc	334220	229,233,999,872	48,350,998,528
Harris Corporation	334220	5,900,000,256	553,000,000
LG Electronics Inc	334220	55,400,000,000	2,230,000,000
Nokia Corporation	334220	28,584,306,688	-1,844,945,536
Sony Mobile Communications AB	334220	5,250,000,000	
Telefon AB LM Ericsson (Ericsson)	334220	23,768,832,000	-4,156,945,152

ALPHABETICAL INDEX

3M Company
AB Volvo
ABB Ltd
Abbott Laboratories
Abengoa SA
Abertis Infraestructuras SA
ACC Companies (The)
Accenture plc
Acciona SA
Acer Inc
ACS Actividades de Construccion y Servicios SA
Activision Blizzard Inc
Adobe Systems Inc
Advanced Micro Devices Inc (AMD)
Advanced Semiconductor Engineering Inc
AECOM
Aecon Group Inc
AF AB
Agfa-Gevaert NV
Agilent Technologies Inc
Air Products and Chemicals Inc
Airbus SE
Aisin Seiki Co Ltd
Akzo Nobel NV
Albany Molecular Research Inc
Alcon Inc
ALFA SAB de CV
Allergan plc
Alphabet Inc
Alps Electric Co Ltd
Alstom SA
Altana AG
Amazon Lab126 Inc
Ambitech Engineering Corporation
Amdocs Limited
Amey plc
Amgen Inc
Analog Devices Inc
Apple Inc
Applied Materials Inc
Arcadis NV
Areva SA
Arkema
ARRIS Group Inc
Artelia
ARUP Group Limited
Associated Consulting Engineers
Astellas Pharma Inc
AstraZeneca plc
ASUSTeK Computer Inc
Atmel Corporation
ATS Automation Tooling Systems Inc
AU Optronics Corp
Audi AG
Aurecon Group Brand (Pte) Ltd
Autodesk Inc
Autoliv Inc
Avaya Holdings Corp
Babcock & Wilcox Enterprises Inc
BAE Systems plc
Baker Huges, A GE Company
Balfour Beatty plc
Baran Group Ltd
BASF New Business GmbH
BASF SE
Bausch & Lomb Inc
Baxter International Inc
Bayer AG
Bayer Corporation
Bayer HealthCare Pharmaceuticals Inc
Beca Group Limited
Bechtel Group Inc
Beckman Coulter Inc
Becton Dickinson & Company
Belden Inc
Benchmark Electronics Inc
Bilfinger SE
Bilfinger Tebodin BV
Biogen Inc
BIOS-BIOENERGYSYSTEME GmbH
Black & Veatch Holding Company
BMC Software Inc
BMW (Bayerische Motoren Werke AG)
Boeing Company (The)
Bombardier Inc
Boston Scientific Corporation
Bouygues SA
BP plc
Bristol-Myers Squibb Co
Burns & McDonnell Inc
BuroHappold Ltd
BYD Company Limited
CA Inc (CA Technologies)
Cadence Design Systems Inc
Calsonic Kansei Corporation
CannonDesign
Canon Inc
Cardno Limited
Casio Computer Co Ltd
Caterpillar Inc
CDM Smith Inc
Celanese Corporation
Celestica Inc
CGI Group Inc
CH2M HILL Inc
CHA Consulting Inc
Chevron Corporation
Chicago Bridge & Iron Company NV (CB&I)
China Chengda Engineering Co Ltd
China Energy Engineering Corporation Limited
China HuanQiu Contracting & Engineering Corporation
China National Machinery Industry Corporation
China National Materials Co Ltd
China Petroleum Engineering & Construction Corporation

China Petroleum Pipeline Engineering Co Ltd
China Power Engineering Consulting Group Corporation
China Railway Construction Corporation Limited (CRCC)
China State Construction Engineering Corp (CSCEC)
Chiyoda Corporation
Cisco Systems Inc
Citrix Systems Inc
Clariant International Ltd
Compal Electronics Inc
ConocoPhillips Company
Corning Inc
COWI A/S
Cray Inc
CRB
CSL Limited
Cummins Inc
Daelim Industrial Co Ltd
Daewoo Shipbuilding & Marine Engineering Co Ltd
Daihatsu Motor Co Ltd
Daimler AG
Daimler Trucks North America LLC
Dana Incorporated
Dar Al-Handasah Consultants (Shair and Partners)
Dassault Aviation SA
Dassault Systemes SA
Deere & Company (John Deere)
Dell EMC
Dell Technologies Inc
Denso Corporation
DIC Corporation
Diebold Nixdorf Inc
DLZ Corporation
DNV GL Group AS
Dongfeng Motor Corporation
Doosan Heavy Industries & Construction Co Ltd
Dorsch Gruppe
DowDupont Inc
Downer EDI Limited
Dyson Limited
Eastman Chemical Company
Eaton Corporation plc
ECC
Eisai Co Ltd
Electronic Arts Inc (EA)
Eli Lilly and Company
Embraer SA
Emerson Electric Co
Empresas ICA SAB de CV
ENERCON GmbH
Engility Holdings Inc
ENGlobal Corporation
Eni SpA
Eptisa
Essilor International SA
Evonik Industries AG
Exxon Mobil Corporation (ExxonMobil)
ExxonMobil Chemical Company Inc
Faurecia SA

FAW Group Corporation (First Automotive Works)
FCA US LLC
Federal-Mogul LLC
Ferrovial SA
Flex Ltd
FLIR Systems Inc
Fluor Corporation
Fomento de Construcciones y Contratas SA (FCC)
Ford Motor Co
FuelCell Energy Inc
FUJIFILM Holdings Corporation
Fujitsu Laboratories Ltd
Fujitsu Limited
Fujitsu Technology Solutions (Holding) BV
Gannett Fleming Inc
GE Aviation
GE Global Research
GE Healthcare
Gemalto NV
Genentech Inc
General Dynamics Corporation
General Electric Company (GE)
General Motors Company (GM)
Georg Fischer Ltd
Geosyntec Consultants Inc
Ghafari Associates LLC
GHD
Gilead Sciences Inc
GKN plc
GlaxoSmithKline plc
Globalvia Inversiones SAU
GM Korea
Golder Associates Corporation
Granite Construction Incorporated
GS Engineering & Construction Corporation
Gulf Interstate Engineering Company
Gulfstream Aerospace Corporation
Halliburton Company
Harris Corporation
Harsco Corporation
Hatch Group
HDR Inc
Hewlett Packard Enterprise Company
Hewlett Packard Laboratories (HP Labs)
HGST Inc
Hill-Rom Holdings Inc
Hitachi High Technologies America Inc
Hitachi Limited
HKS Inc
HNTB Corporation
HOCHTIEF AG
HOK
Hon Hai Precision Industry Company Ltd
Honda Motor Co Ltd
Honeywell International Inc
Hoya Corporation
HTC Corporation
Huawei Technologies Co Ltd

Huntsman Corporation
Hyundai Engineering & Construction Company Ltd
Hyundai Motor Company
IBM Global Business Services
IBM Research
IDOM
ILF Consulting Engineers Austria GmbH
Illinois Tool Works Inc
IMI plc
Infineon Technologies AG
Ingenium Group Inc
Ingersoll-Rand plc
Innolux Corporation
Integral Group Inc
Intel Corporation
Intellectual Ventures Management LLC
International Business Machines Corporation (IBM)
Intertek Group plc
Intuit Inc
IPS - Integrated Project Service LLC
IQVIA Holdings Inc
Isuzu Motors Limited
ITT Inc
Jabil Inc
Jacobs Engineering Group Inc
Jaguar Land Rover Limited
JGC Corporation
Johnson & Johnson
Johnson Controls International plc
Juniper Networks Inc
Kaneka Corporation
Kawasaki Heavy Industries Ltd
KBR Inc
KEO International Consultants WLL
KEPCO Engineering & Construction Company Inc
Khatib & Alami
Kia Motors Corporation
Kiewit Corporation
Kimley-Horn and Associates Inc
Kleinfelder Group Inc (The)
Konami Holdings Corporation
Koninklijke Philips NV (Royal Philips)
Kumho Industrial Co Ltd
L3 Technologies Inc
Lahmeyer International GmbH
Langan Engineering and Environmental Services Inc
Lanxess AG
Larsen & Toubro Limited (L&T)
Lauren Engineers & Constructors Inc
Layne Christensen Company
Lear Corporation
Lenovo Group Limited
Leo A Daly Company
LG Display Co Ltd
LG Electronics Inc
Linde AG
Lite-On Technology Corporation
Lockheed Martin Corporation

Louis Berger Group Inc (The)
LyondellBasell Industries NV
Magna International Inc
Magneti Marelli SpA
Marathon Oil Corporation
Mason & Hanger
Matrix Service Company
Maxim Integrated Products Inc
Mazda Motor Corporation
McAfee Inc
McDermott International Inc
Medtronic plc
Mentor Graphics Inc
Merck & Co Inc
Merck KGaA
Merck Serono SA
Meritor Inc
Michael Baker International LLC
Micron Technology Inc
Microsoft Corporation
Middough Inc
Mitsubishi Corporation
Mitsubishi Electric Corporation
Mitsubishi Motors Corp
Mitsui Chemicals Inc
Molex LLC
Monsanto Company
Mott MacDonald Limited
MWH Global Inc
NCR Corporation
NEC Corporation
NEC Laboratories America Inc
NetApp Inc
Nidec Corporation
Nikon Corporation
Nintendo Co Ltd
Nippon Koei Group
Nissan Motor Co Ltd
Nitto Denko Corporation
Nokia Bell Labs
Nokia Corporation
Northrop Grumman Corporation
Novartis AG
Novo-Nordisk AS
Novozymes
NTT DATA Corporation
NV5 Global Inc
NVIDIA Corporation
OAO Lukoil
Oracle Corporation
Oriental Consultants Global Co Ltd
PACCAR Inc
Page Southerland Page Inc
Palo Alto Research Center Incorporated (PARC)
Panasonic Corporation
PAREXEL International Corporation
Parsons Corporation
Paul C Rizzo Associates Inc

PCL Construction Group Inc
Petrobras (Petroleo Brasileiro SA)
PetroChina Company Limited
Petroleos Mexicanos (Pemex)
Peugeot SA (Groupe PSA)
Pfizer Inc
Pharmaceutical Product Development LLC
Pininfarina SpA
Pioneer Corporation
Plexus Corp
PM Group
Porsche Automobil Holding SE
Power Construction Corporation of China (PowerChina)
POWER Engineers Inc
Poyry PLC
PTC Inc
Qualcomm Incorporated
QuTech
Ramboll Environ Inc
Ramboll Group A/S
Raytheon Company
Renault SA
Rheinmetall AG
Ricardo plc
Ricoh Company Ltd
Robert Bosch GmbH
Roche Holding AG
Rockwell Automation Inc
Rohm Co Ltd
Rolls-Royce plc
Royal Dutch Shell plc
Royal HaskoningDHV
Saab AB
Safran SA
SAIC Motor Corporation Limited
Salini Impregilo SpA
Samsung Electronics Co Ltd
SanDisk Corporation
Sanmina Corporation
Sanofi Genzyme
Sanofi SA
SAP SE
Sargent & Lundy LLC
SAS Institute Inc
Sasol Limited
Saudi Aramco (Saudi Arabian Oil Co)
Schlumberger Limited
Schneider Electric SE
Science Applications International Corporation (SAIC)
Seagate Technology plc
Seiko Epson Corporation
Sembcorp Industries Ltd
Sembcorp Marine Ltd
Sener Ingenieria y Sistemas SA
SEPCO Electric Power Construction Corporation
Shanghai Construction Group Co Ltd
Sharp Corporation
Sheladia Associates Inc

Shin-Etsu Chemical Co Ltd
Showa Denko KK
Siemens AG
Siemens Corporate Technology
Siemens Gamesa Renewable Energy SA
Siemens Healthineers
Singapore Technologies Engineering Limited
Sino-Thai Engineering & Construction PCL
SK Engineering & Construction Co Ltd
Skidmore Owings & Merrill LLP
SMEC Holdings Limited
Smith & Nephew plc
Smiths Group plc
SNC-Lavalin Group Inc
Solvay SA
Sony Corporation
Sony Mobile Communications AB
SpaceX (Space Exploration Technologies Corporation)
Spirit AeroSystems Holdings Inc
SSOE Group
Stanley Black & Decker Inc
Stanley Consultants Inc
Statoil ASA
Stellar Group Inc (The)
STMicroelectronics NV
Stryker Corporation
STV Group Incorporated
Subaru Corporation
Sumitomo Chemical Co Ltd
Suzuki Motor Corporation
Symantec Corporation
Syngenta AG
Synopsys Inc
Taisei Corporation
Taiwan Semiconductor Manufacturing Co Ltd (TSMC)
Takeda Pharmaceutical Company Limited
Take-Two Interactive Software Inc
Tata Motors Limited
Tate & Lyle plc
TechnipFMC plc
Tecnica y Proyectos SA (TYPSA)
Teledyne Technologies Inc
Telefon AB LM Ericsson (Ericsson)
Tellabs Inc
Tenneco Inc
Terex Corporation
Tesla Inc
Texas Instruments Inc (TI)
Textron Inc
Thornton Tomasetti Inc
Toshiba Corporate R&D Center
Toshiba Corporation
Total SA
Toyoda Gosei Co Ltd
Toyota Motor Corporation
TPV Technology Limited
TRC Companies Inc
Trevi-Finanziaria Industriale SpA (Trevi Group)

Tutor Perini Corporation
UCB SA
Union Carbide Corporation
Unisys Corp
United Microelectronics Corp
United Technologies Corporation
UniversalPegasus International Inc
UTStarcom Inc
Valeo SA
VEPICA Grupo Internacional SL
VeriSign Inc
Vestas Wind Systems A/S
VINCI SA
Visteon Corporation
Volkswagen AG (VW)
Volvo Car Corporation
VSE Corporation
VTech Holdings Limited
Waldemar S Nelson and Company Inc
Wanxiang Group Corporation
Waymo LLC
Western Digital Corporation
Westinghouse Electric Company LLC
Whirlpool Corporation
William Demant Holding Group
Wipro Limited
WL Meinhardt Group Pty Ltd
WS Atkins plc
WSP Global Inc
WSP Opus
X Development LLC
Xerox Corporation
ZF Friedrichshafen AG (ZF)
ZTE Corporation

INDEX OF U.S. HEADQUARTERS LOCATION BY STATE

To help you locate members of the firms geographically, the city and state of the headquarters of each company are in the following index.

ARIZONA
ACC Companies (The); Phoenix

CALIFORNIA
Activision Blizzard Inc; Santa Monica
Adobe Systems Inc; San Jose
Advanced Micro Devices Inc (AMD); Santa Clara
AECOM; Los Angeles
Agilent Technologies Inc; Santa Clara
Alphabet Inc; Mountain View
Amazon Lab126 Inc; Sunnyvale
Amgen Inc; Thousand Oaks
Apple Inc; Cupertino
Applied Materials Inc; Santa Clara
Atmel Corporation; San Jose
Autodesk Inc; San Rafael
Avaya Holdings Corp; Santa Clara
Bechtel Group Inc; San Francisco
Beckman Coulter Inc; Brea
Cadence Design Systems Inc; San Jose
Chevron Corporation; San Ramon
Cisco Systems Inc; San Jose
ECC; Burlingame
Electronic Arts Inc (EA); Redwood City
Genentech Inc; South San Francisco
Gilead Sciences Inc; Foster City
Granite Construction Incorporated; Watsonville
Hewlett Packard Enterprise Company; Palo Alto
Hewlett Packard Laboratories (HP Labs); Palo Alto
HGST Inc; San Jose
Integral Group Inc; Oakland
Intel Corporation; Santa Clara
Intuit Inc; Mountain View
Jacobs Engineering Group Inc; Dallas
Juniper Networks Inc; Sunnyvale
Kleinfelder Group Inc (The); San Diego
Maxim Integrated Products Inc; San Jose
McAfee Inc; Santa Clara
NetApp Inc; Sunnyvale
NVIDIA Corporation; Santa Clara
Oracle Corporation; Redwood City
Palo Alto Research Center Incorporated (PARC); Palo Alto
Parsons Corporation; Pasadena
Qualcomm Incorporated; San Diego
SanDisk Corporation; Milpitas
Sanmina Corporation; San Jose
SpaceX (Space Exploration Technologies Corporation); Hawthorne
Symantec Corporation; Mountain View

Synopsys Inc; Mountain View
Teledyne Technologies Inc; Thousand Oaks
Tesla Inc; Palo Alto
Tutor Perini Corporation; Sylmar
Waymo LLC; Mountain View
Western Digital Corporation; San Jose
X Development LLC; Mountain View

COLORADO
CH2M HILL Inc; Englewood
MWH Global Inc; Broomfield

CONNECTICUT
FuelCell Energy Inc; Danbury
Stanley Black & Decker Inc; New Britain
Terex Corporation; Westport
TRC Companies Inc; Windsor
United Technologies Corporation; Farmington
Xerox Corporation; Norwalk

FLORIDA
Citrix Systems Inc; Fort Lauderdale
Harris Corporation; Melbourne
Jabil Inc; St. Petersburg
NV5 Global Inc; Hollywood
Stellar Group Inc (The); Jacksonville

GEORGIA
ARRIS Group Inc; Suwanee
Geosyntec Consultants Inc; Atlanta
Gulfstream Aerospace Corporation; Savannah
NCR Corporation; Atlanta

IDAHO
Micron Technology Inc; Boise
POWER Engineers Inc; Hailey

ILLINOIS
Abbott Laboratories; Abbott Park
Ambitech Engineering Corporation; Downers Grove
Baxter International Inc; Deerfield
Boeing Company (The); Chicago
Caterpillar Inc; Deerfield
Deere & Company (John Deere); Moline
Hill-Rom Holdings Inc; Chicago
Hitachi High Technologies America Inc; Schaumburg
Illinois Tool Works Inc; Glenview
Molex LLC; Lisle
Sargent & Lundy LLC; Chicago
Skidmore Owings & Merrill LLP; Chicago
Tenneco Inc; Lake Forest

INDIANA
Cummins Inc; Columbus
Eli Lilly and Company; Indianapolis

IOWA
Stanley Consultants Inc; Muscatine

KANSAS
Black & Veatch Holding Company; Overland Park
Spirit AeroSystems Holdings Inc; Wichita

LOUISIANA
Waldemar S Nelson and Company Inc; New Orleans

MARYLAND
Lockheed Martin Corporation; Bethesda
Sheladia Associates Inc; Rockville

MASSACHUSETTS
Analog Devices Inc; Norwood
Biogen Inc; Cambridge
Boston Scientific Corporation; Marlborough
CDM Smith Inc; Boston
Dell EMC; Hopkinton
General Electric Company (GE); Boston
PAREXEL International Corporation; Waltham
PTC Inc; Needham
Raytheon Company; Waltham
Sanofi Genzyme; Cambridge

MICHIGAN
DowDupont Inc; Midland
FCA US LLC; Auburn Hills
Federal-Mogul LLC; Southfield
Ford Motor Co; Dearborn
General Motors Company (GM); Detroit
Ghafari Associates LLC; Dearborn
Lear Corporation; Southfield
Meritor Inc; Troy
Stryker Corporation; Kalamazoo
Visteon Corporation; Van Buren Township
Whirlpool Corporation; Benton Harbor

MINNESOTA
3M Company; St. Paul

MISSOURI
Amdocs Limited; Chesterfield
Belden Inc; St. Louis
Burns & McDonnell Inc; Kansas City
CRB; Kansas City
Emerson Electric Co; St. Louis
HNTB Corporation; Kansas City
HOK; St. Louis
Monsanto Company; St. Louis

NEBRASKA
HDR Inc; Omaha
Kiewit Corporation; Omaha
Leo A Daly Company; Omaha

NEW JERSEY
Bausch & Lomb Inc; Bridgewater
Bayer Corporation; Whippany
Bayer HealthCare Pharmaceuticals Inc; Wayne
Becton Dickinson & Company; Franklin Lakes
Honeywell International Inc; Morris Plains
Johnson & Johnson; New Brunswick
Langan Engineering and Environmental Services Inc; Parsippany
Louis Berger Group Inc (The); Morristown
Merck & Co Inc; Kenilworth
NEC Laboratories America Inc; Princeton
Nokia Bell Labs; Murray Hill
Siemens Corporate Technology; Princeton

NEW YORK
Albany Molecular Research Inc; Albany
Bristol-Myers Squibb Co; New York
CA Inc (CA Technologies); New York
CannonDesign; New York
CHA Consulting Inc; Albany
Corning Inc; Corning
GE Global Research; Niskayuna
IBM Global Business Services; Armonk
IBM Research; Yorktown Heights
International Business Machines Corporation (IBM); Armonk
ITT Inc; White Plains
L3 Technologies Inc; New York
Pfizer Inc; New York
Take-Two Interactive Software Inc; New York
Thornton Tomasetti Inc; New York

NORTH CAROLINA
Babcock & Wilcox Enterprises Inc; Charlotte
IQVIA Holdings Inc; Durham
Kimley-Horn and Associates Inc; Cary
Pharmaceutical Product Development LLC; Wilmington
SAS Institute Inc; Cary

OHIO
Dana Incorporated; Maumee
Diebold Nixdorf Inc; North Canton
DLZ Corporation; Columbus
GE Aviation; Cincinnati
Middough Inc; Cleveland
SSOE Group; Toledo

OKLAHOMA
Matrix Service Company; Tulsa

OREGON
Daimler Trucks North America LLC; Portland
FLIR Systems Inc; Wilsonville
Mentor Graphics Inc; Wilsonville

PENNSYLVANIA
Air Products and Chemicals Inc; Allentown
Gannett Fleming Inc; Camp Hill
Harsco Corporation; Camp Hill
IPS - Integrated Project Service LLC; Blue Bell
Michael Baker International LLC; Pittsburgh
Paul C Rizzo Associates Inc; Pittsburgh
STV Group Incorporated; Douglassville
Unisys Corp; Blue Bell
Westinghouse Electric Company LLC; Cranberry Township

RHODE ISLAND
Textron Inc; Providence

TENNESSEE
Eastman Chemical Company; Kingsport

TEXAS
Alcon Inc; Fort Worth
Baker Huges, A GE Company; Houston
Benchmark Electronics Inc; Angleton
BMC Software Inc; Houston
Celanese Corporation; Irving
ConocoPhillips Company; Houston
Dell Technologies Inc; Round Rock
ENGlobal Corporation; Houston
Exxon Mobil Corporation (ExxonMobil); Irving
ExxonMobil Chemical Company Inc; Spring
Fluor Corporation; Irving
Gulf Interstate Engineering Company; Houston
Halliburton Company; Houston
HKS Inc; Dallas
Huntsman Corporation; The Woodlands
KBR Inc; Houston
Lauren Engineers & Constructors Inc; Abilene
Layne Christensen Company; The Woodlands
Marathon Oil Corporation; Houston
McDermott International Inc; Houston
Page Southerland Page Inc; Houston
Schlumberger Limited; Houston
Tellabs Inc; Dallas
Texas Instruments Inc (TI); Dallas
Union Carbide Corporation; Houston
UniversalPegasus International Inc; Houston

VIRGINIA
Engility Holdings Inc; Chantilly
General Dynamics Corporation; Falls Church
Mason & Hanger; Glen Allen
Northrop Grumman Corporation; Falls Church
Ramboll Environ Inc; Arlington
Science Applications International Corporation (SAIC); McLean
VeriSign Inc; Reston
VSE Corporation; Alexandria

WASHINGTON
Cray Inc; Seattle
Intellectual Ventures Management LLC; Bellevue
Microsoft Corporation; Redmond
PACCAR Inc; Bellevue

WISCONSIN
Plexus Corp; Neenah
Rockwell Automation Inc; Milwaukee

INDEX OF NON-U.S. HEADQUARTERS LOCATION BY COUNTRY

AUSTRALIA
Aurecon Group Brand (Pte) Ltd; Docklands
Cardno Limited; Fortitude Valley
CSL Limited; Parkville
Downer EDI Limited; North Ryde
GHD; Sydney
SMEC Holdings Limited; Melbourne
WL Meinhardt Group Pty Ltd; Melbourne

AUSTRIA
BIOS-BIOENERGYSYSTEME GmbH; Graz
ILF Consulting Engineers Austria GmbH; Rum/Innsbruck

BELGIUM
Agfa-Gevaert NV; Mortsel
Solvay SA; Brussels
UCB SA; Brussels

BRAZIL
Embraer SA; Sao Paulo
Petrobras (Petroleo Brasileiro SA); Rio de Janeiro

CANADA
Aecon Group Inc; Toronto
ATS Automation Tooling Systems Inc; Cambridge
Bombardier Inc; Montreal
Celestica Inc; Toronto
CGI Group Inc; Montreal
Golder Associates Corporation; Mississauga
Hatch Group; Mississauga
Ingenium Group Inc; Toronto
Magna International Inc; Aurora
PCL Construction Group Inc; Edmonton
SNC-Lavalin Group Inc; Montreal
WSP Global Inc; Montreal

CHINA
BYD Company Limited; Shenzhen
China Chengda Engineering Co Ltd; Chengdu
China Energy Engineering Corporation Limited; Beijing
China HuanQiu Contracting & Engineering Corporation; Beijing
China National Machinery Industry Corporation; Beijing
China National Materials Co Ltd; Beijing
China Petroleum Engineering & Construction Corporation; Beijing
China Petroleum Pipeline Engineering Co Ltd; Langfang
China Power Engineering Consulting Group Corporation; Beijing
China Railway Construction Corporation Limited (CRCC); Beijing
Dongfeng Motor Corporation; Wuhan

FAW Group Corporation (First Automotive Works); Changchun
Huawei Technologies Co Ltd; Shenzhen
Lenovo Group Limited; Beijing
PetroChina Company Limited; Beijing
Power Construction Corporation of China (PowerChina); Beijing
SAIC Motor Corporation Limited; Shanghai
SEPCO Electric Power Construction Corporation; Jinan City
Shanghai Construction Group Co Ltd; Shanghai
Wanxiang Group Corporation; Hangzhou
ZTE Corporation; Shenzhen

DENMARK
COWI A/S; Kongens Lyngby
Novo-Nordisk AS; Bagsværd
Novozymes; Bagsvaerd
Ramboll Group A/S; Copenhagen
Vestas Wind Systems A/S; Aarhus
William Demant Holding Group; Smorum

FINLAND
Nokia Corporation; Espoo
Poyry PLC; Vantaa

FRANCE
Alstom SA; Cedex
Areva SA; Paris
Arkema; Colombes
Artelia; Lyon
Bouygues SA; Paris
Dassault Aviation SA; Paris
Dassault Systemes SA; Velizy-Villacoublay
Essilor International SA; Paris
Faurecia SA; Nanterre
Peugeot SA (Groupe PSA); Paris
Renault SA; Billancourt Cedex
Safran SA; Paris
Sanofi SA; Paris
Schneider Electric SE; Rueil Malmaison
Total SA; Paris
Valeo SA; Paris
VINCI SA; Cedex

GERMANY
Altana AG; Wesel
Audi AG; Ingolstadt
BASF New Business GmbH; Ludwigshafen
BASF SE; Ludwigshafen
Bayer AG; Leverkusen
Bilfinger SE; Mannheim
BMW (Bayerische Motoren Werke AG); Munich
Daimler AG; Stuttgart
Dorsch Gruppe; Offenbach am Main
ENERCON GmbH; Bremen
Evonik Industries AG; Essen
HOCHTIEF AG; Essen

Infineon Technologies AG; Neubiberg
Lahmeyer International GmbH; Bad Vilbel
Lanxess AG; Cologne
Linde AG; Munich
Merck KGaA; Darmstadt
Merck Serono SA; Darmstadt
Porsche Automobil Holding SE; Stuttgart
Rheinmetall AG; Düsseldorf
Robert Bosch GmbH; Stuttgart
SAP SE; Walldorf
Siemens AG; Munich
Siemens Healthineers; Erlangen
Volkswagen AG (VW); Wolfsburg
ZF Friedrichshafen AG (ZF); Friedrichshafen

GREECE
Associated Consulting Engineers; Athens

HONG KONG
China State Construction Engineering Corp (CSCEC); Wanchai
TPV Technology Limited; Kowloon
UTStarcom Inc; Hong Kong
VTech Holdings Limited; Hong Kong

INDIA
Larsen & Toubro Limited (L&T); Mumbai
Tata Motors Limited; Mumbai
Wipro Limited; Bangalore

IRELAND
Medtronic plc; Dublin
Accenture plc; Dublin
Allergan plc; Coolock, Dublin
Eaton Corporation plc; Dublin
Ingersoll-Rand plc; Dublin
Johnson Controls International plc; Cork
PM Group; Dublin
Seagate Technology plc; Dublin

ISRAEL
Baran Group Ltd; Beit-Dagan

ITALY
Eni SpA; Rome
Magneti Marelli SpA; Milano
Pininfarina SpA; Cambiano
Salini Impregilo SpA; Milan
Trevi-Finanziaria Industriale SpA (Trevi Group); Cesena

JAPAN
Aisin Seiki Co Ltd; Kariya
Alps Electric Co Ltd; Tokyo
Astellas Pharma Inc; Tokyo
Calsonic Kansei Corporation; Saitama
Canon Inc; Tokyo

Casio Computer Co Ltd; Tokyo
Chiyoda Corporation; Yokohama
Daihatsu Motor Co Ltd; Osaka
Denso Corporation; Kariya
DIC Corporation; Tokyo
Eisai Co Ltd; Tokyo
FUJIFILM Holdings Corporation; Tokyo
Fujitsu Laboratories Ltd; Kawasaki-shi
Fujitsu Limited; Tokyo
Hitachi Limited; Tokyo
Honda Motor Co Ltd; Tokyo
Hoya Corporation; Tokyo
Isuzu Motors Limited; Tokyo
JGC Corporation; Yokohama
Kaneka Corporation; Osaka
Kawasaki Heavy Industries Ltd; Kobe
Konami Holdings Corporation; Tokyo
Mazda Motor Corporation; Hiroshima
Mitsubishi Corporation; Tokyo
Mitsubishi Electric Corporation; Tokyo
Mitsubishi Motors Corp; Tokyo
Mitsui Chemicals Inc; Tokyo
NEC Corporation; Tokyo
Nidec Corporation; Kyoto
Nikon Corporation; Tokyo
Nintendo Co Ltd; Kyoto
Nippon Koei Group; Tokyo
Nissan Motor Co Ltd; Kanagawa
Nitto Denko Corporation; Osaka
NTT DATA Corporation; Tokyo
Oriental Consultants Global Co Ltd; Tokyo
Panasonic Corporation; Osaka
Pioneer Corporation; Tokyo
Ricoh Company Ltd; Tokyo
Rohm Co Ltd; Kyoto
Seiko Epson Corporation; Nagano
Sharp Corporation; Sakai City, Osaka
Shin-Etsu Chemical Co Ltd; Tokyo
Showa Denko KK; Tokyo
Sony Corporation; Tokyo
Subaru Corporation; Tokyo
Sumitomo Chemical Co Ltd; Tokyo
Suzuki Motor Corporation; Hamamatsu
Taisei Corporation; Tokyo
Takeda Pharmaceutical Company Limited; Tokyo
Toshiba Corporate R&D Center; Kawasaki-shi
Toshiba Corporation; Tokyo
Toyoda Gosei Co Ltd; Kiyosu
Toyota Motor Corporation; Toyota

KOREA
Daelim Industrial Co Ltd; Seoul
Daewoo Shipbuilding & Marine Engineering Co Ltd; Geoje
Doosan Heavy Industries & Construction Co Ltd; Changwon
GM Korea; Incheon
GS Engineering & Construction Corporation; Seoul
Hyundai Engineering & Construction Company Ltd; Seoul
Hyundai Motor Company; Seoul
KEPCO Engineering & Construction Company Inc; Yongin
Kia Motors Corporation; Seoul
Kumho Industrial Co Ltd; Jeollanam-do
LG Display Co Ltd; Seoul
LG Electronics Inc; Seoul
Samsung Electronics Co Ltd; Suwon-si
SK Engineering & Construction Co Ltd; Seoul

KUWAIT
KEO International Consultants WLL; Safat

LEBANON
Dar Al-Handasah Consultants (Shair and Partners); Beirut
Khatib & Alami; Beirut

MEXICO
ALFA SAB de CV; San Pedro Garza García
Empresas ICA SAB de CV; Mexico City
Petroleos Mexicanos (Pemex); Mexico City

NEW ZEALAND
Beca Group Limited; Auckland
WSP Opus; Wellington

NORWAY
DNV GL Group AS; Hovik
Statoil ASA; Stavanger

RUSSIA
OAO Lukoil; Moscow

SAUDI ARABIA
Saudi Aramco (Saudi Arabian Oil Co); Dhahran

SINGAPORE
Flex Ltd; Singapore
Sembcorp Industries Ltd; Singapore
Sembcorp Marine Ltd; Singapore
Singapore Technologies Engineering Limited; Singapore

SOUTH AFRICA
Sasol Limited; Sandton

SPAIN
Abengoa SA; Sevilla
Abertis Infraestructuras SA; Barcelona
Acciona SA; Alcobendas
ACS Actividades de Construccion y Servicios SA; Madrid
Eptisa; Madrid
Ferrovial SA; Madrid
Fomento de Construcciones y Contratas SA (FCC); Barcelona
Globalvia Inversiones SAU; Madrid

IDOM; Bilbao
Sener Ingenieria y Sistemas SA; Getxo (Biscay)
Siemens Gamesa Renewable Energy SA; Zamudio
Tecnica y Proyectos SA (TYPSA); Madrid

SWEDEN
AB Volvo; Gothenburg
AF AB; Stockholm
Autoliv Inc; Stockholm
Saab AB; Bromma
Telefon AB LM Ericsson (Ericsson); Stockholm
Volvo Car Corporation; Goteborg

SWITZERLAND
ABB Ltd; Zurich
Clariant International Ltd; Muttenz
Georg Fischer Ltd; Schaffhausen
Novartis AG; Basel
Roche Holding AG; Basel
STMicroelectronics NV; Geneva
Syngenta AG; Basel

TAIWAN
Acer Inc; Taipei City
Advanced Semiconductor Engineering Inc; Kaohsiung
ASUSTeK Computer Inc; Taipei
AU Optronics Corp; Hsinchu
Compal Electronics Inc; Taipei
Hon Hai Precision Industry Company Ltd; Tu-Chen City, Taipei
HTC Corporation; Taoyuan
Innolux Corporation; Taipei City
Lite-On Technology Corporation; Taipei
Taiwan Semiconductor Manufacturing Co Ltd (TSMC); Hsinchu
United Microelectronics Corp; Hsinchu

THAILAND
Sino-Thai Engineering & Construction PCL; Bangkok

THE NETHERLANDS
Airbus SE; Leiden
Akzo Nobel NV; Arnhem
Arcadis NV; Amsterdam
Bilfinger Tebodin BV; The Hague
Chicago Bridge & Iron Company NV (CB&I); The Hague
Fujitsu Technology Solutions (Holding) BV; Maarssen
Gemalto NV; Amsterdam
Koninklijke Philips NV (Royal Philips); Amsterdam
LyondellBasell Industries NV; Rotterdam
QuTech; Delft
Royal Dutch Shell plc; The Hague
Royal HaskoningDHV; Amersfoort

UNITED KINGDOM
Amey plc; Oxford
ARUP Group Limited; London
AstraZeneca plc; Cambridge
BAE Systems plc; London
Balfour Beatty plc; London
BP plc; London
BuroHappold Ltd; Bath
Dyson Limited; Malmesbury
GE Healthcare; Chalfont St. Giles
GKN plc; Worcestershire
GlaxoSmithKline plc; Middlesex
IMI plc; Birmingham
Intertek Group plc; London
Jaguar Land Rover Limited; Coventry
Mott MacDonald Limited; Croydon
Ricardo plc; West Sussex
Rolls-Royce plc; London
Smith & Nephew plc; London
Smiths Group plc; London
Sony Mobile Communications AB; London
Tate & Lyle plc; London
TechnipFMC plc; London
WS Atkins plc; Epsom

VENEZUELA
VEPICA Grupo Internacional SL; Baruta Caracas, Miranda

Individual Profiles
On Each Of
THE ENGINEERING & RESEARCH 500

3M Company

www.3m.com

NAIC Code: 339100

TYPES OF BUSINESS:
Health Care Products
Specialty Materials & Textiles
Industrial Products
Safety, Security & Protection Products
Display & Graphics Products
Consumer & Office Products
Electronics & Communications Products
Fuel Cell Technology

BRANDS/DIVISIONS/AFFILIATES:
3M Purification Inc
Thinsulate
Scotch
Command
Filtrete
Scott Safety

CONTACTS:
Note: Officers with more than one job title may be intentionally listed here more than once.

Inge Thulin, CEO
Marlene McGrath, Senior VP, Divisional
Ippocratis Vrohidis, Chief Accounting Officer
John Banovetz, Chief Technology Officer
Michael Roman, COO
James Bauman, Executive VP, Divisional
Ashish Khandpur, Executive VP, Divisional
Joaquin Delgado, Executive VP, Divisional
Julie Bushman, Executive VP, Divisional
Michael Vale, Executive VP, Divisional
Frank Little, Executive VP, Divisional
Hak Shin, Executive VP
Ivan Fong, General Counsel
Jon Lindekugel, Senior VP, Divisional
Eric Hammes, Senior VP, Divisional
Paul Keel, Senior VP, Divisional

GROWTH PLANS/SPECIAL FEATURES:

3M Company is involved in the research, manufacturing and marketing of a variety of products. Its operations are organized in five segments: industrial, safety and graphics, electronics and energy, healthcare and consumer. The industrial segment serves the automotive, electronics, appliance, paper, printing, food, beverage and construction markets. Its major industrial products include Thinsulate acoustic insulation and 3M paint finishing and detail products. Also, 3M Purification, Inc. provides a line of filtration products. The safety and graphics segment serves a range of markets, with major product offerings including personal protection, traffic safety, border and civil security solutions, commercial graphics sheeting, architectural surface and lighting solutions, cleaning products and roofing granules for asphalt shingles. The electronics and energy segment serves customers with telecommunications networks, electrical products, power generation and distribution and infrastructure protection. Major products include LCD computers and televisions, hand-held mobile devices, notebook PCs and automotive displays. The healthcare segment serves medical clinics, hospitals, pharmaceuticals, dental and orthodontic practitioners, health information systems and food manufacturing and testing. Products include medical and surgical supplies, skin health, infection prevention, inhalation and transdermal drug delivery systems. The consumer segment serves markets such as consumer retail, office retail, home improvement and building maintenance. Major products include the Scotch tape, Command adhesive and Filtrete filtration family lines of products. During 2017, the firm sold its safety prescription eyewear business, its identity management business, its tolling and automated license/number plate recognition business and its electronic monitoring business. It acquired Scott Safety, a manufacturer of self-contained breathing apparatus systems, gas and flame detection instruments and other safety devices.

The company offers employees medical and dental insurance, domestic partner benefits, tuition reimbursement, flexible spending accounts, disability coverage, 401(k) and adoption assistance.

FINANCIAL DATA:
Note: Data for latest year may not have been available at press time.

In U.S. $	2017	2016	2015	2014	2013	2012
Revenue	31,657,000,000	30,109,000,000	30,274,000,000	31,821,000,000	30,871,000,000	29,904,000,000
R&D Expense	1,850,000,000	1,735,000,000	1,763,000,000	1,770,000,000	1,715,000,000	1,634,000,000
Operating Income	7,234,000,000	7,223,000,000	6,946,000,000	7,135,000,000	6,666,000,000	6,483,000,000
Operating Margin %	22.85%	23.98%	22.94%	22.42%	21.59%	21.67%
SGA Expense	6,572,000,000	6,111,000,000	6,182,000,000	6,469,000,000	6,384,000,000	6,102,000,000
Net Income	4,858,000,000	5,050,000,000	4,833,000,000	4,956,000,000	4,659,000,000	4,444,000,000
Operating Cash Flow	6,240,000,000	6,662,000,000	6,420,000,000	6,626,000,000	5,817,000,000	5,300,000,000
Capital Expenditure	1,373,000,000	1,420,000,000	1,461,000,000	1,493,000,000	1,665,000,000	1,484,000,000
EBITDA	9,414,000,000	8,726,000,000	8,407,000,000	8,576,000,000	8,078,000,000	7,810,000,000
Return on Assets %	13.70%	15.39%	15.10%	15.29%	13.81%	13.57%
Return on Equity %	44.44%	45.89%	38.94%	32.38%	26.56%	26.93%
Debt to Equity	1.05	1.04	0.75	0.51	0.25	0.28

CONTACT INFORMATION:
Phone: 651 733-1110   Fax: 651 733-9973
Toll-Free: 800-364-3577
Address: 3M Center, St. Paul, MN 55144 United States

STOCK TICKER/OTHER:
Stock Ticker: MMM
Employees: 91,584
Parent Company:

Exchange: NYS
Fiscal Year Ends: 12/31

SALARIES/BONUSES:
Top Exec. Salary: $1,526,595   Bonus: $
Second Exec. Salary: $839,575   Bonus: $

OTHER THOUGHTS:
Estimated Female Officers or Directors: 7
Hot Spot for Advancement for Women/Minorities: Y

Sales, profits and employees may be estimates. Financial information, benefits and other data can change quickly and may vary from those stated here.

AB Volvo

NAIC Code: 336120

www.volvo.com

TYPES OF BUSINESS:
Truck Manufacturer
Engines
Buses
Aerospace Products
Construction Equipment
Financial Services
Intelligent Transport Systems
Overhaul & Repair Services

BRANDS/DIVISIONS/AFFILIATES:
Volvo Group
Volvo
Renault
UD
Mack
Eicher
Dongfeng
Zhejiang Geely Holding Group Co Ltd

CONTACTS:
Note: Officers with more than one job title may be intentionally listed here more than once.

Martin Lundstedt, CEO
Jan Ohlsson, Exec. VP-Oper.
Olof Persson, Pres.
Jan Gurander, CFO
Kerstin Renard, Exec. VP-Corp. Human Resources
Lars Stenqvist, Exec. VP-IT
Sofia Frandberg, General Counsel
Mikael Bratt, Exec. VP-Group Truck Oper.
Karin Falk, Exec. VP-Corp. Strategy
Marten Wikforss, Exec. VP-Corp. Comm.
Anders Osberg, Exec. VP-Corp. Finance & Control
Niklas Gustavsson, Exec. VP-Public & Environmental Affairs
Martin Weissburg, Exec. VP-Volvo Construction Equipment
Torbjorn Homstrom, Exec. VP-Group Trucks Tech.
Dennis Slagle, Exec. VP-Group Trucks Sales & Mktg., Americas
Carl-Henric Svanberg, Chmn.
Peter Karlsten, Exec. VP-Group Trucks Sales & Mktg., EMEA

GROWTH PLANS/SPECIAL FEATURES:

AB Volvo, also called the Volvo Group, is a world leader in the manufacture of trucks and heavy machinery, including buses; construction equipment; and marine, industrial and aerospace components. The Volvo Group has six product-related business areas: trucks, buses, construction equipment, Volvo Penta, financial services and governmental sales. The truck division's brands include Volvo, Renault, UD, Mack, Eicher and Dongfeng which mainly manufacture medium-heavy to heavy long-haul trucks marketed in 140 countries worldwide. This business area also includes joint ventures and trucks for the Asia market, which is designed to meet the specific needs of the Group's truck customers in the value truck segment. The buses division develops, manufactures and sells hybrid, single-decker and double-decker buses, and also offers a network of services such as spare parts handling, financial, traffic information systems and repair contracts. Construction equipment develops, manufactures and sells large road machinery, including hydraulic wheeled and crawler excavators; simulators; expander bolts; filters; lubricants; batteries; and other remanufactured products. Volvo Penta develops, manufactures and sells engines and drive systems for marine duties. It also supplies engines for various industrial applications. Financial services offers customer financing, insurance, treasury, real estate and related services operations. The governmental sales division is responsible for the Group's sales to government authorities and organizations. In December 2017, Zhejiang Geely Holding Group Co. Ltd. became AB Volvo's largest shareholder by number of shares after acquiring an 8.2% stake.

FINANCIAL DATA:
Note: Data for latest year may not have been available at press time.

In U.S. $	2017	2016	2015	2014	2013	2012
Revenue		35,648,470,000	36,900,180,000	33,409,060,000	32,189,810,000	35,853,090,000
R&D Expense		1,727,554,000	1,814,575,000	1,966,656,000	1,785,765,000	1,746,800,000
Operating Income		2,715,014,000	2,407,075,000	1,381,004,000	1,087,470,000	2,219,100,000
Operating Margin %		7.61%	6.52%	4.13%	3.37%	6.18%
SGA Expense		3,776,980,000	3,951,140,000	3,879,469,000	4,057,998,000	4,004,746,000
Net Income		1,552,331,000	1,777,972,000	247,839,200	423,062,400	1,303,429,000
Operating Cash Flow		2,073,277,000	3,053,181,000	1,031,620,000	1,309,451,000	450,455,700
Capital Expenditure		1,124,663,000	1,041,184,000	1,019,459,000	1,440,868,000	1,728,380,000
EBITDA		4,468,072,000	4,674,703,000	2,717,258,000	2,946,323,000	3,847,589,000
Return on Assets %		3.40%	3.97%	.57%	1.04%	3.19%
Return on Equity %		14.61%	18.57%	2.71%	4.43%	12.96%
Debt to Equity		0.87	0.89	1.37	1.09	0.92

CONTACT INFORMATION:
Phone: 46 31660000 Fax: 46 31665170
Toll-Free:
Address: Volvo Bergegardsvag 1, Torslanda, Gothenburg, SE-405 08 Sweden

STOCK TICKER/OTHER:
Stock Ticker: VOLVF Exchange: PINX
Employees: 84,653 Fiscal Year Ends: 12/31
Parent Company:

SALARIES/BONUSES:
Top Exec. Salary: $ Bonus: $
Second Exec. Salary: $ Bonus: $

OTHER THOUGHTS:
Estimated Female Officers or Directors: 5
Hot Spot for Advancement for Women/Minorities: Y

Sales, profits and employees may be estimates. Financial information, benefits and other data can change quickly and may vary from those stated here.

ABB Ltd

NAIC Code: 335313

www.abb.com

TYPES OF BUSINESS:
Diversified Engineering Services
Power Transmission & Distribution Systems
Control & Automation Technology Products
Industrial Robotics
Energy Trading Software

BRANDS/DIVISIONS/AFFILIATES:
SVIA
Yumi Robot

CONTACTS:
Note: Officers with more than one job title may be intentionally listed here more than once.

Ulrich Spiesshofer, CEO
Eric Elzvik, CFO
Jean-Christophe Deslarzes, Head-Human Resources
Diane de Saint Victor, General Counsel
Brice Koch, Head-Power Systems Div.
Bernhard Jucker, Head-Power Prod. Div.
Veli-Matti Reinikkala, Head-Process Automation Div.
Tarak Mehta, Head-Low Voltage Prod. Div.
Peter Voser, Chmn.
Frank Duggan, Head-Global Markets

GROWTH PLANS/SPECIAL FEATURES:

ABB Ltd. is a global leader in power and automation technologies for utility and industrial companies. The firm provides a broad range of products, systems and services that improve power grid reliability, increase industrial productivity and enhance energy efficiency. ABB operates in approximately 100 countries and divides its business into four divisions: power grids, electrification products, discrete automation & motion and process automation. The power grids division focuses on the changing needs of utility customers with ABB's complete power & automation offering for transmission and distribution delivered from a single source: power & automation for the grid. The electrification products division combines ABB's low- and medium-voltage businesses. Its products help customers improve productivity, use energy efficiently and increase safety. Products and systems in this division provide protection, control & measurement for electrical installations, enclosures, switchboards, electronics and electromechanical devices for industrial machines and plants. The discrete automation & motion division, as well as the process automation division, address customer needs and operational efficiency. Discrete automation & motion products and services include drive products and systems for industrial, commercial and residential applications. Drives provide speed, torque and motion control for equipment such as fans, pumps, compressors, conveyors, centrifuges, mixers, hoists, cranes, extruders, printing and textile machines. Process automation provides engineered solutions, products and services for process control, safety, instrumentation, plant electrification and energy management for the key process industry sectors of chemical, oil & gas, marine, mining, minerals, metals, cement and pulp & paper. In May 2016, the firm acquired SVIA, a provider of robot automation cells for machine tending. ABB recently introduced a low-cost, advanced industrial robot arm called YuMi, suitable for collaboration with human workers in small parts assembly.

FINANCIAL DATA:
Note: Data for latest year may not have been available at press time.

In U.S. $	2017	2016	2015	2014	2013	2012
Revenue	34,312,000,000	33,828,000,000	35,481,000,000	39,830,000,000	41,848,000,000	39,336,000,000
R&D Expense	1,365,000,000	1,300,000,000	1,406,000,000	1,499,000,000	1,470,000,000	1,464,000,000
Operating Income	3,294,000,000	3,098,000,000	3,154,000,000	3,649,000,000	4,428,000,000	4,158,000,000
Operating Margin %	9.60%	9.15%	8.88%	9.16%	10.58%	10.57%
SGA Expense	5,607,000,000	5,349,000,000	5,574,000,000	6,067,000,000	6,094,000,000	5,756,000,000
Net Income	2,213,000,000	1,899,000,000	1,933,000,000	2,594,000,000	2,787,000,000	2,704,000,000
Operating Cash Flow	3,799,000,000	3,843,000,000	3,818,000,000	3,845,000,000	3,653,000,000	3,779,000,000
Capital Expenditure	949,000,000	831,000,000	876,000,000	1,026,000,000	1,106,000,000	1,293,000,000
EBITDA	4,609,000,000	4,195,000,000	4,286,000,000	5,563,000,000	5,774,000,000	5,313,000,000
Return on Assets %	5.34%	4.69%	4.48%	5.58%	5.73%	6.09%
Return on Equity %	15.68%	13.62%	12.57%	14.84%	15.66%	16.54%
Debt to Equity	0.45	0.43	0.41	0.45	0.40	0.44

CONTACT INFORMATION:
Phone: 41-43-317-7111 Fax: 41-43-317-4420
Toll-Free:
Address: Affolternstrasse 44, Zurich, CH-8050 Switzerland

SALARIES/BONUSES:
Top Exec. Salary: $1,745,995 Bonus: $2,509,814
Second Exec. Salary: $1,039,794 Bonus: $1,044,992

STOCK TICKER/OTHER:
Stock Ticker: ABB
Employees: 132,300
Parent Company:

Exchange: NYS
Fiscal Year Ends: 12/31

OTHER THOUGHTS:
Estimated Female Officers or Directors: 2
Hot Spot for Advancement for Women/Minorities: Y

Abbott Laboratories

NAIC Code: 325412

www.abbott.com

TYPES OF BUSINESS:
Nutritional Products Manufacturing
Immunoassays
Diagnostics
Consumer Health Products
Medical & Surgical Devices
Generic Pharmaceutical Products
LASIK Devices

BRANDS/DIVISIONS/AFFILIATES:
Zone Perfect
EAS
Alere Inc

CONTACTS:
Note: Officers with more than one job title may be intentionally listed here more than once.

Miles White, CEO
Jared Watkin, Senior VP, Divisional
Brian Yoor, CFO
Robert Funck, Chief Accounting Officer
Robert Ford, Executive VP, Divisional
Daniel Salvadori, Executive VP, Divisional
John Capek, Executive VP, Divisional
Stephen Fussell, Executive VP, Divisional
Brian Blaser, Executive VP, Divisional
Hubert Allen, Executive VP
Sean Shrimpton, Senior VP, Divisional
Roger Bird, Senior VP, Divisional
Andrew Lane, Senior VP, Divisional
Joseph Manning, Senior VP, Divisional
Sharon Bracken, Senior VP, Divisional
Charles Brynelsen, Senior VP, Divisional

GROWTH PLANS/SPECIAL FEATURES:

Abbott Laboratories develops, manufactures and sells healthcare products and technologies, marketed in over 150 countries. The firm operates in four segments: established pharmaceutical, diagnostics, nutrition and cardiovascular and neuromodulation products. The established pharmaceutical segment includes a broad line of branded generic pharmaceuticals manufactured worldwide and marketed and sold outside the U.S. in emerging markets. These products are primarily sold directly to wholesalers, distributors, government agencies, healthcare facilities, pharmacies and independent retailers from Abbott-owned distribution centers and public warehouses. This segment's principal therapeutic offerings include gastroenterology, women's health, cardiovascular, metabolic, pain, central nervous system, respiratory and vaccination products. The diagnostics segment includes a line of diagnostic systems and tests manufactured, marketed and sold worldwide. These products are primarily marketed and sold directly to blood banks, hospitals, commercial laboratories, clinics, physicians' offices, government agencies, alternate care testing sites and plasma protein therapeutic companies from Abbot-owned distribution centers, public warehouses and third-party distributors. This segment's products include: core laboratory systems in the areas of immunoassay, clinical chemistry, hematology and transfusions; molecular diagnostics systems; point of care systems; rapid diagnostic systems; and informatics and automation solutions for use in laboratories. The nutrition segment offers a line of pediatric and adult nutritional products manufactured, marketed and sold worldwide. This segment's products include: various forms of prepared infant formula and follow-on formula; adult and other pediatric nutritional products; nutritional products used in enteral feeding in healthcare institutions; and Zone Perfect and EAS family of nutritional food brands. In October 2017, Abbott acquired Alere, Inc., a global manufacturer of rapid point-of-care diagnostic tests.

Abbott offers comprehensive insurance benefits and employee assistance programs.

FINANCIAL DATA:
Note: Data for latest year may not have been available at press time.

In U.S. $	2017	2016	2015	2014	2013	2012
Revenue	27,390,000,000	20,853,000,000	20,405,000,000	20,247,000,000	21,848,000,000	39,873,910,000
R&D Expense	2,235,000,000	1,422,000,000	1,405,000,000	1,345,000,000	1,452,000,000	4,610,182,000
Operating Income	1,726,000,000	3,185,000,000	2,867,000,000	2,599,000,000	2,629,000,000	8,084,515,000
Operating Margin %	6.30%	15.27%	14.05%	12.83%	12.03%	20.27%
SGA Expense	9,117,000,000	6,672,000,000	6,785,000,000	6,530,000,000	6,936,000,000	12,059,500,000
Net Income	477,000,000	1,400,000,000	4,423,000,000	2,284,000,000	2,576,000,000	5,962,920,000
Operating Cash Flow	5,570,000,000	3,203,000,000	2,966,000,000	3,675,000,000	3,324,000,000	9,314,401,000
Capital Expenditure	1,135,000,000	1,121,000,000	1,110,000,000	1,077,000,000	1,145,000,000	1,795,289,000
EBITDA	6,156,000,000	3,197,000,000	4,818,000,000	4,216,000,000	4,397,000,000	9,638,224,000
Return on Assets %	.74%	2.98%	10.71%	5.42%	4.67%	9.35%
Return on Equity %	1.85%	6.70%	20.69%	9.78%	9.92%	23.31%
Debt to Equity	0.88	1.00	0.27	0.15	0.13	0.67

CONTACT INFORMATION:
Phone: 847 937-6100 Fax: 847 937-1511
Toll-Free:
Address: 100 Abbott Park Rd., Abbott Park, IL 60064-6400 United States

STOCK TICKER/OTHER:
Stock Ticker: ABT
Employees: 75,000
Parent Company:

Exchange: NYS
Fiscal Year Ends: 12/31

SALARIES/BONUSES:
Top Exec. Salary: $644,231 Bonus: $5,000,000
Second Exec. Salary: $1,900,000 Bonus: $

OTHER THOUGHTS:
Estimated Female Officers or Directors: 5
Hot Spot for Advancement for Women/Minorities: Y

Sales, profits and employees may be estimates. Financial information, benefits and other data can change quickly and may vary from those stated here.

Abengoa SA

NAIC Code: 237130

www.abengoa.es

TYPES OF BUSINESS:
Specialty Engineering and Construction
Ethanol Production
Recycling & Waste Management Services
Bioenergy
IT Services
Construction-Plants & Infrastructure
Solar Energy Generation

BRANDS/DIVISIONS/AFFILIATES:

CONTACTS: Note: Officers with more than one job title may be intentionally listed here more than once.
Joaquin Fernandez De Pierola Marin, CEO
Victor Pastor Fernandez, CFO
Avaro Polo Guerrero, Dir.-Human Resources
Alfonso Gonzalez Dominguez, Exec. VP-Eng. & Industrial Construction
Luis Fernandez Mateo, Dir.-Organization, Quality & Budgets
M.A. Jimenez-Velasco Mazario, General Sec.
Izaskun Artucha Corta, Dir.-Strategy & Corp. Dev.
Barbara Zubiria Furest, Dir.-Investor Rel.
Vicente Jorro de Inza, Dir.-Finance
Javier Garoz Neira, Exec. VP-Biofuels
Javier Molina Montes, Exec. VP-Industrial Recycling
Santiago Seage Medela, Exec. VP-Solar
Juan Carlos Jimenez Lora, Dir.-Planning & Control
Gonzalo Fernandez De Araoz, Chmn.
Alfonso Gonzalez Dominguez, Pres., Latin America Bus. Group

GROWTH PLANS/SPECIAL FEATURES:
Abengoa SA is a Spanish technology company that offers solutions for sustainability in the infrastructures, energy and water sectors. For infrastructure sectors, the firm provides engineering and construction services and solutions in relation to: energy transmission, energy distribution, rail electrification, singular installations and all types of industrial plants. This division is also engaged in the manufacture of steel structures, electrical ancillary and electronic equipment. Within the energy sector, Abengoa creates facilities that convert energy from renewable sources into electricity, as well as from conventional energy sources. It also constructs transmission lines that support electricity networks. Within the water sector, the company recycles and recovers industrial waste, preventing the need for extracting natural resources. It specializes in water management and treatment; and designs, constructs and operates facilities for treating water, making it potable or for water desalination. This division also provides related water services and solutions for other water infrastructures worldwide. During 2018, Abengoa agreed to sell its 16.47% stake in Atlantica Yield; and agreed to sell its 56% stake in the Ghana desalination plant.

FINANCIAL DATA: Note: Data for latest year may not have been available at press time.

In U.S. $	2017	2016	2015	2014	2013	2012
Revenue		1,864,770,000	7,107,464,000	8,830,259,000	9,084,529,000	9,611,583,000
R&D Expense		7,898,442	9,743,387	10,760,950		
Operating Income		-2,673,193,000	-440,546,800	1,126,631,000	428,434,900	956,603,100
Operating Margin %		-143.35%	-6.19%	12.75%	4.71%	9.95%
SGA Expense		912,572,500	1,896,131,000	1,872,100,000	936,496,300	
Net Income		-9,421,147,000	-1,498,528,000	154,723,500	125,274,800	154,870,500
Operating Cash Flow		-404,603,700	-1,477,752,000	22,951,910	914,606,500	546,723,800
Capital Expenditure		282,899,100	2,693,824,000	3,185,504,000	2,327,030,000	4,847,069,000
EBITDA		-1,657,339,000	409,293,900	1,474,318,000	1,605,163,000	1,539,112,000
Return on Assets %		-57.48%	-5.79%	.54%	.48%	.63%
Return on Equity %			-160.98%	9.05%	8.48%	10.49%
Debt to Equity			14.04	5.47	3.58	4.06

CONTACT INFORMATION:
Phone: 34 954937000 Fax:
Toll-Free:
Address: C/ Energia Solar 1, Palmas Altas, Sevilla, 41014 Spain

STOCK TICKER/OTHER:
Stock Ticker: ABGOF   Exchange: PINX
Employees: 27,572   Fiscal Year Ends: 12/31
Parent Company:

SALARIES/BONUSES:
Top Exec. Salary: $1,341,105   Bonus: $4,080,121
Second Exec. Salary: $1,341,105   Bonus: $4,080,121

OTHER THOUGHTS:
Estimated Female Officers or Directors: 4
Hot Spot for Advancement for Women/Minorities: Y

Abertis Infraestructuras SA

NAIC Code: 561210

www.abertis.com

TYPES OF BUSINESS:
Transport & Communications
Airports

BRANDS/DIVISIONS/AFFILIATES:
Autopista Central
A4 Holding SpA

GROWTH PLANS/SPECIAL FEATURES:
Abertis Infraestructuras SA is an international group of toll-road operators, managing thousands of miles of high-quality, high-capacity roads worldwide. Abertis has 5,000 road miles under management, and 33 fully-consolidated concessions operating through its electronic tolling technology services. Approximately 33% of the company's 2017 business was derived in France; 31% in Spain; 12% in Brazil; 12% in Chile; 6% in Italy; and 6% in other countries, including the Americas. Assets of the firm include wholly-owned Autopista Central, a highway in Chile that forms part of the Ruta 5; and 51.4%-owned A4 Holding SpA, which manages motorway concession in Europe. In February 2018, Atlantia SpA offered to acquire Abertis.

CONTACTS:
Note: Officers with more than one job title may be intentionally listed here more than once.

Francisco Jose Aljaro Navarro, CEO
Salvador Alemany Mas, Pres.
Jose Maria Coronas Guinart, Sec.
Salvador Alemany Mas, Chmn.

FINANCIAL DATA:
Note: Data for latest year may not have been available at press time.

In U.S. $	2017	2016	2015	2014	2013	2012
Revenue	7,202,192,000	6,695,739,000	5,790,393,000	6,657,883,000	6,221,983,000	5,203,135,000
R&D Expense						
Operating Income	2,541,706,000	2,402,565,000	862,473,800	2,311,287,000	2,124,676,000	1,593,270,000
Operating Margin %	35.29%	35.88%	14.89%	34.71%	34.14%	30.62%
SGA Expense						
Net Income	1,108,218,000	982,459,500	2,321,510,000	808,959,200	761,720,400	1,265,072,000
Operating Cash Flow	2,953,198,000	2,509,645,000	1,888,345,000	2,365,522,000	2,186,064,000	1,890,930,000
Capital Expenditure	1,398,808,000	1,397,923,000	1,098,053,000	1,378,879,000	1,116,307,000	839,931,800
EBITDA	4,330,682,000	4,283,077,000	1,013,293,000	4,022,396,000	3,609,902,000	3,551,209,000
Return on Assets %	2.94%	2.79%	7.02%	2.34%	2.15%	3.95%
Return on Equity %	29.39%	23.27%	58.58%	19.60%	16.74%	29.67%
Debt to Equity	6.61	4.38	4.08	4.66	4.19	4.03

CONTACT INFORMATION:
Phone: 34 932305000 Fax: 34 932305001
Toll-Free:
Address: Avinguda de Pedralbes, 17, Barcelona, 08034 Spain

STOCK TICKER/OTHER:
Stock Ticker: ABRTY
Employees: 15,046
Parent Company:

Exchange: PINX
Fiscal Year Ends: 12/31

SALARIES/BONUSES:
Top Exec. Salary: $ Bonus: $
Second Exec. Salary: $ Bonus: $

OTHER THOUGHTS:
Estimated Female Officers or Directors:
Hot Spot for Advancement for Women/Minorities:

Sales, profits and employees may be estimates. Financial information, benefits and other data can change quickly and may vary from those stated here.

ACC Companies (The)

NAIC Code: 237310

www.accbuilt.com

TYPES OF BUSINESS:
Heavy Construction & Civil Engineering
Construction Materials-Concrete, Sand & Gravel
Design Services
Mining
Ready-Mix Concrete
Technical Services

BRANDS/DIVISIONS/AFFILIATES:
American Civil Constructors Inc
Saiia Construction Company LLC

CONTACTS: Note: Officers with more than one job title may be intentionally listed here more than once.
David Mathews, CEO
Randy Maher, COO
Ryan Evans, CFO
Nicole R. Smith, Controller
Norm Watkins, Dir.-Safety
Mark Krumm, Pres., Arizona Area
Robert Terril, Pres., Nevada Area
Shane Haycock, VP-Nevada Area

GROWTH PLANS/SPECIAL FEATURES:
The ACC Companies solves challenges that accompany complex construction projects via equipment and technology for government and commercial clients throughout the U.S. ACC operates through two wholly-owned subsidiaries: American Civil Constructors, Inc. and Saiia Construction Company, LLC. Together, these companies provide specialized services for infrastructure and industrial projects which are categorized into three groups: civil infrastructure, mining and industrial. Civil infrastructure services include the construction of streets, highways, bridges, tunnels and airport facility projects, as well as flood control and drainage services. This division specializes in the areas of mass grading, underground utilities, structural concrete, paving and bridge construction. Mining services include the outsourcing of services to mine owners and operators. These services range from infrastructure work to greenfield site development, overburden removal and turnkey production mining. All work from this division is completed according to Mine Safety and Health Administration (MSHA) regulations, and provides on-going, in-house training for all employees to ensure current MSHA rules, safety and inspection knowledge is intact. The industrial services group provides a full range of site development and site maintenance services to companies in the power generation, pulp and paper, and waste management industries. It creates innovative solutions for safe and efficient building, managing and decommissioning of large operations, with minimal environmental impact. Based in Phoenix, Arizona, the firm has offices in Colorado, California, Nevada, Utah and Alabama.

The ACC Companies offers its employees medical, dental, vision, prescription, short/long-term disability and AD&D coverage; 401(k); flexible spending accounts; vacation leave; and various employee assistance programs.

FINANCIAL DATA: Note: Data for latest year may not have been available at press time.

In U.S. $	2017	2016	2015	2014	2013	2012
Revenue						
R&D Expense						
Operating Income						
Operating Margin %						
SGA Expense						
Net Income						
Operating Cash Flow						
Capital Expenditure						
EBITDA						
Return on Assets %						
Return on Equity %						
Debt to Equity						

CONTACT INFORMATION:
Phone: 602-437-5400   Fax: 602-437-1681
Toll-Free:
Address: 3333 E. Camelback Rd., Ste. 240, Phoenix, AZ 85018 United States

STOCK TICKER/OTHER:
Stock Ticker: Private
Employees: 510
Parent Company:

Exchange:
Fiscal Year Ends: 12/31

SALARIES/BONUSES:
Top Exec. Salary: $ Bonus: $
Second Exec. Salary: $ Bonus: $

OTHER THOUGHTS:
Estimated Female Officers or Directors: 1
Hot Spot for Advancement for Women/Minorities:

Sales, profits and employees may be estimates. Financial information, benefits and other data can change quickly and may vary from those stated here.

Accenture plc

NAIC Code: 541512

www.accenture.com

TYPES OF BUSINESS:
IT Consulting
Computer Operations Outsourcing
Supply Chain Management
Technology Research
Software Development
Human Resources Consulting
Management Consulting
Research & Development

BRANDS/DIVISIONS/AFFILIATES:
Accenture Consulting
1QBit

CONTACTS:
Note: Officers with more than one job title may be intentionally listed here more than once.

Pierre Nanterme, CEO
Jo Deblaere, COO
David P. Rowland, CFO
Roxanne Taylor, Chief Mktg. & Comm. Officer
Ellyn J. Shook, Chief Leadership & Human Resources Officer
Robert E. Sell, Chief Comm., Media & Technology Officer
Martin I. Cole, Group CEO-Tech.
Sander vant Noordende, Group CEO-Prod.
Richard Lumb, Group CEO-Financial Services
Stephen J Rohleder, Group CEO-Health & Public Service
Michael J Salvino, Group CEO-Business Process Outsourcing
Julie Spellman Sweet, General Counsel
David C. Thomlinson, Chief Oper. & Geographic Strategy Officer
Shawn Collinson, Chief Strategy Officer
Michael R. Sutcliff, Group CEO-Accenture Digital
Robert E. Sell, Group CEO-Comm., Media & Tech.
Mark A. Knickrehm, Group CEO-Accenture Strategy
Gianfranco Casati, Group CEO-Growth Markets
Adrian Lajtha, Chief Leadership Officer
Jean-Marc Ollagnier, Group CEO-Resources
Pierre Nanterme, Chmn.

GROWTH PLANS/SPECIAL FEATURES:

Accenture plc is a leading provider of management consulting, technology and outsourcing services, with operations in over 200 cities in 53 countries. The firm operates through five groups: communications, media and technology; financial services; health and public service; products; and resources. Communications, media and technology serves the communications, electronics, high technology, media and entertainment industries. These industries include most of the world's leading wireline, wireless, cable and satellite communications and service providers. Accenture's financial services group serves the banking, capital markets and insurance industries. Professionals within these industries work with clients to address growth, cost and profitability, pressures, consolidation, regulatory changes and the need to continually adapt to new, digital technologies. The health and public service group serves healthcare payers and providers, as well as government departments and agencies, public service organizations, educational institutions and non-profit organizations around the world. The products group serves interconnected consumer-relevant industries such as consumer goods, retail, travel services, industrial manufacturers and suppliers, pharmaceutical and biotechnology companies. Product offerings help clients transform their organizations and increase relevance in the digital world. The resources group serves the chemicals, energy, forest products, metals and mining, utilities and related industries. It works with clients to develop and execute innovative strategies, improve operations, manage complex change initiatives and integrate digital technologies designed to help differentiate themselves in the marketplace. In addition, Accenture Consulting provides technology, business and management consulting services. In November 2017, the firm invested a minority stake in 1QBit, a quantum computing firm in Vancouver, British Columbia.

Accenture offers its employees medical, dental, long-term disability, life and AD&D coverage; legal coverage; profit sharing; 401(k); and adoption assistance.

FINANCIAL DATA:
Note: Data for latest year may not have been available at press time.

In U.S. $	2017	2016	2015	2014	2013	2012
Revenue	36,765,480,000	34,797,660,000	32,914,420,000	31,874,680,000	30,394,280,000	29,777,990,000
R&D Expense						
Operating Income	4,632,609,000	4,810,445,000	4,435,869,000	4,282,497,000	4,066,638,000	3,873,239,000
Operating Margin %	12.60%	13.82%	13.47%	13.43%	13.37%	13.00%
SGA Expense	6,397,883,000	5,466,982,000	5,373,370,000	5,401,969,000	5,317,537,000	5,114,462,000
Net Income	3,445,149,000	4,111,892,000	3,053,581,000	2,941,498,000	3,281,878,000	2,553,510,000
Operating Cash Flow	4,973,039,000	4,575,115,000	4,092,137,000	3,486,085,000	3,303,128,000	4,256,852,000
Capital Expenditure	515,919,000	496,566,000	395,017,000	321,870,000	369,593,000	371,974,000
EBITDA	5,433,366,000	6,348,882,000	5,071,031,000	4,936,065,000	4,946,357,000	4,512,780,000
Return on Assets %	15.91%	21.15%	16.87%	16.90%	19.57%	15.76%
Return on Equity %	41.74%	60.07%	51.46%	55.02%	72.08%	63.64%
Debt to Equity						

CONTACT INFORMATION:
Phone: 353-1-646-2000 Fax:
Toll-Free:
Address: 1 Grand Canal Sq., Dublin, 2 Ireland

SALARIES/BONUSES:
Top Exec. Salary: $957,585   Bonus: $1,000,000
Second Exec. Salary: $1,136,125   Bonus: $

STOCK TICKER/OTHER:
Stock Ticker: ACN   Exchange: NYS
Employees: 425,000   Fiscal Year Ends: 08/31
Parent Company:

OTHER THOUGHTS:
Estimated Female Officers or Directors: 6
Hot Spot for Advancement for Women/Minorities: Y

Sales, profits and employees may be estimates. Financial information, benefits and other data can change quickly and may vary from those stated here.

Acciona SA

NAIC Code: 237310

www.acciona.es

TYPES OF BUSINESS:
Heavy Construction
Infrastructure Services
Road Concessions
Logistics Services
Airport Services
Passenger Ferries
Urban & Environmental Services
Alternative Energy Installation

BRANDS/DIVISIONS/AFFILIATES:
Acciona Agua
Andes Airport Services

CONTACTS: Note: Officers with more than one job title may be intentionally listed here more than once.
Jose Manuel Entrecanales, CEO
Carlos Arilla de Juana, CFO
Arantza Ezpeleta Puras, Chief Technology Officer
Jorge Vega-Penichet, General Counsel
Juan Muro-Lara, Chief Corp. Dev. Officer
Joaquin Mollinedo, Chief Institutional Rel. Officer
Juan Muro-Lara, Chief Investor Rel. Officer
Alfonso Callejo, Chief Corp. Resources Officer
Pedro Martinez, Pres., Acciona Infrastructure
Luis Castilla, Pres., Acciona Agua
Rafael Mateo, CEO-Acciona Energy
Carmen Becerril, Chief Intl Officer

GROWTH PLANS/SPECIAL FEATURES:

Acciona SA develops and manages infrastructure and related projects in Spain and internationally, with a presence in more than 30 countries. The company operates two main business lines: energy and infrastructure. The energy business is focused on the development of renewable energy facilities, primarily through the installation of wind farms and solar arrays. It is also active in the design and manufacture of wind turbine generators, the production of biofuels and the development of charging infrastructure for electric vehicles. The infrastructure business includes five divisions: water, services, industrial, construction and concessions. The water division, through Acciona Agua, is engineers, constructs and managest drinking water plants, sewage treatment plants and reverse-osmosis desalination plants. The division has built more than 70 desalination plants across the globe. The services division handles the needs of a variety of customers from many sectors through a broad range of services, such as cleaning, ancillary services, technical, energy, environmental maintenance, urban management, handling, production and design, catering and security. The industrial division focuses on range of industrial processes, such as engineering, acquisition of equipment and operations and management, as well as installation of projects. The construction division builds roads, bridges, railways, dams, canals, sewer systems, hospitals, seaports and airports. Last, the concessions division is engaged in the private development of infrastructures worldwide. Currently, this segment manages 25 concessions distributed around Spain, Canada, Mexico, Chile, Australia, New Zealand and Brazil, and in the sectors of transport infrastructure (roads, railways, ports and irrigation) and social infrastructure (hospitals and universities). During 2017, the firm acquired Andes Airport Services, the main handling services provider at Santiago de Chile airport; and announced plans to build and own three photovoltaic plants in Egypt in a 50-50 alliance with Swicorp's renewable energy platform.

FINANCIAL DATA: Note: Data for latest year may not have been available at press time.

In U.S. $	2017	2016	2015	2014	2013	2012
Revenue	8,957,957,000	7,381,534,000	8,080,620,000	8,025,021,000	8,159,017,000	8,664,032,000
R&D Expense						
Operating Income	753,882,500	509,254,400	751,731,400	665,020,200	90,625,850	869,903,000
Operating Margin %	8.41%	6.89%	9.30%	8.28%	1.11%	10.04%
SGA Expense						
Net Income	271,840,500	434,662,500	256,025,100	228,394,100	-2,435,687,000	233,891,900
Operating Cash Flow	606,445,000	1,016,328,000	843,381,000	1,000,263,000	976,946,800	929,787,100
Capital Expenditure	949,354,200	975,865,100	254,537,100	518,834,800	522,223,400	928,886,800
EBITDA	1,228,283,000	1,614,108,000	1,125,649,000	1,014,288,000	1,053,121,000	1,290,835,000
Return on Assets %	1.27%	2.12%	1.29%	1.12%	-10.77%	.94%
Return on Equity %	5.79%	9.61%	6.03%	5.59%	-46.63%	3.58%
Debt to Equity	1.49	1.56	1.81	1.75	1.93	1.33

CONTACT INFORMATION:
Phone: 34 916632850 Fax: 34 916632851
Toll-Free:
Address: Ave. De Europa, 18, Parque Empresarial La Moreleja, Alcobendas, Madrid 28108 Spain

STOCK TICKER/OTHER:
Stock Ticker: ACXIF
Employees: 37,403
Parent Company:

Exchange: PINX
Fiscal Year Ends: 12/31

SALARIES/BONUSES:
Top Exec. Salary: $ Bonus: $
Second Exec. Salary: $ Bonus: $

OTHER THOUGHTS:
Estimated Female Officers or Directors: 2
Hot Spot for Advancement for Women/Minorities:

Sales, profits and employees may be estimates. Financial information, benefits and other data can change quickly and may vary from those stated here.

Acer Inc

NAIC Code: 334111

www.acer.com.tw

TYPES OF BUSINESS:
Computer Manufacturing
PCs & Accessories
Components
Software

BRANDS/DIVISIONS/AFFILIATES:
BYOC
Acer

GROWTH PLANS/SPECIAL FEATURES:
Acer, Inc. is a Taiwanese firm that manufactures and distributes IT, digital display, computer and other types of connected products. Acer organizes its business in two segments: the core business, which includes the research, design, marketing, sale and support of IT products; and the value creation business, encompassing the firm's trademarked BYOC (build your own cloud) and eBusiness operations. All products are marketed under the Acer brand name. The firm operates in approximately 70 countries worldwide, and markets its products to more than 160 countries.

CONTACTS:
Note: Officers with more than one job title may be intentionally listed here more than once.

Jason Chen, CEO
Jason Chen, Pres.
Jason Chen, Chmn.

FINANCIAL DATA:
Note: Data for latest year may not have been available at press time.

In U.S. $	2017	2016	2015	2014	2013	2012
Revenue	8,095,632,000	7,940,365,000	8,999,802,000	11,248,570,000	12,287,420,000	14,654,570,000
R&D Expense	85,225,290	69,892,140	71,285,470	86,129,890	105,489,400	97,861,130
Operating Income	125,208,400	40,687,600	32,024,560	92,383,390	-389,288,800	34,962,160
Operating Margin %	1.54%	.51%	.35%	.82%	-3.16%	.23%
SGA Expense	662,001,800	690,950,500	755,149,100	820,324,700	1,017,074,000	1,340,982,000
Net Income	96,065,610	-167,194,200	20,597,090	61,096,930	-700,106,700	-99,298,020
Operating Cash Flow	-251,189,900	282,221,300	-29,532,460	191,872,800	-295,164,800	20,163,940
Capital Expenditure	10,960,460	5,791,395	11,279,270	11,348,900	19,416,290	33,879,420
EBITDA	161,796,200	90,657,780	89,545,330	160,409,100	-297,183,100	51,083,520
Return on Assets %	1.74%	-2.90%	.33%	.93%	-9.83%	-1.22%
Return on Equity %	4.89%	-7.93%	.95%	3.06%	-31.26%	-3.86%
Debt to Equity	0.05			0.15	0.28	0.05

CONTACT INFORMATION:
Phone: 886-2-2696-1234 Fax:
Toll-Free:
Address: 1/Fl, No. 88, Section 1, Xintai 5th Rd., Taipei City, 221 Taiwan

STOCK TICKER/OTHER:
Stock Ticker: ACEIY
Employees: 7,970
Parent Company:

Exchange: GREY
Fiscal Year Ends: 12/31

SALARIES/BONUSES:
Top Exec. Salary: $ Bonus: $
Second Exec. Salary: $ Bonus: $

OTHER THOUGHTS:
Estimated Female Officers or Directors:
Hot Spot for Advancement for Women/Minorities:

ACS Actividades de Construccion Y Servicios SA

www.grupoacs.com
NAIC Code: 237310

TYPES OF BUSINESS:
Heavy Construction
Engineering Services
Civic Construction & Infrastructure
Industrial Services
Facility Maintenance
Passenger Transportation
Transportation Concessions
Water Treatment & Desalination Plants

BRANDS/DIVISIONS/AFFILIATES:
Dragados SA
Hochtief AG
Iridium Concesiones de Infraestructuras
Cimic Group
Turner Construction Company

CONTACTS: Note: Officers with more than one job title may be intentionally listed here more than once.
Marcelino Fernandez Verdes, CEO
Antonio Garcia Ferrer, Co-Vice Chmn.
Pablo Vallhona Vadell, Co-Vice Chmn.
Florentino Perez Rodriguez, Chmn.

GROWTH PLANS/SPECIAL FEATURES:

ACS, Actividades de Construccion Y Servicios SA is a leading Spanish construction and services group that takes part in the development of key sectors for the economy, including infrastructure and energy. ACS operates through three business segments: construction, industrial services and services. The construction segment engages in a variety of projects, including: civil works such as highways, railways, maritime and airports; building works such as residential, social infrastructure and facilities; and mining, offering contracts for the provision of mining services and the infrastructure required for mining activities. Construction subsidiaries include Dragados SA, Hochtief AG, Iridium Concesiones de Infraestructuras, Cimic Group and Turner Construction Company, which together have projects in more than 30 countries worldwide. The industrial services segment provides applied industrial engineering, with projects in more than 50 countries. This business is focused on the development, construction, maintenance and operation of energy, industrial and mobility infrastructures through a large group of companies. This group's activities include: networks, such as electricity, gas and water network maintenance services; specialized products, such as construction, installation and maintenance for high-voltage electricity lines, telecommunications systems, railway installations, electricity facilities, mechanical assemblies and heating/cooling systems; control systems, including the installation and operation of control systems for industrial and municipal services; and integrated projects, including the execution of engineering, procurement and construction (EPC) projects for the design, construction and commissioning of projects connected to the energy sector. Last, the services business is divided into three categories: services for people, covering the assistance needs and resources for elderly citizens, dependent people, disabled people and children up to age three; services for buildings, including maintenance, energy efficiency, cleaning, security, logistics and auxiliary services; and services for the city and environment, including managing public lighting, environmental services and airport services.

FINANCIAL DATA: Note: Data for latest year may not have been available at press time.

In U.S. $	2017	2016	2015	2014	2013	2012
Revenue		39,486,300,000	43,128,580,000	43,074,490,000	47,386,350,000	47,415,570,000
R&D Expense						
Operating Income		1,553,318,000	1,547,181,000	1,189,880,000	2,277,386,000	1,915,377,000
Operating Margin %		3.93%	3.58%	2.76%	4.80%	4.03%
SGA Expense						
Net Income		927,432,200	895,702,500	885,536,800	866,335,300	-2,378,965,000
Operating Cash Flow		1,732,424,000	2,481,362,000	1,017,589,000	1,249,491,000	1,604,819,000
Capital Expenditure		725,572,400	891,627,400	1,041,035,000	1,579,791,000	2,160,120,000
EBITDA		2,187,977,000	2,520,286,000	2,207,447,000	3,769,036,000	3,729,292,000
Return on Assets %		2.18%	1.94%	1.81%	1.72%	-4.30%
Return on Equity %		21.44%	22.47%	22.75%	23.68%	-64.47%
Debt to Equity		1.36	2.11	1.95	2.20	2.16

CONTACT INFORMATION:
Phone: 34 913439200 Fax: 34 913439456
Toll-Free:
Address: Avda. Pio XII, No. 102, Madrid, 28036 Spain

STOCK TICKER/OTHER:
Stock Ticker: ACSAF Exchange: PINX
Employees: 169,766 Fiscal Year Ends: 12/31
Parent Company:

SALARIES/BONUSES:
Top Exec. Salary: $ Bonus: $
Second Exec. Salary: $ Bonus: $

OTHER THOUGHTS:
Estimated Female Officers or Directors:
Hot Spot for Advancement for Women/Minorities:

Sales, profits and employees may be estimates. Financial information, benefits and other data can change quickly and may vary from those stated here.

Activision Blizzard Inc

NAIC Code: 0

www.activisionblizzard.com

TYPES OF BUSINESS:
Electronic Games, Apps & Entertainment
League-Based, Live Gaming Competition
Apps
TV Distribution of Gaming Events
Merchandising
Licensing Game Content for Movies
Licensing Content to Comic Books

BRANDS/DIVISIONS/AFFILIATES:
Activision Publishing Inc
Blizzard Entertainment Inc
King Digital Entertainment
Call of Duty
World of Warcraft
Overwatch
Overwatch League
Candy Crush

CONTACTS:
Note: Officers with more than one job title may be intentionally listed here more than once.

Riccardo Zacconi, CEO, Subsidiary
Eric Hirshberg, CEO, Subsidiary
Michael Morhaime, CEO, Subsidiary
Robert Kotick, CEO
Spencer Neumann, CFO
Brian Kelly, Chairman of the Board
Stephen Wereb, Chief Accounting Officer
Collister Johnson, COO
Thomas Tippl, Director
Christopher Walther, Other Executive Officer
Dennis Durkin, Other Executive Officer
Brian Stolz, Other Executive Officer

GROWTH PLANS/SPECIAL FEATURES:
Activision Blizzard, Inc. is a leading international publisher and developer of subscription-based massively multiplayer online role-playing games (MMORPGs) and other PC-based, console, handheld and mobile games. The firm develops and distributes content and services across all major gaming platforms, including video game consoles, personal computers (PCs) and mobile devices. Activision operates through four business segments: Activision Publishing, Inc.; Blizzard Entertainment, Inc.; King Digital Entertainment; and other. Activision Publishing is a developer and publisher of interactive software products and entertainment content, particularly in console gaming. Key product franchises include: Call of Duty, Destiny and Skylanders. Blizzard Entertainment develops and publishes interactive software products and entertainment content, particularly in PC gaming. Its content is primarily delivered through retail channels or digital downloads, including subscriptions, full-game sales and in-game purchases. This division's key product franchises include World of Warcraft, a subscription-based MMORPG; StarCraft, a real-time strategy PC franchise; Diablo, an action-role-playing franchise; Hearthstone, an online collectible card franchise; Heroes of the Storm, a free-to-play team brawler; and Overwatch, a team-based, first-person shooter. In addition, Overwatch League sells tickets to fans who watch teams competing at live events or via TV broadcasting. King Digital develops and publishes interactive entertainment content and services, particularly on mobile platforms such as Android and iOS, but distributes its content and services on online social platforms as well. King's games are free. Its product franchises include Candy Crush, Farm Heroes, Pet Rescue and Bubble Witch. Last, the other segment includes Activision's: Major League Gaming business, which focuses on e-sports; Activision Blizzard Studios, which creates original film and television content; and Activision Blizzard Distribution, consisting of operations in Europe that provide warehousing, logistics and sales distribution services to third-party publishers of interactive entertainment software.

FINANCIAL DATA:
Note: Data for latest year may not have been available at press time.

In U.S. $	2017	2016	2015	2014	2013	2012
Revenue	7,017,000,000	6,608,000,000	4,664,000,000	4,408,000,000	4,583,000,000	4,856,000,000
R&D Expense	1,069,000,000	958,000,000	646,000,000	571,000,000	584,000,000	604,000,000
Operating Income	1,309,000,000	1,412,000,000	1,319,000,000	1,183,000,000	1,372,000,000	1,451,000,000
Operating Margin %	18.65%	21.36%	28.28%	26.83%	29.93%	29.88%
SGA Expense	2,138,000,000	1,844,000,000	1,114,000,000	1,129,000,000	1,096,000,000	1,139,000,000
Net Income	273,000,000	966,000,000	892,000,000	835,000,000	1,010,000,000	1,149,000,000
Operating Cash Flow	2,213,000,000	2,155,000,000	1,192,000,000	1,292,000,000	1,264,000,000	1,345,000,000
Capital Expenditure	155,000,000	136,000,000	111,000,000	107,000,000	74,000,000	73,000,000
EBITDA	2,508,000,000	2,562,000,000	1,813,000,000	1,529,000,000	1,692,000,000	1,787,000,000
Return on Assets %	1.51%	5.88%	5.87%	5.80%	7.16%	8.18%
Return on Equity %	2.93%	11.19%	11.51%	12.05%	11.26%	10.31%
Debt to Equity	0.46	0.53	0.50	0.59	0.70	

CONTACT INFORMATION:
Phone: 310 255-2000 Fax: 310 255-2100
Toll-Free:
Address: 3100 Ocean Park Blvd., Santa Monica, CA 90405 United States

STOCK TICKER/OTHER:
Stock Ticker: ATVI Exchange: NAS
Employees: 9,600 Fiscal Year Ends: 12/31
Parent Company:

SALARIES/BONUSES:
Top Exec. Salary: $2,375,858 Bonus: $
Second Exec. Salary: $1,360,000 Bonus: $

OTHER THOUGHTS:
Estimated Female Officers or Directors:
Hot Spot for Advancement for Women/Minorities:

Sales, profits and employees may be estimates. Financial information, benefits and other data can change quickly and may vary from those stated here.

Adobe Systems Inc

www.adobe.com

NAIC Code: 0

TYPES OF BUSINESS:
Computer Software, Multimedia, Graphics & Publishing
Document Management Software
Photo Editing & Management Software
Graphic Design Software

BRANDS/DIVISIONS/AFFILIATES:
Adobe Creative Suite
Adobe Creative Cloud
Adobe Dreamweaver
Adobe Photoshop
Adobe InDesign
Adobe Acrobat
Adobe PostScript
Adobe Stock

CONTACTS:
Note: Officers with more than one job title may be intentionally listed here more than once.

Shantanu Narayen, CEO
Mark Garrett, CFO
John Murphy, Chief Accounting Officer
Ann Lewnes, Chief Marketing Officer
Abhay Parasnis, Chief Technology Officer
John Warnock, Co-Founder
Charles Geschke, Director
Donna Morris, Executive VP, Divisional
Matthew Thompson, Executive VP, Divisional
Scott Belsky, Executive VP, Divisional
Bryan Lamkin, Executive VP
Bradley Rencher, Executive VP
Michael Dillon, General Counsel

GROWTH PLANS/SPECIAL FEATURES:

Adobe Systems, Inc. is one of the largest software companies in the world. It offers a line of creative, business, web and mobile software and services used by creative professionals and developers for creating, managing, delivering, optimizing and engaging with content across multiple operating systems, devices and media. The company operates in three segments: digital media, digital marketing and print and publishing. The digital media division focuses on professional imaging and video products, including the widely used Adobe Creative Suite and Adobe Creative Cloud. Products in this segment also include Adobe Dreamweaver, Adobe Photoshop and Adobe InDesign. Digital media's document services business is built around the Adobe Acrobat family of products, the Adobe Reader and a set of integrated cloud-based document services. Adobe PDF documents can be viewed, printed or filled out using the free Adobe Reader. The digital marketing segment consists of the firm's online marketing services including the firm's Adobe Marketing Cloud. The print and publishing segment addresses market opportunities ranging from technical and business publishing to legacy type printing. This segment's Adobe PostScript and Adobe PDF printing technologies provide advanced functionality. Adobe Stock, is an online marketplace for photos, graphics and videos. Creative Cloud members can access digital content through Adobe Stock. Creative Cloud also offers members access to online services to sync, store and share files; participate in Adobe's Behance community of more than 5 million creative professionals; publish and deliver digital content via app stores; develop mobile apps; and create and manage websites.

The firm offers employees life, disability, medical, dental, vision and prescription drug insurance; adoption assistance; employee assistance program; product discounts; and a 401(k).

FINANCIAL DATA:
Note: Data for latest year may not have been available at press time.

In U.S. $	2017	2016	2015	2014	2013	2012
Revenue	7,301,505,000	5,854,430,000	4,795,511,000	4,147,065,000	4,055,240,000	4,403,677,000
R&D Expense	1,224,059,000	975,987,000	862,730,000	844,353,000	826,631,000	742,823,000
Operating Income	2,168,095,000	1,492,094,000	904,654,000	432,568,000	449,220,000	1,177,274,000
Operating Margin %	29.69%	25.48%	18.86%	10.43%	11.07%	26.73%
SGA Expense	2,822,298,000	2,487,907,000	2,215,161,000	2,195,640,000	2,140,578,000	1,951,141,000
Net Income	1,693,954,000	1,168,782,000	629,551,000	268,395,000	289,985,000	832,775,000
Operating Cash Flow	2,912,853,000	2,199,728,000	1,469,502,000	1,287,482,000	1,151,686,000	1,499,580,000
Capital Expenditure	208,040,000	262,238,000	207,715,000	165,904,000	256,095,000	300,777,000
EBITDA	2,538,040,000	1,837,115,000	1,277,438,000	734,698,000	744,876,000	1,486,047,000
Return on Assets %	12.43%	9.56%	5.59%	2.53%	2.84%	8.78%
Return on Equity %	21.32%	16.20%	9.13%	3.97%	4.33%	13.37%
Debt to Equity	0.22	0.25	0.27	0.13	0.22	0.22

CONTACT INFORMATION:
Phone: 408 536-6000   Fax: 408 536-6799
Toll-Free: 800-833-6687
Address: 345 Park Ave., San Jose, CA 95110 United States

STOCK TICKER/OTHER:
Stock Ticker: ADBE
Employees: 15,706
Parent Company:

Exchange: NAS
Fiscal Year Ends: 11/30

SALARIES/BONUSES:
Top Exec. Salary: $1,000,000   Bonus: $
Second Exec. Salary: $720,192   Bonus: $

OTHER THOUGHTS:
Estimated Female Officers or Directors: 5
Hot Spot for Advancement for Women/Minorities: Y

Sales, profits and employees may be estimates. Financial information, benefits and other data can change quickly and may vary from those stated here.

Advanced Micro Devices Inc (AMD)

NAIC Code: 334413

www.amd.com

TYPES OF BUSINESS:
Microprocessors
Semiconductors
Chipsets
Wafer Manufacturing
Multimedia Graphics

BRANDS/DIVISIONS/AFFILIATES:
Direct Connect Architecture
AMD PRO
AMD Ryzen PRO
AMD EPYC
AMD Opteron
AMD Embedded R-Series
AMD Embedded G-Series
AMD Embedded Radeon

CONTACTS:
Note: Officers with more than one job title may be intentionally listed here more than once.

Lisa Su, CEO
Devinder Kumar, CFO
Darla Smith, Chief Accounting Officer
Mark Papermaster, Chief Technology Officer
John Caldwell, Director
Forrest Norrod, General Manager, Divisional
James Anderson, General Manager, Divisional
Harry Wolin, Senior VP

GROWTH PLANS/SPECIAL FEATURES:

Advanced Micro Devices, Inc. (AMD) is a global semiconductor company that provides processing products for the computing, graphics and consumer electronics markets. The company operates through two segments: computing and graphics; and enterprise, embedded and semi-custom. The computing and graphics segment includes desktop and notebook processors and chipsets, graphics processing units (GPUs), professional GPUs and licensing portions of AMD's intellectual property portfolio. This division supplies microprocessors for the commercial and consumer markets based on the industry standard x86 architecture and its Direct Connect Architecture; chipsets for desktop and notebook PCs, professional workstations and servers. This segment also offers graphics products for use in various computing devices and entertainment platforms, including desktop PCs, notebook PCs, 2-in-1s and professional workstations. The enterprise, embedded and semi-custom segment includes server and embedded processors, semi-custom system-on-chip (SoC) products, engineering services and royalties. This division's commercial products include: enterprise-class desktop and notebook PC solutions sold as AMD PRO and AMD Ryzen PRO; microprocessors for server platforms sold as AMD EPYC and AMD Opteron; and embedded processors sold as AMD Embedded R-Series, AMD Embedded G-Series and AMD Embedded Radeon. In addition, semi-custom products are specifically tailored for clients, with AMD leveraging its core graphics processing technology into the game console market by licensing it in game consoles such as the Microsoft Xbox, Nintendo Wii and Sony PlayStation series. The company primarily markets its products under the AMD brand name.

FINANCIAL DATA:
Note: Data for latest year may not have been available at press time.

In U.S. $	2017	2016	2015	2014	2013	2012
Revenue	5,329,000,000	4,272,000,000	3,991,000,000	5,506,000,000	5,299,000,000	5,422,000,000
R&D Expense	1,160,000,000	1,008,000,000	947,000,000	1,072,000,000	1,201,000,000	1,354,000,000
Operating Income	152,000,000	-470,000,000	-352,000,000	149,000,000	133,000,000	-956,000,000
Operating Margin %	2.85%	-11.00%	-8.81%	2.70%	2.50%	-17.63%
SGA Expense	511,000,000	460,000,000	482,000,000	604,000,000	626,000,000	823,000,000
Net Income	43,000,000	-497,000,000	-660,000,000	-403,000,000	-83,000,000	-1,183,000,000
Operating Cash Flow	68,000,000	90,000,000	-226,000,000	-98,000,000	-148,000,000	-338,000,000
Capital Expenditure	113,000,000	77,000,000	96,000,000	95,000,000	84,000,000	133,000,000
EBITDA	339,000,000	-159,000,000	-319,000,000	-18,000,000	339,000,000	-782,000,000
Return on Assets %	1.25%	-15.45%	-19.19%	-9.94%	-1.99%	-26.42%
Return on Equity %	8.37%	-24850.00%		-110.25%	-15.34%	-111.18%
Debt to Equity	2.16	3.44		10.88	3.67	3.78

CONTACT INFORMATION:
Phone: 408 749-4000 Fax:
Toll-Free:
Address: 2485 Augustine Dr., Santa Clara, CA 95054 United States

STOCK TICKER/OTHER:
Stock Ticker: AMD
Employees: 9,100
Parent Company:

Exchange: NAS
Fiscal Year Ends: 12/31

SALARIES/BONUSES:
Top Exec. Salary: $924,997 Bonus: $
Second Exec. Salary: $611,328 Bonus: $

OTHER THOUGHTS:
Estimated Female Officers or Directors: 3
Hot Spot for Advancement for Women/Minorities: Y

Advanced Semiconductor Engineering Inc

www.aseglobal.com

NAIC Code: 334413

TYPES OF BUSINESS:
Semiconductor Manufacturing
Semiconductor Packaging Services
Design & Testing Services

BRANDS/DIVISIONS/AFFILIATES:
Universal Scientific Industrial Co Ltd
ASE Electronics Inc
ISE Labs Inc

CONTACTS:
Note: Officers with more than one job title may be intentionally listed here more than once.

Jason C.S. Chang, CEO
Tien Wu, COO
Richard H.P. Chang, Pres.
Joseph Tung, CFO
Joseph Su, Mgr.-Investor Rel.
Raymond Lo, Pres., Kaohsiung Plant Area
Jason C.S. Chang, Chmn.
Rutherford Chang, Pres., ASE China

GROWTH PLANS/SPECIAL FEATURES:
Advanced Semiconductor Engineering, Inc. (ASE Group) is a leading provider of semiconductor packaging (also called assembly, which is the process of turning bare semiconductors into finished semiconductors) as well as semiconductor testing services. ASE Group semiconductor assembly products are available in a variety of formats, including dual-in-line packages, quad packages, ball-grid arrays (BGAs), pin grid arrays (PGAs), chip scale packages (CSPs), system-in-package (SiPs), 3D packages, wafer bumping, flip chips and lead-free packages. These assemblies are used to connect the integrated circuit, or die, to the printed circuit board, protecting the die and facilitating electrical connections and heat dissipation. The firm provides services at all stages of the semiconductor manufacturing process except circuit design and wafer fabrication, which is done through ASE Group member, Universal Scientific Industrial Co. Ltd. Its service capabilities include front-end engineering testing, which is the testing of prototypes that takes place before volume production, including software development, electrical verification, reliability analysis and failure analysis; wafer probing, testing each chip on a wafer for defects packaging; and final testing, which makes sure that the product is functional before being sent to customers or assembled into electronic products. Company affiliates and subsidiaries include Universal Scientific Industrial Co. Ltd., which provides design manufacturing services from board design to systems assembly; ASE Electronics, Inc., a supplier of substrates and packaging material; and U.S.-based ISE Labs, Inc., a front-end engineering test firm. ASE Group has operations in Taiwan, South Korea, Japan, China, Hong Kong, Singapore and Malaysia as well as the Americas and Europe.

FINANCIAL DATA:
Note: Data for latest year may not have been available at press time.

In U.S. $	2017	2016	2015	2014	2013	2012
Revenue	9,909,625,000	9,378,828,000	9,666,058,000	8,754,697,000	7,501,533,000	6,618,185,000
R&D Expense	400,785,200	388,657,000	373,181,100	351,075,900	309,280,800	268,661,800
Operating Income	860,439,100	911,273,000	849,043,600	1,034,489,000	755,412,400	606,004,400
Operating Margin %	8.68%	9.71%	8.78%	11.81%	10.07%	9.15%
SGA Expense	537,959,200	515,014,800	488,349,600	463,794,500	396,892,400	374,908,000
Net Income	835,820,400	728,841,200	682,845,000	758,422,400	525,589,600	446,666,800
Operating Cash Flow	1,618,301,000	1,777,879,000	1,963,503,000	1,564,826,000	1,408,985,000	990,069,400
Capital Expenditure	854,250,300	928,999,800	1,049,891,000	1,364,612,000	1,005,010,000	1,371,481,000
EBITDA	2,115,416,000	2,035,722,000	1,947,545,000	1,952,981,000	1,608,657,000	1,433,319,000
Return on Assets %	6.32%	5.90%	5.72%	7.16%	5.77%	5.56%
Return on Equity %	13.30%	13.79%	13.24%	16.52%	13.32%	12.42%
Debt to Equity	0.14	0.30	0.42	0.16	0.24	0.30

CONTACT INFORMATION:
Phone: 886 287805489   Fax: 886 227576121
Toll-Free:
Address: 26 Chin Third Rd., Nantze Export Processing Zone, Kaohsiung, 811 Taiwan

STOCK TICKER/OTHER:
Stock Ticker: ASX
Employees: 68,100
Parent Company:

Exchange: NYS
Fiscal Year Ends: 12/31

SALARIES/BONUSES:
Top Exec. Salary: $ Bonus: $
Second Exec. Salary: $ Bonus: $

OTHER THOUGHTS:
Estimated Female Officers or Directors:
Hot Spot for Advancement for Women/Minorities: Y

Sales, profits and employees may be estimates. Financial information, benefits and other data can change quickly and may vary from those stated here.

AECOM

NAIC Code: 237310

www.aecom.com

TYPES OF BUSINESS:
Engineering & Design Services
Transportation Projects
Environmental Projects
Power & Mining Support
Consulting
Economic Development Consulting

BRANDS/DIVISIONS/AFFILIATES:

GROWTH PLANS/SPECIAL FEATURES:
AECOM designs, builds, finances and operates infrastructure assets for governments, businesses and organizations in more than 150 countries. The firm provides planning, consulting, architectural and engineering design services to clients in major end markets such as transportation, facilities, environmental, energy, water and government markets. AECOM also provides: construction services, such as building, energy, infrastructure and industrial construction; and program and facilities management and maintenance, training, logistics, consulting, technical assistance and systems integration and IT services primarily for the U.S. government, but also for national governments around the world. Based in the U.S., the firm has additional offices in New York, London, Moscow, Hong Kong, Abu Dhabi and Brisbane.

CONTACTS:
Note: Officers with more than one job title may be intentionally listed here more than once.

Lara Poloni, CEO, Geographical
Daniel Tishman, CEO, Subsidiary
Michael Burke, CEO
Randall Wotring, COO
W. Rudd, Executive VP
Carla Christofferson, Executive VP
Mary Finch, Executive VP
John Vollmer, President, Divisional
Daniel McQuade, President, Divisional
Fredrick Werner, President, Divisional
Steve Morriss, President, Geographical
Chuan-Sheng Chiao, President, Geographical

FINANCIAL DATA:
Note: Data for latest year may not have been available at press time.

In U.S. $	2017	2016	2015	2014	2013	2012
Revenue	18,203,400,000	17,410,820,000	17,989,880,000	8,356,783,000	8,153,495,000	8,218,180,000
R&D Expense						
Operating Income	550,411,000	527,736,000	421,213,000	322,268,000	352,670,000	389,606,000
Operating Margin %	3.02%	3.03%	2.34%	3.85%	4.32%	4.74%
SGA Expense	133,309,000	115,088,000	113,975,000	80,908,000	97,318,000	80,903,000
Net Income	339,390,000	96,109,000	-154,845,000	229,854,000	239,243,000	-58,567,000
Operating Cash Flow	696,654,000	814,155,000	764,433,000	360,625,000	408,598,000	433,352,000
Capital Expenditure	86,354,000	191,386,000	69,426,000	62,852,000	52,117,000	62,874,000
EBITDA	939,123,000	782,447,000	747,422,000	451,024,000	474,917,000	165,553,000
Return on Assets %	2.41%	.69%	-1.53%	3.89%	4.22%	-1.02%
Return on Equity %	9.21%	2.83%	-5.53%	10.92%	11.41%	-2.59%
Debt to Equity	0.92	1.11	1.30	0.42	0.53	0.41

CONTACT INFORMATION:
Phone: 213 593-8000   Fax: 213 593-8730
Toll-Free:
Address: 1999 Avenue of the Stars, Ste. 2600, Los Angeles, CA 90067 United States

STOCK TICKER/OTHER:
Stock Ticker: ACM
Employees: 87,000
Parent Company:

Exchange: NYS
Fiscal Year Ends: 09/30

SALARIES/BONUSES:
Top Exec. Salary: $1,354,812   Bonus: $
Second Exec. Salary: $731,925   Bonus: $20,000

OTHER THOUGHTS:
Estimated Female Officers or Directors: 6
Hot Spot for Advancement for Women/Minorities: Y

Sales, profits and employees may be estimates. Financial information, benefits and other data can change quickly and may vary from those stated here.

Aecon Group Inc

NAIC Code: 237310

www.aecon.com

TYPES OF BUSINESS:
Construction
Infrastructure Development
Utility Systems
Steam Power Generation
Renovation

BRANDS/DIVISIONS/AFFILIATES:
Aecon Water Infrastructure
Aecon Constructors
Yellowline Asphalt Products Ltd
Aecon Atlantic Industrial Inc
Aecon Industrial
Aecon Utilities
Aecon Mining
Aecon Concessions

CONTACTS: Note: Officers with more than one job title may be intentionally listed here more than once.
David Smales, CFO
John Beck, Director
Brian Tobin, Director
L. Brian Swartz, Executive VP, Divisional
Yonni Fushman, Executive VP
Steven Nackan, President, Divisional

GROWTH PLANS/SPECIAL FEATURES:

Aecon Group, Inc. is one of Canada's largest construction and infrastructure development companies. The firm operates in four principal segments through its network of subsidiaries: infrastructure, energy, mining and concessions. The infrastructure segment provides all aspects of construction for both public and private infrastructure, including roads, highways, bridges, airport facilities, dams, tunnels, marine facilities, transit systems and power projects. This segment also offers design, project management and construction management services; and utility infrastructure services for gas projects, hydro distribution networks, telecommunication networks, water mains and sewers. Just a few of the many subsidiaries within this segment include Aecon Water Infrastructure, Aecon Constructors and Yellowline Asphalt Products, Ltd. The energy segment offers a range of services for designing, building, and commissioning power generation plants, including oil and gas facilities, cogeneration plants, hydroelectric facilities, natural gas power plants, nuclear plants and waste heat recovery systems. Some of the subsidiaries in this segment include Aecon Atlantic Industrial, Inc.; Aecon Industrial; Aecon Utilities; Bremar; QX; and Tristar. The mining segment is comprised of three subsidiaries: Aecon Mining, Canonbie Contracting Limited and Aecon Mining Construction Management, Inc. These companies are involved in the extraction and refinement of natural resources ranging from oil and gas reserves, potash and uranium, as well as high-grade deposits of base and precious metals. Last, the concession segment is comprised of subsidiary Aecon Concessions, which engages in the development, financing and operation of infrastructure of domestic and international public-private partnership projects, as well as other infrastructure development projects requiring private finance solutions. In August 2017, the firm announced it had engaged financial advisors to explore a potential sale of the company.

Aecon Group offers its employees medical and dental insurance, an employee stock purchase program, a pension plan and tuition reimbursement.

FINANCIAL DATA: Note: Data for latest year may not have been available at press time.

In U.S. $	2017	2016	2015	2014	2013	2012
Revenue	2,224,121,000	2,547,073,000	2,313,185,000	2,072,198,000	2,432,507,000	2,335,946,000
R&D Expense						
Operating Income	30,865,640	50,210,070	47,707,490	34,690,450	47,123,260	86,160,920
Operating Margin %	1.38%	1.97%	2.06%	1.67%	1.93%	3.68%
SGA Expense	147,870,000	146,703,100	134,638,900	118,852,200	117,323,800	124,606,400
Net Income	22,335,310	37,064,600	54,440,740	23,814,510	32,182,320	61,813,710
Operating Cash Flow	156,493,900	21,312,720	46,060,240	59,296,080	106,239,400	54,598,490
Capital Expenditure	33,679,740	31,699,560	41,822,430	46,897,340	46,736,420	94,767,340
EBITDA	117,382,500	120,049,900	168,030,900	112,063,400	120,874,400	142,466,100
Return on Assets %	1.24%	2.41%	3.70%	1.57%	1.96%	3.79%
Return on Equity %	3.69%	6.35%	9.99%	4.83%	7.18%	15.14%
Debt to Equity	0.57	0.33	0.37	0.41	0.63	1.02

CONTACT INFORMATION:
Phone: 416 293-7004 Fax: 416 293-0271
Toll-Free: 877-232-2677
Address: 20 Carlson Ct., Ste. 800, Toronto, ON M9W 7K6 Canada

STOCK TICKER/OTHER:
Stock Ticker: ARE
Employees: 12,000
Parent Company:

Exchange: TSE
Fiscal Year Ends: 12/31

SALARIES/BONUSES:
Top Exec. Salary: $ Bonus: $
Second Exec. Salary: $ Bonus: $

OTHER THOUGHTS:
Estimated Female Officers or Directors: 2
Hot Spot for Advancement for Women/Minorities:

Sales, profits and employees may be estimates. Financial information, benefits and other data can change quickly and may vary from those stated here.

AF AB

NAIC Code: 541330

www.afconsult.com

TYPES OF BUSINESS:
Engineering Services

BRANDS/DIVISIONS/AFFILIATES:
Gottlieb Paludan Architects

CONTACTS:
Note: Officers with more than one job title may be intentionally listed here more than once.

Jonas Gustavsson, CEO
Stefan Johansson, CFO
Emma Claesson, VP-Human Resources

GROWTH PLANS/SPECIAL FEATURES:

AF AB is an engineering and consulting company for the energy, industrial and infrastructure markets. The firm consists of four divisions: industry, infrastructure, energy and digital solutions. The industry and infrastructure divisions are established in Scandinavia, and the digital solutions division is based in within the Swedish market. The energy division provides AF's entire service offering outside of Scandinavia. All of the company's divisions participate in international projects, and they always work together to create strong teams for each AF client. For the industry sector includes the automotive, defence, security, engineering, food processing, forestry, mining, oil and gas, pharmaceuticals and telecommunications industries, providing process and production development solutions as well as IT and product development services and solutions. Within the infrastructure market, AF provides engineering and consulting services primarily in relation to property, roads and railways. For the energy sector, AF offers engineering and consulting solutions in relation to hydropower, nuclear power, renewable energy, thermal power, transmission and distribution. AF's digital solutions cover fields of expertise such as product development, IT, customized business systems, communications system management and civilian security within the automotive, telecoms, defense and life science sectors, as well as for production facilities and industrial and energy plants. Headquartered in Sweden, the firm has additional offices in more than 30 countries, and has performed projects in more than 100 countries worldwide. In January 2018, AF acquired Gottlieb Paludan Architects, expanding its architecture and design services in Denmark.

FINANCIAL DATA:
Note: Data for latest year may not have been available at press time.

In U.S. $	2017	2016	2015	2014	2013	2012
Revenue	1,540,250,000	1,218,630,000	1,214,897,232	7,085,829,958	1,028,179,700	890,937,000
R&D Expense						
Operating Income						
Operating Margin %						
SGA Expense						
Net Income	90,531,400	78,270,000	74,608,418	68,190,761	64,491,443	54,273,600
Operating Cash Flow						
Capital Expenditure						
EBITDA						
Return on Assets %						
Return on Equity %						
Debt to Equity						

CONTACT INFORMATION:
Phone: 46-10-505-00-00   Fax: 46-10-505-00-10
Toll-Free:
Address: Frosundaleden 2, Stockholm, SE-169 99 Sweden

STOCK TICKER/OTHER:
Stock Ticker: AF-B   Exchange: OMX
Employees: 9,865   Fiscal Year Ends:
Parent Company:

SALARIES/BONUSES:
Top Exec. Salary: $ Bonus: $
Second Exec. Salary: $ Bonus: $

OTHER THOUGHTS:
Estimated Female Officers or Directors:
Hot Spot for Advancement for Women/Minorities:

Agfa-Gevaert NV

NAIC Code: 333316

www.agfa.com

TYPES OF BUSINESS:
Imaging Equipment
Commercial Printing Equipment & Products
Image Publishing Software
Consumer Photographic Products
Medical Imaging Systems
X-Ray Films

BRANDS/DIVISIONS/AFFILIATES:
Agfa Graphics
Agfa HealthCare
Agfa Specialty Products

CONTACTS:
Note: Officers with more than one job title may be intentionally listed here more than once.

Christian Reinaudo, CEO
Christian Reinaudo, Pres.
Dirk De Man, CFO
Luc Thijs, Pres., Agfa HealthCare
Luc Delagaye, Pres., Agfa Materials
Stefaan Vanhooren, Pres., Agfa Graphics
Julien De Wilde, Chmn.

GROWTH PLANS/SPECIAL FEATURES:

Agfa-Gevaert NV is a leading imaging equipment company that develops, produces and markets analog and digital systems as well as IT solutions primarily for the printing and healthcare sectors. Agfa has three main divisions: Agfa Graphics, Agfa HealthCare and Agfa Specialty Products. Agfa Graphics provides pre-press services for printing, such as scanning images and designing layouts for anything from books and magazines to billboards and CDs. In addition, the company's commercial printing systems provide commercial, newspaper and packaging printers, including computer-to-film and computer-to-plate systems as well as equipment and consumables. Agfa also supplies digital proofing systems, large-format printing, digital inkjet presses and the professional software that controls the entire prepress process. Agfa HealthCare supplies both analog and digital imaging solutions as well as diagnosis and communications equipment. The company's digital networks and information systems streamline the distribution, storage and management of digital images and optimize the workflow of the entire hospital organization. The Agfa Specialty Products division provides large-scale film-based products and technology solutions for the business-to-business (B2B) market, such as motion picture film, microfilm and film for non-destructive testing as well as materials for smart cards, conductive polymers, synthetic paper and membranes for gas separation. The company also provides solutions for aerial photography, printed circuit boards, identification cards and many other applications.

FINANCIAL DATA:
Note: Data for latest year may not have been available at press time.

In U.S. $	2017	2016	2015	2014	2013	2012
Revenue		3,132,950,000	3,267,554,000	3,235,447,000	3,537,998,000	3,817,086,000
R&D Expense		174,121,400	177,826,100	180,295,900	180,295,900	201,289,200
Operating Income		254,390,100	239,571,200	208,698,700	282,792,900	166,712,000
Operating Margin %		8.11%	7.33%	6.45%	7.99%	4.36%
SGA Expense		631,035,600	644,619,500	627,330,900	664,378,000	716,243,900
Net Income		86,443,230	76,564,010	61,745,170	50,631,040	-50,631,040
Operating Cash Flow		175,356,300	184,000,600	186,470,400	132,134,700	39,516,910
Capital Expenditure		54,335,750	45,691,420	45,691,420	49,396,130	54,335,750
EBITDA		242,041,100	198,819,400	201,289,200	243,276,000	116,080,900
Return on Assets %		2.94%	2.50%	1.95%	1.51%	-1.41%
Return on Equity %		31.60%	38.62%	23.92%	6.59%	-4.36%
Debt to Equity		0.34	0.60	1.34	0.98	0.44

CONTACT INFORMATION:
Phone: 32 34442111   Fax: 32 34447094
Toll-Free:
Address: Septestraat 27, Mortsel, B-2640 Belgium

STOCK TICKER/OTHER:
Stock Ticker: AFGVF
Employees: 10,329
Parent Company:

Exchange: GREY
Fiscal Year Ends: 12/31

SALARIES/BONUSES:
Top Exec. Salary: $ Bonus: $
Second Exec. Salary: $ Bonus: $

OTHER THOUGHTS:
Estimated Female Officers or Directors:
Hot Spot for Advancement for Women/Minorities:

Sales, profits and employees may be estimates. Financial information, benefits and other data can change quickly and may vary from those stated here.

Agilent Technologies Inc

NAIC Code: 334515

www.home.agilent.com

TYPES OF BUSINESS:
Test Equipment
Communications Test Equipment
Integrated Circuits Test Equipment
Bioanalysis Equipment
Laboratory Automation and Robotics
Bioinstrumentation
Software Products
Informatics Products

BRANDS/DIVISIONS/AFFILIATES:
Agilent CrossLab
Agilent Technologies Research Laboratories
Multiplicom NV
Cobalt Light Systems

CONTACTS:
Note: Officers with more than one job title may be intentionally listed here more than once.

Didier Hirsch, CFO
Koh Hwee, Chairman of the Board
Rodney Gonsalves, Chief Accounting Officer
Michael Tang, General Counsel
Mark Doak, President, Divisional
Jacob Thaysen, President, Divisional
Patrick Kaltenbach, President, Divisional
Henrik Ancher-Jensen, President, Divisional
Michael McMullen, President
Dominique Grau, Senior VP, Divisional

GROWTH PLANS/SPECIAL FEATURES:

Agilent Technologies, Inc. is a measurement technology company with three business segments: life sciences and applied markets; diagnostics and genomics; and Agilent CrossLab. The life sciences and applied markets segment provides application-focused solutions, including instruments and software that enable customers to identify, quantify and analyze the physical and biological properties of substances. Product categories include liquid chromatography systems and components; gas chromatography systems and components; inductively coupled plasma mass spectrometry instruments; atomic absorption instruments; and liquid chromatography mass spectrometry systems among others. The diagnostics and genomics segment consists of reagent partnership, pathology, companion diagnostics, genomics and the nucleic acid contract manufacturing businesses. This segment provides solutions including reagents, instruments, software and consumables for customers in the clinical and life sciences research areas. The Agilent CrossLab segment comprises the operations of Agilent Technologies Research Laboratories as well as consumables and services. Product categories in consumables include GC and LC columns, sample preparation products, custom chemistries, and a large selection of laboratory instrument supplies. Services include startup, operational, training and compliance support, as well as asset management and consultation services that help increase customer productivity. During 2017, the firm acquired Multiplicom NV, a diagnostic company with genetic testing technology and products; and Cobalt Light Systems, a provider of differentiated Raman spectroscopic instruments for the pharmaceutical industry, applied markets and public safety. In early-2018, it agreed to acquire Advanced Analytical Technologies, Inc. as well as Lasergen, Inc.

Agilent offers its employees medical, dental, vision, life and disability plans; 401(k) and pension plans; an employee assistance plan; onsite fitness centers; tuition reimbursement; training and development programs; and recreational sports leagues.

FINANCIAL DATA:
Note: Data for latest year may not have been available at press time.

In U.S. $	2017	2016	2015	2014	2013	2012
Revenue	4,472,000,000	4,202,000,000	4,038,000,000	6,981,000,000	6,782,000,000	6,858,000,000
R&D Expense	339,000,000	329,000,000	330,000,000	719,000,000	704,000,000	668,000,000
Operating Income	841,000,000	615,000,000	522,000,000	831,000,000	951,000,000	1,119,000,000
Operating Margin %	18.80%	14.63%	12.92%	11.90%	14.02%	16.31%
SGA Expense	1,229,000,000	1,253,000,000	1,189,000,000	2,043,000,000	1,880,000,000	1,817,000,000
Net Income	684,000,000	462,000,000	401,000,000	504,000,000	724,000,000	1,153,000,000
Operating Cash Flow	889,000,000	793,000,000	491,000,000	711,000,000	1,152,000,000	1,228,000,000
Capital Expenditure	176,000,000	139,000,000	98,000,000	205,000,000	195,000,000	194,000,000
EBITDA	1,094,000,000	862,000,000	799,000,000	1,143,000,000	1,338,000,000	1,445,000,000
Return on Assets %	8.42%	6.04%	4.38%	4.68%	6.82%	11.76%
Return on Equity %	15.07%	10.98%	8.47%	9.52%	13.83%	24.29%
Debt to Equity	0.37	0.45	0.39	0.52	0.51	0.40

CONTACT INFORMATION:
Phone: 408 345-8886 Fax:
Toll-Free: 877-424-4536
Address: 5301 Stevens Creek Blvd., Santa Clara, CA 95051 United States

STOCK TICKER/OTHER:
Stock Ticker: A
Employees: 21,400
Parent Company:

Exchange: NYS
Fiscal Year Ends: 10/31

SALARIES/BONUSES:
Top Exec. Salary: $1,095,833 Bonus: $
Second Exec. Salary: $627,500 Bonus: $

OTHER THOUGHTS:
Estimated Female Officers or Directors: 6
Hot Spot for Advancement for Women/Minorities: Y

Sales, profits and employees may be estimates. Financial information, benefits and other data can change quickly and may vary from those stated here.

Air Products and Chemicals Inc

www.airproducts.com

NAIC Code: 325120

TYPES OF BUSINESS:
Industrial Gases & Chemicals
Respiratory Therapy & Home Medical Equipment
Specialty Resins
Hydrogen Refinery
Natural Gas Liquefaction
Semiconductor Materials

BRANDS/DIVISIONS/AFFILIATES:

CONTACTS: Note: Officers with more than one job title may be intentionally listed here more than once.
M. Crocco, CFO
Seifollah Ghasemi, Chairman of the Board
Russell Flugel, Chief Accounting Officer
Samir Serhan, Executive VP
Corning Painter, Executive VP, Divisional
Sean Major, Executive VP
Mary Afflerbach, Other Executive Officer
Jennifer Grant, Other Executive Officer

GROWTH PLANS/SPECIAL FEATURES:

Air Products and Chemicals, Inc. (APC) provides products, services and solutions such as atmospheric gases, process and specialty gases, and equipment primarily for global energy, electronics, chemicals, metals and manufacturing customers. The company's atmospheric gases include oxygen, nitrogen, argon and rare gases; process gases include hydrogen, helium, carbon dioxide, carbon monoxide, syngas and specialty gases; and equipment for the production or processing of gases include air separation units and non-cryogenic generators. APC is a major supplier of hydrogen and has built leading positions in markets such as helium, refinery hydrogen, semiconductor materials, natural gas liquefaction and advanced coatings/adhesives. The company supplies industrial gases and equipment throughout the Americas, Europe, the Middle East, Africa and Asia, to customers in many industries, including those in metals, glass, chemical processing, electronics, energy production/refining, food processing, metallurgical industries, medical and general manufacturing. Gases are distributed to customers through a variety of modes: liquid bulk, packaged, on-site facilities located adjacent to customers' facilities or via pipeline systems. APC has more than 50 subsidiaries worldwide. In February 2018, the firm agreed to acquire ACP Europe SA, an independent carbon dioxide business.

FINANCIAL DATA: Note: Data for latest year may not have been available at press time.

In U.S. $	2017	2016	2015	2014	2013	2012
Revenue	8,187,600,000	9,524,400,000	9,894,900,000	10,439,000,000	10,180,400,000	9,611,700,000
R&D Expense	57,800,000	132,000,000	138,800,000	141,400,000	133,700,000	126,400,000
Operating Income	1,741,200,000	2,181,600,000	1,877,000,000	1,639,600,000	1,532,800,000	1,518,800,000
Operating Margin %	21.26%	22.90%	18.96%	15.70%	15.05%	15.80%
SGA Expense	726,100,000	855,700,000	962,900,000	1,064,800,000	1,088,800,000	946,800,000
Net Income	3,000,400,000	631,100,000	1,277,900,000	991,700,000	994,200,000	1,167,300,000
Operating Cash Flow	1,567,900,000	2,627,500,000	2,437,800,000	2,187,100,000	1,567,400,000	1,798,700,000
Capital Expenditure	1,039,700,000	1,055,800,000	1,614,800,000	1,684,200,000	1,524,200,000	1,521,000,000
EBITDA	2,402,500,000	3,173,600,000	2,773,400,000	2,436,500,000	2,399,200,000	2,277,000,000
Return on Assets %	16.43%	3.55%	7.25%	5.56%	5.71%	7.47%
Return on Equity %	34.95%	8.80%	17.48%	13.76%	14.70%	19.02%
Debt to Equity	0.33	0.69	0.54	0.65	0.71	0.70

CONTACT INFORMATION:
Phone: 610 481-4911 Fax: 610 481-5900
Toll-Free:
Address: 7201 Hamilton Blvd., Allentown, PA 18195 United States

STOCK TICKER/OTHER:
Stock Ticker: APD
Employees: 18,600
Parent Company:

Exchange: NYS
Fiscal Year Ends: 09/30

SALARIES/BONUSES:
Top Exec. Salary: $448,462 Bonus: $1,100,000
Second Exec. Salary: $1,200,000 Bonus: $

OTHER THOUGHTS:
Estimated Female Officers or Directors: 4
Hot Spot for Advancement for Women/Minorities: Y

Sales, profits and employees may be estimates. Financial information, benefits and other data can change quickly and may vary from those stated here.

Plunkett Research, Ltd.

Airbus SE
NAIC Code: 336411

www.airbusgroup.com

TYPES OF BUSINESS:
Aircraft Manufacturing
Helicopter Manufacturing
Transport Aircraft
Military Aircraft
Defense Communications Systems
Satellites
Space Systems
Maintenance Services

BRANDS/DIVISIONS/AFFILIATES:
ArianeGroup
A320
A330-200F
Beluga
Hforce
ArianeGroup
Airbus SAS
Airbus Group SE

CONTACTS:
Note: Officers with more than one job title may be intentionally listed here more than once.

Thomas Enders, CEO
Tom Williams, COO
Harald Wilhelm, CFO
Eric Shulz, Exec. VP-Mktg.& Sales
Thierry Baril, Chief Human Resources Officer
Marwan Lahoud, Chief Strategy Officer
Fabrice Bregier, CEO-Airbus
Bernhard Gerwert, CEO-Airbus Defense & Space
Guillaume Faury, CEO-Airbus Helicopters
Francois Auque, Exec. VP-Space Systems
Denis Ranque, Chmn.

GROWTH PLANS/SPECIAL FEATURES:

Airbus SE designs, manufactures and delivers aerospace products, services and solutions to customers on a global scale. The company's commercial aircraft include: passenger aircraft, comprising the A320, A330, A350 XWB and A380 family lines; corporate jets comprise the ACJ family of aircraft; and freighters comprise the A330-200F, A330P2F and Beluga lines of aircraft. Airbus offers maintenance engineering, upgrade services, flight operations support and services, training support and services, technical data services and solutions, as well as support and services for airport operators. Airbus' line of helicopters includes: civil helicopters such as light single, light twin, medium, heavy and corporate helicopters; military helicopters such as light, medium, heavy, specialized and HForce; and corporate helicopters. This division also provides care services, military missions support and services, as well as safety support services. The defense division comprises the following aircraft lines: A400M, A330 MRTT, Eurofighter, C295 and unmanned aerial vehicles (UAVs). Its services and solutions include security, cyber security, communications security (both aerial and on land). Last, the space division provides earth observation products and services, telecommunications satellites, human spaceflight products and services, launchers, satellite navigation systems, space exploration products and services, space delta highway products and services, Airbus Aerial data collection technologies and products, as well as other types of space-related equipment and intelligence offerings. This division's ArianeGroup, a 50/50 joint venture with Safran SA, produces orbital propulsion systems and equipment. During 2017, Airbus SAS merged with Airbus Group SE, becoming Airbus SE. In March 2018, Airbus SE sold Plant Holdings, Inc., which held the Airbus DS Communications, Inc. business, to Motorola Solutions. The divestment is part of the portfolio reshaping within the previously-combined Airbus defense and space division.

FINANCIAL DATA:
Note: Data for latest year may not have been available at press time.

In U.S. $	2017	2016	2015	2014	2013	2012
Revenue	82,450,790,000	82,221,100,000	79,589,520,000	74,974,690,000	73,175,430,000	69,747,340,000
R&D Expense	3,466,374,000	3,667,663,000	4,272,765,000	4,187,557,000	3,902,295,000	3,880,067,000
Operating Income	3,381,165,000	2,477,216,000	3,694,831,000	3,823,261,000	2,763,714,000	2,333,967,000
Operating Margin %	4.10%	3.01%	4.64%	5.09%	3.77%	3.34%
SGA Expense	3,011,929,000	3,362,642,000	3,273,729,000	3,211,984,000	3,597,273,000	3,536,763,000
Net Income	3,547,877,000	1,228,729,000	3,329,299,000	2,893,379,000	1,809,133,000	1,516,461,000
Operating Cash Flow	5,487,911,000	5,395,293,000	4,445,652,000	3,161,352,000	2,384,599,000	4,742,029,000
Capital Expenditure	3,158,883,000	3,778,804,000	3,610,857,000	3,146,534,000	3,641,730,000	4,038,134,000
EBITDA	9,119,761,000	5,071,748,000	7,893,502,000	7,193,312,000	5,485,441,000	5,252,044,000
Return on Assets %	2.55%	.91%	2.65%	2.47%	1.58%	1.36%
Return on Equity %	33.79%	20.67%	41.39%	25.92%	13.67%	12.75%
Debt to Equity	0.67	2.40	1.06	0.88	0.35	0.33

CONTACT INFORMATION:
Phone: 31 715245600   Fax: 31 715232807
Toll-Free:
Address: P.O. Box 32008, Leiden, 2303 DA Netherlands

STOCK TICKER/OTHER:
Stock Ticker: EADSF
Employees: 129,442
Parent Company:

Exchange: PINX
Fiscal Year Ends: 12/31

SALARIES/BONUSES:
Top Exec. Salary: $ Bonus: $
Second Exec. Salary: $ Bonus: $

OTHER THOUGHTS:
Estimated Female Officers or Directors: 1
Hot Spot for Advancement for Women/Minorities:

Sales, profits and employees may be estimates. Financial information, benefits and other data can change quickly and may vary from those stated here.

Aisin Seiki Co Ltd

NAIC Code: 336300

www.aisin.co.jp

TYPES OF BUSINESS:
Automobile Parts Manufacturing
Sewing & Embroidery Machines
Air Conditioners
Hospital & Biotechnology Equipment
Lasers & Laser Imaging Technology

BRANDS/DIVISIONS/AFFILIATES:
Aisin Europe Manufacturing (UK) Ltd
Aisin Europe SA
Advics South Africa Pty Ltd
Aisin Asia Pte Ltd
AT India Auto Parts Pvt Ltd
Aisin Tianlin Body Parts Co Ltd
Aisin Al Brasil Industria Automotiva Ltda
Aisin Holdings of America Inc

CONTACTS:
Note: Officers with more than one job title may be intentionally listed here more than once.

Yasumori Ihara, Pres.
Shinzo Kobuki, Exec. VP
Takashi Morita, Exec. VP
Makoto Mitsuya, Exec. VP
Toshikazu Nagura, Exec. VP
Kanshiro Toyoda, Chmn.

GROWTH PLANS/SPECIAL FEATURES:

Aisin Seiki Co., Ltd. primarily develops and manufactures automotive parts and household appliance products. The firm operates in three business units: automotive parts, lifestyle- and energy-related products, and wellness-related products. The automotive parts business manufactures and sells drivetrains, auto body parts, brakes, chassis, engines and information technology auto-related products. The lifestyle- and energy-related business manufactures and sells sewing machines, beds, gas heat pumps and more. The wellness-related business manufactures and sells: fiber laser, a processing laser that uses a femto-second pulse to enable processing that minimally causes heat damage to the peripheral area and micro-fabrication of transparent and ultra-hard materials, which are traditionally difficult to work with. This division is also developing a 3-wheel personal mobility vehicle that resembles a combination of an upright scooter and a Segway. Aisin Seiki comprises 205+ subsidiaries, approximately 80 in Japan and more than 125 overseas, including the Americas, Asia, Europe and Australia. Subsidiaries include: Aisin Europe Manufacturing (UK) Ltd.; Aisin Europe SA; Advics South Africa Pty. Ltd.; Aisin Asia Pte. Ltd.; AT India Auto Parts Pvt. Ltd.; Aisin Tianlin Body Parts Co., Ltd.; Aisin Al Brasil Industria Automotiva Ltda.; and Aisin Holdings of America, Inc. In April 2018, Aisin Seiki announced plans to restructure production lines at Tangshan Aisin Gear Co., Ltd., currently a manual transmission production factory in China, and begin manufacturing automatic transmissions there beginning in August 2019. The plant is to reach an automatic transmission production capacity of 12.5 million units in 2020.

FINANCIAL DATA:
Note: Data for latest year may not have been available at press time.

In U.S. $	2017	2016	2015	2014	2013	2012
Revenue	30,240,220,000	30,214,070,000	27,612,920,000	26,292,300,000	23,569,630,000	21,466,070,000
R&D Expense						
Operating Income	1,720,840,000	3,086,072,000	2,796,991,000	2,831,917,000	2,346,693,000	1,994,140,000
Operating Margin %	5.69%	10.21%	10.12%	10.77%	9.95%	9.28%
SGA Expense	2,610,388,000	445,183,600	407,909,500	394,242,600	367,691,500	357,825,600
Net Income	934,712,200	903,428,400	720,309,300	839,286,400	722,172,500	517,020,700
Operating Cash Flow	3,678,144,000	2,722,126,000	2,233,753,000	2,670,076,000	2,388,141,000	1,558,515,000
Capital Expenditure	2,623,757,000	2,484,787,000	2,240,851,000	1,820,328,000	1,859,055,000	1,352,180,000
EBITDA	3,832,812,000	3,564,608,000	3,272,117,000	3,211,729,000	2,826,942,000	2,538,392,000
Return on Assets %	3.23%	3.34%	2.80%	3.72%	3.58%	2.73%
Return on Equity %	8.57%	8.55%	7.14%	9.68%	9.76%	7.83%
Debt to Equity	0.31	0.28	0.27	0.30	0.31	0.41

CONTACT INFORMATION:
Phone: 81-566-24-8441 Fax:
Toll-Free:
Address: 2-1, Asahi-machi, Kariya, Kariya, 448-8650 Japan

STOCK TICKER/OTHER:
Stock Ticker: ASEKF   Exchange: PINX
Employees: 99,389   Fiscal Year Ends: 03/31
Parent Company:

SALARIES/BONUSES:
Top Exec. Salary: $ Bonus: $
Second Exec. Salary: $ Bonus: $

OTHER THOUGHTS:
Estimated Female Officers or Directors:
Hot Spot for Advancement for Women/Minorities:

Sales, profits and employees may be estimates. Financial information, benefits and other data can change quickly and may vary from those stated here.

Akzo Nobel NV

NAIC Code: 325510

www.akzonobel.com

TYPES OF BUSINESS:
Paint and Coating Manufacturing

GROWTH PLANS/SPECIAL FEATURES:
Akzo Nobel NV is a global paints and coatings company. Paints and coatings include aesthetics, anti-fouling/fouling control, coil coatings, concrete repair and protection, decorative paints, lacquers, fillers/wall treatments, haptics, linings, metal care, powder, specialty coatings, temperature resistant and wood finishes. Akzo Nobel's paints and coatings serve the following industries: aerospace, architecture, construction, automotive, chemical industry, domestic appliances, electronics, furniture, flooring, marine, mining, oil and gas, packaging, power, water and wood. Just a few of the company's numerous brands include Alba, Coral, Dulux, Expancel, Flexa, Interlux, Rexene, Trimetal and Zweihorn. In March 2018, a consortium led by private equity fund Carlye Group agreed to buy the specialty chemical business of the firm for $12.6 billion (€10.1 billion).

BRANDS/DIVISIONS/AFFILIATES:
Alba
Coral
Dulux
Expancel
Flexa
Rexene
Trimetal
Zweihorn

CONTACTS:
Note: Officers with more than one job title may be intentionally listed here more than once.

Thierry Vanlancker, CEO
Ruud Joosten, COO
Marten Booisma, Human Resources
Sven Dumoulin, General Counsel
Conrad Keijzer, Managing Dir.-Performance Coatings
Ruud Joosten, Managing Dir.-Decorative Paints
Werner Fuhrmann, Managing Dir.-Specialty Chemicals

FINANCIAL DATA:
Note: Data for latest year may not have been available at press time.

In U.S. $	2017	2016	2015	2014	2013	2012
Revenue	11,869,890,000	17,531,920,000	18,349,430,000	17,654,180,000	18,017,240,000	19,005,160,000
R&D Expense						
Operating Income	1,018,795,000	1,875,818,000	1,942,503,000	1,218,850,000	1,354,689,000	1,064,487,000
Operating Margin %	8.58%	10.69%	10.58%	6.90%	7.51%	5.60%
SGA Expense						
Net Income	1,027,440,000	1,197,856,000	1,208,970,000	674,257,200	894,070,000	-2,678,505,000
Operating Cash Flow	1,196,621,000	1,601,670,000	1,402,850,000	1,001,507,000	884,190,800	910,123,800
Capital Expenditure	756,995,800	782,928,700	803,922,000	726,123,100	822,445,600	1,020,030,000
EBITDA	1,832,597,000	2,719,257,000	2,787,177,000	1,877,053,000	2,022,772,000	-654,498,800
Return on Assets %	5.13%	6.03%	6.06%	3.37%	4.25%	-11.46%
Return on Equity %	13.39%	14.88%	15.95%	9.59%	11.59%	-26.93%
Debt to Equity	0.39	0.40	0.33	0.43	0.47	0.49

CONTACT INFORMATION:
Phone: 31-26-366-4433 Fax:
Toll-Free:
Address: Velperweg 76, Arnhem, 6824 BM Netherlands

STOCK TICKER/OTHER:
Stock Ticker: AKZOY   Exchange: PINX
Employees: 35,700   Fiscal Year Ends: 12/31
Parent Company:

SALARIES/BONUSES:
Top Exec. Salary: $ Bonus: $
Second Exec. Salary: $ Bonus: $

OTHER THOUGHTS:
Estimated Female Officers or Directors:
Hot Spot for Advancement for Women/Minorities:

Sales, profits and employees may be estimates. Financial information, benefits and other data can change quickly and may vary from those stated here.

Albany Molecular Research Inc

www.amriglobal.com

NAIC Code: 541711

TYPES OF BUSINESS:
Contract Drug Discovery & Development
Pharmaceutical
Biotechnology
Drug Discovery
Drug Production
Analytical Services

BRANDS/DIVISIONS/AFFILIATES:
Carlyl Group (The)
GTCR LLC

GROWTH PLANS/SPECIAL FEATURES:
Albany Molecular Research, Inc. (AMRI) is a global contract research and manufacturing organization that serves the pharmaceutical and biotechnology industries to improve patient outcomes and quality of life. With locations in North America, Europe and Asia, AMRI's provides scientific expertise and technology to offer discovery, development, analytical services, active pharmaceutical ingredient (API) manufacturing and drug products. The company's capabilities span the entire drug continuum, including target discovery, lead finding, lead optimization, candidate selection, pre-clinical, Phases 1-3, product approval, generic research and development and ANDA development and approval. AMRI has 27 locations across nine countries, and a client base of more than 1,500 across three continents. In August 2017, AMRI was taken private by The Carlyle Group and affiliates of GTCR, LLC.

CONTACTS:
Note: Officers with more than one job title may be intentionally listed here more than once.

William Marth, CEO
Stephen Leonard, Sr. VP-Operations
Felicia Ladin, CFO
Joseph D. Sangregorio, Sr. VP-Human Resources
Jimmy Wang, Sr. VP
Margalit Fine, Executive VP, Divisional
Lori Henderson, General Counsel
Milton Boyer, Senior VP, Divisional
Christopher Conway, Senior VP, Divisional
Steven Hagen, Senior VP

FINANCIAL DATA:
Note: Data for latest year may not have been available at press time.

In U.S. $	2017	2016	2015	2014	2013	2012
Revenue	600,000,000	570,449,984	402,356,000	276,571,008	246,575,008	226,686,000
R&D Expense						
Operating Income						
Operating Margin %						
SGA Expense						
Net Income		-70,171,000	-2,301,000	-3,278,000	12,680,000	-3,777,000
Operating Cash Flow						
Capital Expenditure						
EBITDA						
Return on Assets %						
Return on Equity %						
Debt to Equity						

CONTACT INFORMATION:
Phone: 518 512-2000   Fax: 518-512-2020
Toll-Free:
Address: 26 Corporate Cir., Albany, NY 12212 United States

STOCK TICKER/OTHER:
Stock Ticker: Private
Employees: 3,100
Parent Company:

Exchange:
Fiscal Year Ends: 12/31

SALARIES/BONUSES:
Top Exec. Salary: $ Bonus: $
Second Exec. Salary: $ Bonus: $

OTHER THOUGHTS:
Estimated Female Officers or Directors: 3
Hot Spot for Advancement for Women/Minorities: Y

Sales, profits and employees may be estimates. Financial information, benefits and other data can change quickly and may vary from those stated here.

Alcon Inc

NAIC Code: 325412

www.alcon.com

TYPES OF BUSINESS:
Eye Care Products
Ophthalmic Products & Equipment
Contact Lens Care Products
Surgical Instruments

BRANDS/DIVISIONS/AFFILIATES:
Novartis AG
Pataday
AcrySof
Systane
Opti-Free

CONTACTS:
Note: Officers with more than one job title may be intentionally listed here more than once.

Mike Ball, CEO
David Endicott, COO
David Murray, CFO
Kim Adler, VP-Global Communications
Merrick McCracken, Sr. VP-Human Resources
Sabri Markabi, Chief Medical Officer
Ed McGough, Sr. VP-Tech. Oper.
Ed McGough, Sr. VP-Global Mfg.
Christina Ackerman, General Counsel
Bettina Maunz, Head-Comm.
Robert Karsunky, Sr. VP-Finance
Sergio Duplan, Pres., Latin America & Caribbean
Stuart Raetzman, Pres., Europe, Middle East & Africa
Robert Warner, Pres., U.S. & Canada
Roy Acosta, Pres., Asia
Sue Whitfill, Head-Global Quality

GROWTH PLANS/SPECIAL FEATURES:

Alcon, Inc., a subsidiary of Novartis AG, is a leading eye care products company. Its portfolio spans three key ophthalmic categories: pharmaceutical, surgical and consumer eye care products. The divisions develop, manufacture and market ophthalmic pharmaceuticals, surgical equipment and devices, contact lens care products and other consumer eye care products that treat diseases and conditions of the eye. The company's products include prescription and over-the-counter drugs, contact lens solutions, surgical instruments, intraocular lenses and office systems for ophthalmologists. Its brand names include Pataday solution for eye allergies, AcrySof intraocular lenses, Systane lubricant drops for dry eyes and the Opti-Free system for contact lens care. The firm also has research and development laboratories in Germany, the U.S., Switzerland and Spain.

Alcon offers its employees 401(k) and retirement plans; medical, dental, vision, life, disability and AD&D insurance; paid time off; a wellness program, including onsite or discounted fitness centers, flu shots and Weight Watchers discounts; and an employ

FINANCIAL DATA:
Note: Data for latest year may not have been available at press time.

In U.S. $	2017	2016	2015	2014	2013	2012
Revenue	13,000,000,000	11,000,000,000	10,800,000,000	10,827,000,000	10,496,000,000	10,200,000,000
R&D Expense						
Operating Income						
Operating Margin %						
SGA Expense						
Net Income			1,117,900,000	1,597,000,000	1,232,000,000	
Operating Cash Flow						
Capital Expenditure						
EBITDA						
Return on Assets %						
Return on Equity %						
Debt to Equity						

CONTACT INFORMATION:
Phone: 800-757-9785 Fax:
Toll-Free: 817-568-6725
Address: 6201 S. Freeway, Fort Worth, TX 76134-2001 United States

SALARIES/BONUSES:
Top Exec. Salary: $ Bonus: $
Second Exec. Salary: $ Bonus: $

STOCK TICKER/OTHER:
Stock Ticker: Subsidiary   Exchange:
Employees: 19,000   Fiscal Year Ends: 12/31
Parent Company: Novartis AG

OTHER THOUGHTS:
Estimated Female Officers or Directors: 3
Hot Spot for Advancement for Women/Minorities: Y

Sales, profits and employees may be estimates. Financial information, benefits and other data can change quickly and may vary from those stated here.

ALFA SAB de CV

NAIC Code: 325110

www.alfa.com.mx

TYPES OF BUSINESS:
Petrochemicals
Synthetic Fibers
Frozen Food
Aluminum Automobile Components
Telecommunications Services
Oil & Natural Gas Exploration & Production

BRANDS/DIVISIONS/AFFILIATES:
Sigma
Nemak
Alpek
Newpek
Alestra
Axtel
Corpus Christi Polymers LLC

CONTACTS:
Note: Officers with more than one job title may be intentionally listed here more than once.

Alvaro Fernandez Garza, Pres.
Paulino Rodriguez Mendivil, Sr. VP-Human Capital
Carlos Jimenez, Sr. VP-Legal & Corp. Affairs
Alejandro M. Elizondo Barragan, Sr. VP-Bus. Dev.
Ochoa Reyes, Dir.-Investor Rels.
Armando Garza Sada, Chmn.

GROWTH PLANS/SPECIAL FEATURES:

ALFA SAB de CV, through its subsidiaries, operates petrochemical, food processing, automotive and telecommunication businesses. Based in Monterrey, Mexico, the company operates more than 130 plants in Mexico and 27 other countries across the Americas, Europe and Asia. Primary subsidiaries include the following. Sigma, a producer of cooked and cured meats such as ham, sausages and bacon; dairy products such as cheese, yogurt, cream and butter; and a variety of refrigerated and frozen foods. Sigma comprises 70 plants in 14 countries. Nemak provides innovative light-weighting solutions for the automotive industry. The firm specializes in the development and manufacturing of aluminum heads and blocks for gas and diesel engines; transmission cases; and structural components and parts for electric vehicles. Nemak comprises 38 plants located in 16 countries. Alpek is a producer of polyester (PTA, PET and fibers), as well as petrochemicals such as polypropylene, expandable polystyrene, caprolactam and ammonium sulfate. Alpek has 23 plants located in six countries. Axtel provides information technology and communication services for the enterprise, government and residential markets through its Alestra and Axtel brands. Alpek's main services include data centers, data security, networks management, consultancy, systems integration, cloud, internet, Pay-TV and voice. Last, Newpek, is engaged in the hydrocarbons industry within Mexico and the U.S., and also provides oil and gas services to these related markets. ALFA owns 51% of the combined entity's stock. In early-2018, ALFA agreed to sell approximately 1,900 acres of its Eagle Ford Shale (Texas) acreage to Sundance Energy, Inc. for $19 million. That March, ALFA formed a joint venture with Alpek, Indorama Ventures Holdings LP and Far Eastern Investment (Holding) Limited called Corpus Christi Polymers, LLC, to acquire the integrated PTA-PET plant currently under construction in Corpus Christi, Texas.

FINANCIAL DATA:
Note: Data for latest year may not have been available at press time.

In U.S. $	2017	2016	2015	2014	2013	2012
Revenue	17,616,190,000	16,293,700,000	14,325,810,000	12,713,310,000	11,284,050,000	11,101,640,000
R&D Expense						
Operating Income	1,013,732,000	1,464,970,000	1,238,297,000	948,342,800	900,701,100	904,084,200
Operating Margin %	5.75%	8.99%	8.64%	7.45%	7.98%	8.14%
SGA Expense	2,374,323,000	2,270,942,000	1,755,979,000	1,354,490,000	1,127,596,000	1,065,645,000
Net Income	-113,752,300	128,948,900	209,535,000	-112,975,900	328,667,100	498,824,200
Operating Cash Flow	1,908,055,000	2,068,617,000	1,691,920,000	1,328,479,000	1,095,816,000	1,143,624,000
Capital Expenditure	1,174,350,000	1,445,891,000	964,704,100	800,315,100	676,524,100	484,293,200
EBITDA	1,506,123,000	1,819,316,000	1,464,915,000	666,762,800	1,192,431,000	1,423,540,000
Return on Assets %	-.57%	.75%	1.51%	-1.02%	3.71%	6.15%
Return on Equity %	-2.82%	3.37%	6.42%	-3.64%	10.92%	20.48%
Debt to Equity	2.05	1.79	1.63	1.47	0.83	0.90

CONTACT INFORMATION:
Phone: 81-8748-1111 Fax: 81-8748-2552
Toll-Free:
Address: Ave. Gomez Morin 1111, Sur Colonia Carrizalejo, San Pedro Garza García, NL 666254 Mexico

STOCK TICKER/OTHER:
Stock Ticker: ALFA A
Employees: 45,443
Parent Company:

Exchange: MEX
Fiscal Year Ends: 12/31

SALARIES/BONUSES:
Top Exec. Salary: $ Bonus: $
Second Exec. Salary: $ Bonus: $

OTHER THOUGHTS:
Estimated Female Officers or Directors:
Hot Spot for Advancement for Women/Minorities:

Sales, profits and employees may be estimates. Financial information, benefits and other data can change quickly and may vary from those stated here.

Plunkett Research, Ltd.

Allergan plc
NAIC Code: 325412

www.allergan.com

TYPES OF BUSINESS:
Pharmaceutical Development
Eye Care Supplies
Dermatological Products
Neuromodulator Products
Obesity Intervention Products
Urologic Products
Medical Aesthetics

BRANDS/DIVISIONS/AFFILIATES:
Alloderm
Botox
Estrace
Zenpep
Keller Medical Inc
Zeltiq Aesthetics Inc
Coolsculpting
LifeCell Corporation

CONTACTS: Note: Officers with more than one job title may be intentionally listed here more than once.
Brenton Saunders, CEO
Maria Hilado, CFO
Paul Bisaro, Chairman of the Board
James DArecca, Chief Accounting Officer
Robert Stewart, COO
William Meury, Executive VP, Divisional
Charles Mayr, Other Executive Officer
Patrick Eagan, Other Executive Officer
Karen Ling, Other Executive Officer
Robert Bailey, Other Executive Officer

GROWTH PLANS/SPECIAL FEATURES:
Allergan plc is a global pharmaceutical company focused on developing, manufacturing and commercializing branded pharmaceutical, device, biologic, surgical and regenerative medicine products. The firm's portfolio features seven franchises in therapeutic categories: dermatology & medical aesthetics, central nervous system, eye care, women's health, urology, gastroenterology and anti-infective. Because of the differences between the types of products Allergan operates its business in three segments: U.S. specialized therapeutics, U.S. general medicine and international. The U.S. specialized therapeutics segment includes sales and expenses relating to branded products within the U.S., including medical aesthetics, medical dermatology, eye care and neuroscience and urology therapeutic products. The U.S. general medicine segment includes sales and expenses relating to branded products within the U.S. that do not fall into the U.S. specialized category, including central nervous system, gastrointestinal, women's health, anti-infectives and diversified brands. The international segment includes sales and expenses relating to products sold outside the U.S. Branded products include: Alloderm, a regenerative medicine; Botox cosmetics, for facial aesthetics; Estrace cream, a hormone cream for women's health; Lumigan/Ganfort, for eye care; Namenda XR, for the central nervous system; and Zenpep, for gastrointestinal purposes. The majority of Allergan's branded drug delivery research and development activities take place in Irvine, California. During 2017, the firm acquired: Keller Medical, Inc., a medical device company and developer of the Keller Funnel; Zeltiq Aesthetics, Inc., which develops and commercializes products utilizing its proprietary controlled-cooling technology platform Coolsculpting; and LifeCell Corporation, a regenerative medicine company.

U.S. employees of the firm receive medical, long-term care, dental, vision and prescription drug coverage; life, AD&D, business travel accident and disability insurance; group legal services; tuition reimbursement; flexible spending accounts; domestic par

FINANCIAL DATA: Note: Data for latest year may not have been available at press time.

In U.S. $	2017	2016	2015	2014	2013	2012
Revenue	15,940,700,000	14,570,600,000	15,071,000,000	13,062,300,000	8,677,600,000	5,914,900,000
R&D Expense	2,100,100,000	2,575,700,000	2,358,500,000	1,085,900,000	616,900,000	401,800,000
Operating Income	-541,200,000	-1,076,600,000	-2,230,900,000	-518,100,000	479,500,000	470,300,000
Operating Margin %	-3.39%	-7.38%	-14.80%	-3.96%	5.52%	7.95%
SGA Expense	5,016,700,000	4,740,300,000	4,679,600,000	3,593,200,000	2,047,800,000	1,171,300,000
Net Income	-4,125,500,000	14,973,400,000	3,915,200,000	-1,630,500,000	-750,400,000	97,300,000
Operating Cash Flow	5,873,400,000	1,425,300,000	4,530,000,000	2,243,000,000	1,213,500,000	665,800,000
Capital Expenditure	964,200,000	333,400,000	609,600,000	274,700,000	307,900,000	146,500,000
EBITDA	-1,922,200,000	5,094,600,000	2,758,400,000	1,528,100,000	646,100,000	940,400,000
Return on Assets %	-3.56%	11.09%	3.91%	-4.33%	-4.07%	.93%
Return on Equity %	-6.28%	20.56%	7.36%	-8.61%	-11.22%	2.63%
Debt to Equity	0.37	0.42	0.56	0.52	0.89	1.63

CONTACT INFORMATION:
Phone: 441 295 2244 Fax: 714 246-4971
Toll-Free: 800-347-4500
Address: Clonshaugh Business & Tech Park, Coolock, Dublin, D17 E400 Ireland

STOCK TICKER/OTHER:
Stock Ticker: AGN
Employees: 16,700
Parent Company:

Exchange: NYS
Fiscal Year Ends: 12/31

SALARIES/BONUSES:
Top Exec. Salary: $1,232,822   Bonus: $
Second Exec. Salary: $873,973   Bonus: $

OTHER THOUGHTS:
Estimated Female Officers or Directors: 2
Hot Spot for Advancement for Women/Minorities: Y

Sales, profits and employees may be estimates. Financial information, benefits and other data can change quickly and may vary from those stated here.

Alphabet Inc

NAIC Code: 519130

www.google.com

TYPES OF BUSINESS:
Search Engine-Internet
Paid Search Listing Advertising Services
Online Software and Productivity Tools
Online Video and Photo Services
Travel Booking
Analytical Tools
Venture Capital
Online Maps

BRANDS/DIVISIONS/AFFILIATES:
Google LLC
Access
Calico
CapitalG
GV
Nest
Verily
Waymo

CONTACTS:
Note: Officers with more than one job title may be intentionally listed here more than once.

Sundar Pichai, CEO, Subsidiary
Larry Page, CEO
Ruth Porat, CFO
John Hennessy, Chairman of the Board
Sergey Brin, Director
Diane Greene, Director
David Drummond, Other Executive Officer
James Campbell, Vice President

GROWTH PLANS/SPECIAL FEATURES:

Alphabet, Inc. owns a collection of businesses, the largest of which is Google, LLC, an information company offering a leading online search and advertising platform. Alphabet states that its primary job is to make the internet available to as many people as possible, and does this by tailoring hardware and software experiences that suit the needs of emerging markets, mainly through Android and Chrome. Google's core products include Search, Android, Maps, Chrome, YouTube, GooglePlay and Gmail, each of which have more than 1 billion monthly active users. Within Google, Alphabet's investments in machine learning are what enable the firm to continually innovate and build Google products, making them smarter and more useful over time. Machine learning also dramatically improves the energy efficiency of the company's data centers. Alphabet's other businesses include Access, Calico, CapitalG, GV, Nest, Verily, Waymo and X, all of which are not primarily engaged in the company's main internet offerings. Across these businesses, machine learning has the capability of doing things like helping self-driving cars better detect and respond to others on the road, or aiding clinicians in detecting diabetic retinopathy. Therefore, these firms utilize technology to try and solve big problems across many industries. They are early-stage businesses with the goal to become thriving ones in the medium- to long-term. In September 2017, Alphabet created an intermediate holding company, XXVI Holdings, Inc., to complete its corporate reorganization structure. The changes also included a conversion from Google, Inc. to Google, LLC, and placing all the other companies under Alphabet, not Google. Each of the companies became subsidiaries of Alphabet, and on equal footing with Google.

FINANCIAL DATA:
Note: Data for latest year may not have been available at press time.

In U.S. $	2017	2016	2015	2014	2013	2012
Revenue	110,855,000,000	90,272,000,000	74,989,000,000	66,001,000,000	59,825,000,000	50,175,000,000
R&D Expense	16,625,000,000	13,948,000,000	12,282,000,000	9,831,999,000	7,952,000,000	6,793,000,000
Operating Income	28,882,000,000	23,716,000,000	19,360,000,000	16,496,000,000	13,966,000,000	12,760,000,000
Operating Margin %	26.05%	26.27%	25.81%	24.99%	23.34%	25.43%
SGA Expense	19,765,000,000	17,470,000,000	15,183,000,000	13,982,000,000	12,049,000,000	9,988,000,000
Net Income	12,662,000,000	19,478,000,000	16,348,000,000	14,444,000,000	12,920,000,000	10,737,000,000
Operating Cash Flow	37,091,000,000	36,036,000,000	26,024,000,000	22,376,000,000	18,659,000,000	16,619,000,000
Capital Expenditure	13,184,000,000	10,212,000,000	9,915,000,000	10,959,000,000	7,358,000,000	3,273,000,000
EBITDA	34,217,000,000	30,418,000,000	24,818,000,000	22,339,000,000	18,518,000,000	16,432,000,000
Return on Assets %	6.94%	12.36%	11.36%	11.93%	12.62%	12.90%
Return on Equity %	8.68%	15.01%	14.07%	15.06%	16.24%	16.53%
Debt to Equity	0.02	0.02	0.01	0.03	0.02	0.04

CONTACT INFORMATION:
Phone: 650 253-0000   Fax: 650 253-0001
Toll-Free:
Address: 1600 Amphitheatre Pkwy., Mountain View, CA 94043 United States

STOCK TICKER/OTHER:
Stock Ticker: GOOG
Employees: 72,053
Parent Company:

Exchange: NAS
Fiscal Year Ends: 12/31

SALARIES/BONUSES:
Top Exec. Salary: $1,250,000   Bonus: $
Second Exec. Salary: $650,000   Bonus: $

OTHER THOUGHTS:
Estimated Female Officers or Directors: 3
Hot Spot for Advancement for Women/Minorities: Y

Sales, profits and employees may be estimates. Financial information, benefits and other data can change quickly and may vary from those stated here.

Alps Electric Co Ltd

NAIC Code: 335313

www.alps.com

TYPES OF BUSINESS:
Electronic Components Manufacturing
Automotive Parts Manufacturing

BRANDS/DIVISIONS/AFFILIATES:
Alpine Electronics Inc
Alps Logistics Co Ltd
GlidePoint

CONTACTS:
Note: Officers with more than one job title may be intentionally listed here more than once.

Toshihiro Kuriyama, Pres.
Nobuhiko Komeya, Sr. Managing Dir.
Shuji Takamura, Managing Dir.
Takashi Kimoto, Managing Dir.
Masataka Kataoka, Chmn.

GROWTH PLANS/SPECIAL FEATURES:

Alps Electric Co., Ltd. is primarily engaged in the manufacture and sale of more than 40,000 electronic components used in a variety of applications. The company operates in four divisions: automotive, home & mobile, healthcare and environment & energy. The automotive division provides custom products and modules such as control panels and steering modules for specific vehicle models, as well as components compatible for any vehicle. The home & mobile division provides switches, potentiometers, sensors and other components through to multi-input devices like touch panels and GlidePoint trackpad technology to home, mobile and personal computer (PC) markets. The healthcare division offers light, temperature, humidity and various other types of sensors for the detection of environmental changes to assist health maintenance. For example, the light, temperature and humidity products help prevent heat disorders; and switches, card connectors, switches and other components support the evolution of healthcare equipment. Last, the environment & energy division serves environment and energy markets with sensors that enable power usage visualization, as well as sensors for measuring parameters such as temperature, illuminance and carbon dioxide levels in indoor and outdoor environments. These can be combined with communication modules essential for xEMS to build smart networks. Alps Electric leads a group of 100 companies, including: Alpine Electronics, Inc., which develops, manufactures and sells audio products for automotive, information and communication products; and Alps Logistics Co., Ltd., a provider of global integrated logistics services specializing in electronic components.

FINANCIAL DATA:
Note: Data for latest year may not have been available at press time.

In U.S. $	2017	2016	2015	2014	2013	2012
Revenue	7,017,533,000	7,211,087,000	6,974,232,000	6,375,648,000	5,090,582,000	4,904,975,000
R&D Expense						
Operating Income	413,396,700	487,497,700	498,742,300	265,781,600	63,825,230	141,336,000
Operating Margin %	5.89%	6.76%	7.15%	4.16%	1.25%	2.88%
SGA Expense						
Net Income	325,321,400	363,648,200	323,635,200	133,324,000	-65,902,740	38,895,100
Operating Cash Flow	387,581,500	502,683,100	606,586,600	537,572,200	231,088,100	218,241,100
Capital Expenditure	442,342,100	332,923,400	284,702,800	226,616,400	308,859,700	287,991,400
EBITDA	773,951,900	928,107,000	776,048,100	530,259,000	258,114,400	344,876,100
Return on Assets %	5.99%	6.88%	6.41%	2.96%	-1.58%	.96%
Return on Equity %	14.44%	19.12%	21.91%	11.25%	-6.09%	3.61%
Debt to Equity	0.10	0.08	0.25	0.62	0.56	0.22

CONTACT INFORMATION:
Phone: 81-33726-1211 Fax: 81-33728-1741
Toll-Free:
Address: 1-7 Yukigaya Otsuka-cho, Ota-Ku, Tokyo, 145-8501 Japan

STOCK TICKER/OTHER:
Stock Ticker: APELY   Exchange: PINX
Employees: 5,588   Fiscal Year Ends: 03/31
Parent Company:

SALARIES/BONUSES:
Top Exec. Salary: $ Bonus: $
Second Exec. Salary: $ Bonus: $

OTHER THOUGHTS:
Estimated Female Officers or Directors:
Hot Spot for Advancement for Women/Minorities:

Sales, profits and employees may be estimates. Financial information, benefits and other data can change quickly and may vary from those stated here.

Alstom SA

NAIC Code: 333611

www.alstom.com

TYPES OF BUSINESS:
Equipment-Electric Power Distribution
Energy & Transport Infrastructure
Power Plant Machinery
Rail Transport Services
Rail Transport Manufacturing
Technical Consulting & Power Plant Refurbishment

BRANDS/DIVISIONS/AFFILIATES:
Nomad Holdings
EasyMile
EZ10
Aptis

CONTACTS:
Note: Officers with more than one job title may be intentionally listed here more than once.

Henri Poupart-Lafarge, CEO
Thierry Best, COO
Jean-Baptiste Eymeoud, Sr. VP-Finance
Keith Carr, Group General Counsel
Jerome Pecresse, Exec. VP
Philippe Cochet, Exec. VP
Gregoire Poux-Guillaume, Exec. VP

GROWTH PLANS/SPECIAL FEATURES:

Alstom SA develops and markets a complete range of systems, equipment and services in the railway sector. The company manages solutions such as high-speed trains, metros and tramways; offers customized services such as maintenance and modernization; and provides solutions for infrastructure and signaling. Components for all types of railway vehicles include bogies, motors, traction systems, switchgear, auxiliary converters, traction transformers, cariboni feeding systems and dispen dampers. Its solutions, services and infrastructure are offered separately, bundled or fully-integrated. Alstom is present in more than 60 countries, and is headquartered in France. In January 2017, the firm acquired Nomad Holdings, a provider of passenger and fleet digital connectivity solutions to the railway sector. In that same month, Alstom invested over $15 million in EasyMile, a start-up company developing the EZ10 electric driverless shuttle, an electric vehicle that operates from a transport hub within a confined precinct and can transport up to 12 passengers. In March 2017, the company, in conjunction with NTL, launched Aptis, a fully electric public transport bus that offers all the advantages of a tram.

FINANCIAL DATA: Note: Data for latest year may not have been available at press time.

In U.S. $	2017	2016	2015	2014	2013	2012
Revenue	9,022,204,000	8,497,370,000	7,610,709,000	25,030,260,000	25,030,260,000	24,616,560,000
R&D Expense	216,108,100	167,946,800	138,309,200	905,184,100	910,123,800	842,204,100
Operating Income	519,894,300	451,974,600	392,699,300	1,758,502,000	1,806,664,000	1,320,112,000
Operating Margin %	5.76%	5.31%	5.15%	7.02%	7.21%	5.36%
SGA Expense	665,612,900	661,908,200	612,512,100	2,345,082,000	2,154,906,000	2,101,805,000
Net Income	356,887,100	3,705,945,000	-887,895,500	686,606,300	990,392,400	903,949,200
Operating Cash Flow	495,196,200	-2,664,922,000	376,645,500	789,103,200	1,344,810,000	266,739,100
Capital Expenditure	271,678,700	634,740,300	933,586,900	1,042,258,000	911,358,700	1,003,976,000
EBITDA	601,398,000	422,336,900	-407,518,100	1,835,066,000	2,100,570,000	2,158,611,000
Return on Assets %	2.06%	12.80%	-2.25%	1.79%	2.55%	2.41%
Return on Equity %	8.32%	80.96%	-15.66%	11.05%	17.17%	17.26%
Debt to Equity	0.43	0.55	0.77	0.87	0.92	1.00

CONTACT INFORMATION:
Phone: 33 14149200   Fax: 33 14149248
Toll-Free:
Address: 3 Ave. Andre Malraux, Cedex, 75795 France

STOCK TICKER/OTHER:
Stock Ticker: ALSMY   Exchange: PINX
Employees: 32,779   Fiscal Year Ends: 03/31
Parent Company:

SALARIES/BONUSES:
Top Exec. Salary: $ Bonus: $
Second Exec. Salary: $ Bonus: $

OTHER THOUGHTS:
Estimated Female Officers or Directors: 4
Hot Spot for Advancement for Women/Minorities: Y

Sales, profits and employees may be estimates. Financial information, benefits and other data can change quickly and may vary from those stated here.

Altana AG

NAIC Code: 325510

www.altana.com

TYPES OF BUSINESS:
Specialty Chemical Manufacturing
Imaging Products
Electrical Insulation
Coatings
Inks

BRANDS/DIVISIONS/AFFILIATES:
BYK Additives & Instruments
ECKART Effect Pigments
ELANTAS Electrical Insulation
ACTEGA Coatings & Sealants
BYK-Chemie
BYK-Gardner
Melior Innovations Inc

CONTACTS: *Note: Officers with more than one job title may be intentionally listed here more than once.*

Martin Babilas, CEO
Stefan Genten, CFO
Roland Peter, Pres., Coatings & Sealants
Christoph Schlunken, Pres., Additives & Instruments Div.
Wolfgang Schutt, Pres., Effect Pigments Div.
Guido Forstbach, Pres., Electrical Insulation
Klaus-Jurgen Schmieder, Chmn.

GROWTH PLANS/SPECIAL FEATURES:

Altana AG is an international chemicals company that develops, manufactures and markets products for a range of targeted, highly specialized applications. The company serves customers in the coatings, paint, plastics, printing, cosmetics, electrical and electronics industries. Altana has 48 operational companies and 50 service and research labs all over the world. The firm operates through four divisions: BYK Additives & Instruments, ECKART Effect Pigments, ELANTAS Electrical Insulation and ACTEGA Coatings & Sealants. BYK Additives & Instruments offers a range of chemical additives, produced by subsidiary BYK-Chemie, that help to improve and regulate the quality and processability of coatings and plastics. This division also offers testing and measuring equipment, produced by subsidiary BYK-Gardner, allowing manufacturers to predetermine the color, gloss and other physical properties of paints and plastics products. ECKART Effect Pigments develops and produces metallic effect and pearlescent pigments as well as gold-bronze and zinc pigments, used to produce certain optical effects in paints, inks, cosmetics and coatings. ELANTAS Electrical Insulation produces insulating materials used in electrical and electronics applications, including electric motors, household appliances, cars, generators, transformers, capacitors, televisions, computers, wind mills, circuit boards and sensors. ACTEGA Coatings & Sealants develops and produces specialty coatings, sealants, adhesives and printing inks used primarily by the graphic arts and packaging industries. In addition, due to Altana's investment in Melior Innovations, Inc., a technology company in Houston, Texas, the partnership develops a wide range of surface products. In November 2017, Altana announced plans to invest $50 million to expand BYK's additives and measuring instruments capabilities at its Gonzales, Texas facility.

FINANCIAL DATA: *Note: Data for latest year may not have been available at press time.*

In U.S. $	2017	2016	2015	2014	2013	2012
Revenue	2,691,550,000	2,553,570,000	2,349,043,510	2,240,022,625	2,447,310,000	2,253,120,000
R&D Expense						
Operating Income						
Operating Margin %						
SGA Expense						
Net Income	281,095,000	221,343,000	180,230,600	344,645,896	210,266,100	208,829,000
Operating Cash Flow						
Capital Expenditure						
EBITDA						
Return on Assets %						
Return on Equity %						
Debt to Equity						

CONTACT INFORMATION:
Phone: 49-281-670-8
Fax: 49-281-670-10999
Toll-Free:
Address: Abelstrasse 43, Wesel, 46483 Germany

STOCK TICKER/OTHER:
Stock Ticker: ALT
Employees: 6,115
Parent Company:
Exchange: Frankfurt
Fiscal Year Ends: 12/31

SALARIES/BONUSES:
Top Exec. Salary: $
Bonus: $
Second Exec. Salary: $
Bonus: $

OTHER THOUGHTS:
Estimated Female Officers or Directors: 3
Hot Spot for Advancement for Women/Minorities: Y

Sales, profits and employees may be estimates. Financial information, benefits and other data can change quickly and may vary from those stated here.

Amazon Lab126 Inc

www.lab126.com

NAIC Code: 541712

TYPES OF BUSINESS:
Research and Development in the Physical, Engineering and Life Sciences (except Biotechnology)

BRANDS/DIVISIONS/AFFILIATES:
Amazon.com Inc
Kindle
Kindle Touch
Kindle Voyage
Kindle Oasis
Amazon Dash
Amazon Fire TV
Amazon Echo

CONTACTS: *Note: Officers with more than one job title may be intentionally listed here more than once.*
Gregg Zehr, Pres.

GROWTH PLANS/SPECIAL FEATURES:
Amazon Lab126, Inc., a subsidiary of Amazon.com, Inc., operates as a lab focusing on research, innovation and development of consumer electronic products. The Lab126 name originated from the arrow in the Amazon logo, which draws a line from A to Z; the 1 stands for A and the 26 stands for Z. Since the launch of Amazon's first e-reader, the Kindle, in 2007, the firm has expanded its product range and added Kindle Keyboard, Kindle Touch, Kindle Paperwhite e-readers, Kindle Fire tablets, Kindle Voyage and Kindle Oasis to its portfolio. In addition, the company also offers Amazon Fire TV, a streaming media player which can be connected to a HDTV and supports services such as Hulu, Netflix, Pandora, YouTube and Spotify; and Amazon Echo, which is an audio streaming device offering immersive, omni-directional audio and powered by Alexa app (a cloud-based service). Through the app, the device interacts with a user's voice, which it can recognize across the room and can play music, answer questions, read audiobooks, news, report traffic and weather and controls lights and other switches. The device is compatible with WeMo, Wink, Samsung and other smart home devices. The Amazon Dash is a handheld, push-button consumer goods ordering device. The customer can either scan the barcode of the product or voice request it into their Amazon shopping cart. Additionally, the one-click button allows shoppers to reorder their favorite, frequently used products. Lab126 is headquartered in Sunnyvale, California.

FINANCIAL DATA: *Note: Data for latest year may not have been available at press time.*

In U.S. $	2017	2016	2015	2014	2013	2012
Revenue						
R&D Expense						
Operating Income						
Operating Margin %						
SGA Expense						
Net Income						
Operating Cash Flow						
Capital Expenditure						
EBITDA						
Return on Assets %						
Return on Equity %						
Debt to Equity						

CONTACT INFORMATION:
Phone: 650-456-1100 Fax:
Toll-Free:
Address: 1100 Enterprise Way, Sunnyvale, CA 94089 United States

SALARIES/BONUSES:
Top Exec. Salary: $ Bonus: $
Second Exec. Salary: $ Bonus: $

STOCK TICKER/OTHER:
Stock Ticker: Subsidiary   Exchange:
Employees: 3,000   Fiscal Year Ends:
Parent Company: Amazon.com Inc

OTHER THOUGHTS:
Estimated Female Officers or Directors:
Hot Spot for Advancement for Women/Minorities:

Sales, profits and employees may be estimates. Financial information, benefits and other data can change quickly and may vary from those stated here.

Ambitech Engineering Corporation

NAIC Code: 541330

ambitech.com

TYPES OF BUSINESS:
Engineering Services

BRANDS/DIVISIONS/AFFILIATES:
Zachry Holdings Inc

CONTACTS:
Note: Officers with more than one job title may be intentionally listed here more than once.

Allan R. Koenig, CEO
G. Richard Hutter, Pres.
Christopher J. Hunt, VP-Finance

GROWTH PLANS/SPECIAL FEATURES:
Ambitech Engineering Corporation provides full-service engineering design services with deep expertise in front-end loading/front-end engineering (FEL/FEED) design work. For clients wanting the option of an integrated services delivery model, Ambitech can provide a way to transition from FEED into a fully-integrated, construction-led EPC model (engineering, procurement and construction). The firm's FEL stages include: project identification, scope development, project definition, project execution, startup and operation. Ambitech has been in business for more than 35 years, with expertise in the following industries: energy, chemical, food/beverage, pharmaceuticals, biotechnology and manufacturing. The firm is headquartered in Chicago, with additional offices in Oklahoma, Texas, Missouri, Indiana, Illinois and Louisiana in the U.S., as well as an office in the Philippines. Ambitech operates as a subsidiary of Zachry Holdings, Inc.

FINANCIAL DATA:
Note: Data for latest year may not have been available at press time.

In U.S. $	2017	2016	2015	2014	2013	2012
Revenue						
R&D Expense						
Operating Income						
Operating Margin %						
SGA Expense						
Net Income						
Operating Cash Flow						
Capital Expenditure						
EBITDA						
Return on Assets %						
Return on Equity %						
Debt to Equity						

CONTACT INFORMATION:
Phone: 630-963-5800
Fax: 630-963-8099
Toll-Free: 855-378-1173
Address: 1411 Opus Place, Ste. 200, Downers Grove, IL 60515 United States

STOCK TICKER/OTHER:
Stock Ticker: Private
Employees: 500
Parent Company: Zachry Holdings Inc

Exchange:
Fiscal Year Ends:

SALARIES/BONUSES:
Top Exec. Salary: $
Bonus: $
Second Exec. Salary: $
Bonus: $

OTHER THOUGHTS:
Estimated Female Officers or Directors:
Hot Spot for Advancement for Women/Minorities:

Sales, profits and employees may be estimates. Financial information, benefits and other data can change quickly and may vary from those stated here.

Amdocs Limited

www.amdocs.com

NAIC Code: 0

TYPES OF BUSINESS:
Software-Customer Services & Business Operations
Customer Relationship Management Software
Billing Management Software
Directory Publishing Systems
Technical & Support Services
Managed Services

BRANDS/DIVISIONS/AFFILIATES:
Amdocs CES
Amdocs CES 10
Amdocs CES 10.2
Amdocs Optima

CONTACTS:
Note: Officers with more than one job title may be intentionally listed here more than once.
Eli Gelman, CEO
Tamar Dagim, CFO, Subsidiary
Robert Minicucci, Chairman of the Board
Matthew Smith, Other Corporate Officer
Rajat Raheja, President, Subsidiary
Shuky Sheffer, Senior VP, Subsidiary

GROWTH PLANS/SPECIAL FEATURES:

Amdocs Limited provides software products and services primarily to communications, media and entertainment industry service providers worldwide. The firm offers an integrated approach to customer management to clients based on its proprietary Amdocs CES (customer experience solutions) software portfolio. Amdocs CES is an open, service-orientated architecture intended to provide the functionality, scalability, modularity and adaptability required by service providers. To this end, the firm's solutions consist of billing and customer engagement and relationship management systems, revenue management, network planning and resource management and directory sales and publishing systems for publishers of both traditional and internet-based directories as well as system implementation, integration, support and maintenance services. Amdocs CES 10 is a cloud-enabled portfolio that spans BSS/OSS (business support systems/operational support systems) and network solutions in order to deliver contextualized and personalized customer experiences across all channels. Amdocs CES 10.2 empowers business and product marketers to define new services and rapidly launch new customer offers. Amdocs Optima is a converged, multi-tenant, smart digital commerce, billing and customer management platform enabling swift and secure monetization of products and services. The firm's network functions virtualization offerings enable service lifecycle management in a hybrid physical and virtual network; and its Internet of Things (IoT) suite enables service providers to offer intuitive, flexible and innovative IoT products and services. Amdocs' solutions are designed to support a variety of lines of business, including wireline, cable and satellite, as well as a range of communications services such as video, data, internet protocol, electronic and mobile commerce. The company focuses on expanding its solutions and services to providers in emerging markets, including Latin America, India and Southeast Asia.

FINANCIAL DATA:
Note: Data for latest year may not have been available at press time.

In U.S. $	2017	2016	2015	2014	2013	2012
Revenue	3,867,155,000	3,718,229,000	3,643,538,000	3,563,637,000	3,345,854,000	3,246,903,000
R&D Expense	259,097,000	252,292,000	254,944,000	257,896,000	240,266,000	242,063,000
Operating Income	517,333,000	483,141,000	528,948,000	495,648,000	481,552,000	442,472,000
Operating Margin %	13.37%	12.99%	14.51%	13.90%	14.39%	13.62%
SGA Expense	472,778,000	464,883,000	440,085,000	445,134,000	418,574,000	424,671,000
Net Income	436,826,000	409,331,000	446,163,000	422,122,000	412,439,000	391,371,000
Operating Cash Flow	636,112,000	620,234,000	772,622,000	709,258,000	670,547,000	514,069,000
Capital Expenditure	133,392,000	130,086,000	120,503,000	111,569,000	106,724,000	122,053,000
EBITDA	729,397,000	698,156,000	691,341,000	655,805,000	619,810,000	604,313,000
Return on Assets %	8.16%	7.61%	8.40%	8.34%	8.61%	8.43%
Return on Equity %	12.33%	11.82%	12.98%	12.65%	13.07%	12.92%
Debt to Equity						

CONTACT INFORMATION:
Phone: 314-212-7000 Fax: 314-212-7500
Toll-Free:
Address: 1390 Timberlake Manor Pkwy., Chesterfield, MO 63017 United States

STOCK TICKER/OTHER:
Stock Ticker: DOX
Employees: 25,561
Parent Company:

Exchange: NAS
Fiscal Year Ends: 09/30

SALARIES/BONUSES:
Top Exec. Salary: $ Bonus: $
Second Exec. Salary: $ Bonus: $

OTHER THOUGHTS:
Estimated Female Officers or Directors: 1
Hot Spot for Advancement for Women/Minorities: Y

Sales, profits and employees may be estimates. Financial information, benefits and other data can change quickly and may vary from those stated here.

Amey plc

NAIC Code: 541330

www.amey.co.uk

TYPES OF BUSINESS:
Engineering Services
Facilities Management
Design Services
Consulting Services
Asset Management
Infrastructure Services
Highway Design Services
IT Services

BRANDS/DIVISIONS/AFFILIATES:
Grupo Ferrovial SA

GROWTH PLANS/SPECIAL FEATURES:
Amey plc, a subsidiary operating in the service division of the Spanish company Grupo Ferrovial SA, provides business and infrastructure support services through locations across the U.K. The firm works alongside its customers, local authorities and other related businesses and professionals to help keep towns and cities running smoothly. Amey supplies important utilities like water, gas and electricity to homes; maintains roads, railways and airports; keeps facilities running smoothly; improves social housing and schools; and supports the country's defense and justice services. These services include consulting, engineering, strategic consulting, transport, utilities, environmental, waste, facilities management, justice, defense and investments.

The firm offers its employees life, dental, travel and personal accident insurance; parental leave; paid time off; and a pension plan.

CONTACTS:
Note: Officers with more than one job title may be intentionally listed here more than once.

Andy Milner, CEO
Andrew Nelson, CFO
Wayne Robertson, Head-Legal
John Faulkner, Dir.-Strategy & Development
Valerie Hughes-D'Aeth, Dir.-Communications
Andy Milner, Managing Dir.-Consulting, Rail & Strategic Highway
Gillian Duggan, Managing Dir.-Built Environment
Dan Holland, Managing Dir.-Utilities & Defense
Nick Gregg, Managing Dir.-Gov't
Ian Tyler, Chmn.

FINANCIAL DATA:
Note: Data for latest year may not have been available at press time.

In U.S. $	2017	2016	2015	2014	2013	2012
Revenue	3,300,000,000	3,187,370,000	3,753,260,000	3,501,722,776	3,189,383,510	1,879,789,127
R&D Expense						
Operating Income						
Operating Margin %						
SGA Expense						
Net Income		-32,698,900	39,877,000	138,775,832	101,431,558	
Operating Cash Flow						
Capital Expenditure						
EBITDA						
Return on Assets %						
Return on Equity %						
Debt to Equity						

CONTACT INFORMATION:
Phone: 44-1865-713-100   Fax: 44-1865-713-357
Toll-Free:
Address: Edmund Halley Rd., The Sherard Bldg., Oxford, OX4 4DQ United Kingdom

STOCK TICKER/OTHER:
Stock Ticker: Subsidiary
Employees: 19,000
Parent Company: Grupo Ferrovial SA

Exchange:
Fiscal Year Ends: 12/31

SALARIES/BONUSES:
Top Exec. Salary: $ Bonus: $
Second Exec. Salary: $ Bonus: $

OTHER THOUGHTS:
Estimated Female Officers or Directors: 2
Hot Spot for Advancement for Women/Minorities:

Sales, profits and employees may be estimates. Financial information, benefits and other data can change quickly and may vary from those stated here.

Amgen Inc

www.amgen.com

NAIC Code: 325412

TYPES OF BUSINESS:
Drugs-Diversified
Oncology Drugs
Nephrology Drugs
Inflammation Drugs
Neurology Drugs

BRANDS/DIVISIONS/AFFILIATES:
Embrel
Neulasta
Aranesp
Prolia
Sensipar
XGEVA
EPOGEN
EVENITY

CONTACTS:
Note: Officers with more than one job title may be intentionally listed here more than once.

Robert Bradway, CEO
David Meline, CFO
Esteban Santos, Executive VP, Divisional
Sean Harper, Executive VP, Divisional
Anthony Hooper, Executive VP, Divisional
Cynthia Patton, Other Executive Officer
Lori Johnston, Senior VP
David Piacquad, Senior VP, Divisional
Jonathan Graham, Senior VP

GROWTH PLANS/SPECIAL FEATURES:

Amgen, Inc. is a global biotechnology medicines company that discovers, develops, manufactures and markets human therapeutics based on cellular and molecular biology. Its products are used for treatment in the fields of supportive cancer care, nephrology and inflammation. Amgen's current (early-2018) primary pipeline products include: Prolia (denosumab), XGEVA (denosumab) and EVENITY (romosozumab), each for bone health; Repatha (evolucumab), for cardiovascular purposes; Aimovig (erenumab), for the prevention of migraines; Aranesp (darbepoetin alfa), BLINCYTO (blinatumomab), KYPROLIS (carfilzomib) and Vectibix (panitumumab), for oncology/hematology purposes; and Sensipar/Mimpara (cinacalcet), AMJEVITA (adalimumab-atto), AMGEVITA (biosimilar adalimumab), ABP 980 and MVASI (bevacizumab-awwb), each for nephrology purposes. Primary marketed products include: Embrel, for the treatment of adults with rheumatoid arthritis, psoriatic arthritis and plaque psoriasis; Neulasta, to help reduce the chance of infection due to a low white blood cell count in patients with certain types of cancer; Aranesp, to treat a lower-than-normal number of red blood cells caused by chronic kidney disease (CKD); Prolia, to treat postmenopausal women with osteoporosis at high risk for fracture; Sensipar/Mimpara, to treat secondary hyperparathyroidism (sHPT); XGEVA, to prevent skeletal-related events (SREs) in patients with bone metastases from solid tumors; and EPOGEN, to treat anemia caused by CKD. Amgen's product sales to three large wholesalers—AmerisourceBergen Corporation, McKesson Corporation and Cardinal Health, Inc.—each individually accounted for more than 10% of total revenues in 2017. On a combined basis, they accounted for 96% of U.S. gross product sales, and 81% of worldwide gross revenue (in 2017).

Amgen offers its employees health, disability and life insurance; paid time off; home and auto insurance; tuition reimbursement; childcare services; telecommuting options; and recreation/fitness classes.

FINANCIAL DATA:
Note: Data for latest year may not have been available at press time.

In U.S. $	2017	2016	2015	2014	2013	2012
Revenue	22,849,000,000	22,991,000,000	21,662,000,000	20,063,000,000	18,676,000,000	17,265,000,000
R&D Expense	3,562,000,000	3,840,000,000	4,070,000,000	4,297,000,000	4,083,000,000	3,380,000,000
Operating Income	9,973,000,000	9,794,000,000	8,470,000,000	6,191,000,000	5,867,000,000	5,577,000,000
Operating Margin %	43.64%	42.59%	39.10%	30.85%	31.41%	32.30%
SGA Expense	4,870,000,000	5,062,000,000	4,846,000,000	4,699,000,000	5,184,000,000	4,801,000,000
Net Income	1,979,000,000	7,722,000,000	6,939,000,000	5,158,000,000	5,081,000,000	4,345,000,000
Operating Cash Flow	11,177,000,000	10,354,000,000	9,077,000,000	8,555,000,000	6,291,000,000	5,882,000,000
Capital Expenditure	664,000,000	837,000,000	649,000,000	1,003,000,000	693,000,000	689,000,000
EBITDA	12,856,000,000	12,528,000,000	11,181,000,000	8,748,000,000	7,573,000,000	7,150,000,000
Return on Assets %	2.51%	10.35%	9.87%	7.63%	8.43%	8.42%
Return on Equity %	7.18%	26.64%	25.76%	21.54%	24.69%	22.81%
Debt to Equity	1.35	1.01	1.04	1.17	1.34	1.26

CONTACT INFORMATION:
Phone: 805 447-1000   Fax: 805 447-1010
Toll-Free: 800-772-6436
Address: 1 Amgen Center Dr., Thousand Oaks, CA 91320 United States

SALARIES/BONUSES:
Top Exec. Salary: $1,555,962   Bonus: $
Second Exec. Salary: $1,050,173   Bonus: $

STOCK TICKER/OTHER:
Stock Ticker: AMGN
Employees: 19,200
Parent Company:

Exchange: NAS
Fiscal Year Ends: 12/31

OTHER THOUGHTS:
Estimated Female Officers or Directors: 4
Hot Spot for Advancement for Women/Minorities: Y

Sales, profits and employees may be estimates. Financial information, benefits and other data can change quickly and may vary from those stated here.

Analog Devices Inc

NAIC Code: 334413

www.analog.com

TYPES OF BUSINESS:
Integrated Circuits-Analog & Digital
MEMS Products
DSP Products
Accelerometers & Gyroscopes

BRANDS/DIVISIONS/AFFILIATES:
Linear Technology Corporation
OneTree Microdevices Inc

CONTACTS:
Note: Officers with more than one job title may be intentionally listed here more than once.

Vincent Roche, CEO
Prashanth Mahendra-Rajah, CFO
Ray Stata, Chairman of the Board
Eileen Wynne, Chief Accounting Officer
Peter Real, Chief Technology Officer
Margaret Seif, Other Executive Officer
Yusuf Jamal, Senior VP, Divisional
John Hassett, Senior VP, Divisional
Jean Philibert, Senior VP, Divisional
Martin Cotter, Senior VP, Divisional
Steve Pietkiewicz, Senior VP, Divisional
Gregory Henderson, Senior VP, Divisional

GROWTH PLANS/SPECIAL FEATURES:

Analog Devices, Inc. (ADI) designs, manufactures and markets a broad line of high-performance analog, mixed-signal and digital signal processing (DSP) integrated circuits (ICs). The company's analog and mixed-signal products comprise converters, amplifiers and radio frequency (RF), power management and other analog. Converters translate real-world analog signals into digital data, and vice-versa. Amplifiers are used to condition analog signals and minimize noise, while RF products are designed to operate as wireless devices. Power management products include any device that can be plugged into a wall outlet or run on battery, such as converters, battery chargers, charge pumps and regulators. Other analog products include micro-electromechanical devices (MEMS), such as accelerometers, as well as anything else that uses analog technology. ADI's analog technology base includes an advanced IC technology known as surface micromachining, which is used to produce MEMS semiconductor products. DSP products are typically preprogrammed to execute software associated with processing digitized real-time, real-world data for applications such as wireless telecommunications or image processing. The company's products are used in a wide variety of electronic equipment, including industrial process control, factory automation systems, smart munitions, base stations, central office equipment, wireless telephones, computers, cars, CAT scanners, digital cameras and DVD players. ADI's portfolio includes several thousand analog ICs, with as many as several hundred customers per design. ADI's products are used by more than 125,000 customers worldwide. The firm has manufacturing facilities in the U.S., Ireland and Southeast Asia; and more than 50 design facilities worldwide. During 2017, ADI acquired Linear Technology Corporation, a designer, manufacturer and marketer of high-performance analog ICs; and OneTree Microdevices, Inc., a supplier of mixed signal solutions for cable access.

ADI offers its employees medical, dental and vision coverage; life insurance; dependent and health care spending accounts; a retirement plan; and an education assistance plan.

FINANCIAL DATA:
Note: Data for latest year may not have been available at press time.

In U.S. $	2017	2016	2015	2014	2013	2012
Revenue	5,107,503,000	3,421,409,000	3,435,092,000	2,864,773,000	2,633,689,000	2,701,142,000
R&D Expense	968,602,000	653,816,000	637,459,000	559,686,000	513,255,000	512,003,000
Operating Income	1,104,597,000	1,041,796,000	830,841,000	789,806,000	782,923,000	832,479,000
Operating Margin %	21.62%	30.44%	24.21%	27.56%	29.72%	30.81%
SGA Expense	691,046,000	461,438,000	478,972,000	454,676,000	396,233,000	396,519,000
Net Income	727,259,000	861,664,000	696,878,000	629,320,000	673,487,000	651,236,000
Operating Cash Flow	1,112,592,000	1,280,895,000	907,798,000	871,602,000	912,345,000	814,542,000
Capital Expenditure	204,098,000	127,397,000	153,960,000	177,913,000	123,074,000	132,176,000
EBITDA	1,663,384,000	1,255,468,000	1,059,384,000	906,099,000	952,841,000	949,788,000
Return on Assets %	4.99%	11.46%	10.01%	9.50%	11.22%	11.95%
Return on Equity %	9.48%	16.83%	14.17%	13.25%	15.12%	16.36%
Debt to Equity	0.74	0.33	0.09	0.18	0.18	0.19

CONTACT INFORMATION:
Phone: 781 329-4700 Fax: 781 326-8703
Toll-Free: 800-262-5643
Address: One Technology Way, Norwood, MA 02062 United States

STOCK TICKER/OTHER:
Stock Ticker: ADI
Employees: 10,000
Parent Company:

Exchange: NAS
Fiscal Year Ends: 10/31

SALARIES/BONUSES:
Top Exec. Salary: $878,000 Bonus: $
Second Exec. Salary: $35,962 Bonus: $500,000

OTHER THOUGHTS:
Estimated Female Officers or Directors: 3
Hot Spot for Advancement for Women/Minorities: Y

Sales, profits and employees may be estimates. Financial information, benefits and other data can change quickly and may vary from those stated here.

Apple Inc

www.apple.com

NAIC Code: 334220

TYPES OF BUSINESS:
Electronics Design and Manufacturing
Software
Computers and Tablets
Retail Stores
Smartphones
Online Music Store
Apps Store
Home Entertainment Software & Systems

BRANDS/DIVISIONS/AFFILIATES:
iPhone
iPad
Apple Watch
Apple TV
iOS
watchOS
HomePod
AirPower

CONTACTS:
Note: Officers with more than one job title may be intentionally listed here more than once.

Timothy Cook, CEO
Luca Maestri, CFO
Arthur Levinson, Chairman of the Board
Chris Kondo, Chief Accounting Officer
Jeffery Williams, COO
Kate Adams, General Counsel
Katherine Adams, General Counsel
Philip Schiller, Senior VP, Divisional
Craig Federighi, Senior VP, Divisional
Angela Ahrendts, Senior VP, Divisional
Johny Srouji, Senior VP, Divisional
Eduardo Cue, Senior VP, Divisional
Daniel Riccio, Senior VP, Divisional

GROWTH PLANS/SPECIAL FEATURES:

Apple, Inc. designs, manufactures and markets personal computers, portable digital music players and mobile communication devices and sells a variety of related software, services, peripherals and networking applications. The company's products and services include iPhone, iPad, Mac, Apple Watch, Apple TV; a portfolio of consumer and professional software applications; iOS, macOS, watchOS and tvOS operating systems; iCloud, Apple Pay and a variety of accessory, service and support offerings. iPhone is the company's line of smartphones based on its iOS operating system. iCloud stores music, photos, contacts, calendars, mail, documents and more, keeping them up-to-date and available across multiple iOS devices, Mac and Windows personal computers and Apple TV. Other products include apple-branded and third-party accessories; the HomePod wireless speaker; AirPower, a wireless charging accessory; and iPod touch, a flash memory-based digital music and medial player that works with the iTunes store, App Store, iBooks store and Apple Music (collectively referred to as digital content and services) for purchasing and playing digital content and apps. One of Apple's goal is to double revenues from digital services, such as the App Store and Apple Music, from $25 billion in 2016 to $50 billion in 2020. The firm had 499 brick and mortar stores in 22 countries as of December 2017, but also sells its products worldwide through online stores and direct sales force, as well as through third-party cellular network carriers, wholesalers, retailers and value-added resellers. In March 2018, Apple agreed to acquire Texture, a digital magazine subscription service by Next Issue Media, LLC, which gives users unlimited access to their favorite titles for a monthly subscription fee.

Apple offers benefits such as medical, life, long-term care and disability insurance; employee stock purchase and 401(k) plans; paid vacations/holidays; and employee discounts, tuition assistance, counseling services and more.

FINANCIAL DATA:
Note: Data for latest year may not have been available at press time.

In U.S. $	2017	2016	2015	2014	2013	2012
Revenue	229,234,000,000	215,639,000,000	233,715,000,000	182,795,000,000	170,910,000,000	156,508,000,000
R&D Expense	11,581,000,000	10,045,000,000	8,067,000,000	6,041,000,000	4,475,000,000	3,381,000,000
Operating Income	61,344,000,000	60,024,000,000	71,230,000,000	52,503,000,000	48,999,000,000	55,241,000,000
Operating Margin %	26.76%	27.83%	30.47%	28.72%	28.66%	35.29%
SGA Expense	15,261,000,000	14,194,000,000	14,329,000,000	11,993,000,000	10,830,000,000	10,040,000,000
Net Income	48,351,000,000	45,687,000,000	53,394,000,000	39,510,000,000	37,037,000,000	41,733,000,000
Operating Cash Flow	63,598,000,000	65,824,000,000	81,266,000,000	59,713,000,000	53,666,000,000	50,856,000,000
Capital Expenditure	12,795,000,000	13,548,000,000	11,488,000,000	9,813,000,000	9,076,000,000	9,402,000,000
EBITDA	76,569,000,000	73,333,000,000	84,505,000,000	61,813,000,000	57,048,000,000	58,518,000,000
Return on Assets %	13.87%	14.92%	20.44%	18.00%	19.33%	28.54%
Return on Equity %	36.86%	36.90%	46.24%	33.61%	30.63%	42.84%
Debt to Equity	0.72	0.58	0.44	0.25	0.13	

CONTACT INFORMATION:
Phone: 408 996-1010 Fax: 408 974-2483
Toll-Free: 800-692-7753
Address: 1 Infinite Loop, Cupertino, CA 95014 United States

STOCK TICKER/OTHER:
Stock Ticker: AAPL Exchange: NAS
Employees: 123,000 Fiscal Year Ends: 09/30
Parent Company:

SALARIES/BONUSES:
Top Exec. Salary: $3,000,000 Bonus: $
Second Exec. Salary: $1,019,231 Bonus: $

OTHER THOUGHTS:
Estimated Female Officers or Directors:
Hot Spot for Advancement for Women/Minorities:

Sales, profits and employees may be estimates. Financial information, benefits and other data can change quickly and may vary from those stated here.

Applied Materials Inc

www.appliedmaterials.com

NAIC Code: 333242

TYPES OF BUSINESS:
Semiconductor Manufacturing Equipment
LCD Display Technology Equipment
Automation Software
Energy Generation & Conversion Technologies

BRANDS/DIVISIONS/AFFILIATES:

CONTACTS:
Note: Officers with more than one job title may be intentionally listed here more than once.

Gary Dickerson, CEO
Daniel Durn, CFO
James Morgan, Chairman Emeritus
Omkaram Nalamasu, Chief Technology Officer
Thomas Iannotti, Director
Thomas Larkins, General Counsel
Ali Salehpour, General Manager, Divisional
Steve Ghanayem, Senior VP, Divisional
Prabu Raja, Senior VP, Divisional
Ginetto Addiego, Senior VP, Divisional
Charles Read, Vice President

GROWTH PLANS/SPECIAL FEATURES:

Applied Materials, Inc. (AMI), a global leader in the semiconductor industry, provides manufacturing equipment, services and software to the global semiconductor, flat panel display, solar photovoltaic (PV) and related industries. AMI operates in three segments: semiconductor systems, applied global services and display and adjacent markets. The semiconductor systems division, accounting for 65% of the firm's 2017 revenue, develops, manufactures and sells a range of manufacturing equipment used to fabricate semiconductor chips or integrated circuits. Technologies found in this segment are transistor and interconnect, patterning and packaging, and imaging and process control. The applied global services segment (21%) provides integrated solutions to optimize equipment and fab performance and productivity, including spares, upgrades, services, remanufactured earlier generation equipment and factory automation software for semiconductor, display and other products. Its services encompass the following components: fabrication services, automation systems and software, sub-fabrication systems and equipment, parts programs and abatement control systems. The display and adjacent market segment (13%) is comprised of products for manufacturing liquid crystal displays (LCDs), organic light-emitting diodes (OLEDs), and other display technologies for TVs, personal computers (PCs), tablets, smart phones, and other consumer-oriented devices as well as equipment for flexible substrates. The segment offers a variety of technologies and products, including: array testing, defect review, chemical vapor deposition, physical vapor deposition and flexible technologies.

The company offers employees medical, life, AD&D, disability and business travel accident insurance; flexible spending accounts; an employee assistance program; health appraisals; a 401(k) plan; a stock purchase plan; and credit union membership.

FINANCIAL DATA:
Note: Data for latest year may not have been available at press time.

In U.S. $	2017	2016	2015	2014	2013	2012
Revenue	14,537,000,000	10,825,000,000	9,659,000,000	9,072,000,000	7,509,000,000	8,719,000,000
R&D Expense	1,774,000,000	1,540,000,000	1,451,000,000	1,428,000,000	1,320,000,000	1,237,000,000
Operating Income	3,868,000,000	2,152,000,000	1,618,000,000	1,525,000,000	769,000,000	1,000,000,000
Operating Margin %	26.60%	19.87%	16.75%	16.80%	10.24%	11.46%
SGA Expense	890,000,000	819,000,000	883,000,000	890,000,000	902,000,000	1,076,000,000
Net Income	3,434,000,000	1,721,000,000	1,377,000,000	1,072,000,000	256,000,000	109,000,000
Operating Cash Flow	3,609,000,000	2,466,000,000	1,163,000,000	1,800,000,000	623,000,000	1,851,000,000
Capital Expenditure	345,000,000	253,000,000	215,000,000	241,000,000	197,000,000	162,000,000
EBITDA	4,336,000,000	2,557,000,000	2,072,000,000	1,918,000,000	855,000,000	833,000,000
Return on Assets %	20.19%	11.51%	9.66%	8.50%	2.12%	.83%
Return on Equity %	41.45%	23.20%	17.78%	14.33%	3.57%	1.35%
Debt to Equity	0.56	0.43	0.43	0.24	0.27	0.26

CONTACT INFORMATION:
Phone: 408 727-5555   Fax: 408 727-9943
Toll-Free:
Address: 3050 Bowers Ave., Santa Clara, CA 95052 United States

STOCK TICKER/OTHER:
Stock Ticker: AMAT   Exchange: NAS
Employees: 16,700   Fiscal Year Ends: 10/31
Parent Company:

SALARIES/BONUSES:
Top Exec. Salary: $1,000,000   Bonus: $
Second Exec. Salary: $138,462   Bonus: $500,000

OTHER THOUGHTS:
Estimated Female Officers or Directors: 2
Hot Spot for Advancement for Women/Minorities: Y

Sales, profits and employees may be estimates. Financial information, benefits and other data can change quickly and may vary from those stated here.

Arcadis NV

NAIC Code: 541330

www.arcadis.com/index.aspx

TYPES OF BUSINESS:
Engineering Services
Consulting Services
Project Management
Environmental Services
Infrastructure Construction Management
Power Generation Facilities
Industrial & Residential Development

BRANDS/DIVISIONS/AFFILIATES:
Malcolm Pirnie Inc
SEAMS

CONTACTS:
Note: Officers with more than one job title may be intentionally listed here more than once.

Pter Oosterveer, CEO
Sarah Kuijlaars, CFO
Bartheke Weerstra, General Counsel
Roland van Dijk, Global Dir.-Corp. Dev.
Rob Mooren, Global Dir.-Infrastructure Solutions
Stephanie Hottenhuis, Dir.-Europe
Eleanor Allen, Global Dir.-Water Solutions
Manoel Antonio Amarante Avelino da Silva, CEO-ARCADIS Latin America
Gary Coates, CEO-Arcadis U.S.

GROWTH PLANS/SPECIAL FEATURES:

Arcadis NV, based in the Netherlands, is an international provider of consulting, engineering and project management services for the environment, infrastructure, water and buildings sectors, with projects in more than 70 countries. The company develops, designs, implements, maintains and operates projects for private and public-sector clients through four divisions: environment, infrastructure, water and buildings. The environment division, accounting for 21% of its revenue (2017), provides consulting on environmental policy for companies and governments, conducts environmental impact assessments and supports environmental management and environmentally conscious engineering practices. The division provides soil and groundwater contamination testing and develops cost-effective solutions for the remediation of contaminated soil and water. The infrastructure division (26%) consults, designs and manages the construction of infrastructure projects, including railroads, highways, harbors, waterways, dikes and retention ponds. The company also develops utilities for rail signaling, safety, communications and energy supply; constructs bridges and tunnels; and develops small power plants, wind farms and hydroelectric facilities. The water division (13%) oversees projects through the entire water cycle, from the supply of clean drinking water to wastewater treatment and water management services. It operates primarily through Malcolm Pirnie, Inc. Last, the buildings division (40%) develops and maintains buildings, including offices, stores, commercial properties, schools, museums, prisons, stadiums and railway stations. The firm oversaw the 160-story project development of the famous Burj Khalifa project, which is now the world's tallest man-made structure. To carry out the activities of these divisions, Arcadis works from more than 350 offices in over 40 countries. In January 2018, Arcadis acquired software and analytics firm, SEAMS.

Arcadis offers its U.S. employees medical, dental and vision coverage; flexible spending accounts; an employee assistance program; 401(k); and a discount stock purchase plan.

FINANCIAL DATA:
Note: Data for latest year may not have been available at press time.

In U.S. $	2017	2016	2015	2014	2013	2012
Revenue	3,975,017,000	4,110,700,000	4,222,499,000	3,253,869,000	3,106,918,000	3,142,165,000
R&D Expense						
Operating Income	157,723,100	153,986,300	193,705,700	181,435,700	185,920,900	185,223,200
Operating Margin %	3.96%	3.74%	4.58%	5.57%	5.98%	5.89%
SGA Expense	264,716,400	270,648,800	263,052,900	208,829,600	188,740,200	205,117,400
Net Income	88,748,800	81,004,720	124,757,300	116,004,400	122,686,400	111,379,600
Operating Cash Flow	186,632,200	171,988,700	211,012,900	172,232,000	172,997,600	195,155,500
Capital Expenditure	73,259,410	79,982,220	65,904,320	47,030,060	39,809,580	42,975,870
EBITDA	255,800,400	243,653,800	331,616,000	263,006,000	266,201,900	245,931,000
Return on Assets %	2.57%	2.30%	3.71%	4.38%	5.75%	5.41%
Return on Equity %	7.27%	6.53%	10.63%	12.63%	17.58%	18.20%
Debt to Equity	0.48	0.70	0.68	0.56	0.54	0.56

CONTACT INFORMATION:
Phone: 31 202011011   Fax: 31 202011002
Toll-Free:
Address: Gustav Mahlerplein 97-103, Amsterdam, 1082 MS Netherlands

STOCK TICKER/OTHER:
Stock Ticker: ARCVF
Employees: 25,612
Parent Company:

Exchange: PINX
Fiscal Year Ends: 12/31

SALARIES/BONUSES:
Top Exec. Salary: $ Bonus: $
Second Exec. Salary: $ Bonus: $

OTHER THOUGHTS:
Estimated Female Officers or Directors: 4
Hot Spot for Advancement for Women/Minorities: Y

Plunkett Research, Ltd.

Areva SA
NAIC Code: 332410

www.areva.com

TYPES OF BUSINESS:
Nuclear Power Generation Equipment
Nuclear Power Plant Design, Construction & Maintenance
Electrical Transmission & Distribution Products
Electrical & Electronic Interconnect Systems
Uranium Mining & Processing
Forged Steel Equipment
Solar Thermal Technology (CSP)

BRANDS/DIVISIONS/AFFILIATES:
AREVA NC
AREVA NP
AREVA Gabon
AREVA Mongol
AREVA Resources Namibia
SOMAIR
AREVA Australia Holdings Pty Ltd
AREVA Projects

CONTACTS: *Note: Officers with more than one job title may be intentionally listed here more than once.*
Philippe Knoche, CEO
Luc Oursel, Pres.
Olivier Wantz, Sr. VP-Mining

GROWTH PLANS/SPECIAL FEATURES:
AREVA SA is a leading producer of nuclear reactors. The Commissariat a l'Energie Atomique (CEA), the French atomic energy commission, owns a major interest in the company. AREVA operates in five divisions: mining, front-end, reactors & services, back-end and nuclear engineering. The mining division handles the uranium ore exploration, mining and processing operations of the company. This division has 13 mining facilities worldwide, including AREVA Gabon, AREVA Mongol, AREVA Resources Namibia, SOMAIR and AREVA Australia Holdings Pty Ltd. Through the front-end division, and wholly-owned subsidiary AREVA NC, the company manages concentration, conversion and enrichment of uranium ore as well as nuclear fuel design and fabrication. The reactors & services division offers design and construction services for nuclear reactors and other non-carbon dioxide emitting power generation systems. Through AREVA NP, the firm designs and constructs nuclear power plants and research reactors and offers instrumentation and control, modernization and maintenance services, components manufacture and the supply of nuclear fuel. The back-end division provides treatment and recycling of used fuel as well as cleanup of nuclear facilities. The nuclear engineering division operates through AREVA Projects, which provides a wide range of solutions including project management, consulting expertise, construction, testing, engineering and design. In January 2017, the firm sold its stake in its offshore wind activities to Gamesa Corporation, part of transformation plan that includes AREVA refocusing its business solely on nuclear fuel cycle activities.

FINANCIAL DATA: *Note: Data for latest year may not have been available at press time.*

In U.S. $	2017	2016	2015	2014	2013	2012
Revenue		13,583,940	5,185,359,000	10,316,380,000	11,471,020,000	11,614,270,000
R&D Expense		16,053,740	138,309,200	285,262,700	361,826,700	391,464,400
Operating Income		-522,364,100	-761,935,400	-3,266,319,000	14,818,840	146,953,500
Operating Margin %		-3845.45%	-14.69%	-31.66%	.12%	1.26%
SGA Expense		166,712,000	267,974,000	622,391,300	747,116,500	810,096,600
Net Income		-821,210,700	-2,516,733,000	-5,969,523,000	-522,364,100	-122,255,400
Operating Cash Flow		-734,767,500	447,035,000	234,631,600	1,299,118,000	880,486,100
Capital Expenditure		8,644,323	797,747,600	1,421,374,000	1,756,033,000	2,597,002,000
EBITDA		-508,780,200	-789,103,200	-1,008,916,000	959,519,900	1,231,199,000
Return on Assets %		-2.30%	-6.91%	-15.59%	-1.33%	-.31%
Return on Equity %				-241.57%	-8.59%	-1.76%
Debt to Equity					1.21	1.06

CONTACT INFORMATION:
Phone: 33-1-34-96-00-00 Fax: 33-1-34-96-00-01
Toll-Free:
Address: 33 rue La Fayette, Paris, 75442 France

STOCK TICKER/OTHER:
Stock Ticker: ARVCF
Employees: 36,469
Parent Company:

Exchange: PINX
Fiscal Year Ends: 12/31

SALARIES/BONUSES:
Top Exec. Salary: $ Bonus: $
Second Exec. Salary: $ Bonus: $

OTHER THOUGHTS:
Estimated Female Officers or Directors: 3
Hot Spot for Advancement for Women/Minorities: Y

Sales, profits and employees may be estimates. Financial information, benefits and other data can change quickly and may vary from those stated here.

Arkema

NAIC Code: 325180

www.arkema.com

TYPES OF BUSINESS:
Chemicals, Manufacturing
Vinyl Products
Industrial Chemicals
Performance Products
Plexiglas
Agrochemicals
Nanomaterials

BRANDS/DIVISIONS/AFFILIATES:

CONTACTS:
Note: Officers with more than one job title may be intentionally listed here more than once.

Thierry Le Henaff, CEO
Thierry Lemonnier, CFO
Michel Delaborde, Exec. VP-Human Resources
Pierre Chanoine, Exec. VP-Strategy
Michel Delaborde, Exec. VP-Corp. Comm.
Luc Benoit-Cattin, VP-Industry
Marc Schuller, Exec. VP-Business
Pierre Chanoine, Exec. VP-Business
Thierry Le Henaff, Chmn.
Denis Tual, Head-Goods & Svcs. Purchasing

GROWTH PLANS/SPECIAL FEATURES:

Arkema manufactures and markets a broad range of chemicals. The company's product solutions include adhesives, air conditioning, refrigeration, plastics, additives, bio-based materials, paints, coatings and composites. These products are grouped into the following chemical families: acrylics, coating resins, fluorochemicals, fluoropolymers, glass-coating solutions, hydrogen peroxide, molecular sieves, organic peroxides, PMMA acrylic glass, photocure resins, plastic additives, rheology additives, specialty additives, specialty polyamides, surfactants, additives, technical fluids and thiochemicals. Arkema's products serve markets such as construction, electronics/electrical, food, agrochemical, oil and gas, packaging, paper, renewable energies, transportation, water, health, beauty and sports. Based in France, the firm has worldwide operations in North America, South America, Europe, the Middle East, Africa, Asia-Pacific and Oceania. In March 2018, Arkema and Hexcel Corporation signed a strategic alliance to develop thermoplastic composite solutions for the aerospace sector, combining the expertise of Hexcel in carbon fiber and that of Arkema in PEKK (polyetherketoneketone).

FINANCIAL DATA:
Note: Data for latest year may not have been available at press time.

In U.S. $	2017	2016	2015	2014	2013	2012
Revenue	10,281,810,000	9,304,997,000	9,487,762,000	7,350,145,000	7,530,440,000	7,897,207,000
R&D Expense	290,202,300	274,148,500	258,094,800	191,410,000	177,826,100	182,765,700
Operating Income	1,043,493,000	891,600,200	702,660,000	552,001,800	472,968,000	803,922,000
Operating Margin %	10.14%	9.58%	7.40%	7.51%	6.28%	10.17%
SGA Expense	897,774,700	853,318,200	819,975,800	523,599,000	513,719,800	533,478,200
Net Income	711,304,300	527,303,700	351,947,500	206,228,900	207,463,800	271,678,700
Operating Cash Flow	1,244,783,000	1,013,856,000	1,059,547,000	626,096,000	576,699,800	616,216,800
Capital Expenditure	566,820,600	595,223,400	608,807,400	600,163,000	593,988,500	917,533,200
EBITDA	1,662,180,000	1,499,173,000	1,284,300,000	848,378,600	873,076,700	1,250,957,000
Return on Assets %	6.18%	4.80%	3.66%	2.71%	3.04%	4.04%
Return on Equity %	13.33%	10.53%	7.67%	5.71%	7.31%	9.83%
Debt to Equity	0.50	0.32	0.48	0.33	0.52	0.46

CONTACT INFORMATION:
Phone: 33 149008080   Fax: 33 149008396
Toll-Free:
Address: 420, rue d'Estienne d'Orves, Colombes, 92700 France

STOCK TICKER/OTHER:
Stock Ticker: ARKAF
Employees: 19,779
Parent Company:

Exchange: PINX
Fiscal Year Ends: 12/31

SALARIES/BONUSES:
Top Exec. Salary: $ Bonus: $
Second Exec. Salary: $ Bonus: $

OTHER THOUGHTS:
Estimated Female Officers or Directors:
Hot Spot for Advancement for Women/Minorities:

Sales, profits and employees may be estimates. Financial information, benefits and other data can change quickly and may vary from those stated here.

ARRIS Group Inc

NAIC Code: 334210

www.arrisi.com

TYPES OF BUSINESS:
Communications Equipment-Cable Systems
Optical & Radio Frequency Transmission Equipment
Internet Access Products
Support & Testing Products
Motorola Home Business

BRANDS/DIVISIONS/AFFILIATES:

CONTACTS:
Note: Officers with more than one job title may be intentionally listed here more than once.

David Potts, CFO
Robert Stanzione, Chairman of the Board
Philip Baldock, Chief Information Officer
Bruce McClelland, Director
Stephen McCaffery, Managing Director, Divisional
Daniel Whalen, President, Divisional
Daniel Rabinovitsj, President, Divisional
Timothy OLoughlin, President, Divisional
Lawrence Robinson, President, Divisional
James Brennan, Senior VP, Divisional
Victoria Brewster, Senior VP, Divisional
Patrick Macken, Senior VP

GROWTH PLANS/SPECIAL FEATURES:
ARRIS Group, Inc. provides entertainment, communications and networking technology on a global scale. The company's offerings combine hardware, software and services to enable advanced video experiences and constant connectivity. ARRIS operates through three segments: customer premises equipment (CPE); network & cloud (N&C); and enterprise networks. CPE products are divided into two categories: broadband equipment, which includes DSL (digital subscriber line) and cable modems, and broadband gateways; and video equipment, including set-top boxes and video gateways. N&C products are divided into two categories: networks, which include a cable modem termination system, a converged cable access platform, a passive optical network, video systems and access technologies; and software and services, which includes software products that enable providers to securely deliver content and advertising services across multi-screen devices on and off their networks, network management products that collect information from the broadband network and apply analytics, customer experience management solutions, global professional services and global technical services. Last, the enterprise networks segment provides campus network Ethernet switches for next-generation and campus IP networks, Wi-Fi access points, smart wireless services/software, mobile apps, system management and system control products. ARRIS' intellectual property portfolio consists of approximately 3,691 issued patents (both U.S. and foreign), not including the firm's 1,439 current patent protection applications pending (U.S. and foreign). In December 2017, the firm acquired the Ruckus Wireless and ICX Switch businesses from Brocade Communication Systems, Inc. for $61.5 million. In February 2018, ARRIS agreed to sell its manufacturing facility in Taipei City, Taiwan to Pegatron Corporation.

FINANCIAL DATA:
Note: Data for latest year may not have been available at press time.

In U.S. $	2017	2016	2015	2014	2013	2012
Revenue	6,614,392,000	6,829,118,000	4,798,332,000	5,322,921,000	3,620,902,000	1,353,663,000
R&D Expense	539,094,000	584,909,000	534,168,000	556,575,000	425,825,000	170,706,000
Operating Income	276,369,000	271,054,000	240,230,000	378,832,000	65,034,000	100,239,000
Operating Margin %	4.17%	3.96%	5.00%	7.11%	1.79%	7.40%
SGA Expense	475,369,000	454,190,000	417,085,000	410,568,000	338,252,000	161,338,000
Net Income	92,027,000	18,100,000	92,181,000	327,211,000	-48,760,000	53,459,000
Operating Cash Flow	533,837,000	362,495,000	343,872,000	459,281,000	570,846,000	84,401,000
Capital Expenditure	84,494,000	72,286,000	89,230,000	56,588,000	71,443,000	21,507,000
EBITDA	578,902,000	598,961,000	481,359,000	617,870,000	226,891,000	150,340,000
Return on Assets %	1.19%	.29%	2.07%	7.53%	-1.70%	3.86%
Return on Equity %	2.89%	.72%	5.29%	21.74%	-4.27%	5.69%
Debt to Equity	0.66	0.68	0.83		0.86	1.28

CONTACT INFORMATION:
Phone: 678 473-2000 Fax:
Toll-Free:
Address: 3871 Lakefield Dr., Suwanee, GA 30024 United States

SALARIES/BONUSES:
Top Exec. Salary: $825,000 Bonus: $
Second Exec. Salary: $675,000 Bonus: $

STOCK TICKER/OTHER:
Stock Ticker: ARRS
Employees: 7,020
Parent Company:

Exchange: NAS
Fiscal Year Ends: 12/31

OTHER THOUGHTS:
Estimated Female Officers or Directors: 2
Hot Spot for Advancement for Women/Minorities:

Sales, profits and employees may be estimates. Financial information, benefits and other data can change quickly and may vary from those stated here.

Artelia

NAIC Code: 541330

www.arteliagroup.com

TYPES OF BUSINESS:
Engineering Services

BRANDS/DIVISIONS/AFFILIATES:
ACCROPODE
ECOPODE
SANAE
Artelia Italia
Auxitec Ingenierie

CONTACTS:
Note: Officers with more than one job title may be intentionally listed here more than once.

Benoit Clocheret, CEO
Alain Bentejac, Joint Pres.
Jacques Gaillard, Joint Pres.

GROWTH PLANS/SPECIAL FEATURES:

Artelia is a leading French independent engineering firm operating in the construction, infrastructure and environment sectors. Arterlia conducts its assignments in nine markets: building construction, water, environment, energy, maritime, urban development, transportation, industry and multi-site projects. Its four business lines consists of project management, engineering, consultancy and turnkey contracts and public private partnerships (PPPs). The project management business line supervises large-scale building and rehabilitation projects on behalf of investors such as public authorities, international funding agencies, private developers and industrial groups. The engineering business line provides design, planning, organization and construction supervision for buildings and infrastructure projects. It can also work as an owner's assistant during design and construction stages of a project. This division also acts as designer in design-build consortiums or PPPs, and aids with the commissioning, operation and maintenance of structures. The consultancy division, prior to implementing projects, performs technical and environmental studies; strategic, institutional, economic and financial studies; and planning, assistance and assessment assignments concerning public policies or private investments. This division is frequently commissioned by international institutions, banks, industries and private investors to perform due diligence audits for existing or planned sites. The turnkey contracts and PPPs division aims to limit the risks involved while ensuring complete transparency in terms of costs, and takes an active role in the partnership relations. Artelia has a portfolio of a dozen patents and trademarks in key technologies resulting from the group's research and development work. These patents concern breakwater protection, marine energy and waste management. Its most famous patents include breakwater technologies ACCROPODE and ECOPODE. Subsidiary SANAE, within Artelia's building construction and industrial facilities sectors, designs health care buildings. During 2017, Artelia acquired Intertecno and merged it with its subsidiary, Artelia Italia; and acquired Auxitec Ingenierie, an industrial engineering firm.

FINANCIAL DATA:
Note: Data for latest year may not have been available at press time.

In U.S. $	2017	2016	2015	2014	2013	2012
Revenue	575,000,000	547,851,000	442,479,000	415,324,000	386,251,320	
R&D Expense						
Operating Income						
Operating Margin %						
SGA Expense						
Net Income						
Operating Cash Flow						
Capital Expenditure						
EBITDA						
Return on Assets %						
Return on Equity %						
Debt to Equity						

CONTACT INFORMATION:
Phone: 33-1-55-84-10-10   Fax: 33-1-55-84-11-11
Toll-Free:
Address: 2, Ave. Lacassagne, CEDEX 03, Lyon, 69425 France

STOCK TICKER/OTHER:
Stock Ticker: Private   Exchange:
Employees: 4,900   Fiscal Year Ends:
Parent Company:

SALARIES/BONUSES:
Top Exec. Salary: $ Bonus: $
Second Exec. Salary: $ Bonus: $

OTHER THOUGHTS:
Estimated Female Officers or Directors:
Hot Spot for Advancement for Women/Minorities:

Sales, profits and employees may be estimates. Financial information, benefits and other data can change quickly and may vary from those stated here.

ARUP Group Limited

NAIC Code: 541330

www.arup.com

TYPES OF BUSINESS:
Engineering Consulting Services

BRANDS/DIVISIONS/AFFILIATES:

CONTACTS:
Note: Officers with more than one job title may be intentionally listed here more than once.

Gregory Hodkinson, Chmn.

GROWTH PLANS/SPECIAL FEATURES:

ARUP Group Ltd. provides design, planning, engineering, consultancy and technical services to a broad international market. The firm is known for its structural design of the Sydney Opera House. Its service structure consists of building design, economics, planning, infrastructure, management consulting and specialist technical services. ARUP provides these services to markets such as arts & culture, aviation, commercial property, education, energy, government, healthcare, highways, hotels/leisure, maritime, mining, rail, residential, resources/waste, retail, science, industry, sport and water. The building design division provides services such as acoustic consulting, airport planning, architecture, building physics, modelling, civil engineering, cost management, facade engineering, fluid dynamics, geotechnics, landscape architecture, lighting design, mechanical engineering, operations consulting, project management, renewable energy, research, seismic design, sustainable buildings, theater consulting and wind engineering. The economics & planning division provides airport planning, architecture, energy strategy, international development, master planning, site development, town planning, transaction advice and transport consulting. The infrastructure division provides bridge engineering, IT and communications systems, geographic information systems, hydrogeology, intelligent transport solutions, interchange design, maritime engineering, public health engineering, rail engineering, resilience/security and risk, structural engineering, tunnel design and well as water and wind engineering. The management consulting division provides audio/visual and multimedia, cost management, IT and communications systems, operations consulting, operational readiness, activation and transition, organizational behavior, program management, smart cities and transaction advice. The specialist technical services division provides carbon management, advanced technology and research, catastrophe insurance, operations consulting, research and more. ARUP has more than 90 offices across 35+ countries, and has participated in projects in over 160 countries.

FINANCIAL DATA:
Note: Data for latest year may not have been available at press time.

In U.S. $	2017	2016	2015	2014	2013	2012
Revenue	1,880,460,000	1,542,980,000	1,602,914,590	1,493,408,180	1,565,410,000	
R&D Expense						
Operating Income						
Operating Margin %						
SGA Expense						
Net Income	59,402,700	23,172,200	12,163,800	42,309,135		
Operating Cash Flow						
Capital Expenditure						
EBITDA						
Return on Assets %						
Return on Equity %						
Debt to Equity						

CONTACT INFORMATION:
Phone: 44-20-7636-1531 Fax: 44-20-7580-3924
Toll-Free:
Address: 13 Fitzroy St., London, W1T 4BQ United Kingdom

STOCK TICKER/OTHER:
Stock Ticker: Private Exchange:
Employees: 13,346 Fiscal Year Ends: 03/31
Parent Company:

SALARIES/BONUSES:
Top Exec. Salary: $ Bonus: $
Second Exec. Salary: $ Bonus: $

OTHER THOUGHTS:
Estimated Female Officers or Directors:
Hot Spot for Advancement for Women/Minorities:

Sales, profits and employees may be estimates. Financial information, benefits and other data can change quickly and may vary from those stated here.

Associated Consulting Engineers

www.ace-intl.com

NAIC Code: 541330

TYPES OF BUSINESS:
Engineering Consulting Services

BRANDS/DIVISIONS/AFFILIATES:
Sir Frederick Snow and Partners Ltd
IMEG Limited

CONTACTS:
Note: Officers with more than one job title may be intentionally listed here more than once.
Anis El-Sayed, Managing Dir.

GROWTH PLANS/SPECIAL FEATURES:
Associated Consulting Engineers (ACE) provides architectural and engineering solutions across a broad spectrum of professional practices, and to both public and private customers. ACE has offices throughout the Middle East, Europe and Africa, and operates in over 20 countries. Its consulting division serves the following industries: architecture, building development, contract management, project services, environmental management systems, infrastructure, utilities, plan development, industrial development, landscape architecture, planning and urban development, sustainable development and transportation. These services cover all aspects, including inception, conceptual design, detailed design, implementation, commissioning, operation, maintenance and hand over upon completion. Its engineering division serves the following industries: automation and instrumentation, electrical, environmental, geotechnical, mechanical, structural and other ancillary engineering services. These services also cover all aspects from inception to hand over upon completion. Recent projects of the firm involve the airport, architecture, dams, education, harbors, hospitals, industrial, roads, urban, oil and gas, infrastructure, touristic and resort, restoration, environmental and governmental sectors. Subsidiaries of the firm include Sir Frederick Snow and Partners Ltd., a firm of consultancy engineers; and IMEG Limited, an oil and gas consulting firm.

FINANCIAL DATA:
Note: Data for latest year may not have been available at press time.

In U.S. $	2017	2016	2015	2014	2013	2012
Revenue						
R&D Expense						
Operating Income						
Operating Margin %						
SGA Expense						
Net Income						
Operating Cash Flow						
Capital Expenditure						
EBITDA						
Return on Assets %						
Return on Equity %						
Debt to Equity						

CONTACT INFORMATION:
Phone: 30-210-6105090   Fax: 30-210-6197182
Toll-Free:
Address: 4 Frangoklissias, Marousi, Athens, 15125 Greece

STOCK TICKER/OTHER:
Stock Ticker: Private
Employees:
Parent Company:

Exchange:
Fiscal Year Ends:

SALARIES/BONUSES:
Top Exec. Salary: $ Bonus: $
Second Exec. Salary: $ Bonus: $

OTHER THOUGHTS:
Estimated Female Officers or Directors:
Hot Spot for Advancement for Women/Minorities:

Sales, profits and employees may be estimates. Financial information, benefits and other data can change quickly and may vary from those stated here.

Astellas Pharma Inc

NAIC Code: 325412

www.astellas.com

TYPES OF BUSINESS:
Drugs, Manufacturing
Immunological Pharmaceuticals
Over-the-Counter Products
Reagents
Genomic Research
Venture Capital
Drug Licensing

BRANDS/DIVISIONS/AFFILIATES:
Ocata Therapeutics Inc

CONTACTS:
Note: Officers with more than one job title may be intentionally listed here more than once.

Kenji Yasukawa, CEO
Yoshihiko Hantanaka, Pres.
Yoshiro Miyokawa, Exec. VP
Shinichi Tsukamoto, Sr. Corp. Exec. Officer
Masao Yoshida, Sr. Corp. Exec. Officer
Masaru Imahori, Sr. Corp. Exec. VP
Yoshihiko Hatanaka, Chmn.

GROWTH PLANS/SPECIAL FEATURES:

Astellas Pharma, Inc. is one of the largest pharmaceutical manufacturers in Japan. The company's business comprises research, development, manufacturing, technology and medical representatives. The research department explores, optimizes and develops global research activities. The development department engages in clinical trials. The activities within manufacturing and technology department include the industrialization of research, and the manufacturing of products. The medical department supplies information on drug usage. Wholly-owned Ocata Therapeutics, Inc. is a clinical stage biotechnology company focused on the development and commercialization of new therapies in the field of regenerative medicine. Regenerative medicine is the process of replacing or regenerating human cells, tissues or organs to restore or establish normal function. Astellas has more than 35 new molecular/biological entities in its pipeline (as of 2017), and over 100 ongoing collaborative research projects. The firm has its own distribution channels in more than 50 countries worldwide, and develops business across the four main regions of Japan, the Americas, Europe/Middle East/Africa, and Asia/Oceania. Japan derives 36.7% of annual sales; the Americas derive 31.4%; EMEA derives 25.2%; and Asia/Oceania derives 6.7%. In April 2018, Astellas sold certain Agensys research facilities located in Santa Monica, California, USA, to Kite, a Gilead company.

FINANCIAL DATA:
Note: Data for latest year may not have been available at press time.

In U.S. $	2017	2016	2015	2014	2013	2012
Revenue	12,219,720,000	12,788,390,000	11,619,700,000	10,619,610,000	9,368,465,000	9,030,996,000
R&D Expense	1,938,970,000	2,102,339,000	1,924,669,000	1,783,678,000		
Operating Income	2,575,172,000	2,503,251,000	2,014,925,000	1,721,660,000	1,433,454,000	1,225,266,000
Operating Margin %	21.07%	19.57%	17.34%	16.21%	15.30%	13.56%
SGA Expense	4,385,849,000	4,661,441,000	4,215,782,000	3,698,696,000		
Net Income	2,037,461,000	1,804,425,000	1,265,661,000	846,599,700	771,855,800	728,805,800
Operating Cash Flow	2,195,007,000	2,922,834,000	1,748,519,000	1,996,059,000	1,342,948,000	1,608,674,000
Capital Expenditure	453,214,100	1,100,401,000	756,158,000	523,066,900	629,262,200	597,419,500
EBITDA	3,237,712,000	3,098,426,000	2,405,767,000	1,750,857,000	1,702,991,000	1,795,202,000
Return on Assets %	12.08%	10.78%	7.88%	5.86%	5.82%	5.71%
Return on Equity %	17.28%	15.03%	10.50%	7.79%	7.96%	7.67%
Debt to Equity						

CONTACT INFORMATION:
Phone: 81-3-3244-3000 Fax:
Toll-Free:
Address: 2-5-1 Nihonbashi-Honcho, Chuo-ku, Tokyo, 103-8411 Japan

STOCK TICKER/OTHER:
Stock Ticker: ALPMY
Employees: 17,202
Parent Company:

Exchange: PINX
Fiscal Year Ends: 03/31

SALARIES/BONUSES:
Top Exec. Salary: $ Bonus: $
Second Exec. Salary: $ Bonus: $

OTHER THOUGHTS:
Estimated Female Officers or Directors:
Hot Spot for Advancement for Women/Minorities:

AstraZeneca plc

NAIC Code: 325412

www.astrazeneca.com

TYPES OF BUSINESS:
Drugs-Diversified
Pharmaceutical Research & Development

BRANDS/DIVISIONS/AFFILIATES:
Viela Bio Inc

CONTACTS:
Note: Officers with more than one job title may be intentionally listed here more than once.

Pascal Soriot, CEO
Marc Dunoyer, CFO
Fiona Cicconi, Exec. VP-Human Resources
Briggs Morrison, Chief Medical Officer
Jeff Pott, General Counsel
David Smith, Exec. VP-Global Oper.
Katarina Ageborg, Chief Compliance Officer
Menelas (Mene) Pangalos, Exec. VP-Innovative Medicines & Early Dev.
Bahija Jallal, Exec. VP-MedImmune
Briggs Morrison, Exec. VP-Global Medicines Dev.
Leif Johansson, Chmn.
Mark Mallon, Exec. VP-Intl

GROWTH PLANS/SPECIAL FEATURES:

AstraZeneca plc is a leading global pharmaceutical company that discovers, develops, manufactures and markets prescription pharmaceuticals, biologics and vaccines. The firm's products are utilized for the treatment or prevention of diseases in the cardiovascular, renal, metabolism, oncology, respiratory, inflammation, autoimmunity, neuroscience and infection categories. AstraZeneca's cardiovascular, renal and metabolism (CVRM) division addresses metabolic risks in relation to CVRM. It focuses on unmet needs concerning atherosclerosis, heart failure, chronic kidney disease (CKD) and diabetes. The oncology division seeks to redefine the treatment paradigm to eliminate cancer as a cause of death, with a concentration on four scientific platforms: haematology, WEE1 inhibition, AKT inhibition and selective oestrogen receptor downregulation. These platforms concentrate on four key diseases: haematologic cancer, ovarian cancer, lung cancer and breast cancer. The respiratory division focuses on the unmet medical needs of those with asthma and chronic obstructive pulmonary disease (COPD) via tailored therapies, devices and support tools. The inflammation and autoimmunity division develops novel treatments for a wide range of related diseases, including lupus. The neuroscience division is committed to discovering and developing compounds that improve patient care in relation to neurodegenerative diseases, analgesia and psychiatry, including Alzheimer's disease and opioid-induced constipation. Last, the infection and vaccines division develops and implements scientific advancement in relation to infections and vaccines, primarily to protect patients against the burdens of influenza, respiratory syncytial virus (RSV) and bacterial infections (primarily those resistant to current antibiotics). In February 2018, AstraZeneca announced plans to spin off six molecules from its early-stage inflammation and autoimmunity programs into an independent biotech company to be called Viela Bio, Inc. The new firm will focus on developing medicines for severe autoimmune diseases by targeting the underlying causes of each disease.

FINANCIAL DATA:
Note: Data for latest year may not have been available at press time.

In U.S. $	2017	2016	2015	2014	2013	2012
Revenue	22,465,000,000	23,002,000,000	24,708,000,000	26,095,000,000	25,711,000,000	27,973,000,000
R&D Expense	5,757,000,000	5,890,000,000	5,997,000,000	5,579,000,000	4,821,000,000	5,243,000,000
Operating Income	2,157,000,000	3,572,000,000	2,614,000,000	1,350,000,000	3,712,000,000	7,178,000,000
Operating Margin %	9.60%	15.52%	10.57%	5.17%	14.43%	25.66%
SGA Expense	10,233,000,000	9,739,000,000	11,451,000,000	13,324,000,000	12,512,000,000	10,159,000,000
Net Income	2,868,000,000	3,406,000,000	2,825,000,000	1,233,000,000	2,556,000,000	6,297,000,000
Operating Cash Flow	3,578,000,000	4,145,000,000	3,324,000,000	7,058,000,000	7,400,000,000	6,948,000,000
Capital Expenditure	1,620,000,000	2,314,000,000	2,788,000,000	2,752,000,000	2,058,000,000	4,619,000,000
EBITDA	6,771,000,000	6,589,000,000	6,390,000,000	4,946,000,000	8,345,000,000	11,194,000,000
Return on Assets %	4.55%	5.55%	4.75%	2.15%	4.67%	11.84%
Return on Equity %	19.23%	20.42%	14.82%	5.75%	10.88%	26.80%
Debt to Equity	1.04	0.97	0.76	0.42	0.36	0.39

CONTACT INFORMATION:
Phone: 44 2037495000   Fax: 44 1223352858
Toll-Free:
Address: 1 Francis Crick Ave., Cambridge, CB2 0AA United Kingdom

SALARIES/BONUSES:
Top Exec. Salary: $1,737,644   Bonus: $2,728,956
Second Exec. Salary: $1,032,616   Bonus: $1,459,906

STOCK TICKER/OTHER:
Stock Ticker: AZN
Employees: 61,100
Parent Company:

Exchange: NYS
Fiscal Year Ends: 12/31

OTHER THOUGHTS:
Estimated Female Officers or Directors: 3
Hot Spot for Advancement for Women/Minorities: Y

Sales, profits and employees may be estimates. Financial information, benefits and other data can change quickly and may vary from those stated here.

ASUSTeK Computer Inc

NAIC Code: 334111

www.asus.com

TYPES OF BUSINESS:
Computer Manufacturing
Computer Components & Accessories
Networking Devices
Wireless Communication Products
Smart Phones
Personal Computers
Computer Monitors
Computers for Video Game Players

BRANDS/DIVISIONS/AFFILIATES:
ASUS NovaGo
ZenFone 5 Series
ROG
AREZ

GROWTH PLANS/SPECIAL FEATURES:
ASUSTeK Computer, Inc. (ASUS) participates in the 3C industry (computing, consumer electronics and communications). The company manufactures personal computers (PCs), monitors, mobile phones, networking equipment, notebook computers, storage devices, PC components, personal palmtop computers (PDAs), gaming devices, wearables and server equipment generally marketed under the ASUS brand. ASUS also produces commercial desk tops, commercial notebooks and servers and workstations. Moreover, the company manufactures PC components such as barebones; graphic cards; motherboards; multi-media products, such as audio cards, digital media players and TV tuners; and DVD and Blu-ray drives. Products recently-released include: ASUS NovaGo, a gigabit LTE-capable laptop designed for connected mobility, providing users with an always-on, always-connected experience; the ZenFone 5 Series, a 6.2-inch dual-camera smartphone with a 90% screen-to-body ratio in a compact size; the 2018 ROG line of products designed to enable gamers to create their own battle station and enjoy totally immersive gaming experiences, and including laptop, desktop, keyboard, controller, projection light and accessories; and AREZ, a brand identity for ASUS Radeon RX graphics cards.

CONTACTS: Note: Officers with more than one job title may be intentionally listed here more than once.
Jerry Shen, CEO
Jerry Tsao, COO
Jonathan Tsang, Co-Pres.

FINANCIAL DATA:
Note: Data for latest year may not have been available at press time.

In U.S. $	2017	2016	2015	2014	2013	2012
Revenue	14,806,600,000	15,926,940,000	16,115,710,000	16,288,790,000	15,806,970,000	15,308,770,000
R&D Expense	509,436,400	453,748,100	442,065,500	387,867,600	374,162,000	291,331,900
Operating Income	434,502,600	639,801,900	716,721,000	740,726,800	676,789,100	745,121,200
Operating Margin %	2.93%	4.01%	4.44%	4.54%	4.28%	4.86%
SGA Expense	1,082,895,000	1,166,076,000	1,157,409,000	1,102,249,000	995,180,400	1,048,860,000
Net Income	530,379,900	655,182,200	583,352,200	664,315,000	731,853,500	765,032,200
Operating Cash Flow	-47,113,650	1,682,233,000	-360,566,900	894,021,800	1,019,554,000	757,284,200
Capital Expenditure	83,183,290	195,761,400	33,648,260	56,732,330	86,847,860	104,032,900
EBITDA	490,907,900	694,521,700	775,802,200	846,432,200	778,454,700	1,008,290,000
Return on Assets %	4.38%	5.50%	4.98%	6.00%	7.61%	9.24%
Return on Equity %	8.71%	11.00%	10.33%	13.03%	16.42%	18.60%
Debt to Equity			0.01			

CONTACT INFORMATION:
Phone: 886 228943447   Fax:
Toll-Free:
Address: Li-Te Rd., No. 15, Peitou, Taipei, Taiwan

STOCK TICKER/OTHER:
Stock Ticker: AKCPF   Exchange: GREY
Employees: 14,000   Fiscal Year Ends: 09/30
Parent Company:

SALARIES/BONUSES:
Top Exec. Salary: $ Bonus: $
Second Exec. Salary: $ Bonus: $

OTHER THOUGHTS:
Estimated Female Officers or Directors:
Hot Spot for Advancement for Women/Minorities:

Sales, profits and employees may be estimates. Financial information, benefits and other data can change quickly and may vary from those stated here.

Atmel Corporation

www.atmel.com/about/corporate/default.aspx

NAIC Code: 334413

TYPES OF BUSINESS:
Semiconductor Manufacturing
Non-Volatile Memory & Logic Integrated Circuits
Mixed-Signal Semiconductors
RF Semiconductors
Microcontrollers
Military & Aerospace Products

BRANDS/DIVISIONS/AFFILIATES:
Microchip Technology Incorporated

CONTACTS: Note: Officers with more than one job title may be intentionally listed here more than once.
Steve Sanghi, CEO
Stephen Skaggs, CFO
Tsung-Ching Wu, Director
Reza Kazerounian, General Manager, Divisional
Peter Schuman, Other Corporate Officer
Scott Wornow, Other Executive Officer
Robert Valiton, Senior VP

GROWTH PLANS/SPECIAL FEATURES:
Atmel Corporation designs and manufactures microcontrollers, capacitive touch solutions, advanced logic, mixed-signal, nonvolatile memory and radio frequency (RF) components. The company provides the electronics industry with intelligent and connected solutions, primarily to industrial, automotive, consumer, communications and computing markets. Atmel's products include applications for the following industries: automotive, including body, car access, infotainment and under the hood; building automation, including fire/safety, comfort, control and telecare; home appliances, including refrigeration, cooking, washing, motor control and safety critical touch interfaces; home entertainment, including video and remote controls; industrial automation, including human machine interface, sensors, instruments and communications; lighting, including various ballasts, controls, TV backlight, high-voltage edge-lit and solid-state lighting; Internet of Things, including secure provisioning; smart energy, including meters, data concentrators and in-home display units; mobile electronics, including mobile phones, tablets, portable game consoles, cameras, portable audio players and GPS asset tracking; PC peripherals, including small I/O devices, mass storage devices and PC accessories; and wearables, including small badges. Atmel operates as a wholly-owned subsidiary of Microchip Technology Incorporated.

FINANCIAL DATA: Note: Data for latest year may not have been available at press time.

In U.S. $	2017	2016	2015	2014	2013	2012
Revenue	1,200,000,000	1,200,000,000	1,172,455,936	1,413,334,016	1,386,446,976	1,432,109,952
R&D Expense						
Operating Income						
Operating Margin %						
SGA Expense						
Net Income			26,891,000	32,195,000	-22,055,000	30,445,000
Operating Cash Flow						
Capital Expenditure						
EBITDA						
Return on Assets %						
Return on Equity %						
Debt to Equity						

CONTACT INFORMATION:
Phone: 408 441-0311   Fax:
Toll-Free:
Address: 1600 Technology Dr., San Jose, CA 95110 United States

STOCK TICKER/OTHER:
Stock Ticker: Subsidiary   Exchange:
Employees: 5,200   Fiscal Year Ends: 12/31
Parent Company: Microchip Technology Incorporated

SALARIES/BONUSES:
Top Exec. Salary: $ Bonus: $
Second Exec. Salary: $ Bonus: $

OTHER THOUGHTS:
Estimated Female Officers or Directors: 1
Hot Spot for Advancement for Women/Minorities:

Sales, profits and employees may be estimates. Financial information, benefits and other data can change quickly and may vary from those stated here.

ATS Automation Tooling Systems Inc

www.atsautomation.com

NAIC Code: 333517

TYPES OF BUSINESS:
Machine Tool Manufacturing
Testing Equipment
Manufacturing Consulting
Photovoltaic Cells Manufacturing
Photovoltaic Cells Installation & Design
Photovoltaic Cells Research & Development

BRANDS/DIVISIONS/AFFILIATES:
ATS SmartVision
ATS SuperTrak
ATS850
sortimat Discovery
sortimat Spaceline

CONTACTS:
Note: Officers with more than one job title may be intentionally listed here more than once.

Andrew Hider, CEO
Maria Perrella, CFO
David McAusland, Chairman of the Board
Ronald Keyser, Chief Information Officer
Tom Kramer, Executive VP, Divisional
Stewart Mccuaig, General Counsel
Eric Kiisel, Senior VP, Divisional
Simon Roberts, Senior VP, Divisional
Helmut Hock, Senior VP, Divisional
Carl Galloway, Treasurer
Charles Gyles, Vice President, Divisional
Tom Hayes, Vice President, Divisional
Jeff Brennan, Vice President, Divisional
Chris Hart, Vice President, Divisional
Eric Wallace, Vice President, Divisional
Thomas Wildt, Vice President, Divisional

GROWTH PLANS/SPECIAL FEATURES:
ATS Automation Tooling Systems, Inc. produces various automated manufacturing and electronics systems to advance factory automation solutions for global manufacturers. The company's ATS SmartVision technology uses programmable software to control virtually any industry-standard third-party camera and lighting system, and perform high-precision parts defect identification, measurement, sorting and robotic guidance. In relation to material handling platforms, the ATS SuperTrak pallet conveyor system is a high-speed pallet transport that comprises enhanced capabilities and flexibilities; the ATS850 cleanroom conveyor is designed for applications where high reliability, cleanliness and non-contact queuing are process requirements; the sortimat Discovery rotary indexing machine assembles market-ready products in large quantities and accommodates between 12 and 20 stations as standard; and the sortimat Spaceline chassis provides high performance and flexibility while meeting challenging manufacturing requirements. For life science sectors, ATS offers solutions for medical devices, pharmaceuticals and diagnostics, including auto injectors, meters, catheters, blood collection, infusion sets, inhalers, sensors, data tracking, microarrays, biosensors and more. For the transportation industry, it offers solutions for the automotive, powertrain and aerospace sectors, including assembly automation, quality assurance, lithium ion batteries, testing and transmission control. For the energy sector, ATS' solutions include solar automation, nuclear automation and battery manufacturing automation. For the consumer goods and electronic sectors, the company's solutions include high-volume assembly, packaging, computers, peripherals, printers/ink jet cartridges and telecommunications devices. Based in Canada, ATS has worldwide locations in the U.S., Europe and Asia.

FINANCIAL DATA:
Note: Data for latest year may not have been available at press time.

In U.S. $	2017	2016	2015	2014	2013	2012
Revenue	801,350,800	824,130,000	742,034,900	541,705,200	468,567,600	471,947,600
R&D Expense						
Operating Income	57,023,380	60,845,820	53,104,240	48,381,290	44,902,890	47,760,600
Operating Margin %	7.11%	7.38%	7.15%	8.93%	9.58%	10.11%
SGA Expense	141,673,400	144,221,200	141,116,900	95,635,350	73,936,580	78,773,680
Net Income	27,739,990	31,353,940	43,569,560	49,284,980	11,915,180	-47,235,830
Operating Cash Flow	101,387,200	28,347,210	63,826,400	49,882,680	21,144,670	-20,632,580
Capital Expenditure	14,187,870	12,414,590	14,194,210	8,801,427	9,906,460	5,956,401
EBITDA	76,623,860	84,519,220	85,346,020	63,194,610	54,603,250	57,476,020
Return on Assets %	2.55%	3.05%	5.49%	9.15%	2.61%	-8.71%
Return on Equity %	5.23%	6.47%	10.10%	13.57%	3.85%	-13.38%
Debt to Equity	0.47	0.48	0.50			

CONTACT INFORMATION:
Phone: 519 653-4483 Fax: 519 653-6520
Toll-Free:
Address: 730 Fountain St. N., Bldg. 2, Cambridge, ON N3H 4R7 Canada

STOCK TICKER/OTHER:
Stock Ticker: ATA   Exchange: TSE
Employees: 2,500   Fiscal Year Ends: 03/31
Parent Company:

SALARIES/BONUSES:
Top Exec. Salary: $ Bonus: $
Second Exec. Salary: $ Bonus: $

OTHER THOUGHTS:
Estimated Female Officers or Directors: 2
Hot Spot for Advancement for Women/Minorities: Y

Sales, profits and employees may be estimates. Financial information, benefits and other data can change quickly and may vary from those stated here.

AU Optronics Corp

www.auo.com

NAIC Code: 334419

TYPES OF BUSINESS:
LCD (Liquid Crystal Display) Unit Screens Manufacturing
Information Technology Displays
Television Displays
Consumer Product Displays
Solar Module Design, Production & Installation
Silicon Wafer Production

BRANDS/DIVISIONS/AFFILIATES:
M Setek Co Ltd
AUO SunPower Sdn Bhd
AUO Crystal Corp
AUO Green Energy America Corp
AUO Green Energy Europe BV
AUO Crystal (Malaysia) Sdn Bhd
BenQ Solar

CONTACTS: Note: Officers with more than one job title may be intentionally listed here more than once.
Shuang-Lang (Paul) Peng, CEO
Kuo-Hsin Tsai, Pres.
Benjamin Tseng, CFO
F.C. (Fwu-Chyi) Hsiang, Exec. VP
Michael Tsai, Sr. VP
James C.P. Chen, VP

GROWTH PLANS/SPECIAL FEATURES:
AU Optronics Corp. (AUO), based in Taiwan, designs, manufactures, assembles and markets thin-film transistor liquid crystal display (TFT-LCD) panels used in various electronics such as laptops, cellular phones, digital cameras and LCD televisions, among others. Additionally, the firm has expanded into the solar photovoltaic (PV) manufacturing sector. AUO's screens are purchased by original equipment manufacturers (OEMs) and companies that design and assemble products based on customer specifications. Its operations consist of two segments: display business and solar business. The company organizes its display manufacturing into three sections, each with its own production, R&D and sales and marketing operations: video displays, which includes applications in LCD TVs, desktop monitors and other related equipment; mobile displays, focused on smartphones, notebooks and audio video products; and touch panel products, including its e-paper technology. AUO's solar business consists of a controlling interest in M. Setek Co., Ltd., which produces polysilicon and single crystal silicon wafers and ingots in Japan; a joint venture with SunPower Corp. (AUO SunPower Sdn Bhd), which operates a solar cell manufacturing plant in Malaysia; and AUO Crystal Corp., which is responsible for the design and installation of PV modules and systems. Other subsidiaries in this segment include AUO Green Energy America Corp.; AUO Green Energy Europe BV; and AUO Crystal (Malaysia) Sdn Bhd. AUO markets its solar PV products and services under the BenQ Solar brand worldwide. The firm owns more than 17,600 patents worldwide, as well as over 23,600 patent applications.

AUO offers its employees onsite wellness and fitness centers; profit sharing; onsite cafeteria, convenience store, bakery and coffee shop discounts; and subsidized travel and entertainment discounts.

FINANCIAL DATA: Note: Data for latest year may not have been available at press time.

In U.S. $	2017	2016	2015	2014	2013	2012
Revenue	11,635,620,000	11,228,260,000	12,294,740,000	13,926,740,000	14,205,980,000	12,913,130,000
R&D Expense	336,235,000	309,829,400	303,791,300	312,417,900	291,052,600	347,025,300
Operating Income	1,335,396,000	442,533,200	597,807,700	756,266,700	282,934,300	-1,291,913,000
Operating Margin %	11.47%	3.94%	4.86%	5.43%	1.99%	-10.00%
SGA Expense	411,065,200	445,998,500	457,609,900	586,460,300	585,522,700	648,902,000
Net Income	1,453,802,000	340,002,300	247,097,100	558,416,400	129,794,300	-1,863,411,000
Operating Cash Flow	2,878,410,000	1,252,033,000	2,115,507,000	2,162,910,000	1,693,761,000	1,218,508,000
Capital Expenditure	1,503,922,000	1,583,375,000	1,151,300,000	588,975,900	925,042,700	1,496,374,000
EBITDA	2,683,862,000	1,828,347,000	1,976,721,000	2,761,210,000	2,513,105,000	888,712,900
Return on Assets %	10.19%	2.47%	1.72%	3.60%	.75%	-9.47%
Return on Equity %	24.05%	6.29%	4.63%	11.14%	2.64%	-30.80%
Debt to Equity	0.52	0.67	0.43	0.55	0.85	1.13

CONTACT INFORMATION:
Phone: 886 35008800　　Fax: 886 35643370
Toll-Free:
Address: 1 Li-Hsin Rd. 2, Hsin-chu Science Park, Hsinchu, 30078 Taiwan

STOCK TICKER/OTHER:
Stock Ticker: AUO
Employees: 63,499
Parent Company:

Exchange: NYS
Fiscal Year Ends: 12/31

SALARIES/BONUSES:
Top Exec. Salary: $　　Bonus: $
Second Exec. Salary: $　　Bonus: $

OTHER THOUGHTS:
Estimated Female Officers or Directors:
Hot Spot for Advancement for Women/Minorities:

Sales, profits and employees may be estimates. Financial information, benefits and other data can change quickly and may vary from those stated here.

Audi AG

NAIC Code: 336111

www.audi.com

TYPES OF BUSINESS:
Automobile Manufacturing
Luxury & Sports Cars
Automobile Customization & Accessories
Engine Manufacturing
Automotive Electronics

BRANDS/DIVISIONS/AFFILIATES:
Lamborghini
Ducati
Audi Sport GmbH
A8
Audi e-tron
Audi Aicon
Audi Elaine
Volkswagen AG

CONTACTS:
Note: Officers with more than one job title may be intentionally listed here more than once.

Rupert Stadler, CEO
Alexander Seitz, Dir.-Finance
Bram Schot, Dir.-Mktg. & Sales
Wendelin Gobel, Dir.-Human Resources
Peter Mertens, Dir.-Tech. Dev.
Frank Dreves, Dir.-Prod.
Bernd Martens, Dir.-Procurement
Matthias Muller, Chmn.
Ulf Berkenhagen, Dir.-Purchasing

GROWTH PLANS/SPECIAL FEATURES:

Audi AG, a publicly-listed subsidiary of Volkswagen AG, is a Germany-based designer and manufacturer of high-end luxury cars. The firm holds participations in companies such as sports car manufacturer Lamborghini, motorcycle manufacturer Ducati, and vehicle upgrade and technology firm Audi Sport GmbH. Audi AG's current models (early-2018) include the A1, A3, A4, A5, A6, A7, A8, Q2, Q3, Q5, Q7, TT and RS/R8. The A1 is a 2-door Sportback sedan; A3 comes in 2- or 4-door sedan formats, as well as a convertible; A4 comes in 4-door sedan and extended length formats; A5 is an elegant 2-door sport-style vehicle; A6 is a 4-door sedan; A7 is a 4-door Sportback sedan; A8 is a 4-door luxury vehicle; Q2 is a 4-door urban model with geometrical design elements; Q3 is a 4-door compact and agile vehicle; Q5 is a 4-door, all-wheel drive car; Q7 is a 4-door model with a focus on comfort; TT is a 2-door sports car; and the RS series of sport vehicles in various formats and styles. The Audi e-tron, the company's first fully electric SUV is due in 2018, with a range of up to 310 miles (500 kilometers). Under current development (early 2018) is: the Audi Aicon, an autonomous model, with no steering wheel or pedals; and the Audi Elaine, an electric-powered SUV coupe that will also make highly-automated driving possible. Audi's quattro technology offers dynamics and safety in conditions where 2-wheel-drive vehicles lose traction, such as slippery or unpaved roads. In collaboration with Berlin-based PTScientists, the company plans to launch a private moon mission, scheduled for a 2019 touchdown. The Audi lunar quattro vehicles will be built with lightweight construction materials, equipped with quattro technology, and driven by a solar-supplied-e-tron engine.

FINANCIAL DATA:
Note: Data for latest year may not have been available at press time.

In U.S. $	2017	2016	2015	2014	2013	2012
Revenue	74,252,270,000	73,250,760,000	72,143,050,000	66,421,750,000	61,596,980,000	60,227,470,000
R&D Expense						
Operating Income	6,774,680,000	6,025,094,000	5,971,992,000	6,359,752,000	6,212,799,000	6,643,780,000
Operating Margin %	9.12%	8.22%	8.27%	9.57%	10.08%	11.03%
SGA Expense	7,387,192,000	7,989,825,000	7,930,549,000	6,769,740,000	6,430,142,000	6,322,705,000
Net Income	4,390,082,000	2,451,283,000	5,191,534,000	5,392,823,000	4,891,452,000	5,290,326,000
Operating Cash Flow	7,623,058,000	9,282,769,000	8,895,009,000	9,164,218,000	8,370,174,000	7,587,246,000
Capital Expenditure	6,316,530,000	6,279,484,000	5,922,597,000	5,297,735,000	4,437,007,000	4,022,080,000
EBITDA	10,481,860,000	7,762,602,000	9,892,811,000	10,760,950,000	6,768,505,000	6,645,015,000
Return on Assets %	5.69%	3.36%	7.81%	9.10%	9.25%	11.06%
Return on Equity %	13.57%	8.64%	20.99%	23.56%	23.97%	31.18%
Debt to Equity	0.01	0.01	0.01	0.01	0.01	

CONTACT INFORMATION:
Phone: 49-800-2834444 Fax:
Toll-Free:
Address: Ettinger Straße, Ingolstadt, D-85045 Germany

STOCK TICKER/OTHER:
Stock Ticker: AUDVF
Employees: 60,457
Parent Company: Volkswagen AG

Exchange: PINX
Fiscal Year Ends: 12/31

SALARIES/BONUSES:
Top Exec. Salary: $ Bonus: $
Second Exec. Salary: $ Bonus: $

OTHER THOUGHTS:
Estimated Female Officers or Directors:
Hot Spot for Advancement for Women/Minorities:

Sales, profits and employees may be estimates. Financial information, benefits and other data can change quickly and may vary from those stated here.

Aurecon Group Brand (Pte) Ltd

www.aurecongroup.com

NAIC Code: 541330

TYPES OF BUSINESS:
Engineering Services
Design
Consulting
Building
Engineering

BRANDS/DIVISIONS/AFFILIATES:
Aspirata
Aurecon Hatch
Aurecon Advisory
Geostrada Engineering Materials Laboratory
IMIS
JK Aurecon
JKTech

CONTACTS: Note: Officers with more than one job title may be intentionally listed here more than once.
Giam Swiegers, Global CEO
Gustav Rohde, COO
Andrew Muller, CFO
Carl Duckinson, CIO
Teddy Daka, Chmn.

GROWTH PLANS/SPECIAL FEATURES:
Aurecon Group Brand (Pte) Ltd. provides engineering, management and specialist technical services for public and private sector clients globally. Its office network extends across 24 countries, and the firm has been involved in projects in more than 34 countries, including Africa, Asia Pacific, the Middle East and the Americas. Its brands and subsidiaries include Aspirata, a program of health and safety services encompassing microbiological and chemical laboratory testing; Aurecon Hatch, a joint venture with Hatch that provides project management services and site infrastructure design to organizations working in coal, cement, agriculture, seaboard bulk materials handling and heavy haul rail; Aurecon Advisory, a specialist entity in Australia and New Zealand for delivering services on projects such as future infrastructure performance, capital due diligence and operational modelling; Geostrada Engineering Materials Laboratory, which provides commercial and site laboratory testing services for engineering and infrastructure related developments; IMIS, a specialist statistical traffic research and consultancy business; and JK Aurecon, an alliance between Aurecon and mining services company JKTech, which delivers client solutions that reduce total costs on resources projects. Aurecon's specializes in markets such as aviation, construction, data & telecommunications, defense, energy, government, international development assistance, manufacturing, oil and gas, property, resources, transport and water.

FINANCIAL DATA: Note: Data for latest year may not have been available at press time.

In U.S. $	2017	2016	2015	2014	2013	2012
Revenue	1,200,000,000	1,100,000,000	1,007,611,000			
R&D Expense						
Operating Income						
Operating Margin %						
SGA Expense						
Net Income						
Operating Cash Flow						
Capital Expenditure						
EBITDA						
Return on Assets %						
Return on Equity %						
Debt to Equity						

CONTACT INFORMATION:
Phone: 61-3-9975-3000   Fax: 61-3-9975-3444
Toll-Free:
Address: 850 Collins Street, Level 8, Docklands, VIC 3008 Australia

STOCK TICKER/OTHER:
Stock Ticker: Private
Employees: 6,798
Parent Company:

Exchange:
Fiscal Year Ends:

SALARIES/BONUSES:
Top Exec. Salary: $ Bonus: $
Second Exec. Salary: $ Bonus: $

OTHER THOUGHTS:
Estimated Female Officers or Directors:
Hot Spot for Advancement for Women/Minorities:

Sales, profits and employees may be estimates. Financial information, benefits and other data can change quickly and may vary from those stated here.

Autodesk Inc

www.autodesk.com

NAIC Code: 0

TYPES OF BUSINESS:
Computer Software-Design & Drafting
Computer Assisted Design Software
Mapping & Infrastructure Management Technology
Film & Media Production Software

BRANDS/DIVISIONS/AFFILIATES:
AutoCAD
AutoCAD LT
Product Design Collection
M&E Collection
3ds Max
Maya
CAM Solutions
BIM 360

CONTACTS:
Note: Officers with more than one job title may be intentionally listed here more than once.

Paul Underwood, Chief Accounting Officer
Crawford Beveridge, Director
Pascal Di Fronzo, Other Executive Officer
Andrew Anagnost, President
Steven Blum, Senior VP, Divisional
R. Herren, Senior VP
Carmel Galvin, Senior VP

GROWTH PLANS/SPECIAL FEATURES:

Autodesk, Inc. is a design software and services company. The firm offers products and solutions to customers in the architectural, manufacturing, geospatial mapping, engineering, construction and digital media markets. Its products are available in multiple languages and are utilized by over 200 million customers worldwide. Autodesk products include: AutoCAD software, a customizable and extensible computer-aided design (CAD) application for professional design, drafting, detailing and visualization; AutoCAD LT software for professional drafting and detailing, and includes document sharing capability without the need for software customization or advanced functionality found in AutoCAD; architecture, engineering and construction (AEC), a collection that helps Autodesk customers design, engineer and construct higher-quality, more predictable building and civil infrastructure projects; Product Design Collection, which offers connected tools to help customers make great products and compete in the manufacturing landscape; the M&E Collection, which offers end-to-end tools for entertainment creation; 3ds Max software, which provides 3D modeling, animation and rendering solutions that enable game developers, design visualization professionals and visual effects artists to digitally create realistic images, animations and complex scenes; Maya software, providing 3D modeling, animation, effects, rendering and compositing solutions for film and video artists, game developers and other professionals; Revit software, for energy-efficient building information modeling; Inventor, offering flexible tools for 3D mechanical design, simulation, analysis, tooling, visualization and documentation; CAM Solutions, a computer-aided manufacturing software that offers solutions for computer numeric control machining, inspection and modeling for manufacturing; Fusion 360, a 3D, CAD, CAM and computer-aided engineering (CAE) tool that connects an entire product development process on a single cloud-based platform; BIM 360, a construction management software; and Shotgun, a cloud-based software for review and production tracking in the media and entertainment industry.

FINANCIAL DATA:
Note: Data for latest year may not have been available at press time.

In U.S. $	2017	2016	2015	2014	2013	2012
Revenue	2,031,000,000	2,504,100,000	2,512,200,000	2,273,900,000	2,312,200,000	
R&D Expense	766,100,000	790,000,000	725,200,000	611,100,000	600,000,000	
Operating Income	-419,100,000	1,300,000	123,800,000	297,600,000	349,800,000	
Operating Margin %	-20.63%	.05%	4.92%	13.08%	15.12%	
SGA Expense	1,310,300,000	1,308,900,000	1,281,300,000	1,090,900,000	1,123,900,000	
Net Income	-582,100,000	-330,500,000	81,800,000	228,800,000	247,400,000	
Operating Cash Flow	169,700,000	414,000,000	708,100,000	563,500,000	559,100,000	
Capital Expenditure	76,000,000	72,400,000	75,500,000	64,200,000	56,400,000	
EBITDA	-279,900,000	147,100,000	269,700,000	426,500,000	477,600,000	
Return on Assets %	-11.28%	-6.33%	1.72%	5.13%	6.56%	
Return on Equity %	-49.47%	-17.21%	3.65%	10.63%	12.60%	
Debt to Equity	1.48	0.91	0.33	0.33	0.36	

CONTACT INFORMATION:
Phone: 415 507-5000   Fax: 415 507-5100
Toll-Free:
Address: 111 McInnis Pkwy., San Rafael, CA 94903 United States

STOCK TICKER/OTHER:
Stock Ticker: ADSK
Employees: 9,000
Parent Company:

Exchange: NAS
Fiscal Year Ends: 01/31

SALARIES/BONUSES:
Top Exec. Salary: $1,108,461   Bonus: $1,000
Second Exec. Salary: $574,385   Bonus: $

OTHER THOUGHTS:
Estimated Female Officers or Directors: 4
Hot Spot for Advancement for Women/Minorities: Y

Sales, profits and employees may be estimates. Financial information, benefits and other data can change quickly and may vary from those stated here.

Autoliv Inc

www.autoliv.com

NAIC Code: 336300

TYPES OF BUSINESS:
Automotive Safety Products Manufacturing
Seat Belts
Airbags
Seat Components
Steering Wheels
Child Seats
Safety Electronics
Anti-Whiplash Systems

BRANDS/DIVISIONS/AFFILIATES:
Zenuity
Veoneer Inc

CONTACTS: Note: Officers with more than one job title may be intentionally listed here more than once.
Jan Carlson, CEO
Jan Carlson, Pres.
Mats Backman, CFO
Thomas Jonsson, Group VP-Communications
Karin Eliasson, Group VP-Human Resources
Jan Olsson, VP-Research & Eng.
Steve Fredin, CTO
Johan Lofvenholm, VP-Eng.
Svante Mogefors, VP-Mfg. & Quality
Anthony J. Nellis, Interim General Counsel
Thomas Jonsson, VP-Corp. Comm.
Mats Wallin, VP-Finance
Steve Fredin, Pres., Autoliv Americas
Jonas Nilsson, Pres., Autoliv Europe
Steven Rode, Pres., Electronics
Jan Carlson, Chmn.
George Chang, Pres., Autoliv Asia
Henrick Arrland, VP-Purchasing

GROWTH PLANS/SPECIAL FEATURES:
Autoliv, Inc. develops, manufactures and supplies automotive safety equipment and systems to the automotive industry. The company operates through two business segments: passive safety and electronics. Passive safety systems are primarily meant to improve vehicle safety, and include modules and components for frontal-impact airbag protection systems, side-impact airbag protection systems, seatbelts, steering wheels, inflator technologies, battery cable cutters, pedestrian protection systems and child seats. The electronics segment produces restraint control electronics and crash sensors for deployment of airbags and seatbelt pretensioners, active safety sensors and software for both advanced driver assistance systems (ADAS) and autonomous driving (AD) solutions, as well as brake control systems. Joint venture Zenuity (with Volvo Car Corporation) develops advanced driver assist systems and autonomous driving technologies. Including all of its joint venture operations, Autolive has approximately 78 production facilities in 25 countries. More than half of the firm's 2017 sales revenue consisted of airbag and steering wheel products, with 27% consisting of seatbelt products, 10% consisting of restraint control products, 7% consisting of active safety products and 5% consisting of brake control system projects. Business is conducted in the following geographic regions: Europe, the Americas, China, Japan and the rest of Asia (ROA). In March 2018, the firm announced plans to spin off its electronics business into a new company called Veoneer, Inc.

FINANCIAL DATA: Note: Data for latest year may not have been available at press time.

In U.S. $	2017	2016	2015	2014	2013	2012
Revenue	10,382,600,000	10,073,600,000	9,169,601,000	9,240,500,000	8,803,400,000	8,266,700,000
R&D Expense	740,900,000	651,000,000	523,800,000	535,600,000	489,300,000	455,400,000
Operating Income	839,500,000	847,700,000	727,800,000	722,600,000	761,400,000	705,400,000
Operating Margin %	8.08%	8.41%	7.93%	7.81%	8.64%	8.53%
SGA Expense	489,700,000	476,100,000	411,500,000	414,900,000	389,900,000	366,700,000
Net Income	427,100,000	567,100,000	456,800,000	467,800,000	485,800,000	483,100,000
Operating Cash Flow	935,900,000	868,400,000	750,500,000	712,700,000	837,900,000	688,500,000
Capital Expenditure	580,100,000	507,900,000	490,700,000	456,000,000	385,600,000	365,400,000
EBITDA	993,500,000	1,249,200,000	1,059,900,000	1,035,800,000	1,052,900,000	983,500,000
Return on Assets %	5.08%	7.19%	6.10%	6.48%	7.16%	7.61%
Return on Equity %	11.07%	15.90%	13.27%	12.62%	12.55%	13.62%
Debt to Equity	0.32	0.35	0.43	0.44	0.07	0.14

CONTACT INFORMATION:
Phone: 46-8-587-20-600   Fax:
Toll-Free:
Address: Klarabergsviadukten 70, Stockholm, SE-107 24 Sweden

STOCK TICKER/OTHER:
Stock Ticker: ALV
Employees: 70,300
Parent Company:

Exchange: NYS
Fiscal Year Ends: 12/31

SALARIES/BONUSES:
Top Exec. Salary: $1,710,065   Bonus: $
Second Exec. Salary: $757,999   Bonus: $

OTHER THOUGHTS:
Estimated Female Officers or Directors: 1
Hot Spot for Advancement for Women/Minorities:

Sales, profits and employees may be estimates. Financial information, benefits and other data can change quickly and may vary from those stated here.

Avaya Holdings Corp

NAIC Code: 334210

www.avaya.com

TYPES OF BUSINESS:
Telecommunications Systems
Telecommunications Software
Consulting Services
Networking Systems & Software
Network Maintenance, Management & Security Services
Systems Planning & Integration
Unified Communications Systems

BRANDS/DIVISIONS/AFFILIATES:
Silver Lake Partners
TPC Capital

CONTACTS:
Note: Officers with more than one job title may be intentionally listed here more than once.

James Chirico, CEO
William Watkins, Chairman of the Board
Shefali Shah, Chief Administrative Officer
William Rowe, General Manager, Divisional
Jaroslaw Glembocki, Senior VP, Divisional
Nicholas Nikolopoulos, Senior VP, Divisional
Laurent Philonenko, Senior VP, Divisional
Patrick OMalley, Senior VP

GROWTH PLANS/SPECIAL FEATURES:

Avaya Holdings Corp. operates as a holding company which, through its subsidiary Avaya Inc, is a leading global provider of unified communications solutions, customer experience management and cloud services. The company's unified communications solutions include conferencing and infrastructure solutions that support real-time engagement by integrating voice, video, data, messaging, conferencing, mobility and more. Its customer experience management solution is designed with a discipline of treating customer relationships as assets in order to transform them into loyal customers via persistent conversation and consistent experience via context. This product offers an omnichannel assisted experience, an omnichannel automated experience and actionable insights. Avaya's cloud services include a subscription-based hosted service in the cloud for high-performance video conferencing, voice over internet protocol (IP), unified communications and remote collaboration. The firm's cloud solutions for partners and service providers enable them to deliver cloud services for every size enterprise, including unified communications, contact center applications and video. The solutions can integrate with other applications by using open standards, APIs and other capabilities. They can be customized for BYOD and deliver standards-based endpoint support. Its multi-tenant capabilities enable partners to optimize their infrastructure for the entire customer base. Partners include channel partners, technology partners, consultants and more. Avaya is owned by private equity firms Silver Lake Partners and TPG Capital. In November 2017, Avaya obtained U.S. Bankruptcy Court approval for its reorganization plan.

FINANCIAL DATA:
Note: Data for latest year may not have been available at press time.

In U.S. $	2017	2016	2015	2014	2013	2012
Revenue	3,272,000,000	3,702,000,000	4,081,000,000	4,371,000,000	4,708,000,000	5,171,000,000
R&D Expense	229,000,000	275,000,000	338,000,000	379,000,000	445,000,000	464,000,000
Operating Income	284,000,000	331,000,000	434,000,000	362,000,000	367,000,000	266,000,000
Operating Margin %	8.67%	8.94%	10.63%	8.28%	7.79%	5.14%
SGA Expense	1,282,000,000	1,413,000,000	1,432,000,000	1,531,000,000	1,521,000,000	1,630,000,000
Net Income	-182,000,000	-730,000,000	-168,000,000	-253,000,000	-376,000,000	-354,000,000
Operating Cash Flow	291,000,000	113,000,000	215,000,000	39,000,000	151,000,000	44,000,000
Capital Expenditure	59,000,000	96,000,000	124,000,000	135,000,000	124,000,000	127,000,000
EBITDA	374,000,000	126,000,000	725,000,000	629,000,000	500,000,000	650,000,000
Return on Assets %	-5.52%	-12.18%	-3.04%	-4.00%	-5.29%	-5.07%
Return on Equity %						
Debt to Equity						

CONTACT INFORMATION:
Phone: 908-953-6000 Fax:
Toll-Free: 866-462-8292
Address: 4655 Great American Pkwy., Santa Clara, CA 95054 United States

STOCK TICKER/OTHER:
Stock Ticker: AVYA Exchange: NYS
Employees: 15,953 Fiscal Year Ends: 09/30
Parent Company:

SALARIES/BONUSES:
Top Exec. Salary: $ Bonus: $
Second Exec. Salary: $ Bonus: $

OTHER THOUGHTS:
Estimated Female Officers or Directors: 1
Hot Spot for Advancement for Women/Minorities:

Babcock & Wilcox Enterprises Inc

www.babcock.com

NAIC Code: 332410

TYPES OF BUSINESS:
Power Generation Systems
Steam Generators
Environmental Equipment
Engineering & Construction Services
Power Plants
Emissions Reduction Equipment
Waste-to-Energy & Biomass Energy Systems
Boiler Cleaning Equipment

BRANDS/DIVISIONS/AFFILIATES:
Babcock & Wilcox MEGTEC Holdings Inc
SPIG SpA
Babcock & Wilcox Beijing Company Ltd
Thermax Babcock & Wilcox Energy Solutions
Halley & Mellowes Pty Ltd
Universal Acoustic & Emission Technologies Inc

CONTACTS:
Note: Officers with more than one job title may be intentionally listed here more than once.

Jenny Apker, CFO
Daniel Hoehn, Chief Accounting Officer
J. Hall, General Counsel
Elias Gedeon, Other Executive Officer
Leslie Kass, President
Mark Low, Senior VP, Divisional
Jimmy Morgan, Senior VP, Divisional
James Muckley, Senior VP, Divisional
Mark Carano, Senior VP, Divisional

GROWTH PLANS/SPECIAL FEATURES:

Babcock & Wilcox Enterprises, Inc. (B&W) is a leading technology-based provider of advanced fossil and renewable power generation and environmental equipment for power and industrial uses. The company operates in three business units: power, renewable and industrial environmental. The power segment supplies boilers fired with fossil fuels, such as coal, oil and natural gas, or renewable fuels such as biomass, municipal solid waste and concentrated solar energy. The renewable segment offers a range of products and services to support steam generating and associated environmental and auxiliary equipment, such as replacement parts, field engineering services, training, operations and maintenance, aftermarket solutions and customized services. The industrial environmental segment caters to a broad range of industries and provides products such as air emissions control solutions, oxidizers, solvent and distillation systems, precipitators, scrubbers, heat recovery systems and other specialized industrial processes and systems. Wholly-owned subsidiary Babcock & Wilcox MEGTEC Holdings, Inc. supplies ovens and dryers, specialized coating lines and material handling systems for energy storage, membrane production, digital printing and other advanced manufacturing processes. Subsidiary SPIG S.p.A. provides custom-engineered cooling systems, services and aftermarket products such as air-cooled (dry) cooling systems, mechanical draft wet cooling towers and natural draft wet cooling hyperbolic towers. Joint ventures of the firm include Babcock & Wilcox Beijing Company Ltd.; Thermax Babcock & Wilcox Energy Solutions Pvt. Ltd.; and Halley & Mellowes Pty. Ltd. In January 2017, the firm acquired Universal Acoustic & Emission Technologies, Inc., a provider of custom-engineered acoustic, emission and filtration solutions.

B&W offers employees medical, dental, vision, personal accident and life insurance; health and wellness programs; employee assistance programs; a Thrift Plan/401(k); and tuition reimbursement.

FINANCIAL DATA:
Note: Data for latest year may not have been available at press time.

In U.S. $	2017	2016	2015	2014	2013	2012
Revenue	1,557,735,000	1,578,263,000	1,757,295,000	1,589,719,000	1,767,651,000	2,039,100,000
R&D Expense	9,412,000	10,406,000	16,543,000	18,747,000	21,043,000	26,018,000
Operating Income	-169,333,000	-78,438,000	51,646,000	-35,084,000	211,368,000	191,760,000
Operating Margin %	-10.87%	-4.96%	2.93%	-2.20%	11.95%	9.40%
SGA Expense	259,799,000	247,149,000	239,968,000	241,699,000	204,070,000	247,931,000
Net Income	-379,824,000	-115,649,000	19,141,000	-26,529,000	174,527,000	140,753,000
Operating Cash Flow	-189,833,000	2,273,000	170,399,000	-28,672,000	16,400,000	58,195,000
Capital Expenditure	14,278,000	22,450,000	35,397,000	17,926,000	11,588,000	25,074,000
EBITDA	-241,349,000	-64,760,000	56,196,000	-18,735,000	235,981,000	229,641,000
Return on Assets %	-26.64%	-7.24%	1.20%	-1.88%	13.46%	
Return on Equity %	-103.45%	-17.79%	2.65%	-4.33%	32.87%	
Debt to Equity	0.51					

CONTACT INFORMATION:
Phone: 434 522-6800   Fax:
Toll-Free:
Address: 13024 Ballantyne Corp. Pl., Ste. 700, Charlotte, NC 28277 United States

STOCK TICKER/OTHER:
Stock Ticker: BW
Employees: 5,000
Parent Company:

Exchange: NYS
Fiscal Year Ends: 12/31

SALARIES/BONUSES:
Top Exec. Salary: $978,500   Bonus: $
Second Exec. Salary: $424,325   Bonus: $

OTHER THOUGHTS:
Estimated Female Officers or Directors: 3
Hot Spot for Advancement for Women/Minorities: Y

BAE Systems plc

www.baesystems.com

NAIC Code: 336410

TYPES OF BUSINESS:
Defense and Aerospace Systems
Military Vehicles
Military Aircraft
Naval Vessels & Submarines
Satellite Manufacturing
Electronic Systems
Advanced Materials & Technologies
Security & Surveillance Technology

BRANDS/DIVISIONS/AFFILIATES:
BAE Systems Applied Intelligence
BAE Systems Australia
BAE Systems India
BAE Systems Saudi Arabia

CONTACTS:
Note: Officers with more than one job title may be intentionally listed here more than once.

Charles Woodburn, CEO
Peter Lynas, CFO
Claire Divver, Dir.-Communications
Karin Hoeing, Dir.-Human Resources
Nigel Whitehead, CTO
Phillip Bramwell, General Counsel
Alan Garwood, Dir.-Bus. Dev.
Claire Divver, Dir.-Comm.
Nigel Whitehead, Managing Dir.-Programs & Support
Tom Arseneault, COO-BAE Systems, Inc.
Kevin Taylor, Dir.-Strategy
Jerry Demuro, CEO
Roger Carr, Chmn.
Guy Griffiths, Managing Dir.-Intl

GROWTH PLANS/SPECIAL FEATURES:

BAE Systems plc is a global defense, aerospace and security company, with products and services covering air, land and naval forces, as well as advanced electronics, security, IT and support services. The firm operates through 11 global businesses. The air sector business delivers information and air power to customers in the U.K. and overseas. BAE Systems Applied Intelligence delivers solutions that protect and enhance critical assets in the intelligence sector. These solutions combine large-scale data exploitation, security and integration. BAE Systems Australia supplies communications, electronic warfare systems, military air support, air defense, mission support systems and intelligence, surveillance and reconnaissance (ISR) to the Australian Defence Force. BAE Systems India manufactures defense systems in India, for the purpose of providing support to armed services. BAE Systems Saudi Arabia supports customers in the air, land, command and control and naval sectors, and supplies solutions in mechanical engineering, electronics repair/manufacturing, IT, logistics and manpower development. The electronics systems business offers a broad portfolio of products, from flight and engine controls to electronic warfare and night vision systems, surveillance and reconnaissance sensors, secure networked communications equipment, and power and energy management systems. The intelligence and security business offers solutions that enable militaries and governments to carry out their missions across air, land, sea, space and cyber domains. The platforms and services business designs, develops, produces, supports, maintains, modernizes and upgrades armored combat vehicles, naval guns, surface ship combatants, vessels, missile launchers, artillery systems and protective wear. The maritime business designs and manufactures naval ships and submarines, as well as combat systems and equipment. The regional aircraft business provides regional aircraft and support services to regional airlines worldwide. Last, the shared services business provides capabilities and support to BAE Systems' internal customers, including shared technology and tailored solutions.

U.S. employees receive health coverage and 401(k).

FINANCIAL DATA:
Note: Data for latest year may not have been available at press time.

In U.S. $	2017	2016	2015	2014	2013	2012
Revenue	26,096,000,000	25,338,270,000	23,909,700,000	21,976,930,000	24,019,370,000	25,400,940,000
R&D Expense						
Operating Income	1,891,468,000	2,268,908,000	1,917,106,000	1,538,242,000	1,008,403,000	3,939,610,000
Operating Margin %	7.24%	8.95%	8.01%	6.99%	4.19%	15.50%
SGA Expense						
Net Income	1,216,351,000	1,300,385,000	1,307,506,000	1,053,981,000	239,282,200	1,521,151,000
Operating Cash Flow	2,701,894,000	1,750,463,000	894,459,500	952,855,700	-156,672,800	3,095,001,000
Capital Expenditure	677,966,100	697,906,300	588,235,300	458,624,100	383,136,300	572,568,000
EBITDA	3,174,761,000	2,667,711,000	2,730,380,000	2,653,468,000	3,136,305,000	3,247,401,000
Return on Assets %	3.75%	4.24%	4.60%	3.74%	.80%	4.70%
Return on Equity %	20.88%	28.41%	38.00%	28.33%	4.73%	26.83%
Debt to Equity	0.85	1.28	1.26	1.55	0.74	0.79

CONTACT INFORMATION:
Phone: 44 1252373232   Fax: 44 1252383991
Toll-Free:
Address: 6 Carlton Gardens, London, SW1Y 5AD United Kingdom

STOCK TICKER/OTHER:
Stock Ticker: BAESF   Exchange: PINX
Employees: 83,200   Fiscal Year Ends: 12/31
Parent Company:

SALARIES/BONUSES:
Top Exec. Salary: $1,130,893   Bonus: $2,247,543
Second Exec. Salary: $1,157,955   Bonus: $1,867,255

OTHER THOUGHTS:
Estimated Female Officers or Directors: 4
Hot Spot for Advancement for Women/Minorities: Y

Sales, profits and employees may be estimates. Financial information, benefits and other data can change quickly and may vary from those stated here.

Baker Huges, A GE Company

NAIC Code: 213112

www.bhge.com

TYPES OF BUSINESS:
Oil Field Services
Specialty Chemicals
Process Equipment
Geophysical Services
Drilling Fluids
Drill Bits
Data Management

BRANDS/DIVISIONS/AFFILIATES:
General Electric Company
Baker Hughes Inc

CONTACTS:
Note: Officers with more than one job title may be intentionally listed here more than once.

Lorenzo Simonelli, CEO
Brian Worrell, CFO
Jeffrey Immelt, Chairman of the Board
Derek Mathieson, Chief Marketing Officer
Martin Craighead, Director
John Rice, Director
William Marsh, Other Executive Officer
Uwem Ukpong, Other Executive Officer
Roderick Christie, President, Divisional
Maria Borras, President, Divisional
Matthias Heilmann, President, Divisional
Neil Saunders, President, Divisional
Kurt Camilleri, Vice President

GROWTH PLANS/SPECIAL FEATURES:

Baker Hughes, A GE Company (formerly Baker Hughes, Inc.) is a full-stream provider of integrated oil and gas development products, services and digital solutions, with operations in more than 120 countries. These streams include upstream, midstream and downstream. The firm helps its customers acquire, transport and refine hydrocarbons more efficiently, productively, safely and cost-effectively. Baker Hughes utilizes people, machines and the cloud to break down silos and reduce waste and risk. The upstream division offers technology and digital capabilities to achieve better levels of upstream productivity, from evaluation to drilling to completion and production. The midstream division offers equipment and service solutions for liquid natural gas (LNG), pipeline and storage inspection, asset condition monitoring and data analytics to improve power and compression efficiency. The downstream division provides a range of chemical, mechanical, digital and service solutions for refinery and petrochemical operations. Baker Hughes' industrial solutions can be applied to a wide range of industries, from turnkey power generation systems to control and sensing products. These solutions include power turbines and advanced data management tools. The company is headquartered in Houston, Texas and in London, England. In July 2017, Baker Hughes, Inc. was acquired by General Electric Company, creating a new company that delivers industry-leading equipment, services and digital solutions across the entire spectrum of oil and gas development. Baker Hughes, A GE Company trades publicly on the New York Stock Exchange under symbol BHGE.

FINANCIAL DATA:
Note: Data for latest year may not have been available at press time.

In U.S. $	2017	2016	2015	2014	2013	2012
Revenue	17,259,000,000	23,110,000,000	16,688,000,000			
R&D Expense						
Operating Income	678,000,000	-369,000,000	2,380,000,000			
Operating Margin %	3.92%	-1.59%	14.26%			
SGA Expense	2,535,000,000	2,955,000,000	2,115,000,000			
Net Income	-73,000,000	-904,000,000	-606,000,000			
Operating Cash Flow	-799,000,000	262,000,000	1,277,000,000			
Capital Expenditure	665,000,000	424,000,000	607,000,000			
EBITDA	1,781,000,000	-579,000,000	2,910,000,000			
Return on Assets %	-.18%	-4.16%				
Return on Equity %	-.49%	-6.15%				
Debt to Equity	0.42					

CONTACT INFORMATION:
Phone: 713 439-8600   Fax: 713 739-8699
Toll-Free:
Address: 17021 Aldine Westfiled Rd., Houston, TX 77073-5101 United States

SALARIES/BONUSES:
Top Exec. Salary: $768,173   Bonus: $
Second Exec. Salary: $737,740   Bonus: $

STOCK TICKER/OTHER:
Stock Ticker: BHGE   Exchange: NYS
Employees: 32,000   Fiscal Year Ends: 12/31
Parent Company: General Electric Company

OTHER THOUGHTS:
Estimated Female Officers or Directors:
Hot Spot for Advancement for Women/Minorities: Y

Sales, profits and employees may be estimates. Financial information, benefits and other data can change quickly and may vary from those stated here.

Balfour Beatty plc

NAIC Code: 237990

www.balfourbeatty.com

TYPES OF BUSINESS:
Subway Construction
Engineering Services
Railway Services
Property Management
Utility & Roadway Infrastructure Management

BRANDS/DIVISIONS/AFFILIATES:

CONTACTS: Note: Officers with more than one job title may be intentionally listed here more than once.
Leo Quinn, CEO
Philip Harrison, CFO
Chris Vaughan, General Counsel
Peter Zinkin, Dir.-Planning & Dev.
Mark Layman, CEO-Construction
George Pierson, CEO-Professional Services
Ian Rylatt, CEO-Infrastructure Investments
Kevin Craven, CEO-Services
Philip Aiken, Chmn.

GROWTH PLANS/SPECIAL FEATURES:
Balfour Beatty plc provides engineering, construction and financial services for rail, road, power and building projects worldwide. It is one of the largest fixed rail infrastructure contracting companies in the world. Balfour Beatty divides its business into three categories: construction services, support services and infrastructure investments. Construction services include building design, civil and ground engineering, rail engineering, refurbishment and fit-out and mechanical and electrical services. The firm has an established presence in the U.K. and U.S. through its subsidiaries and is expanding its business into Hong Kong and the Middle East. Balfour Beatty provides ongoing operation and maintenance of assets after construction and offers business services outsourcing through its support services division. The division encompasses the company's utilities, facilities management, rail renewals and highway management activities. The infrastructure investments segment is a leader in the public private partnership (PPP) contracts sector. It maintains concessions in the U.K., primarily in the education, health and roads/street lighting sectors; in the U.S., primarily involved in the military housing market; and in Singapore.

FINANCIAL DATA: Note: Data for latest year may not have been available at press time.

In U.S. $	2017	2016	2015	2014	2013	2012
Revenue	9,850,448,000	9,860,419,000	9,905,996,000	10,346,100,000	12,455,490,000	13,506,620,000
R&D Expense						
Operating Income	4,272,896	-150,975,600	-457,199,800	-608,175,500	-149,551,300	-106,822,400
Operating Margin %	.04%	-1.53%	-4.61%	-5.87%	-1.20%	-.79%
SGA Expense						
Net Income	239,282,200	34,183,160	-293,405,500	-85,457,910	-49,850,450	62,669,140
Operating Cash Flow	54,123,340	-193,704,600	-183,734,500	-529,839,000	-249,252,200	-338,983,000
Capital Expenditure	143,854,100	74,063,520	118,216,800	183,734,500	170,915,800	105,398,100
EBITDA	273,465,300	146,702,800	-193,704,600	-287,708,300	233,585,000	321,891,500
Return on Assets %	3.48%	.51%	-4.18%	-1.09%	-.60%	.76%
Return on Equity %	18.53%	3.03%	-20.06%	-5.30%	-2.99%	3.47%
Debt to Equity	0.62	0.95	1.02	0.76	0.81	

CONTACT INFORMATION:
Phone: 44 2072166800 Fax: 44 2072166950
Toll-Free:
Address: 5 Churchill Pl., Canary Wharf, London, E14 5HU United Kingdom

STOCK TICKER/OTHER:
Stock Ticker: BAFBF
Employees: 20,238
Parent Company:

Exchange: PINX
Fiscal Year Ends: 12/31

SALARIES/BONUSES:
Top Exec. Salary: $1,139,439   Bonus: $828,942
Second Exec. Salary: $569,719   Bonus: $410,198

OTHER THOUGHTS:
Estimated Female Officers or Directors: 2
Hot Spot for Advancement for Women/Minorities:

Baran Group Ltd

www.barangroup.com

NAIC Code: 237000

TYPES OF BUSINESS:
Civil Engineering and Heavy Construction
Technology Development
Telecommunications

BRANDS/DIVISIONS/AFFILIATES:
InTime Software Systems Ltd
ICM-Russia

CONTACTS:
Note: Officers with more than one job title may be intentionally listed here more than once.

Sharon Zaid, CEO
Izek Frank, Deputy CEO
Sasson Shilo, CFO
Dan Ben Harosh, VP-Human Resources
Haim Assael, General Counsel
Arik Shaked, Mgr.-Bus. Dev.
Dan Shenbach, CEO-Baran Israel
Issac Friedman, Gen. Mgr.-Infrastructure & Construction Div.
Meir Dor, Chmn.
Steven Senter, CEO-Baran Intl

GROWTH PLANS/SPECIAL FEATURES:

Baran Group, Ltd. is an Israeli firm that provides engineering, construction, telecommunication and technology solutions to a range of market segments. These markets include manufacturing, power & renewable energy, petroleum, water supply, sewage/hazardous waste, transportation, telecommunications, building, green construction and process industries. Baran offers seven primary solutions to its clients, including: feasibility studies, which offers a variety of services during the early stages of the life cycle of a project; engineering & design, which provides engineering in the process, civil, electrical, mechanical and piping fields; permitting & validation, including risk, evaluation of impacts, master plans, urban planning, building permits, business licenses, operating/populating permits, toxin permits, engineering plans and facility licenses; turnkey, including activities in Turkey such as engineering and design for industry, communications, gas, petroleum, power and water sectors; EPCM, providing engineering, procurement, construction and management services worldwide, including the preparation of tender documents, evaluating bidders and advisory/consultation services; project financing, offering the financing of long-term infrastructure, industrial projects and public services based on a non-recourse or limited recourse financial structure where project debt and equity used to finance the project are paid back from cash-flow, generated by the project; and PPP, which is a type of arrangement in which the private sector builds an infrastructure project, operates it and eventually transfers ownership of the project to the government. Additional business of the Baran Group include the following subsidiaries: InTime Software Systems Ltd., a developer of artificial intelligence (AI) and knowledge management software with real-time decision support capabilities; and ICM-Russia (which stands for investments, construction and management), a full-service Russian engineering company formed to provide engineering, construction and technological equipment and services in relation to the Tikhvin Freight Car Building Plant, as well as for other projects.

FINANCIAL DATA:
Note: Data for latest year may not have been available at press time.

In U.S. $	2017	2016	2015	2014	2013	2012
Revenue				133,172,082	141,943,896	
R&D Expense						
Operating Income						
Operating Margin %						
SGA Expense						
Net Income				-17,542,695	4,252,774	
Operating Cash Flow						
Capital Expenditure						
EBITDA						
Return on Assets %						
Return on Equity %						
Debt to Equity						

CONTACT INFORMATION:
Phone: 972 39775000   Fax: 972 39775001
Toll-Free:
Address: 5 Menachem Begin Ave., Beit-Dagan, 50200 Israel

STOCK TICKER/OTHER:
Stock Ticker: BRANF
Employees: 1,454
Parent Company:

Exchange: GREY
Fiscal Year Ends: 12/31

SALARIES/BONUSES:
Top Exec. Salary: $ Bonus: $
Second Exec. Salary: $ Bonus: $

OTHER THOUGHTS:
Estimated Female Officers or Directors:
Hot Spot for Advancement for Women/Minorities:

Sales, profits and employees may be estimates. Financial information, benefits and other data can change quickly and may vary from those stated here.

BASF New Business GmbH

NAIC Code: 541712

www.basf-new-business.com

TYPES OF BUSINESS:
Chemistry & Materials Research
Organic LED Technology
Organic Photovoltaic Materials
Time Temperature Indicators
Waste Heat Recovery
Probiotics

BRANDS/DIVISIONS/AFFILIATES:
BASF SE
BASF Venture Capital GmbH
BASF 3D Printing Solutions GmbH

CONTACTS:
Note: Officers with more than one job title may be intentionally listed here more than once.

Wolfgang Hormuth, Dir.-Strategy & Scouting
Joachim Rosch, VP-Foresight
Carla Siedel, VP-E-Power Mgmt.
Dejana Drew, Dir.-Medical Industry
Felix Gorth, Dir.-Organic Electronics
Kurt Bock, Chmn.

GROWTH PLANS/SPECIAL FEATURES:
BASF New Business GmbH is a subsidiary of BASF SE that strives to discover new business areas for the BASF group. BASF New Business tracks down a businesses' long-term trends and innovative subjects, and then analyzes the growth potential to see if it would fit within the BASF group for the purpose of establishing new growth fields for BASF. Current growth fields are expected to show high sales potential by 2020 and beyond. Focusing on chemistry-based materials, technologies and system solutions new to BASF, the company promotes technological progress by developing new products. BASF New Business comprises two divisions: scouting and incubation, which identifies, evaluates and develops new businesses; and business build up, which is responsible for developing new growth fields. Subsidiary BASF Venture Capital GmbH invests in startup companies to bring the innovative technologies for novel materials to BASF. BASF industries include agriculture, automotive/transportation, chemicals, construction, electronics, energy/resources, furniture/wood, home care/cleaning, nutrition, packaging, print, paints/coatings, personal care/hygiene, pharmaceuticals, plastics/rubber, pulp/paper and textiles. During 2017, the firm established a wholly-owned subsidiary, BASF 3D Printing Solutions GmbH, to establish and expand the business with materials, system solutions, components and services in the field of 3D printing.

FINANCIAL DATA:
Note: Data for latest year may not have been available at press time.

In U.S. $	2017	2016	2015	2014	2013	2012
Revenue						
R&D Expense						
Operating Income						
Operating Margin %						
SGA Expense						
Net Income						
Operating Cash Flow						
Capital Expenditure						
EBITDA						
Return on Assets %						
Return on Equity %						
Debt to Equity						

CONTACT INFORMATION:
Phone: 49-621-60-76811 Fax: 49-621-60-76818
Toll-Free:
Address: Benckiserplatz 1 BE01, Ludwigshafen, 67059 Germany

SALARIES/BONUSES:
Top Exec. Salary: $ Bonus: $
Second Exec. Salary: $ Bonus: $

STOCK TICKER/OTHER:
Stock Ticker: Subsidiary   Exchange:
Employees: 80   Fiscal Year Ends: 12/31
Parent Company: BASF SE

OTHER THOUGHTS:
Estimated Female Officers or Directors: 2
Hot Spot for Advancement for Women/Minorities:

Sales, profits and employees may be estimates. Financial information, benefits and other data can change quickly and may vary from those stated here.

BASF SE

NAIC Code: 325199

www.basf.com

TYPES OF BUSINESS:
Chemicals Manufacturing
Agricultural Products
Oil & Gas Production
Plastics
Coatings
Nanotechnology Research
Nutritional Products
Agricultural Biotechnology

BRANDS/DIVISIONS/AFFILIATES:
Wintershall AG
Rolic AG
Wintershall DEA

CONTACTS:
Note: Officers with more than one job title may be intentionally listed here more than once.

Hans-Ulrich Engel, CFO
Andreas Kreimeyer, Exec. Dir.-Research
Wayne T. Smith, Head-Chemical Eng.
Margret Suckale, Dir.-Industrial Rel.
Martin Brudermuller, Vice Chmn-Exec. Board
Kurt Bock, Chmn.
Harold Schwager, Head-Procurement

GROWTH PLANS/SPECIAL FEATURES:

BASF SE is a chemical manufacturing company that serves customers in more than 200 countries. The firm operates in five business segments: chemicals, performance products, agricultural solutions, functional materials and solutions and oil and gas. The chemicals segment manufactures inorganic, petrochemical and intermediate chemicals for the pharmaceutical, construction, textile and automotive industries. The performance products segment produces pigments, printing supplies, coatings and polymers for the automotive, oil, packaging, textile, detergent, sanitary care, construction and chemical industries. BASF also employs chemical nanotechnology to produce pigments used to color coatings, paints, plastics and sunscreen. The firm's agricultural solutions segment produces genetically engineered plants, nutritional supplements, herbicides, fungicides and insecticides for use in agriculture, public health and pest control. The functional materials and solutions segment develops automotive and industrial catalysts, construction chemicals and coatings and refinishes for the automotive and construction markets. The oil and gas segment, operated through Wintershall AG, focuses on petroleum and natural gas exploration and production in Europe, the Middle East, North Africa, South America, Russia and the Caspian Sea. In early-2017, BASF acquired Rolic AG, a specialist in light management for advanced liquid crystal display (LCD) and organic light-emitting diode (OLED) displays. That October, the firm agreed to acquire the seed and herbicide businesses from Bayer for approximately $7 billion. In December, BASF and LetterOne signed a letter of intent to merge their oil and gas subsidiaries and businesses in a joint venture that would operate under the name Wintershall DEA. More than 65% would be held by BASF, with the remaining 30+% held by LetterOne.

FINANCIAL DATA:
Note: Data for latest year may not have been available at press time.

In U.S. $	2017	2016	2015	2014	2013	2012
Revenue	79,620,390,000	71,068,690,000	86,997,700,000	91,785,420,000	91,349,500,000	97,222,710,000
R&D Expense	2,331,497,000	2,300,625,000	2,411,766,000	2,326,558,000	2,266,048,000	2,156,141,000
Operating Income	9,844,649,000	7,760,133,000	7,586,011,000	8,445,504,000	8,552,941,000	11,606,860,000
Operating Margin %	12.36%	10.91%	8.71%	9.20%	9.36%	11.93%
SGA Expense	11,946,460,000	11,238,850,000	11,720,470,000	10,931,360,000	10,853,570,000	11,158,590,000
Net Income	7,505,743,000	5,008,768,000	4,923,559,000	6,365,926,000	5,979,402,000	6,025,094,000
Operating Cash Flow	10,848,630,000	9,529,750,000	11,664,900,000	8,592,458,000	9,718,690,000	8,314,605,000
Capital Expenditure	4,934,674,000	5,118,674,000	7,177,258,000	6,540,048,000	5,754,649,000	5,123,614,000
EBITDA	15,788,240,000	13,070,220,000	13,461,680,000	14,345,870,000	13,419,700,000	16,944,110,000
Return on Assets %	7.82%	5.50%	5.60%	7.59%	7.52%	7.77%
Return on Equity %	18.51%	12.93%	13.62%	18.83%	18.73%	20.02%
Debt to Equity	0.45	0.40	0.37	0.45	0.41	0.37

CONTACT INFORMATION:
Phone: 49 621600 Fax: 49 6216042525
Toll-Free: 800-526-1072
Address: 38 Carl-Bosch St., Ludwigshafen, GM 67056 Germany

SALARIES/BONUSES:
Top Exec. Salary: $2,278,878 Bonus: $5,168,780
Second Exec. Salary: $1,515,454 Bonus: $3,438,257

STOCK TICKER/OTHER:
Stock Ticker: BASFY
Employees: 115,490
Parent Company:

Exchange: PINX
Fiscal Year Ends: 12/31

OTHER THOUGHTS:
Estimated Female Officers or Directors: 2
Hot Spot for Advancement for Women/Minorities: Y

Bausch & Lomb Inc

NAIC Code: 339100

www.bausch.com

TYPES OF BUSINESS:
Supplies-Eye Care
Contact Lens Products
Ophthalmic Pharmaceuticals
Surgical Products

BRANDS/DIVISIONS/AFFILIATES:
Valeant Pharmaceuticals International Inc
Biotrue
Bausch + Lomb
PureVision
ReNu
Alaway
Alrex
PreserVision

CONTACTS: Note: Officers with more than one job title may be intentionally listed here more than once.
Robert Bertolini, Pres.
John R. Barr, Pres., Surgical Bus.
Mariano Garcia-Valino, Corp. VP
Sheila A. Hopkins, Pres., Vision Care Bus.
Rodney William Unsworth, Pres., Asia Pacific
Joseph C. Papa, Chmn.-Valeant

GROWTH PLANS/SPECIAL FEATURES:

Bausch & Lomb, Inc. (B&L), owned by Valeant Pharmaceuticals International, Inc., is a world leader in the development, marketing and manufacturing of eye care products. The firm's products are marketed in more than 100 countries, and include contact lenses, contact lens care, dry eye products, allergy/redness relief, Rx pharmaceutical, eye vitamins, surgical products and vision accessories. B&L's contact lenses are for people who are nearsighted, farsighted, have astigmatism or presbyopia; they are soft hydrophilic discs that float on the cornea of the eye. Brands include Biotrue, Bausch + Lomb, PureVision, SofLens and Boston Multivision GP. Lens care products include Biotrue eye solution, PeroxiClear cleaning solution, ReNu solution and drops and Boston One Step cleaner and drops as well as Sensitive Eyes solutions. Dry eye product brands include Soothe eye drops, THERA PEARL Eye mask, Advanced Eye Relief and Muro 128 solutions. Allergy and redness relief product brands include Alaway, Opcon and Advanced Relief. Rx pharmaceutical product brands include Alrex, Lotemax, Retisert, BEPREVE, TIMOPTIC, PROLENSA, Vyzulta, Besivance, Zylet, LACRISERT, Istalol, Macugen Visudyne and Zirgan. Eye wash brands include Advanced and Collyrium. Eye vitamins are marketed under the PreserVision brand. Surgical product brands include enVista, Crystalens, Trulign, Akreos and SofPort. Last, vision accessories include magnifiers, cleaning kits, eyewear cleaning products and lens cases, all under the B&L name.

The company offers employees medical and dental coverage, a 401(k) account plan, a vacation buy/sell program, flexible spending accounts and education reimbursement.

FINANCIAL DATA: Note: Data for latest year may not have been available at press time.

In U.S. $	2017	2016	2015	2014	2013	2012
Revenue	4,871,000,000	4,927,000,000	4,603,000,000	3,160,000,000	3,100,000,000	3,040,000,000
R&D Expense						
Operating Income						
Operating Margin %						
SGA Expense						
Net Income	1,440,000,000	1,483,000,000				
Operating Cash Flow						
Capital Expenditure						
EBITDA						
Return on Assets %						
Return on Equity %						
Debt to Equity						

CONTACT INFORMATION:
Phone: 585-338-6000   Fax: 585-338-6896
Toll-Free: 800-553-5340
Address: 400 Somerset Corporate Blvd, Bridgewater, NJ 08807 United States

STOCK TICKER/OTHER:
Stock Ticker: Subsidiary   Exchange:
Employees: 12,000   Fiscal Year Ends: 12/31
Parent Company: Valeant Pharmaceuticals International Inc

SALARIES/BONUSES:
Top Exec. Salary: $ Bonus: $
Second Exec. Salary: $ Bonus: $

OTHER THOUGHTS:
Estimated Female Officers or Directors: 1
Hot Spot for Advancement for Women/Minorities: Y

Sales, profits and employees may be estimates. Financial information, benefits and other data can change quickly and may vary from those stated here.

Baxter International Inc

www.baxter.com

NAIC Code: 339100

TYPES OF BUSINESS:
Medical Equipment Manufacturing
Supplies-Intravenous & Renal Dialysis Systems
Medication Delivery Products & IV Fluids
Biopharmaceutical Products
Plasma Collection & Processing
Vaccines
Software
Contract Research

BRANDS/DIVISIONS/AFFILIATES:
RECOTHROM
PREVELEAK

CONTACTS: Note: Officers with more than one job title may be intentionally listed here more than once.
Jose Almeida, CEO
James Saccaro, CFO
Caroline Karp, Chief Accounting Officer
Sean Martin, General Counsel
Andrew Frye, President, Divisional
Giuseppe Accogli, President, Divisional
Cristiano Franzi, President, Divisional
Brik Eyre, President, Geographical
Jeanne Mason, Senior VP, Divisional
Scott Pleau, Senior VP, Divisional

GROWTH PLANS/SPECIAL FEATURES:
Baxter International, Inc., through its subsidiaries, provides a broad portfolio of essential healthcare products. These offerings include: acute and chronic dialysis therapies; sterile intravenous (IV) solutions; infusion systems and devices; parenteral nutrition therapies; inhaled anesthetics; generic injectable pharmaceuticals; and surgical hemostat and sealant products. In addition, Baxter's renal portfolio addresses the needs of patients with kidney failure or kidney disease. This portfolio includes innovative technologies and therapies for peritoneal dialysis, in-center and home hemodialysis, continuous renal replacement therapy, multi-organ extracorporeal support therapy, and additional dialysis services. Baxter's scientists are currently pursuing a range of next-generation monitors, dialyzers, devices, dialysis solutions and connectivity technology for home patients. Baxter manufactures its products in over 20 countries, and sells them in more than 100 countries. The firm's business is organized into the following geographic regions of: Americas (North and South), EMEA (Europe, Middle East and Africa) and APAC (Asia-Pacific). Each of these regions provide a wide range of essential healthcare products across the company's entire portfolio, with approximately 60% of annual revenue generated outside the U.S. Baxter maintains approximately 50 manufacturing facilities in the U.S., Europe, Asia-Pacific, Latin America and Canada (as of December 2017). In March 2018, the firm acquired two hemostat and sealant products from Mallinckrodt plc: RECOTHROM, a stand-alone recombinant thrombin; and PREVELEAK, a surgical sealant used in vascular reconstruction.

FINANCIAL DATA: Note: Data for latest year may not have been available at press time.

In U.S. $	2017	2016	2015	2014	2013	2012
Revenue	10,561,000,000	10,163,000,000	9,968,000,000	16,671,000,000	15,259,000,000	14,190,000,000
R&D Expense	617,000,000	647,000,000	603,000,000	1,421,000,000	1,246,000,000	1,156,000,000
Operating Income	1,258,000,000	724,000,000	449,000,000	2,707,000,000	2,668,000,000	2,821,000,000
Operating Margin %	11.91%	7.12%	4.50%	16.23%	17.48%	19.88%
SGA Expense	2,587,000,000	2,739,000,000	3,094,000,000	4,029,000,000	3,681,000,000	3,324,000,000
Net Income	717,000,000	4,965,000,000	968,000,000	2,497,000,000	2,012,000,000	2,326,000,000
Operating Cash Flow	1,837,000,000	1,654,000,000	1,647,000,000	3,215,000,000	3,198,000,000	3,106,000,000
Capital Expenditure	634,000,000	719,000,000	911,000,000	1,898,000,000	1,525,000,000	1,161,000,000
EBITDA	2,063,000,000	5,843,000,000	1,333,000,000	3,611,000,000	3,527,000,000	3,714,000,000
Return on Assets %	4.39%	27.18%	4.12%	9.64%	8.69%	11.78%
Return on Equity %	8.23%	57.94%	11.41%	30.11%	26.12%	34.40%
Debt to Equity	0.38	0.33	0.44	0.93	0.96	0.80

CONTACT INFORMATION:
Phone: 847 948-2000　　Fax: 847 948-2964
Toll-Free: 800-422-9837
Address: 1 Baxter Pkwy., Deerfield, IL 60015 United States

STOCK TICKER/OTHER:
Stock Ticker: BAX
Employees: 48,000
Parent Company:

Exchange: NYS
Fiscal Year Ends: 12/31

SALARIES/BONUSES:
Top Exec. Salary: $1,300,000　　Bonus: $
Second Exec. Salary: $521,479　　Bonus: $500,000

OTHER THOUGHTS:
Estimated Female Officers or Directors: 6
Hot Spot for Advancement for Women/Minorities: Y

Sales, profits and employees may be estimates. Financial information, benefits and other data can change quickly and may vary from those stated here.

Bayer AG

NAIC Code: 325412

www.bayer.com

TYPES OF BUSINESS:
- Chemicals Manufacturing
- Pharmaceuticals
- Animal Health Products
- Health Care Products
- Crop Science
- Plant Biotechnology
- Over-the-Counter Drugs
- Personal Care Products

BRANDS/DIVISIONS/AFFILIATES:
- Claritin
- Bayer Aspirin
- Aleve
- Bepanthen/Bepanthol
- Canesten
- Dr. Scholl's
- Coppertone

CONTACTS:
Note: Officers with more than one job title may be intentionally listed here more than once.

Johannes Dietsch, CFO
Hartmut Klusik, Human Resources
Werner Baumann, Chmn.

GROWTH PLANS/SPECIAL FEATURES:

Bayer AG is a German life science company with core competencies in the areas of healthcare and agriculture. With the company's innovative products, Bayer contributes to finding solutions to some of the major challenges confronting these sectors. It seeks to improve quality of life by preventing, alleviating and treating diseases; and the firm helps to provide a reliable supply of high-quality food, feed and plant-based raw materials. Bayer develops new molecules for use in innovative products. Its research and development activities are based on the biochemical processes in living organisms. The company groups its business into four divisions. The pharmaceuticals division focuses on prescription products, especially for cardiology and women's healthcare, and on specialty therapeutics in the areas of oncology, hematology and ophthalmology. This division also includes a radiology unit, which markets contrast-enhanced diagnostic imaging equipment together with contrast agents. The consumer health division markets non-prescription products in dermatology, dietary supplement, analgesic, gastrointestinal, allergy, cold and flu, foot care, sun protection and cardiovascular risk prevention categories. These products include globally-known brands such as Claritin, Bayer Aspirin, Aleve, Bepanthen/Bepanthol, Canesten, Dr. Scholl's and Coppertone. The crop science division comprises businesses in seeds, crop protection and non-agricultural pest control. Last, the animal health division offers products and services for the prevention and treatment of diseases in companion and farm animals. In October 2017, the firm agreed to sell its seed and herbicide businesses to BASF SE for approximately $7 billion. As for the proposed Bayer and Monsanto merger, in December 2017, the Committee on Foreign Investment in the U.S. concluded that there were no unresolved national security concerns related to the transaction; therefore, the merger was expected to be complete in early-2018.

FINANCIAL DATA:
Note: Data for latest year may not have been available at press time.

In U.S. $	2017	2016	2015	2014	2013	2012
Revenue	43,240,140,000	57,755,190,000	57,205,660,000	52,161,080,000	49,590,010,000	49,099,760,000
R&D Expense	5,562,004,000	5,762,059,000	5,286,621,000	4,413,544,000	3,939,342,000	3,720,764,000
Operating Income	7,545,260,000	9,055,546,000	8,401,047,000	7,072,291,000	6,191,805,000	6,517,820,000
Operating Margin %	17.44%	15.67%	14.68%	13.55%	12.48%	13.27%
SGA Expense	16,229,100,000	18,190,130,000	17,862,880,000	15,756,130,000	14,773,150,000	14,637,310,000
Net Income	9,059,251,000	5,595,347,000	5,075,453,000	4,230,779,000	3,938,107,000	3,020,574,000
Operating Cash Flow	10,044,700,000	11,224,040,000	8,508,484,000	7,174,788,000	6,385,685,000	5,596,581,000
Capital Expenditure	2,921,782,000	3,183,581,000	3,108,252,000	2,927,956,000	2,663,686,000	2,382,128,000
EBITDA	10,016,300,000	13,103,560,000	11,906,940,000	10,467,040,000	9,948,381,000	8,978,982,000
Return on Assets %	9.32%	5.80%	5.70%	5.63%	6.21%	4.69%
Return on Equity %	21.85%	16.59%	18.52%	16.78%	16.27%	12.98%
Debt to Equity	0.33	0.52	0.67	0.90	0.26	0.36

CONTACT INFORMATION:
Phone: 49 214301   Fax: 49 2143066328
Toll-Free: 800-269-2377
Address: Bayerwerk Gebaeude W11, Leverkusen, GM D-51368 Germany

STOCK TICKER/OTHER:
Stock Ticker: BAYRY   Exchange: PINX
Employees: 99,820   Fiscal Year Ends: 12/31
Parent Company: Capital Group International Inc

SALARIES/BONUSES:
Top Exec. Salary: $1,363,000   Bonus: $1,828,000
Second Exec. Salary: $899,000   Bonus: $1,051,000

OTHER THOUGHTS:
Estimated Female Officers or Directors: 1
Hot Spot for Advancement for Women/Minorities:

Sales, profits and employees may be estimates. Financial information, benefits and other data can change quickly and may vary from those stated here.

Bayer Corporation

www.bayer.us

NAIC Code: 325412

TYPES OF BUSINESS:
Chemicals Manufacturing
Animal Health Products
Over-the-Counter Drugs
Diagnostic Products
Coatings, Adhesives & Sealants
Polyurethanes & Plastics
Herbicides, Fungicides & Insecticides

BRANDS/DIVISIONS/AFFILIATES:
Capital Group International Inc
Bayer AG
Elmiron
Aleve
Bayer
Alka-Seltzer Plus
Bactine
One-A-Day

CONTACTS:
Note: Officers with more than one job title may be intentionally listed here more than once.

Philip Blake, CEO
Dan Apel, CFO
Lars Benecke, General Counsel
Stefan Scholz, VP-Corp. Auditing
Philip Blake, Head-Bayer Representative, U.S.
Mark Torsten Minuth, VP-Mergers & Acquisitions
Tracy Spagnol, VP
Marjin Dekkers, Chmn.

GROWTH PLANS/SPECIAL FEATURES:

Bayer Corporation., the U.S. subsidiary of chemical and pharmaceutical giant Bayer AG, operates through four divisions: pharmaceuticals, consumer health, crop science and animal health. The pharmaceuticals division consists of women's healthcare, general medicine, diagnostic imaging, hematology/neurology and oncology. Products within this division include Elmiron, Angeliq and Refludan. The consumer health unit manufactures analgesics (Aleve and Bayer), cold and cough treatments (Alka-Seltzer Plus and Neo-Synephrine), digestive relief products (Phillips' Milk of Magnesia), topical skin preparations (Domeboro and Bactine) and vitamins (One-A-Day and Flintstones). The crop science manufactures crop protection, environmental science and bioscience products, such as herbicides, fungicides and insecticides. The animal health unit focuses on research and development of animal health and pest control products, both for companion animals and farm animals. Parent Bayer AG itself is a subsidiary of Capital Group International, Inc.

The company offers its employees life, disability, medical, dental and vision coverage; prescription drug reimbursement; a 401(k); and adoption assistance.

FINANCIAL DATA:
Note: Data for latest year may not have been available at press time.

In U.S. $	2017	2016	2015	2014	2013	2012
Revenue	6,350,000,000	6,300,000,000	6,150,000,000	6,100,000,000	6,050,000,000	6,000,000,000
R&D Expense						
Operating Income						
Operating Margin %						
SGA Expense						
Net Income						
Operating Cash Flow						
Capital Expenditure						
EBITDA						
Return on Assets %						
Return on Equity %						
Debt to Equity						

CONTACT INFORMATION:
Phone: 862-404-3000 Fax: 781-356-0165
Toll-Free:
Address: 100 Bayer Blvd., Whippany, NJ 07981-0915 United States

STOCK TICKER/OTHER:
Stock Ticker: Subsidiary   Exchange:
Employees: 13,450   Fiscal Year Ends: 12/31
Parent Company: Capital Group International Inc

SALARIES/BONUSES:
Top Exec. Salary: $ Bonus: $
Second Exec. Salary: $ Bonus: $

OTHER THOUGHTS:
Estimated Female Officers or Directors: 1
Hot Spot for Advancement for Women/Minorities:

Bayer HealthCare Pharmaceuticals Inc

www.pharma.bayer.com

NAIC Code: 325412

TYPES OF BUSINESS:
Pharmaceuticals Discovery, Development & Manufacturing
Gynecology & Andrology Treatments
Contraceptives
Cancer Treatments
Multiple Sclerosis Treatments
Circulatory Disorder Treatments
Diagnostic & Radiopharmaceutical Agents
Proteomics

BRANDS/DIVISIONS/AFFILIATES:
Bayer AG
Betaferon
Glucobay
Kogenare
Adalat
Nexavar
Avalox
Seresto

CONTACTS:
Note: Officers with more than one job title may be intentionally listed here more than once.

Habib J. Dable, Pres.
Michael Devoy, Head-Medical Affairs & Pharmacovigilance
Oliver Renner, Head-Global Corp. Comm.

GROWTH PLANS/SPECIAL FEATURES:
Bayer HealthCare Pharmaceuticals, Inc. is the pharmaceutical division and subsidiary of Bayer AG. With operations in over 100 countries, the firm manufactures prescription drugs and therapeutic products for seven main disease groups: cardiovascular and blood disorders, cancer, eye conditions, women's health, men's health, other treatment areas and radiology. Cardiovascular and blood disorders include high blood pressure, pulmonary hypertension, heart attack, stroke, hemophilia and thrombosis. Cancer includes gastrointestinal stromal tumors, colorectal cancer, liver cancer, prostate cancer, renal cell carcinoma and thyroid cancer. Eye conditions include age-related macular degeneration, diabetic macular edema, myopic choroidal neovascularization and retinal vein occlusion. Women's health includes contraception, gynecological therapy, endometriosis, menopausal complaints and premenstrual dysphoric disorder. Men's health includes erectile dysfunction and testosterone deficiency. Other treatment areas include multiple sclerosis, diabetes and infectious diseases. Last, the radiology group studies medical images in order to provide a formal assessment and recommendation to the treating doctor who then discusses the results with the patient during a follow-up appointment. Radiology's diagnostic imaging techniques include computer tomography (CT), magnetic resonance imaging (MRI), contrast agents and injectors. Bayer HealthCare has research and development facilities in Germany, the U.S., Norway and Finland; production facilities in the U.S., Europe, Latin America and Asia; and innovation centers in the U.S., China, Singapore and Japan. The firm has developed the following drugs: Betaferon, which reduces the frequency of MS episodes; Glucobay, used to regulate blood sugar control for diabetes; Kogenare, used for the treatment of hemophilia; Adalat, used for treating high blood pressure; Nexavar, a kidney and liver cancer fighting therapy; Avalox/Avelox, a respiratory tract infection treatment; Yasmin, birth control; Xarelto, for venous and arterial thrombosis; and Mirena, a hormonal contraceptive intrauterine delivery system. Bayer HealthCare has also developed Seresto, a flea and tick collar for cats and dogs in the U.S.

FINANCIAL DATA:
Note: Data for latest year may not have been available at press time.

In U.S. $	2017	2016	2015	2014	2013	2012
Revenue	14,500,000,000	14,000,000,000	15,473,026,160	22,641,486,063	15,489,765,000	13,000,000,000
R&D Expense						
Operating Income						
Operating Margin %						
SGA Expense						
Net Income						
Operating Cash Flow						
Capital Expenditure						
EBITDA						
Return on Assets %						
Return on Equity %						
Debt to Equity						

CONTACT INFORMATION:
Phone: 973-694-4100   Fax: 973-487-2003
Toll-Free:
Address: 6 West Belt Rd., Wayne, NJ 07470-6806 United States

STOCK TICKER/OTHER:
Stock Ticker: Subsidiary
Employees: 39,000
Parent Company: Bayer AG
Exchange:
Fiscal Year Ends: 12/31

SALARIES/BONUSES:
Top Exec. Salary: $ Bonus: $
Second Exec. Salary: $ Bonus: $

OTHER THOUGHTS:
Estimated Female Officers or Directors:
Hot Spot for Advancement for Women/Minorities:

Sales, profits and employees may be estimates. Financial information, benefits and other data can change quickly and may vary from those stated here.

Beca Group Limited

www.beca.com

NAIC Code: 541330

TYPES OF BUSINESS:
Engineering Consulting Services

BRANDS/DIVISIONS/AFFILIATES:
Beca AMEC
CH2M Beca
Erasito Beca
Beca Warnes

CONTACTS:
Note: Officers with more than one job title may be intentionally listed here more than once.

Greg Lowe, CEO
Don Lyon, COO
Mark Fleming, CFO
Damian Pedreschi, CMO
Laurent Sylvestre, Chief People Officer
Craig Price, CTO
David Carter, Chmn.

GROWTH PLANS/SPECIAL FEATURES:

Beca Group Limited provides engineering consultancy services for buildings, government, industrial, power, transport and water sectors. The firm is one of the largest employee-owned consultancies in the Asia Pacific, with 20 offices across the world. Beca offers a broad line of services, including airport, architecture, building, business performance, civil and marine, environmental, geotechnical, industrial, planning, power and energy, project and cost management, structural engineering, survey and geographic information systems, transportation, valuation and water and waste. The buildings division includes projects such as airport buildings, correctional facilities, civic facilities, advanced technology environments, defense, laboratory and research facilities, education, hotels and resorts, healthcare, mixed-use developments, commercial offices, residential, retail and sports facilities. The government division provides safe, secure and cost-efficient solutions for projects and services such as correctional facilities, defense, education, healthcare and civic facilities. The industrial division provides engineering services to industrial markets such as chemicals, food and beverage, mining and metals, oil and gas, pulp and paper and wood products. The power division provides creative, cost-effective advice and solutions across many services within the power market sector, including power generation, as well as power transmission and distribution. The transport division provides services for the following market sectors: airport infrastructure, rail, land development, ports and coastal areas and road and transport. The water division has provided design services and advice to the water market in the Asia-Pacific region for more than 30 years, and is engaged in environmental commissions and solutions. The firm's joint ventures include: Beca AMEC, a multi-disciplinary consulting practice; CH2M Beca, a consulting engineering services company serving the water/wastewater industry; Erasito Beca, offering infrastructure, industrial and buildings services throughout the Fiji and Pacific region; and Beca Warnes, offering engineering design, structural assessments, building services engineering and integrated design within Thailand and southeast Asia.

FINANCIAL DATA:
Note: Data for latest year may not have been available at press time.

In U.S. $	2017	2016	2015	2014	2013	2012
Revenue				327,335,000	331,802,000	
R&D Expense						
Operating Income						
Operating Margin %						
SGA Expense						
Net Income						
Operating Cash Flow						
Capital Expenditure						
EBITDA						
Return on Assets %						
Return on Equity %						
Debt to Equity						

CONTACT INFORMATION:
Phone: 64-9-300-9000   Fax: 64-9-300-9300
Toll-Free:
Address: 21 Pitt St., Auckland, 1010 New Zealand

STOCK TICKER/OTHER:
Stock Ticker: Private
Employees: 3,198
Parent Company:

Exchange:
Fiscal Year Ends:

SALARIES/BONUSES:
Top Exec. Salary: $ Bonus: $
Second Exec. Salary: $ Bonus: $

OTHER THOUGHTS:
Estimated Female Officers or Directors:
Hot Spot for Advancement for Women/Minorities:

Sales, profits and employees may be estimates. Financial information, benefits and other data can change quickly and may vary from those stated here.

Bechtel Group Inc

www.bechtel.com

NAIC Code: 237000

TYPES OF BUSINESS:
Heavy Construction
Civic Engineering
Outsourcing
Financial Services
Atomic Propulsion Systems Engineering
Airport Construction
Electric Power Plant Construction
Nuclear Power Plant Construction

BRANDS/DIVISIONS/AFFILIATES:

CONTACTS: Note: Officers with more than one job title may be intentionally listed here more than once.
Brendan Bechtel, CEO
Jack Futcher, COO
Peter Dawson, CFO
Michael Bailey, General Counsel
Charlene Wheeless, Head-Corp. Affairs
Anette Sparks, Controller
Steve Katzman, Pres., Asia
Jose Ivo, Pres., Americas
Charlene Wheeless, Head-Sustainability Svcs.
Michael Wilkinson, Head-Risk Mgmt.
Brendan Bechtel, Chmn.
David Welch, Pres., EMEA

GROWTH PLANS/SPECIAL FEATURES:

Bechtel Group, Inc. is one of the world's largest engineering companies. The privately-owned firm offers engineering, construction and project management services, with a broad project portfolio including road and rail systems, airports and seaports, nuclear power plants, petrochemical facilities, mines, defense and aerospace facilities, environmental cleanup projects, telecommunication networks, pipelines and oil fields development. Bechtel has four main business units: infrastructure; nuclear, security and environmental; oil, gas and chemicals; and mining and metals. The infrastructure segment oversees projects pertaining to hydroelectric power plants, ports, harbors, bridges, airports and airport systems, commercial and light-industrial buildings, wireless sites, railroads, rapid-transit and rail systems. The nuclear, security and environmental includes missile defense infrastructure, scientific and national security facility operations, environmental restoration and recovery, commercial and U.S. navy nuclear reactor services and chemical weapons dematerialization projects. The oil, gas and chemicals segment offers integrated design, procurement, construction and project management of oil, gas and natural gas facilities. The mining and metal segment encompasses mining and metal projects across six continents including procurement, construction, engineering and solutions for mining of coal, ferrous, industrial and nonferrous metals. The firm has participated in such notable endeavors as the construction of the Hoover Dam, the creation of the Bay Area Rapid Transit system in San Francisco, the massive James Bay Hydroelectric Project in Quebec and the quelling of oil field fires in Kuwait following the Persian Gulf War. Bechtel also constructed the Trans-Alaska Oil Pipeline, covering 800 miles between the Prudhoe Bay oil field and Valdez. In August 2017, Bechtel was selected to build the first expressway, a 294-mile route in Kenya.

The firm offers employees benefits including medical, dental and vision coverage; short- and long-term disability; flexible spending accounts; an employee assistance program; life insurance; and a 401(k) plan.

FINANCIAL DATA: Note: Data for latest year may not have been available at press time.

In U.S. $	2017	2016	2015	2014	2013	2012
Revenue	33,100,000,000	32,900,000,000	32,300,000,000	37,200,000,000	39,400,000,000	37,900,000,000
R&D Expense						
Operating Income						
Operating Margin %						
SGA Expense						
Net Income						
Operating Cash Flow						
Capital Expenditure						
EBITDA						
Return on Assets %						
Return on Equity %						
Debt to Equity						

CONTACT INFORMATION:
Phone: 415-768-1234   Fax: 415-768-9038
Toll-Free:
Address: 50 Beale St., San Francisco, CA 94105-1895 United States

STOCK TICKER/OTHER:
Stock Ticker: Private   Exchange:
Employees: 58,000   Fiscal Year Ends: 12/31
Parent Company:

SALARIES/BONUSES:
Top Exec. Salary: $ Bonus: $
Second Exec. Salary: $ Bonus: $

OTHER THOUGHTS:
Estimated Female Officers or Directors: 4
Hot Spot for Advancement for Women/Minorities: Y

Sales, profits and employees may be estimates. Financial information, benefits and other data can change quickly and may vary from those stated here.

Beckman Coulter Inc

NAIC Code: 334510

www.beckmancoulter.com

TYPES OF BUSINESS:
Electromedical and Electrotherapeutic Apparatus Manufacturing
Chemistry Systems
Genetic Analysis/Nucleic Acid Testing
Biomedical Research Supplies
Immunoassay Systems
Cellular Systems
Discovery & Automation Systems

BRANDS/DIVISIONS/AFFILIATES:
Danaher Corporation
ClearLLab Regeants
DxC 700 AU

CONTACTS:
Note: Officers with more than one job title may be intentionally listed here more than once.

J. Robert Hurley, CEO
Pedro Diaz, Dir.-Research
John Blackwood, Sr. VP-Product Mgmt.
Jeff Linton, Sr. VP
Ken Hyek, Dir.-Service Oper.
Allan Harris, Sr. VP-Strategy & Bus. Dev.
Jerry Battenberg, VP-Finance
Clair O'Donovan, Sr. VP-Quality & Regulatory Affairs
Jennifer Honeycutt, Pres., Life Sciences
Richard Creager, Sr. VP
Michael K. Samoszuk, VP
Brian Burnett, Sr. VP-Global Oper.

GROWTH PLANS/SPECIAL FEATURES:

Beckman Coulter, Inc., a wholly-owned subsidiary of Danaher Corporation, designs, develops, manufactures and markets biomedical testing instrument systems, tests and supplies that automate complex biomedical tests. The company operates two divisions: diagnostics and life sciences. The diagnostics division offers diagnostic systems for use in laboratories, hospitals and critical care settings to make treatment decisions, monitor patients and help physicians diagnose many diseases including cancer, HIV and heart conditions. The company's installed base systems provide essential biomedical information to enhance healthcare all around the world. The life sciences division manufactures research instruments used to study complex biological problems including causes of disease and potential new therapies or drugs. The firm operates in over 130 countries worldwide. Its customer base predominately consists of hospital and laboratories, scientists and large biopharma companies. In 2017, the firm received U.S. FDA marketing approval of ClearLLab Reagents (T1, T2, B1, B2, M) test for use with flow cytometry to aid in the detection of several leukemia and lymphomas; and received FDA clearance for its DxC 700 AU chemistry analyzer for mid- to high-volume clinical laboratories.

Employee benefits include medical, dental and vision coverage; a wellness program; a 401(k) and company retirement plan; life insurance; disability income protection; credit union membership; and employee discounts.

FINANCIAL DATA:
Note: Data for latest year may not have been available at press time.

In U.S. $	2017	2016	2015	2014	2013	2012
Revenue	5,100,000,000	5,050,000,000	5,000,000,000	4,700,000,000	4,100,000,000	3,750,000,000
R&D Expense						
Operating Income						
Operating Margin %						
SGA Expense						
Net Income						
Operating Cash Flow						
Capital Expenditure						
EBITDA						
Return on Assets %						
Return on Equity %						
Debt to Equity						

CONTACT INFORMATION:
Phone: 714-993-5321 Fax: 800-232-3828
Toll-Free: 800-526-3821
Address: 250 S. Kraemer Blvd., Brea, CA 92821 United States

STOCK TICKER/OTHER:
Stock Ticker: Subsidiary Exchange:
Employees: 11,900 Fiscal Year Ends: 12/31
Parent Company: Danaher Corporation

SALARIES/BONUSES:
Top Exec. Salary: $ Bonus: $
Second Exec. Salary: $ Bonus: $

OTHER THOUGHTS:
Estimated Female Officers or Directors: 5
Hot Spot for Advancement for Women/Minorities: Y

Sales, profits and employees may be estimates. Financial information, benefits and other data can change quickly and may vary from those stated here.

Becton Dickinson & Company

NAIC Code: 339100

www.bd.com

TYPES OF BUSINESS:
Medical Equipment-Injection/Infusion
Drug Delivery Systems
Infusion Therapy Products
Diabetes Care Products
Surgical Products
Microbiology Products
Diagnostic Products
Consulting Services

BRANDS/DIVISIONS/AFFILIATES:
BD Medical
BD Life Sciences
BD Hypak
Alaris
BD Vacutainer
CR Bard Inc

CONTACTS:
Note: Officers with more than one job title may be intentionally listed here more than once.

Vincent Forlenza, CEO
Gary DeFazio, Secretary
Christopher Reidy, CFO
John Gallagher, Chief Accounting Officer
James Borzi, Executive VP, Divisional
Linda Tharby, Executive VP
Alberto Mas, Executive VP
Roland Goette, Executive VP
James Lim, Executive VP
Thomas Polen, President
Alexandre Conroy, President, Divisional
Nabil Shabshab, President, Divisional

GROWTH PLANS/SPECIAL FEATURES:

Becton, Dickinson & Company (BD) is a global medical technology company engaged in the development, manufacture and sale of medical supplies, devices, laboratory equipment and diagnostic products. These offerings are primarily used by healthcare institutions, life science researchers, clinical laboratories, the pharmaceutical industry and the general public. The company operates in two worldwide business segments: BD Medical and BD Life Sciences. BD Medical offers products, including specially designed devices for diabetes care; pre-fillable drug delivery systems; and infusion therapy products. It also offers anesthesia and surgical products, ophthalmic surgery devices, critical care systems, elastic support products, respiratory ventilation and diagnostic equipment and thermometers. BD Life Sciences offers products for safe collection and transport of diagnostics specimens; instruments and reagent systems to detect a broad range of infectious diseases; and research and clinical tools that facilitate the study of cells in order to get a comprehensive understanding of normal and disease processes. Some of the products are integrated systems for specimen collection, molecular testing systems for infectious diseases and fluorescence-activated cell sorters and analyzers. BD's most popular international products include: BD Hypak pre-fillable syringe systems; Alaris infusion pumps; and BD Vacutainer blood-collection products. Manufacturing operations outside the U.S. include Bosnia/Herzegovina, Brazil, Canada, China, Dominican Republic, France, Germany, Hungary, India, Ireland, Israel, Italy, Japan, Mexico, Netherlands, Singapore, Spain and the U.K. Products are marketed and distributed in the U.S. and internationally through distribution channels, and directly to end-users by BD and independent sales representatives. In December 2017, BD acquired C.R. Bard, Inc., a medical supplies manufacturer.

The firm offers employees medical, dental, vision and prescription drug coverage; a flexible spending account; an employee assistance program; and at select locations, onsite services such as fitness centers, walking trails, banks and cafeterias.

FINANCIAL DATA:
Note: Data for latest year may not have been available at press time.

In U.S. $	2017	2016	2015	2014	2013	2012
Revenue	12,093,000,000	12,483,000,000	10,282,000,000	8,446,000,000	8,054,000,000	7,708,382,000
R&D Expense	774,000,000	828,000,000	632,000,000	550,000,000	494,000,000	471,755,000
Operating Income	1,833,000,000	2,158,000,000	1,500,000,000	1,606,000,000	1,255,000,000	1,557,885,000
Operating Margin %	15.15%	17.28%	14.58%	19.01%	15.58%	20.21%
SGA Expense	2,925,000,000	3,005,000,000	2,563,000,000	2,145,000,000	2,422,000,000	1,923,354,000
Net Income	1,100,000,000	976,000,000	695,000,000	1,185,000,000	1,293,000,000	1,169,927,000
Operating Cash Flow	2,550,000,000	2,559,000,000	1,730,000,000	1,746,000,000	1,505,000,000	1,760,228,000
Capital Expenditure	727,000,000	718,000,000	633,000,000	653,000,000	588,000,000	553,644,000
EBITDA	2,585,000,000	2,576,000,000	2,001,000,000	2,219,000,000	1,849,000,000	2,118,004,000
Return on Assets %	3.25%	3.72%	3.53%	9.63%	10.99%	10.73%
Return on Equity %	10.01%	13.19%	11.37%	23.47%	28.17%	26.10%
Debt to Equity	1.44	1.38	1.58	0.74	0.74	0.90

CONTACT INFORMATION:
Phone: 201 847-6800　Fax:
Toll-Free: 800-284-6845
Address: 1 Becton Dr., Franklin Lakes, NJ 07417 United States

STOCK TICKER/OTHER:
Stock Ticker: BDX
Employees: 50,928
Parent Company:

Exchange: NYS
Fiscal Year Ends: 09/30

SALARIES/BONUSES:
Top Exec. Salary: $1,153,750　Bonus: $
Second Exec. Salary: $778,230　Bonus: $

OTHER THOUGHTS:
Estimated Female Officers or Directors: 6
Hot Spot for Advancement for Women/Minorities: Y

Sales, profits and employees may be estimates. Financial information, benefits and other data can change quickly and may vary from those stated here.

Belden Inc

www.belden.com

NAIC Code: 334417

TYPES OF BUSINESS:
Cable & Wire Connectors Manufacturing
Electronic Products
Broadcasting Equipment
Aerospace & Automotive Electronics
Enclosures

BRANDS/DIVISIONS/AFFILIATES:
Thinklogical Holdings LLC

CONTACTS:
Note: Officers with more than one job title may be intentionally listed here more than once.

John Stroup, CEO
Henk Derksen, CFO
Douglas Zink, Chief Accounting Officer
Dhrupad Trivedi, Executive VP, Divisional
Glenn Pennycook, Executive VP, Divisional
Roel Vestjens, Executive VP, Divisional
Brian Anderson, General Counsel
Dean McKenna, Senior VP, Divisional
Ross Rosenberg, Senior VP, Divisional
Paul Turner, Senior VP, Divisional

GROWTH PLANS/SPECIAL FEATURES:

Belden, Inc. designs, manufactures and markets signal transmission products, including cable, connectivity and networking components. The company is divided into four segments that offer various solutions: broadcast, enterprise connectivity, industrial and network security. Broadcast solutions derived 30.4% of 2017 revenues, and provides production, distribution and connectivity systems for the television broadcast, cable, satellite and internet protocol television (IPTV) industries. Products are used in a variety of applications, including live production signal management, program playout for broadcasters, monitoring for pay-TV operators and broadband connectivity. Broadcast products include camera mounted fiber solutions, interfaces and routers, broadcast and audio-visual cable solutions, monitoring systems, playout systems, outside plant connectivity products and other cable and connectivity products. The enterprise connectivity segment (26.4%) provides infrastructure and connectivity solutions for enterprise customers. Products include fiber and copper connectivity products; fiber optic and copper cable products; and wiring racks, panels and enclosures as well as interconnecting hardware, intelligent patching devices and cable management solutions for complete end-to-end network structured wiring systems. The industrial segment (26.3%) provides high performance networking components and machine connectivity products, including physical network and fieldbus infrastructure components and on-machine connectivity systems customized to end-user and original equipment manufacturer needs. This division's industrial cable products are used in discrete manufacturing and process operations involving the connection of computers, programmable controllers, robots, operator interfaces, motor drives, sensors, printers and other devices. Last, the network security segment (16.9%) provides the following solutions: controls for protecting enterprises against cyberattacks; automating IT regulatory compliance; and improving operational efficiency. During 2017, Belden acquired Thinklogical Holdings, LLC; and sold its 50% stake in Chinese load-moment indicator systems joint venture, Xuzhou Hirschmann Electronics Co. Ltd.

FINANCIAL DATA:
Note: Data for latest year may not have been available at press time.

In U.S. $	2017	2016	2015	2014	2013	2012
Revenue	2,388,643,000	2,356,672,000	2,309,222,000	2,308,265,000	2,069,193,000	1,840,739,000
R&D Expense	134,330,000	140,601,000	148,311,000	113,914,000	83,277,000	65,410,000
Operating Income	234,690,000	247,784,000	138,783,000	159,164,000	192,340,000	132,469,000
Operating Margin %	9.82%	10.51%	6.00%	6.89%	9.29%	7.19%
SGA Expense	461,022,000	494,224,000	527,288,000	487,945,000	378,009,000	345,926,000
Net Income	93,210,000	128,003,000	66,204,000	74,449,000	103,313,000	194,490,000
Operating Cash Flow	255,300,000	314,794,000	236,410,000	194,028,000	164,601,000	139,388,000
Capital Expenditure	64,261,000	53,974,000	54,969,000	45,459,000	40,209,000	41,010,000
EBITDA	384,340,000	393,377,000	289,125,000	265,864,000	294,595,000	116,435,000
Return on Assets %	1.52%	3.16%	2.01%	2.47%	3.87%	8.89%
Return on Equity %	4.02%	9.85%	8.11%	9.05%	12.53%	25.82%
Debt to Equity	1.08	1.10	2.12	2.18	1.63	1.39

CONTACT INFORMATION:
Phone: 314 854-8000
Fax: 314 854-8001
Toll-Free: 800-235-3361
Address: 1 N. Brentwood Blvd., 15/Fl, St. Louis, MO 63105 United States

STOCK TICKER/OTHER:
Stock Ticker: BDC
Employees: 8,400
Parent Company:
Exchange: NYS
Fiscal Year Ends: 12/31

SALARIES/BONUSES:
Top Exec. Salary: $875,000   Bonus: $
Second Exec. Salary: $551,391   Bonus: $

OTHER THOUGHTS:
Estimated Female Officers or Directors: 2
Hot Spot for Advancement for Women/Minorities: Y

Sales, profits and employees may be estimates. Financial information, benefits and other data can change quickly and may vary from those stated here.

Benchmark Electronics Inc

NAIC Code: 334418

www.bench.com

TYPES OF BUSINESS:
Printed Circuit Assembly (Electronic Assembly) Manufacturing
Design & Engineering
Printed Circuit Boards

BRANDS/DIVISIONS/AFFILIATES:

CONTACTS: Note: Officers with more than one job title may be intentionally listed here more than once.
Roop Lakkaraju, CFO
David Scheible, Chairman of the Board
Scott Hicar, Chief Information Officer
Jan Janick, Chief Technology Officer
Paul Tufano, Director
Michael Buseman, Executive VP, Divisional
Nathalie Carruthers, Other Executive Officer
Lisa Weeks, Vice President, Divisional

GROWTH PLANS/SPECIAL FEATURES:
Benchmark Electronics, Inc. provides contract-manufacturing services for complex printed circuit boards (PCBs) and related electronics systems and subsystems. Benchmark primarily serves original equipment manufacturers (OEMs) of computers and related products for business enterprises, medical devices, industrial control equipment, testing and instrumentation products and telecommunications equipment. The firm provides comprehensive and integrated design and manufacturing services, from initial product design to volume production and direct order fulfillment. In addition, the company offers specialized engineering services such as advanced design, software development, industrial design, assembly automation, PCB layout, prototyping and test development. Benchmark provides many of its manufacturing services on a turnkey basis, whereby it purchases customer-specified components from its suppliers, assembles the components on finished PCBs, performs post-production testing and provides production and testing documentation. The company offers its customers a range of traditional and more advanced manufacturing technologies, encompassing processes such as pin-thru-hole, surface mount, chip-on-board, fine pitch, flip chip and ball grid array. The firm has manufacturing facilities in seven countries worldwide, operating several surface mount production lines where electrical components are soldered directly onto PCBs. Benchmark operates domestic facilities in Alabama, Arizona, California, Minnesota, New Hampshire and Texas, totaling approximately 1.4 million square feet. Operations outside the U.S., totaling roughly 2.3 million square feet, include facilities in China, Malaysia, Mexico, the Netherlands, Romania and Thailand.

FINANCIAL DATA: Note: Data for latest year may not have been available at press time.

In U.S. $	2017	2016	2015	2014	2013	2012
Revenue	2,466,811,000	2,310,415,000	2,540,873,000	2,797,061,000	2,506,467,000	2,468,150,000
R&D Expense						
Operating Income	87,231,000	88,177,000	106,830,000	104,157,000	87,153,000	86,787,000
Operating Margin %	3.53%	3.81%	4.20%	3.72%	3.47%	3.51%
SGA Expense	130,401,000	113,448,000	111,744,000	115,700,000	99,331,000	89,951,000
Net Income	-31,965,000	64,047,000	95,401,000	82,442,000	111,159,000	56,607,000
Operating Cash Flow	145,842,000	272,520,000	146,804,000	136,661,000	99,077,000	151,147,000
Capital Expenditure	54,506,000	32,334,000	38,062,000	45,389,000	28,737,000	49,035,000
EBITDA	130,859,000	132,631,000	142,707,000	148,189,000	159,053,000	112,732,000
Return on Assets %	-1.56%	3.29%	5.34%	4.94%	7.03%	3.77%
Return on Equity %	-2.37%	4.76%	7.30%	6.54%	9.39%	5.02%
Debt to Equity	0.14	0.15	0.16			

CONTACT INFORMATION:
Phone: 979 849-6550   Fax:
Toll-Free:
Address: 3000 Technology Dr., Angleton, TX 77515 United States

STOCK TICKER/OTHER:
Stock Ticker: BHE
Employees: 9,900
Parent Company:

Exchange: NYS
Fiscal Year Ends: 12/31

SALARIES/BONUSES:
Top Exec. Salary: $1,000,000   Bonus: $
Second Exec. Salary: $420,000   Bonus: $

OTHER THOUGHTS:
Estimated Female Officers or Directors: 2
Hot Spot for Advancement for Women/Minorities:

Sales, profits and employees may be estimates. Financial information, benefits and other data can change quickly and may vary from those stated here.

Bilfinger SE

NAIC Code: 237000

www.bilfingerberger.com

TYPES OF BUSINESS:
Heavy Construction

BRANDS/DIVISIONS/AFFILIATES:
Bilfinger arnholdt
Bilfinger Chemserv
Bilfinger Deutsch Babcock Middle East
Bilfinger Industrial Automation Services
Bilfinger Maintenance
Bilfinger Personalmanagement
Bilfinger ROB Group
Bilfinger Salamis Inc

CONTACTS:
Note: Officers with more than one job title may be intentionally listed here more than once.
Tom Blades, Chmn.

GROWTH PLANS/SPECIAL FEATURES:
Bilfinger SE provides industrial services for the process industry. The company's portfolio covers the entire value chain, including consulting, engineering, manufacturing, assembly, maintenance, plant expansion and turnarounds, as well as environmental technologies and digital applications. Bilfinger operates in two business segments: engineering and technologies; and maintenance, modifications and operations. The engineering and technologies segment provides the following services: advises, designs, develops, builds, manufactures and assembles; assumes responsibility for project management; supplies components; and commissions plants. Its customized and pioneering solutions are not only used in the design, development and erection of new plants, but for the modification, expansion and shut-down of existing ones. The maintenance, modifications and operations segment services comprise the entire life cycle of an industrial plant, from commissioning to maintenance, including the efficiency enhancement, expansion, conversion and/or shut-down. With Bilfinger being active on a global scale, primarily in the regions of Continental Europe, Northwest Europe, North America and the Middle East, this division operates through many subsidiaries. A few subsidiaries include: Bilfinger arnholdt, Bilfinger Chemserv, Bilfinger Deutsche Babcock Middle East, Bilfinger Industrial Automation Services, Bilfinger Maintenance, Bilfinger Personalmanagement, Bilfinger ROB Group and Bilfinger Salamis, Inc. Primary customers of the firm include chemical/petrochemical, energy, oil and gas, pharmaceutical, biopharmaceutical, metallurgy and cement sectors.

FINANCIAL DATA:
Note: Data for latest year may not have been available at press time.

In U.S. $	2017	2016	2015	2014	2013	2012
Revenue	4,994,196,000	5,246,610,000	8,003,779,000	9,505,298,000	10,391,220,000	10,507,550,000
R&D Expense						
Operating Income	-57,299,520	-82,244,560	196,102,700	216,725,500	342,685,700	497,172,100
Operating Margin %	-1.14%	-1.56%	2.45%	2.28%	3.29%	4.73%
SGA Expense	487,539,800	596,705,300	835,535,600	996,196,500	328,854,800	360,962,200
Net Income	-109,288,900	334,164,800	-603,497,300	-88,172,100	213,391,300	339,474,900
Operating Cash Flow	-102,497,000	-276,988,800	152,634,000	80,268,720	199,560,400	276,247,900
Capital Expenditure	87,554,650	86,072,760	99,780,190	171,157,600	210,304,000	205,117,400
EBITDA	-39,763,890	-138,926,600	349,230,700	216,972,500	604,979,100	762,182,300
Return on Assets %	-2.31%	5.86%	-8.75%	-1.14%	2.58%	3.77%
Return on Equity %	-5.79%	17.31%	-28.62%	-3.49%	8.27%	14.40%
Debt to Equity	0.36	0.30	0.35	0.27	0.24	0.39

CONTACT INFORMATION:
Phone: 49 6214590 Fax: 49 6214592366
Toll-Free:
Address: Carl-Reiß-Platz 1-5, Mannheim, 68165 Germany

STOCK TICKER/OTHER:
Stock Ticker: BFLBF
Employees: 35,644
Parent Company:

Exchange: GREY
Fiscal Year Ends: 12/31

SALARIES/BONUSES:
Top Exec. Salary: $ Bonus: $
Second Exec. Salary: $ Bonus: $

OTHER THOUGHTS:
Estimated Female Officers or Directors:
Hot Spot for Advancement for Women/Minorities:

Sales, profits and employees may be estimates. Financial information, benefits and other data can change quickly and may vary from those stated here.

Bilfinger Tebodin BV

NAIC Code: 541330

www.tebodin.bilfinger.com

TYPES OF BUSINESS:
Engineering Services

BRANDS/DIVISIONS/AFFILIATES:
Bilfinger SE

CONTACTS:
Note: Officers with more than one job title may be intentionally listed here more than once.

Niels van Rhenen, CEO
Arjan van der Vliet, CFO

GROWTH PLANS/SPECIAL FEATURES:
Bilfinger Tebodin BV (formerly Tebodin BV) is the global consultancy and engineering arm of industrial services provider Bilfinger SE. Bilfinger Tebodin's services are divided into: design and engineering, project management, procurement, construction management and consultancy. Design and engineering services include conceptual, basic and detailed design and engineering solutions in relation to: civil, structure and architecture; building; pipelines and infrastructure; electrical; instrumentation and process control; energy; piping; logistics; mechanical; and process. Project management services include: engineering, procurement and construction management; estimating and cost control; scheduling and progress control; quality and safety assurance; commissioning management and assistance; and program management. Procurement services include project purchasing, European tenders; non-production-related purchasing, performance-based maintenance, tendering and contract management. Construction management services include: quality, health, safety and environment management; site management; construction supervision; and planning, cost and progress control. Last, consultancy services include asset management and reliability, license to operate, process integrity and safety, performance and compliance management, and business consulting. Bilfinger Tebodin's markets include industrial, health & nutrition, pharma, energy, environment, chemicals, infrastructure, oil and gas, and property. The firm has global operations in North America, Europe and the Middle East. In February 2018, Tebodin took on its parent's name, becoming Bilfinger Tebodin BV.

FINANCIAL DATA:
Note: Data for latest year may not have been available at press time.

In U.S. $	2017	2016	2015	2014	2013	2012
Revenue						
R&D Expense						
Operating Income						
Operating Margin %						
SGA Expense						
Net Income						
Operating Cash Flow						
Capital Expenditure						
EBITDA						
Return on Assets %						
Return on Equity %						
Debt to Equity						

CONTACT INFORMATION:
Phone: 31-70-348-09-11   Fax:
Toll-Free:
Address: Laan van Nieuw Oost-indie 25, The Hague, 2593 BJ Netherlands

STOCK TICKER/OTHER:
Stock Ticker: Subsidiary
Employees: 3,200
Parent Company: Bilfinger SE

Exchange:
Fiscal Year Ends:

SALARIES/BONUSES:
Top Exec. Salary: $ Bonus: $
Second Exec. Salary: $ Bonus: $

OTHER THOUGHTS:
Estimated Female Officers or Directors:
Hot Spot for Advancement for Women/Minorities:

Sales, profits and employees may be estimates. Financial information, benefits and other data can change quickly and may vary from those stated here.

Biogen Inc

www.biogen.com

NAIC Code: 325412

TYPES OF BUSINESS:
Drugs-Immunology, Neurology & Oncology
Autoimmune & Inflammatory Disease Treatments
Drugs-Multiple Sclerosis
Drugs-Cancer

BRANDS/DIVISIONS/AFFILIATES:
TECFIDERA
AVONEX
PLEGRIDY
SPINRAZA
FUMADERM
RITUXAN
GAZYVA
OCREVUS

CONTACTS:
Note: Officers with more than one job title may be intentionally listed here more than once.

Michel Vounatsos, CEO
Jeffrey Capello, CFO
Gregory Covino, Chief Accounting Officer
Alfred Sandrock, Chief Medical Officer
Stelios Papadopoulos, Director
Kenneth Dipietro, Executive VP, Divisional
Adriana Karaboutis, Executive VP, Divisional
Michael Ehlers, Executive VP, Divisional
Paul McKenzie, Executive VP, Divisional
Chirfi Guindo, Executive VP
Ginger Gregory, Executive VP
Susan Alexander, Executive VP

GROWTH PLANS/SPECIAL FEATURES:

Biogen, Inc. is a biotechnology company focused on discovering, developing, manufacturing and marketing therapies for people living with serious neurological and neurodegenerative diseases. The company's core growth areas in relation to these diseases include multiple sclerosis (MS), neuroimmunology, Alzheimer's disease, dementia, movement disorders, and neuromuscular disorders such as spinal muscular atrophy (SMA) and amyotrophic lateral sclerosis (ALS). Biogen announced plans to invest in emerging growth areas such as pain, ophthalmology, neuropsychiatry and acute neurology, as well as discovering potential treatments for rare and genetic disorders. The firm also manufactures and commercializes biosimilars of advanced biologics. Biogen's marketed products include: TECFIDERA, AVONEX, PLEGRIDY, TYSABRI, ZINBRYTA and FAMPRYA for the treatment of MS; SPINRAZA for the treatment of SMA; and FUMADERM for the treatment of severe plaque psoriasis. In addition, the company has certain business and financial rights with respect to: RITUXAN for the treatment of non-Hodgkin's lymphoma, chronic lymphocytic leukemia (CLL) and other conditions; GAZYVA for the treatment of CLL and follicular lymphoma; OCREVUS for the treatment of primary progressive MS and relapsing MS and other potential anti-CD20 therapies under a collaboration agreement with Genentech, Inc., which is wholly-owned by Roche Group.

Biogen offers employees medical, dental and vision insurance; tuition reimbursement; flexible spending accounts; and an employee assistance program.

FINANCIAL DATA:
Note: Data for latest year may not have been available at press time.

In U.S. $	2017	2016	2015	2014	2013	2012
Revenue	12,273,900,000	10,134,300,000	9,424,600,000	8,507,935,000	5,806,182,000	5,516,461,000
R&D Expense	2,373,600,000	1,973,300,000	2,012,800,000	1,893,422,000	1,444,053,000	1,334,919,000
Operating Income	5,345,100,000	3,894,000,000	3,675,700,000	2,721,374,000	1,364,047,000	1,838,484,000
Operating Margin %	43.54%	38.42%	39.00%	31.98%	23.49%	33.32%
SGA Expense	1,935,500,000	2,402,700,000	2,113,100,000	2,232,342,000	1,797,408,000	1,595,360,000
Net Income	2,539,100,000	3,702,800,000	3,547,000,000	2,934,784,000	1,862,341,000	1,380,033,000
Operating Cash Flow	4,551,000,000	4,522,400,000	3,716,100,000	2,942,115,000	2,345,078,000	1,879,897,000
Capital Expenditure	1,962,800,000	727,700,000	643,000,000	287,751,000	3,509,000,000	261,182,000
EBITDA	6,460,600,000	5,875,700,000	5,463,200,000	4,664,283,000	3,044,219,000	2,257,253,000
Return on Assets %	10.91%	17.47%	20.97%	22.42%	16.93%	14.39%
Return on Equity %	20.51%	34.42%	35.15%	30.21%	23.90%	20.61%
Debt to Equity	0.47	0.53	0.69	0.05	0.06	0.09

CONTACT INFORMATION:
Phone: 617-679-2000　　Fax: 619 679-2617
Toll-Free:
Address: 225 Binney St., Cambridge, MA 02142 United States

STOCK TICKER/OTHER:
Stock Ticker: BIIB　　　Exchange: NAS
Employees: 7,400　　　Fiscal Year Ends: 12/31
Parent Company:

SALARIES/BONUSES:
Top Exec. Salary: $519,231　　Bonus: $1,500,000
Second Exec. Salary: $491,827　　Bonus: $1,170,177

OTHER THOUGHTS:
Estimated Female Officers or Directors: 4
Hot Spot for Advancement for Women/Minorities: Y

BIOS-BIOENERGYSYSTEME GmbH

www.bios-bioenergy.at

NAIC Code: 541330

TYPES OF BUSINESS:
Biomass Plant Design & Development
Research Services
Software Development

BRANDS/DIVISIONS/AFFILIATES:
EU-UltraLowDust
SUNSTORE 4
Sector
Enercom
BioMaxEff
BIOSTROM Erzeugungs GmbH

CONTACTS:
Note: Officers with more than one job title may be intentionally listed here more than once.
Claudia Benesch, Managing Dir.

GROWTH PLANS/SPECIAL FEATURES:
BIOS-BIOENERGYSYSTEME GmbH is engaged in the research, development, design and optimization of processes and plants for heat and power production from biomass fuels. The company has completed or is currently working on projects in Belgium, Germany, the U.K., France, Greece, Ireland, Italy, Croatia, Montenegro, Norway, Russia, Switzerland, Hungary, Belarus, South Africa, Honduras, Canada and the U.S. It provides solutions that cover the entire field of thermal biomass utilization (combustion, gasification and combined heat and power systems). BIOS is actively engaged in several biomass research and development projects, including EU-UltraLowDust, a project to develop small-scale biomass combustion technologies; SUNSTORE 4, a hybrid solar/biomass district heating system; Sector, a project to produce biomass energy pellets by torrefaction; Enercom, a plant that will produce energy, fuels and fertilizers from biomass residues and sewage sludge; and BioMaxEff, cost efficient biomass boiler systems with maximum annual efficiency and lowest emissions. The firm is an industrial partner of the Austrian Bioenergy Competence Centre (Bioenergy 2020+ GmbH), which conducts energetic biomass utilization R&D projects. The company is also a 10% shareholder in BIOSTROM Erzeugungs GmbH, a biomass co-generation heating plant in Vorarlberg, Austria that burns waste wood and has an electric capacity of 1,100 kilowatts, a thermal capacity of 6.2 megawatts (MW) and a chilling capacity of 2.4 MW.

FINANCIAL DATA:
Note: Data for latest year may not have been available at press time.

In U.S. $	2017	2016	2015	2014	2013	2012
Revenue	5,700,000	5,600,000	5,500,000	4,647,250		
R&D Expense						
Operating Income						
Operating Margin %						
SGA Expense						
Net Income						
Operating Cash Flow						
Capital Expenditure						
EBITDA						
Return on Assets %						
Return on Equity %						
Debt to Equity						

CONTACT INFORMATION:
Phone: 43-316-481-300 Fax: 43-316-481-300-4
Toll-Free:
Address: Hedwig-Katschinka-Straße 4, Graz, A-8020 Austria

STOCK TICKER/OTHER:
Stock Ticker: Private Exchange:
Employees: 30 Fiscal Year Ends:
Parent Company:

SALARIES/BONUSES:
Top Exec. Salary: $ Bonus: $
Second Exec. Salary: $ Bonus: $

OTHER THOUGHTS:
Estimated Female Officers or Directors: 3
Hot Spot for Advancement for Women/Minorities: Y

Sales, profits and employees may be estimates. Financial information, benefits and other data can change quickly and may vary from those stated here.

Black & Veatch Holding Company

NAIC Code: 541330

www.bv.com

TYPES OF BUSINESS:
Heavy & Civil Engineering, Construction
Infrastructure & Energy Services
Environmental & Hydrologic Engineering
Consulting Services
IT Services
Power Plant Engineering and Construction
LNG and Gas Processing Plant Engineering
Climate Change Services

BRANDS/DIVISIONS/AFFILIATES:
Atonix Digital
ASSET360

CONTACTS:
Note: Officers with more than one job title may be intentionally listed here more than once.

Steven L. Edwards, CEO
Martin G. Travers, Pres.
Karen L. Daniel, CFO
Lori Kelleher, Chief Human Resources Officer
James R. Lewis, Chief Admin. Officer
Timothy W. Triplett, General Counsel
Cindy Wallis-Lage, Pres., Water
O.H. Oskvig, CEO-Energy Business
William R. Van Dyke, Pres., Federal Svcs.
Steven L. Edwards, Chmn.
Hoe Wai Cheong, Sr. VP-Water-Asia Pacific
John E. Murphy, Pres., Construction & Procurement

GROWTH PLANS/SPECIAL FEATURES:

Black & Veatch Holding Company (B&V) is an employee-owned engineering, consulting and construction company, with more than 100 offices worldwide. The company specializes in the following markets: banking/finance, data centers, governments, mining, oil & gas, power, smart cities, telecommunications and water. B&V divides its service offerings into eight categories. Asset management services span from single asset evaluation to enterprise optimization and efficiency, with specific services including: ISO 55000 assessment and implementation, enterprise asset management system implementation or optimization, capital prioritization and risk management. Consulting services include advanced metering infrastructure, customer engagement, operations, infrastructure investment, infrastructure transactions, utility rates and regulatory support. Data analytic services include B&V's Atonix Digital software subsidiary, which focuses on software development, sales and delivery. Atonix Digital's ASSET360 data analytics platform is cloud-based and captures, integrates and analyzes data from infrastructure systems, assets and devices to enable more-informed decisions and actions. EPC & Design services include design engineering, procurement and expediting, construction and construction management, quality control/quality assurance, startup and training. Operations services include: preparation of facility-specific operations manuals; process control optimization and troubleshooting; on-site technical support for completion of facility startup and commissioning; assessments, including facility operations, of staffing and maintenance; laboratory design and on-site laboratory reviews; and equipment specification development. Physical & Cyber Security solutions include a security risk framework offering organizational maturity assessment or remediation; program management office; application security architecture planning; policy and procedure development, physical and cyber security solution implementation and integration; and penetration testing. Program & Construction management services include engineering, procurement and construction coordination, management software, process design/implementation, permitting and site design. Last, Sustainability services include solutions for enterprise sustainability and utility sustainability, from concept through execution.

FINANCIAL DATA:
Note: Data for latest year may not have been available at press time.

In U.S. $	2017	2016	2015	2014	2013	2012
Revenue	3,400,000,000	3,200,000,000	3,030,000,000	3,600,000,000	3,560,000,000	3,279,000,000
R&D Expense						
Operating Income						
Operating Margin %						
SGA Expense						
Net Income						
Operating Cash Flow						
Capital Expenditure						
EBITDA						
Return on Assets %						
Return on Equity %						
Debt to Equity						

CONTACT INFORMATION:
Phone: 913-458-2000   Fax: 913-458-2934
Toll-Free:
Address: 11401 Lamar Ave., Overland Park, KS 66211 United States

STOCK TICKER/OTHER:
Stock Ticker: Private   Exchange:
Employees: 10,000   Fiscal Year Ends: 12/31
Parent Company:

SALARIES/BONUSES:
Top Exec. Salary: $ Bonus: $
Second Exec. Salary: $ Bonus: $

OTHER THOUGHTS:
Estimated Female Officers or Directors: 4
Hot Spot for Advancement for Women/Minorities: Y

Sales, profits and employees may be estimates. Financial information, benefits and other data can change quickly and may vary from those stated here.

BMC Software Inc

www.bmc.com

NAIC Code: 0

TYPES OF BUSINESS:
Computer Software-Mainframe Related
Systems Management Software
e-Business Software
Consulting & Training Services

BRANDS/DIVISIONS/AFFILIATES:
Boxer Parent Company Inc
Remedy Service Management Suite
Remedyforce

CONTACTS:
Note: Officers with more than one job title may be intentionally listed here more than once.

Peter Leav, CEO
Stephen B. Solcher, CFO
Dan Streetman, Exec. VP-Global Mktg. & Sales
Scott Crowder, CTO
Hollie Castro, Sr. VP-Admin.
Patrick K. Tagtow, General Counsel
Steve Goddard, Sr. VP-Bus. Oper.
Ken Berryman, Sr. VP-Strategy & Corp. Dev.
Ann Duhon, Mgr.-Comm.
Derrick Vializ, VP-Investor Rel.
T. Cory Bleuer, Chief Acct. Officer
Patrick K. Tagtow, Chief Compliance Officer
Paul Avenant, Sr. VP-Solutions

GROWTH PLANS/SPECIAL FEATURES:
BMC Software, Inc. is a software vendor company that provides system management, service management and automation solutions primarily for large companies. Its software products span mainframe systems, IT service management, cloud management, IT operations, workload automation and IT automation. The firm offers digital enterprise management, which includes digital service management, digital infrastructure optimization, digital enterprise automations and digital service assurance. The digital service management enhances employee productivity through automation and compliance tracking. Products in this unit include the Remedy Service Management Suite and Remedyforce. The digital infrastructure optimization solutions focus on offering services to match digital infrastructure, such as servers, private and hybrid clouds and virtual infrastructures. Digital enterprise automations allow users to centrally orchestrate the automation of services and significantly reduce delivery time across a range of technologies, including networks, mobile devices, middleware, cloud, big data, apps and applications. The digital service assurance combines sophisticated data collection and analytic capabilities allowing businesses to take action based on customer online posts and complaints. BMC's customers include manufacturers, telecommunication companies, financial service providers, educational institutions, retailers, distributors, hospitals, government agencies and channel partners, including resellers, distributors and system integrators. Over 10,000 customers worldwide use BMC products, including 82% of Fortune 500 companies. BMC has 470 patents granted or pending, $2 billion in revenue and employs thousands of people in 30 countries. The firm operates as a subsidiary of Boxer Parent Company, Inc.

FINANCIAL DATA:
Note: Data for latest year may not have been available at press time.

In U.S. $	2017	2016	2015	2014	2013	2012
Revenue	2,500,000,000	2,300,000,000	2,250,000,000	2,205,000,000	2,201,000,000	2,172,000,000
R&D Expense						
Operating Income						
Operating Margin %						
SGA Expense						
Net Income						
Operating Cash Flow						
Capital Expenditure						
EBITDA						
Return on Assets %						
Return on Equity %						
Debt to Equity						

CONTACT INFORMATION:
Phone: 713 918-8800
Fax: 713 918-8000
Toll-Free: 800-841-2031
Address: 2101 Citywest Blvd., Houston, TX 77042 United States

STOCK TICKER/OTHER:
Stock Ticker: Subsidiary
Employees: 6,700
Parent Company:
Exchange:
Fiscal Year Ends: 03/31

SALARIES/BONUSES:
Top Exec. Salary: $
Bonus: $
Second Exec. Salary: $
Bonus: $

OTHER THOUGHTS:
Estimated Female Officers or Directors: 2
Hot Spot for Advancement for Women/Minorities: Y

BMW (Bayerische Motoren Werke AG)

www.bmw.com

NAIC Code: 336111

TYPES OF BUSINESS:
Automobile Manufacturing
Financial Services
Motorcycles
Software
Consulting Services
Fleet Management
IT Solutions
Engines

BRANDS/DIVISIONS/AFFILIATES:
MINI
Rolls-Royce Motor Cars
BMW Motoren
Bavaria Wirtschaftsagentur GmbH
BMW Technik
X2
X3
i3

CONTACTS:
Note: Officers with more than one job title may be intentionally listed here more than once.

Harald Krueger, CEO
Nicolas Peter, CFO
Ian Robertson, Dir.-Sales & Mktg.
Milagros Caina Carreiro-Andree, Dir.-Human Resources
Frank-Peter Arndt, Head-Prod.
Herbert Diess, Dir.-Dev.
Friedrich Eichner, Dir.-Finance
Harald Kruger, Dir.-MINI, Motorcycles, Rolls-Royce & After Sales
Peter Schwarzenbauer, Head-MINI, Rolly-Royce & Aftersales
Harald Krueger, Chmn.
Klaus Draeger, Chief Purchasing & Supplier Network Officer

GROWTH PLANS/SPECIAL FEATURES:
BMW (Bayerische Motoren Werke AG), based in Munich, Germany, is a leading vehicle manufacturer in Europe, with brands including BMW, MINI and Rolls-Royce Motor Cars. The company operates in three primary business segments: automobiles, motorcycles and financial services. The company's automobile models include the 1 Series; the 2 Series; the 3 Series; the 4 Series, the 5 Series; the 6 Series; the 7 Series; the X1, X2, X3, X4, X5 and X6 sport utilities; the M2, M3, M4, M5, M6, X5 M and X6 M; and the BMW i electric and hybrid vehicles, i3, i8 coupe and i8 roadster. The company also manufactures specialty vehicles such as the BMW X5 armored security vehicle. Additionally, BMW produces the MINI brand of cars (Cooper, Cooper D and Cooper S) and Rolls-Royce Motor Cars (Phantom, Ghost and Wraith). BMW brand motorcycles include: Sport models HP4 RACE, S 1000 RR and R 1200 RS; Tour models K 1600 B, K 1600 Grand America, K1600 GTL, K 1600 GT, R 1200 RT and F 800 GT; Roadster models R 1200 R, S 1000 R, F 800 R and G 310 R; Heritage model R nineT; Adventure models R 1200, S 100, F 800, F 700 and G 310; and Urban Mobility models C 650 GT, C evolution and C 400 X. The financial services segment manages vehicle-related financial services, including financing and leasing, asset management, insurance, dealer financing and company car pools. Other group activities include Bavaria Wirtschaftsagentur GmbH, which provides insurance and other services to the firm; BMW Technik, which works to develop innovative automobile technologies; and BMW Motoren, which manufactures engines. The firm operates approximately 30 production and assembly facilities in 14 countries and has a global sales network in over 140 countries.

FINANCIAL DATA:
Note: Data for latest year may not have been available at press time.

In U.S. $	2017	2016	2015	2014	2013	2012
Revenue	121,857,800,000	116,282,200,000	113,827,200,000	99,287,460,000	93,924,280,000	94,899,850,000
R&D Expense						
Operating Income	12,083,530,000	11,489,540,000	11,706,880,000	11,263,550,000	9,831,066,000	10,269,460,000
Operating Margin %	9.91%	9.88%	10.28%	11.34%	10.46%	10.82%
SGA Expense	11,805,680,000	11,309,240,000	10,660,920,000	9,745,857,000	8,959,224,000	8,652,968,000
Net Income	10,644,870,000	8,475,142,000	7,865,099,000	7,159,970,000	6,562,276,000	6,293,067,000
Operating Cash Flow	7,297,044,000	3,918,348,000	1,185,507,000	3,596,038,000	4,462,941,000	6,268,369,000
Capital Expenditure	8,782,633,000	7,190,842,000	7,272,346,000	7,531,675,000	8,235,571,000	6,465,954,000
EBITDA	19,621,380,000	18,711,260,000	17,940,680,000	16,731,710,000	15,041,120,000	14,505,170,000
Return on Assets %	4.51%	3.80%	3.89%	3.95%	3.93%	3.99%
Return on Equity %	17.03%	15.31%	15.97%	15.95%	16.16%	17.77%
Debt to Equity	0.90	1.05	0.99	1.01	0.98	1.14

CONTACT INFORMATION:
Phone: 49 893820   Fax: 49 8938214661
Toll-Free:
Address: Petuelring 130, Munich, 80788 Germany

STOCK TICKER/OTHER:
Stock Ticker: BMWM5N   Exchange: MEX
Employees: 129,932   Fiscal Year Ends: 12/31
Parent Company:

SALARIES/BONUSES:
Top Exec. Salary: $ Bonus: $
Second Exec. Salary: $ Bonus: $

OTHER THOUGHTS:
Estimated Female Officers or Directors: 5
Hot Spot for Advancement for Women/Minorities: Y

Sales, profits and employees may be estimates. Financial information, benefits and other data can change quickly and may vary from those stated here.

Boeing Company (The)

NAIC Code: 336411

www.boeing.com

TYPES OF BUSINESS:
Aircraft Manufacturing
Aerospace Technology & Manufacturing
Military Aircraft
Satellite Manufacturing
Communications Products & Services
Air Traffic Management Technology
Financing Services
Research & Development

BRANDS/DIVISIONS/AFFILIATES:
Boeing Capital Corporation
737
747
767
777
787
Cuberg Inc

CONTACTS:
Note: Officers with more than one job title may be intentionally listed here more than once.

Kevin McAllister, CEO, Divisional
Diana Sands, Senior VP, Divisional
Stanley Deal, CEO, Divisional
Leanne Caret, CEO, Divisional
Gregory Smith, CFO
Robert Verbeck, Chief Accounting Officer
Theodore Colbert, Chief Information Officer
Gregory Hyslop, Chief Technology Officer
Dennis Muilenburg, Director
J. Luttig, Executive VP
Bertrand-Marc Allen, President, Subsidiary
Heidi Capozzi, Senior VP, Divisional
Timothy Keating, Senior VP, Divisional
Philip Musser, Senior VP, Divisional
Jenette Ramos, Senior VP, Divisional

GROWTH PLANS/SPECIAL FEATURES:

The Boeing Company is one of the world's major aerospace firms. The company operates through four segments: commercial airplanes; defense, space & security (BDS); global services; and Boeing Capital Corporation (BCC). The commercial airplanes segment develops, produces and markets commercial jet aircraft. Its aircraft includes the 737 narrow-body model, as well as the 747, 767, 777 and 787 wide-body models. The BDS segment researches, develops, produces and modifies manned and un-manned military aircraft and weapons systems for global strike, vertical lift, and mobility/surveillance and engagement purposes. This division also researches, develops, produces and modifies the following products: strategic defense and intelligence systems, including missile and defense systems, C4ISR (command, control, communications, computers, intelligence, surveillance and reconnaissance) and related intelligence systems; and satellite systems, including government and commercial satellites. BDS' primary customer is the U.S. Department of Defense. The global services segment provides services to Boeing's commercial and defense customers, offering aviation services support, aircraft modifications, spare parts, training, maintenance documents, data analytics and information-based services. Last, BCC seeks to ensure that Boeing customers have the financing they need to buy and take delivery of their Boeing product. This subsidiary manages Boeing's overall financing exposure, including equipment under operating leases, finance leases, notes and other receivables, as well as assets held for sale or re-lease, among other investments. In early-2018, Boeing (49.99%) formed a joint venture with Adient plc (50.01%) to develop and manufacture airline seats for new installations or retrofit to be based in Kaiserslautern, Germany, and distributed through Boeing subsidiary Aviall in Seattle; and invested in California-based Cuberg, Inc., a startup developing next-generation battery technology for potential aerospace and industrial applications.

The company offers its employees medical, dental, life, AD&D and disability insurance; flexible spending accounts; pension and retirement savings plans; tuition assistance; and onsite and on-the-job training.

FINANCIAL DATA:
Note: Data for latest year may not have been available at press time.

In U.S. $	2017	2016	2015	2014	2013	2012
Revenue	93,392,000,000	94,571,000,000	96,114,000,000	90,762,000,000	86,623,000,000	81,698,000,000
R&D Expense	3,179,000,000	4,627,000,000	3,331,000,000	3,047,000,000	3,071,000,000	3,298,000,000
Operating Income	10,123,000,000	5,597,000,000	7,234,000,000	7,265,000,000	6,403,000,000	6,127,000,000
Operating Margin %	10.83%	5.91%	7.52%	8.00%	7.39%	7.49%
SGA Expense	4,094,000,000	3,616,000,000	3,525,000,000	3,767,000,000	3,956,000,000	3,717,000,000
Net Income	8,197,000,000	4,895,000,000	5,176,000,000	5,446,000,000	4,585,000,000	3,900,000,000
Operating Cash Flow	13,344,000,000	10,499,000,000	9,363,000,000	8,858,000,000	8,179,000,000	7,508,000,000
Capital Expenditure	1,870,000,000	2,613,000,000	2,450,000,000	2,236,000,000	2,238,000,000	1,710,000,000
EBITDA	12,546,000,000	7,843,000,000	9,327,000,000	9,445,000,000	8,537,000,000	8,272,000,000
Return on Assets %	8.98%	5.30%	5.34%	5.67%	5.04%	4.60%
Return on Equity %	1397.78%	136.80%	68.95%	46.21%	44.14%	82.96%
Debt to Equity	27.55	11.71	1.37	0.93	0.54	1.52

CONTACT INFORMATION:
Phone: 312 544-2000 Fax:
Toll-Free:
Address: 100 N. Riverside Plz., Chicago, IL 60606 United States

STOCK TICKER/OTHER:
Stock Ticker: BA Exchange: NYS
Employees: 150,500 Fiscal Year Ends: 12/31
Parent Company:

SALARIES/BONUSES:
Top Exec. Salary: $1,690,769 Bonus: $
Second Exec. Salary: $1,095,385 Bonus: $

OTHER THOUGHTS:
Estimated Female Officers or Directors: 7
Hot Spot for Advancement for Women/Minorities: Y

Sales, profits and employees may be estimates. Financial information, benefits and other data can change quickly and may vary from those stated here.

Bombardier Inc

www.bombardier.com

NAIC Code: 336411

TYPES OF BUSINESS:
Aircraft Manufacturing
Railway Vehicles & Equipment
Business, Passenger & Civil Aircraft
Jet Leasing & Charters
Railroad Car Leasing & Management
Amphibious Aircraft

BRANDS/DIVISIONS/AFFILIATES:
FLEXX
Learjet
Challenger
Global
C Series
CRJ Series
Q Series

CONTACTS:
Note: Officers with more than one job title may be intentionally listed here more than once.

Alain Bellemare, CEO
Nico Buchholz, Senior VP, Divisional
John Di Bert, CFO
Laurent Beaudoin, Chairman Emeritus
Pierre Beaudoin, Chairman of the Board
J. R. Bombardier, Director
Jean-Louis Fontaine, Director
Dimitrios Vounassis, Other Executive Officer
FranCois Caza, Other Executive Officer
David Coleal, President, Divisional
Frederick Cromer, President, Divisional
Laurent Troger, President, Divisional
Daniel Brennan, Senior VP, Divisional
Daniel Desjardins, Senior VP

GROWTH PLANS/SPECIAL FEATURES:
Bombardier, Inc. manufactures both planes and trains. The company's products and services are divided into four groups: transportation, business aircraft, commercial aircraft and aerostructures and engineering services. Transportation products and services include rail vehicles, including automated people movers, automated monorails, light rail vehicles, metros, commuter and regional trains, intercity trains, high-speed trains and locomotives. This division's propulsion and control solutions include propulsion converters, traction drives and various related electronics. Its FLEXX line of bogies are structures underneath a rail vehicle to which axles are attached via bearings. Its rail control solutions include advanced rail control systems, signaling systems, computer-based interlocking systems, automatic train protection and train operation systems, and wayside equipment. The business aircraft group manufactures, sells and supports business jets. Its Learjet, Challenger and Global lines of jet aircraft comprise more than 4,700 aircraft in operation in over 115 countries. This division has a worldwide network of training facilities, service centers, mobile response trucks, parts and component repair/overhaul facilities and more. Its customer service support and solutions are available 24/7/365. Commercial aircraft include: the C Series, optimized for the 100-to-150-seat market; the CRJ Series, for the 60-to-100-seat segment; and the Q Series, a twin-engine, medium-range turboprop. Last, the aerostructures and engineering services group designs, manufactures and provides aftermarket support for primary metallic and composite structures such as fuselages, engine nacelles, wings, one-piece pressure bulkheads, doors and horizontal stabilizers. This division also produces various system components, including electrical harnesses, tubing and ducting.

FINANCIAL DATA:
Note: Data for latest year may not have been available at press time.

In U.S. $	2017	2016	2015	2014	2013	2012
Revenue	16,218,000,000	16,339,000,000	18,172,000,000	20,111,000,000	18,151,000,000	16,768,000,000
R&D Expense	240,000,000	287,000,000	355,000,000	347,000,000	293,000,000	299,000,000
Operating Income	508,000,000	297,000,000	405,000,000	872,000,000	783,000,000	757,000,000
Operating Margin %	3.13%	1.81%	2.22%	4.33%	4.31%	4.51%
SGA Expense	1,194,000,000	1,133,000,000	1,213,000,000	1,358,000,000	1,417,000,000	1,443,000,000
Net Income	-516,000,000	-1,022,000,000	-5,347,000,000	-1,260,000,000	564,000,000	588,000,000
Operating Cash Flow	531,000,000	137,000,000	20,000,000	847,000,000	1,380,000,000	1,348,000,000
Capital Expenditure	1,389,000,000	1,255,000,000	1,879,000,000	1,982,000,000	2,357,000,000	2,140,000,000
EBITDA	203,000,000	-61,000,000	-4,591,000,000	-286,000,000	1,433,000,000	1,142,000,000
Return on Assets %	-2.27%	-4.60%	-21.26%	-4.42%	2.04%	2.36%
Return on Equity %				-142.05%	36.82%	92.16%
Debt to Equity					3.36	5.44

CONTACT INFORMATION:
Phone: 514 861-9481 Fax: 514 861-7053
Toll-Free:
Address: 800 Rene-Levesque Blvd. W., Montreal, QC H3B 1Y8 Canada

STOCK TICKER/OTHER:
Stock Ticker: BBD.A Exchange: TSE
Employees: 69,500 Fiscal Year Ends: 12/31
Parent Company:

SALARIES/BONUSES:
Top Exec. Salary: $ Bonus: $
Second Exec. Salary: $ Bonus: $

OTHER THOUGHTS:
Estimated Female Officers or Directors: 3
Hot Spot for Advancement for Women/Minorities: Y

Sales, profits and employees may be estimates. Financial information, benefits and other data can change quickly and may vary from those stated here.

Boston Scientific Corporation

NAIC Code: 339100

www.bostonscientific.com

TYPES OF BUSINESS:
Supplies-Surgery
Interventional Medical Products
Catheters
Guide wires
Stents
Oncology Research

BRANDS/DIVISIONS/AFFILIATES:
Emcision Limited
Securus Medical Group Inc
nVision Medical Corporation

CONTACTS:
Note: Officers with more than one job title may be intentionally listed here more than once.

Michael Mahoney, CEO
John Sorenson, Senior VP, Divisional
Daniel Brennan, CFO
Edward Mackey, Executive VP, Divisional
Ian Meredith, Executive VP
Kevin Ballinger, Executive VP
Joseph Fitzgerald, Executive VP
Michael Phalen, Executive VP
Desiree Ralls-Morrison, General Counsel
David Pierce, President, Divisional
Maulik Nanavaty, President, Divisional
Jeffrey Mirviss, President, Divisional
Arthur Butcher, President, Divisional
Warren Wang, President, Geographical
Eric Thepaut, President, Geographical
Wendy Carruthers, Senior VP, Divisional

GROWTH PLANS/SPECIAL FEATURES:

Boston Scientific Corporation is a global developer, manufacturer and marketer of medical devices used in a broad range of interventional medical specialties. The firm comprises seven core businesses organized into three segments: cardiovascular, rhythm management and MedSurg. The cardiovascular segment has two business units: the interventional cardiology business develops and manufactures technologies for diagnosing and treating coronary artery disease and other cardiovascular disorders, including structural heart conditions; and the peripheral interventions business develops and manufactures products to diagnose and treat peripheral arterial diseases, including a broad line of medical devices used in percutaneous transluminal angioplasty (PTA) and peripheral vascular diseases, as well as products to diagnose, treat and ease various forms of cancer. The rhythm management segment has two business units: the cardiac rhythm management business develops and manufactures a variety of implantable devices that monitor the heart and deliver electricity to treat cardiac abnormalities; and the electrophysiology business develops and manufactures less-invasive medical technologies used in the diagnosis and treatment of rate and rhythm disorders of the heart, including a broad portfolio of therapeutic and diagnostic catheters and a variety of equipment used in the electrophysiology lab. Last, the MedSurg segment has three business units: the endoscopy business develops and manufactures devices to diagnose and treat a range of gastrointestinal and pulmonary conditions with innovative, less-invasive technologies; the urology and pelvic health business develops and manufactures devices to treat various urological and pelvic conditions for both male and female anatomies; and the neuromodulation business develops and manufactures devices to treat various neurological movement disorders and manage chronic pain. In early-2018, Boston Scientific acquired EMcision Limited; Securus Medical Group, Inc.; and nVision Medical Corporation. It agreed to acquire NxThera.

The firm offers employees medical, dental, vision and life insurance; educational assistance; and flexible spending accounts.

FINANCIAL DATA:
Note: Data for latest year may not have been available at press time.

In U.S. $	2017	2016	2015	2014	2013	2012
Revenue	9,048,001,000	8,386,000,000	7,477,000,000	7,380,000,000	7,143,000,000	7,249,000,000
R&D Expense	997,000,000	920,000,000	876,000,000	817,000,000	861,000,000	886,000,000
Operating Income	1,611,000,000	1,319,000,000	946,000,000	902,000,000	884,000,000	931,000,000
Operating Margin %	17.80%	15.72%	12.65%	12.22%	12.37%	12.84%
SGA Expense	3,294,000,000	3,178,000,000	2,987,000,000	3,013,000,000	2,814,000,000	2,688,000,000
Net Income	104,000,000	347,000,000	-239,000,000	-119,000,000	-121,000,000	-4,068,000,000
Operating Cash Flow	1,426,000,000	972,000,000	600,000,000	1,269,000,000	1,082,000,000	1,260,000,000
Capital Expenditure	319,000,000	376,000,000	247,000,000	259,000,000	245,000,000	226,000,000
EBITDA	2,006,000,000	1,225,000,000	439,000,000	432,000,000	790,000,000	-3,163,000,000
Return on Assets %	.56%	1.91%	-1.35%	-.70%	-.71%	-21.16%
Return on Equity %	1.51%	5.31%	-3.74%	-1.83%	-1.80%	-44.64%
Debt to Equity	0.54	0.80	0.89	0.59	0.64	0.61

CONTACT INFORMATION:
Phone: 508 683-4000 Fax: 508 647-2200
Toll-Free: 888-272-1001
Address: 300 Boston Scientific Way, Marlborough, MA 01752-1234 United States

STOCK TICKER/OTHER:
Stock Ticker: BSX Exchange: NYS
Employees: 27,000 Fiscal Year Ends: 12/31
Parent Company:

SALARIES/BONUSES:
Top Exec. Salary: $1,179,452 Bonus: $
Second Exec. Salary: $652,998 Bonus: $

OTHER THOUGHTS:
Estimated Female Officers or Directors: 5
Hot Spot for Advancement for Women/Minorities: Y

Sales, profits and employees may be estimates. Financial information, benefits and other data can change quickly and may vary from those stated here.

Bouygues SA

NAIC Code: 237130

www.bouygues.fr

TYPES OF BUSINESS:
Construction & Telecommunications
Construction
Road Building
Property Development
Precasting
Cellular Phone Service
Media Operation
Research & Development

BRANDS/DIVISIONS/AFFILIATES:
Bouygues Construction
Bouygues Immobilier
Colas
Buoygues Telecom
Bbox Miami
TF1
TMC
LCI

CONTACTS:
Note: Officers with more than one job title may be intentionally listed here more than once.

Martin Bouygues, CEO
Jean-Claude Tostivin, Sr. VP-Admin.
Jean Francois Guillemin, Corp. Sec.
Olivier Bouygues, Deputy CEO
Philippe Marien, Chmn.-Bourgues Telecom

GROWTH PLANS/SPECIAL FEATURES:
Buoygues SA, based in Paris, France, was founded in 1952 as a construction and industrial works company. Operating through its subsidiaries, the firm provides services to three sectors: construction, telecoms and media. The construction sector operates through three subsidiaries: Bouygues Construction, which is dedicated to electrical contracting, building, energy services and civil works; Bouygues Immobilier, committed to property development; and Colas, dedicated to building roads and other complementary activities, such as safety, road marking and signaling services. The telecom sector operates through subsidiary Buoygues Telecom, a mobile telephone operator comprising a 4G+ network, with a subscriber base of 17.8 million customers. Its Bbox Miami offering is a TV box operating under the Android operating system, combines traditional TV content with apps and content from the web within a highly seamless interface. The media sector operates through TF1, a leading private media group in freeview television within France. TF1 produces five complementary freeview TV channels TF1, TMC, TFX, TF1 Series films and rolling news channel, LCI, that together claimed an average 27.7% audience share in 2017. Buoygues maintains operations in Europe, Central and South America, North America, Asia, the Middle East and Africa.

FINANCIAL DATA:
Note: Data for latest year may not have been available at press time.

In U.S. $	2017	2016	2015	2014	2013	2012
Revenue	39,414,500,000	33,608,600,000	36,995,483,800	37,234,898,478	46,193,335,211	44,296,705,342
R&D Expense						
Operating Income						
Operating Margin %						
SGA Expense						
Net Income	1,299,680,000	771,206,000	557,826,750	561,322,800	-1,048,710,129	853,836,721
Operating Cash Flow						
Capital Expenditure						
EBITDA						
Return on Assets %						
Return on Equity %						
Debt to Equity						

CONTACT INFORMATION:
Phone: 33-1-44-20-10-00
Fax: 33-1-30-60-4861
Toll-Free:
Address: 32 Ave. Hoche, Paris, 75008 France

STOCK TICKER/OTHER:
Stock Ticker: EN
Employees: 115,530
Parent Company:

Exchange: Paris
Fiscal Year Ends: 12/31

SALARIES/BONUSES:
Top Exec. Salary: $ Bonus: $
Second Exec. Salary: $ Bonus: $

OTHER THOUGHTS:
Estimated Female Officers or Directors: 5
Hot Spot for Advancement for Women/Minorities: Y

Sales, profits and employees may be estimates. Financial information, benefits and other data can change quickly and may vary from those stated here.

BP plc

NAIC Code: 211111

www.bp.com

TYPES OF BUSINESS:
Oil & Gas Exploration & Production
Refining
Renewable & Alternative Energy
Lubricants
Natural Gas
Photovoltaic Modules
Gas Stations & Convenience Stores

BRANDS/DIVISIONS/AFFILIATES:
BP
Aral
Castrol
Butamax
Lightsource BP

CONTACTS:
Note: Officers with more than one job title may be intentionally listed here more than once.

Bob Dudley, CEO
Brian Gilvary, CFO
Helmut Schuster, Dir.-Human Resources
Bernard Looney, COO-Prod.
Rupert Bondy, General Counsel
Andy Hopwood, COO-Strategy & Regions, Upstream
Dev Sanyal, Chief of Staff
Katrina Landis, Exec. VP-Corp. Bus. Activities
Bob Fryer, Exec. VP-Safety & Operational Risk
Lamar McKay, Chief Exec.-Upstream
Carl-Henric Svanberg, Chmn.

GROWTH PLANS/SPECIAL FEATURES:

BP plc is one of the world's largest integrated oil companies, with proven reserves of 18.4 million barrels of oil equivalent (as of April 2018). Barrels of oil equivalent produced per day is 1.7 million. The firm's core brands include BP, Aral and Castrol. The company operates through four segments: upstream, downstream, alternative energy and BP ventures. Upstream manages BP's upstream activities, including oil and gas exploration, field development and production; and midstream activities, including the management of crude oil and natural gas pipelines, processing and export terminals and liquefied natural gas (LNG) processing facilities. Downstream focuses on refining, marketing and transporting crude oil and petroleum products to wholesale and retail customers. This segment also includes the firm's aromatics and acetyls businesses. The alternative energy segment comprises BP's investments in renewables, with a focus on biofuels, biopower, wind energy and solar energy. The biofuels unit is operated through 50/50 joint venture Butamax (with DuPont), which has developed technology that converts sugars from corn into bio-isobutanol, which can be blended with gasoline. The biopower unit creates biopower by burning bagasse, the fiber that remains after crushing sugarcane stalks. The wind energy unit comprises interests in 14 sites in the U.S., comprising a net generating capacity of 1,432 megawatts (MW). The solar energy unit operates through joint venture Lightsource BP (with Lightsource), which develops, acquires and manages large-scale solar projects and smart energy solutions worldwide, with a commissioned 1.3 gigawatts of solar capacity and manages approximately 2GW via long-term contracts. Last, the BP ventures segment identifies and invests in private, high-growth technology companies that aid in accelerating innovation across the entire energy spectrum. This division's focus is on: advanced mobility, power and storage, carbon management, bio and low carbon products, and digital transformation.

FINANCIAL DATA:
Note: Data for latest year may not have been available at press time.

In U.S. $	2017	2016	2015	2014	2013	2012
Revenue	241,418,000,000	183,008,000,000	222,894,000,000	353,568,000,000	379,136,000,000	375,580,000,000
R&D Expense						
Operating Income	7,526,000,000	-5,692,000,000	-9,097,000,000	9,837,000,000	16,190,000,000	12,956,000,000
Operating Margin %	3.11%	-3.11%	-4.08%	2.78%	4.27%	3.44%
SGA Expense	10,508,000,000	10,495,000,000	11,553,000,000	12,696,000,000	13,070,000,000	13,357,000,000
Net Income	3,389,000,000	115,000,000	-6,482,000,000	3,780,000,000	23,451,000,000	11,582,000,000
Operating Cash Flow	18,931,000,000	10,691,000,000	19,133,000,000	32,754,000,000	21,100,000,000	20,397,000,000
Capital Expenditure	16,562,000,000	16,701,000,000	18,648,000,000	22,546,000,000	24,520,000,000	23,078,000,000
EBITDA	24,185,000,000	14,848,000,000	8,345,000,000	23,159,000,000	46,564,000,000	34,298,000,000
Return on Assets %	1.25%	.04%	-2.37%	1.28%	7.74%	3.90%
Return on Equity %	3.49%	.11%	-6.21%	3.13%	18.93%	10.07%
Debt to Equity	0.56	0.54	0.47	0.41	0.31	0.32

CONTACT INFORMATION:
Phone: 44 2074964000 Fax: 44 2074964570
Toll-Free:
Address: 1 St. James's Sq., London, SW1Y 4PD United Kingdom

SALARIES/BONUSES:
Top Exec. Salary: $1,854,000 Bonus: $1,491,000
Second Exec. Salary: $1,071,073 Bonus: $870,246

STOCK TICKER/OTHER:
Stock Ticker: BP Exchange: NYS
Employees: 74,500 Fiscal Year Ends: 12/31
Parent Company:

OTHER THOUGHTS:
Estimated Female Officers or Directors: 3
Hot Spot for Advancement for Women/Minorities: Y

Sales, profits and employees may be estimates. Financial information, benefits and other data can change quickly and may vary from those stated here.

Bristol-Myers Squibb Co

NAIC Code: 325412

www.bms.com

TYPES OF BUSINESS:
Drugs-Diversified
Medical Imaging Products
Nutritional Products

BRANDS/DIVISIONS/AFFILIATES:
Opdivo
Eliquis
Orencia
Sprycel
Yervoy
Empliciti
Baraclude
Reyataz

CONTACTS: Note: Officers with more than one job title may be intentionally listed here more than once.
Giovanni Caforio, CEO
Charles Bancroft, CFO
Joseph Caldarella, Chief Accounting Officer
Paul von Autenried, Chief Information Officer
Thomas Lynch, Chief Scientific Officer
Murdo Gordon, Executive VP
Sandra Leung, General Counsel
Ann Judge, Other Executive Officer
Louis Schmukler, President, Divisional
John Elicker, Senior VP, Divisional

GROWTH PLANS/SPECIAL FEATURES:

Bristol-Myers Squibb Company (BMS) discovers, develops, licenses, manufactures, markets, distributes and sells pharmaceuticals and other healthcare-related products. The company manufactures drugs across multiple therapeutic classes, including: cardiovascular; virology, including immunodeficiency virus infection; oncology; and immunoscience. The firm's pharmaceutical products include chemically-synthesized drugs, or small molecules, and an increasing portion of products produced from biological processes typically involving recombinant DNA technology, or biologics. Small molecule drugs are typically administered orally in the form of a pill, although there are other drug delivery mechanisms that are also used. Biologics are typically administered to patients through injections or by intravenous infusion. BMS' approved indications include: Opdivo, for several anti-cancer indications; Eliquis, for stroke prevention in atrial fibrillation and the prevention and treatment of venous thromboembolism (VTE) disorders; Orencia, a fusion protein with novel immunosuppressive activity for adult patients with active rheumatoid arthritis and prostate specific antigen; Sprycel, a multi-targeted tyrosine kinase inhibitor for adults with Philadelphia chromosome-positive chronic myelogenous leukemia (CML); Yervoy, a monoclonal antibody for adults and pediatric patients with unresectable or metastatic melanoma; Empliciti, a humanized monoclonal antibody for multiple myeloma; Baraclude, a selective inhibitor of the hepatitis B virus; Sustiva, a non-nucleoside reverse transcriptase inhibitor for human immunodeficiency virus (HIV), as well as bulk efavirenz; Reyataz, a protease inhibitor for HIV; Daklinza, an oral small molecule NS5A replication complex inhibitor for hepatitis C virus (HCV); and Sunvepra, an oral small molecule NS3 protease inhibitor for HCV. 2017 revenues included 55% being derived from the U.S., 24% from Europe, 7% from Japan and 14% from other countries.

BMS offers employees medical and dental insurance; pension and 401(k) plans; short- and long-term disability coverage; travel accident insurance; an employee assistance plan; and adoption assistance.

FINANCIAL DATA: Note: Data for latest year may not have been available at press time.

In U.S. $	2017	2016	2015	2014	2013	2012
Revenue	20,776,000,000	19,427,000,000	16,560,000,000	15,879,000,000	16,385,000,000	17,621,000,000
R&D Expense	6,411,000,000	4,940,000,000	5,920,000,000	4,534,000,000	3,731,000,000	3,904,000,000
Operating Income	3,612,000,000	4,630,000,000	1,890,000,000	2,591,000,000	3,096,000,000	4,090,000,000
Operating Margin %	17.38%	23.83%	11.41%	16.31%	18.89%	23.21%
SGA Expense	4,687,000,000	4,911,000,000	4,841,000,000	4,822,000,000	4,939,000,000	5,017,000,000
Net Income	1,007,000,000	4,457,000,000	1,565,000,000	2,004,000,000	2,563,000,000	1,960,000,000
Operating Cash Flow	5,275,000,000	2,850,000,000	1,832,000,000	3,148,000,000	3,545,000,000	6,941,000,000
Capital Expenditure	1,055,000,000	1,215,000,000	820,000,000	526,000,000	537,000,000	548,000,000
EBITDA	6,116,000,000	6,464,000,000	2,637,000,000	3,051,000,000	3,853,000,000	3,203,000,000
Return on Assets %	2.99%	13.61%	4.77%	5.54%	6.88%	5.69%
Return on Equity %	7.21%	29.28%	10.74%	13.35%	17.81%	13.25%
Debt to Equity	0.59	0.35	0.45	0.48	0.52	0.48

CONTACT INFORMATION:
Phone: 212 546-4000 Fax: 212 546-4020
Toll-Free:
Address: 345 Park Ave., New York, NY 10154 United States

STOCK TICKER/OTHER:
Stock Ticker: BMY
Employees: 25,000
Parent Company:

Exchange: NYS
Fiscal Year Ends: 12/31

SALARIES/BONUSES:
Top Exec. Salary: $796,154   Bonus: $1,400,000
Second Exec. Salary: $1,587,500   Bonus: $

OTHER THOUGHTS:
Estimated Female Officers or Directors: 4
Hot Spot for Advancement for Women/Minorities: Y

Burns & McDonnell Inc

NAIC Code: 541330

www.burnsmcd.com

TYPES OF BUSINESS:
Engineering Services
Construction
Consulting
Environmental Consulting
Architecture & Design
Energy Transmission

BRANDS/DIVISIONS/AFFILIATES:

GROWTH PLANS/SPECIAL FEATURES:
Burns & McDonnell, Inc. provides engineering, architectural, construction, environmental and consulting services across the U.S. and worldwide. The company's services include architecture, commissioning, construction, consulting, engineering, operations, maintenance, planning, program management and studies. Burns & McDonnell serves the following industries: aviation, commercial, retail, industrial, construction, environmental, government, military, municipal, manufacturing, oil & gas, power, transportation and water. The firm's offices are located in the U.S., Canada, Mexico, England, Qatar, United Arab Emirates and the Philippines.

The firm offers employees health and life insurance, short- and long-term disability, flexible spending accounts, personal time off, eight paid holidays, educational seminars and tuition assistance. The company is 100% employee-owned through its employee

CONTACTS:
Note: Officers with more than one job title may be intentionally listed here more than once.

Gregory M. Graves, CEO
Denny Scott, CFO
Mark Taylor, Treas.
Don Greenwood, Pres., Construction
Ray Kowalik, VP
John Nobles, Pres., Process & Industrial

FINANCIAL DATA:
Note: Data for latest year may not have been available at press time.

In U.S. $	2017	2016	2015	2014	2013	2012
Revenue	2,450,000,000	2,400,000,000	2,700,000,000	2,645,000,000	2,300,000,000	1,500,000,000
R&D Expense						
Operating Income						
Operating Margin %						
SGA Expense						
Net Income						
Operating Cash Flow						
Capital Expenditure						
EBITDA						
Return on Assets %						
Return on Equity %						
Debt to Equity						

CONTACT INFORMATION:
Phone: 816-333-9400   Fax: 816-822-3028
Toll-Free:
Address: 9400 Ward Parkway, Kansas City, MO 64114 United States

STOCK TICKER/OTHER:
Stock Ticker: Private   Exchange:
Employees: 5,499   Fiscal Year Ends: 12/31
Parent Company:

SALARIES/BONUSES:
Top Exec. Salary: $ Bonus: $
Second Exec. Salary: $ Bonus: $

OTHER THOUGHTS:
Estimated Female Officers or Directors:
Hot Spot for Advancement for Women/Minorities:

Sales, profits and employees may be estimates. Financial information, benefits and other data can change quickly and may vary from those stated here.

BuroHappold Ltd

NAIC Code: 541330

www.burohappold.com

TYPES OF BUSINESS:
Engineering Services
Engineering
Consultancy

BRANDS/DIVISIONS/AFFILIATES:
Happold LLP

GROWTH PLANS/SPECIAL FEATURES:
BuroHappold Ltd. provides engineering, design, planning and project management consulting services for all aspects of buildings, infrastructure and the environment. Its services within its buildings division include design for construction, green design, reuse of buildings, reuse of sites, operational effectiveness of buildings and portfolio and campus performance. Services within its cities division include city diagnostics and strategy, environments and resource management optimization, infrastructure and city system optimization, development strategies and master planning and program delivery and organization. Sectors that BuroHappold serve include aviation, commercial office, culture, energy, higher education, rail, scientific, transport, water, civic, commercial, residential, health care, hospitality, retail, sports and entertainment, as well as waste. Based in Bath, England, the firm has additional offices in the U.S., China, India, Saudi Arabia, the UAE, Germany, Italy, Nordics, Poland, Russia and the U.K. BuroHappold is a subsidiary of Happold, LLP.

CONTACTS:
Note: Officers with more than one job title may be intentionally listed here more than once.

Neil Squibbs, CEO
James Bruce, COO
James Brude, CFO
Misti Melville, HR Director
Mike Cook, Chmn.

FINANCIAL DATA:
Note: Data for latest year may not have been available at press time.

In U.S. $	2017	2016	2015	2014	2013	2012
Revenue	231,914,000	197,933,000	220,130,000	198,965,000	184,336,000	188,671,000
R&D Expense						
Operating Income						
Operating Margin %						
SGA Expense						
Net Income						
Operating Cash Flow						
Capital Expenditure						
EBITDA						
Return on Assets %						
Return on Equity %						
Debt to Equity						

CONTACT INFORMATION:
Phone: 44-1225-320-600   Fax:
Toll-Free:
Address: Camden Mill, 230 Lower Bristol Rd., Bath, BA2 3DQ United Kingdom

STOCK TICKER/OTHER:
Stock Ticker: Subsidiary
Employees: 1,669
Parent Company: Happold LLP

Exchange:
Fiscal Year Ends:

SALARIES/BONUSES:
Top Exec. Salary: $ Bonus: $
Second Exec. Salary: $ Bonus: $

OTHER THOUGHTS:
Estimated Female Officers or Directors:
Hot Spot for Advancement for Women/Minorities:

BYD Company Limited

NAIC Code: 336111

www.byd.com.cn

TYPES OF BUSINESS:
Automobile Manufacturing
Cellular Telephone Equipment Manufacturing
Battery Manufacturing
Advanced Battery Technologies
Hybrid and Electric Cars
Contract Electronics Manufacturing

BRANDS/DIVISIONS/AFFILIATES:
BYD Auto Company Limited
Shenzhen BYD Automobile Company Limited
Berkshire Hathaway Inc

CONTACTS:
Note: Officers with more than one job title may be intentionally listed here more than once.

Chuan-fu Wang, CEO
Chuan-Fu Wang, Pres.
Jing-Sheng, CFO
Lian Yubo, VP
Chuan-Fu Wang, Chmn.

GROWTH PLANS/SPECIAL FEATURES:

BYD Company Limited, based in China, is involved in the design and production of automobiles as well as contract electronics manufacturing. The company operates in three divisions: automobiles, new energy and IT. The automobile division, operating as BYD Auto Company Limited, manufactures low to high-end vehicles, auto molding, auto parts, Dual Mode (DM) electric cars and all-electric cars. BYD's all-electric compact crossover, the BYD e6, can travel about 250 miles and has zero emissions. Through Shenzhen BYD Automobile Company Limited, the firm manufactures buses and coaches for the Chinese market. In addition to the development of BYD's electric vehicles, the new energy division has developed energy storage solutions based on its Fe battery technology and solar energy stations. Additionally, it has developed solar farms, LED lighting and electric forklifts. BYD's IT division produces rechargeable batteries, battery chargers, electro acoustic components, connectors, keypads, microelectronics, cell phone accessories and opto-electronics. It is a major manufacturer of cell phone handsets as well as batteries for iPods and iPhones. BYD has manufacturing facilities located across China and branch offices in the U.S. (Illinois and California), Europe, Japan, South Korea, India, Taiwan and Hong Kong. Berkshire Hathaway, Inc., owns a 24.6% stake in the company. In late-2017, the firm announced plans to open a factory in Ontario, Canada to manufacture electric vehicles.

FINANCIAL DATA:
Note: Data for latest year may not have been available at press time.

In U.S. $	2017	2016	2015	2014	2013	2012
Revenue	16,881,800,000	16,492,130,000	12,752,670,000	9,275,870,000	8,425,905,000	7,468,046,000
R&D Expense						
Operating Income	1,131,413,000	1,357,753,000	628,800,400	228,809,500	253,052,000	142,606,500
Operating Margin %	6.70%	8.23%	4.93%	2.46%	3.00%	1.90%
SGA Expense	1,866,681,000	1,759,507,000	1,320,240,000	1,061,386,000	849,004,900	748,625,900
Net Income	648,158,000	805,265,300	450,029,600	69,099,760	88,152,350	12,970,720
Operating Cash Flow	1,014,981,000	-294,166,500	612,393,300	6,067,837	388,302,200	885,466,900
Capital Expenditure	2,355,243,000	2,080,596,000	1,958,935,000	1,367,273,000	918,719,700	693,373,500
EBITDA	2,398,420,000	2,453,910,000	1,710,038,000	1,049,686,000	872,890,700	719,248,500
Return on Assets %	2.51%	3.87%	2.69%	.50%	.76%	.12%
Return on Equity %	7.65%	12.09%	9.79%	1.84%	2.57%	.38%
Debt to Equity	0.19	0.18	0.34	0.43	0.39	0.34

CONTACT INFORMATION:
Phone: 86-755-89888888 Fax: 86-755-84202222
Toll-Free:
Address: BYD Rd., No. 3009, Pingshan, Shenzhen, Guangdong 518118 China

STOCK TICKER/OTHER:
Stock Ticker: BYDDF Exchange: PINX
Employees: 194,000 Fiscal Year Ends: 12/31
Parent Company:

SALARIES/BONUSES:
Top Exec. Salary: $ Bonus: $
Second Exec. Salary: $ Bonus: $

OTHER THOUGHTS:
Estimated Female Officers or Directors:
Hot Spot for Advancement for Women/Minorities:

Sales, profits and employees may be estimates. Financial information, benefits and other data can change quickly and may vary from those stated here.

CA Inc (CA Technologies)

www.ca.com

NAIC Code: 0

TYPES OF BUSINESS:
Computer Software, Business Management & ERP
Enterprise Management Software
Security Software
Storage Software
Application Development Software
Business Intelligence Software
Application Life Cycle Management
Consulting Services

BRANDS/DIVISIONS/AFFILIATES:
CA Technologies
Automic Holding GmbH
Veracode Inc
zIT Consulting

CONTACTS:
Note: Officers with more than one job title may be intentionally listed here more than once.

Michael Gregoire, CEO
Kieran McGrath, CFO
Arthur Weinbach, Chairman of the Board
Anthony Radesca, Chief Accounting Officer
Lauren Flaherty, Chief Marketing Officer
Jacob Lamm, Executive VP, Divisional
Paul Pronsati, Executive VP, Divisional
Michael Bisignano, Executive VP
Adam Elster, President, Divisional
Ayman Sayed, President

GROWTH PLANS/SPECIAL FEATURES:

CA, Inc., operating as CA Technologies, designs, markets and licenses enterprise IT management software, which allows businesses to run and manage critical aspects of their IT operations and data center managers and programmers to automate their daily functions. The company operates in three segments: enterprise solutions, mainframe solutions and services. Enterprise solutions includes products designed for distributed and cloud computing environments and run on industry standard servers. Areas of focus are: agile management, which enables customers to more effectively plan and manage the software development process and the business of IT service delivery; DevOps, which comprises a range of solutions that allow customers to deliver and manage applications and IT infrastructure; and security, which includes a set of solutions to address concern regarding external and internal threats to their business environments and the critical data they contain. Mainframe solutions are designed for the IBM z Systems mainframe platform, which runs many of CA Technologies' largest customers' mission-critical business applications. Mainframe solutions' areas of focus include application development, databases, database management, security, compliance and systems/operations management. Last, the services segment helps customers reach their IT and business goals by enabling the rapid implementation and adoption of CA Technologies' mainframe and enterprise solutions. This division comprises approximately 1,000 certified consultants, architects, project managers and advisors located in 30 countries, and works with them throughout the entire solution lifecycle. During 2017, the firm acquired Automic Holding GmbH, a provider of business process and IT automation software; Veracode, Inc., which provides cloud-based security testing solutions for web, mobile and third-party applications across the software development lifecycle; and zIT Consulting, which makes software that helps administrators optimize the workloads on IBM System z data center mainframes.

CA offers employees medical, dental, life, disability and long-term care insurance; and 401(k), discount stock and employee assistance programs.

FINANCIAL DATA:
Note: Data for latest year may not have been available at press time.

In U.S. $	2017	2016	2015	2014	2013	2012
Revenue	4,036,000,000	4,025,000,000	4,262,000,000	4,515,000,000	4,643,000,000	4,814,000,000
R&D Expense	586,000,000	560,000,000	603,000,000	587,000,000	490,000,000	510,000,000
Operating Income	1,154,000,000	1,147,000,000	1,185,000,000	1,301,000,000	1,357,000,000	1,389,000,000
Operating Margin %	28.59%	28.49%	27.80%	28.81%	29.22%	28.85%
SGA Expense	1,403,000,000	1,373,000,000	1,437,000,000	1,545,000,000	1,681,000,000	1,856,000,000
Net Income	775,000,000	783,000,000	846,000,000	914,000,000	955,000,000	951,000,000
Operating Cash Flow	1,039,000,000	1,022,000,000	982,000,000	1,013,000,000	1,408,000,000	1,478,000,000
Capital Expenditure	47,000,000	48,000,000	53,000,000	105,000,000	215,000,000	252,000,000
EBITDA	1,455,000,000	1,497,000,000	1,564,000,000	1,519,000,000	1,839,000,000	1,820,000,000
Return on Assets %	6.43%	6.86%	6.97%	7.47%	7.93%	7.79%
Return on Equity %	13.84%	13.83%	14.32%	16.15%	17.40%	17.26%
Debt to Equity	0.48	0.36	0.22	0.22	0.23	0.23

CONTACT INFORMATION:
Phone: 800 225-5224   Fax: 631 342-6800
Toll-Free: 800-225-5224
Address: 520 Madison Ave., New York, NY 10022 United States

STOCK TICKER/OTHER:
Stock Ticker: CA
Employees: 11,800
Parent Company:

Exchange: NAS
Fiscal Year Ends: 03/31

SALARIES/BONUSES:
Top Exec. Salary: $445,266   Bonus: $560,000
Second Exec. Salary: $1,000,000   Bonus: $

OTHER THOUGHTS:
Estimated Female Officers or Directors: 4
Hot Spot for Advancement for Women/Minorities: Y

Sales, profits and employees may be estimates. Financial information, benefits and other data can change quickly and may vary from those stated here.

Cadence Design Systems Inc

NAIC Code: 0

www.cadence.com

TYPES OF BUSINESS:
Software-Electronic Design Automation
Training & Support Services
Design & Methodology Services

BRANDS/DIVISIONS/AFFILIATES:
nusemi inc

CONTACTS:
Note: Officers with more than one job title may be intentionally listed here more than once.

Lip-Bu Tan, CEO
John Wall, CFO
John Shoven, Chairman of the Board
James Cowie, General Counsel
Anirudh Devgan, President
Neil Zaman, Senior VP, Divisional
Surendra Babu Mandava, Senior VP, Divisional
Thomas Beckley, Senior VP, Divisional

GROWTH PLANS/SPECIAL FEATURES:

Cadence Design Systems, Inc. is a leading provider of system design enablement solutions and electronic design automation software/hardware used by semiconductor and electronic system customers to develop and design integrated circuits (ICs) and electronic devices. It licenses, sells and leases its hardware technology and provides design and methodology services throughout the world to help manage and accelerate electronic product development processes. Cadence combines its design technologies into platforms for five major design activities: functional verification, digital IC and signoff, custom IC, system interconnect and analysis, and IP. Functional verification products are used to verify that the circuitry designed by customers will perform as intended. Digital IC design offerings are used by customers to create logical representations of a digital circuit or an IC that can be verified for correctness prior to implementation. Once the logic is verified, the design is converted to a format ready for silicon manufacturing. This division's signoff offering is comprised of tools used to signoff the design as ready for manufacture by a silicon foundry, which provides certification for this step. Custom IC design and verification offerings are used to create schematic and physical representations of circuits down to the transistor level for analog, mixed-signal, custom digital, memory and radio frequency designs. System interconnect and analysis offerings are used to develop PCBs and IC packages. IP offerings consist of pre-verified, customizable functional blocks which customers integrate into their system-on-a-chips to accelerate the development process and to reduce the risk of errors in the design process. In November 2017, the firm expanded its high-speed communications IP portfolio by acquiring nusemi inc, which focuses on the development of ultra-high-speed Serializer/Deserializer communications IP.

Cadence employees receive medical, dental, vision, short/long-term and life insurance; retiree health access; a 401(k); an employee stock purchase plan; and tuition reimbursement.

FINANCIAL DATA:
Note: Data for latest year may not have been available at press time.

In U.S. $	2017	2016	2015	2014	2013	2012
Revenue	1,943,032,000	1,816,083,000	1,702,091,000	1,580,932,000	1,460,116,000	1,326,424,000
R&D Expense	804,223,000	735,340,000	637,567,000	603,006,000	534,022,000	454,085,000
Operating Income	333,361,000	285,856,000	289,941,000	216,896,000	207,006,000	211,785,000
Operating Margin %	17.15%	15.74%	17.03%	13.71%	14.17%	15.96%
SGA Expense	553,342,000	520,300,000	512,414,000	513,307,000	499,471,000	454,354,000
Net Income	204,101,000	203,086,000	252,417,000	158,898,000	164,243,000	439,948,000
Operating Cash Flow	470,740,000	444,879,000	378,200,000	316,722,000	367,605,000	315,994,000
Capital Expenditure	57,901,000	53,712,000	44,808,000	39,810,000	44,929,000	35,966,000
EBITDA	456,234,000	380,411,000	414,072,000	330,757,000	294,885,000	312,230,000
Return on Assets %	9.03%	9.13%	9.07%	5.63%	6.96%	21.73%
Return on Equity %	23.58%	19.17%	18.63%	12.76%	15.85%	66.34%
Debt to Equity	0.65	0.86	0.25	0.26		

CONTACT INFORMATION:
Phone: 408 943-1234
Fax: 408 428-5001
Toll-Free: 800-746-6223
Address: 2655 Seely Ave., Bldg. 5, San Jose, CA 95134 United States

STOCK TICKER/OTHER:
Stock Ticker: CDNS
Employees: 7,100
Parent Company:
Exchange: NAS
Fiscal Year Ends: 12/31

SALARIES/BONUSES:
Top Exec. Salary: $700,000 Bonus: $
Second Exec. Salary: $322,500 Bonus: $250,000

OTHER THOUGHTS:
Estimated Female Officers or Directors: 2
Hot Spot for Advancement for Women/Minorities:

Calsonic Kansei Corporation

www.calsonickansei.co.jp

NAIC Code: 336300

TYPES OF BUSINESS:
Automobile Parts Manufacturing
Modular Assemblies
Retail Parts & Accessories
Industrial & Construction Equipment

BRANDS/DIVISIONS/AFFILIATES:
Nissan Motor Co Ltd

CONTACTS:
Note: Officers with more than one job title may be intentionally listed here more than once.

Hiroshi Moriya, CEO
Hiroshi Moriya, Pres.
Shigeo Shingyoji, Exec. VP
Kosaku Hosokawa, Exec. VP
Koji Furukawa, Sr. VP
Akira Fujisaki, Exec. VP

GROWTH PLANS/SPECIAL FEATURES:

Calsonic Kansei Corporation manufactures automotive parts and accessories, with a focus on integrated modular assemblies such as cockpits, front-ends and exhaust systems. With over 60 manufacturing and distribution centers across North America, Europe, China and Asia, Calsonic Kansei has more than 33 consolidated subsidiaries in its global network. The company's production base in Japan provides manufacturing through nearly 20 facilities. Modules offer automakers reduced costs and lighter composite weights and provide drivers with engineered efficiencies that increase ease of use and comfort. Calsonic Kansei's cockpit modules integrate instrument panels, air conditioning systems, airbags, electric controls, audio systems, steering columns and other related components in one consolidated unit. Other modules include front-end modules that combine in one unit a radiator, condenser, internal air cooler and oil cooler. Other Calsonic Kansei automotive components and products include air conditioners, exhaust systems and keyless entry devices. The company's sales division sells retail automotive parts and accessories, as well as electronic toll collection devices. Moreover, Calsonic Kansei markets industrial and construction equipment including control units, instrument clusters, radiators and mufflers. In March 2017, KKR & Co. LP agreed to acquire 95.21% of Calsonic Kansei's shares, including Nissan Motor Co. Ltd.'s 41% ownership stake, for approximately $4.5 billion. After the acquisition, KKR will implement a series of procedures to acquire the remaining common shares of the firm.

FINANCIAL DATA:
Note: Data for latest year may not have been available at press time.

In U.S. $	2017	2016	2015	2014	2013	2012
Revenue	10,000,000,000	9,704,868,864	8,896,336,896	8,464,439,296	7,010,364,928	7,207,803,392
R&D Expense						
Operating Income						
Operating Margin %						
SGA Expense						
Net Income		207,453,808	192,739,648	233,417,776	58,036,572	232,514,848
Operating Cash Flow						
Capital Expenditure						
EBITDA						
Return on Assets %						
Return on Equity %						
Debt to Equity						

CONTACT INFORMATION:
Phone: 81 486602111 Fax:
Toll-Free:
Address: 2-1917 Nisshin, Kita-ku, Saitama, 331-8501 Japan

STOCK TICKER/OTHER:
Stock Ticker: CLKNF
Employees: 22,424
Parent Company: Nissan Motor Co Ltd

Exchange: GREY
Fiscal Year Ends: 03/31

SALARIES/BONUSES:
Top Exec. Salary: $ Bonus: $
Second Exec. Salary: $ Bonus: $

OTHER THOUGHTS:
Estimated Female Officers or Directors:
Hot Spot for Advancement for Women/Minorities:

Sales, profits and employees may be estimates. Financial information, benefits and other data can change quickly and may vary from those stated here.

CannonDesign

NAIC Code: 541330

www.cannondesign.com

TYPES OF BUSINESS:
Engineering Consulting Services
Consultancy
Engineering

BRANDS/DIVISIONS/AFFILIATES:

CONTACTS: Note: Officers with more than one job title may be intentionally listed here more than once.
Bradley A. Lukanic, CEO

GROWTH PLANS/SPECIAL FEATURES:

CannonDesign provides architectural design and engineering services to clients in the business, educational, science, technology and health sectors. Its single-firm, multi-office methodology gathers the best expertise and talent around the globe to confront each challenge. Within the corporate/commercial design industry, CannonDesign develops master plans, workplace strategy, interior design, real estate strategy, architecture and change management solutions that support the strategic objectives of its clients. For the sports industry, the firm offers master planning, engineering, architecture, environmental graphics, as well as design-led construction services. The facilities include community centers, professional venues, collegiate recreation & wellness centers and athletic facilities. The design services for civic industry are offered for facilities, such as libraries, museums, veteran medical centers, courthouses and recreation centers. Within the educational industry, the company designs and engineers buildings and spaces that provide the essential tools for achieving the goals and visions of those institutions, whether Pre-K through 12th grade or college and university. CannonDesign's Science and Technology Practice assists discovery organizations in conceiving transformational business strategies, developing organizational change mechanisms, leveraging human capital, harnessing state-of-the-art technologies and synchronizing them with optimum working and learning environments. Within the health industry, CannonDesign provides design solutions, advisory services, interior environments, engineering systems and facility optimization services in order to maximize the physical spaces and operational processes. The firm's Facility Optimization Solutions (FOS) team is a market responsive consultancy focused on advancing solutions to the greatest challenges faced by clients and society. Office locations include Abu Dhabi, Baltimore, Boston, Buffalo, Chicago, Columbus, Dallas, Denver, Houston, Los Angeles, Montreal, Mumbai, New York, Phoenix, Pittsburgh, San Francisco, St. Louis, Toronto and Washington D.C.

FINANCIAL DATA: Note: Data for latest year may not have been available at press time.

In U.S. $	2017	2016	2015	2014	2013	2012
Revenue						
R&D Expense						
Operating Income						
Operating Margin %						
SGA Expense						
Net Income						
Operating Cash Flow						
Capital Expenditure						
EBITDA						
Return on Assets %						
Return on Equity %						
Debt to Equity						

CONTACT INFORMATION:
Phone: 212-972-9800 Fax: 212-972-9191
Toll-Free:
Address: 2170 Whitehaven Rd., Grand Island, New York, NY 14072 United States

STOCK TICKER/OTHER:
Stock Ticker: Private Exchange:
Employees: 1,004 Fiscal Year Ends:
Parent Company:

SALARIES/BONUSES:
Top Exec. Salary: $ Bonus: $
Second Exec. Salary: $ Bonus: $

OTHER THOUGHTS:
Estimated Female Officers or Directors:
Hot Spot for Advancement for Women/Minorities:

Sales, profits and employees may be estimates. Financial information, benefits and other data can change quickly and may vary from those stated here.

Canon Inc

NAIC Code: 333316

www.canon.com

TYPES OF BUSINESS:
Photographic and Photocopying Equipment Manufacturing
Printers & Scanners
Semiconductor Production Equipment
Cameras, Film & Digital
Optics & Lenses
X-Ray Equipment
Fax Machines
Photovoltaic Cells

BRANDS/DIVISIONS/AFFILIATES:
Canon Medical Systems Corporation

CONTACTS: Note: Officers with more than one job title may be intentionally listed here more than once.
Fujio Mitarai, CEO
Toshizo Tanaka, CFO
Ryuichi Ebinuma, Group Exec.-R&D Core Tech.
Toshiaki Ikoma, CTO
Haruhisa Honda, Exec.-Prod. Eng.
Sachio Kageyama, Group Exec.-Mfg.
Kenichi Nagasawa, Group Exec.-Legal & Intellectual Property
Kunio Watanabe, Sr. Managing Dir.-Corp. Planning Dev.
Shigeyuki Matsumoto, Exec.-Device Tech. Dev.
Masaki Nakaoka, CEO-Office Imaging Prod.
Yasou Mitsuhashi, Sr. Managing Dir.
Hideki Ozawa, Pres.
Fujio Mitarai, Chmn.
Yoroku Adachi, Pres.
Toshio Homma, Exec.-Procurement

GROWTH PLANS/SPECIAL FEATURES:
Canon, Inc. manufactures office multi-function devices. The firm sells its products primarily under the Canon brand and through sales subsidiaries, each of which are responsible for marketing and distribution to retail dealers in their assigned territories. Canon's business strategy is to develop innovative, high value-added products incorporating advanced technologies. The company operates through four business segments: office, imaging systems, medical systems, and industry and other. The office segment manufactures, markets and services multi-function devices, printers, copying machines for personal and office use and production print products for print professionals. The imaging systems segment manufactures and markets digital cameras and digital camcorders, as well as lenses and various related accessories. The medical systems segment markets diagnostic imaging systems, including computed tomography (CT), magnetic resonance imaging (MRI), ultrasound and X-ray systems, as well as clinical laboratory systems and healthcare information and communication technologies (ICT) solutions, and provides them to customers in more than 140 countries worldwide. These systems offer technology that enables fast diagnosis and early stage treatment. Last, the industry and other segment includes investments for: memory devices in relation to semiconductor lithography equipment; i-line steppers for semiconductors in relation Internet of Things (IoT) devices; and for the production of automobile electronics. This division also aims to capture a larger share of the smartphone market by taking advantage of organic light-emitting diode (OLED) panel manufacturing activities. The majority of Canon's 2017 sales were generated outside Japan, 78.3%; with 27.1% generated in the Americas; 25.2% in Europe; and 26% generated in Asia and Oceania, respectively. In early-2018, Canon renamed its Toshiba Medical subsidiary to Canon Medical Systems Corporation, a manufacturer of computed tomography, diagnostic ultrasound systems and related service parts.

Canon offers medical, dental, vision and life insurance; flexible spending accounts; and employee assistance and educational assistance programs.

FINANCIAL DATA: Note: Data for latest year may not have been available at press time.

In U.S. $	2017	2016	2015	2014	2013	2012
Revenue	38,010,200,000	31,688,900,000	35,404,050,000	34,723,790,000	34,762,250,000	32,418,370,000
R&D Expense	3,074,837,000	2,816,993,000	3,060,369,000	2,878,508,000	2,853,773,000	2,761,915,000
Operating Income	3,404,052,000	2,132,160,000	3,309,204,000	3,386,333,000	3,142,137,000	3,017,105,000
Operating Margin %	8.95%	6.72%	9.34%	9.75%	9.03%	9.30%
SGA Expense	12,085,400,000	10,644,600,000	11,651,520,000	11,076,990,000	10,758,520,000	9,592,379,000
Net Income	2,253,801,000	1,403,484,000	2,051,509,000	2,373,738,000	2,147,224,000	2,092,081,000
Operating Cash Flow	5,501,743,000	4,660,732,000	4,422,620,000	5,439,976,000	4,729,290,000	3,578,135,000
Capital Expenditure	1,765,269,000	1,928,182,000	2,356,512,000	2,034,302,000	2,172,303,000	2,945,882,000
EBITDA	5,744,206,000	4,619,042,000	5,788,606,000	6,029,616,000	5,807,034,000	5,605,664,000
Return on Assets %	4.68%	3.14%	4.95%	5.85%	5.62%	5.69%
Return on Equity %	8.55%	5.24%	7.40%	8.65%	8.36%	8.72%
Debt to Equity	0.17	0.21				

CONTACT INFORMATION:
Phone: 81 337582111   Fax: 81 354825135
Toll-Free:
Address: 30-2, Shimomaruko 3-chome, Ohta-ku, Tokyo, 146-8501 Japan

STOCK TICKER/OTHER:
Stock Ticker: CAJ
Employees: 197,673
Parent Company:

Exchange: NYS
Fiscal Year Ends: 12/31

SALARIES/BONUSES:
Top Exec. Salary: $ Bonus: $
Second Exec. Salary: $ Bonus: $

OTHER THOUGHTS:
Estimated Female Officers or Directors:
Hot Spot for Advancement for Women/Minorities:

Sales, profits and employees may be estimates. Financial information, benefits and other data can change quickly and may vary from those stated here.

Plunkett Research, Ltd.

Cardno Limited

NAIC Code: 541330

www.cardno.com

TYPES OF BUSINESS:
Engineering Services
Consulting Services

BRANDS/DIVISIONS/AFFILIATES:
SureSearch

CONTACTS:
Note: Officers with more than one job title may be intentionally listed here more than once.

Michael Alscher, Interim CEO
Ross Thompson, Mgr.-Group Oper.
Roger Collins-Woolcock, Gen. Mgr.-Australia & New Zealand
Paul Gardiner, Gen. Mgr.-Americas & Software
Kylie Sprott, Mgr.-Group Svcs. Div.
Michael Alscher, Chmn.
Michael Renshaw, Exec. Gen. Mgr.-Intl

GROWTH PLANS/SPECIAL FEATURES:

Cardno Limited provides a range of engineering, design and consulting services. Through more than 130 offices globally, the company works on projects in over 100 countries. The firm's primary focus is on providing professional services associated with the planning, design and delivery of physical and social infrastructure to help build new communities and to improve living standards in developing and developed countries around the world. Cardno offers services in 10 market sectors: buildings, land, coastal and ocean, environment, international development, management services, energy and resources, transportation, water and defense. Its services cover project feasibility, planning and design, software implementation, construction management, development assistance and management consulting. Cardno's recent projects include the Victorian desalination plant, the Fiji Women's Fund, subsurface engineering services on London's gateway, upgrading the Pacific Highway, mitigation the wetlands on Highway 31, a school construction rehabilitation program, a mixed-use development in New South Wales (Australia), and structural engineering services on Tysons' Corner Center. In April 2018, Cardno acquired SureSearch, a utility location and management business with offices in NSW, Sydney and the Illawarra, in Australia.

FINANCIAL DATA: Note: Data for latest year may not have been available at press time.

In U.S. $	2017	2016	2015	2014	2013	2012
Revenue	913,414,300	927,433,800	1,104,393,000	1,013,953,000	925,768,600	745,591,400
R&D Expense						
Operating Income	-34,219,800	-140,531,300	-128,076,100	81,732,820	84,044,270	82,851,260
Operating Margin %	-3.74%	-15.15%	-11.59%	8.06%	9.07%	11.11%
SGA Expense	425,505,200	453,838,400	548,198,800	488,269,500	438,670,200	330,558,400
Net Income	6,663,301	-151,393,400	-112,751,800	60,686,600	60,302,140	57,606,210
Operating Cash Flow	-2,977,087	43,795,730	37,377,090	65,717,280	74,353,390	56,410,870
Capital Expenditure	9,537,864	15,871,070	19,633,400	17,081,940	15,729,710	12,347,180
EBITDA	-8,806,990	-104,688,200	-89,800,380	110,076,900	105,081,200	99,924,660
Return on Assets %	.94%	-17.22%	-10.95%	6.37%	7.41%	9.04%
Return on Equity %	1.55%	-31.78%	-20.26%	11.19%	13.14%	16.37%
Debt to Equity	0.17	0.27	0.58	0.39	0.37	0.35

CONTACT INFORMATION:
Phone: 07 3369 9822 Fax: 07 3369 9722
Toll-Free:
Address: Level 11, Green Square North Tower, 515 St. Paul's, Fortitude Valley, QLD 4006 Australia

STOCK TICKER/OTHER:
Stock Ticker: COLDF   Exchange: PINX
Employees: 8,100
Parent Company: Fiscal Year Ends: 06/30

SALARIES/BONUSES:
Top Exec. Salary: $ Bonus: $
Second Exec. Salary: $ Bonus: $

OTHER THOUGHTS:
Estimated Female Officers or Directors: 2
Hot Spot for Advancement for Women/Minorities:

Sales, profits and employees may be estimates. Financial information, benefits and other data can change quickly and may vary from those stated here.

Casio Computer Co Ltd

NAIC Code: 334111

www.casio.com

TYPES OF BUSINESS:
Computer Manufacturing
Timepieces
Calculators
Cellular Phones
Electronic Music Instruments
LCDs
Digital Cameras
Factory Automation Equipment

BRANDS/DIVISIONS/AFFILIATES:
Yamagata Casio Co Ltd
Casio Electronic Manufacturing Co Ltd
Casio Europe GmbH
Computer (Hong Kong) Ltd
Casio America Inc
Casio Middle East FZE
G'xEYE
G-SHOCK

CONTACTS:
Note: Officers with more than one job title may be intentionally listed here more than once.

Kazuo Kashio, CEO
Kazuo Kashio, Pres.
Susumu Takashima, Dir.-R&D
Akira Kashio, Sr. Gen. Mgr.-System Prod.
Toshiyuki Yamagishi, Sr. Gen. Mgr.-Corp. Mgmt.
Makoto Kobayashi, Gen. Mgr.-Sec.
Akinori Takagi, Managing Dir.-Investor Rel.
Shin Takano, Sr. Gen. Mgr.-Finance
Toshio Kashio, CEO-Casio America
Fumitsune Murakami, Sr. Managing Dir.

GROWTH PLANS/SPECIAL FEATURES:
Casio Computer Co., Ltd. makes a wide range of electronic products and other equipment. The company's products include calculators; label printers; cash registers; projectors; digital cameras, including the G'xEYE for tough shooting situations; timepieces, such as the shock resistant G-SHOCK, as well digital and analog watches and clocks; handheld terminals, such as the IT-G500 Series barcode scanner with an liquid crystal display (LCD) touchscreen; and electronic musical instruments, such as keyboards. Casio's other businesses include small LCDs for mobile devices, stamp makers for creating one-of-a-kind rubber stamps, as well as bump processing services (a technology through which electrodes are formed for liquid crystal driver chips), wafer-level packaging (WLP) processing consignments and molds. Consumer electronics account for approximately 84.9% of the firm's fiscal 2017 sales; system equipment, 12.4 %; and others, 2.7%. The firm operates through several subsidiaries, including domestic-based Yamagata Casio Co., Ltd.; Casio Electronic Manufacturing Co., Ltd.; Casio Techno Co., Ltd.; Casio Information Systems Co., Ltd.; CXD NEXT Co., Ltd. and Casio Human Systems Co, Ltd.; and international subsidiaries Casio Europe GmbH; Computer (Hong Kong) Ltd.; Casio America, Inc.; Casio Middle East FZE, among many others. In April 2018, Casio Computer completed construction on a new watch plant in Japan, bringing the manufacturing of components and finished products under a single roof.

FINANCIAL DATA:
Note: Data for latest year may not have been available at press time.

In U.S. $	2017	2016	2015	2014	2013	2012
Revenue	2,992,482,000	3,281,703,000	3,152,497,000	2,997,587,000	2,774,017,000	2,810,323,000
R&D Expense	61,477,550	61,570,710	66,955,470	77,808,830	73,765,610	69,070,250
Operating Income	453,912,800	563,974,300	519,088,900	438,168,400	342,342,100	243,925,900
Operating Margin %	15.16%	17.18%	16.46%	14.61%	12.34%	8.67%
SGA Expense	340,711,800	395,621,400	396,012,700	341,811,100	313,564,400	323,728,400
Net Income	171,511,100	290,609,300	245,947,500	148,956,600	110,639,100	23,812,190
Operating Cash Flow	260,108,100	304,732,600	286,519,500	373,644,500	88,298,860	100,549,700
Capital Expenditure	83,501,030	96,385,330	78,358,490	81,302,410	95,640,030	85,643,750
EBITDA	313,052,000	473,393,000	409,306,900	307,937,400	265,735,100	102,422,200
Return on Assets %	5.11%	8.39%	7.11%	4.34%	3.22%	.66%
Return on Equity %	9.24%	15.35%	13.56%	9.16%	7.59%	1.69%
Debt to Equity	0.36	0.38	0.37	0.24	0.45	0.72

CONTACT INFORMATION:
Phone: 81-5334-4111 Fax:
Toll-Free:
Address: 6-2, Hon-machi 1-chome, Shibuya-ku, Tokyo, 151-8543 Japan

STOCK TICKER/OTHER:
Stock Ticker: CSIOF   Exchange: PINX
Employees: 12,358   Fiscal Year Ends: 03/31
Parent Company:

SALARIES/BONUSES:
Top Exec. Salary: $ Bonus: $
Second Exec. Salary: $ Bonus: $

OTHER THOUGHTS:
Estimated Female Officers or Directors:
Hot Spot for Advancement for Women/Minorities:

Sales, profits and employees may be estimates. Financial information, benefits and other data can change quickly and may vary from those stated here.

Caterpillar Inc

NAIC Code: 333120

www.cat.com

TYPES OF BUSINESS:
Machinery-Earth Moving & Agricultural
Diesel and Turbine Engines
Financing
Fuel Cell Manufacturing
Rail Car Maintenance
Engine & Equipment Remanufacturing
Locomotive Manufacturing and Maintenance

BRANDS/DIVISIONS/AFFILIATES:
Cat
Caterpillar Financial Services Corporation
Caterpillar Insurance Holdings Inc

CONTACTS:
Note: Officers with more than one job title may be intentionally listed here more than once.

D. Umpleby, CEO
Bradley Halverson, CFO
Jananne Copeland, Chief Accounting Officer
David Calhoun, Director
Suzette Long, General Counsel
Cheryl Johnson, Other Executive Officer
Thomas Pellette, President, Divisional
Denise Johnson, President, Divisional
Robert Charter, President, Divisional
Bob De Lange, President, Divisional

GROWTH PLANS/SPECIAL FEATURES:

Caterpillar, Inc. is a leading manufacturer of construction and mining equipment. The company's principal lines of business are: machinery, energy and transportation; and financial products. The machinery, energy and transportation segment comprises the firm's construction industries division, the resource industries division, and the energy and transportation division. The construction industries division supports customers via machinery in infrastructure, forestry and building construction. The majority of its machine sales are made in the heavy and general construction, rental, quarry and aggregates markets and mining. The resource industries division supports customers using machinery for mining, quarry, waste and material handling applications. This division manufactures high productivity equipment for both surface and underground mining operations worldwide. The equipment is used to extract and haul copper, iron ore, coal, oil sands, aggregates, gold and other minerals and ores. The energy and transportation division supports customers in oil and gas, power generation, marine, rail and industrial applications. Products and services include reciprocating engines, generator sets, marine propulsion systems, gas turbines, the remanufacturing of Cat-branded engines and components, as well as the remanufacturing services for other companies. The financial products segment includes: Caterpillar Financial Services Corporation, which provides retail and wholesale financing alternatives for Caterpillar products to customers and dealers globally; and Caterpillar Insurance Holdings, Inc., which offers property/casualty, life and health insurance products, among other services. Caterpillar's machines are distributed through a worldwide organization of dealers, 48 in the U.S. and 123 outside the U.S., serving 192 countries. During 2017, after more than 90 years of being headquartered in Peoria, the firm moved to Deerfield, Illinois.

Employees of the company receive benefits including health coverage, 401(k), an employee assistance program and flexible spending accounts.

FINANCIAL DATA:
Note: Data for latest year may not have been available at press time.

In U.S. $	2017	2016	2015	2014	2013	2012
Revenue	45,462,000,000	38,537,000,000	47,011,000,000	55,184,000,000	55,656,000,000	65,875,000,000
R&D Expense	1,905,000,000	1,951,000,000	2,165,000,000	2,135,000,000	2,046,000,000	2,466,000,000
Operating Income	5,052,000,000	1,689,000,000	3,843,000,000	5,952,000,000	6,355,000,000	9,950,000,000
Operating Margin %	11.11%	4.38%	8.17%	10.78%	11.41%	15.10%
SGA Expense	5,177,000,000	4,686,000,000	5,199,000,000	5,697,000,000	5,547,000,000	5,919,000,000
Net Income	754,000,000	-67,000,000	2,102,000,000	3,695,000,000	3,789,000,000	5,681,000,000
Operating Cash Flow	5,702,000,000	5,608,000,000	6,675,000,000	8,057,000,000	10,191,000,000	5,241,000,000
Capital Expenditure	2,336,000,000	2,928,000,000	3,261,000,000	3,379,000,000	4,446,000,000	5,076,000,000
EBITDA	8,136,000,000	4,274,000,000	6,995,000,000	9,354,000,000	9,407,000,000	12,313,000,000
Return on Assets %	.99%	-.08%	2.57%	4.35%	4.34%	6.65%
Return on Equity %	5.61%	-.47%	13.32%	19.67%	19.76%	37.35%
Debt to Equity	1.74	1.73	1.70	1.65	1.28	1.58

CONTACT INFORMATION:
Phone: 309 675-1000   Fax: 309 675-4332
Toll-Free:
Address: 510 Lake Cook Rd., Ste. 100, Deerfield, IL 60015 United States

SALARIES/BONUSES:
Top Exec. Salary: $1,600,008   Bonus: $
Second Exec. Salary: $729,768   Bonus: $500,000

STOCK TICKER/OTHER:
Stock Ticker: CAT   Exchange: NYS
Employees: 95,400   Fiscal Year Ends: 12/31
Parent Company:

OTHER THOUGHTS:
Estimated Female Officers or Directors: 11
Hot Spot for Advancement for Women/Minorities: Y

Sales, profits and employees may be estimates. Financial information, benefits and other data can change quickly and may vary from those stated here.

CDM Smith Inc

www.cdm.com

NAIC Code: 237000

TYPES OF BUSINESS:
Water and Sewer Line and Related Structures Construction
Water Management
Environmental Services
Design Services
Information Management & Technology
Consulting
Facilities Design
Geotechnical Services

BRANDS/DIVISIONS/AFFILIATES:

CONTACTS: Note: Officers with more than one job title may be intentionally listed here more than once.
Timothy B. Wall, CEO
Anthony B. Bouchard, Pres.
Thierry Desmaris, Exec. VP-Finance
Julia Forgas, Exec. VP-Mktg. & Communications
Timothy B. Wall, Chmn.

GROWTH PLANS/SPECIAL FEATURES:

CDM Smith, Inc. is a full-service engineering and construction firm. The company partners with related professionals and clients to navigate, discuss and understand challenges, and to develop and provide solutions. CDM's solutions are divided into: water, environment, transportation, energy and facilities. CDM's water solutions include planning, consulting and engineering for water and resource management. The company takes a holistic approach concerning the environment with innovative technology and broad knowledge of regulations and compliance strategies. This solutions division is committed to protecting air, water and wildlife, whether by designing remediation systems, restoring fragile ecosystems or managing greenhouse gasses for cities. Transportation solutions include funding, building and/or rebuilding transportation infrastructure, for the improvement of transportation-related mobility. Energy solutions include the development and management of energy across every industry sector. CDM's energy solutions take an approach that is efficient, economical and environmentally responsible, and include solutions for urban systems, combined heat and power, minimizing energy use and utilizing renewable sources. Solutions related to facilities involve planning, developing and implementing innovative, sustainable and cost-efficient facilities for clients, their employees and their communities. This division's portfolio has engineered and constructed LEED-certified recycling centers, water reclamation facilities and earthquake-resistant hospitals, and has also rehabilitated schools and more. In early-2018, CDM created an industrial unit that operates as its own business. Its design and construction teams help clients expedite project delivery, optimize water management and streamline compliance in order to drive business growth and capture market share. Based in the U.S., CDM has global offices across Canada, Europe, Asia, Africa, the Middle East and Latin America.

The firm offers medical, dental, vision, disability, life and AD&D insurance; and 401(k), profit sharing and flexible spending programs.

FINANCIAL DATA: Note: Data for latest year may not have been available at press time.

In U.S. $	2017	2016	2015	2014	2013	2012
Revenue	1,330,000,000	1,300,000,000	1,280,000,000	1,260,000,000	1,100,000,000	1,000,000,000
R&D Expense						
Operating Income						
Operating Margin %						
SGA Expense						
Net Income		912,700,000				
Operating Cash Flow						
Capital Expenditure						
EBITDA						
Return on Assets %						
Return on Equity %						
Debt to Equity						

CONTACT INFORMATION:
Phone: 617-452-6000 Fax: 617-345-3901
Toll-Free:
Address: 75 State St., Ste. 701, Boston, MA 02109 United States

STOCK TICKER/OTHER:
Stock Ticker: Private
Employees: 5,000
Parent Company:

Exchange:
Fiscal Year Ends: 12/31

SALARIES/BONUSES:
Top Exec. Salary: $ Bonus: $
Second Exec. Salary: $ Bonus: $

OTHER THOUGHTS:
Estimated Female Officers or Directors:
Hot Spot for Advancement for Women/Minorities:

Sales, profits and employees may be estimates. Financial information, benefits and other data can change quickly and may vary from those stated here.

Celanese Corporation

www.celanese.com

NAIC Code: 325211

TYPES OF BUSINESS:
Manufacturing-Acetyl Intermediate Chemicals
Industrial Products
Technical & High-Performance Polymers
Sweeteners & Sorbates
Ethanol Production
Food Ingredients
Cellulose Derivative Fibers

BRANDS/DIVISIONS/AFFILIATES:

CONTACTS: Note: Officers with more than one job title may be intentionally listed here more than once.
Mark Rohr, CEO
Scott Richardson, CFO
Kevin Oliver, Chief Accounting Officer
Peter Edwards, Executive VP
Scott Sutton, Executive VP
Shannon Jurecka, Other Executive Officer

GROWTH PLANS/SPECIAL FEATURES:
Celanese Corporation is a producer of industrial chemicals and advanced materials. The firm manufactures acetyl products, which are intermediate chemicals for nearly all major industries, and produces high-performance engineered polymers. The company operates through two business segments: materials solutions and the acetyl chain. Together, these segments utilize raw materials, technology, integrated systems and research resources in order to increase efficiency and respond to market needs. Materials solutions is further divided into two units: advanced engineered materials, which includes polyoxymethylene, ultra-high molecular weight polyethylene, polybutylene terephthalate, long-fiber thermoplastics and liquid crystal polymers; and consumer specialties, which includes acetate tow, acetate flake, acetate film, acesulfame potassium, potassium sorbate, sorbic acid and sweetener systems. These materials are used for fuel system components, automotive safety systems, medical applications, industrial applications, battery separators, consumer electronics, filtration, films, packaging, confections, telecommunications and more. The acetyl chain segment is further divided into two units: industrial specialties, which includes conventional emulsions, vinyl acetate ethylene emulsions, ethylene vinyl acetate resins/compounds and low-density polyethylene resins; and acetyl intermediates, which includes acetic acid, vinyl acetate monomer, acetaldehyde, ethyl acetate, formaldehyde, butyl acetate and ethanol. These materials are used for paints, coatings, adhesives, textiles, paper finishing, packaging, lamination, medical applications, automotive parts, pharmaceuticals, inks and more. Headquartered in Irving, Texas, the company's operations are primarily located in North America, Europe and Asia, consisting of 30 global production facilities and eight affiliate production facilities. In December 2017, the firm agreed to acquire Omni Plastics and its subsidiaries, which is based in the U.S., with additional offices in Mexico City.

FINANCIAL DATA: Note: Data for latest year may not have been available at press time.

In U.S. $	2017	2016	2015	2014	2013	2012
Revenue	6,140,000,000	5,389,000,000	5,674,000,000	6,802,000,000	6,510,000,000	6,418,000,000
R&D Expense	72,000,000	78,000,000	119,000,000	86,000,000	85,000,000	102,000,000
Operating Income	967,000,000	902,000,000	682,000,000	752,000,000	937,000,000	532,000,000
Operating Margin %	15.74%	16.73%	12.01%	11.05%	14.39%	8.28%
SGA Expense	456,000,000	416,000,000	506,000,000	758,000,000	311,000,000	507,000,000
Net Income	843,000,000	900,000,000	304,000,000	624,000,000	1,101,000,000	605,000,000
Operating Cash Flow	803,000,000	893,000,000	862,000,000	962,000,000	762,000,000	722,000,000
Capital Expenditure	267,000,000	246,000,000	520,000,000	678,000,000	377,000,000	410,000,000
EBITDA	1,507,000,000	1,445,000,000	970,000,000	1,386,000,000	2,100,000,000	1,162,000,000
Return on Assets %	9.42%	10.62%	3.49%	6.99%	12.22%	6.90%
Return on Equity %	30.79%	36.24%	11.70%	22.62%	49.71%	39.40%
Debt to Equity	1.14	1.11	1.03	0.92	1.06	1.69

CONTACT INFORMATION:
Phone: 972 443-4000   Fax: 972 332-9373
Toll-Free:
Address: 222 West Las Colinas Blvd, Ste 900N, Irving, TX 75039-5421 United States

STOCK TICKER/OTHER:
Stock Ticker: CE
Employees: 7,293
Parent Company:

Exchange: NYS
Fiscal Year Ends: 12/31

SALARIES/BONUSES:
Top Exec. Salary: $1,155,000   Bonus: $
Second Exec. Salary: $645,231   Bonus: $

OTHER THOUGHTS:
Estimated Female Officers or Directors: 1
Hot Spot for Advancement for Women/Minorities: Y

Celestica Inc

www.celestica.com

NAIC Code: 334418

TYPES OF BUSINESS:
Contract Electronics Manufacturing
Product Design
Engineering and Design
Distribution Services

BRANDS/DIVISIONS/AFFILIATES:
Atrenne Integrated Solutions Inc

CONTACTS:
Note: Officers with more than one job title may be intentionally listed here more than once.

Mandeep Chawla, CFO
Todd Cooper, COO
William Etherington, Director
Robert Mionis, Director
Nicolas Pujet, Other Executive Officer
John Lawless, President, Divisional
Michael McCaughey, President, Divisional
Elizabeth DelBianco, Secretary

GROWTH PLANS/SPECIAL FEATURES:

Celestica, Inc. provides design, manufacturing and supply chain solutions globally to customers engaged in the advanced technology solutions (ATS) and connectivity/cloud solutions (CCS) end markets. The company operates a network of sites in various geographies with specialized end-to-end supply chain capabilities tailored to meet specific market and customer product lifecycle requirements. Celestica offers a range of services, including design and development, engineering, supply chain management, new product introduction, component sourcing, electronics manufacturing/assembly/test, complex mechanical assembly, systems integration, precision machining, order fulfillment, logistics and after-market repair and return solutions. The firm's ATS end market division derives 32% of annual revenue (2017), and consists of aerospace, defense, industrial, smart energy, healthcare, semiconductor and consumer businesses. Its CCS end market division derives 68% of annual revenue, and consists of Celestica's communications and enterprise end markets. Products and services provided from these divisions serve a wide variety of applications, including: servers; networking and telecommunications equipment; storage systems; converged systems; optical equipment; aerospace and defense electronics; healthcare products and applications; semiconductor equipment; and a range of industrial and alternative energy products. In April 2018, the firm acquired Atrenne Integrated Solutions, Inc., an advanced, vertically-integrated, component and system provider serving aerospace, defense, computing, communications and other technology-driven industries.

FINANCIAL DATA:
Note: Data for latest year may not have been available at press time.

In U.S. $	2017	2016	2015	2014	2013	2012
Revenue	6,110,500,000	6,016,500,000	5,639,200,000	5,631,300,000	5,796,100,000	6,507,200,000
R&D Expense	26,200,000	24,900,000	23,200,000	19,700,000	17,400,000	15,200,000
Operating Income	179,500,000	188,600,000	151,200,000	172,800,000	137,600,000	177,100,000
Operating Margin %	2.93%	3.13%	2.68%	3.06%	2.37%	2.72%
SGA Expense	203,200,000	211,100,000	207,500,000	210,300,000	222,300,000	237,000,000
Net Income	105,000,000	136,300,000	66,900,000	108,200,000	118,000,000	117,700,000
Operating Cash Flow	127,000,000	173,300,000	196,300,000	241,500,000	149,400,000	312,400,000
Capital Expenditure	102,600,000	64,100,000	62,800,000	61,300,000	52,800,000	105,900,000
EBITDA	219,000,000	246,600,000	183,700,000	196,400,000	205,300,000	197,100,000
Return on Assets %	3.64%	5.01%	2.57%	4.14%	4.45%	4.18%
Return on Equity %	8.10%	11.70%	5.38%	7.73%	8.68%	8.46%
Debt to Equity	0.12	0.15	0.22			

CONTACT INFORMATION:
Phone: 416 448-2211   Fax: 416 448-4810
Toll-Free: 888-899-9998
Address: 844 Don Mills Rd., Toronto, ON M3C 1V7 Canada

STOCK TICKER/OTHER:
Stock Ticker: CLS
Employees: 26,400
Parent Company:

Exchange: NYS
Fiscal Year Ends: 12/31

SALARIES/BONUSES:
Top Exec. Salary: $925,342   Bonus: $
Second Exec. Salary: $475,000   Bonus: $

OTHER THOUGHTS:
Estimated Female Officers or Directors: 4
Hot Spot for Advancement for Women/Minorities: Y

Sales, profits and employees may be estimates. Financial information, benefits and other data can change quickly and may vary from those stated here.

CGI Group Inc

NAIC Code: 541512

www.cgi.com

TYPES OF BUSINESS:
IT Consulting
Systems Management Services
Systems Development & Integration
Business Process Outsourcing

BRANDS/DIVISIONS/AFFILIATES:

CONTACTS:
Note: Officers with more than one job title may be intentionally listed here more than once.

George Schindler, CEO
David Henderson, President, Divisional
Francois Boulanger, CFO
Julie Godin, Chief Administrative Officer
Serge Godin, Co-Founder
Lorne Gorber, Executive VP, Divisional
Daniel Rocheleau, Executive VP
Benoit Dube, Executive VP
Doug Mccuaig, President, Divisional
George Mattackal, President, Divisional
Steve Thorn, President, Divisional
Heikki Nikku, President, Divisional
Jean-Michel Baticle, President, Geographical
Mark Boyajian, President, Geographical
Michael Keating, Senior VP, Divisional

GROWTH PLANS/SPECIAL FEATURES:

CGI Group, Inc. is one of the largest independent information technology (IT) services companies in the world, with delivery centers located on five continents. The firm offers services to clients in a variety of sectors, including financial, communications, government, healthcare, utilities, consumer services, transportation, oil/gas, logistics, postal, retail and manufacturing. CGI's services are divided into six primary categories: systems integration, infrastructure services, IT outsourcing, application, business consulting and business process services. Systems integration services include business intelligence, enterprise application integration, enterprise architecture services, enterprise content management, geospatial solutions, information security services and mobile computing. Infrastructure services include energy-efficient green data centers, cloud computing and managed security services, all supported by an enterprise service management toolset. IT outsourcing services include operations management, allowing business executives to retain control over IT strategies while benefiting from reduced operating costs and risks without compromising service delivery to end users and their clients. Application services include application development, management testing, portfolio management and modernization. This division's end-to-end services provide the technology and industry expertise, solutions, skills, frameworks and processes clients need to successfully build, run and evolve their enterprise applications. Business consulting includes agile services, change management, CIO advisory, cybersecurity, data analytics, digital enterprise, project management and industry-specific services. Last, business process services includes business-to-business (B2B) operations support, business-to-consumer (B2C) operations support, purchase management, revenue management and supplier payments. CGI Group employs more than 72,000 professionals at hundreds of locations worldwide, serving 5,000 clients.

CGI provides its employees with various benefits, including wellness programs, counseling services, a savings plan, a share purchase plan and a profit participation plan.

FINANCIAL DATA:
Note: Data for latest year may not have been available at press time.

In U.S. $	2017	2016	2015	2014	2013	2012
Revenue	8,596,961,000	8,468,699,000	8,154,654,000	8,323,180,000	7,994,153,000	3,783,158,000
R&D Expense						
Operating Income	1,258,349,000	1,238,474,000	1,167,919,000	1,085,930,000	850,030,900	435,632,200
Operating Margin %	14.63%	14.62%	14.32%	13.04%	10.63%	11.51%
SGA Expense	6,093,183,000	5,943,765,000	5,764,549,000	5,927,028,000	5,759,298,000	2,666,806,000
Net Income	820,606,400	847,178,800	774,915,500	681,286,600	361,331,700	104,264,000
Operating Cash Flow	1,076,934,000	1,056,737,000	1,022,045,000	931,300,000	532,110,200	486,137,200
Capital Expenditure	173,550,500	211,239,800	153,665,500	205,467,300	169,173,200	85,781,210
EBITDA	1,476,576,000	1,529,401,000	1,462,862,000	1,326,134,000	929,427,600	424,908,400
Return on Assets %	8.96%	9.10%	8.49%	7.77%	4.27%	1.73%
Return on Equity %	16.34%	17.03%	17.65%	19.00%	12.19%	4.56%
Debt to Equity	0.28	0.26	0.31	0.52	0.57	0.93

CONTACT INFORMATION:
Phone: 514 841-3200   Fax: 514 841-3299
Toll-Free:
Address: 1350 Rene-Levesque Blvd. W., 15/Fl, Montreal, QC H3G 1T4 Canada

STOCK TICKER/OTHER:
Stock Ticker: GIB   Exchange: NYS
Employees: 72,000   Fiscal Year Ends: 09/30
Parent Company:

SALARIES/BONUSES:
Top Exec. Salary: $1,375,000   Bonus: $
Second Exec. Salary: $1,182,556   Bonus: $

OTHER THOUGHTS:
Estimated Female Officers or Directors: 4
Hot Spot for Advancement for Women/Minorities: Y

Sales, profits and employees may be estimates. Financial information, benefits and other data can change quickly and may vary from those stated here.

CH2M HILL Inc

www.ch2m.com

NAIC Code: 541330

TYPES OF BUSINESS:
Engineering Services-Consultation
Environmental Engineering & Consulting
Nuclear Management Services
Water & Electrical Utility Services
Decommissioning & Decontamination
Facilities Design & Construction
Project Financing & Procurement
Nanotechnology Research

BRANDS/DIVISIONS/AFFILIATES:
Jacobs Engineering Group Inc

CONTACTS:
Note: Officers with more than one job title may be intentionally listed here more than once.

Jacqueline Hinman, CEO
Jacqueline Hinman, Pres.
Elisa M. Speranza, Pres., Oper. & Maintenance Bus. Group
Patrick O'Keefe, Sr. VP-Corp. Affairs
John Corsi, VP-Global Media & Public Rel.
Michael E McKelvy, Pres., Gov't, Environment & Infrastructure Div.
Michael A. Szomjassy, Pres., Energy, Water & Facilities Div.
Robert W. Bailey, Pres., Water Bus. Group
Terry A. Ruhl, Pres., Transportation Bus. Group
Jacqueline C. Rast, Pres., Int'l Div.

GROWTH PLANS/SPECIAL FEATURES:
CH2M HILL, Inc. provides engineering, consulting, design, construction, procurement, operations, maintenance and program and project management services to clients in the public and private sectors. The firm conducts business in more than 50 countries worldwide, serving 5,000 clients. CH2M partners with governments, cities and businesses in order to meet their biggest engineering challenges, including transportation, water, environment, nuclear, oil and gas, industry and urban environments. The company's design division focuses on sustainable, economical and smart technologies for designing infrastructure, campuses, buildings, labs, plants and infrastructure. The consulting division helps clients to make decisions concerning sustainable plans, management practices, investments in infrastructure, resources and operations. The construction management division focuses on cost estimating, schedule compliance, financial performance, change management and safety/risk management. The program management division works with clients to coordinate multiple, related projects so they can realize their goals. The operations management division provides expertise concerning an engaged workforce, facilities management and operations management. Last, the project management division manages and guides projects from conception to completion. Based in the U.S., the firm has offices in Canada, Latin America, the U.K., Poland, India, United Arab Emirates, Qatar, Saudi Arabia, Singapore, Australia, New Zealand, China, Hong Kong, Malaysia, Thailand, Philippines and South Korea. In December 2017, CH2M was acquired by Jacobs Engineering Group, Inc., an international technical professional services company.

FINANCIAL DATA:
Note: Data for latest year may not have been available at press time.

In U.S. $	2017	2016	2015	2014	2013	2012
Revenue	5,200,000,000	5,235,944,000	5,361,500,000	5,410,000,000	5,877,800,000	6,160,553,000
R&D Expense						
Operating Income						
Operating Margin %						
SGA Expense						
Net Income		15,000,000	80,400,000	-181,500,000	118,000,000	93,000,000
Operating Cash Flow						
Capital Expenditure						
EBITDA						
Return on Assets %						
Return on Equity %						
Debt to Equity						

CONTACT INFORMATION:
Phone: 720-286-2000 Fax:
Toll-Free: 888-242-6445
Address: 9191 S. Jamaica St., Englewood, CO 80112 United States

STOCK TICKER/OTHER:
Stock Ticker: Subsidiary
Employees: 20,000
Parent Company: Jacobs Engineering Group Inc
Exchange:
Fiscal Year Ends: 12/31

SALARIES/BONUSES:
Top Exec. Salary: $ Bonus: $
Second Exec. Salary: $ Bonus: $

OTHER THOUGHTS:
Estimated Female Officers or Directors: 3
Hot Spot for Advancement for Women/Minorities: Y

Sales, profits and employees may be estimates. Financial information, benefits and other data can change quickly and may vary from those stated here.

CHA Consulting Inc

www.chacompanies.com

NAIC Code: 541330

TYPES OF BUSINESS:
Engineering Services
Engineering
Design

BRANDS/DIVISIONS/AFFILIATES:
CHA Tech Services LLC
Gryphon International Engineering Services Inc
American Fire Protection LLC
PDT Architects
Novara GeoSolutions

CONTACTS:
Note: Officers with more than one job title may be intentionally listed here more than once.

Mike Carroll, CEO
Dom Bernardo, CFO
David Ulm, Sr. VP-Mktg.

GROWTH PLANS/SPECIAL FEATURES:

CHA Consulting, Inc. is a full-service engineering and construction management firm, operating throughout the U.S., as well as in Canada. The company provides a wide range of planning and design services to public, private and institutional clients. Its services include architecture, asset management, aviation design/planning, civil engineering, construction engineering, electrical, energy solutions, safety (environmental and health), geospatial innovation, geotechnical, land development, security, mechanical, program management, sports master planning/architecture, structures, survey, sustainability, technology solutions, transportation engineering/planning and water/wastewater. Markets served by CHA include aviation, environmental, facilities, manufacturing, energy, sports, transportation, utility infrastructure and water. CHA's subsidiary and affiliate companies include: CHA Tech Services, LLC, a provider of construction management services; Gryphon International Engineering Services, Inc., a multi-discipline consulting engineering design firm dedicated to the thermal power and energy industry; American Fire Protection, LLC, a highly-specialized provider of fire protection engineering services worldwide; PDT Architects, a full-service, community-based architectural, interior design and planning company; and Novara GeoSolutions, which supplies the energy industry with software solutions and consulting services to manage the full data lifecycle of pipeline assets. The company is headquartered in Albany, New York, with offices located throughout the U.S. Gryphon International Engineering is based in Ontario, Canada.

FINANCIAL DATA:
Note: Data for latest year may not have been available at press time.

In U.S. $	2017	2016	2015	2014	2013	2012
Revenue	290,000,000					
R&D Expense						
Operating Income						
Operating Margin %						
SGA Expense						
Net Income						
Operating Cash Flow						
Capital Expenditure						
EBITDA						
Return on Assets %						
Return on Equity %						
Debt to Equity						

CONTACT INFORMATION:
Phone: 518-453-4500
Fax: 518-458-1735
Toll-Free:
Address: 575 Broadway, Ste. 301, Albany, NY 12207 United States

STOCK TICKER/OTHER:
Stock Ticker: Private
Employees: 1,000
Parent Company:
Exchange:
Fiscal Year Ends:

SALARIES/BONUSES:
Top Exec. Salary: $
Bonus: $
Second Exec. Salary: $
Bonus: $

OTHER THOUGHTS:
Estimated Female Officers or Directors:
Hot Spot for Advancement for Women/Minorities:

Chevron Corporation

www.chevron.com

NAIC Code: 211111

TYPES OF BUSINESS:
Oil & Gas Exploration & Production
Power Generation
Petrochemicals
Gasoline Retailing
Coal Mining
Fuel & Oil Additives
Convenience Stores
Pipelines

BRANDS/DIVISIONS/AFFILIATES:
Texaco
Chevron
Chevron Phillips Chemical Company LLC

CONTACTS: Note: Officers with more than one job title may be intentionally listed here more than once.
Michael Wirth, Chairman of the Board
Jeanette Ourada, Controller
Joseph Geagea, Executive VP, Divisional
James Johnson, Executive VP, Divisional
Pierre Breber, Executive VP, Divisional
R Pate, General Counsel
Mary Francis, Other Executive Officer
Mark Nelson, Vice President, Divisional
Patricia Yarrington, Vice President

GROWTH PLANS/SPECIAL FEATURES:
Chevron Corporation is an integrated energy company that conducts petroleum, mining and chemical operations as well as power generation and energy services. The firm is divided into two operations: upstream operations, consisting of exploring, developing and producing crude oil and natural gas; and downstream operations, consisting of refining, marketing and transportation of crude oil and refined products as well as the manufacturing and marketing of commodity petrochemicals, fuel and plastics. The company maintains a refining network capable of processing more than 1.8 million barrels of crude oil per day. Its marketing operations in the USA consist of 7,800 Chevron and Texaco branded motor vehicle fuel retail outlets. Outside the USA, the firm supplies approximately 6,000 branded service stations, including affiliates. Chevron's transportation infrastructure includes an owned and operated system of crude oil, refined products, chemicals, natural gas liquids and natural gas pipelines in the USA. The company also has direct or indirect interests in other USA and international pipelines. Its chemical operations include the manufacturing and marketing of fuel and lubricating oil additives and commodity petrochemicals through joint venture Chevron Phillips Chemical Company, LLC. The power generation business develops and operates commercial power projects. In October 2017, the firm canceled plans to sell its wholly-owned indirect subsidiaries in Bangladesh to Himalaya Energy Co. Ltd.

Employee benefits include health and dental coverage, retirement and savings plans, disability and life insurance, adoption benefits, domestic partner benefits, counseling services, dependent care reimbursements and fitness memberships.

FINANCIAL DATA: Note: Data for latest year may not have been available at press time.

In U.S. $	2017	2016	2015	2014	2013	2012
Revenue	134,674,000,000	110,215,000,000	129,925,000,000	200,494,000,000	220,156,000,000	230,590,000,000
R&D Expense						
Operating Income	2,480,000,000	-6,216,000,000	-3,710,000,000	19,726,000,000	27,213,000,000	35,013,000,000
Operating Margin %	1.84%	-5.63%	-2.85%	9.83%	12.36%	15.18%
SGA Expense	4,448,000,000	4,684,000,000	4,443,000,000	4,494,000,000	4,510,000,000	4,724,000,000
Net Income	9,195,000,000	-497,000,000	4,587,000,000	19,241,000,000	21,423,000,000	26,179,000,000
Operating Cash Flow	20,515,000,000	12,846,000,000	19,456,000,000	31,475,000,000	35,002,000,000	38,812,000,000
Capital Expenditure	13,404,000,000	18,109,000,000	29,504,000,000	35,407,000,000	37,985,000,000	30,938,000,000
EBITDA	28,877,000,000	17,498,000,000	17,327,000,000	36,519,000,000	41,399,000,000	59,745,000,000
Return on Assets %	3.57%	-.18%	1.72%	7.40%	8.80%	11.83%
Return on Equity %	6.26%	-.33%	2.98%	12.65%	15.00%	20.30%
Debt to Equity	0.22	0.24	0.22	0.15	0.13	0.08

CONTACT INFORMATION:
Phone: 925 842-1000 Fax:
Toll-Free:
Address: 6001 Bollinger Canyon Rd., San Ramon, CA 94583 United States

SALARIES/BONUSES:
Top Exec. Salary: $1,863,500 Bonus: $
Second Exec. Salary: $1,231,050 Bonus: $

STOCK TICKER/OTHER:
Stock Ticker: CVX
Employees: 55,200
Parent Company:

Exchange: NYS
Fiscal Year Ends: 12/31

OTHER THOUGHTS:
Estimated Female Officers or Directors: 5
Hot Spot for Advancement for Women/Minorities: Y

Sales, profits and employees may be estimates. Financial information, benefits and other data can change quickly and may vary from those stated here.

Chicago Bridge & Iron Company NV (CB&I)

NAIC Code: 237000

www.cbi.com

TYPES OF BUSINESS:
Heavy Construction & Civil Engineering
Specialty Engineering & Procurement Services
Liquid & Gas Storage Facilities
Maintenance & Support Services

BRANDS/DIVISIONS/AFFILIATES:

CONTACTS:
Note: Officers with more than one job title may be intentionally listed here more than once.

Patrick K. Mullen, CEO
James W. Sabin, Exec. VP-Global Oper.
Phillip K. Asheman, Pres.
Michael S. Taff, CFO
Daniel M. McCarthy, Exec. VP-Tech.
Beth A. Bailey, Chief Admin. Officer
Richard E. Chandler, Jr., Chief Legal Officer
Patrick K. Mullen, Exec. VP-Corp. Dev.
E. Chip Ray, Exec. VP
Luke V. Scorsone, Exec. VP
L. Richard Flury, Chmn.

GROWTH PLANS/SPECIAL FEATURES:

Chicago Bridge & Iron Company NV (CB&I), a global engineering, procurement and construction company, provides specialty construction for liquid and gas storage facilities. The company has active projects in more than 70 countries. CB&I has four business units, operating both independently and on an integrated basis. The engineering & construction unit offers engineering, procurement and construction services for major energy infrastructure facilities. The fabrication services unit provides fabrication and erection of steel plate structures, fabrication of piping systems and process modules, manufacturing and distribution of pipe and fittings, as well as engineered products for the oil and gas, petrochemical, power generation, water and wastewater, and mining and mineral processing industries. The technology unit provides licensed process technologies, catalysts, specialized equipment and engineered products for use in petrochemical facilities, oil refineries, coal gasification plants and gas processing plants; and offers process planning and project development services, as well as a comprehensive program of aftermarket support. Last, the capital services unit provides maintenance, environmental, infrastructure and program management services for government and private sector customers. Services in this segment include decommissioning and decontamination; environmental engineering and consulting; energy efficiency and sustainability; and program management. Additionally, it offers numerous complementary products and services, including low-temperature or cryogenic tanks and systems primarily used by petroleum, chemical, petrochemical and other companies to store, transport and handle liquefied gases. In August 2017, the firm announced its intention to sell its technology business by year's end.

The firm offers its U.S. employees medical, dental and vision plans; employee and dependent life insurance options; a 401(k) plan; profit sharing; a stock purchase program; and an education assistance plan.

FINANCIAL DATA:
Note: Data for latest year may not have been available at press time.

In U.S. $	2017	2016	2015	2014	2013	2012
Revenue	6,673,330,000	10,679,560,000	12,929,500,000	12,974,930,000	11,094,530,000	5,485,206,000
R&D Expense						
Operating Income	-229,234,000	631,404,000	1,065,045,000	997,068,000	756,771,000	437,712,000
Operating Margin %	-3.43%	5.91%	8.23%	7.68%	6.82%	7.97%
SGA Expense	275,421,000	349,874,000	387,027,000	405,208,000	379,485,000	227,948,000
Net Income	-1,458,193,000	-313,169,000	-504,415,000	543,607,000	454,120,000	301,655,000
Operating Cash Flow	-909,353,000	654,458,000	-56,214,000	264,047,000	-112,836,000	202,504,000
Capital Expenditure	46,168,000	52,462,000	78,852,000	117,624,000	151,317,000	72,279,000
EBITDA	-199,970,000	-9,392,000	-255,697,000	1,172,530,000	871,464,000	530,093,000
Return on Assets %	-21.11%	-3.67%	-5.42%	5.79%	6.62%	7.91%
Return on Equity %	-196.37%	-18.27%	-21.22%	21.39%	24.46%	23.70%
Debt to Equity		0.91	0.89	0.57	0.69	0.58

CONTACT INFORMATION:
Phone: 31 703732010 Fax: 31 703732750
Toll-Free:
Address: Prinses Beatrixlaan 35, The Hague, 2595 Netherlands

STOCK TICKER/OTHER:
Stock Ticker: CBI
Employees: 42,100
Parent Company:

Exchange: NYS
Fiscal Year Ends: 12/31

SALARIES/BONUSES:
Top Exec. Salary: $1,304,000 Bonus: $
Second Exec. Salary: $707,682 Bonus: $

OTHER THOUGHTS:
Estimated Female Officers or Directors: 2
Hot Spot for Advancement for Women/Minorities: Y

Sales, profits and employees may be estimates. Financial information, benefits and other data can change quickly and may vary from those stated here.

China Chengda Engineering Co Ltd

www.chengda.com

NAIC Code: 541330

TYPES OF BUSINESS:
Engineering Services

BRANDS/DIVISIONS/AFFILIATES:

CONTACTS: Note: Officers with more than one job title may be intentionally listed here more than once.
Jing Huang, Pres.

GROWTH PLANS/SPECIAL FEATURES:

China Chengda Engineering Co., Ltd. is an international engineering corporation engaged in engineering design activities. In China, the firm's engineering projects have included infrastructure construction such as petrochemical, natural gas chemical, salt chemical, coal chemical, fine chemical, power generation, pharmaceutical, goods and grains, architecture, municipal works and environmental protection. Internationally, the firm has completed projects in construction management test run and start-up assistance for customers in countries and regions such as Pakistan, Sudan, Indonesia and Hong Kong. The scope of the firm's capabilities and business also includes the design and construction of a soda ash plant using chlorine-alkali process and co-production process technologies; fertilizer technology plants that produce and process ammonia with natural gas, heavy oil and coal as raw materials; synthetic material and plastic technologies for engineering companies undertaking the design of synthesis resin, synthesis rubber, synthesis fiber and plastics projects; utility plants such as coal-fired power stations, power substations and distribution, transformation stations, waste heat boiler and recovery project water intake, purified water and circulating water works projects; and architectural design and structure discipline services.

FINANCIAL DATA: Note: Data for latest year may not have been available at press time.

In U.S. $	2017	2016	2015	2014	2013	2012
Revenue						
R&D Expense						
Operating Income						
Operating Margin %						
SGA Expense						
Net Income						
Operating Cash Flow						
Capital Expenditure						
EBITDA						
Return on Assets %						
Return on Equity %						
Debt to Equity						

CONTACT INFORMATION:
Phone: 86 28 65531100 Fax: 86 28 65530000
Toll-Free:
Address: Tianfu Ave., No. 279, Middle Section, Chengdu, SC China

STOCK TICKER/OTHER:
Stock Ticker: Government-Owned
Employees:
Parent Company:

Exchange:
Fiscal Year Ends:

SALARIES/BONUSES:
Top Exec. Salary: $ Bonus: $
Second Exec. Salary: $ Bonus: $

OTHER THOUGHTS:
Estimated Female Officers or Directors:
Hot Spot for Advancement for Women/Minorities:

Sales, profits and employees may be estimates. Financial information, benefits and other data can change quickly and may vary from those stated here.

China Energy Engineering Corporation Limited

en.ceec.net.cn

NAIC Code: 541330

TYPES OF BUSINESS:
Engineering Services
Energy Solutions

BRANDS/DIVISIONS/AFFILIATES:
Guangxi Water & Power Group Co Ltd
Northwest Power Construction
Guangdong Power Engineering Corporation
Hunan Thermal Power Construction Company
China Petroleum Engineering & Construction Corp

GROWTH PLANS/SPECIAL FEATURES:
China Energy Engineering Corporation provides comprehensive solutions for the power industry in China and globally. The firm offers customers one-stop integrated engineering and full lifecycle project management services. Its business segments consist of: survey, design and consultancy; construction, engineering and contracting; equipment manufacturing; civil explosives and cement production; and investment and other businesses. China Energy operates through more than 30 subsidiaries, including Guangxi Water & Power Group Co. Ltd., Northwest Power Construction, Guangdong Power Engineering Corporation, Hunan Thermal Power Construction Company, and China Petroleum Engineering and Construction Corporation (CPECC).

CONTACTS: Note: Officers with more than one job title may be intentionally listed here more than once.

Yanzhang Ding, CEO
Jianping Wang, Chmn.

FINANCIAL DATA: Note: Data for latest year may not have been available at press time.

In U.S. $	2017	2016	2015	2014	2013	2012
Revenue	34,577,700,000	33,400,000,000	32,735,000,000	29,820,800,000	24,996,700,000	
R&D Expense						
Operating Income						
Operating Margin %						
SGA Expense						
Net Income	776,258,000	645,000,000	674,135,000	349,190,000	218,703,000	
Operating Cash Flow						
Capital Expenditure						
EBITDA						
Return on Assets %						
Return on Equity %						
Debt to Equity						

CONTACT INFORMATION:
Phone: 86-10-59099999
Fax: 86-10-59098888
Toll-Free:
Address: 26 Xidawang Rd., Bldg. 1, Chaoyang Dist., Beijing, Beijing 100022 China

STOCK TICKER/OTHER:
Stock Ticker: 3669
Employees: 130,295
Parent Company:
Exchange: Hong Kong
Fiscal Year Ends:

SALARIES/BONUSES:
Top Exec. Salary: $
Bonus: $
Second Exec. Salary: $
Bonus: $

OTHER THOUGHTS:
Estimated Female Officers or Directors:
Hot Spot for Advancement for Women/Minorities:

China HuanQiu Contracting & Engineering Corporation

hqcec.cnpc.com.cn/hqcecen/
NAIC Code: 541330

TYPES OF BUSINESS:
Engineering Services

BRANDS/DIVISIONS/AFFILIATES:
HQC (Guangdong) Company
Sixth Construction Company of Huanqiu
Huanqiu Lanzhou Company
Huanqiu Liaoning Company
Huanqiu Shanghai Company
Huanqiu North China Institute
Huanqiu Project Management Company
Huanqiu Equipment Manufacture Company

CONTACTS:
Note: Officers with more than one job title may be intentionally listed here more than once.

Shihong Wang, CEO

GROWTH PLANS/SPECIAL FEATURES:
China Huanqiu Contracting & Engineering Corporation (HQC), through its subsidiaries, provides project consultancy, management, engineering, procurement, construction and commissioning services. It offers these services to a broad range of sectors including chemical, storage and handling facilities, oil and gas, light, telecommunications, food, engineering, geotechnical, traffic, thermoelectric, architecture, water supply and drainage, fabrication and steel. The firm operates through a number of subsidiaries. HQC (Guangdong) Company is a specialization international engineering company for petrochemical sectors. Sixth Construction Company of Huanqiu is a general contractor of petrochemical project construction in China. Huanqiu Lanzhou Company and Huanqiu Xinjiang Company both provide project consultation, design, supervision, construction cost estimation and project management. Huanqiu Liaoning Company designs and constructs medium- and large-sized projects. Both Huanqiu Shanghai Company and Huanqiu Shenghuan Company are engineering firms qualified to design chemical, petrochemical and pharmaceutical projects. Huanqiu North China Institute is certified to provide chemical and construction project consultation services. Huanqiu Project Management Company is a project management, consultation and bidding agency that also provides construction supervision. Huanqiu Singapore Company is a joint venture with Sembcorp Marine Engineering Co., engaged in design and construction for sea- and land-based petrochemical projects. Huanqui Saudi Company designs, procures and manages construction, and also manages the import and export of equipment and material for medium- and large-sized overseas projects. Huanqiu Equipment Manufacture Company produces 8,000 tons of pressure vessels and non-standard equipment, as well as 15,000 tons of metal structures annually.

FINANCIAL DATA:
Note: Data for latest year may not have been available at press time.

In U.S. $	2017	2016	2015	2014	2013	2012
Revenue						
R&D Expense						
Operating Income						
Operating Margin %						
SGA Expense						
Net Income						
Operating Cash Flow						
Capital Expenditure						
EBITDA						
Return on Assets %						
Return on Equity %						
Debt to Equity						

CONTACT INFORMATION:
Phone: 86-10-58676688　　Fax: 86-10-6441-5884
Toll-Free:
Address: No. 1, Chongda Rd., Gaonguang Hi-Tech Indust. Park, Beijing, 100012 China

STOCK TICKER/OTHER:
Stock Ticker: Government-Owned
Employees: 9,500
Parent Company:
Exchange:
Fiscal Year Ends:

SALARIES/BONUSES:
Top Exec. Salary: $　　Bonus: $
Second Exec. Salary: $　　Bonus: $

OTHER THOUGHTS:
Estimated Female Officers or Directors:
Hot Spot for Advancement for Women/Minorities:

Sales, profits and employees may be estimates. Financial information, benefits and other data can change quickly and may vary from those stated here.

China National Machinery Industry Corporation

www.sinomach.com.cn
NAIC Code: 541330

TYPES OF BUSINESS:
Engineering Services

BRANDS/DIVISIONS/AFFILIATES:
SINOMACH
China National Erzhong Group Company
China National Machinery & Equipment I/E Corp
China United Engineering Corporation
China National Automotive Industry International
SINOMACH Finance Co Ltd

CONTACTS: Note: Officers with more than one job title may be intentionally listed here more than once.
Xu Jian, Pres.
Ren Hongbin, Chmn.

GROWTH PLANS/SPECIAL FEATURES:
China National Machinery Industry Corporation, known as SINOMACH, is a state-owned enterprise run directly by the central government. The firm provides research and development (R&D), manufacturing and project contracting services to equipment manufacturing industries worldwide. SINOMACH undertakes projects in the fields of scientific and technological R&D, technology and equipment development, industrial planning, standards setting, consultation, engineering studies, monitoring and testing. The R&D and manufacture of machinery and equipment is one of the top priority businesses for SINOMACH. It has state-level research institutes in all specialties and fields, and holds many patents. The equipment R&D and manufacturing division offers equipment such as heavy, petrochemical, general-purpose, farming, construction, forestry, power and environmental protection as well as machine tools, electrical equipment, power plants, meters and machinery components. The company offers contractor services in relation to power engineering, automotive engineering, factory construction and transport engineering, as well as port, dock and ship engineering. In the trade and services field, SINOMACH exports mechanical and electrical products to foreign countries, and also introduces advanced technologies and products from outside China. Export fields include the trade of machinery, electrical products, automobiles and exhibitions. SINOMACH also provides financial and asset management services and solutions. The firm comprises more than 40 wholly-owned and majority-owned subsidiaries, of which 12 are publicly listed. Just a few subsidiaries include China National Erzhong Group Company, China National Machinery & Equipment I/E Corporation, China United Engineering Corporation, China National Automotive Industry International Corporation and SINOMACH Finance Co. Ltd. SINOMACH has a market presence in over 170 countries and regions worldwide.

FINANCIAL DATA: Note: Data for latest year may not have been available at press time.

In U.S. $	2017	2016	2015	2014	2013	2012
Revenue						
R&D Expense						
Operating Income						
Operating Margin %						
SGA Expense						
Net Income						
Operating Cash Flow						
Capital Expenditure						
EBITDA						
Return on Assets %						
Return on Equity %						
Debt to Equity						

CONTACT INFORMATION:
Phone: 86-10-82688888   Fax: 86-10-82688811
Toll-Free:
Address: No.3 Danling St., Haidian District, Beijing, 100080 China

STOCK TICKER/OTHER:
Stock Ticker: Government-Owned   Exchange:
Employees: 160,000   Fiscal Year Ends:
Parent Company:

SALARIES/BONUSES:
Top Exec. Salary: $ Bonus: $
Second Exec. Salary: $ Bonus: $

OTHER THOUGHTS:
Estimated Female Officers or Directors:
Hot Spot for Advancement for Women/Minorities:

Sales, profits and employees may be estimates. Financial information, benefits and other data can change quickly and may vary from those stated here.

China National Materials Co Ltd

www.sinoma-ltd.cn

NAIC Code: 541330

TYPES OF BUSINESS:
Engineering Services

BRANDS/DIVISIONS/AFFILIATES:
CBMI Construction Co Ltd
Sinoma (Suzhou) Construction Co Ltd
Sinoma (Handan) Construction Co Ltd
Sinoma Cement Co Ltd
Xinjiang Tianshan Cement Joint-Stock Co
Ningxia Building Materials Group Co Ltd
Taishan Fiberglass Inc
Sinoma Wind Power Blade Co Ltd

CONTACTS:
Note: Officers with more than one job title may be intentionally listed here more than once.

Jianxin Peng, Pres.
Kaijun Yu, CFO
Zhijiang Liu, Chmn.

GROWTH PLANS/SPECIAL FEATURES:
China National Materials Co. Ltd. (Sinoma) is a cement equipment and engineering service provider and China's leading non-metal materials manufacturer. The firm is a central government-administered enterprise directly under the administration of the State-owned Assets Supervision and Administration Commission of the State Council of the People's Republic of China. Sinoma divides its activities into three business platforms: Cement Engineering, Cement Equipment and Fiber Glass Products. Through the Cement Engineering division, the firm owns three of the largest construction companies in China: CBMI Construction Co., Ltd.; Sinoma (Suzhou) Construction Co., Ltd.; and Sinoma (Handan) Construction Co., Ltd. General contracting has become the company's core business, and occupies more than 70% of revenue. The Cement Equipment division focuses on the production and sell of cement, clinkers and standard sands. This division operates primarily through Sinoma Cement Co., Ltd.; Xinjiang Tianshan Cement Joint-Stock Co., Ltd.; Ningxia Building Materials Group Co., Ltd.; Gansu Qilianshan Cement Group Co., Ltd.; and China National Building Materials Group Co., ltd. Zambia Industrial Park. The Glass Fiber division focuses on the production and sell of glass fiber and glass fiber products, such as roving, glass fiber mats, electronic yarn, chopped strands and woven roving. This division operates primarily through Taishan Fiberglass, Inc.; and Sinoma Wind Power Blade Co., Ltd.

FINANCIAL DATA:
Note: Data for latest year may not have been available at press time.

In U.S. $	2017	2016	2015	2014	2013	2012
Revenue	9,083,647,000	8,061,473,000	8,488,958,000	8,811,875,000	8,301,266,000	7,375,407,000
R&D Expense						
Operating Income	1,059,227,000	524,445,200	314,189,800	453,676,400	520,625,200	422,738,200
Operating Margin %	11.66%	6.50%	3.70%	5.14%	6.27%	5.73%
SGA Expense	1,164,331,000	1,036,039,000	1,102,286,000	1,148,816,000	1,159,235,000	971,561,500
Net Income	279,275,500	93,313,880	123,068,900	80,835,850	63,359,640	75,527,020
Operating Cash Flow		1,050,074,000	1,150,558,000	903,390,100	79,205,760	271,538,100
Capital Expenditure		341,411,800	200,691,400	253,075,800	483,974,200	808,144,400
EBITDA	986,555,600	1,101,430,000	1,130,498,000	1,226,831,000	1,171,157,000	1,028,316,000
Return on Assets %	1.67%	.56%	.75%	.52%	.43%	.56%
Return on Equity %	9.89%	3.67%	5.32%	4.02%	3.50%	4.29%
Debt to Equity	0.80	0.69	0.59	0.95	1.41	1.51

CONTACT INFORMATION:
Phone: 86-10-68139666   Fax: 86-10-68139688
Toll-Free:
Address: Guohai Plaza Tower 2, 8/Fl, 17 Fuxing Rd., Haidian Dist., Beijing, 100036 China

STOCK TICKER/OTHER:
Stock Ticker: CASDY
Employees: 58,637
Parent Company:

Exchange: PINX
Fiscal Year Ends: 12/31

SALARIES/BONUSES:
Top Exec. Salary: $ Bonus: $
Second Exec. Salary: $ Bonus: $

OTHER THOUGHTS:
Estimated Female Officers or Directors:
Hot Spot for Advancement for Women/Minorities:

China Petroleum Engineering & Construction Corporation

cpecc.cnpc.com.cn/cpecc
NAIC Code: 541330

TYPES OF BUSINESS:
Engineering Services
Engineering
Construction

BRANDS/DIVISIONS/AFFILIATES:
China National Petroleum Corporation
China-Mozambique Oil Engineering Company

CONTACTS:
Note: Officers with more than one job title may be intentionally listed here more than once.
Dongjin Wang, Managing Dir.

GROWTH PLANS/SPECIAL FEATURES:
China Petroleum Engineering & Construction Corporation (CPECC) provides oil engineering, manufacturing, construction and lump-sum contracting. The firm's five business divisions include engineering design, construction and erection, engineering manufacture, engineering procurement and technical services. CPECC manages projects such as production facilities for oil and gas fields, refineries, petrochemical plants, fertilizer plants, gas treatment plants, oil and gas storage, long-distance pipelines, electricity and communication facilities, industrial and civil construction, roads and bridges and municipal works. It also provides consultation, feasibility studies, assessment, design, construction and supervision of petroleum and petrochemical projects as well as importing and exporting the technologies, equipment and materials necessary for overseas projects. CPECC is a subsidiary of China National Petroleum Corporation. Joint venture China-Mozambique Oil Engineering Company (with Mozambique ENHL) was established to develop Mozambique's oil and natural gas industry through its own resources. CPECC is a subsidiary of China National Petroleum Corporation.

FINANCIAL DATA:
Note: Data for latest year may not have been available at press time.

In U.S. $	2017	2016	2015	2014	2013	2012
Revenue						
R&D Expense						
Operating Income						
Operating Margin %						
SGA Expense						
Net Income						
Operating Cash Flow						
Capital Expenditure						
EBITDA						
Return on Assets %						
Return on Equity %						
Debt to Equity						

CONTACT INFORMATION:
Phone: 86-10-5819-2777　Fax: 86-10-5819-2600
Toll-Free:
Address: No. 28, Gulouwai Ave, Dongcheng District, Beijing, 100120 China

STOCK TICKER/OTHER:
Stock Ticker: Government-Owned　Exchange:
Employees:　Fiscal Year Ends:
Parent Company: China National Petroleum Corporation

SALARIES/BONUSES:
Top Exec. Salary: $　Bonus: $
Second Exec. Salary: $　Bonus: $

OTHER THOUGHTS:
Estimated Female Officers or Directors:
Hot Spot for Advancement for Women/Minorities:

Sales, profits and employees may be estimates. Financial information, benefits and other data can change quickly and may vary from those stated here.

China Petroleum Pipeline Engineering Co Ltd

cpp.cnpc.com.cn

NAIC Code: 541330

TYPES OF BUSINESS:
Engineering Services

BRANDS/DIVISIONS/AFFILIATES:
China National Petroleum Corporation
CPP LONGWAY Engineering Project Management Co
China Petroleum Pipeline Inspection Technologies
China Petroleum Pipeline College

CONTACTS:
Note: Officers with more than one job title may be intentionally listed here more than once.
Yilin Wang, Chmn.

GROWTH PLANS/SPECIAL FEATURES:
China Petroleum Pipeline Engineering Co., Ltd. (CPP) specializes in pipeline engineering and construction, primarily for the oil and gas industry. The firm is a subsidiary of China National Petroleum Corporation, and is also referred to as China Petroleum Pipeline Bureau. CPP has built much of the cross-country pipeline infrastructure in China, and has several large-scale projects worldwide. The company's core services include engineering, procurement and construction (EPC) project management, supervision, construction scientific research, engineering, procurement, construction, anti-corrosion and pipe fittings. More than 25 EPC projects have been operated successfully in 14 foreign countries such as Sudan, Libya, Kazakhstan and more. Supervision on petrochemical engineering makes certain that projects are carried out in accordance with various standards, per country/region. Construction scientific research is conducted through 17 professional institutes, as well as study and test platforms, workstations and more. CPP's engineering division comprises comprehensive first-rank qualification for engineering design issued by China. The firm owns a specialized procurement company which caters to the pipeline industry, with the ability to undertake 20 pipeline projects simultaneously, and with the ability to form and manage 150 warehouses and transfer stations. The construction division includes the fields of pipelines, storage tanks, underground caverns, large compressor stations, liquefied natural gas (LNG) receiving stations, spherical tanks, communication engineering, oilfield surface construction, refinery construction and more. The anti-corrosion division specializes in anti-corrosion and anti-corrosion technology, owning 28 anti-corrosive production lines, including removable skid operating lines. Last, CPP owns a pipe fitting manufacturing company capable of producing fittings such as bends, tees and quick-opening closures in a variety of diameters. Among CPP's more than 25 subsidiaries include CPP LONGWAY Engineering Project Management Co., Ltd.; China Petroleum Pipeline Inspection Technologies Co., Ltd.; and China Petroleum Pipeline College.

FINANCIAL DATA:
Note: Data for latest year may not have been available at press time.

In U.S. $	2017	2016	2015	2014	2013	2012
Revenue						
R&D Expense						
Operating Income						
Operating Margin %						
SGA Expense						
Net Income						
Operating Cash Flow						
Capital Expenditure						
EBITDA						
Return on Assets %						
Return on Equity %						
Debt to Equity						

CONTACT INFORMATION:
Phone: 86-316-2075403 Fax: 86-316-2073756
Toll-Free:
Address: No. 22, Jinguang Rd., Langfang, 065000 China

STOCK TICKER/OTHER:
Stock Ticker: Government-Owned
Employees: 2,705
Parent Company:

Exchange:
Fiscal Year Ends:

SALARIES/BONUSES:
Top Exec. Salary: $ Bonus: $
Second Exec. Salary: $ Bonus: $

OTHER THOUGHTS:
Estimated Female Officers or Directors:
Hot Spot for Advancement for Women/Minorities:

Sales, profits and employees may be estimates. Financial information, benefits and other data can change quickly and may vary from those stated here.

China Power Engineering Consulting Group Corporation

www.cpecc.net
NAIC Code: 541330

TYPES OF BUSINESS:
Engineering Consulting Services
Engineering

BRANDS/DIVISIONS/AFFILIATES:
China Power Engineering Consulting Group Co Ltd
CGGC-UN Power Co Ltd
China Energy Engineering Group Co Ltd

CONTACTS:
Note: Officers with more than one job title may be intentionally listed here more than once.
Wu Chun Li, Pres.

GROWTH PLANS/SPECIAL FEATURES:
China Power Engineering Consulting Group Corporation (CPECC) is a power engineering integrative service provider for both domestic and foreign markets. CPECC's lines of business include survey and design, consulting, EPC (engineering, procurement and consulting), and investment and financing. Within survey and design, the company has participated and completed middle- and long-term planning for power industry development and national research works such as energy conservation and emission reduction, shut-down and build-up of programs and target configuration of national grid connection; it has also provided implementation schemes. Consulting consists of power project consultation and evaluation, thermal power project consulting, grid project consulting and nuclear power consulting. EPC consists of engineering designs for projects such as coal-fired power plants, gas turbine power plants, power transmission lines and substations as well as civil constructions. Investment & financing includes consulting and financial services on investments in coal-fired power plants, hydro power stations, solar power projects and wind power projects. CPECC has eight R&D centers for conventional power technology, nuclear power technology, air-cooling technology, direct current transmission technology, integrated gasification combined cycle (IGCC) technology, smart grid technology, power plant cooling tower technology and information technology. Its wholly-owned subsidiaries and affiliates include regional (Northeast China, East China, Central Southern China, Northwest China, Southwest China, and North China) electric power design institutes: CGGC-UN Power Co. Ltd., an integrated service provider for various distributed energy solutions and key equipment, including marine energy engineering and ship power; and China Energy Engineering Group Co. Ltd. (CEEC), offering survey, design, consultancy, construction, equipment, civil explosives, cement production and other manufacturing businesses. CPECC is a wholly-owned subsidiary of China Power Engineering Consulting Group Co. Ltd.

FINANCIAL DATA:
Note: Data for latest year may not have been available at press time.

In U.S. $	2017	2016	2015	2014	2013	2012
Revenue						
R&D Expense						
Operating Income						
Operating Margin %						
SGA Expense						
Net Income						
Operating Cash Flow						
Capital Expenditure						
EBITDA						
Return on Assets %						
Return on Equity %						
Debt to Equity						

CONTACT INFORMATION:
Phone: 86-10-58388888 Fax:
Toll-Free:
Address: 65 Andre Rd., Beijing, 100120 China

SALARIES/BONUSES:
Top Exec. Salary: $ Bonus: $
Second Exec. Salary: $ Bonus: $

STOCK TICKER/OTHER:
Stock Ticker: Subsidiary Exchange:
Employees: Fiscal Year Ends:
Parent Company: China Power Engineering Consulting Group Co Ltd

OTHER THOUGHTS:
Estimated Female Officers or Directors:
Hot Spot for Advancement for Women/Minorities:

Sales, profits and employees may be estimates. Financial information, benefits and other data can change quickly and may vary from those stated here.

China Railway Construction Corporation Limited (CRCC)

www.crcc.cn
NAIC Code: 237990

TYPES OF BUSINESS:
Transportation Infrastructure Construction
Design and Engineering
Highway and Bridge Construction
Railway Construction

BRANDS/DIVISIONS/AFFILIATES:

GROWTH PLANS/SPECIAL FEATURES:
China Railway Construction Corporation Limited (CRCC) is a major construction corporation under the administration of the State-owned Assets Supervision and Administration Commission of the State Council of China (SASAC). CRCC, one of the world's largest integrated construction groups, is a major engineering contractor in China and ranks among the world's biggest construction firms in terms of revenue and number of employees. The firm covers contracting, design consultation, industrial manufacturing, real estate development, logistics, trade of goods and materials as well as capital operations. CRCC has developed mainly from construction management into a comprehensive group of transportation infrastructure research, planning, survey, design, construction, supervision, maintenance and operations. This enables the company to provide its clients one-stop integrated services. CRCC has established its leadership position in project design and construction fields in plateau railways, high-speed railways, highways, bridges, tunnels and urban rail traffic.

CONTACTS: Note: Officers with more than one job title may be intentionally listed here more than once.

Zhuang Shangbiao, Pres.
Meng Fengchao, Chmn.

FINANCIAL DATA: Note: Data for latest year may not have been available at press time.

In U.S. $	2017	2016	2015	2014	2013	2012
Revenue	108,541,900,000	100,308,800,000	95,720,170,000	94,354,150,000	93,528,690,000	77,194,880,000
R&D Expense						
Operating Income	4,364,493,000	3,432,962,000	3,861,498,000	3,213,701,000	2,786,997,000	2,284,140,000
Operating Margin %	4.02%	3.42%	4.03%	3.40%	2.97%	2.95%
SGA Expense	4,875,575,000	4,505,538,000	4,230,108,000	4,159,589,000	4,021,272,000	3,610,548,000
Net Income	2,559,371,000	2,231,405,000	2,015,569,000	1,808,009,000	1,648,840,000	1,351,455,000
Operating Cash Flow	4,049,185,000	5,919,377,000	8,029,313,000	1,049,190,000	-1,484,560,000	883,815,600
Capital Expenditure	4,818,535,000	4,752,450,000	4,326,514,000	3,393,014,000	2,812,498,000	1,673,648,000
EBITDA	6,294,407,000	5,747,798,000	5,457,065,000	5,140,340,000	4,623,492,000	4,051,727,000
Return on Assets %	2.03%	1.92%	1.92%	1.93%	2.00%	1.87%
Return on Equity %	11.44%	11.52%	12.48%	13.19%	13.52%	12.40%
Debt to Equity	0.63	0.86	0.70	0.86	0.88	0.43

CONTACT INFORMATION:
Phone: 86 1052688600 Fax: 86 1052688302
Toll-Free:
Address: No. 40 Fuxing Rd. East, Beijing, 100855 China

STOCK TICKER/OTHER:
Stock Ticker: CWYCY
Employees: 249,624
Parent Company:

Exchange: PINX
Fiscal Year Ends: 12/31

SALARIES/BONUSES:
Top Exec. Salary: $ Bonus: $
Second Exec. Salary: $ Bonus: $

OTHER THOUGHTS:
Estimated Female Officers or Directors:
Hot Spot for Advancement for Women/Minorities:

Sales, profits and employees may be estimates. Financial information, benefits and other data can change quickly and may vary from those stated here.

China State Construction Engineering Corp (CSCEC)

www.cscec.com.cn
NAIC Code: 531100

TYPES OF BUSINESS:
Construction & Real Estate Development
Contract Engineering
Property Development
Infrastructure Design and Construction
Real Estate Investments

BRANDS/DIVISIONS/AFFILIATES:
China State Construction International Co
China Construction Development Co Ltd
China Construction Decoration Engineering Co
CSCEC Property Management Co
China Construction American Co

CONTACTS:
Note: Officers with more than one job title may be intentionally listed here more than once.

Xiangming Wang, Pres.
Mao Zhibing, Chief Engineer
Zeng Zhaohe, General Counsel
Liu Jie, Leader-Discipline Inspection
Liu Jinzhang, VP
Kong Qingping, VP
Wang Xiangming, VP
Qing Guan, Chmn.

GROWTH PLANS/SPECIAL FEATURES:

China State Construction Engineering Corporation (CSCEC) is a Chinese state-owned enterprise that primarily engages in real estate, construction and contract engineering. The firm is China's leading international contracting agent and one of the largest house builders in the world, conducting business operations in over 20 countries. The company also conducts design and planning, property development, machinery leasing, project supervision, property management and trading activities. CSCEC has worked on office buildings, public facilities, airports, hotels, educational institutions, sports facilities, residential complexes, hospitals and military buildings. Its technologies are used for many applications, such as constructing high-rises, installing large industrial works, complex deep pit support and dewatering activities, concrete manufacturing, project management and general contracting of international projects. Specific projects by CSCEC have included the Hada Express Way, Wuhan Railway Station, Shaanxi LanShang Expressway, the Tianjin Cihan Ferris Wheel, the Beijing Subway Line 4, Hongheyan Nuclear Station and China World Trade Center. The company has various domestic affiliated companies, such as China State Construction International Co., China Construction Development Co. Ltd., China Construction Decoration Engineering Co. and CSCEC Property Management Co. The firm also has various international affiliated companies such as China Construction (South Pacific) Development Co. Pte. Ltd. in Singapore, and China Construction American Co. in New Jersey, USA.

FINANCIAL DATA:
Note: Data for latest year may not have been available at press time.

In U.S. $	2017	2016	2015	2014	2013	2012
Revenue		5,886,906,000	4,830,194,000	4,387,654,000	3,464,294,000	2,518,092,000
R&D Expense						
Operating Income		631,153,300	538,568,300	473,853,600	349,759,300	218,921,000
Operating Margin %		10.72%	11.15%	10.79%	10.09%	8.69%
SGA Expense		140,916,800	126,831,600	131,623,600	129,515,000	90,409,730
Net Income		653,578,200	529,107,700	440,479,300	353,175,500	271,551,100
Operating Cash Flow		365,303,300	38,232,680	-215,173,300	-415,164,200	-425,497,300
Capital Expenditure		22,644,730	54,206,540	65,546,420	48,178,030	51,241,660
EBITDA		892,604,600	718,658,700	609,477,500	479,755,900	384,164,000
Return on Assets %		6.56%	6.07%	5.88%	6.29%	6.66%
Return on Equity %		22.02%	20.27%	19.20%	18.67%	18.53%
Debt to Equity		0.77	0.80	0.71	0.76	0.74

CONTACT INFORMATION:
Phone: 86-10-880-82888 Fax:
Toll-Free:
Address: 15 Sanlihe Rd., Haidan District, Wanchai, Hong Kong

STOCK TICKER/OTHER:
Stock Ticker: CCOHY Exchange: PINX
Employees: 11,084 Fiscal Year Ends: 12/31
Parent Company:

SALARIES/BONUSES:
Top Exec. Salary: $ Bonus: $
Second Exec. Salary: $ Bonus: $

OTHER THOUGHTS:
Estimated Female Officers or Directors:
Hot Spot for Advancement for Women/Minorities:

Sales, profits and employees may be estimates. Financial information, benefits and other data can change quickly and may vary from those stated here.

Chiyoda Corporation

www.chiyoda-corp.com

NAIC Code: 541330

TYPES OF BUSINESS:
Engineering & Construction Services
Plant Lifecycle Engineering
Computer-Aided Engineering
Risk Management
Pollution Prevention Systems
Industrial Equipment-Online Procurement

BRANDS/DIVISIONS/AFFILIATES:
Chiyoda System Technologies Corporation
Chiyoda U-Tech Co Ltd
Chiyoda Oceania Pty Ltd
Chiyoda Almana Engineering LLC
L&T-Chiyoda Limited
Xodus Group (Holdings) Ltd

CONTACTS:
Note: Officers with more than one job title may be intentionally listed here more than once.

Masaji Santo, CEO
Shogo Shibuya, Pres.
Hirotsugu Hayashi, CFO
Masao Ishikawa, Dir.-Technology & Engineering
Hiroshi Ogawa, Sr. Managing Exec. Officer-Project Oper.
Keiichi Nakagaki, Sr. Exec. VP-Corp. Planning, Mgmt. & Finance
Hiroshi Ogawa, Sr. Exec. VP-Global Project Mgmt.
Katsuo Nagasaka, Exec. VP-Bus. Dev.
Masahiko Kojima, Sr. VP-Corp. Planning, Mgmt. & Finance
Katsuo Nagasaka, Chmn.

GROWTH PLANS/SPECIAL FEATURES:

Chiyoda Corporation is a Japanese engineering firm that operates in the energy sector covering the oil and gas industry, as well as chemicals, environment, energy conservation, industrial facilities and life science. The company engages in numerous engineering, procurement and construction (EPC) and other type of projects worldwide. Chiyoda's wide range of services include planning, engineering, procurement, construction, operation and maintenance of any type of process plant and social infrastructure. Its capabilities include project lifecycle engineering, advanced engineering technology, technology development, artificial intelligence solutions and asset holding solutions. Business fields Chiyoda is engaged in includes liquefied natural gas (LNG), gas, oil, petrochemical, metal, medicine, biochemistry, general chemistry, environment, new energy, infrastructure and many others. The firm has number of affiliate companies and domestic and overseas subsidiaries including: Chiyoda System Technologies Corporation; Chiyoda U-Tech Co., Ltd; Chiyoda Oceania Pty. Ltd.; Chiyoda U-Tech Co., Ltd.; Chiyoda Almana Engineering, LLC; L&T-Chiyoda Limited; and Xodus Group (Holdings) Ltd.

FINANCIAL DATA:
Note: Data for latest year may not have been available at press time.

In U.S. $	2017	2016	2015	2014	2013	2012
Revenue	5,624,605,000	5,697,298,000	4,480,892,000	4,156,391,000	3,716,397,000	2,372,601,000
R&D Expense						
Operating Income	146,087,200	149,198,800	199,990,700	196,376,000	233,966,800	225,442,500
Operating Margin %	2.59%	2.61%	4.46%	4.72%	6.29%	9.50%
SGA Expense						
Net Income	-383,044,500	31,442,150	102,748,300	125,274,800	149,776,400	133,817,800
Operating Cash Flow	-40,758,340	517,290,900	-224,939,500	-160,024,200	131,796,200	518,120,000
Capital Expenditure	19,564,000	24,287,310	36,072,300	49,142,910	66,349,920	27,929,940
EBITDA	-204,667,400	181,861,400	254,378,600	249,599,400	275,135,100	245,826,400
Return on Assets %	-8.30%	.64%	2.22%	2.95%	4.01%	3.99%
Return on Equity %	-23.13%	1.66%	5.47%	6.98%	9.01%	8.88%
Debt to Equity		0.05	0.04	0.05	0.05	

CONTACT INFORMATION:
Phone: 81-45-225-7777 Fax:
Toll-Free:
Address: 4-6-2 Minatomirai, Nishi-ku, Yokohama, 220-8765 Japan

SALARIES/BONUSES:
Top Exec. Salary: $ Bonus: $
Second Exec. Salary: $ Bonus: $

STOCK TICKER/OTHER:
Stock Ticker: CHYCF
Employees: 1,519
Parent Company:

Exchange: PINX
Fiscal Year Ends: 03/31

OTHER THOUGHTS:
Estimated Female Officers or Directors:
Hot Spot for Advancement for Women/Minorities:

Cisco Systems Inc

NAIC Code: 0

www.cisco.com

TYPES OF BUSINESS:
Computer Networking Equipment
Routers & Switches
Real-Time Conferencing Technology
Server Virtualization Software
Data Storage Products
Security Products
Teleconference Systems and Technology
Unified Communications Systems

BRANDS/DIVISIONS/AFFILIATES:
Cisco Unified Computing System
Cisco Umbrella
AppDynamics Inc

CONTACTS:
Note: Officers with more than one job title may be intentionally listed here more than once.

Charles Robbins, CEO
Prat Bhatt, Chief Accounting Officer
Karen Walker, Chief Marketing Officer
Chris Dedicoat, Executive VP, Divisional
Kelly Kramer, Executive VP
David Goeckeler, Executive VP
Mark Chandler, General Counsel

GROWTH PLANS/SPECIAL FEATURES:

Cisco Systems, Inc. designs and sells broad lines of products, provides services and delivers integrated solutions to develop and connect networks around the world, building the internet. The company is organized into three geographic segments: the Americas; Europe, Middle East and Africa; and Asia Pacific, Japan and China. Its products and technologies are grouped into: switching, next-generation network (NGN) routing, collaboration, data center, wireless and security. Switching is an integral networking technology used in campuses, branch offices and data centers. It is used within buildings in local-area networks (LANs) and across great distances in wide-area networks (WANs). Switching products offer forms of connectivity to end users, workstations, IP phones, wireless access points and servers. NGN routing technology interconnects public and private wireline and mobile networks for mobile, data, voice and video applications. This division's portfolio of hardware and software solutions consists of physical and virtual routers, as well as routing and optical systems. Collaboration integrates voice, video, data and mobile applications on fixed and mobile networks across a wide range of devices and related IT equipment. Data center's Cisco Unified Computing System enables fast IT and scalability for workloads, data analytics and cloud-native applications and infrastructures. Wireless access via wireless fidelity (Wi-Fi) is a technology that provides indoor/outdoor coverage with seamless roaming for voice, video and data applications. Security aims to protect the digital economy of Cisco customers. Its Cisco Umbrella cloud-based secure internet gateway offering is tailored to provide safe internet access to users to do not use their corporate networks to connect to remote data centers. During 2017, the firm acquired AppDynamics, Inc, which offers an integrated suite of software application and IT infrastructure monitoring and analytics products.

FINANCIAL DATA:
Note: Data for latest year may not have been available at press time.

In U.S. $	2017	2016	2015	2014	2013	2012
Revenue	48,005,000,000	49,247,000,000	49,161,000,000	47,142,000,000	48,607,000,000	46,061,000,000
R&D Expense	6,059,000,000	6,296,000,000	6,207,000,000	6,294,000,000	5,942,000,000	5,488,000,000
Operating Income	12,729,000,000	12,928,000,000	11,254,000,000	9,763,000,000	11,301,000,000	10,369,000,000
Operating Margin %	26.51%	26.25%	22.89%	20.70%	23.24%	22.51%
SGA Expense	11,177,000,000	11,433,000,000	11,861,000,000	11,437,000,000	11,802,000,000	11,969,000,000
Net Income	9,609,000,000	10,739,000,000	8,981,000,000	7,853,000,000	9,983,000,000	8,041,000,000
Operating Cash Flow	13,876,000,000	13,570,000,000	12,552,000,000	12,332,000,000	12,894,000,000	11,491,000,000
Capital Expenditure	964,000,000	1,146,000,000	1,227,000,000	1,275,000,000	1,160,000,000	1,126,000,000
EBITDA	15,434,000,000	15,746,000,000	14,209,000,000	12,711,000,000	14,161,000,000	13,357,000,000
Return on Assets %	7.64%	9.13%	8.21%	7.61%	10.34%	8.99%
Return on Equity %	14.81%	17.42%	15.43%	13.56%	18.08%	16.32%
Debt to Equity	0.38	0.38	0.35	0.36	0.21	0.31

CONTACT INFORMATION:
Phone: 408 526-4000 Fax: 408 526-4100
Toll-Free: 800-553-6387
Address: 170 W. Tasman Dr., San Jose, CA 95134 United States

STOCK TICKER/OTHER:
Stock Ticker: CSCO
Employees: 72,900
Parent Company:

Exchange: NAS
Fiscal Year Ends: 07/31

SALARIES/BONUSES:
Top Exec. Salary: $1,187,308 Bonus: $
Second Exec. Salary: $735,000 Bonus: $

OTHER THOUGHTS:
Estimated Female Officers or Directors: 10
Hot Spot for Advancement for Women/Minorities: Y

Sales, profits and employees may be estimates. Financial information, benefits and other data can change quickly and may vary from those stated here.

Citrix Systems Inc

www.citrix.com

NAIC Code: 0

TYPES OF BUSINESS:
Computer Software-Application Server
Consulting Services
Training & Technical Support
Online Services

BRANDS/DIVISIONS/AFFILIATES:
XenApp
XenDesktop
XenMobile
Citrix Workspace Suite
Citrix Receiver
NetScaler ADC
NetScaler SD-WAN
LogMeIn Inc

CONTACTS:
Note: Officers with more than one job title may be intentionally listed here more than once.

David Henshall, CEO
Mark Coyle, CFO
Robert Calderoni, Chairman of the Board
Jessica Soisson, Chief Accounting Officer
Timothy Minahan, Chief Marketing Officer
Mark Ferrer, Executive VP

GROWTH PLANS/SPECIAL FEATURES:

Citrix Systems, Inc. designs, develops and markets products that allow applications to be delivered, supported and shared on demand. The firm's desktop virtualization solutions, XenApp and XenDesktop, reduce the complexity and cost of desktop management by virtualizing the desktop and applications in the datacenter. XenApp runs the business logic of applications on a central server, transmitting only screen pixels, keystrokes and mouse movements through an encrypted channel to users' computers. XenDesktop streams desktop images through multiple virtual machines. Citrix Systems' enterprise mobility management solutions are designed to increase productivity and security with mobile device management, mobile application management, mobile content management, secure network gateway and enterprise-grade mobile apps in one comprehensive solution, XenMobile. Citrix Workspace Suite delivers user experience solutions for any app or desktop using a universal client, Citrix Receiver, which is available on tablets, smartphones, PCs, Macs or thin clients. NetScaler ADC is a software-defined application delivery controller (ADC) and load balancer designed to improve application performance and reliability for mobile, remote and branch users. NetScaler SD-WAN increased the security, performance and reliability of traditional enterprise applications, software-as-a-service (SaaS) applications and virtual desktops for remote users. In early-2017 Citrix spun off its GoTo family of products and merged it into wholly-owned subsidiary LogMeIn, Inc. As a result, GetGo, Inc., which comprises the GoTo product line, operates as a subsidiary of LogMeIn.

Citrix offers employees medical, dental, prescription and vision benefits; on-site fitness centers; 401(k); and paid time off.

FINANCIAL DATA:
Note: Data for latest year may not have been available at press time.

In U.S. $	2017	2016	2015	2014	2013	2012
Revenue	2,824,686,000	3,418,265,000	3,275,594,000	3,142,856,000	2,918,434,000	2,586,123,000
R&D Expense	415,801,000	489,265,000	563,975,000	553,817,000	516,338,000	450,571,000
Operating Income	645,910,000	776,904,000	450,496,000	322,735,000	380,717,000	390,778,000
Operating Margin %	22.86%	22.72%	13.75%	10.26%	13.04%	15.11%
SGA Expense	1,308,677,000	1,563,382,000	1,538,027,000	1,600,187,000	1,476,916,000	1,306,088,000
Net Income	-20,719,000	536,112,000	319,361,000	251,723,000	339,523,000	352,547,000
Operating Cash Flow	908,276,000	1,115,830,000	1,034,548,000	845,981,000	928,343,000	818,527,000
Capital Expenditure	88,280,000	160,512,000	172,228,000	179,093,000	175,042,000	150,718,000
EBITDA	771,970,000	910,751,000	748,909,000	634,308,000	648,217,000	605,651,000
Return on Assets %	-.33%	9.03%	5.81%	4.69%	6.78%	7.92%
Return on Equity %	-1.12%	23.00%	15.40%	9.16%	10.54%	12.04%
Debt to Equity	2.14		0.67	0.59		

CONTACT INFORMATION:
Phone: 954 267-3000   Fax: 954 267-9319
Toll-Free: 800-424-8749
Address: 851 W. Cypress Creek Rd., Fort Lauderdale, FL 33309 United States

STOCK TICKER/OTHER:
Stock Ticker: CTXS
Employees: 9,600
Parent Company:

Exchange: NAS
Fiscal Year Ends: 12/31

SALARIES/BONUSES:
Top Exec. Salary: $1,000,000   Bonus: $
Second Exec. Salary: $937,500   Bonus: $

OTHER THOUGHTS:
Estimated Female Officers or Directors: 2
Hot Spot for Advancement for Women/Minorities:

Sales, profits and employees may be estimates. Financial information, benefits and other data can change quickly and may vary from those stated here.

Clariant International Ltd

NAIC Code: 325510

www.clariant.com

TYPES OF BUSINESS:
Paint and Coating Manufacturing
Chemical Additives
Pigments & Dyes
Color & Additive Concentrates
Textile, Leather & Paper Chemicals

BRANDS/DIVISIONS/AFFILIATES:

CONTACTS:
Note: Officers with more than one job title may be intentionally listed here more than once.
Hariolf Kottmann, CEO
Gunter von Au, Chmn.

GROWTH PLANS/SPECIAL FEATURES:
Clariant International, Ltd. is a leading developer, producer and marketer of specialty chemicals, with more than 100 group companies on five continents. The firm's businesses are organized into seven divisions: additives, catalysts, industrial and consumer specialties, masterbatches, oil and mining services, pigments and functional materials. Additives include plastic, coating and printing ink ingredients such as flame retardants, high performance waxes and polymer additives. The catalysts division manufactures catalysts used in the production of industrial chemicals, plastics and fuels. Additionally, these products enable the use of alternative raw materials such as natural gas, coal and biomass, as chemical and energy feedstocks, instrumental to the reduction of emissions from industrial processes and combustion engines. The industrial and consumer specialties unit provides specialty chemicals for the consumer care and industrial markets. The masterbatches division offers color and additive concentrates and technical compounds for the plastics industry. Clariant's oil and mining services division offers products and services to the oil, refinery and mining industries. The pigments division provides organic pigments, pigment preparations and dyes used in coatings, printing, plastics and other products. The functional materials unit focuses on the development of functional polymers and functional chemicals. New businesses that Clariant is venturing into include: electronic materials, which focuses on creating sustainable solutions for the electronics manufacturing industry; food ingredients, offering tailor-made solutions, via technological and nutritional formulation, to the food and beverage industry; and biotech and bio-based chemicals, with a focus on innovation and progress based on using sustainable renewable resources. In November 2017, the company terminated its proposed merger with U.S.-based Huntsman Corporation.

FINANCIAL DATA:
Note: Data for latest year may not have been available at press time.

In U.S. $	2017	2016	2015	2014	2013	2012
Revenue		6,079,669,000	6,038,077,000	6,359,373,000	6,317,782,000	6,278,269,000
R&D Expense		214,197,300	212,117,700	221,475,900	206,918,800	181,963,800
Operating Income		442,951,800	539,652,500	530,294,400	531,334,200	474,145,600
Operating Margin %		7.28%	8.93%	8.33%	8.41%	7.55%
SGA Expense		1,183,284,000	1,106,340,000	1,090,743,000	1,075,146,000	1,158,329,000
Net Income		263,067,600	238,112,600	158,048,500	-20,795,860	225,635,100
Operating Cash Flow		671,706,200	521,976,000	347,290,800	312,977,700	486,623,100
Capital Expenditure		349,370,400	416,957,000	335,853,100	331,693,900	366,007,100
EBITDA		740,332,500	687,303,100	821,436,400	814,157,800	745,531,500
Return on Assets %		3.19%	2.97%	1.88%	-.22%	2.33%
Return on Equity %		10.37%	9.11%	5.71%	-.70%	7.37%
Debt to Equity		0.77	0.76	0.67	0.67	0.82

CONTACT INFORMATION:
Phone: 41 614695111 Fax: 41 614695901
Toll-Free:
Address: Rothausstrasse 61, Muttenz, 4132 Switzerland

SALARIES/BONUSES:
Top Exec. Salary: $ Bonus: $
Second Exec. Salary: $ Bonus: $

STOCK TICKER/OTHER:
Stock Ticker: CLZNF Exchange: PINX
Employees: 17,213 Fiscal Year Ends: 12/31
Parent Company:

OTHER THOUGHTS:
Estimated Female Officers or Directors:
Hot Spot for Advancement for Women/Minorities:

Compal Electronics Inc

www.compal.com

NAIC Code: 334418

TYPES OF BUSINESS:
Contract Electronics Manufacturing
Personal Music Players
Monitors
Notebook Computers
LCD Televisions
Automotive Electronics

BRANDS/DIVISIONS/AFFILIATES:
Worldwide Logistics Group
Bizcom Electronics Inc
Compal (Vietnam) Co Ltd
Auscom Engineering Inc

CONTACTS:
Note: Officers with more than one job title may be intentionally listed here more than once.
Ray Chen, Gen. Mgr.
Ray Chen, Pres.
Rock Hsu, Chmn.

GROWTH PLANS/SPECIAL FEATURES:

Compal Electronics, Inc., headquartered in Taiwan, is a world leading contract manufacturer of notebook computers, liquid crystal displays (LCD) and smart devices. Compal specializes in manufacturing high-quality electronics marketed under its clients' brands. The company has established branches in China, Brazil, Mexico, Vietnam, Poland and the U.S. Compal's in-house research and development groups enable it to produce innovative and high-quality products at a rapid pace, with the capability to process most orders in 48 hours. The firm's 15 manufacturing facilities in China, Vietnam and Mexico are state-of-the-art and certified for ISO-9001 international quality standards and ISO-14001 and OHSAS 18000 international environmental standards. Compal makes a wide variety of products including notebook computers, data center equipment, LCD screens, monitors, portable music players, smart lamps, smart refrigerators, baby monitors, point-of-sale solutions and even adult medical-monitoring devices. Subsidiaries include Bizcom Electronics, Inc.; Compal (Vietnam) Co., Ltd.; and Auscom Engineering, Inc. Compal Electronics itself is owned by Worldwide Logistics Group.

Compal offers its employees company trips, an onsite fitness center, shuttle services, a pension plan and health insurance.

FINANCIAL DATA:
Note: Data for latest year may not have been available at press time.

In U.S. $	2017	2016	2015	2014	2013	2012
Revenue	30,286,150,000	26,162,950,000	28,909,400,000	28,854,640,000	23,636,030,000	23,299,710,000
R&D Expense	393,689,700	408,114,500	417,948,700	413,218,900	385,904,100	376,829,800
Operating Income	314,184,300	377,482,800	385,971,900	398,326,200	315,058,300	343,510,000
Operating Margin %	1.03%	1.44%	1.33%	1.38%	1.33%	1.47%
SGA Expense	244,548,100	179,817,300	171,003,800	127,821,300	258,142,000	296,825,400
Net Income	196,169,300	277,419,600	296,312,000	239,997,300	84,179,300	218,739,200
Operating Cash Flow	-74,414,060	43,934,010	325,301,300	1,153,169,000	18,751,300	-391,935,800
Capital Expenditure	128,458,400	142,465,100	208,427,100	237,566,500	210,132,000	287,128,700
EBITDA	491,081,200	570,874,300	588,114,900	604,299,200	504,614,800	528,784,400
Return on Assets %	1.61%	2.40%	2.45%	1.96%	.76%	2.18%
Return on Equity %	5.53%	7.75%	8.47%	7.17%	2.44%	6.03%
Debt to Equity	0.20	0.22	0.13	0.20	0.14	

CONTACT INFORMATION:
Phone: 886-2-87978588 Fax: 886-2-26585001
Toll-Free:
Address: 581 Ruiguang Rd., Neihu, Taipei, 11492 Taiwan

STOCK TICKER/OTHER:
Stock Ticker: CMPFF
Employees: 67,160
Parent Company: Worldwide Logistics Group

Exchange: GREY
Fiscal Year Ends: 12/31

SALARIES/BONUSES:
Top Exec. Salary: $ Bonus: $
Second Exec. Salary: $ Bonus: $

OTHER THOUGHTS:
Estimated Female Officers or Directors:
Hot Spot for Advancement for Women/Minorities:

Sales, profits and employees may be estimates. Financial information, benefits and other data can change quickly and may vary from those stated here.

ConocoPhillips Company

www.conocophillips.com

NAIC Code: 211111

TYPES OF BUSINESS:
Oil & Gas Exploration & Production
Natural Gas Distribution
Oil Sands
Pipelines

BRANDS/DIVISIONS/AFFILIATES:

CONTACTS:
Note: Officers with more than one job title may be intentionally listed here more than once.

Ryan Lance, CEO
Don Wallette, CFO
Glenda Schwarz, Chief Accounting Officer
Alan Hirshberg, Executive VP, Divisional
Matthew Fox, Executive VP, Divisional
Janet Carrig, General Counsel
Andrew Lundquist, Senior VP, Divisional
Ellen DeSanctis, Vice President, Divisional
James McMorran, Vice President, Divisional

GROWTH PLANS/SPECIAL FEATURES:

ConocoPhillips Company explores for, produces, transports and markets crude oil bitumen, natural gas, liquefied natural gas (LNG) and natural gas liquids. Its net proved reserves total approximately 6 million barrels of oil equivalent (MBOE). In all, ConocoPhillips produces, on average, about 1,500 MBOE per day. The firm reports under six geographic segments, dividing operations in over 17 countries: Alaska, lower 48, Canada, Europe and North Africa, Asia Pacific and Middle East and other international. The Alaska segment primarily explores for, produces, transports and markets crude oil, natural gas and LNG. Alaska contributes approximately 19% of the firm's worldwide liquids productions and less than 1% of its natural gas production. The lower 48 segment (covering Gulf Coast, mid-continent, Rockies and San Juan) holds onshore and offshore acreage utilized for liquids and natural gas production. Canadian operations mainly consist of natural gas fields and oil sands developments. Europe and North Africa consists of Norway, the U.K., Greenland and Libya, contributing to liquids and natural gas production. The Asia Pacific and Middle East segment accounts for about 14% of the company's liquids production and 42% of its natural gas. Finally, other international includes exploration activities in Colombia, Angola and Chile. In addition, ConocoPhillips owns and licenses the Optimized Cascade technology for liquefying natural gas, which provides cost-effective, high-value natural gas liquefaction solutions. The Optimized Cascade process has been licensed by owners of 24 additional LNG trains. In 2017, ConocoPhillips sold oil sands assets in Canada, as well as natural gas fields in the U.S., to Cenovus Energy, Inc. for $16 billion.

Employee benefits in the U.S. include medical and dental coverage, short- and long-term disability, life and AD&D insurance, 401(k) and flexible spending accounts.

FINANCIAL DATA:
Note: Data for latest year may not have been available at press time.

In U.S. $	2017	2016	2015	2014	2013	2012
Revenue	29,106,000,000	24,308,000,000	30,280,000,000	52,988,000,000	56,029,000,000	60,093,000,000
R&D Expense						
Operating Income	2,360,000,000	-4,217,000,000	-4,804,000,000	8,299,000,000	13,310,000,000	14,942,000,000
Operating Margin %	8.10%	-17.34%	-15.86%	15.66%	23.75%	24.86%
SGA Expense	561,000,000	723,000,000	953,000,000	735,000,000	854,000,000	1,106,000,000
Net Income	-855,000,000	-3,615,000,000	-4,428,000,000	6,869,000,000	9,156,000,000	8,428,000,000
Operating Cash Flow	7,077,000,000	4,403,000,000	7,572,000,000	16,735,000,000	16,087,000,000	13,922,000,000
Capital Expenditure	4,591,000,000	4,869,000,000	10,050,000,000	17,085,000,000	15,537,000,000	14,172,000,000
EBITDA	5,328,000,000	4,777,000,000	2,710,000,000	18,367,000,000	22,492,000,000	23,106,000,000
Return on Assets %	-1.04%	-3.86%	-4.13%	5.85%	7.78%	6.23%
Return on Equity %	-2.60%	-9.67%	-9.66%	13.20%	18.29%	14.88%
Debt to Equity	0.55	0.74	0.58	0.43	0.40	0.43

CONTACT INFORMATION:
Phone: 281 293-1000 Fax:
Toll-Free:
Address: 600 N. Dairy Ashford, Houston, TX 77079 United States

STOCK TICKER/OTHER:
Stock Ticker: COP
Employees: 18,400
Parent Company:

Exchange: NYS
Fiscal Year Ends: 12/31

SALARIES/BONUSES:
Top Exec. Salary: $1,700,000 Bonus: $
Second Exec. Salary: $1,241,000 Bonus: $

OTHER THOUGHTS:
Estimated Female Officers or Directors: 5
Hot Spot for Advancement for Women/Minorities: Y

Sales, profits and employees may be estimates. Financial information, benefits and other data can change quickly and may vary from those stated here.

Corning Inc

www.corning.com

NAIC Code: 327212

TYPES OF BUSINESS:
Glass & Optical Fiber Manufacturing
Glass Substrates for LCDs
Optical Switching Products
Photonic Modules & Components
Networking Devices
Semiconductor Materials
Laboratory Supplies
Emissions Control Products

BRANDS/DIVISIONS/AFFILIATES:
Eagle XG
Iris
Vascade
LEAF
ClearCurve
InfiniCor
Gorilla

CONTACTS:
Note: Officers with more than one job title may be intentionally listed here more than once.

Wendell Weeks, CEO
Jeffrey Evenson, Other Executive Officer
R. Tripeny, CFO
Edward Schlesinger, Chief Accounting Officer
Lisa Ferrero, Chief Administrative Officer
David Morse, Chief Technology Officer
Clark Kinlin, Executive VP
James Clappin, Executive VP, Divisional
Eric Musser, Executive VP, Divisional
Martin Curran, Executive VP
Lewis Steverson, General Counsel
Lawrence McRae, Other Corporate Officer
Christine Pambianchi, Senior VP, Divisional

GROWTH PLANS/SPECIAL FEATURES:

Corning, Inc. is an international technology-based corporation. The firm operates in five business segments: display technologies, optical communications, specialty materials, environmental technologies and life sciences. The display technologies segment manufactures glass substrates for active matrix liquid crystal displays (LCDs), used in notebook computers, flat panel desktop monitor and LCD televisions. Its Eagle XG glass is an LCD glass substrate free of heavy metals; and its Eagle XG slim glass and Iris glass products enables lighter-weight portable devices and thinner televisions and monitors. The optical communications segment is divided into carrier network and enterprise network. The carrier network products include: Vascade submarine optical fibers for use in submarine networks; LEAF optical fiber for long-haul, regional and metropolitan networks; SMF-28e single mode optical fiber for additional transmission wavelengths in metropolitan and access networks; and ClearCurve fiber for use in multiple dwelling units. Enterprise network products include ClearCurve ultra-bendable multimode fiber for data centers and other enterprise network applications; InfiniCor fibers for local area networks; and ClearCurve VSDN ultra-bendable optical fiber designed to support emerging high-speed interconnects between computers and other consumer electronics devices. The specialty materials segment offers products such as glass windows for space shuttles and optical components for high-tech industries and includes the firm's Gorilla glass product line of protective cover glass for portable display devices. The environmental technologies segment produces ceramic products for emissions and pollution control, such as gasoline/diesel substrate and filter products. The life sciences segment manufactures laboratory products such as consumables (plastic vessels, specialty surfaces and media), as well as general labware and equipment used for cell culture research, bioprocessing, genomics, drug discovery, microbiology and chemistry. In December 2017, the firm agreed to acquire all of 3M's communication markets division for approximately $900 million.

FINANCIAL DATA:
Note: Data for latest year may not have been available at press time.

In U.S. $	2017	2016	2015	2014	2013	2012
Revenue	10,116,000,000	9,390,000,000	9,111,000,000	9,715,000,000	7,819,000,000	8,012,000,000
R&D Expense	860,000,000	742,000,000	769,000,000	815,000,000	710,000,000	745,000,000
Operating Income	1,630,000,000	1,468,000,000	1,307,000,000	1,993,000,000	1,513,000,000	1,551,000,000
Operating Margin %	16.11%	15.63%	14.34%	20.51%	19.35%	19.35%
SGA Expense	1,467,000,000	1,472,000,000	1,523,000,000	1,211,000,000	1,126,000,000	1,165,000,000
Net Income	-497,000,000	3,695,000,000	1,339,000,000	2,472,000,000	1,961,000,000	1,728,000,000
Operating Cash Flow	2,004,000,000	2,521,000,000	2,809,000,000	4,709,000,000	2,787,000,000	3,206,000,000
Capital Expenditure	1,804,000,000	1,130,000,000	1,250,000,000	1,076,000,000	1,019,000,000	1,801,000,000
EBITDA	2,970,000,000	5,046,000,000	2,810,000,000	4,891,000,000	3,595,000,000	3,225,000,000
Return on Assets %	-2.14%	12.74%	4.23%	8.12%	6.77%	6.03%
Return on Equity %	-4.10%	22.42%	6.93%	11.76%	9.19%	8.11%
Debt to Equity	0.35	0.23	0.23	0.16	0.15	0.15

CONTACT INFORMATION:
Phone: 607 974-9000   Fax: 607 974-8688
Toll-Free:
Address: 1 Riverfront Plaza, Corning, NY 14831 United States

SALARIES/BONUSES:
Top Exec. Salary: $1,370,971   Bonus: $
Second Exec. Salary: $750,173   Bonus: $

STOCK TICKER/OTHER:
Stock Ticker: GLW   Exchange: NYS
Employees: 40,700   Fiscal Year Ends: 12/31
Parent Company:

OTHER THOUGHTS:
Estimated Female Officers or Directors: 1
Hot Spot for Advancement for Women/Minorities: Y

Sales, profits and employees may be estimates. Financial information, benefits and other data can change quickly and may vary from those stated here.

Plunkett Research, Ltd.

COWI A/S
NAIC Code: 541330

www.cowi.com

TYPES OF BUSINESS:
Engineering Consulting Services
Engineering
Consultancy
Design

BRANDS/DIVISIONS/AFFILIATES:

CONTACTS: Note: Officers with more than one job title may be intentionally listed here more than once.
Lars-Peter Sobye, CEO
Rasmus Odum, Exec. VP
Tomas Bergendahl, CFO
Steen Riisgaard, Chmn.

GROWTH PLANS/SPECIAL FEATURES:
COWI A/S is a consulting group for the engineering, economics and environmental science sectors. The firm is involved in more than 14,000 projects at any given moment on a global basis. COWI's services within economics, management and planning include analysis and tools, financial analysis and law, evaluation and impact assessment, organizational development and social studies, communication, transport planning and modelling, public transport, spatial planning and urban development. Within water and environment, services include health, safety and environment, water supply and wastewater, water and natural resources management, environmental impact assessment and monitoring, solid waste management, contaminated sites and strategic environmental consultancy. Within geographical information and IT, the firm provides 3D visualization and modelling, maps, geodata products, data capture, surveying, property rights and land administration. Within railways, roads and airport, COWI provides consultancy on roads, highways, railways, light rails, metros and airports. Within bridge, tunnel and marine structures, it serves bridges, tunnels, offshore wind farms, marine/coastal and geotechnical engineering, operation and maintenance, risk management, analysis and service life design. Within buildings, it provides building design, sustainable and green buildings, fire engineering, hospitals, healthcare, project management consultancy, high-rise, master planning, urban development, refurbishment and retrofit. It also serves the industry and energy sectors. COWI's projects include hotel apartments in Copenhagen; a Keflavik International Airport in Iceland; environmental assessment in the Sahara Forest; a bio-reactor for fermentation; an immersed tunnel for the Hong Kong-Zhuhai-Macao fixed link; and business sector advocacy in Ghana.

FINANCIAL DATA: Note: Data for latest year may not have been available at press time.

In U.S. $	2017	2016	2015	2014	2013	2012
Revenue	989,391,000	841,645,000	816,474,000	867,395,000	974,402,000	908,529,000
R&D Expense						
Operating Income						
Operating Margin %						
SGA Expense						
Net Income	23,162,500	18,564,700	19,178,400	28,407,100	25,836,400	-30,839,600
Operating Cash Flow						
Capital Expenditure						
EBITDA						
Return on Assets %						
Return on Equity %						
Debt to Equity						

CONTACT INFORMATION:
Phone: 45-56-40-00-00 Fax: 45-56-40-99-99
Toll-Free:
Address: Parallelvej 2, Kongens Lyngby, 2800 Denmark

STOCK TICKER/OTHER:
Stock Ticker: Private Exchange:
Employees: 6,599 Fiscal Year Ends: 12/31
Parent Company:

SALARIES/BONUSES:
Top Exec. Salary: $ Bonus: $
Second Exec. Salary: $ Bonus: $

OTHER THOUGHTS:
Estimated Female Officers or Directors:
Hot Spot for Advancement for Women/Minorities:

Sales, profits and employees may be estimates. Financial information, benefits and other data can change quickly and may vary from those stated here.

Cray Inc

NAIC Code: 334111

www.cray.com

TYPES OF BUSINESS:
Computer Manufacturing
Custom Computers
Software Design

BRANDS/DIVISIONS/AFFILIATES:
Cray XC
Cray CS
Cray Urika-GX
Shasta
Cray Sonexion
Cray DataWarp Applications Accelerator

CONTACTS:
Note: Officers with more than one job title may be intentionally listed here more than once.

Peter Ungaro, CEO
Brian Henry, CFO
Stephen Kiely, Chairman of the Board
Charles Fairchild, Chief Accounting Officer
Michael Piraino, General Counsel
Charles Morreale, Senior VP, Divisional
Efstathios Papaefstathiou, Senior VP, Divisional

GROWTH PLANS/SPECIAL FEATURES:

Cray, Inc. is a global leader in the design, development and production of high-performance computer (HPC) systems, more commonly known as supercomputers, for government, industry and academic institutions. The company manufactures a standard supercomputer product line and also designs and manufactures customized computers and storage and data management solutions. Cray supercomputers feature an interconnection system that allows users to network dozens of processors with multiple cores. Its key product lines include its Cray XC series, Cray CS series, Cray Urika-GX and next-generation Shasta supercomputers. The XC series adaptive supercomputing architecture provides both extreme scalability and sustained performance. Its platform ensures that uses can precisely configure the machines that will meet their specific requirements and remain confident they can upgrade and enhance the systems to address future demands. Crazy XC40, XC40-AC and XC40-LC supercomputers are enabled by a robust Intel Xeon processor road map, Aries high performance interconnect and flexible Dragonfly network topology, providing low latency and scalable global bandwidth to satisfy the most challenging multi-petaflops applications. The Cray CS cluster supercomputer series are industry-standards based, highly customizable and expressly designed to handle the broadest range of medium- to large-scale simulation and data analytics worldwide. The Cray Urika-GX platform is an agile analytics platform for production-class big data analytics workloads. Cray's Shasta supercomputer system is flexible to accommodate a variety of leading processor, networking and memory technologies. In the storage and data management market, the firm offers its flagship Cray Sonexion storage system, which combines next-generation hardware and software technology into a modular design that scales from terabytes to petabytes; and the Cray DataWarp Applications Accelerator, which addresses disk-based storage input/output issues by providing a new tier of storage featuring solid-state-drive and in-memory flash that is integrated with Cray XC supercomputing resources.

FINANCIAL DATA:
Note: Data for latest year may not have been available at press time.

In U.S. $	2017	2016	2015	2014	2013	2012
Revenue	392,509,000	629,809,000	724,689,000	561,606,000	525,749,000	421,058,000
R&D Expense	98,777,000	112,130,000	96,563,000	94,048,000	87,728,000	64,303,000
Operating Income	-57,080,000	9,139,000	41,004,000	9,200,000	21,650,000	28,988,000
Operating Margin %	-14.54%	1.45%	5.65%	1.63%	4.11%	6.88%
SGA Expense	89,007,000	98,946,000	88,116,000	81,166,000	74,948,000	57,887,000
Net Income	-133,829,000	10,615,000	27,537,000	62,323,000	32,223,000	161,241,000
Operating Cash Flow	-73,341,000	-52,313,000	147,756,000	-58,109,000	-87,350,000	156,892,000
Capital Expenditure	17,467,000	7,503,000	7,467,000	17,193,000	13,136,000	10,843,000
EBITDA	-36,020,000	24,632,000	59,851,000	26,158,000	35,408,000	177,577,000
Return on Assets %	-20.07%	1.50%	4.09%	9.93%	5.78%	40.64%
Return on Equity %	-28.91%	2.08%	5.81%	15.02%	8.99%	63.56%
Debt to Equity						

CONTACT INFORMATION:
Phone: 206 701-2000 Fax: 206 701-2500
Toll-Free: 877-272-9462
Address: 901 Fifth Ave., Ste. 1000, Seattle, WA 98164 United States

STOCK TICKER/OTHER:
Stock Ticker: CRAY   Exchange: NAS
Employees: 1,312   Fiscal Year Ends: 12/31
Parent Company:

SALARIES/BONUSES:
Top Exec. Salary: $520,000   Bonus: $
Second Exec. Salary: $400,000   Bonus: $

OTHER THOUGHTS:
Estimated Female Officers or Directors: 2
Hot Spot for Advancement for Women/Minorities: Y

Sales, profits and employees may be estimates. Financial information, benefits and other data can change quickly and may vary from those stated here.

CRB

www.crbusa.com

NAIC Code: 541330

TYPES OF BUSINESS:
Engineering Consulting Services
Engineering
Design
Construction

BRANDS/DIVISIONS/AFFILIATES:

GROWTH PLANS/SPECIAL FEATURES:
CRB is a global service provider of engineers, architects, constructors and consultants that deliver solutions to life science and advanced technology clients. The firm's services include architecture, design, commissioning and qualification, construction, consulting, engineering, operations improvement, planning, process simulation, process utilities, project management, regulatory compliance, staff augmentation, sustainability and strategic facility planning. Markets served include biotechnology, food/beverage, pharmaceuticals, science and technology. CRB is headquartered in Kansas City, Missouri, with 12 offices across the U.S., as well as one in Switzerland and one in Puerto Rico. Each office has full multi-disciplinary teams to support a wide range of project types and sizes.

The company offers its employees health, dental and vision care; life, AD&D and long-term care insurance; short- and long-term disability; 401K and tax savings plans; and paid time off.

CONTACTS:
Note: Officers with more than one job title may be intentionally listed here more than once.

Jeff Biskup, CEO
Ryan Schroeder, Pres.

FINANCIAL DATA:
Note: Data for latest year may not have been available at press time.

In U.S. $	2017	2016	2015	2014	2013	2012
Revenue						
R&D Expense						
Operating Income						
Operating Margin %						
SGA Expense						
Net Income						
Operating Cash Flow						
Capital Expenditure						
EBITDA						
Return on Assets %						
Return on Equity %						
Debt to Equity						

CONTACT INFORMATION:
Phone: 816-880-9800   Fax:
Toll-Free:
Address: 1251 NW Briarcliff Pkwy., Ste. 500, Kansas City, MO 64116 United States

STOCK TICKER/OTHER:
Stock Ticker: Private
Employees: 1,000
Parent Company:

Exchange:
Fiscal Year Ends:

SALARIES/BONUSES:
Top Exec. Salary: $ Bonus: $
Second Exec. Salary: $ Bonus: $

OTHER THOUGHTS:
Estimated Female Officers or Directors:
Hot Spot for Advancement for Women/Minorities:

Sales, profits and employees may be estimates. Financial information, benefits and other data can change quickly and may vary from those stated here.

CSL Limited

NAIC Code: 325414

www.csl.com.au

TYPES OF BUSINESS:
Human Blood-Plasma Collection
Plasma Products
Immunohematology Products
Vaccines
Pharmaceutical Marketing
Antivenom
Drugs-Cancer

BRANDS/DIVISIONS/AFFILIATES:
CSL Plasma
Seqirus

CONTACTS:
Note: Officers with more than one job title may be intentionally listed here more than once.

Paul Perreault, CEO
Andrew Cuthbertson, Chief Scientific Officer
Mary Sontrop, Exec. VP-Mfg. & Planning
Greg Boss, General Counsel
Ingolf Sieper, Exec. VP-Commercial Oper.
Karen Etchberger, Exec. VP-Quality & Bus. Svcs.
John Shine, Chmn.

GROWTH PLANS/SPECIAL FEATURES:

CSL Limited develops, manufactures and markets pharmaceutical products of biological origin in 30 countries worldwide. The company focuses on rare and serious diseases and influenza vaccines. Within the rare and serious diseases division, CSL's innovations are used around the world to treat immunodeficiencies, bleeding disorders, hereditary angioedema, Alpha-1 antitrypsin deficiency and neurological disorders. The CSL Plasma division is one of the world's largest and most efficient plasma collection networks, with more than 140 centers in the U.S. and Europe, as well as production facilities in the U.S., Germany, Switzerland and Australia. Within the influenza vaccines division, joint venture Seqirus (with Novartis), is a leading influenza company with corporate offices in the U.K., and manufacturing plants in the U.S., the U.K., Germany and Australia. Seqirus is a transcontinental partner in pandemic preparedness and a major contributor to the prevention and control of influenza globally. CSL's current product pipeline (as of April 2018) includes 14 research/pre-clinical products, 12 clinical development products and 11 registration/post-launch products. These products include immunoglobulins, specialty products, breakthrough medicines, vaccines, inactivated polio vaccines, hemophilia products and transplant products.

CSL Limited offers its employees flexible work arrangements, an employee share plan, tuition reimbursement and technology training.

FINANCIAL DATA:
Note: Data for latest year may not have been available at press time.

In U.S. $	2017	2016	2015	2014	2013	2012
Revenue	6,680,298,000	6,180,855,000	5,520,429,000	4,398,656,000	4,145,521,000	3,443,262,000
R&D Expense	651,591,100	641,984,700	467,941,000	384,556,700	357,407,200	275,728,200
Operating Income	-378,958,800	-512,813,800	136,124,600	35,042,150	769,916,000	-116,660,200
Operating Margin %	-5.67%	-8.29%	2.46%	.79%	18.57%	-3.38%
SGA Expense	2,885,459,000	2,647,115,000	2,097,593,000	1,671,305,000	846,790,300	1,369,476,000
Net Income	1,350,438,000	1,299,449,000	1,394,620,000	1,077,649,000	1,018,543,000	763,184,400
Operating Cash Flow						
Capital Expenditure	868,990,000	591,676,000	418,487,100	331,375,100	376,918,800	241,475,700
EBITDA	1,960,125,000	1,932,648,000	1,977,043,000	1,527,178,000	1,437,584,000	1,108,660,000
Return on Assets %	15.77%	18.06%	23.94%	21.17%	21.38%	18.05%
Return on Equity %	45.93%	47.57%	51.79%	42.05%	39.32%	27.78%
Debt to Equity	1.21	1.20	0.82	0.59	0.55	0.32

CONTACT INFORMATION:
Phone: 61-3-9389-1911　　Fax: 61-3-9389-1434
Toll-Free:
Address: 45 Poplar Rd., Parkville, VIC 3052 Australia

STOCK TICKER/OTHER:
Stock Ticker: CMXHF　　Exchange: PINX
Employees: 16,000　　Fiscal Year Ends: 06/30
Parent Company:

SALARIES/BONUSES:
Top Exec. Salary: $　　Bonus: $
Second Exec. Salary: $　　Bonus: $

OTHER THOUGHTS:
Estimated Female Officers or Directors: 4
Hot Spot for Advancement for Women/Minorities: Y

Sales, profits and employees may be estimates. Financial information, benefits and other data can change quickly and may vary from those stated here.

Plunkett Research, Ltd.

Cummins Inc
NAIC Code: 336300

www.cummins.com

TYPES OF BUSINESS:
Automotive Products, Motors & Parts Manufacturing
Engines
Filtration Systems
Power Generation Systems
Alternators
Air Handling Systems
Filtration & Emissions Solutions
Fuel Systems

BRANDS/DIVISIONS/AFFILIATES:
Stamford
AVK
Markon
Fleetguard
Brammo Inc

CONTACTS:
Note: Officers with more than one job title may be intentionally listed here more than once.

N. Linebarger, CEO
Peter Anderson, VP, Divisional
Christopher Clulow, Chief Accounting Officer
Marya Rose, Chief Administrative Officer
Sherry Aaholm, Chief Information Officer
Jennifer Rumsey, Chief Technology Officer
Richard Freeland, Director
Sharon Barner, General Counsel
Jill Cook, Other Executive Officer
Livingston Satterthwaite, President, Divisional
Tracy Embree, President, Divisional
Norbert Nusterer, President, Divisional
Donald Jackson, Treasurer
Mark Smith, Vice President, Divisional
Thaddeaus Ewald, Vice President, Divisional
Mark Osowick, Vice President, Divisional
Steven Chapman, Vice President, Geographical

GROWTH PLANS/SPECIAL FEATURES:
Cummins, Inc. designs, manufactures, distributes and services diesel and natural gas engines; electric power generation systems; and engine-related component products, including filtration and emissions solutions, fuel systems, controls and air handling systems. The company's operations are divided into four segments: engine, power generation, components and distribution. The engine segment, which generates 34% of Cummins' net sales, manufactures and markets diesel and natural gas-powered engines, parts and services under the Cummins brand name for the heavy- and medium-duty truck, bus, recreational vehicle, light-duty automotive, agricultural, construction, mining, marine, oil and gas, rail and governmental equipment markets. The power generation segment, accounting for 16% the firm's sales, designs and manufactures components of power generation systems, including engines, controls, alternators, transfer switches and switchgear. Products are marketed principally under the Stamford, AVK and Markon brands and include diesel and alternative-fuel electrical generator sets for commercial, institutional and consumer applications, such as office buildings, hospitals, factories, municipalities, utilities, universities, boats and homes. The components segment (23% of sales) produces filters, silencers and intake and exhaust systems and commercial turbochargers. It produces and sells Fleetguard branded filtration products in over 160 countries. The distribution segment (27% of sales) consists of 28 company-owned groups and 10 joint ventures that distribute the company's products and services in more than 90 distribution territories. Cummins serves customers through a combined network of approximately 500 wholly-owned and independent distributor locations and over 7,500 dealer locations in more than 190 countries and territories. In late-2017, Cummins acquired Brammo, Inc., which designs and develops battery packs for mobile and stationary applications. In January 2018, it acquired Johnson Matthey's automotive battery systems business.

The firm offers employees life, medical and dental insurance; flexible spending accounts; and an employee stock purchase plan.

FINANCIAL DATA:
Note: Data for latest year may not have been available at press time.

In U.S. $	2017	2016	2015	2014	2013	2012
Revenue	20,428,000,000	17,509,000,000	19,110,000,000	19,221,000,000	17,301,000,000	17,334,000,000
R&D Expense	752,000,000	636,000,000	735,000,000	754,000,000	713,000,000	728,000,000
Operating Income	1,997,000,000	1,765,000,000	2,043,000,000	2,018,000,000	1,753,000,000	1,866,000,000
Operating Margin %	9.77%	10.08%	10.69%	10.49%	10.13%	10.76%
SGA Expense	2,390,000,000	2,046,000,000	2,092,000,000	2,098,000,000	1,922,000,000	1,920,000,000
Net Income	999,000,000	1,394,000,000	1,399,000,000	1,651,000,000	1,483,000,000	1,645,000,000
Operating Cash Flow	2,277,000,000	1,935,000,000	2,059,000,000	2,266,000,000	2,089,000,000	1,532,000,000
Capital Expenditure	587,000,000	594,000,000	799,000,000	798,000,000	740,000,000	777,000,000
EBITDA	3,029,000,000	2,529,000,000	2,604,000,000	2,953,000,000	2,567,000,000	2,664,000,000
Return on Assets %	6.03%	9.24%	9.05%	10.82%	10.87%	13.58%
Return on Equity %	14.13%	19.52%	18.46%	21.63%	21.01%	27.20%
Debt to Equity	0.21	0.22	0.21	0.20	0.22	0.10

CONTACT INFORMATION:
Phone: 812 377-5000 Fax:
Toll-Free:
Address: 500 Jackson St., Columbus, IN 47202 United States

STOCK TICKER/OTHER:
Stock Ticker: CMI Exchange: NYS
Employees: 55,400 Fiscal Year Ends: 12/31
Parent Company:

SALARIES/BONUSES:
Top Exec. Salary: $1,375,000 Bonus: $
Second Exec. Salary: $848,000 Bonus: $

OTHER THOUGHTS:
Estimated Female Officers or Directors: 2
Hot Spot for Advancement for Women/Minorities: Y

Sales, profits and employees may be estimates. Financial information, benefits and other data can change quickly and may vary from those stated here.

Daelim Industrial Co Ltd

NAIC Code: 237000

www.daelim.co.kr

TYPES OF BUSINESS:
Heavy Construction and Engineering
Petrochemicals Distribution

BRANDS/DIVISIONS/AFFILIATES:
Daelim Corporation
Daelim Motor Co Ltd
Daelim Educational Foundation
Daelim Energy Co Ltd

CONTACTS: *Note: Officers with more than one job title may be intentionally listed here more than once.*
Sang Shin Park, CEO

GROWTH PLANS/SPECIAL FEATURES:
Daelim Industrial Co., Ltd., founded in 1939, is a construction, engineering and petrochemical firm operating in three segments: building and housing, civil works and plants. The building and housing segment is engaged in the construction, redevelopment and remodeling of offices and apartments; cultural and assembly facilities; commercial buildings, such as markets and department stores; educational facilities; medical and sports facilities, including the King Abdul Aziz University Hospital in Saudi Arabia; and others, such as the Seoul Court House Complex and the U.S. Embassy in Bangladesh. Some of the division's projects include constructing the main stadium for the 1988 Seoul Olympics, the Sejong Performing Arts Center and the main campus of the Arabian Gulf University in Bahrain, as well as work on the Meyongdong Cathedral, the Daelim Contemporary Art Museum and the main building of the Bank of Korea. The civil works segment has three broad categories of projects. The first combines expressways, airports, airfields and bridges. The second encompasses railroads, subways and tunnels. The third is engaged in the construction of dams, irrigation infrastructure and harbors and marine facilities. Some of the division's pending projects include the Yi Sun-Sin Bridge in Korea, and a container terminal in Vietnam. The plants segment constructs chemical plants, such as oil refineries and petrochemical processing facilities, implementing projects in the Middle East, Southeast Asia, Africa and China. Daelem's affiliate firms are engaged in the fields of engineering and construction, petrochemicals, manufacturing, trading, information technology, leisure, education, culture and energy. A few of these affiliates include: Daelim Corporation, Daelim Motor Co. Ltd., Daelim Educational Foundation and Daelim Energy Co. Ltd.

FINANCIAL DATA: *Note: Data for latest year may not have been available at press time.*

In U.S. $	2017	2016	2015	2014	2013	2012
Revenue	1,155,110,000	8,153,719,000	7,872,299,000	7,263,028,818	9,512,626,947	9,767,300,000
R&D Expense						
Operating Income						
Operating Margin %						
SGA Expense						
Net Income	459,302,000	242,611,000	180,553,952	-437,069,808	-23,994,000	372,600,000
Operating Cash Flow						
Capital Expenditure						
EBITDA						
Return on Assets %						
Return on Equity %						
Debt to Equity						

CONTACT INFORMATION:
Phone: 82-2-2011-7114 Fax: 82-2-2011-8000
Toll-Free:
Address: 146-12 Susong-Dong, Jongno-Gu, Seoul, 110-732 South Korea

STOCK TICKER/OTHER:
Stock Ticker: 210
Employees: 4,158
Parent Company:

Exchange: Seoul
Fiscal Year Ends: 12/31

SALARIES/BONUSES:
Top Exec. Salary: $ Bonus: $
Second Exec. Salary: $ Bonus: $

OTHER THOUGHTS:
Estimated Female Officers or Directors:
Hot Spot for Advancement for Women/Minorities:

Sales, profits and employees may be estimates. Financial information, benefits and other data can change quickly and may vary from those stated here.

Daewoo Shipbuilding & Marine Engineering Co Ltd

www.dsme.co.kr
NAIC Code: 336611

TYPES OF BUSINESS:
Ship Building
Offshore Oil Rig Construction
Submarine Building
Wind Power Turbines
Robotic Technology

BRANDS/DIVISIONS/AFFILIATES:
DSME Shandong Co Ltd
Samwoo Heavy Industries Co Ltd
Shinhan Heavy Industries Co Ltd

CONTACTS: Note: Officers with more than one job title may be intentionally listed here more than once.
Sung Leep Jung, CEO
Gap-Jung Kim, CFO
Kim Gap-Jung, VP
Mun Gyu-Sang, VP
Ryu Wan-Soo, VP
Jung Bang-Eon, VP

GROWTH PLANS/SPECIAL FEATURES:
Daewoo Shipbuilding & Marine Engineering Co., Ltd. (DSME) builds vessels, drilling rigs, offshore platforms, floating oil production units, destroyers and submarines. DSME's primary subsidiaries include: DSME Shandong Co. Ltd., which is engaged in the R&D, manufacturing and sales of large vessel blocks, as well as land and offshore infrastructure; Samwoo Heavy Industries Co. Ltd., which produces blocks, hatch covers, rudder and on/offshore products; and Shinhan Heavy Industries Co. Ltd., a major shipbuilder as well as the world's largest living quarter module maker for offshore facilities and topside production platforms. DSME also offers ship repair and refurbishment services. Its commercial vessels include tankers, liquefied natural gas (LNG) and liquefied petroleum gas (LPG) carriers, passenger ferries, container ships, roll-on roll-off (RORO) carriers, chemical carriers, product tankers and others. Specialty vessels include submarines, destroyers, submarine rescue vehicles and AUVs (Autonomous Underwater Vehicles). DSME is one of the only companies in Korea that builds submarines. Offshore plants include fixed platforms, rigs and offshore oil and gas exploration and production plants. The firm is engaged in a variety of R&D projects, including developing robotic technologies for painting and welding applications. It also engages in ship and ocean R&D, such as researching special and multipurpose propellers, developing noise and vibration reduction systems and software and developing automation systems for offshore platforms and ships. DSME maintains shipyards in Korea and Romania and overseas branch offices in Japan, China, Greece, the U.K., Norway, Angola, the UAE and Australia as well as U.S. offices in Houston, Texas.

FINANCIAL DATA: Note: Data for latest year may not have been available at press time.

In U.S. $	2017	2016	2015	2014	2013	2012
Revenue	9,000,000,000	9,460,200,000	11,335,600,128	11,739,235,328	11,448,250,368	10,656,321,536
R&D Expense						
Operating Income						
Operating Margin %						
SGA Expense						
Net Income		-2,485,230,000	-2,991,283,968	-704,029,440	-571,238,848	116,207,048
Operating Cash Flow						
Capital Expenditure						
EBITDA						
Return on Assets %						
Return on Equity %						
Debt to Equity						

CONTACT INFORMATION:
Phone: 055-735-2114   Fax:
Toll-Free:
Address: 3370, Geoje-daero, Gyeongsangnam-do, Geoje, 53302 South Korea

STOCK TICKER/OTHER:
Stock Ticker: DWOTF   Exchange: GREY
Employees: 13,120   Fiscal Year Ends: 12/31
Parent Company:

SALARIES/BONUSES:
Top Exec. Salary: $ Bonus: $
Second Exec. Salary: $ Bonus: $

OTHER THOUGHTS:
Estimated Female Officers or Directors:
Hot Spot for Advancement for Women/Minorities:

Sales, profits and employees may be estimates. Financial information, benefits and other data can change quickly and may vary from those stated here.

Daihatsu Motor Co Ltd

NAIC Code: 336111

www.daihatsu.com

TYPES OF BUSINESS:
Automobile Manufacturing
Industrial Engines

BRANDS/DIVISIONS/AFFILIATES:
Toyota Motor Corporation
Daihatsu Motor Kyushu Co Ltd
Daihatsu Business Support & Engineering Center
Daihatsu Credit Co Ltd
Daihatsu Transportation Co Ltd
Aoi Machine Industry Co Ltd
Daihatsu Metal Co Ltd
Akashi-Kikai Industry Co Ltd

CONTACTS:
Note: Officers with more than one job title may be intentionally listed here more than once.

Soichiro Okudaira, Pres.
Tatsuya Kaneko, Exec. VP
Takashi Nomoto, Sr. Managing Exec. Officer
Yasunori Nakawaki, Sr. Managing Exec. Officer
Naoto Kitagawa, Sr. Managing Exec. Officer

GROWTH PLANS/SPECIAL FEATURES:

Daihatsu Motor Co., Ltd., headquartered in Osaka, Japan, develops, manufactures and sells mini vehicles that offer fuel efficiency, affordability and added value. Mini vehicles are super-small-sized cars unique to Japan. Their overall length is approximately 11 feet or less, with an overall width of less than 5 feet and a height of less than 6.5 feet. Daihatsu's mini cars are among the world's smallest class of vehicles, but can accommodate four adults, steadily drive at 62 miles per hour (100 km/h) and offer a level of safety equal to compact cars. The firm has been manufacturing mini vehicles since it was established in 1949, with plants located in Osaka, Shiga and Kyoto, and a parts center located in Nishinomiya. Wholly-owned subsidiaries include Daihatsu Motor Kyushu Co. Ltd., which develops, designs, produces, sells and repairs automobiles, industrial vehicles and other types of vehicles and their parts; Daihatsu Business Support & Engineering Center Corp., which sells automotive accessories and materials, is engaged in research and development for automobiles and machines, and provides facility maintenance; Daihatsu Credit Co. Ltd., offering sales and lease financing; and Daihatsu Transportation Co. Ltd., providing cargo and vehicle transportation services. Majority-owned subsidiaries include Aoi Machine Industry Co. Ltd., which manufactures stamped vehicle and agricultural equipment body parts; Daihatsu Metal Co. Ltd., a manufacturer of vehicle parts, diesel engine parts for marine and land vehicles, as well as hydraulic components and machinery; Akashi-Kikai Industry Co. Ltd., which manufactures vehicle control devices, engine parts, transmissions and hydraulic components; and Kanbishi Co. Ltd., which manufactures die cast parts, automobile door locks, switches and other functional parts. Daihatsu is a wholly-owned subsidiary of Toyota Motor Corporation.

FINANCIAL DATA:
Note: Data for latest year may not have been available at press time.

In U.S. $	2017	2016	2015	2014	2013	2012
Revenue	16,750,000,000	16,570,347,520	17,813,338,112	18,755,971,072	17,302,329,344	15,992,079,360
R&D Expense						
Operating Income						
Operating Margin %						
SGA Expense						
Net Income		410,830,496	901,978,240	1,068,504,448	994,245,504	809,142,464
Operating Cash Flow						
Capital Expenditure						
EBITDA						
Return on Assets %						
Return on Equity %						
Debt to Equity						

CONTACT INFORMATION:
Phone: 81-72-751-8811 Fax:
Toll-Free:
Address: 1-1 Daihatsu-cho Ikeda-shi, Osaka, 563-8651 Japan

SALARIES/BONUSES:
Top Exec. Salary: $ Bonus: $
Second Exec. Salary: $ Bonus: $

STOCK TICKER/OTHER:
Stock Ticker: Subsidiary
Employees: 12,596
Parent Company: Toyota Motor Corporation

Exchange:
Fiscal Year Ends: 03/31

OTHER THOUGHTS:
Estimated Female Officers or Directors:
Hot Spot for Advancement for Women/Minorities:

Plunkett Research, Ltd.

Daimler AG
NAIC Code: 336111

www.daimler.com

TYPES OF BUSINESS:
Automobile Manufacturing
Financial Services & Insurance
Commercial Vehicles, Trucks & Buses
Aerospace & Defense Technology

GROWTH PLANS/SPECIAL FEATURES:
Daimler AG develops, manufactures, distributes and sells a wide range of automotive products, mainly passenger cars, trucks, vans and buses. Daimler distributes over 100 products in 200 countries worldwide. It also provides financial and other services relating to its automotive businesses in more than 40 countries. The company reports in five segments: Mercedes-Benz cars, Daimler trucks, Daimler financial services, Mercedes-Benz vans and Daimler buses. The Mercedes-Benz cars segment designs, produces and sells Mercedes-Benz and Mercedes-AMG passenger cars, Maybach luxury sedans and smart micro compact cars. The Daimler trucks segment manufactures trucks and specialty vehicles under the Mercedes-Benz, Freightliner, Western Star, Fuso, Thomas and BharatBenz; it also maintains the components brand, Detroit. Daimler financial services primarily provides financing, leasing, insurance and fleet management services. Mercedes-Benz vans comprises the Citan urban delivery vehicle, the Sprinter and Vito medium- and heavy-duty vans, as well as the V-Class MPV van. Daimler buses includes the Mercedes-Benz and Setra brands. Daimler offers products and services primarily in Western Europe and in the NAFTA region, including the U.S., Canada and Mexico. In addition, Daimler's Mercedes me package of innovative services includes access to vehicles via smartphone and personalized home pages with relevant topics concerning entertainment, travel and lifestyle. Subsidiary moovel NA, help people navigate cities in real-time, connects users to transportation solutions no matter where they are and provides mobile payment solutions as needed. In December 2016, the firm acquired Athlon Car Lease International, a leading fleet management company in Europe, for $1.2 billion. In January 2017, Daimler announced a partnership with Uber, where they will join forces to bring more autonomous vehicles on the road through R&D and network operations.

BRANDS/DIVISIONS/AFFILIATES:
moovel NA
Mercedes-Benz
Daimler
Mercedes-AMG
Maybach
Freightliner
BharatBenz
Athlon Car Lease International

CONTACTS:
Note: Officers with more than one job title may be intentionally listed here more than once.

Dieter Zetsche, CEO
Bodo Uebber, Dir.-Finance
Thomas Weber, Dir.-Group Research
Andreas Renschler, Dir.-Mfg.
Cristine Hohmann-Dennhardt, Dir.-Legal Affairs & Integrity
Bodo Uebber, Dir.-Controlling
Thomas Weber, Dir.-Mercedes-Benz Cars Dev.
Wolfgang Bernhard, Dir.-Trucks
Dieter Zetsche, Chmn.
Andreas Renschler, Dir.-Procurement

FINANCIAL DATA:
Note: Data for latest year may not have been available at press time.

In U.S. $	2017	2016	2015	2014	2013	2012
Revenue	202,931,700,000	189,262,500,000	184,577,300,000	160,379,400,000	145,696,400,000	141,145,800,000
R&D Expense	7,332,856,000	6,491,887,000	5,878,140,000	5,596,581,000	5,064,338,000	5,160,661,000
Operating Income	16,033,990,000	14,910,220,000	15,489,390,000	11,705,650,000	9,645,830,000	9,912,569,000
Operating Margin %	7.90%	7.87%	8.39%	7.29%	6.62%	7.02%
SGA Expense	20,714,270,000	19,320,060,000	19,581,860,000	18,354,370,000	18,202,470,000	17,812,250,000
Net Income	12,997,360,000	10,528,790,000	10,402,830,000	8,597,396,000	8,449,208,000	7,526,736,000
Operating Cash Flow	-2,040,060,000	4,582,726,000	274,148,500	-1,573,267,000	4,056,657,000	-1,358,394,000
Capital Expenditure	12,544,150,000	10,907,900,000	9,059,251,000	7,788,535,000	8,529,477,000	8,220,751,000
EBITDA	25,388,380,000	22,966,730,000	23,129,740,000	19,618,910,000	19,006,400,000	16,683,540,000
Return on Assets %	4.22%	3.70%	4.14%	3.88%	4.12%	3.91%
Return on Equity %	17.25%	15.29%	17.32%	16.12%	15.80%	14.59%
Debt to Equity	1.14	1.13	1.05	1.11	0.98	0.92

CONTACT INFORMATION:
Phone: 49 7111792543   Fax: 49 7111794116
Toll-Free:
Address: Mercedesstrasse 137, Stuttgart, 70546 Germany

STOCK TICKER/OTHER:
Stock Ticker: DAI N
Employees: 289,530
Parent Company:

Exchange: MEX
Fiscal Year Ends: 12/31

SALARIES/BONUSES:
Top Exec. Salary: $ Bonus: $
Second Exec. Salary: $ Bonus: $

OTHER THOUGHTS:
Estimated Female Officers or Directors: 6
Hot Spot for Advancement for Women/Minorities: Y

Sales, profits and employees may be estimates. Financial information, benefits and other data can change quickly and may vary from those stated here.

Daimler Trucks North America LLC

www.daimler-trucksnorthamerica.com

NAIC Code: 336120

TYPES OF BUSINESS:

Truck Manufacturing
Custom-Built Chassis
Van & Bus Manufacturing
Automobile Parts Manufacturing
Specialty Vehicle Manufacturing
Military Vehicle Manufacturing
Used Truck Dealerships
Truck Stops

BRANDS/DIVISIONS/AFFILIATES:

Daimler AG
Freightliner Trucks
Western Star Truck Sales Inc
Detroit Diesel Corporation
Thomas Built Buses
SelecTrucks
Alliance Truck Parts
Daimler Truck Financial

CONTACTS: Note: Officers with more than one job title may be intentionally listed here more than once.

Roger M. Nielsen, CEO
Martin Daum, Pres.
John O'Leary, CFO
Friedrich Baumann, Sr. VP-Aftermarket
Albert Kirchmann, Head-Daimler Truck Asia, Finance & Control

GROWTH PLANS/SPECIAL FEATURES:

Daimler Trucks North America, LLC (Daimler NA), a wholly-owned subsidiary of Daimler AG, is one of the largest manufacturers of medium- and heavy-duty trucks and specialized commercial vehicles in North America. The company is comprised of nine businesses. Freightliner Trucks manufactures Class 5-8 models of Freightliner-branded trucks with pickup and delivery, towing, municipal, construction and long-haul on-highway applications. Western Star Truck Sales, Inc. manufactures the Western Star brand of trucks, which are targeted at small and medium fleets, as well as owner-operators, with a focus on vocational and extreme-duty segments. Detroit Diesel Corporation manufactures a full portfolio of heavy-duty and mid-range diesel engines, as well as transmissions, axles, safety systems and telematics products for the on-highway and vocational commercial truck markets. Thomas Built Buses designs and builds school buses, including light- and medium-duty lines. Freightliner Custom Chassis Corporation manufactures premium chassis for recreational vehicles, walk-in vans, delivery vehicles, commercial vehicles, shuttle buses and school buses. SelecTrucks is Daimler Trucks' remarketing retail distributor, engaged in selling Freightliner-branded used trucks through retail locations in the U.S. and Canada. Alliance Truck Parts offers new and remanufactured parts to the commercial transportation industry. It has more than 30 product lines for all makes and all models of trucks and buses. Daimler Truck Financial offers financing for commercial vehicles such as Freightliner, Western Star, SelecTrucks, Thomas Built Buses, Mitsubishi Fuso and Sprinter. The firm customizes its financing solutions with a broad range of loan, lease and payment options. Daimler Truck Financial is a business unit of Mercedes-Benz Financial Services USA, LLC. Last, Elite Support are certified delivers that sell, maintain and repair Freightliner and Western Star trucks.

FINANCIAL DATA: Note: Data for latest year may not have been available at press time.

In U.S. $	2017	2016	2015	2014	2013	2012
Revenue	36,712,725,000	34,964,500,000	42,743,096,100	40,869,330,000	40,766,550,522	40,657,746,460
R&D Expense						
Operating Income						
Operating Margin %						
SGA Expense						
Net Income		1,943,440,000	2,930,071,200	2,136,131,100	3,013,038,603	2,429,568,652
Operating Cash Flow						
Capital Expenditure						
EBITDA						
Return on Assets %						
Return on Equity %						
Debt to Equity						

CONTACT INFORMATION:

Phone: 503-745-8000   Fax: 503-745-8921
Toll-Free:
Address: 4747 N. Channel Ave., Portland, OR 97217 United States

STOCK TICKER/OTHER:

Stock Ticker: Subsidiary   Exchange:
Employees: 22,000   Fiscal Year Ends: 12/31
Parent Company: Daimler AG

SALARIES/BONUSES:

Top Exec. Salary: $ Bonus: $
Second Exec. Salary: $ Bonus: $

OTHER THOUGHTS:

Estimated Female Officers or Directors:
Hot Spot for Advancement for Women/Minorities:

Sales, profits and employees may be estimates. Financial information, benefits and other data can change quickly and may vary from those stated here.

Dana Incorporated

NAIC Code: 336300

www.dana.com

TYPES OF BUSINESS:
Automotive Products, Motors & Parts Manufacturing
Engine Systems
Fluid Systems
Heavy Vehicle Technologies
Brake Components
Chassis & Drive Train Components
Filtration Products
Financial Services

BRANDS/DIVISIONS/AFFILIATES:

CONTACTS: Note: Officers with more than one job title may be intentionally listed here more than once.
Jonathan Collins, CFO
Keith Wandell, Chairman of the Board
James Kamsickas, Director
Mark Wallace, Executive VP
Douglas Liedberg, General Counsel
Robert Pyle, President, Divisional
Aziz Aghili, President, Divisional
Dwayne Matthews, President, Divisional

GROWTH PLANS/SPECIAL FEATURES:

Dana Incorporated supplies high technology driveline, sealing, thermal management and fluid-power products for global vehicle manufacturers. The company operates 139 facilities in 33 countries. Dana divides its operations into four segments: light vehicle, commercial vehicle, off-highway and power technologies. The light vehicle segment manufactures axles, driveshafts differentials, torque couplings, modular assemblies, drive units, power transfer units and electric vehicle (EV) gearboxes for the light vehicle market. The commercial vehicle segment manufactures parts for the medium/heavy duty vehicle market, including medium duty trucks, heavy duty trucks, buses and specialty vehicles. Products include axles, driveshafts and tire inflation systems. The off-highway segment manufactures axels, driveshafts, transmissions, torque converters, industrial gear boxes, tire inflation systems, hydraulic valves/pumps/motors and electronic controls for off-highway use such as construction, earth moving, agriculture, mining, forestry, rail and material handling. Last, the power technologies segment manufactures parts for the light vehicle, medium/heavy vehicle and off-highway markets. Products include gaskets, cover modules, heat shields, engine sealing systems, cooling and heat transfer products. Major customers of the company include: Ford Motor Company; Toyota Motor Company; General Motors Company; PACCAR, Inc.; Daimler AG; Deere & Company, Manitou Group; Cummins, Inc.; and Volkswagen AG, among others. In March 2018, Dana agreed to combine with the driveline division of GKN plc to create Dana plc, a global leader in driveline systems. The total consideration will be composed of $1.6 billion to GKN plc, and Dana shareholders would own about 52.75% of the company and GKN shareholders would own about 47.25%. The firm would be domiciled in the U.K., and will continue to trade on NYSE under DAN.

FINANCIAL DATA: Note: Data for latest year may not have been available at press time.

In U.S. $	2017	2016	2015	2014	2013	2012
Revenue	7,209,000,000	5,826,000,000	6,060,000,000	6,617,000,000	6,769,000,000	7,224,000,000
R&D Expense						
Operating Income	540,000,000	430,000,000	444,000,000	492,000,000	436,000,000	466,000,000
Operating Margin %	7.49%	7.38%	7.32%	7.43%	6.44%	6.45%
SGA Expense	511,000,000	406,000,000	391,000,000	411,000,000	410,000,000	434,000,000
Net Income	111,000,000	640,000,000	159,000,000	319,000,000	244,000,000	300,000,000
Operating Cash Flow	554,000,000	384,000,000	406,000,000	510,000,000	577,000,000	339,000,000
Capital Expenditure	393,000,000	322,000,000	260,000,000	234,000,000	209,000,000	164,000,000
EBITDA	715,000,000	510,000,000	579,000,000	591,000,000	729,000,000	725,000,000
Return on Assets %	2.11%	13.93%	3.43%	6.20%	-.25%	5.14%
Return on Equity %	10.23%	67.90%	17.58%	30.93%	-1.28%	25.94%
Debt to Equity	1.73	1.37	2.13	1.49	1.67	0.73

CONTACT INFORMATION:
Phone: 419 887-3000   Fax: 419 535-4643
Toll-Free: 800-537-8823
Address: 3939 Technology Dr., Maumee, OH 43537 United States

STOCK TICKER/OTHER:
Stock Ticker: DAN   Exchange: NYS
Employees: 24,900   Fiscal Year Ends: 12/31
Parent Company:

SALARIES/BONUSES:
Top Exec. Salary: $1,122,500   Bonus: $
Second Exec. Salary: $587,500   Bonus: $

OTHER THOUGHTS:
Estimated Female Officers or Directors:
Hot Spot for Advancement for Women/Minorities: Y

Sales, profits and employees may be estimates. Financial information, benefits and other data can change quickly and may vary from those stated here.

Dar Al-Handasah Consultants (Shair and Partners)

dar.dargroup.com
NAIC Code: 541330

TYPES OF BUSINESS:
Engineering Services

BRANDS/DIVISIONS/AFFILIATES:

CONTACTS: Note: Officers with more than one job title may be intentionally listed here more than once.
Talal Shair, Chmn.

GROWTH PLANS/SPECIAL FEATURES:
Dar Al-Handasah Consultants (Shair and Partners) is a planning, design, management and supervision consultancy with more than 950 clients from over 63 countries. Dar operates from 40 offices worldwide, with principal design centers located in Beirut, Amman, Manama and Baghdad. It serves both public and private sectors via planning and design, built environment, industry, water, power, transportation, telecommunications, oil and gas, environment and project management. Planning and design provides urban design, infrastructure planning, district cooling and heating, landscape architecture and solid waste management. Built environment consists of building civic structures such as hotels, universities and schools, and high-rise buildings. It serves markets such as commercial, governmental, educational, correctional, healthcare, hospitality, convention centers, residential, sports, entertainment, religious and tall buildings. Industry involves designing and supervising the construction of plants, developing industrial parks and counseling governments on their industrial potential. Markets within this division include pharmaceuticals, food and beverage processing, cement, bulk material handling and storage, fertilizer, potash and other. The water division consists of specialists in hydrology, hydraulics and treatment, covering the full water-use cycle from source to reuse and disposal. Power provides evaluation, design and supervision of power projects, including generation, transmission and distribution as well as renewable energy. Transportation includes land, air and sea, with road, highway, railway and airport projects all undertaken by the firm. Telecommunications plans, designs and integrates the deployment of infrastructure cabling solutions, data centers and security systems. Oil and gas involves onshore and offshore crude oil production, fuel pumping facilities and fuel and gas pipelines. Environment services involves document preparation and permit applications as well as construction management. Project management provides construction consultancy from inception to completion and operation and maintenance of completed facilities.

FINANCIAL DATA: Note: Data for latest year may not have been available at press time.

In U.S. $	2017	2016	2015	2014	2013	2012
Revenue						
R&D Expense						
Operating Income						
Operating Margin %						
SGA Expense						
Net Income						
Operating Cash Flow						
Capital Expenditure						
EBITDA						
Return on Assets %						
Return on Equity %						
Debt to Equity						

CONTACT INFORMATION:
Phone: 961-1790002 Fax: 961-1869011
Toll-Free:
Address: Verdun St., Dar Al-Handasah Bldg., Beirut, 1107 2230 Lebanon

STOCK TICKER/OTHER:
Stock Ticker: Private
Employees: 9,850
Parent Company:

Exchange:
Fiscal Year Ends:

SALARIES/BONUSES:
Top Exec. Salary: $ Bonus: $
Second Exec. Salary: $ Bonus: $

OTHER THOUGHTS:
Estimated Female Officers or Directors:
Hot Spot for Advancement for Women/Minorities:

Sales, profits and employees may be estimates. Financial information, benefits and other data can change quickly and may vary from those stated here.

Plunkett Research, Ltd.

Dassault Aviation SA
NAIC Code: 336411

www.dassault-aviation.com

TYPES OF BUSINESS:
Aircraft Manufacturing
Business Jets
Military Aircraft
Unmanned Combat Aircraft
Aerospace Technology

BRANDS/DIVISIONS/AFFILIATES:
Dassault Group
Dassalt Falcon Jet Corp
Dassault Procurement Services inc
Dassault Falcon Service SARL
Sogitec Industries SA
Dassault Falcon
Rafale
nEUROn Uninhabited Combat Aircraft Vehicle

CONTACTS: Note: Officers with more than one job title may be intentionally listed here more than once.
Eric Trappier, CEO
Loik Segalen, COO
Denis Dasse, CFO
Jean-Jacques Cara, Sr. VP-Human Resources
Jean Sass, Chief Digital Officer
Didier Gondoin, Sr. VP-Eng.
Benoit Berger, Exec. VP-Industrial Oper.
Stephane Fort, Sr. VP-Corp. Comm. & Institutional Rel.
Alain Bonny, Sr. VP-Military Customer Support
Olivier Villa, Sr. VP-Civil Aircraft
Gerald Maria, Sr. VP-Total Quality
Eric Trappier, Chmn.
Benoit Dussaugey, Exec. VP-Intl
Benoit Berger, Exec. VP-Procurement & Purchasing

GROWTH PLANS/SPECIAL FEATURES:
Dassault Aviation SA designs, engineers and produces civil and military aircraft, and is one of the largest producers of business jets in the world. It is part of the Dassault Group and operates in three divisions: Dassault Falcon, defense and space. The Dassault Falcon family of luxury business jets includes the Falcon 7X, a mid-size craft with three engines; the Falcon 8X, a large-cabin, long range tri-jet; the Falcon 2000, a large business jet with two engines; the Falcon 2000LXS, which flies 4,000 nautical miles (nm) while cruising at Mach .80; and the Falcon 900, a large business jet with three engines. The Falcon 6x, a 5,500-nm aircraft scheduled to make its first flight in early 2021, and begin deliveries in 2022. The firm's defense division includes the production of the Rafale and Maritime Falcon lines of aircraft, as well as acting as the primary contractor for the European nEUROn Uninhabited Combat Aircraft Vehicle (UCAV) project. Dassault's space division develops pyrotechnics equipment for space and military aircraft, aerospace telemetry systems and manned and unmanned vehicles for space travel. The firm operates through a number of subsidiaries, including: Dassault Falcon Jet Corp., which is responsible for customizing Falcon interiors in the U.S.; Dassault Procurement Services, Inc., which purchases aviation equipment for Falcon aircraft; Dassault Falcon Service SARL, which provides business aviation services, including maintenance, management and technical for Falcon business jets, and also owns and operates business aircrafts; and Sogitec Industries SA, which designs, develops and manufactures instruction, simulation and training products for aerospace and defense systems. Dassault has created more than 100 prototypes in the last century, with over 10,000 aircraft delivered to 90 countries.

FINANCIAL DATA: Note: Data for latest year may not have been available at press time.

In U.S. $	2017	2016	2015	2014	2013	2012
Revenue		4,526,659,000	5,165,996,000	4,544,914,000	5,671,942,000	4,872,300,000
R&D Expense						
Operating Income		357,689,700	423,384,100	396,200,200	622,623,400	662,673,900
Operating Margin %		7.90%	8.19%	8.71%	10.97%	13.60%
SGA Expense						
Net Income		468,065,400	174,685,700	349,275,100	567,340,500	629,595,700
Operating Cash Flow		1,219,482,000	1,599,094,000	-342,333,700	137,670,700	751,702,900
Capital Expenditure		132,821,300	188,041,200	112,864,000	78,425,010	74,664,730
EBITDA		685,450,400	210,854,800	544,428,200	922,280,200	1,012,628,000
Return on Assets %		2.92%	1.27%	2.82%	4.49%	4.95%
Return on Equity %		10.69%	3.59%	6.14%	9.32%	11.07%
Debt to Equity		0.32	0.30	0.21	0.04	0.05

CONTACT INFORMATION:
Phone: 33 153769300   Fax: 33 153769320
Toll-Free:
Address: 9 Rond-Point des Champs-Elysees, Marcel Dassault, Paris, 75008 France

STOCK TICKER/OTHER:
Stock Ticker: DUAVF
Employees: 11,942
Parent Company: Dassault Group

Exchange: PINX
Fiscal Year Ends: 12/31

SALARIES/BONUSES:
Top Exec. Salary: $ Bonus: $
Second Exec. Salary: $ Bonus: $

OTHER THOUGHTS:
Estimated Female Officers or Directors:
Hot Spot for Advancement for Women/Minorities:

Sales, profits and employees may be estimates. Financial information, benefits and other data can change quickly and may vary from those stated here.

Dassault Systemes SA

www.3ds.com

NAIC Code: 0

TYPES OF BUSINESS:
Computer Software-Product Lifecycle Management
3D Imaging Software

BRANDS/DIVISIONS/AFFILIATES:
CATIA
SOLIDWORKS
DELMIA
SIMULIA
BIOVIA
3DVIA
EXALEAD
3DEXCITE

CONTACTS:
Note: Officers with more than one job title may be intentionally listed here more than once.

Bernard Charles, CEO
Dominique Florack, Pres.
Pascal Daloz, CFO
Laurence Barthes, Chief People Officer
Dominique Florack, Sr. Exec. VP-R&D
Pascal Daloz, Exec. VP-Brands
Pascal Daloz, Exec. VP-Corp. Dev.
Sylvain Laurent, Exec. VP-Bus. Transformation & Asia Pacific Market
Bruno Latchague, Sr. Exec. VP-Americas Market & Global Sales Oper.
Charles Edelstenne, Chmn.
Philippe Forestier, Exec. VP-Global Affairs & Communities

GROWTH PLANS/SPECIAL FEATURES:
Dassault Systemes SA is a global provider of product lifecycle management (PLM) software and 3D rendering software. The company's software applications and services enable businesses to digitally define and simulate products, providing a 3D vision for the lifecycle of products from conception to maintenance. Its products facilitate the design, simulation and production of complex systems such as cars, aircraft and dams, as well as the manufacturing facilities used to produce them. PLM software aims to offer customers a competitive advantage in the market by reducing product introduction costs, managing supplier networks, extending design expertise globally and accelerating time to market. Its applications are also employed to design and manufacture products for everyday life, from tableware and household appliances to jewelry. The firm's software brands include CATIA, which creates and simulates digital products; SOLIDWORKS, a 3D software that trains engineering and design teams; NETVIBES, a real-time monitoring and analysis dashboard; DELMIA, which simulates manufacturing processes; SIMULIA, for virtual testing; and ENOVIA, for online global collaborative lifecycle management. For science driven companies, Dassault offers the biological, chemical and material modeling and simulation BIOVIA and GEOVIA portfolios. Additions to Dassault's brand lineup include 3DVIA platform, which is dedicated to extending 3D content creation to new businesses and consumers; EXALEAD, a cloud view platform focused on search and other search-based applications where companies can discover, search and manage information assets; and 3DEXCITE, a platform that creates real-time visualizations for product experiences. During 2017, Dassault Systemes acquired Exa Corporation, a developer and distributor of computer-aided engineering software; and agreed to acquire No Magic, Inc., a software developer offering solutions that enable object oriented design and development capabilities.

FINANCIAL DATA:
Note: Data for latest year may not have been available at press time.

In U.S. $	2017	2016	2015	2014	2013	2012
Revenue		3,773,353,000	3,506,452,000	2,833,214,000	2,551,462,000	2,504,806,000
R&D Expense		667,472,600	608,182,500	505,890,500	463,739,600	454,614,800
Operating Income		850,268,000	781,949,400	580,558,900	629,506,800	621,829,400
Operating Margin %		22.53%	22.30%	18.77%	24.34%	24.69%
SGA Expense		1,460,926,000	1,363,226,000	1,158,176,000	1,010,829,000	982,868,200
Net Income		552,238,900	496,650,900	359,654,500	435,030,500	413,471,600
Operating Cash Flow		767,791,300	782,016,100	616,776,200	625,907,100	699,323,300
Capital Expenditure		69,963,450	53,815,850	56,055,970	52,347,550	50,169,180
EBITDA		1,040,600,000	1,051,994,000	775,311,800	821,684,900	813,718,500
Return on Assets %		6.74%	7.13%	6.36%	9.04%	9.40%
Return on Equity %		12.20%	12.54%	10.48%	14.16%	15.11%
Debt to Equity		0.25	0.28	0.11	0.13	0.01

CONTACT INFORMATION:
Phone: 33 161626162
Fax: 33 170734363
Toll-Free:
Address: 10 rue Marcel Dassault, CS 40501, Velizy-Villacoublay, 78140 France

STOCK TICKER/OTHER:
Stock Ticker: DASTY
Employees: 11,803
Parent Company:

Exchange: PINX
Fiscal Year Ends: 12/31

SALARIES/BONUSES:
Top Exec. Salary: $
Bonus: $
Second Exec. Salary: $
Bonus: $

OTHER THOUGHTS:
Estimated Female Officers or Directors: 2
Hot Spot for Advancement for Women/Minorities: Y

Deere & Company (John Deere)

NAIC Code: 333111

www.deere.com

TYPES OF BUSINESS:
Construction & Agricultural Equipment
Commercial & Consumer Equipment
Forestry Equipment
Financing

BRANDS/DIVISIONS/AFFILIATES:
John Deere
Wirtgen Group Holding GmbH

CONTACTS:
Note: Officers with more than one job title may be intentionally listed here more than once.

Samuel Allen, CEO
Rajesh Kalathur, CFO
Marc Howze, Chief Administrative Officer
John May, Chief Information Officer
James Field, President, Divisional
Markwart Pentz, President, Divisional
Max Guinn, President, Divisional
Cory Reed, President, Divisional
Jean Gilles, Senior VP, Divisional
Mary Jones, Senior VP

GROWTH PLANS/SPECIAL FEATURES:

Deere & Company is known for its John Deere brand name. The firm conducts business in three divisions: agriculture and turf; construction and forestry; and financial services. The agriculture and turf segment manufactures and distributes farm, lawn and garden equipment including tractors; combines; harvesters; tillage, seeding and soil preparation machinery; sprayers; hay and forage equipment; material handling equipment; integrated agricultural management systems technology; mowers; golf course equipment; utility tractors; landscape and irrigation equipment; and other outdoor power products. The construction and forestry division offers equipment and service parts used in construction, earthmoving, material handling and timber harvesting, including backhoe loaders, crawler dozers and loaders, four-wheel-drive loaders, excavators and more. The financial services segment primarily finances sales and leases by John Deere dealers of new and used agriculture and turf equipment and construction and forestry equipment. In addition, the segment provides wholesale financing to dealers of the foregoing equipment, finances retail revolving charge accounts and operating loans, and offers crop risk mitigation products and extended equipment warranties. Sales are generally conducted through 2,359 dealer locations (largely independently-owned and operated), 1,532 of which sell agricultural equipment and about 424 of which sell construction, earthmoving, material handling and/or forestry equipment. In December 2017, the firm acquired Wirtgen Group Holding GmbH, a manufacturer of road construction equipment, and was merged into the construction and forestry segment.

FINANCIAL DATA:
Note: Data for latest year may not have been available at press time.

In U.S. $	2017	2016	2015	2014	2013	2012
Revenue	27,006,200,000	24,132,800,000	26,481,700,000	33,784,800,000	35,253,900,000	33,733,900,000
R&D Expense	1,367,700,000	1,389,100,000	1,425,100,000	1,452,000,000	1,477,300,000	1,433,600,000
Operating Income	1,321,800,000	476,100,000	1,079,000,000	3,179,300,000	4,093,800,000	3,521,500,000
Operating Margin %	4.89%	1.97%	4.07%	9.41%	11.61%	10.43%
SGA Expense	3,253,600,000	2,951,700,000	3,056,300,000	3,608,400,000	3,809,500,000	3,662,000,000
Net Income	2,159,100,000	1,523,900,000	1,940,000,000	3,161,700,000	3,537,300,000	3,064,700,000
Operating Cash Flow	2,199,800,000	3,764,300,000	3,740,300,000	3,525,900,000	3,254,300,000	1,167,700,000
Capital Expenditure	2,592,300,000	2,955,100,000	2,826,100,000	2,659,300,000	2,375,300,000	2,121,000,000
EBITDA	4,906,300,000	3,729,700,000	4,842,500,000	5,955,400,000	7,365,000,000	6,521,400,000
Return on Assets %	3.48%	2.62%	3.25%	5.23%	6.10%	5.86%
Return on Equity %	26.85%	22.96%	24.53%	32.70%	41.35%	44.92%
Debt to Equity	2.70	3.64	3.53	2.69	2.10	3.28

CONTACT INFORMATION:
Phone: 309 765-8000   Fax: 309 765-9929
Toll-Free:
Address: 1 John Deere Plaza, Moline, IL 61265 United States

STOCK TICKER/OTHER:
Stock Ticker: DE   Exchange: NYS
Employees: 56,800   Fiscal Year Ends: 10/31
Parent Company:

SALARIES/BONUSES:
Top Exec. Salary: $1,500,000   Bonus: $
Second Exec. Salary: $700,553   Bonus: $

OTHER THOUGHTS:
Estimated Female Officers or Directors: 7
Hot Spot for Advancement for Women/Minorities: Y

Dell EMC

NAIC Code: 334112

www.emc.com/en-us/index.htm

TYPES OF BUSINESS:
Networked Computer Storage Systems
Virtual Server Software
Management Protection Software
Consulting Services
Storage Management Services

BRANDS/DIVISIONS/AFFILIATES:
Dell Technologies Inc

GROWTH PLANS/SPECIAL FEATURES:
Dell EMC provides the essential infrastructure for organizations to build their digital future, transform information technology (IT) and protect information assets. The company enables enterprise customers' digital and IT transformation through the hybrid cloud and big data solutions built on a data center infrastructure that incorporates industry-leading converged infrastructure, servers, storage and cybersecurity technologies. Dell EMC works with organizations around the globe, in every industry, in both the public and private sectors, and of every size, including startups and Fortune Global 500 entities. The company services customers across 180 countries. Dell EMC operates as a subsidiary of Dell Technologies, Inc.

CONTACTS: Note: Officers with more than one job title may be intentionally listed here more than once.
Michael Dell, CEO
Robert Mee, CEO, Divisional
Tom Sweet, CFO
Jeremy Burton, CMO
Steve Price, Chief Human Resources Officer
Howard Elias, COO, Divisional
Bask Iyer, CIO
Erin McSweeney, Executive VP, Divisional
Paul Dacier, Executive VP
Harry You, Executive VP
Jeremy Burton, President, Divisional
Amit Yoran, President, Divisional
William Scannell, President, Divisional
William Teuber, Vice Chairman

FINANCIAL DATA: Note: Data for latest year may not have been available at press time.

In U.S. $	2017	2016	2015	2014	2013	2012
Revenue	27,500,000,000	25,000,000,000	24,704,000,000	24,440,000,512	23,221,999,616	21,713,901,568
R&D Expense						
Operating Income						
Operating Margin %						
SGA Expense						
Net Income		-2,100,000,000	1,990,000,000	2,713,999,872	2,888,999,936	2,732,613,120
Operating Cash Flow						
Capital Expenditure						
EBITDA						
Return on Assets %						
Return on Equity %						
Debt to Equity						

CONTACT INFORMATION:
Phone: 508 435-1000 Fax: 508 435-5222
Toll-Free:
Address: 176 South St., Hopkinton, MA 01748 United States

STOCK TICKER/OTHER:
Stock Ticker: Subsidiary
Employees: 71,250
Parent Company: Dell Technologies Inc

Exchange:
Fiscal Year Ends: 02/28

SALARIES/BONUSES:
Top Exec. Salary: $ Bonus: $
Second Exec. Salary: $ Bonus: $

OTHER THOUGHTS:
Estimated Female Officers or Directors: 2
Hot Spot for Advancement for Women/Minorities: Y

Sales, profits and employees may be estimates. Financial information, benefits and other data can change quickly and may vary from those stated here.

Dell Technologies Inc

NAIC Code: 334111

www.delltechnologies.com/en-us/index.htm

TYPES OF BUSINESS:
Computer Manufacturing
Direct Sales
Technical & Support Services
Online Music Service
Web Hosting Services
Printers & Accessories
Personal Music Players
Storage Devices

BRANDS/DIVISIONS/AFFILIATES:
Dell
Dell EMC
Pivotal
RSA
Secureworks
VirtuStream
Vmware

CONTACTS: Note: Officers with more than one job title may be intentionally listed here more than once.
Michael Dell, CEO
Thomas Sweet, CFO
Maya McReynolds, Chief Accounting Officer
Jeremy Burton, Chief Marketing Officer
Richard Rothberg, General Counsel
Karen Quintos, Other Executive Officer
Rory Read, Other Executive Officer
Steven Price, Other Executive Officer
Marius Haas, Other Executive Officer
William Scannell, President, Divisional
Howard Elias, President, Divisional
Jeffrey Clarke, Vice Chairman, Divisional

GROWTH PLANS/SPECIAL FEATURES:
Dell Technologies, Inc. is a multinational information technology corporation. The firm provides transformational devices, processes and services in order to modernize data centers, drive progress and help clients thrive within the digital era. Dell's products are divided into four groups. Within the digital transformation group, Dell's solutions for the Internet of Things (IoT), cloud-native applications and big data empower companies to reinvent their businesses and transform their IT infrastructure. IoT products are sensor-enabled equipment and smart devices that connect the physical world with the digital world, optimizing operations and delivering enhanced customer experience. Cloud-native applications transform businesses IT into modern and digital enterprises. Big data and analytics help businesses keep up with customer expectations via systems, smart devices and software. The IT transformation group comprises a hybrid cloud IT model modernizes data centers, automates IT processes and transforms operations; a converged infrastructure which streamlines operations and presents an on-demand business culture; and offers all-flash storage architecture. The workforce transformation group provides innovative devices for employees, digital workplace and data security solutions. Last, the security transformation group offers security operations solutions to mitigate advanced threats; identity and access management solutions; perimeter and endpoint security solutions; and governance, risk and compliance solutions. Brands by Dell Technologies include Dell, Dell EMC, Pivotal, RSA, Secureworks, VirtuStream and VMware.

Dell offers employees medical, dental, vision, life, disability, auto and home insurance; 401(k); and discounts and various assistance programs.

FINANCIAL DATA: Note: Data for latest year may not have been available at press time.

In U.S. $	2017	2016	2015	2014	2013	2012
Revenue	3,199,000,000					
R&D Expense	659,000,000					
Operating Income	737,000,000					
Operating Margin %	23.03%					
SGA Expense	1,350,000,000					
Net Income	492,000,000					
Operating Cash Flow						
Capital Expenditure						
EBITDA	737,000,000					
Return on Assets %	1.90%					
Return on Equity %	7.42%					
Debt to Equity						

CONTACT INFORMATION:
Phone: 512 338-4400   Fax: 512 283-6161
Toll-Free: 800-289-3355
Address: One Dell Way, Round Rock, TX 78682 United States

SALARIES/BONUSES:
Top Exec. Salary: $686,539   Bonus: $2,170,832
Second Exec. Salary: $950,000   Bonus: $

STOCK TICKER/OTHER:
Stock Ticker: DVMT   Exchange: NYS
Employees: 138,000   Fiscal Year Ends: 01/31
Parent Company: Silver Lake Partners

OTHER THOUGHTS:
Estimated Female Officers or Directors: 1
Hot Spot for Advancement for Women/Minorities: Y

Sales, profits and employees may be estimates. Financial information, benefits and other data can change quickly and may vary from those stated here.

Denso Corporation

NAIC Code: 336300

www.denso.com/global/en.html

TYPES OF BUSINESS:
Automobile Parts Manufacturer
Engine Components
Automotive Electrical Systems
Automotive Electronic Systems
Thermal Systems
Small Motors
Semiconductors
Industrial Robots

BRANDS/DIVISIONS/AFFILIATES:
DENSO
Denso Pres Tech Inc

CONTACTS: Note: Officers with more than one job title may be intentionally listed here more than once.
Koji Arima, CEO
Nobuaki Katoh, Pres.
Hikaru Sugi, Exec. VP
Hiromi Tokuda, Exec. VP
Koji Kobayashi, Exec. VP
Masahiko Miyaki, Exec. VP
Nobuaki Katoh,

GROWTH PLANS/SPECIAL FEATURES:
Denso Corporation is a global automotive supplier of advanced technology, systems and components. The company has 190 subsidiaries worldwide, including Japan (62), North America (28), Europe (35), Asia (13) and South America/others (2). Denso's products and services are divided into the mobility and industry/home categories. Mobility products and services include electronics, powertrain, thermal, information, safety, service parts, accessories and customer services. These products and services include electronic control units (ECUs), semiconductors, heat/cool generation and control, sensing systems, prediction systems, connectivity systems, protection systems and more. Industry/home's products and services include air conditioning equipment, industrial robots, barcode systems, QR code systems home energy management systems and carbon dioxide refrigerant heat pumps for water supply systems. All of the company's products are marketed under the DENSO brand name. In March 2018, Denso announced plans to integrate two of its subsidiaries into a single company, Denso Pres Tech, Inc., which will manufacture metal press-worked parts used in automobiles. The integrated company will enhance mass production technologies and manufacturing capabilities, and will be based in Aichi, Japan.

FINANCIAL DATA: Note: Data for latest year may not have been available at press time.

In U.S. $	2017	2016	2015	2014	2013	2012
Revenue	42,175,780,000	42,151,320,000	40,150,800,000	38,158,420,000	33,360,570,000	29,389,140,000
R&D Expense						
Operating Income	3,041,029,000	3,402,236,000	3,336,417,000	4,884,545,000	3,382,197,000	2,305,497,000
Operating Margin %	7.21%	8.07%	8.30%	12.80%	10.13%	7.84%
SGA Expense	4,017,068,000	3,838,411,000	3,721,483,000	702,068,200	695,202,200	547,773,400
Net Income	2,400,028,000	2,275,489,000	2,407,136,000	2,677,362,000	1,692,584,000	831,917,300
Operating Cash Flow	4,357,919,000	5,150,569,000	3,569,555,000	4,311,524,000	3,491,476,000	1,646,003,000
Capital Expenditure	3,208,636,000	3,208,310,000	3,396,833,000	2,933,576,000	2,109,242,000	1,616,071,000
EBITDA	5,700,242,000	5,523,896,000	5,602,786,000	5,822,098,000	4,379,011,000	3,260,844,000
Return on Assets %	5.05%	4.73%	5.31%	6.82%	4.78%	2.55%
Return on Equity %	8.00%	7.57%	8.58%	11.50%	8.42%	4.48%
Debt to Equity	0.08	0.06	0.10	0.11	0.15	0.23

CONTACT INFORMATION:
Phone: 81 566255511   Fax:
Toll-Free:
Address: 1-1 Showa-cho, Kariya, 448-8661 Japan

STOCK TICKER/OTHER:
Stock Ticker: DNZOF   Exchange: PINX
Employees: 151,775   Fiscal Year Ends: 03/31
Parent Company:

SALARIES/BONUSES:
Top Exec. Salary: $ Bonus: $
Second Exec. Salary: $ Bonus: $

OTHER THOUGHTS:
Estimated Female Officers or Directors:
Hot Spot for Advancement for Women/Minorities:

Sales, profits and employees may be estimates. Financial information, benefits and other data can change quickly and may vary from those stated here.

DIC Corporation

NAIC Code: 325910

www.dic.co.jp

TYPES OF BUSINESS:

Inks, Pigments & Printing Supplies
Packaging Materials
Synthetic Resins
Building Materials
Plastic Additives
Coatings & Finishes
Health Foods

BRANDS/DIVISIONS/AFFILIATES:

Sun Chemicals Corporation

CONTACTS: Note: Officers with more than one job title may be intentionally listed here more than once.

Kaoru Ino, CEO
Yoshiyuki Nakanishi, Pres.
Toshifumi Tamaki, Gen. Mgr.-R&D & Central Research Labs
Akira Konishi, Gen. Mgr.-Prod. Admin.
Tetsuro Agawa, Gen. Mgr.-Tech. Admin.
Kazou Kudo, Head-General Affairs & Legal
Masayuki Saito, Exec. VP-Finance & Acct.
Yoshiaki Masuda, Managing Dir.-DIC Asia Pacific Pte Ltd.
Hitoshi Wakabayashi, Gen. Mgr.-Fine Chemicals Prod.
Toshio Hasumi, CEO
Rudi Lenz, CEO
Toshio Kanbe, Gen. Mgr.-Purchasing & Logistics

GROWTH PLANS/SPECIAL FEATURES:

DIC Corporation is a manufacturer of inks and pigments, printing supplies and other chemical products. The company operates through more than 170 subsidiaries, including 32 domestic and 139 overseas, as of December 2017. DIC is organized into five business divisions: printing inks, polymers, fine chemicals, compounds and application materials. The printing Inks segment is a leader in the production of printing inks. Operating internationally through Sun Chemicals Corporation, the company produces a range of inks, including offset, gravure, flexo and news inks, as well as coatings, adhesives, presensitized plates and other printing supplies. The polymers segment is divided into general polymers and specialty polymers, producing synthetic resins for a broad array of industries. Products include a range of resins, including alkyd, unsaturated polyester, waterborne, acrylic, phenolic, epoxy, ultraviolet-curable and polyurethane. This segment additionally offers plasticizers, polystyrene and flourochemicals. The fine chemicals segment makes organic pigments, liquid crystal materials, alkyl phenols, metal carboxylates and sulfurized chemicals all for use in digital devices. The compounds division offers products that respond to needs arising from growth in such key global markets as digital printing, automobiles and electronics. Liquid compound products include Jet inks, coatings for optical films and inks for printed electronics. Solid compounds include plastic colorants, PPS compounds and high-performance optical materials. The applications materials segment produces applied products, divided into the categories of liquid compounds (jet inks and textile colorants), solid compounds (plastic colorants and high-performance optical materials) and processed products (sheet molding compounds, labels and stickers).

FINANCIAL DATA: Note: Data for latest year may not have been available at press time.

In U.S. $	2017	2016	2015	2014	2013	2012
Revenue	7,354,454,000	7,000,541,000	7,639,268,000	7,733,166,000	6,556,559,000	
R&D Expense	115,772,300	104,397,200	113,312,800			
Operating Income	526,206,500	1,014,645,000	1,023,002,000	1,017,310,000	853,474,900	
Operating Margin %	7.15%	14.49%	13.39%	13.15%	13.01%	
SGA Expense	117,346,800	138,168,400	138,401,300	130,883,200	123,924,000	
Net Income	359,633,000	323,896,000	348,369,700	234,712,100	177,603,900	
Operating Cash Flow	504,900,300	582,299,300	271,222,300	432,047,700	385,997,800	
Capital Expenditure	312,875,000	291,401,200	298,938,000	312,893,600	247,857,300	
EBITDA	840,907,500	800,633,500	907,527,500	744,428,900	641,764,500	
Return on Assets %	4.83%	4.50%	4.72%	3.13%	2.78%	
Return on Equity %	13.00%	12.85%	14.60%	10.08%	15.96%	
Debt to Equity	0.55	0.51	0.62	0.69	1.58	

CONTACT INFORMATION:

Phone: 81-3-6733-3000 Fax:
Toll-Free:
Address: 7-20, Nihonbashi 3-chome, Chuo-ku, Tokyo, 103-8233 Japan

SALARIES/BONUSES:

Top Exec. Salary: $ Bonus: $
Second Exec. Salary: $ Bonus: $

STOCK TICKER/OTHER:

Stock Ticker: DICCF Exchange: PINX
Employees: 20,628 Fiscal Year Ends: 12/31
Parent Company:

OTHER THOUGHTS:

Estimated Female Officers or Directors:
Hot Spot for Advancement for Women/Minorities:

Diebold Nixdorf Inc

NAIC Code: 334118

www.dieboldnixdorf.com/en-us

TYPES OF BUSINESS:
Computer Manufacturing
Self-Service Terminals
Security Systems
Technical Services
Software
Electronic Voting Machines

BRANDS/DIVISIONS/AFFILIATES:

CONTACTS: Note: Officers with more than one job title may be intentionally listed here more than once.
Gerrard Schmid, CEO
Christopher Chapman, CFO
Jurgen Wunram, COO
Gary Greenfield, Director
Jonathan Leiken, Other Executive Officer
Ulrich Naher, Senior VP, Divisional
Alan Kerr, Senior VP, Divisional
Olaf Heyden, Senior VP, Divisional

GROWTH PLANS/SPECIAL FEATURES:

Diebold Nixdorf, Inc. provides connected commerce services, software and technology to enable millions of finance transactions each day. The company designs and delivers always-on and highly-secure solutions to financial institutions that bridge the physical and digital capabilities of monetary transactions. Diebold Nixdorf's solutions include automated teller machines (ATMs), transaction security, remote management capabilities and technician experts/repairers. The firm's global ATMs help financial institutions grow revenue, reduce costs and increase convenience and security for the banks' customers by migrating routine transactions. Diebold Nixdorf's advisory services team collaborates with clients to help define the ideal customer experience, modify processes, refine existing staffing models and deploy technology to meet branch automation objectives. In-lobby teller terminals provide automation technology by combining the speed and accuracy of a self-service terminal with intelligence from the bank's core systems, as well as the ability to complete higher value transactions away from the teller line. The company also offers hardware-agnostic, omni-channel software solutions for ATMs as well as other self-service applications, including configurable, enterprise-wide software that automates and migrates financial services across channels. Security solutions include: physical security systems such as pneumatic tube systems for drive-up lanes, as well as video and audio capabilities for remote transactions; barrier systems such as vaults, safes, depositories, bullet-resistive items and under-counter equipment; electronic security and monitoring systems such as video management, web-based solutions, fire detection, managed access control and more. Diebold Nixdorf sells and services its financial self-service solutions, retail solutions and security systems worldwide through wholly-owned subsidiaries, alliances, joint ventures and independent distributors located in more than 130 countries.

FINANCIAL DATA: Note: Data for latest year may not have been available at press time.

In U.S. $	2017	2016	2015	2014	2013	2012
Revenue	4,609,300,000	3,316,300,000	2,419,300,000	3,051,053,000	2,857,491,000	2,991,693,000
R&D Expense	155,500,000	110,200,000	86,900,000	93,617,000	92,315,000	85,881,000
Operating Income	-79,500,000	-149,700,000	76,900,000	170,182,000	-48,653,000	139,293,000
Operating Margin %	-1.72%	-4.51%	3.17%	5.57%	-1.70%	4.65%
SGA Expense	933,700,000	761,200,000	488,200,000	515,551,000	596,694,000	510,979,000
Net Income	-233,100,000	-33,000,000	73,700,000	114,417,000	-181,605,000	78,454,000
Operating Cash Flow	37,100,000	28,400,000	36,700,000	186,906,000	124,224,000	135,508,000
Capital Expenditure	69,400,000	39,500,000	52,300,000	61,453,000	35,447,000	62,819,000
EBITDA	193,800,000	-2,100,000	142,300,000	276,081,000	-7,979,000	226,400,000
Return on Assets %	-4.43%	-.87%	3.21%	5.05%	-7.60%	3.07%
Return on Equity %	-43.92%	-6.57%	15.61%	20.28%	-25.81%	9.58%
Debt to Equity	3.80	2.85	1.48	0.90	0.80	0.76

CONTACT INFORMATION:
Phone: 330 490-4000   Fax:
Toll-Free: 800-999-3600
Address: 5995 Mayfair Rd., North Canton, OH 44720 United States

SALARIES/BONUSES:
Top Exec. Salary: $963,382   Bonus: $
Second Exec. Salary: $598,446   Bonus: $

STOCK TICKER/OTHER:
Stock Ticker: DBD
Employees: 25,000
Parent Company:

Exchange: NYS
Fiscal Year Ends: 12/31

OTHER THOUGHTS:
Estimated Female Officers or Directors:
Hot Spot for Advancement for Women/Minorities: Y

Sales, profits and employees may be estimates. Financial information, benefits and other data can change quickly and may vary from those stated here.

DLZ Corporation

NAIC Code: 541330

dlz.com

TYPES OF BUSINESS:
Engineering Services
Engineering
Architecture
Construction
Consulting

BRANDS/DIVISIONS/AFFILIATES:
DLZ Hydrokinetic Company
India Hydropower Development Company LLC

CONTACTS: Note: Officers with more than one job title may be intentionally listed here more than once.
Vikram Rajadhyaksha, CEO
Joseph Zwierzynski, COO
Shyam Rajadhyaksha, CFO
Hollie Linton, Dir.-Ohio Mktg.
Ram Rajadhyaksha, Corporate Secretary
Vikram Rajadhyaksha, Chmn.

GROWTH PLANS/SPECIAL FEATURES:
DLZ Corporation provides consulting services to the engineering, architecture and construction industries. It has 22 offices that partners with clients to develop the best solutions to achieve the goals of any project. This includes architecture, construction management, energy, environmental, geotechnical, landscape architecture, planning, program management, survey, transportation and water. Market sectors of the firm include criminal justice, education, federal/state/local governments as well as private sectors. Just a few of the firm's many projects include the Maumee River Crossing bridge in Toledo, Ohio; the Lucas Oil Stadium in Indianapolis, Indiana; the Main Street Bridge in Columbus, Ohio; and the Intercity Bus Transportation Facility in St. Ignace, Michigan. DLZ Hydrokinetic Company is engaged in research and development of innovative hydrokinetic technology. The firm has formed India Hydropower Development Company, LLC in partnership with Infrastructure India Plc, which focuses on the development of hydropower projects in India.

The firm offers its employees health and life insurance; healthcare and dependent care savings account; flexible work hours; short-and long-term disability; 401(k) plan; tuition reimbursement; wellness program including gym reimbursement; vacation and sic

FINANCIAL DATA: Note: Data for latest year may not have been available at press time.

In U.S. $	2017	2016	2015	2014	2013	2012
Revenue	100,000,000					
R&D Expense						
Operating Income						
Operating Margin %						
SGA Expense						
Net Income						
Operating Cash Flow						
Capital Expenditure						
EBITDA						
Return on Assets %						
Return on Equity %						
Debt to Equity						

CONTACT INFORMATION:
Phone: 216-771-1090　　Fax: 216-771-0034
Toll-Free:
Address: 6121 Huntley Rd., Columbus, OH 44113 United States

SALARIES/BONUSES:
Top Exec. Salary: $　　Bonus: $
Second Exec. Salary: $　　Bonus: $

STOCK TICKER/OTHER:
Stock Ticker: Private　　Exchange:
Employees: 600　　Fiscal Year Ends:
Parent Company:

OTHER THOUGHTS:
Estimated Female Officers or Directors:
Hot Spot for Advancement for Women/Minorities:

Sales, profits and employees may be estimates. Financial information, benefits and other data can change quickly and may vary from those stated here.

DNV GL Group AS

NAIC Code: 541330

www.dnvgl.com

TYPES OF BUSINESS:
Engineering Services

BRANDS/DIVISIONS/AFFILIATES:
Det Norske Veritas Holding AS

CONTACTS:
Note: Officers with more than one job title may be intentionally listed here more than once.

Remi Eriksen, CEO
Henrick O. Madsen, Pres.
Thomas Vogth-Eriksen, CFO
Ulrike Haugen, Chief Communications Officer
Gro Gotteberg, Human Resources Officer
Adeline Yap, Sr. Comm. Officer
Tor Svensen, CEO-Maritime
Knut Orbeck-Nilssen, Pres., Maritime
Elisabeth Torstad, CEO-Oil & Gas
David Walker, CEO-Energy
Leif-Arne Langoy, Chmn.

GROWTH PLANS/SPECIAL FEATURES:
DNV GL Group AS, based in Norway, is a leading classification society (which maintains the organization and upholds the technical standards of ships and offshore structures) with a focus on additional business areas. DNV GL enables organizations to advance the safety and sustainability of their businesses. With 300 sites in more than 100 countries, the firm serves five primary sectors: maritime, oil & gas, energy, business assurance and software. For the maritime industry, DNV GL is a leading classification society and advisor, enhancing safety, quality, energy efficiency and environmental performance of the global shipping industry across all vessel types and offshore structures. For the oil and gas industry, the firm provides technical advisory services, integrated services within technical and marine assurance, risk management, as well as offshore classification in order to enable safe, reliable and enhanced performance in projects and operations. For the energy industry, DNV GL delivers testing and advisory services to the energy value chain, including renewables and energy efficiency. This division's expertise spans onshore and offshore wind power, solar, conventional generation, transmission/distribution, smart grids and sustainable energy use and regulations. For the business assurance industry, DNV GL is a leading certification firm that helps businesses assure the performance of their organizations, products, people, facilities and supply chains through certification, verification, assessment and training services. The software segment provides ecologically-focused software for the energy, process and maritime industries. This division's solutions support a variety of business-critical activities, including design and engineering, risk assessment, asset integrity and optimization, QHSE (quality health safety environment) and ship management. In December 2017, Det Norske Veritas Holding AS acquired Mayfair's 36.5% share in DNV GL, giving Det Norske full ownership of the company.

FINANCIAL DATA:
Note: Data for latest year may not have been available at press time.

In U.S. $	2017	2016	2015	2014	2013	2012
Revenue	2,369,300,000	2,415,760,000	2,671,000,000	2,901,440,000	2,487,710,000	2,242,790,000
R&D Expense						
Operating Income						
Operating Margin %						
SGA Expense						
Net Income	7,421,170	-25,045,800	115,793,000	135,122,000	109,574,000	103,621,000
Operating Cash Flow						
Capital Expenditure						
EBITDA						
Return on Assets %						
Return on Equity %						
Debt to Equity						

CONTACT INFORMATION:
Phone: 47-6757-9900 Fax:
Toll-Free:
Address: Veritasveien 1, Hovik, 1363 Norway

STOCK TICKER/OTHER:
Stock Ticker: Private Exchange:
Employees: 12,715 Fiscal Year Ends:
Parent Company: Det Norske Veritas Holding AS

SALARIES/BONUSES:
Top Exec. Salary: $ Bonus: $
Second Exec. Salary: $ Bonus: $

OTHER THOUGHTS:
Estimated Female Officers or Directors: 7
Hot Spot for Advancement for Women/Minorities: Y

Sales, profits and employees may be estimates. Financial information, benefits and other data can change quickly and may vary from those stated here.

Dongfeng Motor Corporation

NAIC Code: 336111

www.dfmc.com.cn

TYPES OF BUSINESS:
Automobile Manufacturing
Truck & Bus Manufacturing
Auto Parts & Components Manufacturing

BRANDS/DIVISIONS/AFFILIATES:
ix5

GROWTH PLANS/SPECIAL FEATURES:

Dongfeng Motor Corporation (DFM) is one of China's leading automakers. Established as a state-owned company in 1969, DFM was restructured in the 1990s and has since sought out numerous joint ventures as well as integrating its development with international automotive companies. Subsequently, the firm has become one of the Chinese automotive companies most heavily vested in foreign partnerships. DFM's products are categorized into two groups: commercial vehicles and passenger vehicles. Commercial vehicles include various types of heavy duty trucks, semis, buses, motor coaches, sanitation vehicles, hybrids and tankers. Passenger vehicles include sedans, compact cars, sport utility vehicles (SUVs), vans and mini vans. In 2018, DFM introduced its ix5 crossover vehicle which will be launched on the Chinese market by year's end, and was made in conjunction with Baidu Apollo, a software platform for auto manufacturing partners to develop their own autonomous driving systems via on-vehicle and hardware platforms.

CONTACTS:
Note: Officers with more than one job title may be intentionally listed here more than once.

Zhu Yanfeng, CEO
Jun Seki, Pres.
Cai Wei, VP
Fan Zhong, Exec. Dir.
Li Shaozhu, Exec. Dir.
Hu Xindong, Joint Sec.
Susan Lo Yee Har, Joint Sec.

FINANCIAL DATA:
Note: Data for latest year may not have been available at press time.

In U.S. $	2017	2016	2015	2014	2013	2012
Revenue	18,444,100,000	17,621,700,000	19,576,351,777	13,028,413,251	6,069,000,000	991,900,000
R&D Expense						
Operating Income						
Operating Margin %						
SGA Expense						
Net Income	2,074,800,000	2,000,100,000	1,786,529,167	2,143,345,698	1,714,700,000	1,480,800,000
Operating Cash Flow						
Capital Expenditure						
EBITDA						
Return on Assets %						
Return on Equity %						
Debt to Equity						

CONTACT INFORMATION:
Phone: 86-719-8226-962 Fax: 86-719-8226-845
Toll-Free:
Address: 29 Baiye Rd., Wuhan, Hubei 430015 China

STOCK TICKER/OTHER:
Stock Ticker: 489
Employees: 146,843
Parent Company:

Exchange: Hong Kong
Fiscal Year Ends: 12/31

SALARIES/BONUSES:
Top Exec. Salary: $ Bonus: $
Second Exec. Salary: $ Bonus: $

OTHER THOUGHTS:
Estimated Female Officers or Directors: 1
Hot Spot for Advancement for Women/Minorities:

Doosan Heavy Industries & Construction Co Ltd

www.doosanheavy.com

NAIC Code: 237130

TYPES OF BUSINESS:

Power and Communication Line and Related Structures Construction
Power Plant Construction
Desalination Plant Construction
Civil Works Projects
Architecture Works Projects
Casting & Forging
Material Handling Systems

BRANDS/DIVISIONS/AFFILIATES:

Doosan Power Systems
Doosan Babcock
Doosan Skoda Power
Doosan Lentjes
Doosan Enpure
Doosan IMGB
Doosan Turbomachinery Services
ACT Independent Turbo Services

CONTACTS: Note: Officers with more than one job title may be intentionally listed here more than once.

Geewon Park, CEO
Myungwoo Kim, Pres.
Hyounghee Choi, COO
Ji Taik Chung, Vice Chmn.

GROWTH PLANS/SPECIAL FEATURES:

Doosan Heavy Industries & Construction Co., Ltd., established in 1962, is an engineering, procurement and construction contractor. The firm offers a range of services ranging from the manufacturing of castings and forgings, power generation systems and desalination facilities to the construction of power plants. U.K. subsidiary Doosan Power Systems provides integrated power solutions, including the construction of power plants, and the manufacture of boilers, turbines and equipment for nuclear and wind power stations. U.K.-based Doosan Babcock specializes in delivering power generation systems using state-of-the-art technologies related to boilers, oxyfuel and other areas. Czech Republic-based Doosan Skoda Power produces turbines, having delivered more than 450 turbines to customers in 62 countries. German-based Doosan Lentjes provides cutting-edge proprietary technologies for circulating fluidized bed boiler units, air quality control systems, selective catalytic reduction DeNOx systems and fabric filters. This subsidiary also plans and builds waste-to-energy plants. U.K.-based Doosan Enpure is a process engineering company with expertise in design, technology and project delivery for water and wastewater sectors. Romania-based Doosan IMGB is the country's largest maker of power generation systems, industrial machinery and castings and forgings. In September 2017, Doosan Heavy acquired ACT Independent Turbo Services, a U.S. gas turbine service company, which was renamed Doosan Turbomachinery Services.

FINANCIAL DATA: Note: Data for latest year may not have been available at press time.

In U.S. $	2017	2016	2015	2014	2013	2012
Revenue	13,567,080,000	12,977,750,000	15,137,150,000	16,933,700,000	17,943,180,000	8,993,165,000
R&D Expense	175,039,700	179,015,400	262,851,000	259,688,000	252,869,700	34,153,200
Operating Income	864,772,600	739,068,500	57,978,650	829,742,000	894,975,900	555,664,700
Operating Margin %	6.37%	5.69%	.38%	4.89%	4.98%	6.17%
SGA Expense	473,772,100	432,686,600	644,497,300	647,354,800	680,182,000	276,395,900
Net Income	-272,805,300	-159,505,600	-970,147,800	-88,440,150	64,664,660	35,539,450
Operating Cash Flow	401,050,700	903,845,600	-69,474,220	564,043,800	140,530,400	343,578,700
Capital Expenditure	518,602,400	504,060,500	600,279,700	591,652,700	620,080,400	326,922,000
EBITDA	1,057,473,000	746,734,800	-320,030,600	957,158,000	1,231,108,000	385,380,700
Return on Assets %	-1.17%	-.65%	-3.78%	-.34%	.33%	.28%
Return on Equity %	-8.67%	-4.93%	-25.61%	-2.03%	1.49%	.82%
Debt to Equity	1.46	1.33	1.70	1.44	1.51	0.57

CONTACT INFORMATION:

Phone: 82 552786114 Fax: 82 552645551
Toll-Free:
Address: 22 Doosan Volvo-ro, Seongsan-Gu, Changwon, Gyeongnam 51711 South Korea

STOCK TICKER/OTHER:

Stock Ticker: DOHFF
Employees: 8,400
Parent Company:

Exchange: GREY
Fiscal Year Ends:

SALARIES/BONUSES:

Top Exec. Salary: $ Bonus: $
Second Exec. Salary: $ Bonus: $

OTHER THOUGHTS:

Estimated Female Officers or Directors:
Hot Spot for Advancement for Women/Minorities:

Dorsch Gruppe

NAIC Code: 541330

www.dorsch.de

TYPES OF BUSINESS:
Engineering Consulting Services
Consulting
Engineering

BRANDS/DIVISIONS/AFFILIATES:
RAG-Stiftung Investment Company
RAG-Stiftung Beteiligungsgesellschaft GmbH
Dorsch International Consultants GmbH
Dorsch Gruppe BDC
Dorsch Gruppe DC Asia
Dorsch Gruppe DC India
Dorsch Gruppe DC-Abu Dhabi

CONTACTS: *Note: Officers with more than one job title may be intentionally listed here more than once.*
Olaf Hoffmann, CEO

GROWTH PLANS/SPECIAL FEATURES:
Dorsch Gruppe is a consulting and engineering firm for industrial clients, private investors and public institutions. It is one of Germany's largest independent planning and consulting companies, located in more than 40 countries. Dorsch Gruppe services include construction engineering, both civil and structural; airports, involving planning and equipment; transport and infrastructure, including roads and railways; water and environment, including water supply, sanitary engineering, hydraulic engineering, hydroinformatics, landfills and hazardous waste, geotechnical engineering, environmental planning and water loss reduction; renewable energy, including green building technology and photovoltaic; project management; construction supervision; interdisciplinary services, including organizational advisory services, international cooperation and feasibility studies; architecture; urban development; industrial engineering, such as buildings, industrial plants and oil and gas; and marinal engineering, such as studies and assessments, guidelines, specifications, manuals, marine operations planning, design, technical bid evaluation, risk & safety environment and third party verification. Affiliates of the firm include Dorsch International Consultants GmbH, Dorsch Gruppe BDC, Dorsch Gruppe DC Asia, Dorsch Gruppe DC India and Dorsch Gruppe DC-Abu Dhabi. RAG-Stiftung Beteiligungsgesellschaft GmbH, an investment arm of RAG-Stiftung Investment Company, holds a 70% stake in the Dorsch Gruppe.

FINANCIAL DATA: *Note: Data for latest year may not have been available at press time.*

In U.S. $	2017	2016	2015	2014	2013	2012
Revenue						
R&D Expense						
Operating Income						
Operating Margin %						
SGA Expense						
Net Income						
Operating Cash Flow						
Capital Expenditure						
EBITDA						
Return on Assets %						
Return on Equity %						
Debt to Equity						

CONTACT INFORMATION:
Phone: 49-69-130257-0   Fax: 49-69-130257-32
Toll-Free:
Address: Berliner St. 74-76, Offenbach am Main, 63065 Germany

STOCK TICKER/OTHER:
Stock Ticker: Private   Exchange:
Employees: 2,000   Fiscal Year Ends:
Parent Company: RAG-Stiftung Investment Company

SALARIES/BONUSES:
Top Exec. Salary: $ Bonus: $
Second Exec. Salary: $ Bonus: $

OTHER THOUGHTS:
Estimated Female Officers or Directors:
Hot Spot for Advancement for Women/Minorities:

Sales, profits and employees may be estimates. Financial information, benefits and other data can change quickly and may vary from those stated here.

DowDupont Inc

NAIC Code: 325199

www.dow-dupont.com/home/default.aspx

TYPES OF BUSINESS:
Specialty Chemicals Manufacturer
Electronic & Functional Materials
Coatings & Infrastructure
Agricultural Sciences
Performance Materials
Performance Plastics
Feedstocks & Energy

BRANDS/DIVISIONS/AFFILIATES:
Dow Corning Corporation
DuPont

CONTACTS:
Note: Officers with more than one job title may be intentionally listed here more than once.

Edward Breen, CEO
Charles Kalil, Other Corporate Officer
Howard Ungerleider, CFO
Andrew Liveris, Chairman of the Board
Ronald Edmonds, Co-Controller
Jeanmarie Desmond, Co-Controller
James Collins, COO, Divisional
Christopher Doyle, COO, Divisional
James Fitterling, COO, Divisional
Stacy Fox, General Counsel

GROWTH PLANS/SPECIAL FEATURES:

DowDuPont, Inc., formed by the 2017 merger between Dow and DuPont, the company operates through three divisions: agriculture, materials science and specialty products. The agriculture division offers a complete portfolio of products and technologies, as well as a pipeline of germplasm, traits and crop protection. Its solutions include various herbicides, fungicides, insecticides, pasture and land management, seed-applied technologies, structural pest management and turf and ornamental pest management. Its seeds solutions apply to alfalfa, canola, cereals, corn, cotton, rice, silage inoculants, sorghum, soybeans, sunflowers and wheat. The materials science division is further divided into three categories: performance materials and coatings, offering technology platforms that empower DowDuPont customers to create ingredients and solutions with performance and process enhancements for home and beauty care applications; industrial intermediates and infrastructure, which enable unique properties in manufacturing processes, infrastructure markets and downstream finished goods; and packaging and specialty plastics, comprising plastic portfolios that offer solutions and technologies for addressing consumer and brand owner demand for increased packaging convenience, food waste reduction and the global development of telecommunications and electric transmission and distribution infrastructure. Last, the specialty products division is divided into six categories: electronics and imaging, serving the semiconductor, advanced chip packaging, circuit board, electronic and other industries; industrial biosciences, offering solutions that improve the performance, productivity and sustainability of customer products; nutrition and health, offering sustainable, bio-based ingredients; safety and construction, offering high-performance fibers and foams, aramid papers, non-woven structures, membranes and filtration technologies and more; sustainable solutions, offering operations management consulting, services and technologies; and transportation and advanced polymers, providing high-performance engineering resins, adhesives, lubricants and parts to engineers and designers in the transportation, electronics and medical markets.

FINANCIAL DATA:
Note: Data for latest year may not have been available at press time.

In U.S. $	2017	2016	2015	2014	2013	2012
Revenue	62,484,000,000	48,158,000,000	48,778,000,000	58,167,000,000	57,080,000,000	56,786,000,000
R&D Expense	2,110,000,000	1,584,000,000	1,598,000,000	1,647,000,000	1,747,000,000	1,708,000,000
Operating Income	4,926,000,000	5,085,000,000	5,954,000,000	5,514,000,000	4,254,000,000	3,947,000,000
Operating Margin %	7.88%	10.55%	12.20%	9.47%	7.45%	6.95%
SGA Expense	4,021,000,000	3,304,000,000	2,971,000,000	3,106,000,000	3,024,000,000	2,861,000,000
Net Income	1,460,000,000	4,318,000,000	7,685,000,000	3,772,000,000	4,787,000,000	1,182,000,000
Operating Cash Flow	8,695,000,000	5,478,000,000	7,516,000,000	6,502,000,000	7,823,000,000	4,075,000,000
Capital Expenditure	3,570,000,000	3,991,000,000	3,826,000,000	3,572,000,000	2,302,000,000	2,614,000,000
EBITDA	6,244,000,000	8,133,000,000	13,397,000,000	8,995,000,000	10,586,000,000	5,632,000,000
Return on Assets %	1.07%	5.36%	10.66%	4.92%	6.33%	1.19%
Return on Equity %	2.31%	16.70%	36.65%	16.48%	22.16%	4.71%
Debt to Equity	0.29	0.78	0.75	1.02	0.73	1.18

CONTACT INFORMATION:
Phone: 989 636-1000 Fax: 989 636-3518
Toll-Free: 800-422-8193
Address: 2030 Dow Ctr., Midland, MI 48674 United States

STOCK TICKER/OTHER:
Stock Ticker: DWDP
Employees: 56,000
Parent Company:

Exchange: NYS
Fiscal Year Ends: 12/31

SALARIES/BONUSES:
Top Exec. Salary: $1,930,800 Bonus: $
Second Exec. Salary: $1,134,578 Bonus: $

OTHER THOUGHTS:
Estimated Female Officers or Directors: 3
Hot Spot for Advancement for Women/Minorities: Y

Sales, profits and employees may be estimates. Financial information, benefits and other data can change quickly and may vary from those stated here.

Downer EDI Limited

NAIC Code: 541330

www.downergroup.co.nz/

TYPES OF BUSINESS:
Engineering Services
Construction Services
Railroad Infrastructure Management

BRANDS/DIVISIONS/AFFILIATES:
Hawkins
Spotless Group Holdings Limited
Envista

CONTACTS:
Note: Officers with more than one job title may be intentionally listed here more than once.

Grant Fenn, CEO
Michael Ferguson, CFO
Steve Schofield, Human Resources
Peter Tompkins, General Counsel
David Cattell, CEO-Downer Infrastructure
Ross Spicer, CEO-Downer Rail
David Overall, CEO-Downer Mining
Campbell Mason, Chief Risk Officer
Michael Harding, Chmn.

GROWTH PLANS/SPECIAL FEATURES:
Downer EDI Limited supports customers through the full life of their assets, from initial feasibility and design through to production, operations and eventual decommissioning. The firm's construction and manufacturing capabilities meet the diverse needs of its customers in a variety of industries. Downer engages in roads, transport infrastructure, transport solutions, renewables, industrial plants, facilities management, rail, bridges, power/gas, communications, minerals processing, non-residential building, light rail, buses, airports, ports, water, oil/gas, mining services and defense. The company has over 300 sites across Australia and New Zealand. In 2017, Downer acquired Hawkins, a leading builder in New Zealand; and acquired a majority-stake (88%) in Spotless Group Holdings Limited, a provider of integrated facility services in Australia and New Zealand. In March 2018, the firm acquired Envista, a provider of strategy, architecture and delivery services in complex and sensitive environments.

FINANCIAL DATA:
Note: Data for latest year may not have been available at press time.

In U.S. $	2017	2016	2015	2014	2013	2012
Revenue	5,626,796,000	5,292,738,000	5,448,466,000	5,699,463,000	6,479,835,000	6,138,956,000
R&D Expense						
Operating Income	182,446,600	187,417,500	236,660,200	238,925,000	253,708,700	190,013,200
Operating Margin %	3.24%	3.54%	4.34%	4.19%	3.91%	3.09%
SGA Expense	2,157,437,000	2,142,602,000	2,023,534,000	2,185,128,000	2,383,059,000	2,223,336,000
Net Income	140,970,900	140,271,800	163,262,100	167,729,700	158,430,300	87,585,240
Operating Cash Flow	342,990,300	347,805,800	377,864,100	453,147,200	351,355,300	283,084,300
Capital Expenditure	187,572,800	179,495,100	161,398,000	304,825,600	276,259,400	295,584,400
EBITDA	397,980,600	421,592,200	442,097,100	477,022,100	511,370,900	402,285,800
Return on Assets %	3.11%	4.16%	5.06%	5.14%	4.73%	2.60%
Return on Equity %	6.92%	8.29%	10.44%	12.06%	12.71%	7.06%
Debt to Equity	0.18	0.28	0.23	0.16	0.26	0.30

CONTACT INFORMATION:
Phone: 61-2-9468-9700 Fax: 61-2-9813-8915
Toll-Free: 800-369-637
Address: 39 Delhi Rd., North Ryde, NSW 2113 Australia

STOCK TICKER/OTHER:
Stock Ticker: DNERY   Exchange: GREY
Employees: Fiscal Year Ends: 06/30
Parent Company:

SALARIES/BONUSES:
Top Exec. Salary: $ Bonus: $
Second Exec. Salary: $ Bonus: $

OTHER THOUGHTS:
Estimated Female Officers or Directors: 3
Hot Spot for Advancement for Women/Minorities: Y

Sales, profits and employees may be estimates. Financial information, benefits and other data can change quickly and may vary from those stated here.

Dyson Limited

NAIC Code: 335210

www.dyson.co.uk

TYPES OF BUSINESS:
Vacuum Cleaner Manufacturing
Artificial Intelligence
Hair Dryers and Air Filters
Robotics
Advanced, Solid-State Battery Technologies
Research and Development
Consumer and Household Goods
Electric Car Technologies

BRANDS/DIVISIONS/AFFILIATES:
Dyson Supersonic
Air Multiplier
Dyson Airblade
CSYS
Cu-Beam

CONTACTS:
Note: Officers with more than one job title may be intentionally listed here more than once.

Jim Rowan, CEO
Jake Dyson, VP
James Dyson, Chmn.

GROWTH PLANS/SPECIAL FEATURES:

Dyson Limited is a British technology company that designs and manufactures vacuum cleaners, hair dryers, hand dryers, fans, heaters and lighting. Owner and Inventor James Dyson built an industrial cyclone tower that separated particles from the air using centrifugal force. More than 5,000 prototypes later, the Dyson bagless vacuum cleaner was invented. Today, there are Dyson machines in over 65 countries worldwide, and Dyson Limited employs more than 1,000 engineers and scientists engaged in research, design and development. Vacuum cleaner products include uprights, cylinders, cordless, handheld, robot and parts. The Dyson Supersonic handheld hair dryer comprises a motor uniquely position in the handle. The digital motor spins on average six times faster than other hair dryer motors at one inaudible frequency, at one-third less weight. Its 13-blade impeller generates pressure, propelling 13 liters of air up to the amplifier every second. With the motor in the handle, there is space in the head for this Air Multiplier technology. Hand dryers, primarily used in bathrooms, replace the need for towels after washing one's hands. Dyson Airblade hand dryers are hygienic, quiet and use 430-miles-per-hour sheets of air to scrape water from hands, drying them in just 10-12 seconds. Room fans are therefore bladeless, safe and clean; bladeless purifiers remove allergens and pollutants; bladeless heaters provide fast, even room heating; and bladeless humidifiers provide hygienic humidification with even room coverage. Lighting products include the CSYS desk lamp with heat pipe technology to cool light emitting diodes (LEDs), providing powerful lighting precisely where it is needed; and the Cu-Bean suspended light, which also utilizes heat pipe technology, hangs from the ceiling primarily in office locations. Dyson announced plans (as of February 2018) to design three new electric vehicles over the next decade, each of which will also adopt a solid-state battery pack.

FINANCIAL DATA:
Note: Data for latest year may not have been available at press time.

In U.S. $	2017	2016	2015	2014	2013	2012
Revenue	4,358,690,000	3,598,180,000	2,521,760,000			
R&D Expense						
Operating Income						
Operating Margin %						
SGA Expense						
Net Income		785,000,000	465,000,000			
Operating Cash Flow						
Capital Expenditure						
EBITDA						
Return on Assets %						
Return on Equity %						
Debt to Equity						

CONTACT INFORMATION:
Phone: Fax: 01666 827 200
Toll-Free: 0800-298-0298
Address: Tetbury Hill, Malmesbury, Wiltshire SN16 0RP United Kingdom

STOCK TICKER/OTHER:
Stock Ticker: Private   Exchange:
Employees: 7,350   Fiscal Year Ends: 03/31
Parent Company:

SALARIES/BONUSES:
Top Exec. Salary: $ Bonus: $
Second Exec. Salary: $ Bonus: $

OTHER THOUGHTS:
Estimated Female Officers or Directors:
Hot Spot for Advancement for Women/Minorities:

Sales, profits and employees may be estimates. Financial information, benefits and other data can change quickly and may vary from those stated here.

Eastman Chemical Company

NAIC Code: 325220

www.eastman.com

TYPES OF BUSINESS:
Chemicals, Fibers & Plastics
Coatings, Adhesives & Additives
Performance & Intermediate Chemicals
Acetate Fibers & Textiles
Gasification Services
Food Safety Diagnostics
Logistics Services
PET, Polyethylene & Polymers

BRANDS/DIVISIONS/AFFILIATES:
Estrobond
Estron
Chromspun

CONTACTS:
Note: Officers with more than one job title may be intentionally listed here more than once.

Curtis Espeland, CFO
Scott King, Chief Accounting Officer
Stephen Crawford, Chief Technology Officer
Mark Costa, Director
Brad Lich, Executive VP
David Golden, Other Executive Officer
Mark Cox, Other Executive Officer
Perry Stuckey, Other Executive Officer
Damon Warmack, Senior VP, Divisional
Lucian Boldea, Senior VP, Divisional

GROWTH PLANS/SPECIAL FEATURES:
Eastman Chemical Company manufactures and sells a broad portfolio of chemicals, plastics and fibers through 48 manufacturing sites in 14 countries. The firm has four operating segments: additives & functional products (AFP); fibers; advanced materials; and chemical intermediates. The AFP segment manufactures chemicals for products in the coatings, tires, consumables, building and construction, industrial applications including solar energy markets, animal nutrition, care chemicals, crop protection, and energy markets. Key technology platforms in this segment are cellulose esters, polyester polymers, insoluble sulfur, hydrocarbon resins, alkylamine derivatives and propylene derivatives. The fibers segment manufactures Estron acetate and Estrobond triacetin plasticizers for use in cigarette filters; Estron natural and Chromspun solution-dyed acetate yarns for the apparel, home furnishing and industrial fabrics industries; and cellulose acetate and acetyl raw materials for other acetate fiber producers. The advanced materials segment produces specialized co-polyesters, cellulosic plastics, aftermarket window films, polyvinyl butyral sheets and resins used in industries including transportation, consumables, building and construction. The chemical intermediates segment sells excess intermediates beyond our specialty needs for use in markets such as industrial chemicals and processing, building and construction, health and wellness and agrochemicals. Key technology platforms include acetyls, oxos, plasticizers, polyesters and alkylamines.

The company offers employees health, life, dependent life and disability insurance; a 401(k); and an employee stock purchase plan.

FINANCIAL DATA:
Note: Data for latest year may not have been available at press time.

In U.S. $	2017	2016	2015	2014	2013	2012
Revenue	9,549,000,000	9,008,000,000	9,648,000,000	9,527,000,000	9,350,000,000	8,102,000,000
R&D Expense	215,000,000	219,000,000	251,000,000	227,000,000	193,000,000	198,000,000
Operating Income	1,540,000,000	1,428,000,000	1,567,000,000	1,239,000,000	1,938,000,000	920,000,000
Operating Margin %	16.12%	15.85%	16.24%	13.00%	20.72%	11.35%
SGA Expense	699,000,000	703,000,000	762,000,000	755,000,000	645,000,000	644,000,000
Net Income	1,384,000,000	854,000,000	848,000,000	751,000,000	1,165,000,000	437,000,000
Operating Cash Flow	1,657,000,000	1,385,000,000	1,612,000,000	1,408,000,000	1,297,000,000	1,128,000,000
Capital Expenditure	649,000,000	626,000,000	652,000,000	596,000,000	488,000,000	470,000,000
EBITDA	2,120,000,000	1,910,000,000	1,979,000,000	1,643,000,000	2,298,000,000	1,157,000,000
Return on Assets %	8.79%	5.49%	5.35%	5.38%	9.93%	4.90%
Return on Equity %	27.86%	20.15%	22.76%	20.55%	34.57%	18.15%
Debt to Equity	1.13	1.39	1.67	2.06	1.12	1.62

CONTACT INFORMATION:
Phone: 423 229-2000 Fax: 423 229-2145
Toll-Free:
Address: 200 S. Wilcox Dr., Kingsport, TN 37662 United States

STOCK TICKER/OTHER:
Stock Ticker: EMN
Employees: 14,000
Parent Company:

Exchange: NYS
Fiscal Year Ends: 12/31

SALARIES/BONUSES:
Top Exec. Salary: $1,139,436   Bonus: $
Second Exec. Salary: $751,506   Bonus: $

OTHER THOUGHTS:
Estimated Female Officers or Directors: 2
Hot Spot for Advancement for Women/Minorities: Y

Sales, profits and employees may be estimates. Financial information, benefits and other data can change quickly and may vary from those stated here.

Eaton Corporation plc

NAIC Code: 336300

www.eaton.com

TYPES OF BUSINESS:
Hydraulic Products
Electrical Power Distribution & Control Equipment
Truck Transmissions & Axles
Engine Components
Aerospace & Military Components

BRANDS/DIVISIONS/AFFILIATES:

CONTACTS: Note: Officers with more than one job title may be intentionally listed here more than once.
Craig Arnold, CEO
Richard H. Fearon, CFO
Ramanath Ramakrishnan, CTO
Mark M. McGuire, General Counsel
Richard H. Fearon, Chief Planning Officer
Donald J. McGrath, Sr. VP-Comm.
Donald H. Bullock, Jr., Sr. VP-Investor Rel.
Ken D. Semelsberger, Controller
Uday Yadav, Pres., Aerospace Group
Curtis J. Hutchins, Pres., Asia Pacific Region
Craig Arnold, COO-Industrial Sector
Thomas S. Gross, COO-Electrical Sector
Frank C. Campbell, Pres., EMEA
Pavan Pattada, Sr. VP-Supply Chain Mgmt.

GROWTH PLANS/SPECIAL FEATURES:
Eaton Corporation plc is a global power management company, selling its products to customers in more than 175 countries. Customers are engaged in the aerospace, buildings, data center, food/beverage, government, military, healthcare, machine building, mining, metals, minerals, oil/gas, rail, utilities and vehicle industries. Eaton provides energy solutions that help these customers effectively manage electrical, hydraulic and mechanical power more efficiently, safely and sustainably. The firm's wide array of products include aerospace actuators, motion controls, backup power, IT power distribution, clutches, brakes, conduits, cable/wire management, cylinders, differentials, traction control, ducting solutions, electrical circuit protection, electronic components, engine solutions, filtration solutions, fuel systems, emissions, furniture, golf grips, hoses, tubing, fittings/connectors, hydraulic power units, heat exchangers, industrial controls, automation solutions, sensors, lighting, low- and medium-voltage power distribution, motors, generators, plastics, pumps, emergency communication systems, airflow management, steering systems, transmissions, grid solutions and much more. Based in Ireland, the firm has worldwide offices in the U.S., Canada and more.

FINANCIAL DATA: Note: Data for latest year may not have been available at press time.

In U.S. $	2017	2016	2015	2014	2013	2012
Revenue		19,747,000,000	20,855,000,000	22,552,000,000	22,046,000,000	16,311,000,000
R&D Expense	584,000,000	589,000,000	625,000,000	647,000,000	644,000,000	439,000,000
Operating Income	-17,905,000,000	2,253,000,000	2,342,000,000	2,449,000,000	2,147,000,000	1,530,000,000
Operating Margin %		11.40%	11.22%	10.85%	9.73%	9.38%
SGA Expense	3,565,000,000	3,505,000,000	3,596,000,000	3,810,000,000	3,886,000,000	2,894,000,000
Net Income	2,985,000,000	1,922,000,000	1,979,000,000	1,793,000,000	1,861,000,000	1,217,000,000
Operating Cash Flow	2,666,000,000	2,552,000,000	2,371,000,000	1,878,000,000	2,285,000,000	1,664,000,000
Capital Expenditure	520,000,000	497,000,000	506,000,000	632,000,000	614,000,000	593,000,000
EBITDA	-16,991,000,000	3,182,000,000	3,267,000,000	3,432,000,000	3,152,000,000	2,057,000,000
Return on Assets %	9.46%	6.25%	6.13%	5.19%	5.21%	4.53%
Return on Equity %	18.56%	12.77%	12.77%	11.00%	11.67%	10.79%
Debt to Equity	0.41	0.45	0.51	0.50	0.53	0.64

CONTACT INFORMATION:
Phone: 440-523-5000 Fax:
Toll-Free:
Address: Eaton House, 30 Pembroke Rd., Dublin, 4 Ireland

STOCK TICKER/OTHER:
Stock Ticker: ETN
Employees: 95,000
Parent Company:

Exchange: NYS
Fiscal Year Ends: 12/31

SALARIES/BONUSES:
Top Exec. Salary: $1,125,002 Bonus: $
Second Exec. Salary: $906,100 Bonus: $

OTHER THOUGHTS:
Estimated Female Officers or Directors: 4
Hot Spot for Advancement for Women/Minorities: Y

Sales, profits and employees may be estimates. Financial information, benefits and other data can change quickly and may vary from those stated here.

ECC

NAIC Code: 541330

www.ecc.net

TYPES OF BUSINESS:
Engineering Consulting Services

BRANDS/DIVISIONS/AFFILIATES:
Nordlys Environmental LP
Watermark ECC LLC
ECC/Quantum Murray LP
Parks Closure Group LLC

CONTACTS:
Note: Officers with more than one job title may be intentionally listed here more than once.

Paul Sabharwal, Chmn.

GROWTH PLANS/SPECIAL FEATURES:

ECC is an engineering and construction firm that delivers design-build, construction, environmental remediation, engineering and design management, energy, munitions response and international development solutions. The employee-owned firm is headquartered in the Bay Area of California, with offices throughout the U.S., as well as in Germany, Guam, Italy, Kuwait and the U.K. ECC has executed billions in design-build and construction projects. The company provides cradle-to-grave environmental remediation services with a broad diversity of remedial technologies to remediate a full range of contaminants, including printed circuit boards, petroleum hydrocarbons, asbestos, metals and other inorganics and volatile/semi-volatile organic compounds as well as explosives and explosive residues. Services in engineering and design management include: comprehensive project planning, project engineering and submittal management, A/E partnering and lifecycle design management, LEED (leadership in energy and environmental design) and commissioning management and CADD (computer-aided design and drafting)/BIM (building information modeling). Energy solutions include upgrading distribution systems; renovating facilities; installing renewable sources; and developing, constructing, owning and operating energy projects. The munitions response segment undertakes the demining operations, battlefield area clearance, range maintenance and weapons demilitarization. In addition, joint venture Nordlys Environmental, LP is a global environmental remediation and construction company based in Nova Scotia, Canada; joint venture Watermark ECC, LLC provides remediation, operation, maintenance, long-term management, construction and design/build services in the U.S.; joint venture ECC/Quantum Murray, LP is based in Toronto, Canada, and provides remediation construction contractor services; and joint venture Parks Closure Group, LLC offers remediation, engineering and nuclear criticality services.

FINANCIAL DATA:
Note: Data for latest year may not have been available at press time.

In U.S. $	2017	2016	2015	2014	2013	2012
Revenue						
R&D Expense						
Operating Income						
Operating Margin %						
SGA Expense						
Net Income						
Operating Cash Flow						
Capital Expenditure						
EBITDA						
Return on Assets %						
Return on Equity %						
Debt to Equity						

CONTACT INFORMATION:
Phone: 650-347-1555　　Fax: 650-347-8789
Toll-Free:
Address: 1240 Bayshore Highway, Burlingame, CA 94010 United States

STOCK TICKER/OTHER:
Stock Ticker: Private　　Exchange:
Employees:　　Fiscal Year Ends:
Parent Company:

SALARIES/BONUSES:
Top Exec. Salary: $　　Bonus: $
Second Exec. Salary: $　　Bonus: $

OTHER THOUGHTS:
Estimated Female Officers or Directors:
Hot Spot for Advancement for Women/Minorities:

Sales, profits and employees may be estimates. Financial information, benefits and other data can change quickly and may vary from those stated here.

Eisai Co Ltd

NAIC Code: 325412

www.eisai.co.jp

TYPES OF BUSINESS:
Pharmaceuticals Manufacturing
Over-the-Counter Pharmaceuticals
Pharmaceutical Production Equipment
Diagnostic Products
Food Additives
Personal Health Care Products
Vitamins & Nutritional Supplements

BRANDS/DIVISIONS/AFFILIATES:
Halaven
Lenvima
Fycompa
BELVIQ
Aricept
Pariet
Humira

CONTACTS:
Note: Officers with more than one job title may be intentionally listed here more than once.

Haruo Naito, CEO
Haruo Naito, Pres.
Yasushi Okada, CTO
Takashi Owa, Chief Innovation Officer
Hideki Hayashi, CIO
Hideki Hayashi, Chief Prod. Creation Officer
Kenta Takahashi, General Counsel
Hideto Ueda, Chief Compliance Officer
Noboru Naoe, VP-Strategy & Planning Dept.
Noboru Naoe, Pres., Eisai Japan
Hideshi Honda, Pres., Asia Region
Yutaka Tsuchiya, Deputy Pres., Global Prod. Emergency Mgmt.
Lonnel Coats, Pres., Americas Region
Gary Hendler, CEO
Takafumi Asano, Pres., Demand Chain Systems

GROWTH PLANS/SPECIAL FEATURES:
Eisai Co., Ltd. primarily develops, manufactures and distributes medical products. The firm operates six production plants in Japan, the U.K., China and India; seven laboratories in Japan, the U.S. and the U.K.; and overseas sales offices in the U.S., U.K., Germany, France, China and South Korea. Eisai positions dementia-related and neurological diseases (neurology) and cancer (oncology) as its two strategic areas in which it can find unmet needs of patients and become a front-runner in helping them. Therefore, the neurology group and the oncology group aggregate all functions from research and development via the sales of Eisai products. The firm seeks to grow four global brands: Halaven, Lenvima, Fycompa and BELVIQ. Halaven, an anti-cancer agent discovered and developed in-house, and has been approved for the treatment of breast cancer and malignant soft tissue sarcoma in over 60 countries. Lenvima, another anti-cancer agent discovered and developed in-house, and has been approved for the treatment of thyroid cancer in over 50 countries. In neurology, Fycompa, discovered and developed in-house, is available in Europe, the Americas, Asia and Japan. BELVIQ is used for the treatment of chronic weight management, and is available in the U.S. In addition, Aricept (for Alzheimer's and dementia), is approved and marketed Japan, the U.S., Europe and Asia. Other major products include Pariet, a proton-pump inhibitor available in Japan by EA Pharma; and Humira, a fully-human anti-TNF-a monoclonal antibody available in Japan, South Korea and Taiwan.

FINANCIAL DATA:
Note: Data for latest year may not have been available at press time.

In U.S. $	2017	2016	2015	2014	2013	2012
Revenue	5,022,331,000	5,104,546,000	5,109,605,000	5,593,004,000	5,344,476,000	6,036,194,000
R&D Expense	1,047,867,000	1,139,436,000	1,228,871,000			
Operating Income	475,470,500	357,173,500	264,738,200	662,446,500	656,446,800	892,034,700
Operating Margin %	9.46%	6.99%	5.18%	11.84%	12.28%	14.77%
SGA Expense	1,673,905,000	1,796,320,000	1,812,428,000			
Net Income	366,666,700	511,766,400	402,962,600	307,015,100	449,739,200	545,099,700
Operating Cash Flow	706,642,400	890,786,300	708,235,500	798,276,500	681,768,300	844,270,600
Capital Expenditure	186,333,200	373,318,400	171,650,800	205,915,800	184,712,100	181,544,600
EBITDA	814,188,600	820,029,800	649,403,800	1,046,031,000	1,203,736,000	1,399,609,000
Return on Assets %	3.92%	5.41%	4.32%	3.40%	4.83%	5.70%
Return on Equity %	6.79%	9.37%	7.81%	6.73%	10.86%	14.22%
Debt to Equity	0.27	0.35	0.34	0.38	0.50	0.71

CONTACT INFORMATION:
Phone: 81 338173700   Fax:
Toll-Free:
Address: 4-6-10 Koishikawa, Bunkyo-ku, Tokyo, 112-8088 Japan

STOCK TICKER/OTHER:
Stock Ticker: ESALY
Employees: 9,877
Parent Company:

Exchange: PINX
Fiscal Year Ends: 03/31

SALARIES/BONUSES:
Top Exec. Salary: $ Bonus: $
Second Exec. Salary: $ Bonus: $

OTHER THOUGHTS:
Estimated Female Officers or Directors:
Hot Spot for Advancement for Women/Minorities:

Sales, profits and employees may be estimates. Financial information, benefits and other data can change quickly and may vary from those stated here.

Electronic Arts Inc (EA)

NAIC Code: 0

www.ea.com

TYPES OF BUSINESS:
Computer Software, Electronic Games, Apps & Entertainment
Online Interactive Games
E-Commerce Sales
Mobile Games
Apps

BRANDS/DIVISIONS/AFFILIATES:
Battlefield
Mass Effect
Need for Speed
Sims vs Zombies (The)
Origin
Respawn Entertainment LLC
Titanfall

CONTACTS:
Note: Officers with more than one job title may be intentionally listed here more than once.

Andrew Wilson, CEO
Blake Jorgensen, CFO
Lawrence Probst, Chairman of the Board
Kenneth Barker, Chief Accounting Officer
Christopher Bruzzo, Chief Marketing Officer
Kenneth Moss, Chief Technology Officer
Matt Bilbey, Executive VP, Divisional
Joel Linzner, Executive VP, Divisional
Laura Miele, Other Executive Officer
Vijayanthimala Singh, Other Executive Officer
Patrick Soderlund, Other Executive Officer
Jacob Schatz, Senior VP

GROWTH PLANS/SPECIAL FEATURES:

Electronic Arts, Inc. (EA) develops, markets, publishes and distributes games, content and services that can be played by consumers on a variety of platforms. These platforms include consoles such as PlayStation and Xbox, personal computers (PCs), mobile phones and tablets. Some of the company's games are based on its wholly-owned intellectual property, including Battlefield, Mass Effect, Need for Speed, The Sims vs. Zombies; and some games leverage content that EA licenses from others, such as FIFA, Madden NFL and Star Wars. EA also publishes and distributes games developed by third parties. The company's products and services can be purchased through multiple distribution channels, including physical and online retailers, platform providers (console manufacturers, providers of free-to-download PC games and mobile carriers) and through EA's own digital distribution platform, Origin. In November 2017, the firm agreed to acquire Respawn Entertainment, LLC, a leading independent game development studio and creators of AAA shooter and action games including the critically-acclaimed Titanfall franchise

EA offers its employees health care coverage, employee assistance programs, onsite childcare, employee discount programs, business travel accident insurance, retirement savings/pension and free EA games.

FINANCIAL DATA:
Note: Data for latest year may not have been available at press time.

In U.S. $	2017	2016	2015	2014	2013	2012
Revenue	4,845,000,000	4,396,000,000	4,515,000,000	3,575,000,000	3,797,000,000	4,143,000,000
R&D Expense	1,205,000,000	1,109,000,000	1,094,000,000	1,125,000,000	1,153,000,000	1,212,000,000
Operating Income	1,224,000,000	898,000,000	945,000,000	-3,000,000	84,000,000	62,000,000
Operating Margin %	25.26%	20.42%	20.93%	-.08%	2.21%	1.49%
SGA Expense	1,112,000,000	1,028,000,000	1,033,000,000	1,090,000,000	1,142,000,000	1,228,000,000
Net Income	967,000,000	1,156,000,000	875,000,000	8,000,000	98,000,000	76,000,000
Operating Cash Flow	1,383,000,000	1,223,000,000	1,067,000,000	712,000,000	324,000,000	277,000,000
Capital Expenditure	123,000,000	93,000,000	95,000,000	97,000,000	106,000,000	172,000,000
EBITDA	1,425,000,000	1,102,000,000	1,176,000,000	264,000,000	432,000,000	254,000,000
Return on Assets %	13.09%	17.51%	14.75%	.14%	1.85%	1.45%
Return on Equity %	25.93%	35.94%	32.06%	.34%	4.14%	3.02%
Debt to Equity	0.24	0.29	0.01	0.23	0.24	0.21

CONTACT INFORMATION:
Phone: 650 628-1500 Fax: 650 628-1414
Toll-Free:
Address: 209 Redwood Shores Parkway, Redwood City, CA 94065 United States

STOCK TICKER/OTHER:
Stock Ticker: EA
Employees: 8,800
Parent Company:

Exchange: NAS
Fiscal Year Ends: 03/31

SALARIES/BONUSES:
Top Exec. Salary: $1,083,846   Bonus: $
Second Exec. Salary: $762,981   Bonus: $

OTHER THOUGHTS:
Estimated Female Officers or Directors: 2
Hot Spot for Advancement for Women/Minorities:

Sales, profits and employees may be estimates. Financial information, benefits and other data can change quickly and may vary from those stated here.

Eli Lilly and Company

NAIC Code: 325412

www.lilly.com

TYPES OF BUSINESS:
Pharmaceuticals Discovery & Development
Veterinary Products

BRANDS/DIVISIONS/AFFILIATES:
Humulin
Trajenta
Alimta
Cyramza
Effient
Rumensin
Coban
Interceptor Plus

CONTACTS:
Note: Officers with more than one job title may be intentionally listed here more than once.

David Ricks, CEO
Alfonso Zulueta, Pres., Divisional
Joshua Smiley, CFO
Donald Zakrowski, Chief Accounting Officer
Jan Lundberg, Executive VP, Divisional
Michael Harrington, General Counsel
Melissa Barnes, Other Executive Officer
Enrique Conterno, President, Divisional
Jeffrey Simmons, President, Divisional
Susan Mahony, President, Divisional
Myles ONeill, President, Divisional
Leigh Pusey, Senior VP, Divisional
Johna Norton, Senior VP, Divisional
Stephen Fry, Senior VP, Divisional

GROWTH PLANS/SPECIAL FEATURES:

Eli Lilly and Company discovers, develops, manufactures and markets human pharmaceutical and animal health products. Human pharmaceutical products are grouped into five divisions: endocrinology, neuroscience, oncology, immunology and cardiovascular. Endocrinology products include: Humalog, Humulin, Basaglar, Trajenta, Jentadueto, Jardiance, Trulicity and Glyxambi, for the treatment of diabetes; Forteo and Evista, for osteoporosis in women; and Humatrope, for human growth hormone deficiency. Neuroscience products include: Cymbalta and Prozac, for major depressive disorder; Zyprexa, for schizophrenia; Strattera, for attention-deficit hyperactivity disorder; and Amyvid, a radioactive diagnostic agent for brain imaging of people with cognitive decline. Oncology products include: Alimta, for non-small cell lung cancer; Erbitux, for colorectal cancers; Gemzar, for pancreatic cancer/metastatic breast cancer/ovarian cancer/bladder cancer; Cyramza, for advanced or metastatic gastric cancer; Portrazza, to treat epidermal growth factor receptor expressing squamous non-small cell lung cancer; Lartruvo, for soft tissue carcinoma; and Verzenio, for advanced/metastatic breast cancer. Immunology products include: Olumiant, for adults with moderately-to-severe active rheumatoid arthritis; and Taltz, for moderate-to-severe plaque psoriasis and active psoriatic arthritis. Cardiovascular products include: Cialis, for erectile dysfunction; and Effient, for reduction of thrombotic cardiovascular events. Animal health products are grouped into two divisions: food animals and companion animals. Food animal products include: Rumensin, a cattle feed additive; Coban, Maxiban and Monteban, anticoccidial agents for use in poultry; Posilac, a protein supplement; Paylean and Optaflexx, leanness and/or performance enhancers; and Tylan and Denagard, antibiotics. Companion animal products include Trifexis and Comfortis chewable tablets are manufactured for flea prevention; Interceptor Plus, a chewable for the prevention of heartworm disease; and Duramune, Bronchi-Shield, Fel-O and Rabvac, vaccines.

Eli Lilly offers employees life, health, prescription drug and dental insurance; domestic partner benefits; an employee assistance program; paid maternity leave; a 401(k); flexible spending accounts; adoption assistance; and tuition reimbursement.

FINANCIAL DATA:
Note: Data for latest year may not have been available at press time.

In U.S. $	2017	2016	2015	2014	2013	2012
Revenue	22,871,300,000	21,222,100,000	19,958,700,000	19,615,600,000	23,113,100,000	22,603,400,000
R&D Expense	6,394,400,000	5,273,900,000	5,331,400,000	4,933,800,000	5,588,400,000	5,278,100,000
Operating Income	3,121,200,000	3,714,600,000	2,916,100,000	2,903,000,000	5,400,400,000	4,940,800,000
Operating Margin %	13.64%	17.50%	14.61%	14.79%	23.36%	21.85%
SGA Expense	7,285,500,000	6,578,700,000	6,674,000,000	6,846,300,000	7,216,200,000	7,588,000,000
Net Income	-204,100,000	2,737,600,000	2,408,400,000	2,390,500,000	4,684,800,000	4,088,600,000
Operating Cash Flow	5,615,600,000	4,851,000,000	2,772,800,000	4,367,100,000	5,735,000,000	5,304,800,000
Capital Expenditure	2,163,600,000	1,092,000,000	1,626,200,000	1,565,900,000	1,093,300,000	1,044,200,000
EBITDA	3,989,700,000	5,055,800,000	4,378,900,000	4,528,100,000	7,495,000,000	7,048,200,000
Return on Assets %	-.48%	7.36%	6.62%	6.60%	13.45%	12.01%
Return on Equity %	-1.59%	19.15%	16.08%	14.48%	28.92%	28.88%
Debt to Equity	0.85	0.59	0.54	0.34	0.23	0.37

CONTACT INFORMATION:
Phone: 317 276-2000   Fax:
Toll-Free:
Address: Lilly Corporate Center, Indianapolis, IN 46285 United States

STOCK TICKER/OTHER:
Stock Ticker: LLY   Exchange: NYS
Employees: 41,975   Fiscal Year Ends: 12/31
Parent Company:

SALARIES/BONUSES:
Top Exec. Salary: $1,400,000   Bonus: $
Second Exec. Salary: $1,089,134   Bonus: $

OTHER THOUGHTS:
Estimated Female Officers or Directors: 8
Hot Spot for Advancement for Women/Minorities: Y

Embraer SA

NAIC Code: 336411

www.embraer.com

TYPES OF BUSINESS:
Aircraft Manufacturing
Commuter Aircraft
Business Jets
Aircraft Maintenance
Military Aircraft
Agricultural Aircraft
Aircraft Leasing
After-Sales Service

BRANDS/DIVISIONS/AFFILIATES:
E-Jets
ERJ 145
Legacy
Lineage 1000E
A-20 Super Tucano
KC-390
Agricultural Airplane Ipanema

CONTACTS:
Note: Officers with more than one job title may be intentionally listed here more than once.

Paulo Cesar De Souza Silva, CEO
Frederico P. F. Curado, Pres.
Jose Antonio de Almeida Filippo, CFO
Mauro Kern, Jr., Exec. VP-Eng.
Jose Antonio de Almeida Filippo, Investor Rel. Officer
Paulo Cesar de Souza e Silva, Pres., Commercial Aviation
Luiz Carlos Siqueira Aguiar, Pres., Defense & Security
Flavio Rimoli, Exec. VP-Corp. Svcs.
Jackson Schneider, Exec. VP-Institutional Rel. & Sustainability

GROWTH PLANS/SPECIAL FEATURES:

Embraer SA manufactures commercial aircraft for the global market. Originally a government-controlled company producing aircraft for the Brazilian Air Force, the firm is now one of the leading global manufacturers of commercial aircraft. Embraer offers four product segments: commercial aviation, executive aviation, defense and security and agricultural aviation. Its commercial jets business produces next-generation E-Jets and ERJ 145 jets. E-Jets feature ultra-high by-pass ratio geared turbofan PW engines, 4-G fly-by-wire control, e-Enabled architecture and spacious cabins. E-Jet models include E195-E2, E190-E2 and E175-E2. The ERJ family of jets comprise 37 to 50 seats, with each being built specifically for use in regional networks. As of February 2018, more than 1,000 ERJ's have been delivered. Some 70 operators fly the ERJ 145. ERJ models include ERJ 145, ERJ 145 XR, ERJ 140 and ERJ 135. Each jet is built specifically for use in regional networks and seats 37-50 passengers. The executive aviation segment produces the Phenom 100 and 300 light jets; the midsize Legacy 500; the mid-light Legacy 450; the large Legacy 650E; and the ultra-large Lineage 1000E. This division's global jet fleet exceeds 1,100 aircraft, which are in operation in more than 70 countries. The defense and security segment produces the A-29 Super Tucano light attack and advanced trainer, as well as the multi-mission KC-390 military airlift. This division provides a full line of integrated solutions and applications such as command and control center radars, ISR (intelligence, surveillance and reconnaissance) and space. These solutions and applications also include integrated systems for information, communications, border monitoring and surveillance as well as aircraft for authorities' transportation and special missions. Last, the agricultural aviation segment produces the Agricultural Airplane Ipanema, which runs on ethanol. Embraer takes care of the full lifecycle of its aircraft.

FINANCIAL DATA:
Note: Data for latest year may not have been available at press time.

In U.S. $	2017	2016	2015	2014	2013	2012
Revenue	5,839,300,000	6,217,500,000	5,928,100,000	6,288,800,000	6,235,000,000	6,177,900,000
R&D Expense	49,200,000	47,600,000	41,700,000	47,100,000	74,700,000	77,300,000
Operating Income	503,200,000	385,000,000	392,000,000	543,400,000	731,500,000	621,800,000
Operating Margin %	8.61%	6.19%	6.61%	8.64%	11.73%	10.06%
SGA Expense	486,100,000	501,200,000	543,600,000	627,400,000	664,900,000	762,500,000
Net Income	246,800,000	166,100,000	69,200,000	334,700,000	342,000,000	347,800,000
Operating Cash Flow	757,300,000	-20,500,000	862,500,000	482,300,000	564,600,000	694,800,000
Capital Expenditure	708,200,000	897,500,000	769,100,000	699,100,000	754,200,000	580,400,000
EBITDA	848,400,000	733,000,000	830,000,000	829,700,000	1,033,200,000	1,017,000,000
Return on Assets %	2.09%	1.42%	.62%	3.25%	3.48%	3.79%
Return on Equity %	6.23%	4.37%	1.84%	9.17%	10.07%	11.10%
Debt to Equity	1.02	0.93	0.98	0.74	0.70	0.65

CONTACT INFORMATION:
Phone: 55 1239271216 Fax: 55 1239226070
Toll-Free:
Address: Ave. Brigadeiro Faria Lima, 2170, Sao Paulo, SP 12227-901 Brazil

STOCK TICKER/OTHER:
Stock Ticker: ERJ
Employees: 20,348
Parent Company:

Exchange: NYS
Fiscal Year Ends: 12/31

SALARIES/BONUSES:
Top Exec. Salary: $ Bonus: $
Second Exec. Salary: $ Bonus: $

OTHER THOUGHTS:
Estimated Female Officers or Directors:
Hot Spot for Advancement for Women/Minorities:

Sales, profits and employees may be estimates. Financial information, benefits and other data can change quickly and may vary from those stated here.

Emerson Electric Co

www.emerson.com

NAIC Code: 334513

TYPES OF BUSINESS:
Engineering & Technology Products & Services
Industrial Automation Products
Power Products
Air Conditioning & Refrigeration Products
Appliances & Tools

BRANDS/DIVISIONS/AFFILIATES:
Paradigm
ProSys Inc
Cooper-Atkins

CONTACTS:
Note: Officers with more than one job title may be intentionally listed here more than once.

David Farr, CEO
Frank Dellaquila, CFO
Michael Baughman, Chief Accounting Officer
K Bell, Chief Marketing Officer
Steven Pelch, COO
Michael Train, Executive VP, Divisional
Robert Sharp, Executive VP, Divisional
Sara Bosco, General Counsel
Edward Monser, President
Mark Bulanda, Senior VP, Divisional

GROWTH PLANS/SPECIAL FEATURES:
Emerson Electric Co. designs and supplies technology products and engineering services to a wide range of industrial, commercial and consumer markets worldwide. The company is organized into two business segments: automation solutions and commercial & residential solutions. The automation solutions segment enables process, hybrid and discrete manufacturers to maximize production, protect personnel and the environment, and optimize their energy efficiency and operating costs through a broad offering of integrated solutions and products. These include measurement and analytical instrumentation, industrial valves and equipment, and process control systems. The commercial & residential solutions segment provides products that promote energy efficiency, enhance household and commercial comfort, and protect food quality and sustainability through heating, air conditioning and refrigeration technology, as well as a broad range of tools and appliance solutions. During 2017, Emerson sold its Leroy-Somer, SSB Wind Systems and Control Techniques businesses to Nidec Corporation; and acquired Paradigm, a provider of software solutions to the oil and gas industry. In 2018, the firm acquired ProSys, Inc., a global supplier of software and services that increase production and safety for the chemical, oil/gas, pulp/paper and refining industries; acquired Cooper-Atkins, which manufactures temperature management and environmental measurement devices, as well as wireless monitoring solutions for foodservice, healthcare and industrial markets; and agreed to acquire Textron, Inc.'s tools and test equipment business for approximately $810 million.

FINANCIAL DATA:
Note: Data for latest year may not have been available at press time.

In U.S. $	2017	2016	2015	2014	2013	2012
Revenue	15,264,000,000	14,522,000,000	22,304,000,000	24,537,000,000	24,669,000,000	24,412,000,000
R&D Expense						
Operating Income	2,650,000,000	2,798,000,000	3,864,000,000	4,443,000,000	3,941,000,000	4,332,000,000
Operating Margin %	17.36%	19.26%	17.32%	18.10%	15.97%	17.74%
SGA Expense	3,618,000,000	3,464,000,000	5,184,000,000	5,715,000,000	5,648,000,000	5,436,000,000
Net Income	1,518,000,000	1,635,000,000	2,710,000,000	2,147,000,000	2,004,000,000	1,968,000,000
Operating Cash Flow	1,912,000,000	2,881,000,000	2,529,000,000	3,692,000,000	3,649,000,000	3,053,000,000
Capital Expenditure	476,000,000	447,000,000	685,000,000	767,000,000	678,000,000	665,000,000
EBITDA	3,172,000,000	3,090,000,000	5,176,000,000	4,397,000,000	4,249,000,000	4,179,000,000
Return on Assets %	7.34%	7.46%	11.71%	8.78%	8.25%	8.25%
Return on Equity %	18.64%	20.89%	29.78%	20.73%	19.19%	19.02%
Debt to Equity	0.43	0.53	0.53	0.35	0.38	0.36

CONTACT INFORMATION:
Phone: 314 553-2000
Fax: 314 553-3527
Toll-Free:
Address: 8000 W. Florissant Ave., St. Louis, MO 63136 United States

STOCK TICKER/OTHER:
Stock Ticker: EMR
Employees: 103,500
Parent Company:
Exchange: NYS
Fiscal Year Ends: 09/30

SALARIES/BONUSES:
Top Exec. Salary: $1,300,000   Bonus: $2,500,000
Second Exec. Salary: $750,000   Bonus: $1,150,000

OTHER THOUGHTS:
Estimated Female Officers or Directors: 2
Hot Spot for Advancement for Women/Minorities: Y

Empresas ICA SAB de CV

NAIC Code: 237310

www.ica.com.mx

TYPES OF BUSINESS:
Heavy Construction
Civic Construction
Industrial Construction
Transportation Infrastructure Management
Residential Construction
Design & Engineering Services
Airport Operations

BRANDS/DIVISIONS/AFFILIATES:
ICA Fluor
San Martin
PRET
Los Portales
ACTICA
Vive Ica
OMA
Proactiva

GROWTH PLANS/SPECIAL FEATURES:

Empresas ICA SAB de CV (ICA) is one of Mexico's largest engineering, procurement and construction companies. The firm specializes in the following activities: roadways, ports, airports, water, energy, underground works, mass transit, social buildings, industry, oil and gas, mining, real estate development and pre-cast construction. Through majority-owned subsidiary ICA Fluor, the firm builds industrial factories such as refineries, petrochemical plants, cement factories, automotive factories and electrical generation plants. ICA participated in the operating concessioned tunnel (the Acapulco tunnel), and in the management and operation of a water treatment plant in Ciudad Acuna and other water supply systems, including the Aqueduct II water supply system. Other subsidiaries the firm owns are: San MartÃn, PRET, Los Portales, ACTICA, Vive Ica, OMA, Proactiva, Facchina and Rodio Kronsa, all vital portions of its operations. During 2017, the firm filed a Form 15 with the Securities and Exchange Commission to voluntarily de-register its ordinary shares, and began a restructuring plan.

CONTACTS:
Note: Officers with more than one job title may be intentionally listed here more than once.

Guadalupe Phillips Margain, CEO
Alonso Quintana Kawage, Pres.
Pablo Garcia, VP-Finance
Porfirio Gonzalez Alvarez, CEO-GACN
Diego Quintana Kawage, Exec. VP-Industrial Construction & Airports
Bernardo Quintana Isaac, Chmn.

FINANCIAL DATA:
Note: Data for latest year may not have been available at press time.

In U.S. $	2017	2016	2015	2014	2013	2012
Revenue		1,131,471,000	1,837,124,000	1,977,650,000	1,639,242,000	2,636,815,000
R&D Expense						
Operating Income		134,025,500	-380,145,800	191,716,200	170,329,200	178,623,200
Operating Margin %		11.84%	-20.69%	9.69%	10.39%	6.77%
SGA Expense		107,581,400	169,528,100	170,028,100	167,066,800	199,771,800
Net Income		-491,987,300	-1,132,681,000	-167,691,100	78,886,270	62,651,910
Operating Cash Flow		342,256,000	398,640,200	139,877,500	9,343,498	304,316,900
Capital Expenditure		9,397,573	77,719,800	38,847,220	19,787,690	32,179,260
EBITDA		-162,144,700	-465,814,000	149,646,800	226,943,100	343,656,400
Return on Assets %		-8.06%	-18.02%	-2.75%	1.35%	1.08%
Return on Equity %			-310.89%	-17.38%	8.03%	6.72%
Debt to Equity				2.91	1.55	2.42

CONTACT INFORMATION:
Phone: 52 5552729991   Fax: 52 5252712431
Toll-Free:
Address: Blvd. Manuel Avila Camacho 36, Mexico City, DF 11000 Mexico

STOCK TICKER/OTHER:
Stock Ticker: ICAYY
Employees: 31,302
Parent Company:

Exchange: PINX
Fiscal Year Ends: 12/31

SALARIES/BONUSES:
Top Exec. Salary: $ Bonus: $
Second Exec. Salary: $ Bonus: $

OTHER THOUGHTS:
Estimated Female Officers or Directors:
Hot Spot for Advancement for Women/Minorities: Y

ENERCON GmbH

www.enercon.de

NAIC Code: 333611

TYPES OF BUSINESS:
Wind Turbine Manufacturing

BRANDS/DIVISIONS/AFFILIATES:
ENERCON Storm Control
ENERCON SCADA

CONTACTS:
Note: Officers with more than one job title may be intentionally listed here more than once.

Hans-Dieter Kettwig, Co-Managing Dir.
Simon-Hermann Wobben, Co-Managing Dir.
Bernard Fink, Manager-Sales
Stefan Hartage, Head-Electrical Engineering Development

GROWTH PLANS/SPECIAL FEATURES:

ENERCON GmbH, founded in 1984, designs and manufactures wind turbines. To support turbine installation, the firm operates mobile cranes of up to 1,600 tons, special transporters for blades and towers and hundreds of service vehicles. The firm's turbines have featured gearless systems since 1992, allowing the turbines to operate with fewer rotating parts, resulting in almost frictionless performance. ENERCON offers turbine configurations rated from 900 kilowatts to 7.56 megawatts. Generally, all of ENERCON's turbine systems feature independent pitch control for each of the three rotor blades, as well as integrated lighting protection, and typically operate at speeds around 12-20 revolutions per minute (rpm), with some capable of operating as slow as six rpm and some as fast as 34 rpm. In order to prevent the shut-downs caused by high winds that other turbines systems may suffer from, the firm has developed ENERCON Storm Control software, which causes the rotor blades to rotate slightly out of sync with the wind, thus preventing damage by reducing the rotation speed rather than ceasing rotation altogether. To connect the turbines to a power grid, the company offers ENERCON SCADA, an upgradable and adaptable monitoring and control interface. Each turbine also comes equipped with a modem to signal a central data transmission facility of any malfunction. The firm's service and support division operates over 300 stations worldwide. In addition, Elektric Schaltanlagenfertigung GmbH produces the company's inverter system, which converts voltage, frequency and power into wind energy, while also corresponding to grid specifications. ENERCON's inverter core technology is contained in all ENERCON wind energy converters. ENERCON has production facilities in Germany, as well as in Austria, France, Canada, Turkey, Brazil, Sweden and Portugal. As of December 2017, the company has installed over 26,300 wind turbines in over 30 countries with an installed capacity exceeding 43 gigawatts.

FINANCIAL DATA:
Note: Data for latest year may not have been available at press time.

In U.S. $	2017	2016	2015	2014	2013	2012
Revenue	5,000,000,000	5,267,800,000	4,510,000,000	5,955,850,000	4,600,015,500	4,376,989,500
R&D Expense						
Operating Income						
Operating Margin %						
SGA Expense						
Net Income						
Operating Cash Flow						
Capital Expenditure						
EBITDA						
Return on Assets %						
Return on Equity %						
Debt to Equity						

CONTACT INFORMATION:
Phone: 49 421 24415100   Fax: 49 421 2441539
Toll-Free:
Address: Terrhof 59, Bremen, D-28199 Germany

SALARIES/BONUSES:
Top Exec. Salary: $ Bonus: $
Second Exec. Salary: $ Bonus: $

STOCK TICKER/OTHER:
Stock Ticker: Private   Exchange:
Employees: 20,000   Fiscal Year Ends: 12/31
Parent Company:

OTHER THOUGHTS:
Estimated Female Officers or Directors:
Hot Spot for Advancement for Women/Minorities:

Sales, profits and employees may be estimates. Financial information, benefits and other data can change quickly and may vary from those stated here.

Engility Holdings Inc

NAIC Code: 541330

www.engilitycorp.com

TYPES OF BUSINESS:
Engineering Services
IT Services
Defense Training
Technical Consulting Services
Supply Chain & Logistics Services
Business Process Outsourcing
US Government Contractor

BRANDS/DIVISIONS/AFFILIATES:

CONTACTS:
Note: Officers with more than one job title may be intentionally listed here more than once.

Lynn Dugle, CEO
Wayne Rehberger, CFO
David Savner, Co-Chairman
Peter Marino, Co-Chairman
Thomas Miiller, General Counsel
Susan Balaguer, Other Executive Officer

GROWTH PLANS/SPECIAL FEATURES:

Engility Holdings, Inc. offers a broad range of technical services to solve its customers' difficult challenges. The firm's core capabilities are categorized into six groups: systems engineering and integration, cybersecurity, high-performance computing, enterprise modernization, mission operations support, and readiness and training. The systems engineering and integration group provides engineering and integration solutions that support the acquisition and sustainment lifecycle of customer programs. These solutions include technology, information assurance, modeling and simulation, as well as architecture analysis and modernization. The cybersecurity group modernizes and develops new systems with cyber resiliency at its core. Its offerings include vulnerability assessments and penetration testing, independent test and evaluation, cybersecurity systems engineering, cyber quick reaction range capability and cyber hunting. The high-performance computing group collaborates with scientists, technologists and decision-makers across the Federal government, industry and academia to apply complex science to challenges, with services including architecture and infrastructure design, data management, analytics, integration, testing and systems operation/optimization/sustainment. The enterprise modernization group provides enterprise services and systems that optimize client operations, increase cost efficiencies and improve mission effectiveness. These offerings include architecture analysis and modernization, IT services and solutions and agile software development and integration. The mission and operations support group provides solutions that give customers flexibility, efficiency and effectiveness in accomplishing their critical missions, including the following areas: artificial intelligence, space launch/space flight, law enforcement, intelligence analysis, air traffic management, engineering, fabrication and communication data exchange. Last, the readiness and training group helps clients prepare to meet the challenges of complex environments and missions, with services and solutions that include training development, learning and knowledge management and a turnkey modular shooting range.

FINANCIAL DATA:
Note: Data for latest year may not have been available at press time.

In U.S. $	2017	2016	2015	2014	2013	2012
Revenue	1,931,887,000	2,076,423,000	2,085,623,000	1,367,091,000	1,407,372,000	1,655,344,000
R&D Expense						
Operating Income	133,767,000	132,341,000	102,652,000	82,920,000	108,156,000	97,518,000
Operating Margin %	6.92%	6.37%	4.92%	6.06%	7.68%	5.89%
SGA Expense	142,391,000	166,238,000	203,262,000	114,890,000	84,635,000	142,440,000
Net Income	-35,191,000	-10,807,000	-235,352,000	35,423,000	49,527,000	-350,373,000
Operating Cash Flow	97,673,000	94,405,000	48,418,000	102,359,000	150,840,000	58,158,000
Capital Expenditure	9,691,000	21,446,000	19,610,000	5,436,000	3,336,000	2,164,000
EBITDA	178,339,000	179,138,000	161,087,000	103,873,000	121,055,000	-310,781,000
Return on Assets %	-1.66%	-.48%	-13.85%	3.45%	5.06%	-27.68%
Return on Equity %	-5.18%	-1.56%	-40.57%	7.90%	12.29%	-48.04%
Debt to Equity	1.41	1.50	1.60	0.59	0.43	0.75

CONTACT INFORMATION:
Phone: 703-748-1400 Fax: 703-708-5700
Toll-Free:
Address: 4803 Stonecroft Blvd., Chantilly, VA 20151 United States

STOCK TICKER/OTHER:
Stock Ticker: EGL   Exchange: NYS
Employees: 9,100   Fiscal Year Ends:
Parent Company:

SALARIES/BONUSES:
Top Exec. Salary: $692,308   Bonus: $425,000
Second Exec. Salary: $641,346   Bonus: $

OTHER THOUGHTS:
Estimated Female Officers or Directors:
Hot Spot for Advancement for Women/Minorities:

Sales, profits and employees may be estimates. Financial information, benefits and other data can change quickly and may vary from those stated here.

ENGlobal Corporation

NAIC Code: 541330

www.englobal.com

TYPES OF BUSINESS:
Engineering Services
Petrochemicals Industry Support Services
Control & Instrumentation Systems
Consulting & Inspection Services
Project Management

BRANDS/DIVISIONS/AFFILIATES:
ENGlobal US Inc
ENGlobal Government Services Inc
ENGlobal International Inc
ENGlobal Emerging Markets Inc

CONTACTS:
Note: Officers with more than one job title may be intentionally listed here more than once.

William Coskey, CEO
Mark Hess, CFO
Tami Walker, General Counsel
Michael Patton, Senior VP
Bruce Williams, Senior VP

GROWTH PLANS/SPECIAL FEATURES:

ENGlobal Corporation is an international provider of engineering services and systems to the energy market. The firm operates in two primary segments: engineering, procurement & construction management (EPCM) and automation. The EPCM segment offers a range of services relating to the development, management and execution of projects requiring professional engineering primarily to the energy industry and to the U.S. government. Its services include feasibility studies, engineering, design, procurement and construction management. This segment also includes the technical services group, which provides engineering, design, installation and operation and maintenance of various government, public sector and international facilities. Its customers include pipeline, refining, utility, chemical, petroleum, petrochemical, oil and gas and power industries throughout the U.S. The automation segment provides services related to the design, fabrication and implementation of process distributed control and analyzer systems, advanced automation and information technology projects. This segment's customers include members of both domestic and foreign energy related industries. ENGlobal caters to the engineering and construction, automation integration, automation engineering and subsea controls and integration markets. Subsidiaries of the firm include ENGlobal U.S., Inc.; ENGlobal Government Services, Inc.; ENGlobal International, Inc.; and ENGlobal Emerging Markets, Inc.

Employees receive medical, dental and vision coverage; life insurance; flexible spending accounts; and educational reimbursement.

FINANCIAL DATA:
Note: Data for latest year may not have been available at press time.

In U.S. $	2017	2016	2015	2014	2013	2012
Revenue	55,765,000	59,224,000	79,605,000	107,900,000	168,963,000	227,916,000
R&D Expense						
Operating Income	-6,143,000	-3,238,000	2,100,000	6,880,000	-778,000	-6,519,000
Operating Margin %	-11.01%	-5.46%	2.63%	6.37%	-.46%	-2.86%
SGA Expense	12,581,000	13,350,000	14,168,000	16,568,000	22,080,000	25,239,000
Net Income	-16,258,000	-2,342,000	10,536,000	6,031,000	-2,989,000	-33,601,000
Operating Cash Flow	-5,104,000	9,565,000	-2,847,000	3,767,000	10,666,000	-4,874,000
Capital Expenditure	713,000	64,000	1,005,000	438,000	836,000	666,000
EBITDA	-5,173,000	-2,095,000	3,556,000	9,206,000	1,291,000	-19,268,000
Return on Assets %	-44.12%	-4.84%	20.28%	12.37%	-4.80%	-36.74%
Return on Equity %	-56.18%	-6.09%	30.51%	23.41%	-12.51%	-80.19%
Debt to Equity						

CONTACT INFORMATION:
Phone: 281 878-1000   Fax: 281 821-5488
Toll-Free:
Address: 654 N. Sam Houston Pkwy E., Ste. 400, Houston, TX 77060 United States

SALARIES/BONUSES:
Top Exec. Salary: $236,913   Bonus: $11,256
Second Exec. Salary: $216,299   Bonus: $16,884

STOCK TICKER/OTHER:
Stock Ticker: ENG
Employees: 279
Parent Company:

Exchange: NAS
Fiscal Year Ends: 12/31

OTHER THOUGHTS:
Estimated Female Officers or Directors: 2
Hot Spot for Advancement for Women/Minorities: Y

Eni SpA

NAIC Code: 211111

www.eni.com

TYPES OF BUSINESS:
Oil & Gas-Exploration & Production
Engineering & Construction Services
Oilfield Services
Refining & Transportation
Petrochemicals
Petroleum & Energy Research
Electricity Generation
Gas Stations

BRANDS/DIVISIONS/AFFILIATES:
Sardegna Matrica

CONTACTS: Note: Officers with more than one job title may be intentionally listed here more than once.
Claudio Descalzi, CEO
Alessandro Puliti, Chief Dev., Oper. & Technology Officer
Massimo Mondazzi, CFO
Giuseppe Ricci, Chief Refining & Mktg. Officer
Luca Bertelli, Chief Exploration Officer
Massimo Mantovani, General Counsel
Stefano Lucchini, Sr. Exec. VP-Public Affairs & Comm.
Roberto Ulissi, Sr. Exec. VP-Corp. Affairs & Governance
Claudio Descalzi, COO-Exploration & Prod.
Angelo Fanelli, COO-Refining & Mktg.
Marco Petracchini, Sr. Exec. VP-Internal Audit
Emma Marcegaglia, Chmn.
Marco Alvera, Sr. Exec. VP-Midstream

GROWTH PLANS/SPECIAL FEATURES:
Eni SpA is a diversified energy company that is approximately 30%-owned by the Italian government. The firm conducts business in more than 70 countries. Eni operates in three divisions: upstream, mid-downstream and new energy solutions. The upstream division comprises the Zohr gas field located off the Egyptian coast, which began production in December 2017; the Nooros field in Egypt, which reached 0.187 barrels of oil equivalent (boe) per day, and 0.091 barrels of gas equivalent per day during 2017; and three upstream activities in Italy (Basilicata, Ravenna and Gela), from which oil is extracted from 24 wells with an 80,000 boe/d. The mid-downstream division includes: the wholesale and retail supply and sale of natural gas; the purchase and sale of liquefied natural gas (LNG); and the production and sale of electricity. This division is also engaged in refining with new biorefineries and chemical manufacturers to provide solutions for green chemistry. It converts traditional refineries to those capable of processing biological raw materials to provide fuel; and chemical materials are used to make packaging, toys, food containers and other products. Joint venture Sardegna Matrica, with Versalis Eni-Novamont, produces bio-plastic and bio-lubricant products, food additives and cosmetics made from vegetable sources-green chemistry. The new energy solutions division is engaged in and invests in de-carbonization, natural gas advocacy and renewables for the purpose of reducing direct emissions of CO2 across all sectors. In March 2018, Eni agreed to sell a 10% stake in the Shorouk concession, offshore Egypt, where Zohr's gas field is located, to Mubadala Petroleum. Eni currently holds a 60% stake in the concession, with Rosneft holding 30% and BP holding 10%.

FINANCIAL DATA: Note: Data for latest year may not have been available at press time.

In U.S. $	2017	2016	2015	2014	2013	2012
Revenue	82,638,500,000	68,860,680,000	83,652,350,000	135,650,400,000	141,639,700,000	157,104,400,000
R&D Expense						
Operating Income	5,920,126,000	2,472,276,000	-3,410,803,000	9,484,058,000	10,606,580,000	17,885,110,000
Operating Margin %	7.16%	3.59%	-4.07%	6.99%	7.48%	11.38%
SGA Expense	3,644,200,000	3,697,300,000	3,430,561,000	6,590,679,000	6,546,223,000	5,752,180,000
Net Income	4,166,564,000	-1,807,898,000	-10,846,160,000	1,594,260,000	6,372,101,000	9,617,427,000
Operating Cash Flow	12,493,520,000	9,475,413,000	14,699,050,000	18,659,390,000	13,616,040,000	15,276,990,000
Capital Expenditure	10,720,200,000	11,336,410,000	14,270,540,000	15,115,220,000	15,806,760,000	16,692,190,000
EBITDA	24,961,100,000	18,132,080,000	19,432,440,000	30,899,750,000	37,094,030,000	42,495,490,000
Return on Assets %	2.81%	-1.12%	-6.25%	.90%	3.71%	5.51%
Return on Equity %	6.67%	-2.79%	-15.75%	2.18%	8.78%	13.58%
Debt to Equity	0.42	0.38	0.37	0.32	0.35	0.32

CONTACT INFORMATION:
Phone: 39 252041730 Fax: 39 252041765
Toll-Free:
Address: Piazzale Enrico Mattei, 1, Rome, 00144 Italy

STOCK TICKER/OTHER:
Stock Ticker: E
Employees: 33,356
Parent Company:

Exchange: NYS
Fiscal Year Ends: 12/31

SALARIES/BONUSES:
Top Exec. Salary: $1,350,000 Bonus: $1,755,000
Second Exec. Salary: $ Bonus: $

OTHER THOUGHTS:
Estimated Female Officers or Directors: 1
Hot Spot for Advancement for Women/Minorities: Y

Eptisa

www.eptisa.com

NAIC Code: 541330

TYPES OF BUSINESS:
Engineering Consulting Services

BRANDS/DIVISIONS/AFFILIATES:
Eptisa Servicios de Ingeneieria SL
Eptisa Tecnologias de la Informacion SA
Eptisa Romania SRL

CONTACTS:
Note: Officers with more than one job title may be intentionally listed here more than once.

Luis Villarroya Alonso, CEO
Angel Corcostegui Guraya, Chmn.

GROWTH PLANS/SPECIAL FEATURES:
Eptisa is an international engineering, architecture and information technology company. The firm carries out complex projects in over 45 countries in the fields of transport; water and environment; buildings, energy and industry; institutional, economic and social development; instrumentation and monitoring; and information technology. The transport division provides services including feasibility studies, environmental impact assessment, detailed design, quality control and works supervision, contract management, general consultancy services and technical assistance, as well as project management. Transport sectors include railways, roads, airports and ports. The water and environment division collaborates with administrations on hydrological and environmental plans to improve management of natural resources. Service areas include hydrological planning, hydraulic infrastructure, water treatment plants, natural environments, industrial environments, solid wastes and spatial planning. The buildings, energy and industry divisions unite to offer architecture and engineering services for building management from its design, technical assistance and project management to the turnkey execution of the work. This division provides services to the health, logistics and distribution, hotel, energy and major events sectors. The institutional, economic and social development division focuses on social and environmental sustainability, budget support, public financial management and other specialized services. The instrumentation and monitoring division consists of urban works, including metropolitan tunnels, sewers and drains; and hydraulic works, including the monitoring of large dams from construction through filling and operational phases. The information technology division is focused on telecommunication and utilities, database management, enterprise content management, geographic information systems and geomarketing. Eptisa is comprised of the following subsidiaries: Eptisa Servicios de Ingeneieria SL, the firm's flagship that primarily provides engineering and information technologies; Eptisa Tecnologias de la Informacion SA, which provides technological consulting services; and Eptisa Romania SRL, an engineering and consultancy company for the Romanian market.

FINANCIAL DATA:
Note: Data for latest year may not have been available at press time.

In U.S. $	2017	2016	2015	2014	2013	2012
Revenue	110,000,000	105,356,000	100,000,000			
R&D Expense						
Operating Income						
Operating Margin %						
SGA Expense						
Net Income						
Operating Cash Flow						
Capital Expenditure						
EBITDA						
Return on Assets %						
Return on Equity %						
Debt to Equity						

CONTACT INFORMATION:
Phone: 34-915-949-500   Fax: 34-914-465-546
Toll-Free:
Address: C/ Emilio Munoz 35-37, Madrid, 28037 Spain

STOCK TICKER/OTHER:
Stock Ticker: Private
Employees: 1,800
Parent Company:

Exchange:
Fiscal Year Ends:

SALARIES/BONUSES:
Top Exec. Salary: $ Bonus: $
Second Exec. Salary: $ Bonus: $

OTHER THOUGHTS:
Estimated Female Officers or Directors:
Hot Spot for Advancement for Women/Minorities:

Sales, profits and employees may be estimates. Financial information, benefits and other data can change quickly and may vary from those stated here.

Essilor International SA

www.essilor.com

NAIC Code: 339100

TYPES OF BUSINESS:
Supplies-Ophthalmic Products
Corrective Lenses
Lens Treatments
Ophthalmic Instruments
Technical Consulting

BRANDS/DIVISIONS/AFFILIATES:
Eyezen
Essilor
Varilux
Crizal
Xperio
Optifog
Transitions
Bolon

CONTACTS:
Note: Officers with more than one job title may be intentionally listed here more than once.

Hubert Sagnieres, CEO
Laurent Vacherot, Pres.
Jean-Luc Schuppiser, Corp. Sr. VP-R&D
Patrick Poncin, Corp. Sr. VP-Global Eng.
Kevin Rupp, Exec. VP-Admin., Essilor Of America
Carol Xueref, Corp. Sr. VP-Legal Affairs & Dev.
Claude Brignon, Corp. Sr. VP-Worldwide Oper.
Kate Philipps, VP-Corp. Comm.
Veronique Gillet, Sr. VP-Investor Rel.
Kevin Rupp, Exec. VP-Finance, Essilor Of America
Eric Bernard, Pres., Essilor China
Norbert Gorny, Pres., Satisloh
Jean Carrier-Guillomet, Pres., Essilor of America
Eric Leonard, Pres., European Region
Hubert Sagnieres, Chmn.
Tadeu Alves, Pres., Latin America

GROWTH PLANS/SPECIAL FEATURES:
Essilor International SA is a global designer, manufacturer and distributor of ophthalmic and optical products. The firm divides its operations into three segments: corrective lenses, sunglasses and readers and equipment and instruments. Corrective lenses treat common sight problems such as myopia, hyperopia, astigmatism and presbyopia. This segment's innovations include the e-SPF index, the Eyezen range of lenses and technologies that filter blue-violet light, all of which also benefit Essilor's other activities. The sunglasses and readers segment sells more than 140 million pairs of sunglasses, readers and eyewear annually. Its technologies enable the company to offer sunlenses worldwide, with or without prescription. The equipment and instrument segment contributes to Essilor's technical advances by mastering technologies in lens manufacturing and the instruments used for taking measurements. This division designs, manufactures and distributes innovative products, technologies and services for opticians, optometrists and ophthalmologists in relation to optical and vision care instruments, measurement, edging/mounting tools. In addition, this segment provides a range of diagnostic equipment for preventive healthcare organizations. Primary brands of the firm include Essilor, Varilux, Crizal, Eyezen, Xperio, Optifog, Transitions, Bolon, Costa, Foster Grant, Kodak Lens and Osse. Essilor operates in more than 100 countries, supplies products through a global network of 490 prescription laboratories and 33 production sites, producing millions of lenses annually. In January 2017, Luxottica Group SpA, a manufacturer and retailer of prescription and fashion eyeglass frames and sunglasses, agreed to be merged with and into Essilor. Essilor would become a holding company under new name EssilorLuxottica via a hive-down of all of its operating activities into a wholly-owned company called Essilor International. In March 2018, the proposed merger had been cleared by the U.S. Federal Trade Commission without conditions, and had already been unconditionally approved in the EU and 13 other countries.

FINANCIAL DATA:
Note: Data for latest year may not have been available at press time.

In U.S. $	2017	2016	2015	2014	2013	2012
Revenue	9,249,425,000	8,786,337,000	8,293,611,000	7,001,902,000	6,254,786,000	6,160,741,000
R&D Expense	267,974,000	264,269,300	264,269,300	232,161,800	202,524,100	199,902,400
Operating Income	1,326,286,000	1,552,273,000	1,460,891,000	1,509,052,000	1,042,258,000	1,007,789,000
Operating Margin %	14.33%	17.66%	17.61%	21.55%	16.66%	16.35%
SGA Expense	2,278,397,000	2,161,081,000	2,072,168,000	1,688,113,000	1,413,964,000	1,407,612,000
Net Income	974,338,800	1,003,976,000	934,821,800	1,147,225,000	732,297,700	721,193,400
Operating Cash Flow	1,522,636,000	1,474,475,000	1,474,475,000	1,274,420,000	1,041,023,000	1,037,316,000
Capital Expenditure	380,350,200	363,061,600	403,813,400	286,497,600	366,766,300	297,867,300
EBITDA	2,011,657,000	1,970,906,000	1,941,268,000	2,065,993,000	1,347,280,000	1,291,358,000
Return on Assets %	6.19%	6.46%	6.65%	10.11%	8.18%	8.93%
Return on Equity %	11.96%	13.11%	14.25%	21.42%	15.98%	16.71%
Debt to Equity	0.25	0.20	0.33	0.30	0.16	0.14

CONTACT INFORMATION:
Phone: 33-1-49-77-42-16   Fax: 33-1-49-77-44-20
Toll-Free:
Address: 147 rue de Paris,, Paris, 94220 France

STOCK TICKER/OTHER:
Stock Ticker: ESLOF
Employees: 63,676
Parent Company:

Exchange: PINX
Fiscal Year Ends: 12/31

SALARIES/BONUSES:
Top Exec. Salary: $ Bonus: $
Second Exec. Salary: $ Bonus: $

OTHER THOUGHTS:
Estimated Female Officers or Directors: 5
Hot Spot for Advancement for Women/Minorities: Y

Sales, profits and employees may be estimates. Financial information, benefits and other data can change quickly and may vary from those stated here.

Evonik Industries AG

NAIC Code: 325110

www.evonik.com

TYPES OF BUSINESS:
Petrochemicals
Industrial Engineering
Electricity Generation
Real Estate
Renewable Energy-Biomass
Paints and Coatings

BRANDS/DIVISIONS/AFFILIATES:
Evonik Nutrition & Care GmbH
Evonik Resource Efficiency GmbH
Evonik Performance Materials GmbH
Evonik Technology & Infrastructure GmbH
RAG Foundation
Gabriel Acquisitions GmbH
Dr Straetmans GmbH
HPNow ApS

CONTACTS:
Note: Officers with more than one job title may be intentionally listed here more than once.

Christian Kullmann, CEO
Ute Wolf, CFO
Thomas Wessel, Chief Human Resources Officer

GROWTH PLANS/SPECIAL FEATURES:

Evonik Industries AG is an international industrial group with plants in 25 countries and activities in more than 100 countries worldwide. The firm operates through three primary operating subsidiaries: Evonik Nutrition & Care GmbH, Evonik Resource Efficiency GmbH and Evonik Performance Materials GmbH. Evonik Nutrition & Care's product lines involve animal nutrition, health care, baby care, personal care, household care, rigid and flexible foams for comfort and insulation purposes, as well as oleochemical and silicone based specialties to industrial markets. Evonik Resource Efficiency specializes in chemicals for industrial applications, including energy-efficient systems for the automotive, paints and coatings, adhesives, construction and other industries. Business lines in this segment include active oxygens, catalysts, coating additives, coating and adhesive resins, crosslinkers, high performance polymers, oil additives, silanes and silica. Evonik Performance Materials is comprised of intermediates, agrochemicals and polymer additives, functional solutions, acrylic monomers and acrylic polymers. This segment's high-volume intermediates and solutions allow its customers to make plastics, biofuels and agrochemicals. Additionally, Evonik Technology & Infrastructure GmbH provides customers from the chemical industry the backing needed to be free to perform their core businesses. Its business lines include utilities, waste management, technical service, process technology and engineering, logistics and site management. Evonik Industries is headquartered in Germany, is 67.9%-owned by RAG Foundation; 14 % by Gabriel Acquisitions GmbH; and 18.1% free float. During 2017, the firm formed a joint venture with Koninklijke DSM NV to produce omega-3 fatty acid products from natural marine algae for animal nutrition, a breakthrough innovation; acquired Dr. Straetmans GmbH, which develops and markets alternative preservatives for the cosmetic industry; and invested a minority stake in Danish hydrogen peroxide startup HPNow ApS, which has developed a technology for producing H2O2 in a fully automatic system using water, air and an electric current.

FINANCIAL DATA:
Note: Data for latest year may not have been available at press time.

In U.S. $	2017	2016	2015	2014	2013	2012
Revenue	17,806,070,000	15,722,790,000	16,679,840,000	15,951,250,000	15,898,150,000	16,830,500,000
R&D Expense	565,585,700	540,887,700	535,948,000	510,015,100	486,551,900	485,317,000
Operating Income	1,669,589,000	2,074,638,000	2,390,773,000	1,723,925,000	1,767,147,000	2,236,410,000
Operating Margin %	9.37%	13.19%	14.33%	10.80%	11.11%	13.28%
SGA Expense	2,997,111,000	2,718,022,000	2,642,693,000	2,333,967,000	2,377,189,000	2,332,732,000
Net Income	885,425,700	1,042,258,000	1,223,789,000	701,425,100	2,536,492,000	1,437,427,000
Operating Cash Flow	1,915,335,000	2,170,960,000	2,433,994,000	1,316,407,000	1,337,400,000	1,753,563,000
Capital Expenditure	1,284,300,000	1,170,688,000	1,131,171,000	1,352,219,000	1,331,226,000	1,260,836,000
EBITDA	2,706,908,000	2,593,297,000	3,025,513,000	2,206,772,000	2,168,490,000	3,462,669,000
Return on Assets %	3.62%	4.60%	6.06%	3.59%	12.61%	6.92%
Return on Equity %	9.49%	11.14%	14.23%	8.60%	30.45%	18.33%
Debt to Equity	0.49	0.42	0.18	0.09	0.09	0.20

CONTACT INFORMATION:
Phone: 49-201-177-01 Fax: 49-201-177-3475
Toll-Free:
Address: Rellinghauser Strasse 1-11, Essen, 45128 Germany

STOCK TICKER/OTHER:
Stock Ticker: EVKIF   Exchange: PINX
Employees: 35,803   Fiscal Year Ends: 12/31
Parent Company:

SALARIES/BONUSES:
Top Exec. Salary: $ Bonus: $
Second Exec. Salary: $ Bonus: $

OTHER THOUGHTS:
Estimated Female Officers or Directors: 1
Hot Spot for Advancement for Women/Minorities:

Sales, profits and employees may be estimates. Financial information, benefits and other data can change quickly and may vary from those stated here.

Exxon Mobil Corporation (ExxonMobil)

NAIC Code: 211111

www.exxonmobil.com

TYPES OF BUSINESS:
Oil & Gas Exploration & Production
Gas Refining & Supply
Fuel Marketing
Power Generation
Chemicals
Petroleum Products
Convenience Stores

BRANDS/DIVISIONS/AFFILIATES:
ExxonMobil
Esso
Exxon
XTO
Mobil

CONTACTS: Note: Officers with more than one job title may be intentionally listed here more than once.
Darren Woods, CEO
Neil Chapman, Senior VP
Andrew Swiger, CFO
David Rosenthal, Chief Accounting Officer
James Spellings, Other Corporate Officer
Bryan Milton, President, Divisional
Sara Ortwein, President, Subsidiary
Liam Mallon, President, Subsidiary
John Verity, President, Subsidiary
Stephen Greenlee, President, Subsidiary
Neil Duffin, President, Subsidiary
Bradley Corson, President, Subsidiary
Robert Franklin, President, Subsidiary
Jeffrey Woodbury, Secretary
Jack Williams, Senior VP
Mark Albers, Senior VP
Michael Dolan, Senior VP

GROWTH PLANS/SPECIAL FEATURES:
Exxon Mobil Corporation (ExxonMobil) is one of the largest international petroleum and natural gas exploration and production companies in the world. Its principal business is energy, involving exploration for and production of crude oil and natural gas; the manufacture of petroleum products; and the transportation and sale of crude oil, natural gas and petroleum products. The company has hundreds of affiliates, many with names that include ExxonMobil, Esso, Exxon, XTO or Mobil. Overall, the firm divides its business units into three areas: upstream, downstream and chemical. The upstream business focuses on conventional oil, heavy oil, shale gas, deepwater, liquefied natural gas (LNG), Arctic and sour gas projects. The downstream business is concerned with refining crude oil and other feedstocks into fuels, lubricants and other chemicals and delivering it to customers through a global distributor network. The chemical business is focused on the production of olefins, such as ethylene and propylene, and polyolefins, such as polyethylene and polypropylene. In addition, it manufactures specialty chemicals for use in water treatment, coatings, lubricants and oil drilling fluids. In late-2017, the firm signed production sharing contracts with the government of Mauritania for three deepwater offshore blocks; and acquired a 25% stake in Mozambique's gas-rich Area 4 block from Eni and assume responsibility for midstream operations. In January 2018, ExxonMobil signed a petroleum agreement with the government of Ghana to acquire exploration and production rights for the Deepwater Cape Three Points block, with exploration activities, including acquisition of seismic data and analysis, expected to begin by year's end.

U.S. employee benefits include health, dental and vision coverage; life insurance; education assistance; childcare, elder care and adoption assistance; and spousal relocation assistance.

FINANCIAL DATA: Note: Data for latest year may not have been available at press time.

In U.S. $	2017	2016	2015	2014	2013	2012
Revenue	237,162,000,000	218,608,000,000	259,488,000,000	394,105,000,000	420,836,000,000	453,123,000,000
R&D Expense						
Operating Income	12,074,000,000	936,000,000	12,883,000,000	34,082,000,000	40,301,000,000	49,881,000,000
Operating Margin %	5.09%	.42%	4.96%	8.64%	9.57%	11.00%
SGA Expense	10,956,000,000	10,799,000,000	11,501,000,000	12,598,000,000	12,877,000,000	13,877,000,000
Net Income	19,710,000,000	7,840,000,000	16,150,000,000	32,520,000,000	32,580,000,000	44,880,000,000
Operating Cash Flow	30,066,000,000	22,082,000,000	30,344,000,000	45,116,000,000	44,914,000,000	56,170,000,000
Capital Expenditure	15,402,000,000	16,163,000,000	26,490,000,000	32,952,000,000	33,669,000,000	34,271,000,000
EBITDA	39,168,000,000	30,730,000,000	40,325,000,000	69,213,000,000	74,902,000,000	94,941,000,000
Return on Assets %	5.80%	2.35%	4.70%	9.34%	9.57%	13.50%
Return on Equity %	11.10%	4.63%	9.35%	18.66%	19.17%	28.02%
Debt to Equity	0.13	0.17	0.11	0.06	0.03	0.04

CONTACT INFORMATION:
Phone: 972 444-1000   Fax: 972 444-1348
Toll-Free:
Address: 5959 Las Colinas Blvd., Irving, TX 75039 United States

STOCK TICKER/OTHER:
Stock Ticker: XOM   Exchange: NYS
Employees: 71,100   Fiscal Year Ends: 12/31
Parent Company:

SALARIES/BONUSES:
Top Exec. Salary: $1,200,000   Bonus: $1,848,000
Second Exec. Salary: $1,430,000   Bonus: $1,603,000

OTHER THOUGHTS:
Estimated Female Officers or Directors: 2
Hot Spot for Advancement for Women/Minorities: Y

ExxonMobil Chemical Company Inc

www.exxonmobilchemical.com

NAIC Code: 325110

TYPES OF BUSINESS:
Plastics & Rubber Manufacturing
Petrochemicals
Catalyst Technology
Polypropylene

BRANDS/DIVISIONS/AFFILIATES:
Exxon Mobil Corporation
ExxonMobile Chemical Technology Licensing LLC
Exxcore
Enable

CONTACTS:
Note: Officers with more than one job title may be intentionally listed here more than once.

Neil A. Chapman, Pres.
Sherman J. Glass Jr., Pres., ExxonMobil Refining & Amp
Donald D. Humphreys, Sr. VP

GROWTH PLANS/SPECIAL FEATURES:

ExxonMobil Chemical Company, Inc., a subsidiary of Exxon Mobil Corporation, is a global leader in the petrochemicals industry. The firm applies proprietary technology to create products that improve the quality of life for people worldwide. Its products and services are divided into three units: polymers, chemicals and fluids, and technology licensing and catalysts. These units produce sustainable solutions in relation to olefins, aromatics, fluids, synthetic rubber, polyethylene, polypropylene, plasticizers, synthetic lubricant base-stocks, additives for fuels and lubricants, and zeolite catalysts. The company's products span a variety of markets, but most can be grouped into the following areas: automotive, packaging, construction/industrial and personal care. ExxonMobile Chemical's technology division focuses on developing new products with environmentally-preferred characteristics, including tire innerliners made with Exxcore, a vulcanized allow resin that holds air longer; and Enable metallocene polyethylene chemicals, which significantly reduces waste and energy consumption across a wide range of film applications. Technologies are available for licensing through ExxonMobile Chemical Technology Licensing, LLC. In October 2017, the firm announced plans to invest more than $20 billion over the next 10 years to build and expand manufacturing facilities in the U.S. Gulf region. These projects are expected to create more than 45,000 jobs, including 12,000 full-time jobs, and covers 11 major chemical, refining, lubricant and liquefied natural gas projects along the Texas and Louisiana coasts. That same year, ExxonMobile Chemical acquired one of the world's largest aromatics facilities on Jurong Island in Singapore; and began production on the first of two new 650,000 tons-per-year high-performance polyethylene lines at its plastics plant in Mont Belvieu, Texas.

FINANCIAL DATA:
Note: Data for latest year may not have been available at press time.

In U.S. $	2017	2016	2015	2014	2013	2012
Revenue						
R&D Expense						
Operating Income						
Operating Margin %						
SGA Expense						
Net Income	4,518,000,000	4,615,000,000	4,418,000,000	4,315,000,000	3,828,000,000	3,898,000,000
Operating Cash Flow						
Capital Expenditure						
EBITDA						
Return on Assets %						
Return on Equity %						
Debt to Equity						

CONTACT INFORMATION:
Phone: 281-870-6000 Fax: 281-870-6661
Toll-Free:
Address: 22777 Springwoods Village Pkwy., Spring, TX 77389-1425 United States

STOCK TICKER/OTHER:
Stock Ticker: Subsidiary
Employees: 18,000
Parent Company: Exxon Mobil Corporation
Exchange:
Fiscal Year Ends: 12/31

SALARIES/BONUSES:
Top Exec. Salary: $ Bonus: $
Second Exec. Salary: $ Bonus: $

OTHER THOUGHTS:
Estimated Female Officers or Directors:
Hot Spot for Advancement for Women/Minorities:

Sales, profits and employees may be estimates. Financial information, benefits and other data can change quickly and may vary from those stated here.

Faurecia SA

NAIC Code: 336300

www.faurecia.com

TYPES OF BUSINESS:
Automobile Part Manufacturing
Vehicle Component Modules
Vehicle Seats
Vehicle Doors
Exhaust Systems
Front End Modules
Acoustic Engineering & Equipment

BRANDS/DIVISIONS/AFFILIATES:

CONTACTS:
Note: Officers with more than one job title may be intentionally listed here more than once.

Patrick Koller, CEO
Hagen Wiesner, Exec. VP-Oper.
Michel Favre, CFO
Jean-Pierre Sounillac, Exec. VP-Human Resources
Frank Imbert, Exec. VP
Herve Guyot, Exec. VP-Group Strategy
Kate Phillips, Exec. VP-Group Comm.
Herve Guyot, Exec. VP-Automotive Exteriors
Christophe Schmitt, Exec. VP-Emission Control Tech.
Patrick Koller, Exec. VP-Automotive Seating
Jean-Michel Renaude, Exec. VP-Interior Systems

GROWTH PLANS/SPECIAL FEATURES:

Faurecia SA, headquartered in France, is a global supplier of vehicle equipment. The firm has approximately 110 production facilities and 13 research and development centers throughout Western Europe, Central Europe, North America, South America and Asia. It divides its design and assembly operations into three business groups: seating, interiors and clean mobility. The seating group produces the full line of components that go into automotive seating: frames, mechanisms, mechatronics, foam pads, trim covers, accessories and electronic/pneumatic systems. Faurecia develops state-of-the-art technologies for enhanced seat performance, including mechanisms, cover technology, comfort systems and integrated safety. It also assembles complete seats, both front and rear, for just-in-time delivery to its customers' plants. The interiors group develops, produces and supplies: instrument panels and center consoles, cockpits, door panels and modules, acoustic products and modules, and decorative components. Faurecia is currently developing and integrating renewable, bio-based materials as part of a long-term campaign to produce lighter components. One of its technologies combines natural hemp fibers with a polypropylene resin to yield a 25% weight reduction over glass-reinforced polypropylene. Last, the clean mobility group contributes to the reduction of pollutant emissions by supplying carmakers with solutions in emissions control, as well as acoustic treatment, weight reduction and energy heat recovery. Its selective catalytic reduction systems curb nitrogen oxide emissions from diesel engines, eliminating up to 95% of engine NOx emissions; and its exhaust heat recovery system can capture up to 75% of the energy typically lost as heat when warming the cabin and engine. In February 2018, the firm announced plans to submit a proposal to its shareholders to convert as a European company and renamed as Societas Europaea, SE.

FINANCIAL DATA:
Note: Data for latest year may not have been available at press time.

In U.S. $	2017	2016	2015	2014	2013	2012
Revenue	24,922,450,000	23,105,660,000	23,179,630,000	23,251,870,000	22,263,580,000	21,443,480,000
R&D Expense	327,249,400	357,504,500	343,797,100	290,819,700	313,665,400	295,882,800
Operating Income	1,445,454,000	1,187,236,000	1,026,328,000	835,659,100	664,748,500	634,369,900
Operating Margin %	5.79%	5.13%	4.42%	3.59%	2.98%	2.95%
SGA Expense	840,228,200	822,692,600	786,880,400	800,587,800	741,189,000	703,771,500
Net Income	753,538,000	787,621,400	459,137,100	204,623,500	108,177,500	175,726,800
Operating Cash Flow	1,991,405,000	1,601,299,000	1,542,641,000	1,281,089,000	1,145,249,000	334,041,300
Capital Expenditure	1,491,146,000	1,290,350,000	1,150,436,000	1,040,530,000	972,609,900	1,017,560,000
EBITDA	2,200,104,000	1,879,029,000	1,658,969,000	1,345,921,000	1,143,644,000	1,118,699,000
Return on Assets %	5.53%	6.28%	3.94%	1.90%	1.06%	1.85%
Return on Equity %	19.76%	23.88%	18.07%	10.29%	6.24%	11.57%
Debt to Equity	0.49	0.54	0.40	0.59	0.86	1.27

CONTACT INFORMATION:
Phone: 33 172367000   Fax: 33 172367007
Toll-Free:
Address: 2 rue Hennape, Nanterre, 92000 France

STOCK TICKER/OTHER:
Stock Ticker: FURCF
Employees: 98,608
Parent Company:

Exchange: PINX
Fiscal Year Ends: 12/31

SALARIES/BONUSES:
Top Exec. Salary: $ Bonus: $
Second Exec. Salary: $ Bonus: $

OTHER THOUGHTS:
Estimated Female Officers or Directors: 1
Hot Spot for Advancement for Women/Minorities:

Sales, profits and employees may be estimates. Financial information, benefits and other data can change quickly and may vary from those stated here.

FAW Group Corporation (First Automotive Works)
www.faw.com

NAIC Code: 336111

TYPES OF BUSINESS:
Automobile Manufacturing
Parts Manufacturing
Truck Manufacturing

BRANDS/DIVISIONS/AFFILIATES:
First Automotive Works
FAW Jiefang Truck Co Ltd
FAW Bus and Coach Co Ltd
FAW Assets Operation and Management Co Ltd
FAW Jilin Automobile Co Ltd
FAW Group Import and Export Corporation
FAW Foundry Co Ltd
FAW Tool and Die Co Ltd

CONTACTS:
Note: Officers with more than one job title may be intentionally listed here more than once.

Xianping Xu, Pres.
Tieqi Teng, Chief Acct.
Xianping Xu, Chmn.

GROWTH PLANS/SPECIAL FEATURES:

FAW Group Corporation is a state-owned Chinese vehicle manufacturer. Founded in 1953 as First Automotive Works, it became one of the first vehicle producers in China, starting with the 1956 rollout of Jiefang trucks and the 1958 launch of Hongqi cars. FAW has sold nearly 20 million vehicles worldwide, with product including light-, medium- and heavy-duty trucks; automobiles; municipal buses; luxury tourist coaches; custom bus chassis; and mini-vehicles. Headquartered in Changchun, Jilin Province, the firm's domestic production facilities, subsidiaries and engineering development/test centers are located in 18 locations throughout China. Manufacturing plants are located in Jilin, Liaoning, Heilongjiang, Shandong, Guangxi, Hainan, Sichuan and Yunnan provinces, as well as in the municipality of Tianjin. Wholly-owned subsidiaries include FAW Jiefang Truck Co. Ltd.; FAW Bus and Coach Co. Ltd.; FAW Assets Operation and Management Co. Ltd.; FAW Jilin Automobile Co. Ltd.; FAW Group Import and Export Corporation; FAW Foundry Co. Ltd.; FAW Tool and Die Co. Ltd.; and MMI Planning & Engineering Group.

FINANCIAL DATA:
Note: Data for latest year may not have been available at press time.

In U.S. $	2017	2016	2015	2014	2013	2012
Revenue	68,174,700,000	62,852,000,000	80,194,000,000	80,194,500,000	68,500,000,000	64,886,000,000
R&D Expense						
Operating Income						
Operating Margin %						
SGA Expense						
Net Income		3,253,000,000	4,248,000,000	3,000,000,000	2,285,816,000	2,622,000,000
Operating Cash Flow						
Capital Expenditure						
EBITDA						
Return on Assets %						
Return on Equity %						
Debt to Equity						

CONTACT INFORMATION:
Phone: 86-431-8590-0715 Fax: 86-431-8761-4780
Toll-Free:
Address: Dongfeng St., No. 3025, Changchun, 130011 China

SALARIES/BONUSES:
Top Exec. Salary: $ Bonus: $
Second Exec. Salary: $ Bonus: $

STOCK TICKER/OTHER:
Stock Ticker: Government-Owned
Employees: 132,083
Parent Company:
Exchange:
Fiscal Year Ends: 03/31

OTHER THOUGHTS:
Estimated Female Officers or Directors:
Hot Spot for Advancement for Women/Minorities:

Sales, profits and employees may be estimates. Financial information, benefits and other data can change quickly and may vary from those stated here.

FCA US LLC
www.fcanorthamerica.com/company/AboutUs/Pages/AboutUs.aspx
NAIC Code: 336111

TYPES OF BUSINESS:
Automobile Manufacturing
Research & Development
Nanotechnology-Coatings
Light Truck Manufacturing
Financial Services

BRANDS/DIVISIONS/AFFILIATES:
Fiat Chrysler Automobiles NV
Chrysler
Jeep
Dodge
Ram
Fiat
Alfa Romeo
Uconnect

CONTACTS:
Note: Officers with more than one job title may be intentionally listed here more than once.

Sergio Marchionne, CEO
Ralph V. Gilles, Sr. VP-Prod. Design
Mark M. Chernoby, Sr. VP-Eng.
Mauro Pino, Sr. VP-Mfg. & World Class Mfg.
Peter Grady, VP-Network Dev. & Fleet
Marjorie Loeb, General Counsel
Barbara J. Pilarski, VP-Bus. Dev.
Gualberto Ranieri, Sr. VP-Comm.
Laurie A. Macaddino, VP-Audit
Doug D. Betts, Sr. VP-Quality
Alistair Gardner, Pres.
Reid Bigland, Head-U.S. Sales
Sergio Marchionne, Chmn.
Steven G. Beahm, Sr. VP-Supply Chain Mgmt.

GROWTH PLANS/SPECIAL FEATURES:
FCA US, LLC, also known as Fiat Chrysler, is a North American automaker headquartered in Michigan. It is a member of the Fiat Chrysler Automobiles NV family of companies. FCA US designs, engineers, manufactures and sells vehicles under the Chrysler, Jeep, Dodge, Ram, Fiat and Alfa Romeo brands, as well as the street and racing technology (SRT) performance vehicle designation. The company also distributes the Alfa Romeo model and Mopar parts and accessories. FCA is one of the largest automakers in the world based on total annual vehicle sales, shipping 2.4 million vehicles in 2017 from its 36 worldwide manufacturing sites. The 2018 Fiat 124 Spider Lusso vehicle offers classic Italian roadster style and performance. The 2018 Chrysler Pacifica minivan and 2018 Dodge Durango large SUV received awards for ranking as best buy vehicles. Engineering breakthroughs made by the company include: Uconnect, which allows drivers to easily adjust seat or cabin temperature, select a new music station or make a call without taking their eyes from the road; various fuel efficiency features in relation to power, transmissions, engines and electrified propulsion systems; and design, development and vehicle integration of technologies in relation to customer safety and security.

The firm offers employees medical, prescription, vision and dental coverage; life insurance; discounted auto and home insurance; discount new vehicle purchase programs; and educational and personal development programs.

FINANCIAL DATA:
Note: Data for latest year may not have been available at press time.

In U.S. $	2017	2016	2015	2014	2013	2012
Revenue	11,750,000,000	12,000,000,000	11,676,910,000	10,913,000,000	72,140,000,000	65,800,000,000
R&D Expense						
Operating Income						
Operating Margin %						
SGA Expense						
Net Income		1,985,015,213	1,747,498,195	1,587,005,793	2,760,000,000	1,700,000,000
Operating Cash Flow						
Capital Expenditure						
EBITDA						
Return on Assets %						
Return on Equity %						
Debt to Equity						

CONTACT INFORMATION:
Phone: 248-576-5741 Fax:
Toll-Free: 800-992-1997
Address: 1000 Chrysler Dr., Auburn Hills, MI 48326-2766 United States

STOCK TICKER/OTHER:
Stock Ticker: Private Exchange:
Employees: 83,800 Fiscal Year Ends: 12/31
Parent Company: Fiat Chrysler Automobiles NV

SALARIES/BONUSES:
Top Exec. Salary: $ Bonus: $
Second Exec. Salary: $ Bonus: $

OTHER THOUGHTS:
Estimated Female Officers or Directors: 3
Hot Spot for Advancement for Women/Minorities: Y

Sales, profits and employees may be estimates. Financial information, benefits and other data can change quickly and may vary from those stated here.

Federal-Mogul LLC

NAIC Code: 336300

www.federalmogul.com

TYPES OF BUSINESS:
Aftermarket Products & Services
Powertrain Products
Sealing Systems
Vehicle Safety & Performance Products

BRANDS/DIVISIONS/AFFILIATES:
Icahn Enterprises LP

CONTACTS:
Note: Officers with more than one job title may be intentionally listed here more than once.

Brad Norton, Co-CEO
Rainer Jueckstock, Co-CEO
Rainer Jueckstock, CEO, Divisional
Jerome Rouquet, Sr. VP
Martin Hendricks, President, Divisional
Scott Pepin, Senior VP, Divisional
Jerome Rouquet, Senior VP
John Patouhas, Vice President

GROWTH PLANS/SPECIAL FEATURES:

Federal-Mogul, LLC is a global supplier of vehicle and industrial products for fuel economy, alternative energies and safety systems. The company operates two divisions: powertrain and motor parts. Powertrain focuses on original equipment (OE) products for automotive, heavy duty and industrial applications. This segment offers its customers a diverse array of market-leading products for OE applications, including pistons, piston rings, piston pins, cylinder liners, valve seats and guides, ignition products, dynamic seals, bonded piston seals, combustion & exhaust gaskets, static gaskets/seals, rigid heat shields, engine bearings, industrial bearings, brushings, washers, plus element resistant systems protection sleeving products, acoustic shielding and flexible heat shields. The motor parts segment sells and distributes a broad portfolio of products manufactured by Powertrain. Motor parts' products include brake disc pads, brake linings, brake linings, brake blocks, brake system components, chassis products, wipers and other product lines to OE and aftermarket customers. Federal-Mogul maintains manufacturing facilities and distribution centers in 24 countries. In April 2018, parent company Icahn Enterprises LP announced plans to sell the firm to Tenneco, Inc. for $2.5 billion.

The firm offers employees medical, dental, prescription drug, vision and hearing insurance; flexible spending accounts; life and AD&D insurance; disability coverage; a 401(k) plan; tuition assistance; and a pension plan.

FINANCIAL DATA:
Note: Data for latest year may not have been available at press time.

In U.S. $	2017	2016	2015	2014	2013	2012
Revenue	7,500,000,000	7,434,000,000	7,418,999,808	7,317,000,192	6,785,999,872	6,664,000,000
R&D Expense						
Operating Income						
Operating Margin %						
SGA Expense						
Net Income		90,000,000	-110,000,000	-168,000,000	41,000,000	-117,000,000
Operating Cash Flow						
Capital Expenditure						
EBITDA						
Return on Assets %						
Return on Equity %						
Debt to Equity						

CONTACT INFORMATION:
Phone: 248 354-7700 Fax: 248 354-8950
Toll-Free:
Address: 27300 West 11 Mile Rd., Southfield, MI 48034 United States

STOCK TICKER/OTHER:
Stock Ticker: Subsidiary
Employees: 53,000
Parent Company: Icahn Enterprises LP
Exchange:
Fiscal Year Ends: 12/31

SALARIES/BONUSES:
Top Exec. Salary: $ Bonus: $
Second Exec. Salary: $ Bonus: $

OTHER THOUGHTS:
Estimated Female Officers or Directors: 1
Hot Spot for Advancement for Women/Minorities:

Sales, profits and employees may be estimates. Financial information, benefits and other data can change quickly and may vary from those stated here.

Ferrovial SA

NAIC Code: 488119

www.ferrovial.com/en

TYPES OF BUSINESS:
Airport Operations
Construction
Infrastructure Services
Toll Roads
Civil Engineering

BRANDS/DIVISIONS/AFFILIATES:
Cintra

CONTACTS:
Note: Officers with more than one job title may be intentionally listed here more than once.

Inigo Meiras, CEO
Ernesto Lopez Mozo, CFO
Maria Dionis, Dir.-Human Resources
Federico Florez, CIO
Santiago Ortiz, Sec.
Santiago Olivares, CEO-Ferrovial Svcs.
Enrique Diaz-Rato, CEO-Cintra
Alejandro de la Joya, CEO-Ferrovial Agroman
Jorge Gil, CEO-Ferrovial Airports
Rafael del Pino, Chmn.

GROWTH PLANS/SPECIAL FEATURES:

Ferrovial SA is a leading infrastructure and industrial group with a presence in over 25 countries worldwide. The company has four business units: airports, toll roads, services and construction. Ferrovial's airports segment is one of the leading private airport operators in the world, conducting business largely through London Heathrow Airports (LHR), handling flights from 138 airlines every year, carrying approximately 90 million passengers. LHR manages four airports in the U.K.: Heathrow, Southampton, Glasgow and Aberdeen. Cintra is the firm's toll road and car parks business division and subsidiary. It manages a total of 27 toll roads in Spain, Portugal, Ireland, Colombia, Australia, Greece, Canada, the U.K. and the U.S. Ferrovial's services segment provides maintenance and operation of public and private infrastructures for transport, environment, industry, natural resources (oil, gas and mining) and utilities (water and electricity). This division also provides facility management services. Last, the construction business covers all aspects of civil engineering and building, including roads, tunnels, railways, residential/non-residential buildings, airports, dams, gas/oil pipelines, water treatment plants, canals, hydroelectric plants and docks and port infrastructures. This segment has accumulated more than 80 years' experience, 50 years of international activity in 50 countries across 5 continents, and more than 675 projects.

FINANCIAL DATA:
Note: Data for latest year may not have been available at press time.

In U.S. $	2017	2016	2015	2014	2013	2012
Revenue	15,075,700,000	13,286,330,000	11,979,800,000	10,869,620,000	10,084,220,000	9,491,467,000
R&D Expense						
Operating Income	687,841,200	743,411,800	952,110,500	912,593,500	865,667,300	874,311,600
Operating Margin %	4.56%	5.59%	7.94%	8.39%	8.58%	9.21%
SGA Expense						
Net Income	560,646,100	464,323,600	889,130,400	496,431,100	897,774,700	876,781,400
Operating Cash Flow	1,580,676,000	1,447,307,000	1,395,441,000	1,764,677,000	1,600,435,000	1,457,186,000
Capital Expenditure	166,712,000	218,577,900	218,577,900	142,013,900	118,550,700	145,718,600
EBITDA	1,150,930,000	1,165,749,000	1,268,246,000	1,213,910,000	1,153,400,000	1,144,755,000
Return on Assets %	1.95%	1.54%	2.83%	1.66%	3.22%	3.14%
Return on Equity %	8.18%	6.45%	12.27%	7.05%	12.79%	12.05%
Debt to Equity	1.36	1.40	1.10	1.53	1.34	1.27

CONTACT INFORMATION:
Phone: 34 915862500   Fax: 34 915862677
Toll-Free:
Address: Principe de Vergara, 135, Madrid, 28002 Spain

STOCK TICKER/OTHER:
Stock Ticker: FRRVY
Employees: 95,978
Parent Company:

Exchange: PINX
Fiscal Year Ends: 12/31

SALARIES/BONUSES:
Top Exec. Salary: $ Bonus: $
Second Exec. Salary: $ Bonus: $

OTHER THOUGHTS:
Estimated Female Officers or Directors:
Hot Spot for Advancement for Women/Minorities:

Flex Ltd

www.flextronics.com

NAIC Code: 334418

TYPES OF BUSINESS:
Printed Circuit Assembly (Electronic Assembly) Manufacturing
Telecommunications Equipment Manufacturing
Engineering, Design & Testing Services
Logistics Services
Camera Modules
Medical Devices
LCD Displays
Original Design Manufacturing (ODM)

BRANDS/DIVISIONS/AFFILIATES:

CONTACTS: Note: Officers with more than one job title may be intentionally listed here more than once.
Michael McNamara, CEO
Francois Barbier, Pres.
Christopher Collier, CFO
Paul Baldassari, Chief Human Resources Officer
Mark Kemp, Pres., Medical
Mike Dennison, Pres-Consumer Technologies
Erik Volkerink, CTO
Christopher Obey, Pres., Automotive
Christopher Cook, Pres., Power Solutions
Jeannine Sargent, Pres., Energy
Jonathan Hoak, General Counsel
Francois Barbier, Pres., Global Oper. & Components
David Mark, Chief Strategy Officer
Renee Brotherton, VP-Corp. Comm.
Christopher Collier, Chief Accounting Officer
Paul Humphries, Pres., High Reliability Solutions
Caroline Dowling, Pres., Integrated Network Solutions
Doug Britt, Pres., Industrial & Emerging Solutions
Mike Dennison, Pres., High Velocity Solutions
Tom Linton, Chief Procurement & Supply Chain Officer

GROWTH PLANS/SPECIAL FEATURES:
Flex Ltd. is a provider of innovative design, engineering, manufacturing and supply chain services and solutions that span from conceptual sketch to full-scale production. The company offers packaged consumer electronics and industrial products for original equipment manufacturers (OEMs) through its four business segments: high reliability solutions (HRS), consumer technologies group (CTG), industrial and emerging industries (IEI) and communications and enterprise compute (CEC). HRS is comprised of Flex's medical business, including consumer health, digital health, disposables, drug delivery, diagnostics, life sciences and imaging equipment; automotive business, including vehicle electronics, connectivity and clean technologies; and defense and aerospace businesses, which focus on commercial aviation, defense and military. CTG includes Flex's mobile devices, consumer electronics and connectivity devices. IEI is comprised of semiconductor and capital equipment, office solutions, household industrial and lifestyle, industrial automation and kiosks, energy and metering and lighting. Last, CEC includes radio access base stations, remote radio heads and small cells for wireless infrastructure; optical, routing, broadcasting and switching products for the data and video networks; server and storage platforms for both enterprise and cloud-based deployments; next generation storage and security appliance products; and rack level solutions, converged infrastructure and software-defined product solutions. Flex is headquartered in Singapore, with locations established throughout the U.S., South America, Europe, the U.K., India, Australia, Japan, Indonesia, Philippines, South Korea, Israel, China and more.

FINANCIAL DATA: Note: Data for latest year may not have been available at press time.

In U.S. $	2017	2016	2015	2014	2013	2012
Revenue	23,862,930,000	24,418,890,000	26,147,920,000	26,108,610,000	23,569,480,000	29,387,660,000
R&D Expense						
Operating Income	502,210,000	587,206,000	668,832,000	536,533,000	331,484,000	580,809,000
Operating Margin %	2.10%	2.40%	2.55%	2.05%	1.40%	1.97%
SGA Expense	937,339,000	954,890,000	844,473,000	874,796,000	805,235,000	880,636,000
Net Income	319,564,000	444,081,000	600,801,000	365,594,000	277,051,000	488,765,000
Operating Cash Flow	1,149,909,000	1,136,445,000	794,034,000	1,216,460,000	1,115,430,000	804,268,000
Capital Expenditure	525,111,000	510,634,000	347,413,000	609,643,000	488,993,000	437,191,000
EBITDA	1,111,870,000	1,102,573,000	1,209,322,000	1,001,076,000	897,841,000	1,102,732,000
Return on Assets %	2.55%	3.69%	4.97%	3.16%	2.56%	4.31%
Return on Equity %	12.25%	18.00%	26.56%	16.58%	12.22%	21.34%
Debt to Equity	1.09	1.05	0.86	0.95	0.73	0.94

CONTACT INFORMATION:
Phone: 65 6890-7188   Fax: 65 6543-1888
Toll-Free:
Address: 2 Changi South Lane, Singapore, 486123 Singapore

STOCK TICKER/OTHER:
Stock Ticker: FLEX
Employees: 200,000
Parent Company:

Exchange: NAS
Fiscal Year Ends: 03/31

SALARIES/BONUSES:
Top Exec. Salary: $1,250,000   Bonus: $
Second Exec. Salary: $316,955   Bonus: $625,000

OTHER THOUGHTS:
Estimated Female Officers or Directors: 4
Hot Spot for Advancement for Women/Minorities: Y

Sales, profits and employees may be estimates. Financial information, benefits and other data can change quickly and may vary from those stated here.

Plunkett Research, Ltd.

FLIR Systems Inc

NAIC Code: 334511

www.flir.com

TYPES OF BUSINESS:
Search, Detection, Navigation, Guidance, Aeronautical, and Nautical System and Instrument Manufacturing
Infrared Camera Systems

BRANDS/DIVISIONS/AFFILIATES:
FLIR
Extech
Raymarine
DroneSense

CONTACTS:
Note: Officers with more than one job title may be intentionally listed here more than once.

James Cannon, CEO
Earl Lewis, Chairman of the Board
Brian Harding, Chief Accounting Officer
Travis Merrill, Chief Marketing Officer
Carol Lowe, Executive VP
Todd Duchene, General Counsel
Paul Sale, Other Executive Officer
Shane Harrison, Senior VP, Divisional
Jeffrey Frank, Senior VP, Divisional

GROWTH PLANS/SPECIAL FEATURES:

FLIR Systems, Inc. designs, manufactures, markets and distributes technologies that enhance perception and awareness. FLIR operates in six segments: surveillance, instruments, OEM (original equipment manufacturers) and emerging markets, maritime, security and detection. Surveillance provides advanced imaging and sensor systems to government customers and markets where high performance is required. Instruments provides devices that image, measure and assess thermal energy, gases and other environmental elements for industrial, commercial, and scientific applications under the FLIR and Extech brands. The OEM and emerging markets segment provides thermal imaging camera cores and components that are utilized by third parties to create thermal and other types of imaging systems. The maritime segment develops and manufactures electronics and imaging instruments for the recreational and commercial maritime market under the FLIR and Raymarine brands. The security segment develops and manufactures a variety of cameras and video recording systems for use in commercial, critical infrastructure and border surveillance applications. The segment sells products under the FLIR brand. The detection segment offers sensors, instruments and integrated platform solutions for the detection, identification and suppression of chemical, biological, radiological, nuclear and explosives threats for military force protection, homeland security, first responders and commercial applications. The firm conducts manufacturing, research and development, and sales and administration in 98 facilities worldwide. Its major operations are located in the U.S., the U.K., Sweden, Estonia, Canada, the U.K. and Belgium. In February 2018, FLIR sold is Lorex brand, as well as its consumer and small/medium-sized visible-spectrum security products business. That April, FLIR completed a strategic investment in DroneSense, makers of a unique software platform that serves public safety organizations in utilizing unmanned aircraft systems.

FLIR offers employees medical, dental, short-term disability and domestic partner insurance; 401(k); and various employee assistance programs.

FINANCIAL DATA:
Note: Data for latest year may not have been available at press time.

In U.S. $	2017	2016	2015	2014	2013	2012
Revenue	1,800,434,000	1,662,167,000	1,557,067,000	1,530,654,000	1,496,372,000	1,405,358,000
R&D Expense	170,735,000	147,537,000	132,892,000	142,751,000	147,696,000	137,762,000
Operating Income	314,174,000	297,149,000	307,125,000	275,627,000	266,575,000	303,330,000
Operating Margin %	17.44%	17.87%	19.72%	18.00%	17.81%	21.58%
SGA Expense	373,867,000	322,435,000	313,544,000	331,995,000	322,739,000	290,298,000
Net Income	107,223,000	166,626,000	241,686,000	200,261,000	177,015,000	222,398,000
Operating Cash Flow	308,252,000	312,280,000	275,814,000	226,244,000	354,965,000	285,545,000
Capital Expenditure	42,109,000	35,940,000	68,234,000	61,262,000	52,061,000	58,089,000
EBITDA	366,879,000	351,541,000	369,066,000	321,367,000	305,873,000	363,286,000
Return on Assets %	3.94%	6.63%	10.15%	8.52%	7.83%	10.28%
Return on Equity %	6.10%	10.01%	14.83%	12.42%	11.01%	13.99%
Debt to Equity	0.22	0.29	0.05	0.22	0.23	0.15

CONTACT INFORMATION:
Phone: 503 498-3547
Fax: 503 684-5452
Toll-Free:
Address: 27700 SW Parkway Ave., Wilsonville, OR 97070 United States

STOCK TICKER/OTHER:
Stock Ticker: FLIR
Employees: 3,436
Parent Company:

Exchange: NAS
Fiscal Year Ends: 12/31

SALARIES/BONUSES:
Top Exec. Salary: $390,385
Bonus: $3,496,869
Second Exec. Salary: $764,492
Bonus: $632,600

OTHER THOUGHTS:
Estimated Female Officers or Directors:
Hot Spot for Advancement for Women/Minorities:

Sales, profits and employees may be estimates. Financial information, benefits and other data can change quickly and may vary from those stated here.

Fluor Corporation

NAIC Code: 237000

www.fluor.com

TYPES OF BUSINESS:
Heavy Construction and Engineering
Power Plant Construction and Management
Facilities Management
Procurement Services
Consulting Services
Project Management
Asset Management
Staffing Services

BRANDS/DIVISIONS/AFFILIATES:
Stork Holding BV

CONTACTS: Note: Officers with more than one job title may be intentionally listed here more than once.
David Seaton, CEO
Mark Landry, Senior VP, Divisional
Bruce Stanski, CFO
Robin Chopra, Chief Accounting Officer
Garry Flowers, Executive VP
Ray Barnard, Executive VP, Divisional
Jose Luis Bustamante, Executive VP, Divisional
Carlos Hernandez, Executive VP
James Brittain, President, Divisional
Taco de Haan, President, Divisional
Nestoras Koumouris, President, Divisional
Thomas DAgostino, President, Divisional

GROWTH PLANS/SPECIAL FEATURES:

Fluor Corporation, through its subsidiaries, is a global provider of integrated engineering, procurement, fabrication, construction and maintenance services, with representatives in over 100 countries. Besides being a primary service provider to the U.S. federal government, Fluor serves a diverse set of industries, including oil and gas, chemical and petrochemicals, transportation, mining and metals, power, life sciences and manufacturing. The firm operates in four business segments: energy, chemicals and mining (ECM); industrial, infrastructure and power (IIP); government; and diversified services. ECM focuses on opportunities in the upstream, downstream, chemical, petrochemical, offshore and onshore oil and gas production, liquefied natural gas, pipeline, metals and mining markets. IIP provides design, engineering, procurement, construction and project management services to the transportation, life sciences, advanced manufacturing, water and power sectors. The government segment is a provider of engineering, construction, logistics, base and facilities operations and maintenance, contingency response and environmental and nuclear services to U.S. and international governments. The diversified services segment includes Stork Holding BV, which provides facility startup and management, plant and facility maintenance, operations support and asset management services to the oil and gas, chemicals, life sciences, mining and metals, consumer products and manufacturing industries. This division also comprises Fluor's equipment and temporary staffing businesses and power services.

Fluor offers its employees health, dental, vision, life and accident insurance; disability coverage; savings and retirement plans; a tax savings account; and educational assistance.

FINANCIAL DATA: Note: Data for latest year may not have been available at press time.

In U.S. $	2017	2016	2015	2014	2013	2012
Revenue	19,520,970,000	19,036,520,000	18,114,050,000	21,531,580,000	27,351,570,000	27,577,140,000
R&D Expense						
Operating Income	426,303,000	599,243,000	926,367,000	1,216,322,000	1,190,043,000	733,987,000
Operating Margin %	2.18%	3.14%	5.11%	5.64%	4.35%	2.66%
SGA Expense	192,187,000	191,073,000	168,329,000	182,711,000	175,148,000	151,010,000
Net Income	191,377,000	281,401,000	412,512,000	510,909,000	667,711,000	456,330,000
Operating Cash Flow	601,971,000	705,919,000	849,132,000	642,574,000	788,906,000	628,378,000
Capital Expenditure	283,107,000	235,904,000	240,220,000	324,704,000	288,487,000	254,747,000
EBITDA	679,348,000	842,202,000	961,060,000	1,427,184,000	1,411,584,000	974,124,000
Return on Assets %	2.06%	3.34%	5.21%	6.18%	8.04%	5.51%
Return on Equity %	5.91%	9.19%	13.50%	14.87%	18.81%	13.54%
Debt to Equity	0.47	0.48	0.33	0.31	0.13	0.15

CONTACT INFORMATION:
Phone: 469 398-7000   Fax: 469 398-7255
Toll-Free:
Address: 6700 Las Colinas Blvd., Irving, TX 75039 United States

STOCK TICKER/OTHER:
Stock Ticker: FLR
Employees: 61,551
Parent Company:

Exchange: NYS
Fiscal Year Ends: 12/31

SALARIES/BONUSES:
Top Exec. Salary: $1,295,029   Bonus: $
Second Exec. Salary: $647,111   Bonus: $220,000

OTHER THOUGHTS:
Estimated Female Officers or Directors: 3
Hot Spot for Advancement for Women/Minorities: Y

Sales, profits and employees may be estimates. Financial information, benefits and other data can change quickly and may vary from those stated here.

Fomento de Construcciones Y Contratas SA (FCC)

www.fcc.es

NAIC Code: 237000

TYPES OF BUSINESS:
Heavy & Civil Engineering Construction
Alternative Energy Development
Integrated Water Management
Cement Manufacturing
Logistics Services
Engineering Services
Railway Concessions

BRANDS/DIVISIONS/AFFILIATES:
Control Empresarial de Capitales SA de CV
FCC Aqualia
FCC Construction
FACC Industrial
FCC Concessiones
Cementos Portland Valderrivas

CONTACTS:
Note: Officers with more than one job title may be intentionally listed here more than once.

Pablo Colio Abril, CEO
Miguel A. Martinez Parra, Dir.-Finance
Antonio Gomez Ciria, Gen. Dir.-Admin.
Jose Manuel Velasco Guardado, Gen. Dir.-Comm.
Juan Bejar, Exec. Chmn.-Cementos Portland Valderrivas SA
Eric Marotel, Managing Dir.-Cemusa
Eduardo Gonzalez Gomez, Gen Dir.-Energy
Miguel Hernanz Sanjuan, Gen. Dir.-Internal Audit

GROWTH PLANS/SPECIAL FEATURES:

Fomento de Construcciones Y Contratas SA (FCC) is a Spanish environmental, water and infrastructure services company serving like-kind sectors worldwide. Nearly half of the firm's annual revenues come from international markets, predominantly in Europe and America, respectively. FCC's environment business division provides waste collection, street cleaning, solid waste treatment, maintenance of green areas, sewage network maintenance and industrial waste solutions and services. Its water business division provides solutions in all phases of the water cycle, whether human, agricultural or industrial, serving the needs of public bodies, private companies and private clients. Its operations are run by subsidiary FCC Aqualia, which provides water services and solutions to millions of water users in 1,100 municipalities in more than 20 countries. FCC has extensive experience in the operation and maintenance of waste water treatment plants and drinking water treatment plants, running more than 500 facilities in Europe, America, Africa and Asia. The infrastructures business division operates through FCC Construction, FCC Industrial, FCC Concessiones and Cementos Portland Valderrivas, which together design, plan, construct and maintain infrastructure. Cementos Portland is a listed company and the top cement producer in Spain. This division's strategy is to focus on projects where FCC Construction contributes its expertise, technical capabilities and civil engineering portfolio, which includes metro, high-speed, roads, bridges, hydraulic and port work, as well as airports and industrial/special building work. FCC operates as a subsidiary of Control Empresarial de Capitales SA de CV. During 2017, the firm was awarded the contract to manage the Pinto light-packaging waste sorting plant in Madrid; and signed the contract to build the Abu Rawash treatment plant in Egypt.

FINANCIAL DATA:
Note: Data for latest year may not have been available at press time.

In U.S. $	2017	2016	2015	2014	2013	2012
Revenue	7,164,949,000	7,349,640,000	7,997,263,000	7,821,960,000	8,306,563,000	13,771,920,000
R&D Expense						
Operating Income	554,007,300	463,446,800	405,841,100	378,310,200	-79,521,600	-74,269,560
Operating Margin %	7.73%	6.30%	5.07%	4.83%	-.95%	-.53%
SGA Expense						
Net Income	145,769,200	-199,529,500	-57,164,910	-894,433,100	-1,860,141,000	-1,269,435,000
Operating Cash Flow	949,472,700	1,265,655,000	741,292,700	751,882,000	944,793,700	866,858,900
Capital Expenditure	336,395,100	373,928,700	418,506,200	486,512,400	552,293,200	640,927,200
EBITDA	990,018,300	736,603,800	996,558,400	877,543,400	443,498,200	716,773,700
Return on Assets %	1.10%	-1.36%	-.34%	-4.88%	-8.53%	-4.87%
Return on Equity %	14.26%	-30.14%	-16.75%	-527.02%	-238.51%	-56.50%
Debt to Equity	4.92	5.83	19.26	19.96	289.08	3.45

CONTACT INFORMATION:
Phone: 34-934-964900   Fax: 34 913594923
Toll-Free:
Address: Balmes 36, Barcelona, 08007 Spain

STOCK TICKER/OTHER:
Stock Ticker: FMOCF   Exchange: PINX
Employees: 56,372   Fiscal Year Ends: 12/31
Parent Company: Control Empresarial de Capitales SA de CV

SALARIES/BONUSES:
Top Exec. Salary: $ Bonus: $
Second Exec. Salary: $ Bonus: $

OTHER THOUGHTS:
Estimated Female Officers or Directors: 2
Hot Spot for Advancement for Women/Minorities: Y

Sales, profits and employees may be estimates. Financial information, benefits and other data can change quickly and may vary from those stated here.

Ford Motor Co

www.ford.com

NAIC Code: 336111

TYPES OF BUSINESS:
Automobile Manufacturing
Automobile Financing
Fuel-Cell & Hybrid Research

BRANDS/DIVISIONS/AFFILIATES:
Ford
Lincoln
Ford Motor Credit Co
Ford Mustang
Ford F150
Ford Focus
Lincoln Navigator SUV
Ford Escape Hybrid SUV

CONTACTS:
Note: Officers with more than one job title may be intentionally listed here more than once.

Nancy Falotico, CEO, Subsidiary
James Farley, Executive VP
James Hackett, CEO
John Lawler, CFO, Divisional
Cathy O'Callaghan, CFO, Geographical
Robert Shanks, CFO
William Ford, Chairman of the Board
Bradley Gayton, Chief Administrative Officer
Hau Thai-Tang, Executive VP, Divisional
David McClelland, Executive VP, Geographical
Marcy Klevorn, Executive VP
Joseph Hinrichs, Executive VP
Steven Armstrong, President, Geographical
Peter Fleet, President, Geographical
Kumar Galhotra, President, Geographical

GROWTH PLANS/SPECIAL FEATURES:
Ford Motor Co. is a designer and manufacturer of automobiles and automotive systems. The firm operates in two segments: automotive and financial services. The automotive segment designs, manufactures, sells and services cars and trucks under the brands Ford and Lincoln. The company sells its vehicles to the public via independently owned dealerships, including roughly 10,608 Ford; 214 Lincoln; and 915 Ford/Lincoln dealerships. These dealerships are in North America, South America, Europe, Asia Pacific and Africa. In addition to new car sales, the firm also sells vehicles to its dealerships for sale to fleet customers, including commercial fleet customers, daily rental car companies and governments, and sells parts and accessories to authorized parts distributors. The firm's financial services segment, operating through Ford Motor Credit Co., offers vehicle-related financing, leasing and insurance. Some of Ford's most popular vehicles include the Ford Mustang sports car, the Ford F150 truck, the compact Ford Focus, the Lincoln Navigator SUV and the Ford Escape Hybrid SUV. The company hopes to quickly introduce fully electric vehicles to the U.S. market. In January 2017, the firm announced the production of 13 new electric vehicles in the next five years, including hybrid versions of the F-150 and Mustang, as well as a fully electric small SUV with a projected EPA-estimated range of over 300 miles. In May 2017, Ford announced that it plans to reduce its global workforce by about 10% as part of an effort to reduce its total cost structure and boost profitability.

FINANCIAL DATA:
Note: Data for latest year may not have been available at press time.

In U.S. $	2017	2016	2015	2014	2013	2012
Revenue	156,776,000,000	151,799,000,000	149,558,000,000	144,077,000,000		
R&D Expense						
Operating Income	4,813,000,000	13,019,000,000	6,981,000,000	7,210,000,000		
Operating Margin %	3.07%	8.57%	4.66%	5.00%		
SGA Expense	11,527,000,000	12,196,000,000	10,763,000,000	11,842,000,000		
Net Income	7,602,000,000	4,596,000,000	7,373,000,000	1,231,000,000		
Operating Cash Flow	18,096,000,000	19,792,000,000	16,226,000,000	14,507,000,000		
Capital Expenditure	7,049,000,000	6,992,000,000	7,196,000,000	7,463,000,000		
EBITDA	17,734,000,000	25,614,000,000	18,991,000,000	16,307,000,000		
Return on Assets %	3.06%	1.98%	3.27%			
Return on Equity %	23.73%	15.89%	25.74%			
Debt to Equity	2.94	3.19	3.13			

CONTACT INFORMATION:
Phone: 313 322-3000   Fax: 313 222-4177
Toll-Free: 800-392-3673
Address: 1 American Rd., Dearborn, MI 48126 United States

SALARIES/BONUSES:
Top Exec. Salary: $1,344,333   Bonus: $1,000,000
Second Exec. Salary: $1,650,000   Bonus: $

STOCK TICKER/OTHER:
Stock Ticker: F   Exchange: NYS
Employees: 201,000   Fiscal Year Ends: 12/31
Parent Company:

OTHER THOUGHTS:
Estimated Female Officers or Directors: 4
Hot Spot for Advancement for Women/Minorities: Y

FuelCell Energy Inc

www.fuelcellenergy.com

NAIC Code: 0

TYPES OF BUSINESS:
Fuel Cell Manufacturing
Power Plants

BRANDS/DIVISIONS/AFFILIATES:
SureSource

CONTACTS: Note: Officers with more than one job title may be intentionally listed here more than once.
Arthur Bottone, CEO
Michael Bishop, CFO
John Rolls, Chairman of the Board
Anthony Rauseo, COO
Jennifer Arasimowicz, General Counsel

GROWTH PLANS/SPECIAL FEATURES:
FuelCell Energy, Inc. delivers proprietary fuel cell power solutions. The company serves utilities, industry and municipal power users on three continents with megawatt-class scalable services that include utility-scale and on-site power generation, carbon capture, local hydrogen production for transportation and industry, and energy storage. FuelCell Energy has generated more than 5.6 million megawatt hours (MWh) of ultra-clean power. It develops, installs and services fuel cell power plants, and provides maintenance under multi-year service agreements. The company also sells power plant equipment without installation and/or maintenance service agreements attached. FuelCell's proprietary SureSource line of carbonate fuel cell technology generates electricity directly from a fuel, such as natural gas or renewable biogas, by reforming the fuel inside the fuel cell to produce hydrogen. The SureSource product line is a global platform based on carbonate fuel cell technology, providing high efficiency with fuel conversion efficiency, fuel flexibility and virtually no pollution since the SureSource plants emit only trace levels of nitrogen oxide, sulfur oxide or particle matter. The company markets the different configurations of its plants to meet specific market needs, including energy supply, energy recovery and energy storage.

FINANCIAL DATA: Note: Data for latest year may not have been available at press time.

In U.S. $	2017	2016	2015	2014	2013	2012
Revenue	95,666,000	108,252,000	163,077,000	180,293,000	187,658,000	120,603,000
R&D Expense	20,398,000	20,846,000	17,442,000	18,240,000	15,717,000	14,354,000
Operating Income	-44,935,000	-46,353,000	-28,892,000	-27,311,000	-29,813,000	-32,129,000
Operating Margin %	-46.97%	-42.81%	-17.71%	-15.14%	-15.88%	-26.64%
SGA Expense	25,916,000	25,150,000	24,226,000	22,797,000	21,218,000	18,220,000
Net Income	-53,903,000	-50,957,000	-29,359,000	-38,125,000	-34,358,000	-35,495,000
Operating Cash Flow	-71,845,000	-46,595,000	-44,274,000	-57,468,000	-16,658,000	-58,659,000
Capital Expenditure	12,351,000	7,726,000	6,930,000	7,079,000	6,551,000	4,453,000
EBITDA	-36,170,000	-40,782,000	-22,351,000	-30,450,000	-26,878,000	-28,341,000
Return on Assets %	-15.73%	-17.48%	-11.67%	-15.94%	-17.50%	-20.63%
Return on Equity %	-52.95%	-51.65%	-33.34%	-94.37%	-3582.06%	-7314.93%
Debt to Equity	0.62	0.71	0.13	0.13		0.27

CONTACT INFORMATION:
Phone: 203 825-6000 Fax: 203 825-6100
Toll-Free:
Address: 3 Great Pasture Rd., Danbury, CT 06813 United States

SALARIES/BONUSES:
Top Exec. Salary: $428,816 Bonus: $
Second Exec. Salary: $333,554 Bonus: $

STOCK TICKER/OTHER:
Stock Ticker: FCEL Exchange: NAS
Employees: 596 Fiscal Year Ends: 10/31
Parent Company:

OTHER THOUGHTS:
Estimated Female Officers or Directors:
Hot Spot for Advancement for Women/Minorities:

FUJIFILM Holdings Corporation

www.fujifilm.com

NAIC Code: 333316

TYPES OF BUSINESS:
Copying Machines
Cameras
Photographic Equipment
Medical Imaging
Office Equipment
Photographic Film & Paper

BRANDS/DIVISIONS/AFFILIATES:
FUJIFILM Corporation
Fuji Xerox Co Ltd
Toyama Chemical Co Ltd
FUJIFILM Business Expert Corporation

CONTACTS:
Note: Officers with more than one job title may be intentionally listed here more than once.

Shigetaka Komori, CEO
Kenji Sukeno, COO
Kouichi Tamai, Chief Innovation Officer
Yuzo Toda, CTO
Kouichi Tamai, Exec. VP
Yuzo Toda, Sr. VP
Toru Takahashi, Sr. VP
Keiji Mihayashi, VP
Shigetaka Komori, Chmn.

GROWTH PLANS/SPECIAL FEATURES:

FUJIFILM Holdings Corporation is a manufacturer of traditional and digital imaging products, including photographic film, as well as pharmaceutical and life science solutions. Its operations are conducted through its 277 subsidiary companies (as of March 2017). The firm provides strategic management of the entire Fujifilm group, including its two major operating companies, FUJIFILM Corporation and Fuji Xerox Co., Ltd. FUJIFILM Holdings has three operating segments: imaging solutions, information solutions and document solutions. The imaging solutions division includes businesses related to color film, digital cameras, lab equipment, color paper, chemicals and services for photofinishing. The information solutions segment is responsible for producing optical devices, life science and medical systems, graphic arts equipment, electronic materials and recording media, flat panel displays and inkjet materials. In addition, the firm owns a 66% interest in Toyama Chemical Co., Ltd., a pharmaceutical development firm focusing its research in the areas of anti-infectives, central nervous system disorders and anti-inflammatory products. The document solutions segment, which is comprised of the operations of Fuji Xerox and its subsidiaries, produces copying machines, printers, fax machines and consumables for document service applications in offices. Wholly-owned FUJIFILM Business Expert Corporation is a shared services company in Japan, which integrates the administrative, human resource and travel agency functions for FUJIFILM Holdings' group of companies. In early-2018, the firm announced plans to build a new manufacturing facility at Toyama Chemical for the manufacture of liposome drugs utilizing proprietary technologies such as its anti-cancer agent FF-10832 for the use of clinical trials and commercial marketing; and agreed to acquire Irvine Scientific Sales Company as well as IS Japan Co., Ltd., each of which are leading companies in cell culture media.

FINANCIAL DATA:
Note: Data for latest year may not have been available at press time.

In U.S. $	2017	2016	2015	2014	2013	2012
Revenue	21,633,720,000	23,212,450,000	23,221,590,000	22,731,070,000	20,632,530,000	20,451,770,000
R&D Expense	1,492,752,000	1,518,847,000	1,501,248,000	1,531,126,000	1,566,527,000	1,615,176,000
Operating Income	1,605,003,000	1,781,060,000	1,606,093,000	1,311,794,000	1,063,127,000	1,052,245,000
Operating Margin %	7.41%	7.67%	6.91%	5.77%	5.15%	5.14%
SGA Expense	5,572,303,000	5,798,584,000	5,850,252,000	5,737,684,000	5,293,768,000	5,416,480,000
Net Income	1,225,135,000	1,148,808,000	1,104,463,000	754,574,300	505,552,500	407,657,900
Operating Cash Flow	2,688,830,000	2,066,974,000	2,456,969,000	2,725,284,000	1,858,124,000	1,258,925,000
Capital Expenditure	903,344,600	802,012,400	777,874,100	883,864,400	1,025,061,000	1,134,451,000
EBITDA	2,955,143,000	2,983,576,000	3,023,831,000	2,820,710,000	2,469,694,000	2,239,445,000
Return on Assets %	3.81%	3.56%	3.49%	2.57%	1.87%	1.60%
Return on Equity %	6.41%	5.75%	5.57%	4.16%	3.02%	2.54%
Debt to Equity	0.21	0.15	0.14	0.15	0.16	0.01

CONTACT INFORMATION:
Phone: 81 362711111   Fax:
Toll-Free:
Address: 7-3 Akasaka 9-chome, Minato-ku, Tokyo, 107-0052 Japan

SALARIES/BONUSES:
Top Exec. Salary: $ Bonus: $
Second Exec. Salary: $ Bonus: $

STOCK TICKER/OTHER:
Stock Ticker: FUJIF   Exchange: PINX
Employees: 78,150   Fiscal Year Ends: 03/31
Parent Company:

OTHER THOUGHTS:
Estimated Female Officers or Directors:
Hot Spot for Advancement for Women/Minorities:

Fujitsu Laboratories Ltd

NAIC Code: 541712

www.fujitsu.com/jp/group/labs/en/

TYPES OF BUSINESS:
Research & Development
Computing Research
RFID Technology
Semiconductors
Security & Encryption Technology
Robotics Research
Nanotechnology Research

BRANDS/DIVISIONS/AFFILIATES:
Fujitsu Limited
Fujitsu Laboratories of America Inc
Fujitsu Laboratories of Europe Limited
Fujitsu Research and Development Center Co Ltd

CONTACTS:
Note: Officers with more than one job title may be intentionally listed here more than once.

Shigeru Sasaki, CEO

GROWTH PLANS/SPECIAL FEATURES:
Fujitsu Laboratories Ltd. is Fujitsu Limited's central research and development unit. Fujitsu Lab's stated goal is to make ubiquitous networking a reality, meaning that communication would be possible anytime, anywhere and with anyone. To this end, the firm divides its research into four target areas. The people, which focuses on developing a system of sensors, interactive interfaces and surveillance programs designed to anticipate and assist user needs. These technologies include cloud devices, sensing and actuation, human-friendly interfaces, front-end systems and personal-area networks and body-area networks. Information via creative intelligence, which includes social intelligence, intelligent optimization and social innovation-oriented technologies. This target area is dedicated to creating widespread systems for easily-accessible and secure information. The connected infrastructure target area aims to develop technologies that provide information and communication technology environments that are capable of quickly adapting to change. Its technologies include platform-as-a-service (PaaS) environments, network services, cloud services and flexible storage systems. The common foundation target area supports Fujitsu Lab's other business units, as well as client needs, through the development of various technologies as product bases, manufacturing technologies for product formations, energy management technologies, networking technologies and green solutions technologies. Global research and development subsidiaries include Fujitsu Laboratories of America, Inc.; Fujitsu Laboratories of Europe Limited; and Fujitsu Research and Development Center Co. Ltd. The firm's various laboratory niches include computer systems, software, information systems technologies, Internet of Things systems, network systems, front technologies, artificial intelligence, security research, devices and materials, applied innovation research and R&D strategy and planning. In late-2017, the firm announced it was setting up a new R&D center in Toronto, Canada to create the next breakthroughs in quantum-inspired computing as part of a new partnership with the University of Toronto.

FINANCIAL DATA:
Note: Data for latest year may not have been available at press time.

In U.S. $	2017	2016	2015	2014	2013	2012
Revenue						
R&D Expense						
Operating Income						
Operating Margin %						
SGA Expense						
Net Income						
Operating Cash Flow						
Capital Expenditure						
EBITDA						
Return on Assets %						
Return on Equity %						
Debt to Equity						

CONTACT INFORMATION:
Phone: 81-44-754-2613 Fax:
Toll-Free:
Address: 4-1-1, Kamikodanaka, Nakahara-ku, Kawasaki-shi, 211-8588 Japan

STOCK TICKER/OTHER:
Stock Ticker: Subsidiary
Employees: 1,200
Parent Company: Fujitsu Limited

Exchange:
Fiscal Year Ends: 03/31

SALARIES/BONUSES:
Top Exec. Salary: $ Bonus: $
Second Exec. Salary: $ Bonus: $

OTHER THOUGHTS:
Estimated Female Officers or Directors:
Hot Spot for Advancement for Women/Minorities:

Sales, profits and employees may be estimates. Financial information, benefits and other data can change quickly and may vary from those stated here.

Fujitsu Limited

NAIC Code: 334111

www.fujitsu.com

TYPES OF BUSINESS:
Computer Manufacturing
Telecommunications Equipment
IT Outsourcing & Consulting Services
Microelectronics
Appliances & Consumer Electronics
Nanotechnology Research
Software Products
Flash Memory Products

BRANDS/DIVISIONS/AFFILIATES:
Fujitsu Semiconductor Limited
Solekia Limited
INESA Intelligent Technology Co Ltd

CONTACTS:
Note: Officers with more than one job title may be intentionally listed here more than once.

Tatsuya Tanaka, Pres.
Hidehiro Tsukano, CFO
Masami Fujita, Sr. Exec. VP
Hideyuki Saso, Sr. Exec. VP
Masahiro Koezuka, Vice Chmn.
Kazuhiko Kato, Exec. VP
Masami Yamamoto, Chmn.

GROWTH PLANS/SPECIAL FEATURES:

Fujitsu Limited is a leading provider of IT products and services globally. The company has three main business segments: technology solutions, which offers IT-driven business solutions, systems platforms and services; ubiquitous solutions, which caters to the personal computers (PCs), mobile phone and mobilewear markets; and device solutions, which consists of operations of Fujitsu Semiconductor Limited. The firm has four lines of services: business services, application services, managed infrastructure services and product support services. Business services segment enables organizations across the private and public sectors to plan, deliver and operate IT and business strategies in complex environments. Its capabilities range from business process outsourcing to rich business, IT effectiveness and sustainability consulting services tackling cost, efficiency and environment issues. Application services improves and transforms customer applications to ensure they are optimized and adaptable for present and future business needs. This division provides application development and integration, as well as application management and outsourcing services, and fully integrates emerging delivery models like software as a service. Applications within this segment include SAP technologies, Oracle, legacy modernization, hybrid cloud, IT management as a service and platform as a service. Managed infrastructure services cut costs and boost efficiency through technological innovation and a focus on high-quality service design, and follows green environmental best practices accordingly. Services within this division include data center services, end user services, network and communication services, technical and maintenance services and service desk. Product support services include computing products, software, network capabilities, electronic devices and other products that ensure the reliability of a company's IT infrastructure. During 2017, the firm acquired Solekia Limited, a technology solutions provider. In March 2018, Fujitsu and INESA (Group) Co. Ltd. formed INESA Intelligent Technology Co., Ltd., a joint venture to provide services and a platform for smart manufacturing solutions in China.

FINANCIAL DATA:
Note: Data for latest year may not have been available at press time.

In U.S. $	2017	2016	2015	2014	2013	2012
Revenue	42,013,180,000	44,152,170,000	44,281,820,000	44,367,850,000	40,821,020,000	41,620,770,000
R&D Expense						2,220,607,000
Operating Income	1,541,662,000	1,531,042,000	1,676,933,000	1,328,182,000	887,628,100	914,803,500
Operating Margin %	3.66%	3.46%	3.78%	2.99%	2.17%	2.19%
SGA Expense	9,796,181,000	10,127,840,000	10,261,760,000	10,495,920,000	10,326,890,000	
Net Income	824,380,500	808,300,800	1,304,490,000	452,860,100	-679,271,600	397,866,600
Operating Cash Flow	2,332,132,000	2,357,854,000	2,609,922,000	1,635,290,000	661,542,800	2,115,064,000
Capital Expenditure	1,849,236,000	1,767,934,000	1,854,938,000	1,667,440,000	1,639,454,000	1,819,713,000
EBITDA	3,080,594,000	3,259,456,000	3,704,593,000	3,058,822,000	1,402,329,000	2,660,220,000
Return on Assets %	2.75%	2.67%	4.40%	1.58%	-2.43%	1.43%
Return on Equity %	10.63%	11.03%	20.54%	7.17%	-8.98%	5.13%
Debt to Equity	0.40	0.49	0.51	0.72	0.34	0.33

CONTACT INFORMATION:
Phone: 81 362522220 Fax:
Toll-Free:
Address: Shiodome City Center, 1-5-2 Higashi-Shimbashi, Tokyo, 105-7123 Japan

STOCK TICKER/OTHER:
Stock Ticker: FJTSY   Exchange: PINX
Employees: 169,000   Fiscal Year Ends: 03/31
Parent Company:

SALARIES/BONUSES:
Top Exec. Salary: $ Bonus: $
Second Exec. Salary: $ Bonus: $

OTHER THOUGHTS:
Estimated Female Officers or Directors: 1
Hot Spot for Advancement for Women/Minorities:

Sales, profits and employees may be estimates. Financial information, benefits and other data can change quickly and may vary from those stated here.

Fujitsu Technology Solutions (Holding) BV

ts.fujitsu.com

NAIC Code: 334111

TYPES OF BUSINESS:
Computer Manufacturing
Servers
Storage Devices
Monitors & Peripherals
Software Distribution
Support Services

BRANDS/DIVISIONS/AFFILIATES:
Fujitsu Limited

CONTACTS:
Note: Officers with more than one job title may be intentionally listed here more than once.

Aidan Walsh, CFO
Heribert Goggerle, Exec. VP-Prod. Oper.
Jurgen Walter, Exec. VP

GROWTH PLANS/SPECIAL FEATURES:
Fujitsu Technology Solutions (Holding) BV manufactures and distributes electronics in the EMEIA (Europe, Middle East, India and Africa) market. As a wholly-owned subsidiary of Fujitsu Limited, the company was established to expand products and sales channels outside of Japan. Fujitsu Tech products are divided into four groups: IT products and systems, product support services, software and electronic devices. IT products and systems include servers, storage systems, integrated systems, client computing devices, peripheral devices, and the made4you family of hardware, software, add-on and extended component lifetime services. Product support services include startup hardware services, product support services (for both hardware and software), infrastructure support and hardware-as-a-service. Software products include operating systems, middleware, applications, partner software and Microsoft software licensing. Electronic devices include electromechanical components, printed circuit boards, integrated circuit packaging, semiconductors and standard components. Services offered by the company include business services such as IT consulting and product compliance; application services such as application management, outsourcing, information management, SAP enterprise management, application development/integration, software-as-a-service, platform-as-a-service, and application lifecycle management; managed infrastructure services such as data center, end-user, technical support, infrastructure and service desk; product support services, including startup services hardware, product support (hardware/software) and infrastructure support; and financial services and remarketing, including financial services, end-of-term services and remarketing services. Fujitsu Tech's solutions include infrastructure, industry, business/technology, cloud and small/medium enterprise solutions.

FINANCIAL DATA:
Note: Data for latest year may not have been available at press time.

In U.S. $	2017	2016	2015	2014	2013	2012
Revenue	18,000,000,000	17,841,000,000	17,208,000,000	20,862,000,000	22,152,100,000	25,816,700,000
R&D Expense						
Operating Income						
Operating Margin %						
SGA Expense						
Net Income		377,787,000	375,339,000	1,795,800,000	-3,586,360,000	666,091,000
Operating Cash Flow						
Capital Expenditure						
EBITDA						
Return on Assets %						
Return on Equity %						
Debt to Equity						

CONTACT INFORMATION:
Phone: 31-346-59-8111 Fax: 31-346-56-1298
Toll-Free:
Address: Het Kwadrant 1, Maarssen, 3606 AZ Netherlands

SALARIES/BONUSES:
Top Exec. Salary: $ Bonus: $
Second Exec. Salary: $ Bonus: $

STOCK TICKER/OTHER:
Stock Ticker: Subsidiary   Exchange:
Employees: 24,112   Fiscal Year Ends: 03/31
Parent Company: Fujitsu Limited

OTHER THOUGHTS:
Estimated Female Officers or Directors:
Hot Spot for Advancement for Women/Minorities:

Sales, profits and employees may be estimates. Financial information, benefits and other data can change quickly and may vary from those stated here.

Gannett Fleming Inc

NAIC Code: 541330

www.gannettfleming.com

TYPES OF BUSINESS:
Engineering Services

BRANDS/DIVISIONS/AFFILIATES:
GANCOM
Gannet Fleming Architects Inc
Gannett Fleming IT
Gannett Fleming Project Development Corporation
Gannett Fleming Valuation and Rate Consultants LLC
GeoDecisions
LDP Group Inc
TerraSure

CONTACTS:
Note: Officers with more than one job title may be intentionally listed here more than once.

Robert Scaer, CEO
Paul Nowicki, COO
Kevin Switala, VP
Robert Scaer, Chmn.

GROWTH PLANS/SPECIAL FEATURES:
Gannett Fleming, Inc. is an engineering infrastructure firm that provides planning, design, technology and construction management services for a diverse range of markets and disciplines. The firm is headquartered in Camp Hill, Pennsylvania, and has a global network of 60+ additional offices. Gannett Fleming offers a myriad of services to its potential clients. These services include acoustics, architecture, business/technology solutions, engineering, environmental management/remediation, geotechnical, IT, program/construction management, project delivery, security/safety, valuation and vertical transportation. Gannet Fleming carries out its business in conjuncture with its subsidiaries and affiliates. GANCOM offers services in the areas of reprographics, digital print, graphic design and information technology. Gannet Fleming Architects, Inc. provides general architectural and related engineering design, planning and site development. Gannett Fleming IT Services provides information technology services for computer consulting services. Gannett Fleming Project Development Corporation provides design/build and construction management services. Gannett Fleming Valuation and Rate Consultants, LLC provides consulting services to public utilities and railroads. GeoDecisions provides computerized mapping and database management. ITEC is a design-build electrical contractor, providing a full suite of electrical engineering, procurement and construction services for turnkey projects. LDP Group, Inc. is a Chicago-based electrical engineering design firm. TerraSure provides environmental risk transfer solutions to property owners, developers and investors dealing with contaminated sites. Last, Vertical Transportation Excellence provide elevator/escalator-related advisory services to aviation, transit, commercial, healthcare and government clients.

FINANCIAL DATA:
Note: Data for latest year may not have been available at press time.

In U.S. $	2017	2016	2015	2014	2013	2012
Revenue	395,000,000	388,000,000	325,000,000	320,000,000	311,600,000	
R&D Expense						
Operating Income						
Operating Margin %						
SGA Expense						
Net Income						
Operating Cash Flow						
Capital Expenditure						
EBITDA						
Return on Assets %						
Return on Equity %						
Debt to Equity						

CONTACT INFORMATION:
Phone: 717-763-7211   Fax:
Toll-Free: 800-233-1055
Address: 207 Senate Ave., Camp Hill, PA 17011 United States

STOCK TICKER/OTHER:
Stock Ticker: Private   Exchange:
Employees: 2,000   Fiscal Year Ends:
Parent Company:

SALARIES/BONUSES:
Top Exec. Salary: $ Bonus: $
Second Exec. Salary: $ Bonus: $

OTHER THOUGHTS:
Estimated Female Officers or Directors:
Hot Spot for Advancement for Women/Minorities:

Sales, profits and employees may be estimates. Financial information, benefits and other data can change quickly and may vary from those stated here.

GE Aviation

www.geaviation.com

NAIC Code: 336412

TYPES OF BUSINESS:
Aircraft Engine and Engine Parts Manufacturing
Gas Turbine Manufacturing
Marine Engines
Engine Maintenance & Parts
Engine Leasing

BRANDS/DIVISIONS/AFFILIATES:
General Electric Company
GE90
F110
CF34
Passport
LM6000
Avionics
Dowty

CONTACTS: Note: Officers with more than one job title may be intentionally listed here more than once.
David L. Joyce, CEO
Anthony Aiello, VP
David Joyce, Pres.
Anne M. Lynch, CFO
Chaker A. Chahrour, VP-Mktg. & Sales
Ernest W. Marshall, Jr., VP-Human Resources
Alan C. Caslavka, VP-Avionics & Digital Sys.
Mohammad Ehteshami, VP-New Prod. Introduction Oper.
Gary Mercer, Chief Engineer
Michael McAlevey, General Counsel
Bill Fitzgerald, VP
Michael R. McAlevey, VP-Bus. Dev.
Jamie Regg, Sr. Exec.-Global Comm. & GE Advantage
Peter Prowitt, Exec. Dir.-Global Gov't Rel.
Jean Lydon-Rodgers, VP
Paul McElhinney, VP
Jeanne M. Rosario, VP
Chris S. Beaufait, Sr. Exec.-China
Colleen Athans, VP

GROWTH PLANS/SPECIAL FEATURES:
GE Aviation, a subsidiary of General Electric Company, produces jet, turboprop and turbo shaft engines, components and integrated systems. The company manufactures its products for commercial, military, business and general aviation aircraft. GE Aviation has a global service network to support these offerings. Commercial engines include GE90, GE9X, GEnx, GP7200, CF6, CFM56, LEAP, CF34 and CT7; and its commercial systems include Avionics computing systems, electrical power components, structures, Dowty-branded propellers and Unison-branded solid-state ignition systems. Military engines include adaptive cycle, F110, F404, F414, T408, T700, T901, F108 and F103/138; and military systems include Avionics computer systems, electrical power components, structures, Dowty propellers and Unison ignition systems. Business and general aviation (B&GA) engines include advanced turboprop, CF34, Passport, CFM56, CF700, CFE738, CJ610 and HF120; and B&GA systems include Avionics computer systems, electrical power components, structures, Dowty propellers and Unison ignition systems. For the marine industry, military gas turbine products include the LM500, LM2500, LM2500+, LM2500+G4 AND LM6000; commercial gas turbine products include the 4.5 MW, 25 MW, 30 MW, 35 MW and 42 MW; and systems for the marine industry include propulsion systems, exhaust energy recovery systems and the firm's optional dry low emissions combustor system. GE Aviation's global supply chain includes approximately 80 facilities in 19 countries, employing more than 27,000 people. The company's Asheville, North Carolina plant was its first site to mass produce ceramic matrix composite (CMC) components for jet engines. In March 2018, the firm invested an additional $105 million in the Asheville plant to meet the growing demand for its CMC products.

FINANCIAL DATA: Note: Data for latest year may not have been available at press time.

In U.S. $	2017	2016	2015	2014	2013	2012
Revenue	27,375,000,000	26,261,000,000	24,660,000,000	23,990,000,000	21,911,000,000	19,997,000,000
R&D Expense						
Operating Income						
Operating Margin %						
SGA Expense						
Net Income	6,642,000,000	6,115,000,000	5,507,000,000	4,973,000,000	4,345,000,000	3,747,000,000
Operating Cash Flow						
Capital Expenditure						
EBITDA						
Return on Assets %						
Return on Equity %						
Debt to Equity						

CONTACT INFORMATION:
Phone: 513-243-2000 Fax:
Toll-Free:
Address: 1 Neumann Way, Cincinnati, OH 45215-6301 United States

STOCK TICKER/OTHER:
Stock Ticker: Subsidiary   Exchange:
Employees: 44,500   Fiscal Year Ends: 12/31
Parent Company: General Electric Company (GE)

SALARIES/BONUSES:
Top Exec. Salary: $ Bonus: $
Second Exec. Salary: $ Bonus: $

OTHER THOUGHTS:
Estimated Female Officers or Directors: 4
Hot Spot for Advancement for Women/Minorities: Y

Sales, profits and employees may be estimates. Financial information, benefits and other data can change quickly and may vary from those stated here.

GE Global Research

www.geglobalresearch.com

NAIC Code: 541712

TYPES OF BUSINESS:
Research & Development
Nuclear & Fossil Fuel Energy Technology
Wind, Solar, Hydroelectric & Biomass Technology
Fuel Cell & Energy Storage Technology
Nanotechnology
Photonics & Optoelectronics
Engine Technology
Biotechnology

BRANDS/DIVISIONS/AFFILIATES:
General Electric Company (GE)

GROWTH PLANS/SPECIAL FEATURES:
GE Global Research (GE Global) is the research and development arm of General Electric Company (GE). GE Global's researchers advance horizontal technologies across GE's offerings, scaling investment across the company in the four core areas of artificial intelligence (AI), additive manufacturing, silicon carbide and edge controls. The researchers are: using AI to enable GE's machines to mimic the ability of humans to react and adapt to changing conditions; unleashing the potential of additive manufacturing in relation to materials development, advanced design and process capabilities and machine engineering across every GE factory; launching the next power electronics revolution by replacing silicon with silicon carbide power devices; at the edge of the industrial internet via GE's local, secure platform, which acts on a machine's data through controls. Moreover, the edge controls platform speaks multiple languages. GE Global's research headquarters are based in the U.S., with an integrated multi-disciplinary R&D center located in Bangalore, India.

CONTACTS:
Note: Officers with more than one job title may be intentionally listed here more than once.

Mark M. Little, Sr. VP-Global Research
Vic Abate, CTO
Michael Idelchik, VP-Advanced Tech. Programs
Xiangli Chen, Gen. Mgr.-GE China Tech. Center
Terry K. Lieb, Dir.-Global Tech., Chemistry & Chemical Eng.
Christine M. Furstoss, Dir.-Global Tech., Mfg. & Materials Tech.
Kenneth G. Herd, Gen. Mgr.-Brazil Tech. Center
James R. Maughan, Dir.-Global Tech. & Research, Americas
A. Nadeem Ishaque, Dir.-Global Tech., Diagnostics & Biomedical Tech.
Danielle Merfield, Dir.-Global Tech., Electrical Tech. & Systems
Michael Ming, Gen. Mgr.-Oil & Gas Tech. Center
Gopi Katragadda, Managing Dir.-GE India Tech. Center
Carlos Hartel, Managing Dir.-GE Global Research Center-Europe

FINANCIAL DATA:
Note: Data for latest year may not have been available at press time.

In U.S. $	2017	2016	2015	2014	2013	2012
Revenue						
R&D Expense						
Operating Income						
Operating Margin %						
SGA Expense						
Net Income						
Operating Cash Flow						
Capital Expenditure						
EBITDA						
Return on Assets %						
Return on Equity %						
Debt to Equity						

CONTACT INFORMATION:
Phone: 518-387-5000 Fax: 518-387-6696
Toll-Free:
Address: 1 Research Cir., Niskayuna, NY 12309 United States

STOCK TICKER/OTHER:
Stock Ticker: Subsidiary
Employees: 3,000
Parent Company: General Electric Company (GE)
Exchange:
Fiscal Year Ends: 12/31

SALARIES/BONUSES:
Top Exec. Salary: $ Bonus: $
Second Exec. Salary: $ Bonus: $

OTHER THOUGHTS:
Estimated Female Officers or Directors: 2
Hot Spot for Advancement for Women/Minorities:

Sales, profits and employees may be estimates. Financial information, benefits and other data can change quickly and may vary from those stated here.

GE Healthcare

NAIC Code: 339100

www3.gehealthcare.com/en

TYPES OF BUSINESS:
Medical Imaging & Information Technology
Magnetic Resonance Imaging Systems
Patient Monitoring Systems
Clinical Information Systems
Nuclear Medicine
Surgery & Vascular Imaging
X-Ray & Ultrasound Bone Densitometers
Clinical & Business Services

BRANDS/DIVISIONS/AFFILIATES:
General Electric Company (GE)
Puridify

CONTACTS:
Note: Officers with more than one job title may be intentionally listed here more than once.

Kieran Murphy, CEO
Monish Patolawala, CFO
Raghu Krishnamoorthy, VP-Human Resources
Jorg Debatin, VP
Michael Harsh, CTO
Keith Newman, General Counsel
Markus Ewert, Exec. VP-Bus. Dev.
Jeff DeMarrais, Chief Comm. Officer
Dee Miller, Chief Quality Officer
Kieran Murphy, CEO
Rachel Duan, CEO
Tom Gentile, CEO-Health Care Systems
Terri Bresenham, CEO
Brian Masterson, VP-Supply Chain

GROWTH PLANS/SPECIAL FEATURES:
GE Healthcare is the healthcare business of General Electric Company (GE), harnessing data and analytics across hardware, software and biotechnology. The firm is a leading provider of medical imaging equipment, with a track record of more than 100 years in the industry across 100 countries. GE Healthcare products include the health cloud, bone and metabolic health, advanced visualization, anesthesia delivery, applied intelligence, computed tomography, diagnostics, EP recording, healthcare IT, hemodynamic recording, interventional image guided systems, life sciences, magnetic resonance imaging, mammography, maternal-infant care, molecular imaging, nuclear imaging agents, patient monitoring, radiography, fluoroscopy, surgical imaging, ultrasound and ventilators. Specialties of the company include: cardiology, offering a suite of solutions that diagnose and fight cardiovascular disease; orthopedics, offering tools and technologies that cover each stage of patient care, from assessment and diagnosis through treatment and follow-up; and an ambulatory surgery center, which provides single source solutions regarding anesthesia delivery, patient monitoring, point-of-care ultrasound, financial and U.S. government supporting services. Other services by GE Healthcare include education and training, healthcare technology management, research, equipment financing and more. In November 2017, GE Healthcare acquired Puridify, a bioprocessing startup that is developing a nanofiber-based platform purification technology for biopharmaceutical production. In April 2018, the firm announced plans to sell its IT business to private equity firm Veritas Capital for $1.05 billion in order to focus on smart diagnostics and connected devices.

FINANCIAL DATA:
Note: Data for latest year may not have been available at press time.

In U.S. $	2017	2016	2015	2014	2013	2012
Revenue	19,116,000,000	18,291,000,000	17,639,000,000	18,299,000,000	18,200,000,000	18,500,000,000
R&D Expense						
Operating Income						
Operating Margin %						
SGA Expense						
Net Income	3,448,000,000	3,161,000,000	2,882,000,000	3,047,000,000	3,048,000,000	2,920,000,000
Operating Cash Flow						
Capital Expenditure						
EBITDA						
Return on Assets %						
Return on Equity %						
Debt to Equity						

CONTACT INFORMATION:
Phone: 44-1494-544-000 Fax:
Toll-Free:
Address: Nightingales Ln., Pollards Wood, Chalfont St. Giles, HP8 4SP United Kingdom

STOCK TICKER/OTHER:
Stock Ticker: Subsidiary Exchange:
Employees: 55,125 Fiscal Year Ends: 12/31
Parent Company: General Electric Company (GE)

SALARIES/BONUSES:
Top Exec. Salary: $ Bonus: $
Second Exec. Salary: $ Bonus: $

OTHER THOUGHTS:
Estimated Female Officers or Directors: 4
Hot Spot for Advancement for Women/Minorities: Y

Sales, profits and employees may be estimates. Financial information, benefits and other data can change quickly and may vary from those stated here.

Gemalto NV

NAIC Code: 334418

www.gemalto.com

TYPES OF BUSINESS:
Computer Storage Equipment-Smart Cards
Smart Card Interfaces, Readers & Chipsets
Smart Card Software & Development Tools
Consulting, Training & Support Services
Online Security Programs

BRANDS/DIVISIONS/AFFILIATES:

CONTACTS:
Note: Officers with more than one job title may be intentionally listed here more than once.

Philippe Vallee, CEO
Virginie Duperat-Vergne, CFO
Philippe Cabanettes, Exec. VP-Human Resources
Serge Barbe, CTO
Jean-Pierre Charlet, General Counsel
Martin McCourt, Exec. VP-Strategy & Innovation
Isabelle Marand, Exec. VP-Corp. Comm.
Eke Bijzitter, Compliance, Governance & Central Officer
Jean-Pierre Charlet, Exec. VP-Risk Prevention & Mgmt.
Alex Mandl, Chmn.

GROWTH PLANS/SPECIAL FEATURES:

Gemalto NV designs and manufactures security software for e-identity documents, chip payment cards, network authentication devices and wireless modules. The company also provides and operates systems to manage confidential data and secure transactions. Gemalto's solutions are categorized into eight groups. The banking & payment group offers a range of digital solutions for secure consumer options to pay, communicate and interact with their banks, including mobile banking, applications, eBanking, eCommerce, credit/debit cards, payments and other services. The government group offers identity solutions and services addressing the government ID management, eGovernment, government infrastructures, road safety, border management and Visa management. This division also comprises Cogent Systems, which offers criminal forensic solutions to public security and law enforcement, as well as secure document issuance, biometrics, document readers, authentication, ID management and data protection products and solutions. The enterprise security group offers advanced identity and data protection solutions for enterprises, including identity and access management, data encryption, crypto management and cloud security. The IoT group offers: reliable connectivity for enterprise IoT devices; reliable security across devices and the cloud; and an agile monetization framework to enable innovative business models through embedded licensing, and a swift time-to-market via an application enablement platform. The mobile group offers a software platform that allows the creation, implementation and secure connection of mobile services between the customer and the business. The software monetization group offers the Sentinel software monetization portfolio, which provides software companies and intelligent device vendors with software licensing, protection and entitlement management solutions. The automotive & mobility services group offers solutions to help the automotive market secure digital mobility services, including connected cars, secure data, ID management and monitoring service usage. Last, the transport group offers contactless technology solutions so that consumers can purchase travel tickets via smartphone or contactless card.

FINANCIAL DATA:
Note: Data for latest year may not have been available at press time.

In U.S. $	2017	2016	2015	2014	2013	2012
Revenue	3,669,783,000	3,860,964,000	3,854,825,000	3,044,233,000	2,949,699,000	2,772,975,000
R&D Expense	244,488,600	232,842,300	232,634,800	177,471,600	177,109,800	174,293,000
Operating Income	69,346,000	434,067,300	289,771,300	369,980,800	350,764,400	297,073,300
Operating Margin %	1.88%	11.24%	7.51%	12.15%	11.89%	10.71%
SGA Expense	876,070,100	798,026,600	807,097,000	598,577,400	582,890,400	573,218,600
Net Income	-523,484,200	229,353,700	165,609,200	272,482,700	318,476,600	248,266,200
Operating Cash Flow	421,792,400	565,553,700	438,527,800	362,519,500	314,626,200	352,066,000
Capital Expenditure	189,936,800	173,489,100	229,955,000	155,181,700	128,395,400	156,745,000
EBITDA	-176,866,600	630,173,600	457,568,700	479,858,800	508,651,700	407,050,000
Return on Assets %	-9.48%	4.10%	3.26%	6.58%	9.15%	7.82%
Return on Equity %	-17.49%	7.20%	5.50%	9.72%	12.67%	11.05%
Debt to Equity	0.32	0.20	0.21	0.16		

CONTACT INFORMATION:
Phone: 3120-562-0680   Fax:
Toll-Free:
Address: Barbara Strozzilaan 382, Amsterdam, 1083 HN Netherlands

STOCK TICKER/OTHER:
Stock Ticker: GTOFF
Employees: 15,000
Parent Company:

Exchange: PINX
Fiscal Year Ends: 12/31

SALARIES/BONUSES:
Top Exec. Salary: $ Bonus: $
Second Exec. Salary: $ Bonus: $

OTHER THOUGHTS:
Estimated Female Officers or Directors: 5
Hot Spot for Advancement for Women/Minorities: Y

Sales, profits and employees may be estimates. Financial information, benefits and other data can change quickly and may vary from those stated here.

Genentech Inc

NAIC Code: 325412

www.gene.com

TYPES OF BUSINESS:
Drug Development & Manufacturing
Genetically Engineered Drugs

BRANDS/DIVISIONS/AFFILIATES:
Roche Holding AG
www.gene.com
HEMLIBRA
Lucentis
TECENTRIQ

CONTACTS:
Note: Officers with more than one job title may be intentionally listed here more than once.

Bill Anderson, CEO
Ed Harrington, CFO
Nancy Vitale, Sr. VP-Human Resources
Richard H. Scheller, Exec. VP-Research
Frederick C. Kentz, Sec.
Timothy Moore, Head-Pharmaceutical Technical Operation Biologics
Severin Schwan, Chmn.

GROWTH PLANS/SPECIAL FEATURES:

Genentech, Inc., a wholly-owned subsidiary of Roche Holding AG, is a biotechnology company that discovers, develops, manufactures and commercializes medicines to treat patients with serious or life-threatening medical conditions. The firm makes medicines by splicing genes into fast-growing bacteria that then produce therapeutic proteins and combat diseases on a molecular level. Genentech uses cutting-edge technologies such as computer visualization of molecules, micro arrays and sensitive assaying techniques to develop, manufacture and market pharmaceuticals for unmet medical needs. For patients, the company's website (www.gene.com) provides access for viewing medicine information, investigational medicines, finding open clinical trials and information on diseases in general. Genentech's range of programs and services help make sure that price is not a barrier for patients. For medical professionals, the website offers information on the medicines that are on the market by Genentech, as well as what is on the current pipeline, compliance, product security and various types of medical resources. Currently (April 2018), there are 38 medicines on the market by the company, and 46 molecules in the pipeline. These medicines and molecules are in various phases in relation to oncology, metabolism, immunology, infectious disease, neuroscience, ophthalmology or other conditions. Approximately half of Genentech's marketed and pipeline products are derived from collaborations with companies and institutions worldwide; therefore, the firm is open to having partners. In early-2018, the U.S. FDA granted breakthrough therapy designation for Genentech's HEMLIBRA (emicizumab-kxwh) in Hemophilia A without inhibitors; the FDA approved Lucentis (ranibizumab injection) 0.3mg pre-filled syringe for diabetic macular edema and diabetic retinopathy; and Phase III IMpower150 study showed Genentech's TECENTRIQ (atezolizumab) and Avastin (bevacizumab) plus carboplatin and paclitaxel helped people with advanced lung cancer live longer.

Genentech provides employees benefits including 401(k); disability, life, AD&D, medical, dental and vision coverage; flexible spending accounts; and paid vacations.

FINANCIAL DATA:
Note: Data for latest year may not have been available at press time.

In U.S. $	2017	2016	2015	2014	2013	2012
Revenue	19,000,000,000	18,000,000,000	17,000,000,000	16,300,000,000		
R&D Expense						
Operating Income						
Operating Margin %						
SGA Expense						
Net Income						
Operating Cash Flow						
Capital Expenditure						
EBITDA						
Return on Assets %						
Return on Equity %						
Debt to Equity						

CONTACT INFORMATION:
Phone: 650-225-1000 Fax: 650-225-6000
Toll-Free: 800-626-3553
Address: 1 DNA Way, South San Francisco, CA 94080-4990 United States

STOCK TICKER/OTHER:
Stock Ticker: Subsidiary
Employees: 14,717
Parent Company: Roche Holding AG

Exchange:
Fiscal Year Ends: 12/31

SALARIES/BONUSES:
Top Exec. Salary: $ Bonus: $
Second Exec. Salary: $ Bonus: $

OTHER THOUGHTS:
Estimated Female Officers or Directors: 1
Hot Spot for Advancement for Women/Minorities: Y

Sales, profits and employees may be estimates. Financial information, benefits and other data can change quickly and may vary from those stated here.

General Dynamics Corporation

www.generaldynamics.com

NAIC Code: 336411

TYPES OF BUSINESS:
Aircraft Manufacturing
Combat Vehicles & Systems
Telecommunications Systems
Naval Vessels & Submarines
Ship Management Services
Information Systems & Technology
Defense Systems & Services
Business Jets

BRANDS/DIVISIONS/AFFILIATES:
Gulfstream Aerospace Corporation
M1A2 Abrams Tank
G500
G600
CSRA Inc

CONTACTS: Note: Officers with more than one job title may be intentionally listed here more than once.
Phebe Novakovic, CEO
Robert Helm, Senior VP, Divisional
Jason Aiken, CFO
William Moss, Chief Accounting Officer
John Casey, Executive VP, Divisional
Mark Roualet, Executive VP, Divisional
S. Johnson, Executive VP, Divisional
Gregory Gallopoulos, General Counsel
Marguerite Gilliland, President, Subsidiary
Mark Burns, President, Subsidiary
Gary Whited, President, Subsidiary
Jeffrey Geiger, President, Subsidiary
Christopher Marzilli, President, Subsidiary
Kimberly Kuryea, Senior VP, Divisional

GROWTH PLANS/SPECIAL FEATURES:
General Dynamics Corporation is one of the world's largest aerospace and defense contractors, with a portfolio of over 60 businesses. Its customers include the U.S. military, other government organizations, armed forces of allied nations and a diverse base of corporate and industrial buyers. The firm's operations are divided into four segments: information systems and technology (IST), marine systems, combat systems and aerospace. The IST group designs, manufactures and delivers tactical and strategic mission systems, information technology and mission services as well as intelligence mission systems to the U.S. Department of Defense and other customers. The marine systems division provides the U.S. Navy with combat vessels, including nuclear submarines, surface combatants and auxiliary ships. The segment also provides ship management services, such as overhaul, repair and lifecycle support services, and builds commercial ships. The combat systems group provides design, development, production, support and enhancement for tracked and wheeled military vehicles, weapons systems and munitions, with product lines including medium armored vehicles, main battle tanks, munitions, rockets and missile components and armament and detection systems. It is the leading builder of armored vehicles and makes products such as the M1A2 Abrams Tank. The aerospace group designs, manufactures and provides services for technologically advanced business jet aircraft under the Gulfstream name. Wholly-owned Gulfstream Aerospace Corporation's new family of business jets, the G500 and G600, can fly 5,000 and 6,200 nautical miles at Mach 0.85 and Mach 0.995, and carry approximately 19 passengers. In April 2018, General Dynamics, as part of its expansion in government information-technology services, acquired CSRA, Inc. That same month, the firm agreed to acquire Hawker Pacific, a provider of integrated aviation solutions across the Asia Pacific and the Middle East.

FINANCIAL DATA: Note: Data for latest year may not have been available at press time.

In U.S. $	2017	2016	2015	2014	2013	2012
Revenue	30,973,000,000	31,353,000,000	31,469,000,000	30,852,000,000	31,218,000,000	31,513,000,000
R&D Expense						
Operating Income	4,177,000,000	4,309,000,000	4,178,000,000	3,889,000,000	3,685,000,000	2,827,000,000
Operating Margin %	13.48%	13.74%	13.27%	12.60%	11.80%	8.97%
SGA Expense	2,010,000,000	1,940,000,000	1,952,000,000	1,984,000,000	2,079,000,000	2,276,000,000
Net Income	2,912,000,000	2,955,000,000	2,965,000,000	2,533,000,000	2,357,000,000	-332,000,000
Operating Cash Flow	3,879,000,000	2,198,000,000	2,499,000,000	3,728,000,000	3,106,000,000	2,687,000,000
Capital Expenditure	428,000,000	392,000,000	569,000,000	521,000,000	440,000,000	450,000,000
EBITDA	4,635,000,000	4,784,000,000	4,682,000,000	4,401,000,000	4,266,000,000	1,329,000,000
Return on Assets %	8.57%	9.11%	8.80%	7.15%	6.75%	-.95%
Return on Equity %	25.98%	27.21%	26.27%	19.24%	18.20%	-2.69%
Debt to Equity	0.34	0.27		0.28	0.26	0.34

CONTACT INFORMATION:
Phone: 703 876-3000
Fax: 703 876-3125
Toll-Free:
Address: 2941 Fairview Park Dr., Ste. 100, Falls Church, VA 22042 United States

STOCK TICKER/OTHER:
Stock Ticker: GD
Employees: 98,800
Parent Company:

Exchange: NYS
Fiscal Year Ends: 12/31

SALARIES/BONUSES:
Top Exec. Salary: $1,585,000   Bonus: $
Second Exec. Salary: $773,750   Bonus: $

OTHER THOUGHTS:
Estimated Female Officers or Directors: 3
Hot Spot for Advancement for Women/Minorities: Y

Sales, profits and employees may be estimates. Financial information, benefits and other data can change quickly and may vary from those stated here.

Plunkett Research, Ltd.

General Electric Company (GE)
NAIC Code: 333000

www.ge.com

TYPES OF BUSINESS:
- Machinery and Equipment Manufacturing
- Energy Systems & Consulting
- Business Leasing & Finance
- Industrial & Electrical Equipment
- Transportation, Aircraft Engines, Rail Systems & Truck Fleet Management
- Real Estate Investments & Finance
- Medical Equipment

BRANDS/DIVISIONS/AFFILIATES:
- GE Additive
- GE Capital
- GE Digital
- GE Lighting
- GE Power
- GE Renewable Energy
- Baker Hughes a GE company
- Drawbridge Health

CONTACTS: Note: Officers with more than one job title may be intentionally listed here more than once.
- John Rice, CEO, Divisional
- Keith Sherin, CEO, Subsidiary
- John Flannery, CEO
- Jeffrey Bornstein, CFO
- Jan Hauser, Chief Accounting Officer
- Alexander Dimitrief, General Counsel
- Brackett Denniston, Secretary

GROWTH PLANS/SPECIAL FEATURES:

General Electric Company (GE) is one of the largest industrial and technology corporations in the world. The firm's businesses include numerous core divisions. GE Additive is engaged in the transformation power of advanced manufacturing to offer solutions concerning modern design and manufacturing challenges. GE Aviation is a global provider of jet engines, components and integrated systems for commercial and military aircraft. GE Capital offers financial services to more than 245 customers in 75 countries, including aircraft leasing, financing, services and consulting. GE Digital offers Predix, an industrial internet platform that connects an organization's physical and digital worlds. GE Healthcare provides medical imaging equipment, and harnesses data and analytics across hardware, software and biotechnology. GE Lighting produces light-emitting diode (LED) lighting solutions. GE Power is a global provider of power generation, delivering 1/3 of the world's electricity. GE Renewable Energy combines onshore and offshore wind, hydro and innovative technologies (such as concentrated solar power) to provide renewable energy. It has installed more than 400 gigawatts of capacity globally. GE Transportation utilizes data science and analytics to create an efficient and reliable digital-rail ecosystem. Baker Hughes, a GE company, is a fullstream business, delivering integrated oilfield products, services and digital solutions. Current, powered by GE, applies advanced energy technologies and digital networks to provide connected lighting, energy efficient solutions. Last, GE Global Research advances horizontal technologies across GE's offerings, scaling investment in the key areas of artificial intelligence, additive manufacturing, silicon carbide power devices and industrial internet edge controls. During 2017, the firm merged its oil and gas business with subsidiary Baker Hughes, a GE company; and created a blood collection company, Drawbridge Health, to develop proprietary technology designed to make it easier for doctor's offices/clinics to collect small samples of blood from patients for testing onsite via handheld device.

FINANCIAL DATA: Note: Data for latest year may not have been available at press time.

In U.S. $	2017	2016	2015	2014	2013	2012
Revenue	122,092,000,000	123,693,000,000	117,386,000,000	148,589,000,000	146,045,000,000	144,796,000,000
R&D Expense						
Operating Income	11,878,000,000	17,833,000,000	16,862,000,000	25,854,000,000	26,267,000,000	32,771,000,000
Operating Margin %	9.72%	14.41%	14.36%	17.39%	17.98%	22.63%
SGA Expense	18,280,000,000	18,377,000,000	17,831,000,000	30,572,000,000	37,819,000,000	
Net Income	-5,786,000,000	8,831,000,000	-6,126,000,000	15,233,000,000	13,057,000,000	13,641,000,000
Operating Cash Flow	10,426,000,000	-244,000,000	19,891,000,000	27,710,000,000	28,579,000,000	31,331,000,000
Capital Expenditure	7,920,000,000	7,199,000,000	7,309,000,000	13,727,000,000	13,458,000,000	15,126,000,000
EBITDA	1,217,000,000	19,052,000,000	16,496,000,000	35,994,000,000	36,029,000,000	39,260,000,000
Return on Assets %	-1.67%	1.90%	-1.07%	2.33%	1.94%	1.94%
Return on Equity %	-8.88%	9.39%	-5.41%	11.77%	10.29%	11.39%
Debt to Equity	1.72	1.39	1.50	1.73	1.85	2.54

CONTACT INFORMATION:
Phone: 203-373-2211 Fax:
Toll-Free:
Address: 41 Farnsworth St., Boston, MA 02210 United States

STOCK TICKER/OTHER:
Stock Ticker: GE Exchange: NYS
Employees: 295,000 Fiscal Year Ends: 12/31
Parent Company:

SALARIES/BONUSES:
Top Exec. Salary: $ Bonus: $
Second Exec. Salary: $ Bonus: $

OTHER THOUGHTS:
Estimated Female Officers or Directors: 10
Hot Spot for Advancement for Women/Minorities: Y

Sales, profits and employees may be estimates. Financial information, benefits and other data can change quickly and may vary from those stated here.

General Motors Company (GM)

www.gm.com

NAIC Code: 336111

TYPES OF BUSINESS:
Automobile Manufacturing
Security & Information Services
Automotive Electronics
Financing & Insurance
Parts & Service
Transmissions
Engines
Locomotives

BRANDS/DIVISIONS/AFFILIATES:
Chevrolet
Buick
Cadillac
GMC
Opel
Vauxhall
Holden

CONTACTS:
Note: Officers with more than one job title may be intentionally listed here more than once.

Mary Barra, CEO
Charles Stevens, CFO
Thomas Timko, Chief Accounting Officer
Vinit Sethi, Director
Mark Reuss, Executive VP, Divisional
Alicia Boler-Davis, Executive VP, Divisional
Craig Glidden, Executive VP
Alan Batey, Executive VP
Matthew Tsien, Executive VP
Carel De Nysschen, Executive VP
Barry Engle, Executive VP
Daniel Ammann, President

GROWTH PLANS/SPECIAL FEATURES:

General Motors Company (GM) is engaged in the worldwide development, production and marketing of cars, trucks, automotive systems and locomotives. The firm's major North American brands include Chevrolet, Buick, Cadillac and GMC. Besides its North American brands, GM markets vehicles internationally under the following brands: Opel, via Adam Opel AG; Vauxhall, via Vauxhall Motors Ltd.; and Holden, via GM. The company is organized into four geographically-based segments: General Motors North America (GMNA), focused on U.S., Canada, and Mexico; General Motors international operations (GMIO), focused primarily on Egypt, Australia, the Middle East and Asia; General Motors Europe (GME), centered on European operations; and General Motors South America (GMSA), with operations primarily in Brazil, Argentina, Colombia and Venezuela. GM's equity ownership stakes through various regional subsidiaries in Asia design, manufacture and market vehicles under the Baojun, Buick, Cadillac, Chevrolet, Jiefang and Wuling brands. The firm has 19,452 dealerships worldwide, with 4,857 locations in North America.

FINANCIAL DATA:
Note: Data for latest year may not have been available at press time.

In U.S. $	2017	2016	2015	2014	2013	2012
Revenue	145,588,000,000	166,380,000,000	152,356,000,000	155,929,000,000	155,427,000,000	152,256,000,000
R&D Expense						
Operating Income	10,016,000,000	9,545,000,000	4,897,000,000	1,650,000,000	5,672,000,000	-3,218,000,000
Operating Margin %	6.87%	5.73%	3.21%	1.05%	3.64%	-2.11%
SGA Expense	9,575,000,000	11,710,000,000	13,405,000,000	12,158,000,000	12,382,000,000	13,593,000,000
Net Income	-3,864,000,000	9,427,000,000	9,687,000,000	3,949,000,000	5,346,000,000	6,188,000,000
Operating Cash Flow	17,328,000,000	16,545,000,000	11,978,000,000	10,058,000,000	12,630,000,000	10,605,000,000
Capital Expenditure	27,633,000,000	29,166,000,000	23,032,000,000	11,867,000,000	9,819,000,000	9,118,000,000
EBITDA	24,699,000,000	22,664,000,000	16,178,000,000	11,887,000,000	15,833,000,000	8,994,000,000
Return on Assets %	-1.78%	4.52%	5.20%	1.63%	2.38%	3.30%
Return on Equity %	-9.84%	22.52%	25.71%	7.48%	11.53%	18.13%
Debt to Equity	0.31	0.21	0.19	0.25	0.16	0.13

CONTACT INFORMATION:
Phone: 313 556-5000   Fax:
Toll-Free:
Address: 300 Renaissance Ctr., Detroit, MI 48265-3000 United States

STOCK TICKER/OTHER:
Stock Ticker: GM
Employees: 135,000
Parent Company:

Exchange: NYS
Fiscal Year Ends: 12/31

SALARIES/BONUSES:
Top Exec. Salary: $1,750,000   Bonus: $
Second Exec. Salary: $1,200,000   Bonus: $

OTHER THOUGHTS:
Estimated Female Officers or Directors: 8
Hot Spot for Advancement for Women/Minorities: Y

Sales, profits and employees may be estimates. Financial information, benefits and other data can change quickly and may vary from those stated here.

Georg Fischer Ltd

NAIC Code: 336300

www.georgfischer.com

TYPES OF BUSINESS:
Automotive Components
Iron Casting
Manufacturing Technology
Machine Tools
Piping Systems
Design
Control systems

BRANDS/DIVISIONS/AFFILIATES:
Central Plastics
JRG Gunzenhauser AG

CONTACTS: Note: Officers with more than one job title may be intentionally listed here more than once.
Yves Serra, CEO
Andreas Muller, CFO
Beat Romer, Head-Corp. Comm.
Daniel Bosiger, Head-Investor Rel.
Josef Edbauer, Head-Automotive
Pietro Lori, Head-Piping Systems
Pascal Boillat, Head-GF AgieCharmilles
Andreas Koopmann, Chmn.

GROWTH PLANS/SPECIAL FEATURES:

Georg Fischer Ltd. is a design and manufacturing firm with over 135 subsidiaries operating through three divisions: casting, piping systems and machining solutions. The casting division designs and manufactures cast components and systems for auto chassis, powertrains and bodies. The firm performs large-scale iron casting, sand and die-casting and pressure die casting of iron and light metals. In addition, the firm sells automotive products such as mounting plates and mounting kits. The piping systems division supplies plastic and metal piping systems for industrial applications, gas and water utilities and construction projects. Products include industrial piping systems, piping system control and regulation products, distribution systems for gas and water, drinking water installation systems and machines and tools for jointing plastic and metal piping systems. The division has a sales presence in over 50 countries to ensure round-the-clock customer support. Subsidiaries within this division include Central Plastics and JRG Gunzenhauser AG. The machining solutions division provides milling and electrical discharge machines, additive manufacturing solutions, laser texturing, automation, tooling and spindles. These machining solutions serve the tool- and mold-making industry, as well as the precision components manufacturing industry. This division's production facilities and research and development centers are located in Switzerland, Sweden and China. In January 2018, the firm agreed to acquire Precicast Industrial Holding SA, a Swiss-based precision casting specialist.

FINANCIAL DATA: Note: Data for latest year may not have been available at press time.

In U.S. $	2017	2016	2015	2014	2013	2012
Revenue	4,250,570,000	3,673,690,000	3,764,608,920	4,069,203,960	4,262,801,797	3,941,220,000
R&D Expense						
Operating Income						
Operating Margin %						
SGA Expense						
Net Income	258,107,000	220,774,000	2,047,675,825	197,294,737	164,126,945	132,395,000
Operating Cash Flow						
Capital Expenditure						
EBITDA						
Return on Assets %						
Return on Equity %						
Debt to Equity						

CONTACT INFORMATION:
Phone: 41 526311111   Fax: 41 526312847
Toll-Free:
Address: Amsler-Laffon-Strasse 9, Schaffhausen, CH-8201 Switzerland

SALARIES/BONUSES:
Top Exec. Salary: $ Bonus: $
Second Exec. Salary: $ Bonus: $

STOCK TICKER/OTHER:
Stock Ticker: GFIN   Exchange: Frankfurt
Employees: 15,835   Fiscal Year Ends: 12/31
Parent Company:

OTHER THOUGHTS:
Estimated Female Officers or Directors: 2
Hot Spot for Advancement for Women/Minorities: Y

Geosyntec Consultants Inc

www.geosyntec.com

NAIC Code: 541330

TYPES OF BUSINESS:
Engineering Consulting Services

BRANDS/DIVISIONS/AFFILIATES:
MMI Engineering
SiREM
Savron
Green Harbor Energy
Geosyntec Europe
Geosyntec Australia & New Zealand

CONTACTS:
Note: Officers with more than one job title may be intentionally listed here more than once.

Rudy Bonaparte, Chmn.

GROWTH PLANS/SPECIAL FEATURES:
Geosyntec Consultants, Inc. is a specialized consulting and engineering firm primarily for private and public sectors. The company's services address new ventures and complex problems in relation to the environment, natural resources and civil infrastructure. Geosyntec's solutions are delivered through six wholly-owned subsidiaries: MMI Engineering, SiREM Lab, Savron, Green Harbor Energy, Geosyntec Europe and Geosyntec Australia & New Zealand. MMI Engineering helps clients manage risks that could affect life, the environment or asset performance via risk management analysis and engineering solutions. SiREM provides a range of products and testing services needed by environmental professionals in order to optimize the remediation of chlorinated solvents and other recalcitrant chemicals. This division's branded products include: KB-1, comprising bioaugmentation cultures; genetrac, for environmental molecular testing; treatability, which evaluates and optimizes remediation performance in a laboratory setting; and SP3, which addresses contaminated sediment issues. Savron is a multi-national provider of sustainable waste management and remediation solutions, specializing in the safe, energy-efficient, environmentally-responsible treatment of a wide range of hazardous materials. Its products provide in situ and ex situ solutions for the treatment of contaminated soils and organic wastes, based on the principles of smoldering combustion. Green Harbor Energy provides environmental management and sustainability services such as consulting, engineering and marketing for the enhanced energy efficiency and cost-effectiveness of its clients. Geosyntec Europe is a specialized consulting and engineering firm that works with Asian private and public-sector clients concerning the natural and built environments. Its services include environmental studies, cleanup, infrastructure assessment, engineering, design, health/environmental/safety management, natural resource assessment, restoration, structural load analysis, fluid dynamics and risk mitigation. Last, Geosyntec Australia & New Zealand offers the same services as Geosyntec Europe, across their respective countries.

FINANCIAL DATA:
Note: Data for latest year may not have been available at press time.

In U.S. $	2017	2016	2015	2014	2013	2012
Revenue						
R&D Expense						
Operating Income						
Operating Margin %						
SGA Expense						
Net Income						
Operating Cash Flow						
Capital Expenditure						
EBITDA						
Return on Assets %						
Return on Equity %						
Debt to Equity						

CONTACT INFORMATION:
Phone: 404-267-1101 Fax:
Toll-Free:
Address: 2002 Sumit Blvd., NE, Ste. 885, Atlanta, GA 30319 United States

STOCK TICKER/OTHER:
Stock Ticker: Private
Employees: 1,200
Parent Company:

Exchange:
Fiscal Year Ends:

SALARIES/BONUSES:
Top Exec. Salary: $ Bonus: $
Second Exec. Salary: $ Bonus: $

OTHER THOUGHTS:
Estimated Female Officers or Directors:
Hot Spot for Advancement for Women/Minorities:

Sales, profits and employees may be estimates. Financial information, benefits and other data can change quickly and may vary from those stated here.

Ghafari Associates LLC

www.ghafari.com

NAIC Code: 541330

TYPES OF BUSINESS:
Engineering Consulting Services

BRANDS/DIVISIONS/AFFILIATES:

CONTACTS:
Note: Officers with more than one job title may be intentionally listed here more than once.

Kouhaila G. Hammer, CEO
Ali Solaksubasi, Pres.
Keith Sherman, CFO
Catherine Noyes, CMO
Christine McDermott, Chief Human Resources Officer
Bob Bell, CIO
Yousif B. Ghafari, Chmn.

GROWTH PLANS/SPECIAL FEATURES:

Ghafari Associates, LLC is an architecture, engineering, consulting, process and construction services organization. With offices in North and South America, the Middle East and India, Ghafari serves a diverse range of clients within markets such as automotive, aviation, commercial, education, energy, food, government/institutional, healthcare and industrial/manufacturing. The company offers in-house capabilities to lead projects through any and all phases of the development process, from planning to start-up and commissioning, regardless of size or scope of complexity. Ghafari's architecture division utilizes the latest technology in conjunction with creativity to design buildings that complement the built environment. Its services include programming, planning, architectural design, interior design and sustainable design. The engineering division applies analytical tools and techniques, coupled with 3D BIM (building information modeling) capabilities. Its engineering services include civil, structural, mechanical, electrical, plumbing, fire protection and security systems. The consulting division provides integrated project delivery and building information modeling (BIM) technologies, project planning and facilitation, transition planning, last planner system facilitation and management, information flow management, value stream mapping, design management and coordination, production system design, planning and execution. The process division offers productivity solutions including industrial, manufacturing, packaging engineering and lean implementation; and equipment solutions including conveyors, paint finishing systems, control systems, equipment set and tool installation. The construction division provides development, design and construction services such as owner's representation, project management, construction management, agency construction management, construction management at cost plus fee as well as at-risk design build. In October 2017, Ghafari opened its newest office in Fort Worth, Texas.

The company offers employees in-house training programs, continuing education and seminars, undergraduate and graduate studies reimbursement as well as professional registration and membership reimbursement.

FINANCIAL DATA:
Note: Data for latest year may not have been available at press time.

In U.S. $	2017	2016	2015	2014	2013	2012
Revenue						
R&D Expense						
Operating Income						
Operating Margin %						
SGA Expense						
Net Income						
Operating Cash Flow						
Capital Expenditure						
EBITDA						
Return on Assets %						
Return on Equity %						
Debt to Equity						

CONTACT INFORMATION:
Phone: 313-441-3000 Fax: 313-441-1545
Toll-Free:
Address: 17101 Michigan Ave., Dearborn, MI 48126-2736 United States

STOCK TICKER/OTHER:
Stock Ticker: Private   Exchange:
Employees: 400   Fiscal Year Ends:
Parent Company:

SALARIES/BONUSES:
Top Exec. Salary: $ Bonus: $
Second Exec. Salary: $ Bonus: $

OTHER THOUGHTS:
Estimated Female Officers or Directors:
Hot Spot for Advancement for Women/Minorities:

Sales, profits and employees may be estimates. Financial information, benefits and other data can change quickly and may vary from those stated here.

GHD

NAIC Code: 541330

www.ghd.com

TYPES OF BUSINESS:
Engineering Services

BRANDS/DIVISIONS/AFFILIATES:

CONTACTS: Note: Officers with more than one job title may be intentionally listed here more than once.
Ashley Wright, CEO
Phillip Bradley, CFO
Elizabeth Harper, CIO
Rob Knott, Chmn.

GROWTH PLANS/SPECIAL FEATURES:
GHD (Gutteridge, Haskins and Davey) is an employee-owned provider of engineering, architecture, environmental and construction services to private and public-sector clients. The firm is one of the world's leading professional services companies operating in the advisory, buildings, digital, energy/resources, environmental, geosciences, project management, transportation and water markets. The advisory division has played a leading role in the development and growth of asset management for more than 35 years, with significant experience in asset management planning and implementation of asset management programs at strategic, tactical and operations levels for over 500 organizations worldwide. The buildings division offers asset and facilities management, building sciences and physics, design documentation, demolition and decommissioning, forensic engineering, geotechnical, instrumentation and control, land development and urban planning, materials technology, mechanical/electrical/fire/life safety, project management, security/information/communication technology, spatial sciences and structures services. The digital division offers data and analytics, design documentation, instrumentation and control, security/information/communication technology and spatial science services. The energy and resources division's services range from feasibility to performance optimization, and include expansion of existing operations, development of new greenfield projects or closure of assets. The environment division offers a broad spectrum of services to help clients develop projects, enhance performance and close and remediate operations, while managing risks and impacts. The geoscience division offers services in relation to dams, geology, geotechnology, hydrogeology, mining, risk management, spatial sciences, tailings (mines & residue) and tunnels. The project management division aims to deliver on time and on budget, with all the necessary approvals for every one of its projects. The transportation division assists clients from initial policy, transportation planning, economics and business case advice, through to concept, procurement, detailed design, construction, operations, maintenance and asset management. Last, the water division's services cover feasibility studies, planning, design, project management, construction and asset management, as well as operational optimization.

FINANCIAL DATA: Note: Data for latest year may not have been available at press time.

In U.S. $	2017	2016	2015	2014	2013	2012
Revenue	1,326,830,000	1,220,000,000	1,270,912,500	1,155,375,000	770,285,000	
R&D Expense						
Operating Income						
Operating Margin %						
SGA Expense						
Net Income						
Operating Cash Flow						
Capital Expenditure						
EBITDA						
Return on Assets %						
Return on Equity %						
Debt to Equity						

CONTACT INFORMATION:
Phone: 61-2-9239-7100 Fax: 61-2-9239-7199
Toll-Free:
Address: 133 Castlereagh St., 15/Fl, Sydney, NSW 2000 Australia

STOCK TICKER/OTHER:
Stock Ticker: Private   Exchange:
Employees: 9,000   Fiscal Year Ends:
Parent Company:

SALARIES/BONUSES:
Top Exec. Salary: $ Bonus: $
Second Exec. Salary: $ Bonus: $

OTHER THOUGHTS:
Estimated Female Officers or Directors:
Hot Spot for Advancement for Women/Minorities:

Gilead Sciences Inc

NAIC Code: 325412

www.gilead.com

TYPES OF BUSINESS:
Viral & Bacterial Infections Drugs
Respiratory & Cardiopulmonary Diseases Drugs

BRANDS/DIVISIONS/AFFILIATES:
Kite Pharma Inc
Cell Design Labs Inc
Sovaldi
Harvoni
Vemlidy
Yescarta
synNotch
Throttle

CONTACTS: Note: Officers with more than one job title may be intentionally listed here more than once.
John Milligan, CEO
Robin Washington, CFO
John Martin, Chairman of the Board
Kevin Young, COO
Gregg Alton, Executive VP, Divisional
Norbert Bischofberger, Executive VP, Divisional

GROWTH PLANS/SPECIAL FEATURES:
Gilead Sciences, Inc. is a research-based biopharmaceutical company that discovers, develops and commercializes innovative medicines in the areas of unmet medical need. The firm's primary areas of focus include human immunodeficiency virus (HIV), acquired immunodeficiency syndrome (AIDS), liver diseases, hematology/oncology and inflammation/respiratory diseases. In relation to HIV/AIDS, Gilead has six single tablet regimens available for treatment. In relation to liver diseases, the company provides products that meet the needs of almost all hepatitis C virus (HCV) patients regardless of disease severity, genotype or prior treatment, and include Sovaldi, Harvoni, Epclusa and Vemlidy, with others in various phases of study. In relation to hematology/oncology, subsidiary Kite Pharma, Inc. is a leader in cellular therapy and provides a foundation from which it will drive continued innovation for people with advanced cancers. Kite's cell therapies express either a CAR (chimeric antigen receptor) or an engineered T cell receptor, depending on the type of cancer. Its Yescarta cell therapy was recently approved by the FDA for the treatment of adult patients with relapsed or refractory large B-cell lymphoma after two or more lines of systemic therapy. EC approval of Yescarta was expected by mid-2018. This segment also comprises Cell Design Labs, Inc., a pre-clinical stage company with expertise in custom cell engineering. Cell Design is developing two proprietary technology platforms: synNotch, a synthetic gene expression system that responds to external cues which can be deployed to engineer CAR T cells that require dual antigen recognition for activation; and Throttle, an on-switch that modulates CAR T cell activity using small molecules. Last, the inflammation/respiratory disease segment is engaged in advancing five ongoing Phase 3 clinical trials of filgotinib, a JAK1 inhibitor for the potential treatment of rheumatoid arthritis; and a Phase 2 study of andecaliximab in combination with nivolumab.

Gilead offers comprehensive benefits.

FINANCIAL DATA: Note: Data for latest year may not have been available at press time.

In U.S. $	2017	2016	2015	2014	2013	2012
Revenue	26,107,000,000	30,390,000,000	32,639,000,000	24,890,000,000	11,201,690,000	9,702,517,000
R&D Expense	3,734,000,000	5,098,000,000	3,014,000,000	2,854,000,000	2,119,756,000	1,759,945,000
Operating Income	14,124,000,000	17,633,000,000	22,193,000,000	15,265,000,000	4,523,999,000	4,010,175,000
Operating Margin %	54.10%	58.02%	67.99%	61.32%	40.38%	41.33%
SGA Expense	3,878,000,000	3,398,000,000	3,426,000,000	2,983,000,000	1,699,431,000	1,461,034,000
Net Income	4,628,000,000	13,501,000,000	18,108,000,000	12,101,000,000	3,074,808,000	2,591,566,000
Operating Cash Flow	11,898,000,000	16,669,000,000	20,329,000,000	12,818,000,000	3,104,988,000	3,194,716,000
Capital Expenditure	590,000,000	748,000,000	747,000,000	557,000,000	190,782,000	397,046,000
EBITDA	15,933,000,000	19,219,000,000	23,445,000,000	16,318,000,000	4,859,817,000	4,251,102,000
Return on Assets %	7.27%	24.81%	41.86%	42.34%	14.06%	13.44%
Return on Equity %	23.53%	72.15%	106.58%	90.05%	29.64%	32.29%
Debt to Equity	1.50	1.39	1.14	0.77	0.34	0.75

CONTACT INFORMATION:
Phone: 650 574-3000 Fax: 650 578-9264
Toll-Free: 800-445-3235
Address: 333 Lakeside Dr., Foster City, CA 94404 United States

STOCK TICKER/OTHER:
Stock Ticker: GILD   Exchange: NAS
Employees: 9,000   Fiscal Year Ends: 12/31
Parent Company:

SALARIES/BONUSES:
Top Exec. Salary: $1,539,462 Bonus: $
Second Exec. Salary: $1,253,208 Bonus: $

OTHER THOUGHTS:
Estimated Female Officers or Directors: 4
Hot Spot for Advancement for Women/Minorities: Y

Sales, profits and employees may be estimates. Financial information, benefits and other data can change quickly and may vary from those stated here.

GKN plc

www.gknplc.com

NAIC Code: 336300

TYPES OF BUSINESS:
- Automobile Parts-Manufacturing & Engineering
- Aerospace Engineering
- Driveshaft System Products
- Powder Metallurgy
- Off Highway Components
- Engineering Support Services
- Helicopters & Military Vehicles
- Propulsion System Components

BRANDS/DIVISIONS/AFFILIATES:
- GKN Aerospace
- GKN Driveline
- GKN Powder Metallurgy
- GKN Sinter Metals
- GKN Hoeganaes
- GKN Wheels and Structures
- GKN Off-Highway Powertrain

CONTACTS:
Note: Officers with more than one job title may be intentionally listed here more than once.

- Nigel Stein, CEO
- Adam Walker, Finance
- Judith Felton, Corp. Sec.
- William Seeger, Jr., Dir.-Finance
- Andrew Reynolds Smith, CEO-Automotive & Power Metallurgy
- Marcus Bryson, CEO-Aerospace & Land Systems
- Michael Turner, Chmn.

GROWTH PLANS/SPECIAL FEATURES:

GKN plc is a global engineering company with operations in 30 countries. The firm operates three primary segments: GKN Aerospace, which supplies aerostructures, engine products, systems and electrical wiring systems to the aerospace industry; GKN Driveline, which supplies automotive driveline systems and solutions to vehicle manufacturers; and GKN Powder Metallurgy, which comprises GKN Sinter Metals, a manufacturer of sintered components, and GKN Hoeganaes, a producer of metal powder used in the manufacture of these components. Additional GKN businesses include GKN Wheels and Structures, and GKN Off-Highway Powertrain, both of which provide products and technologies that deliver the power to harvest crops, move earth, mine resources and handle materials. GKN Wheels and Structures develops tailored product solutions for local markets, with manufacturing facilities in five countries across three continents. Its products include hub systems, spindles, chassis systems, pressed steel, aluminum structural assemblies, modules and a range of wheels designed to operate in challenging environments. GKN Off-Highway Powertrain comprises nine manufacturing facilities and 28 service centers in over 16 countries across five continents. It supplies engineered power management products and systems such as antivibration systems, clutches, driveshafts, gearboxes, hydrostatic ground drives, hitch systems and tractor attachment systems. In April 2017, the firm agreed to acquire Tozmetal Ticaret Ve Sanayi AS, a powder metal part manufacturer based in Istanbul, Turkey.

FINANCIAL DATA:
Note: Data for latest year may not have been available at press time.

In U.S. $	2017	2016	2015	2014	2013	2012
Revenue	13,774,390,000	12,565,160,000	10,299,100,000	9,944,452,000	10,163,790,000	9,272,184,000
R&D Expense						
Operating Income	739,210,900	924,369,700	680,814,700	702,179,200	856,003,400	669,420,300
Operating Margin %	5.36%	7.35%	6.61%	7.06%	8.42%	7.21%
SGA Expense						
Net Income	716,422,100	344,680,300	280,586,800	240,706,400	562,597,900	683,663,300
Operating Cash Flow	677,966,100	948,582,800	1,103,831,000	937,188,400	1,009,828,000	639,510,000
Capital Expenditure	742,059,500	712,149,200	588,235,300	575,416,600	498,504,500	485,685,800
EBITDA	1,801,738,000	1,155,106,000	1,006,979,000	944,310,000	1,271,899,000	1,321,749,000
Return on Assets %	5.64%	2.93%	2.77%	2.61%	6.31%	8.45%
Return on Equity %	21.55%	12.13%	11.78%	10.38%	23.58%	33.97%
Debt to Equity	0.44	0.39	0.46	0.59	0.50	0.59

CONTACT INFORMATION:
Phone: 44 1527517715   Fax: 44 1527517700
Toll-Free:
Address: Ipsley House, Ipsley Church Ln., P.O. Box 55, Worcestershire, B98 OTL United Kingdom

STOCK TICKER/OTHER:
Stock Ticker: GKNLY
Employees: 74,200
Parent Company:

Exchange: PINX
Fiscal Year Ends: 12/31

SALARIES/BONUSES:
Top Exec. Salary: $1,160,803   Bonus: $737,787
Second Exec. Salary: $813,274   Bonus: $522,718

OTHER THOUGHTS:
Estimated Female Officers or Directors: 2
Hot Spot for Advancement for Women/Minorities:

Sales, profits and employees may be estimates. Financial information, benefits and other data can change quickly and may vary from those stated here.

GlaxoSmithKline plc

www.gsk.com

NAIC Code: 325412

TYPES OF BUSINESS:
Prescription Medications
Asthma Drugs
Respiratory Drugs
Antibiotics
Antivirals
Dermatological Drugs
Over-the-Counter & Nutritional Products

BRANDS/DIVISIONS/AFFILIATES:
Sensodyne
Panadol
Horlicks
ViiV Healthcare
Stiefel Laboratories Inc

CONTACTS: Note: Officers with more than one job title may be intentionally listed here more than once.
Emma Walmsley, CEO
David Redfern, Chief Strategy Officer
Simon Dingemans, CFO
Claire Thomas, Sr. VP-Human Resources
Moncef Slaoui, Chmn.-Global R&D & Vaccines
Karenann Terrell, CTO
Roger Connor, Pres., Global Mfg. & Supply
Dan Troy, General Counsel
David Redfern, Chief Strategy Officer
Phil Thomson, Sr. VP-Global Comm.
Simon Bicknell, Sr. VP-Governance, Ethics & Assurance
Deirdre Connelly, Pres., North American Pharmaceuticals
Bill Louv, Sr. VP-Core Bus. Svcs.
Emma Walmsley, Pres., Consumer Health Care Worldwide
Philip Hampton, Chmn.
Abbas Hassain, Pres., Europe, Japan & EMAP
Roger Connor, Pres., Global Mfg. & Supply

GROWTH PLANS/SPECIAL FEATURES:
GlaxoSmithKline plc (GSK) is a leading research-based pharmaceutical company. Its subsidiaries consist of global drug and health companies engaged in the creation, discovery, development, manufacturing and marketing of pharmaceuticals and consumer health products. GSK researches and develops a broad range of innovative products in three primary areas: pharmaceuticals, vaccines and consumer healthcare. The pharmaceuticals division represents 57% of the firm's net revenue in 2017, and develops and makes medicines to treat a broad range of acute and chronic diseases. These medicines are made up of both patent-protected and off patent medicines. The vaccines division (17%) produces pediatric and adult vaccines against a range of infectious diseases. In 2017, it distributed more than 2 million vaccine doses per day to people in over 160 countries. The consumer healthcare division (26%) develops and markets a range of consumer healthcare products based on scientific innovation. Its brands fall within four main categories, wellness, oral health, skin health and nutrition, and include names such as Sensodyne, Panadol and Horlicks. In addition to its primary areas, the firm also researches new options for the care and treatment of people living with HIV/AIDS through subsidiary ViiV Healthcare. Through Stiefel Laboratories, Inc., GSK also offers a portfolio of dermatological products for such conditions as psoriasis, eczema, atopic dermatitis and superficial skin infections. In early-2018, GSK agreed to buy out Novartis' 36.5% stake in consumer healthcare joint venture for $13 billion, in order to hold full ownership of the business; and GSK agreed to transfer its rare disease gene therapy portfolio to Orchard Therapeutics, enabling GSK to continue to invest in the development of its cell and gene therapies, with a focus on oncology.

FINANCIAL DATA: Note: Data for latest year may not have been available at press time.

In U.S. $	2017	2016	2015	2014	2013	2012
Revenue	42,993,880,000	39,722,260,000	34,073,490,000	32,767,410,000	37,751,030,000	37,645,640,000
R&D Expense	6,375,160,000	5,167,355,000	5,070,503,000	4,913,830,000	5,587,523,000	5,651,617,000
Operating Income	8,112,804,000	8,582,823,000	3,743,057,000	6,133,029,000	8,383,421,000	8,782,224,000
Operating Margin %	18.86%	21.60%	10.98%	18.71%	22.20%	23.32%
SGA Expense	13,775,810,000	13,339,980,000	13,149,120,000	11,744,770,000	12,078,050,000	12,446,950,000
Net Income	2,182,025,000	1,298,960,000	11,995,440,000	3,925,367,000	7,742,487,000	6,501,923,000
Operating Cash Flow	9,853,298,000	9,253,668,000	3,659,023,000	7,372,169,000	10,286,280,000	6,231,306,000
Capital Expenditure	3,136,305,000	3,349,950,000	2,707,591,000	2,493,947,000	2,422,732,000	2,164,934,000
EBITDA	8,752,314,000	6,286,854,000	18,337,840,000	7,320,894,000	12,515,310,000	12,650,620,000
Return on Assets %	2.65%	1.62%	17.90%	6.66%	13.01%	11.05%
Return on Equity %	290.15%	29.24%	179.63%	48.95%	84.89%	65.95%
Debt to Equity		13.04	2.99	3.71	2.20	2.52

CONTACT INFORMATION:
Phone: 44 20-8047-5000   Fax: 44 20-8047-7807
Toll-Free: 888-825-5249
Address: 980 Great W. Rd., Brentford, Middlesex, TW8 9GS United Kingdom

STOCK TICKER/OTHER:
Stock Ticker: GSK
Employees: 99,300
Parent Company:

Exchange: NYS
Fiscal Year Ends: 12/31

SALARIES/BONUSES:
Top Exec. Salary: $1,374,448   Bonus: $2,193,420
Second Exec. Salary: $1,110,953   Bonus: $1,605,185

OTHER THOUGHTS:
Estimated Female Officers or Directors: 8
Hot Spot for Advancement for Women/Minorities: Y

Sales, profits and employees may be estimates. Financial information, benefits and other data can change quickly and may vary from those stated here.

Globalvia Inversiones SAU

NAIC Code: 488490

www.globalvia.es

TYPES OF BUSINESS:
Bridge, Tunnel and Highway Operations
Highway Operations
Railway Operations
Infrastructure Concession Management

BRANDS/DIVISIONS/AFFILIATES:

GROWTH PLANS/SPECIAL FEATURES:
Globalvia Inversiones SAU is an infrastructure concession management firm. Established in 2007, Globalvia is led by three international pension funds and manages 27 projects in eight different countries, with a focus on highways and railways. The company manages more than 900 miles of highways and tunnels; and provides private passenger rail transport management services in Spain. In all, the firm's projects include 19 highways and eight railways located in Spain, the U.S., Ireland, Portugal, Andorra, Mexico, Costa Rica and Chile. In October 2018, the firm acquired 100% of A23-Beira Interior (Scutvias) highway in Portugal.

CONTACTS:
Note: Officers with more than one job title may be intentionally listed here more than once.

Javier Perez Fortea, CEO
Alberto Garcia, CFO
Javier Perez Fortea, Dir.-Dev., Construction & Oper.
Jose Felipe Gomez de Barreda, General Counsel
Rafael Nevada, Dir.-Bus. Dev. & Contract Bids
Patricia Coba, Chief Comm. Officer
Carmen Rubio, Dir.-Audit & Risk Control
Luis Sanchez Salmeron, Dir.-Bus. Managing
Maria Luisa Castro, Dir.-Spanish Highways
Javier Galera, Dir.-European Highways
Pablo Pajares, Construction Department

FINANCIAL DATA:
Note: Data for latest year may not have been available at press time.

In U.S. $	2017	2016	2015	2014	2013	2012
Revenue	305,000,000	310,000,000	306,917,638	293,942,985	237,758,763	
R&D Expense						
Operating Income						
Operating Margin %						
SGA Expense						
Net Income						
Operating Cash Flow						
Capital Expenditure						
EBITDA						
Return on Assets %						
Return on Equity %						
Debt to Equity						

CONTACT INFORMATION:
Phone: 34-914-565-850   Fax: 34-915-720-068
Toll-Free:
Address: Paseo Castellana, 141-5 Planta, Edificio Cuzco IV, Madrid, 28046 Spain

STOCK TICKER/OTHER:
Stock Ticker: Joint-Venture   Exchange:
Employees: Fiscal Year Ends:
Parent Company: Fomento De Construcciones Y Contratas SA (FCC)

SALARIES/BONUSES:
Top Exec. Salary: $ Bonus: $
Second Exec. Salary: $ Bonus: $

OTHER THOUGHTS:
Estimated Female Officers or Directors: 3
Hot Spot for Advancement for Women/Minorities: Y

Sales, profits and employees may be estimates. Financial information, benefits and other data can change quickly and may vary from those stated here.

GM Korea

NAIC Code: 336111

www.gm-korea.co.kr

TYPES OF BUSINESS:
Automobile Manufacturing
Auto Marketing

BRANDS/DIVISIONS/AFFILIATES:
General Motors Company (GM)
Chevrolet

GROWTH PLANS/SPECIAL FEATURES:
GM Korea designs, develops, produces and sells vehicles in South Korea. The company has been 96%-owned by General Motors Company since 2002. GM Korea manufactures passenger vehicles, sports cars and light commercial vehicles primarily under the Chevrolet brand. The firm's luxury division also offers Cadillac vehicles. The company offers vehicle kits for assembly at GM facilities in China, Uzbekistan, Mexico, India, Columbia, Russia and other countries. GM Korea exports its products to automakers internationally. Its production facilities are located in Bupyeong, Gunsan, Changwon and Boryeong. In early-2018, GM Korea announced plans to cease production and close its Gunsan plant by the end of May of the same year.

CONTACTS:
Note: Officers with more than one job title may be intentionally listed here more than once.

Kaher Kazem, CEO
Sergio Rocha, Pres.

FINANCIAL DATA:
Note: Data for latest year may not have been available at press time.

In U.S. $	2017	2016	2015	2014	2013	2012
Revenue	12,500,000,000	12,000,000,000	13,500,000,000	13,115,000,000	15,138,191,000	15,400,000,000
R&D Expense						
Operating Income						
Operating Margin %						
SGA Expense						
Net Income		-43,000,000	-92,000,000	-180,000,000	327,000,000	330,000,000
Operating Cash Flow						
Capital Expenditure						
EBITDA						
Return on Assets %						
Return on Equity %						
Debt to Equity						

CONTACT INFORMATION:
Phone: 8280-3000-5000
Fax: 833-2520-4613
Toll-Free:
Address: 233 Chongcheon-dong, Bupyeong-gu, Incheon, 403-714 South Korea

STOCK TICKER/OTHER:
Stock Ticker: Subsidiary
Employees: 17,258
Parent Company: General Motors Company (GM)
Exchange:
Fiscal Year Ends: 12/31

SALARIES/BONUSES:
Top Exec. Salary: $
Bonus: $
Second Exec. Salary: $
Bonus: $

OTHER THOUGHTS:
Estimated Female Officers or Directors:
Hot Spot for Advancement for Women/Minorities:

Golder Associates Corporation

www.golder.com

NAIC Code: 541330

TYPES OF BUSINESS:
Engineering & Environmental Services

BRANDS/DIVISIONS/AFFILIATES:
Alan Auld Group Ltd

CONTACTS:
Note: Officers with more than one job title may be intentionally listed here more than once.

Hisham Mahmoud, CEO
Tom Logan, COO
Lee Anne Lackey, CFO
Caroline Tavares, Global Dir.-Human Resources

GROWTH PLANS/SPECIAL FEATURES:

Golder Associates Corporation is an employee-owned consulting, design and construction services firm for the manufacturing, mining, oil and gas, power, urban development and infrastructure industries. Its services include detailed design and construction, engineering, environment and social assessment, environmental management and compliance, natural resources planning and evaluation, strategic planning/advice and management and water. Detailed design and construction solutions include shallow and deep soil mixing, blast densification, rapid impact compaction/dynamic compaction, mine dewatering, slurry/tailings/backfill management, pumping, grouting and shoring/slope stabilization retaining walls. Engineering services include ground engineering, construction materials engineering, testing and instrumentation, tunneling, pipeline systems, dams and hydropower and waste management. Environmental and social assessment services include impact assessment, cultural heritage, social management and compliance and ecological services. Environmental management and compliance services include atmospheric services, environment, health and safety, industrial hygiene, human health and toxicology, energy, carbon, climate, permitting, sustainability, containment site investigation and clean up. Natural resources planning and evaluation includes geochemical services, mine planning and engineering, mine waste management and backfill systems. Strategic planning/advice and management services include information and graphics, project management, mergers and acquisitions, divestures, due diligence, risk assessment, analysis, landscape architecture, urban design and facility siting. Water services include water and wastewater treatment, coastal and marine solutions, groundwater solutions, surface water and hydrology. Golder Associates has more than 165 offices in Africa, Asia, Australia, Europe, North America and South America. In November 2017, the firm acquired the U.K.-based Alan Auld Group Ltd., a global provider of specialized engineering design and construction services for underground structures.

FINANCIAL DATA:
Note: Data for latest year may not have been available at press time.

In U.S. $	2017	2016	2015	2014	2013	2012
Revenue	1,000,000,000					
R&D Expense						
Operating Income						
Operating Margin %						
SGA Expense						
Net Income						
Operating Cash Flow						
Capital Expenditure						
EBITDA						
Return on Assets %						
Return on Equity %						
Debt to Equity						

CONTACT INFORMATION:
Phone: 905-567-4444 Fax: 905-567-6561
Toll-Free:
Address: 6925 Century Ave., Ste. 100, Mississauga, ON L5N 7K2 Canada

STOCK TICKER/OTHER:
Stock Ticker: Private
Employees: 6,500
Parent Company:
Exchange:
Fiscal Year Ends:

SALARIES/BONUSES:
Top Exec. Salary: $ Bonus: $
Second Exec. Salary: $ Bonus: $

OTHER THOUGHTS:
Estimated Female Officers or Directors:
Hot Spot for Advancement for Women/Minorities:

Sales, profits and employees may be estimates. Financial information, benefits and other data can change quickly and may vary from those stated here.

Granite Construction Incorporated

www.graniteconstruction.com

NAIC Code: 237310

TYPES OF BUSINESS:
Construction, Heavy & Civil Engineering
Infrastructure Projects
Site Preparation Services
Construction Materials Processing
Heavy Construction Equipment

BRANDS/DIVISIONS/AFFILIATES:
Granite Construction Company
Granite Construction Northeast Inc
Granite Infrastructure Constructors Inc
Kenny Construction Company
LiquiForce

CONTACTS:
Note: Officers with more than one job title may be intentionally listed here more than once.

James Roberts, CEO
Laurel Krzeminski, CFO
William Powell, Chairman of the Board
Richard Watts, General Counsel
Kyle Larkin, Other Corporate Officer
James Richards, Other Corporate Officer
Dale Swanberg, Other Corporate Officer

GROWTH PLANS/SPECIAL FEATURES:

Granite Construction Incorporated is one of the largest diversified heavy civil contractors and construction materials producers in the U.S. The firm operates nationwide, serving both public and private sector clients. As of December 2017, Granite had 46 active and 15 inactive permitted quarry properties available for the extraction of sand, gravel and hard rock, all of which are located in the western U.S. In addition, the company owns nearly 2,000 heavy construction equipment, and more than 3,600 trucks, truck-trailers, trailers and vehicles. Granite Construction operates in three segments: construction, large project construction and construction materials. The construction segment performs construction management, as well as various civil construction projects with a large portion of the work focused on new construction and improvement of streets, roads, highways, bridges, site work, underground, power-related facilities, water-related facilities, utilities and other infrastructure projects. The large project construction segment focuses on large, complex infrastructure projects which typically have a longer duration than the firm's construction segment work. Large projects include major highways, mass transit facilities, bridges, tunnels, waterway locks and dams, pipelines, canals, power-related facilities, water-related facilities, utilities and airport infrastructure. The construction materials segment mines and processes aggregates and operates plants that produce construction materials, primarily asphalt, for internal use and for sale to third parties. Wholly-owned subsidiaries of the firm include: Granite Construction Company; Granite Construction Northeast, Inc.; Granite Infrastructure Constructors, Inc.; and Kenny Construction Company. In early-2018, the firm agreed to acquire Layne Christensen Company, a global water management, infrastructure services and drilling company; and acquired LiquiForce, which serves water and wastewater customers in Canada and the U.S. with a variety of underground contracting services.

The company offers employees life, AD&D, medical, dental and vision coverage; 401(k) and stock purchase plans; flexible spending accounts; education reimbursement; and domestic partner benefits.

FINANCIAL DATA:
Note: Data for latest year may not have been available at press time.

In U.S. $	2017	2016	2015	2014	2013	2012
Revenue	2,989,713,000	2,514,617,000	2,371,029,000	2,275,270,000	2,266,901,000	2,083,037,000
R&D Expense						
Operating Income	92,122,000	82,071,000	96,019,000	46,485,000	-14,683,000	49,660,000
Operating Margin %	3.08%	3.26%	4.04%	2.04%	-.64%	2.38%
SGA Expense	222,811,000	219,299,000	207,339,000	203,821,000	199,946,000	185,099,000
Net Income	69,098,000	57,122,000	60,485,000	25,346,000	-36,423,000	45,283,000
Operating Cash Flow	146,195,000	73,146,000	66,978,000	43,142,000	5,380,000	91,790,000
Capital Expenditure	67,695,000	90,970,000	44,179,000	43,428,000	43,682,000	37,622,000
EBITDA	181,608,000	173,103,000	181,993,000	138,008,000	23,256,000	147,733,000
Return on Assets %	3.83%	3.39%	3.72%	1.56%	-2.17%	2.76%
Return on Equity %	7.54%	6.62%	7.40%	3.21%	-4.51%	5.55%
Debt to Equity	0.18	0.25	0.29	0.34	0.35	0.32

CONTACT INFORMATION:
Phone: 831 724-1011   Fax: 831 7617871
Toll-Free:
Address: 585 W. Beach St., Watsonville, CA 95076 United States

STOCK TICKER/OTHER:
Stock Ticker: GVA
Employees: 3,400
Parent Company:

Exchange: NYS
Fiscal Year Ends: 12/31

SALARIES/BONUSES:
Top Exec. Salary: $800,000   Bonus: $
Second Exec. Salary: $475,000   Bonus: $

OTHER THOUGHTS:
Estimated Female Officers or Directors: 2
Hot Spot for Advancement for Women/Minorities:

Sales, profits and employees may be estimates. Financial information, benefits and other data can change quickly and may vary from those stated here.

GS Engineering & Construction Corporation

www.gsconst.co.kr

NAIC Code: 237000

TYPES OF BUSINESS:
Heavy Construction and Civil Engineering

BRANDS/DIVISIONS/AFFILIATES:

CONTACTS:
Note: Officers with more than one job title may be intentionally listed here more than once.

Byeong-Yong Lim, CEO
Myung-Soo Huh, Pres.

GROWTH PLANS/SPECIAL FEATURES:

GS Engineering & Construction Corporation (GS E&C) comprises five main construction divisions: plant, power, architecture, infrastructure and leisure. The plant business constructs refinery, gas, petrochemical, waste and water treatment plants. This division seeks to enter the liquid natural gas (LNG) and unconventional oil and gas business. The power business engages in developing a country's power, communication and railway infrastructure. This division has completed projects for high-voltage substations in South Korea, Asia, Saudi Arabia, Ghana and Tanzania. The architecture business markets and builds various types of buildings for residencies, offices and factories, including public and private sectors. This division also specializes in environmentally-friendly and energy-saving buildings. The infrastructure business constructs roads, railways, water reservoirs, ports, industrial parks and underground structures. This division has also been working on new construction methods which are being applied for projects such as marine suspension bridges and deep underground tunnels. Last, the leisure business provides cultural space, services and facilities, including recreational facilities, stadiums, arenas, high-class hotels, sports facilities and arts centers. GS E&C also comprises a technology division for research and development purposes; a finance division; a procurement and sub-contract management division; and various company and administrative departments. In March 2018, GS E&C formed a 50/50 joint venture with Vansata Group to construct a residential complex for 1,445 households in western Jakarta, Indonesia.

FINANCIAL DATA:
Note: Data for latest year may not have been available at press time.

In U.S. $	2017	2016	2015	2014	2013	2012
Revenue	10,936,700,000	9,856,920,000	9,443,380,000	7,736,233,642	9,284,889,000	8,095,900,000
R&D Expense						
Operating Income						
Operating Margin %						
SGA Expense						
Net Income	-159,228,000	-23,026,900	23,279,100	-73,994,092	-857,566,503	113,100,000
Operating Cash Flow						
Capital Expenditure						
EBITDA						
Return on Assets %						
Return on Equity %						
Debt to Equity						

CONTACT INFORMATION:
Phone: 82-2-2154 1112 Fax:
Toll-Free:
Address: Gran Seoul, 33 Jongro, Jongno-gu, Seoul, 110-130 South Korea

STOCK TICKER/OTHER:
Stock Ticker: 6360   Exchange: Seoul
Employees: 770   Fiscal Year Ends: 12/31
Parent Company:

SALARIES/BONUSES:
Top Exec. Salary: $ Bonus: $
Second Exec. Salary: $ Bonus: $

OTHER THOUGHTS:
Estimated Female Officers or Directors:
Hot Spot for Advancement for Women/Minorities:

Sales, profits and employees may be estimates. Financial information, benefits and other data can change quickly and may vary from those stated here.

Gulf Interstate Engineering Company

NAIC Code: 541330

www.gie.com

TYPES OF BUSINESS:
Engineering Consulting Services

BRANDS/DIVISIONS/AFFILIATES:
Gulf Interstate Field Services
Post Oak Graphics

CONTACTS:
Note: Officers with more than one job title may be intentionally listed here more than once.

Rick Barnard, CEO
Bob Sprick, Sr. VP-Field Srvcs.
H.D. (Doug) Evans, Chmn.

GROWTH PLANS/SPECIAL FEATURES:
Gulf Interstate Engineering Company provides project management, engineering, design, procurement and material and construction management services for oil and gas production, transportation and storage systems. The firm specializes in the project management and engineering of pipeline systems, a focus that covers onshore pipelines, gathering systems, production facilities, pump and compressor stations, storage terminals and loading facilities. Gulf Interstate's services consist of: feasibility and economic studies, including system optimization, capital and operating cost estimates, tariff and cost of service analysis, financial studies, risk and sensitive analysis and facility appraisals; project management, include execution plan and procedures, budget development and cost control, planning and scheduling, contract administration, quality assurance and project execution; right-of-way and land acquisition support, including regulatory and ownership research, permit applications and acquisitions, route selection and aerial photography; engineering, including preliminary engineering, hydraulics and surge analysis, civil/structural design and pipeline risk assessment; geographic information system (GIS), including desktop routing and analysis, progress tracking, geo-processing and construction management; pipeline integrity, including records and data management, data conversion and global positioning system (GPS) acquisition; materials management, including procurement, vendor documentation, logistics, site procurement and site materials management; construction management, including planning and scheduling, contractor pre-qualification, bid solicitation, quality assurance/control and certification and commissioning; and operations and maintenance, including startup assistance, training, operations/maintenance manuals, support and contract maintenance. In addition, affiliate Gulf Interstate Field Services provides construction management and construction inspection services; and affiliate Post Oak Graphics provides complete in-house reprographics and promotion services.

FINANCIAL DATA: Note: Data for latest year may not have been available at press time.

In U.S. $	2017	2016	2015	2014	2013	2012
Revenue						
R&D Expense						
Operating Income						
Operating Margin %						
SGA Expense						
Net Income						
Operating Cash Flow						
Capital Expenditure						
EBITDA						
Return on Assets %						
Return on Equity %						
Debt to Equity						

CONTACT INFORMATION:
Phone: 713-850-3400   Fax: 713-850-3579
Toll-Free:
Address: 16010 Barkers Point Lane, Ste. 600, Houston, TX 77076-9000 United States

STOCK TICKER/OTHER:
Stock Ticker: Private   Exchange:
Employees: Fiscal Year Ends:
Parent Company:

SALARIES/BONUSES:
Top Exec. Salary: $ Bonus: $
Second Exec. Salary: $ Bonus: $

OTHER THOUGHTS:
Estimated Female Officers or Directors:
Hot Spot for Advancement for Women/Minorities:

Sales, profits and employees may be estimates. Financial information, benefits and other data can change quickly and may vary from those stated here.

Gulfstream Aerospace Corporation

www.gulfstream.com

NAIC Code: 336411

TYPES OF BUSINESS:
Aircraft Manufacturing
Business Jets
Support Services
Leasing & Financing

BRANDS/DIVISIONS/AFFILIATES:
General Dynamics Corporation
G280
G500
G550
G600
G650
G650ER

CONTACTS:
Note: Officers with more than one job title may be intentionally listed here more than once.

Mark Burns, Pres.
Daniel G. Clare, CFO
Dan Nale, Sr. VP-Programs, Eng. & Test
Ira Berman, Sr. VP-Admin.
Ira Berman, General Counsel
Dennis Stuligross, Sr. VP-Oper.
Joe Lombardo, Exec. VP-Aerospace Group, General Dynamics
Mark Burns, Pres., Product Support
Scott Neal, Sr. VP-Worldwide Sales & Mktg.
Buddy Sams, Sr. VP-Gov't Programs & Sales

GROWTH PLANS/SPECIAL FEATURES:

Gulfstream Aerospace Corporation, a subsidiary of General Dynamics Corporation, designs, develops, manufactures, markets and provides maintenance and support services for technologically-advanced business jet aircraft. Established in 1958, Gulfstream operates facilities on four continents and employs more than 15,000 people worldwide. The company is also a leading provider of land and expeditionary combat systems, armaments and munitions; shipbuilding and marine systems; and information systems and technologies. Gulfstream's current (as of March 2018) aircraft includes six product lines: the mid-size G280; the ultra-long-range G500, G550, G600 and G650; and the extended reach G650ER, extending the nonstop reach of the industry's highest performance long-range business aircraft to 7,500 nautical miles at Mach 0.85. The maximum operating speed for G650ER is 0.925. Gulfstream also routinely accepts aircraft trade-ins for the sale of new Gulfstream models and resells the used planes on the pre-owned market. The group offers several product enhancements for its planes, including the ultra-high-speed broadband multi-link (BBML) system, which allows customers to access the internet at altitudes up to 51,000 feet; and the enhanced vision system (EVS), a forward-looking infrared (FLIR) camera that projects an infrared real-world image on the pilot's heads-up display, which allows the flight crew to see in conditions of low light and reduced visibility.

Employees of the firm receive tuition reimbursement; relocation assistance; a performance-based incentive plan; a wellness program; flexible spending accounts; and medical, dental, vision, disability and life insurance.

FINANCIAL DATA:
Note: Data for latest year may not have been available at press time.

In U.S. $	2017	2016	2015	2014	2013	2012
Revenue	8,550,000,000	8,500,000,000	8,851,000,000	8,649,000,000	8,118,000,000	6,912,000,000
R&D Expense						
Operating Income						
Operating Margin %						
SGA Expense						
Net Income	1,600,000,000	1,500,000,000	1,706,000,000	1,611,000,000	1,416,000,000	858,000,000
Operating Cash Flow						
Capital Expenditure						
EBITDA						
Return on Assets %						
Return on Equity %						
Debt to Equity						

CONTACT INFORMATION:
Phone: 912-965-3000   Fax: 912-965-3084
Toll-Free:
Address: 500 Gulfstream Rd., Savannah, GA 31407 United States

STOCK TICKER/OTHER:
Stock Ticker: Subsidiary   Exchange:
Employees: 15,000   Fiscal Year Ends: 12/31
Parent Company: General Dynamics Corporation

SALARIES/BONUSES:
Top Exec. Salary: $ Bonus: $
Second Exec. Salary: $ Bonus: $

OTHER THOUGHTS:
Estimated Female Officers or Directors:
Hot Spot for Advancement for Women/Minorities:

Sales, profits and employees may be estimates. Financial information, benefits and other data can change quickly and may vary from those stated here.

Halliburton Company

NAIC Code: 213112

www.halliburton.com

TYPES OF BUSINESS:
Oil Field Services
Software Information Systems
Project Management Consulting

BRANDS/DIVISIONS/AFFILIATES:
Baroid
Sperry
Landmark
Multi-Chem
Artificial Lift
Summit ESP

CONTACTS:
Note: Officers with more than one job title may be intentionally listed here more than once.

Christopher Weber, CFO
David Lesar, Chairman of the Board
Jeffrey Miller, Director
Eric Carre, Executive VP, Divisional
Lawrence Pope, Executive VP, Divisional
Robb Voyles, Executive VP
Joe Rainey, President, Geographical
James Brown, President, Geographical
Myrtle Jones, Senior VP, Divisional
Anne Beaty, Senior VP, Divisional
Charles Geer, Vice President
Timothy McKeon, Vice President

GROWTH PLANS/SPECIAL FEATURES:

Halliburton Company provides products and services to the upstream oil and natural gas industry. The firm serves major national and independent oil and natural gas companies around the world, operating in approximately 70 countries. Halliburton operates through two business segments: drilling and evaluation, and completion and production. The drilling and evaluation segment provides field and reservoir modeling, drilling, evaluation and precise well-bore placement systems that enable customers to model, measure and optimize their well construction activities. This segment consists of Baroid-branded drilling fluid systems, Sperry-branded drilling systems, wireline and perforating services, drill bits and services, Landmark-branded software and services, testing and subsea services, as well as consulting and project management. The completion and production segment delivers cementing, stimulation, intervention, pressure control, specialty chemicals, artificial lift and completion services. This segment consists of brands, services and solutions such as production enhancement, cementing, completion tools, pipeline and process services, production solutions, the Multi-Chem brand of oilfield production and completion chemicals, and the Artificial Lift brand of electrical submersible pumps. Completion tools and services include subsurface safety valves and flow control equipment, surface safety systems, packers and specialty completion equipment, intelligent completion systems, expandable liner hanger systems, sand control systems, well servicing tools and reservoir performance services. Production covers stimulation services, pipeline process services, sand control services and well intervention services. In July 2017, the firm acquired Summit ESP, a provider of electric submersible pump technology and services.

Employee benefits include retirement and savings plans; an employee stock purchase program; life, disability and AD&D insurance; comprehensive health benefits; and a wellness program.

FINANCIAL DATA:
Note: Data for latest year may not have been available at press time.

In U.S. $	2017	2016	2015	2014	2013	2012
Revenue	20,620,000,000	15,887,000,000	23,633,000,000	32,870,000,000	29,402,000,000	28,503,000,000
R&D Expense						
Operating Income	2,009,000,000	636,000,000	2,320,000,000	4,902,000,000	4,138,000,000	4,159,000,000
Operating Margin %	9.74%	4.00%	9.81%	14.91%	14.07%	14.59%
SGA Expense	256,000,000	228,000,000	200,000,000	309,000,000	333,000,000	275,000,000
Net Income	-463,000,000	-5,763,000,000	-671,000,000	3,500,000,000	2,125,000,000	2,635,000,000
Operating Cash Flow	2,468,000,000	-1,703,000,000	2,906,000,000	4,062,000,000	4,447,000,000	3,654,000,000
Capital Expenditure	1,373,000,000	798,000,000	2,184,000,000	3,283,000,000	2,934,000,000	3,566,000,000
EBITDA	2,943,000,000	-5,424,000,000	4,155,000,000	7,028,000,000	6,038,000,000	5,755,000,000
Return on Assets %	-1.77%	-18.02%	-1.93%	11.38%	7.50%	10.31%
Return on Equity %	-5.22%	-46.34%	-4.22%	23.45%	14.48%	18.19%
Debt to Equity	1.25	1.29	0.94	0.48	0.57	0.30

CONTACT INFORMATION:
Phone: 281 871-2699   Fax: 713 759-2635
Toll-Free: 888-669-3920
Address: 3000 N. Sam Houston Pkwy. E., Houston, TX 77032 United States

STOCK TICKER/OTHER:
Stock Ticker: HAL
Employees: 50,000
Parent Company:

Exchange: NYS
Fiscal Year Ends: 12/31

SALARIES/BONUSES:
Top Exec. Salary: $1,312,500   Bonus: $
Second Exec. Salary: $1,175,000   Bonus: $

OTHER THOUGHTS:
Estimated Female Officers or Directors:
Hot Spot for Advancement for Women/Minorities: Y

Sales, profits and employees may be estimates. Financial information, benefits and other data can change quickly and may vary from those stated here.

Harris Corporation

www.harris.com

NAIC Code: 334220

TYPES OF BUSINESS:
Communications Equipment Manufacturing
Wireless Communications Equipment
Healthcare IT Systems
Managed Satellite Communications
Integrated IT Systems

BRANDS/DIVISIONS/AFFILIATES:

CONTACTS: Note: Officers with more than one job title may be intentionally listed here more than once.
William Brown, CEO
Rahul Ghai, CFO
Todd Taylor, Chief Accounting Officer
Scott Mikuen, General Counsel
Dana Mehnert, Other Executive Officer
Christopher Young, President, Divisional
Edward Zoiss, President, Divisional
William Gattle, President, Divisional
Robert Duffy, Senior VP, Divisional
Sheldon Fox, Senior VP, Divisional

GROWTH PLANS/SPECIAL FEATURES:

Harris Corporation is leading technology innovator, solving customers' mission-critical challenges. The company provides solutions that connect, inform and protect, serving government and commercial clients in more than 100 countries. Harris' largest customers comprise various departments and agencies of the U.S. Government and their prime contractors. Harris structures its operations primarily around the products, systems and services it sells, as well as the markets it serves, which are categorized into three divisions: communication systems, space and intelligence systems and electronic systems. The communication systems division serves tactical communication, defense and public safety network markets with products that include tactical ground and airborne radio communications solutions, as well as night vision technology. The space and intelligence systems division provides intelligence, space protection, geospatial, complete Earth observation, universe exploration, positioning/navigation/timing (PNT), and environmental solutions for national security, defense, civil and commercial customers. This division offers advanced sensors, antennas and payloads, as well as ground processing and information analytics. The electronic systems division provides electronic warfare, avionics and command/control/communications/computers/intelligence/surveillance/reconnaissance (C4ISR) solutions for the defense industry; and air traffic management solutions for the civil aviation industry. During 2017, the company sold its government IT services division to Veritas Capital Management, LLC; and sold its Harris CapRock Communications commercial business.

The firm offers employees benefits including medical, dental and vision insurance; a 401(k); paid time off; tuition reimbursement; and health and dependent care spending accounts.

FINANCIAL DATA: Note: Data for latest year may not have been available at press time.

In U.S. $	2017	2016	2015	2014	2013	2012
Revenue	5,900,000,000	7,467,000,000	5,083,000,000	5,012,000,000	5,111,700,000	5,451,300,000
R&D Expense						
Operating Income	1,073,000,000	1,149,000,000	713,000,000	881,900,000	812,200,000	941,100,000
Operating Margin %	18.18%	15.38%	14.02%	17.59%	15.88%	17.26%
SGA Expense	1,016,000,000	1,186,000,000	1,008,000,000	819,600,000	914,500,000	940,900,000
Net Income	553,000,000	324,000,000	334,000,000	534,800,000	113,000,000	30,600,000
Operating Cash Flow	569,000,000	924,000,000	854,000,000	849,200,000	833,000,000	852,900,000
Capital Expenditure	119,000,000	152,000,000	148,000,000	212,600,000	178,200,000	233,800,000
EBITDA	1,388,000,000	1,155,000,000	851,000,000	1,093,300,000	994,300,000	1,215,400,000
Return on Assets %	5.00%	2.57%	3.69%	10.92%	2.16%	.52%
Return on Equity %	18.48%	10.04%	12.78%	31.57%	6.45%	1.37%
Debt to Equity	1.15	1.34	1.48	0.86	1.01	0.97

CONTACT INFORMATION:
Phone: 321 727-9100 Fax: 321 724-3973
Toll-Free: 800-442-7747
Address: 1025 W. NASA Blvd., Melbourne, FL 32919 United States

STOCK TICKER/OTHER:
Stock Ticker: HRS
Employees: 17,000
Parent Company:

Exchange: NYS
Fiscal Year Ends: 06/30

SALARIES/BONUSES:
Top Exec. Salary: $1,237,499 Bonus: $
Second Exec. Salary: $536,250 Bonus: $

OTHER THOUGHTS:
Estimated Female Officers or Directors: 2
Hot Spot for Advancement for Women/Minorities: Y

Harsco Corporation

www.harsco.com

NAIC Code: 541330

TYPES OF BUSINESS:
Engineering Services
Industrial Products Manufacturing
Railroad Equipment Maintenance
Rail Track Construction
Construction Equipment Rental
Outsourced Steel Mill Services

BRANDS/DIVISIONS/AFFILIATES:
Harsco Industrial IKG
Harsco Industrial Air-X-Changers
Harsco Industrial Patterson-Kelley

CONTACTS: Note: Officers with more than one job title may be intentionally listed here more than once.
F. Grasberger, CEO
Peter Minan, CFO
David Everitt, Chairman of the Board
Sam Fenice, Chief Accounting Officer
Russell Hochman, General Counsel
Tracey McKenzie, Other Executive Officer
Jeswant Gill, President, Subsidiary
Scott Gerson, President, Subsidiary

GROWTH PLANS/SPECIAL FEATURES:
Harsco Corporation is a multinational provider of industrial services and engineered products. The company's operations fall into three reportable segments: Harsco Metals & Minerals, Harsco Rail and Harsco Industrial. The Harsco Metals & Minerals segment accounting for 63% of consolidated revenues for 2017, provides onsite, outsourced services to the global metals industries in more than 30 countries, with its largest operations focused in the U.K., the U.S., France, China and Brazil. The division provides its services on a long-term contract basis, supporting each stage of the metal-making process, which includes extracting high-value metallic content from stainless steel by-products. It also specializes in the development of minerals technologies for commercial applications. The Harsco Rail segment (18%) is a global provider of equipment and services to maintain, repair and construct railway track. The company's railway track maintenance services, solutions and specialized track maintenance equipment support private and government-owned railroads and urban transit systems worldwide. The Harsco Industrial segment (19%) consists of Harsco Industrial IKG, Harsco Industrial Air-X-Changers and Harsco Industrial Patterson-Kelley. Harsco Industrial IKG manufactures a varied line of industrial grating products and high-security fences at plants in the U.S. and Mexico. These products include a full range of bar grating configurations, which are used mainly in industrial flooring, as well as safety and security applications in the power, paper, chemical, refining and processing industries. Harsco Industrial Air-X-Changers manufactures air-cooled heat exchangers for the natural gas industry. Harsco Industrial Patterson-Kelley is a leading manufacturer of energy-efficient heat transfer products such as boilers and water heaters for commercial and institutional applications.

FINANCIAL DATA: Note: Data for latest year may not have been available at press time.

In U.S. $	2017	2016	2015	2014	2013	2012
Revenue	1,607,062,000	1,451,223,000	1,723,092,000	2,065,738,000	2,896,520,000	
R&D Expense	4,227,000	4,280,000	4,510,000	6,348,000	9,570,000	
Operating Income	140,090,000	65,312,000	105,195,000	127,352,000	167,755,000	
Operating Margin %	8.71%	4.50%	6.10%	6.16%	5.79%	
SGA Expense	242,023,000	211,168,000	257,026,000	285,252,000	484,980,000	
Net Income	7,822,000	-85,667,000	6,188,000	-24,792,000	-227,941,000	
Operating Cash Flow	176,892,000	159,785,000	121,507,000	225,846,000	188,255,000	
Capital Expenditure	98,314,000	69,340,000	123,552,000	207,978,000	246,147,000	
EBITDA	272,940,000	113,599,000	238,094,000	231,759,000	103,363,000	
Return on Assets %	.49%	-4.69%	.28%	-1.05%	-8.41%	
Return on Equity %	5.86%	-46.57%	2.11%	-5.64%	-33.14%	
Debt to Equity	3.32	6.53	3.15	2.64	1.38	

CONTACT INFORMATION:
Phone: 717-763-7064 Fax: 717-763-6424
Toll-Free:
Address: 350 Poplar Church Rd., Camp Hill, PA 17011 United States

STOCK TICKER/OTHER:
Stock Ticker: HSC Exchange: NYS
Employees: 9,400 Fiscal Year Ends: 12/31
Parent Company:

SALARIES/BONUSES:
Top Exec. Salary: $841,183 Bonus: $
Second Exec. Salary: $499,612 Bonus: $

OTHER THOUGHTS:
Estimated Female Officers or Directors: 3
Hot Spot for Advancement for Women/Minorities: Y

Sales, profits and employees may be estimates. Financial information, benefits and other data can change quickly and may vary from those stated here.

Hatch Group

www.hatch.ca

NAIC Code: 541330

TYPES OF BUSINESS:
Engineering Services

BRANDS/DIVISIONS/AFFILIATES:
g3baxi partnership

CONTACTS:
Note: Officers with more than one job title may be intentionally listed here more than once.

John Bianchini, CEO
Kurt Strobele, Chmn.

GROWTH PLANS/SPECIAL FEATURES:

Hatch Group supplies engineering, project and construction management services, process and business consulting and operational services to the mining, metallurgical, energy and infrastructure industries. It has project experience in more than 150 countries. The mining and metals division provides services to the mining, mineral and metals industries, including coal, industrial minerals, iron, steel, iron ore, light metals, mining and mineral processing and non-ferrous metals. The energy division provides services in hydro, wind, solar, thermal and nuclear power, and also provides transmission and distribution services. The energy subdivision, oil and gas, is experienced in producing regions such as Canada, Australia and the Middle East, with a portfolio that spans both the upstream and downstream sectors. Its key focal points are in conventional gas and sulfur, bitumen extraction and processing, carbon sequestration, shale-to-liquids technologies and liquefied natural gas (LNG) developments. This subdivision provides everything from construction to plant expansions and retrofit projects as well as in-house management, process design, engineering, procurement and construction activities. The infrastructure division undertakes major projects and assignments from concept and feasibility through detailed engineering, procurement and construction-management contracts and operational and maintenance management. It is currently engaged in rapid-transit systems, bulk commodity ports/terminals/tunneling, solid waste and potable water projects as well as desalination plants and bulk-material handling facilities. In May 2017, Hatch acquired g3baxi partnership, an employee-owned oil and gas engineering company founded in the U.K.

FINANCIAL DATA:
Note: Data for latest year may not have been available at press time.

In U.S. $	2017	2016	2015	2014	2013	2012
Revenue						
R&D Expense						
Operating Income						
Operating Margin %						
SGA Expense						
Net Income						
Operating Cash Flow						
Capital Expenditure						
EBITDA						
Return on Assets %						
Return on Equity %						
Debt to Equity						

CONTACT INFORMATION:
Phone: 905-855-7600 Fax: 905-855-8270
Toll-Free:
Address: 2800 Speakman Dr., Sheridan Science & Technology Park, Mississauga, ON L5K 2R7 Canada

STOCK TICKER/OTHER:
Stock Ticker: Private
Employees: 9,000
Parent Company:

Exchange:
Fiscal Year Ends:

SALARIES/BONUSES:
Top Exec. Salary: $ Bonus: $
Second Exec. Salary: $ Bonus: $

OTHER THOUGHTS:
Estimated Female Officers or Directors:
Hot Spot for Advancement for Women/Minorities:

Sales, profits and employees may be estimates. Financial information, benefits and other data can change quickly and may vary from those stated here.

HDR Inc

NAIC Code: 541330

www.hdrinc.com

TYPES OF BUSINESS:
Engineering Services
Architectural Services
Consulting Services

BRANDS/DIVISIONS/AFFILIATES:
HDR/Archer

CONTACTS: Note: Officers with more than one job title may be intentionally listed here more than once.
Eric L. Keen, CEO
Charles L. O'Reilly, Pres.
Eric L. Keen, Vice Chmn.
Doug S. Wignall, Pres., HDR Architecture
Eric L. Keen, Chmn.

GROWTH PLANS/SPECIAL FEATURES:

HDR, Inc. is an architectural, engineering and consulting firm that specializes in managing complex projects and solving engineering and architectural challenges for its clients. The employee-owned firm has 215 locations globally, including operations in all 50 U.S. states and seven countries worldwide. The company offers design-build services and program management for a variety of markets, including community architecture, hospitals and other healthcare projects, science and technology construction, transportation, power, justice and wastewater and water resources. HDR operates in 14 markets, including community, defense & intelligence, development, education, health, industrial, justice, power & energy, science, technology, transportation, waste, water and workplace. The firm's economic and finance services include economic evaluation, forecasting, funding and financial analysis, regulatory and policy analysis, risk management and statistics and data analytics. This division comprises more than 50 economists and financial experts in offices throughout the U.S. and Canada. Repeat clients account for roughly 80% of the company's business. Subsidiary HDR/Archer provides engineering consulting services to public and private sectors, including planning, design and construction management services.

The company offers employees medical, dental and vision coverage; tuition assistance; a 401(k) plan; a flexible spending account; life insurance; and short- & long-term disability.

FINANCIAL DATA: Note: Data for latest year may not have been available at press time.

In U.S. $	2017	2016	2015	2014	2013	2012
Revenue	1,930,000,000	1,927,600,000	1,911,500,000	1,804,700,000	1,762,100,000	
R&D Expense						
Operating Income						
Operating Margin %						
SGA Expense						
Net Income						
Operating Cash Flow						
Capital Expenditure						
EBITDA						
Return on Assets %						
Return on Equity %						
Debt to Equity						

CONTACT INFORMATION:
Phone: 402-399-1000   Fax: 402-548-5015
Toll-Free: 800-366-4411
Address: 8404 Indian Hills Dr., Omaha, NE 68114-4098 United States

STOCK TICKER/OTHER:
Stock Ticker: Private   Exchange:
Employees: 10,000   Fiscal Year Ends: 12/31
Parent Company:

SALARIES/BONUSES:
Top Exec. Salary: $ Bonus: $
Second Exec. Salary: $ Bonus: $

OTHER THOUGHTS:
Estimated Female Officers or Directors: 1
Hot Spot for Advancement for Women/Minorities:

Sales, profits and employees may be estimates. Financial information, benefits and other data can change quickly and may vary from those stated here.

Hewlett Packard Enterprise Company

www.hpe.com

NAIC Code: 334111

TYPES OF BUSINESS:
Electronic Computer Manufacturing

BRANDS/DIVISIONS/AFFILIATES:
Hewlet Packard Labs
Seattle SpinCo Inc

CONTACTS:
Note: Officers with more than one job title may be intentionally listed here more than once.

Antonio Neri, CEO
Patricia Russo, Chairman of the Board
John Schultz, Chief Administrative Officer
Henry Gomez, Chief Marketing Officer
Alan May, Executive VP, Divisional
Timothy Stonesifer, Executive VP
Kirt Karros, Senior VP, Divisional
Jeff Ricci, Senior VP

GROWTH PLANS/SPECIAL FEATURES:

Hewlett Packard Enterprise Company (HPE) develops and delivers technology innovation that fosters business transformation. The firm organizes its business into three segments: enterprise group, financial services and corporate investments. The enterprise group business segment provides secure, software-defined technology and services that enable customers to move data seamlessly across their hybrid information technology (IT) environments. It powers the intelligent edge that runs campus, branch and Internet of Things (IoT) applications. This division's products include industry standard servers, mission-critical servers, storage platforms, switches, routers, wireless local area network (WLAN), network virtualization, security, location-based services and technology services that power a digital business. The financial services business segment enables flexible IT consumption models, financial architectures and customized investment solutions for its customers. These solutions include leasing, financing, IT consumption and utility programs. The corporate investments segment includes Hewlett Packard Labs (HP Labs), which enables fast, fluid transfer of advanced technologies into next-generation products and solutions; and certain cloud-related business incubation projects. HPE has major product development, manufacturing and HP Labs facilities worldwide, including the Americas, Asia Pacific, Europe, the Middle East and Africa. In April 2017, the firm was spun-off from HP, Inc. to Micro Focus International plc, and its software division was separated from HPE and given to its Seattle SpinCo, Inc. subsidiary.

FINANCIAL DATA:
Note: Data for latest year may not have been available at press time.

In U.S. $	2017	2016	2015	2014	2013	2012
Revenue	28,475,000,000	49,759,000,000	51,746,000,000	54,722,000,000	56,924,000,000	60,580,000,000
R&D Expense	1,486,000,000	2,298,000,000	2,338,000,000	2,197,000,000	1,956,000,000	2,120,000,000
Operating Income	1,754,000,000	3,378,000,000	3,138,000,000	3,416,000,000	3,509,000,000	3,998,000,000
Operating Margin %	6.15%	6.78%	6.06%	6.24%	6.16%	6.59%
SGA Expense	4,999,000,000	7,821,000,000	8,250,000,000	8,717,000,000	8,601,000,000	8,678,000,000
Net Income	344,000,000	3,161,000,000	2,461,000,000	1,648,000,000	2,051,000,000	-14,761,000,000
Operating Cash Flow	889,000,000	4,958,000,000	3,661,000,000	6,911,000,000	8,739,000,000	7,240,000,000
Capital Expenditure	3,137,000,000	3,280,000,000	3,344,000,000	3,620,000,000	2,497,000,000	3,475,000,000
EBITDA	3,915,000,000	8,431,000,000	5,470,000,000	6,479,000,000	7,348,000,000	-9,281,000,000
Return on Assets %	.48%	3.92%	3.36%	2.46%	2.98%	
Return on Equity %	1.25%	9.72%	7.00%	4.40%	5.39%	
Debt to Equity	0.43	0.40	0.45	0.01	0.01	

CONTACT INFORMATION:
Phone: 650-857-1501 Fax:
Toll-Free:
Address: 3000 Hanover St., Palo Alto, CA 94304 United States

STOCK TICKER/OTHER:
Stock Ticker: HPE
Employees: 195,000
Parent Company:

Exchange: NYS
Fiscal Year Ends:

SALARIES/BONUSES:
Top Exec. Salary: $1,500,053 Bonus: $
Second Exec. Salary: $753,152 Bonus: $

OTHER THOUGHTS:
Estimated Female Officers or Directors:
Hot Spot for Advancement for Women/Minorities:

Sales, profits and employees may be estimates. Financial information, benefits and other data can change quickly and may vary from those stated here.

Hewlett Packard Laboratories (HP Labs)

www8.hp.com/us/en/hp-labs/index.html

NAIC Code: 541712

TYPES OF BUSINESS:
Electronics Research
Printing & Imaging Technology
Internet & Computing Technology
Cloud Services
Sustainable Technologies

BRANDS/DIVISIONS/AFFILIATES:
Hewlett-Packard Enterprise Company

CONTACTS:
Note: Officers with more than one job title may be intentionally listed here more than once.

Shane Wall, Managing Dir.
John Sontag, Dir.-Systems Research
Martin Sadler, Dir.-Security & Cloud Lab
Chandrakant D. Patel, Chief Engineer
Jaap Suermondt, Dir.-Analytics Lab
Laurel Krieger, VP-Strategy & Oper.
Ruth Bergman, Head-HP Labs Israel
David Lee, Dir.-Networking & Mobility
David Lee, Head-HP Labs China
Eric Hanson, Dir.-Printing & Content Lab

GROWTH PLANS/SPECIAL FEATURES:
Hewlett-Packard Laboratories (HP Labs) is the innovation and research arm of Hewlett Packard Enterprise Company. HP Labs' current areas of research include: emerging compute, immersive experiences, print adjacencies & 3D and security. Within emerging compute, the lab researches the technologies, applications and services that will drive a new era of immersive, seamless collaboration and persistent connectivity at home and at work. It aims to unlock the human potential via ambient computing, sensors, natural language detection, audio/video analytics and new information displays. Within the immersive experiences area, HP Labs seeks to understand people and their practices via wide-scale urbanization and the Internet of Things in order to create and enhance best experiences via future technologies. Within the print adjacencies & 3D research area, HP Labs applies sciences to advanced printing technology to make 3D printing less expensive, faster and open. The same technologies are being used to innovate in areas not yet imagined, from medical diagnostics to next-generation manufacturing. Last, the security area seeks to ensure that connected devices remain secure and resilient in an ever-changing threat environment. Connected devices include PCs, smartphones, printers and home appliances, as well as emerging technologies.

FINANCIAL DATA:
Note: Data for latest year may not have been available at press time.

In U.S. $	2017	2016	2015	2014	2013	2012
Revenue						
R&D Expense						
Operating Income						
Operating Margin %						
SGA Expense						
Net Income						
Operating Cash Flow						
Capital Expenditure						
EBITDA						
Return on Assets %						
Return on Equity %						
Debt to Equity						

CONTACT INFORMATION:
Phone: 650-857-1501　Fax: 650-857-5518
Toll-Free: 800-752-0900
Address: 1501 Page Mill Rd., Palo Alto, CA 94304 United States

SALARIES/BONUSES:
Top Exec. Salary: $　Bonus: $
Second Exec. Salary: $　Bonus: $

STOCK TICKER/OTHER:
Stock Ticker: Subsidiary　Exchange:
Employees: 155　Fiscal Year Ends: 10/31
Parent Company: Hewlett Packard Enterprise Company

OTHER THOUGHTS:
Estimated Female Officers or Directors: 2
Hot Spot for Advancement for Women/Minorities: Y

HGST Inc

www.hgst.com

NAIC Code: 334112

TYPES OF BUSINESS:
Computer Storage Equipment
Hard Drives
Software

BRANDS/DIVISIONS/AFFILIATES:
Western Digital Corporation
Ultrastar
Travelstar
CinemaStar
4U60
InfiniFlash All-Flash
ActiveScale
ActiveScale Cloud Management

CONTACTS: Note: Officers with more than one job title may be intentionally listed here more than once.

Michael D. Cordano, Pres.
Dennis Lee Brown, Sr. VP-Operations
Chelse Ferero, Assistant Gen. Counsel
Dennis Brown, Sr. VP-Oper.
Bill Johns, Sr. VP-Dev.
Steven Craig, VP-Quality
George Horvath, Jr., VP-Real Estate & Site Oper.
Masamitsu Horike, Gen. Mgr.-Japan
Matthew E. Massengill, Chmn.-Western Digital
Renate Quigley, Sr. VP-Supply Chain Mgmt.

GROWTH PLANS/SPECIAL FEATURES:
HGST, Inc., wholly-owned by Western Digital Corporation, manufactures disk drives and components for personal computers, servers and electronic devices. The firm's products offer solutions such as backup, recovery/archive, cloud (both private and hybrid), database acceleration and virtualization. Its products are divided into four groups: hard drives, solid-state drives, platforms and systems. Hard drives include 2.5- and 3.5-inch platforms for enterprises, digital video and mobile devices, high-performance desktop systems and retail kits. Brands within this division include Ultrastar, Travelstar, CinemaStar and Endurastar. Solid-state solutions include the Ultrastar SN200, SS200, SS300 and SA210 series. The platforms group includes: the Ultrastar Data102 and Ultrastar Data60 next-generation disaggregated and software-defined storage systems; the Ultrastar Serv24 and Ultrastar Serv24 storage systems; the 2U24 Flash Storage platform; the 4U60 storage enclosure, delivering high capacity, scalable storage expansion for data centers; and the InfiniFlash All-Flash platform, a foundation for software-defined storage with a density, performance and scalability up to 512TB (terabytes) and up to 2M IOPS (million input/output per second). The systems group includes: the ActiveScale P100 modular object storage system, scaling up from 720 TB to over 19PB (petabytes); the ActiveScale X100 integrated object storage system, scaling from 840TB to 52PB; and the ActiveScale Cloud Management system, which monitors and stores analytics for ActiveScale systems via a cloud interface.

FINANCIAL DATA: Note: Data for latest year may not have been available at press time.

In U.S. $	2017	2016	2015	2014	2013	2012
Revenue	3,300,000,000	3,250,000,000	3,155,000,000	3,150,000,000	3,000,000,000	3,100,000,000
R&D Expense						
Operating Income						
Operating Margin %						
SGA Expense						
Net Income						
Operating Cash Flow						
Capital Expenditure						
EBITDA						
Return on Assets %						
Return on Equity %						
Debt to Equity						

CONTACT INFORMATION:
Phone: 408-717-6000   Fax: 408-256-6770
Toll-Free: 800-801-4618
Address: 3403 Yerba Buena Rd., San Jose, CA 95135 United States

STOCK TICKER/OTHER:
Stock Ticker: Subsidiary
Employees: 41,000
Parent Company: Western Digital Corporation

Exchange:
Fiscal Year Ends: 12/31

SALARIES/BONUSES:
Top Exec. Salary: $ Bonus: $
Second Exec. Salary: $ Bonus: $

OTHER THOUGHTS:
Estimated Female Officers or Directors: 3
Hot Spot for Advancement for Women/Minorities: Y

Sales, profits and employees may be estimates. Financial information, benefits and other data can change quickly and may vary from those stated here.

Plunkett Research, Ltd.

Hill-Rom Holdings Inc
NAIC Code: 339100

www.hill-rom.com

TYPES OF BUSINESS:
Equipment-Hospital Beds & Related Products
Specialized Therapy Products
Rentals

BRANDS/DIVISIONS/AFFILIATES:
Mortara Instrument Inc

CONTACTS: Note: Officers with more than one job title may be intentionally listed here more than once.
John Greisch, CEO
William Dempsey, Chairman of the Board
Kenneth Meyers, Other Executive Officer
Deborah Rasin, Other Executive Officer
Alton Shader, President, Divisional
Francisco Vega, President, Divisional
Paul Johnson, President, Divisional
Andreas Frank, Senior VP, Divisional
Steven Strobel, Senior VP
Carlos Alonso-Marum, Senior VP
Jason Richardson, Vice President

GROWTH PLANS/SPECIAL FEATURES:
Hill-Rom Holdings, Inc. is a global medical technology company. Hill-Rom partners with healthcare providers in more than 100 countries, with a focus on patient care solutions. The firm operates and manages its business within four segments, each aligned by region and/or product type: North America patient support systems, international patient support systems, front line care and surgical solutions. North America patient support systems sells and rents Hill-Rom's specialty frames, surfaces and mobility solutions, as well as its clinical workflow solutions in the U.S. and Canada. Frames and surfaces include medical surgical beds, intensive care unit beds and bariatric patient beds; and mobility solutions include lifts and other devices used to safely move patients. Clinical workflow solutions include communications technologies and software solutions. International patient support systems sells and rents similar products as the North America segment, but in regions outside the U.S. and Canada. Front line care globally sells and rents respiratory care products, and sells medical diagnostic equipment and a varied portfolio of devices that assess, diagnose, treat and manage a wide variety of illnesses and diseases. Surgical solutions sells Hill-Rom's surgical products globally, and include surgical tables, lights and pendants utilized within the operating room setting. This segment also offers a range of positioning devices for use in shoulder, hip, spinal and lithotomy surgeries, as well as platform-neutral positioning accessories for nearly every model of operating room table. In February 2017, the firm acquired Mortara Instrument, Inc., a producer of diagnostic cardiology devices. That June, it agreed to sell its Volker business, which serves the European long-term care bed market, to CoBe Capital.

FINANCIAL DATA: Note: Data for latest year may not have been available at press time.

In U.S. $	2017	2016	2015	2014	2013	2012
Revenue	2,743,700,000	2,655,200,000	1,988,200,000	1,686,100,000	1,716,200,000	1,634,300,000
R&D Expense	133,700,000	133,500,000	91,800,000	71,900,000	70,200,000	66,900,000
Operating Income	310,800,000	270,200,000	124,300,000	159,700,000	160,600,000	191,400,000
Operating Margin %	11.32%	10.17%	6.25%	9.47%	9.35%	11.71%
SGA Expense	876,100,000	853,300,000	664,200,000	548,300,000	549,500,000	496,400,000
Net Income	133,600,000	124,100,000	47,700,000	60,600,000	105,000,000	120,800,000
Operating Cash Flow	311,100,000	281,200,000	213,800,000	210,300,000	263,200,000	261,700,000
Capital Expenditure	97,500,000	83,300,000	121,300,000	62,700,000	65,300,000	77,800,000
EBITDA	482,700,000	437,700,000	201,700,000	231,400,000	270,300,000	281,700,000
Return on Assets %	3.03%	2.84%	1.53%	3.62%	6.53%	8.25%
Return on Equity %	10.33%	10.45%	4.88%	7.27%	12.56%	15.54%
Debt to Equity	1.56	1.57	1.89	0.45	0.26	0.29

CONTACT INFORMATION:
Phone: 3120819-7200 Fax:
Toll-Free:
Address: Two Prudential Plz., Ste. 4100, Chicago, IL 60601 United States

STOCK TICKER/OTHER:
Stock Ticker: HRC
Employees: 10,000
Parent Company:

Exchange: NYS
Fiscal Year Ends: 09/30

SALARIES/BONUSES:
Top Exec. Salary: $1,047,692   Bonus: $
Second Exec. Salary: $502,269   Bonus: $

OTHER THOUGHTS:
Estimated Female Officers or Directors: 1
Hot Spot for Advancement for Women/Minorities: Y

Sales, profits and employees may be estimates. Financial information, benefits and other data can change quickly and may vary from those stated here.

Hitachi High Technologies America Inc

www.hitachi-hightech.com/us/

NAIC Code: 541712

TYPES OF BUSINESS:
Research & Development
Semiconductor Manufacturing Equipment
Biotechnology Products
Industrial Equipment
Electronic & Industrial Materials
Electronic Components & Systems
Nanotechnology Research
Chromatography Systems

BRANDS/DIVISIONS/AFFILIATES:
Hitachi Limited

CONTACTS:
Note: Officers with more than one job title may be intentionally listed here more than once.

Craig Kerkove, CEO
Masahiro Miyazaki, Pres.
Greg Rigby, VP
Tom Grossi, Asst. Dir.-Corp. Business. Dev.
Steve Keough, Head-Media, Central & Eastern U.S.
Monica Degnan, Head-Media, Western U.S.
Phil Bryson, Gen. Mgr.-Nanotechnology Systems Division

GROWTH PLANS/SPECIAL FEATURES:

Hitachi High Technologies America, Inc. (Hitachi Hi-Tech), a subsidiary of Hitachi Limited of Japan, specializes in electronics. The firm operates in eight divisions. The electron microscope engineering division offers service support for Hitachi chromatography, spectroscopy, electron microscopy and semiconductor metrology systems. The electron, ion and probe microscopy division is Hitachi Hi-Tech's nanotechnology arm, providing technologically-advanced solutions to meet the diverse and complex challenges of materials science, biological research and industrial manufacturing. The industrial and IT solutions division provides sustainable solutions in the areas of automated production line equipment, broadband networking, automotive digital solutions and digital home technologies through strategic Tier-1 partnerships. The industrial solutions division provides technologies and services to manufacturers of automotive, communications, electronics and automation production line equipment, as well as to renewable energy product manufacturers. The life sciences division assists researchers in finding solutions to their scientific instrument requirements. The semiconductor etch equipment division supplies state-of-the art dry plasma etch systems to global semiconductor and hard disk drive manufacturers. The semiconductor metrology equipment division provides technologies and services to manufacturers of semiconductor and solar energy products. Last, the systems products division designs and builds system solutions for manufacturers of gaming products, automotive and medical monitors, packet capture application programming (PCAP) solutions for touch, and a new and growing line of smart sensors for industrial applications using embedded technology. Based in the U.S., the firm has locations throughout the country as well as in Mexico City, Mexico.

Hitchai Hi-Tech offers its employees comprehensive health, income protection, retirement and savings protection benefits and plans.

FINANCIAL DATA:
Note: Data for latest year may not have been available at press time.

In U.S. $	2017	2016	2015	2014	2013	2012
Revenue	5,500,000,000	5,521,960,000	5,312,576,056	5,184,890,000	6,118,744,000	
R&D Expense						
Operating Income						
Operating Margin %						
SGA Expense						
Net Income		344,145,000	266,909,722			
Operating Cash Flow						
Capital Expenditure						
EBITDA						
Return on Assets %						
Return on Equity %						
Debt to Equity						

CONTACT INFORMATION:
Phone: 847-273-4141 Fax: 847-273-4407
Toll-Free:
Address: 10 N. Martingale Rd., Ste. 500, Schaumburg, IL 60173-2295 United States

STOCK TICKER/OTHER:
Stock Ticker: Subsidiary
Employees: 464
Parent Company: Hitachi Ltd
Exchange:
Fiscal Year Ends: 03/31

SALARIES/BONUSES:
Top Exec. Salary: $ Bonus: $
Second Exec. Salary: $ Bonus: $

OTHER THOUGHTS:
Estimated Female Officers or Directors: 1
Hot Spot for Advancement for Women/Minorities:

Sales, profits and employees may be estimates. Financial information, benefits and other data can change quickly and may vary from those stated here.

Plunkett Research, Ltd.

Hitachi Limited
NAIC Code: 334111

www.hitachi.com

TYPES OF BUSINESS:
Computer Manufacturing
Consumer Appliances & Electronics
Materials Manufacturing
Financial Services Products
Power & Industrial Systems
Medical & Scientific Equipment
Transportation Systems
Consulting Services

BRANDS/DIVISIONS/AFFILIATES:

CONTACTS:
Note: Officers with more than one job title may be intentionally listed here more than once.

Toshiaki Higashihara, CEO
Hiroaki Nakanishi, Pres.
Shigeru Azuhata, Gen. Mgr.-R&D
Toyoaki Nakamura, Gen. Mgr.-Consumer Bus.
Koji Tanaka, Exec. VP-Power Systems Bus.
Nobuo Mochida, Exec. VP-Prod. Eng.
Tatsuro Ishizuka, CEO-Power Systems Group
Junzo Nakajima, CEO-Asia Pacific

GROWTH PLANS/SPECIAL FEATURES:

Hitachi Limited is a Japan-based electronics company which manufactures communications and electronic equipment, heavy electrical and industrial machinery and consumer electronics. Hitachi divides its products and services into nine segments. The healthcare segment operates through Hitachi Medical Corporation and focuses on increasing national medical expenditure. The power systems segment develops and maximizes the efficiency and reliability of nuclear power plants and transmission/distribution systems. It also provides renewable energy related products, including wind and solar power generation systems. The infrastructure segment provides various advanced infrastructure systems which makes maximum use of IT. This division is engaged in two main business areas: social infrastructure, which includes electric power systems, railways, water supply and sewage systems; and roads and industrial infrastructure, which include systems for steel, chemical, automotive and other production facilities. The information & telecommunication segment offers highly reliable IT platforms such as storage solutions, servers, middleware and telecommunications equipment as well as IT consulting and systems integration services. The electronic systems and equipment segment supplies production and inspection equipment for the semiconductors and other electronic devices essential to providing advanced functions in electronic products. The automotive systems segment supplies technologies and products that cover the fields of environment, safety and information. The consumer products segment offers appliances, air conditioners/heaters, lighting and facility/business spaces comprising all-electric and/or solar power generation systems such as water heaters that use CO_2 natural refrigerants. The financial services segment supplies leases, insurance and other financial services. Last, the high functional materials and components segment produce elements, metals, wires and cables for a variety of fields that combine infrastructure technology and IT.

FINANCIAL DATA:
Note: Data for latest year may not have been available at press time.

In U.S. $	2017	2016	2015	2014	2013	2012
Revenue	85,357,410,000	93,481,510,000	91,065,130,000	89,586,380,000	84,228,350,000	90,049,220,000
R&D Expense						
Operating Income	5,471,483,000	5,914,562,000	5,974,707,000	4,963,769,000	3,931,694,000	3,840,880,000
Operating Margin %	6.41%	6.32%	6.56%	5.54%	4.66%	4.26%
SGA Expense	16,697,210,000	18,076,790,000	18,030,310,000	18,632,640,000	17,468,340,000	18,396,050,000
Net Income	2,154,472,000	1,603,829,000	2,026,104,000	2,468,558,000	1,633,371,000	3,234,386,000
Operating Cash Flow	5,865,307,000	7,566,853,000	4,209,288,000	4,093,591,000	5,436,072,000	4,165,782,000
Capital Expenditure	6,615,363,000	4,527,036,000	8,674,977,000	8,760,658,000	7,208,058,000	6,641,457,000
EBITDA	8,415,204,000	9,789,650,000	9,487,274,000	9,778,964,000	7,352,926,000	9,926,747,000
Return on Assets %	2.08%	1.37%	1.85%	2.54%	1.82%	3.73%
Return on Equity %	8.11%	6.06%	7.77%	11.19%	9.09%	21.61%
Debt to Equity	0.26	0.76	0.71	0.57	0.67	0.78

CONTACT INFORMATION:
Phone: 81 332581111   Fax: 81 332582375
Toll-Free:
Address: 6-6, Marunouchi 1-chome, Chiyoda-ku, Tokyo, 100-8280 Japan

STOCK TICKER/OTHER:
Stock Ticker: HTHIY
Employees: 335,244
Parent Company:

Exchange: PINX
Fiscal Year Ends: 03/31

SALARIES/BONUSES:
Top Exec. Salary: $ Bonus: $
Second Exec. Salary: $ Bonus: $

OTHER THOUGHTS:
Estimated Female Officers or Directors: 1
Hot Spot for Advancement for Women/Minorities:

Sales, profits and employees may be estimates. Financial information, benefits and other data can change quickly and may vary from those stated here.

HKS Inc

www.hksinc.com

NAIC Code: 541330

TYPES OF BUSINESS:
Engineering Consulting Services

BRANDS/DIVISIONS/AFFILIATES:

CONTACTS:
Note: Officers with more than one job title may be intentionally listed here more than once.

Dan Noble, CEO

GROWTH PLANS/SPECIAL FEATURES:
HKS, Inc. is an architectural consulting firm. The firm has worked on projects in over 1,500 cities throughout 92 countries since its inception in 1939. While headquartered in Dallas, Texas, the firm has an additional 24 worldwide offices located in the U.S., the U.K., the U.A.E., Mexico, India, China and Singapore. HKS has a vast suite of capabilities that it offers as services to the client. The firm's architectural services include conceptual and schematic design, design development and construction documentation, assisting with contractor bidding and/or negotiating and construction contract administration. Planning and development offers services that handle issues of site analysis, access, circulation, parking, urban design, local development guidelines and placemaking. Programming services takes the client's goals, objectives and space requirements and develops innovative, imaginative, highly functional and operationally efficient solutions. Project management services includes design-quality management reviews and consultant coordination, budget management, monthly reporting, design scheduling and design-fee cash flow forecasting and trending. Other services offered by HKS include interior design, structural engineering, graphic design, branding, advisory practices, research, sustainable design and architectural design interpretation. In early-2017, HKS was selected to design the new ballpark to be built in Arlington, Texas for the Texas Rangers. The stadium will be a multi-use sports and entertainment venue that will include capabilities for hosting high school, college and international sports, as well as entertainment tours. The facility is expected to open in time for the 2020 Major League Baseball season. That same year, HKS expanded its footprint in New York, with the debut of a hospitality architecture design studio in New York City, its first in the Northeast.

FINANCIAL DATA:
Note: Data for latest year may not have been available at press time.

In U.S. $	2017	2016	2015	2014	2013	2012
Revenue	380,000,000	376,680,000	280,500,000	255,120,000		
R&D Expense						
Operating Income						
Operating Margin %						
SGA Expense						
Net Income						
Operating Cash Flow						
Capital Expenditure						
EBITDA						
Return on Assets %						
Return on Equity %						
Debt to Equity						

CONTACT INFORMATION:
Phone: 214-969-5599 Fax: 214-969-3367
Toll-Free:
Address: 350 N. Saint Paul St., Ste. 100, Dallas, TX 75201 United States

STOCK TICKER/OTHER:
Stock Ticker: Private
Employees: 1,350
Parent Company:

Exchange:
Fiscal Year Ends:

SALARIES/BONUSES:
Top Exec. Salary: $ Bonus: $
Second Exec. Salary: $ Bonus: $

OTHER THOUGHTS:
Estimated Female Officers or Directors:
Hot Spot for Advancement for Women/Minorities:

HNTB Corporation

NAIC Code: 541330

www.hntb.com

TYPES OF BUSINESS:
Engineering Design Services
Financial Planning
Construction
Water Management
Architecture

BRANDS/DIVISIONS/AFFILIATES:

GROWTH PLANS/SPECIAL FEATURES:
HNTB Corporation is an employee-owned provider of infrastructure and architecture services to public and private owners, as well as to contractors. The firm addresses the full life-cycle of infrastructure, delivering a range of related services such as planning, design, program and construction management. HNTB's expertise includes the following industries and applications: architecture, aviation, bridges, construction management, design-build, highways, intelligent transportation systems, program management, tolls, rails, tunnels and water. Based in Missouri, the firm has offices throughout the U.S.

The group offers employees a 401(k), life and disability insurance, flexible spending accounts, adoption assistance and paid time off.

CONTACTS: Note: Officers with more than one job title may be intentionally listed here more than once.
Rob Slimp, CEO
Thomas O'Grady, Pres.
Craig Denson, CFO
Kevin Haboian, Chief Sales Officer
Lindsay Jordan, Human Resources Officer
Steve Haag, CIO
Paul Yarossi, Exec. VP
Rob Slimp, CEO-HNTB Infrastructure
Harvey Hammond, Jr., Chmn.

FINANCIAL DATA: Note: Data for latest year may not have been available at press time.

In U.S. $	2017	2016	2015	2014	2013	2012
Revenue						
R&D Expense						
Operating Income						
Operating Margin %						
SGA Expense						
Net Income						
Operating Cash Flow						
Capital Expenditure						
EBITDA						
Return on Assets %						
Return on Equity %						
Debt to Equity						

CONTACT INFORMATION:
Phone: 816-472-1201   Fax: 816-472-4060
Toll-Free:
Address: 715 Kirk Dr., Kansas City, MO 64105 United States

STOCK TICKER/OTHER:
Stock Ticker: Private   Exchange:
Employees: 3,313   Fiscal Year Ends: 12/31
Parent Company:

SALARIES/BONUSES:
Top Exec. Salary: $ Bonus: $
Second Exec. Salary: $ Bonus: $

OTHER THOUGHTS:
Estimated Female Officers or Directors:
Hot Spot for Advancement for Women/Minorities:

Sales, profits and employees may be estimates. Financial information, benefits and other data can change quickly and may vary from those stated here.

HOCHTIEF AG

NAIC Code: 237000

www.hochtief.de

TYPES OF BUSINESS:
Heavy Construction
Airport Management & Consulting Services
Infrastructure Development
Geothermal Plant Construction
Green Building Engineering Services

BRANDS/DIVISIONS/AFFILIATES:
Turner Construction Company
Flatiron
E E Cruz and Company
HOCHTIEF Solutions AG
CIMIC Group Limited
HOCHTIEF Insurance Broking and Risk
Leighton Holdings Limited

CONTACTS: Note: Officers with more than one job title may be intentionally listed here more than once.
Marcelino Fernandez Verdes, Chmn.

GROWTH PLANS/SPECIAL FEATURES:

HOCHTIEF AG is a construction services provider which designs, builds, finances and operates facilities worldwide. The company operates through three divisions: HOCHTIEF Americas, HOCHTIEF Europe and HOCHTIEF Asia-Pacific. The Americas division includes the activities of subsidiaries in the U.S., Canada and Brazil, including: Turner Construction Company, a U.S. general construction contractor and green building engineering firm; Flatiron, which has a regional presence in the U.S. and Canada, and is among the top 10 suppliers in the U.S. transportation infrastructure construction sector; E. E. Cruz and Company, which specializes in civil construction; and Clark Builders, a general contractor in Canada. The Europe division's leading company, HOCHTIEF Solutions AG, plans, develops, implements, operates and manages real estate and infrastructure facilities, and also operates concessions and projects via public-private partnerships. Other business units and subsidiaries within this division include HOCHTIEF Infrastructure, HOCHTIEF Building, HOCHTIEF PPP Solutions, HOCHTIEF Engineering, HOCHTIEF ViCon, HOCHTIEF Project Development, synexs, HOCHTIEF (UK) Construction, HOCHTIEF Infrastructure Austria, HOCHTIEF Polska, HOCHTIEF CZ and HOCHTIEF (India). The Asia-Pacific division is run by CIMIC Group Limited (formerly Leighton) which operates through various subsidiaries in Australia and Asia, providing building and infrastructure construction, raw materials extraction and processing, concessions, project development, as well as maintenance and services. Other business units and subsidiaries within this division include: CPB Contractors Pty Limited; Leighton Asia, India and Offshore; Thiess Pty Ltd.; Sedgman Pty Limited; UGL Limited; HLG Contracting, LLC; Devine Limited; and Ventia Pty Limited. In addition to these primary divisions, subsidiary HOCHTIEF Insurance Broking and Risk Management Solutions GmbH handles insurance services for the company's operating divisions.

FINANCIAL DATA: Note: Data for latest year may not have been available at press time.

In U.S. $	2017	2016	2015	2014	2013	2012
Revenue		24,584,860,000	26,052,280,000	27,290,200,000	31,728,670,000	31,524,270,000
R&D Expense						
Operating Income		576,796,200	644,935,700	479,433,900	648,763,900	561,227,800
Operating Margin %		2.34%	2.47%	1.75%	2.04%	1.78%
SGA Expense		524,414,000	505,008,800	542,623,900	572,290,000	673,096,400
Net Income		395,765,500	257,214,300	310,809,100	211,410,500	195,249,300
Operating Cash Flow		1,449,024,000	1,401,870,000	933,627,700	255,345,900	1,241,921,000
Capital Expenditure		336,603,800	352,534,000	710,483,100	1,128,169,000	1,499,951,000
EBITDA		1,334,906,000	1,466,312,000	765,102,800	2,374,272,000	2,222,721,000
Return on Assets %		2.34%	1.46%	1.67%	1.07%	.96%
Return on Equity %		16.15%	9.63%	11.32%	6.97%	6.03%
Debt to Equity		0.89	1.09	1.40	1.17	1.03

CONTACT INFORMATION:
Phone: 49 2018240 Fax: 49 2018242777
Toll-Free:
Address: Opernplatz 2, Essen, 45128 Germany

STOCK TICKER/OTHER:
Stock Ticker: HOCFY Exchange: PINX
Employees: 51,490 Fiscal Year Ends: 12/31
Parent Company: ACS Group

SALARIES/BONUSES:
Top Exec. Salary: $ Bonus: $
Second Exec. Salary: $ Bonus: $

OTHER THOUGHTS:
Estimated Female Officers or Directors: 1
Hot Spot for Advancement for Women/Minorities:

Sales, profits and employees may be estimates. Financial information, benefits and other data can change quickly and may vary from those stated here.

HOK

NAIC Code: 541330

www.hok.com

TYPES OF BUSINESS:
Engineering Services

BRANDS/DIVISIONS/AFFILIATES:

CONTACTS: *Note: Officers with more than one job title may be intentionally listed here more than once.*
Bill Hellmuth, CEO

GROWTH PLANS/SPECIAL FEATURES:

HOK is a design, architecture, engineering and planning firm. Founded in St. Louis in 1955, the company now has a network of 23 offices on three continents. HOK offers a multitude of services across various strategic practice areas. These services include architecture, consulting, engineering, interior design, landscape architecture, lighting design, onsite services, planning and urban design, product design, renovation and restoration, strategic accounts, sustainable consulting and visual communications. The strategic practice areas of the firm are aviation and transportation, civic and cultural, commercial, corporate, education, government, healthcare, hospitality, justice, recreation and wellness, residential, retail, science and technology, sports and recreation, entertainment and tall buildings. Recently, HOK partnered with the United Soccer League (USL) in the U.S. to lead a stadium development, design and standards initiative to help house all USL clubs in soccer-specific stadiums across North America by the end of 2025. Current projects (2018) by HOK include a regional transit center and passenger processing facility at Toronto Pearson International Airport; the 80-story Capital Market Authority Tower in Riyadh; the La Guardia Airport central terminal B/Concourse B in New York; and Atlantis Sanya Resort in Hainan, China; the Penn State University Chemical and Biomedical Engineering Building; the modernization of Hartsfield-Jackson Atlanta International Airport; the New York Presbyterian Hospital David H. Koch Center; the International School of Kuala Lumpur, in Malaysia; the Philips Arena renovation in Atlanta, Georgia; the LG Science Park in Seoul's Magok District; the Kentucky International Convention Center; the University of Maryland, Baltimore Health Sciences Facility III; and the Sachibondu Hospital in Zambia, Africa.

FINANCIAL DATA: *Note: Data for latest year may not have been available at press time.*

In U.S. $	2017	2016	2015	2014	2013	2012
Revenue	440,000,000	430,000,000	416,000,000	440,000,000	406,560,000	
R&D Expense						
Operating Income						
Operating Margin %						
SGA Expense						
Net Income						
Operating Cash Flow						
Capital Expenditure						
EBITDA						
Return on Assets %						
Return on Equity %						
Debt to Equity						

CONTACT INFORMATION:
Phone: 314-421-2000 Fax:
Toll-Free:
Address: 10 S. Broadway, Ste. 200, St. Louis, MO 63102 United States

STOCK TICKER/OTHER:
Stock Ticker: Private Exchange:
Employees: 1,700 Fiscal Year Ends:
Parent Company:

SALARIES/BONUSES:
Top Exec. Salary: $ Bonus: $
Second Exec. Salary: $ Bonus: $

OTHER THOUGHTS:
Estimated Female Officers or Directors:
Hot Spot for Advancement for Women/Minorities:

Hon Hai Precision Industry Company Ltd

www.foxconn.com

NAIC Code: 334418

TYPES OF BUSINESS:

Contract Manufacturing of Electronics
Consumer Electronics & Components Manufacturing
Product Design Services
Original Design Manufacturing (ODM)
Optical Technology
Wireless Products Manufacturing

BRANDS/DIVISIONS/AFFILIATES:

Foxconn Technology Group

CONTACTS:
Note: Officers with more than one job title may be intentionally listed here more than once.

Tai-Ming Gou, CEO
Tai-Ming Gou, Chmn.

GROWTH PLANS/SPECIAL FEATURES:

Hon Hai Precision Industry Company, Ltd., which does business under its registered trade name Foxconn Technology Group, is a technology manufacturer that focuses on joint-design and development, manufacturing, assembly and after-sales services for global communication, computer and customer electronics firms. Foxconn is operated by a propriety business model called eCMMS (e-enabled components, modules, moves and services), and is one of the largest multinational electronics and computer components manufacturing service providers in the world. Its primary areas of focus are nanotechnology, heat transfer, wireless connectivity, material sciences, green manufacturing process, new material and optical electric. The firm holds more than 55,000 patents worldwide. Some of Foxconn's most notable contract design and manufacturing products include the Mac Mini, iPod and iPhone for Apple, Inc.; branded motherboards for Intel Corp.; the Wii for Nintendo; the Xbox 360 for Microsoft; Motorola cell phones; and computers for retailers such as Dell and Hewlett-Packard. Other non-branded products include connectors, cables, motherboards, graphics cards and other computer components that are primarily sold to corporate users. Foxconn also provides logistic planning and e-supplying, global supply chain management, computer software development, computer programming and sales channel solutions to its customers. The company has locations across the Americas, Asia and Europe.

FINANCIAL DATA:
Note: Data for latest year may not have been available at press time.

In U.S. $	2017	2016	2015	2014	2013	2012
Revenue	160,590,100,000	148,716,500,000	152,927,300,000	143,750,100,000	134,850,000,000	133,249,000,000
R&D Expense	2,790,308,000	1,744,865,000	1,790,975,000	1,666,852,000	1,589,274,000	1,556,756,000
Operating Income	3,840,814,000	5,968,798,000	5,604,714,000	4,885,578,000	3,729,721,000	3,700,245,000
Operating Margin %	2.39%	4.01%	3.66%	3.39%	2.76%	2.77%
SGA Expense	3,707,235,000	3,258,563,000	3,542,656,000	3,408,464,000	3,370,981,000	5,989,683,000
Net Income	4,733,509,000	5,072,264,000	5,010,985,000	4,453,742,000	3,640,423,000	3,233,218,000
Operating Cash Flow	-1,342,295,000	5,937,450,000	8,267,857,000	6,505,705,000	5,894,147,000	6,134,808,000
Capital Expenditure	2,060,283,000	1,815,290,000	2,423,015,000	944,884,200	1,827,942,000	2,393,269,000
EBITDA	5,922,100,000	8,128,093,000	8,035,951,000	7,281,833,000	6,241,346,000	6,682,561,000
Return on Assets %	4.62%	6.06%	6.15%	5.46%	4.89%	5.02%
Return on Equity %	12.82%	14.25%	15.15%	15.40%	15.12%	15.47%
Debt to Equity	0.17	0.16	0.17	0.17	0.17	0.16

CONTACT INFORMATION:

Phone: 886 222683466   Fax: 886 222686204
Toll-Free:
Address: No. 2, Zihyou Street,, Tu-Chen City, Taipei, 236 Taiwan

STOCK TICKER/OTHER:

Stock Ticker: HNHPF   Exchange: PINX
Employees: 1,300,000   Fiscal Year Ends: 12/31
Parent Company:

SALARIES/BONUSES:

Top Exec. Salary: $ Bonus: $
Second Exec. Salary: $ Bonus: $

OTHER THOUGHTS:

Estimated Female Officers or Directors:
Hot Spot for Advancement for Women/Minorities:

Sales, profits and employees may be estimates. Financial information, benefits and other data can change quickly and may vary from those stated here.

Plunkett Research, Ltd.   357

Honda Motor Co Ltd

NAIC Code: 336111   world.honda.com

TYPES OF BUSINESS:
- Automobile Manufacturing
- Motorcycles
- ATVs & Personal Watercraft
- Generators
- Marine Engines
- Lawn & Garden Equipment
- Fuel Cell & Hybrid Vehicles
- Airplanes

BRANDS/DIVISIONS/AFFILIATES:
- Acura
- Honda
- Civic
- Accord
- Fit
- CR-V
- HondaJet

CONTACTS:
Note: Officers with more than one job title may be intentionally listed here more than once.

Takahiro Hachigo, CEO
Takanobu Ito, Pres.

GROWTH PLANS/SPECIAL FEATURES:

Honda Motor Co. Ltd. develops, produces and manufactures a variety of motor products, ranging from small general-purpose engines and scooters to specialty sports cars. Comprised of 442 company subsidiaries and affiliates in Japan and internationally, Honda operates through four segments: motorcycles, automobiles, financial services and power products/other. The motorcycle unit produces sport, business and commuter model bikes, which utilize air- or water-cooled gasoline engines with 1-6 cylinders, manufactured by the company. This segment also includes the production of all-terrain vehicles (ATVs), personal watercraft and multi-utility vehicles (MUVs). The automobiles segment manufactures vehicles under the Acura and Honda trademarks. Honda models include the Civic, a sub-compact car; the Accord, an intermediate passenger car; the Fit, a compact passenger car; the Odyssey, a minivan; the Accord, Fit/Jazz, Freed, Jade, Legend and Shuttle hybrid cars; and the CR-V, an SUV. Through the financial services segment, the company offers financial services to its customers and dealers through finance subsidiaries in countries including Japan, the U.S., Canada, the U.K., Germany, Brazil and Thailand. This segment's services include retail lending, leasing to customers and wholesale financing to dealers. Through its power products unit, Honda produces tillers, portable generators, general purpose engines, grass cutters, outboard marine engines, water pumps, snow throwers, power carriers, power sprayers, lawn mowers and lawn tractors. In addition, HondaJet manufactures business jets and jet engines; and manufactures advanced humanoid robots, as well as walking assisted devices and stride management systems for people with weakened leg muscles.

U.S. employee benefits include paid time off, credit union access, health care plans, domestic partner benefits, onsite fitness facilities, education reimbursement and retirement plans.

FINANCIAL DATA:
Note: Data for latest year may not have been available at press time.

In U.S. $	2017	2016	2015	2014	2013	2012
Revenue	130,419,200,000	136,027,100,000	124,167,100,000	110,326,500,000	92,024,850,000	74,045,980,000
R&D Expense	6,441,485,000	6,116,099,000	5,647,121,000	5,907,677,000	5,219,583,000	4,842,724,000
Operating Income	7,832,225,000	4,689,547,000	6,247,466,000	6,989,762,000	5,075,555,000	2,155,431,000
Operating Margin %	6.00%	3.44%	5.03%	6.33%	5.51%	2.91%
SGA Expense	14,917,200,000	19,646,670,000	16,028,970,000	15,809,180,000	13,300,770,000	11,899,390,000
Net Income	5,744,075,000	3,209,717,000	4,745,994,000	5,348,491,000	3,420,431,000	1,970,207,000
Operating Cash Flow	8,245,510,000	12,958,780,000	9,506,279,000	11,451,380,000	7,459,885,000	6,870,030,000
Capital Expenditure	5,938,626,000	8,123,337,000	8,227,316,000	17,717,960,000	13,228,960,000	10,070,660,000
EBITDA	15,779,640,000	12,244,370,000	13,505,310,000	14,313,050,000	10,168,780,000	7,439,343,000
Return on Assets %	3.31%	1.87%	2.99%	3.92%	2.88%	1.81%
Return on Equity %	8.77%	4.96%	7.82%	10.47%	7.77%	4.77%
Debt to Equity	0.55	0.55	0.55	0.54	0.53	0.50

CONTACT INFORMATION:
Phone: 81 334231111   Fax:
Toll-Free:
Address: 1-1, 2-chome, Minami-Aoyama, Minato-ku, Tokyo, 107-8556 Japan

STOCK TICKER/OTHER:
Stock Ticker: HMC
Employees: 211,915
Parent Company:

Exchange: NYS
Fiscal Year Ends: 03/31

SALARIES/BONUSES:
Top Exec. Salary: $ Bonus: $
Second Exec. Salary: $ Bonus: $

OTHER THOUGHTS:
Estimated Female Officers or Directors:
Hot Spot for Advancement for Women/Minorities:

Sales, profits and employees may be estimates. Financial information, benefits and other data can change quickly and may vary from those stated here.

Honeywell International Inc

www.honeywell.com

NAIC Code: 336412

TYPES OF BUSINESS:
Aircraft Engine and Engine Parts Manufacturing
Automation & Control Systems
Turboprop Engines
Performance Polymers
Specialty Chemicals
Nuclear Services
Life Sciences

BRANDS/DIVISIONS/AFFILIATES:

CONTACTS:
Note: Officers with more than one job title may be intentionally listed here more than once.

Rajeev Gautam, CEO, Divisional
John Waldron, CEO, Divisional
Gary Michel, CEO, Divisional
Timothy Mahoney, CEO, Subsidiary
Darius Adamczyk, CEO
Thomas Szlosek, CFO
David Cote, Chairman of the Board
Jennifer Mak, Chief Accounting Officer
Anne Madden, General Counsel
Mark James, Senior VP, Divisional
Krishna Mikkilineni, Senior VP, Divisional

GROWTH PLANS/SPECIAL FEATURES:
Honeywell International, Inc. invents and commercializes technologies that address critical challenges related to energy, safety, security, productivity and global urbanization. The firm operates through four segments: aerospace, home and building technologies (HBT), performance materials and technologies (PMT), and safety and productivity solutions (SPS). The aerospace segment supplies products, software and services for aircraft and vehicles that it sells to original equipment manufacturers (OEMs) and other customers in a variety of end markets. These markets include aircraft/aviation, defense and space contractors, and automotive and truck manufacturers. Its products consist of aircraft engines, integrated avionics, systems and service solutions; related products and services for aircraft manufacturers; and turbochargers for the performance improvement and efficiency of passenger cars and commercial vehicles. HBT provides products, software, solutions and technologies that help owners of homes stay connected and in control of their comfort, security and energy use; enable commercial building owners and occupants to ensure their facilities are safe, energy efficient, sustainable and productive; and help electricity, gas and water providers to serve customers and communities. PMT develops and manufactures advanced materials, process technologies and automation solutions. Its products include catalysts, absorbents, equipment and consulting. Last, SPS provides products, software and connected solutions that improve productivity, workplace safety and asset performance. Safety products include equipment and footwear designed for work, play and outdoor activities; and productivity products include gas detection technology, mobile devices, software, supply chain/warehouse automation equipment, sensors, switches and controls.

FINANCIAL DATA:
Note: Data for latest year may not have been available at press time.

In U.S. $	2017	2016	2015	2014	2013	2012
Revenue	40,534,000,000	39,302,000,000	38,581,000,000	40,306,000,000	39,055,000,000	37,665,000,000
R&D Expense						
Operating Income	7,053,000,000	6,482,000,000	6,806,000,000	5,822,000,000	5,493,000,000	4,154,000,000
Operating Margin %	17.40%	16.49%	17.64%	14.44%	14.06%	11.02%
SGA Expense	5,808,000,000	5,469,000,000	5,006,000,000	5,518,000,000	5,190,000,000	5,218,000,000
Net Income	1,655,000,000	4,809,000,000	4,768,000,000	4,239,000,000	3,924,000,000	2,926,000,000
Operating Cash Flow	5,966,000,000	5,498,000,000	5,454,000,000	5,024,000,000	4,335,000,000	3,517,000,000
Capital Expenditure	1,031,000,000	1,095,000,000	1,073,000,000	1,094,000,000	947,000,000	884,000,000
EBITDA	8,333,000,000	7,815,000,000	7,779,000,000	7,060,000,000	6,728,000,000	5,152,000,000
Return on Assets %	2.91%	9.29%	10.06%	9.32%	8.99%	7.16%
Return on Equity %	9.03%	25.54%	26.53%	24.13%	25.78%	24.60%
Debt to Equity	0.72	0.62	0.30	0.34	0.38	0.49

CONTACT INFORMATION:
Phone: 973 455-2000 Fax:
Toll-Free: 877-841-2840
Address: 115 Tabor Rd., Morris Plains, NJ 07950 United States

SALARIES/BONUSES:
Top Exec. Salary: $1,414,615 Bonus: $
Second Exec. Salary: $963,615 Bonus: $

STOCK TICKER/OTHER:
Stock Ticker: HON Exchange: NYS
Employees: 131,000 Fiscal Year Ends: 12/31
Parent Company:

OTHER THOUGHTS:
Estimated Female Officers or Directors: 2
Hot Spot for Advancement for Women/Minorities: Y

Hoya Corporation

NAIC Code: 334413

www.hoya.co.jp

TYPES OF BUSINESS:
Semiconductor Manufacturing Equipment
Glass Semiconductor Components
Medical Equipment
Eyeglass Lenses
Optical Glass
Bio-Compatible Bone Replacement
Laser & UV Light Sources
Nanoimprint Technology

BRANDS/DIVISIONS/AFFILIATES:

GROWTH PLANS/SPECIAL FEATURES:
HOYA Corporation, established in 1941, primarily manufactures innovative high-tech and healthcare products. HOYA operates through two segments: life care and information technology. Life care encompasses healthcare products such as eyeglass lenses; medical related products such as intraocular lenses for cataract surgery, medical endoscopes, surgical equipment and artificial bones and implants; and the operation of HOYA's contact lens retail stores. Information technology focuses on electronics products for the semiconductor industry; LCD panels, glass disks for hard disk drives (HDDs); and optical lenses for digital cameras and smart phones. HOYA comprises more than 100 subsidiaries and affiliates worldwide. In October 2016, the firm agreed to acquire Performance Optics, LLC, including its subsidiaries VISION EASE and Daemyung Optical. Performance Optics is a global ophthalmic lens manufacturer specializing in polycarbonate, photochromic, polarized and high index eyeglass lenses.

CONTACTS:
Note: Officers with more than one job title may be intentionally listed here more than once.

Hiroshi Suzuki, CEO
Eiichiro Ikeda, COO
Hiroshi Suzuki, Pres.
Ryo Hirooka, CFO
Eiichiro Ikeda, Exec. Officer-IT
Taro Hagiwara, CTO

FINANCIAL DATA:
Note: Data for latest year may not have been available at press time.

In U.S. $	2017	2016	2015	2014	2013	2012
Revenue	4,562,260,000	4,799,544,000	4,618,344,000	4,051,398,000	3,840,768,000	3,621,194,000
R&D Expense						
Operating Income	2,066,126,000	2,118,428,000	1,975,769,000	1,584,573,000	1,646,488,000	1,482,504,000
Operating Margin %	45.28%	44.13%	42.78%	39.11%	42.86%	40.93%
SGA Expense	430,575,700	428,703,200	393,152,600	344,382,300	1,179,886,000	1,144,159,000
Net Income	808,086,500	868,036,200	864,579,800	543,972,400	662,371,900	402,636,500
Operating Cash Flow	1,003,000,000	1,228,703,000	1,074,902,000	956,493,400	829,057,200	686,780,400
Capital Expenditure	200,559,000	169,405,600	171,278,200	154,145,700	401,052,800	290,516,100
EBITDA	1,320,123,000	1,430,958,000	1,437,582,000	1,124,334,000	1,139,613,000	824,483,000
Return on Assets %	13.35%	13.57%	12.90%	8.83%	11.91%	7.49%
Return on Equity %	17.27%	17.20%	16.47%	11.59%	16.61%	11.34%
Debt to Equity		0.07	0.06	0.06	0.12	0.15

CONTACT INFORMATION:
Phone: 81339521151　　Fax: 81339520726
Toll-Free:
Address: 20/Fl Nittochi Nishishinjuku Bldg, 6-10-1 Nishi-Shinjuku, Tokyo, 160-8347 Japan

STOCK TICKER/OTHER:
Stock Ticker: HOCPY　　　　　　　Exchange: PINX
Employees: 35,752　　　　　　　Fiscal Year Ends: 03/31
Parent Company:

SALARIES/BONUSES:
Top Exec. Salary: $　　Bonus: $
Second Exec. Salary: $　　Bonus: $

OTHER THOUGHTS:
Estimated Female Officers or Directors:
Hot Spot for Advancement for Women/Minorities:

Sales, profits and employees may be estimates. Financial information, benefits and other data can change quickly and may vary from those stated here.

HTC Corporation

www.htc.com

NAIC Code: 334418

TYPES OF BUSINESS:
Contract Electronics Manufacturing
Mobile Computing & Communications Hardware
Cellular Phones & Smartphones
PDAs
Contract Manufacturing

BRANDS/DIVISIONS/AFFILIATES:
HTC U11
HTC U Ultra
HTC Bolt
VIVE
UA Healthbox

CONTACTS: Note: Officers with more than one job title may be intentionally listed here more than once.
Cher Wang, CEO
Fred Liu, Pres., Eng.
Fred Liu, Pres., Oper.

GROWTH PLANS/SPECIAL FEATURES:
HTC Corporation specializes in designing and manufacturing mobile computing and communications hardware, including cell phones, smartphones and PDAs. The company operates as an original equipment manufacturer (OEM) by providing contract design as well as manufacturing services. The firm's customers include major mobile device brands and wireless service providers. HTC's smartphones include: the HTC U11 innovative phones featuring 3D liquid glass surfaces; the HTC U Ultra next-generation, liquid surface 5.7-inch phone; and the HTC Bolt, comprising a metal unibody that is light, yet water, splash and dust resistant. Accessories include cases, screen protectors, chargers, USB cables and earphones. Virtual reality products include the VIVE line of headsets, systems and related software and accessories. Fitness products include the UA Healthbox wrist band, a connected fitness system created to measure, monitor and manage the factors that determine how the wearer feels. The water-resistant bands include features that measure sleep, resting heart rate, daily activity and workout intensity, all in real-time. In early-2018, HTC sold roughly 2,000 employees who worked in the design and research division, as well as its non-exclusive licenses to smartphone-related intellectual property, to Google for $1.1 billion. HTC will continue to produce its own smartphones, but plans to increase its focus on Internet of Things and virtual reality technologies and products.

FINANCIAL DATA: Note: Data for latest year may not have been available at press time.

In U.S. $	2017	2016	2015	2014	2013	2012
Revenue	2,119,479,000	2,666,797,000	4,151,770,000	6,411,382,000	6,939,938,000	9,236,128,000
R&D Expense	356,211,700	373,851,000	468,375,400	445,161,900	427,972,700	470,175,600
Operating Income	-594,544,900	-498,415,600	-484,600,200	22,817,900	-135,471,100	544,738,000
Operating Margin %	-28.05%	-18.68%	-11.67%	.35%	-1.95%	5.89%
SGA Expense	284,042,400	446,465,400	765,247,400	922,551,900	1,149,743,000	929,508,500
Net Income	-576,809,600	-360,302,400	-529,976,000	50,600,360	-45,166,500	572,553,400
Operating Cash Flow	-648,587,400	-328,210,200	-445,340,400	-11,595,720	-553,804,700	777,643,300
Capital Expenditure	8,971,339	23,094,680	36,883,280	55,188,580	105,043,000	179,874,800
EBITDA	-512,893,600	-382,688,800	-331,214,500	187,330,800	31,207,780	639,488,300
Return on Assets %	-19.92%	-9.08%	-10.59%	.88%	-.71%	7.39%
Return on Equity %	-39.56%	-18.11%	-21.40%	1.87%	-1.67%	18.46%
Debt to Equity						

CONTACT INFORMATION:
Phone: 886 33753252
Fax: 886 33753251
Toll-Free:
Address: 23 Xinghua Rd., Taoyuan, 330 Taiwan

STOCK TICKER/OTHER:
Stock Ticker: HTCCY
Employees: 17,413
Parent Company:

Exchange: GREY
Fiscal Year Ends: 12/31

SALARIES/BONUSES:
Top Exec. Salary: $ Bonus: $
Second Exec. Salary: $ Bonus: $

OTHER THOUGHTS:
Estimated Female Officers or Directors: 2
Hot Spot for Advancement for Women/Minorities:

Sales, profits and employees may be estimates. Financial information, benefits and other data can change quickly and may vary from those stated here.

Plunkett Research, Ltd.

Huawei Technologies Co Ltd

NAIC Code: 334210

www.huawei.com

TYPES OF BUSINESS:
Telecommunications Equipment Manufacturing
Network Equipment
Software
Wireless Technology
Smartphones
5G Wireless Technology

BRANDS/DIVISIONS/AFFILIATES:
Shenzhen Huawei Investment & Holding Co
Huawei Marine Networks
Huaewi Matebook
Huawei Watch 2
NB-IoT

CONTACTS:
Note: Officers with more than one job title may be intentionally listed here more than once.

Ren Zhengfei, Pres.
Ding Yun (Ryan Ding), Chief Prod. & Solutions Officer
Yu Chengdong (Richard Yu), Chief Strategy Officer
Chen Lifang, Corp. Sr. VP-Public Affairs & Comm. Dept.
Guo Ping, Chmn.-Finance Committee
Zhang Ping'an (Alex Zhang), CEO-Huawei Symantec
Hu Houkun (Ken Hu), Chmn.-Huawei USA
Sun Yafang, Chmn.
Wan Biao, Pres., Russia

GROWTH PLANS/SPECIAL FEATURES:
Huawei Technologies Co., Ltd., founded in 1987, is a leading global information and communications technology (ICT) solutions provider. Huawei is one of the world's leading manufacturers of smartphones. The company's ICT portfolio of end-to-end solutions in telecom and enterprise networks, devices and cloud computing are used in more than 170 countries and regions, serving more than one-third of the world's population. Huawei's consumer products include the Huawei brand of mobile smart phones, the Huawei Matebook notebook, the Huawei Watch 2 with 4G connectivity, mobile broadband, and smart home connected devices. The company's business products include switches, routers, WLAN (wireless local area network), servers, storage, cloud computing, network energy services and more. Its carrier products include wireless network, fixed network, cloud core network, carrier software, IT infrastructure and network energy global services. Business solutions and products serve the public safety, government, railway, power grid, finance, media/entertainment and education sectors. Joint venture Huawei Marine Networks (with Global Marine Systems Limited) manufactures submarine cable. Huawei Tech, along with Seven Network Limited, manages a 4G wireless network in Australia. Huawei Tech has research and development sites located in the U.S., Germany, Japan, Canada, Turkey, China, India, Sweden and Russia. The company operates as a subsidiary of Shenzhen Huawei Investment & Holding Co. Ltd. During 2017, Huawei Technologies created an NB-IoT city-aware network using a one network/one platform/N-tier applications model. NB-IoT stands for NarrowBand Internet of Things, and is a low-power, wide-area network radio technology standard that enables a wide range of devices and services to be connected using cellular telecommunications bands. Huawei is one of the world's leading manufacturers of smartphones. The company invests more than $12 billion yearly in research and development, and has one of the world's largest engineering teams. It is investing very heavily in 5G wireless technologies.

FINANCIAL DATA:
Note: Data for latest year may not have been available at press time.

In U.S. $	2017	2016	2015	2014	2013	2012
Revenue	92,080,000,000	78,200,000,000	60,100,000,000	46,000,000,000	39,463,000,000	35,353,000,000
R&D Expense						
Operating Income						
Operating Margin %						
SGA Expense						
Net Income		7,000,000,000	5,700,000,000	4,300,000,000	3,468,000,000	2,469,000,000
Operating Cash Flow						
Capital Expenditure						
EBITDA						
Return on Assets %						
Return on Equity %						
Debt to Equity						

CONTACT INFORMATION:
Phone: 86-755-28780808   Fax: 86-755-28789251
Toll-Free:
Address: Section H, Bantian, Longgang District, Shenzhen, Guangdong 518129 China

STOCK TICKER/OTHER:
Stock Ticker: Subsidiary   Exchange:
Employees: 160,000   Fiscal Year Ends: 12/31
Parent Company: Shenzhen Huawei Investment & Holding Co Ltd

SALARIES/BONUSES:
Top Exec. Salary: $ Bonus: $
Second Exec. Salary: $ Bonus: $

OTHER THOUGHTS:
Estimated Female Officers or Directors: 3
Hot Spot for Advancement for Women/Minorities: Y

Sales, profits and employees may be estimates. Financial information, benefits and other data can change quickly and may vary from those stated here.

Huntsman Corporation

www.huntsman.com

NAIC Code: 325211

TYPES OF BUSINESS:
Chemicals Manufacturing
Polyurethane Manufacturing
Advanced Materials & Surface Technologies
Performance Chemicals
Pigments

BRANDS/DIVISIONS/AFFILIATES:
Huntsman International LLC
Venator Materials PLC

CONTACTS:
Note: Officers with more than one job title may be intentionally listed here more than once.

Troy Keller, Assistant General Counsel
Brandon Gray, Vice President
Anthony Hankins, CEO, Geographical
Sean Douglas, CFO
Peter Huntsman, Chairman of the Board
Randy Wright, Chief Accounting Officer
Nolan Archibald, Director
J. Esplin, Executive VP, Divisional
David Stryker, Executive VP
Monte Edlund, President, Divisional
Scott Wright, President, Divisional
Rohit Aggarwal, President, Divisional
Ronald Gerrard, Senior VP, Divisional
R. Rogers, Senior VP, Divisional
Kevin Hardman, Vice President, Divisional
Pierre Poukens, Vice President, Divisional
Ivan Marcuse, Vice President, Divisional
Delaney Bellinger, Vice President

GROWTH PLANS/SPECIAL FEATURES:

Huntsman Corporation is a global manufacturer of differentiated organic chemical products and inorganic chemical products. The company operates all its businesses through wholly-owned subsidiary Huntsman International, LLC. The firm operates in four business segments: polyurethanes, advanced materials, textile effects and performance products. The polyurethanes segment produces MDI (Methylene diphenyl diisocyanate) products, propylene oxide, polyols, propylene glycol, thermoplastic urethane, aniline and methyl tert-butyl ether products. The advanced materials segment manufactures epoxy resin compounds and formulations; cross-linking, matting and curing agents; and epoxy, acrylic and polyurethane-based adhesives. The textile effects division produces textile chemicals and dyes. Last, the performance products segment is organized around three market groups: performance specialties, performance intermediates and maleic anhydride and licensing. It produces amines, carbonates and certain specialty surfactants; consumes internally produced and third-party-sourced base petrochemicals in the manufacture of its surfactants and ethanolamines products; licenses maleic anhydride manufacturing technology (mainly used in the production of fiberglass reinforced resins); and supplies butane fixed bed catalyst used in the manufacture of maleic anhydrides. In October 2017, the firm announced that it had terminated a proposed merger with Clariant AG, based in Switzerland. Earlier that year, Huntsman spun off its pigments and additives division as Venator Materials PLC in an initial public offering on the New York Stock Exchange under ticker symbol VNTR. Venator is based in the U.K.

FINANCIAL DATA:
Note: Data for latest year may not have been available at press time.

In U.S. $	2017	2016	2015	2014	2013	2012
Revenue	8,358,000,000	9,657,000,000	10,299,000,000	11,578,000,000	11,079,000,000	11,187,000,000
R&D Expense	138,000,000	152,000,000	160,000,000	158,000,000	140,000,000	152,000,000
Operating Income	899,000,000	746,000,000	707,000,000	791,000,000	661,000,000	937,000,000
Operating Margin %	10.75%	7.72%	6.86%	6.83%	5.96%	8.37%
SGA Expense	798,000,000	920,000,000	982,000,000	974,000,000	942,000,000	951,000,000
Net Income	636,000,000	326,000,000	93,000,000	323,000,000	128,000,000	363,000,000
Operating Cash Flow	1,219,000,000	1,088,000,000	575,000,000	760,000,000	708,000,000	774,000,000
Capital Expenditure	282,000,000	421,000,000	663,000,000	601,000,000	471,000,000	412,000,000
EBITDA	1,131,000,000	1,082,000,000	780,000,000	1,054,000,000	917,000,000	1,205,000,000
Return on Assets %	6.54%	3.42%	.89%	3.19%	1.41%	4.13%
Return on Equity %	32.55%	23.89%	5.77%	17.19%	6.82%	21.13%
Debt to Equity	0.86	3.21	3.20	2.77	1.83	1.92

CONTACT INFORMATION:
Phone: 281-719-6000   Fax:
Toll-Free:
Address: 10003 Woodloch Forest Dr., The Woodlands, TX 77380 United States

STOCK TICKER/OTHER:
Stock Ticker: HUN
Employees: 15,000
Parent Company:

Exchange: NYS
Fiscal Year Ends: 12/31

SALARIES/BONUSES:
Top Exec. Salary: $1,700,000   Bonus: $850,000
Second Exec. Salary: $1,325,000   Bonus: $

OTHER THOUGHTS:
Estimated Female Officers or Directors: 2
Hot Spot for Advancement for Women/Minorities:

Hyundai Engineering & Construction Company Ltd

www.hdec.co.kr
NAIC Code: 237000

TYPES OF BUSINESS:
Construction, Heavy & Civil Engineering
Power Plant Construction
Highway & Bridge Construction
Residential Construction
Commercial Construction

BRANDS/DIVISIONS/AFFILIATES:
Hillstate
Hyundai Engineering Co Ltd

CONTACTS:
Note: Officers with more than one job title may be intentionally listed here more than once.
Soo-Hyun Jung, CEO

GROWTH PLANS/SPECIAL FEATURES:

Hyundai Engineering & Construction Company Ltd. (HDEC) is an international construction company based in South Korea. HDEC has expertise in a variety of structures, such as civil works, highways and bridges, housing, shipyards, dams, power plants (including nuclear power), airports, stadiums, hotels and retail complexes. The company is organized into four divisions: infra and environment works, building works, plant works and power and energy works. The infra and environment works division is responsible for the engineering and construction of roads, bridges, harbor, railways, highways and other infrastructure developments across Korea and overseas. Its major projects include the Gyeongbu Expressway, the Honam High-speed Railway, the Soyang Multi-Purpose Dam, Busan Harbor, Pattani-Narathiwat Highway in Thailand and Jaber Causeway Marine Bridge in Kuwait. The building works division builds skyscrapers, sports/leisure facilities, residential housing and other large-scale architectural projects in both the Korean and international markets. Some of its notable projects include Hamad Medical Center in Qatar, the Hwaseong Stadium in Korea, the Jangbogo Antarctic Research Station, the Four Seasons Hotel in Cairo and the National Center for Korean Traditional Performing Arts. The plant works division constructs hydrocarbon processing and industrial plants, including LNG receiving terminals, LNG supply pipelines, nuclear energy power plant, multi-purpose water gate facilities and integrated steel works. Last, the power and energy works division constructs power and desalination plants and overseas operations. This division is also expanding into the renewable energy business with developments in photovoltaic, wind velocity and nuclear energy abroad in Africa, Central America and South America. Subsidiaries of the company include Hyundai Engineering Co., Ltd.; and Hyundai Hillstate, a construction company.

FINANCIAL DATA:
Note: Data for latest year may not have been available at press time.

In U.S. $	2017	2016	2015	2014	2013	2012
Revenue	15,813,200,000	15,577,174,000	15,914,919,000	15,064,930,625	13,490,214,000	12,675,900,000
R&D Expense						
Operating Income						
Operating Margin %						
SGA Expense						
Net Income	188,871,000	605,472,000	549,257,000	363,618,739	487,526,647	485,000,000
Operating Cash Flow						
Capital Expenditure						
EBITDA						
Return on Assets %						
Return on Equity %						
Debt to Equity						

CONTACT INFORMATION:
Phone: 82-2-746-1114   Fax: 82-2-743-8963
Toll-Free:
Address: Bldg 75, Yulgok-ro, Jongno-gu, Seoul, 03058 South Korea

SALARIES/BONUSES:
Top Exec. Salary: $ Bonus: $
Second Exec. Salary: $ Bonus: $

STOCK TICKER/OTHER:
Stock Ticker: 720   Exchange: Seoul
Employees: 59,481   Fiscal Year Ends: 12/31
Parent Company:

OTHER THOUGHTS:
Estimated Female Officers or Directors:
Hot Spot for Advancement for Women/Minorities:

Sales, profits and employees may be estimates. Financial information, benefits and other data can change quickly and may vary from those stated here.

Hyundai Motor Company

NAIC Code: 336111

worldwide.hyundai.com

TYPES OF BUSINESS:
Automobile Manufacturing
Trucks
Buses
Light Commercial Vehicles
Machine Tools
Factory Automation Equipment
Material Handling Equipment
Specialty Vehicle Manufacturing

BRANDS/DIVISIONS/AFFILIATES:
Accent
Sonata
Elantra
Xcient
i30 N
Kia Motors Corporation
Hyundai Motor America
Hyundai Capital Germany GmbH

CONTACTS: *Note: Officers with more than one job title may be intentionally listed here more than once.*

Won Hee Lee, Pres.
Choong Ho Kim, Co-CEO
Mong-koo Chung, Chmn.

GROWTH PLANS/SPECIAL FEATURES:

Hyundai Motor Company, headquartered in South Korea, is one of the world's leading automobile manufacturers. The firm designs and manufactures passenger cars; recreational vehicles; commercial vehicles, including trucks, buses and tractors; and specialty vehicles, including crane trucks, refrigerated vans and tank trucks for fuel and water transport. Popular export models include the Accent, a sub-compact; the Sonata, a mid-size sedan; the Elantra, a compact sedan; the Santa Fe SUV; and the Tucson SUV. Light commercial vehicles include the H-1 cargo van, the Xcient truck and a variety of mini buses. Heavy commercial vehicles include small/medium size HD36L, HD35-78 and HD120 trucks and busses as well as cargo, dump, mixer and tractor trucks. New cars in 2018 include the i30 N, providing the feeling of driving a racecar with up to 275 horsepower and high-performance cornering capabilities; the KONA, a compact SUV; and the IONIQ line of electric and hybrid sedans. Hyundai also makes machine tools for factory automation and material handling and owns approximately 34% of Kia Motors Corporation. Subsidiary Hyundai Motor America oversees U.S. operations, including primary facilities in Alabama, Michigan and California. The subsidiary also distributes Hyundai vehicles in the U.S. In addition to its U.S. operations, the firm has other overseas plants in Brazil, Turkey, the Czech Republic, Russia, India and China, as well as research and development centers in North America, Japan and Europe. The company offers automotive financing services to European customers through joint venture Hyundai Capital Germany GmbH.

FINANCIAL DATA: *Note: Data for latest year may not have been available at press time.*

In U.S. $	2017	2016	2015	2014	2013	2012
Revenue		87,481,570,000	85,902,610,000	83,378,150,000	81,557,810,000	78,906,790,000
R&D Expense		952,067,300	868,080,400	740,509,100	675,135,000	641,388,100
Operating Income		4,851,471,000	5,939,193,000	7,052,766,000	7,767,863,000	7,881,314,000
Operating Margin %		5.54%	6.91%	8.45%	9.52%	9.98%
SGA Expense		3,295,141,000	3,073,318,000	3,116,049,000	3,067,349,000	3,142,365,000
Net Income		5,050,383,000	5,994,678,000	6,862,967,000	7,979,294,000	7,997,968,000
Operating Cash Flow		931,306,800	1,166,198,000	1,981,172,000	1,128,880,000	4,988,030,000
Capital Expenditure		4,091,437,000	8,743,452,000	4,414,661,000	3,888,049,000	3,548,477,000
EBITDA		10,217,680,000	10,754,430,000	11,958,350,000	13,628,430,000	13,597,150,000
Return on Assets %		3.14%	4.10%	5.23%	6.70%	7.41%
Return on Equity %		8.36%	10.72%	13.40%	17.80%	21.10%
Debt to Equity		0.74	0.72	0.65	0.65	0.69

CONTACT INFORMATION:
Phone: 82 234641114 Fax: 82 234643477
Toll-Free:
Address: 12 Heolleung-ro Seocho-gu, Seoul, 06797 South Korea

STOCK TICKER/OTHER:
Stock Ticker: HYMLF
Employees: 61,410
Parent Company:

Exchange: PINX
Fiscal Year Ends: 12/31

SALARIES/BONUSES:
Top Exec. Salary: $ Bonus: $
Second Exec. Salary: $ Bonus: $

OTHER THOUGHTS:
Estimated Female Officers or Directors:
Hot Spot for Advancement for Women/Minorities:

IBM Global Business Services

935.ibm.com/services/us/gbs/consulting/

NAIC Code: 541513

www-

TYPES OF BUSINESS:
Computer Facilities Management Services
Software Applications Management
Computer Operations Outsourcing
Business and IT Consulting
Consulting
Application Management

BRANDS/DIVISIONS/AFFILIATES:
International Business Machines Corporation (IBM)
IBM Global Process Services
IBM Cnnsulting

CONTACTS: Note: Officers with more than one job title may be intentionally listed here more than once.
Mark Foster, Sr. VP-Global Business Services
Robert C. Weber, Sr. VP-Legal & Regulatory Affairs
Bob Moffat, Sr. VP-Integrated Oper.
Colleen Arnold, Sr. VP-Application Mgmt. Services
Bridget van Kralingen, Sr. VP-Global Business Services

GROWTH PLANS/SPECIAL FEATURES:

IBM Global Business Services (GBS) provides consulting, computer application management services and global business process services. These professional services deliver business value and innovation to clients through solutions which leverage industry, technology and business process expertise. GBS positions itself as a digital reinvention partner for clients, combining industry knowledge, functional expertise, and applications with the power of IBM's additional capabilities, such as systems design, artificial intelligence/analytics and cloud computing. GBS services are backed by its globally integrated delivery network and integration with the full array of IBM solutions and services including Watson supercomputing. To deepen its capabilities, in 2016 IBM acquired four consulting and design firms to enhance the GBS global network of 35 digital experience design studios. IBM also announced Watson IoT (internet of things) Consulting Solutions, a new practice that brings together IBM's industry and technical expertise to help clients introduce IoT innovation into their businesses. GBS provides business consulting services focused on bringing to market solutions that help clients shape their digital blueprints and customer experiences, define their cognitive operating models, set their next-generation talent strategies and create new technology visions and architectures in a cloud environment. GBS application management delivers system integration, software application services, maintenance and support. It offers advanced capabilities in areas such as security and privacy, application testing and modernization, cloud application migration and automation. GBS' business process outsourcing service line, delivers finance, procurement, HR, and industry-specific business processes. These services deliver improved business results to clients through the strategic change and/or operation of the client's business processes, applications and infrastructure. GBS is redefining the efficiency and cost profiles of clients' core processes through the application of the power of Watson, cognitive and deep analytics.

FINANCIAL DATA: Note: Data for latest year may not have been available at press time.

In U.S. $	2017	2016	2015	2014	2013	2012
Revenue	16,348,000,000	16,700,000,000	17,166,000,000			
R&D Expense						
Operating Income						
Operating Margin %						
SGA Expense						
Net Income	1,401,000,000	1,732,000,000				
Operating Cash Flow						
Capital Expenditure						
EBITDA						
Return on Assets %						
Return on Equity %						
Debt to Equity						

CONTACT INFORMATION:
Phone: 914-499-1900   Fax: 914-765-7382
Toll-Free: 800-426-4968
Address: 1 New Orchard Rd., Armonk, NY 10504-1722 United States

SALARIES/BONUSES:
Top Exec. Salary: $ Bonus: $
Second Exec. Salary: $ Bonus: $

STOCK TICKER/OTHER:
Stock Ticker: Subsidiary   Exchange:
Employees: 100,000   Fiscal Year Ends: 12/31
Parent Company: International Business Machines Corporation (IBM)

OTHER THOUGHTS:
Estimated Female Officers or Directors: 1
Hot Spot for Advancement for Women/Minorities: Y

Sales, profits and employees may be estimates. Financial information, benefits and other data can change quickly and may vary from those stated here.

IBM Research

www.research.ibm.com

NAIC Code: 541712

TYPES OF BUSINESS:
Research & Development
Computing
Software
Networks, Servers & Embedded Systems
Materials Science
Nanomechanics
Display Technology
Semiconductor & Storage Technology

BRANDS/DIVISIONS/AFFILIATES:
International Business Machines Corporation (IBM)
Hyperledger Project
IBM Quantum Experience

CONTACTS:
Note: Officers with more than one job title may be intentionally listed here more than once.

Arvind Krishna, Sr. VP
T.C. Chen, VP-Science

GROWTH PLANS/SPECIAL FEATURES:
IBM Research is the R&D arm of International Business Machines Corporation (IBM). The company often works with private customers and academic and government research centers. Featured research areas include: blockchain, a distributed ledger technology based on the IBM Research-backed Hyperledger Project with the potential to build trust and security into every business transaction on a global basis; artificial intelligence (AI) and cognitive computing, which focuses on using AI to augment human intelligence and decision-making, via the building of cognitive systems that reason, draw insights and analyze data; and quantum computing, which harnesses the power of nature to address problems unsolvable with today's systems. Quantum computing includes IBM's first quantum computing platform on the cloud, the IBM Quantum Experience, which deliver solutions for business and science challenges where patterns cannot be seen nor explored by current classical computers. These challenges range from drug discovery to machine learning. Quantum computers are based on the properties of quantum physics, and can explore an exponential number of possibilities. Industries served by the firm include aerospace/defense, automotive, banking, chemical/petroleum, consumer products, education, electronics, energy/utilities, finance, government, healthcare, insurance, life sciences, manufacturing, construction, retail, telecommunications, media/entertainment and travel/transport. During 2017, IBM inventors received a record 9,043 patents, marking the company's 25th consecutive year of U.S. patent leadership, crossing the 100,000-patent milestone. Nearly half of the patents granted to IBM in 2017 are pioneering advancements in AI, cloud computing, cybersecurity, blockchain and quantum computing.

FINANCIAL DATA:
Note: Data for latest year may not have been available at press time.

In U.S. $	2017	2016	2015	2014	2013	2012
Revenue						
R&D Expense						
Operating Income						
Operating Margin %						
SGA Expense						
Net Income						
Operating Cash Flow						
Capital Expenditure						
EBITDA						
Return on Assets %						
Return on Equity %						
Debt to Equity						

CONTACT INFORMATION:
Phone: 914-945-3000 Fax: 914-945-2141
Toll-Free:
Address: 1101 Kitchawan Rd., Rte. 134, Yorktown Heights, NY 10598 United States

STOCK TICKER/OTHER:
Stock Ticker: Subsidiary Exchange:
Employees: 3,000 Fiscal Year Ends: 12/31
Parent Company: International Business Machines Corporation (IBM)

SALARIES/BONUSES:
Top Exec. Salary: $ Bonus: $
Second Exec. Salary: $ Bonus: $

OTHER THOUGHTS:
Estimated Female Officers or Directors:
Hot Spot for Advancement for Women/Minorities:

Sales, profits and employees may be estimates. Financial information, benefits and other data can change quickly and may vary from those stated here.

IDOM

NAIC Code: 541330

www.idom.com

TYPES OF BUSINESS:
Engineering Consulting Services

BRANDS/DIVISIONS/AFFILIATES:

CONTACTS: Note: Officers with more than one job title may be intentionally listed here more than once.
Luis Rodriguez Llopis, Pres.

GROWTH PLANS/SPECIAL FEATURES:

IDOM provides engineering services through 11 divisions. The advanced engineering division designs and constructs testing facilities, complex industrial infrastructures and non-conventional structures. The architecture division provides integrated project management service for various building projects, as well as technical support for each project phase. The consulting division offers logistics infrastructure advisory services and solutions; assists in decision-making; advises on project investments; develops IT specific to client needs and requirements; and provides supply chain management support in all areas of the operations process. The energy division provides engineering, construction and maintenance services and solutions in relation to fossil fuel plants, solar power plants, biomass and waste-to-energy plants, wind farms, photovoltaic power stations and geothermal power stations. The environment division provides a wide range of engineering solutions regarding waste, water, sustainable demolition of industrial ruins, contaminated soil/air and green infrastructure. The industry division offers diverse manufacturing services tailored for manufacturing and industrial projects; develops projects for the refining, petrochemical, compressed and liquefied gas sectors; and design and engineering for the metals and minerals sectors. The nuclear division designs, engineers and constructs power plants, thermonuclear reactors; provides engineering, procurement, construction (EPC) and management; and offers project management consultancy. The telecommunications division provides support and services for telecom development, both regional and country, including master plans, feasibility studies, network, infrastructure design, data centers, smart cities and more. The city & territory division plans and designs: new cities, urban transformation, territorial development, smart growth infrastructure and climate change infrastructure. The transport division design, engineers and constructs urban transportation systems, metro systems, roads, rail systems and airports. Last, the water division offers planning, consultancy and infrastructure construction and solutions in connection with water and resources, including treatment facilities, dams, hydropower, rivers, irrigation and flood mitigation.

FINANCIAL DATA: Note: Data for latest year may not have been available at press time.

In U.S. $	2017	2016	2015	2014	2013	2012
Revenue	383,316,000	350,000,000				
R&D Expense						
Operating Income						
Operating Margin %						
SGA Expense						
Net Income						
Operating Cash Flow						
Capital Expenditure						
EBITDA						
Return on Assets %						
Return on Equity %						
Debt to Equity						

CONTACT INFORMATION:
Phone: 34-94-479-7600 Fax: 34-94-476-1804
Toll-Free:
Address: Avda, Zarandoa 23, Bilbao, 48015 Spain

STOCK TICKER/OTHER:
Stock Ticker: Private
Employees: 2,500
Parent Company:

Exchange:
Fiscal Year Ends:

SALARIES/BONUSES:
Top Exec. Salary: $ Bonus: $
Second Exec. Salary: $ Bonus: $

OTHER THOUGHTS:
Estimated Female Officers or Directors:
Hot Spot for Advancement for Women/Minorities:

Sales, profits and employees may be estimates. Financial information, benefits and other data can change quickly and may vary from those stated here.

ILF Consulting Engineers Austria GmbH

www.ilf.com

NAIC Code: 541330

TYPES OF BUSINESS:
Engineering Consulting Services

BRANDS/DIVISIONS/AFFILIATES:

CONTACTS: *Note: Officers with more than one job title may be intentionally listed here more than once.*
Klaus Lasser, CEO
Markus Steiner, CFO
Thomas Fritz, CMO

GROWTH PLANS/SPECIAL FEATURES:
ILF Consulting Engineers Austria GmbH consists of several international and independent engineering and consulting firms that undertake complex industrial and infrastructure projects. The firm's main offices are in Austria and Germany, with more than 40 subsidiary offices strategically-located worldwide. The business areas of focus include: oil and gas, water and environment, energy and climate protection, and transportation and structures. Within oil and gas, ILF has worked on upstream facilities, pipeline systems, underground storage facilities, tank farms and terminals, and refineries and petrochemical plants. The water and environment business area has included projects such as hydropower plants, water transmission systems, water supply and wastewater networks, and water and wastewater treatment plants. Expertise within the energy and climate protection business includes thermal power plants, desalination plants, renewable energy, climate protection, and power transmission and distribution systems. Within the transportation and structures business area, ILF has worked on airports, roads, railways, urban transportation systems, tunnels, caverns, buildings, structures and Alpine resorts. Engineering and consulting services offered by the firm encompass consultancy, design, planning, procurement, supervision, start-up, project management and special services. ILF has executed more than 6,000 projects in more than 150 countries.

FINANCIAL DATA: *Note: Data for latest year may not have been available at press time.*

In U.S. $	2017	2016	2015	2014	2013	2012
Revenue						
R&D Expense						
Operating Income						
Operating Margin %						
SGA Expense						
Net Income						
Operating Cash Flow						
Capital Expenditure						
EBITDA						
Return on Assets %						
Return on Equity %						
Debt to Equity						

CONTACT INFORMATION:
Phone: 43-512-24120   Fax: 43-512-24125900
Toll-Free:
Address: Feldkreuzstrasse 3, Rum/Innsbruck, 6063 Austria

STOCK TICKER/OTHER:
Stock Ticker: Private   Exchange:
Employees: 2,000   Fiscal Year Ends:
Parent Company:

SALARIES/BONUSES:
Top Exec. Salary: $ Bonus: $
Second Exec. Salary: $ Bonus: $

OTHER THOUGHTS:
Estimated Female Officers or Directors:
Hot Spot for Advancement for Women/Minorities:

Illinois Tool Works Inc

NAIC Code: 333249

www.itw.com

TYPES OF BUSINESS:
Industrial Products & Equipment
Steel, Plastic & Paper Products
Power Systems & Electronics
Transportation-Related Components, Fasteners, Fluids & Polymers
Construction-Related Fasteners & Tools
Food Equipment & Adhesives
Decorative Surfacing Materials
Adhesives, Sealants & Lubrication

BRANDS/DIVISIONS/AFFILIATES:

CONTACTS:
Note: Officers with more than one job title may be intentionally listed here more than once.

E. Santi, CEO
Michael Larsen, CFO
Randall Scheuneman, Chief Accounting Officer
Michael Zimmerman, Executive VP
Lei Zhang Schlitz, Executive VP
John Hartnett, Executive VP
Juan Valls, Executive VP
Roland Martel, Executive VP
Steven Martindale, Executive VP
Sundaram Nagarajan, Executive VP
Norman Finch, General Counsel
Mary Lawler, Other Executive Officer
Christopher OHerlihy, Vice Chairman

GROWTH PLANS/SPECIAL FEATURES:

Illinois Tool Works, Inc. is a multinational manufacturer of a diversified range of industrial products and equipment, with operations in 56 countries. It operates in seven primary segments: automotive OEM, test & measurement and electronics, food equipment, polymers and fluids, welding, construction products and specialty products. The automotive OEM segment produces components and fasteners for automotive-related applications. Products include plastic and metal components, fasteners and assemblies for automobiles, light trucks and other industrial uses. The test & measurement and electronics segment produces equipment, consumables and related software for testing and measuring of materials and structures as well as equipment and consumables used in the production of electronic subassemblies and microelectronics. The food equipment division provides commercial food equipment and related services. Products include warewashing equipment; cooking and refrigeration equipment; food processing equipment; and kitchen exhaust, ventilation and pollution control systems. The polymer and fluids segment offers adhesives, sealants, lubrication and cutting fluids, janitorial and hygiene products and fluids and polymers for auto aftermarket maintenance and appearance. The welding segment produces arc welding equipment, consumables and accessories for a wide array of industrial and commercial applications. The construction products segment produces tools, fasteners and other products for construction applications. Products include packaged hardware, fasteners, anchors and other products for retail. Finally, the specialty products segment produces beverage packaging equipment and consumables; product coding and marking equipment and consumables; and appliance components and fasteners.

FINANCIAL DATA:
Note: Data for latest year may not have been available at press time.

In U.S. $	2017	2016	2015	2014	2013	2012
Revenue	14,314,000,000	13,599,000,000	13,405,000,000	14,484,000,000	14,135,000,000	17,924,000,000
R&D Expense						
Operating Income	3,494,000,000	3,064,000,000	2,869,000,000	2,891,000,000	2,516,000,000	2,849,000,000
Operating Margin %	24.40%	22.53%	21.40%	19.95%	17.79%	15.89%
SGA Expense	2,305,000,000	2,415,000,000	2,417,000,000	2,678,000,000	2,815,000,000	3,332,000,000
Net Income	1,687,000,000	2,035,000,000	1,899,000,000	2,946,000,000	1,679,000,000	2,870,000,000
Operating Cash Flow	2,402,000,000	2,302,000,000	2,299,000,000	1,616,000,000	2,528,000,000	2,072,000,000
Capital Expenditure	297,000,000	273,000,000	284,000,000	361,000,000	368,000,000	382,000,000
EBITDA	3,992,000,000	3,615,000,000	3,422,000,000	3,456,000,000	3,199,000,000	4,430,000,000
Return on Assets %	10.54%	13.15%	11.36%	15.65%	8.55%	15.39%
Return on Equity %	38.17%	42.94%	31.53%	35.66%	16.57%	27.89%
Debt to Equity	1.63	1.68	1.32	0.87	0.28	0.43

CONTACT INFORMATION:
Phone: 847 724-7500   Fax: 847 657-4261
Toll-Free:
Address: 155 Harlem Ave., Glenview, IL 60025 United States

STOCK TICKER/OTHER:
Stock Ticker: ITW
Employees: 50,000
Parent Company:

Exchange: NYS
Fiscal Year Ends: 12/31

SALARIES/BONUSES:
Top Exec. Salary: $1,253,684   Bonus: $
Second Exec. Salary: $727,341   Bonus: $

OTHER THOUGHTS:
Estimated Female Officers or Directors: 4
Hot Spot for Advancement for Women/Minorities: Y

Sales, profits and employees may be estimates. Financial information, benefits and other data can change quickly and may vary from those stated here.

IMI plc

NAIC Code: 333996

www.imiplc.com

TYPES OF BUSINESS:
Machinery Manufacturing
Fluid Controls
HVAC Components

BRANDS/DIVISIONS/AFFILIATES:
IMI Critical Engineering
IMI Presicion Engineering
IMI Hydronic Engineering
IMI CCI
IMI Truflo Marine
IMI Norgren
IMI Flow Design
Bimba Manufacturing Company

CONTACTS:
Note: Officers with more than one job title may be intentionally listed here more than once.

Mark Selway, CEO
Daniel Shook, Dir.-Finance
Geoff Tranfield, Dir.-Human Resources
John OShea, Corp. Sec.
Mark Shellenbarger, Global VP-Bus. Dev.
Ivan Ronald, Group Financial Controller
Robert Guerra, Pres., Norgren Americas
Brendan Colgan, Pres., Fluid Power
Peter Spencer, Pres., Indoor Climate
Michael Preinerstorfer, Regional VP-European Sales
Daniel Nowack, Dir.-Global Procurement

GROWTH PLANS/SPECIAL FEATURES:

IMI plc (which stands for Imperial Metal Industries) is an engineering holding firm focused on the movement and control of fluids in critical applications. The company has manufacturing facilities in more than 20 countries, and operates its global network through three divisions: IMI Critical Engineering, IMI Precision Engineering and IMI Hydronic Engineering. IMI Critical Engineering provides critical flow control solutions for the energy and process industries. The main markets for this division are the oil and gas, fossil power, nuclear power, petrochemical and iron and steel markets. The segment's products are sold under brand names such as IMI CCI, IMI Bopp & Reuther, IMI Fluid Kinetics, IMI InterAtiva, IMI NH, IMI Orton, IMI Remosa, IMI STI, IMI SSF, IMI Th Jansen, IMI Truflo Marine, IMI Truflo Rona and IMI Z&J. The IMI Precision Engineering division creates technologies related to the control of air and other fluids for the commercial vehicle, rail, food and beverage, life sciences, energy and pneumatic industries. Products in this division are marketed under brand names such as MI Norgren, IMI Buschjost, IMI FAS, IMI Herion and MI Maxseal. Last, IMI Hydronic Engineering is a global supplier of hydronic distribution systems that provide energy-efficient heating and cooling systems to the residential and commercial building sectors. Its products are marketed under brand names such as IMI TA, IMI Flow Design, IMI Heimeier and IMI Pneumatex brands. In February 2018, IMI acquired Bimba Manufacturing Company, which was merged into the precision engineering division.

FINANCIAL DATA:
Note: Data for latest year may not have been available at press time.

In U.S. $	2017	2016	2015	2014	2013	2012
Revenue	2,493,947,000	2,360,062,000	2,217,633,000	2,409,913,000	2,482,552,000	3,119,214,000
R&D Expense						
Operating Income	316,906,400	303,090,700	318,900,400	387,978,900	425,438,000	479,418,900
Operating Margin %	12.70%	12.84%	14.38%	16.09%	17.13%	15.36%
SGA Expense	754,878,200		642,216,200	666,999,000	674,547,800	805,298,400
Net Income	230,878,800	186,298,200	181,740,500	952,143,500	318,900,400	328,443,200
Operating Cash Flow	304,942,300	358,353,500	345,962,100	167,497,500	454,778,500	301,096,700
Capital Expenditure	99,416,040	100,982,800	100,555,500	100,840,300	76,057,540	66,799,600
EBITDA	380,715,000	360,917,200	362,768,800	458,339,300	489,531,400	589,232,300
Return on Assets %	9.96%	8.20%	8.76%	43.48%	13.07%	13.34%
Return on Equity %	28.17%	24.01%	24.18%	120.42%	36.21%	38.42%
Debt to Equity	0.36	0.63	0.53	0.42	0.34	0.37

CONTACT INFORMATION:
Phone: 44 1217173700
Fax: 44 1217173701
Toll-Free:
Address: Lakeside, Solihull Parkway, Birmingham, B37 7XZ United Kingdom

STOCK TICKER/OTHER:
Stock Ticker: IMIAF
Employees: 10,670
Parent Company:

Exchange: PINX
Fiscal Year Ends: 12/31

SALARIES/BONUSES:
Top Exec. Salary: $1,140,863   Bonus: $2,172,055
Second Exec. Salary: $659,450   Bonus: $770,546

OTHER THOUGHTS:
Estimated Female Officers or Directors: 3
Hot Spot for Advancement for Women/Minorities: Y

Infineon Technologies AG

NAIC Code: 334413

www.infineon.com

TYPES OF BUSINESS:
Semiconductor Manufacturing
Fiber-Optic Components
GPS Microchips
Embedded Memory Products
Broadband Components

BRANDS/DIVISIONS/AFFILIATES:
Infineon Technologies Asia Pacific Pte Ltd
Infineon Technologies Japan KK
Infineon Technologies North America Corp
LS Power Semitech Co Ltd

CONTACTS:
Note: Officers with more than one job title may be intentionally listed here more than once.

Reinhard Ploss, CEO
Dominik Asam, CFO
Arunjai Mittal, Exec. VP-Strategy Dev.
Klaus Walther, Corp. VP-Comm. & Public Authorities & Associations
Reinhard Ploss, Chmn.

GROWTH PLANS/SPECIAL FEATURES:

Infineon Technologies AG designs, develops, manufactures and markets semiconductors and complete system solutions. The company is organized into four principal operating segments: chip card and security, automotive, power management and multimarket and industrial power control. Infineon's chip card and security segment designs, develops, manufactures and markets a wide range of security controllers and security memories for chip card and security applications. These products include security memory integrated circuits (ICs) in prepaid telecom cards and access and transportation cards; contact-based and contactless security microcontroller ICs for identification documents, payment cards, SIM cards and Pay-TV applications; Trusted Platform Module products in computers and networks; and RFID ICs for object identification. The automotive segment designs, develops, manufactures and markets semiconductors safety management, powertrain applications and body and convenience systems. The power management and multimarket segment comprises products such as cellular infrastructure, Light management and LED lighting systems, micro-inverter for photovoltaic rooftop systems, mobile devices (navigation devices, smartphones, tablets) and power supplies for consumer electronic devices. Last, the industrial power control segment's products include charger stations for electric vehicles, energy transmission and conversion (offshore windpark HVDC lines and flexible AC transmission systems), home appliances, industrial drives (air conditioning, automation, drives, elevators, escalators), industrial vehicles (agricultural vehicles, forklifts, heavy construction, hybrid buses, mining vehicles), renewable energy generation, traction (high-speed trains, locomotives, metro trains, trams) and uninterruptable power supplies. Infineon's subsidiaries include Infineon Technologies Asia Pacific Pte. Ltd., Infineon Technologies Japan K.K., Infineon Technologies North America Corp. and LS Power Semitech Co. Ltd.

FINANCIAL DATA:
Note: Data for latest year may not have been available at press time.

In U.S. $	2017	2016	2015	2014	2013	2012
Revenue	8,722,123,000	7,993,529,000	7,156,264,000	5,334,782,000	4,745,734,000	4,821,063,000
R&D Expense	958,285,000	950,875,600	885,425,700	679,196,900	648,324,200	561,881,000
Operating Income	1,213,910,000	942,231,200	718,713,700	648,324,200	429,746,400	561,881,000
Operating Margin %	13.91%	11.78%	10.04%	12.15%	9.05%	11.65%
SGA Expense	1,011,386,000	976,808,500	960,754,800	582,874,400	548,297,100	586,579,100
Net Income	975,573,600	918,768,100	780,458,900	660,673,300	335,893,700	527,303,700
Operating Cash Flow	2,127,738,000	1,594,260,000	1,008,916,000	1,211,440,000	742,176,900	789,103,200
Capital Expenditure	1,262,071,000	1,020,030,000	969,399,100	824,915,500	466,793,500	1,099,064,000
EBITDA	2,232,705,000	1,982,020,000	1,639,952,000	1,299,118,000	1,016,325,000	1,136,111,000
Return on Assets %	8.30%	8.34%	8.32%	8.66%	4.60%	7.25%
Return on Equity %	14.82%	15.36%	14.33%	13.49%	7.40%	12.32%
Debt to Equity	0.26	0.34	0.37	0.03	0.04	0.06

CONTACT INFORMATION:
Phone: 49-89-234-0 Fax: 49-89-2349553431
Toll-Free: 49-800-951-951-951
Address: Am Campeon 1-12, Neubiberg, 85579 Germany

STOCK TICKER/OTHER:
Stock Ticker: IFNNF Exchange: PINX
Employees: 37,479 Fiscal Year Ends: 09/30
Parent Company:

SALARIES/BONUSES:
Top Exec. Salary: $ Bonus: $
Second Exec. Salary: $ Bonus: $

OTHER THOUGHTS:
Estimated Female Officers or Directors:
Hot Spot for Advancement for Women/Minorities:

Sales, profits and employees may be estimates. Financial information, benefits and other data can change quickly and may vary from those stated here.

Ingenium Group Inc

NAIC Code: 541330

theingeniumgroup.com

TYPES OF BUSINESS:
Engineering Consulting Services

BRANDS/DIVISIONS/AFFILIATES:
NORR
Cion/Coulter

GROWTH PLANS/SPECIAL FEATURES:
Ingenium Group, Inc. is an integrated consulting, design-build and partnership solutions firm. The companies that comprise the group are NORR and Cion/Coulter. NORR is a full-service consulting organization that provides architectural, engineering, interiors and planning services on various building types worldwide. Its architectural design work has ranged from spiraling, 40-storey buildings in Kuwait, to fire stations in Canada. Cion/Coulter provides technical services, consulting engineering services and software solutions tailored to the property and facilities management industry. Its key areas of expertise for commercial, industrial, retail, and corporate real estate include: building sciences, drawing and document management, area certification and CADD (computer-aided design and drafting) services and innovative software. Ingenium has offices in Canada, India, the U.K. and the U.S.

CONTACTS:
Note: Officers with more than one job title may be intentionally listed here more than once.

Brian Gerstmar, Pres.

FINANCIAL DATA:
Note: Data for latest year may not have been available at press time.

In U.S. $	2017	2016	2015	2014	2013	2012
Revenue						
R&D Expense						
Operating Income						
Operating Margin %						
SGA Expense						
Net Income						
Operating Cash Flow						
Capital Expenditure						
EBITDA						
Return on Assets %						
Return on Equity %						
Debt to Equity						

CONTACT INFORMATION:
Phone: 416-675-5950   Fax: 416-798-5495
Toll-Free: 800-567-8918
Address: 30 International Blvd., Unit 4, Toronto, ON M9W 1A2 Canada

STOCK TICKER/OTHER:
Stock Ticker: Private   Exchange:
Employees: 900   Fiscal Year Ends:
Parent Company:

SALARIES/BONUSES:
Top Exec. Salary: $ Bonus: $
Second Exec. Salary: $ Bonus: $

OTHER THOUGHTS:
Estimated Female Officers or Directors:
Hot Spot for Advancement for Women/Minorities:

Sales, profits and employees may be estimates. Financial information, benefits and other data can change quickly and may vary from those stated here.

Ingersoll-Rand plc

NAIC Code: 333400

company.ingersollrand.com

TYPES OF BUSINESS:
Refrigeration Systems & Controls
Heating, Ventilation & Air Conditioning (HVAC) Systems
Stationary & Mobile Food Refrigeration Systems
Industrial Products-Compressed Air Systems
Golf Carts & Utility Vehicles
Security Products-Doors & Locks
Electronic & Biometric Access Control Systems & Software
Time, Attendance & Personnel Scheduling Systems

BRANDS/DIVISIONS/AFFILIATES:
Trane
American Standard
Thermo King
Ingersoll Rand
ARO
Club Car
Cameron International Corporation
FRIGOBLOCK

CONTACTS:
Note: Officers with more than one job title may be intentionally listed here more than once.

Michael W. Lamach, CEO
Susan Carter, CFO
Marcia J. Avedon, Sr. VP-Human Resources
Paul Camuit, CIO
Robert L. Katz, General Counsel
Todd Wyman, Sr. VP-Global Oper.
Marcia J. Avedon, Sr. VP-Comm.
Didier Teirlinck, Sr. VP
Robert G. Zafari, Pres., Industrial Tech. Sector
John W. Conover, IV, Sr. VP
Gary Michel, Sr. VP
Michael W. Lamach, Chmn.
Venky Valluri, Chmn.
Todd Wyman, Sr. VP-Integrated Supply Chain

GROWTH PLANS/SPECIAL FEATURES:
Ingersoll-Rand plc primarily manufactures heating and cooling systems and industrial products. The firm operates in two segments: climate and industrial. The climate segment provides energy-efficient solutions globally and includes the Trane and American Standard heating and air conditioning brands. Through these brands, the firm provides heating, ventilation and air conditioning (HVAC) systems as well as commercial and residential building services, parts, support and controls. Through the Thermo King brand, the company transports temperature control solutions. The industrial segment delivers products and services that enhance energy efficiency, productivity and operations. Brands in this segment include: Ingersoll Rand, a provider of compressed air systems and services, power tools, material handling systems; ARO, a fluid management equipment provider; and Club Car, a golf, utility and rough terrain vehicle provider. In addition, Ingersoll-Rand subsidiary Cameron International Corporation manufactures centrifugal compression equipment and provides aftermarket parts and services for global industrial applications, air separation, gas transmission and process gas; and FRIGOBLOCK manufactures and designs transport refrigeration units for trucks and trailers, which it sells primarily in Western Europe.

FINANCIAL DATA:
Note: Data for latest year may not have been available at press time.

In U.S. $	2017	2016	2015	2014	2013	2012
Revenue	14,197,600,000	13,508,900,000	13,300,700,000	12,891,400,000	12,350,500,000	14,034,900,000
R&D Expense						
Operating Income	1,634,300,000	1,573,100,000	1,458,000,000	1,404,700,000	1,105,000,000	1,500,700,000
Operating Margin %	11.51%	11.64%	10.96%	10.89%	8.94%	10.69%
SGA Expense	2,751,700,000	2,606,500,000	2,541,100,000	2,503,900,000	2,570,000,000	2,776,000,000
Net Income	1,302,600,000	1,476,200,000	664,600,000	931,700,000	618,800,000	1,018,600,000
Operating Cash Flow	1,523,500,000	1,500,200,000	851,100,000	973,200,000	1,170,400,000	1,180,900,000
Capital Expenditure	221,300,000	182,500,000	249,600,000	233,500,000	242,200,000	262,600,000
EBITDA	1,987,000,000	2,315,000,000	1,835,000,000	1,767,100,000	1,442,100,000	1,905,700,000
Return on Assets %	7.32%	8.64%	3.90%	5.33%	3.42%	5.46%
Return on Equity %	18.89%	23.69%	11.26%	14.27%	8.70%	14.47%
Debt to Equity	0.41	0.55	0.64	0.62	0.44	0.31

CONTACT INFORMATION:
Phone: 353 18707400 Fax:
Toll-Free:
Address: 170/175 Lakeview Dr., Airside Business Park, Dublin, 2 Ireland

STOCK TICKER/OTHER:
Stock Ticker: IR
Employees: 45,000
Parent Company:

Exchange: NYS
Fiscal Year Ends: 12/31

SALARIES/BONUSES:
Top Exec. Salary: $1,300,000 Bonus: $
Second Exec. Salary: $525,000 Bonus: $500,000

OTHER THOUGHTS:
Estimated Female Officers or Directors: 3
Hot Spot for Advancement for Women/Minorities: Y

Sales, profits and employees may be estimates. Financial information, benefits and other data can change quickly and may vary from those stated here.

Innolux Corporation

NAIC Code: 334419

www.innolux.com

TYPES OF BUSINESS:
LCD (Liquid Crystal Display) Unit Screens Manufacturing
OLED Displays
LCD Televisions
Medical Display Panels
Color Filters

BRANDS/DIVISIONS/AFFILIATES:
Innolux Technology Japan Co Ltd
Innolux Optoelectronics Japan Co Ltd
Innolux Technology Europe BV
Innolux Optoelectronics Europe BV
Innolux Optoelectronics Japan Co Ltd
Innolux Optoelectronics Germany GmbH
Innolux Technology USA Inc
Innolux Optoelectronics USA Inc

CONTACTS:
Note: Officers with more than one job title may be intentionally listed here more than once.

Jyh-Chau Wang, CEO
Chih-Hung Shiao, Pres.
Wen-Jyh Sah, VP
Ching-Lung Ting, VP
Chih-Hung Shiao, VP
Hung-Wen Yang, Associate VP
Jyh-Chau Wang, Chmn.

GROWTH PLANS/SPECIAL FEATURES:

Innolux Corporation manufactures thin-film transistor liquid-crystal displays (TFT-LCD) and touch panels used to enhance resolution, color and brightness in a variety of LCD display products. The company's LCD TV panels are produced with either light-emitting diode (LED) or cold cathode fluorescent lamp (CCFL) technology. Notebook panels are engineered to be lightweight and slender, with LED widescreens, LCD panels and various types of high definition (HD) features. Its monitor panels are also equipped with widescreen displays utilizing full high definition (FHD) resolution and LED backlighting. Medical display panels are used to assist doctors with diagnoses, and possess high image quality while also complying with safety standards. Industrial display applications include panels that offer high resolution, a wide operation temperature range, wide viewing angle, high contrast and fast response. Automotive and avionics display applications meet the needs of top auto manufacturers, and include various viewing angle technologies, high resolutions, integrated touch functions and transflective features. Smart phone/mobile applications are lightweight and slender in style, have touch functions, high resolution, low power consumption, wide viewing angle and narrow bezel features. Consumer electronic applications are used in panels that apply to digital cameras, printers and multi-functional office devices. Innolux operates manufacturing facilities in Taiwan, China and the Netherlands. Its subsidiaries include: Innolux Technology Japan Co. Ltd.; Innolux Optoelectronics Japan Co. Ltd.; Innolux Technology Europe BV; Innolux Optoelectronics Europe BV; Innolux Optoelectronics Germany GmbH; Innolux Technology USA, Inc.; and Innolux Optoelectronics USA, Inc.

The firm offers employees labor and health insurance, cash incentives for three annual festivals and various recreational activities.

FINANCIAL DATA:
Note: Data for latest year may not have been available at press time.

In U.S. $	2017	2016	2015	2014	2013	2012
Revenue	11,078,100,000	8,883,800,000	11,247,354,669	13,957,200,000	13,764,000,000	15,746,300,000
R&D Expense						
Operating Income						
Operating Margin %						
SGA Expense						
Net Income	1,246,190,000	350,025,362	334,085,040	705,800,000	166,100,000	-973,500,000
Operating Cash Flow						
Capital Expenditure						
EBITDA						
Return on Assets %						
Return on Equity %						
Debt to Equity						

CONTACT INFORMATION:
Phone: 886 37586000   Fax:
Toll-Free:
Address: No. 160 Kesyue Rd., Chu-Nan Site Hsinchu, Taipei City, 35053 Taiwan

SALARIES/BONUSES:
Top Exec. Salary: $ Bonus: $
Second Exec. Salary: $ Bonus: $

STOCK TICKER/OTHER:
Stock Ticker: 3481
Employees: 66,107
Parent Company:

Exchange: Taipei
Fiscal Year Ends: 12/31

OTHER THOUGHTS:
Estimated Female Officers or Directors:
Hot Spot for Advancement for Women/Minorities: Y

Integral Group Inc

www.integralgroup.com

NAIC Code: 541330

TYPES OF BUSINESS:
Engineering Consulting Services
Engineering
Design

BRANDS/DIVISIONS/AFFILIATES:

CONTACTS:
Note: Officers with more than one job title may be intentionally listed here more than once.
Kevin Hydes, CEO
Conrad Schartau, COO
Christine Jeffery, CFO
Carl Foster, CIO

GROWTH PLANS/SPECIAL FEATURES:

Integral Group, Inc. is a global network of mechanical, electrical and plumbing engineers, energy analysts, commissioning authorities and sustainability consultants. This network specializes in the design of simple, elegant, cost-effective systems for high-performance buildings. Integral's mission is to accelerate the adoption of sustainable building design moving from green and net zero buildings toward regenerative buildings that mitigate global environment impacts and reduce ecological degradation. The firm's expertise lies in the fields of electrical engineering, lighting design, mechanical engineering, performance engineering, integrated district planning and sustainability consulting. Electrical engineering services include power distribution, sub-stations, generators, grounding analysis, lighting systems, panic and fire alarm systems, access control, telecommunications, audio/visual systems, site infrastructure, electrical and load flow analysis and coordination studies. Lighting services include high performance lighting, control systems, daylighting designs and sustainable lighting design. Mechanical engineering services include building automation and controls design, site services, air quality engineering, field reviews, plumbing design, primary energy design, sound control, special laboratory and medical gas services design, ventilation and environmental impact planning. Performance services include facility assessments, management, construction administration, measurement/verification, analytics, various types of commissioning, turnover and training as well as operations and maintenance. Integrated district planning services include developing energy master plans at campus and district scale, micro-grid resiliency, energy integration with water systems, thermal and electrical energy storage, on-site renewable technologies and ultra-low energy building design. Sustainability services provides LEED (leading energy and environment design) certification and deep green, high performance strategies that focus on health and wellness, comfort as well as a reduction of resource use.

The company offers employees health, dental and vision insurance; paid time off; and various employee programs.

FINANCIAL DATA:
Note: Data for latest year may not have been available at press time.

In U.S. $	2017	2016	2015	2014	2013	2012
Revenue						
R&D Expense						
Operating Income						
Operating Margin %						
SGA Expense						
Net Income						
Operating Cash Flow						
Capital Expenditure						
EBITDA						
Return on Assets %						
Return on Equity %						
Debt to Equity						

CONTACT INFORMATION:
Phone: 510-663-2070 Fax:
Toll-Free:
Address: 427 13th St., Oakland, CA 94612 United States

STOCK TICKER/OTHER:
Stock Ticker: Private
Employees:
Parent Company:
Exchange:
Fiscal Year Ends:

SALARIES/BONUSES:
Top Exec. Salary: $ Bonus: $
Second Exec. Salary: $ Bonus: $

OTHER THOUGHTS:
Estimated Female Officers or Directors:
Hot Spot for Advancement for Women/Minorities:

Sales, profits and employees may be estimates. Financial information, benefits and other data can change quickly and may vary from those stated here.

Intel Corporation

www.intel.com

NAIC Code: 334413

TYPES OF BUSINESS:
Microprocessors
Semiconductors
Circuit Boards
Flash Memory Products
Software Development
Home Network Equipment
Digital Imaging Products
Healthcare Products

BRANDS/DIVISIONS/AFFILIATES:
Mobileye NV

CONTACTS: Note: Officers with more than one job title may be intentionally listed here more than once.
Brian Krzanich, CEO
Robert Swan, CFO
Andy Bryant, Chairman of the Board
Kevin McBride, Chief Accounting Officer
Navin Shenoy, Executive VP
Venkata Renduchintala, Executive VP

GROWTH PLANS/SPECIAL FEATURES:

Intel Corporation designs and manufactures products and technologies that power the cloud and smart connectivity. The company produces computer, networking and communications platforms to a broad set of customers, including original equipment manufacturers (OEMs), original design manufacturers (ODMs), cloud and communications service providers, as well as industrial, communications and automotive equipment manufacturers. Intel's business across the cloud and data center are focused on memory and field-programmable gate array technologies. Its devices include everything smart: personal computers (PCs), sensors, consoles and other edge devices that are connected to the cloud. Memory and programmable solutions make possible new classes of products for the data center and Internet of Things. Intel is a leader in silicon manufacturing process technology, of which its products are manufactured in the company's own facilities. Its intellectual property can be shared across its platforms and operating segments, providing cost reduction and seamless production capabilities. Intel also offers software and services for consumer and corporate environments, as well as for assisting software developers in creating software applications via Intel platforms. Its client computing product group includes platforms for notebooks, 2-in-1 systems, desktops, tablets, phones, wired/wireless connectivity products and mobile communications components. The firm's non-volatile memory solutions (NAND) flash memory products are primarily used in solid-state drives. In August 2017, Intel acquired Mobileye NV, an Israeli developer of autonomous driving systems, for more than $15 billion.

FINANCIAL DATA: Note: Data for latest year may not have been available at press time.

In U.S. $	2017	2016	2015	2014	2013	2012
Revenue	62,761,000,000	59,387,000,000	55,355,000,000	55,870,000,000	52,708,000,000	53,341,000,000
R&D Expense	13,098,000,000	12,740,000,000	12,128,000,000	11,537,000,000	10,611,000,000	10,148,000,000
Operating Income	18,320,000,000	14,760,000,000	14,356,000,000	15,642,000,000	12,531,000,000	14,638,000,000
Operating Margin %	29.19%	24.85%	25.93%	27.99%	23.77%	27.44%
SGA Expense	7,474,000,000	8,397,000,000	7,930,000,000	8,136,000,000	8,088,000,000	8,057,000,000
Net Income	9,601,000,000	10,316,000,000	11,420,000,000	11,704,000,000	9,620,000,000	11,005,000,000
Operating Cash Flow	22,110,000,000	21,808,000,000	19,017,000,000	20,418,000,000	20,776,000,000	18,884,000,000
Capital Expenditure	11,778,000,000	9,625,000,000	7,446,000,000	10,197,000,000	10,747,000,000	11,842,000,000
EBITDA	29,127,000,000	21,459,000,000	23,260,000,000	24,542,000,000	20,887,000,000	22,485,000,000
Return on Assets %	8.11%	9.53%	11.71%	12.70%	10.88%	14.15%
Return on Equity %	14.19%	16.20%	19.52%	20.51%	17.57%	22.66%
Debt to Equity	0.36	0.31	0.32	0.21	0.22	0.25

CONTACT INFORMATION:
Phone: 408 765-8080   Fax: 408 765-2633
Toll-Free: 800-628-8686
Address: 2200 Mission College Blvd., Santa Clara, CA 95054 United States

STOCK TICKER/OTHER:
Stock Ticker: INTC   Exchange: NAS
Employees: 106,000   Fiscal Year Ends: 12/31
Parent Company:

SALARIES/BONUSES:
Top Exec. Salary: $954,000   Bonus: $2,700,000
Second Exec. Salary: $658,300   Bonus: $2,000,000

OTHER THOUGHTS:
Estimated Female Officers or Directors: 10
Hot Spot for Advancement for Women/Minorities: Y

Sales, profits and employees may be estimates. Financial information, benefits and other data can change quickly and may vary from those stated here.

Plunkett Research, Ltd.

Intellectual Ventures Management LLC
www.intellectualventures.com

NAIC Code: 541712

TYPES OF BUSINESS:
Research & Engineering
Intellectual Property
Investments

BRANDS/DIVISIONS/AFFILIATES:
Intellectual Ventures Lab

CONTACTS: Note: Officers with more than one job title may be intentionally listed here more than once.
Nathan Myhrvold, CEO
Larry Froeber, CFO
Nicole Grogan, Chief People Officer
David Kris, General Counsel
Shelby Barnes, Sr. VP-Corp. Comm.
Andy Elder, Exec. VP-Global Licensing
Jim Wallace, Sr. VP-Systems & Tech. Group
Loria Yeadon, Exec. VP-Invention Investment Fund
Casey Tegreene, Exec. VP-Invention Science Fund
Maurizio Vecchione, VP-Global Good

GROWTH PLANS/SPECIAL FEATURES:
Intellectual Ventures Management, LLC is a business concerned with developing and acquiring novel inventions across a variety of fields. The company's roster includes eminent professionals from disciplines ranging from life and physical sciences, mathematics, computer programming, medical technology and more. Through the firm's Invention Science framework, the products of these professionals are developed into possible streams of commercialization through spin-off companies (such as TerraPower and Kymeta), partnerships or product licensing. Such projects are funded through Invention Capital development portfolios. Individuals or groups can approach Intellectual Ventures with novel invention ideas in exchange for funding and development assistance. The company's development arm, Intellectual Ventures Lab, works to prove the viability of certain projects. The firm's patent portfolio includes 95,000 IP assets acquired and nearly 30,000 in active monetization programs, the patent portfolio spans more than 50 technology areas from agriculture to software. Intellectual Ventures has raised over $7.3 billion for its projects since its inception.

FINANCIAL DATA: Note: Data for latest year may not have been available at press time.

In U.S. $	2017	2016	2015	2014	2013	2012
Revenue						
R&D Expense						
Operating Income						
Operating Margin %						
SGA Expense						
Net Income						
Operating Cash Flow						
Capital Expenditure						
EBITDA						
Return on Assets %						
Return on Equity %						
Debt to Equity						

CONTACT INFORMATION:
Phone: 425-467-2300 Fax:
Toll-Free:
Address: 3150 139th Ave. SE, Bldg. 4, Bellevue, WA 98005 United States

STOCK TICKER/OTHER:
Stock Ticker: Private
Employees: 500
Parent Company:

Exchange:
Fiscal Year Ends:

SALARIES/BONUSES:
Top Exec. Salary: $ Bonus: $
Second Exec. Salary: $ Bonus: $

OTHER THOUGHTS:
Estimated Female Officers or Directors: 4
Hot Spot for Advancement for Women/Minorities: Y

Sales, profits and employees may be estimates. Financial information, benefits and other data can change quickly and may vary from those stated here.

International Business Machines Corporation (IBM)

www.ibm.com
NAIC Code: 541513

TYPES OF BUSINESS:
Computer Facilities and Business Process Outsourcing
Supercomputing
Business & Management Consulting
Software & Hardware
Cloud-Based Computer Services
IT Consulting & Outsourcing
Financial Services
Data Analytics and Health Care Analytics

BRANDS/DIVISIONS/AFFILIATES:
IBM Cognitive Solutions
IBM Global Business Services
IBM Technology Services & Cloud Platforms
IBM Systems
IBM Global Financing
Watson
Truven Health Analytics

CONTACTS:
Note: Officers with more than one job title may be intentionally listed here more than once.

James Kavanaugh, CFO
Michelle Browdy, Senior VP, Divisional
Virginia Rometty, Chairman of the Board
Robert Del Bene, Chief Accounting Officer
Diane Gherson, Other Executive Officer
Christina Montgomery, Secretary
Martin Schroeter, Senior VP, Divisional
Kenneth Keverian, Senior VP, Divisional
Erich Clementi, Senior VP, Divisional
John Kelly, Senior VP, Divisional

GROWTH PLANS/SPECIAL FEATURES:

International Business Machines Corporation (IBM) is a global leader in computer facilities management services, business process outsourcing, supercomputing services and advanced computer hardware and software. It is one of the largest technology consulting and services businesses in the world. The firm has reorganized its primary operating segments to better reflect the dominant themes in information technologies today, such as artificial intelligence and cloud computing. Now, IBM operates in primary segments that include: Cognitive Solutions (data analytics, health care analytics, supercomputing, artificial intelligence and machine learning), Global Business Services (offering application management, consulting and business process management), Technology Services & Cloud Platforms (including technical support, infrastructure services, integration software and the operation of one of the world's most advanced cloud services systems), Systems (including IBM's proprietary hardware and software), Global Financing, and Other. Offerings include information management software; operating systems; and Tivoli software for infrastructure management, including security and storage management. The systems units provide IBM's clients with infrastructure technologies to help meet the requirements of hybrid cloud and workloads. The global financing provides loans and leases for that assist in the marketing of IBM computer systems. For future growth, the firm has developed world-class capabilities in supercomputing (including its famous Watson computer), artificial intelligence, machine learning and data analytics, particularly the analysis of massive amounts of health care data and patient outcomes information. IBM is active in over 175 countries worldwide. During 2016, the firm acquired the digital assets of The Weather Company; Ustream, Inc.; Bluewolf Group, LLC; EZ Source; Optevia; ecx.io; IRIS Analytics; Promontory Financial Group; Resilient Systems; Truven Health Analytics; Resource/Ammirati; and Sanovi Technologies.

IBM offers its employees medical, vision and dental insurance; a flexible spending account; short- and long-term disability; a 401(k) plus plan; and an employee stock purchase plan.

FINANCIAL DATA:
Note: Data for latest year may not have been available at press time.

In U.S. $	2017	2016	2015	2014	2013	2012
Revenue	79,139,000,000	79,920,000,000	81,742,000,000	92,793,000,000	99,751,000,000	104,507,000,000
R&D Expense	5,787,000,000	5,751,000,000	5,247,000,000	5,437,000,000	6,226,000,000	6,302,000,000
Operating Income	11,800,000,000	13,105,000,000	15,690,000,000	18,532,000,000	19,600,000,000	21,518,000,000
Operating Margin %	14.91%	16.39%	19.19%	19.97%	19.64%	20.58%
SGA Expense	19,555,000,000	20,479,000,000	19,894,000,000	22,472,000,000	22,975,000,000	23,174,000,000
Net Income	5,753,000,000	11,872,000,000	13,190,000,000	12,022,000,000	16,483,000,000	16,604,000,000
Operating Cash Flow	16,724,000,000	16,958,000,000	17,008,000,000	16,868,000,000	17,485,000,000	19,586,000,000
Capital Expenditure	3,773,000,000	4,150,000,000	4,151,000,000	4,183,000,000	4,140,000,000	4,717,000,000
EBITDA	16,556,000,000	17,341,000,000	20,268,000,000	24,962,000,000	24,604,000,000	27,037,000,000
Return on Assets %	4.73%	10.41%	11.56%	9.86%	13.43%	14.09%
Return on Equity %	32.10%	73.04%	100.95%	69.37%	79.14%	85.15%
Debt to Equity	2.26	1.89	2.34	2.95	1.44	1.27

CONTACT INFORMATION:
Phone: 914-499-1900 Fax: 800-314-1092
Toll-Free: 800-426-4968
Address: 1 New Orchard Rd., Armonk, NY 10504-1722 United States

SALARIES/BONUSES:
Top Exec. Salary: $1,600,000 Bonus: $
Second Exec. Salary: $830,500 Bonus: $

STOCK TICKER/OTHER:
Stock Ticker: IBM Exchange: NYS
Employees: 379,592 Fiscal Year Ends: 12/31
Parent Company:

OTHER THOUGHTS:
Estimated Female Officers or Directors: 6
Hot Spot for Advancement for Women/Minorities: Y

Sales, profits and employees may be estimates. Financial information, benefits and other data can change quickly and may vary from those stated here.

Intertek Group plc

NAIC Code: 541690

www.intertek.com

TYPES OF BUSINESS:
Product Testing and Certification
Safety Consulting

BRANDS/DIVISIONS/AFFILIATES:
Aldo Abela Surveys Limited

CONTACTS: Note: Officers with more than one job title may be intentionally listed here more than once.
Andre Lacroix, CEO
Edward Leigh, CFO
Ken Lee, Exec. VP-Mktg. & Communications
Tony George, VP-Human Resources
Ann-Michele Bowlin, CIO
Julia Thomas, VP-Corp. Dev.
Stefan Butz, Exec. VP-Industry & Assurance
Stefan Butz, Exec. VP-Chemicals & Pharmaceuticals
Gregg Tiemann, Exec. VP-Consumer Goods, Commercial & Electrical
Jay Gutierrez, Exec. VP-Commodities

GROWTH PLANS/SPECIAL FEATURES:
Intertek Group plc is a U.K.-based provider of quality and safety solutions serving a wide range of industries around the world. Its services include: assurance, which enables clients to identify and mitigate the risk in their operations, supply chains and management systems; testing, which evaluates how products and services rate within quality, safety, sustainability and performance standards; inspection, which validates the specifications, value and safety of raw materials, products and assets; and certification, which formally confirms products and services in meeting external and internal standards. Industries served by the firm include chemicals, construction, engineering, energy, commodities, food, healthcare, government, trade, transportation, products and retail. Intertek's network of more than 1,000 laboratories and offices, in more than 100 countries, enables the delivery of its services and bespoke solutions to customers' operations and supply chains on a global scale. In early-2018, the firm acquired Malta-based Aldo Abela Surveys Limited, a provider of quality and quantity cargo inspection services; and agreed to acquire Proasem, a provider of laboratory testing, inspection, metrology and training services, based in Colombia.

FINANCIAL DATA: Note: Data for latest year may not have been available at press time.

In U.S. $	2017	2016	2015	2014	2013	2012
Revenue	3,944,025,000	3,656,174,000	3,085,458,000	2,981,484,000	3,111,238,000	2,925,936,000
R&D Expense						
Operating Income	627,973,200	563,594,900	-403,788,600	393,961,000	441,532,500	403,503,800
Operating Margin %	15.92%	15.41%	-13.08%	13.21%	14.19%	13.79%
SGA Expense						
Net Income	409,343,400	363,196,100	-513,459,600	251,103,800	285,571,800	247,543,100
Operating Cash Flow	641,076,700	597,635,600	491,525,400	415,183,000	383,421,200	332,573,700
Capital Expenditure	160,803,300	150,263,500	159,806,300	155,960,700	206,238,400	163,794,300
EBITDA	752,314,500	680,957,100	-247,970,400	536,248,400	577,553,000	539,239,400
Return on Assets %	13.68%	13.01%	-19.02%	8.92%	10.64%	9.73%
Return on Equity %	44.99%	58.00%	-66.01%	23.30%	29.43%	30.17%
Debt to Equity	0.85	1.43	2.55	0.84	0.98	1.13

CONTACT INFORMATION:
Phone: 44 2073963400   Fax: 44 2073963480
Toll-Free:
Address: 25 Savile Row, London, W1S 2ES United Kingdom

STOCK TICKER/OTHER:
Stock Ticker: IKTSY   Exchange: PINX
Employees: 43,906   Fiscal Year Ends: 12/31
Parent Company:

SALARIES/BONUSES:
Top Exec. Salary: $1,320,325   Bonus: $2,652,044
Second Exec. Salary: $589,660   Bonus: $1,185,016

OTHER THOUGHTS:
Estimated Female Officers or Directors: 4
Hot Spot for Advancement for Women/Minorities: Y

Intuit Inc

www.intuit.com

NAIC Code: 0

TYPES OF BUSINESS:
Computer Software-Financial Management
Business Accounting Software
Consumer Finance Software
Tax Preparation Software
Online Financial Services

BRANDS/DIVISIONS/AFFILIATES:
ProConnect
QuickBooks Online
TurboTax
Lacerte
ProSeries
ProConnect Tax Online
ProFile

CONTACTS:
Note: Officers with more than one job title may be intentionally listed here more than once.

Michelle Clatterbuck, CFO
Brad Smith, Chairman of the Board
Mark Flournoy, Chief Accounting Officer
H. Stansbury, Chief Technology Officer
Daniel Wernikoff, Executive VP
Laura Fennell, Executive VP
Scott Cook, Founder
Sasan Goodarzi, General Manager, Divisional

GROWTH PLANS/SPECIAL FEATURES:

Intuit, Inc. is a provider of software and web-based services, specializing in financial management and tax solutions. The company has three business segments: small business, consumer tax and ProConnect. The small business segment targets small businesses, as well as the accounting professionals who serve them. This division's products include QuickBooks Online, which offers financial management tools; online payroll solutions; online payment solutions; an Intuit developer group, which provides tools that third-party developers need to create online and mobile applications that personalize and add value to QuickBooks; desktop payments solutions; technical support; and financial supplies. The consumer tax segment targets consumers, and includes TurboTax income tax preparation products and services. TurboTax products and services are designed to enable individuals to prepare and file their own federal and state personal income tax returns quickly and accurately. The ProConnect segment targets professional accountants in the U.S. and Canada, who are essential to both small business success and doing the nations' taxes. ProConnect professional tax offerings include Lacerte, ProSeries, ProConnect Tax Online and ProFile. Lacerte is designed for full-service accounting firms who handle more complex returns. ProSeries offers two software versions: ProSeries Professional Edition, designed for year-round tax practices handling moderately complex tax returns; and ProSeries Basic Edition, for the needs of smaller and seasonal tax practices. ProConnect Tax Online is a cloud-based solution designed for year-round practices who prepare moderately complex consumer and small business returns, and integrates with QuickBooks Online offerings. Last, ProFile is Intuit's Canadian tax offering which serves year-round, full-service accounting firms for both consumer and business tax returns. This division's services include year-round document storage and access, collaboration services, e-signature and bank products. In late-2017, the firm agreed to acquire Exactor, Inc. and TSheets.

Intuit employees receive health, dental and life insurance; and 401(k) and employee stock purchase plans.

FINANCIAL DATA:
Note: Data for latest year may not have been available at press time.

In U.S. $	2017	2016	2015	2014	2013	2012
Revenue	5,177,000,000	4,694,000,000	4,192,000,000	4,506,000,000	4,171,000,000	4,151,000,000
R&D Expense	998,000,000	881,000,000	798,000,000	758,000,000	685,000,000	669,000,000
Operating Income	1,395,000,000	1,242,000,000	886,000,000	1,314,000,000	1,233,000,000	1,177,000,000
Operating Margin %	26.94%	26.45%	21.13%	29.16%	29.56%	28.35%
SGA Expense	1,973,000,000	1,807,000,000	1,771,000,000	1,746,000,000	1,641,000,000	1,506,000,000
Net Income	971,000,000	979,000,000	365,000,000	907,000,000	858,000,000	792,000,000
Operating Cash Flow	1,599,000,000	1,401,000,000	1,504,000,000	1,446,000,000	1,366,000,000	1,246,000,000
Capital Expenditure	230,000,000	522,000,000	261,000,000	186,000,000	195,000,000	186,000,000
EBITDA	1,634,000,000	1,476,000,000	970,000,000	1,542,000,000	1,472,000,000	1,443,000,000
Return on Assets %	23.34%	21.24%	7.17%	16.97%	16.87%	16.17%
Return on Equity %	77.21%	56.05%	13.49%	27.44%	27.34%	29.55%
Debt to Equity	0.32	0.42	0.21	0.16	0.14	0.18

CONTACT INFORMATION:
Phone: 650 944-6000 Fax: 650 944-3060
Toll-Free: 800-446-8848
Address: 2700 Coast Ave., Mountain View, CA 94043 United States

SALARIES/BONUSES:
Top Exec. Salary: $1,000,000 Bonus: $
Second Exec. Salary: $750,000 Bonus: $

STOCK TICKER/OTHER:
Stock Ticker: INTU Exchange: NAS
Employees: 8,200 Fiscal Year Ends: 07/31
Parent Company:

OTHER THOUGHTS:
Estimated Female Officers or Directors: 5
Hot Spot for Advancement for Women/Minorities: Y

Sales, profits and employees may be estimates. Financial information, benefits and other data can change quickly and may vary from those stated here.

IPS - Integrated Project Service LLC

www.ipsdb.com

NAIC Code: 541330

TYPES OF BUSINESS:
Engineering Consulting Services
Engineering

BRANDS/DIVISIONS/AFFILIATES:
IPS International
IPS-Mehtalia Pvt Ltd

CONTACTS:
Note: Officers with more than one job title may be intentionally listed here more than once.

Dave Goswami, CEO
Brian T. Morris, CFO

GROWTH PLANS/SPECIAL FEATURES:

IPS-Integrated Project Service, LLC is a multi-national, full-service engineering firm, with nearly 1,100 professionals in the U.S., Canada, Brazil, the U.K., Ireland, Switzerland, Singapore, China and India. IPS specializes in complex facilities in hi-tech and highly regulated industries providing its expertise in the areas of technical consulting, engineering, construction, commissioning and qualification. Industries the company serves include pharmaceutical, biotechnology, mission critical facilities, medical device/novel dosage, higher education, energy and sustainability, healthcare, food and beverage, government, semiconductor and industrial/specialty chemical. IPS is internationally recognized as an expert in advanced aseptic processing and containment, bio-manufacturing, energy and sustainability, science- and risk-based methodologies, laboratories and master planning. The firm's subsidiaries include: IPS International, which provides technical consulting, process engineering and facility design through international subsidiaries in India, Brazil, China, Switzerland, the U.K. and Singapore; and IPS-Mehtalia Pvt. Ltd., an engineering, construction management and compliance company based in India. Affiliate companies include: IES Engineers, a professional services company specializing in environmental compliance; Somma Tech, a pharmaceutical technology firm; and xCell Strategic Consulting, offering a range of development and operations improvement solutions.

The company offers its employees medical, dental and vision coverage; 401(k); continuing education, licensing and registration incentives; paid vacation and personal/sick time; life insurance, flexible spending accounts; and short- and long-term disabilit

FINANCIAL DATA: Note: Data for latest year may not have been available at press time.

In U.S. $	2017	2016	2015	2014	2013	2012
Revenue						
R&D Expense						
Operating Income						
Operating Margin %						
SGA Expense						
Net Income						
Operating Cash Flow						
Capital Expenditure						
EBITDA						
Return on Assets %						
Return on Equity %						
Debt to Equity						

CONTACT INFORMATION:
Phone: 610-828-4090   Fax: 610-828-3656
Toll-Free:
Address: 721 Arbor Way, Ste. 100, Blue Bell, PA 19422 United States

STOCK TICKER/OTHER:
Stock Ticker: Private   Exchange:
Employees: 2,523   Fiscal Year Ends:
Parent Company:

SALARIES/BONUSES:
Top Exec. Salary: $ Bonus: $
Second Exec. Salary: $ Bonus: $

OTHER THOUGHTS:
Estimated Female Officers or Directors:
Hot Spot for Advancement for Women/Minorities:

Sales, profits and employees may be estimates. Financial information, benefits and other data can change quickly and may vary from those stated here.

IQVIA Holdings Inc

NAIC Code: 541711

www.iqvia.com

TYPES OF BUSINESS:
Contract Research
Pharmaceutical, Biotech & Medical Device Research
Consulting & Training Services
Sales & Marketing Services

BRANDS/DIVISIONS/AFFILIATES:
IQVIA CORE
Quintiles IMS Holdings Inc

GROWTH PLANS/SPECIAL FEATURES:
IQVIA Holdings, Inc. (formerly Quintiles IMS Holdings, Inc.) provides integrated information and technology-enabled healthcare services. The company's offerings help clients improve clinical, scientific and commercial results, with operations in more than 100 countries. IQVIA Holdings' range of healthcare information, technology and service solutions span the entire product lifecycle, from clinical to commercial operations. Its information includes more than 530 million comprehensive and anonymous patient records spanning sales, prescription and promotional data; medical claims; electronic medical records; and social media. The firm's proprietary assets develop clinical and commercial capabilities. These assets and capabilities include: healthcare-specific global IT infrastructure, data-enriched clinical development, real-world insights ecosystem and proprietary commercial applications. In November 2017, Quintiles IMS Holdings changed its name to IQVIA Holdings. The company continues to trade on the NYSE, but under a new ticker symbol: IQV.

CONTACTS:
Note: Officers with more than one job title may be intentionally listed here more than once.

Michael Mcdonnell, CFO
Ari Bousbib, Chairman of the Board
Robert Parks, Controller
James Erlinger, Executive VP
Kevin Knightly, President, Divisional
W. Staub, President, Divisional

FINANCIAL DATA:
Note: Data for latest year may not have been available at press time.

In U.S. $	2017	2016	2015	2014	2013	2012
Revenue	9,739,000,000	6,878,000,000	5,737,619,000	5,459,998,000	5,099,545,000	4,865,513,000
R&D Expense						
Operating Income	822,000,000	828,000,000	679,848,000	599,378,000	476,404,000	415,176,000
Operating Margin %	8.44%	12.03%	11.84%	10.97%	9.34%	8.53%
SGA Expense	1,605,000,000	1,011,000,000	920,985,000	882,338,000	860,510,000	817,755,000
Net Income	1,309,000,000	115,000,000	387,205,000	356,383,000	226,591,000	177,546,000
Operating Cash Flow	970,000,000	860,000,000	475,691,000	431,754,000	397,370,000	335,701,000
Capital Expenditure	369,000,000	164,000,000	78,391,000	82,650,000	92,346,000	71,336,000
EBITDA	1,688,000,000	912,000,000	768,529,000	723,791,000	554,128,000	500,087,000
Return on Assets %	5.95%	.91%	10.70%	11.18%	8.14%	7.36%
Return on Equity %	15.63%	2.85%				
Debt to Equity	1.24	0.82				

CONTACT INFORMATION:
Phone: 919-998-2000   Fax:
Toll-Free: 866-267-4479
Address: 4820 Emperor Blvd., Durham, NC 27703 United States

SALARIES/BONUSES:
Top Exec. Salary: $1,600,000   Bonus: $
Second Exec. Salary: $650,000   Bonus: $

STOCK TICKER/OTHER:
Stock Ticker: IQV
Employees: 50,000
Parent Company:

Exchange: NYS
Fiscal Year Ends: 12/31

OTHER THOUGHTS:
Estimated Female Officers or Directors: 3
Hot Spot for Advancement for Women/Minorities: Y

Sales, profits and employees may be estimates. Financial information, benefits and other data can change quickly and may vary from those stated here.

Isuzu Motors Limited

NAIC Code: 336111

www.isuzu.co.jp

TYPES OF BUSINESS:
Automobile Manufacturing
Trucks & Buses
Diesel Engines
Logistics Services

BRANDS/DIVISIONS/AFFILIATES:
mu-X
Panther
Isuzu D-MAX
Erga Mio
Isuzu (China) Holding Co Ltd
Isuzu Malaysia Sendirian Berhad
Isuzu Philippines Corporation
Isuzu Remanufactura de Colombia SAS

CONTACTS: *Note: Officers with more than one job title may be intentionally listed here more than once.*
Masanori Katayama, Pres.
Susumu Hosoi, Chmn.

GROWTH PLANS/SPECIAL FEATURES:

Isuzu Motors Limited, headquartered in Tokyo, manufactures and sells sport-utility vehicles (SUVs), pickups, freight trucks, buses, automobile parts and diesel engines. Its SUV line includes the mu-X in Thailand and the Panther in Indonesia, while its pick-up truck offering is the Isuzu D-MAX, popular throughout Thailand. Commercial truck models come in heavy, medium and light-duty varieties, with models that include tractor-trailers, dump trucks and concrete trucks. Isuzu sells its buses under the Erga brand name, offering a standard-size version and a smaller version known as the Erga Mio, both of which offer natural gas and diesel-run options. The company has focused on the development of fuel-efficient and low-emissions diesel engines for years, and currently produces a wide variety of diesel engine models sold to the automotive, industrial and maritime markets. Additionally, the firm produces snowmobile engines as well as industrial engines, such as cooler power sources for use in construction machinery, boats, agricultural tractors and refrigerated trucks. Isuzu Motors has more than 40 subsidiaries worldwide, and its products are currently sold in more than 100 countries. Its Fujisawa plant performs the company's research and development activities, and handles the assembly of heavy/medium/light-duty trucks. The Tochigi plant manufactures engines. Overseas subsidiaries include Isuzu (China) Holding Co. Ltd.; Isuzu Motors Asia Ltd. (Singapore); Isuzu Malaysia Sendirian Berhad; Isuzu Vietnam Co. Ltd.; PT Isuzu Astra Motor Indonesia: Isuzu Motors Co. (Thailand) Ltd.; Isuzu Philippines Corporation; Isuzu Motors India Private Limited; and Isuzu Motors Saudi Arabia Company Limited, among others. In November 2017, the firm formed a joint venture with National Truck Service SAS, called Isuzu Remanufactura de Colombia SAS, to rebuild used vehicle engines in Colombia.

FINANCIAL DATA: *Note: Data for latest year may not have been available at press time.*

In U.S. $	2017	2016	2015	2014	2013	2012
Revenue	18,196,260,000	17,951,990,000	17,509,240,000	16,404,490,000	15,423,780,000	13,043,360,000
R&D Expense						
Operating Income	1,709,344,000	1,947,951,000	1,896,544,000	1,900,317,000	1,467,589,000	1,112,204,000
Operating Margin %	9.39%	10.85%	10.83%	11.58%	9.51%	8.52%
SGA Expense	603,810,400	617,486,500	576,793,400	479,765,200	418,092,100	390,078,300
Net Income	874,399,100	1,068,344,000	1,090,553,000	1,111,571,000	899,357,200	850,158,400
Operating Cash Flow	1,410,024,000	1,238,793,000	1,411,943,000	1,483,222,000	1,277,483,000	740,804,900
Capital Expenditure						
EBITDA	2,006,251,000	2,309,447,000	2,205,757,000	2,172,694,000	1,646,087,000	1,320,319,000
Return on Assets %	5.08%	6.35%	7.04%	8.33%	7.55%	7.84%
Return on Equity %	11.95%	15.23%	16.86%	20.53%	20.44%	24.54%
Debt to Equity	0.24	0.24	0.18	0.13	0.15	0.30

CONTACT INFORMATION:
Phone: 81 354711141 Fax: 81 354711043
Toll-Free:
Address: 6-26-1 Minami-Oi, Shinagawa-Ku, Tokyo, 140-8722 Japan

STOCK TICKER/OTHER:
Stock Ticker: ISUZF   Exchange: PINX
Employees: 29,430   Fiscal Year Ends: 03/31
Parent Company:

SALARIES/BONUSES:
Top Exec. Salary: $ Bonus: $
Second Exec. Salary: $ Bonus: $

OTHER THOUGHTS:
Estimated Female Officers or Directors:
Hot Spot for Advancement for Women/Minorities:

Sales, profits and employees may be estimates. Financial information, benefits and other data can change quickly and may vary from those stated here.

ITT Inc

NAIC Code: 333131

www.itt.com

TYPES OF BUSINESS:
Engineered Systems

BRANDS/DIVISIONS/AFFILIATES:

CONTACTS: *Note: Officers with more than one job title may be intentionally listed here more than once.*
Denise Ramos, CEO
Thomas Scalera, CFO
Frank Macinnis, Chairman of the Board
Steven Giuliano, Chief Accounting Officer
Luca Savi, Executive VP
Mary Gustafsson, General Counsel
David Malinas, President, Divisional
Farrokh Batliwala, President, Divisional
Victoria Creamer, Senior VP, Divisional

GROWTH PLANS/SPECIAL FEATURES:
ITT, Inc. is a diversified manufacturer of highly-engineered critical components and customized technology solutions for the energy, transportation and industrial markets. The company's components are integral to the operation of systems and manufacturing processes, enabling functionality for applications where reliability and performance are important. ITT operates through three segments: industrial process, consisting of industrial pumping and complementary equipment; motion technologies, consisting of friction and shock/vibration equipment; and connect & control technologies, consisting of connectors and specialized control components which are able to withstand high extreme shock and vibrations, are resistant to dirt and fluids, and provide power and capabilities for equipment and applications. ITT has operations in approximately 35 countries, with 67% of sales being derived from outside the U.S., including 33% from emerging markets (as of December 2017).

The firm offers employees tuition reimbursement; an employee assistance program; scholarship programs; medical, dental and life insurance; and health club discounts.

FINANCIAL DATA: *Note: Data for latest year may not have been available at press time.*

In U.S. $	2017	2016	2015	2014	2013	2012
Revenue	2,585,300,000	2,405,400,000	2,485,600,000	2,654,600,000	2,496,900,000	2,227,800,000
R&D Expense	93,700,000	80,800,000	78,900,000	76,600,000	67,300,000	62,700,000
Operating Income	289,800,000	233,300,000	288,700,000	270,300,000	216,400,000	151,500,000
Operating Margin %	11.20%	9.69%	11.61%	10.18%	8.66%	6.80%
SGA Expense	433,700,000	444,100,000	441,500,000	519,500,000	516,100,000	466,000,000
Net Income	113,500,000	186,100,000	351,800,000	184,500,000	488,500,000	125,400,000
Operating Cash Flow	247,400,000	240,700,000	229,700,000	244,700,000	210,300,000	243,900,000
Capital Expenditure	113,300,000	111,400,000	86,700,000	118,800,000	122,900,000	83,800,000
EBITDA	395,100,000	335,300,000	378,700,000	354,300,000	273,700,000	220,300,000
Return on Assets %	3.10%	5.08%	9.56%	5.00%	13.70%	3.55%
Return on Equity %	7.51%	13.34%	27.30%	15.27%	51.30%	17.95%
Debt to Equity						

CONTACT INFORMATION:
Phone: 914 641-2000 Fax: 914 696-2950
Toll-Free:
Address: 1133 Westchester Ave., White Plains, NY 10604 United States

STOCK TICKER/OTHER:
Stock Ticker: ITT
Employees: 9,500
Parent Company:

Exchange: NYS
Fiscal Year Ends: 12/31

SALARIES/BONUSES:
Top Exec. Salary: $1,000,000   Bonus: $
Second Exec. Salary: $375,884   Bonus: $165,000

OTHER THOUGHTS:
Estimated Female Officers or Directors: 5
Hot Spot for Advancement for Women/Minorities: Y

Sales, profits and employees may be estimates. Financial information, benefits and other data can change quickly and may vary from those stated here.

Jabil Inc
NAIC Code: 334418

www.jabil.com

TYPES OF BUSINESS:
Contract Electronics Manufacturing
Maintenance & Support Services
Custom Design Services

BRANDS/DIVISIONS/AFFILIATES:
Jabil Circuit Inc

CONTACTS:
Note: Officers with more than one job title may be intentionally listed here more than once.

Michael Loparco, CEO, Divisional
Alessandro Parimbelli, CEO, Divisional
Erich Hoch, CEO, Divisional
Steven Borges, CEO, Divisional
Mark Mondello, CEO
Forbes Alexander, CFO
Timothy Main, Chairman of the Board
Meheryar Dastoor, Controller
Thomas Sansone, Director
Courtney Ryan, Executive VP, Divisional
Robert Katz, Executive VP
Bruce Johnson, Other Executive Officer
William Peters, President
Sergio Cadavid, Senior VP

GROWTH PLANS/SPECIAL FEATURES:
Jabil, Inc. (formerly Jabil Circuit, Inc.) is a provider of worldwide electronic manufacturing services and solutions. Through its more than 100 plants in 28 countries, the firm develops and manufactures products that help to connect people, advance technology and more. Jabil divides its operations into two segments: diversified manufacturing services (DMS) and electronics manufacturing services (EMS). DMS is focused on providing engineering solutions and on material sciences and technologies. This segment includes customers primarily in the consumer lifestyles and wearable technologies, defense & aerospace, emerging growth, healthcare, mobility and packaging industries. EMS is focused around leveraging information technology, supply chain design and engineering, technologies largely centered on core electronics, sharing of Jabil's large-scale manufacturing infrastructure and the ability to serve a broad range of end markets. This segment includes customers primarily in the automotive, digital home, industrial and energy, networking and telecommunications, point of sale, printing and storage industries. As of fiscal 2017, Jabil's largest customers include Apple, Inc.; Cisco Systems, Inc.; GoPro, Inc.; Hewlett-Packard Company; Ingenico SA; LM Ericsson Telephone Company; NetApp, Inc.; Nokia Networks; Valeo SA; and Zebra Technologies Corporation. In February 2018, Jabil announced plans to construct a new worldwide headquarters in St. Petersburg, Florida, while also expanding operations at its current site, which is also in St. Petersburg. The campus will bring its local employees together.

FINANCIAL DATA:
Note: Data for latest year may not have been available at press time.

In U.S. $	2017	2016	2015	2014	2013	2012
Revenue	19,063,120,000	18,353,090,000	17,899,200,000	15,762,150,000	18,336,890,000	17,151,940,000
R&D Expense	29,680,000	31,954,000	27,645,000	28,611,000	28,468,000	25,837,000
Operating Income	572,737,000	534,202,000	588,477,000	297,405,000	626,488,000	621,931,000
Operating Margin %	3.00%	2.91%	3.28%	1.88%	3.41%	3.62%
SGA Expense	907,702,000	924,427,000	862,647,000	675,730,000	688,752,000	644,452,000
Net Income	129,090,000	254,095,000	284,019,000	241,313,000	371,482,000	394,687,000
Operating Cash Flow	1,256,643,000	916,207,000	1,240,282,000	498,857,000	1,213,889,000	634,226,000
Capital Expenditure	716,485,000	924,239,000	963,145,000	624,060,000	736,858,000	497,697,000
EBITDA	1,154,712,000	1,220,333,000	1,088,913,000	687,456,000	925,243,000	968,521,000
Return on Assets %	1.20%	2.55%	3.14%	2.73%	4.38%	5.31%
Return on Equity %	5.38%	10.69%	12.46%	10.54%	16.73%	19.87%
Debt to Equity	0.69	0.85	0.58	0.74	0.72	0.78

CONTACT INFORMATION:
Phone: 727 577-9749 Fax: 727 579-8529
Toll-Free:
Address: 10560 Dr. Martin Luther King Jr. St. N., St. Petersburg, FL 33716 United States

STOCK TICKER/OTHER:
Stock Ticker: JBL
Employees: 161,000
Parent Company:

Exchange: NYS
Fiscal Year Ends: 08/31

SALARIES/BONUSES:
Top Exec. Salary: $1,100,000   Bonus: $
Second Exec. Salary: $700,000   Bonus: $

OTHER THOUGHTS:
Estimated Female Officers or Directors:
Hot Spot for Advancement for Women/Minorities: Y

Jacobs Engineering Group Inc

NAIC Code: 237000

www.jacobs.com

TYPES OF BUSINESS:
Engineering & Design Services
Facility Management
Construction & Field Services
Technical Consulting Services
Environmental Services

BRANDS/DIVISIONS/AFFILIATES:
CH2M HILL Companies Ltd

CONTACTS:
Note: Officers with more than one job title may be intentionally listed here more than once.

Steven Demetriou, CEO
Kevin Berryman, CFO
Joseph Mandel, Executive VP, Divisional
Michael Tyler, General Counsel
Robert Pragada, President, Divisional
Terence Hagen, President, Divisional
William Allen, Senior VP

GROWTH PLANS/SPECIAL FEATURES:

Jacobs Engineering Group, Inc. offers technical, professional and construction services to industrial, commercial and governmental clients throughout the Americas, Europe, Asia, India, the Middle East, Africa, the U.K. and Australia. Jacobs provides project services, which include engineering, design and architecture; process, scientific and systems consulting services; operations and maintenance services; and construction services, which include direct-hire construction and management services. Services are offered to industry groups such as oil and gas exploration, production and refining; pharmaceuticals and biotechnology; chemicals and polymers; buildings, which includes projects in the fields of health care and education as well as civic, governmental and other buildings; infrastructure; technology; energy; consumer and forest products; automotive and industrial; and environmental programs. Jacobs also provides pricing studies, project feasibility reports and automation and control system analysis for U.S. government agencies involved in defense and aerospace programs. In addition, the company is one of the leading providers of environmental engineering and consulting services in the U.S. and abroad, providing support in such areas as underground storage tank removal, contaminated soil and water remediation and long-term groundwater monitoring. Jacobs also designs, builds, installs, operates and maintains various types of soil and groundwater cleanup systems. In December 2017, Jacobs Engineering acquired CH2M HILL Companies Ltd., a global engineering company that provides consulting, design, construction and operations services for corporations as well as federal, state and local governments.

Jacobs offers its employees medical, disability, life and AD&D insurance; an employee stock purchase plan; and tuition reimbursement.

FINANCIAL DATA:
Note: Data for latest year may not have been available at press time.

In U.S. $	2017	2016	2015	2014	2013	2012
Revenue	10,022,790,000	10,964,160,000	12,114,830,000	12,695,160,000	11,818,380,000	10,893,780,000
R&D Expense						
Operating Income	392,269,000	338,598,000	445,527,000	528,068,000	668,979,000	596,073,000
Operating Margin %	3.91%	3.08%	3.67%	4.15%	5.66%	5.47%
SGA Expense	1,379,983,000	1,429,233,000	1,522,811,000	1,545,716,000	1,173,340,000	1,130,916,000
Net Income	293,727,000	210,463,000	302,971,000	328,108,000	423,093,000	378,954,000
Operating Cash Flow	574,881,000	680,173,000	484,572,000	721,716,000	448,516,000	299,805,000
Capital Expenditure	118,060,000	77,715,000	88,404,000	132,146,000	127,270,000	102,574,000
EBITDA	527,765,000	431,954,000	598,932,000	699,015,000	773,328,000	705,846,000
Return on Assets %	3.94%	2.77%	3.73%	4.17%	5.99%	5.88%
Return on Equity %	6.68%	4.91%	6.91%	7.55%	10.66%	10.77%
Debt to Equity	0.05	0.09		0.13	0.17	0.09	0.14

CONTACT INFORMATION:
Phone: 214-583-8500   Fax:
Toll-Free:
Address: 1999 Bryan St., Ste. 1200, Dallas, CA 75201 United States

STOCK TICKER/OTHER:
Stock Ticker: JEC
Employees: 43,800
Parent Company:

Exchange: NYS
Fiscal Year Ends: 09/30

SALARIES/BONUSES:
Top Exec. Salary: $1,300,000   Bonus: $
Second Exec. Salary: $684,231   Bonus: $350,000

OTHER THOUGHTS:
Estimated Female Officers or Directors: 1
Hot Spot for Advancement for Women/Minorities: Y

Sales, profits and employees may be estimates. Financial information, benefits and other data can change quickly and may vary from those stated here.

Jaguar Land Rover Limited

NAIC Code: 336111

www.jaguarlandrover.com

TYPES OF BUSINESS:
Automobile Manufacturing
Racing
Financial Services

BRANDS/DIVISIONS/AFFILIATES:
Tata Motors Limited
XE
XF
XJ
F-Type
I-Pace
E-Pace
F-Pace

CONTACTS:
Note: Officers with more than one job title may be intentionally listed here more than once.

Ralf D. Speth, CEO
John Edwards, Managing Dir.-Operations
Kenneth Gregor, CFO
Ian Harnett, Exec. Dir.-Human Resources
Ian Callum, Dir.-Jaguar Design

GROWTH PLANS/SPECIAL FEATURES:

Jaguar Land Rover Limited, founded in 1922 and based in the U.K., manufactures a distinctive line of luxury sedans, sports cars and electric/hybrid vehicles. The company is part of India-based Tata Motors Limited. Jaguar's current line includes six models: the XE, XF, XJ, F-Type, I-Pace, E-Pace and F-Pace. The Jaguar XE is a line of sports saloon cars comprising lightweight aluminum intensive architecture and packed with systems that deliver premium handling and performance. The XF is a sports sedan with a 5.0-liter V8 supercharged engine as well as features such as Bluetooth phone connectivity, a portable audio interface and voice-controlled navigation options. The company's flagship model, the XJ sedan, features a monocoque alloy body shell, a 470 hp supercharged engine and 510 hp engine, Bluetooth wireless technology and automatic climate control. The F-Type is a convertible sports car with 3.0 Litre V6 engines, quick shift transmission and a stiffer body for more precise and intuitive control. The I-Pace is an all-electric performance sport utility vehicle (SUV). The E-Pace is a compact SUV. The F-Pace is a sports car based on the C-X17 crossover concept vehicle, and also includes the lightweight aluminum intensive architecture. In total, Jaguar operates five engineering and production facilities in the Midlands and North West of England, three of which it shares with sister company Land Rover. During 2017, the firm announced the I-Pace concept, its very first all-electric car with a 220-mile range, and will be released for purchase in 2018; announced that the Range Rover Sport P400e, a plug-in hybrid, would be released in 2018; and announced that all new Jaguar and Land Rover models launched from the 2020 model year will have an all-electric or hybrid powertrain option.

FINANCIAL DATA:
Note: Data for latest year may not have been available at press time.

In U.S. $	2017	2016	2015	2014	2013	2012
Revenue	32,783,700,000	25,605,600,000	31,098,153,190	29,784,165,750	26,669,822,970	22,915,241,210
R&D Expense						
Operating Income						
Operating Margin %						
SGA Expense						
Net Income	2,158,600,000	1,613,970,000	2,898,474,170	2,886,848,625	2,835,626,104	1,992,956,859
Operating Cash Flow						
Capital Expenditure						
EBITDA						
Return on Assets %						
Return on Equity %						
Debt to Equity						

CONTACT INFORMATION:
Phone: 44-24-7640-2121 Fax:
Toll-Free:
Address: Abbey Rd., Whitley, Coventry, CV3 4LF United Kingdom

STOCK TICKER/OTHER:
Stock Ticker: Subsidiary
Employees: 40,265
Parent Company: TATA Motors Limited

Exchange:
Fiscal Year Ends: 12/31

SALARIES/BONUSES:
Top Exec. Salary: $ Bonus: $
Second Exec. Salary: $ Bonus: $

OTHER THOUGHTS:
Estimated Female Officers or Directors:
Hot Spot for Advancement for Women/Minorities:

JGC Corporation

NAIC Code: 541330

www.jgc.com

TYPES OF BUSINESS:
Engineering Services

BRANDS/DIVISIONS/AFFILIATES:
JGC Plant Innovation Co Ltd
JGC Catalysts & Chemicals Ltd
JGC China Engineering Co Ltd
JCG Gulf International Co Ltd
JGC Algeria SpA
JGC America Inc

CONTACTS:
Note: Officers with more than one job title may be intentionally listed here more than once.

Masayuki Sato, CEO
Tadashi Ishizuka, Pres.
Takashi Yasuda, Sr. Gen. Mgr.-Tech. Innovation Center
Toru Amemiya, Sr. Gen. Mgr.-Eng.
Masayuki Sato, Exec. VP-Corp. Admin.
Hisakazu Nishiguchi, Sr. Gen. Mgr.-Legal & Compliance Office
Toyohiko Shimada, Sr. Gen. Mgr.-Bus. Planning & Govt.
Toyohiko Shimada, Sr. Gen. Mgr.-Industry Rel.
Masayuki Sato, Exec. VP-Financial Affairs Div.
Tadashi Ishizuka, Exec. VP
Yasumasa Isetani, Sr. Gen. Mgr.-Bus. Promotions
Tadao Takahashi, Pres., JGC Gulf Intl Co. Ltd.
Masato Kato, Pres.
Masayuki Sato, Chmn.
Yutaka Yamazaki, Sr. Gen. Mgr.-Intl Project Div.

GROWTH PLANS/SPECIAL FEATURES:

JGC Corporation provides consulting, planning, design, engineering, procurement, construction (EPC), commissioning and maintenance services for various energy and infrastructure plants and facilities. The company's services are grouped into six categories, including: EPC, O&M (operation and maintenance), business investment and operation, catalysts and fine chemicals, technology innovation and big data solutions. EPC services include feasibility studies, front-end engineering and design (FEED), procurement, construction, commissioning and project management. O&M services include a wide range of operation and maintenance services for all project stages, from feasibility studies through FEED, EPC and commercial operation. Business investment and operation services include investing in businesses engaged in power generation, water production, oil and gas exploration/development, new energy, transportation, medical facilities and agriculture; and providing the full spectrum of EPC contracting services that go along with those investments. Catalysts and fine chemicals services include supplying petroleum refining catalysts to businesses worldwide. This division also manufactures and sells various forms of these substances for other petrochemical plants, as well as for environmental protection purposes. Technology innovation services are offered to businesses which contribute to the preservation of the natural environment and to the promotion advances in social infrastructure. For the environment, these services center around the management of carbon dioxide; and for social purposes, encompass a number of fields, including the utilization of undeveloped resources, nuclear power, life sciences, mineral resources development and urban infrastructure. In addition, this division actively pursues opportunities to develop innovative new technologies jointly with outside partners. Last, big data solutions include Internet of Things (IoT), providing big data solutions which contribute to the enhancement of clients' business value. JGC subsidiaries include, but are not limited to: JGC Plant Innovation Co., Ltd.; JGC Catalysts & Chemicals Ltd.; JGC China Engineering Co., Ltd.; JCG Gulf International Co., Ltd.; JGC Algeria SpA; and JGC America, Inc.

FINANCIAL DATA:
Note: Data for latest year may not have been available at press time.

In U.S. $	2017	2016	2015	2014	2013	2012
Revenue	6,457,537,000	8,197,820,000	7,444,345,000	6,296,078,000	5,819,238,000	5,188,803,000
R&D Expense						
Operating Income	-200,260,900	462,660,700	277,072,900	635,867,400	597,391,500	624,687,900
Operating Margin %	-3.10%	5.64%	3.72%	10.09%	10.26%	12.03%
SGA Expense						
Net Income	-205,487,300	398,667,800	192,174,400	439,519,300	430,212,400	364,365,600
Operating Cash Flow	-269,088,900	-463,611,000	-665,325,100	1,123,309,000	791,969,500	911,561,500
Capital Expenditure	69,899,390	49,720,520	162,567,600	101,453,300	143,804,700	146,730,000
EBITDA	-99,450,350	650,260,900	380,137,900	805,859,900	659,707,500	743,199,200
Return on Assets %	-3.30%	6.07%	2.81%	6.86%	7.99%	7.86%
Return on Equity %	-5.50%	10.61%	5.41%	13.28%	14.75%	14.10%
Debt to Equity	0.03	0.05	0.05	0.03	0.02	0.02

CONTACT INFORMATION:
Phone: 81 456821111   Fax: 81 456821112
Toll-Free:
Address: 2-3-1, Minato Mirai, Nishi-ku, Yokohama, 220-6001 Japan

SALARIES/BONUSES:
Top Exec. Salary: $ Bonus: $
Second Exec. Salary: $ Bonus: $

STOCK TICKER/OTHER:
Stock Ticker: JGCCY
Employees: 7,489
Parent Company:

Exchange: PINX
Fiscal Year Ends: 03/31

OTHER THOUGHTS:
Estimated Female Officers or Directors:
Hot Spot for Advancement for Women/Minorities:

Sales, profits and employees may be estimates. Financial information, benefits and other data can change quickly and may vary from those stated here.

Plunkett Research, Ltd.

Johnson & Johnson
NAIC Code: 325412

www.jnj.com

TYPES OF BUSINESS:
Personal Health Care & Hygiene Products
Sterilization Products
Surgical Products
Pharmaceuticals
Skin Care Products
Baby Care Products
Contact Lenses
Medical Equipment

BRANDS/DIVISIONS/AFFILIATES:
Motrin
Band-Aid
Listerine
Tylenol
Neosporin
Risperdal Consta
Actelion Ltd
Idorsia Ltd

CONTACTS:
Note: Officers with more than one job title may be intentionally listed here more than once.

Alex Gorsky, CEO
Dominic Caruso, CFO
Jorge Mesquita, Chairman of the Board, Divisional
Sandra Peterson, Chairman of the Board, Divisional
Joaquin Duato, Chairman of the Board, Divisional
Ronald Kapusta, Chief Accounting Officer
Paulus Stoffels, Executive VP
Peter Fasolo, Executive VP
Michael Ullmann, General Counsel
Joseph Wolk, Vice President, Divisional

GROWTH PLANS/SPECIAL FEATURES:

Johnson & Johnson, founded in 1886, is one of the world's most comprehensive and well-known researchers, developers and manufacturers of healthcare products. Johnson & Johnson's worldwide operations are divided into three segments: consumer, pharmaceuticals and medical devices. The company's principal consumer goods are personal care and hygiene products, including baby care, skin care, oral care, wound care and women's healthcare products as well as nutritional and over-the-counter pharmaceutical products. Major consumer brands include Motrin, Band-Aid, Listerine, Tylenol, Neosporin, Aveeno and Pepcid AC. The pharmaceutical segment covers a wide spectrum of health fields, including anti-infective, antipsychotic, contraceptive, dermatology, gastrointestinal, hematology, immunology, neurology, oncology, pain management and virology. Among its pharmaceutical products are Risperdal Consta, an antipsychotic used to treat schizophrenia, and Remicade for the treatment of immune mediated inflammatory diseases. In the medical devices segment, Johnson & Johnson makes a number of products including orthopedic joint reconstruction devices, surgical care, advanced sterilization products, blood glucose monitoring devices, diagnostic products and disposable contact lenses. The firm owns more than 260 companies in virtually all countries of the world, and is headquartered in New Brunswick, New Jersey. During 2017, Johnson & Johnson acquired Actelion Ltd., Europe's largest biotech firm by sales and market capitalization, for $30 billion. The deal included the spin-off of Actelion's drug discovery operations and early-stage development assets into a newly-created, Swiss-based biopharmaceutical company, Idorsia Ltd. Johnson & Johnson controls 16% of Idorsia, with the ability to raise the stake to 32% through convertible notes. In March 2018, Johnson & Johnson agreed to sell its LifeScan, Inc. business to Platinum Equity LLC for approximately $2.1 billion.

FINANCIAL DATA:
Note: Data for latest year may not have been available at press time.

In U.S. $	2017	2016	2015	2014	2013	2012
Revenue	76,450,000,000	71,890,000,000	70,074,000,000	74,331,000,000	71,312,000,000	67,224,000,000
R&D Expense	10,962,000,000	9,124,000,000	9,270,000,000	8,672,000,000	8,763,000,000	8,828,000,000
Operating Income	18,714,000,000	21,136,000,000	18,065,000,000	20,959,000,000	18,377,000,000	15,869,000,000
Operating Margin %	24.47%	29.40%	25.77%	28.19%	25.76%	23.60%
SGA Expense	21,420,000,000	19,945,000,000	21,203,000,000	21,954,000,000	21,830,000,000	20,869,000,000
Net Income	1,300,000,000	16,540,000,000	15,409,000,000	16,323,000,000	13,831,000,000	10,853,000,000
Operating Cash Flow	21,056,000,000	18,767,000,000	19,279,000,000	18,471,000,000	17,414,000,000	15,396,000,000
Capital Expenditure	3,513,000,000	3,349,000,000	3,566,000,000	4,013,000,000	3,861,000,000	2,934,000,000
EBITDA	24,249,000,000	24,283,000,000	23,494,000,000	24,991,000,000	20,057,000,000	17,973,000,000
Return on Assets %	.87%	12.04%	11.65%	12.37%	10.88%	9.23%
Return on Equity %	1.99%	23.36%	21.87%	22.70%	19.91%	17.80%
Debt to Equity	0.50	0.31	0.18	0.21	0.17	0.17

CONTACT INFORMATION:
Phone: 732 524-0400   Fax: 732 214-0332
Toll-Free:
Address: 1 Johnson & Johnson Plaza, New Brunswick, NJ 08933 United States

STOCK TICKER/OTHER:
Stock Ticker: JNJ
Employees: 126,400
Parent Company:

Exchange: NYS
Fiscal Year Ends: 12/31

SALARIES/BONUSES:
Top Exec. Salary: $1,600,000   Bonus: $
Second Exec. Salary: $1,173,023   Bonus: $

OTHER THOUGHTS:
Estimated Female Officers or Directors: 4
Hot Spot for Advancement for Women/Minorities: Y

Sales, profits and employees may be estimates. Financial information, benefits and other data can change quickly and may vary from those stated here.

Johnson Controls International plc

www.johnsoncontrols.com/

NAIC Code: 561600

TYPES OF BUSINESS:
Fire & Security Systems & Services
Security Monitoring Services
Specialty Valves
Breathing Apparatus
Metal Tubing

BRANDS/DIVISIONS/AFFILIATES:

CONTACTS:
Note: Officers with more than one job title may be intentionally listed here more than once.

George Oliver, CEO
Brian J. Stief, CFO
Lynn Minella, Exec. VP-Human Resources
Scott Clements, CTO
Judith A. Reinsdorf, General Counsel
Chris Brown, VP-Strategy
Juan Mogollon, Pres., Growth Markets
Colleen Repplier, Pres., Fire & Protection Products
Mike Ryan, Pres., Life Safety & Security Products
George Oliver, Chmn.
Vivek Kamath, Chief Procurement Officer

GROWTH PLANS/SPECIAL FEATURES:

Johnson Controls International plc is global diversified technology and multi-industrial firm that serves a wide range of customers located in more than 150 countries. The company creates intelligent buildings, efficient energy solutions, integrated infrastructure and next-generation transportation systems that work seamlessly together in relation to smart cities and communities. Johnson Controls' products, systems and services are divided into two categories: building technologies and solutions, and power solutions. The building technologies and solutions category sells integrated control systems, security systems, fire-detection systems, equipment and services through an extensive global network of sales and services offices, with operations in about 60 countries. The power solutions category services both automotive original equipment manufacturers (OEMs) and the battery aftermarket by providing advanced battery technology, coupled with systems engineering, marketing and service expertise. This division is a world-leading producer of lead-acid automotive batteries, producing and distributing approximately 154 million batteries annually. The power solutions segment operates approximately 68 wholly- and majority-owned manufacturing and assembly plants, distribution centers and sales offices in 17 countries worldwide. Raw materials used by each of Johnson Controls' businesses include lead, steel, tin, aluminum, urethan chemicals, brass, copper, sulfuric acid, polypropylene and certain fluorochemicals.

FINANCIAL DATA:
Note: Data for latest year may not have been available at press time.

In U.S. $	2017	2016	2015	2014	2013	2012
Revenue	30,172,000,000	37,674,000,000	37,179,000,000	42,828,000,000	42,730,000,000	41,955,000,000
R&D Expense						
Operating Income	3,181,000,000	1,989,000,000	2,461,000,000	2,319,000,000	2,813,000,000	1,780,000,000
Operating Margin %	10.54%	5.27%	6.61%	5.41%	6.58%	4.24%
SGA Expense	6,158,000,000	5,325,000,000	3,986,000,000	4,308,000,000	3,965,000,000	4,438,000,000
Net Income	1,611,000,000	-868,000,000	1,563,000,000	1,215,000,000	1,178,000,000	1,226,000,000
Operating Cash Flow	12,000,000	1,895,000,000	1,600,000,000	2,395,000,000	2,686,000,000	1,559,000,000
Capital Expenditure	1,343,000,000	1,249,000,000	1,135,000,000	1,199,000,000	1,377,000,000	1,831,000,000
EBITDA	4,212,000,000	2,848,000,000	3,299,000,000	3,244,000,000	3,765,000,000	2,647,000,000
Return on Assets %	2.79%	-1.86%	5.00%	3.77%	3.77%	4.04%
Return on Equity %	7.22%	-5.03%	14.41%	10.28%	9.87%	10.85%
Debt to Equity	0.58	0.60	0.55	0.56	0.37	0.46

CONTACT INFORMATION:
Phone: 353-21735-5800
Fax:
Toll-Free:
Address: One Albert Quay, Cork, T12 X8N6 Ireland

STOCK TICKER/OTHER:
Stock Ticker: JCI
Employees: 120,000
Parent Company:

Exchange: NYS
Fiscal Year Ends: 09/30

SALARIES/BONUSES:
Top Exec. Salary: $1,486,833 Bonus: $
Second Exec. Salary: $1,250,000 Bonus: $

OTHER THOUGHTS:
Estimated Female Officers or Directors: 2
Hot Spot for Advancement for Women/Minorities: Y

Sales, profits and employees may be estimates. Financial information, benefits and other data can change quickly and may vary from those stated here.

Juniper Networks Inc

www.juniper.net

NAIC Code: 0

TYPES OF BUSINESS:
Networking Equipment
IP Networking Systems
Internet Routers
Network Security Products
Internet Software
Intrusion Prevention
Application Acceleration

BRANDS/DIVISIONS/AFFILIATES:
ACX
MX
M
PTX
Cloud CPE
NorthStar
Junos
OCX1100

CONTACTS:
Note: Officers with more than one job title may be intentionally listed here more than once.

Rami Rahim, CEO
Kenneth Miller, CFO
Scott Kriens, Chairman of the Board
Terrance Spidell, Chief Accounting Officer
Bikash Koley, Chief Technology Officer
Andy Athreya, Executive VP
Vincent Molinaro, Other Executive Officer
Brian Martin, Senior VP

GROWTH PLANS/SPECIAL FEATURES:

Juniper Networks, Inc. designs, develops and sells products and services for high-performance networks. These products help customers build highly scalable, reliable, secure and cost-effective networks for their businesses. Juniper sells its products in more than 100 countries across three geographic regions: Americas; Europe, Middle East and Africa (EMEA); and Asia Pacific. The company's offerings address high-performance network requirements for global service providers, cloud environments, enterprises, governments and research and public-sector organizations who view the network as critical to its business success. Routing products include the firm's ACX, MX, M, PTX and T series, as well as its Cloud CPE end-to-end solution and NorthStar wide-area network controller. Switching products include the EX and QFX series, as well as the disaggregated version of Junos software, and the OCX1100 open networking switch designed to combine a cloud-optimized open compute project with the Junos operating system. Security products include the SRX series for data center gateway services, and for campus and branch gateway services; the vSRX virtual firewall; advanced malware protection; and Spotlight Secure threat intelligence platform. Juniper's Junos platform enables customers to expand network software into the application space, deploy software clients to control delivery and accelerate the pace of innovation with an ecosystem of developers. Juniper Networks owns over 2,900 issued or pending technology patents.

The firm offers its employees medical, dental, prescription and vision insurance; a savings plan; paid time off and holidays; and a stock purchase plan.

FINANCIAL DATA:
Note: Data for latest year may not have been available at press time.

In U.S. $	2017	2016	2015	2014	2013	2012
Revenue	5,027,200,000	4,990,100,000	4,857,800,000	4,627,100,000	4,669,100,000	4,365,400,000
R&D Expense	980,700,000	1,013,700,000	994,500,000	1,006,200,000	1,043,200,000	1,101,600,000
Operating Income	913,700,000	893,000,000	911,400,000	597,300,000	605,000,000	356,900,000
Operating Margin %	18.17%	17.89%	18.76%	12.90%	12.95%	8.17%
SGA Expense	1,177,700,000	1,197,800,000	1,172,700,000	1,254,700,000	1,293,200,000	1,245,600,000
Net Income	306,200,000	592,700,000	633,700,000	-334,300,000	439,800,000	186,500,000
Operating Cash Flow	1,260,100,000	1,106,000,000	892,500,000	763,400,000	842,300,000	642,400,000
Capital Expenditure	151,200,000	214,700,000	210,300,000	192,900,000	243,100,000	414,000,000
EBITDA	1,138,600,000	1,099,700,000	1,112,000,000	166,700,000	773,800,000	531,400,000
Return on Assets %	3.14%	6.48%	7.44%	-3.56%	4.36%	1.88%
Return on Equity %	6.35%	12.42%	13.35%	-5.47%	6.15%	2.64%
Debt to Equity	0.45	0.42	0.36	0.27	0.13	0.14

CONTACT INFORMATION:
Phone: 408 745-2000   Fax: 408 745-2100
Toll-Free: 888-586-4737
Address: 1133 Innovation Way, Sunnyvale, CA 94089 United States

SALARIES/BONUSES:
Top Exec. Salary: $1,000,000   Bonus: $
Second Exec. Salary: $162,879   Bonus: $500,000

STOCK TICKER/OTHER:
Stock Ticker: JNPR   Exchange: NYS
Employees: 9,832   Fiscal Year Ends: 12/31
Parent Company:

OTHER THOUGHTS:
Estimated Female Officers or Directors: 3
Hot Spot for Advancement for Women/Minorities: Y

Sales, profits and employees may be estimates. Financial information, benefits and other data can change quickly and may vary from those stated here.

Kaneka Corporation

NAIC Code: 325211

www.kaneka.co.jp/kaneka-e

TYPES OF BUSINESS:
Chemicals Manufacturing
Functional & Expandable Plastics
PVC Piping
Food Products
Specialty Fibers
Electronics Products
Biopharmaceuticals
Solar Photovoltaics

BRANDS/DIVISIONS/AFFILIATES:
Kaneka
Papre
Belco
Lachente
Kaneka Coenzyme Q10
Liposorber
Kanekalon
Kaneka Shokuhin Co Ltd

CONTACTS:
Note: Officers with more than one job title may be intentionally listed here more than once.

Mamoru Kadokura, Pres.
Hirosaku Nagano, Sr. Managing Exec. Officer
Tetsuro Hara, Sr. Managing Exec. Officer
Akihiko Iguchi, Managing Exec. Officer
Shinji Mizusawa, Managing Exec. Officer
Kimikazu Sugawara, Chmn.

GROWTH PLANS/SPECIAL FEATURES:

Kaneka Corporation is a Japanese manufacturer of chemical products for commercial and industrial use. The company operates through seven business segments. Kaneka's chemicals segment manufactures caustic soda for use in chemical fibers, paper, pharmaceuticals and aluminum; hydrochloric acid, hypochlorous soda and liquefied chlorine; and a variety of polyvinyl chloride (PVC) products. The functional plastics segment produces a variety of resins and polymers that improve the quality of PVC and other plastic products and the durability of sealing materials for cars, buildings and adhesives. The expandable plastics segment produces a variety of plastic foams for applications such as automobile bumpers, packaging materials and building insulation. Kaneka's foodstuffs segment produces margarines including its Kaneka margarine and shortening; Papre crystalized margarine; Belco, a cacao butter substitute; bakery yeast; Lachente and Franje cream products; and spices. The life science products segment manufactures food product supplement ingredients such as Kaneka Coenzyme Q10, a yeast extract; Kaneka Glavonoid, a polyphenol derived from licorice; and pharmaceutical intermediates for anti-hypertensives, hepatic medicines and antibiotics as well as Liposorber, a low-density lipoprotein (LDL) cholesterol absorption system. The electronic segment produces photovoltaic (PV) systems, optical and heat-resistant polyimide films, super thermal-conductive graphite sheets, and thin-film silicon PV modules. The synthetic fibers segment includes Kanekalon and Kanecaron modacrylic fibers, which are used in wigs and fake fur products; and ULTIMA, a protein fiber made from collagen that resembles human hair. Kaneka operates subsidiaries in Belgium, the U.S., Vietnam, Singapore, Malaysia, Korea, Taiwan, Australia, India and China. In early-2018, the firm acquired the composites portfolio of Henkel Corporation; and acquired a patent for large-scale culturing pluripotent stem cells in Japan. That April, Kaneka entered the dairy market via Kaneka Shokuhin Co., Ltd., selling milk to retailers in the Tokyo and Kansai areas.

FINANCIAL DATA:
Note: Data for latest year may not have been available at press time.

In U.S. $	2017	2016	2015	2014	2013	2012
Revenue	5,107,341,000	5,172,601,000	5,144,298,000	4,888,998,000	4,438,811,000	4,371,986,000
R&D Expense						
Operating Income	308,971,500	356,074,200	229,513,700	231,246,500	147,289,000	122,535,900
Operating Margin %	6.04%	6.88%	4.46%	4.72%	3.31%	2.80%
SGA Expense						
Net Income	190,832,900	195,500,300	167,998,900	127,166,000	86,873,490	50,326,070
Operating Cash Flow	448,285,900	556,214,000	313,042,700	316,042,500	305,338,200	147,587,100
Capital Expenditure	355,878,500	385,979,100	407,993,300	350,633,500	316,191,600	299,338,600
EBITDA	539,668,400	542,547,100	495,025,200	346,935,000	419,135,500	389,696,300
Return on Assets %	3.50%	3.69%	3.34%	2.71%	1.96%	1.17%
Return on Equity %	6.85%	7.10%	6.29%	5.09%	3.66%	2.16%
Debt to Equity	0.19	0.21	0.19	0.17	0.15	0.15

CONTACT INFORMATION:
Phone: 81 662265050   Fax: 81 662265037
Toll-Free:
Address: 2-3-18, Nakanoshima, Kita-ku, Osaka, 530-8288 Japan

STOCK TICKER/OTHER:
Stock Ticker: KANKF
Employees: 3,289
Parent Company:

Exchange: PINX
Fiscal Year Ends: 03/31

SALARIES/BONUSES:
Top Exec. Salary: $ Bonus: $
Second Exec. Salary: $ Bonus: $

OTHER THOUGHTS:
Estimated Female Officers or Directors:
Hot Spot for Advancement for Women/Minorities:

Sales, profits and employees may be estimates. Financial information, benefits and other data can change quickly and may vary from those stated here.

Plunkett Research, Ltd.

Kawasaki Heavy Industries Ltd
NAIC Code: 336999

www.khi.co.jp

TYPES OF BUSINESS:
Recreational Vehicle & Machinery Manufacturing
Motorcycles, ATVs & Personal Watercraft
Helicopter & Aerospace Manufacturing
Industrial Machinery and Robotics
Gas Turbines, Engines & Generators
Locomotives, Ships & Submarines
Plant & Infrastructure Manufacturing
Power Plant Construction

BRANDS/DIVISIONS/AFFILIATES:

GROWTH PLANS/SPECIAL FEATURES:
Kawasaki Heavy Industries, Ltd. manufactures a range of transportation equipment and industrial goods. The firm operates through four main business segments: mobility, energy, industrial equipment and leisure. The mobility segment consists of air unit, which includes airplanes, helicopters and space-related products; rail unit, which manufactures a wide range of rail cars; and marine, which makes marine machinery and ships. The energy segment consists of solutions unit, which includes distributed power generation, energy generation plants, power management systems for electric and thermal energy, nickel-metal hydride batteries production and technologies for renewable energy; and the equipment unit includes advanced products, such as gas turbines, efficient green gas engines, boiler facilities, oil/gas supply systems, industrial steam turbines, absorption chillers and high-end gasoline engines. The industrial equipment segment includes hydraulics components and systems such as motors, valves and pumps for agricultural and industrial use; robotics solutions for variety of industrial applications; industrial facilities and solutions, including cement and fertilizer plants, recycling and waste treatment facilities, construction machinery, technical products for defense and security, airport and material logistics systems, noise reduction hangers and rocket launch complexes. The leisure segment includes motorcycles, ATVs, recreation utility vehicles, utility vehicles, Jet Ski watercraft and general-purpose gasoline engines.

CONTACTS: Note: Officers with more than one job title may be intentionally listed here more than once.
Yoshinori Kanehana, Pres.
Masahiko Hirohata, Gen. Mgr.-Corp. Planning
Hiroshi Takata, Sr. VP
Joji Iki, Sr. VP
Shigeru Murayama, Sr. VP
Kyohei Matsuoka, Sr. VP

FINANCIAL DATA: Note: Data for latest year may not have been available at press time.

In U.S. $	2017	2016	2015	2014	2013	2012
Revenue	14,149,710,000	14,357,150,000	13,845,010,000	12,907,420,000	12,007,460,000	12,146,250,000
R&D Expense	406,437,500	406,288,400	387,609,500	376,355,500	388,569,000	372,088,700
Operating Income	1,244,811,000	1,667,990,000	1,552,655,000	1,373,989,000	1,028,209,000	1,158,860,000
Operating Margin %	8.79%	11.61%	11.21%	10.64%	8.56%	9.54%
SGA Expense	104,723,300	112,418,500	97,643,020	99,059,070	75,740,640	76,076,020
Net Income	244,121,500	428,945,400	481,078,800	359,614,300	287,534,900	217,281,600
Operating Cash Flow	871,194,400	801,742,100	1,189,221,000	1,413,462,000	261,794,300	789,426,200
Capital Expenditure	645,994,100	740,292,500	720,700,600	746,916,400	655,999,700	615,306,600
EBITDA	869,163,500	1,187,563,000	1,235,523,000	960,862,700	919,396,400	949,217,500
Return on Assets %	1.58%	2.80%	3.21%	2.55%	2.18%	1.71%
Return on Equity %	6.03%	10.66%	12.99%	11.00%	9.58%	7.83%
Debt to Equity	0.63	0.65	0.62	0.69	0.75	0.84

CONTACT INFORMATION:
Phone: 81 783719530   Fax: 81 783719568
Toll-Free:
Address: Kobe Crystal Tower,1-3 Higashikawasaki-cho 1-chome, Kobe, 650-8680 Japan

STOCK TICKER/OTHER:
Stock Ticker: KWHIF
Employees: 32,266
Parent Company:

Exchange: PINX
Fiscal Year Ends: 03/31

SALARIES/BONUSES:
Top Exec. Salary: $ Bonus: $
Second Exec. Salary: $ Bonus: $

OTHER THOUGHTS:
Estimated Female Officers or Directors: 1
Hot Spot for Advancement for Women/Minorities:

Sales, profits and employees may be estimates. Financial information, benefits and other data can change quickly and may vary from those stated here.

KBR Inc

NAIC Code: 237000

www.kbr.com

TYPES OF BUSINESS:
Heavy Construction and Engineering
Energy & Petrochemical Projects
Program & Project Management
Consulting & Technology Services
Operations & Maintenance Services
Contract Staffing Services

BRANDS/DIVISIONS/AFFILIATES:
Mantenimiento Marino de Mexico
Brown & Root Industrial Services
Granherne
Energo
GVA
Sigma Bravo Pty Ltd
Aspire Defence

CONTACTS:
Note: Officers with more than one job title may be intentionally listed here more than once.

Mark Sopp, CFO
Loren Carroll, Chairman of the Board
Raymond Carney, Chief Accounting Officer
Kenneth Hill, Executive VP, Divisional
Eileen Akerson, Executive VP
Ian Mackey, Executive VP
John Derbyshire, President, Divisional
Farhan Mujib, President, Divisional
J. Ibrahim, President, Geographical
Gregory Conlon, President, Geographical
William Bright, President, Subsidiary
Stuart Bradie, President

GROWTH PLANS/SPECIAL FEATURES:

KBR, Inc. is a global engineering, construction and services company supporting the hydrocarbons and international government services markets. The company conducts business in over 75 countries and maintains offices throughout the U.S., Australia, Africa, the U.K., Asia and the Middle East. KBR operates in three segments: technology and consulting, engineering and construction, and government services. The technology and consulting division combines proprietary KBR technologies, knowledge-based services and its three brands--Granherne, Energo and GVA--under a single global business. It also provides licensed technologies and consulting services to the oil and gas sectors. The engineering and construction segment leverages the firm's operational and technical abilities as a global provider of engineering, procurement, construction, commissioning and maintenance services for oil and gas, refining, petrochemicals and chemicals customers. The government services division provides full life-cycle support solutions to defense, space, aviation and other programs and missions for government agencies for the U.K., Australian and U.S. KBR covers the full spectrum of defense, space, aviation and other government programs and missions from research and development; through systems engineering; test and evaluation; systems integration; program management; to operations support, maintenance and field logistics. Geographically, the firm's U.S. operations account for 48% of total 2017 revenue; the Middle East, 22%; Europe, 12%; Australia, 8%; Canada, 5%; Africa, 1%; and other, 4%. Joint ventures (50/50) of KBR include: Mantenimiento Marino de Mexico, which provides maintenance and rehabilitation services to PEMEX offshore oil and gas facilities; and Brown & Root Industrial Services, which offers maintenance services, turnarounds and small capital expenditure projects, primarily in North America. In late-2017, KBR acquired Sigma Bravo Pty Ltd., a provider of software development, training, information management and technical support services to the Australian Defence Force. In April 2018, it acquired Carillion's interest in joint venture Aspire Defence, assuming operational control.

FINANCIAL DATA:
Note: Data for latest year may not have been available at press time.

In U.S. $	2017	2016	2015	2014	2013	2012
Revenue	4,171,000,000	4,268,000,000	5,096,000,000	6,366,000,000	7,283,000,000	7,770,000,000
R&D Expense						
Operating Income	195,000,000	-31,000,000	170,000,000	-304,000,000	332,000,000	296,000,000
Operating Margin %	4.67%	-.72%	3.33%	-4.77%	4.55%	3.80%
SGA Expense	147,000,000	143,000,000	155,000,000	239,000,000	249,000,000	222,000,000
Net Income	434,000,000	-61,000,000	203,000,000	-1,262,000,000	229,000,000	144,000,000
Operating Cash Flow	193,000,000	61,000,000	47,000,000	170,000,000	290,000,000	142,000,000
Capital Expenditure	8,000,000	11,000,000	10,000,000	53,000,000	78,000,000	75,000,000
EBITDA	318,000,000	14,000,000	209,000,000	-232,000,000	400,000,000	360,000,000
Return on Assets %	11.10%	-1.61%	5.33%	-25.98%	4.05%	2.51%
Return on Equity %	43.70%	-6.69%	20.22%	-70.91%	8.87%	5.71%
Debt to Equity	0.40	0.90	0.04	0.06		0.03

CONTACT INFORMATION:
Phone: 713 753-3011   Fax: 713 753-5353
Toll-Free:
Address: 601 Jefferson St., Ste. 3400, Houston, TX 77002 United States

STOCK TICKER/OTHER:
Stock Ticker: KBR
Employees: 27,500
Parent Company:

Exchange: NYS
Fiscal Year Ends: 12/31

SALARIES/BONUSES:
Top Exec. Salary: $1,000,022   Bonus: $
Second Exec. Salary: $547,899   Bonus: $

OTHER THOUGHTS:
Estimated Female Officers or Directors: 2
Hot Spot for Advancement for Women/Minorities: Y

KEO International Consultants WLL

NAIC Code: 541330

www.keoic.com

TYPES OF BUSINESS:
Engineering Consulting Services
Consulting
Engineering

BRANDS/DIVISIONS/AFFILIATES:
InSite
C-Quest

GROWTH PLANS/SPECIAL FEATURES:
KEO International Consultants WLL provides architectural design, infrastructure engineering and project and construction management services. The firm offers end-to-end planning and development solutions through the following firms: InSite, for inspired planning, urban design and landscape architecture; and C-Quest, for surveying purposes. KEO International draws expertise from more than 2,500 multi-disciplinary professionals across 60 nations, and serves clients from every major global market. Sectors include commercial, retail, education, environment, government, civic, healthcare, industrial, leisure/hospitality, residential, sports, tall buildings, transportation and water. Based in Kuwait, the firm has offices in Bahrain, Oman, Qatar, Saudi Arabia and the United Arab Emirates.

CONTACTS:
Note: Officers with more than one job title may be intentionally listed here more than once.

Donna Sultan, CEO
Darrel Fergus, CFO
Ann de Villiers, VP-Human Resources

FINANCIAL DATA:
Note: Data for latest year may not have been available at press time.

In U.S. $	2017	2016	2015	2014	2013	2012
Revenue						
R&D Expense						
Operating Income						
Operating Margin %						
SGA Expense						
Net Income						
Operating Cash Flow						
Capital Expenditure						
EBITDA						
Return on Assets %						
Return on Equity %						
Debt to Equity						

CONTACT INFORMATION:
Phone: 965-24651-6000   Fax: 965-2461-6001
Toll-Free:
Address: Free Trade Zone, Future Zone, Flamingo Complex, Bldg. 6, Safat, 13037 Kuwait

STOCK TICKER/OTHER:
Stock Ticker: Private
Employees: 2,500
Parent Company:

Exchange:
Fiscal Year Ends:

SALARIES/BONUSES:
Top Exec. Salary: $ Bonus: $
Second Exec. Salary: $ Bonus: $

OTHER THOUGHTS:
Estimated Female Officers or Directors:
Hot Spot for Advancement for Women/Minorities:

KEPCO Engineering & Construction Company Inc

www.kepco-enc.com

NAIC Code: 541330

TYPES OF BUSINESS:
Engineering Services

BRANDS/DIVISIONS/AFFILIATES:
Korea Electric Power Corporation (KEPCO)

GROWTH PLANS/SPECIAL FEATURES:
KEPCO Engineering & Construction Company, Inc. (KEPCO E&C) designs and develops power plant engineering technology. KEPCO stands for Korea Electric Power Corporation, of which KEPCO E&C is a wholly-owned subsidiary. The firm developed the Korean-model nuclear reactor, as well as various unique technologies in both thermal and nuclear power, and in architectural design. KEPCO E&C specializes in nuclear power plants, transmission and substation facilities, thermal power plants, research and development, and renewables. Renewable activities include flue gas desulfurization, deNOx systems, greenhouse gas mitigation, water pollution control facilities and environmental assessments.

CONTACTS:
Note: Officers with more than one job title may be intentionally listed here more than once.

Bae-Soo Lee, CEO

FINANCIAL DATA:
Note: Data for latest year may not have been available at press time.

In U.S. $	2017	2016	2015	2014	2013	2012
Revenue	459,021,000	420,447,000	582,820,386	722,961,765	669,781,895	
R&D Expense						
Operating Income						
Operating Margin %						
SGA Expense						
Net Income	19,872,500	14,786,400	27,525,028	48,547,139	30,505,590	
Operating Cash Flow						
Capital Expenditure						
EBITDA						
Return on Assets %						
Return on Equity %						
Debt to Equity						

CONTACT INFORMATION:
Phone: 82-544213114 Fax: 82-544216114
Toll-Free:
Address: 269 Hyeoksin-ro, Gimcheon-si, Yongin, 39660 South Korea

STOCK TICKER/OTHER:
Stock Ticker: 52690 Exchange: Seoul
Employees: 2,300 Fiscal Year Ends:
Parent Company: Korea Electric Power Corporation (KEPCO)

SALARIES/BONUSES:
Top Exec. Salary: $ Bonus: $
Second Exec. Salary: $ Bonus: $

OTHER THOUGHTS:
Estimated Female Officers or Directors:
Hot Spot for Advancement for Women/Minorities:

Sales, profits and employees may be estimates. Financial information, benefits and other data can change quickly and may vary from those stated here.

Khatib & Alami

www.khatibalami.com

NAIC Code: 541330

TYPES OF BUSINESS:
Engineering Consulting Services

BRANDS/DIVISIONS/AFFILIATES:

GROWTH PLANS/SPECIAL FEATURES:
Khatib & Alami is a multidisciplinary urban and regional planning, architectural and engineering consulting company. The firm has more than 30 offices worldwide. Khatib & Alami's services include engineering, design, tendering, supervision, project management, design & build, geographic information systems (GIS) and integrated client representative role. The company's divisions include: architecture, specializing in buildings, interior design and city/regional planning; infrastructure, specializing in transportation, water, environment, geotechnical and heavy civil; energy, specializing in oil & gas, power, renewables, energy and utilities; GIS, offering geospatial services and solutions; and project management services, offering project consultancy and sustainability services and solutions.

CONTACTS:
Note: Officers with more than one job title may be intentionally listed here more than once.

Najib Khatib, CEO

FINANCIAL DATA:
Note: Data for latest year may not have been available at press time.

In U.S. $	2017	2016	2015	2014	2013	2012
Revenue						
R&D Expense						
Operating Income						
Operating Margin %						
SGA Expense						
Net Income						
Operating Cash Flow						
Capital Expenditure						
EBITDA						
Return on Assets %						
Return on Equity %						
Debt to Equity						

CONTACT INFORMATION:
Phone: 961-1-843-843 Fax: 961-1-844-400
Toll-Free:
Address: Al Akhtal Assaghir Street, Jnah, Beirut, 1105 2100 Lebanon

STOCK TICKER/OTHER:
Stock Ticker: Private Exchange:
Employees: 6,000 Fiscal Year Ends:
Parent Company:

SALARIES/BONUSES:
Top Exec. Salary: $ Bonus: $
Second Exec. Salary: $ Bonus: $

OTHER THOUGHTS:
Estimated Female Officers or Directors:
Hot Spot for Advancement for Women/Minorities:

Sales, profits and employees may be estimates. Financial information, benefits and other data can change quickly and may vary from those stated here.

Kia Motors Corporation

NAIC Code: 336111

www.kia.com

TYPES OF BUSINESS:
Automobile Manufacturing
Buses
Military Vehicles
Passenger Vehicles

BRANDS/DIVISIONS/AFFILIATES:
Hyundai Motor Company
Picanto
Rio
Optima
Kia Quoris
Kia Soul EV
Sorento
Niro

CONTACTS: Note: Officers with more than one job title may be intentionally listed here more than once.
Hyoung-Keun Lee, CEO
Han-Woo Park, Pres.
Mong-Koo Chung, Chmn.

GROWTH PLANS/SPECIAL FEATURES:
Kia Motors Corporation is one of the largest automobile manufacturers in Korea. It is an affiliate of Hyundai Motor Company, which controls 33.88% of the firm. Kia has the capacity to produce 3.55 million vehicles a year from its manufacturing facilities in Mexico, South Korea, Slovakia, China, Vietnam and the U.S. The majority of Kia's car production is conducted in South Korea, with 44.8%, followed by China, with 25%. Passenger sedans include the Picanto, Rio, Cerato/Forte, cee'd, pro-cee'd, Optima, Cadenza and Kia Quoris models. The Kia Soul EV (electric vehicle) uses a heat pump system that increases driving distance by using recovered waste heat from the coolant water for its electric powertrain. SUVs and multi-purpose vehicles (MPVs) include the Soul, Carens/Rondo, Carnival, Sportage, Sorento and Mohave models. Commercial vehicles include trucks such as the K2500, K2700, K3000S and K4000G models. The company also produces buses and military vehicles. Additionally, Kia is involved in sports marketing, acting as a major sponsor of the Australian Open and the FIFA World Cup. The firm has several subsidiaries, including Kia Motors America, Inc.; Kia Motors Europe, the European sales arm based in Frankfurt; and Kia Motors Mexico. In addition, Kia maintains a manufacturing plant in the U.S. in Georgia, which can produce 370,000 cars annually. The company has more than 3,000 dealers and distributors in 172 countries. In 2016, the firm launched Niro, an eco-friendly compact SUV.

FINANCIAL DATA: Note: Data for latest year may not have been available at press time.

In U.S. $	2017	2016	2015	2014	2013	2012
Revenue	50,009,980,000	49,241,390,000	46,260,110,000	43,995,380,000	44,463,240,000	
R&D Expense	721,723,500	740,247,600	715,647,900	582,534,300	526,174,700	
Operating Income	618,613,800	2,299,374,000	2,199,227,000	2,403,129,000	2,967,866,000	
Operating Margin %	1.23%	4.66%	4.75%	5.46%	6.67%	
SGA Expense	5,482,857,000	5,258,866,000	4,874,115,000	4,377,888,000	4,586,583,000	
Net Income	904,267,100	2,573,228,000	2,457,357,000	2,796,444,000	3,565,679,000	
Operating Cash Flow	2,423,344,000	3,060,142,000	3,152,964,000	2,208,151,000	4,462,021,000	
Capital Expenditure	2,234,187,000	2,216,821,000	4,274,665,000	1,886,456,000	1,629,072,000	
EBITDA	3,004,230,000	4,920,898,000	4,308,102,000	4,867,652,000	5,716,556,000	
Return on Assets %	1.87%	5.68%	6.04%	7.75%	11.13%	
Return on Equity %	3.62%	10.84%	11.26%	14.00%	20.57%	
Debt to Equity	0.18	0.14	0.14	0.12	0.08	

CONTACT INFORMATION:
Phone: 82 234641114   Fax: 82 234646816
Toll-Free:
Address: 12 Heolleung-ro Seocho-gu, Seoul, 06797 South Korea

STOCK TICKER/OTHER:
Stock Ticker: KIMTF
Employees: 49,500
Parent Company: Hyundai Motor Company

Exchange: PINX
Fiscal Year Ends: 12/31

SALARIES/BONUSES:
Top Exec. Salary: $ Bonus: $
Second Exec. Salary: $ Bonus: $

OTHER THOUGHTS:
Estimated Female Officers or Directors:
Hot Spot for Advancement for Women/Minorities:

Sales, profits and employees may be estimates. Financial information, benefits and other data can change quickly and may vary from those stated here.

Kiewit Corporation

NAIC Code: 237310

www.kiewit.com

TYPES OF BUSINESS:
Construction & Engineering Services

BRANDS/DIVISIONS/AFFILIATES:

CONTACTS: Note: Officers with more than one job title may be intentionally listed here more than once.
Bruce E. Grewcock, CEO

GROWTH PLANS/SPECIAL FEATURES:
Kiewit Corporation, based in Omaha, Nebraska and employee-owned, is one of the largest general contractors in the world. The firm is organized into six business divisions, including: building; mining; oil, gas and chemical; power; transportation; and water/wastewater. The building division focuses on office buildings, industrial complexes, education and sports facilities, hotels, hospitals, transportation terminals, science and technology facilities and manufacturing plants, as well as retail and special-use facilities. The segment is Leadership in Energy and Environmental Design (LEED) certified. The mining division specializes in mine management, production, maintenance, contract mining, ore processing and mine infrastructure. The oil, gas and chemical division partners with domestic and international oil and gas firms to develop energy sources. It offers clients a fully-integrated delivery model for engineer-procure-construct (EPC) and startup services for their energy needs. This division focuses on the market sectors of offshore, oil sands, midstream and downstream. The power division helps clients meet the challenge of changing power consumption trends by building run-of-the-river hydroelectric, nuclear and geothermal power plants, as well as cogeneration, combined-cycle and waste-to-energy generation and resource facilities. The transportation division builds highways, bridges, rails and runways in order to connect the world. Its transportation projects have delivered engineering solutions and construction for air, bridge, marine/port, rail, roads and tunnels sectors, among others. Last, water/wastewater performs water supply projects such as roller-compacted concrete, earth-fill and rock-fill dams, reservoirs, water tunnels and canals across North America. Kiewet has hundreds of subsidiaries and offices located in the U.S., Canada and Mexico.

FINANCIAL DATA: Note: Data for latest year may not have been available at press time.

In U.S. $	2017	2016	2015	2014	2013	2012
Revenue	8,700,000,000	8,600,000,000	10,380,000,000	11,000,000,000	10,787,600,000	10,100,000,000
R&D Expense						
Operating Income						
Operating Margin %						
SGA Expense						
Net Income		251,000,000				
Operating Cash Flow						
Capital Expenditure						
EBITDA						
Return on Assets %						
Return on Equity %						
Debt to Equity						

CONTACT INFORMATION:
Phone: 402-342-2052 Fax: 402-271-2829
Toll-Free:
Address: 3555 Farnam St., Omaha, NE 68131 United States

STOCK TICKER/OTHER:
Stock Ticker: Private Exchange:
Employees: 19,900 Fiscal Year Ends:
Parent Company:

SALARIES/BONUSES:
Top Exec. Salary: $ Bonus: $
Second Exec. Salary: $ Bonus: $

OTHER THOUGHTS:
Estimated Female Officers or Directors:
Hot Spot for Advancement for Women/Minorities:

Sales, profits and employees may be estimates. Financial information, benefits and other data can change quickly and may vary from those stated here.

Kimley-Horn and Associates Inc

www.kimley-horn.com

NAIC Code: 541330

TYPES OF BUSINESS:
Engineering
Project Consulting
Environmental Restoration
Wireless Network Development
Water System Management

BRANDS/DIVISIONS/AFFILIATES:

CONTACTS:
Note: Officers with more than one job title may be intentionally listed here more than once.

John C. Atz, CEO
John Atz, Pres.
Julie Beauvais, Dir.-Corp. Comm.
Varner Olmsted, Controller
Richard Adams, VP
Kurt Cooper, Sr. VP

GROWTH PLANS/SPECIAL FEATURES:

Kimley-Horn and Associates, Inc. is an engineering and land-planning firm with more than 80 offices across the U.S. The company offers a variety of design and planning services to clients in the private and public sectors in a wide range of industries. It is a leading engineering firm for multi-family residential and retail properties. For the aviation industry, Kimley-Horn is able to plan, design and administer various construction projects. In the environmental sector, it offers a variety of services, such as planning and feasibility studies, environmental documentation and environmental restoration. The company provides engineering and consulting services to clients in the biomass, solar, wind energy and fossil fuel-based power industries. Solutions for the intelligent transportation segment include intelligent transportation system (ITS) architectures, systems engineering analyses, ITS master planning, deployment plans and feasibility studies. Other transit sector services include bus system planning, regional operations studies, modeling and simulation as well as financial feasibility and cost studies for mass transit systems. Parking services include planning and management of parking projects; design, maintenance and restoration services; and parking technologies. In the wireless communications market, Kimley-Horn offers wireless systems inventory and assessment, network development, wireless camouflage applications and distributed antenna systems. For clients in the water resources and utilities segment, the company offers alternative supplies; flood control; storm water management; wastewater collection; treatment and disposal; water resources permitting; and water supply, treatment and distribution.

The firm offers employees benefits including medical, prescription, dental and vision coverage; a health savings account; a flexible spending account; short- and long-term disability insurance; life insurance; an employee assistance program; tuition reimb

FINANCIAL DATA:
Note: Data for latest year may not have been available at press time.

In U.S. $	2017	2016	2015	2014	2013	2012
Revenue	722,298,000	628,800,000	523,800,000	435,000,000	400,000,000	374,000,000
R&D Expense						
Operating Income						
Operating Margin %						
SGA Expense						
Net Income						
Operating Cash Flow						
Capital Expenditure						
EBITDA						
Return on Assets %						
Return on Equity %						
Debt to Equity						

CONTACT INFORMATION:
Phone: 919-677-2000   Fax: 919-677-2050
Toll-Free: 888-524-4636
Address: 3001 Weston Pkwy., Cary, NC 27513 United States

SALARIES/BONUSES:
Top Exec. Salary: $ Bonus: $
Second Exec. Salary: $ Bonus: $

STOCK TICKER/OTHER:
Stock Ticker: Private
Employees: 3,100
Parent Company:

Exchange:
Fiscal Year Ends: 12/31

OTHER THOUGHTS:
Estimated Female Officers or Directors: 1
Hot Spot for Advancement for Women/Minorities:

Kleinfelder Group Inc (The)

NAIC Code: 541330

www.kleinfelder.com

TYPES OF BUSINESS:
Engineering Consulting Services
Engineering
Architecture
Consulting

BRANDS/DIVISIONS/AFFILIATES:

CONTACTS: Note: Officers with more than one job title may be intentionally listed here more than once.
George J. Pierson, CEO
John A. Murphy, Exec. VP
Patrick Schaffner, Sr. VP-Human Resources

GROWTH PLANS/SPECIAL FEATURES:

The Kleinfelder Group, Inc. provides architectural, engineering and scientific consulting solutions for infrastructure and natural resource needs in the U.S and internationally. Market sectors the firm services include: energy, consisting of oil, gas and power; facilities, consisting of commercial, industrial and institutional; government, consisting of civilian federal agencies, Department of Energy, National Guard, state and local governments, the U.S. Air Force, the U.S. Army Corps of Engineers and the U.S. Navy; transportation, consisting of aviation, marine ports and harbors, rail, mass transit and surface transportation; and water, consisting of dams, levees and water infrastructure. Kleinfelder's services to its clients include architecture and design, construction materials engineering and testing, design engineering, environmental sciences and engineering, facility and operations compliance, geotechnical and geologic engineering, project management, strategic planning, risk management, sustainability and water science and engineering. The firm is headquartered in San Diego, California, with over 70 locations across the U.S., Canada and Australia.

The company offers its employees medical, dental and vision insurance; pharmaceutical services; wellness incentives; long-term care; financial programs; and other benefits.

FINANCIAL DATA: Note: Data for latest year may not have been available at press time.

In U.S. $	2017	2016	2015	2014	2013	2012
Revenue						
R&D Expense						
Operating Income						
Operating Margin %						
SGA Expense						
Net Income						
Operating Cash Flow						
Capital Expenditure						
EBITDA						
Return on Assets %						
Return on Equity %						
Debt to Equity						

CONTACT INFORMATION:
Phone: 619-831-4600   Fax: 619-232-1039
Toll-Free:
Address: 550 West C St., Ste. 1200, San Diego, CA 92101 United States

SALARIES/BONUSES:
Top Exec. Salary: $ Bonus: $
Second Exec. Salary: $ Bonus: $

STOCK TICKER/OTHER:
Stock Ticker: Private   Exchange:
Employees: 2,000   Fiscal Year Ends:
Parent Company:

OTHER THOUGHTS:
Estimated Female Officers or Directors:
Hot Spot for Advancement for Women/Minorities:

Sales, profits and employees may be estimates. Financial information, benefits and other data can change quickly and may vary from those stated here.

Konami Holdings Corporation

NAIC Code: 0

www.konami.co.jp

TYPES OF BUSINESS:
Computer Software, Electronic Games, Apps & Entertainment
Toys
Arcade Games
Mobile Phone Media Content
Sports Clubs
Health & Fitness Products
Casino Games
Casino Management Systems

BRANDS/DIVISIONS/AFFILIATES:
Konami Digital Entertainment Co Ltd
Konami Sports Club Co Ltd
Konami Sports Life Co Ltd
Konami Gaming Inc
Konami Australia Pty Ltd
Konami Amusement Co Ltd
KPE Inc
Internet Revolution Inc

CONTACTS: *Note: Officers with more than one job title may be intentionally listed here more than once.*
Takuya Kozuki, Pres.
Satoshi Sakamoto, CEO
Kagemasa Kozuki, Chmn.

GROWTH PLANS/SPECIAL FEATURES:
Konami Holdings Corporation is based in Japan, and operates four key businesses: digital enterprise, health and fitness, gaming and systems and amusement. The digital entertainment business produces a wide range of digital products, including mobile games, computer and video games, as well as computer and video card games. This division is operated through wholly-owned Konami Digital Entertainment Co. Ltd. The health and fitness business operates health and fitness clubs, and also designs, manufactures and sells fitness machines and health-related products. Subsidiaries within this division include Konami Sports Club Co. Ltd. and Konami Sports Life Co. Ltd. The gaming and systems business designs, manufactures, sells and services gaming machines and casino management systems in the global gaming market. Subsidiaries within this division include Konami Gaming, Inc.; and Konami Australia Pty Ltd. The amusement business handles all business aspects related to arcade games, pachislot and pachinko machines, from design and production to sales. Subsidiaries within this division include Konami Amusement Co. Ltd. and KPE, Inc. Konami Holdings owns an additional 13 businesses, including Internet Revolution, Inc. and Konami Real Estate, Inc., located in Japan; Konami Corporation of America and Konami Gaming, Inc., located in the U.S.; Konami Digital Entertainment BV, located in the U.K.; and Konami Digital Entertainment Limited, Konami Digital Entertainment Pte. Ltd. and Konami Australia Pty Ltd., located in Hong Kong, Singapore and Australia, respectively.

FINANCIAL DATA:
Note: Data for latest year may not have been available at press time.

In U.S. $	2017	2016	2015	2014	2013	2012
Revenue	2,141,997,000	2,328,135,000	2,032,393,000	2,027,157,000	2,105,413,000	2,475,853,000
R&D Expense						
Operating Income	406,409,600	355,505,900	197,941,100	120,616,700	203,791,700	384,684,200
Operating Margin %	18.97%	15.27%	9.73%	5.95%	9.67%	15.53%
SGA Expense	420,225,500	459,213,800	467,738,000	487,879,600	477,985,900	466,284,700
Net Income	241,764,500	97,969,070	92,397,990	35,718,280	122,731,500	214,384,200
Operating Cash Flow	407,667,300	664,579,900	421,594,900	84,097,270	95,360,540	353,223,400
Capital Expenditure	139,454,100	177,743,600	240,069,000	247,391,500	92,481,840	86,267,940
EBITDA	494,801,600	505,356,800	360,406,200	193,981,700	314,216,500	477,464,200
Return on Assets %	7.80%	3.28%	3.13%	1.19%	4.04%	7.16%
Return on Equity %	11.60%	4.88%	4.47%	1.70%	5.97%	11.24%
Debt to Equity	0.08	0.11	0.06	0.15	0.10	0.13

CONTACT INFORMATION:
Phone: 81 357700573   Fax: 81 354123300
Toll-Free:
Address: 9-7-2, Akasaka, Minato-ku, Tokyo, 107-8323 Japan

STOCK TICKER/OTHER:
Stock Ticker: KNMCY
Employees: 5,048
Parent Company:

Exchange: PINX
Fiscal Year Ends: 03/31

SALARIES/BONUSES:
Top Exec. Salary: $2,757,593   Bonus: $
Second Exec. Salary: $ Bonus: $

OTHER THOUGHTS:
Estimated Female Officers or Directors:
Hot Spot for Advancement for Women/Minorities:

Sales, profits and employees may be estimates. Financial information, benefits and other data can change quickly and may vary from those stated here.

Plunkett Research, Ltd. 403

Koninklijke Philips NV (Royal Philips)
NAIC Code: 334310

www.philips.com/global

TYPES OF BUSINESS:
Manufacturing-Electrical & Electronic Equipment
Consumer Electronics & Appliances
Lighting Systems
Medical Imaging Equipment
Semiconductors
Consulting Services
Nanotech Research
MEMS

BRANDS/DIVISIONS/AFFILIATES:
VitalHealth

GROWTH PLANS/SPECIAL FEATURES:
Koninklijke Philips NV (Royal Philips) is a health technology company. The firm focuses on improving people's health and enabling better outcomes across the health continuum from wellness and prevention to diagnosis, treatment and home care. Royal Philips leverages advanced technology and clinical and consumer insights to deliver integrated solutions. The company is a leader in diagnostic imaging, image-guided therapy, patient monitoring and health informatics, as well as in consumer health and home care. In December 2017, the firm acquired VitalHealth, a provider of cloud-based population health management solutions for the delivery of personalized care outside of the hospital.

CONTACTS: Note: Officers with more than one job title may be intentionally listed here more than once.
Frans van Houten, CEO
Abhijit Bhattacharya, CFO
Eric Coutinho, Chief Legal Officer
Jim Andrew, Chief Strategy & Innovation Officer
Deborah DiSanzo, Exec. VP
Pieter Nota, CEO-Phillips Consumer Lifestyle
Eric Rondolat, Exec. VP
J. van der Veer, Chmn.
Patrick Kung, CEO-Greater China

FINANCIAL DATA: Note: Data for latest year may not have been available at press time.

In U.S. $	2017	2016	2015	2014	2013	2012
Revenue	21,956,580,000	30,274,890,000	29,939,000,000	26,415,820,000	28,809,060,000	30,610,780,000
R&D Expense	2,178,370,000	2,495,740,000	2,379,659,000	2,019,067,000	2,140,087,000	2,235,175,000
Operating Income	1,873,348,000	2,327,793,000	1,225,024,000	603,867,700	2,493,270,000	1,271,950,000
Operating Margin %	8.53%	7.68%	4.09%	2.28%	8.65%	4.15%
SGA Expense	6,143,644,000	8,314,605,000	8,673,961,000	7,250,118,000	7,439,058,000	7,737,904,000
Net Income	2,046,235,000	1,788,140,000	796,512,600	512,484,900	1,443,602,000	279,088,200
Operating Cash Flow	3,350,293,000	2,864,976,000	1,743,683,000	1,843,711,000	1,416,434,000	2,680,975,000
Capital Expenditure	1,060,782,000	1,073,131,000	1,181,802,000	1,044,728,000	1,226,259,000	1,310,232,000
EBITDA	3,289,783,000	3,982,563,000	2,927,956,000	2,206,772,000	4,211,020,000	3,172,467,000
Return on Assets %	5.75%	4.57%	2.17%	1.51%	4.20%	.77%
Return on Equity %	13.47%	11.93%	5.72%	3.75%	10.45%	1.92%
Debt to Equity	0.28	0.31	0.35	0.34	0.29	0.33

CONTACT INFORMATION:
Phone: 31 402791111 Fax:
Toll-Free: 877-248-4237
Address: Breitner Center, Amstelplein 2, Amsterdam, 1096 BC Netherlands

STOCK TICKER/OTHER:
Stock Ticker: PHG
Employees: 114,731
Parent Company:

Exchange: NYS
Fiscal Year Ends: 12/31

SALARIES/BONUSES:
Top Exec. Salary: $1,205,000 Bonus: $1,270,166
Second Exec. Salary: $687,500 Bonus: $553,392

OTHER THOUGHTS:
Estimated Female Officers or Directors: 3
Hot Spot for Advancement for Women/Minorities: Y

Sales, profits and employees may be estimates. Financial information, benefits and other data can change quickly and may vary from those stated here.

Kumho Industrial Co Ltd

NAIC Code: 236220

www.kumhoenc.com

TYPES OF BUSINESS:
Commercial and Institutional Building Construction
Research & Development
Sewage Treatment

BRANDS/DIVISIONS/AFFILIATES:
Kumho Asiana Group

CONTACTS:
Note: Officers with more than one job title may be intentionally listed here more than once.

Park Sam Koo, CEO
Bak Sam Koo, CEO-Kumho Asiana Group

GROWTH PLANS/SPECIAL FEATURES:
Kumho Industrial Co. Ltd. provides engineering and construction services in South Korea and internationally. The firm's business activities are divided into four divisions: buildings, civil works, housing and environment/plant. The buildings division designs, develops and constructs buildings in relation to the development of cities, including public, business, education, research, correction, military, airport, sales, culture, medical and various types of overseas buildings and facilities. The civil works division designs, develops and constructs buildings in relation to cities and its respective country, including airports, railways, roads, housing, harbors and various related overseas construction. The housing division designs, develops and constructs residential complexes such as apartments and various types of residential living spaces. Last, the environment/plant division is engaged in industrial development, including energy storage, petrochemicals, industrial facilities and solutions, as well as environmental facilities and solutions. Kumho Industrial is part of the Kumho Asiana Group.

FINANCIAL DATA:
Note: Data for latest year may not have been available at press time.

In U.S. $	2017	2016	2015	2014	2013	2012
Revenue	1,215,410,000	1,124,800,000	1,357,435,200	1,407,472,919	1,389,132,708	1,425,300,000
R&D Expense						
Operating Income						
Operating Margin %						
SGA Expense						
Net Income	89,219,200	29,942,400	-5,416,942	55,757,263	50,959,898	-691,700,000
Operating Cash Flow						
Capital Expenditure						
EBITDA						
Return on Assets %						
Return on Equity %						
Debt to Equity						

CONTACT INFORMATION:
Phone: 82-2-6303-0114 Fax:
Toll-Free:
Address: 4, Sicheong-gil, Naju-si, Jeollanam-do, 1095-4 South Korea

STOCK TICKER/OTHER:
Stock Ticker: 2990
Employees: 3,107
Parent Company: Kumho Asiana Group

Exchange: Seoul
Fiscal Year Ends: 12/31

SALARIES/BONUSES:
Top Exec. Salary: $ Bonus: $
Second Exec. Salary: $ Bonus: $

OTHER THOUGHTS:
Estimated Female Officers or Directors:
Hot Spot for Advancement for Women/Minorities:

Sales, profits and employees may be estimates. Financial information, benefits and other data can change quickly and may vary from those stated here.

L3 Technologies Inc

NAIC Code: 334200

www.l3t.com

TYPES OF BUSINESS:
Electronic Equipment-Specialized Communications
Intelligence, Surveillance & Reconnaissance Systems
Aviation & Aerospace Products
Telemetry Products
Instrumentation Products
Microwave Components
Security Systems
Signal Intelligence Products

BRANDS/DIVISIONS/AFFILIATES:
Open Water Power
Ocean-Server Technology
Adaptive Methods Inc
Doss Aviation Inc
Escola De Aviacao Aerocondor SA
Kigre Inc

CONTACTS:
Note: Officers with more than one job title may be intentionally listed here more than once.

Christopher Kubasik, CEO
Ralph DAmbrosio, CFO
Michael Strianese, Chairman of the Board
Dan Azmon, Chief Accounting Officer
Ann Davidson, General Counsel
Mark Schwarz, President, Divisional
Todd Gautier, President, Divisional
Jeff Miller, President, Divisional
John Mega, President, Divisional

GROWTH PLANS/SPECIAL FEATURES:

L3 Technologies, Inc. is a supplier of products and services used in various aerospace and defense platforms. The company operates through three business segments: electronic systems, aerospace systems and communication systems. The electronic systems segment provides components, products, systems and subsystems and related services. The aerospace systems segment provides products and services for the global intelligence, surveillance and reconnaissance (ISR) market, specializing in signals intelligence (SIGINT) and multi-intelligence platforms, to include full motion video, electro-optical, infrared and synthetic aperture radars, along with other types of information gathering systems. The businesses in this segment provide select command, control and communications (C3) systems products for military and other U.S. Government and select foreign government ISR applications. The communication systems segment provides networked communication systems; secure communications products; radio frequency components; satellite communication terminals; and space, microwave and telemetry products. The firm's customers include the U.S. Department of Defense, the Department of Homeland Security, U.S. intelligence agencies, aerospace and defense contractors, foreign governments and commercial customers. During 2017, L3 acquired Open Water Power, a Massachusetts-based battery startup spun out of MIT; Ocean-Server Technology, a business specializing in lithium-ion battery, sensor and robotic mini-sub products; Adaptive Methods, Inc., a systems engineering company that delivers undersea warfare and anti-submarine warfare capabilities for U.S. military customers; Doss Aviation, Inc., the sole provider of initial flight training for U.S. Air Force pilots, and also trains international military pilots; Escola De Aviacao Aerocondor SA, which trains professional pilots in the field of commercial aviation; and Kigre, Inc., which supplies solid-state laser components, and manufactures specialty laser and filter glass materials for use in a variety of applications.

L3 Technologies offers its employees health, dental and vision insurance; a prescription drug plan; flexible spending accounts; a 401(k) plan; educational assistance; and an employee stock purchase plan.

FINANCIAL DATA:
Note: Data for latest year may not have been available at press time.

In U.S. $	2017	2016	2015	2014	2013	2012
Revenue	9,573,000,000	10,511,000,000	10,466,000,000	12,124,000,000	12,629,000,000	13,146,000,000
R&D Expense						
Operating Income	1,020,000,000	1,008,000,000	890,000,000	1,085,000,000	1,258,000,000	1,351,000,000
Operating Margin %	10.65%	9.58%	8.50%	8.94%	9.96%	10.27%
SGA Expense						
Net Income	677,000,000	710,000,000	-240,000,000	664,000,000	778,000,000	810,000,000
Operating Cash Flow	1,102,000,000	1,041,000,000	1,098,000,000	1,125,000,000	1,263,000,000	1,231,000,000
Capital Expenditure	224,000,000	216,000,000	197,000,000	183,000,000	209,000,000	210,000,000
EBITDA	1,265,000,000	1,225,000,000	701,000,000	1,328,000,000	1,487,000,000	1,642,000,000
Return on Assets %	5.50%	5.92%	-1.85%	4.76%	5.59%	5.52%
Return on Equity %	14.05%	15.94%	-4.97%	11.74%	13.54%	13.39%
Debt to Equity	0.65	0.73	0.72	0.74	0.60	0.66

CONTACT INFORMATION:
Phone: 212 697-1111 Fax: 212 867-5249
Toll-Free:
Address: 600 Third Ave., New York, NY 10016 United States

STOCK TICKER/OTHER:
Stock Ticker: LLL Exchange: NYS
Employees: 45,000 Fiscal Year Ends: 12/31
Parent Company:

SALARIES/BONUSES:
Top Exec. Salary: $1,390,000 Bonus: $
Second Exec. Salary: $905,365 Bonus: $

OTHER THOUGHTS:
Estimated Female Officers or Directors:
Hot Spot for Advancement for Women/Minorities:

Sales, profits and employees may be estimates. Financial information, benefits and other data can change quickly and may vary from those stated here.

Lahmeyer International GmbH

www.lahmeyer.de

NAIC Code: 541330

TYPES OF BUSINESS:
Engineering Services

BRANDS/DIVISIONS/AFFILIATES:
Engie
Tractebel Engineering
W Lahmeyer & Co
Lahmeyer International Qatar LLC
Lahmeyer IDP Consult Inc
Lahmeyer Hydroprojekt GmbH
Hidro Dizayn Group
Lahmeyer and Tractebel Engineering Consultancy LLC

CONTACTS:
Note: Officers with more than one job title may be intentionally listed here more than once.
Martin Seeger, CEO
Michael Stephan, CFO

GROWTH PLANS/SPECIAL FEATURES:
Lahmeyer International GmbH is an international engineering company offering a broad range of planning and consultancy services, primarily to complex infrastructure projects in the energy, hydropower and water resources sectors. The firm is subdivided into two divisions: energy and hydropower and water resources. The energy division is operated through W. Lahmeyer & Co., which provides technical innovations for generating energy. Its competencies include thermal power plants, renewable energies, power transmission and distribution, energy storage, energy management and energy efficiency. Subsidiaries in the energy division include Lahmeyer International Qatar LLC, Lahmeyer International Rus, Lahmeyer Nigeria Ltd. and Lahmeyer IDP Consult, Inc. The hydropower and water resources division provides solutions to sustainable hydropower utilization, development of water and land resources and reliable and environmentally compatible flood protection. Its competencies include hydropower plants, dams, underground structures and hydraulic structures, as well as sustainable land and water resources development. Subsidiaries in the hydropower and water resources division include Lahmeyer Hydroprojekt GmbH, Hidro Dizayn Group, Lahmeyer International (India) Pvt. Ltd. and Lahmeyer Consulting Engineers (Tanzania) Limited. Lahmeyer International is a subsidiary of Tractebel Engineering, which itself is part of the energy services division of Engie. In December 2017, Lahmeyer formed a joint venture with Tractebel called Lahmeyer and Tractebel Engineering Consultancy, LLC, to become more of a local partner to clients in the Sultanate of Oman, as well as in the greater region.

FINANCIAL DATA:
Note: Data for latest year may not have been available at press time.

In U.S. $	2017	2016	2015	2014	2013	2012
Revenue						
R&D Expense						
Operating Income						
Operating Margin %						
SGA Expense						
Net Income						
Operating Cash Flow						
Capital Expenditure						
EBITDA						
Return on Assets %						
Return on Equity %						
Debt to Equity						

CONTACT INFORMATION:
Phone: 49-6101-55-0
Fax: 49-6101-55-2222
Toll-Free:
Address: Friedberger Strasse 173, Bad Vilbel, 61118 Germany

STOCK TICKER/OTHER:
Stock Ticker: Private
Employees: 1,300
Parent Company: Engie
Exchange:
Fiscal Year Ends:

SALARIES/BONUSES:
Top Exec. Salary: $
Bonus: $
Second Exec. Salary: $
Bonus: $

OTHER THOUGHTS:
Estimated Female Officers or Directors:
Hot Spot for Advancement for Women/Minorities:

Sales, profits and employees may be estimates. Financial information, benefits and other data can change quickly and may vary from those stated here.

Langan Engineering and Environmental Services Inc

www.langan.com

NAIC Code: 541330

TYPES OF BUSINESS:
Engineering Consulting Services
Engineering
Consulting
Environment

BRANDS/DIVISIONS/AFFILIATES:
Langan International

CONTACTS:
Note: Officers with more than one job title may be intentionally listed here more than once.

David T. Gockel, CEO
William Kraekel, CFO

GROWTH PLANS/SPECIAL FEATURES:

Langan Engineering and Environmental Services, Inc. (LEES) provides integrated site engineering and environmental consulting services for private developers, property owners and public-sector clients. LEES' industry sectors include airports, redevelopment, colleges and universities, corporate headquarters, entertainment and attraction, energy, environmental, federal/state/local governments, high tech, hospitals and healthcare, infrastructure, industrial/manufacturing/warehouse, K-12 schools, mission critical, data centers, mixed-use, renewable energy, residential, resorts/hospitality/casinos, retail, stadium and arena, tall buildings, waterfront and marine. The company's services include site plans, civil plans, hydrology studies, construction management, value engineering, geotechnical, sub-surface investigations, tunneling/underground/trenchless construction, groundwater control, forensic studies, natural resources and ecological restoration, regulatory compliance and permitting, air quality, industrial hygiene, seismic and ground motion, demolition, traffic and transportation, surveying, 3D scanning, information management, landscape architecture and permitting. LEES is headquartered in New Jersey, with regional offices in New York, Pennsylvania, Connecticut, Virginia, Florida, California, Ohio and North Dakota. Wholly-owned subsidiary Langan International, provides integrated consulting services through international office locations, including Abu Dhabi, Athens, Doha, Dubai, Istanbul, London and Panama.

The company offers its employees medical, dental and vision plans; retirement savings plans; life and accidental insurance; short- and long-term disability; and employee assistance, flexible spending, educational reimbursement programs.

FINANCIAL DATA:
Note: Data for latest year may not have been available at press time.

In U.S. $	2017	2016	2015	2014	2013	2012
Revenue						
R&D Expense						
Operating Income						
Operating Margin %						
SGA Expense						
Net Income						
Operating Cash Flow						
Capital Expenditure						
EBITDA						
Return on Assets %						
Return on Equity %						
Debt to Equity						

CONTACT INFORMATION:
Phone: 973-560-4900   Fax: 973-560-4901
Toll-Free:
Address: 300 Kimball Dr., 4/Fl, Parsippany, NJ 07054-2172 United States

STOCK TICKER/OTHER:
Stock Ticker: Private   Exchange:
Employees: 1,000   Fiscal Year Ends:
Parent Company:

SALARIES/BONUSES:
Top Exec. Salary: $ Bonus: $
Second Exec. Salary: $ Bonus: $

OTHER THOUGHTS:
Estimated Female Officers or Directors:
Hot Spot for Advancement for Women/Minorities:

Lanxess AG

www.lanxess.com

NAIC Code: 325211

TYPES OF BUSINESS:
Plastics Material and Resin Manufacturing
Performance Chemicals
Chemical Intermediates
Engineering Plastics
Performance Rubber

BRANDS/DIVISIONS/AFFILIATES:
Arlanxeo
Chemtura Corporation

CONTACTS:
Note: Officers with more than one job title may be intentionally listed here more than once.

Matthias Zachert, CEO
Michael Pontzen, CFO
Matthias Zachert, Chmn.

GROWTH PLANS/SPECIAL FEATURES:
Lanxess AG is a German specialty chemicals manufacturing company with operations in 25 countries. The firm's products are grouped into five categories: advanced intermediates, performance chemicals, high-performance materials, Arlanxeo performance elastomers and specialty additives. Advanced intermediates are produces by Saltigo and Advanced Industrial Intermediates, a global supplier of industrial chemical intermediates, as well as a key player in the custom synthesis and manufacturing of chemical precursors and specialty active ingredients. Performance chemicals include inorganic pigments, liquid purification technologies and leather and material protection products. The high-performance materials division provides a broad range of engineering plastics and polyurethane systems to major industries worldwide. Arlanxeo is a joint venture between Lanxess and Saudi Aramco, and produces high performance elastomers and tire and specialty rubbers, with a focus on the development, manufacturing and marketing of synthetic high-performance rubber. Last, specialty additive products include the areas of plastic additives and lubricants, as well as rubber additives and colorant additives. During 2017, Lanxess acquired U.S. company, Chemtura Corporation, a leading global supplier of flame retardant and lubricant additives. Chemtura was merged with and into the specialty additives business group.

FINANCIAL DATA:
Note: Data for latest year may not have been available at press time.

In U.S. $	2017	2016	2015	2014	2013	2012
Revenue	11,934,110,000	9,507,521,000	9,758,206,000	9,886,636,000	10,249,700,000	11,230,210,000
R&D Expense	179,061,000	161,772,300	160,537,400	197,584,500	229,692,000	237,101,400
Operating Income	855,788,000	695,250,600	697,720,400	502,605,700	203,759,100	1,058,312,000
Operating Margin %	7.17%	7.31%	7.15%	5.08%	1.98%	9.42%
SGA Expense	1,648,596,000	1,338,635,000	1,288,004,000	1,259,601,000	1,304,058,000	1,360,863,000
Net Income	107,436,600	237,101,400	203,759,100	58,040,460	-196,349,600	634,740,300
Operating Cash Flow	1,071,896,000	850,848,400	854,553,100	984,218,000	791,573,100	1,034,849,000
Capital Expenditure	675,492,100	542,122,600	535,948,000	758,230,700	770,579,700	859,492,700
EBITDA	1,349,749,000	1,150,930,000	1,015,091,000	764,405,200	764,405,200	1,446,072,000
Return on Assets %	.85%	2.24%	2.28%	.66%	-2.21%	7.14%
Return on Equity %	3.59%	7.89%	7.38%	2.31%	-7.55%	23.50%
Debt to Equity	0.97	1.07	0.54	0.78	0.86	0.93

CONTACT INFORMATION:
Phone: 49 221 8885-0   Fax:
Toll-Free:
Address: Kennedyplatz 1, Cologne, 51369 Germany

STOCK TICKER/OTHER:
Stock Ticker: LNXSF
Employees: 18,527
Parent Company:

Exchange: PINX
Fiscal Year Ends: 12/31

SALARIES/BONUSES:
Top Exec. Salary: $ Bonus: $
Second Exec. Salary: $ Bonus: $

OTHER THOUGHTS:
Estimated Female Officers or Directors: 3
Hot Spot for Advancement for Women/Minorities: Y

Sales, profits and employees may be estimates. Financial information, benefits and other data can change quickly and may vary from those stated here.

Larsen & Toubro Limited (L&T)

NAIC Code: 237000

www.larsentoubro.com

TYPES OF BUSINESS:
Heavy Construction and Engineering
Manufacturing Services
Shipbuilding
Construction Equipment Manufacturing
Electronic Engineering Services
IT Services
Financial Services
Insurance

BRANDS/DIVISIONS/AFFILIATES:
L&T Hydrocarbon Engineering
L&T Heavy Engineering
L&T Defence
L&T Valves
L&T Technology Services
L&T Infrastructure Development Projects Ltd
L&T Metro Rail
L&T Finance Holdings

CONTACTS:
Note: Officers with more than one job title may be intentionally listed here more than once.

S. N. Subrahmanyan, Deputy Manag. Dir.
R. Shankar Raman, CFO
Shailendra Roy, Sr. Exec. VP-Corp. Affairs & Power
M. V. Kotwal, Pres., Heavy Eng.
S. N. Subrahmanyan, Sr. Exec. VP-Infrastructure & Construction
A. M. Naik, Exec. Chmn.

GROWTH PLANS/SPECIAL FEATURES:

Larsen & Toubro Limited (L&T) is a technology, engineering, construction and manufacturing company based in India, with operations around the world. The company operates in 16 divisions. Construction includes buildings, factories, transport infrastructure, heavy civil infrastructure, water plants and facilities, renewable energy plants and facilities, and power transmission and distribution plants and facilities. Wholly-owned L&T Hydrocarbon Engineering serves the oil and gas sector worldwide, delivering engineering and construction solutions across the hydrocarbon spectrum, including up-, mid- and downstream, as well as pipelines. Power provides concept-to-commissioning solutions for supercritical thermal power plants. Metallurgical and material handling undertakes EPC (engineering, procurement, construction) projects for ferrous and non-ferrous metal industries, as well as bulk material and ash handling systems. L&T Heavy Engineering manufactures and supplies custom designed equipment and critical piping to process industries. Shipbuilding offers total solutions, from concept to design, for new builds as well as repair and retrofit for defense and commercial vessels. Electrical and automation offers products, and solutions for electricity distribution and control. Construction and mining machinery manufactures, distributes and provides after-sales support for construction and mining equipment. L&T Valves is a flow-control solutions provider for critical global needs. EWAC Alloys is a market leader in maintenance and repair welding. L&T Infotech is a global IT services and solutions provider. L&T Technology Services designs and develops solutions through the entire development chain across multiple industries. L&T Infrastructure Development Projects Ltd. is an infrastructure developer in India. L&T Metro Rail is building the Hyderabad Metro Rail, one of the world's largest projects of its kind. L&T Finance Holdings provides financial products and services, covering mutual funds, infrastructure finance and home loans. L&T Realty is the residential and commercial real estate arm of L&T.

FINANCIAL DATA:
Note: Data for latest year may not have been available at press time.

In U.S. $	2017	2016	2015	2014	2013	2012
Revenue	16,763,790,000	15,742,120,000	14,112,080,000	13,057,380,000	11,426,840,000	9,864,639,000
R&D Expense						
Operating Income	2,226,458,000	2,228,692,000	1,983,212,000	1,904,874,000	1,670,826,000	1,189,500,000
Operating Margin %	13.28%	14.15%	14.05%	14.58%	14.62%	12.05%
SGA Expense	1,138,844,000	942,806,000	840,245,400	719,287,800	715,871,900	319,127,400
Net Income	926,631,600	780,808,800	730,849,900	751,891,200	798,469,500	725,271,300
Operating Cash Flow	956,329,900	-495,263,500	-102,594,300	-1,068,066,000	-576,747,500	-972,570,200
Capital Expenditure	456,888,200	807,433,300	1,062,831,000	1,068,761,000	1,201,357,000	1,120,072,000
EBITDA	2,744,205,000	2,839,690,000	1,917,836,000	2,126,640,000	1,921,927,000	1,481,034,000
Return on Assets %	2.74%	2.41%	2.61%	3.13%	3.97%	4.39%
Return on Equity %	12.82%	11.99%	12.12%	13.69%	16.46%	17.24%
Debt to Equity	1.34	1.67	1.59	1.47	1.39	1.23

CONTACT INFORMATION:
Phone: 91-22-67525656   Fax: 91-22-67525893
Toll-Free:
Address: L&T House, N.M. Marg, Ballard Estate, Mumbai, 400 001 India

STOCK TICKER/OTHER:
Stock Ticker: LTORY
Employees: 41,466
Parent Company:

Exchange: PINX
Fiscal Year Ends: 03/31

SALARIES/BONUSES:
Top Exec. Salary: $ Bonus: $
Second Exec. Salary: $ Bonus: $

OTHER THOUGHTS:
Estimated Female Officers or Directors:
Hot Spot for Advancement for Women/Minorities:

Sales, profits and employees may be estimates. Financial information, benefits and other data can change quickly and may vary from those stated here.

Lauren Engineers & Constructors Inc

www.laurenec.com

NAIC Code: 541330

TYPES OF BUSINESS:
Engineering Consulting Services
Engineering

BRANDS/DIVISIONS/AFFILIATES:

CONTACTS: Note: Officers with more than one job title may be intentionally listed here more than once.
C. Cleve Whitener III, CEO
Randy Lipps, Pres.
Matt Higgins, CFO
C. Cleve Whitener III, Chmn.

GROWTH PLANS/SPECIAL FEATURES:

Lauren Engineers & Constructors, Inc. provides comprehensive engineering, procurement and construction (EPC) services to the heavy industrial sector throughout North America and select international markets. The company designs and constructs highly-specialized facilities in the chemicals and polymers, power, oil and gas, and refining industries. Lauren Engineers & Constructors' services include EPC, engineering, fabrication, modularization, field services, project management and safety. Current projects are engaged in power generation, refining, petrochemicals, oil and gas midstream, oil and gas upstream, chemical processing and modularization. Some of the firm's customers have been General Electric; Dominion; Southern Company; Siemens Westinghouse; DAK Americas; Procter & Gamble; BAE Systems; Holly Corporation; Navajo Refining; Flying J, Inc.; and Alon, USA. Headquartered in Abilene, Texas, Lauren Engineers & Constructors has fabrication facilities in Abilene, as well as in Catoosa, Oklahoma.

FINANCIAL DATA: Note: Data for latest year may not have been available at press time.

In U.S. $	2017	2016	2015	2014	2013	2012
Revenue						
R&D Expense						
Operating Income						
Operating Margin %						
SGA Expense						
Net Income						
Operating Cash Flow						
Capital Expenditure						
EBITDA						
Return on Assets %						
Return on Equity %						
Debt to Equity						

CONTACT INFORMATION:
Phone: 325-670-9660 Fax: 325-670-9663
Toll-Free:
Address: 901 S. First St., Abilene, TX 79602 United States

SALARIES/BONUSES:
Top Exec. Salary: $ Bonus: $
Second Exec. Salary: $ Bonus: $

STOCK TICKER/OTHER:
Stock Ticker: Private   Exchange:
Employees: Fiscal Year Ends:
Parent Company:

OTHER THOUGHTS:
Estimated Female Officers or Directors:
Hot Spot for Advancement for Women/Minorities:

Sales, profits and employees may be estimates. Financial information, benefits and other data can change quickly and may vary from those stated here.

Layne Christensen Company

NAIC Code: 237110

www.laynechristensen.com

TYPES OF BUSINESS:
Construction & Civil Engineering Services
Water Treatment Plant Development
Drilling Services
Oil & Gas Field Services
Unconventional Natural Gas Production

BRANDS/DIVISIONS/AFFILIATES:
Layne Inliner LLC
Inliner

CONTACTS:
Note: Officers with more than one job title may be intentionally listed here more than once.

David Brown, Chairman of the Board
Lisa Curtis, Chief Accounting Officer
Michael Caliel, Director
Steven Crooke, General Counsel
Larry Purlee, President, Subsidiary
Kevin Maher, Senior VP, Divisional
J. Anderson, Senior VP

GROWTH PLANS/SPECIAL FEATURES:

Layne Christensen Company is a global water management and services and drilling company, providing integrated solutions to address the world's toughest water, mineral and energy challenges. The firm's customers include government agencies, investor-owned utilities, industrial companies, global mining companies, consulting engineering firms, oil & gas companies, power companies and agribusinesses. Layne Christensen operates on a geographically dispersed basis, with approximately 52 sales and operations offices located throughout the Americas. The company operates in three business segments: water resources, inliner and mineral services. Water resources provides customers with sustainable solutions for water supply system development and technology. The inliner segment is a full-service rehabilitation company offering a wide range of solutions for wastewater, storm water and process sewer pipeline networks. Its proprietary Inliner cured-in-place pipe allows the company to rehabilitate aging and deteriorated infrastructure and provide structural building, as well as infiltration and inflow reduction. Subsidiary Layne Inliner, LLC began as the first U.S. licensee of the Inliner technology in 1991, and has expanded to own and operate Inliner technologies and products. Last, the mineral services segment extracts rock and soil samples for analysis of mineral content and grade for clients considering in investing in mineral mining firms. In February 2018, Layne agreed to be acquired by Granite Construction Incorporated in a stock-for-stock transaction, subject to shareholder and other customary closing conditions. That same month, the firm sold its heavy civil business.

FINANCIAL DATA:
Note: Data for latest year may not have been available at press time.

In U.S. $	2017	2016	2015	2014	2013	2012
Revenue	601,972,000	683,010,000	797,601,000	859,283,000	1,075,624,000	
R&D Expense						
Operating Income	-24,191,000	-27,912,000	-56,481,000	-59,945,000	-25,174,000	
Operating Margin %	-4.01%	-4.08%	-7.08%	-6.97%	-2.34%	
SGA Expense	97,202,000	108,159,000	122,240,000	146,457,000	163,962,000	
Net Income	-52,236,000	-44,777,000	-110,151,000	-128,639,000	-36,651,000	
Operating Cash Flow	12,972,000	-307,000	-23,102,000	-1,131,000	24,751,000	
Capital Expenditure	21,818,000	25,668,000	16,211,000	34,409,000	77,503,000	
EBITDA	-7,022,000	-561,000	-5,291,000	-10,916,000	50,969,000	
Return on Assets %	-11.29%	-8.65%	-18.47%	-17.63%	-4.53%	
Return on Equity %	-49.54%	-28.90%	-46.80%	-36.63%	-8.50%	
Debt to Equity	1.97	1.23	0.72	0.37	0.24	

CONTACT INFORMATION:
Phone: 281-475-2600 Fax: 281-475-2733
Toll-Free: 855-529-6301
Address: 1800 Hughes Landing Blvd. Ste. 800, The Woodlands, TX 77380 United States

STOCK TICKER/OTHER:
Stock Ticker: LAYN Exchange: NAS
Employees: 2,491 Fiscal Year Ends: 01/31
Parent Company:

SALARIES/BONUSES:
Top Exec. Salary: $660,000 Bonus: $
Second Exec. Salary: $400,000 Bonus: $

OTHER THOUGHTS:
Estimated Female Officers or Directors:
Hot Spot for Advancement for Women/Minorities:

Sales, profits and employees may be estimates. Financial information, benefits and other data can change quickly and may vary from those stated here.

Lear Corporation

NAIC Code: 336300

www.lear.com

TYPES OF BUSINESS:
- Automobile Components
- Automotive Interiors
- Electrical Systems
- Instrument Panels
- Seat Systems
- Flooring Systems
- Entertainment & Wireless Systems
- Keyless Entry Systems

BRANDS/DIVISIONS/AFFILIATES:
EXO Technologies

CONTACTS:
Note: Officers with more than one job title may be intentionally listed here more than once.

- Raymond Scott, CEO
- Jeffrey Vanneste, CFO
- Henry Wallace, Chairman of the Board
- Amy Doyle, Chief Accounting Officer
- Terrence Larkin, Executive VP, Divisional
- Shari Burgess, Other Executive Officer
- Frank Orsini, President, Divisional
- Jay Kunkel, President, Divisional
- Jeneanne M. Hanley, President, Divisional
- Thomas DiDonato, Senior VP, Divisional
- Melvin Stephens, Senior VP, Divisional

GROWTH PLANS/SPECIAL FEATURES:

Lear Corporation is one of the world's largest automotive interior systems suppliers. The firm serves every major automotive manufacturer, including General Motors, Ford, BMW, Fiat Chrysler and Daimler. The company currently operates 151 facilities in 22 countries. Its business is conducted through two segments: seating and e-systems. The seating segment consists of the design, engineering, just-in-time assembly and delivery of complete seat systems as well as the manufacture of all major seat components, including seat structures and mechanisms, seat covers, seat forms and headrests. The segment produces seat systems that are fully assembled and ready for installation in automobiles and light trucks. These include luxury and performance automotive seating required by premium automakers, including Alfa Romeo, Audi, Lamborghini, BMW, Cadillac, Ferrari, Jaguar Land Rover, Lincoln, Maserati, Mercedes-Benz and Porsche. The e-systems segment consists of the design, manufacture, assembly and supply of electrical distribution systems, electronic modules and related components and software for light vehicles globally. Its electrical distribution systems route electrical signals and manage electrical power within the vehicle for traditional vehicle architectures, as well as high power and hybrid electric systems. Electronics control various functions within the vehicle, and include body control modules, smart junction boxes, gateway modules, wireless control modules, lighting control modules and audio amplifiers. Connectivity capabilities facilitate secure, wireless communication between the vehicle's systems and external networks, as well as other vehicles. As of December 2017, the company had 18 operating joint ventures located in five countries, of which 14 operated in Asia and four in North America. During 2017, Lear Corporation acquired Grupo Antolin's automotive seating business; and in January 2018, it acquired Israel-based EXO Technologies, a developer of differentiated GPS technology providing high-accuracy positioning solutions for autonomous and connected vehicle applications.

FINANCIAL DATA:
Note: Data for latest year may not have been available at press time.

In U.S. $	2017	2016	2015	2014	2013	2012
Revenue	20,467,000,000	18,557,600,000	18,211,400,000	17,727,300,000	16,234,000,000	14,567,000,000
R&D Expense						
Operating Income	1,608,300,000	1,427,200,000	1,186,800,000	929,200,000	736,600,000	705,200,000
Operating Margin %	7.85%	7.69%	6.51%	5.24%	4.53%	4.84%
SGA Expense	635,200,000	621,900,000	580,500,000	529,900,000	528,700,000	479,300,000
Net Income	1,313,400,000	975,100,000	745,500,000	672,400,000	431,400,000	1,282,800,000
Operating Cash Flow	1,783,100,000	1,619,300,000	1,271,100,000	927,800,000	820,100,000	729,800,000
Capital Expenditure	594,500,000	528,300,000	485,800,000	424,700,000	460,600,000	458,300,000
EBITDA	2,040,100,000	1,799,000,000	1,466,000,000	1,165,800,000	964,000,000	938,300,000
Return on Assets %	11.79%	10.10%	8.03%	7.69%	5.22%	16.87%
Return on Equity %	35.73%	32.58%	25.33%	22.39%	13.20%	43.31%
Debt to Equity	0.47	0.62	0.65	0.49	0.34	0.17

CONTACT INFORMATION:
Phone: 248 447-1500 Fax:
Toll-Free: 800-413-5327
Address: 21557 Telegraph Rd., Southfield, MI 48033 United States

STOCK TICKER/OTHER:
Stock Ticker: LEA
Employees: 148,400
Parent Company:

Exchange: NYS
Fiscal Year Ends: 12/31

SALARIES/BONUSES:
Top Exec. Salary: $1,354,500 Bonus: $
Second Exec. Salary: $855,098 Bonus: $

OTHER THOUGHTS:
Estimated Female Officers or Directors: 1
Hot Spot for Advancement for Women/Minorities:

Sales, profits and employees may be estimates. Financial information, benefits and other data can change quickly and may vary from those stated here.

Plunkett Research, Ltd.

Lenovo Group Limited
NAIC Code: 334111

www.lenovo.com

TYPES OF BUSINESS:
Computer Manufacturing
Servers
Notebook Computers
Handheld Computers
Peripherals
Cellular Phones

BRANDS/DIVISIONS/AFFILIATES:
P Series
ThinkPad
ideapad
YOGA
Lenovo

CONTACTS: Note: Officers with more than one job title may be intentionally listed here more than once.
Yuanqing Yang, CEO
Gianfranco Lanci, Pres.
Wai Ming Wong, CFO
David Roman, CMO
Gao Lan, Sr. VP-Human Resources
Arthur Hu, CIO
Zhiqiang He, CTO
Jay Clemens, Sr. VP-Legal
Jun Liu, Sr. VP
Gerry P. Smith, Sr. VP
Peter Hortensius, Sr. VP
Gianfranco Lanci, Sr. VP
Yuanqing Yang, Chmn.
Xudong Chen, Sr. VP
Gerry P. Smith, Sr. VP-Global Supply Chain

GROWTH PLANS/SPECIAL FEATURES:
Lenovo Group Limited is one of the largest PC manufacturers in China. The company manufactures its own line of laptops, tablets, desktops, workstations, servers, storage and networking, accessories and software, marketing its products in more than 160 countries. Its P Series workstation is designed to run powerful applications with stability and speed, and are created with tools for industries such as oil/gas, energy, engineering, architecture, media/entertainment, finance, medical and science. Lenovo's ThinkPad P Series mobile workstations fuse the portability of ThinkPad with the power of a workstation, and feature ISV-certified applications, fast graphics and processing, and cutting-edge technology to handle compute-sensitive needs, all within a light and thin package. Lenovo tower servers deliver performance and room for expansion at affordable prices. The firm's ThinkStation P Series towers deliver the latest generation of Intel Xeon processors which are combined with NVIDIA Quadro graphics, and come in a variety of widths and sizes. The company's laptop and 2-in-1 brands include ThinkPad, ideapad, YOGA and Lenovo; its phones, tablets and smart devices include video reality devices, Android phones and tablets, Windows tablets, convertibles and smart home products. Gaming products include laptops, towers, desktops, accessories and AR/VR (augmented reality/virtual reality). Other products include servers, storage solutions, networking solutions, software, monitors, docking, chargers, batteries, mice, keyboards, cables, adapters, cases/bags, audio accessories and more. Services offered by the Lenovo include warranty support, technical support, accidental damage protection, asset tagging and transition services. Lenovo operates throughout China, Asia Pacific, Europe, the Middle East, Africa and the Americas.

The firm offers employees retirement and savings plans; discounts on fitness centers; and an employee discount program, which allows employees, as well as their friends and families, to buy discounted Lenovo computers and accessories.

FINANCIAL DATA: Note: Data for latest year may not have been available at press time.

In U.S. $	2017	2016	2015	2014	2013	2012
Revenue	43,034,730,000	44,912,100,000	46,295,590,000	38,707,130,000	33,873,400,000	29,574,440,000
R&D Expense	1,361,691,000	1,491,370,000	1,220,919,000	732,454,000	623,987,000	453,334,000
Operating Income	211,204,000	650,987,000	1,275,598,000	1,028,211,000	799,959,000	583,990,000
Operating Margin %	.49%	1.44%	2.75%	2.65%	2.36%	1.97%
SGA Expense	4,532,621,000	4,481,580,000	4,185,296,000	3,302,984,000	2,734,789,000	2,421,072,000
Net Income	535,084,000	-128,146,000	828,715,000	817,228,000	635,148,000	472,992,000
Operating Cash Flow	2,119,822,000	292,261,000	238,492,000	1,432,058,000	19,530,000	1,939,956,000
Capital Expenditure	627,884,000	751,263,000	902,794,000	675,344,000	441,312,000	329,193,000
EBITDA	1,430,248,000	642,368,000	1,696,022,000	1,396,603,000	1,110,322,000	836,971,000
Return on Assets %	2.05%	-.49%	3.64%	4.63%	3.87%	3.56%
Return on Equity %	15.14%	-3.61%	23.36%	28.79%	25.26%	22.54%
Debt to Equity	0.72	0.83	0.46		0.11	

CONTACT INFORMATION:
Phone: 86-10-5886-8888   Fax:
Toll-Free:
Address: No. 6 Chuang Ye Rd., Haidian District, Beijing, 100085 China

SALARIES/BONUSES:
Top Exec. Salary: $ Bonus: $
Second Exec. Salary: $ Bonus: $

STOCK TICKER/OTHER:
Stock Ticker: LNVGF   Exchange: PINX
Employees: 52,000   Fiscal Year Ends: 03/31
Parent Company:

OTHER THOUGHTS:
Estimated Female Officers or Directors: 2
Hot Spot for Advancement for Women/Minorities:

Sales, profits and employees may be estimates. Financial information, benefits and other data can change quickly and may vary from those stated here.

Leo A Daly Company

NAIC Code: 541330

www.leoadaly.com

TYPES OF BUSINESS:
Engineering Services
Engineering
Design
Architecture
Management

BRANDS/DIVISIONS/AFFILIATES:
Lockwood Andrews & Newman Inc

GROWTH PLANS/SPECIAL FEATURES:
Leo A Daly Company is an architecture, engineering, planning, interior design and program management firm. Its portfolio includes projects in more than 91 countries, all 50 U.S. states and Washington, D.C. Daly's services are extended through subsidiary Lockwood, Andrews & Newman, Inc. to markets such as aviation, civic, corporate/commercial, education, federal, food, distribution, manufacturing, gaming, entertainment, healthcare, hospitality, residential, science, technology, senior living and venues. Daly's projects include: 1776 Eye Street, a 245,000-square-foot Washington D.C. renovation project; a design for an international airport in China; the Allegro at Boynton Beach, a 136-unit assisted living community in Florida; and Tucson, Arizona's Casino Del Sol. Leo A Daly is headquartered in Nebraska, USA, with additional domestic offices in Atlanta, Dallas, Houston, Las Vegas, Los Angeles, Miami, Minneapolis, Omaha, West Palm Beach and Washington, D.C.; and internationally in Beijing, Hong Kong, Abu Dhabi, Dammam, Doha and Riyadh.

CONTACTS:
Note: Officers with more than one job title may be intentionally listed here more than once.

Leo A. Daly III, CEO
Dennis W. Petersen, Pres.
James B. Brader, CFO
Stephen W. Held, CIO
John J. Kraskiewicz, Sr. VP

FINANCIAL DATA:
Note: Data for latest year may not have been available at press time.

In U.S. $	2017	2016	2015	2014	2013	2012
Revenue	160,000,000	156,510,000	140,000,000			
R&D Expense						
Operating Income						
Operating Margin %						
SGA Expense						
Net Income						
Operating Cash Flow						
Capital Expenditure						
EBITDA						
Return on Assets %						
Return on Equity %						
Debt to Equity						

CONTACT INFORMATION:
Phone: 402-391-8111 Fax: 42-391-8564
Toll-Free:
Address: 8600 Indian Hills Dr., Omaha, NE 68114-4039 United States

STOCK TICKER/OTHER:
Stock Ticker: Private
Employees: 800
Parent Company:

Exchange:
Fiscal Year Ends:

SALARIES/BONUSES:
Top Exec. Salary: $ Bonus: $
Second Exec. Salary: $ Bonus: $

OTHER THOUGHTS:
Estimated Female Officers or Directors:
Hot Spot for Advancement for Women/Minorities:

Sales, profits and employees may be estimates. Financial information, benefits and other data can change quickly and may vary from those stated here.

LG Display Co Ltd

NAIC Code: 334419

www.lgdisplay.com

TYPES OF BUSINESS:
LCD (Liquid Crystal Display) Unit Screens Manufacturing
OLED Manufacturing

BRANDS/DIVISIONS/AFFILIATES:

CONTACTS:
Note: Officers with more than one job title may be intentionally listed here more than once.
Sang-Beom Han, CEO
Yong-Kee Hwang, Pres.
Cheol Dong Jeong, Chief Prod. Officer
Yong Kee Hwang, Head-TV Bus.

GROWTH PLANS/SPECIAL FEATURES:

LG Display Co., Ltd. operates in the digital display business and is headquartered in Seoul, South Korea. LG Display develops and manufactures TFT-LCD (thin-film transistor liquid crystal display) and OLED (organic light-emitting diode) panels for use in televisions, notebook computers, desktop monitors, tablet computers and mobile devices. The firm is a world-leading supplier of ultra-high-definition television panels. The company also manufactures display panels for industrial and other applications, including entertainment systems, automotive displays, portable navigation devices and medical diagnostic equipment. During 2017, LG Display sold 142.2 million display panels that were nine inches or larger, comprising an approximate 28% global market share based on sales revenue for the same year. A TFT-LCD panel consists of two thing glass substrates and polarizer films between which a layer of liquid crystals is deposited and behind which a light source unit is mounted. The frontplane glass substrate is fitted with a color filter, and the backplane glass substrate has many thin film transistors formed on its surface. An OLED panel consists of a thin film of organic material encased between anode and cathode electrodes. When a current is applied, light is emitted directly from the organic material. Because a separate backlight is not needed, OLED panels can be lighter and thinner than TFT-LCD panels. LG Display currently operates 12 fabrication facilities, six assembly facilities, and an R&D center. The firm typically ships its display panels to original equipment manufacturer clients on a contract basis, who use them in products they assemble for end-brand customers.

FINANCIAL DATA:
Note: Data for latest year may not have been available at press time.

In U.S. $	2017	2016	2015	2014	2013	2012
Revenue		24,758,590,000	26,514,600,000	24,713,240,000	25,252,720,000	
R&D Expense		1,059,292,000	1,137,720,000	1,087,617,000	1,023,566,000	
Operating Income		1,209,360,000	1,399,454,000	1,166,504,000	844,582,000	
Operating Margin %		4.88%	5.27%	4.72%	3.34%	
SGA Expense		1,084,973,000	1,353,489,000	1,176,841,000	1,288,472,000	
Net Income		846,999,500	902,898,600	844,715,600	398,055,100	
Operating Cash Flow		3,401,126,000	2,547,013,000	2,675,872,000	3,348,690,000	
Capital Expenditure		3,868,393,000	2,484,471,000	3,116,158,000	3,416,920,000	
EBITDA		4,159,106,000	4,612,271,000	4,525,029,000	4,505,970,000	
Return on Assets %		3.82%	4.24%	4.04%	1.84%	
Return on Equity %		7.21%	8.18%	8.20%	4.09%	
Debt to Equity		0.31	0.23	0.28	0.28	

CONTACT INFORMATION:
Phone: 82-2-3777-1010   Fax: 82-2-3777-0785
Toll-Free:
Address: LG Twin Tower, 128, Yeoui-daero, Yeongdeungpo-gu, Seoul, 07336 South Korea

STOCK TICKER/OTHER:
Stock Ticker: LPL
Employees: 49,094
Parent Company:

Exchange: NYS
Fiscal Year Ends: 12/31

SALARIES/BONUSES:
Top Exec. Salary: $ Bonus: $
Second Exec. Salary: $ Bonus: $

OTHER THOUGHTS:
Estimated Female Officers or Directors:
Hot Spot for Advancement for Women/Minorities:

LG Electronics Inc

www.lg.com

NAIC Code: 334220

TYPES OF BUSINESS:
Manufacturing-Electronics
Cellular Handsets
Telecommunications Equipment
Computer Products
Home Appliances & Electronics
Security Systems
Displays
Audio Systems

BRANDS/DIVISIONS/AFFILIATES:
LG Electronics Institute of Technology
LG Display Co Ltd
LG Electronics USA Inc
Zenith

CONTACTS:
Note: Officers with more than one job title may be intentionally listed here more than once.

Seong-jin Cho, CEO
Young-Ha Lee, Co-Pres.
David Jung, CFO
Hyun-Hoi Ha, Pres.

GROWTH PLANS/SPECIAL FEATURES:

LG Electronics, Inc. is a Korean manufacturer of telecommunications equipment, home appliances, televisions, audio equipment, security systems and computer products. The company has four lines of business: home entertainment, mobile communications, home appliance and air solution, and vehicle components. The home entertainment division manufactures plasma screen, liquid crystal display (LCD), high definition, flat panel, projection TVs and speakers as well notebook computers, optical storage devices, monitors and DVDs. Its mobile communications division produces UMTS (WCDMA), CDMA and GSM mobile handsets, the popular being G Series, K Series, V Series and X Series phones. The division also manufactures wireline telephones, wireless telephone networking equipment, Voice-over Internet Protocol (VoIP) equipment and telecommunications mainframes. LG's home appliance and air solution division manufactures home appliances for home ubiquitous networking, including refrigerators, dish washers, washers and dryers, ovens, built-in-appliances, vacuum cleaners, robot vacuum cleaners, dehumidifiers, air purifiers and air conditioners. In addition, the company is a leading global supplier of home appliance components such as washing machine motors. The firm's vehicle component division includes in-vehicle infotainment, HVAC and motor and vehicle engineering. The firm's 80 subsidiaries include Zenith, LG Display Co. Ltd. and LG Electronics USA, Inc. The firm has offices throughout Asia, Europe, Africa, the Middle East, South America and North America. LG maintains a focus on R&D activities, with operations worldwide, including the LG Electronics Institute of Technology in Seoul, Korea.

FINANCIAL DATA:
Note: Data for latest year may not have been available at press time.

In U.S. $	2017	2016	2015	2014	2013	2012
Revenue	55,400,000,000	51,720,720,384	52,787,486,720	55,152,513,024	54,311,419,904	47,603,904,512
R&D Expense						
Operating Income						
Operating Margin %						
SGA Expense						
Net Income	2,230,000,000	46,180,288	116,201,768	373,049,984	165,126,560	62,376,460
Operating Cash Flow						
Capital Expenditure						
EBITDA						
Return on Assets %						
Return on Equity %						
Debt to Equity						

CONTACT INFORMATION:
Phone: 82 237771114 Fax:
Toll-Free: 800-243-0000
Address: LG Twin Towers, 128 Yeoui-daero, Yeongdeungpo-gu, Seoul, 150-721 South Korea

SALARIES/BONUSES:
Top Exec. Salary: $ Bonus: $
Second Exec. Salary: $ Bonus: $

STOCK TICKER/OTHER:
Stock Ticker: 66570
Employees: 2,215,000
Parent Company:

Exchange: Korea
Fiscal Year Ends: 12/31

OTHER THOUGHTS:
Estimated Female Officers or Directors:
Hot Spot for Advancement for Women/Minorities:

Sales, profits and employees may be estimates. Financial information, benefits and other data can change quickly and may vary from those stated here.

Linde AG

www.the-linde-group.com

NAIC Code: 325120

TYPES OF BUSINESS:
Industrial Gas Manufacturing
Engineering & Construction-Gas & Chemical Plants
Plant Components Manufacturing
Microelectronics Manufacturing Equipment
Olefin Plants
Logistics & Supply Chain Solutions
Welding Products

BRANDS/DIVISIONS/AFFILIATES:

CONTACTS:
Note: Officers with more than one job title may be intentionally listed here more than once.
Wolfgang Reitzle, Pres.
Wolfgang Reitzle, Chmn.

GROWTH PLANS/SPECIAL FEATURES:

Linde AG is a leading industrial gas and engineering company operating in more than 100 countries worldwide. The company is a leader in plant engineering and construction, including hydrogen production facilities. Linde is divided into two primary segments: industrial gases and healthcare, and engineering. The industrial gases and healthcare division supplies oxygen, nitrogen, argon, hydrogen, acetylene, carbon monoxide and carbon dioxide; shielding gases for welding applications; rare gases and calibration gas mixtures; and high-purity gases and mixtures to customers in the medical, industrial, commercial and research fields. The engineering division constructs various types of processing facilities, including hydrogen, oxygen and olefin as well as plants for natural gas treatment. The division also manufactures plant components; liquefied gas tanks; vacuum-brazed heat exchangers; coil-wound heat exchangers and reactors; and catalysts. This segment holds over 1,000 process engineering patents with a portfolio of 4,000 completed projects. In August 2017, the shareholders of both Linde AG and Praxair, Inc. approved their proposed merger. The new company, to be named Linde, would become the biggest player in the industrial-gas suppliers market. That same year, Linde's annual report described Gist as a discontinued operation due to a proposal to sell it.

FINANCIAL DATA:
Note: Data for latest year may not have been available at press time.

In U.S. $	2017	2016	2015	2014	2013	2012
Revenue	21,132,900,000	20,929,140,000	22,159,110,000	21,051,400,000	20,567,310,000	18,869,320,000
R&D Expense	138,309,200	149,423,300	163,007,200	130,899,800	113,611,100	124,725,200
Operating Income	2,242,585,000	2,375,954,000	2,438,934,000	2,153,671,000	2,546,371,000	2,305,565,000
Operating Margin %	10.61%	11.35%	11.00%	10.23%	12.38%	12.21%
SGA Expense	4,944,553,000	5,071,748,000	5,402,702,000	4,895,157,000	4,854,405,000	4,516,041,000
Net Income	1,770,851,000	1,425,078,000	1,418,904,000	1,360,863,000	1,626,368,000	1,543,629,000
Operating Cash Flow	4,332,041,000	4,248,068,000	4,437,007,000	3,705,945,000	3,882,536,000	3,114,426,000
Capital Expenditure	2,049,940,000	2,174,665,000	2,338,907,000	2,416,706,000	2,669,861,000	2,208,007,000
EBITDA	4,786,485,000	4,935,908,000	4,914,915,000	4,819,828,000	5,002,593,000	4,788,955,000
Return on Assets %	4.17%	3.27%	3.29%	3.28%	3.97%	4.00%
Return on Equity %	9.97%	7.91%	8.21%	8.42%	10.18%	10.12%
Debt to Equity	0.43	0.44	0.57	0.62	0.64	0.68

CONTACT INFORMATION:
Phone: 49-89-35757-01 Fax: 49-89-35757-1075
Toll-Free:
Address: Klosterhofstrasse 1, Munich, 80331 Germany

STOCK TICKER/OTHER:
Stock Ticker: LNEGY   Exchange: PINX
Employees: 58,381   Fiscal Year Ends: 12/31
Parent Company:

SALARIES/BONUSES:
Top Exec. Salary: $ Bonus: $
Second Exec. Salary: $ Bonus: $

OTHER THOUGHTS:
Estimated Female Officers or Directors:
Hot Spot for Advancement for Women/Minorities:

Sales, profits and employees may be estimates. Financial information, benefits and other data can change quickly and may vary from those stated here.

Lite-On Technology Corporation

NAIC Code: 335313

www.liteon.com

TYPES OF BUSINESS:
Switchgear and Switchboard Apparatus Manufacturing
Computer Hardware
Computer Accessories
Networking Products
LED Lamps
Personal Digital Assistants
Portable Navigation Devices

BRANDS/DIVISIONS/AFFILIATES:
Lite-On Group Co Ltd
V2X
mmWave
Lite-On Skyla

CONTACTS:
Note: Officers with more than one job title may be intentionally listed here more than once.

Warren Chen, CEO
Danny Liao, Pres.
Warren Chen, CEO-Lite-On Group
Raymond Soong, Chmn.-Lite-On Group
Danny Liao, Sr. VP-Procurement

GROWTH PLANS/SPECIAL FEATURES:

Lite-On Technology Corporation is a leading manufacturer of electronic application products to the smart city, home, building, factory, mobile device and healthcare markets. The company's smart products are categorized into three business units, including power conversion, mobile mechanics and storage. Smart city products, solutions and services include communication networking, smart lighting, smart surveillance, sensing and smart signage. Smart car products and solutions include: the V2X (vehicle-to-everything) communication platform, which can report any safety concern to the driver in real-time and brake automatically when necessary; the automotive mmWave radar, which can detect and track surrounding cars, pedestrians and objects within an approximate, light-emitting diode (LED) car light module design/manufacture; and a camera module for autonomous vehicles, comprising a 650-foot range. Smart home and building products and solutions cover fields like smart control, energy management, security and automation. This business unit provides hardware design service, as well as integration service for device software, app and application cloud for the smart home, smart building and smart industry sectors. Smart factory products include Internet of Things (IoT) manufacturing and production solutions, including visualized control, monitored manufacturing and interconnection with green manufacturing processes. Smart mobile device products and solutions include smartphones with advanced camera module technology, including panoramic and portable image capabilities. Last, smart healthcare products and solutions include the Lite-On Skyla, which helps doctors and patients obtain diagnostic and medical results quickly. The company's biomedical research and development center in Singapore, focuses on in-vitro diagnostics. The Lite-On is the largest affiliate of electronics conglomerate Lite-On Group Co., Ltd. In February 2018, Lite-On agreed to sell its camera module business to LuxVisions Innovation Limited, per regulatory approval.

Lite-On offers employees life, medical, accident, hospitalization and business travel insurance.

FINANCIAL DATA:
Note: Data for latest year may not have been available at press time.

In U.S. $	2017	2016	2015	2014	2013	2012
Revenue	7,320,765,000	7,832,807,000	7,401,437,000	7,868,981,000	7,274,704,000	7,371,354,000
R&D Expense	218,904,500	208,249,000	204,258,400	217,420,700	212,557,300	194,896,700
Operating Income	284,689,500	433,629,900	295,227,500	243,242,700	342,635,000	371,626,300
Operating Margin %	3.88%	5.53%	3.98%	3.09%	4.71%	5.04%
SGA Expense	441,843,100	424,628,500	460,670,300	503,169,200	485,463,900	478,469,800
Net Income	89,710,800	321,278,500	246,439,600	220,466,700	298,708,500	257,083,500
Operating Cash Flow	380,537,700	495,155,500	530,630,900	482,152,800	705,869,800	443,365,800
Capital Expenditure	151,263,400	134,077,400	184,167,700	307,848,600	216,308,600	162,258,500
EBITDA	343,663,200	682,631,900	609,560,600	549,376,300	655,822,700	673,366,000
Return on Assets %	1.31%	4.47%	3.38%	3.01%	4.29%	3.77%
Return on Equity %	3.59%	12.39%	9.56%	8.73%	12.26%	10.86%
Debt to Equity		0.15	0.21	0.18	0.25	0.28

CONTACT INFORMATION:
Phone: 886 287982888 Fax: 886 287982866
Toll-Free:
Address: 392 Ruey Kuang Rd., 22/Fl, Neihu, Taipei, Taiwan

SALARIES/BONUSES:
Top Exec. Salary: $ Bonus: $
Second Exec. Salary: $ Bonus: $

STOCK TICKER/OTHER:
Stock Ticker: LTOTY   Exchange: GREY
Employees: 77,497   Fiscal Year Ends: 12/31
Parent Company:

OTHER THOUGHTS:
Estimated Female Officers or Directors:
Hot Spot for Advancement for Women/Minorities:

Lockheed Martin Corporation

www.lockheedmartin.com

NAIC Code: 336411

TYPES OF BUSINESS:
Aircraft Manufacturing
Military Aircraft
Defense Electronics
Systems Integration & Technology Services
Communications Satellites & Launch Services
Undersea, Shipboard, Land & Airborne Systems & Subsystems

BRANDS/DIVISIONS/AFFILIATES:

CONTACTS:
Note: Officers with more than one job title may be intentionally listed here more than once.
Marillyn Hewson, CEO
Brian Colan, Chief Accounting Officer
Frank St John, Executive VP, Divisional
Orlando Carvalho, Executive VP, Divisional
Dale Bennett, Executive VP, Divisional
Richard Ambrose, Executive VP, Divisional
Bruce Tanner, Executive VP
Maryanne Lavan, General Counsel
John Mollard, Treasurer

GROWTH PLANS/SPECIAL FEATURES:
Lockheed Martin Corporation is a global security and aerospace company engaged in the research, design, development, manufacture, integration and sustainment of advanced technology systems, products and services. It serves domestic and international customers with products and services that have defense, civil and commercial applications, with principal customers including agencies of the U.S. government (69% of 2017 sales). The company operates in four segments: aeronautics, missiles and fire control (MFC), rotary and mission systems (RMS) and space. The aeronautics segment, accounting for 39% of the firm's revenue, is engaged in the design, R&D, systems integration, production, sustainment, support and upgrade of advanced military aircraft, air and unmanned vehicles and related technologies. Major products include the F-35 Lightning strike fighter, the F-22 stealth fighter and the C-130 tactical airlifter. The MFC segment (14%) provides: air and missile defense systems; tactical missiles and air-to-ground precision strike weapon systems; logistics; fire control systems; mission operations support, readiness, engineering support and integration services; manned and unmanned ground vehicles; and energy management solutions. The RMS division (28%) provides: design, manufacture, service and support for a variety of military and commercial helicopters; ship and submarine mission and combat systems; mission systems and sensors for rotary and fixed-wing aircraft; sea and land-based missile defense systems; radar systems; the Littoral Combat Ship; simulation and training services; and unmanned systems and technologies. Last, the space segment (19%) is engaged in the R&D, design, engineering and production of satellites, strategic and defensive missile systems and space transportation systems. In September 2017, Lockheed agreed to sell 40 F-35 fighter jets to South Korea for delivery between 2018 and 2021, for approximately $7 billion.

FINANCIAL DATA:
Note: Data for latest year may not have been available at press time.

In U.S. $	2017	2016	2015	2014	2013	2012
Revenue	51,048,000,000	47,248,000,000	46,132,000,000	45,600,000,000	45,358,000,000	47,182,000,000
R&D Expense						
Operating Income	5,921,000,000	5,549,000,000	5,436,000,000	5,592,000,000	4,505,000,000	4,434,000,000
Operating Margin %	11.59%	11.74%	11.78%	12.26%	9.93%	9.39%
SGA Expense						
Net Income	2,002,000,000	5,302,000,000	3,605,000,000	3,614,000,000	2,981,000,000	2,745,000,000
Operating Cash Flow	6,476,000,000	5,189,000,000	5,101,000,000	3,866,000,000	4,546,000,000	1,561,000,000
Capital Expenditure	1,177,000,000	1,063,000,000	939,000,000	845,000,000	836,000,000	942,000,000
EBITDA	7,115,000,000	6,764,000,000	6,492,000,000	6,592,000,000	5,495,000,000	5,443,000,000
Return on Assets %	4.24%	10.93%	8.36%	9.86%	7.96%	7.17%
Return on Equity %	483.57%	230.12%	110.97%	86.89%	120.27%	527.88%
Debt to Equity		9.45	4.61	1.81	1.25	157.89

CONTACT INFORMATION:
Phone: 301 897-6000   Fax: 301 897-6083
Toll-Free:
Address: 6801 Rockledge Dr., Bethesda, MD 20817 United States

STOCK TICKER/OTHER:
Stock Ticker: LMT   Exchange: NYS
Employees: 97,000   Fiscal Year Ends: 12/31
Parent Company:

SALARIES/BONUSES:
Top Exec. Salary: $1,688,269   Bonus: $
Second Exec. Salary: $995,962   Bonus: $

OTHER THOUGHTS:
Estimated Female Officers or Directors: 5
Hot Spot for Advancement for Women/Minorities: Y

Louis Berger Group Inc (The)

www.louisberger.com

NAIC Code: 541330

TYPES OF BUSINESS:
Engineering Services
Civil Engineering
Environmental Engineering
Transportation Infrastructure
Project Management
Consulting Services
Hydrologic Engineering
Seismic & Geotechnical Services

BRANDS/DIVISIONS/AFFILIATES:
Berger Group Holdings Inc
Louis Berger Power KSA

CONTACTS:
Note: Officers with more than one job title may be intentionally listed here more than once.

Jim Stamatis, CEO
James G. Bach, COO
Thomas Lewis, Pres.
Meg Lassarat, CFO
Susan Knauf, Chief Learning Officer
Thomas Nicastro, Corp. Compliance & Ethics Officer
Andrew V. Bailey II, Group VP
Charles Bell, Group VP

GROWTH PLANS/SPECIAL FEATURES:

The Louis Berger Group, Inc. (Berger) is an infrastructure engineering, environmental science and economic development company with offices throughout the U.S., and in more than 50 countries worldwide. The firm helps infrastructure and development clients solve their complex challenges through its team of 6,000 engineers, economists, scientists, managers and planners. Berger serves the agriculture, buildings, facilities, defense/security, economic, institutional development, environment, mining, minerals, power/energy, transportation and water markets. Its services include alternative project delivery, architecture, capacity building assistance, technical assistance, construction services, economics services, financial services, emergency/disaster management, engineering, environmental services, heritage resource management, operations and maintenance, planning and program management. Berger is privately-owned by Berger Group Holdings, Inc. In April 2018, Berger announced a joint venture, Louis Berger Power KSA, with Riyadh-based KFB Holding Group to support innovative power projects in Kingdom of Saudi Arabia (KSA).

The firm offers employees medical and dental coverage, life and travel insurance, a new employee hiring referral award, tuition reimbursement, flexible spending accounts, a cafeteria plan and registration fee payment for professional licenses.

FINANCIAL DATA:
Note: Data for latest year may not have been available at press time.

In U.S. $	2017	2016	2015	2014	2013	2012
Revenue	1,250,000,000	1,000,000,000	1,000,000,000	1,200,000,000	1,000,000,000	960,000,000
R&D Expense						
Operating Income						
Operating Margin %						
SGA Expense						
Net Income						
Operating Cash Flow						
Capital Expenditure						
EBITDA						
Return on Assets %						
Return on Equity %						
Debt to Equity						

CONTACT INFORMATION:
Phone: 973-407-1000   Fax: 973-267-6468
Toll-Free:
Address: 412 Mt. Kemble Ave., Morristown, NJ 07960 United States

STOCK TICKER/OTHER:
Stock Ticker: Private
Employees: 6,000
Parent Company: Berger Group Holdings Inc

Exchange:
Fiscal Year Ends: 06/30

SALARIES/BONUSES:
Top Exec. Salary: $ Bonus: $
Second Exec. Salary: $ Bonus: $

OTHER THOUGHTS:
Estimated Female Officers or Directors: 1
Hot Spot for Advancement for Women/Minorities:

Sales, profits and employees may be estimates. Financial information, benefits and other data can change quickly and may vary from those stated here.

LyondellBasell Industries NV

NAIC Code: 325110

www.lyondellbasell.com

TYPES OF BUSINESS:
- Polymers & Petrochemicals
- Intermediate & Performance Chemicals
- Petroleum Products
- Refining
- Biofuels
- Automotive Parts
- Medical Applications
- Durable Textiles

BRANDS/DIVISIONS/AFFILIATES:
- Lyondell Chemical Co
- Basell AF SCA

CONTACTS:
Note: Officers with more than one job title may be intentionally listed here more than once.

- Bhavesh V. Patel, CEO
- Thomas Aebischer, CFO
- Massimo Covezzi, Sr. VP-R&D
- Daniel Coombs, Exec. VP-Global Manu., Projects, Refining & Technology
- Karen Swindler, Sr. VP-Mfg.-Americas
- Craig Glidden, Chief Legal Officer
- Sam Smolik, VP-Oper. Excellence
- Sergey Vasnetsov, Sr. VP-Strategic Planning & Transactions
- David Harpole, Contact-Media
- Douglas J. Pike, Contact-Investor Rel.
- Pat Quarles, Sr. VP-Intermediates & Derivatives
- Kevin Brown, Sr. VP-Refining
- Sam Smolik, VP-Health, Safety & Environment
- Bhavesh V. Patel, Chmn.
- Tim Roberts, Sr. VP-Olefins & Polyolefins Americas

GROWTH PLANS/SPECIAL FEATURES:

LyondellBasell Industries N.V. is one of the world's largest producers and marketers of polymers, petrochemicals and fuels. The company was formed from the merger of Basell AF SCA, a chemical manufacturing company and polypropylene producer, and Lyondell Chemical Co., a leading manufacturer of chemicals and plastics and a refiner of crude oil. It is one of the world's leading providers of propylene oxide, generating sales from more than 100 countries, and has 57 manufacturing sites in 18 countries. The firm operates in five segments: olefins & polyolefins Americas; olefins & polyolefins Europe, Asia & international; intermediates & derivatives; refining; and technology. Through the olefin & polyolefin divisions, the firm is one of the world's largest producers of ethylene, propylene, polyethylene, polypropylene and polypropylene compounds. The intermediates & derivatives division, one of the largest producers of propylene oxide, produces products used in the creation of insulation, home furnishings, adhesives and sealants, aircraft deicers, cosmetics and more. The refining segment offers clients automotive and industrial engine lube oils; biofuels; heating oil; and automotive, aviation and diesel fuels. The technology segment is responsible for process licensing, catalyst sales and other services. LyondellBasell owns approximately 5,300 patents and patent applications worldwide.

FINANCIAL DATA:
Note: Data for latest year may not have been available at press time.

In U.S. $	2017	2016	2015	2014	2013	2012
Revenue	34,484,000,000	29,183,000,000	32,735,000,000	45,608,000,000	44,062,000,000	45,352,000,000
R&D Expense	106,000,000	99,000,000	102,000,000	127,000,000	150,000,000	172,000,000
Operating Income	5,460,000,000	5,060,000,000	6,122,000,000	5,736,000,000	5,102,000,000	4,676,000,000
Operating Margin %	15.83%	17.33%	18.70%	12.57%	11.57%	10.31%
SGA Expense	859,000,000	833,000,000	828,000,000	806,000,000	870,000,000	909,000,000
Net Income	4,879,000,000	3,836,000,000	4,476,000,000	4,174,000,000	3,857,000,000	2,848,000,000
Operating Cash Flow	5,206,000,000	5,606,000,000	5,842,000,000	6,048,000,000	4,835,000,000	4,787,000,000
Capital Expenditure	1,547,000,000	2,243,000,000	1,440,000,000	1,499,000,000	1,561,000,000	1,060,000,000
EBITDA	7,158,000,000	6,619,000,000	7,566,000,000	7,083,000,000	6,326,000,000	5,823,000,000
Return on Assets %	19.63%	16.58%	18.99%	16.13%	14.93%	12.09%
Return on Equity %	64.99%	60.83%	60.11%	40.03%	32.56%	26.18%
Debt to Equity	0.95	1.38	1.17	0.81	0.46	0.38

CONTACT INFORMATION:
Phone: 31-10-275-5500 Fax: 31-10-275-5589
Toll-Free:
Address: Delftseplein 27E, Rotterdam, 3013 AK Netherlands

STOCK TICKER/OTHER:
Stock Ticker: LYB
Employees: 13,300
Parent Company:
Exchange: NYS
Fiscal Year Ends: 12/31

SALARIES/BONUSES:
Top Exec. Salary: $1,341,827 Bonus: $
Second Exec. Salary: $725,000 Bonus: $

OTHER THOUGHTS:
Estimated Female Officers or Directors: 3
Hot Spot for Advancement for Women/Minorities: Y

Sales, profits and employees may be estimates. Financial information, benefits and other data can change quickly and may vary from those stated here.

Magna International Inc

NAIC Code: 336300

www.magna.com

TYPES OF BUSINESS:
Automobile Parts Manufacturer
Vehicle Assembly Services
Seating & Interior Products
Closure Systems
Body & Chassis Systems
Mirror, Lighting & Glass Systems
Exterior Decorative Systems
Solar Photovoltaic Components

BRANDS/DIVISIONS/AFFILIATES:
Cosma International of America Inc
Magna Exteriors and Interiors Corp
Magna Seating Inc
Magna Steyr AG & Co KG
Magna Powertrain Inc
Magna Structural Systems Inc

CONTACTS:
Note: Officers with more than one job title may be intentionally listed here more than once.

Donald Walker, CEO
William Young, Chairman of the Board
James Tobin, Chief Marketing Officer
Seetarama Kotagiri, Chief Technology Officer
Tommy Skudutis, COO, Divisional
Francis Seguin, Executive VP
Vincent Galifi, Executive VP
Jeffrey Palmer, Executive VP
Marc Neeb, Executive VP
Indira Samarasekera, Independent Director
Cynthia Niekamp, Independent Director
Guenther Apfalter, President, Geographical

GROWTH PLANS/SPECIAL FEATURES:

Magna International, Inc. is a global supplier of high-tech automotive components, systems and complete modules. Its services span the design, engineering and manufacture of a full range of interior and exterior systems as well as providing complete vehicle assembly services to major automotive manufacturers. The company's operations include 335 manufacturing facilities and 96 product development, engineering and sales centers located in 28 countries across three geographic segments: North America, Europe and the rest of the world. Through its divisions and subsidiaries, the company provides services in four main product areas. These include: body exteriors & structures, consisting of the body, chassis, exteriors and roof systems; power & vision, consisting of powertrain, electronics, vision systems and closures; seating systems; and complete vehicles, consisting of vehicle engineering and contract manufacturing. Magna's primary operating subsidiaries include Cosma International of America, Inc.; Magna Powertrain, Inc.; Magna Seating, Inc.; Magna Exteriors and Interiors Corp.; Magna Steyr AG & Co. KG; and Magna Structural Systems, Inc. Among its customers are Fiat/Chrysler Group, Daimler AG, General Motors, BMW, Volkswagen and Ford Motor Company. In early-2018, Magna opened a new composites center in Esslingen, Germany, to help European automakers meet stringent emissions requirements with lightweight structures and exterior components made of advanced materials; opened a new seat facility in South Carolina, which will supply the BMW group; and formed a joint venture in China with GAC Component Co., Ltd., to begin production of composite liftgates in late-2018 for a global automaker's crossover vehicle.

The company provides its employees with a range of benefits, including profit sharing, an employee assistance program, job counseling and training and an employee disaster relief fund.

FINANCIAL DATA:
Note: Data for latest year may not have been available at press time.

In U.S. $	2017	2016	2015	2014	2013	2012
Revenue	38,946,000,000	36,445,000,000	32,134,000,000	36,641,000,000	34,835,000,000	30,837,000,000
R&D Expense						
Operating Income	2,808,000,000	2,665,000,000	2,325,000,000	2,421,000,000	1,869,000,000	1,507,000,000
Operating Margin %	7.20%	7.31%	7.23%	6.60%	5.36%	4.88%
SGA Expense	1,668,000,000	1,601,000,000	1,448,000,000	1,707,000,000	1,616,000,000	1,519,000,000
Net Income	2,206,000,000	2,031,000,000	2,013,000,000	1,882,000,000	1,561,000,000	1,433,000,000
Operating Cash Flow	3,329,000,000	3,386,000,000	2,332,000,000	2,792,000,000	2,567,000,000	2,206,000,000
Capital Expenditure	1,858,000,000	1,807,000,000	1,591,000,000	1,586,000,000	1,169,000,000	1,274,000,000
EBITDA	4,262,000,000	3,936,000,000	3,511,000,000	3,476,000,000	3,002,000,000	2,585,000,000
Return on Assets %	9.19%	9.60%	10.63%	10.41%	8.89%	9.01%
Return on Equity %	21.01%	21.68%	22.84%	20.58%	16.38%	16.28%
Debt to Equity	0.28	0.24	0.26	0.09	0.01	0.01

CONTACT INFORMATION:
Phone: 905 726-2462
Fax:
Toll-Free:
Address: 337 Magna Dr., Aurora, ON L4G 7K1 Canada

SALARIES/BONUSES:
Top Exec. Salary: $325,000 Bonus: $
Second Exec. Salary: $325,000 Bonus: $

STOCK TICKER/OTHER:
Stock Ticker: MGA
Employees: 131,225
Parent Company:
Exchange: NYS
Fiscal Year Ends: 12/31

OTHER THOUGHTS:
Estimated Female Officers or Directors: 2
Hot Spot for Advancement for Women/Minorities:

Sales, profits and employees may be estimates. Financial information, benefits and other data can change quickly and may vary from those stated here.

Magneti Marelli SpA

NAIC Code: 336300

www.magnetimarelli.com

TYPES OF BUSINESS:
Automotive Components
Power Train Systems
Motor Sport Components
Lighting
Automotive Performance Research Equipment

BRANDS/DIVISIONS/AFFILIATES:
Fiat Chrysler Automobiles NV
FCA Italy SpA
Freechoice
Magneti Marelli Checkstar Service Network
LeddarTech Inc

CONTACTS: Note: Officers with more than one job title may be intentionally listed here more than once.
Pietro Gorlier, CEO
Eugenio Razelli, Pres.
G. Rosso, CTO
A.C. Ferrara, Head-Mfg.
G. Acossato, General Counsel
A. Tanganelli, Head-Bus. Dev.
M. Bellone, Head-Comm.
M. Mamavello, Coordinator-Purchasing

GROWTH PLANS/SPECIAL FEATURES:
Magneti Marelli SpA designs and manufactures high-tech systems and components for the automotive sector. The firm has 86 production units and 14 research and development centers across 19 countries. Magneti Marelli has supplied major car manufacturers such as Renault, Citroen, Peugeot, the Fiat Group, Ford, Volkswagen, Audi, Seat, BMW, DaimlerChrysler, GM-Opel, Volvo, Saab, Nissan, Toyota and Daewoo. Magneti Marelli operates through eight business segments. Automotive lighting comprises front and rear lighting systems and body electronics. Powertrain comprises engine control systems for gasoline, diesel and multi-fuel engines; and automated manual transmission Freechoice gearboxes. Electronic systems include instrument clusters, as well as infotainment and telematics. Suspension systems include suspension systems, shock absorbers and dynamic systems. Exhaust systems include exhaust systems, catalytic converters and silencing systems. Plastic components and modules include dashboard and center consoles, bumpers and fuel systems. Aftermarket parts and services is a commercial division dedicated to spare parts and services, relying on an organized network of over 5,000 authorized workshops spread throughout the world under the Magneti Marelli Checkstar Service Network brand. Finally, the motorsport segment designs and produces electronic and electro-mechanical systems for 2- and 4-wheels racing vehicles. Specific products in this division include data acquisition, display, lap trigger, electronic control systems, engine components, power supply systems, software and technological excellences. The motorsport department is engaged in the research and production of kinetic energy recovery systems (KERS) for Formula 1 and other motorsports series. Magneti Marelli is a subsidiary of FCA Italy SpA, the Italian branch of Fiat Chrysler Automobiles NV. In September 2017, Magneti acquired a stake in LeddarTech, Inc., a global leader in solid state LiDAR (light detection and ranging) sensing technology. That December, parent Fiat Chrysler announced plans to spin off Magneti Marelli by the end of 2018.

FINANCIAL DATA: Note: Data for latest year may not have been available at press time.

In U.S. $	2017	2016	2015	2014	2013	2012
Revenue	8,400,000,000	8,323,120,000	8,263,066,700	7,349,550,000	8,323,457,820	7,928,061,412
R&D Expense						
Operating Income						
Operating Margin %						
SGA Expense						
Net Income		321,236,521	359,020,750	230,665,860	191,088,300	95,236,985
Operating Cash Flow						
Capital Expenditure						
EBITDA						
Return on Assets %						
Return on Equity %						
Debt to Equity						

CONTACT INFORMATION:
Phone: 39-02-9722-7454   Fax: 39-02-9722-7510
Toll-Free:
Address: Viale Aldo Borletti 61/63, Milano, 20011 Italy

STOCK TICKER/OTHER:
Stock Ticker: Subsidiary   Exchange:
Employees: 43,000   Fiscal Year Ends: 12/31
Parent Company: Fiat Chrysler Automobiles NV

SALARIES/BONUSES:
Top Exec. Salary: $ Bonus: $
Second Exec. Salary: $ Bonus: $

OTHER THOUGHTS:
Estimated Female Officers or Directors: 1
Hot Spot for Advancement for Women/Minorities:

Sales, profits and employees may be estimates. Financial information, benefits and other data can change quickly and may vary from those stated here.

Marathon Oil Corporation

NAIC Code: 211111

www.marathonoil.com

TYPES OF BUSINESS:
Oil & Gas Exploration & Production
Oil Sands
Integrated Gas Operations

BRANDS/DIVISIONS/AFFILIATES:

CONTACTS:
Note: Officers with more than one job title may be intentionally listed here more than once.

Dennis Reilley, Director
Lee Tillman, Director
Thomas Little, Executive VP, Divisional
Dane Whitehead, Executive VP
Reginald Hedgebeth, General Counsel
Patrick Wagner, Senior VP, Divisional
Catherine Krajicek, Vice President, Divisional
Gary Wilson, Vice President

GROWTH PLANS/SPECIAL FEATURES:

Marathon Oil Corporation is a Houston-based international energy firm operating in two segments: U.S. E&P and International E&P, each of which explores for, produces and markets crude oil and condensate, natural gas liquids (NGLs) and natural gas. The U.S. E&P segment comprises the unconventional resource plays of: Eagle Ford, located in south Texas, with 32 central gathering and treating facilities across the field that support more than 1,500 producing wells; Bakken, located in North Dakota and eastern Montana, with acreage within the McKenzie, Mountrail and Dunn counties of North Dakota; Oklahoma, with a focus on delineation and leasehold protection in the Meramec play in the STACK, and delineation of the Woodford and Springer plays in the SCOOP; and Northern Delaware, with development in the Wolfcamp and Bone Spring plays in the Permian Basin. Other properties in the U.S. primarily consist of assets in the Gulf of Mexico, including the Gunflint field where Marathon holds an 18% non-operated working interest. The International E&P segment has assets in the following six areas. Equatorial Guinea, with a 63% operated working interest under a production sharing contract in the Alba field, as well as an 80% operated working interest in Block D. Equatorial Guinea-Gas Processing, with a 52% interest in Alba Plant LLC, which operates an onshore liquified petroleum gas (LPG) processing plant on Bioko Island; 60% of Equatorial Guinea LNG Holdings Limited, which operates a 4-million-tons-per-annum (mtpa) liquefied natural gas (LNG) production facility; and 45% of Atlantic Methanol Production Company LLC, which operates a methanol plant. U.K. assets include: minority working interests in various Brae fields, as well as the Foinaven fields. Libya comprises a 16% non-operated working interest in the Waha concessions; Kurdistan comprises non-operated interests in two blocks in Erbil; and Gabon holds 100% in the Tchicuate block.

FINANCIAL DATA:
Note: Data for latest year may not have been available at press time.

In U.S. $	2017	2016	2015	2014	2013	2012
Revenue	4,373,000,000	4,031,000,000	5,522,000,000	10,846,000,000	14,501,000,000	15,688,000,000
R&D Expense						
Operating Income	-218,000,000	-1,397,000,000	-2,204,000,000	1,397,000,000	4,906,000,000	6,206,000,000
Operating Margin %	-4.98%	-34.65%	-39.91%	12.88%	33.83%	39.55%
SGA Expense	400,000,000	484,000,000	590,000,000	654,000,000	687,000,000	555,000,000
Net Income	-5,723,000,000	-2,140,000,000	-2,204,000,000	3,046,000,000	1,753,000,000	1,582,000,000
Operating Cash Flow	2,193,000,000	1,073,000,000	1,565,000,000	5,487,000,000	5,270,000,000	4,017,000,000
Capital Expenditure	1,974,000,000	1,245,000,000	3,476,000,000	5,160,000,000	4,766,000,000	4,940,000,000
EBITDA	2,295,000,000	1,539,000,000	331,000,000	4,499,000,000	8,006,000,000	8,823,000,000
Return on Assets %	-21.55%	-6.75%	-6.45%	8.50%	4.94%	4.74%
Return on Equity %	-39.13%	-11.85%	-11.13%	15.09%	9.31%	8.92%
Debt to Equity	0.46	0.37	0.39	0.25	0.33	0.35

CONTACT INFORMATION:
Phone: 713 629-6600   Fax:
Toll-Free: 866-462-7284
Address: 5555 San Felipe Rd., Houston, TX 77056 United States

SALARIES/BONUSES:
Top Exec. Salary: $1,050,000   Bonus: $
Second Exec. Salary: $575,000   Bonus: $

STOCK TICKER/OTHER:
Stock Ticker: MRO   Exchange: NYS
Employees: 2,117   Fiscal Year Ends: 12/31
Parent Company:

OTHER THOUGHTS:
Estimated Female Officers or Directors: 5
Hot Spot for Advancement for Women/Minorities: Y

Sales, profits and employees may be estimates. Financial information, benefits and other data can change quickly and may vary from those stated here.

Mason & Hanger

NAIC Code: 541330

www.ha-inc.com

TYPES OF BUSINESS:
Engineering Consulting Services
Design
Engineering
Environment

BRANDS/DIVISIONS/AFFILIATES:
Day & Zimmermann Company

CONTACTS:
Note: Officers with more than one job title may be intentionally listed here more than once.

Benjamin A. Lilly, Pres.
Jared B. Jamison, VP-Operations
Catherine H. Gettys, VP-Mktg. & Bus. Dev.

GROWTH PLANS/SPECIAL FEATURES:

Mason & Hanger, a Day & Zimmermann Company, provides architectural and engineering services for federal projects. The firm has served in the U.S. for nearly two centuries, being founded in 1827 as a railroad-engineering and construction company. Today, Mason & Hanger has served the federal government on thousands of projects in 48 states and 163 countries. It specializes in the worldwide design of secure, mission-driven facilities. Mission-driven facilities include command and control centers, embassies, consulates, communication facilities, data centers, headquarter facilities, secure office buildings, training facilities, shooting ranges, aviation pavements and systems, military planning, blast/explosives facilities and munitions/weapons facilities. The firm's energy and sustainability services include energy auditing, energy modeling, performance contracting consulting, commissioning/retro-commissioning, building sciences, renewable energy systems, sustainability management, LEED services, building envelop services and new zero energy and water solutions. Security design services include physical and technical security, energy security, resiliency, security consulting/assessment, blast design and mitigation, mitigation for other threats, holistic security design and specialty facilities.

FINANCIAL DATA:
Note: Data for latest year may not have been available at press time.

In U.S. $	2017	2016	2015	2014	2013	2012
Revenue						
R&D Expense						
Operating Income						
Operating Margin %						
SGA Expense						
Net Income						
Operating Cash Flow						
Capital Expenditure						
EBITDA						
Return on Assets %						
Return on Equity %						
Debt to Equity						

CONTACT INFORMATION:
Phone: 804-285-4171   Fax: 804-217-8520
Toll-Free:
Address: 4880 Sadler Rd., Ste. 300, Glen Allen, VA 23060 United States

STOCK TICKER/OTHER:
Stock Ticker: Private   Exchange:
Employees: 158   Fiscal Year Ends:
Parent Company: Day & Zimmermann Company

SALARIES/BONUSES:
Top Exec. Salary: $ Bonus: $
Second Exec. Salary: $ Bonus: $

OTHER THOUGHTS:
Estimated Female Officers or Directors:
Hot Spot for Advancement for Women/Minorities:

Sales, profits and employees may be estimates. Financial information, benefits and other data can change quickly and may vary from those stated here.

Matrix Service Company

www.matrixservicecompany.com

NAIC Code: 237100

TYPES OF BUSINESS:
Heavy Construction for Utilities and Energy
Plant Maintenance Services
Storage Tank Services
Petrochemical Industry Services

BRANDS/DIVISIONS/AFFILIATES:
Matrix PDM Engineering
Matrix NAC
Matrix Service
Matrix Applied Technologies
Houston Interests LLC

CONTACTS:
Note: Officers with more than one job title may be intentionally listed here more than once.

John Hewitt, CEO
Kevin Cavanah, CFO
Rick Bennett, Chief Information Officer
Joseph Montalbano, COO
Bradley Rinehart, President, Divisional
Jason Turner, President, Subsidiary
James Ryan, President, Subsidiary
Nancy Austin, Vice President, Divisional
Justin Sheets, Vice President, Divisional

GROWTH PLANS/SPECIAL FEATURES:

Matrix Service Company and its subsidiaries provide engineering, fabrication, construction, repair and maintenance services, primarily to the petroleum, pipeline, bulk storage terminal and industrial gas markets. Matrix operates in four segments: electrical infrastructure; oil, gas & chemical; industrial; and storage solutions. The electrical infrastructure segment primarily encompasses high voltage services to investor-owned utilities, such as construction of new substations, upgrades of existing substations, short-run transmission line installations, upgrades and maintenance and storm restoration services. The oil, gas & chemical segment includes plant maintenance services, construction in the downstream petroleum industry and industrial cleaning services. The industrial segment encompasses work in the mining and minerals industry, thermal vacuum chambers and bulk material processing. The storage solutions segment includes new construction of crude and refined products, aboveground storage tanks as well as planned and emergency maintenance services for those tanks. Matrix targets a wide array of specialty markets, comprising the areas of liquefied natural gas (LNG)/industrial gas/liquefied petroleum gas (LPG), specialty tanks and vessels, power projects, fabrication and material handling. Matrix Service's primary subsidiaries include: Matrix PDM Engineering, a provider of multi-discipline engineering worldwide; Matrix NAC and Matrix Service, both of which provide full-service construction, maintenance and repair services to energy, power and industrial customers across North America; and Matrix Applied Technologies, which sells above-ground storage tank products and process heaters worldwide. In December 2016, the firm acquired Houston Interests, LLC, a provider of consulting, engineering, design, construction services and systems integration. The company was merged into Matrix PDM.

Matrix offers employee benefits including life, AD&D, medical, vision, dental and cancer insurance; short- and long-term disability; flexible spending accounts; retirement benefits; employee assistance and wellness programs; tuition reimbursement; and an

FINANCIAL DATA:
Note: Data for latest year may not have been available at press time.

In U.S. $	2017	2016	2015	2014	2013	2012
Revenue	1,197,509,000	1,311,917,000	1,343,135,000	1,263,089,000	892,574,000	739,046,000
R&D Expense						
Operating Income	4,859,000	40,882,000	8,802,000	58,607,000	36,714,000	31,635,000
Operating Margin %	.40%	3.11%	.65%	4.63%	4.11%	4.28%
SGA Expense	76,144,000	85,109,000	78,568,000	77,866,000	57,988,000	47,983,000
Net Income	-183,000	28,863,000	17,157,000	35,810,000	24,008,000	17,188,000
Operating Cash Flow	-18,746,000	30,326,000	24,438,000	76,988,000	57,084,000	2,941,000
Capital Expenditure	11,908,000	13,939,000	15,773,000	23,589,000	23,231,000	13,534,000
EBITDA	26,259,000	61,946,000	32,908,000	76,765,000	49,498,000	42,789,000
Return on Assets %	-.03%	5.09%	3.01%	7.31%	6.54%	5.46%
Return on Equity %	-.05%	9.46%	5.97%	13.80%	10.68%	8.36%
Debt to Equity	0.13		0.03	0.04		

CONTACT INFORMATION:
Phone: 866-367-5879   Fax: 918-838-8810
Toll-Free:
Address: 5100 E. Skelly Dr., Ste. 500, Tulsa, OK 74135 United States

STOCK TICKER/OTHER:
Stock Ticker: MTRX
Employees: 4,001
Parent Company:

Exchange: NAS
Fiscal Year Ends: 06/30

SALARIES/BONUSES:
Top Exec. Salary: $750,000   Bonus: $
Second Exec. Salary: $491,127   Bonus: $

OTHER THOUGHTS:
Estimated Female Officers or Directors: 1
Hot Spot for Advancement for Women/Minorities:

Sales, profits and employees may be estimates. Financial information, benefits and other data can change quickly and may vary from those stated here.

Maxim Integrated Products Inc

www.maximintegrated.com

NAIC Code: 334413

TYPES OF BUSINESS:
Integrated Circuits-Analog & Mixed Signal
High-Frequency Design Processes
Custom Manufacturing
Power Conversion Chips
Environmental Management & Monitoring Systems
Data Interface and Interconnection
Wireless & RF Receivers and Transmitters
Data Storage

BRANDS/DIVISIONS/AFFILIATES:

CONTACTS:
Note: Officers with more than one job title may be intentionally listed here more than once.

Tunc Doluca, CEO
Bruce Kiddoo, CFO
William Sullivan, Chairman of the Board
Sumeet Gagneja, Chief Accounting Officer
Edwin Medlin, General Counsel
Vivek Jain, Senior VP, Divisional
Christopher Neil, Senior VP, Divisional
Bryan Preeshl, Senior VP, Divisional
David Loftus, Vice President, Divisional

GROWTH PLANS/SPECIAL FEATURES:

Maxim Integrated Products, Inc. designs, develops, manufactures and markets analog and mixed-signal integrated circuits (ICs). Maxim's ICs connect the analog and digital world by detecting, measuring, amplifying and converting real-world signals into the digital signals necessary for computer processing. It produces electronic interface products to interact with people, through audio, video, touchpad, key pad and security devices; the physical world, through motion, time, temperature and humidity sensors; power sources, via conversion, charging, supervision and regulation systems; and other digital systems, including wireless, storage and fiber optic systems. Its products serve five major end-markets: automotive, which includes infotainment, powertrain, body electronics and safety/security products; communications and data center, which includes base station, data center, data storage, network/Datacom, server, telecom and other communications products; computing, including desktop computers, notebook computers, as well as peripherals and other computer products; consumer, including smartphones, digital cameras, handheld computers, home entertainment, appliances, mobility/fitness wearables and other consumer products; and industrial, including automatic test equipment, control/automation, electrical instrumentation, financial terminals, medical, military/aerospace, security, utility/meters and other industrial products.

Maxim employees receive medical, dental and vision insurance; an educational assistance program; health and transportation flexible spending accounts; an employee assistance program; business travel accident insurance; health club membership discounts; we

FINANCIAL DATA:
Note: Data for latest year may not have been available at press time.

In U.S. $	2017	2016	2015	2014	2013	2012
Revenue	2,295,615,000	2,194,719,000	2,306,864,000	2,453,663,000	2,441,459,000	2,403,529,000
R&D Expense	453,977,000	467,161,000	521,772,000	558,168,000	534,819,000	552,379,000
Operating Income	714,747,000	526,512,000	427,974,000	465,820,000	616,077,000	571,677,000
Operating Margin %	31.13%	23.98%	18.55%	18.98%	25.23%	23.78%
SGA Expense	291,511,000	288,899,000	308,065,000	324,734,000	324,282,000	321,273,000
Net Income	571,613,000	227,475,000	206,038,000	354,810,000	454,912,000	386,727,000
Operating Cash Flow	773,657,000	721,885,000	693,706,000	776,107,000	817,935,000	756,722,000
Capital Expenditure	51,421,000	69,369,000	75,816,000	132,523,000	216,672,000	264,348,000
EBITDA	879,039,000	771,149,000	727,370,000	710,413,000	823,213,000	782,773,000
Return on Assets %	12.98%	5.37%	4.77%	8.50%	11.85%	10.64%
Return on Equity %	26.52%	10.34%	8.73%	14.37%	18.02%	15.31%
Debt to Equity	0.67	0.46	0.43	0.41	0.20	

CONTACT INFORMATION:
Phone: 408 601-1000　　Fax: 408 737-7194
Toll-Free:
Address: 160 Rio Robles, San Jose, CA 95134 United States

STOCK TICKER/OTHER:
Stock Ticker: MXIM　　　　　　　Exchange: NAS
Employees: 7,040　　　　　　　Fiscal Year Ends: 06/30
Parent Company:

SALARIES/BONUSES:
Top Exec. Salary: $660,000　　Bonus: $
Second Exec. Salary: $420,000　　Bonus: $75,000

OTHER THOUGHTS:
Estimated Female Officers or Directors: 1
Hot Spot for Advancement for Women/Minorities:

Sales, profits and employees may be estimates. Financial information, benefits and other data can change quickly and may vary from those stated here.

Mazda Motor Corporation

NAIC Code: 336111

www.mazda.com

TYPES OF BUSINESS:
Automobile Manufacturing
Commercial Vans & Trucks
Hydrogen Engine Technology

BRANDS/DIVISIONS/AFFILIATES:
Demio
Axela
Atenza
CX-5
Roadster
Flair
Scrum
Bongo

CONTACTS: Note: Officers with more than one job title may be intentionally listed here more than once.
Masamichi Kogai, CEO
Masamichi Kogai, Pres.
Yasuhiro Aoyama, Dir.-Sales & Mktg
Kiyoshi Fujiwara, Gen. Mgr.-R&D
Mitsuo Hitomi, Dir.-IT
Masafumi Nakano, Managing Exec. Officer-Prod. & Brand Quality
Kiyotaka Shobuda, Gen. Mgr.-Eng.
Koji Kurosawa, Sec.
Akira Marumoto, Exec. VP-Corp. Planning & American Oper.
Yuji Nakamine, Sr. Managing Exec. Officer-Corp. Comm.
Seita Kanai, Vice Chmn.
Nobuhide Inamoto, Sr. Managing Exec. Officer-China & Domestic Sales
Koji Kurosawa, Pres.
Keishi Egawa, Managing Exec. Officer-Latin America
Seita Kanai, Chmn.
Yuji Nakamine, Sr. Managing Exec. Officer-EMEA, Asia & Oceania
Kazuki Imai, Managing Exec. Officer-Purchasing

GROWTH PLANS/SPECIAL FEATURES:
Mazda Motor Corporation, established in 1920, is one of Japan's largest automakers. Mazda manufactures passenger and commercial vehicles through its production facilities located in Japan, China, Thailand, Mexico, Vietnam and Russia. Mazda's research and development sites are located in Japan, the U.S., Germany and China. The company has been exporting cars to the U.S. and Europe for nearly 40 years, while Mazda cars and trucks are currently sold in approximately 140 countries. Overseas sales account for over two-thirds of the firm's annual revenues. Current passenger vehicle models (early 2018) include Demio, Axela, Atenza, CX-3, CX-5, CX-8, Roadster, Premacy and Biante. Additional passenger vehicle models which are sold outside Japan include the Mazda2 sedan, the CX-4 compact crossover, the CX-9 seven-passenger SUV and the BT-50 mid-sized pickup truck. Micro-mini vehicle models include Flair, Flair Wagon, Scrum Wagon, Carol and Flair Crossover. Commercial vehicle models include the Bongo van, Bongo truck, Familia van, Titan flatbed, Scrum van and Scrum truck. Special needs features can be configured through the Demio, Premacy, Biante, Flair Wagon and CX-5 models. Mazda produced more than 1.5 million units in 2017, with an expectation of increasing production to more than 1.6 million units in 2018.

FINANCIAL DATA: Note: Data for latest year may not have been available at press time.

In U.S. $	2017	2016	2015	2014	2013	2012
Revenue	29,945,620,000	31,736,570,000	28,264,380,000	25,081,410,000	20,544,720,000	18,940,360,000
R&D Expense						
Operating Income	1,170,924,000	2,112,680,000	1,890,144,000	1,696,674,000	502,478,100	-360,704,300
Operating Margin %	3.91%	6.65%	6.68%	6.76%	2.44%	-1.90%
SGA Expense						
Net Income	873,672,500	1,252,273,000	1,479,486,000	1,264,198,000	319,582,700	-1,003,661,000
Operating Cash Flow	1,500,811,000	2,448,016,000	1,904,779,000	1,270,533,000	456,800,800	-84,758,720
Capital Expenditure	835,727,700	820,560,900	1,268,195,000	1,109,493,000	708,114,400	651,052,800
EBITDA	2,051,537,000	2,411,189,000	2,719,518,000	1,565,493,000	1,053,820,000	232,718,500
Return on Assets %	3.69%	5.35%	6.73%	6.42%	1.76%	-5.84%
Return on Equity %	9.40%	14.74%	20.75%	23.45%	7.10%	-23.98%
Debt to Equity	0.26	0.37	0.56	0.79	1.04	1.31

CONTACT INFORMATION:
Phone: 81 822821111 Fax:
Toll-Free:
Address: 3-1 Shinchi, Fuchu-cho, Aki-gun, Hiroshima, 100-0011 Japan

STOCK TICKER/OTHER:
Stock Ticker: MZDAF
Employees: 48,849
Parent Company:

Exchange: PINX
Fiscal Year Ends: 03/31

SALARIES/BONUSES:
Top Exec. Salary: $ Bonus: $
Second Exec. Salary: $ Bonus: $

OTHER THOUGHTS:
Estimated Female Officers or Directors:
Hot Spot for Advancement for Women/Minorities:

Sales, profits and employees may be estimates. Financial information, benefits and other data can change quickly and may vary from those stated here.

Plunkett Research, Ltd.

McAfee Inc

www.mcafee.com
NAIC Code: 0

TYPES OF BUSINESS:
Computer Software, Security & Anti-Virus
Virus Protection Software
Network Management Software

BRANDS/DIVISIONS/AFFILIATES:
TPG Capital
Intel Corporation
Thoma Bravo LLC

GROWTH PLANS/SPECIAL FEATURES:
McAfee, LLC is a cybersecurity company. The firm creates security solutions for business and consumer customers. Its solutions work with other companies' products and therefore helps businesses orchestrate cyber environments that are integrated and secure. McAfee's products enable the protection, detection and correction of threats on both sides of the spectrum: between McAfee and the business or consumer, simultaneously and collaboratively. Since McAfee products protect consumers across all connected devices, homes and businesses can be monitored in real-time, whether at home/office or away. Moreover, McAfee works with other security players in an effort to unite against cybercriminal activities. During 2017, Intel Corporation converted Intel Security into a joint venture between itself, TPG Capital and Thoma Bravo, LLC called McAfee, LLC. TPG is the majority holder, Intel owns 49% and Thoma owns a minimal stake.

CONTACTS: Note: Officers with more than one job title may be intentionally listed here more than once.

Christopher Young, CEO
Michael Fey, CTO
Bryan Reed Barney, Exec. VP-Prod. Dev.
Ari Jaaksi, Sr. VP
Louis Riley, General Counsel
Tom Fountain, Sr. VP
Edward Hayden, Sr. VP-Finance & Acct.
Steve Redman, Exec. VP-Global Sales
Ken Levine, Sr. VP
Gert-Jan Schenk, Pres., EMEA
Barry McPherson, Exec. VP-Worldwide Delivery & Support Svcs.
Jean-Claude Broido, Pres., McAfee Japan
Barry McPherson, Exec. VP-Supply Chain & Facilities

FINANCIAL DATA: Note: Data for latest year may not have been available at press time.

In U.S. $	2017	2016	2015	2014	2013	2012
Revenue	2,681,000,000	2,450,000,000	2,375,000,000	2,216,000,000	2,190,000,000	2,072,000,000
R&D Expense						
Operating Income						
Operating Margin %						
SGA Expense						
Net Income						
Operating Cash Flow						
Capital Expenditure						
EBITDA						
Return on Assets %						
Return on Equity %						
Debt to Equity						

CONTACT INFORMATION:
Phone: 972-963-8000   Fax:
Toll-Free: 855-380-6445
Address: 2821 Mission College Blvd., Santa Clara, CA 95054 United States

STOCK TICKER/OTHER:
Stock Ticker: Joint Venture
Employees: 8,001
Parent Company:

Exchange:
Fiscal Year Ends: 12/31

SALARIES/BONUSES:
Top Exec. Salary: $ Bonus: $
Second Exec. Salary: $ Bonus: $

OTHER THOUGHTS:
Estimated Female Officers or Directors: 3
Hot Spot for Advancement for Women/Minorities: Y

Sales, profits and employees may be estimates. Financial information, benefits and other data can change quickly and may vary from those stated here.

McDermott International Inc

www.mcdermott.com

NAIC Code: 541330

TYPES OF BUSINESS:
Engineering Services
Marine Construction
Procurement Services
Project Management

BRANDS/DIVISIONS/AFFILIATES:

CONTACTS:
Note: Officers with more than one job title may be intentionally listed here more than once.

Stuart Spence, CFO
Gary Luquette, Chairman of the Board
Christopher Krummel, Chief Accounting Officer
David Dickson, Director
Brian McLaughlin, Senior VP, Divisional
Jonathan Kennefick, Senior VP, Divisional
Andrew Leys, Vice President, Divisional
Linh Austin, Vice President, Geographical
Hugh Cuthbertson, Vice President, Geographical
Scott Munro, Vice President, Geographical

GROWTH PLANS/SPECIAL FEATURES:

McDermott International, Inc. is a multinational engineering and construction services company specializing in offshore construction for oil and gas exploration projects. The firm operates in approximately 20 countries and divides its operations into three primary geographic segments: Asia Pacific, Americas/Europe/Africa and the Middle East. In the Asia Pacific segment, the company offers engineering, procurement, construction and installation (EPCI) services to energy companies primarily in Australia, Indonesia, Vietnam, Malaysia, India and Thailand. This division's primary fabrication facility in this region is located on Batam Island, Indonesia. The Americas/Europe/Africa segment serves customers primarily in the U.S., Brazil, Mexico, Trinidad, the North Sea, West Africa and East Africa. The Middle East segment includes the Caspian region, serving customers in Saudi Arabia, the United Arab Emirates, Qatar, Kuwait, India, Azerbaijan and Russia. All of the segments focus on the fabrication and installation of fixed and floating structures and the installation of pipelines and subsea systems. Its fabrication facilities construct a full range of offshore structures, from conventional jacket-type fixed platforms to intermediate water and deepwater platform configurations. Project installation is performed by major construction vessels stationed throughout the various regions, which McDermott either owns or operates. McDermott vessels offer a variety of complex installation services, including structural lifting/lowering and pipelay services.

FINANCIAL DATA:
Note: Data for latest year may not have been available at press time.

In U.S. $	2017	2016	2015	2014	2013	2012
Revenue	2,984,768,000	2,635,983,000	3,070,275,000	2,300,889,000	2,658,932,000	3,641,624,000
R&D Expense	4,946,000					
Operating Income	331,406,000	207,615,000	161,752,000	-20,688,000	-343,665,000	335,641,000
Operating Margin %	11.10%	7.87%	5.26%	-.89%	-12.92%	9.21%
SGA Expense	198,973,000	178,752,000	217,239,000	208,564,000	201,171,000	205,974,000
Net Income	178,546,000	34,117,000	-17,983,000	-75,994,000	-516,913,000	206,653,000
Operating Cash Flow	135,804,000	178,179,000	55,272,000	6,960,000	-256,611,000	209,784,000
Capital Expenditure	118,811,000	228,079,000	102,851,000	321,187,000	283,962,000	286,310,000
EBITDA	432,108,000	310,292,000	280,033,000	92,216,000	-240,618,000	455,115,000
Return on Assets %	5.54%	1.03%	-.52%	-2.43%	-16.83%	6.53%
Return on Equity %	10.76%	2.24%	-1.20%	-5.35%	-31.93%	11.65%
Debt to Equity	0.29	0.45	0.55	0.58	0.03	0.04

CONTACT INFORMATION:
Phone: 281 870-5000   Fax: 281 870-5095
Toll-Free:
Address: 757 N. Eldridge Pkwy., Houston, TX 77079 United States

SALARIES/BONUSES:
Top Exec. Salary: $850,000   Bonus: $
Second Exec. Salary: $477,750   Bonus: $

STOCK TICKER/OTHER:
Stock Ticker: MDR
Employees: 12,400
Parent Company:

Exchange: NYS
Fiscal Year Ends: 12/31

OTHER THOUGHTS:
Estimated Female Officers or Directors: 4
Hot Spot for Advancement for Women/Minorities: Y

Medtronic plc

NAIC Code: 334510

www.medtronic.com

TYPES OF BUSINESS:
Equipment-Defibrillators & Pacing Products
Neurological Devices
Diabetes Management Devices
Ear, Nose & Throat Surgical Equipment
Pain Management Devices
Cardiac Surgery Equipment

BRANDS/DIVISIONS/AFFILIATES:

CONTACTS: Note: Officers with more than one job title may be intentionally listed here more than once.
Omar Ishrak, CEO
Mark Ploof, Sr. VP-Global Operations
Karen Parkhill, CFO
Karen L. Parkhill, CFO
Carol A. Surface, -Chief Human Resources Officer
Michael Coyle, Executive VP
Hooman Hakami, Executive VP
Robert Hoedt, Executive VP
Bradley Lerman, General Counsel
Richard Kuntz, Other Executive Officer
Carol Surface, Other Executive Officer
Geoffrey Martha, President, Divisional
Bob White, President, Divisional
Chris Lee, President, Geographical
Omar Ishrak, Chmn.

GROWTH PLANS/SPECIAL FEATURES:

Medtronic plc is a global leader in medical device technology, serving physicians, clinicians and patients in approximately 160 countries worldwide. Its operations consist of four primary segments: the cardiac and vascular group, which includes the cardiac rhythm and heart failure disease management (CRHF), as well as coronary, structural heart and endovascular therapies; the restorative therapies group, which includes the spinal, brain, specialty and pain therapies; the minimally invasive therapies group, which includes surgical and patient monitoring and recovery solutions; and the diabetes group, which includes intensive insulin management, non-intensive diabetes therapies and diabetes services and solutions. Products in the CRHF division manage cardiac rhythm disorders and include pacemakers, implantable defibrillators, ablation products and products for the treatment of atrial fibrillation (AF). The coronary, structural heart and endovascular therapies makes technology that supports the interventional treatment of coronary artery disease to help improve blood flow, and includes products such as stents, guide wires, and catheters. The spinal division offers medical devices used to treat spinal and cranial conditions. The neuromodulation division develops devices for the treatment of neurological, urological and gastroenterological disorders. The surgical technologies division develops and manufactures minimally invasive products to treat ear, nose and throat and neurological diseases. The patient monitoring and recovery develops and markets sensors, monitors and temperature management products, as well as products and therapies for complication-free recovery. The diabetes unit develops integrated diabetes management systems, insulin pump therapies, continuous glucose monitoring systems and therapy management software.

The firm offers employees health care and disability, adoption and elder care assistance, retirement plans and stock options.

FINANCIAL DATA: Note: Data for latest year may not have been available at press time.

In U.S. $	2017	2016	2015	2014	2013	2012
Revenue	29,710,000,000	28,833,000,000	20,261,000,000	17,005,000,000	16,590,000,000	16,184,000,000
R&D Expense	2,193,000,000	2,224,000,000	1,640,000,000	1,477,000,000	1,557,000,000	1,490,000,000
Operating Income	6,313,000,000	6,067,000,000	4,675,000,000	4,999,000,000	4,878,000,000	4,847,000,000
Operating Margin %	21.24%	21.04%	23.07%	29.39%	29.40%	29.94%
SGA Expense	9,711,000,000	9,469,000,000	6,904,000,000	5,847,000,000	5,698,000,000	5,623,000,000
Net Income	4,028,000,000	3,538,000,000	2,675,000,000	3,065,000,000	3,467,000,000	3,617,000,000
Operating Cash Flow	6,880,000,000	5,218,000,000	4,902,000,000	4,959,000,000	4,883,000,000	4,470,000,000
Capital Expenditure	1,254,000,000	1,046,000,000	571,000,000	396,000,000	457,000,000	499,000,000
EBITDA	8,613,000,000	8,542,000,000	5,458,000,000	4,934,000,000	5,221,000,000	5,327,000,000
Return on Assets %	4.03%	3.42%	3.69%	8.42%	10.20%	11.39%
Return on Equity %	7.87%	6.72%	7.36%	16.08%	19.37%	21.86%
Debt to Equity	0.51	0.58	0.63	0.53	0.52	0.43

CONTACT INFORMATION:
Phone: 3531-438-1700 Fax:
Toll-Free:
Address: 20 On Hatch, Lower Hatch St., Dublin, 2

STOCK TICKER/OTHER:
Stock Ticker: MDT
Employees: 91,000
Parent Company:

Exchange: NYS
Fiscal Year Ends: 04/30

SALARIES/BONUSES:
Top Exec. Salary: $620,192 Bonus: $1,000,000
Second Exec. Salary: $1,593,770 Bonus: $

OTHER THOUGHTS:
Estimated Female Officers or Directors: 5
Hot Spot for Advancement for Women/Minorities: Y

Sales, profits and employees may be estimates. Financial information, benefits and other data can change quickly and may vary from those stated here.

Mentor Graphics Inc

NAIC Code: 0

www.mentor.com

TYPES OF BUSINESS:
Software-Component Design, Simulation & Testing
Electronic Design Automation Tools
Consulting Services

BRANDS/DIVISIONS/AFFILIATES:
Siemens AG

CONTACTS:
Note: Officers with more than one job title may be intentionally listed here more than once.

Walden Rhines, CEO
Gregory Hinckley, CFO
Richard Trebing, VP-Finance
Brian Derrick, VP-Mktg.
Vicky Sargent, Chief Human Resources Officer
Ananthan Thandri, CIO
Michael Ellow, Senior VP, Divisional
Brian Derrick, Vice President, Divisional
Dean Freed, Vice President

GROWTH PLANS/SPECIAL FEATURES:
Mentor Graphics, Inc. is a supplier of electronic design automation (EDA) systems, advanced computer software and emulation hardware products used to automate the design, analysis and testing of electronic hardware and embedded systems and components. These products are primarily marketed to large companies in the military, aerospace, communications, computer, consumer electronics, semiconductor, networking, multimedia and transportation industries. The company's offerings are divided into five categories: EDA, systems, automotive, thermal simulation and test and embedded. EDA products and solutions include virtual prototyping, high-level synthesis, low-power optics and analytics, functional verification, AMS integrated circuit (IC) design flow, MEMS (micro-electro-mechanical systems) design flow, IC design, IC manufacturing, IC test, intellectual property and field-programmable gate array (FPGA). Systems include electrical, networks, harness, system modeling and design management, printed circuit board (PCB) design, IC package design and PCB manufacturing/assembly/test. Automotive products and solutions include connectivity, electrification, autonomous and architecture. Thermal simulation and test products and solutions include computer-aided design (CAD)-embedded computational fluid dynamics (CFD), electronics cooling CFD, semiconductor device thermal testing and one-dimensional CFD. Last, embedded products include software and IoT solutions. Mentor offers support services, including software updates, a support center, support forums, technical support and shared product ideas. In March 2017, Mentor Graphics was acquired by Siemens AG, and subsequently ceased from being publicly-traded.

Employees of Mentor receive health coverage, an adoption program and flexible time off.

FINANCIAL DATA:
Note: Data for latest year may not have been available at press time.

In U.S. $	2017	2016	2015	2014	2013	2012
Revenue	1,200,000,000	1,180,988,032	1,244,132,992	1,156,372,992	1,088,727,040	1,014,638,016
R&D Expense						
Operating Income						
Operating Margin %						
SGA Expense						
Net Income		96,277,000	147,139,008	155,258,000	138,736,000	83,872,000
Operating Cash Flow						
Capital Expenditure						
EBITDA						
Return on Assets %						
Return on Equity %						
Debt to Equity						

CONTACT INFORMATION:
Phone: 503 685-7000   Fax: 503 685-1202
Toll-Free: 800-592-2210
Address: 8005 SW Boeckman Rd., Wilsonville, OR 97070 United States

STOCK TICKER/OTHER:
Stock Ticker: Subsidiary
Employees: 5,558
Parent Company: Siemens AG

Exchange:
Fiscal Year Ends: 01/31

SALARIES/BONUSES:
Top Exec. Salary: $ Bonus: $
Second Exec. Salary: $ Bonus: $

OTHER THOUGHTS:
Estimated Female Officers or Directors:
Hot Spot for Advancement for Women/Minorities:

Merck & Co Inc

NAIC Code: 325412

www.merck.com

TYPES OF BUSINESS:
Drugs-Diversified
Anti-Infective & Anti-Cancer Drugs
Dermatologicals
Cardiovascular Drugs
Animal Health Products

BRANDS/DIVISIONS/AFFILIATES:
Merck Sharp & Dohme Corp

CONTACTS:
Note: Officers with more than one job title may be intentionally listed here more than once.

Kenneth Frazier, CEO
Ashley Watson, Other Executive Officer
Robert Davis, CFO
Rita Karachun, Chief Accounting Officer
Mirian Graddick-Weir, Executive VP, Divisional
Michael Holston, Executive VP
Julie Gerberding, Executive VP
Sanat Chattopadhyay, Executive VP
Adam Schechter, Executive VP
Roger Perlmutter, Executive VP
Richard DeLuca, Executive VP

GROWTH PLANS/SPECIAL FEATURES:
Merck & Co., Inc., known as Merck Sharp & Dohme Corp. outside of the U.S. and Canada, is a global healthcare company that develops and manufactures medicines, vaccines and biologics. The firm operates through four segments: pharmaceutical, animal health, healthcare services and alliances. Pharmaceutical, the company's primary segment, markets human health pharmaceutical and vaccine products either directly or through joint ventures. Merck & Co. markets and develops human health pharmaceutical products for the treatment of bone, respiratory, dermatology, immunology, cardiovascular, diabetes, obesity, infectious disease, neurological, ophthalmology and oncology conditions. These products are sold primarily to drug wholesalers and retailers, hospitals, government agencies and managed healthcare providers such as health maintenance organizations (HMOs), pharmacy benefit managers and other institutions. Vaccine products are primarily sold to physicians, wholesalers, physician distributors and government entities. This segment also offers certain women's health products, including contraceptives and fertility treatments. The animal health segment offers vaccine, anti-infective and anti-parasitic products for disease prevention, treatment and control in farm and companion animals. The healthcare services segment provides services and solutions that focus on engagement, health analytics and clinical services to improve the value of care delivered to patients. The alliances segment consists of revenue derived from the company's relationship with AstraZeneca LP. Merck continues to pursue opportunities for establishing external alliances to complement its internal research capabilities, including research collaborations as well as licensing preclinical and clinical compounds and technology platforms. In February 2018, Merck agreed to acquire Viralytics, an Australian public company focused on oncolytic immunotherapy treatments for a range of cancers.

FINANCIAL DATA:
Note: Data for latest year may not have been available at press time.

In U.S. $	2017	2016	2015	2014	2013	2012
Revenue	40,122,000,000	39,807,000,000	39,498,000,000	42,237,000,000	44,033,000,000	47,267,000,000
R&D Expense	10,208,000,000	10,124,000,000	6,704,000,000	7,180,000,000	7,503,000,000	8,168,000,000
Operating Income	7,309,000,000	6,030,000,000	7,547,000,000	6,683,000,000	7,665,000,000	9,877,000,000
Operating Margin %	18.21%	15.14%	19.10%	15.82%	17.40%	20.89%
SGA Expense	9,830,000,000	9,762,000,000	10,313,000,000	11,606,000,000	11,911,000,000	12,776,000,000
Net Income	2,394,000,000	3,920,000,000	4,442,000,000	11,920,000,000	4,404,000,000	6,168,000,000
Operating Cash Flow	6,447,000,000	10,376,000,000	12,421,000,000	7,860,000,000	11,654,000,000	10,022,000,000
Capital Expenditure	1,888,000,000	1,614,000,000	1,283,000,000	2,317,000,000	1,548,000,000	1,954,000,000
EBITDA	11,912,000,000	10,793,000,000	12,448,000,000	24,706,000,000	13,334,000,000	16,431,000,000
Return on Assets %	2.61%	3.97%	4.43%	11.68%	4.15%	5.83%
Return on Equity %	6.43%	9.24%	9.51%	24.22%	8.56%	11.46%
Debt to Equity	0.62	0.60	0.53	0.38	0.41	0.30

CONTACT INFORMATION:
Phone: 908 423-1000
Fax: 908 735-1253
Toll-Free:
Address: 2000 Galloping Hill Rd., Kenilworth, NJ 07033 United States

STOCK TICKER/OTHER:
Stock Ticker: MRK
Employees: 68,000
Parent Company:
Exchange: NYS
Fiscal Year Ends: 12/31

SALARIES/BONUSES:
Top Exec. Salary: $1,572,212   Bonus: $
Second Exec. Salary: $1,083,750   Bonus: $

OTHER THOUGHTS:
Estimated Female Officers or Directors: 4
Hot Spot for Advancement for Women/Minorities: Y

Sales, profits and employees may be estimates. Financial information, benefits and other data can change quickly and may vary from those stated here.

Merck KGaA

NAIC Code: 325412

www.emdgroup.com/en/company.html

TYPES OF BUSINESS:
Pharmaceuticals
Over-the-Counter Drugs & Vitamins
Generic Drugs
Chemicals
LCD Components
Reagents & Diagnostics
Nanotechnology Research

BRANDS/DIVISIONS/AFFILIATES:
EMD Serono

CONTACTS: Note: Officers with more than one job title may be intentionally listed here more than once.
Stefan Oschmann, CEO
Marcus Kuhnert, CFO
Stefan Oschmann, Head-Patents & Scientific Svcs
Kai Beckmann, Head-Site Oper.
Walter Huber, Head-Group Comm.
Bernd Reckmann, CEO-Chemicals
Stefan Oschmann, Chmn.

GROWTH PLANS/SPECIAL FEATURES:

Merck KGaA, headquartered in Germany, is a science and technology company engaged in research and discovery. The firm's business segments include healthcare, life science and performance materials. The healthcare segment consists of Merck's biopharma, consumer health, allergopharma and biosimilars businesses. Biopharma primarily engages in prescription medicines in relation to neurodegenerative diseases, oncology, fertility, endocrinology and cardiometabolic diseases, and also produces general medicines. Consumer health comprises over-the-counter pharmaceuticals to address mobility, women's and children's health, cough, cold and everyday health protection. Allergopharma comprises products for diagnostic testing and the treatment of allergies. Biosimilars focuses on the development of biosimilars. Merck operates its healthcare business in the U.S. and Canada as EMD Serono. The life science segment provides: in-vitro diagnostic manufacturers with raw materials, equipment and services for their assay development, scale-up and manufacturing needs; expertise, products and solutions to biotech clients, from discovery to commercialization; environmental testing services; testing solutions for the food/beverage and industrial industries; government and academic research, from concept inception to pre-clinical development; manufacturing solutions that support pharmaceutical and biopharmaceutical manufacturers; and quality control services and solutions. Last, the performance materials segment offers a wide range of products and solutions to the following industries: architecture, automotive, cosmetic, display, pigment, functional technology, optoelectronic and semiconductor. In April 2018, Merck agreed to sell its consumer health business to Procter & Gamble Co. for approximately $4.2 billion. The proceeds will increase flexibility and strengthen Merck's three primary business segments.

FINANCIAL DATA: Note: Data for latest year may not have been available at press time.

In U.S. $	2017	2016	2015	2014	2013	2012
Revenue	18,150,960,000	17,795,060,000	14,396,659,712	12,890,383,360	12,435,664,896	12,522,864,640
R&D Expense						
Operating Income						
Operating Margin %						
SGA Expense						
Net Income	3,084,780,000	1,898,320,000	1,249,495,680	1,297,130,624	1,347,455,744	635,171,520
Operating Cash Flow						
Capital Expenditure						
EBITDA						
Return on Assets %						
Return on Equity %						
Debt to Equity						

CONTACT INFORMATION:
Phone: 49 6151720   Fax: 49 6151722000
Toll-Free:
Address: Frankfurter St. 250, Darmstadt, 64293 Germany

SALARIES/BONUSES:
Top Exec. Salary: $ Bonus: $
Second Exec. Salary: $ Bonus: $

STOCK TICKER/OTHER:
Stock Ticker: MRK   Exchange: Frankfurt
Employees: 50,500   Fiscal Year Ends: 12/31
Parent Company:

OTHER THOUGHTS:
Estimated Female Officers or Directors:
Hot Spot for Advancement for Women/Minorities:

Sales, profits and employees may be estimates. Financial information, benefits and other data can change quickly and may vary from those stated here.

Merck Serono SA

NAIC Code: 325412

www.merckserono.com

TYPES OF BUSINESS:
Biopharmaceuticals Development
Fertility Drugs
Neurology Drugs
Growth & Metabolism Drugs
Dermatology Drugs
Oncology Research

BRANDS/DIVISIONS/AFFILIATES:
Merck KGaA
EMD Serono Inc
Rebif
GONAL-f
Ovidrel
Cetrotide
Saizen
Serostim

CONTACTS: Note: Officers with more than one job title may be intentionally listed here more than once.
Belen Garijo Lopez, Pres.
Thierry Hulot, Head-Global Mfg. & Supply
Thomas Gunning, Head-Legal
Meeta Gulyani, Head-Strategy & Global Franchises
Patrice Grand, Head-Communications
Susan Herbert, Head-Global Bus. Dev. & Strategy
Sascha Becker, Sr. VP
Elchin Ergun, Head-Global Commercial
Annalisa Jenkins, Head-Global Dev. & Medical

GROWTH PLANS/SPECIAL FEATURES:
Merck Serono SA is a biopharmaceutical company, and an operating subsidiary of Merck KGaA. The firm discovers, develops, manufactures and commercializes prescription medicines of chemical and biological origin in specialist indications. For neurodegenerative diseases, the company has developed drugs such as Rebif, a modifying drug that treats relapsing forms of multiple sclerosis; and Erbitux, an antibody that targets the epidermal growth factor receptor for treating squamous cell carcinoma of the head and neck, and metastatic colorectal cancer. Merck Serono also develops fertility drugs for various stages of the reproductive cycle and recombinant versions of various hormones to treat infertility, such as GONAL-f (follitropin alfa for injection), Ovidrel pre-filled syringe (choriogonadotropin alfa injection) and Cetrotide (cetrorelix acetate for injection). For metabolic endocrinology, products include Saizen (somatropin-rDNA origin-for injection), and Serostim (somatropin-rDNA origin-for injection). For oncology, BAVENCIO (avelumab) is indicated for the treatment of adults and pediatric patients 12 years and older with metastatic Merkel cell carcinoma, as well as patients with locally-advanced or metastatic urothelial carcinoma. EMD Serono's diversified pipeline includes multiple, high-priority projects currently in development to deliver new and innovative products to people living with unmet patient needs. The company's research and development translational innovation platforms focus on using emerging science and tools to apply precision medicine to develop personalized therapies for patients. Merck Serono is headquartered in Darmstadt, Germany, with additional offices in Boston, Massachusetts, and markets its products in more than 150 countries. In Canada and the U.S., Merck Serono operates as EMD Serono, Inc.

FINANCIAL DATA: Note: Data for latest year may not have been available at press time.

In U.S. $	2017	2016	2015	2014	2013	2012
Revenue	7,000,000,000	6,900,000,000	6,800,000,000	6,690,000,000		
R&D Expense						
Operating Income						
Operating Margin %						
SGA Expense						
Net Income						
Operating Cash Flow						
Capital Expenditure						
EBITDA						
Return on Assets %						
Return on Equity %						
Debt to Equity						

CONTACT INFORMATION:
Phone: 49-6151-72-0 Fax: 49-6151-72-2000
Toll-Free:
Address: Frankfurter St. 250, Darmstadt, 64293 Germany

STOCK TICKER/OTHER:
Stock Ticker: Subsidiary Exchange:
Employees: 4,775 Fiscal Year Ends: 12/31
Parent Company: Merck KGaA

SALARIES/BONUSES:
Top Exec. Salary: $ Bonus: $
Second Exec. Salary: $ Bonus: $

OTHER THOUGHTS:
Estimated Female Officers or Directors: 5
Hot Spot for Advancement for Women/Minorities: Y

Meritor Inc

www.meritor.com

NAIC Code: 336300

TYPES OF BUSINESS:
Auto Parts Manufacturer
Drivetrain Systems & Components
Exhaust Systems
Braking Systems
Driveline Systems & Axles
Undercarriage Systems
Third-Party Logistics (3PL) Services

BRANDS/DIVISIONS/AFFILIATES:

CONTACTS: Note: Officers with more than one job title may be intentionally listed here more than once.
Kevin Nowlan, CFO
Timothy Heffron, Chief Information Officer
Paul Bialy, Controller
William Newlin, Director
April Miller, Other Executive Officer
Cheri Lantz, Other Executive Officer
Chris Villavarayan, President, Divisional
Joseph Plomin, President, Divisional
Jeffrey Craig, President
Mike Lei, Treasurer
Carl Anderson, Vice President, Divisional

GROWTH PLANS/SPECIAL FEATURES:

Meritor, Inc., headquartered in Troy, Michigan, is a global supplier of a broad range of integrated systems, modules and components serving commercial truck, trailer and specialty original equipment manufacturers (OEMs) and certain aftermarkets. The company has 26 manufacturing facilities and 25 engineering facilities, sales offices, warehouses and services centers in the U.S., Europe, South America, Canada, Mexico and the Asia Pacific regions. The firm's primary operating segments are commercial truck and industrial, and aftermarket and trailer. The commercial truck and industrial segment supplies drivetrain systems and components, including axles, drivelines and braking and suspension systems, primarily for medium- and heavy-duty trucks in North America, South America, Europe and Asia Pacific. Its industrial components include drivetrain systems for off-highway, military, construction, bus and coach, fire and emergency and other industrial applications. This segment also includes all of the firm's aftermarket businesses in Asia-Pacific and South America, including all on- and off-highway activities. The aftermarket and trailer segment supplies axles, brakes, drivelines, suspension parts and other replacement and remanufactured parts to commercial vehicle aftermarket customers. This segment also supplies a wide variety of undercarriage products and systems for trailer applications in North America. During 2017, the firm acquired the product portfolio and related technologies of Fabco Holdings, Inc.

The company offers employees medical, dental and vision insurance; life and AD&D insurance; flexible spending accounts; disability coverage; a retirement plan; a 401(k); and business travel accident insurance.

FINANCIAL DATA: Note: Data for latest year may not have been available at press time.

In U.S. $	2017	2016	2015	2014	2013	2012
Revenue	3,347,000,000	3,199,000,000	3,505,000,000	3,766,000,000	3,701,000,000	4,418,000,000
R&D Expense						
Operating Income	228,000,000	219,000,000	164,000,000	230,000,000	37,000,000	205,000,000
Operating Margin %	6.81%	6.84%	4.67%	6.10%	.99%	4.64%
SGA Expense	235,000,000	240,000,000	299,000,000	235,000,000	346,000,000	258,000,000
Net Income	324,000,000	573,000,000	64,000,000	249,000,000	-22,000,000	52,000,000
Operating Cash Flow	176,000,000	204,000,000	97,000,000	215,000,000	-96,000,000	77,000,000
Capital Expenditure	95,000,000	93,000,000	79,000,000	77,000,000	54,000,000	89,000,000
EBITDA	303,000,000	286,000,000	229,000,000	297,000,000	104,000,000	268,000,000
Return on Assets %	12.28%	24.44%	2.72%	9.81%	-.86%	2.01%
Return on Equity %	1136.84%					
Debt to Equity	2.79					

CONTACT INFORMATION:
Phone: 248 435-1000 Fax:
Toll-Free:
Address: 2135 W. Maple Rd., Troy, MI 48084 United States

STOCK TICKER/OTHER:
Stock Ticker: MTOR
Employees: 8,000
Parent Company:

Exchange: NYS
Fiscal Year Ends: 09/30

SALARIES/BONUSES:
Top Exec. Salary: $900,000 Bonus: $
Second Exec. Salary: $500,000 Bonus: $

OTHER THOUGHTS:
Estimated Female Officers or Directors: 3
Hot Spot for Advancement for Women/Minorities: Y

Sales, profits and employees may be estimates. Financial information, benefits and other data can change quickly and may vary from those stated here.

Michael Baker International LLC

NAIC Code: 541330

www.mbakerintl.com

TYPES OF BUSINESS:
Engineering Services
Infrastructure Projects
Facilities Management
Consulting Services
Regulatory Compliance Services

BRANDS/DIVISIONS/AFFILIATES:
DC Capital Partners LLC
Sallyport Global Holdings

CONTACTS:
Note: Officers with more than one job title may be intentionally listed here more than once.

Brian A. Lutes, CEO
Dale R. Spaulding, COO
James M. Kempton, CFO
Leanne Anderson, CCO
Penny Mercadante, Chief Human Resources Officer
Martin J. Miner, CTO
James McKnight, Chief Legal Officer
Thomas J. Campbell, Chmn.
Nicholas Gross, COO-Intl

GROWTH PLANS/SPECIAL FEATURES:

Michael Baker International, LLC provides engineering design and related consulting services for public and private sector clients worldwide. The firm operates in two business divisions: engineering, planning and consulting; and Sallyport Global Holdings. The engineering, planning and consulting division encompasses the complete life-cycle of planning, environmental assessment, engineering design, construction management and facilities maintenance for projects worldwide. Its markets include highways, bridges, airports, rail and mass transit systems, domestic and overseas government facilities, commercial facilities, water and wastewater infrastructure, energy infrastructure and urban planning and development. Sallyport provides full life-cycle support services facilitating client operations in challenging, remote, austere environments; and specializes in supporting clients conducting business in areas of natural disaster, conflict or unrest. This division customizes its solutions to meet the specific needs and requirements of its clients, and aims to offer solutions that readily adapt to emergent political, security, regulatory or environmental risks. Sallyport's logistics stability unit provides services to reduce customer costs, increase efficiencies and ensure continuous mission-readiness. Its technical and physical security services include access control, intrusion detection, surveillance, program management, staffing, training, consulting, systems integration, maintenance and monitoring. Michael Baker operates through more than 90 offices in the U.S. and internationally. It is privately-owned by DC Capital Partners, LLC.

Michael Baker International offers its employees health, wellness, life/disability and retirement benefits; paid time off; and health and dependent care plans.

FINANCIAL DATA:
Note: Data for latest year may not have been available at press time.

In U.S. $	2017	2016	2015	2014	2013	2012
Revenue	670,000,000	665,000,000	660,000,000	650,000,000	630,000,000	593,396,992
R&D Expense						
Operating Income						
Operating Margin %						
SGA Expense						
Net Income						
Operating Cash Flow						
Capital Expenditure						
EBITDA						
Return on Assets %						
Return on Equity %						
Debt to Equity						

CONTACT INFORMATION:
Phone: 412 269-6300   Fax: 412 375-3909
Toll-Free: 800-553-1153
Address: 500 Grant St., Ste. 5400, Pittsburgh, PA 15219 United States

STOCK TICKER/OTHER:
Stock Ticker: Private   Exchange:
Employees: 3,000   Fiscal Year Ends: 12/31
Parent Company: DC Capital Partners LLC

SALARIES/BONUSES:
Top Exec. Salary: $ Bonus: $
Second Exec. Salary: $ Bonus: $

OTHER THOUGHTS:
Estimated Female Officers or Directors: 1
Hot Spot for Advancement for Women/Minorities:

Sales, profits and employees may be estimates. Financial information, benefits and other data can change quickly and may vary from those stated here.

Micron Technology Inc

NAIC Code: 334413

www.micron.com

TYPES OF BUSINESS:
Components-Semiconductor Memory
PCs & Peripherals
Flash Memory Devices

BRANDS/DIVISIONS/AFFILIATES:
IM Flash Technologies LLC
3D Xpoint

CONTACTS: Note: Officers with more than one job title may be intentionally listed here more than once.
Sanjay Mehrotra, CEO
Ernie Maddock, CFO
Robert Switz, Chairman of the Board
Scott Deboer, Executive VP, Divisional
Sumit Sadana, Executive VP
April Arnzen, Senior VP, Divisional
Steven Thorsen, Senior VP, Divisional
Joel Poppen, Senior VP, Divisional

GROWTH PLANS/SPECIAL FEATURES:

Micron Technology, Inc. designs, develops, manufactures and markets semiconductor memory products and personal computer (PC) systems. Its broad portfolio of high-performance memory technologies, including DRAM, NAND Flash and NOR Flash is the basis for solid-state drives, modules, multi-chip packages and other system solutions. Micron's memory solutions enable the world's most innovative computing, consumer enterprise storage, networking, mobile, embedded and automotive applications. Its 3D XPoint memory technology is non-volatile memory and transistor-less, and creates a three-dimensional checkerboard where memory cells sit at the intersection of word lines and bit lines, allowing the cells to be addressed individually. The company sells these products from its wholly-owned manufacturing facilities and through its joint venture companies. Manufacturing facilities are located in the U.S., China, Japan, Malaysia, Singapore and Taiwan. Micron operates its business through four segments: compute and networking business unit (CNBU), which includes memory products sold into computer, networking, graphics and cloud server markets; storage business unit (SBU), which includes memory products sold into enterprise, client, cloud and removable storage markets, as well as products sold to Intel through its IM Flash Technologies, LLC joint venture; mobile business unit (MBU), which includes memory products sold into smartphone, tablet and other mobile device markets; and embedded business unit (EBU), which includes memory products sold into automotive, industrial, connected home and consumer electronics markets.

Micron employees receive medical, dental, vision and life insurance; short- and long-term disability coverage; business travel accident coverage; and educational assistance.

FINANCIAL DATA: Note: Data for latest year may not have been available at press time.

In U.S. $	2017	2016	2015	2014	2013	2012
Revenue	20,322,000,000	12,399,000,000	16,192,000,000	16,358,000,000	9,073,000,000	8,234,000,000
R&D Expense	1,824,000,000	1,617,000,000	1,540,000,000	1,371,000,000	931,000,000	918,000,000
Operating Income	5,864,000,000	231,000,000	2,984,000,000	3,370,000,000	359,000,000	-570,000,000
Operating Margin %	28.85%	1.86%	18.42%	20.60%	3.95%	-6.92%
SGA Expense	743,000,000	659,000,000	719,000,000	707,000,000	562,000,000	620,000,000
Net Income	5,089,000,000	-276,000,000	2,899,000,000	3,045,000,000	1,190,000,000	-1,032,000,000
Operating Cash Flow	8,153,000,000	3,168,000,000	5,208,000,000	5,699,000,000	1,811,000,000	2,114,000,000
Capital Expenditure	4,734,000,000	5,817,000,000	4,021,000,000	2,658,000,000	1,244,000,000	1,699,000,000
EBITDA	9,658,000,000	3,136,000,000	5,647,000,000	5,188,000,000	3,320,000,000	1,566,000,000
Return on Assets %	16.18%	-1.06%	12.43%	14.63%	7.11%	-7.09%
Return on Equity %	33.15%	-2.26%	25.12%	30.58%	14.13%	-12.76%
Debt to Equity	0.53	0.75	0.51	0.46	0.48	0.39

CONTACT INFORMATION:
Phone: 208 368-4000   Fax: 208 368-4435
Toll-Free:
Address: 8000 S. Federal Way, Boise, ID 83707-0006 United States

STOCK TICKER/OTHER:
Stock Ticker: MU
Employees: 34,100
Parent Company:

Exchange: NAS
Fiscal Year Ends: 08/31

SALARIES/BONUSES:
Top Exec. Salary: $912,692   Bonus: $
Second Exec. Salary: $630,000   Bonus: $

OTHER THOUGHTS:
Estimated Female Officers or Directors: 2
Hot Spot for Advancement for Women/Minorities:

Sales, profits and employees may be estimates. Financial information, benefits and other data can change quickly and may vary from those stated here.

Microsoft Corporation

www.microsoft.com

NAIC Code: 0

TYPES OF BUSINESS:
Computer Software, Operating Systems, Languages & Development Tools
Enterprise Software
Game Consoles
Operating Systems
Software as a Service (SAAS)
Search Engine and Advertising
E-Mail Services
Instant Messaging

BRANDS/DIVISIONS/AFFILIATES:
Office 365
Dynamics
SQL
Windows
Visual Studio
Azure
LinkedIn Corporation
Xbox

CONTACTS:
Note: Officers with more than one job title may be intentionally listed here more than once.

Satya Nadella, CEO
Amy Hood, CFO
John Thompson, Chairman of the Board
Frank Brod, Chief Accounting Officer
Christopher Capossela, Chief Marketing Officer
William Gates, Co-Founder
Margaret Johnson, Executive VP, Divisional
Kathleen Hogan, Executive VP, Divisional
Jean-Philippe Courtois, Executive VP
Bradford Smith, Other Executive Officer

GROWTH PLANS/SPECIAL FEATURES:

Microsoft Corporation develops, license and supports software products, services and devices. It is a technology company that builds best-in-class platforms and productivity services for a mobile-first, cloud-first world. The firm's products include operating systems; cross-device productivity applications; server applications; business solution applications; desktop and server management tools; software development tools; video games; and training and certification of computer system integrators and developers. Microsoft also designs, manufactures and sells devices such as personal computers (PCs), tablets, gaming and entertainment consoles, phones, other intelligent devices and related accessories that integrate with its cloud-based offerings. The company operates its business in two segments: productivity and business processes, which consists of products and services in its portfolio of productivity, communication and information services through its devices and platforms; intelligent cloud, which consists of the company's public, private and hybrid server products and cloud services that can power modern businesses; and more personal computing, which consists of products and services geared towards harmonizing the interests of end users, developers and IT professionals across all devices. Products offered through the productivity and business processes segment include Office 365 and Dynamics. Products offered through the intelligent cloud segment include SQL servers, Windows servers, Visual Studio, system centers and Azure, as well as enterprise and consulting services. The more personal computing segment primarily consists of Windows, including Windows OEM licensing and other non-volume licensing of the Windows operating system; Devices, including Microsoft Surface, PC accessories, and other intelligent devices; Gaming, including Xbox hardware, software and services, comprising Xbox Live transactions, subscriptions and advertising, video games and third-party video game royalties; and search advertising. In December 2016, Microsoft completed its acquisition of LinkedIn Corporation, the world's largest online professional network.

Microsoft offers its employees health, dental and vision coverage; onsite health screenings; adoption assistance; childcare service discounts; a 401(k) plan; an employee stock purchase plan; and tuition assistance.

FINANCIAL DATA:
Note: Data for latest year may not have been available at press time.

In U.S. $	2017	2016	2015	2014	2013	2012
Revenue	89,950,000,000	85,320,000,000	93,580,000,000	86,833,000,000	77,849,000,000	73,723,000,000
R&D Expense	13,037,000,000	11,988,000,000	12,046,000,000	11,381,000,000	10,411,000,000	9,811,000,000
Operating Income	22,632,000,000	21,292,000,000	28,172,000,000	27,886,000,000	26,764,000,000	27,956,000,000
Operating Margin %	25.16%	24.95%	30.10%	32.11%	34.37%	37.92%
SGA Expense	20,020,000,000	19,260,000,000	20,324,000,000	20,632,000,000	20,425,000,000	18,426,000,000
Net Income	21,204,000,000	16,798,000,000	12,193,000,000	22,074,000,000	21,863,000,000	16,978,000,000
Operating Cash Flow	39,507,000,000	33,325,000,000	29,080,000,000	32,231,000,000	28,833,000,000	31,626,000,000
Capital Expenditure	8,129,000,000	8,343,000,000	5,944,000,000	5,485,000,000	4,257,000,000	2,305,000,000
EBITDA	34,149,000,000	27,616,000,000	25,245,000,000	33,629,000,000	31,236,000,000	25,614,000,000
Return on Assets %	9.75%	9.08%	6.99%	14.02%	16.58%	14.76%
Return on Equity %	29.37%	22.09%	14.35%	26.16%	30.09%	27.50%
Debt to Equity	1.05	0.56	0.34	0.22	0.15	0.16

CONTACT INFORMATION:
Phone: 425 882-8080   Fax: 425 936-7329
Toll-Free: 800-642-7676
Address: One Microsoft Way, Redmond, WA 98052 United States

SALARIES/BONUSES:
Top Exec. Salary: $1,450,000   Bonus: $
Second Exec. Salary: $852,917   Bonus: $

STOCK TICKER/OTHER:
Stock Ticker: MSFT   Exchange: NAS
Employees: 124,000   Fiscal Year Ends: 06/30
Parent Company:

OTHER THOUGHTS:
Estimated Female Officers or Directors: 4
Hot Spot for Advancement for Women/Minorities: Y

Middough Inc

NAIC Code: 541330

www.middough.com

TYPES OF BUSINESS:
Engineering Services
Engineering
Design
Consultancy

BRANDS/DIVISIONS/AFFILIATES:

CONTACTS: Note: Officers with more than one job title may be intentionally listed here more than once.
Ronald R. Ledin, CEO
Carl E. Wendell, COO
Vincent W. Shemo, CFO

GROWTH PLANS/SPECIAL FEATURES:

Middough, Inc., founded in 1950 by Willian Vance Middough, is a private engineering, architectural and management services company. Its services range from consulting to major projects, serving both small- and large-scale organizations. The company's engineering services consists of field inspections, electrical, industrial, metallurgical, mechanical, environmental, civil and chemical process engineering, piping, instrumentation and process controls, energy management and machine design. Its architectural services include facility planning and design, codes and compliance, energy conservation studies, automated security systems and control, laser scanning and surveying, laboratory planning, life cycle cost analysis and process and equipment layout among others. Its management services include pre-construction services, procurement, project controls, equipment and material management, environment, health and safety. Middough serves the following industries: agribusiness, chemical, energy, facilities, food/consumer products, industrial gas, manufacturing, oil and gas, pharmaceutical/biotechnology, refining, utilities, and research and development. The firm has major offices in Cleveland, Chicago, Houston, Philadelphia and Toledo, as well as additional offices nationally. Middough's newest office opened in early-2018, in the northwest Indiana area.

Middough offers its employees medical, prescription, dental, vision, life, AD&D, travel accident and short/long term disability coverage; 401(k); paid time off; and various employee assistance programs.

FINANCIAL DATA: Note: Data for latest year may not have been available at press time.

In U.S. $	2017	2016	2015	2014	2013	2012
Revenue						
R&D Expense						
Operating Income						
Operating Margin %						
SGA Expense						
Net Income						
Operating Cash Flow						
Capital Expenditure						
EBITDA						
Return on Assets %						
Return on Equity %						
Debt to Equity						

CONTACT INFORMATION:
Phone: 216-367-6000 Fax: 216-367-6020
Toll-Free:
Address: 1901 E. 13th St., Ste. 400, Cleveland, OH 44114 United States

STOCK TICKER/OTHER:
Stock Ticker: Private   Exchange:
Employees: 522   Fiscal Year Ends:
Parent Company:

SALARIES/BONUSES:
Top Exec. Salary: $ Bonus: $
Second Exec. Salary: $ Bonus: $

OTHER THOUGHTS:
Estimated Female Officers or Directors:
Hot Spot for Advancement for Women/Minorities:

Sales, profits and employees may be estimates. Financial information, benefits and other data can change quickly and may vary from those stated here.

Mitsubishi Corporation

NAIC Code: 333000

www.mitsubishicorp.com

TYPES OF BUSINESS:
Machinery Manufacturing
Automobile Manufacturing
Metals Mining & Production
Chemicals
Food Products & Commodities
Petroleum Exploration & Production
IT Services & Equipment
Machinery Manufacturing

BRANDS/DIVISIONS/AFFILIATES:
Vegetalia Inc

CONTACTS:
Note: Officers with more than one job title may be intentionally listed here more than once.

Takehiko Kakiuchi, CEO
Ken Kobayashi, Pres.
Hideyuki Nabeshima, Sr. Exec. VP-Admin.
Hideyuki Nabeshima, Sr. Exec. VP-Legal
Hideto Nakahara, Sr. Exec. VP-Global Strategy & Bus. Dev.
Hideyuki Nabeshima, Sr. Exec. VP-Corporate Communications
Jun Yanai, Sr. Exec. VP
Jun Kinukawa, Sr. Exec. VP
Takahisa Miyauchi, Sr. Exec. VP
Nobuaki Kojima, Exec. VP
Ken Kobayashi, Chmn.

GROWTH PLANS/SPECIAL FEATURES:

Mitsubishi Corporation is one of Japan's largest general trading companies, with customers in virtually every industry, including energy, metals, machinery, chemicals, food and general merchandise. The company's consolidated subsidiaries and affiliates fall into seven business groups: industrial finance, logistics and development; energy; metals; machinery; chemicals; living essentials; and global environment and infrastructure. The industrial finance, logistics and development group consists of three smaller divisions: asset finance and investment, real estate and logistics. The energy business group's operations include crude oil, petroleum, liquefied natural gas (LNG) and carbon production and marketing. The metals group is involved in the mining of coal and ferrous and non-ferrous metals as well as steel production. The machinery group manufactures power and electrical systems, transportation infrastructure, defense systems, aeronautical systems and automotive parts. The chemicals group manufactures raw materials for synthetic resins, chemical fertilizers, inorganic raw materials, industrial salts, plastics, electronics materials and life science products. The living essentials group produces food products, food commodities, textiles and other consumer products, including health care products. The global environment and infrastructure group develops power generation, water and transportation projects as well as handles lithium-ion batteries for various uses, including electric cars. Mitsubishi has more than 200 offices and subsidiaries in 90 countries and regions worldwide. In December 2017, the firm invested in Vegetalia, Inc., a startup venture specializing in providing information and communication technology for the agriculture sector.

FINANCIAL DATA:
Note: Data for latest year may not have been available at press time.

In U.S. $	2017	2016	2015	2014	2013	2012
Revenue	59,863,620,000	64,520,050,000	71,450,430,000	71,130,690,000	55,606,240,000	51,852,360,000
R&D Expense						46,394,630
Operating Income	3,788,075,000	420,365,200	1,348,714,000	2,097,298,000	1,541,522,000	4,758,208,000
Operating Margin %	6.32%	.65%	1.88%	2.94%	2.77%	9.17%
SGA Expense	8,668,345,000	9,464,953,000	9,304,557,000	2,420,468,000	8,290,992,000	128,209,400
Net Income	4,101,854,000	-1,391,793,000	3,731,824,000	3,366,490,000	3,354,090,000	4,228,144,000
Operating Cash Flow	5,431,377,000	6,522,313,000	7,436,781,000	3,554,835,000	3,757,341,000	5,087,228,000
Capital Expenditure	1,491,103,000	2,320,310,000	2,865,092,000	4,621,837,000	5,384,396,000	3,847,503,000
EBITDA	8,076,607,000	1,905,804,000	7,707,808,000	3,818,241,000	4,663,695,000	5,660,518,000
Return on Assets %	2.87%	-.94%	2.45%	2.38%	2.66%	3.80%
Return on Equity %	9.25%	-2.94%	7.53%	7.81%	9.36%	13.46%
Debt to Equity	0.84	0.99	0.86	0.92	1.05	1.07

CONTACT INFORMATION:
Phone: 81 332102121 Fax:
Toll-Free:
Address: 3-1 Marunouchi 2-chome, Chiyoda-ku, Tokyo, 100-8086 Japan

STOCK TICKER/OTHER:
Stock Ticker: MSBHY
Employees: 63,058
Parent Company:

Exchange: PINX
Fiscal Year Ends: 03/31

SALARIES/BONUSES:
Top Exec. Salary: $ Bonus: $
Second Exec. Salary: $ Bonus: $

OTHER THOUGHTS:
Estimated Female Officers or Directors: 1
Hot Spot for Advancement for Women/Minorities:

Sales, profits and employees may be estimates. Financial information, benefits and other data can change quickly and may vary from those stated here.

Mitsubishi Electric Corporation

www.mitsubishielectric.com

NAIC Code: 335311

TYPES OF BUSINESS:
Electrical and Electronic Equipment Manufacturer
Power Plant Manufacturing, Nuclear & Fossil
Wind & Solar Generation Systems
Consumer Electronics
Telecommunications & Computer Equipment
Industrial Automation Systems
Chips & Memory Devices
Semiconductors

BRANDS/DIVISIONS/AFFILIATES:
Mitsubishi Corporation

CONTACTS:
Note: Officers with more than one job title may be intentionally listed here more than once.

Masaki Sakuyama, CEO
Kenichiro Yamanishi, Pres.
Kazuhiko Tsutsumi, Exec. Officer-R&D
Masaharu Moriyaso, Exec. Officer-Total Productivity Mgmt.
Tsuyoshi Nakamura, Exec. Officer-Legal Affairs & Compliance
Noritomo Hashimoto, Sr. VP-Corp. Strategic Planning & Oper.
Takayuki Sueki, Exec. Officer-Global Strategic Planning & Mktg.
Masayuki Ichige, Exec. Officer-Govt & External & Public Rel.
Masayuki Ichige, Exec. Officer-Auditing
Yoshiaki Nakatani, Exec. Officer-Energy & Industrial Systems
Takashi Sasakawa, Exec. Officer-Electronic Systems
Mitsuo Muneyuki, Exec. VP-Export Control & Building Systems
Masaki Sakuyama, Exec. VP-Semiconductors & Device
Kenichiro Yamanishi, Chmn.

GROWTH PLANS/SPECIAL FEATURES:
Mitsubishi Electric Corporation, a subsidiary of Mitsubishi Corporation, is a global manufacturer, distributor and marketer of electrical and electronic equipment. This equipment is used in information processing and communications, space development and satellite communications, consumer electronics, industrial technology, energy, transportation and building equipment. The company has five primary business segments: energy & electric systems, home appliances, information & communication systems, industrial automation systems and electronic devices. The energy & electric systems segment manufactures nuclear and fossil fuel power generation plants and monitoring systems as well as wind turbines, solar panels and other electricity generators; turbine generators and hydraulic turbine generators; proton beam radiation treatment systems; elevators; security systems; railway systems; and large-scale display systems. The home appliances segment manufactures home electronics such as air conditioners, flat-screen televisions, DVD players, computers and computer monitors. The information & communication systems segment includes mobile phones, satellites, aerospace communication systems, digital closed-circuit television systems, enterprise information technology networks and internet servers. The industrial automation systems segment includes the manufacturing of programmable logic controllers, circuit breakers and robotics that are created and customized for multiple industrial uses. The electronic devices segment makes power modules, high-frequency devices, optical devices, LCD devices and microcomputers. Other business activities include procurement, logistics, real estate, advertising and finance. Currently, the firm is building a high-voltage direct current (HVDC) facility at its transmission and distribution center in Amagasaki, Japan, with a target for more than $500 million in global orders for HVDC-Diamond systems by 2020.

FINANCIAL DATA:
Note: Data for latest year may not have been available at press time.

In U.S. $	2017	2016	2015	2014	2013	2012
Revenue	39,488,230,000	40,938,640,000	40,677,710,000	37,771,190,000	33,468,840,000	34,112,770,000
R&D Expense	1,723,160,000	1,742,426,000	1,673,449,000	1,525,666,000	1,467,505,000	1,453,279,000
Operating Income	2,548,426,000	2,884,796,000	3,391,029,000	2,226,225,000	1,693,432,000	2,342,296,000
Operating Margin %	6.45%	7.04%	8.33%	5.89%	5.05%	6.86%
SGA Expense	7,727,082,000	7,697,336,000	7,365,037,000	6,866,424,000	6,045,184,000	5,825,256,000
Net Income	1,960,993,000	2,128,694,000	2,186,454,000	1,429,784,000	647,633,700	1,044,000,000
Operating Cash Flow	3,409,261,000	3,416,033,000	3,524,437,000	4,103,661,000	770,933,500	700,391,300
Capital Expenditure	1,557,341,000	1,697,885,000	1,860,984,000	1,414,571,000	1,401,388,000	1,484,498,000
EBITDA	4,108,981,000	4,352,711,000	4,501,547,000	3,600,568,000	1,859,419,000	3,336,519,000
Return on Assets %	5.10%	5.62%	6.11%	4.37%	2.04%	3.33%
Return on Equity %	10.85%	12.41%	13.94%	10.86%	5.71%	10.26%
Debt to Equity	0.11	0.15	0.11	0.13	0.23	0.30

CONTACT INFORMATION:
Phone: 81 332182111 Fax: 81 332182431
Toll-Free:
Address: Tokyo Bldg. 2-7-3 Marunouchi, Chiyoda-ku, Tokyo, 100-8310 Japan

STOCK TICKER/OTHER:
Stock Ticker: MIELY
Employees: 135,160
Parent Company: Mitsubishi Corporation

Exchange: PINX
Fiscal Year Ends: 03/31

SALARIES/BONUSES:
Top Exec. Salary: $ Bonus: $
Second Exec. Salary: $ Bonus: $

OTHER THOUGHTS:
Estimated Female Officers or Directors:
Hot Spot for Advancement for Women/Minorities:

Sales, profits and employees may be estimates. Financial information, benefits and other data can change quickly and may vary from those stated here.

Mitsubishi Motors Corp

NAIC Code: 336111

www.mitsubishi-motors.com

TYPES OF BUSINESS:
- Automobile Manufacturing
- Automobile Parts
- Agricultural Machinery & Industrial Engines
- Automotive Sales
- Financial Services

BRANDS/DIVISIONS/AFFILIATES:
- Renault-Nissan
- Mitsubishi Corporation
- Pajero Montero
- Triton
- Outlander
- Attrage
- i-MiEV
- Nissan Motor Co Ltd

GROWTH PLANS/SPECIAL FEATURES:
Mitsubishi Motors Corp. (MMC) designs, manufactures, sells and distributes automobiles, trucks, buses and parts. It also designs, manufactures, sells and imports agricultural machinery and industrial engines. The Mitsubishi brand includes the Pajero Montero, Triton, Outlander, Delica, Lancer, Mirage, Attrage, i-MiEV, eK and Minicab-MiEV models. The firm has seven car manufacturing facilities; five engine, transmission and parts manufacturing facilities; and six research & development centers. In June 2016, the company became majority-owned by Nissan Motor Co. Ltd. (34%), and is now a part of the Renault-Nissan Alliance. Mitsubishi Corporation maintains a 20% stake in MMC. Renault-Nissan owns a major share of the firm's stock.

CONTACTS:
Note: Officers with more than one job title may be intentionally listed here more than once.

Osamu Masuko, CEO
Tetsuro Aikawa, COO
Ryugo Nakao, Managing Dir.-Prod. Projects & Strategy
Hiizu Ichikawa, Exec. VP-Corp. Planning
Shuichi Aoto, Managing Dir.-Corp. Affairs
Hiizu Ichikawa, Exec. VP-Finance
Shuichi Aoto, Chief Bus. Ethics Officer
Seiji Izumisawa, Head-Quality Affairs Group
Osamu Masuko, Chmn.
Hiroshi Harunari, Exec. VP-Overseas Oper.
Shuichi Aoto, Head-Procurement Group

FINANCIAL DATA:
Note: Data for latest year may not have been available at press time.

In U.S. $	2017	2016	2015	2014	2013	2012
Revenue	17,762,550,000	21,127,710,000	20,316,080,000	19,502,600,000	16,909,940,000	16,837,090,000
R&D Expense	537,348,600	419,340,400	419,759,600	342,034,700	324,361,900	326,029,400
Operating Income	549,441,100	1,818,195,000	1,747,950,000	1,612,847,000	1,041,597,000	1,011,589,000
Operating Margin %	3.09%	8.60%	8.60%	8.26%	6.15%	6.00%
SGA Expense	1,815,987,000	2,009,614,000	2,126,533,000	2,117,133,000	1,717,142,000	1,576,309,000
Net Income	-1,849,488,000	676,122,600	1,100,894,000	975,069,900	353,810,400	222,917,800
Operating Cash Flow	-426,951,800	1,841,727,000	1,649,041,000	1,960,527,000	1,604,500,000	1,112,223,000
Capital Expenditure	633,538,300	642,817,300	797,447,400	844,932,000	573,625,900	674,976,700
EBITDA	-1,031,442,000	1,575,657,000	1,828,349,000	1,730,492,000	1,251,584,000	1,044,531,000
Return on Assets %	-13.60%	4.81%	7.55%	6.98%	2.73%	1.81%
Return on Equity %	-29.16%	10.91%	19.70%	23.76%	12.71%	9.65%
Debt to Equity			0.04	0.13	0.33	0.65

CONTACT INFORMATION:
Phone: 81 334561111 Fax:
Toll-Free:
Address: 33-8, Shiba 5-chome, Minato-ku, Tokyo, 108-8410 Japan

SALARIES/BONUSES:
Top Exec. Salary: $ Bonus: $
Second Exec. Salary: $ Bonus: $

STOCK TICKER/OTHER:
Stock Ticker: MMTOF Exchange: PINX
Employees: 29,604 Fiscal Year Ends: 03/31
Parent Company: Nissan Motor Co Ltd

OTHER THOUGHTS:
Estimated Female Officers or Directors:
Hot Spot for Advancement for Women/Minorities:

Mitsui Chemicals Inc

NAIC Code: 325110

www.mitsuichem.com/index.htm

TYPES OF BUSINESS:
Petrochemical Producer
Agrochemicals
Industrial Products
Pharmaceuticals & Medical
Packaging
Dyes & Pigments
Phenols

BRANDS/DIVISIONS/AFFILIATES:
Chiba Chemicals Manufacturing LLP
Chiba Phenol Co Ltd
DM NovaFoam Ltd
Mitsui Chemicals Europe GmbH
Mitsui Chemicals Asia Pacific Ltd
Mitsui Chemicals America Inc
SUNVIEO

CONTACTS: Note: Officers with more than one job title may be intentionally listed here more than once.
Tsutomu Tannowa, CEO
Toshikazu Tanaka, Pres.

GROWTH PLANS/SPECIAL FEATURES:
Mitsui Chemicals, Inc. is a Japanese chemical manufacturer that specializes in petrochemicals, phenols and specialty polymers. The company operates through four business groups: healthcare, mobility, food and packaging, and basic materials. The healthcare group produces healthcare materials, personal care materials and nonwovens. The mobility group produces elastomers, performance compounds and performance polymers. The food and packaging group produces coatings and engineering materials, packaging films, industrial films, functional sheets and agricultural chemicals. The basic materials group produces phenols, purified terephthalic acid (PTA), polyethylene terephthalate (PET), industrial chemicals, polyurethane, petrochemicals and feedstocks. This division is also responsible for the company's licensing activities. Mitsui has six domestic manufacturing sites: Kashima Works, Ichihara Works (which includes the Mobara Factory), Nagoya Works, Osaka Works, Iwakuni-Ohtake Works and Omuta Works. Among Mitsui's many subsidiaries, include: (domestic) Chiba Chemicals Manufacturing LLP, Chiba Phenol Co. Ltd. and DM NovaFoam Ltd.; and (overseas) Mitsui Chemicals Europe GmbH, Mitsui Chemicals Asia Pacific Ltd., Tianjin Cosmo Polyurethane Co. Ltd. and Mitsui Chemicals America, Inc. In December 2017, the firm acquired Asahi Kasei Corporation's SUNVIEO business of thermoplastic styrene elastomers (TPS), which are primarily used in the automotive industry as a replacement for polyvinyl chloride and vulcanized rubber.

FINANCIAL DATA: Note: Data for latest year may not have been available at press time.

In U.S. $	2017	2016	2015	2014	2013	2012
Revenue	11,293,850,000	12,520,010,000	14,440,810,000	14,589,590,000	13,100,620,000	13,545,970,000
R&D Expense						
Operating Income	951,639,700	660,760,300	391,652,700	231,963,900	39,966,460	200,894,400
Operating Margin %	8.42%	5.27%	2.71%	1.58%	.30%	1.48%
SGA Expense						
Net Income	604,052,500	213,927,700	160,806,800	-234,190,400	-75,917,650	-9,381,405
Operating Cash Flow	935,718,300	1,359,354,000	543,012,900	405,030,800	172,461,300	403,409,700
Capital Expenditure	386,603,400	385,559,900	349,133,600	498,341,700	485,252,500	345,714,600
EBITDA	1,263,071,000	899,618,100	851,909,900	419,014,400	464,384,200	802,711,000
Return on Assets %	5.01%	1.71%	1.21%	-1.81%	-.62%	-.07%
Return on Equity %	15.59%	5.82%	4.54%	-6.89%	-2.19%	-.26%
Debt to Equity	0.67	0.88	0.90	1.10	0.85	0.80

CONTACT INFORMATION:
Phone: 81-3-6253-2100   Fax: 81-3-6253-4245
Toll-Free:
Address: Shiodome City Ctr., 5-2 Higashi-Shimbashi 1-chome, Minato-ku, Tokyo, 105-7117 Japan

STOCK TICKER/OTHER:
Stock Ticker: MITUY
Employees: 13,423
Parent Company:

Exchange: PINX
Fiscal Year Ends: 03/31

SALARIES/BONUSES:
Top Exec. Salary: $ Bonus: $
Second Exec. Salary: $ Bonus: $

OTHER THOUGHTS:
Estimated Female Officers or Directors:
Hot Spot for Advancement for Women/Minorities:

Sales, profits and employees may be estimates. Financial information, benefits and other data can change quickly and may vary from those stated here.

Molex LLC

NAIC Code: 334417

www.molex.com

TYPES OF BUSINESS:
Electronic Connector Manufacturing
Transportation Products
Commercial Products
Micro Products
Automation & Electrical Products
Integrated Products
Global Sales & Marketing Organization

BRANDS/DIVISIONS/AFFILIATES:
Koch Industries Inc
Molex

GROWTH PLANS/SPECIAL FEATURES:
Molex, LLC, a subsidiary of Koch Industries, Inc., is a manufacturer and supplier of electronic components. The firm designs, manufactures and sells thousands of products, including 3D semiconductors, 3D custom circuitry, antennas, application tooling, audio-balanced armature, automation, cables, cable assemblies, capillary tubing, micro components, connectors, edgecards, sockets, electrical rubber solutions, power distribution electricals, grips, portable lighting, reels, test and control electronics, wiring devices, noise suppression sheets, flexible circuit solutions, FPGA computing systems, hoods, IT infrastructure solutions, lighting products, optical solutions, printed circuit board (PCB) assemblies, product traceability, sensor solutions, user interface and wireless solutions. Molex also provides manufacturing services to integrate specific components into a customer's product. The company's products are utilized across a wide range of industries, including data communications, consumer electronics, industrial, automotive, commercial vehicle, medical and other. Molex is a registered trademark of Molex, LLC in the U.S., and is present in more than 40 countries.

CONTACTS:
Note: Officers with more than one job title may be intentionally listed here more than once.

Martin P. Slark, CEO
Joseph William Nelligan, Jr., COO
K. Travis George, CFO
Gary J. Matula, CIO
Robert J. Zeitler, General Counsel
Tim Ruff, Sr. VP-Bus. Dev. & Corp. Strategy
David D. Johnson, Treas.
John H. Krehbiel, Jr., Co-Chmn.
Junichi Kaji, Pres., Global Mirco Prod. Div.
J. Michael Nauman, Pres., Global Integrated Prod. Div.
Joseph Nelligan, Pres., Commercial Prod. Division

FINANCIAL DATA:
Note: Data for latest year may not have been available at press time.

In U.S. $	2017	2016	2015	2014	2013	2012
Revenue	4,100,000,000	4,000,000,000	3,900,000,000	3,862,540,000	3,620,446,976	3,489,189,120
R&D Expense						
Operating Income						
Operating Margin %						
SGA Expense						
Net Income						
Operating Cash Flow						
Capital Expenditure						
EBITDA						
Return on Assets %						
Return on Equity %						
Debt to Equity						

CONTACT INFORMATION:
Phone: 630 969-4550   Fax: 630 969-1352
Toll-Free: 800-786-6539
Address: 2222 Wellington Ct., Lisle, IL 60532-1682 United States

STOCK TICKER/OTHER:
Stock Ticker: Subsidiary   Exchange:
Employees: 35,983   Fiscal Year Ends: 06/30
Parent Company: Koch Industries Inc

SALARIES/BONUSES:
Top Exec. Salary: $ Bonus: $
Second Exec. Salary: $ Bonus: $

OTHER THOUGHTS:
Estimated Female Officers or Directors: 2
Hot Spot for Advancement for Women/Minorities:

Monsanto Company

www.monsanto.com

NAIC Code: 325320

TYPES OF BUSINESS:
Agricultural Biotechnology Products & Chemicals Manufacturing
Herbicides
Seeds
Genetic Products
Lawn & Garden Products

BRANDS/DIVISIONS/AFFILIATES:
DEKALB
Asgrow
Deltapine
De Ruiter
Roundup Ready
SmartStax
YieldGard
Bollgard II

CONTACTS:
Note: Officers with more than one job title may be intentionally listed here more than once.

Hugh Grant, CEO
Pierre Courduroux, CFO
Nicole Ringenberg, Chief Accounting Officer
Robert Fraley, Executive VP
Steven Mizell, Executive VP
Kerry Preete, Executive VP
David Snively, Executive VP
Janet Holloway, Other Executive Officer
Brett Begemann, President
Michael Stern, Vice President
Duraiswami Narian, Vice President

GROWTH PLANS/SPECIAL FEATURES:
Monsanto Company is a global provider of agricultural products for farmers. The company operates in two principal business segments: seeds and genomics and agricultural productivity. The seeds and genomics segment is responsible for producing seed brands and patenting genetic traits that enable seeds to resist insects, disease, drought and weeds. Major germplasm brands for row crop seeds produced by Monsanto include DEKALB corn seeds, Asgrow soybean seeds and Deltapine cotton seeds. Fruit and vegetable seeds, such as tomato, pepper, eggplant, melon, cucumber, pumpkin, squash, beans, broccoli, onions and lettuce, are sold under the Seminis and De Ruiter brands. The company's genetic trait products include Roundup Ready and Roundup Ready 2 Yield for soybeans; SmartStax, YieldGard and YieldGardVT for corn; and Bollgard II for cotton. The segment also focuses on cereal grain seeds and biotech wheat products. Monsanto's agricultural productivity segment produces herbicide products such as Harness, which is used for corn and cotton. Its most significant trademark is the Roundup branded products. Monsanto markets its seeds and commercial herbicides through a variety of channels and directly to farmers. Residential herbicides are marketed through the Scotts Miracle-Gro Company. As of January 24, 2018, the proposed merger acquisition of Monsanto by global chemicals giant, Bayer AG, was still undergoing regulatory approval procedures.

Monsanto offers its employees medical, dental, vision and life insurance; disability coverage; and a 401(k) plan.

FINANCIAL DATA:
Note: Data for latest year may not have been available at press time.

In U.S. $	2017	2016	2015	2014	2013	2012
Revenue	14,640,000,000	13,502,000,000	15,001,000,000	15,855,000,000	14,861,000,000	13,504,000,000
R&D Expense	1,607,000,000	1,512,000,000	1,580,000,000	1,725,000,000	1,533,000,000	1,517,000,000
Operating Income	3,361,000,000	2,672,000,000	3,916,000,000	4,075,000,000	3,570,000,000	3,138,000,000
Operating Margin %	22.95%	19.78%	26.10%	25.70%	24.02%	23.23%
SGA Expense	2,969,000,000	2,833,000,000	2,686,000,000	2,774,000,000	2,550,000,000	2,390,000,000
Net Income	2,260,000,000	1,336,000,000	2,314,000,000	2,740,000,000	2,482,000,000	2,045,000,000
Operating Cash Flow	3,226,000,000	2,588,000,000	3,108,000,000	3,054,000,000	2,740,000,000	3,051,000,000
Capital Expenditure	1,311,000,000	992,000,000	1,015,000,000	1,408,000,000	829,000,000	723,000,000
EBITDA	4,086,000,000	3,154,000,000	4,310,000,000	4,766,000,000	4,216,000,000	3,801,000,000
Return on Assets %	11.00%	6.41%	10.54%	12.85%	12.14%	10.20%
Return on Equity %	41.19%	23.18%	31.13%	26.81%	20.35%	17.49%
Debt to Equity	1.12	1.64	1.20	0.95	0.16	0.17

CONTACT INFORMATION:
Phone: 314 694-1000   Fax: 314 694-1057
Toll-Free:
Address: 800 N. Lindbergh Blvd., St. Louis, MO 63167 United States

STOCK TICKER/OTHER:
Stock Ticker: MON   Exchange: NYS
Employees: 20,500   Fiscal Year Ends: 08/31
Parent Company:

SALARIES/BONUSES:
Top Exec. Salary: $1,702,897   Bonus: $
Second Exec. Salary: $1,023,923   Bonus: $

OTHER THOUGHTS:
Estimated Female Officers or Directors: 6
Hot Spot for Advancement for Women/Minorities: Y

Mott MacDonald Limited

NAIC Code: 541330

www.mottmac.com

TYPES OF BUSINESS:
Engineering & Development Consultancy
Engineering
Consultancy

BRANDS/DIVISIONS/AFFILIATES:

CONTACTS: Note: Officers with more than one job title may be intentionally listed here more than once.
Mike Haigh, Managing Dir.
Ed Roud, Dir.-Finance
Keith Howells, Chmn.

GROWTH PLANS/SPECIAL FEATURES:
Mott MacDonald Limited is a global management, engineering and development consultancy for public and private clients worldwide. It strives to save customers money and time, reduce risks, increase efficiency, maximize sustainable outcomes and advance best practice through innovative thinking and cross-sector mobilization strategies. Mott MacDonald consists of designers, engineers, project and program managers, consultants, environmentalists, planners, economists, infrastructure finance advisors, public/private partnership experts, technology experts, safety advisors and health and education specialists. It has more than 150 offices in 50 countries. Its primary business sectors are buildings, education, environment, health, industry, international development, oil and gas, power, digital infrastructure, transport, urban development and water. Some of the firm's projects include London's Crossrail commuter line, South Africa's Department for Environmental Affairs headquarters, Bangladesh's English in Action education program offering learning opportunities to 25 million adults and children and Tsuen Wan New Town storm water drainage tunnel in Hong Kong. Recently-completed projects (in early-2018) include the expanded north terminal at the Macau International Airport, the Hong Kong-Zhuhai-Macau Bridge and the Sheffield Lower Don Valley flood defense project (U.K.).

FINANCIAL DATA: Note: Data for latest year may not have been available at press time.

In U.S. $	2017	2016	2015	2014	2013	2012
Revenue	850,000,000	830,487,000	952,579,000	834,387,553	902,556,000	851,185,000
R&D Expense						
Operating Income						
Operating Margin %						
SGA Expense						
Net Income		51,477,300	49,312,200	50,242,062	24,127,771	
Operating Cash Flow						
Capital Expenditure						
EBITDA						
Return on Assets %						
Return on Equity %						
Debt to Equity						

CONTACT INFORMATION:
Phone: 44-20-8774-2000 Fax:
Toll-Free:
Address: Mott MacDonald House, 8-10 Sydenham Rd., Croydon, Surrey CR0 2EE United Kingdom

STOCK TICKER/OTHER:
Stock Ticker: Private   Exchange:
Employees: 16,000   Fiscal Year Ends:
Parent Company:

SALARIES/BONUSES:
Top Exec. Salary: $ Bonus: $
Second Exec. Salary: $ Bonus: $

OTHER THOUGHTS:
Estimated Female Officers or Directors:
Hot Spot for Advancement for Women/Minorities:

Sales, profits and employees may be estimates. Financial information, benefits and other data can change quickly and may vary from those stated here.

MWH Global Inc

NAIC Code: 237110

www.mwhglobal.com/

TYPES OF BUSINESS:
Engineering & Construction Services
Environmental Engineering
Water & Waste Treatment Analysis
Facilities Development
Infrastructure Asset Management
Consulting
Government Relations & Lobbying
Software & IT Services

BRANDS/DIVISIONS/AFFILIATES:
Stantec Inc

CONTACTS:
Note: Officers with more than one job title may be intentionally listed here more than once.

David G. Barnes, CFO
Jeff D'Agosta, General Counsel
Meg Vanderlaan, Chief Comm. Officer
Daniel McConville, Pres., Bus. Solutions Group
Joseph D. Adams, Pres., Energy & Industry
Paul F. Boulos, Pres., Innovyze
Bruce K. Howard, Exec. VP
Wim Drossaert, Pres., Europe & Africa Gov't & Infrastructure

GROWTH PLANS/SPECIAL FEATURES:

MWH Global, Inc., a subsidiary of Stantec, Inc., helps manage water purity and availability in a sustainable way for the health, livelihood and security of people worldwide. The firm's more than 7,000 employees operate on six continents, providing innovative, sustainable solutions to challenging projects in communities. Markets served by MWH include energy/power, industrial/commercial, international development, mining, oil and gas, ports/waterways/coastal, transportation and water/wastewater. Its services include analytics and research, construction, construction management, digital enterprise, engineering and design, environmental/health/safety management, industry training, management consulting, program management and sustainability/climate change. MWH also partners with companies that offer additional expertise in software solutions (Innovyze) and management consulting (Hawksley Consulting). Some of the company's projects include (or have included) the San Vicente Dam Raise, Wanapum Dam Spillway, Canterbury Earthquake Recovery Programme, American Municipal Power Hydropower Projects, Technical Assistance Facility for Sustainable Energy for All Initiative, Drainage Asset Management Services and Alewife Reservation Stormwater Wetland.

FINANCIAL DATA:
Note: Data for latest year may not have been available at press time.

In U.S. $	2017	2016	2015	2014	2013	2012
Revenue	1,950,000,000	1,945,000,000	1,900,000,000	1,850,000,000	1,725,000,000	1,600,000,000
R&D Expense						
Operating Income						
Operating Margin %						
SGA Expense						
Net Income						
Operating Cash Flow						
Capital Expenditure						
EBITDA						
Return on Assets %						
Return on Equity %						
Debt to Equity						

CONTACT INFORMATION:
Phone: 303-533-1900   Fax: 303-533-1901
Toll-Free:
Address: 370 Interlocken Crescent, Ste. 300, Broomfield, CO 80021 United States

STOCK TICKER/OTHER:
Stock Ticker: Subsidiary
Employees: 7,000
Parent Company: Stantec Inc

Exchange:
Fiscal Year Ends: 09/30

SALARIES/BONUSES:
Top Exec. Salary: $ Bonus: $
Second Exec. Salary: $ Bonus: $

OTHER THOUGHTS:
Estimated Female Officers or Directors: 2
Hot Spot for Advancement for Women/Minorities: Y

NCR Corporation

NAIC Code: 334118

www.ncr.com

TYPES OF BUSINESS:
Computer Manufacturing
Barcode Scanning Equipment
Automatic Teller Machines (ATMs)
Transaction Processing Equipment
Point-of-Sale & Store Automation
Data Warehousing
Printer Consumables

BRANDS/DIVISIONS/AFFILIATES:

CONTACTS: Note: Officers with more than one job title may be intentionally listed here more than once.
William Nuti, CEO
Robert Fishman, CFO
Paul Langenbahn, COO
Daniel Campbell, Executive VP, Divisional
J. Ciminera, Executive VP, Divisional
Edward Gallagher, General Counsel
Andrea Ledford, Other Executive Officer
Adrian Button, Senior VP, Divisional

GROWTH PLANS/SPECIAL FEATURES:
NCR Corporation is a global technology company that provides information technology and related services to various industries, enabling client companies to interact more efficiently with customers. The company offers financial-oriented self-service technologies, such as ATMs, cash dispensers, self-checkout kiosks and software solutions. Its operations are divided into three operating segments: software, services and hardware. The software segment includes a portfolio of industry-based software applications and application suites for the financial services, retail, hospitality and small business industries. Moreover, the firm offers other industry-oriented software applications including cash management software, video banking software, fraud and loss prevention applications, check and document imaging, remote-deposit capture and customer-facing digital banking applications for the financial services industry; and secure electronic and mobile payment solutions, sector-specific point of sale software applications, and back-office inventory and store and restaurant management applications for the retail and hospitality industries. The services segment provides global end-to-end services solutions including assessment and preparation, staging, installation, implementation, and maintenance and support for its hardware solutions. The firm also provides systems management and complete managed services for its product offerings. In addition, it provides servicing for third party networking products and computer hardware from select manufacturers. The hardware solutions segment includes its suite of financial-oriented self-service ATM-related hardware, and its retail- and hospitality-oriented point of sale terminal, self-checkout kiosk and related hardware. The company also offers other self-service kiosks, such as self-check in kiosks for airlines, and wayfinding solutions for buildings and campuses. In December 2017, NCR completed the sale of all dedicated assets of its former interactive printer solutions located in the Middle East and Africa.

FINANCIAL DATA: Note: Data for latest year may not have been available at press time.

In U.S. $	2017	2016	2015	2014	2013	2012
Revenue	6,516,000,000	6,543,000,000	6,373,000,000	6,591,000,000	6,123,000,000	5,730,000,000
R&D Expense	256,000,000	242,000,000	230,000,000	263,000,000	203,000,000	219,000,000
Operating Income	676,000,000	614,000,000	197,000,000	457,000,000	666,000,000	232,000,000
Operating Margin %	10.37%	9.38%	3.09%	6.93%	10.87%	4.04%
SGA Expense	932,000,000	926,000,000	1,042,000,000	1,012,000,000	871,000,000	894,000,000
Net Income	232,000,000	270,000,000	-178,000,000	191,000,000	443,000,000	146,000,000
Operating Cash Flow	747,000,000	855,000,000	638,000,000	523,000,000	229,000,000	-294,000,000
Capital Expenditure	294,000,000	227,000,000	229,000,000	258,000,000	226,000,000	160,000,000
EBITDA	999,000,000	893,000,000	386,000,000	602,000,000	865,000,000	390,000,000
Return on Assets %	1.60%	2.88%	-2.24%	2.28%	6.11%	2.44%
Return on Equity %	17.39%	31.23%	-14.04%	10.49%	29.37%	14.27%
Debt to Equity	4.08	4.31	4.49	1.85	1.87	1.51

CONTACT INFORMATION:
Phone: 937 445-5000
Fax: 937 445-5541
Toll-Free: 800-225-5627
Address: 864 Spring St. NW, Atlanta, GA 30308 United States

SALARIES/BONUSES:
Top Exec. Salary: $1,000,000 Bonus: $
Second Exec. Salary: $750,000 Bonus: $

STOCK TICKER/OTHER:
Stock Ticker: NCR
Employees: 33,500
Parent Company:

Exchange: NYS
Fiscal Year Ends: 12/31

OTHER THOUGHTS:
Estimated Female Officers or Directors: 3
Hot Spot for Advancement for Women/Minorities: Y

Sales, profits and employees may be estimates. Financial information, benefits and other data can change quickly and may vary from those stated here.

NEC Corporation

www.nec.com

NAIC Code: 334111

TYPES OF BUSINESS:
Computer Manufacturing
Lithium-Ion Batteries
Servers & Supercomputers
Telecommunications & Wireless Equipment
Nanotube Research
Broadband & Networking Equipment
Operating Systems & Application Software
Cloud Computing

BRANDS/DIVISIONS/AFFILIATES:
FlexProcess for Ever Changing Business
Express 5800
DX2000

CONTACTS:
Note: Officers with more than one job title may be intentionally listed here more than once.

Takashi Niino, CEO
Nobuhiro Endo, Pres.
Isamu Kawashima, CFO
Katsumi Emura, CTO
Takashi Niino, Chief Strategy Officer
Toshiyuki Mineno, Exec. VP
Kuniaki Okada, Exec. VP
Manabu Kinoshita, Exec. VP
Tomonori Nishimura, Exec. VP
Nobuhiro Endo, Chmn.
Junji Yasui, Chief Supply Chain Officer

GROWTH PLANS/SPECIAL FEATURES:

NEC Corporation is a leading global provider of internet, broadband network and enterprise business solutions. Operating through more than 235 subsidiaries, the firm markets its services towards the aerospace, education, government, healthcare, retail and telecommunications industries. NEC is divided into four business segments: public, enterprise, telecom carrier and system platform. The public business provides solutions for governments both domestic and foreign, public institutions, financial institutions and more through networking and sensing technologies. These include air traffic control and airport systems, cloud storage, fiber optic devices and public safety solutions. The enterprise business, catering to large enterprises, consists of IT solutions for manufacturing, retail, distribution and customer services, both internationally and domestically. More specifically, the company can offer original equipment manufacturing services, its proprietary FlexProcess for Ever Changing Business and a digital signage solution. The telecom carrier business supplies to telecom carriers network implantation equipment, network control platform systems and operating services. Finally, the system platform business offers a range of solutions for small to medium businesses, including mobile terminals, network equipment, computer equipment, software products, service platforms and more. The company also offers storage solutions such as cloud or its Express5800 and DX2000 servers. In April 2017, the firm sold its 61% controlling interest in NEC Tokin to KEMET Corporation, making NEC Tokin a wholly-owned subsidiary of KEMET.

FINANCIAL DATA:
Note: Data for latest year may not have been available at press time.

In U.S. $	2017	2016	2015	2014	2013	2012
Revenue	24,827,980,000	26,282,660,000	27,347,840,000	28,350,230,000	28,615,700,000	28,291,750,000
R&D Expense						
Operating Income	532,960,700	999,683,300	1,193,255,000	989,314,400	1,068,073,000	686,994,600
Operating Margin %	2.14%	3.80%	4.36%	3.48%	3.73%	2.42%
SGA Expense	6,506,550,000					
Net Income	254,425,200	640,478,900	533,836,400	314,346,900	283,529,000	-1,027,269,000
Operating Cash Flow	861,980,700	911,393,800	819,051,600	876,877,200	1,339,184,000	781,227,900
Capital Expenditure	420,057,800	380,454,700	479,178,300	948,248,600	564,263,100	532,821,000
EBITDA	1,576,775,000	1,607,481,000	1,884,982,000	1,751,994,000	1,623,794,000	973,216,000
Return on Assets %	1.05%	2.68%	2.23%	1.32%	1.18%	-4.25%
Return on Equity %	3.31%	8.50%	7.54%	4.79%	4.45%	-15.59%
Debt to Equity	0.40	0.40	0.46	0.68	0.55	0.75

CONTACT INFORMATION:
Phone: 81 334541111 Fax:
Toll-Free: 800-268-3997
Address: 7-1, Shiba 5-Chome, Minato-ku, Tokyo, 108-8001 Japan

STOCK TICKER/OTHER:
Stock Ticker: NIPNF
Employees: 98,726
Parent Company:

Exchange: GREY
Fiscal Year Ends: 03/31

SALARIES/BONUSES:
Top Exec. Salary: $ Bonus: $
Second Exec. Salary: $ Bonus: $

OTHER THOUGHTS:
Estimated Female Officers or Directors:
Hot Spot for Advancement for Women/Minorities:

Sales, profits and employees may be estimates. Financial information, benefits and other data can change quickly and may vary from those stated here.

NEC Laboratories America Inc

NAIC Code: 541712

www.nec-labs.com

TYPES OF BUSINESS:
Communications Technology
Electronics
Broadband & Mobile Networking
Computing
Software
Storage Technologies
Security Systems
Quantum Computing

BRANDS/DIVISIONS/AFFILIATES:
NEC Corporation

CONTACTS:
Note: Officers with more than one job title may be intentionally listed here more than once.

Sanjay Palnitkar, Sr. Mgr-IT
Kaoru Yano, Chmn.-NEC Corp.

GROWTH PLANS/SPECIAL FEATURES:

NEC Laboratories America, Inc. is the U.S.-based research facility in NEC Corporation's global network of research laboratories. Operating through two laboratories, located in Princeton, New Jersey and Cupertino, California, the company focuses on nine areas of research. The computer security department focuses on novel technologies for information and system security which provide solutions related to research innovations such as automated security intelligence and mobile application management. The data science department focuses on building novel big data solutions to support complex system management for power plants, manufacture plants, transportation and social infrastructure. The energy management department addresses challenges associated with efficiency, environment and economics related to an interconnected energy infrastructure. The integrated systems department focuses on accelerating enterprise workloads on computing clusters that include various types of heterogeneity in computing, interconnect, networking and storage units. The machine learning department develops solutions such as deep learning, support vector machines and semantic analysis in order to interpret multi-modal data and complex situations. The media analytics department aims to solve challenges in computer vision, including image-based recognition, object detection, tracking, segmentation and 3D reconstruction. The mobile communications and networking department focuses on two areas: technologies for improving the capacity, coverage and scalability of next-generation 5G cellular networks; and end-to-end solution creation via wireless sensing formats and communication technologies. The optical networking and sensing department researches into the next-generation of optical networks and sensing systems that will power ICT-based (information and communication technologies) social solutions for the future. These solutions include optics, photonics, multi-dimensional optical processing, optical transmission systems and software. Last, the systems research department seeks to build service platforms that simplify complex computer systems management, as well as new information technology for innovative applications.

NEC Labs offers employees medical, dental, vision, life, AD&D and disability insurance; 401(k); and various employee-assistance programs.

FINANCIAL DATA:
Note: Data for latest year may not have been available at press time.

In U.S. $	2017	2016	2015	2014	2013	2012
Revenue						
R&D Expense						
Operating Income						
Operating Margin %						
SGA Expense						
Net Income						
Operating Cash Flow						
Capital Expenditure						
EBITDA						
Return on Assets %						
Return on Equity %						
Debt to Equity						

CONTACT INFORMATION:
Phone: 609-520-1555 Fax: 609-951-2481
Toll-Free:
Address: 4 Independence Way, Ste. 200, Princeton, NJ 08540 United States

STOCK TICKER/OTHER:
Stock Ticker: Subsidiary
Employees: 120
Parent Company: NEC Corporation

Exchange:
Fiscal Year Ends: 03/31

SALARIES/BONUSES:
Top Exec. Salary: $ Bonus: $
Second Exec. Salary: $ Bonus: $

OTHER THOUGHTS:
Estimated Female Officers or Directors:
Hot Spot for Advancement for Women/Minorities:

NetApp Inc

NAIC Code: 334112

www.netapp.com

TYPES OF BUSINESS:
Data Management Solutions
Storage Solutions
Data Protection Software Products
Data Protection Platform Products
Storage Security Products
Data Retention & Archive Software Products
Storage Management & Application Software
Management Tools

BRANDS/DIVISIONS/AFFILIATES:
All Flash FAS
AFF A-Series
ONTAP Cloud
NetApp OnCommand
SolidFire All-Flash Arrays
EF-Series
FlexPod

CONTACTS:
Note: Officers with more than one job title may be intentionally listed here more than once.

George Kurian, CEO
Ronald Pasek, CFO
T. Nevens, Chairman of the Board
Henri Richard, Executive VP, Divisional
Joel Reich, Executive VP, Divisional
Matthew Fawcett, General Counsel

GROWTH PLANS/SPECIAL FEATURES:

NetApp, Inc. provides software, systems and services to manage and store customer data. The company enables enterprises, service providers, governmental organizations and partners to deploy and evolve their IT environments. NetApp's data management and storage offerings help improve business productivity, performance and profitability. The company's all-flash arrays include the following. All-Flash FAS an all-flash system to support seamless data management across flash, disk and cloud resources. Its AFF A-Series supply enterprise class scale-out all flash storage, harnessing the power of ONTAP and OnCommand software to deliver advanced data management and protection, as well as high efficiency, performance and availability. ONTAP Cloud storage data management allows customers to build an enterprise storage service on Amazon Web Services elastic cloud compute with elastic block storage, and also supports the Microsoft Azure public cloud. NetApp OnCommand storage management software incorporates a broad range of data management tools for NetApp and multivendor storage. SolidFire All-Flash Arrays deliver fully-automated agility and guaranteed application performance at web scale so that customers can achieve the next-generation data center. The EF-Series all-flash arrays deliver fast, consistent response times to accelerate high-performance databases and data analytics. NetApp hybrid flash storage serves customers who want the option to deploy the speed of flash storage where they need it while using more affordable hard disk drives (HDDs) to address capacity requirements. NetApp hybrid arrays include the FAS series and the E-series storage systems. FlexPod is a converged infrastructure for large enterprises worldwide. Other products offered by the firm include data management software, object storage software, backup and data protection solutions and various other storage solutions.

NetApp offers medical, dental and vision coverage; short- and long-term disability; 401(k); employee stock purchase and employee assistance programs; flexible spending accounts; and tuition reimbursement.

FINANCIAL DATA:
Note: Data for latest year may not have been available at press time.

In U.S. $	2017	2016	2015	2014	2013	2012
Revenue	5,519,000,000	5,546,000,000	6,122,700,000	6,325,100,000	6,332,400,000	6,233,200,000
R&D Expense	779,000,000	861,000,000	919,300,000	917,300,000	904,200,000	828,200,000
Operating Income	707,000,000	413,000,000	716,500,000	822,600,000	609,500,000	756,300,000
Operating Margin %	12.81%	7.44%	11.70%	13.00%	9.62%	12.13%
SGA Expense	1,904,000,000	2,099,000,000	2,197,400,000	2,179,200,000	2,247,400,000	2,128,900,000
Net Income	509,000,000	229,000,000	559,900,000	637,500,000	505,300,000	605,400,000
Operating Cash Flow	986,000,000	974,000,000	1,268,100,000	1,349,600,000	1,386,300,000	1,462,600,000
Capital Expenditure	175,000,000	160,000,000	175,300,000	221,400,000	303,300,000	407,100,000
EBITDA	943,000,000	673,000,000	1,062,000,000	1,110,900,000	1,002,900,000	1,080,200,000
Return on Assets %	5.21%	2.35%	6.01%	6.23%	4.86%	6.71%
Return on Equity %	17.98%	7.27%	15.55%	14.99%	11.13%	14.97%
Debt to Equity	0.26	0.51	0.43	0.26	0.21	

CONTACT INFORMATION:
Phone: 408 822-6000 Fax: 408 822-4501
Toll-Free: 877-263-8277
Address: 495 East Java Dr., Sunnyvale, CA 94089 United States

SALARIES/BONUSES:
Top Exec. Salary: $530,962 Bonus: $400,000
Second Exec. Salary: $875,000 Bonus: $

STOCK TICKER/OTHER:
Stock Ticker: NTAP Exchange: NAS
Employees: 10,100 Fiscal Year Ends: 04/30
Parent Company:

OTHER THOUGHTS:
Estimated Female Officers or Directors: 4
Hot Spot for Advancement for Women/Minorities: Y

Sales, profits and employees may be estimates. Financial information, benefits and other data can change quickly and may vary from those stated here.

Plunkett Research, Ltd.

Nidec Corporation
NAIC Code: 334112

www.nidec.com

TYPES OF BUSINESS:
Motor Manufacturing
Brushless DC Motors
Brushless DC Fans
Camera Shutters
Hard Drive Pivot Assemblies
Card Readers

BRANDS/DIVISIONS/AFFILIATES:
Vamco International Inc
LGB Elettropompe Srl
Secoup Holding GmbH

CONTACTS:
Note: Officers with more than one job title may be intentionally listed here more than once.

Shigenobu Nagamori, CEO
Shigenobu Nagamori, Pres.
Hiroshi Kobe, Chief Sales Officer
Mikio Katayama, Chief Technology Officer
Kenji Sawamura, Exec. VP
Bunsei Kure, Exec. VP
Akira Sato, Exec. VP
Tadaaki Hamada, First Sr. VP
Shigenobu Nagamori, Chmn.

GROWTH PLANS/SPECIAL FEATURES:
Nidec Corporation, based in Japan, manufactures electric motors and related components, with a focus on brushless DC (direct current) motors. Brushless DC motors are a type of electric motor that use electronically controlled commutation systems, rather than mechanical commutation systems, which provide higher efficiency, longer operating life and higher dynamic response characteristics. The firm operates in five business groups: small precision motors; automotive, appliance, commercial and industrial products; machinery; electronic and optical components; and others. Small precision motors include brushless DC motors for hard disk drives and laser printers; brushless DC fans for game machine consoles, personal computers and automobiles; and other small precision motors for mobile phones, DVD recorders and other products. Automotive, appliance, commercial and industrial products include automotive motors for power steering systems and other applications; home appliances motors for air conditioners, washing machines and refrigerators; and industrial motors for machine tools and water heater systems. Machinery products include transfer robots (for LCD panels and semiconductor wafers), card readers, high-speed pressing machines and power transmission systems. Electronic and optical components include shutters and lens units for digital cameras, precision plastic moldings and plastic metal casings. The firm's other offerings include logistics services and music box products. Nidec operates manufacturing and sales facilities through approximately 230 domestic and foreign subsidiaries. During 2017, the firm acquired Merson Electric Company's motors, drives and electric power generation business; Vamco International, Inc., a manufacturer of high-speed servo feeding equipment; LGB Elettropompe Srl, an Italian commercial pump and motor manufacturer; and Secoup Holding GmbH, a German compressor manufacturer.

FINANCIAL DATA:
Note: Data for latest year may not have been available at press time.

In U.S. $	2017	2016	2015	2014	2013	2012
Revenue	11,173,010,000	10,977,180,000	9,580,632,000	8,152,684,000	6,607,695,000	6,356,624,000
R&D Expense	491,960,200	484,237,000	420,896,200	352,226,600	319,340,400	279,951,600
Operating Income	1,307,351,000	1,160,220,000	1,036,128,000	792,509,800	164,216,500	680,734,100
Operating Margin %	11.70%	10.56%	10.81%	9.72%	2.48%	10.70%
SGA Expense	870,672,600	870,719,300	799,152,300	722,321,700	789,640,400	516,778,500
Net Income	1,040,814,000	855,319,600	710,042,900	525,470,500	74,510,900	379,457,800
Operating Cash Flow	1,209,735,000	1,375,163,000	855,925,100	812,549,000	1,027,446,000	528,339,900
Capital Expenditure	640,190,100	763,163,800	540,730,400	375,414,600	571,716,100	386,118,900
EBITDA	1,826,002,000	1,735,532,000	1,511,496,000	1,234,135,000	501,183,200	982,718,500
Return on Assets %	7.29%	6.70%	6.04%	5.19%	.88%	5.26%
Return on Equity %	13.86%	12.16%	12.06%	12.08%	2.03%	11.22%
Debt to Equity	0.19	0.17	0.24	0.57	0.35	0.27

CONTACT INFORMATION:
Phone: 81 759221111   Fax: 81 759356101
Toll-Free:
Address: 338 Tonoshiro-cho, Kuze Minami-ku, Kyoto, 601-8205 Japan

SALARIES/BONUSES:
Top Exec. Salary: $ Bonus: $
Second Exec. Salary: $ Bonus: $

STOCK TICKER/OTHER:
Stock Ticker: NJDCY   Exchange: PINX
Employees: 96,602   Fiscal Year Ends: 03/31
Parent Company:

OTHER THOUGHTS:
Estimated Female Officers or Directors:
Hot Spot for Advancement for Women/Minorities:

Sales, profits and employees may be estimates. Financial information, benefits and other data can change quickly and may vary from those stated here.

Nikon Corporation

NAIC Code: 333316

www.nikon.com

TYPES OF BUSINESS:
Digital Cameras and Equipment
Lenses
Semiconductor Testing Equipment
Image Processing Software
Microscopes and Binoculars

BRANDS/DIVISIONS/AFFILIATES:
Nikon CeLL innovation Co Ltd
Nikon Image Space
SnapBridge

CONTACTS: Note: Officers with more than one job title may be intentionally listed here more than once.
Kazuo Ushida, Pres.
Masashi Oka, CFO
Hiroshi Ohki, Pres., Core Tech.
Kenichi Kanazawa, Pres., Bus. Admin.
Takaharu Honda, Gen. Mgr.-Corp. Planning
Takaharu Honda, Head-Corp. Comm.
Takaharu Honda, Head-Investor Rel.
Norio Hashizume, Gen. Mgr.-Finance & Acct.
Nobuyoshi Gokyu, Pres.
Yasuyuki Okamoto, Pres., Imaging Co.
Kunio Kawabata, Pres., Precision Equipment Co.
Toshiyuki Masai, Pres., Instruments Co.

GROWTH PLANS/SPECIAL FEATURES:
Nikon Corporation is a Japanese company specializing in optical technology, and is a leading provider of cameras and camera-related products. The company's products are divided into the following primary business segments: precision equipment, imaging products, healthcare and industrial metrology and others. Nikon's precision equipment segment develops and produces semiconductor lithography systems that produce semiconductors, as well as FPD lithography systems for manufacturing liquid crystal display (LCD) panels and organic LCD panels (OLED). The imaging products segment develops technologies used in its digital cameras, binoculars, Fieldscopes and loupes, as well as laser rangefinders for use in golf. This division also offers: image-editing software; the Nikon Image Space, an online photo sharing service; and the SnapBridge app, which seamlessly connects a Nikon camera and smart device. The healthcare business segment provides solutions for solving problems in the bioscience and medical fields, supporting various fields globally such as advanced research, early development of regenerative medicine and retinal diagnostic imaging for prevention, diagnosis, treatment and prognosis management. Wholly-owned subsidiary, Nikon CeLL innovation Co., Ltd. is engaged in the manufacturing of cells for clinical and regenerative medicine purposes. Last, the industrial metrology and others segment offers products and technologies ranging from everyday products such as ophthalmic lenses to cutting-edge technologies related to outer space and highly sophisticated industries. Nikon's global network includes locations in the Americas, Europe, Asia, Oceania, the Middle East and Africa. In early-2018, Nikon sold its coordinate measuring machines business in order to focus on optical 3D metrology and X-ray/CT inspection systems solutions.

Nikon offers its U.S. employees benefits including life, disability, health, dental and vision plans as well as an employee assistance program.

FINANCIAL DATA: Note: Data for latest year may not have been available at press time.

In U.S. $	2017	2016	2015	2014	2013	2012
Revenue	6,980,371,000	7,666,434,000	7,991,262,000	9,135,048,000	9,413,947,000	8,558,329,000
R&D Expense						
Operating Income	545,668,000	341,922,900	404,443,800	586,379,800	475,144,400	746,050,000
Operating Margin %	7.81%	4.45%	5.06%	6.41%	5.04%	8.71%
SGA Expense	2,306,205,000					
Net Income	36,957,340	206,744,900	171,082,600	436,221,400	395,556,200	552,496,800
Operating Cash Flow	906,856,700	980,193,900	664,328,300	1,063,769,000	483,417,200	140,423,000
Capital Expenditure	283,342,700	204,555,600	208,095,800	304,453,200	576,253,100	333,268,200
EBITDA	382,392,400	677,315,100	698,863,500	1,104,146,000	925,852,500	1,115,847,000
Return on Assets %	.40%	2.31%	1.91%	5.16%	4.92%	7.01%
Return on Equity %	.73%	3.99%	3.28%	9.02%	9.18%	14.41%
Debt to Equity	0.21	0.15	0.15	0.18	0.13	0.15

CONTACT INFORMATION:
Phone: 81-3-6433-3600 Fax:
Toll-Free:
Address: Shinagawa Intercity Tower C, 2-15-3, Konan, Minato-ku, Tokyo, 108-6290 Japan

SALARIES/BONUSES:
Top Exec. Salary: $ Bonus: $
Second Exec. Salary: $ Bonus: $

STOCK TICKER/OTHER:
Stock Ticker: NINOF
Employees: 25,729
Parent Company:

Exchange: PINX
Fiscal Year Ends: 03/31

OTHER THOUGHTS:
Estimated Female Officers or Directors:
Hot Spot for Advancement for Women/Minorities:

Sales, profits and employees may be estimates. Financial information, benefits and other data can change quickly and may vary from those stated here.

Plunkett Research, Ltd.

Nintendo Co Ltd
NAIC Code: 334111

www.nintendo.com

TYPES OF BUSINESS:
Video Game Hardware & Software
Electronic Games
Online Games

BRANDS/DIVISIONS/AFFILIATES:
Nintendo DS
Nintendo DSi
Nintendo 3DS
Wii
Wii U
Legend of Zelda (The)
Donkey Kong
Pokemon

CONTACTS: Note: Officers with more than one job title may be intentionally listed here more than once.
Tatsumi Kimishima, Managing Dir.
Satoru Iwata, Pres.
Genyo Takeda, Gen. Manager-Integrated R&D Div.
Genyo Takeda, Chief Dir.-Total Dev.
Tatsumi Kimishima, Managing Dir.-Nintendo of America
Genyo Takeda, Head-European PR

GROWTH PLANS/SPECIAL FEATURES:
Nintendo Co., Ltd. develops, manufactures and sells home entertainment products globally. Based in Kyoto, Japan, Nintendo is comprised of 27 subsidiaries and five associated companies located in the U.S., Canada, Korea, Australia and several European countries. Its main products are the video game systems and related software and merchandise for the Nintendo DS (dual screen), Nintendo DSi, Nintendo 3DS and Nintendo Switch. Nintendo currently focuses on selling the Nintendo Switch. The Switch is a home console that can transition to a portable handheld that can be taken anywhere. The included controllers attach to the console while in handheld mode, and can be removed and used separately with compatible games in TV or tabletop modes. The system's features include built-in amiibo support, motion controls and HD Rumble to makes games more immersive, and the Nintendo Switch Online service. The firm's home game station product was the Wii, a motion sensitive game station that picks up user movements with the controller. The Wii's successor, Wii U features a touch screen, camera and microphone in addition to motion sensors on its controller. Well-known video game titles from the company include Mario Brothers, Donkey Kong, Pokemon, Animal Crossing, Splatoon and The Legend of Zelda. Other operations of the company include the manufacture and sale of poker and Japanese-style playing cards (Karuta) and Pokemon animation products in addition to the management of services for electronic registration of in-home console machines and intellectual property rights.

FINANCIAL DATA: Note: Data for latest year may not have been available at press time.

In U.S. $	2017	2016	2015	2014	2013	2012
Revenue	4,556,503,000	4,699,637,000	5,121,856,000	5,326,309,000	5,919,713,000	6,033,650,000
R&D Expense						
Operating Income	273,551,300	306,335,000	230,762,100	-432,504,200	-339,202,600	-347,680,300
Operating Margin %	6.00%	6.51%	4.50%	-8.12%	-5.73%	-5.76%
SGA Expense						
Net Income	955,599,000	153,763,700	389,817,400	-216,340,600	66,135,640	-402,496,800
Operating Cash Flow	177,948,600	514,160,600	561,701,200	-215,334,500	-376,281,000	-884,619,100
Capital Expenditure	97,428,740	43,506,620	42,686,790	182,038,400	53,922,120	186,128,200
EBITDA	351,490,600	391,475,700	314,710,300	-340,106,200	-221,473,800	-231,013,600
Return on Assets %	7.41%	1.24%	3.14%	-1.68%	.50%	-2.87%
Return on Equity %	8.50%	1.41%	3.66%	-1.97%	.58%	-3.49%
Debt to Equity						

CONTACT INFORMATION:
Phone: 81 756629614   Fax: 81 756629540
Toll-Free: 1-800-255-3700
Address: 11-1 Kamitoba, Hokotate-cho, Minami-ku, Kyoto, 601-8116 Japan

STOCK TICKER/OTHER:
Stock Ticker: NTDOF
Employees: 5,166
Parent Company:

Exchange: PINX
Fiscal Year Ends: 03/31

SALARIES/BONUSES:
Top Exec. Salary: $ Bonus: $
Second Exec. Salary: $ Bonus: $

OTHER THOUGHTS:
Estimated Female Officers or Directors:
Hot Spot for Advancement for Women/Minorities:

Sales, profits and employees may be estimates. Financial information, benefits and other data can change quickly and may vary from those stated here.

Nippon Koei Group

www.nipponkoei.com

NAIC Code: 541330

TYPES OF BUSINESS:
Engineering Consulting Services

BRANDS/DIVISIONS/AFFILIATES:
Nippon Koei Co Ltd
Koei Research & Consulting Inc
Nippon Keoi Latin America-Caribbean Co Ltd
PhilKoei International Inc
Nippon Koei India
PT IndoKoei International
ThaiKoei International Co Ltd
VEC Consultant JSC

GROWTH PLANS/SPECIAL FEATURES:
Nippon Koei Group is a Japanese consulting firm that provides services in the field of technical assistance to developing countries. The services offered by the firm cover such needed areas as water, energy, urban and regional development, transportation, agricultural and rural development, environment, climate change, information and communication technology, geosphere engineering, and project and program management. The Nippon Koei Group's global network includes: Nippon Koei Co. Ltd.; Koei Research & Consulting, Inc.; Nippon Keoi Latin America-Caribbean Co., Ltd.; PhilKoei International, Inc.; Nippon Koei India; PT IndoKoei International; ThaiKoei International Co., Ltd.; and VEC Consultant JSC. Additionally, the firm operates the Nippon Koei Group Human Resources Database system, a facility for the online search and management of qualified and eligible consultants for future projects of Nippon Koei Group.

CONTACTS: Note: Officers with more than one job title may be intentionally listed here more than once.

Noriaki Hirose, Pres.

FINANCIAL DATA:
Note: Data for latest year may not have been available at press time.

In U.S. $	2017	2016	2015	2014	2013	2012
Revenue	901,983,000	798,046,000	749,469,286	725,609,030	63,152,533	
R&D Expense						
Operating Income						
Operating Margin %						
SGA Expense						
Net Income	29,274,500	18,063,400	39,030,756	27,473,299	-17,537,282	
Operating Cash Flow						
Capital Expenditure						
EBITDA						
Return on Assets %						
Return on Equity %						
Debt to Equity						

CONTACT INFORMATION:
Phone: 81 3-3238-8030   Fax: 81 3-3238-8326
Toll-Free:
Address: 4 Kojimachi, 5-chome, Chiyoda-ku, Tokyo, 102-8539 Japan

STOCK TICKER/OTHER:
Stock Ticker: 1954   Exchange: Tokyo
Employees: 4,566   Fiscal Year Ends: 06/30
Parent Company:

SALARIES/BONUSES:
Top Exec. Salary: $ Bonus: $
Second Exec. Salary: $ Bonus: $

OTHER THOUGHTS:
Estimated Female Officers or Directors:
Hot Spot for Advancement for Women/Minorities:

Sales, profits and employees may be estimates. Financial information, benefits and other data can change quickly and may vary from those stated here.

Nissan Motor Co Ltd

NAIC Code: 336111

www.nissan-global.com

TYPES OF BUSINESS:
Automobile Manufacturing
Research & Development
Industrial Machinery
Marine Equipment
Logistics Services
Alternative Fuels Research
Financial Services

BRANDS/DIVISIONS/AFFILIATES:
Versa
Sentra
Altima
370Z
NV
QX80
GO
mi-DO

CONTACTS:
Note: Officers with more than one job title may be intentionally listed here more than once.

Hiroto Saikawa, CEO
Carlos Ghosn, Pres.
Joseph G. Peter, CFO
Carlos Ghosn, Chmn.

GROWTH PLANS/SPECIAL FEATURES:

Nissan Motor Co., Ltd. develops, manufactures, sells and services automotive products in over 160 countries. The company's products, which are sold both in Japan and overseas (principally in North America and Europe), include passenger cars, zero emission vehicles, busses and trucks, along with related components. Brands include Nissan, Infiniti and Datsun. Nissan's model offerings include Versa, Sentra, Altima, Maxima, 370Z, GT-R, Juke, Rogue, Murano, Pathfinder, Armada, Frontier, Titan, NV and Leaf. Nissan's commercial vehicle models include NV200 Compact Cargo, NV Cargo, NV200 Taxi and NV Passenger. Infiniti models include Q50, Q70, Q60, QX30, QX50, QX60, QX70 and QX80. The Datsun brand offers hatchback vehicles GO, redi-GO and GO+, as well as the on-DO 4-door sedan and the mi-DO mini SUV. Through Nissan Marine, the firm also produces/sells pleasure boats, operates a marina business and exports outboard engines. The company operates offices and production plants in Japan, Africa, North America, Australia, Europe, Asia and the Middle East. Nissan and Renault SA, a French company, manage an alliance that allows each company to maintain its distinct corporate culture and brand identity while enduring the challenges of market globalization and the accelerating change of technology. Renault-Nissan ranks as one of the world's leading automotive groups, and the two companies operate a joint venture factory in the eastern Indian city of Chennai. Renault SA owns approximately 43% of Nissan. Nissan, an allied firm, promotes intensive research and development in alternative fuel technologies. In January 2018, Nissan announced that Infiniti will introduce new vehicles with electrified powertrains beginning in 2021, and that electrified vehicles will comprise more than half of Infiniti's global sales by 2025.

FINANCIAL DATA:
Note: Data for latest year may not have been available at press time.

In U.S. $	2017	2016	2015	2014	2013	2012
Revenue	109,186,200,000	113,559,900,000	105,973,600,000	97,657,170,000	89,710,950,000	87,656,290,000
R&D Expense						
Operating Income	8,890,321,000	9,501,128,000	7,466,118,000	6,369,983,000	6,655,748,000	6,874,557,000
Operating Margin %	8.14%	8.36%	7.04%	6.52%	7.41%	7.84%
SGA Expense	7,257,789,000	7,909,829,000	7,669,378,000	6,571,856,000	4,580,679,000	4,602,777,000
Net Income	6,181,284,000	4,880,203,000	4,262,847,000	3,624,315,000	3,190,293,000	3,180,855,000
Operating Cash Flow	12,441,520,000	8,636,232,000	6,453,764,000	6,783,333,000	3,641,672,000	6,486,837,000
Capital Expenditure	12,053,660,000	12,912,150,000	9,974,418,000	9,354,770,000	6,614,450,000	5,828,638,000
EBITDA	16,958,660,000	14,818,580,000	13,963,710,000	11,508,690,000	10,394,220,000	10,644,360,000
Return on Assets %	3.70%	3.04%	2.88%	2.82%	2.86%	3.13%
Return on Equity %	13.84%	10.96%	9.97%	9.63%	9.94%	11.20%
Debt to Equity	0.94	0.79	0.79	0.83	0.81	0.79

CONTACT INFORMATION:
Phone: 81 455235523 Fax:
Toll-Free:
Address: 1-1, Takashima 1-chome, Nishi-ku, Kanagawa, 220-8686 Japan

STOCK TICKER/OTHER:
Stock Ticker: NSANF
Employees: 152,421
Parent Company:

Exchange: PINX
Fiscal Year Ends: 03/31

SALARIES/BONUSES:
Top Exec. Salary: $ Bonus: $
Second Exec. Salary: $ Bonus: $

OTHER THOUGHTS:
Estimated Female Officers or Directors:
Hot Spot for Advancement for Women/Minorities:

Sales, profits and employees may be estimates. Financial information, benefits and other data can change quickly and may vary from those stated here.

Nitto Denko Corporation

NAIC Code: 322220

www.nitto.com

TYPES OF BUSINESS:
Industrial Adhesive Tapes
Semiconductor Materials
Drug Delivery Systems
Water Treatment Membranes
Semiconductor Machinery

BRANDS/DIVISIONS/AFFILIATES:
Nitto Denko America Inc
Nitto Denko Avecia Inc
Hydranautics
Nitto Denko Automotive Inc

CONTACTS:
Note: Officers with more than one job title may be intentionally listed here more than once.

Hideo Takasaki, CEO
Yukio Nagira, Pres.
Kaoru Aizawa, Sr. Exec. VP
Hideo Takasaki, Sr. Exec. VP
Yoichiro Sakuma, Exec. VP
Toshihiko Omote, Exec. VP

GROWTH PLANS/SPECIAL FEATURES:

Nitto Denko Corporation primarily manufactures industrial adhesive tapes for the electronics, automotive, healthcare, packaging and construction industries. The company produces industrial, electronic and functional products. Industrial products include double-coated adhesive tapes, masking tapes, surface protective materials, sealing materials and label printing systems. Its electronics products include liquid crystal display (LCD)-related items, general and advanced device resins, printed circuit boards and semiconductor package adhesive sheets. Functional products include medical items such as transdermal therapeutic patches; polymer separation membranes used for water purification and treatment; and plastic engineering products such as information equipment and porous film materials used in cars, electronics and home appliances. Nitto's recent method of sintering neodymium magnet material allows it to control a non-uniform orientation of the magnetic field in the sintered material so as to locally concentrate the field. This process aims to improve the performance of electric motors by 20% to 30%, while also contributing to motor miniaturization efforts. Nitto Denko America, Inc. manufactures semiconductor encapsulating materials, materials and systems for semiconductor processing and flexible printed circuits. Other North American subsidiaries include Nitto Denko Avecia, Inc., a developer of oligo therapeutics for the drug development industry; Hydranautics, a producer of membranes for water treatment; and Nitto Denko Automotive, Inc., a producer of structural, acoustic and sealing products for the automotive industry. Nitto Denko also operates through subsidiaries in Europe, East Asia and Southeast Asia. During 2017, the firm closed its European technical center in Lausanne, Switzerland.

FINANCIAL DATA:
Note: Data for latest year may not have been available at press time.

In U.S. $	2017	2016	2015	2014	2013	2012
Revenue	7,152,134,000	7,388,243,000	7,688,122,000	6,985,607,000	6,294,150,000	5,660,881,000
R&D Expense	282,895,500	299,236,100	263,089,200			
Operating Income	926,355,600	908,701,400	960,080,200	673,141,400	639,770,900	526,281,000
Operating Margin %	12.95%	12.29%	12.48%	9.63%	10.16%	9.29%
SGA Expense	1,018,418,000	1,071,735,000	1,070,794,000			
Net Income	591,140,400	760,974,500	725,507,800	475,293,500	408,421,900	289,416,800
Operating Cash Flow	1,117,375,000	1,310,397,000	1,113,108,000	729,327,400	634,917,100	544,922,700
Capital Expenditure	402,254,500	587,358,000	496,823,200			
EBITDA	1,324,716,000	1,416,620,000	1,421,930,000	1,060,322,000	939,892,000	815,735,100
Return on Assets %	7.43%	9.71%	9.51%	6.70%	6.29%	4.75%
Return on Equity %	10.00%	13.32%	13.70%	10.06%	9.48%	7.28%
Debt to Equity					0.10	0.12

CONTACT INFORMATION:
Phone: 8 1357402101 Fax:
Toll-Free: 800-356-4880
Address: 33/Fl, Grnad Front Osaka, 4-20, Ofuka-cho, Kita-ku, Osaka, 530-0001 Japan

STOCK TICKER/OTHER:
Stock Ticker: NDEKY
Employees: 29,617
Parent Company:

Exchange: PINX
Fiscal Year Ends: 03/31

SALARIES/BONUSES:
Top Exec. Salary: $ Bonus: $
Second Exec. Salary: $ Bonus: $

OTHER THOUGHTS:
Estimated Female Officers or Directors:
Hot Spot for Advancement for Women/Minorities:

Sales, profits and employees may be estimates. Financial information, benefits and other data can change quickly and may vary from those stated here.

Nokia Bell Labs

www.bell-labs.com

NAIC Code: 541712

TYPES OF BUSINESS:
Research & Development-Communications
Physical Science
Computer Science & Software
Mathematics Research
Optical & Wireless Networking Technologies
Nanotechnology Research

BRANDS/DIVISIONS/AFFILIATES:
Nokia Corporation

CONTACTS:
Note: Officers with more than one job title may be intentionally listed here more than once.

Marcus Weldon, Pres.

GROWTH PLANS/SPECIAL FEATURES:
Nokia Bell Labs is a research and scientific development company headquartered in Murray Hill, New Jersey. Winner of eight Nobel prizes and a dozen U.S. Medals of Science, it designs products and services at the forefront of communications technology and conducts fundamental research in the following fields: physical technologies, computer science and software, mathematical/algorithmic sciences, optical and wireless networking, security solutions and government research. Its research programs are grouped into six categories: algorithms, analytics and security, which comprises coding, mathematics networks, statistical and data sciences, computational/algorithmic sciences and quantum computing/communications; applications and platforms, including information systems, distributed systems/controls and software engineering; fixed networks, including network architecture and design, and network dynamics and operations; IP and optical networking, which includes transport systems and solutions; new materials and devices, including thermal management, energy harvesting/storage and materials science; and wireless, including modulation and multiplexing. Bell Labs operates as a subsidiary of Nokia Corporation.

FINANCIAL DATA:
Note: Data for latest year may not have been available at press time.

In U.S. $	2017	2016	2015	2014	2013	2012
Revenue						
R&D Expense						
Operating Income						
Operating Margin %						
SGA Expense						
Net Income						
Operating Cash Flow						
Capital Expenditure						
EBITDA						
Return on Assets %						
Return on Equity %						
Debt to Equity						

CONTACT INFORMATION:
Phone: 908-582-8500 Fax: 908-508-2576
Toll-Free:
Address: 600-700 Mountain Ave., Murray Hill, NJ 07974 United States

STOCK TICKER/OTHER:
Stock Ticker: Subsidiary
Employees: 748
Parent Company: Nokia Corporation

Exchange:
Fiscal Year Ends: 12/31

SALARIES/BONUSES:
Top Exec. Salary: $ Bonus: $
Second Exec. Salary: $ Bonus: $

OTHER THOUGHTS:
Estimated Female Officers or Directors:
Hot Spot for Advancement for Women/Minorities:

Sales, profits and employees may be estimates. Financial information, benefits and other data can change quickly and may vary from those stated here.

Nokia Corporation

NAIC Code: 334220

company.nokia.com/en

TYPES OF BUSINESS:
Smartphones and Cellphones
Network Systems & Services
Internet Software & Services
Multimedia Equipment
Digital Music
Digital Map Information
Mobile Applications

BRANDS/DIVISIONS/AFFILIATES:
OZO
Unium

CONTACTS:
Note: Officers with more than one job title may be intentionally listed here more than once.

Rajeev Suri, CEO
Rajeev Suri, Pres.
Louise Pentland, Chief Legal Officer
Juha Rutkiranta, Exec. VP-Oper.
Kai Oistamo, Chief Dev. Officer
Stephen Elop, Exec. VP-Devices & Svcs.
Timo Toikkanen, Exec. VP-Mobile Phones
Jo Harlow, Exec. VP-Smart Devices
Risto Siilasmaa, Chmn.

GROWTH PLANS/SPECIAL FEATURES:

Nokia Corporation is a leading supplier of services and software for the converging internet and communications industries. The company consists of two business segments: Nokia Networks and Nokia Technologies. Nokia Networks is the firm's infrastructure business that offers smart, virtual networks with one seamless service. Networks weaves together mobile broadband, fixed access, internet protocol routing, optical technologies, as well as cloud applications and services. Nokia Technologies is focused on advanced technology and licensing. Its primary product includes the OZO virtual reality camera, designed and built for professional content creators. Nokia Technologies expects to establish a virtual reality ecosystem (format, player licensing, new virtual reality experiences) to manage virtual reality workflows and content for end-user experiences, including production, distribution and consumption of virtual reality digital content. Nokia has approximately 20,000 patent families. In March 2018, the firm acquired Unium, a Seattle-based software company specializing in solving complex wireless networking problems for us in mission-critical and residential Wi-Fi applications.

FINANCIAL DATA:
Note: Data for latest year may not have been available at press time.

In U.S. $	2017	2016	2015	2014	2013	2012
Revenue	28,584,310,000	29,161,010,000	15,435,060,000	15,722,790,000	15,694,390,000	37,264,440,000
R&D Expense	6,070,785,000	6,055,966,000	2,625,404,000	3,078,614,000	3,234,212,000	5,905,308,000
Operating Income	721,183,600	-449,504,800	2,119,094,000	1,874,583,000	1,265,776,000	-686,606,300
Operating Margin %	2.52%	-1.54%	13.72%	11.92%	8.06%	-1.84%
SGA Expense	4,464,176,000	4,716,096,000	2,040,060,000	2,017,832,000	2,063,524,000	5,142,137,000
Net Income	-1,844,946,000	-945,935,900	3,045,272,000	4,275,236,000	-759,465,500	-3,835,610,000
Operating Cash Flow	2,236,410,000	-1,795,549,000	626,096,000	1,574,502,000	88,913,040	-437,155,800
Capital Expenditure	742,176,900	589,048,900	387,759,600	384,054,900	502,605,700	569,290,400
EBITDA	1,963,496,000	669,317,600	2,468,572,000	556,941,400	1,597,965,000	-1,296,648,000
Return on Assets %	-3.47%	-2.32%	11.74%	14.96%	-2.23%	-9.39%
Return on Equity %	-8.24%	-5.00%	25.80%	45.91%	-8.46%	-31.16%
Debt to Equity	0.21	0.18	0.19	0.29	0.50	0.63

CONTACT INFORMATION:
Phone: 358-10-44-88-000   Fax: 358-10-44-81-002
Toll-Free:
Address: Kearaportti 3, Espoo, FI-02610 Finland

STOCK TICKER/OTHER:
Stock Ticker: NOK
Employees: 102,687
Parent Company:

Exchange: NYS
Fiscal Year Ends: 12/31

SALARIES/BONUSES:
Top Exec. Salary: $666,667   Bonus: $1,778,105
Second Exec. Salary: $1,390,900   Bonus: $

OTHER THOUGHTS:
Estimated Female Officers or Directors: 4
Hot Spot for Advancement for Women/Minorities: Y

Sales, profits and employees may be estimates. Financial information, benefits and other data can change quickly and may vary from those stated here.

Northrop Grumman Corporation

www.northropgrumman.com

NAIC Code: 336411

TYPES OF BUSINESS:
Aircraft Manufacturing
Shipbuilding & Engineering
Aircraft Manufacturing
Electronic Systems & Components
Hardware & Software Manufacturing
Design & Engineering Services
IT Systems & Services
Nuclear-Powered Aircraft Carriers & Submarines

BRANDS/DIVISIONS/AFFILIATES:

CONTACTS:
Note: Officers with more than one job title may be intentionally listed here more than once.

Wesley Bush, CEO
Kathy Warden, Pres.
Kenneth Bedingfield, CFO
Michael Hardesty, Chief Accounting Officer
Patrick Antkowiak, Chief Technology Officer
Sheila Cheston, General Counsel
Denise Peppard, Other Executive Officer
David Perry, Other Executive Officer
Christopher Jones, President, Divisional
Mark Caylor, President, Divisional
Janis Pamiljans, President, Divisional
Shawn Purvis, President, Divisional
Jennifer McGarey, Secretary
Lesley Kalan, Vice President, Divisional
Lisa Davis, Vice President, Divisional

GROWTH PLANS/SPECIAL FEATURES:

Northrop Grumman Corporation (NGC) is a global aerospace and defense technology company. It has three primary segments: aerospace systems, mission systems and technology services. The aerospace systems segment designs, develops, integrates and produces manned aircraft, autonomous systems, spacecraft, high-energy laser systems, microelectronics and other systems/subsystems. This division's customers, primarily the Department of Defense (DoD) and other U.S. government agencies, use these systems in mission areas such as intelligence, surveillance and reconnaissance, strike operations, communications, earth observation, space science and space exploration. The mission systems segment provides advanced end-to-end mission solutions and multifunction systems for DoD, intelligence community, international, federal civil and commercial customers. Its major products and services include C4ISR (command, control, communications and computer (C4)/intelligence, surveillance and reconnaissance (ISR)) systems; radar, electro-optical/infrared and acoustic sensors; electronic warfare systems; cyber solutions; space systems; intelligence processing systems; air and missile defense integration; navigation; and shipboard missile and encapsulated payload launch systems. Last, the technology services segment provides logistics solutions supporting the full life cycle of platforms and systems for global defense and federal-civil customers. Its offerings include software and system sustainment, modernization of platforms and associated subsystems, advanced training solutions and integrated logistics support. In September 2017, Northrup agreed to acquire rocket motor and satellite firm Orbital ATK for $7.8 billion; the transaction was expected to be completed by mid-2018. Upon completion, Orbital ATK will become a new business sector named Northrop Grumman Innovation Systems. In March 2018, the government of Poland signed a letter of offer and acceptance with the U.S. government to purchase Northrop's integrated air and missile defense battle command system.

FINANCIAL DATA:
Note: Data for latest year may not have been available at press time.

In U.S. $	2017	2016	2015	2014	2013	2012
Revenue	25,803,000,000	24,508,000,000	23,526,000,000	23,979,000,000	24,661,000,000	25,218,000,000
R&D Expense						
Operating Income	3,299,000,000	3,193,000,000	3,076,000,000	3,196,000,000	3,123,000,000	3,130,000,000
Operating Margin %	12.78%	13.02%	13.07%	13.32%	12.66%	12.41%
SGA Expense	2,655,000,000	2,584,000,000	2,566,000,000	2,405,000,000	2,256,000,000	2,450,000,000
Net Income	2,015,000,000	2,200,000,000	1,990,000,000	2,069,000,000	1,952,000,000	1,978,000,000
Operating Cash Flow	2,613,000,000	2,813,000,000	2,162,000,000	2,593,000,000	2,483,000,000	2,640,000,000
Capital Expenditure	928,000,000	920,000,000	471,000,000	561,000,000	364,000,000	331,000,000
EBITDA	3,884,000,000	3,680,000,000	3,558,000,000	3,681,000,000	3,615,000,000	3,687,000,000
Return on Assets %	6.65%	8.78%	7.79%	7.81%	7.37%	7.61%
Return on Equity %	32.74%	40.81%	31.19%	23.17%	19.39%	19.92%
Debt to Equity	2.04	1.34	1.16	0.81	0.55	0.41

CONTACT INFORMATION:
Phone: 703 280-2900 Fax: 310 201-3023
Toll-Free:
Address: 2980 Fairview Park Dr., Falls Church, VA 22042 United States

STOCK TICKER/OTHER:
Stock Ticker: NOC Exchange: NYS
Employees: 67,000 Fiscal Year Ends: 12/31
Parent Company:

SALARIES/BONUSES:
Top Exec. Salary: $1,548,577 Bonus: $
Second Exec. Salary: $807,116 Bonus: $

OTHER THOUGHTS:
Estimated Female Officers or Directors: 9
Hot Spot for Advancement for Women/Minorities: Y

Sales, profits and employees may be estimates. Financial information, benefits and other data can change quickly and may vary from those stated here.

Novartis AG

NAIC Code: 325412

www.novartis.com

TYPES OF BUSINESS:
Drugs-Diversified
Therapeutic Drug Discovery
Therapeutic Drug Manufacturing
Generic Drugs
Over-the-Counter Drugs
Ophthalmic Products
Nutritional Products
Veterinary Products

BRANDS/DIVISIONS/AFFILIATES:
Sandoz
Alcon
Novartis Institutes for BioMedical Research
Global Drug Development
Novartis Technical Operations
Novartis Business Services

CONTACTS:
Note: Officers with more than one job title may be intentionally listed here more than once.

Vasant Narasimhan, CEO
Harry Kirsch, CFO
Steffen Lang, Global Dir.-Technical Operations
Steven Baert, Head-Human Resources
Mark C. Fishman, Pres., Novartis Institute for Biomedical Research
Bertrand Bodson, Chief Digital Officer
Peter Kornicker, Chief Compliance Officer
Felix Ehrat, General Counsel
Paul van Arkel, Head-Corp. Strategy & External Affairs
Michele Galen, Head-Comm.
Kevin Buehler, Head-Alcon
David Epstein, Head-Novartis Pharmaceuticals
George Gunn, Head-Novartis Animal Health
Jeffrey George, Head-Sandoz Div.
Joerg Reinhardt, Chmn.

GROWTH PLANS/SPECIAL FEATURES:
Novartis AG researches, develops and manufactures pharmaceuticals, as well as a large number of consumer and animal healthcare products. The company has a diverse portfolio, operating through three primary divisions: innovative medicines, which develops, manufactures, distributes and sells innovative patent-protected prescription medicines; Sandoz, which develops, manufactures, distributes and sells generic pharmaceuticals and biosimilars; and Alcon, which develops, manufactures, distributes and sells surgical and vision care products. Each of these divisions are supported by the following cross-divisional organizational units: Novartis Institutes for BioMedical Research, Global Drug Development, Novartis Technical Operations (NTO) and Novartis Business Services (NBS). Novartis Institutes for BioMedical Research is the innovation engine of Novartis. It supports the innovative medicines division and collaborates with the Sandoz division. Global Drug Development oversees all drug development activities for the innovative medicines division and biosimilars portfolio. NTO centralizes management of Novartis' manufacturing operations across the innovative medicines and Sandoz divisions. NBS delivers integrated solutions to all Novartis divisions and units worldwide. Headquartered in Switzerland, the company's products are sold in approximately 155 countries worldwide. In March 2018, Novartis agreed to sell its 36.5% stake in GlaxoSmithKline plc's consumer healthcare joint venture, to GlaxoSmithKline for $13 billion. That April, Novartis agreed to acquire AveXis, Inc., a U.S.-based gene-therapy company, for $8.7 billion.

FINANCIAL DATA:
Note: Data for latest year may not have been available at press time.

In U.S. $	2017	2016	2015	2014	2013	2012
Revenue	50,135,000,000	49,436,000,000	50,387,000,000	53,634,000,000	58,831,000,000	57,561,000,000
R&D Expense	8,972,000,000	9,039,000,000	8,935,000,000	9,086,000,000	9,852,000,000	9,332,000,000
Operating Income	6,660,000,000	6,341,000,000	6,928,000,000	9,698,000,000	10,910,000,000	11,511,000,000
Operating Margin %	13.28%	12.82%	13.74%	18.08%	18.54%	19.99%
SGA Expense	14,997,000,000	14,192,000,000	14,247,000,000	14,993,000,000	17,609,000,000	17,290,000,000
Net Income	7,703,000,000	6,712,000,000	17,783,000,000	10,210,000,000	9,175,000,000	9,505,000,000
Operating Cash Flow	12,621,000,000	11,475,000,000	11,897,000,000	13,897,000,000	13,174,000,000	14,194,000,000
Capital Expenditure	2,746,000,000	2,879,000,000	3,505,000,000	3,404,000,000	3,571,000,000	3,068,000,000
EBITDA	9,776,000,000	8,524,000,000	8,803,000,000	12,976,000,000	16,343,000,000	16,887,000,000
Return on Assets %	5.85%	5.12%	13.84%	8.11%	7.32%	7.86%
Return on Equity %	10.33%	8.83%	24.06%	14.07%	12.79%	14.08%
Debt to Equity	0.31	0.23	0.21	0.19	0.15	0.19

CONTACT INFORMATION:
Phone: 41 613241111
Fax: 41 613248001
Toll-Free:
Address: Lichtstrasse 35, Basel, 4056 Switzerland

STOCK TICKER/OTHER:
Stock Ticker: NVS
Employees: 118,393
Parent Company:

Exchange: NYS
Fiscal Year Ends: 12/31

SALARIES/BONUSES:
Top Exec. Salary: $2,183,565   Bonus: $2,047,092
Second Exec. Salary: $1,120,000   Bonus: $873,600

OTHER THOUGHTS:
Estimated Female Officers or Directors: 4
Hot Spot for Advancement for Women/Minorities: Y

Sales, profits and employees may be estimates. Financial information, benefits and other data can change quickly and may vary from those stated here.

Novo-Nordisk AS

NAIC Code: 325412

www.novonordisk.com

TYPES OF BUSINESS:
Drugs-Diabetes
Hormone Replacement Therapy
Growth Hormone Drugs
Hemophilia Drugs
Insulin Delivery Systems
Educational & Training Services

BRANDS/DIVISIONS/AFFILIATES:
Tresiba
Xultophy
Ryzodeg
Fiasp

CONTACTS: Note: Officers with more than one job title may be intentionally listed here more than once.
Lars Jorgensen, CEO
Kare Schulz, Pres.
Jesper Brandgaard, CFO
Mads Krogsgaard Thomsen, Chief Science Officer
Helge Lund, Chmn.

GROWTH PLANS/SPECIAL FEATURES:
Novo Nordisk AS is a global healthcare company engaged in the discovery, development, manufacturing and marketing pharmaceutical products. As a leader in diabetes care, it has one of the broadest diabetes product portfolios in the industry, including new generation insulins, a full portfolio of modern insulins as well as a human once-daily GLP-1 analog. In addition, Novo Nordisk has a leading position within hemophilia care, growth hormone therapy and hormone replacement therapy. Operations are divided into two segments: diabetes and obesity care, and biopharmaceuticals. The diabetes and obesity care segment covers insulin, GLP-1 (glucagon-like peptide), other protein-related products (such as glucagon, protein-related delivery systems and needles) and oral antidiabetic drugs. The biopharmaceuticals segment covers the therapy areas of hemophilia care, growth hormone therapy and hormone replacement therapy. Novo products include: Tresiba (insulin degludec) is a once-daily new-generation insulin launched in more than 50 countries, including the U.S.; Xultophy, a once-daily single-injection combination of insulin degludec (Tresiba) and liraglutide (Victoza), which is marketed in 18 countries, including the U.S.; Ryzodeg, a soluble formulation of insulin degludec and insulin aspart, which is marketed in 18 countries; and Fiasp, a fast-acting insulin aspart, launched in 17 countries and was due to launch in the U.S. during 2018. The major production facilities owned by Novo Nordisk are located in Denmark, and internationally in the U.S., France, China and Brazil. Active pharmaceutical ingredient (API) production is located in Denmark, primarily in Kalundorg, with secondary locations in Hillerod and Gentofte, although two API production sites in the U.S. are currently being established, and expected to commence operation in 2020. Construction of a new facility in Hillerod, Denmark, for producing medicines for the treatment of diabetes and obesity is expected to commence operation in 2019.

FINANCIAL DATA: Note: Data for latest year may not have been available at press time.

In U.S. $	2017	2016	2015	2014	2013	2012
Revenue	18,495,470,000	18,509,380,000	17,871,370,000	14,705,170,000	13,838,490,000	12,920,140,000
R&D Expense	2,320,545,000	2,411,452,000	2,253,316,000	2,278,816,000	1,942,839,000	1,804,408,000
Operating Income	8,108,327,000	7,897,700,000	7,610,737,000	5,583,945,000	5,101,919,000	4,770,247,000
Operating Margin %	43.83%	42.66%	42.58%	37.97%	36.86%	36.92%
SGA Expense	5,319,336,000	5,354,937,000	5,326,787,000	4,431,124,000	4,452,319,000	4,115,845,000
Net Income	6,313,855,000	6,279,909,000	5,772,383,000	4,384,925,000	4,170,158,000	3,548,873,000
Operating Cash Flow	6,816,910,000	8,000,199,000	6,339,852,000	5,247,802,000	4,295,673,000	3,678,363,000
Capital Expenditure	1,432,001,000	1,368,913,000	1,060,754,000	717,822,200	603,401,200	599,758,300
EBITDA	8,602,607,000	8,454,240,000	7,701,313,000	6,221,126,000	5,860,641,000	5,347,154,000
Return on Assets %	38.15%	40.06%	41.28%	35.93%	37.03%	32.87%
Return on Equity %	80.20%	82.23%	79.89%	63.91%	60.53%	54.89%
Debt to Equity						

CONTACT INFORMATION:
Phone: 45 44448888 Fax: 45 44490555
Toll-Free:
Address: Novo Alle, Bagsvã¦rd, 2880 Denmark

SALARIES/BONUSES:
Top Exec. Salary: $4,900,000   Bonus: $1,700,000
Second Exec. Salary: $1,970,492   Bonus: $993,526

STOCK TICKER/OTHER:
Stock Ticker: NVO   Exchange: NYS
Employees: 42,500   Fiscal Year Ends: 12/31
Parent Company:

OTHER THOUGHTS:
Estimated Female Officers or Directors: 3
Hot Spot for Advancement for Women/Minorities: Y

Sales, profits and employees may be estimates. Financial information, benefits and other data can change quickly and may vary from those stated here.

Novozymes

www.novozymes.com

NAIC Code: 325414

TYPES OF BUSINESS:
Industrial Enzyme & Microorganism Production
Biopharmaceuticals
Enzymes
Microbiology

BRANDS/DIVISIONS/AFFILIATES:

GROWTH PLANS/SPECIAL FEATURES:
Novozymes is a biotechnology company specializing in enzyme and microorganism production. The firm's solutions improve industrial manufacturing processes by saving energy, water and raw materials, while also reducing waste and emissions. Enzymes are proteins that act as catalysts, which speed up the transformation process of substances, causing them to transform from one substance into another. Enzymes are used in a variety of products, including ethanol, sugar, beer and bread, as well as in laundry detergents. Microorganisms have natural properties which can be useful in several industrial processes, helping farmers increase yields and protect crops. Novozyme's products provide solutions for the following broad industry categories: agriculture, household care, forest products, bioenergy, leather, textile, food and beverages, pharmaceuticals and wastewater. Based in Copenhagen, Denmark, the firm has production sites in Argentina, Brazil, Canada, China, Denmark, India and the U.S., as well as affiliates and sales offices in more than 30 countries.

CONTACTS: *Note: Officers with more than one job title may be intentionally listed here more than once.*

Peder Holk Nielsen, CEO
Thomas Videbaek, COO
Peder Holk Nielsen, Pres.
Per Falholt, Exec. VP-R&D
Thomas Videbaek, Exec. VP-Bus. Dev
Andrew Fordyce, Exec. VP-Bus. Oper.
Jorgen Buhl Rasmussen, Chmn.
Thomas Nagy, Exec. VP-Supply Chain Oper.

FINANCIAL DATA: *Note: Data for latest year may not have been available at press time.*

In U.S. $	2017	2016	2015	2014	2013	2012
Revenue	2,406,153,000	2,341,740,000	2,318,557,000	2,063,056,000	1,944,992,000	1,860,211,000
R&D Expense	316,769,100	308,820,800	313,954,100	304,846,800	253,017,800	252,852,300
Operating Income	681,061,800	653,408,600	643,142,200	521,104,200	480,369,600	454,537,900
Operating Margin %	28.30%	27.90%	27.73%	25.25%	24.69%	24.43%
SGA Expense	405,689,600	402,709,000	405,192,800	374,724,700	380,851,500	369,094,700
Net Income	516,467,700	505,042,100	467,453,800	418,274,300	364,292,700	333,659,000
Operating Cash Flow	672,782,400	635,856,300	552,897,000	749,283,900	430,362,100	456,690,600
Capital Expenditure	280,174,200	201,354,500	170,720,800	119,719,800	130,151,800	195,724,500
EBITDA	822,970,300	815,684,500	791,343,000	720,802,800	589,988,600	556,539,900
Return on Assets %	16.84%	16.73%	15.58%	14.46%	13.91%	13.91%
Return on Equity %	27.13%	26.16%	24.71%	22.63%	21.34%	21.94%
Debt to Equity	0.11	0.14	0.10	0.11	0.15	0.18

CONTACT INFORMATION:
Phone: 45 44460000   Fax: 45 44469999
Toll-Free:
Address: Krogshoejvej 36, Bagsvaerd, 2880 Denmark

SALARIES/BONUSES:
Top Exec. Salary: $ Bonus: $
Second Exec. Salary: $ Bonus: $

STOCK TICKER/OTHER:
Stock Ticker: NVZMF
Employees: 6,245
Parent Company:

Exchange: PINX
Fiscal Year Ends: 12/31

OTHER THOUGHTS:
Estimated Female Officers or Directors: 3
Hot Spot for Advancement for Women/Minorities: Y

Sales, profits and employees may be estimates. Financial information, benefits and other data can change quickly and may vary from those stated here.

NTT DATA Corporation

NAIC Code: 541512

www.nttdata.com

TYPES OF BUSINESS:
IT Services
Systems Integration
Consulting Services
Bioinformatics
Telecom Consulting

BRANDS/DIVISIONS/AFFILIATES:
Japan Telegraph & Telephone Corporation
NTT DATA Business Solutions Australia Pty Ltd
NTT DATA Business Solutions Malaysia Sdn Bhd
NTT DATA Business Solutions Singapore Pte Ltd

CONTACTS:
Note: Officers with more than one job title may be intentionally listed here more than once.

Toshio Iwamoto, CEO
Toshio Iwamoto, Pres.
Toru Yamashita, Counselor
Masanori Shiina, Exec. VP
Hironobu Sagae, Sr. VP

GROWTH PLANS/SPECIAL FEATURES:

NTT DATA Corporation, originally formed as a division of Japan Telegraph & Telephone Corporation, is one of the largest information technology providers in Japan. The firm offers a wide array of IT and related services with operations in over 50 countries. NTT DATA's services include advisory services, application development and management, enterprise application services, business intelligence and analytics, infrastructure services and outsourcing services. These services feature SAP solutions, Oracle solutions, cloud solutions, big data solutions, manufacturer-to-manufacturer solutions and application development technologies. Industry sectors that NTT serves include automotive, banking/financial, consumer products, education, electronics/high-tech, energy/utilities, public, healthcare, life sciences, insurance, manufacturing, media/entertainment, natural resources, retail service providers, telecommunications, transportation/logistics and wholesale/distribution. Primary subsidiaries include NTT DATA Business Solutions Australia Pty Ltd., NTT DATA Business Solutions Malaysia Sdn Bhd and NTT DATA Business Solutions Singapore Pte Ltd. Former parent Japan Telegraph and Telephone Corporation still controls a majority stake in the firm, even though it is a publicly-traded company.

FINANCIAL DATA:
Note: Data for latest year may not have been available at press time.

In U.S. $	2017	2016	2015	2014	2013	2012
Revenue	16,140,050,000	15,044,690,000	14,084,330,000	12,518,840,000	12,129,130,000	11,656,210,000
R&D Expense						
Operating Income	1,091,010,000	939,864,000	782,681,200	583,035,300	798,360,400	749,170,900
Operating Margin %	6.75%	6.24%	5.55%	4.65%	6.58%	6.42%
SGA Expense						
Net Income	611,943,400	590,395,100	312,828,400	233,864,400	419,172,700	289,416,800
Operating Cash Flow	2,222,396,000	2,168,353,000	1,713,062,000	2,184,871,000	1,502,953,000	1,772,377,000
Capital Expenditure	1,472,704,000	1,167,896,000	1,351,565,000	1,403,661,000	1,087,600,000	1,262,186,000
EBITDA	2,471,083,000	2,433,780,000	2,111,729,000	1,840,004,000	2,073,971,000	2,103,661,000
Return on Assets %	3.20%	3.44%	1.83%	1.56%	2.90%	2.06%
Return on Equity %	8.53%	8.36%	4.43%	3.78%	6.92%	5.04%
Debt to Equity	0.41	0.43	0.45	0.49	0.44	0.56

CONTACT INFORMATION:
Phone: 81 355468202 Fax: 81 355462405
Toll-Free:
Address: Toyosu Ctr. Bldg., 3-3 Toyosu 3-chome, Koto-ku, Tokyo, 135-6033 Japan

STOCK TICKER/OTHER:
Stock Ticker: NTDTY   Exchange: PINX
Employees: 31,739   Fiscal Year Ends: 03/31
Parent Company: Japan Telegraph & Telephone Corporation

SALARIES/BONUSES:
Top Exec. Salary: $ Bonus: $
Second Exec. Salary: $ Bonus: $

OTHER THOUGHTS:
Estimated Female Officers or Directors:
Hot Spot for Advancement for Women/Minorities:

Sales, profits and employees may be estimates. Financial information, benefits and other data can change quickly and may vary from those stated here.

NV5 Global Inc

NAIC Code: 541330

www.nv5.com

TYPES OF BUSINESS:
Construction Engineering Services

BRANDS/DIVISIONS/AFFILIATES:

CONTACTS: Note: Officers with more than one job title may be intentionally listed here more than once.
Dickerson Wright, CEO
Michael Rama, CFO
MaryJo OBrien, Chief Administrative Officer
Donald Alford, Executive VP
Richard Tong, Executive VP
Alexander Hockman, President

GROWTH PLANS/SPECIAL FEATURES:
NV5 Global, Inc. provides professional and technical engineering and consulting services. The firm offers solutions to public and private sector clients in the energy, transportation, water, government, hospitality, education, healthcare, commercial and residential markets. NV5 helps these clients plan, design, build, test, certify and manage a variety of projects. The company's solutions include, but are not limited to, construction quality assurance, surveying/mapping, design, consulting, program and construction management, permitting, planning, forensic engineering, litigation support, condition assessment and compliance certification. NV5's service capabilities are organized into five verticals: infrastructure, engineering and support services; construction quality assurance; program management; energy services; and environmental services. The firm is headquartered in Hollywood, Florida, and operates its business from 89 U.S. locations, as well as four locations abroad. Its primary clients include U.S. federal, state, municipal and local government agencies, as well as military and defense clients.

NV5 offers its employees medical, dental, vision, life and disability insurance plans; 401(k) and financial consulting; paid time off; and an employee assistance program.

FINANCIAL DATA: Note: Data for latest year may not have been available at press time.

In U.S. $	2017	2016	2015	2014	2013	2012
Revenue	333,034,000	223,910,000	154,655,000	108,382,000	68,232,000	60,576,000
R&D Expense						
Operating Income	26,568,000	18,403,000	13,699,000	8,243,000	3,896,000	2,357,000
Operating Margin %	7.97%	8.21%	8.85%	7.60%	5.70%	3.89%
SGA Expense	125,558,000	82,949,000	51,611,000	34,950,000	29,406,000	27,843,000
Net Income	24,006,000	11,607,000	8,492,000	4,893,000	2,759,000	1,293,000
Operating Cash Flow	17,625,000	15,213,000	5,972,000	1,420,000	3,421,000	1,536,000
Capital Expenditure	2,239,000	985,000	601,000	825,000	533,000	554,000
EBITDA	39,696,000	24,631,000	17,167,000	10,231,000	5,410,000	3,825,000
Return on Assets %	9.06%	6.92%	10.16%	9.76%	7.37%	4.46%
Return on Equity %	14.62%	10.14%	14.59%	15.19%	13.73%	11.81%
Debt to Equity	0.31	0.14	0.07	0.09	0.08	0.33

CONTACT INFORMATION:
Phone: 954 495-2112 Fax: 954 495-2101
Toll-Free:
Address: 200 South Park Rd., Ste. 350, Hollywood, FL 33021 United States

STOCK TICKER/OTHER:
Stock Ticker: NVEE
Employees: 1,532
Parent Company:

Exchange: NAS
Fiscal Year Ends: 12/31

SALARIES/BONUSES:
Top Exec. Salary: $483,462 Bonus: $
Second Exec. Salary: $360,385 Bonus: $

OTHER THOUGHTS:
Estimated Female Officers or Directors:
Hot Spot for Advancement for Women/Minorities:

Sales, profits and employees may be estimates. Financial information, benefits and other data can change quickly and may vary from those stated here.

Plunkett Research, Ltd.

NVIDIA Corporation

NAIC Code: 334413

www.nvidia.com

TYPES OF BUSINESS:
Printed Circuit Assembly (Electronic Assembly) Manufacturing
Graphics Processors
Graphics Software

BRANDS/DIVISIONS/AFFILIATES:
GeForce
Quadro
Tesla
GRID
Tegra
DRIVE
SHIELD

CONTACTS: *Note: Officers with more than one job title may be intentionally listed here more than once.*
Jen-Hsun Huang, CEO
Colette Kress, CFO
Michael Mccaffery, Chairman of the Board
Michael Byron, Chief Accounting Officer
Ajay Puri, Executive VP, Divisional
Debora Shoquist, Executive VP, Divisional
Tim Teter, General Counsel

GROWTH PLANS/SPECIAL FEATURES:

NVIDIA Corporation designs, develops and markets a family of 3D graphics processors, graphics processing units (GPUs) and related software. The company serves virtually all markets that rely on high-quality visuals in PC applications, including manufacturing, science, e-business, entertainment and education. It has two product groups: the GPU and Tegra processors. GPUs, each with billions of transistors, are the engine of visual computing and among the world's most complex processors. Products include GeForce, Quadro, Tesla and GRID. GeForce processors enhance the gaming experience on PCs by improving the visual quality of graphics. Quadro is for professional workstations. Tesla is a GPU-accelerated computing processor used to accelerate scientific, analytics, engineering, consumer and enterprise applications. GRID uses GPUs to deliver graphics performance remotely, from the cloud. GRID's uses include gaming, professional applications provided as a service and improving Citrix and VMware installations. Tegra processors are architected to deliver a superior visual and multimedia experience on tablets, smartphones and gaming devices while consuming minimal power. Tegra is also sold to original equipment manufacturers for devices where graphics and overall performance are of great importance. The processors are primarily designed to enable the firm's branded DRIVE and SHIELD platforms. DRIVE automotive computers provide supercomputing capabilities to make driving safer and more enjoyable. SHIELD is a family of devices designed to harness the power of mobile-cloud in order to revolutionize gaming. NVIDIA's research and development in visual computing has yielded approximately 7,300 patent assets, including inventions essential to modern computing.

Employees of NVIDIA receive medical, dental and vision coverage; a 529 college savings plan; a 401(K) plan; an employee assistance program; flex spending accounts; and discounts with Apple, Microsoft and AT&T.

FINANCIAL DATA: *Note: Data for latest year may not have been available at press time.*

In U.S. $	2017	2016	2015	2014	2013	2012
Revenue	6,910,000,000	5,010,000,000	4,681,507,000	4,130,162,000	4,280,159,000	
R&D Expense	1,463,000,000	1,331,000,000	1,359,725,000	1,335,834,000	1,147,282,000	
Operating Income	1,937,000,000	878,000,000	758,989,000	496,227,000	648,239,000	
Operating Margin %	28.03%	17.52%	16.21%	12.01%	15.14%	
SGA Expense	663,000,000	602,000,000	480,763,000	435,702,000	430,822,000	
Net Income	1,666,000,000	614,000,000	630,587,000	439,990,000	562,536,000	
Operating Cash Flow	1,672,000,000	1,175,000,000	905,656,000	835,146,000	824,172,000	
Capital Expenditure	176,000,000	86,000,000	122,381,000	255,186,000	183,309,000	
EBITDA	2,150,000,000	987,000,000	1,021,094,000	759,845,000	891,568,000	
Return on Assets %	19.35%	8.42%	8.72%	6.44%	9.40%	
Return on Equity %	32.56%	13.81%	14.21%	9.47%	12.53%	
Debt to Equity	0.35	0.02	0.31		0.30	

CONTACT INFORMATION:
Phone: 408 486-2000   Fax: 408 486-2200
Toll-Free:
Address: 2701 San Tomas Expressway, Santa Clara, CA 95050 United States

STOCK TICKER/OTHER:
Stock Ticker: NVDA   Exchange: NAS
Employees: 7,282   Fiscal Year Ends: 01/31
Parent Company:

SALARIES/BONUSES:
Top Exec. Salary: $999,985   Bonus: $
Second Exec. Salary: $949,640   Bonus: $

OTHER THOUGHTS:
Estimated Female Officers or Directors: 3
Hot Spot for Advancement for Women/Minorities: Y

Sales, profits and employees may be estimates. Financial information, benefits and other data can change quickly and may vary from those stated here.

OAO Lukoil

www.lukoil.com

NAIC Code: 211111

TYPES OF BUSINESS:
Oil & Gas Exploration & Production
Petroleum Refining
Pipeline Operations
Gas Stations
Ocean Terminals & Oil Tankers
Natural Gas & Petrochemical Processing Plants

BRANDS/DIVISIONS/AFFILIATES:

CONTACTS: Note: Officers with more than one job title may be intentionally listed here more than once.
Vagit Alekperov, CEO
Vagit Alekperov, Pres.
Alexander Matytsyn, VP-Finance
Vadim Vorobyev, VP-Sales & Supplies
Anatoly Moskalenko, VP-Human Resources
Ivan Maslyaev, General Counsel
Lyubov Khoba, Chief Acct.
Sergei Kukura, First VP-Finance & Economics
Gennady Fedotov, VP-Economics & Planning
Sergei Malyukov, VP-Internal Control & Audit
Ravil Maganov, First Exec. VP-OAO LUKOIL Exploration & Production
Valery Grayfer, Chmn.
Valery Subbotin, VP-Supplies & Sales

GROWTH PLANS/SPECIAL FEATURES:
OAO Lukoil operates in oil and gas exploration and production as well as the production and sale of petroleum products. The company represents 2% of the global output of crude oil and around 1% of the proved hydrocarbon reserves. Lukoil's proved hydrocarbon reserves are 16.4 billion barrels of oil equivalent (boe) per year, 2.2 million barrels of hydrocarbon per day, 1.3 million barrels of oil refining per day and 917,000 tons of lubricants production per year. The firm owns and operates nearly 5,400 filling stations. Lukoil's upstream business develops new fields and enhances mature fields through advanced technologies, increased production drilling and a number of EOR (enhanced oil recovery) operations such as thermal recovery, gas injection, chemical injection and low-salinity water flooding. Current upstream activities are located in Western Siberia, Timan-Pechora, Northern Caspian Sea and Uzbekistan. The downstream business comprises four refineries in Russia (Perm, Volgograd, Nizhny Novgorod and Ukhta), three in Europe (Italy, Romania and Bulgaria), and a 45% stake in one in the Netherlands, comprising a total capacity of 82.1 million tons per year. Lukoil also processes gas and natural gas liquids (NGLs), with a natural and petroleum gas throughput being 3.9 billion cubic meters (bcm) per year, and the output of NGLs being 1.3 million tons in 2016. It markets oils and lubricants in over 100 countries, and its production facilities include seven owned sites, two joint venture sites and 24 contracted plants. The company's petrochemical facilities are located in Russia, Bulgaria and Italy, and make pyrolysis and organic synthesis products, fuel fractions and polymer materials. Lukoil's aggregate power generation capacity is 5.8 gigawatts, with a commercial power generation accounting for 73% and a supply power generation for 27%.

FINANCIAL DATA: Note: Data for latest year may not have been available at press time.

In U.S. $	2017	2016	2015	2014	2013	2012
Revenue		84,322,410,000	92,743,370,000	129,277,100,000	75,037,690,000	68,198,630,000
R&D Expense						
Operating Income		6,761,592,000	7,513,115,000	7,961,955,000	6,794,409,000	6,894,790,000
Operating Margin %		8.01%	8.10%	6.15%	9.05%	10.10%
SGA Expense		3,164,378,000	2,720,959,000	3,459,536,000	2,041,824,000	1,840,081,000
Net Income		3,335,990,000	4,696,574,000	4,255,821,000	4,154,732,000	5,392,343,000
Operating Cash Flow		12,135,210,000	13,695,570,000	13,960,100,000	8,725,893,000	9,309,191,000
Capital Expenditure		8,060,795,000	9,700,542,000	13,130,630,000	8,384,793,000	6,158,758,000
EBITDA		10,072,560,000	12,650,060,000	14,549,240,000	8,860,105,000	9,356,235,000
Return on Assets %		4.12%	5.18%	5.37%	7.79%	11.28%
Return on Equity %		6.41%	7.53%	7.43%	10.71%	15.23%
Debt to Equity		0.19	0.24	0.14	0.12	0.08

CONTACT INFORMATION:
Phone: 7 4956274444   Fax: 7 4956257016
Toll-Free:
Address: 11 Sretensky Blvd., Moscow, 101000 Russia

STOCK TICKER/OTHER:
Stock Ticker: LUKOY
Employees: 105,500
Parent Company:

Exchange: PINX
Fiscal Year Ends: 12/31

SALARIES/BONUSES:
Top Exec. Salary: $ Bonus: $
Second Exec. Salary: $ Bonus: $

OTHER THOUGHTS:
Estimated Female Officers or Directors: 1
Hot Spot for Advancement for Women/Minorities:

Sales, profits and employees may be estimates. Financial information, benefits and other data can change quickly and may vary from those stated here.

Oracle Corporation

NAIC Code: 0

www.oracle.com

TYPES OF BUSINESS:
Computer Software, Data Base & File Management
e-Business Applications Software
Internet-Based Software
Consulting Services
Human Resources Management Software
CRM Software
Middleware

BRANDS/DIVISIONS/AFFILIATES:
Moat
Apiary
Wercker

CONTACTS: Note: Officers with more than one job title may be intentionally listed here more than once.
Lawrence Ellison, Chairman of the Board
William West, Chief Accounting Officer
Mark Hurd, Co-CEO
Safra Catz, Co-CEO
Jeffrey Henley, Director
Dorian Daley, Executive VP
Thomas Kurian, President, Divisional

GROWTH PLANS/SPECIAL FEATURES:
Oracle Corporation is a leading enterprise software company, providing hardware products and services to over 400,000 customers throughout the world. The firm markets its integrated hardware and software systems directly to corporations. Oracle's products can be categorized into three broad areas: cloud and on-premises software, hardware systems and services. The cloud and on-premise software business represents 80% of total 2017 fiscal revenues, and includes the cloud software-as-a-service (SaaS), platform-as-a-service and internet-as-a-service offerings; and the on-premise software license offerings, license updates and product support offerings. Hardware systems (11%) is comprised of hardware systems products and hardware systems support services for on-premise IT environments. Its Oracle engineered systems are core to the firm's on-premise and cloud-based infrastructure offerings, and are pre-integrated products designed to integrate multiple Oracle technology components in order to work together to deliver enhanced performance, availability, security and operational efficiency relative to the customer's products. Services (9%) offers consulting services, enhanced support services and education services. During 2017, the firm acquired Moat, an always-on mobile we analytics application; Apiary, which creates a comprehensive API integration cloud; and Wercker, a software firm that helps developers build and deploy applications and microservices. That December, it agreed to acquire Aconex Limited, a provider of mobile and web-based collaboration technologies.

Oracle offers employees a 401(k) plan; employee assistance and employee stock purchase plans; and a Live and Work Well program.

FINANCIAL DATA: Note: Data for latest year may not have been available at press time.

In U.S. $	2017	2016	2015	2014	2013	2012
Revenue	37,728,000,000	37,047,000,000	38,226,000,000	38,275,000,000	37,180,000,000	37,121,000,000
R&D Expense	6,159,000,000	5,787,000,000	5,524,000,000	5,151,000,000	4,850,000,000	4,523,000,000
Operating Income	13,276,000,000	13,104,000,000	14,289,000,000	14,983,000,000	14,432,000,000	14,057,000,000
Operating Margin %	35.18%	35.37%	37.38%	39.14%	38.81%	37.86%
SGA Expense	9,373,000,000	9,039,000,000	8,732,000,000	8,605,000,000	8,400,000,000	8,253,000,000
Net Income	9,335,000,000	8,901,000,000	9,938,000,000	10,955,000,000	10,925,000,000	9,981,000,000
Operating Cash Flow	14,126,000,000	13,561,000,000	14,336,000,000	14,921,000,000	14,224,000,000	13,743,000,000
Capital Expenditure	2,021,000,000	1,189,000,000	1,391,000,000	580,000,000	650,000,000	648,000,000
EBITDA	15,766,000,000	15,418,000,000	16,838,000,000	17,526,000,000	17,626,000,000	16,644,000,000
Return on Assets %	7.55%	7.98%	9.87%	12.72%	13.64%	13.14%
Return on Equity %	18.45%	18.55%	20.80%	23.93%	24.73%	23.91%
Debt to Equity	0.89	0.84	0.82	0.48	0.41	0.30

CONTACT INFORMATION:
Phone: 650 506-7000   Fax: 650 506-7200
Toll-Free: 800-392-2999
Address: 500 Oracle Pkwy., Redwood City, CA 94065 United States

STOCK TICKER/OTHER:
Stock Ticker: ORCL   Exchange: NYS
Employees: 138,000   Fiscal Year Ends: 05/31
Parent Company:

SALARIES/BONUSES:
Top Exec. Salary: $950,000   Bonus: $
Second Exec. Salary: $950,000   Bonus: $

OTHER THOUGHTS:
Estimated Female Officers or Directors: 6
Hot Spot for Advancement for Women/Minorities: Y

Sales, profits and employees may be estimates. Financial information, benefits and other data can change quickly and may vary from those stated here.

Oriental Consultants Global Co Ltd

NAIC Code: 541330

www.ocglobal.jp

TYPES OF BUSINESS:
Engineering Consulting Services
Consulting
Engineering

BRANDS/DIVISIONS/AFFILIATES:
ACKG Ltd

CONTACTS: *Note: Officers with more than one job title may be intentionally listed here more than once.*
Eiji Yonezawa, Pres.

GROWTH PLANS/SPECIAL FEATURES:
Oriental Consultants Global Co. Ltd., a wholly-owned subsidiary of ACKG Ltd., provides consulting services for sustainable development worldwide in approximately 150 countries. The firm offers sustainable consulting services in a broad range of areas. The urban and regional planning/social policy services include city scape planning, formulation of master plans for development as well as feasibility studies, regional design management, implementation and maintenance, policy evaluation and economic analysis. The transportation services include analyzing impacts of developing projects, analysis for reducing traffic congestion and conducting traffic surveys. The development of renewable energy/environment management services consists of installation of solar, small hydraulic and wind power energy generation facilities, environmental assessments documentation and field surveys. The landscapes services include development plans, structural design and landscape designs to conserve regional resources. The tourism planning services encompasses market research, participatory workshops, tourism promotion, tourist facility planning, and feasibility studies. The roads and expressways services include development safe road construction plans as well as infrastructures, such as bridges, tunnels and underground structures. Maintenance services are offered for aging tunnels, roads, bridges including inspection and monitoring surveys, seismic strengthening designs and investigations for asset management. Disaster management services consists of tsunami simulations, prevention, evaluation, countermeasures, disaster reconstruction and risk management. Water management services include flood control measures, such as bank protection and construction of levees, developing forecasting, warning and information dissemination systems, river patrol systems, as well as relief and evacuation schemes. The port and harbors services include planning, maintenance, designing and reconstruction of ports, fishery and related facilities. Planning, design, development and maintenance services are also offered for rail transport, including intercity rail links, high-speed trains, subways, light rail transits and monorails; and airports and air traffic control systems.

FINANCIAL DATA: *Note: Data for latest year may not have been available at press time.*

In U.S. $	2017	2016	2015	2014	2013	2012
Revenue						
R&D Expense						
Operating Income						
Operating Margin %						
SGA Expense						
Net Income						
Operating Cash Flow						
Capital Expenditure						
EBITDA						
Return on Assets %						
Return on Equity %						
Debt to Equity						

CONTACT INFORMATION:
Phone: 81-3-6311-7551   Fax: 81-3-6311-8011
Toll-Free:
Address: Tokyo Opera City Tower 9F, 20-2, Nishishinjuku 3-chome, Shinjuku-ku, Tokyo, 151-0071 Japan

STOCK TICKER/OTHER:
Stock Ticker: Subsidiary   Exchange:
Employees: 426   Fiscal Year Ends:
Parent Company: ACKG Ltd

SALARIES/BONUSES:
Top Exec. Salary: $ Bonus: $
Second Exec. Salary: $ Bonus: $

OTHER THOUGHTS:
Estimated Female Officers or Directors:
Hot Spot for Advancement for Women/Minorities:

Sales, profits and employees may be estimates. Financial information, benefits and other data can change quickly and may vary from those stated here.

PACCAR Inc

NAIC Code: 336120

www.paccar.com

TYPES OF BUSINESS:
Truck Manufacturing
Premium Truck Manufacturer
Parts Distribution
Finance, Lease and Insurance Services

BRANDS/DIVISIONS/AFFILIATES:
Kenworth Truck Company
DAF Trucks
Peterbilt Motors
PACCAR Financial Services
Carco
Braden
Gearmatic

CONTACTS: Note: Officers with more than one job title may be intentionally listed here more than once.
Ronald Armstrong, CEO
Douglas Grandstaff, VP
Harrie Schippers, CFO
Mark Pigott, Chairman of the Board
Michael Barkley, Chief Accounting Officer
A Ley, Chief Information Officer
Gary Moore, Executive VP
T. Quinn, General Manager, Divisional
Michael Dozier, General Manager, Subsidiary
Preston Feight, President, Subsidiary
Darrin Siver, Senior VP
Robert Bengston, Senior VP, Divisional
Marco Davila, Vice President
Jack LeVier, Vice President, Divisional

GROWTH PLANS/SPECIAL FEATURES:
PACCAR, Inc. is a leading manufacturer of premium light-, medium- and heavy-duty trucks. The firm operates in three major divisions: trucks, parts and financial services. Truck division subsidiaries include Kenworth Truck Company, Peterbilt Motors and DAF Trucks. The vehicles are used worldwide for over-the-road and off-highway hauling of freight, petroleum, wood products, construction and other materials. The Kenworth and Peterbilt nameplates are manufactured and distributed by separate divisions in the U.S. and foreign plants in Canada, Mexico and Australia. Headquartered in the Netherlands, DAF Trucks comprises the European component of PACCAR, with distribution throughout Europe, Asia and Africa. Products and services are available worldwide, with customer call centers operating continuously. Substantially all trucks and related parts are sold to independent dealers, and this division accounts for 76% of net sales. The parts division includes the distribution of aftermarket parts for trucks and related commercial vehicles in the U.S., Canada, Europe, Australia, Mexico and South America. Aftermarket truck parts are sold and delivered to the company's independent dealers through the firm's 17 strategically-located distribution centers. The parts segment accounts for 17% of net sales. The company's financial services segment (7% of net sales), which operates through wholly-owned subsidiary PACCAR Financial Services, maintains a presence in over 24 countries. This division provides financing and leasing arrangements, mainly for its manufactured trucks. The company's share of the U.S. and Canadian Class 8 truck market is roughly 28.5%. In addition, other businesses (less than 1% of net sales) consists of a manufacturing division, which makes industrial winches in two U.S. plants and markets them under the Braden, Carco and Gearmatic nameplates.

FINANCIAL DATA: Note: Data for latest year may not have been available at press time.

In U.S. $	2017	2016	2015	2014	2013	2012
Revenue	19,456,400,000	1,186,700,000	18,671,300,000	18,534,400,000	16,661,000,000	16,596,800,000
R&D Expense	264,700,000	247,200,000	239,800,000	215,600,000	251,400,000	279,300,000
Operating Income	2,293,200,000	-13,772,000,000	2,001,800,000	1,671,900,000	1,364,800,000	1,300,200,000
Operating Margin %	11.78%	-1160.52%	10.72%	9.02%	8.19%	7.83%
SGA Expense	555,000,000	540,200,000	541,500,000	561,400,000	559,500,000	571,600,000
Net Income	1,675,200,000	521,700,000	1,604,000,000	1,358,800,000	1,171,300,000	1,111,600,000
Operating Cash Flow	2,715,800,000	2,300,800,000	2,556,000,000	2,123,600,000	2,375,700,000	1,519,000,000
Capital Expenditure	1,846,600,000	1,964,900,000	1,725,200,000	1,537,300,000	1,872,800,000	1,803,400,000
EBITDA	3,436,000,000	2,262,300,000	3,374,500,000	3,074,500,000	2,666,900,000	2,488,200,000
Return on Assets %	7.60%	2.49%	7.68%	6.57%	5.95%	6.21%
Return on Equity %	22.59%	7.60%	23.42%	20.29%	18.76%	19.83%
Debt to Equity	0.73	0.88	0.83	0.82	0.90	0.77

CONTACT INFORMATION:
Phone: 425 468-7400   Fax: 425 468-8216
Toll-Free:
Address: 777 106th Ave. NE, Bellevue, WA 98004 United States

STOCK TICKER/OTHER:
Stock Ticker: PCAR
Employees: 23,000
Parent Company:

Exchange: NAS
Fiscal Year Ends: 12/31

SALARIES/BONUSES:
Top Exec. Salary: $1,347,308   Bonus: $
Second Exec. Salary: $697,116   Bonus: $

OTHER THOUGHTS:
Estimated Female Officers or Directors:
Hot Spot for Advancement for Women/Minorities:

Sales, profits and employees may be estimates. Financial information, benefits and other data can change quickly and may vary from those stated here.

Page Southerland Page Inc

pagethink.com

NAIC Code: 541330

TYPES OF BUSINESS:
Engineering Consulting Services

BRANDS/DIVISIONS/AFFILIATES:

GROWTH PLANS/SPECIAL FEATURES:
Page Southerland Page, Inc. is a multidisciplinary architecture and engineering firm with offices in the U.S., and abroad. The firm's work has primarily consisted of complex projects that integrate its disciplines. Services offered by Page include architecture, engineering, interiors, planning and consulting in the fields of sustainability, branding, commissioning and programming. Core markets the firm has worked in include academic, civic/government, corporate/commercial, healthcare, housing/hospitality, science and technology.

CONTACTS:
Note: Officers with more than one job title may be intentionally listed here more than once.

Arturo Chavez, Sr. Principle
Robert E. Burke, Sr. Principle
Mattia J. Flabiano III, Senior Principle
Thomas McCarthy, Sr. Principle
Lawrence W. Speck, Sr. Principle
Michael J. Mace, Sr. Principle
John N. Cryer, Chmn.

FINANCIAL DATA:
Note: Data for latest year may not have been available at press time.

In U.S. $	2017	2016	2015	2014	2013	2012
Revenue	147,000,000	141,390,000	121,980,000	100,000,000	99,750,000	
R&D Expense						
Operating Income						
Operating Margin %						
SGA Expense						
Net Income						
Operating Cash Flow						
Capital Expenditure						
EBITDA						
Return on Assets %						
Return on Equity %						
Debt to Equity						

CONTACT INFORMATION:
Phone: 713-871-8484 Fax:
Toll-Free:
Address: 1100 Louisiana, Ste. One, Houston, TX 77002 United States

STOCK TICKER/OTHER:
Stock Ticker: Private   Exchange:
Employees: 400   Fiscal Year Ends:
Parent Company:

SALARIES/BONUSES:
Top Exec. Salary: $ Bonus: $
Second Exec. Salary: $ Bonus: $

OTHER THOUGHTS:
Estimated Female Officers or Directors:
Hot Spot for Advancement for Women/Minorities:

Sales, profits and employees may be estimates. Financial information, benefits and other data can change quickly and may vary from those stated here.

Palo Alto Research Center Incorporated (PARC)

www.parc.com

NAIC Code: 541712

TYPES OF BUSINESS:
Research & Development-Office Technology
Computing
Software
Networks
Materials Science
Renewable Energy Technology
Biomedical Science
Environmental Technologies

BRANDS/DIVISIONS/AFFILIATES:
Xerox Corporation

CONTACTS:
Note: Officers with more than one job title may be intentionally listed here more than once.

Tolga Kurtoglu, CEO
Rob McHenry, COO
Mats Bergstrom, CFO
Russell Williams, VP-Human Resources
Walt Johnson, VP-Intelligent Systems Laboratory
Mike Steep, Sr. VP-Global Bus. Oper.
John Pauksta, VP-Finance
Rob McHenry, VP-Public Sector Oper.
Scott Elrod, VP-Hardware Systems Laboratory
Teresa Lunt, VP

GROWTH PLANS/SPECIAL FEATURES:

Palo Alto Research Center Incorporated (PARC) is a research and development (R&D) firm owned and operated by Xerox Corporation. The company practices open innovation, and provides custom R&D services, technology, expertise, best practices and intellectual to Fortune 500 and Global 1000 companies, startups and government agencies and partners. PARC's services and solutions create new business options, accelerate time to market and reduces risk for its clients. They also enhance internal capabilities and help clients overcome the barriers between ideation and implementation. The firm engages in co-developing technology, customizing technology, creating/discovering offerings from the ground up, enables access to missing or specialized expertise and intellectual property, and enables access to capital-intensive infrastructure. PARC'S current focus areas include big data, biomedical devices, clean water, cleantech and energy, content-centric networking, health and wellness, innovation services, intelligent automation, intelligent software systems, optics, optoelectronics and printed and flexible electronics. The company is comprised of 180 physical, computer and social scientists and engineers, as well as staff from approximately 35 countries.

Xerox employees receive benefits including paid holidays, health care, life insurance, retirement savings plans, employee assistance programs and child and elder care resources.

FINANCIAL DATA:
Note: Data for latest year may not have been available at press time.

In U.S. $	2017	2016	2015	2014	2013	2012
Revenue						
R&D Expense						
Operating Income						
Operating Margin %						
SGA Expense						
Net Income						
Operating Cash Flow						
Capital Expenditure						
EBITDA						
Return on Assets %						
Return on Equity %						
Debt to Equity						

CONTACT INFORMATION:
Phone: 650-812-4000 Fax: 650-812-4028
Toll-Free:
Address: 3333 Coyote Hill Rd., Palo Alto, CA 94304 United States

SALARIES/BONUSES:
Top Exec. Salary: $ Bonus: $
Second Exec. Salary: $ Bonus: $

STOCK TICKER/OTHER:
Stock Ticker: Subsidiary
Employees: 175
Parent Company: Xerox Corporation

Exchange:
Fiscal Year Ends: 12/31

OTHER THOUGHTS:
Estimated Female Officers or Directors: 1
Hot Spot for Advancement for Women/Minorities: Y

Sales, profits and employees may be estimates. Financial information, benefits and other data can change quickly and may vary from those stated here.

Panasonic Corporation

www.panasonic.com

NAIC Code: 334310

TYPES OF BUSINESS:
Audio & Video Equipment, Manufacturing
Lithium Rechargeable Batteries
Home Appliances
Electronic Components
Cellular Phones
Medical Equipment
Photovoltaic Equipment
Telecommunications Equipment

BRANDS/DIVISIONS/AFFILIATES:
PanaHome
Technics
Panasonic System Solutions Co North America
Connected Solutions Company of North America
Panasonic System Communications Co North America
Panasonic Media Entertainment Company
Panasonic Factory Solutions Company of America

CONTACTS:
Note: Officers with more than one job title may be intentionally listed here more than once.

Kazuhiro Tsuga, Pres.
Shusaku Nagae, Chmn.

GROWTH PLANS/SPECIAL FEATURES:
Panasonic Corporation produces consumer, professional and industrial electronics products under brand names such as Panasonic, Technics and PanaHome. The company owns 496 consolidated companies around the world and operates in four business segments: Appliances Company, Eco Solutions Company, Connected Solutions Company and Automotive & Industrial Systems Company. The Appliances Company develops and manufactures home appliances, personal-care products, consumer electronics as well as commercial-use heating/refrigeration/air-conditioning equipment. The Eco Solutions Company develops, manufactures and sells lighting fixtures, lamps, lighting devices, wiring devices, distribution panelboards, housing-related materials and equipment, solar photovoltaic power generation systems, storage batteries, ventilation fans, and nursing care equipment and services as well as the provision of business solutions in various areas. The Connected Solutions Company focuses on the development, manufacturing and sales of products as well as system integration, installation, support and maintenance in the areas of aviation, manufacturing, entertainment, retail and logistics. The Automotive & Industrial Systems Company is engaged in the development, manufacture and sales of automotive infotainment and electronics products (such as car-use-multimedia-related equipment and electrical components), energy products (such as lithium-ion batteries and primary batteries) and industrial devices (such as electronic components, electromechanical control components, electronic materials, semiconductors, display and electric motors). In January 2018, Panasonic announced the establishment of Panasonic System Solutions Company of North America, which will consolidate four existing divisions of Panasonic Corporation of North America: Connected Solutions Company North America; Panasonic System Communications Company of North America, a provider of security camera systems, ruggedized personal computers and POS systems; Panasonic Media Entertainment Company, which provides projectors, broadcast-use cameras and other products to the entertainment industry; and Panasonic Factory Solutions Company of America, whose products include surface mounted machines for circuit board manufacturing, welding robots and factory systems management software.

FINANCIAL DATA:
Note: Data for latest year may not have been available at press time.

In U.S. $	2017	2016	2015	2014	2013	2012
Revenue	68,415,390,000	70,371,880,000	71,874,760,000	72,075,100,000	68,036,570,000	73,096,860,000
R&D Expense						4,846,441,000
Operating Income	3,201,193,000	3,872,825,000	3,557,975,000	2,842,501,000	1,499,311,000	407,350,500
Operating Margin %	4.67%	5.50%	4.95%	3.94%	2.20%	.55%
SGA Expense	17,169,070,000	16,750,600,000	16,824,210,000	16,699,810,000	16,044,540,000	10,793,960,000
Net Income	1,391,466,000	1,800,410,000	1,672,117,000	1,122,061,000	-7,026,738,000	-7,193,703,000
Operating Cash Flow	3,590,554,000	3,714,179,000	4,578,564,000	5,421,558,000	3,155,860,000	-343,683,600
Capital Expenditure	3,184,405,000	2,252,991,000	2,088,336,000	1,879,402,000	2,982,747,000	4,252,543,000
EBITDA	5,304,481,000	4,740,228,000	4,532,793,000	5,209,791,000	-311,328,500	-4,158,077,000
Return on Assets %	2.57%	3.34%	3.21%	2.27%	-12.57%	-10.70%
Return on Equity %	9.11%	10.95%	10.64%	8.56%	-47.23%	-34.40%
Debt to Equity	0.60	0.41	0.39	0.36	0.52	0.48

CONTACT INFORMATION:
Phone: 81 669081121   Fax:
Toll-Free:
Address: 1006 Oaza Kadoma, Kadoma City, Osaka, 571-8501 Japan

STOCK TICKER/OTHER:
Stock Ticker: PCRFF   Exchange: PINX
Employees: 271,789   Fiscal Year Ends: 03/31
Parent Company:

SALARIES/BONUSES:
Top Exec. Salary: $ Bonus: $
Second Exec. Salary: $ Bonus: $

OTHER THOUGHTS:
Estimated Female Officers or Directors:
Hot Spot for Advancement for Women/Minorities:

Sales, profits and employees may be estimates. Financial information, benefits and other data can change quickly and may vary from those stated here.

PAREXEL International Corporation

www.parexel.com

NAIC Code: 541711

TYPES OF BUSINESS:
Clinical Trial & Data Management
Biostatistical Analysis & Reporting
Medical Communications Services
Clinical Pharmacology Services
Consulting Services

BRANDS/DIVISIONS/AFFILIATES:
Pamplona Capital Management LLP
PAREXEL Access

CONTACTS:
Note: Officers with more than one job title may be intentionally listed here more than once.

Jamie Macdonald, CFO
Sybrand Pretorius, Chief Scientific Officer
Simon Harford, Sr. VP
Michele Fournier, VP-Interim Human Resources
Josef Von Rickenbach, Founder
Michelle Graham, Other Executive Officer
Xavier Flinois, President, Divisional
Gadi Saarony, Senior VP, Divisional
Roland Andersson, Senior VP, Divisional
Joshua Schultz, Senior VP, Divisional
David Godwin, Senior VP, Divisional
Douglas Batt, Senior VP

GROWTH PLANS/SPECIAL FEATURES:
PAREXEL International Corporation is a leading biopharmaceutical outsourcing services company. The firm provides comprehensive drug development capabilities, including phase I-IV clinical research services, integrated eClinical technologies and advanced commercialization services. Operating in more than 80 locations throughout 51 countries, PAREXEL has four business segments: clinical research, informatics, consulting and PAREXEL Access. The clinical research segment offers the following solutions and services: early phase, phase I-IV, ForeSite clinical trial methodology, global data operations, medical writing, quantitative clinical development, clinical trial supplies/logistics, customer care services, genomic medicine and clinical adjudication. The informatics segment offers the following solutions and services: regulatory and clinical technology, patient technology, clinical trial supplies/logistics, Perceptive cloud, asset transfer, PAREXEL's education services and customer care services. The consulting segment offers: integrated product development, regulatory compliance, risk management, regulatory outsourcing, regulatory information management, IDMP (identification of medicinal products) solutions and market access consulting. Last, the PAREXEL Access segment provides a simplified and complete solution that can help identify, generate, evaluate and communicate the evidence of product value, which helps accelerate time to market, de-risk the reimbursement and market access process. Access' services include real world evidence, drug safety services, market access consulting, medical communications and outsourced field-based medical teams. In September 2017, PAREXEL was taken private by Pamplona Capital Management, LLP.

FINANCIAL DATA:
Note: Data for latest year may not have been available at press time.

In U.S. $	2017	2016	2015	2014	2013	2012
Revenue	2,500,000,000	2,426,299,904	2,330,274,048	2,266,341,888	1,995,965,952	1,618,233,984
R&D Expense						
Operating Income						
Operating Margin %						
SGA Expense						
Net Income		154,900,000	147,820,992	129,094,000	95,972,000	63,158,000
Operating Cash Flow						
Capital Expenditure						
EBITDA						
Return on Assets %						
Return on Equity %						
Debt to Equity						

CONTACT INFORMATION:
Phone: 781 487-9900
Fax: 781 487-0525
Toll-Free:
Address: 195 West St., Waltham, MA 02451 United States

STOCK TICKER/OTHER:
Stock Ticker: Private
Employees: 18,660
Parent Company: Pamplona Capital Management LLP
Exchange:
Fiscal Year Ends: 06/30

SALARIES/BONUSES:
Top Exec. Salary: $
Bonus: $
Second Exec. Salary: $
Bonus: $

OTHER THOUGHTS:
Estimated Female Officers or Directors: 1
Hot Spot for Advancement for Women/Minorities: Y

Parsons Corporation

www.parsons.com

NAIC Code: 541330

TYPES OF BUSINESS:
Civil Engineering
Construction Management
Facility Operations and Maintenance
Environmental Services
Analytical, Technical and Training Services
Transportation Infrastructure Project Design and Construction

BRANDS/DIVISIONS/AFFILIATES:
Williams Electric Company Inc

CONTACTS: Note: Officers with more than one job title may be intentionally listed here more than once.
Charles L. Harrington, CEO
Michael Loose, Sr. VP-Oper.
George L. Ball, CFO
Charles L. Harrington, Chmn.

GROWTH PLANS/SPECIAL FEATURES:
Parsons Corporation is an employee-owned engineering, construction, technical and professional services firm. The company offers design, design-build, program/construction management, and other professional services to federal, regional and local government agencies as well as to private industrial customers worldwide. Parsons' solutions include asset management, construction, construction engineering, inspection, cybersecurity, disaster response, intelligent transportation systems, mission support, planning, positive train control, smart cities, technology, toll services, traffic incident management, vehicle inspection and vehicle compliance. The firm has expertise in relation to airports, environmental builds, environment, communications, defense, energy, chemicals, infrastructure, intelligence, ports & harbors, rail transit systems, roads, bridges, tunnels, security, water and wastewater. Parsons is headquartered in Pasadena, California, but has additional offices throughout the U.S., Bahrain, Canada, France, Hong Kong, Oman, Qatar, Saudi Arabia, Turkey, United Arab Emirates, the U.K. and Ireland. In October 2017, the firm acquired Williams Electric Company, Inc., a privately-held company specializing in control system integration, electrical and general contracting, and energy infrastructure solutions.

Parsons offers its employees medical and life insurance, tuition reimbursement, an ESOP for eligible employees, a 401(k) and membership to a Federal Credit Union.

FINANCIAL DATA: Note: Data for latest year may not have been available at press time.

In U.S. $	2017	2016	2015	2014	2013	2012
Revenue	3,016,000,000	3,039,000,000	3,219,000,000	3,098,000,000	2,992,000,000	3,001,000,000
R&D Expense						
Operating Income						
Operating Margin %						
SGA Expense						
Net Income	156,000,000	144,000,000	164,000,000	159,000,000	144,000,000	143,000,000
Operating Cash Flow						
Capital Expenditure						
EBITDA						
Return on Assets %						
Return on Equity %						
Debt to Equity						

CONTACT INFORMATION:
Phone: 626-440-2000 Fax: 626-440-2630
Toll-Free:
Address: 100 W. Walnut St., Pasadena, CA 91124 United States

STOCK TICKER/OTHER:
Stock Ticker: Private
Employees: 14,000
Parent Company:

Exchange:
Fiscal Year Ends:

SALARIES/BONUSES:
Top Exec. Salary: $ Bonus: $
Second Exec. Salary: $ Bonus: $

OTHER THOUGHTS:
Estimated Female Officers or Directors:
Hot Spot for Advancement for Women/Minorities:

Sales, profits and employees may be estimates. Financial information, benefits and other data can change quickly and may vary from those stated here.

Paul C Rizzo Associates Inc

www.rizzoassoc.com

NAIC Code: 541330

TYPES OF BUSINESS:
Engineering Consulting Services

BRANDS/DIVISIONS/AFFILIATES:
Rizzo Associates Czech a s
Nuclear Structural Engineering Pty Ltd
Fall Line Testing & inspection LLC

CONTACTS:
Note: Officers with more than one job title may be intentionally listed here more than once.

Paul C. Rizzo, Chmn.

GROWTH PLANS/SPECIAL FEATURES:
Paul C. Rizzo Associates, Inc. specializes in all aspects of civil engineering and earth science fields for the power generation, dam, mining, infrastructure and tunneling markets. Rizzo's services include: engineering design, construction management, nuclear power plant siting studies, seismology, specialty structures, geotechnology, geophysics, hydraulic engineering, health/safety, hydrology, RAM (reliability, availability and maintainability) and more. Projects of the firm include dams and water resources, power generation, tunneling, mining, infrastructure and specialty markets. Rizzo is headquartered in Pennsylvania, U.S., with locations throughout the U.S., and internationally such as Peru, Chile, UAE, Australia, Czech Republic, Italy, the U.K. and Russia. Subsidiaries of the firm include: Rizzo Associates Czech, a.s., which offers seismic and structural related services; Nuclear Structural Engineering Pty, Ltd., which provides specialized structural engineering services; and Fall Line Testing & inspection, LLC, which offers construction materials testing.

FINANCIAL DATA:
Note: Data for latest year may not have been available at press time.

In U.S. $	2017	2016	2015	2014	2013	2012
Revenue						
R&D Expense						
Operating Income						
Operating Margin %						
SGA Expense						
Net Income						
Operating Cash Flow						
Capital Expenditure						
EBITDA						
Return on Assets %						
Return on Equity %						
Debt to Equity						

CONTACT INFORMATION:
Phone: 412-856-9700 Fax: 412-856-9749
Toll-Free:
Address: 500 Penn Center Blvd., Pittsburgh, PA 15214 United States

STOCK TICKER/OTHER:
Stock Ticker: Private   Exchange:
Employees: Fiscal Year Ends:
Parent Company:

SALARIES/BONUSES:
Top Exec. Salary: $ Bonus: $
Second Exec. Salary: $ Bonus: $

OTHER THOUGHTS:
Estimated Female Officers or Directors:
Hot Spot for Advancement for Women/Minorities:

PCL Construction Group Inc

www.pcl.com

NAIC Code: 237000

TYPES OF BUSINESS:
Heavy Construction
Financial and Accounting Reporting
Development, Support and Project Management
Engineering Services

BRANDS/DIVISIONS/AFFILIATES:
Melloy Industrial Services Inc
PCL Energy Inc
PCL Civil Constructors Inc
PCL Industrial Services Inc
PCL Constructors Pacific Rim Pty Ltd
PCL Constructors Bahamas Ltd

CONTACTS:
Note: Officers with more than one job title may be intentionally listed here more than once.

Dave Filipchuk, CEO
Gordon Panas, CFO
Steve Richards, General Counsel
Lee Clayton, VP-Global Strategic Initiatives
Gordon Stephenson, VP-Corp. Finance
Luis Ventoza, COO-Civil Infrastructure
Ian Johnson, COO-Heavy Industrial
Rob Hoimberg, COO-Buildings
Paul Douglas, Chmn.

GROWTH PLANS/SPECIAL FEATURES:

PCL Construction Group, Inc., founded in 1906, is an employee-owned group of construction companies throughout Canada, Australia, the U.S. and the Caribbean. The firm focuses on three main areas of construction: buildings construction, civil infrastructure and heavy industrial. The buildings construction segment conducts projects throughout North America and is able to work on an array of projects including commercial; institutional; educational; residential; adaptive reuse, which entails upgrading and converting an existing facility; cultural consideration, including onsite and on-the-job employment and training opportunities; green building; high-tech projects, for meeting cleanliness protocols in the medical, biotech and research working environments; and historical preservation, including repair, exterior masonry and renovations combining typical construction methods with scenic construction technology. PCL's building operations include larger projects, such as airports, sports facilities and office towers, and smaller projects, such as renovations, restorations and repairs. The civil infrastructure segment undertakes various civil structure projects including bridges, overpasses, tunnels, interchanges, water treatment facilities and light rail transportation projects. The heavy industrial division offers construction assistance to the petrochemical, oil and gas, pulp and paper, mining and power and generation industries. Subsidiaries include Melloy Industrial Services, Inc.; PCL Energy, Inc.; PCL Civil Constructors, Inc.; PCL Industrial Services, Inc.; PCL Constructors Pacific Rim Pty Ltd.; and PCL Constructors Bahamas Ltd.

The firm offers employees medical, vision and dental insurance; flexible spending accounts; a prescription drug plan; a 401(k); a profit sharing bonus; and an employee assistance program.

FINANCIAL DATA:
Note: Data for latest year may not have been available at press time.

In U.S. $	2017	2016	2015	2014	2013	2012
Revenue	8,250,000,000	8,200,000,000	7,232,900,000	7,300,000,000	7,500,000,000	
R&D Expense						
Operating Income						
Operating Margin %						
SGA Expense						
Net Income						
Operating Cash Flow						
Capital Expenditure						
EBITDA						
Return on Assets %						
Return on Equity %						
Debt to Equity						

CONTACT INFORMATION:
Phone: 780-733-5000 Fax: 780-733-5075
Toll-Free:
Address: 9915 56th Ave. NW, Edmonton, AB T6E 5L7 Canada

STOCK TICKER/OTHER:
Stock Ticker: Private
Employees: 4,500
Parent Company:

Exchange:
Fiscal Year Ends:

SALARIES/BONUSES:
Top Exec. Salary: $ Bonus: $
Second Exec. Salary: $ Bonus: $

OTHER THOUGHTS:
Estimated Female Officers or Directors:
Hot Spot for Advancement for Women/Minorities:

Sales, profits and employees may be estimates. Financial information, benefits and other data can change quickly and may vary from those stated here.

Petrobras (Petroleo Brasileiro SA)

NAIC Code: 211111

www.petrobras.com.br

TYPES OF BUSINESS:
Oil & Gas Exploration & Production
Oil Refineries
Service Stations
Transportation & Pipelines
Energy Trading

BRANDS/DIVISIONS/AFFILIATES:
Petrobras
Petrobras Distribuidora SA

CONTACTS:
Note: Officers with more than one job title may be intentionally listed here more than once.

Pedro Parente, CEO
Ivan de Souza, CFO
Hugo Repsold Junior, Human Resources Director

GROWTH PLANS/SPECIAL FEATURES:

Petroleo Brasileiro SA, known as Petrobras, is owned largely by the Brazilian government and is one of the world's largest energy companies. It refines, produces and distributes oil and oil-based products both nationally and internationally. Petrobras serves sectors such as exploration and production, refining, marketing, transportation, petrochemicals, oil; and natural gas, electricity, gas and chemical biofuels. The firm divides company activities into eight business sectors. Oil and gas exploration and production researches, identifies, develops, produces and incorporates oil and natural gas reserves in Brazil. It currently produces roughly 2.14 million barrels of oil per day. The refining business includes 13 oil refineries. Transportation and trade includes the firm's oil and liquid natural gas (LNG) pipeline and tanker business. Distribution, operated through subsidiary Petrobras Distribuidora SA, distributes petroleum byproducts in Brazil through roughly 8,176 service stations. Petrochemicals and fertilizers produces paraffins and naphtha for use in a variety of applications, including plastics, paints and cosmetics. In addition, it converts natural gas to urea, ammonia and other products to be used as feedstock in various industries. Biofuel production produces biodiesel and ethanol from four plants, two are owned and two are in partnerships. Renewable energy generation capacity is equivalent to 25.4 megawatts (MW) of hydroelectric power, 1.1 MW of solar capacity and 105.8 MW of wind capacity. These assets are owned or in joint venture partnerships. Natural gas supply is offered to the Brazilian market from one of three terminals of Petrobras: Pecem, Bay of All Saints or Guanabara Bay. Petrobas' portfolio also consists of 184 ship vessels (56 owned), 20 thermoelectric plants and three fertilizer factories. In December 2017, the firm began the binding phase of the sale process of its 90% interest in Transportadora Associada de Gas (TAG).

FINANCIAL DATA:
Note: Data for latest year may not have been available at press time.

In U.S. $	2017	2016	2015	2014	2013	2012
Revenue		81,405,000,000	97,314,000,000	143,657,000,000	141,462,000,000	144,103,000,000
R&D Expense		523,000,000	630,000,000	1,099,000,000	1,132,000,000	1,143,000,000
Operating Income		14,932,000,000	16,514,000,000	17,486,000,000	18,451,000,000	19,187,000,000
Operating Margin %		18.34%	16.96%	12.17%	13.04%	13.31%
SGA Expense		7,282,000,000	7,978,000,000	11,777,000,000	9,886,000,000	11,859,000,000
Net Income		-4,838,000,000	-8,450,000,000	-7,367,000,000	11,094,000,000	11,034,000,000
Operating Cash Flow		26,114,000,000	25,913,000,000	26,632,000,000	26,289,000,000	27,888,000,000
Capital Expenditure		14,085,000,000	21,653,000,000	34,808,000,000	45,110,000,000	
EBITDA		16,553,000,000	6,928,000,000	7,333,000,000	29,271,000,000	27,628,000,000
Return on Assets %		-2.02%	-3.18%	-2.37%	3.39%	3.38%
Return on Equity %		-6.81%	-9.31%	-5.56%	7.01%	6.42%
Debt to Equity		1.41	1.70	1.03	0.71	0.52

CONTACT INFORMATION:
Phone: 55 2132244477 Fax: 55 2 132246055
Toll-Free:
Address: 65 Ave. Republica do Chile, Rio de Janeiro, RJ 20031-912 Brazil

STOCK TICKER/OTHER:
Stock Ticker: PBR
Employees: 68,829
Parent Company:

Exchange: NYS
Fiscal Year Ends: 12/31

SALARIES/BONUSES:
Top Exec. Salary: $ Bonus: $
Second Exec. Salary: $ Bonus: $

OTHER THOUGHTS:
Estimated Female Officers or Directors: 1
Hot Spot for Advancement for Women/Minorities:

PetroChina Company Limited

www.petrochina.com.cn

NAIC Code: 211111

TYPES OF BUSINESS:
Oil & Gas Exploration & Production
Chemicals, Lubricants & Petroleum Products
Oil Refining, Transportation & Marketing
Gas Stations

BRANDS/DIVISIONS/AFFILIATES:

CONTACTS: Note: Officers with more than one job title may be intentionally listed here more than once.
Wang Dongjin, Pres.
Sun Longde, Acting Sec.
Wang Yilin, Chmn.

GROWTH PLANS/SPECIAL FEATURES:
PetroChina Company Limited, headquartered in Beijing, is one of the largest oil and gas producers and distributors in China. The company is involved in a broad range of petroleum and natural gas related activities, including the exploration, development, production and marketing of crude oil and natural gas; the refining of crude oil and petroleum products as well as the production and marketing of basic petrochemical products, derivative chemical products and other chemical products. The firm also focuses on marketing of refined oil products and trading, the transmission of natural gas, crude oil and refined oil products as well as the sale of natural gas. PetroChina operates in four business segments: exploration and production, refining and chemicals, marketing and natural gas and pipeline. The exploration and production segment is engaged in the exploration, development, production and marketing of crude oil and natural gas. The refining and chemicals segment is engaged in the refining of crude oil and petroleum products, production and marketing of primary petrochemical products and derivative petrochemical products and other chemical products. The marketing segment is engaged in the marketing of refined products and the trading business. The natural gas and pipeline segment is engaged in the transmission of natural gas, crude oil and refined products and the sale of natural gas. The company's estimated proved reserves in 2016 totaled approximately 7,437.8 million barrels of crude oil and approximately 78,711.8 billion cubic feet (Bcf) of natural gas.

FINANCIAL DATA: Note: Data for latest year may not have been available at press time.

In U.S. $	2017	2016	2015	2014	2013	2012
Revenue		257,719,000,000	275,016,800,000	363,882,400,000	359,923,500,000	349,909,300,000
R&D Expense						
Operating Income		8,847,607,000	11,683,640,000	26,208,100,000	29,320,200,000	27,141,330,000
Operating Margin %		3.43%	4.24%	7.20%	8.14%	7.75%
SGA Expense		30,589,750,000	30,180,910,000	30,959,210,000	31,151,760,000	28,830,710,000
Net Income		1,252,331,000	5,661,072,000	17,082,200,000	20,656,850,000	18,381,870,000
Operating Cash Flow		42,267,010,000	41,650,650,000	56,819,050,000	45,988,780,000	38,140,230,000
Capital Expenditure		29,779,720,000	35,278,650,000	49,350,810,000	48,941,010,000	50,865,810,000
EBITDA		44,869,860,000	44,480,780,000	56,126,970,000	57,351,730,000	53,031,290,000
Return on Assets %		.32%	1.48%	4.51%	5.74%	5.64%
Return on Equity %		.66%	3.01%	9.28%	11.79%	11.16%
Debt to Equity		0.31	0.36	0.31	0.26	0.27

CONTACT INFORMATION:
Phone: 86 1059986223   Fax: 86 1062099557
Toll-Free:
Address: 9 Dongzhimen N. St., Dongcheng District, Beijing, 100007 China

STOCK TICKER/OTHER:
Stock Ticker: PTR
Employees: 508,757
Parent Company: China National Petroleum Corporation (CNPC)

Exchange: NYS
Fiscal Year Ends: 12/31

SALARIES/BONUSES:
Top Exec. Salary: $793,000   Bonus: $
Second Exec. Salary: $646,000   Bonus: $

OTHER THOUGHTS:
Estimated Female Officers or Directors:
Hot Spot for Advancement for Women/Minorities:

Sales, profits and employees may be estimates. Financial information, benefits and other data can change quickly and may vary from those stated here.

Petroleos Mexicanos (Pemex)

www.pemex.com

NAIC Code: 211111

TYPES OF BUSINESS:
Oil & Gas Exploration & Production
Oil & Gas Transportation & Storage
Gas Stations
Refining
Petrochemicals

BRANDS/DIVISIONS/AFFILIATES:
Pemex Transformacion Industrial
Pemex Etileno
Pemex Fertilizantes
Pemex Logistica
Pemex Drilling and Services

CONTACTS:
Note: Officers with more than one job title may be intentionally listed here more than once.

Carlos Alberto Trevino Medino, Managing Dir.
David Ruelas Rodriguez, CFO
Rodrigo Becerra Mizuno, CIO
Victor Diaz Solis, Dir.-Admin.
Marco Sanchez, General Counsel
Elena del Carmen Tanus Meouchi, Dir.-Finance
Tame Miguel Dominguez, CEO-Pemex Refining
Gustavo Hernandez Garcia, CEO-Pemex Exploration & Prod.
Alejandro Martinez Sibaja, CEO-Pemex Gas & Basic Petrochemicals
Manuel Sanchez Guzman, CEO-Pemex Petrochemicals
Jose Manuel Carrera Panizzo, CEO-Pemex Int'l
Francisco Arturo Heriquez Autrey, Dir.-Procurement & Supply

GROWTH PLANS/SPECIAL FEATURES:
Petroleos Mexicanos (Pemex) is Mexico's national petroleum company and an essential source of revenue for the country's government. Pemex, under Mexican Law, has the exclusive right to explore, exploit, refine/produce, transport and sell crude oil, natural gas and other petroleum derivatives in Mexico. Pemex stores, markets, transports and distributes its gas and petroleum products. The company operates through five business subsidiaries. Pemex Transformacion Industrial operates six refineries, nine gas processing plants and eight petrochemical facilities, providing hydrocarbons, petroleum (gas, diesel, turbo gas, combustion gas and liquid gas) and petrochemicals for the residential, industrial, electric, maritime, aero and automobile sectors. Pemex Etileno produces polyethylene, ethylene oxide and mixed glycols for the consumer goods, textile, plastics, pharmaceuticals, dairy, film, soaps and bottling industries. Pemex Fertilizantes produces ammonia and chemical solutions for the agriculture, textile, plastics, automotive, film and paper sectors. Pemex Logistica transports hydrocarbons and petrochemicals, storage, maintenance and port services and solutions. Pemex Drilling and Services provides well-drilling and repair services and solutions. In total, Pemex has 83 land and marine terminals, as well as oil and gas pipelines, maritime vessels and varying fleets of ground transportation in order to supply more than 10,000 service stations throughout the country. Additionally, Pemex's wealth management division acquires, divests and maintains the properties and production of the firm's subsidiaries.

FINANCIAL DATA:
Note: Data for latest year may not have been available at press time.

In U.S. $	2017	2016	2015	2014	2013	2012
Revenue	70,604,000,000	52,190,400,000	67,471,900,000	83,036,000,000	103,653,000,000	126,600,000,000
R&D Expense						
Operating Income						
Operating Margin %						
SGA Expense						
Net Income	-14,194,000,000	-9,238,520,000	-39,225,046,643	-17,920,000,000	-10,960,000,000	200,000,000
Operating Cash Flow						
Capital Expenditure						
EBITDA						
Return on Assets %						
Return on Equity %						
Debt to Equity						

CONTACT INFORMATION:
Phone: 52-55-1944--2500   Fax: 52-55-1944-8768
Toll-Free:
Address: Avenida Marina Nacional 329, Mexico City, 11311 Mexico

STOCK TICKER/OTHER:
Stock Ticker: Government-Owned
Employees: 127,941
Parent Company:
Exchange:
Fiscal Year Ends: 12/31

SALARIES/BONUSES:
Top Exec. Salary: $ Bonus: $
Second Exec. Salary: $ Bonus: $

OTHER THOUGHTS:
Estimated Female Officers or Directors:
Hot Spot for Advancement for Women/Minorities:

Sales, profits and employees may be estimates. Financial information, benefits and other data can change quickly and may vary from those stated here.

Peugeot SA (Groupe PSA)

NAIC Code: 336111

www.groupe-psa.com

TYPES OF BUSINESS:
Automobile Manufacturing
Automotive Equipment & Components
Transportation & Logistics Services
Motorcycles
Financial Services
Industrial Equipment
Engines
Clean Diesel & Hybrid Engine Technology

BRANDS/DIVISIONS/AFFILIATES:
Peugeot
Citroen
DS Automobiles
Free2 Move
PSA Powertrain
Banque PSA Finance
Mister Auto
Adam Opel AG

CONTACTS: Note: Officers with more than one job title may be intentionally listed here more than once.

Carlos Tavares, Chmn.-Managing Board
Jean-Baptiste De Chatillon, CFO
Yannick Bezard, Dir.-Sales
Xavier Chereau, Exec. VP-Human Resources
Guillaume Faury, Exec. VP-R&D
Pierre Todorov, Corp. Sec.
Denis Martin, Exec. VP-Industrial Oper.
Yves Bonnefont, Exec. VP-Strategy
Jonathan Goodman, Exec. VP-Corp. Comm.
Olivier Sartoris, Investors Rel. Mgr.
Frederic Saint-Geours, VP-Finance
Frederic Saint Geours, Exec. VP-Brands
Christian Peugeot, Exec. VP- Public Affairs & External Rel.
Carlos Gomes, Sr. VP-Latin America
Bernd Schantz, Sr. VP- Russia, Ukraine & CIS
Carlos Tavares, Chmn.
Gregoire Olivier, Exec. VP-Asia
Yannick Bezard, VP-Purchasing

GROWTH PLANS/SPECIAL FEATURES:

Peugeot SA, operating as Groupe PSA, is a leading automobile manufacturer in Europe, producing cars and light commercial vehicles under the Peugeot, Citroen, DS Automobiles, Opel and Vauxhall brand names. Groupe PSA firm sold more than 3.5 million vehicles in 2017, which includes vehicles sold in Europe, Latin America, China, Southeast Asia, Middle East, Africa, Eurasia and India/Pacific. Style ranges include small, super-mini, city, sport utility and hatchback passenger vehicles. Peugot's 3008 model is an SUV; Citrogen's C3 is a third-generation connected vehicle; the DS 4 is a crossback model; and the Opel/Vauxhall Ampera-e is a 100% electric vehicle. In addition to vehicles, Groupe PSA owns Free2Move, a worldwide mobility service provider offering shared vehicle, scooter or bike services; PSA Powertrain, which adapts the engines and components made by the Group for sale to other vehicle brands and manufacturers; Banque PSA Finance, which provides financing for vehicles sold by the three brands in 18 network countries; Mister Auto, an automotive spare parts e-commerce site, managing nearly 12,000 daily orders; and Europar, offering a range of multi-brand spare parts and accessories for the maintenance and repair of vehicles over three years old. During 2017, Groupe PSA acquired the Opel and Vauxhall line of vehicles from General Motors.

FINANCIAL DATA: Note: Data for latest year may not have been available at press time.

In U.S. $	2017	2016	2015	2014	2013	2012
Revenue	80,528,050,000	66,721,830,000	67,519,570,000	66,199,460,000	66,795,920,000	68,470,450,000
R&D Expense	2,763,714,000	2,364,840,000	2,294,450,000	2,500,679,000	2,327,793,000	2,527,847,000
Operating Income	4,928,499,000	3,994,912,000	3,374,991,000	1,117,587,000	-218,577,900	-711,304,300
Operating Margin %	6.12%	5.98%	4.99%	1.68%	-.32%	-1.03%
SGA Expense	7,272,346,000	6,385,685,000	6,885,821,000	7,303,218,000	7,925,609,000	7,894,737,000
Net Income	2,382,128,000	2,136,383,000	1,110,178,000	-871,841,700	-2,861,271,000	-6,186,866,000
Operating Cash Flow	6,516,585,000	7,989,825,000	14,859,590,000	5,018,647,000	2,012,892,000	1,749,858,000
Capital Expenditure	5,087,802,000	4,413,544,000	3,665,193,000	3,083,554,000	3,184,816,000	4,604,955,000
EBITDA	6,984,613,000	6,100,423,000	5,384,179,000	3,263,849,000	2,611,821,000	1,967,201,000
Return on Assets %	3.75%	3.67%	1.62%	-1.16%	-3.72%	-7.48%
Return on Equity %	14.18%	14.90%	9.06%	-8.74%	-27.74%	-42.35%
Debt to Equity	0.32	0.35	0.40	0.69	1.17	0.79

CONTACT INFORMATION:
Phone: 33-1-40-66-55-11   Fax:
Toll-Free:
Address: 75, Ave. de la Grande-Armee, Paris, 75116 France

STOCK TICKER/OTHER:
Stock Ticker: PUGOY
Employees: 186,220
Parent Company:

Exchange: PINX
Fiscal Year Ends: 12/31

SALARIES/BONUSES:
Top Exec. Salary: $ Bonus: $
Second Exec. Salary: $ Bonus: $

OTHER THOUGHTS:
Estimated Female Officers or Directors: 3
Hot Spot for Advancement for Women/Minorities: Y

Sales, profits and employees may be estimates. Financial information, benefits and other data can change quickly and may vary from those stated here.

Pfizer Inc

NAIC Code: 325412

www.pfizer.com

TYPES OF BUSINESS:
Pharmaceuticals
Infusion Technologies

BRANDS/DIVISIONS/AFFILIATES:
Prevnar 13
Xeljanz
Eliquis
Lyrica
Enbrel
Lipitor
Premarin
Celebrex

CONTACTS:
Note: Officers with more than one job title may be intentionally listed here more than once.

Ian Read, CEO
Margaret Madden, Other Executive Officer
Frank DAmelio, CFO
Loretta Cangialosi, Chief Accounting Officer
Freda Lewis-Hall, Chief Medical Officer
Rady Johnson, Chief Risk Officer
Albert Bourla, COO
Sally Susman, Executive VP, Divisional
Laurie Olson, Executive VP, Divisional
Charles Hill, Executive VP, Divisional
Douglas Lankler, Executive VP
Alexander Mackenzie, Executive VP
Angela Hwang, President, Divisional
John Young, President, Divisional
Mikael Dolsten, President, Divisional

GROWTH PLANS/SPECIAL FEATURES:
Pfizer, Inc. is a research-based, global pharmaceutical company that discovers, develops, manufactures and markets healthcare products. Pfizer operates in two business segments: innovative health and essential health. The innovative health segment focuses on developing and commercializing novel, value-creating medicines and vaccines that significantly improve patients' lives, as well as products for consumer healthcare. Key therapeutic areas within this division include internal medicine, vaccines, oncology, inflammation/immunology, rare diseases and consumer healthcare. Leading brands within this segment include Prevnar 13, Xeljanz, Eliquis, Lyrica, Enbrel, Ibrance, Xtandi and several over-the-counter (OTC) consumer products. The essential health segment comprises legacy brands that have lost or will soon lose market exclusivity in both developed and emerging markets. These branded products include generics, generic sterile injectable products and biosimilars. This division also includes a research and development organization, as well as the company's manufacturing business. Brands within this segment include Lipitor, Premarin, Norvasc, Lyrica (within Europe, Russia, Turkey, Israel and Central Asia countries), Celebrex, Viagra and Inflectra/Remsima, as well as several sterile injectable products.

FINANCIAL DATA:
Note: Data for latest year may not have been available at press time.

In U.S. $	2017	2016	2015	2014	2013	2012
Revenue	52,546,000,000	52,824,000,000	48,851,000,000	49,605,000,000	51,584,000,000	58,986,000,000
R&D Expense	7,657,000,000	7,872,000,000	7,690,000,000	8,393,000,000	6,678,000,000	7,870,000,000
Operating Income	14,107,000,000	13,730,000,000	12,976,000,000	13,499,000,000	16,366,000,000	17,991,000,000
Operating Margin %	26.84%	25.99%	26.56%	27.21%	31.72%	30.50%
SGA Expense	14,784,000,000	14,837,000,000	14,809,000,000	14,097,000,000	14,355,000,000	16,616,000,000
Net Income	21,308,000,000	7,215,000,000	6,960,000,000	9,135,000,000	22,003,000,000	14,570,000,000
Operating Cash Flow	16,470,000,000	15,901,000,000	14,512,000,000	16,883,000,000	17,765,000,000	17,054,000,000
Capital Expenditure	2,217,000,000	1,999,000,000	1,496,000,000	1,583,000,000	1,465,000,000	1,327,000,000
EBITDA	20,376,000,000	15,294,000,000	15,321,000,000	19,137,000,000	23,540,000,000	21,215,000,000
Return on Assets %	12.40%	4.25%	4.13%	5.35%	12.29%	7.79%
Return on Equity %	32.57%	11.61%	10.23%	12.38%	27.93%	17.83%
Debt to Equity	0.47	0.52	0.44	0.44	0.39	0.38

CONTACT INFORMATION:
Phone: 212 733-2323 Fax: 212 573-7851
Toll-Free:
Address: 235 E. 42nd St., New York, NY 10017 United States

STOCK TICKER/OTHER:
Stock Ticker: PFE Exchange: NYS
Employees: 96,500 Fiscal Year Ends: 12/31
Parent Company:

SALARIES/BONUSES:
Top Exec. Salary: $1,956,750 Bonus: $
Second Exec. Salary: $1,356,750 Bonus: $

OTHER THOUGHTS:
Estimated Female Officers or Directors: 7
Hot Spot for Advancement for Women/Minorities: Y

Sales, profits and employees may be estimates. Financial information, benefits and other data can change quickly and may vary from those stated here.

Pharmaceutical Product Development LLC

www.ppdi.com

NAIC Code: 541711

TYPES OF BUSINESS:
Contract Research
Drug Discovery & Development Services
Clinical Data Consulting Services
Medical Marketing & Information Support Services
Drug Discovery Services
Medical Device Development

BRANDS/DIVISIONS/AFFILIATES:
Carlyle Group (The)
Hellman & Friedman

CONTACTS:
Note: Officers with more than one job title may be intentionally listed here more than once.

David Simmons, CEO
Christine A. Dingivan, Chief Medical Officer
B. Judd Hartman, General Counsel
William W. Richardson, Sr. VP-Global Bus. Dev.
Randy Buckwalter, Head-Media
Luke Heagle, Head-Investor Rel.
Lee E. Babiss, Chief Science Officer
David Johnston, Exec. VP-Global Lab Svcs.
David Simmons, Chmn.
Paul Colvin, Exec. VP-Global Clinical Dev.

GROWTH PLANS/SPECIAL FEATURES:
Pharmaceutical Product Development, LLC (PPD), jointly owned by The Carlyle Group and Hellman & Friedman, provides drug discovery and development services to pharmaceutical, biotechnology, medical device, academic and government organizations. PPD's services are divided into seven segments: early development, which offers a range of early development services, phase 1 clinical trial services and non-clinical consulting; clinical development, which helps advance drug research and development for products; PPD Laboratories, which provides comprehensive lab services; post-approval, which provides post-approval studies and late-stage clinical trials management; PPD Consulting, which acts as a consulting partner that assists companies with their biopharmaceutical product's success from pre-clinical through post-approval; functional service partnerships, provides customizable outsourcing solutions, including full-time equivalent models, units-based contracts and geographical-aligned agreements; and technology/innovation/performance, which helps companies deliver life-changing medicines, cutting-edge technologies, real-time analytics and customized training. Therapeutic areas of studies include cardiovascular, critical care, dermatology, dental pain research, endocrine and metabolics, gastroenterology, hemotology and oncology, immunology, infectious diseases, neuroscience, ophthalmology, respiratory and urology. PPD is headquartered in North Carolina, USA, with nearly 90 additional offices spanning 47 countries.

FINANCIAL DATA:
Note: Data for latest year may not have been available at press time.

In U.S. $	2017	2016	2015	2014	2013	2012
Revenue	1,350,000,000	1,300,000,000	1,200,000,000	1,222,000,000	1,023,100,000	749,100,032
R&D Expense						
Operating Income						
Operating Margin %						
SGA Expense						
Net Income						
Operating Cash Flow						
Capital Expenditure						
EBITDA						
Return on Assets %						
Return on Equity %						
Debt to Equity						

CONTACT INFORMATION:
Phone: 910-251-0081   Fax: 910-762-5820
Toll-Free:
Address: 929 N. Front St., Wilmington, NC 28401-3331 United States

STOCK TICKER/OTHER:
Stock Ticker: Private
Employees: 20,000
Parent Company: Carlyle Group (The)

Exchange:
Fiscal Year Ends: 12/31

SALARIES/BONUSES:
Top Exec. Salary: $ Bonus: $
Second Exec. Salary: $ Bonus: $

OTHER THOUGHTS:
Estimated Female Officers or Directors: 2
Hot Spot for Advancement for Women/Minorities:

Sales, profits and employees may be estimates. Financial information, benefits and other data can change quickly and may vary from those stated here.

Pininfarina SpA

NAIC Code: 541330

www.pininfarina.it

TYPES OF BUSINESS:

Automotive Design & Engineering Services
Aeronautics Design
Mass Transit Design
Consumer Products Design
Retractable Roof Systems
Engineering Services
Prototype Testing
Automobile Design

BRANDS/DIVISIONS/AFFILIATES:

Mahindra Group
Pininfarina Extra Srl
Pininfarina Automotive Engineering Shanghai Co
Pininfarina Deutschland Holding GmbH
Pininfarina Deutschland GmbH
Pininfarina of America Corp
Goodmind Srl

CONTACTS:
Note: Officers with more than one job title may be intentionally listed here more than once.

Silvio Pietro Angori, CEO
Andrea Maria Benedetto, VP-Prod. Dev.
Gabriella Isoardi, Dir.-Legal
Silvio Pietro Angori, Interim Dir.-Comm. & Image
Gianfranco Albertini, Gen. Mgr.-Investor Rel.
Fabio Filippini, Dir.-Design
Paolo Pininfarina, Chmn.

GROWTH PLANS/SPECIAL FEATURES:

Pininfarina SpA specializes in providing automotive and general manufacturers with services through all stages of product development, from planning, designing and development to engineering, manufacturing and end product consultation. The firm's wholly-owned subsidiaries include Pininfarina Extra Srl, Pininfarina Automotive Engineering Shanghai Co. Ltd., Pininfarina Deutschland Holding GmbH, Pininfarina Deutschland GmbH and Pininfarina of America Corp. Pininfarina also has a 20% stake in Goodmind Srl. In the aerodynamics and aeroacoustics industry, the company designs the interior and exterior forms of its vehicles using its own automotive wind tunnels. It does design work for trains, planes and boats, as well as non-transportation products such as shoes, cellular phones, coffee machines, ski boots and watches. The company's customers include car makers such as Ferrari, GM, Lancia, Maserati, Fiat, Alfa Romeo, Hyundai, Peugeot, Citroen, Jaguar, Daewoo, Honda, Brillance, Chery, JAC, Ford Europe, Volvo, Mitsubishi Europe and Rolls-Royce; industrial vehicle makers, including BMC; bus and truck makers, including BredaMenarinibus, IVECO and Hispano; railway makers, including AnsaldoBreda, Bombardier and Eurostar; nautical and aeronautical clients, including Beneteau, Derecktor Shipyards, Ferretti Yachts and BAE Systems; and other clients, including Leitner Ropeways, Poma and Solex. The Mahindra Group owns a majority stake in Pininfarina (76.06%).

FINANCIAL DATA:
Note: Data for latest year may not have been available at press time.

In U.S. $	2017	2016	2015	2014	2013	2012
Revenue	954,010,200	730,161,909	881,114,017	95,104,800	89,200,000	78,700,000
R&D Expense						
Operating Income						
Operating Margin %						
SGA Expense						
Net Income	1,571,600	240,772,937	-213,090,409	-11,322,000	-13,100,000	41,600,000
Operating Cash Flow						
Capital Expenditure						
EBITDA						
Return on Assets %						
Return on Equity %						
Debt to Equity						

CONTACT INFORMATION:

Phone: 39-011-9438111 Fax:
Toll-Free:
Address: Via Nazionale, 30, Cambiano, TO 10020 Italy

STOCK TICKER/OTHER:

Stock Ticker: PINF
Employees: 1,005
Parent Company: Mahindra Group

Exchange: Milan
Fiscal Year Ends: 12/31

SALARIES/BONUSES:

Top Exec. Salary: $ Bonus: $
Second Exec. Salary: $ Bonus: $

OTHER THOUGHTS:

Estimated Female Officers or Directors: 2
Hot Spot for Advancement for Women/Minorities:

Pioneer Corporation

NAIC Code: 334310

pioneer.jp/en/

TYPES OF BUSINESS:
Consumer Electronics
Audio/Video Equipment
CD/DVD Players
Automotive Electronics
Telecommunications Equipment
Research & Development
Software Development

BRANDS/DIVISIONS/AFFILIATES:
Pioneer Digital Design and Manufacturing Corp
Anyo Pioneer Motor Info Tech Co Ltd

CONTACTS:
Note: Officers with more than one job title may be intentionally listed here more than once.

Susumu Kotani, CEO
Susumu Kotani, Pres.
Masanori Koshoubu, Gen. Mgr.-R&D
Hideki Okayasu, Sr. Mgr. Dir.-Gen. Admin. Div.
Masanori Koshoubu, Mgr. Dir.-Legal & Intellectual Property Div.
Mikio Ono, Gen. Mgr.-Corp. Planning Div.
Hideki Okayasu, Sr. Mgr. Dir.-Corp. Comm.
Hideki Okayasu, Sr. Mgr. Dir.-Finance & Acct. Div.
Satoshi Matsumoto, Mgr. Dir.-Quality Assurance Div.
Mikio Ono, Gen. Mgr.-Home Audiovisual Bus.
Tatsuo Takeuchi, Gen. Mgr.-Intl Bus. Div.

GROWTH PLANS/SPECIAL FEATURES:

Pioneer Corporation, headquartered in Japan, is a leading manufacturer of consumer electronics. The firm operates primarily in three segments: home electronics, others and new businesses. The home electronics segment manufactures home theater components, such as Blu-ray disc players, surround sound systems, audiovisual components, Blu-ray and DVD drives for computers, professional disc jockey equipment and professional speakers. The others segment focuses on factory automation systems, home telephones, speaker devices, cyber conference system solutions and map software. Pioneer's new businesses segment produces bicycle GPS systems; organic electroluminescent lighting, electronics manufacturing services and components; medical and healthcare equipment; electric and autonomous vehicle products; and horizontal vertical transforming (HVT) speakers. The firm is part of two joint ventures: optical disk developer Pioneer Digital Design and Manufacturing Corporation (with Sharp Corporation); and Anyo Pioneer Motor Information Technology Co., Ltd., a Chinese car navigation systems developer (with Shanghai Automotive Industry Corporation Group). In October 2017, the firm announced that it was developing a new type of lidar (laser radar) technology utilized within a swiveling, microscopic mirror for autonomous vehicles. The mirror will help driverless cars see and locate surrounding objects.

FINANCIAL DATA:
Note: Data for latest year may not have been available at press time.

In U.S. $	2017	2016	2015	2014	2013	2012
Revenue	3,602,404,000	4,188,839,000	4,673,710,000	4,639,939,000	4,209,437,000	4,068,875,000
R&D Expense						
Operating Income	38,820,570	68,045,460	72,461,340	104,052,600	55,869,200	116,582,800
Operating Margin %	1.07%	1.62%	1.55%	2.24%	1.32%	2.86%
SGA Expense						
Net Income	-47,084,040	6,810,137	136,314,500	4,946,898	-182,150,200	34,190,420
Operating Cash Flow	182,727,800	179,728,000	322,004,900	319,005,100	10,983,790	169,675,800
Capital Expenditure						
EBITDA	217,030,000	309,139,200	477,026,300	309,483,900	160,229,200	310,760,200
Return on Assets %	-1.74%	.23%	4.45%	.16%	-6.17%	1.16%
Return on Equity %	-6.00%	.78%	16.79%	.71%	-24.36%	4.33%
Debt to Equity	0.21	0.29	0.09		0.17	0.11

CONTACT INFORMATION:
Phone: 81-3-6634-8777   Fax:
Toll-Free:
Address: 28-8, Honkomagome 2-chome, Bunkyo-ku, Tokyo, 113-0021 Japan

STOCK TICKER/OTHER:
Stock Ticker: PNCOF
Employees: 19,404
Parent Company:

Exchange: PINX
Fiscal Year Ends: 03/31

SALARIES/BONUSES:
Top Exec. Salary: $ Bonus: $
Second Exec. Salary: $ Bonus: $

OTHER THOUGHTS:
Estimated Female Officers or Directors:
Hot Spot for Advancement for Women/Minorities:

Sales, profits and employees may be estimates. Financial information, benefits and other data can change quickly and may vary from those stated here.

Plexus Corp

NAIC Code: 334418

www.plexus.com

TYPES OF BUSINESS:
Telephone Apparatus Manufacturing
Hardware & Software Design
Printed Circuit Board Design
Prototyping Services
Material Procurement & Management
Logistics Services

BRANDS/DIVISIONS/AFFILIATES:

CONTACTS:
Note: Officers with more than one job title may be intentionally listed here more than once.

Todd Kelsey, CEO
Patrick Jermain, CFO
Dean Foate, Chairman of the Board
Angelo Ninivaggi, Chief Administrative Officer
Steven Frisch, COO
Ronnie Darroch, Executive VP, Divisional
Oliver Mihm, President, Divisional
Yong Lim, President, Geographical

GROWTH PLANS/SPECIAL FEATURES:

Plexus Corp. is a global provider of electronic manufacturing services (EMS). The company also provides global logistics management, aftermarket service and repair. It provides these services to more than 140 branded products companies in the networking, communications, healthcare, life sciences, industrial, commercial, security and defense and aerospace market sectors. Plexus' services include product development and design services, such as project management, feasibility studies, product conceptualization and product verification testing; prototyping and new product introduction services, including prototype assembly; test equipment development services, including testing for printed circuit assemblies, subassemblies, system assemblies and finished products; material sourcing and procurement services; agile manufacturing services, including printed circuit board assembly, basic assembly, system integration and mechatronic integration; fulfillment and logistic services; and aftermarket support. The company offers customers the ability to outsource all stages of the product realization process, including product specifications; development, design and design verification; regulatory compliance support; prototyping and new product introduction; manufacturing test equipment development; materials sourcing, procurement and supply-chain management; product assembly, manufacturing, configuration and test; order fulfillment; logistics; and service and repair. Plexus has 22 active facilities, totaling approximately 3.5 million square feet. Facilities are located strategically throughout the world to support its global supply chain as well as manufacturing and engineering needs of its customers.

The firm offers employees medical, dental and vision coverage; flexible spending accounts; tuition reimbursement; employee assistance programs; a 401(k); and performance-based salary increases.

FINANCIAL DATA:
Note: Data for latest year may not have been available at press time.

In U.S. $	2017	2016	2015	2014	2013	2012
Revenue	2,528,052,000	2,556,004,000	2,654,290,000	2,378,249,000	2,228,031,000	2,306,732,000
R&D Expense						
Operating Income	129,908,000	106,473,000	117,127,000	111,887,000	96,623,000	104,159,000
Operating Margin %	5.13%	4.16%	4.41%	4.70%	4.33%	4.51%
SGA Expense	125,947,000	120,886,000	122,423,000	113,682,000	116,562,000	115,754,000
Net Income	112,062,000	76,427,000	94,332,000	87,213,000	82,259,000	62,089,000
Operating Cash Flow	171,734,000	127,738,000	76,572,000	88,432,000	207,647,000	157,503,000
Capital Expenditure	38,538,000	31,123,000	35,076,000	65,284,000	108,122,000	63,697,000
EBITDA	180,731,000	149,443,000	168,637,000	153,484,000	147,097,000	156,509,000
Return on Assets %	5.98%	4.40%	5.69%	5.70%	5.76%	4.57%
Return on Equity %	11.53%	8.68%	11.62%	11.78%	12.20%	10.28%
Debt to Equity	0.02	0.20	0.30	0.33	0.36	0.40

CONTACT INFORMATION:
Phone: 920 722-3451   Fax: 920 751-5395
Toll-Free:
Address: One Plexus Way, Neenah, WI 54957 United States

STOCK TICKER/OTHER:
Stock Ticker: PLXS
Employees: 14,000
Parent Company:

Exchange: NAS
Fiscal Year Ends: 10/31

SALARIES/BONUSES:
Top Exec. Salary: $840,000   Bonus: $
Second Exec. Salary: $524,038   Bonus: $

OTHER THOUGHTS:
Estimated Female Officers or Directors: 2
Hot Spot for Advancement for Women/Minorities:

Sales, profits and employees may be estimates. Financial information, benefits and other data can change quickly and may vary from those stated here.

PM Group

www.pmgroup-global.com

NAIC Code: 541330

TYPES OF BUSINESS:
Engineering Consulting Services

BRANDS/DIVISIONS/AFFILIATES:
PM Devereux

CONTACTS:
Note: Officers with more than one job title may be intentionally listed here more than once.

Dave Murphy, CEO
Larry Westman, CFO
Dan Flinter, Chmn.

GROWTH PLANS/SPECIAL FEATURES:

PM Group is an engineering, architecture and project management firm serving multi-national clients throughout the world. The firm has been in operation for nearly 45 years and has 18 locations worldwide. PM Group collaborates with many of the world's leading private companies and major public-sector organizations. Currently, the group is actively involved with projects in 30 countries throughout Europe, Asia, the U.S. and the Middle East. Services offered by PM Group include: location selection and strategic project planning; project and construction management; engineering consulting and design; architecture, master-planning and interior design; managed service; sustainability; environment, health and safety; commissioning and qualification; outsourcing of professional and technical personnel; development consulting; and standard disposables design. Sectors served by PM Group include pharmaceuticals, food/beverage, consumer health, advanced manufacturing technology, data centers/mission-critical facilities, energy, medical technology, international finance, education, healthcare, R&D, commercial/retail, and infrastructure/transportation. Just a few of the firm's key projects include: Alexion, a biologics manufacturing development facility in Ireland; Boston Scientific, a medical technology manufacturing hub in Malaysia; IFF, a flavors production facility in China; GSK Vaccines, a vaccine manufacturing facility in Belgium; and AGI, an aviation components manufacturing facility in Poland. Subsidiary PM Devereux is a design practice providing a wide range of architectural, master-planning and design services primarily in the healthcare, science and technology, education and commercial sectors.

FINANCIAL DATA:
Note: Data for latest year may not have been available at press time.

In U.S. $	2017	2016	2015	2014	2013	2012
Revenue	360,000,000	353,996,000	324,484,000	396,997,050	403,297,750	
R&D Expense						
Operating Income						
Operating Margin %						
SGA Expense						
Net Income						
Operating Cash Flow						
Capital Expenditure						
EBITDA						
Return on Assets %						
Return on Equity %						
Debt to Equity						

CONTACT INFORMATION:
Phone: 353-1-404-0700 Fax: 353-1-459-9785
Toll-Free:
Address: Killakee House, Belgard Square, Tallaght, Dublin, 24 Ireland

STOCK TICKER/OTHER:
Stock Ticker: Private Exchange:
Employees: 2,200 Fiscal Year Ends:
Parent Company:

SALARIES/BONUSES:
Top Exec. Salary: $ Bonus: $
Second Exec. Salary: $ Bonus: $

OTHER THOUGHTS:
Estimated Female Officers or Directors:
Hot Spot for Advancement for Women/Minorities:

Sales, profits and employees may be estimates. Financial information, benefits and other data can change quickly and may vary from those stated here.

Porsche Automobil Holding SE

NAIC Code: 336111

www.porsche-se.com

TYPES OF BUSINESS:
Automobile Manufacturing
Sports Cars
Apparel & Accessories

BRANDS/DIVISIONS/AFFILIATES:
Volkswagen Group
Audi
SEAT
SKODA
Bentley
Bugatti
Lamborghini
Porsche

CONTACTS:
Note: Officers with more than one job title may be intentionally listed here more than once.
Hans Dieter Potsch, CFO
Matthias Muller, Dir.-Strategy & Corp. Dev.
Philipp von Hagen, Dir.-Investment Management
Wolfgang Porsche, Chmn.

GROWTH PLANS/SPECIAL FEATURES:
Porsche Automobil Holding SE is a German-based holding company comprised of 12 brands from seven European countries. Primarily, Porsche holds the majority (50.7%) of the ordinary shares in the Volkswagen Group, which is one of the world's leading automobile manufacturers. The firm's 12 brands include: Volkswagen Passenger Cars, Audi, SEAT, SKODA, Bentley, Bugatti, Lamborghini, Porsche, Ducati, Volkswagen Commercial Vehicles, Scania and MAN. The company also retains interest in after-sales of automobiles, parts distribution and the investment in the automotive value chain, which encompasses vehicle related services, supporting the developments and production process and offering its technological resources. In addition to its 12 brands, Porche Automobil owns interests in other auto-related businesses, including: a 100% stake in Planung Transport Verkehr AG, a German provider of software for traffic planning and traffic management, as well as transport logistics; a minority stake in the U.S.-technology company, INRIX, Inc.; and in two 3D printing specialists, Markforged, Inc. and Suerat Technologies, Inc., each based in the U.S. Additionally, Porsche Beteiligung GmbH is a wholly-owned subsidiary of the company.

FINANCIAL DATA:
Note: Data for latest year may not have been available at press time.

In U.S. $	2017	2016	2015	2014	2013	2012
Revenue		1,234,903				
R&D Expense						
Operating Income		1,731,335,000	-563,115,900	4,059,127,000	3,199,635,000	9,707,575,000
Operating Margin %		140200.00%				
SGA Expense		37,047,100	25,932,970			
Net Income		1,696,757,000	-337,128,600	3,739,287,000	2,973,647,000	9,654,474,000
Operating Cash Flow		-119,785,600	739,707,100	384,054,900	821,210,700	249,450,500
Capital Expenditure						
EBITDA		1,735,039,000	-534,713,200	4,059,127,000	3,199,635,000	9,707,575,000
Return on Assets %		4.90%	-.93%	9.80%	7.70%	24.36%
Return on Equity %		4.99%	-.96%	10.09%	7.94%	30.39%
Debt to Equity			0.01	0.01		

CONTACT INFORMATION:
Phone: 49-711-911-0   Fax: 49-711-911-25777
Toll-Free:
Address: Porscheplatz 1, Stuttgart, 70435 Germany

STOCK TICKER/OTHER:
Stock Ticker: POAHY   Exchange: PINX
Employees: 30   Fiscal Year Ends: 07/31
Parent Company:

SALARIES/BONUSES:
Top Exec. Salary: $ Bonus: $
Second Exec. Salary: $ Bonus: $

OTHER THOUGHTS:
Estimated Female Officers or Directors:
Hot Spot for Advancement for Women/Minorities:

Sales, profits and employees may be estimates. Financial information, benefits and other data can change quickly and may vary from those stated here.

Power Construction Corporation of China (PowerChina)

http://en.powerchina.cn/
NAIC Code: 541330

TYPES OF BUSINESS:
Engineering Consulting Services

BRANDS/DIVISIONS/AFFILIATES:

CONTACTS: *Note: Officers with more than one job title may be intentionally listed here more than once.*
Yan Zhiyong, Chmn.

GROWTH PLANS/SPECIAL FEATURES:
Power Construction Corporation of China (PowerChina) provides a range of services in the fields of hydropower, thermal power, new energy and infrastructure. The state-owned company's services include planning, investigation, design, consultancy, construction, mechanical/electrical installation and equipment manufacturing. PowerChina provides global engineering, procurement and construction (EPC) services, particularly in relation to the development of hydropower, water works, thermal power, new energy and transmission and distribution projects. The firm possesses state-of-the-art technology in dam engineering and construction, and specializes in the installation of turbine-generator units, foundation design, construction of extra-large underground caverns, engineering/treatment of high earth/rock slopes, dredging and hydraulic fill works, construction of airport runways, design and construction of thermal and hydropower plants, design and installation of power grids, and much more. The firm is also engaged in real estate and investment. April 2018, PowerChina signed a memorandum of understanding with PT Indonesia Kayan Hydropower Energy to jointly build hydropower plants along the Kayan River in North Kalimantan. The two firms will develop five hydropower facilities with a total electricity generation capacity of 9,000 megawatts.

FINANCIAL DATA: *Note: Data for latest year may not have been available at press time.*

In U.S. $	2017	2016	2015	2014	2013	2012
Revenue	49,000,000,000	48,869,000,000	43,600,000,000	26,441,200,000	23,047,600,000	20,289,800,000
R&D Expense						
Operating Income						
Operating Margin %						
SGA Expense						
Net Income		974,491,000	806,684,000	737,355,000	740,391,000	669,615,000
Operating Cash Flow						
Capital Expenditure						
EBITDA						
Return on Assets %						
Return on Equity %						
Debt to Equity						

CONTACT INFORMATION:
Phone: 8610-58368779   Fax: 8610-68599504
Toll-Free:
Address: No.22, Chegongzhuang West Rd., Haidian Dist., Beijing, 100048 China

STOCK TICKER/OTHER:
Stock Ticker: Government-Owned
Employees: 210,000
Parent Company:

Exchange:
Fiscal Year Ends:

SALARIES/BONUSES:
Top Exec. Salary: $ Bonus: $
Second Exec. Salary: $ Bonus: $

OTHER THOUGHTS:
Estimated Female Officers or Directors:
Hot Spot for Advancement for Women/Minorities:

Sales, profits and employees may be estimates. Financial information, benefits and other data can change quickly and may vary from those stated here.

POWER Engineers Inc

www.powereng.com

NAIC Code: 541330

TYPES OF BUSINESS:
Engineering Consulting Services
Engineering
Design
Consulting

BRANDS/DIVISIONS/AFFILIATES:
Sega Inc
Zephyr Environmental Corporation

CONTACTS:
Note: Officers with more than one job title may be intentionally listed here more than once.

Bret Moffett, CEO

GROWTH PLANS/SPECIAL FEATURES:

POWER Engineers, Inc. is a global consulting engineering firm specializing in the delivery of integrated solutions for the energy, food, beverage, facilities, communications, environmental and federal markets. POWER's capabilities include: power delivery, power generation, plant/facility construction, automation systems, information systems, packaging design, telecom services, fiber optic infrastructure, feasibility studies, routing studies, energy facility licensing, permitting, construction monitoring, compliance inspection, air quality testing, resources management, geosciences engineering, industrial hygiene, remediation, exploration/production, gathering/processing, pipelines, storage, liquid natural gas (LNG) operations, oil and gas distribution and microgrids. POWER is headquartered in Idaho, with locations throughout the U.S., as well as internationally, in Canada and South Africa. In mid-2017, the firm acquired Sega, Inc., a Kansas-based power generation and power distribution company. In January 2018, POWER acquired Texas-based Zephyr Environmental Corporation, a full-service environmental, health and safety firm offering consulting, training and data systems services to clients worldwide.

The company offers its employees medical, dental and vision coverage; long-term disability; employee assistance; a 401(k); as well as wellness and education and training programs.

FINANCIAL DATA:
Note: Data for latest year may not have been available at press time.

In U.S. $	2017	2016	2015	2014	2013	2012
Revenue						
R&D Expense						
Operating Income						
Operating Margin %						
SGA Expense						
Net Income						
Operating Cash Flow						
Capital Expenditure						
EBITDA						
Return on Assets %						
Return on Equity %						
Debt to Equity						

CONTACT INFORMATION:
Phone: 208-788-3456   Fax: 208-788-2082
Toll-Free:
Address: 3940 Glenbrook Dr., Hailey, ID 83333 United States

STOCK TICKER/OTHER:
Stock Ticker: Private   Exchange:
Employees: 2,100   Fiscal Year Ends:
Parent Company:

SALARIES/BONUSES:
Top Exec. Salary: $ Bonus: $
Second Exec. Salary: $ Bonus: $

OTHER THOUGHTS:
Estimated Female Officers or Directors:
Hot Spot for Advancement for Women/Minorities:

Sales, profits and employees may be estimates. Financial information, benefits and other data can change quickly and may vary from those stated here.

Poyry PLC

NAIC Code: 541330

www.poyry.com

TYPES OF BUSINESS:
Engineering Consulting Services
Consulting
Engineering

BRANDS/DIVISIONS/AFFILIATES:

CONTACTS: Note: Officers with more than one job title may be intentionally listed here more than once.
Martin a Porta, CEO
Juuso Pajunen, CFO
Henrik Ehrnrooth, Chmn.

GROWTH PLANS/SPECIAL FEATURES:
Poyry PLC, based in Finland, is a consulting and engineering company. Its business operations consist of energy, industry, regional operations and management consulting. The energy business group provides technical consulting, engineering, supervision and project management within the areas of hydro power, thermal power, nuclear power, renewables and transmission and distribution. It participates in both new build and rehabilitation projects, and also helps clients to effectively manage their assets throughout the entire business life-cycle. The industry business group provides technical consulting, engineering, project management and implementation services in the areas of process industries and across the entire investment life-cycle. Sectors include pulp and paper, mining and metals as well as chemicals and biorefining. Regional operations deliver engineering and technical advice to the energy, industry, transportation and water sectors. Management consulting provides strategic advisory services to the world's capital and resource intensive industries. Its expertise is based on market-led insights and quantitative models as well as an understanding of sector-specific strategies and technologies. Projects of the firm involve the fields of energy, forest industry, management consulting, chemicals and biorefining, mining and minerals, transportation, water and real estate.

FINANCIAL DATA: Note: Data for latest year may not have been available at press time.

In U.S. $	2017	2016	2015	2014	2013	2012
Revenue	625,644,000	560,698,000	609,082,000	647,058,216	737,258,780	1,024,150,000
R&D Expense						
Operating Income						
Operating Margin %						
SGA Expense						
Net Income	6,708,040	-13,485,600	6,555,240	-30,265,500	3,579,160	-31,979,800
Operating Cash Flow						
Capital Expenditure						
EBITDA						
Return on Assets %						
Return on Equity %						
Debt to Equity						

CONTACT INFORMATION:
Phone: 358-10-3311
Fax: 358-10-33-21818
Toll-Free:
Address: P.O.Box 4, Jaakonkatu 3, Vantaa, FI-01621 Finland

STOCK TICKER/OTHER:
Stock Ticker: Private
Employees: 4,637
Parent Company:

Exchange:
Fiscal Year Ends:

SALARIES/BONUSES:
Top Exec. Salary: $
Bonus: $
Second Exec. Salary: $
Bonus: $

OTHER THOUGHTS:
Estimated Female Officers or Directors:
Hot Spot for Advancement for Women/Minorities:

Sales, profits and employees may be estimates. Financial information, benefits and other data can change quickly and may vary from those stated here.

Plunkett Research, Ltd.

PTC Inc

NAIC Code: 0

www.ptc.com

TYPES OF BUSINESS:
Computer Software-Engineering & Manufacturing
Engineering Consulting Services
Enterprise Publishing Software
Product Data Management

BRANDS/DIVISIONS/AFFILIATES:
PTC Windchill
PTC Servigistics
PTC Creo View
PTC Creo
PTC Mathcad
PTC Servigistics
ThingWorx
Vuforia

CONTACTS: Note: Officers with more than one job title may be intentionally listed here more than once.

James Heppelmann, CEO
Robert Schechter, Chairman of the Board
Matthew Cohen, Executive VP, Divisional
Anthony Dibona, Executive VP, Divisional
Andrew Miller, Executive VP
Barry Cohen, Executive VP
Aaron Von Staats, General Counsel

GROWTH PLANS/SPECIAL FEATURES:

PTC, Inc. develops markets and supports product development software and related services designed to aid companies in designing products and managing product information. PTC serves customers in the aerospace and defense, airlines, automotive, consumer products, electronics, footwear and apparel, industrial equipment, medical devices, smart cities, oil and gas and retail industries. The firm has two business segments: solutions group and technology platform group. The solutions group consists of the product lifecycle management (PLM), computer-aided design (CAD) and service lifecycle management (SLM) products. The PLM products manage product configuration information through each stage of the product lifecycle and communicate and collaborate across the entire enterprise. Some of the products in this category are PTC Windchill and PTC Creo View. CAD products include PTC Creo and PTC Mathcad and can be used to create conceptual and detailed designs, analyze designs, perform engineering calculations and leverage the information created downstream using 2D, 3D, parametric and direct modeling. The SLM products offer service parts planning and optimization, service knowledge management, support product service and maintenance requirements and service analytics. Products in this category are PTC Servigistics and PTC Arbortext. The technology platform group includes Internet of Things (IoT), analytics and augmented reality business. The IoT products, such as ThingWorx, platform designed to build and run IoT applications; Vuforia, an augmented reality technology platform; and ThingWorx Machine Learning, a predictive intelligence tool focused on providing connectivity and data intelligence optimization.

The firm provides its employees with tuition reimbursement; medical, dental and vision plans; life insurance; a 401(k) plan; and short- and long-term disability coverage.

FINANCIAL DATA: Note: Data for latest year may not have been available at press time.

In U.S. $	2017	2016	2015	2014	2013	2012
Revenue	1,164,039,000	1,140,533,000	1,255,242,000	1,356,967,000	1,293,541,000	1,255,679,000
R&D Expense	236,059,000	229,331,000	227,513,000	226,496,000	221,918,000	214,960,000
Operating Income	48,840,000	39,259,000	151,357,000	224,982,000	179,521,000	153,024,000
Operating Margin %	4.19%	3.44%	12.05%	16.57%	13.87%	12.18%
SGA Expense	518,013,000	513,080,000	505,509,000	499,679,000	492,577,000	495,264,000
Net Income	6,239,000	-54,465,000	47,557,000	160,194,000	143,769,000	-35,398,000
Operating Cash Flow	134,590,000	183,168,000	179,903,000	304,552,000	224,683,000	217,975,000
Capital Expenditure	25,444,000	26,189,000	30,628,000	25,275,000	29,328,000	31,413,000
EBITDA	127,736,000	49,244,000	125,700,000	271,574,000	209,761,000	191,953,000
Return on Assets %	.26%	-2.38%	2.15%	7.95%	7.94%	-2.06%
Return on Equity %	.72%	-6.39%	5.54%	17.99%	16.68%	-4.37%
Debt to Equity	0.80	0.89	0.71	0.68	0.26	0.45

CONTACT INFORMATION:
Phone: 781 370-5000   Fax: 781 370-6000
Toll-Free: 877-275-4782
Address: 140 Kendrick St., Needham, MA 02494 United States

STOCK TICKER/OTHER:
Stock Ticker: PTC   Exchange: NAS
Employees: 5,800   Fiscal Year Ends: 09/30
Parent Company:

SALARIES/BONUSES:
Top Exec. Salary: $800,000   Bonus: $
Second Exec. Salary: $625,000 Bonus: $

OTHER THOUGHTS:
Estimated Female Officers or Directors: 1
Hot Spot for Advancement for Women/Minorities:

Sales, profits and employees may be estimates. Financial information, benefits and other data can change quickly and may vary from those stated here.

Qualcomm Incorporated

www.qualcomm.com

NAIC Code: 334413

TYPES OF BUSINESS:
- Telecommunications Equipment
- Digital Wireless Communications Products
- Integrated Circuits
- Mobile Communications Systems
- Wireless Software & Services
- E-Mail Software
- Code Division Multiple Access

BRANDS/DIVISIONS/AFFILIATES:
RF360 Holdings Singapore Pte Ltd

CONTACTS:
Note: Officers with more than one job title may be intentionally listed here more than once.

Steven Mollenkopf, CEO
George Davis, CFO
Matthew Grob, Chief Technology Officer
James Thompson, Chief Technology Officer
Michelle Sterling, Executive VP, Divisional
Brian Modoff, Executive VP, Divisional
Donald Rosenberg, Executive VP
Alexander Rogers, Executive VP
Cristiano Amon, President

GROWTH PLANS/SPECIAL FEATURES:

Qualcomm Incorporated provides digital wireless communications products, technologies and services. Its operations are divided into three segments: Qualcomm CDMA Technologies (QCT), Qualcomm Technology Licensing (QTL) and Qualcomm Strategic Initiatives (QSI). QCT designs application-specific integrated circuits based on Code Division Multiple Access (CDMA), Orthogonal Frequency-Division Multiple Access (OFDMA), Time Division Multiple Access (TDMA) and other technologies for use in voice and data communications, networking, application processing, multimedia functions and GPS products. QTL grants licenses and provides rights to use portions of Qualcomm's intellectual property portfolio to third-party manufacturers of wireless products and networking equipment. QSI makes strategic investments in various companies and technologies that Qualcomm believes will open new opportunities for its technologies. Joint venture (with TDK Corporation), RF360 Holdings Singapore Pte. Ltd., delivers radio frequency (RF) front-end modules and RF filters into fully integrated systems for mobile devices and fast-growing business segments such as the Internet of Things, drones, robotics, automotive applications and more. In April 2018, Qualcomm extended the offering period of its previously-announced cash tender offer to purchase all the outstanding common shares of NXP Semiconductors NV, pursuant to an October 2016 purchase agreement between the two companies.

U.S. employees of the company receive medical, dental and vision insurance; dependent/health care reimbursement accounts; tuition reimbursement; a 401(k); and an employee stock purchase plan.

FINANCIAL DATA:
Note: Data for latest year may not have been available at press time.

In U.S. $	2017	2016	2015	2014	2013	2012
Revenue	22,291,000,000	23,554,000,000	25,281,000,000	26,487,000,000	24,866,000,000	19,121,000,000
R&D Expense	5,485,000,000	5,151,000,000	5,490,000,000	5,477,000,000	4,967,000,000	3,915,000,000
Operating Income	4,356,000,000	6,269,000,000	7,069,000,000	8,034,000,000	7,561,000,000	5,786,000,000
Operating Margin %	19.54%	26.61%	27.96%	30.33%	30.40%	30.25%
SGA Expense	2,658,000,000	2,385,000,000	2,344,000,000	2,290,000,000	2,518,000,000	2,324,000,000
Net Income	2,466,000,000	5,705,000,000	5,271,000,000	7,967,000,000	6,853,000,000	6,109,000,000
Operating Cash Flow	4,693,000,000	7,400,000,000	5,506,000,000	8,887,000,000	8,778,000,000	5,998,000,000
Capital Expenditure	690,000,000	539,000,000	994,000,000	1,185,000,000	1,048,000,000	1,284,000,000
EBITDA	4,975,000,000	8,558,000,000	7,805,000,000	9,933,000,000	9,234,000,000	7,549,000,000
Return on Assets %	4.18%	11.06%	10.60%	16.93%	15.48%	15.38%
Return on Equity %	7.88%	18.05%	14.93%	21.17%	19.68%	20.20%
Debt to Equity	0.63	0.31	0.31			

CONTACT INFORMATION:
Phone: 858 587-1121
Fax: 858 658-2100
Toll-Free:
Address: 5775 Morehouse Dr., San Diego, CA 92121 United States

STOCK TICKER/OTHER:
Stock Ticker: QCOM
Employees: 33,000
Parent Company:

Exchange: NAS
Fiscal Year Ends: 09/30

SALARIES/BONUSES:
Top Exec. Salary: $889,438   Bonus: $1,375,000
Second Exec. Salary: $542,324   Bonus: $1,000,000

OTHER THOUGHTS:
Estimated Female Officers or Directors: 2
Hot Spot for Advancement for Women/Minorities: Y

Sales, profits and employees may be estimates. Financial information, benefits and other data can change quickly and may vary from those stated here.

QuTech

NAIC Code: 334111

qutech.nl

TYPES OF BUSINESS:
Electronic Computer Manufacturing

BRANDS/DIVISIONS/AFFILIATES:
Delft Univeristy of Technology
Netherlands Organization for Applied Scientific

CONTACTS: *Note: Officers with more than one job title may be intentionally listed here more than once.*
Ronald Hanson, Scientific Dir.

GROWTH PLANS/SPECIAL FEATURES:
QuTech, which stands for quantum technology, is engaged in the researching and engineering of quantum computing and quantum internet technologies. Quantum technology is a key future energy technology based on the fields of physics and engineering, and transitions some of the properties of quantum mechanics into practical computing/internet applications. Founded in 2014 by Delft University of Technology and the Netherlands Organization for Applied Scientific Research (TNO), the center has transformed from a being university-based research division to a quantum science technology engineering entity. QuTech's research roadmap includes the following. Fault-tolerant quantum computing (FT), due to a 2015 contract with Intel Corporation to establish a 10-year collaboration on FT, which involves electron spin quantum bits (known as qubits) in silicon quantum dots, superconducting transmon qubits, cyrogenic electronics to control and measure the qubits, interconnects between classical control circuitry and the qubits, and quantum computer architecture. A qubit is a unit of quantum information. Next, quantum internet and networked computing (QINC), which demonstrates the feasibility of device-independent quantum key distribution-the ultimate security attainable for communication. Topological quantum computing, which is focused on material science and novel device geometries leading to topological qubits. QuTech shared development, in which TNO scientists and engineers contribute to the goals of other roadmaps, with many technologies developed in 2015. These shared developments have also contributed to QuTech's roadmap on the reciprocated receiving end. Last, quantum internet and networked computing currently seeks to build an optically-connected network of many small quantum computers, which would enable the exchange of qubits between any of the connected quantum processors in order to solve problems that cannot be seen nor captured via classical computers.

FINANCIAL DATA: *Note: Data for latest year may not have been available at press time.*

In U.S. $	2017	2016	2015	2014	2013	2012
Revenue						
R&D Expense						
Operating Income						
Operating Margin %						
SGA Expense						
Net Income						
Operating Cash Flow						
Capital Expenditure						
EBITDA						
Return on Assets %						
Return on Equity %						
Debt to Equity						

CONTACT INFORMATION:
Phone: 31-15-27-86-133   Fax:
Toll-Free:
Address: Lorentzweg 1, Delft, 2628 CJ Netherlands

STOCK TICKER/OTHER:
Stock Ticker: Private   Exchange:
Employees: 164   Fiscal Year Ends:
Parent Company:

SALARIES/BONUSES:
Top Exec. Salary: $ Bonus: $
Second Exec. Salary: $ Bonus: $

OTHER THOUGHTS:
Estimated Female Officers or Directors:
Hot Spot for Advancement for Women/Minorities:

Sales, profits and employees may be estimates. Financial information, benefits and other data can change quickly and may vary from those stated here.

Ramboll Environ Inc

NAIC Code: 541330

www.ramboll-environ.com

TYPES OF BUSINESS:
Engineering Consulting Services
Consulting

BRANDS/DIVISIONS/AFFILIATES:
Ramboll Group A/S

CONTACTS: *Note: Officers with more than one job title may be intentionally listed here more than once.*
Stephen T. Washburn, CEO
Thomas R. Vetrano, Pres.

GROWTH PLANS/SPECIAL FEATURES:

Ramboll Environ, Inc. is a consulting firm that focuses on resolving environmental and human health issues. Air quality management services include air quality compliance and permitting, air toxics health risk assessment, ambient air emissions monitoring programs, carbon emissions trading and footprinting, indoor air quality, noise and acoustics and regional planning services. Compliance, strategy and transaction services include building performance and property loss, environmental due diligence, environment, health and safety (EHS) management, product safety and toxicological sciences. Impact assessment services include environmental and social impact assessment (ESIA) and planning serving sectors, such as commercial and residential real estate, urban and regional planning, industry, infrastructure, mining and mineral processing, waste, power generation and renewables and oil and gas exploration and production. Laboratory services consist of chemical testing, ecological toxicity testing, regulatory compliance services, environmental analysis and measurement of chemicals in air, sediment, soil, freshwater and marine water environments. Resource and waste management services include landfill engineering and development, hazardous, radioactive and solid waste management, disposal facilities and operations and waste quality surveys and analytics among others. Site solutions services include site investigation and remediation, net environmental benefit analysis, decommissioning and closure and risk assessment. Water services are offered across the water cycle from water resources and supply, processing and treatment, to sewerage and discharge. Ecological services include expertise in ecotoxicology and ecological risk assessment, nature restoration, natural resource consulting, nature survey and monitoring, ecosystem services and marine sciences. Ramboll Environ operates as a subsidiary of Ramboll Group A/S. In April 2018, the firm acquired MMG, an engineering consultancy specializing in the design of hospital logistics systems, and the use of automated guided vehicles in hospitals.

Ramboll Environ offers medical, dental, vision insurance; annual leave, medical leave; life/accident/disability insurance; retirement savings and pension plans; and incentive and educational assistance programs.

FINANCIAL DATA: *Note: Data for latest year may not have been available at press time.*

In U.S. $	2017	2016	2015	2014	2013	2012
Revenue	415,071,000	349,659,000	280,783,000			
R&D Expense						
Operating Income						
Operating Margin %						
SGA Expense						
Net Income						
Operating Cash Flow						
Capital Expenditure						
EBITDA						
Return on Assets %						
Return on Equity %						
Debt to Equity						

CONTACT INFORMATION:
Phone: 703-516-2300   Fax: 703-516-2345
Toll-Free:
Address: 4350 N. Fairfax Dr., Ste. 300, Arlington, VA 22203 United States

STOCK TICKER/OTHER:
Stock Ticker: Private
Employees: 13,000
Parent Company: Ramboll Group A/S

Exchange:
Fiscal Year Ends:

SALARIES/BONUSES:
Top Exec. Salary: $ Bonus: $
Second Exec. Salary: $ Bonus: $

OTHER THOUGHTS:
Estimated Female Officers or Directors:
Hot Spot for Advancement for Women/Minorities:

Plunkett Research, Ltd.

Ramboll Group A/S

NAIC Code: 541330

www.ramboll.com

TYPES OF BUSINESS:
Engineering Consulting Services
Engineering
Consulting

BRANDS/DIVISIONS/AFFILIATES:
Ramboll Foundation
MMG

CONTACTS: Note: Officers with more than one job title may be intentionally listed here more than once.
Jens-Peter Saul, CEO

GROWTH PLANS/SPECIAL FEATURES:
Ramboll Group A/S provides consulting engineering, design and management consultancy services. It offers these services in the areas of buildings, transport, water, environment and health, energy, planning and urban design, and management consulting. The buildings unit includes acoustics, architecture, building physics, client consultancy, digital design, electrical engineering, façade engineering, facilities engineering, ground engineering, landscape architecture, lighting design, master planning, urban development, mechanical engineering, pharma and biotech consultancy, refurbishment, structural engineering, survey, sustainability and technical due diligence. Transport includes acoustics and noise, aviation, bridge engineering, contracts, management, landscape architecture, ports and marine structures, rail engineering, road and motorway engineering, risk and safety, transport planning, traffic engineering and safety, and tunnel engineering. Water includes climate adaptation and flood risk management, water and waste water infrastructure, waste water process and treatment, water supply and leakage and water resource management. The environment and health unit focuses on air quality management, ecological services, impact assessment, resource and waste management and laboratory services. Energy includes wind energy, waste-to-energy, thermal power, district energy, power transmission, asset management, renewable energy and energy strategy. The planning and urban design unit focuses on a holistic approach to urban development with emphasis on architecture, economics, mobility, physical planning and utilities and resources. Last, the management consulting unit covers all social and economic impacts of a project, stakeholder insights to drive transformational actions, and digital business strategies. Headquartered in Denmark, the firm has nearly 300 global offices in 35 countries throughout Australasia, the Americas, Asia, Europe and Africa. Ramboll is privately-held by Ramboll Foundation. In April 2018, Ramboll acquired German hospital logistics company, MMG.

FINANCIAL DATA: Note: Data for latest year may not have been available at press time.

In U.S. $	2017	2016	2015	2014	2013	2012
Revenue	1,727,580,000	1,503,270,000	1,550,270,000	1,353,730,000	1,438,370,000	
R&D Expense						
Operating Income						
Operating Margin %						
SGA Expense						
Net Income	23,500,200	25,069,400	11,170,300	26,856,100	26,408,500	
Operating Cash Flow						
Capital Expenditure						
EBITDA						
Return on Assets %						
Return on Equity %						
Debt to Equity						

CONTACT INFORMATION:
Phone: 45-5161-1000 Fax: 45-5161-1001
Toll-Free:
Address: Hannemanns Alle 53, Copenhagen, DK-2300 Denmark

SALARIES/BONUSES:
Top Exec. Salary: $ Bonus: $
Second Exec. Salary: $ Bonus: $

STOCK TICKER/OTHER:
Stock Ticker: Private Exchange:
Employees: 13,000 Fiscal Year Ends:
Parent Company: Ramboll Foundation

OTHER THOUGHTS:
Estimated Female Officers or Directors:
Hot Spot for Advancement for Women/Minorities:

Sales, profits and employees may be estimates. Financial information, benefits and other data can change quickly and may vary from those stated here.

Raytheon Company

www.raytheon.com

NAIC Code: 336414

TYPES OF BUSINESS:
Guided Missile and Space Vehicle Manufacturing
Commercial Electronics
Technical Services
Communications & Information Systems
Sensors & Surveillance Equipment
Missile Systems
Software Engineering
Cybersecurity Solutions

BRANDS/DIVISIONS/AFFILIATES:
Forcepoint

CONTACTS:
Note: Officers with more than one job title may be intentionally listed here more than once.

Thomas Kennedy, CEO
Anthony OBrien, CFO
Michael Wood, Controller
Wesley Kremer, President, Divisional
Rebecca Rhoads, President, Divisional
David Wajsgras, President, Divisional
Randa Newsome, Vice President, Divisional
Frank Jimenez, Vice President
Taylor Lawrence, Vice President
Richard Yuse, Vice President

GROWTH PLANS/SPECIAL FEATURES:

Raytheon Company offers electronics, mission systems integration and mission support services to defense, homeland security and other government markets worldwide. Raytheon operates through five segments: integrated defense systems (IDS); intelligence, information and systems (IIS); missile systems (MS); space and airborne systems (SAS); and Forcepoint. IDS provides air and missile defense; radar solutions; naval combat and ship electronic systems; command, control, communications, computers and intelligence solutions; and international and domestic Air Traffic Management systems. IIS provides technical and professional services to intelligence, defense, federal and commercial customers worldwide. IIS specializes in global intelligence, surveillance and reconnaissance (ISR), navigation, DoD (Department of Defense) space and weather solutions; cybersecurity, analytics, training, logistics, mission support and engineering and sustainment solutions. MS develops and produces missile and combat systems, including weapon systems, projectiles, kinetic kill vehicles, directed energy effectors and advanced combat sensor solutions for the armed forces of the U.S. and other allied nations. SAS designs and develops sensor and communication systems for advanced missions, including ISR, precision engagement, unmanned aerial operations and space. This segment provides electro-optical/infrared sensors, airborne radars for surveillance and fire control applications, lasers, precision guidance systems, signals intelligence systems, processors, electronic warfare systems, communication systems and space-qualified systems for civil and military applications. Forcepoint develops cybersecurity products serving commercial and government organizations, and include user and data security solutions, as well as cloud access and network security solutions. Its government organizations solutions include a suite of cross domain and insider threat technologies to access and transfer data, including streaming video, across multiple domains.

Employees receive medical, dental, prescription drug and vision care coverage; health care reimbursement accounts; life and AD&D insurance; short- and long-term disability; a retirement program; adoption assistance; and educational assistance.

FINANCIAL DATA:
Note: Data for latest year may not have been available at press time.

In U.S. $	2017	2016	2015	2014	2013	2012
Revenue	25,348,000,000	24,069,000,000	23,247,000,000	22,826,000,000	23,706,000,000	24,414,000,000
R&D Expense	734,000,000	755,000,000	706,000,000	500,000,000	465,000,000	704,000,000
Operating Income	3,318,000,000	3,240,000,000	3,013,000,000	3,179,000,000	2,938,000,000	2,989,000,000
Operating Margin %	13.08%	13.46%	12.96%	13.92%	12.39%	12.24%
SGA Expense	2,220,000,000	2,127,000,000	1,954,000,000	1,852,000,000	1,771,000,000	1,629,000,000
Net Income	2,024,000,000	2,211,000,000	2,074,000,000	2,244,000,000	1,996,000,000	1,888,000,000
Operating Cash Flow	2,745,000,000	2,852,000,000	2,359,000,000	2,184,000,000	2,378,000,000	1,957,000,000
Capital Expenditure	611,000,000	625,000,000	457,000,000	380,000,000	329,000,000	415,000,000
EBITDA	3,868,000,000	3,777,000,000	3,509,000,000	3,635,000,000	3,412,000,000	3,435,000,000
Return on Assets %	6.64%	7.45%	7.25%	8.33%	7.58%	7.18%
Return on Equity %	20.21%	21.89%	21.10%	21.82%	20.94%	23.29%
Debt to Equity	0.47	0.53	0.52	0.55	0.42	0.58

CONTACT INFORMATION:
Phone: 788 522-3000 Fax: 781 522-3001
Toll-Free:
Address: 870 Winter St., Waltham, MA 02451 United States

STOCK TICKER/OTHER:
Stock Ticker: RTN
Employees: 63,000
Parent Company:

Exchange: NYS
Fiscal Year Ends: 12/31

SALARIES/BONUSES:
Top Exec. Salary: $1,299,979 Bonus: $
Second Exec. Salary: $971,943 Bonus: $

OTHER THOUGHTS:
Estimated Female Officers or Directors: 4
Hot Spot for Advancement for Women/Minorities: Y

Sales, profits and employees may be estimates. Financial information, benefits and other data can change quickly and may vary from those stated here.

Renault SA

NAIC Code: 336111

www.renault.com

TYPES OF BUSINESS:
Automobile Manufacturing
Financial Services
Commercial Vehicles
Scooters
Farm Machinery
Automotive Maintenance Service

BRANDS/DIVISIONS/AFFILIATES:
Renault
Renault Samsung Motors
Dacia
Renault-Nissan BV
AvtoVAZ OAO
Daimler AG
Nissan Motor Co Ltd
Renault Minute

CONTACTS:
Note: Officers with more than one job title may be intentionally listed here more than once.

Carlos Ghosn, CEO
Thierry Bollore, COO
Cotilde Delbos, CFO
Thierry Koskas, Exec. VP-Sales & Mktg.
Marie-Francoise Damesin, Exec. VP-Human Resources
Philippe Klein, Exec. VP-Prod. Planning, Plan & Programs
Jean-Michel Billig, Exec. VP-Eng. & Quality
Jose Vicente de los Mosoz Obispo, Exec. VP-Mfg.
Philippe Klein, Exec. VP-Corp. Planning
Mouna Sepehri, Exec. VP-Office of CEO
Stefan Mueller, Exec. VP
Carlos Ghosn, Chmn.
Gerard Leclercq, Exec. VP-Supply Chain

GROWTH PLANS/SPECIAL FEATURES:

Renault SA is a leading automobile manufacturer in France. The company's automobile division consists of the Renault, Renault Samsung Motors (RSM) and Dacia brands based in France, South Korea and Romania, respectively. It designs, develops and markets a line of small- to mid-size cars, including hatchbacks and minivans, as well as light commercial vehicles and two-wheelers, such as scooters. Some of Renault's brands include the Twingo, Clio, Captur, Scenic, Espace, Laguna, Latitude, Kadjar and Talisman. RSM models include SM5, SM3, QM3, SM3 ZE, QM5, SM7 and SM6. Dacia's models include the Duster, an SUV; Logan, available in a 4-door sedan; and Sandero, a 4-door hatchback. Renault's sales and finance division is comprised of RCI Banque and its subsidiaries, which provide sales, services and cash management for the group. Renault SA operates a host of automotive maintenance locations under the names Renault Minute and Motrio. There are more than 750 Renault Minute centers throughout France. Motrio offers a range of multi-branded parts for the maintenance and light engineering of vehicles, as well as at-your-service auto repair shops throughout the country. Through its joint venture Renault-Nissan BV, Renault owns approximately 43.4% of Japan-based Nissan Motor Co. Ltd. Nissan, in turn, owns approximately 15% of Renault. In addition, the French government has a 19.73% stake in the company. The firm has a partnership and 25% stake in Russian automaker AvtoVAZ OAO, as well as a 1.55% stake in automaker Daimler AG of Germany.

FINANCIAL DATA:
Note: Data for latest year may not have been available at press time.

In U.S. $	2017	2016	2015	2014	2013	2012
Revenue	72,575,270,000	63,280,150,000	55,974,460,000	50,698,950,000	50,547,060,000	50,964,460,000
R&D Expense	3,198,400,000	2,926,721,000	2,562,425,000	2,125,269,000	2,237,645,000	2,364,840,000
Operating Income	4,759,318,000	4,052,953,000	2,864,976,000	1,986,959,000	1,533,750,000	900,244,500
Operating Margin %	6.55%	6.40%	5.11%	3.91%	3.03%	1.76%
SGA Expense	7,222,949,000	6,588,209,000	5,950,999,000	5,452,099,000	5,269,332,000	5,599,052,000
Net Income	6,315,296,000	4,222,135,000	3,486,132,000	2,333,967,000	723,653,400	2,188,249,000
Operating Cash Flow	7,041,419,000	5,419,991,000	7,430,413,000	4,905,036,000	4,411,075,000	4,786,485,000
Capital Expenditure	4,446,887,000	3,824,496,000	3,458,964,000	3,100,842,000	3,394,749,000	3,515,770,000
EBITDA	11,871,130,000	9,700,166,000	7,929,314,000	6,653,660,000	5,913,952,000	7,461,286,000
Return on Assets %	4.82%	3.54%	3.27%	2.41%	.77%	2.38%
Return on Equity %	16.00%	11.64%	10.76%	7.98%	2.48%	7.32%
Debt to Equity	0.14	0.13	0.18	0.28	0.29	0.25

CONTACT INFORMATION:
Phone: 33 176840404 Fax:
Toll-Free:
Address: 13-15 Quai Alponse le Gallo, Billancourt Cedex, 92513 France

STOCK TICKER/OTHER:
Stock Ticker: RNSDF
Employees: 181,344
Parent Company:

Exchange: PINX
Fiscal Year Ends: 12/31

SALARIES/BONUSES:
Top Exec. Salary: $ Bonus: $
Second Exec. Salary: $ Bonus: $

OTHER THOUGHTS:
Estimated Female Officers or Directors: 7
Hot Spot for Advancement for Women/Minorities: Y

Sales, profits and employees may be estimates. Financial information, benefits and other data can change quickly and may vary from those stated here.

Rheinmetall AG

NAIC Code: 336300

www.rheinmetall.de

TYPES OF BUSINESS:
Automotive Components Manufacturing
Military Vehicles
Weapons & Ammunition
Defense Electronics
Air Defense Systems
Command & Control Systems
Reconnaissance Systems
Training & Simulator Operations

BRANDS/DIVISIONS/AFFILIATES:
Rheinmetall Defence AG
Rheinmetall Automotive AG

CONTACTS:
Note: Officers with more than one job title may be intentionally listed here more than once.

Armin Papperger, CEO
Helmut P. Merch, CFO
Horst Binnig, Chmn.-Automotive

GROWTH PLANS/SPECIAL FEATURES:
Rheinmetall AG, established in 1889, provides environmentally-friendly mobility and threat security technology. The company operates through two business segments: Rheinmetall Defence AG and Rheinmetall Automotive AG. Rheinmetall Defence provides innovative products for German and international armed forces, and offers systems and partial system solutions as well as a wide range of services in the areas of mobility, reconnaissance, management, effectiveness and protection. This division's products and services include armored vehicles, vehicle systems, weapons/ammunition, turret systems, weapon stations, protection systems, air defense systems, C4I systems, electro-optics, simulation/training, unmanned vehicles, infantry, naval applications, airborne applications aviation systems, tracked vehicles, military trucks, services vehicle systems, propulsion systems, ammunition disposal, manufacturing and testing. Rheinmetall Automotive provides air supply, emission control and pump products and component systems. It also develops, manufactures and supplies aftermarket pistons, engine blocks and plain bearings. Based in Dusseldorf, Germany, the firm has additional locations throughout Europe, the U.K., Asia, America, Africa and Australia.

FINANCIAL DATA:
Note: Data for latest year may not have been available at press time.

In U.S. $	2017	2016	2015	2014	2013	2012
Revenue		6,917,928,000	6,400,504,000	5,789,227,000	5,696,609,000	5,808,985,000
R&D Expense						
Operating Income		411,222,800	321,074,900	86,443,230	196,349,600	311,195,600
Operating Margin %		5.94%	5.01%	1.49%	3.44%	5.35%
SGA Expense		274,148,500	266,739,100	246,980,700	232,161,800	391,464,400
Net Income		246,980,700	186,470,400	22,228,260	35,812,200	234,631,600
Operating Cash Flow		548,297,100	418,632,200	125,960,100	240,806,100	443,330,300
Capital Expenditure		349,477,600	382,820,000	350,712,500	235,866,500	288,967,400
EBITDA		723,653,400	608,807,400	385,289,900	402,578,500	616,216,800
Return on Assets %		3.37%	2.74%	.35%	.59%	3.90%
Return on Equity %		12.58%	11.56%	1.51%	2.22%	13.77%
Debt to Equity		0.13	0.50	0.67	0.42	0.42

CONTACT INFORMATION:
Phone: 49-211-473-01 Fax: 49-21-473-4727
Toll-Free:
Address: Rheinmetall Platz 1, Düsseldorf, 40476 Germany

STOCK TICKER/OTHER:
Stock Ticker: RNMBF
Employees: 22,386
Parent Company:

Exchange: PINX
Fiscal Year Ends: 12/31

SALARIES/BONUSES:
Top Exec. Salary: $ Bonus: $
Second Exec. Salary: $ Bonus: $

OTHER THOUGHTS:
Estimated Female Officers or Directors:
Hot Spot for Advancement for Women/Minorities:

Sales, profits and employees may be estimates. Financial information, benefits and other data can change quickly and may vary from those stated here.

Ricardo plc

NAIC Code: 541330

www.ricardo.com

TYPES OF BUSINESS:
Engineering and Research
Consulting and Technical Services
Software

BRANDS/DIVISIONS/AFFILIATES:
Ricardo Software
Ricardo Knowledge

CONTACTS:
Note: Officers with more than one job title may be intentionally listed here more than once.

Dave Shemmans, CEO
Mark Garrett, COO
Ian Gibson, CFO
Terry Morgan, Chmn.

GROWTH PLANS/SPECIAL FEATURES:

Ricardo plc is a global engineering, strategic and environmental consultancy. Ricardo specializes in the areas of transport and security; energy; and scarce resources and waste. The transport and security sector provides engineering and product development services, compliance services and manufacturing services to the motorsport, aerospace, defense and other high-performance industries. The energy sector is concerned with low-cost sustainability and engineering services for conventional and renewable power generation, energy storage and distribution. The scarce resources and waste sector delivers environmental consulting focused on air quality, chemical risk, climate change, resource efficiency and water and waste management. In addition, Ricardo Software markets and supports a range of design and analysis software products for powertrain development and vehicle integration processes. The company's Ricardo Knowledge platform offers customers an easy online interactive portal to ask technical questions or find technical assistance and training. In March 2018, the firm sold its Chicago facility to Power Solutions International (PSI), and relocated its heavy-duty test operations to Detroit.

FINANCIAL DATA:
Note: Data for latest year may not have been available at press time.

In U.S. $	2017	2016	2015	2014	2013	2012
Revenue	501,495,500	473,436,800	366,756,900	336,419,300	327,161,400	281,156,500
R&D Expense						
Operating Income	52,414,180	49,708,020	33,898,300	34,895,310	31,477,000	26,491,950
Operating Margin %	10.45%	10.49%	9.24%	10.37%	9.62%	9.42%
SGA Expense	131,890,000	138,014,500	112,092,300	99,131,180	105,113,200	91,439,970
Net Income	35,322,600	36,462,040	26,491,950	27,346,530	24,213,070	21,506,910
Operating Cash Flow	21,791,770	33,328,590	38,456,060	30,764,850	41,731,950	31,904,290
Capital Expenditure	16,949,150	20,937,190	22,646,350	14,955,140	17,661,300	15,667,280
EBITDA	72,924,090	69,933,060	49,138,300	48,711,010	45,007,830	38,028,770
Return on Assets %	7.69%	9.13%	8.34%	10.57%	10.00%	9.13%
Return on Equity %	16.81%	20.03%	16.63%	18.50%	17.92%	16.83%
Debt to Equity	0.38	0.39	0.39			

CONTACT INFORMATION:
Phone: 44 1273455611   Fax: 44 1273464124
Toll-Free:
Address: Shoreham Technical Ctr., Shoreham-by-Sea, West Sussex, BN43 5FG United Kingdom

STOCK TICKER/OTHER:
Stock Ticker: RCDOF   Exchange: GREY
Employees: 2,718   Fiscal Year Ends: 06/30
Parent Company:

SALARIES/BONUSES:
Top Exec. Salary: $675,118   Bonus: $
Second Exec. Salary: $434,411   Bonus: $

OTHER THOUGHTS:
Estimated Female Officers or Directors:
Hot Spot for Advancement for Women/Minorities:

Ricoh Company Ltd

NAIC Code: 333316

www.ricoh.com

TYPES OF BUSINESS:
Photographic and Photocopying Equipment Manufacturing
Network Systems
Printers, Copiers & Fax Machines
PCs & Servers
Accessories
Digital Cameras
Electronic Devices
Managed Print Services

BRANDS/DIVISIONS/AFFILIATES:
Ricoh USA Inc
Ricoh Europe plc
Ricoh Asia Pacific Pte Ltd

CONTACTS:
Note: Officers with more than one job title may be intentionally listed here more than once.

Yoshinori Yamashita, CEO
Shiro Sasaki, Exec. VP
Nobuo Inaba, Exec. VP
Yohzoh Matsuura, Exec. VP
Yoshinori Yamashita, Exec. VP
Shiro Kondo, Chmn.

GROWTH PLANS/SPECIAL FEATURES:
Ricoh Company, Ltd. manufactures and markets office automation equipment, electronic devices and photographic instruments. The firm operates its business through six segments. The office printing segment produces and/or provides multi-functional printers, copiers, laser printers, digital duplicators, wide format, facsimile, scanners, related parts and supplies, services, support and software. The office service segment produces and/or provides personal computers, servers, network equipment, related services, support, software and service/solutions related to documents. The commercial printing segment produces and/or provides cut sheet printers, continuous-feed printers, related parts and supplies, services, support and software. The industrial printing segment produces and/or provides inkjet heads, imaging systems and industrial printers. The thermal media segment offers thermal heating products and solutions in relation to printing technology and printheads. Last, the other segment produces and/or provides optical equipment, electronic components, semiconductor devices, digital cameras, industrial cameras and 3D printing, as well as related environment and healthcare products and solutions. Based in Tokyo, Japan, the company has regional headquarters covering the Americas, Europe/MiddleEast/Africa and Asia/Pacific/China via subsidiaries Ricoh USA, Inc.; Ricoh Europe plc and Ricoh Asia Pacific Pte. Ltd.

FINANCIAL DATA:
Note: Data for latest year may not have been available at press time.

In U.S. $	2017	2016	2015	2014	2013	2012
Revenue	18,901,610,000	20,579,730,000	20,793,200,000	20,455,530,000	17,928,980,000	17,733,160,000
R&D Expense						
Operating Income	309,623,600	769,126,200	1,078,489,000	1,121,157,000	725,414,600	201,416,100
Operating Margin %	1.63%	3.73%	5.18%	5.48%	4.04%	1.13%
SGA Expense	7,037,386,000	7,447,420,000	7,370,533,000	7,013,975,000	6,435,020,000	6,554,043,000
Net Income	32,504,190	586,687,200	638,736,800	678,386,500	302,468,800	-415,129,500
Operating Cash Flow	822,610,500	930,296,300	955,319,600	1,368,493,000	1,160,108,000	104,397,200
Capital Expenditure	952,487,500	1,050,363,000	1,043,264,000	1,006,363,000	920,393,200	817,728,800
EBITDA	1,354,584,000	2,001,183,000	2,119,564,000	2,174,530,000	1,410,984,000	616,536,300
Return on Assets %	.12%	2.28%	2.57%	2.94%	1.39%	-1.95%
Return on Equity %	.32%	5.82%	6.48%	7.55%	3.77%	-5.08%
Debt to Equity	0.60	0.54	0.52	0.43	0.53	0.63

CONTACT INFORMATION:
Phone: 81 362785241   Fax: 81 335439086
Toll-Free:
Address: 8-13-1 Ginza, Chuo-ku, Tokyo, 104-8222 Japan

STOCK TICKER/OTHER:
Stock Ticker: RICOF
Employees: 109,361
Parent Company:

Exchange: PINX
Fiscal Year Ends: 03/31

SALARIES/BONUSES:
Top Exec. Salary: $ Bonus: $
Second Exec. Salary: $ Bonus: $

OTHER THOUGHTS:
Estimated Female Officers or Directors:
Hot Spot for Advancement for Women/Minorities:

Sales, profits and employees may be estimates. Financial information, benefits and other data can change quickly and may vary from those stated here.

Robert Bosch GmbH

NAIC Code: 336300

www.bosch.com

TYPES OF BUSINESS:
Automobile Components Manufacturing
Software and Machine to Machine Data
Motor, Control & Motion Products
Chassis Systems
Electronics & Multimedia
Energy, Fuel & Body Systems
Security Systems
Power Tools

BRANDS/DIVISIONS/AFFILIATES:
Bosch Mahle TurboSystems
Bosch Engineering
Bosch Boxberg Proving Ground
Bosch Battery Systems
Bosch Rexroth
Bosch Packaging Technology

CONTACTS: Note: Officers with more than one job title may be intentionally listed here more than once.
Volkmar Denner, Dir.-Research
Volkmar Denner, Dir.-Prod. Planning
Volkmar Denner, Dir.-Eng.
Stefan Asenkerschbaumer, Dir.-Bus. Admin.
Christoph Kubel, Dir.-Legal Svcs., Taxes & Internal Auditing
Stefan Asenkerschbaumer, Dir.-Corp. Planning
Volkmar Denner, Dir.-Corp. Comm.
Stefan Asenkerschbaumer, Dir.-Finance & Controlling
Wolf-Henning Scheider, Dir.-Coordination Automotive Tech.
Uwe Raschke, Dir.-Consumer Goods & User Experience
Werner Struth, Dir.-North & South America
Volkmar Denner, Chmn.
Peter Tyroller, Dir.-Asia Pacific
Stefan Asenkerschbaumer, Dir.-Purchasing & Logistics

GROWTH PLANS/SPECIAL FEATURES:
Robert Bosch GmbH is one of the world's leading manufacturers of automotive components. It has operations in roughly 60 countries through over 440 subsidiaries. The company operates in four business sectors: mobility solutions, industrial technology, consumer goods and energy and building technology. Mobility solutions supplies independent parts to the automotive industry, including gasoline systems, diesel systems, chassis systems control, electrical drives, starter motors, generators, multimedia, automotive electronics, automotive aftermarket parts and steering systems. Subsidiaries and joint ventures (JVs) in this segment include Bosch Mahle TurboSystems, Bosch Engineering, Bosch Boxberg Proving Ground and Bosch Battery Systems. Industrial technology incorporates the drive, control technology and packaging technology divisions. Subsidiary Bosch Rexroth provides drive and control technologies for mobile applications, machinery applications/engineering and factory automation. Bosch Packaging Technology is a leading supplier in the field of processing and packaging technology, developing and producing solutions for the pharmaceutical, food and confectionary industries. Consumer goods provides a wide spectrum of products and solutions in the areas of power tools and household appliances. Energy and building technology offers products and solutions such as HVAC (heating, ventilating and air conditioning), solar energy and security systems. In January 2018, the firm opened a new global Internet of Things (IoT) campus in Berlin, Germany; and agreed to acquire a minority stake (5%) in HERE Technologies, a global provider of digital mapping and location services.

Bosch USA offers employees benefits including medical, dental and vision coverage; long-term care insurance; life and AD&D insurance; travel accident insurance; paid vacations; short- and long-term disability coverage; and an educational assistance progra

FINANCIAL DATA: Note: Data for latest year may not have been available at press time.

In U.S. $	2017	2016	2015	2014	2013	2012
Revenue	93,512,400,000	77,058,200,000	77,152,300,000	54,586,000,000	51,372,000,000	49,849,000,000
R&D Expense						
Operating Income						
Operating Margin %						
SGA Expense						
Net Income	3,921,810,000	2,805,000,000	4,178,000,000	2,941,000,000	1,395,000,000	2,569,000,000
Operating Cash Flow						
Capital Expenditure						
EBITDA						
Return on Assets %						
Return on Equity %						
Debt to Equity						

CONTACT INFORMATION:
Phone: 49-711-400-40990   Fax: 49-711-400-40999
Toll-Free:
Address: Postfach 10 60 50, Stuttgart, 70049 Germany

STOCK TICKER/OTHER:
Stock Ticker: Private
Employees: 402,000
Parent Company:

Exchange:
Fiscal Year Ends: 12/31

SALARIES/BONUSES:
Top Exec. Salary: $ Bonus: $
Second Exec. Salary: $ Bonus: $

OTHER THOUGHTS:
Estimated Female Officers or Directors: 3
Hot Spot for Advancement for Women/Minorities: Y

Sales, profits and employees may be estimates. Financial information, benefits and other data can change quickly and may vary from those stated here.

Roche Holding AG

www.roche.com

NAIC Code: 325412

TYPES OF BUSINESS:
Pharmaceuticals Manufacturing
Antibiotics
Diagnostics
Cancer Drugs
Virology Products
HIV/AIDS Treatments
Transplant Drugs

BRANDS/DIVISIONS/AFFILIATES:
F Hoffmann-La Roche Ltd
Genentech Inc
Chugai Pharmaceutical Co Ltd
Flatiron Health
Ignyta Inc

CONTACTS:
Note: Officers with more than one job title may be intentionally listed here more than once.

Severin Schwan, CEO
Alan Hippe, CFO
Cristina A. Wilbur, Head-Human Resources
John C. Reed, Head-Roche Pharmaceutical Research & Early Dev.
Alan Hippe, CIO
Gottlieb Keller, General Counsel
Daniel ODay, COO-Pharmaceuticals
Stephen Feldhaus, Head-Comm.
Richard Scheller, Head-Genentech Research & Early Dev.
Roland Diggelmann, COO-Diagnostics
Sophie Kornowski-Bonnet, Head-Roche Partnering
Christoph Franz, Chmn.
Osamu Nagayama, CEO

GROWTH PLANS/SPECIAL FEATURES:

Roche Holding AG, also referred to as F. Hoffmann-La Roche Ltd. and based in Switzerland, is a world-leading healthcare and biotechnology company. The firm occupies an industry-leading position in the global diagnostics market and ranks as one of the top producers of pharmaceuticals, with recognition in the areas of oncology, autoimmune disease and metabolic disorder treatments, virology and transplantation medicine. The company's operations currently extend to over 100 countries, with additional alliances and research and development agreements with corporate and institutional partners furthering Roche's collective reach. It operates in two divisions: pharmaceuticals, which generates the majority of the firm's annual sales; and diagnostics. The pharmaceuticals division focuses on translating science into breakthrough medicines for patients, with research at Roche and wholly-owned Genentech, Inc. in the U.S., as well as Chugai Pharmaceutical Co., Ltd. in Japan. This segment has more than 150 worldwide partners engaged in clinical development, manufacturing and commercial operations, with a focus on oncology, immunology, ophthalmology, infectious diseases and neuroscience. More than half of the compounds in this division's product pipeline are biopharmaceuticals. The diagnostics division performs blood, tissue and other types of patient samples, as well as in vitro diagnostics for the purpose of obtaining information in relation to improved disease management and patient care. Diagnostic services and solutions provide prevention, screening, diagnosis, prognosis, stratification, treatment and monitoring capabilities in regard to diseases. In April 2018, the firm acquired Flatiron Health, specializing in U.S. cancer data analytics. Earlier that year, Roche acquired an additional stake of Ignyta, Inc., for a total 84.71% holding. Ignyta develops precisely-targeted therapeutics guided by diagnostic tests to patients with cancer.

FINANCIAL DATA:
Note: Data for latest year may not have been available at press time.

In U.S. $	2017	2016	2015	2014	2013	2012
Revenue	55,419,920,000	54,730,540,000	52,408,680,000	51,850,310,000	50,546,410,000	49,331,930,000
R&D Expense	11,741,340,000	11,990,890,000	9,962,255,000	10,288,750,000	9,638,879,000	9,932,102,000
Operating Income	13,520,430,000	14,628,850,000	14,370,980,000	14,650,680,000	17,027,650,000	14,687,070,000
Operating Margin %	24.39%	26.72%	27.42%	28.25%	33.68%	29.77%
SGA Expense	13,800,130,000	11,286,950,000	12,000,250,000	12,997,410,000	11,456,440,000	12,053,280,000
Net Income	8,976,532,000	9,957,057,000	9,215,684,000	9,703,347,000	11,608,250,000	9,918,585,000
Operating Cash Flow	18,741,230,000	15,597,930,000	15,857,880,000	16,563,900,000	16,399,610,000	15,602,090,000
Capital Expenditure	4,380,647,000	5,349,734,000	4,273,549,000	3,466,670,000	2,967,569,000	2,501,742,000
EBITDA	17,385,340,000	18,550,950,000	17,352,060,000	16,933,030,000	19,101,000,000	17,412,370,000
Return on Assets %	11.24%	12.55%	11.70%	13.54%	17.58%	15.09%
Return on Equity %	34.29%	42.66%	43.69%	48.00%	66.08%	71.75%
Debt to Equity	0.59	0.71	0.81	0.98	0.85	1.23

CONTACT INFORMATION:
Phone: 41-61-688-1111   Fax: 41-61-691-9391
Toll-Free:
Address: Grenzacherstrasse 124, Basel, 4070 Switzerland

STOCK TICKER/OTHER:
Stock Ticker: RHHBY
Employees: 94,052
Parent Company:

Exchange: PINX
Fiscal Year Ends: 12/31

SALARIES/BONUSES:
Top Exec. Salary: $ Bonus: $
Second Exec. Salary: $ Bonus: $

OTHER THOUGHTS:
Estimated Female Officers or Directors: 4
Hot Spot for Advancement for Women/Minorities: Y

Plunkett Research, Ltd.

Rockwell Automation Inc
NAIC Code: 334513

www.rockwellautomation.com

TYPES OF BUSINESS:
Architecture & Software Products
Control Products & Services

BRANDS/DIVISIONS/AFFILIATES:
FactoryTalk
A-B
Allen-Bradley
Rockwell Software
Odos Imaging

CONTACTS: Note: Officers with more than one job title may be intentionally listed here more than once.
Patrick Goris, CFO
John Miller, Vice President
Keith Nosbusch, Chairman of the Board
David Dorgan, Chief Accounting Officer
Christopher Nardecchia, Chief Information Officer
Sujeet Chand, Chief Technology Officer
Rebecca House, General Counsel
Blake Moret, President
Frank Kulaszewicz, Senior VP
John Mcdermott, Senior VP
Theodore Crandall, Senior VP
Elik Fooks, Senior VP
Robert Murphy, Senior VP, Divisional
Susan Schmitt, Senior VP, Divisional
Steven Etzel, Vice President

GROWTH PLANS/SPECIAL FEATURES:
Rockwell Automation, Inc. is a global provider of industrial automation power, control and information products and services. It operates in two segments: architecture and software (A&S); and control products and solutions (CP&S). The A&S operating segment contains all elements of the company's integrated control and information architecture capable of connecting the customer's entire manufacturing enterprise. The division's integrated architecture and Logix controllers perform multiple types of control and monitoring applications, including discrete, batch, continuous process, drive system, motion and machine safety across various industrial machinery, plants and processes; and supply real time information to supervisory software and plant-wide information systems. Products include control platforms, software, I/O devices, communication networks, high performance rotary and linear motion control systems, electronic operator interface devices, condition based monitoring systems, sensors, industrial computers and machine safety components. These products are marketed primarily under the FactoryTalk, A-B, Allen-Bradley and Rockwell Software brand names. The CP&S segment's portfolio includes low voltage and medium voltage electro-mechanical and electronic motor starters, motor and circuit protection devices, AC/DC variable frequency drives, contractors, push buttons, signaling devices, termination and protection devices, relays and timers and condition sensors. The segment also offers value-added packaged solutions that range from configured drives and motor control centers to automation and information solutions where Rockwell provides design, integration and start-up services for custom-engineered hardware and software systems. Additionally, the CP&S segment provides life-cycle support services designed to help maximize a customer's automation investment, including multi-vendor customer technical support and repair, asset management, training and maintenance. In December 2017, Rockwell acquired Odos Imaging, a Scottish technology company that provides three-dimensional, time-of-flight sensing systems for industrial imaging applications.

FINANCIAL DATA: Note: Data for latest year may not have been available at press time.

In U.S. $	2017	2016	2015	2014	2013	2012
Revenue	6,311,300,000	5,879,500,000	6,307,900,000	6,623,500,000	6,351,900,000	6,259,400,000
R&D Expense						
Operating Income	1,033,200,000	1,001,700,000	1,180,400,000	1,184,600,000	1,032,500,000	1,019,200,000
Operating Margin %	16.37%	17.03%	18.71%	17.88%	16.25%	16.28%
SGA Expense	1,591,500,000	1,467,400,000	1,506,400,000	1,570,100,000	1,537,700,000	1,491,700,000
Net Income	825,700,000	729,700,000	827,600,000	826,800,000	756,300,000	737,000,000
Operating Cash Flow	1,034,000,000	947,300,000	1,187,700,000	1,033,300,000	1,014,800,000	718,700,000
Capital Expenditure	141,700,000	116,900,000	122,900,000	141,000,000	146,200,000	139,600,000
EBITDA	1,282,500,000	1,186,600,000	1,353,700,000	1,346,000,000	1,187,000,000	1,164,600,000
Return on Assets %	11.56%	10.79%	13.08%	13.67%	13.15%	13.47%
Return on Equity %	35.44%	34.33%	33.64%	31.49%	34.03%	40.87%
Debt to Equity	0.46	0.76	0.66	0.34	0.35	0.48

CONTACT INFORMATION:
Phone: 414 382-2000 Fax: 414 382-8520
Toll-Free:
Address: 1201 S. 2nd St., Milwaukee, WI 53204 United States

SALARIES/BONUSES:
Top Exec. Salary: $950,000   Bonus: $
Second Exec. Salary: $652,000   Bonus: $

STOCK TICKER/OTHER:
Stock Ticker: ROK   Exchange: NYS
Employees: 22,000   Fiscal Year Ends: 09/30
Parent Company:

OTHER THOUGHTS:
Estimated Female Officers or Directors: 1
Hot Spot for Advancement for Women/Minorities:

Sales, profits and employees may be estimates. Financial information, benefits and other data can change quickly and may vary from those stated here.

Rohm Co Ltd

NAIC Code: 334418

www.rohm.com

TYPES OF BUSINESS:
Electronic Components Manufacturing
Integrated Circuits
Discrete Semiconductor Devices
Passive Components
Resistors & Capacitors
Display Devices
LED Displays

BRANDS/DIVISIONS/AFFILIATES:

CONTACTS: Note: Officers with more than one job title may be intentionally listed here more than once.
Satoshi Sawamura, CEO
Satoshi Sawamura, Pres.

GROWTH PLANS/SPECIAL FEATURES:
Rohm Co., Ltd. is a Japanese manufacturer of electronic components and component systems. Rohm makes components for a number of applications, including car electronics, mobile phones, flat-panel display (FPD) TVs and DVD players and recorders. The firm's products are grouped into seven categories. The integrated circuit (IC) products category includes memory, amplifiers, power management, clocks/timers, switches, multiplexers, data converters, sensors, micro-electro-mechanical systems (MEMS), digital power, display drivers, motor/actuator drivers, interfaces, communication large-scale integration (LSI), audio/video, speech synthesis LSI and microcontrollers. The discrete semiconductors category includes transistors and diodes. The power devices category includes silicon carbide (SiC) power devices, insulated-gate bipolar transistors (IGBTs) and intelligent power modules (IPMs). The passive devices category includes resistors and tantalum capacitors. The modules product category includes power modules, wireless communication modules, printheads and battery-less radio modules. The opto devices category includes light-emitting diode (LED) devices, LED displays, laser diodes and optical sensors. Last, the commercial products category includes chipsets and reference boards for the general embedded systems market, power management ICs (integrated circuits), clock generators ICs and input-output hubs.

FINANCIAL DATA: Note: Data for latest year may not have been available at press time.

In U.S. $	2017	2016	2015	2014	2013	2012
Revenue	3,279,393,000	3,282,998,000	3,379,654,000	3,084,470,000	2,724,148,000	2,838,196,000
R&D Expense						
Operating Income	296,515,800	313,359,400	361,477,500	220,197,500	-8,580,213	59,185,770
Operating Margin %	9.04%	9.54%	10.69%	7.13%	-.31%	2.08%
SGA Expense						
Net Income	246,245,600	239,295,700	421,986,200	298,965,900	-488,764,700	-150,046,600
Operating Cash Flow	627,883,400	735,056,900	674,315,300	550,903,700	470,840,400	343,376,200
Capital Expenditure	368,939,800	505,040,100	375,172,400	260,443,500	474,520,300	388,559,700
EBITDA	680,212,500	672,806,100	682,886,200	458,617,500	-106,689,000	433,463,800
Return on Assets %	3.22%	3.07%	5.59%	4.41%	-7.30%	-2.15%
Return on Equity %	3.69%	3.52%	6.40%	5.02%	-8.41%	-2.47%
Debt to Equity						

CONTACT INFORMATION:
Phone: 81 753112121 Fax: 81 753150172
Toll-Free:
Address: 21 Saiin Mizosaki-cho, Ukyo-ku, Kyoto, 615-8585 Japan

STOCK TICKER/OTHER:
Stock Ticker: ROHCY
Employees: 25,000
Parent Company:

Exchange: PINX
Fiscal Year Ends: 03/31

SALARIES/BONUSES:
Top Exec. Salary: $ Bonus: $
Second Exec. Salary: $ Bonus: $

OTHER THOUGHTS:
Estimated Female Officers or Directors:
Hot Spot for Advancement for Women/Minorities:

Rolls-Royce plc

NAIC Code: 336412

www.rolls-royce.com

TYPES OF BUSINESS:
Aircraft Engine and Engine Parts Manufacturing
Power Generation Solutions
Marine Propulsion Systems
Aftermarket & Support Services

BRANDS/DIVISIONS/AFFILIATES:
Rolls-Royce North America Inc
Rolls-Royce AB
Rolls-Royce Marine Power Operations Limited
Trent

CONTACTS:
Note: Officers with more than one job title may be intentionally listed here more than once.

D. Warren East, CEO
Simon Kirby, COO
Stephen Daintith, CFO
Ben Story, Dir.-Mktg.
Harry Holt, Dir.-Human Resources
Paul Stein, CTO
Rob Webb, General Counsel
Alain Michaelis, Dir.-Oper.
Miles Cowdry, Dir.-Corp. Dev.
Lawrie Haynes, Pres., Nuclear & Marine
Andrew Heath, Pres., Energy
John Paterson, Pres., Marine & Industrial Power Systems
Ian Davis, Chmn.
James M. Guyette, CEO
Tony Wood, Pres., Aerospace

GROWTH PLANS/SPECIAL FEATURES:

Rolls-Royce plc designs and produces engines and power systems for civilian aerospace, defense aerospace, marine and nuclear markets worldwide. In civilian aerospace, its customers include airlines, business aviation and helicopter Rolls-Royce plc designs and produces engines and power systems for civilian aerospace, defense aerospace, marine and nuclear markets worldwide. In civilian aerospace, its customers include airlines, business aviation and helicopter manufacturers, offering various types of aircraft engines as well as aftermarket services, training and other related services. Rolls-Royce's defense aerospace operations serve armed forces customers in more than 100 countries with offerings such as aircraft engines, service packages for managing engines throughout their lifecycle, operator support and advanced technology for aerospace systems. This division's products are primarily utilized in combat jets, rotary aircraft, transporters for military/maritime/regional purposes, tankers, patrol aircraft, tactical aircraft, trainers, reconnaissance aircraft and unmanned aerial vehicles (UAVs). Within the marine sector, the company serves more than 4,000 customers, including 70 navies, with equipment installed on over 30,000 vessels operating around the world. Its equipment includes intelligent software and technologies for marine awareness, automation and control products, cranes, deck machinery, diesel and gas engines, electrical power systems, gas turbines, propulsion systems, propulsors, reduction gears and stabilization and maneuvering systems. The firm's nuclear products and services include submarine nuclear propulsion products, instrumentation and control systems, small modular reactors, nuclear steam supply systems, safety/licensing and environmental engineering. Services include operation management, repairs and overhauls and customer training. Rolls-Royce has subsidiaries and joint ventures operating in Africa, the Americas, Asia Pacific, Europe and the Middle East. A few of these include Rolls-Royce North America, Inc.; Rolls-Royce AB; and Rolls-Royce Marine Power Operations Limited. In January 2018, the firm announced it would be operating a new jet engine testbed at the Alliance Airport in Fort Worth, Texas. The facility will carry out endurance test runs for Rolls-Royce Trent engines.

FINANCIAL DATA:
Note: Data for latest year may not have been available at press time.

In U.S. $	2017	2016	2015	2014	2013	2012
Revenue	23,226,040,000	21,300,380,000	19,548,500,000	19,564,160,000	22,095,140,000	17,320,890,000
R&D Expense	1,132,317,000	1,307,506,000	1,165,076,000	1,129,469,000	972,795,900	838,911,800
Operating Income	1,646,489,000	-103,973,800	1,992,594,000	1,845,891,000	1,958,411,000	1,709,158,000
Operating Margin %	7.08%	-.48%	10.19%	9.43%	8.86%	9.86%
SGA Expense	1,740,493,000	3,144,851,000	1,508,332,000	1,600,911,000	1,884,347,000	1,408,631,000
Net Income	5,992,024,000	-5,742,772,000	118,216,800	98,276,600	1,947,016,000	3,248,825,000
Operating Cash Flow	2,577,980,000	2,009,685,000	1,558,183,000	1,853,012,000	2,905,569,000	1,787,495,000
Capital Expenditure	2,486,825,000	1,731,947,000	1,274,747,000	1,602,336,000	1,669,278,000	975,644,500
EBITDA	8,323,600,000	-4,992,166,000	1,482,695,000	1,283,293,000	3,727,389,000	4,710,155,000
Return on Assets %	15.14%	-16.84%	.37%	.30%	6.63%	13.20%
Return on Equity %	104.79%	-117.27%	1.45%	1.15%	23.38%	43.01%
Debt to Equity	0.55	1.71	0.57	0.34	0.38	0.20

CONTACT INFORMATION:
Phone: 44 2072229020 Fax: 44 2072279170
Toll-Free:
Address: 62 Buckingham Gate, London, SW1E 6AT United Kingdom

STOCK TICKER/OTHER:
Stock Ticker: RYCEF Exchange: PINX
Employees: 49,900 Fiscal Year Ends: 12/31
Parent Company:

SALARIES/BONUSES:
Top Exec. Salary: $ Bonus: $
Second Exec. Salary: $ Bonus: $

OTHER THOUGHTS:
Estimated Female Officers or Directors: 4
Hot Spot for Advancement for Women/Minorities: Y

Sales, profits and employees may be estimates. Financial information, benefits and other data can change quickly and may vary from those stated here.

Royal Dutch Shell plc

www.shell.com

NAIC Code: 211111

TYPES OF BUSINESS:
Oil & Gas-Exploration & Production
Gas Stations
Refineries
Solar & Wind Power
Chemicals
Consulting & Technology Services
Hydrogen & Fuel Cell Technology

BRANDS/DIVISIONS/AFFILIATES:

CONTACTS:
Note: Officers with more than one job title may be intentionally listed here more than once.
Ben van Beurden, CEO
Jessica Uhl, CFO
Ronan Cassidy, Chief Human Resources Officer
Harry Brekelmans, Dir.-Projects & Tech. Div.
Peter Rees, Dir.-Legal
Marvin Odum, Dir.-Upstream Americas
John Abbot, Dir.-Downstream
Andrew Brown, Dir.-Upstream Intl
Charles O. Holliday, Chmn.

GROWTH PLANS/SPECIAL FEATURES:

Royal Dutch Shell plc (Shell) is one of the world's largest oil and gas groups, with operations in over 70 countries. Shell's worldwide retail network includes thousands of gasoline stations, serving more than 20 million customer visits per day. The company's business segments include integrated gas and new energies, upstream, downstream and projects and technology. The integrated gas and new energies segment manages LNG activities and the conversion of natural gas into GTL fuels and other products. It includes natural gas exploration and extraction, production and transportation of LNG and the operation of the upstream and midstream infrastructure necessary to deliver gas to market. It markets and trades crude oil, natural gas, LNG, electricity, carbon-emission rights and also sells and markets LNG as a fuel for heavy-duty vehicles and marine vessels. The upstream division searches for and recovers crude oil, natural gas, and natural gas liquids. It also operates the infrastructure necessary to deliver oil and gas to market. The downstream segment manages Shell's manufacturing, distribution, trading activities and marketing activities for oil products and chemicals, including the refining, supply and shipping of crude oil. This segment oversees the sale of a range of products including fuels, lubricants, heating oil, bitumen, sulphur and liquefied petroleum gas (LPG) for home, transport and industrial use as well as petrochemicals for industrial customers. The projects and technology segment manages the firm's major projects and drives research to develop new technology innovations. It also provides technical services to both the upstream and downstream segments. In late-2017, the firm sold its LPG marketing business in Hong Kong and Macau; sold its U.K. North Sea assets; and sold its entire Gabon onshore oil and gas interests. In January 2018, Royal Dutch terminated its proposed sale of A/S Dansk Shell

FINANCIAL DATA:
Note: Data for latest year may not have been available at press time.

In U.S. $	2017	2016	2015	2014	2013	2012
Revenue	305,179,000,000	233,591,000,000	264,960,000,000	421,105,000,000	451,235,000,000	467,153,000,000
R&D Expense	922,000,000	1,014,000,000	1,093,000,000	1,222,000,000	1,318,000,000	1,314,000,000
Operating Income	15,481,000,000	2,367,000,000	-3,261,000,000	19,879,000,000	26,870,000,000	37,499,000,000
Operating Margin %	5.07%	1.01%	-1.23%	4.72%	5.95%	8.02%
SGA Expense	10,509,000,000	12,101,000,000	11,956,000,000	13,965,000,000	14,675,000,000	14,616,000,000
Net Income	12,977,000,000	4,575,000,000	1,939,000,000	14,874,000,000	16,371,000,000	26,592,000,000
Operating Cash Flow	35,650,000,000	20,615,000,000	29,810,000,000	45,044,000,000	40,440,000,000	46,140,000,000
Capital Expenditure	20,845,000,000	22,116,000,000	26,131,000,000	31,854,000,000	40,145,000,000	32,576,000,000
EBITDA	48,395,000,000	32,606,000,000	29,754,000,000	53,573,000,000	55,669,000,000	65,588,000,000
Return on Assets %	3.17%	1.21%	.55%	4.18%	4.56%	7.53%
Return on Equity %	6.81%	2.61%	1.15%	8.45%	8.88%	14.85%
Debt to Equity	0.38	0.44	0.32	0.22	0.20	0.15

CONTACT INFORMATION:
Phone: 31 703779111   Fax: 31 703773953
Toll-Free:
Address: Carel van Bylandtlaan 16, The Hague, 2596 HR Netherlands

STOCK TICKER/OTHER:
Stock Ticker: RDS.A
Employees: 86,000
Parent Company:

Exchange: NYS
Fiscal Year Ends: 12/31

SALARIES/BONUSES:
Top Exec. Salary: $1,840,006   Bonus: $3,704,710
Second Exec. Salary: $982,983   Bonus: $1,296,649

OTHER THOUGHTS:
Estimated Female Officers or Directors: 1
Hot Spot for Advancement for Women/Minorities: Y

Royal HaskoningDHV

NAIC Code: 541330

www.royalhaskoningdhv.com

TYPES OF BUSINESS:
Engineering Consulting Services
Engineering
Consultancy
Design
Management

BRANDS/DIVISIONS/AFFILIATES:
ELC Consulting & Engineering
First Marine International
InterVISTAS Consulting Group
Netherlands Airport Consultants B V
Ocean Shipping Consultants

CONTACTS: Note: Officers with more than one job title may be intentionally listed here more than once.
Erik Oostwegel, CEO
Nynke Dalstra, CFO
Cindy Meervis, Dir.-Human Resources

GROWTH PLANS/SPECIAL FEATURES:
Royal HaskoningDHV is an international engineering and project management consultancy firm headquartered in the Netherlands. It comprises more than 6,000 colleagues across 150 countries, catering to markets such as aviation, buildings, energy, industry, infrastructure, maritime, mining, rural areas, urban areas and water. Its services include architecture, building physics, asset management, aviation services, building structural design and technology, coastal and river engineering and management, energy and power, environmental and sustainability services, flood risk management, modelling and design, health and safety, industrial processes and engineering, information technology and data management, infrastructure design, investment services, legal consultancy, marine design and construction services, maritime structures, mining services, oil and gas services, permits and licenses, port and shipping studies, nautical services, ports planning, process and chemical industry services, procurement and contracting, real estate services and management, renewable energy services, tourism services, transport services, wastewater management services, water for industry, water management and water supply. Some of the firm's projects include the restoration of Mississippi Coast Barrier Islands U.S., Dutch Steel Bridges, the cultivation of oysters to combat coastal erosion in Bangladesh, the Camau Power Plant and the Pembrokeshire Onshore Wind Farm. Subsidiaries of the firm are ELC Consulting & Engineering, an environmental and geotechnical engineering consultancy; First Marine International, a marine industry consulting services company; InterVISTAS Consulting Group, a management consultancy specializing in aviation, transport and tourism; Netherlands Airport Consultants B V (NACO) an independent airport consultancy and engineering firm; and Ocean Shipping Consultants, an economic consultancy specializing in shipping economics and port development among others.

FINANCIAL DATA: Note: Data for latest year may not have been available at press time.

In U.S. $	2017	2016	2015	2014	2013	2012
Revenue	700,664,000	654,577,000	722,598,800	559,529,100	574,278,900	927,018,000
R&D Expense						
Operating Income						
Operating Margin %						
SGA Expense						
Net Income	15,389,000	12,707,000	13,106,100	6,798,000	-3,398,100	-26,297,500
Operating Cash Flow						
Capital Expenditure						
EBITDA						
Return on Assets %						
Return on Equity %						
Debt to Equity						

CONTACT INFORMATION:
Phone: 31-88-348-20-00 Fax: 31-88-348-28-01
Toll-Free:
Address: Laan 1914 no 35, Amersfoort, 3818 EX Netherlands

STOCK TICKER/OTHER:
Stock Ticker: Private Exchange:
Employees: 6,000 Fiscal Year Ends:
Parent Company:

SALARIES/BONUSES:
Top Exec. Salary: $ Bonus: $
Second Exec. Salary: $ Bonus: $

OTHER THOUGHTS:
Estimated Female Officers or Directors:
Hot Spot for Advancement for Women/Minorities:

Saab AB

NAIC Code: 336411

www.saabgroup.com

TYPES OF BUSINESS:
Aircraft Manufacturing
Security System Development
Electronic Warfare
Aeronautics Training

BRANDS/DIVISIONS/AFFILIATES:
Kockums
Combitech
Avionics Systems
Aerostructures
Vricon
Saab Technology Centre

CONTACTS:
Note: Officers with more than one job title may be intentionally listed here more than once.

Hakan Buskhe, CEO
Micael Johansson, Deputy CEO
Hakan Buskhe, Pres.
Magnus Ornberg, CFO
Lena Eliasson, Head-Human Resources
Pontus De Laval, CTO
Gorgen Johansson, Sr. VP
Annika Baremo, General Counsel
Dan Jangblad, Chief Strategy Officer
Magnus Ornberg, Head-Group Finance
Lennart Sindahl, Exec. VP
Gunilla Fransson, Sr. VP
Micael Johansson, Exec. VP
Lars-Erik Wige, Sr. VP
Marcus Wallenberg, Chmn.

GROWTH PLANS/SPECIAL FEATURES:

Saab AB is a Sweden-based aerospace and defense company. The firm designs and manufactures military/civilian aircraft, aeronautical systems and defense/security technology. Saab operates in six segments: aeronautics, dynamics, surveillance, support and services, industrial products and services, and Kockums. Aeronautics engages in advanced development of military and civil aviation technology, as well as long-term future studies of manned and unmanned aircraft for new systems and future development. Dynamics offers products such as ground combat weapons, missile systems, torpedoes, unmanned underwater vehicles and signature management systems for armed forces, as well as niche products for the civil and defense market. Surveillance provides solutions for safety and security, for surveillance and decision support, and for threat detection and protection. Its products and solutions cover airborne, ground-based and naval radar; electronic warfare; combat systems; traffic management systems; and C4I (command, control, communications, computers and intelligence) systems. Support and services offers support solutions for all of Saab's markets, including technical maintenance and logistics and products/solutions/services for military and civil missions in locations with limited infrastructure. Industrial products and services comprises the business units Combitech, Avionics Systems, Aerostructures and Vricon, as well as the development of product ideas that fall outside of Saab's core business. Combitech is one of the Nordic region's largest technology consulting firms; Avionics Systems designs and builds instrument panels for experimental aircraft; Aerostructures designs and manufactures aircraft; and Vricon creates high resolution elevation products and accurate immersive 3D products. Last, Kockums provides design, construction and in-service support for advanced naval systems such as surface combatants and submarines to the Swedish Armed Forces and other countries worldwide. Kockums has operations in Karlskrona, Malmo, Musko and Singapore. In January 2018, Saab expanded its activities in Finland by establishing a new development center, the Saab Technology Centre, in Tampere.

FINANCIAL DATA:
Note: Data for latest year may not have been available at press time.

In U.S. $	2017	2016	2015	2014	2013	2012
Revenue		3,380,602,000	3,209,984,000	2,777,948,000	2,804,279,000	2,834,978,000
R&D Expense		187,975,200	184,787,200	175,577,400	208,048,000	247,485,000
Operating Income		211,472,200	189,392,100	154,914,300	138,974,100	207,221,500
Operating Margin %		6.25%	5.90%	5.57%	4.95%	7.30%
SGA Expense		421,763,600	399,565,500	396,495,500	404,288,400	402,163,100
Net Income		133,778,900	160,818,000	136,140,400	87,493,500	184,669,200
Operating Cash Flow		490,483,100	42,270,820	-84,187,410	-80,527,080	41,326,220
Capital Expenditure		199,428,500	164,478,300	114,650,700	72,143,770	79,228,260
EBITDA		203,088,800	214,778,300	185,377,600	130,708,900	238,629,400
Return on Assets %		2.96%	4.21%	4.01%	2.57%	5.08%
Return on Equity %		8.71%	11.28%	9.84%	5.67%	11.61%
Debt to Equity		0.42	0.37	0.18	0.09	

CONTACT INFORMATION:
Phone: 46 84630000   Fax: 46 84630152
Toll-Free:
Address: Gustavslundsvagen 42, Bromma, SE-102 22 Sweden

STOCK TICKER/OTHER:
Stock Ticker: SAABF
Employees: 14,716
Parent Company:

Exchange: PINX
Fiscal Year Ends: 12/31

SALARIES/BONUSES:
Top Exec. Salary: $ Bonus: $
Second Exec. Salary: $ Bonus: $

OTHER THOUGHTS:
Estimated Female Officers or Directors: 7
Hot Spot for Advancement for Women/Minorities: Y

Safran SA

NAIC Code: 336412

www.safran-group.com

TYPES OF BUSINESS:
Aircraft Engine and Engine Parts Manufacturing
Aircraft Equipment
Defense Security Equipment
Defense Electronics
Aerospace Propulsion

BRANDS/DIVISIONS/AFFILIATES:
Ariane 5
ArianeGroup
Kalray

CONTACTS:
Note: Officers with more than one job title may be intentionally listed here more than once.

Philippe Petitcolin, CEO
Bernard Delpit, CFO
Eric Bachelet, Corp. VP-Research & Tech.
Marc Ventre, Deputy CEO-Oper.
Jean-Pierre Cojan, Exec. VP-Strategy
Ross McInnes, Deputy CEO-Finance
Philippe Petitcolin, Pres., Defense-Security
Jean-Lin Fournereaux, Corp. VP-Space
Yves Leclere, Exec. VP-Transformation
Ross McInnes, Chmn.
Bruno Cotte, Exec. VP-Intl

GROWTH PLANS/SPECIAL FEATURES:

Safran SA is a Paris-based international group of high-technology companies. The group has industrial, design and commercial operations in more than 30 countries. Safran operates in three divisions: aviation, space and defense. Aviation supplies engines and equipment to all main producers of civil and military airplanes and helicopters. Its propulsion systems meet all the requirements of airplane and helicopter manufacturers: performance, reliability, cost-effectiveness and environmental-friendliness. Its systems and equipment products include nacelles and thrust reversers, landing systems, wheels and brakes, wiring, power transmissions and more. Space produces rocket technology for the design and production of rocket and satellite propulsion systems and related equipment. It applies all enabling technologies for both solid and liquid (cryogenic) propulsion. The Ariane 5 launcher can boost up to 10,300 kilos of geostationary transfer orbit (GTO), enabling it to handle even the largest geostationary satellites on the market, orbiting at an altitude of about 22,500 miles. The ArianeGroup is a 50/50 joint venture company between Airbus Group and Safran. Defense produces equipment for naval, land and air defense. Products and technologies include navigation systems, optronics, drones, fire control systems, avionics and weapons systems. The defense division offers innovative systems and equipment such as navigation, missile propulsion, guidance, optronics, drones and avionics. While most of Safran's operations are based in France, it also has locations in other parts of Europe, the Americas, Africa, the Middle East and Asia-Pacific. During 2017, the firm acquired a stake in Kalray, a European leader in new-generation processors for critical onboard systems. In addition, Safran and Zodiac Aerospace withdrew its early-2017 acquisition/merger agreement and entered into a new business combination agreement (for a lesser amount) which had yet to be finalized as of March 12, 2018.

FINANCIAL DATA:
Note: Data for latest year may not have been available at press time.

In U.S. $	2017	2016	2015	2014	2013	2012
Revenue		20,353,680,000	22,351,750,000	18,577,890,000	17,893,750,000	16,813,210,000
R&D Expense						
Operating Income		3,880,067,000	3,684,952,000	1,864,704,000	1,716,516,000	1,621,428,000
Operating Margin %		19.06%	16.48%	10.03%	9.59%	9.64%
SGA Expense						
Net Income		2,356,196,000	-523,599,000	-155,597,800	1,711,576,000	1,607,844,000
Operating Cash Flow		3,066,265,000	3,399,689,000	2,910,667,000	2,641,458,000	1,996,839,000
Capital Expenditure		1,718,985,000	2,196,893,000	1,996,839,000	1,762,207,000	1,300,353,000
EBITDA		4,076,416,000	1,021,265,000	1,095,359,000	3,666,428,000	3,481,193,000
Return on Assets %		6.40%	-1.55%	-.50%	5.90%	5.96%
Return on Equity %		31.41%	-7.13%	-1.95%	21.82%	23.60%
Debt to Equity		0.36	0.31	0.26	0.19	0.37

CONTACT INFORMATION:
Phone: 33 140608080   Fax: 33 40608102
Toll-Free:
Address: 2 Blvd. du General Martial Valin, Paris, 75724 France

SALARIES/BONUSES:
Top Exec. Salary: $ Bonus: $
Second Exec. Salary: $ Bonus: $

STOCK TICKER/OTHER:
Stock Ticker: SAFRF   Exchange: PINX
Employees: 66,490   Fiscal Year Ends: 12/31
Parent Company:

OTHER THOUGHTS:
Estimated Female Officers or Directors: 5
Hot Spot for Advancement for Women/Minorities: Y

Sales, profits and employees may be estimates. Financial information, benefits and other data can change quickly and may vary from those stated here.

SAIC Motor Corporation Limited

NAIC Code: 336111

www.saicmotor.com

TYPES OF BUSINESS:

Automobile Manufacturing
Motorcycle Manufacturing
Bus Manufacturing
Car Rental Services
Tractor & Heavy Equipment Manufacturing
Parts Manufacturing, Distribution & Retailing
Consumer Finance & Leasing
Insurance

BRANDS/DIVISIONS/AFFILIATES:

General Motors India Private Limited
SAIC USA Inc
SAIC Europe GmbH
SAIC Motor-CP Co ltd
SAIC Hong Kong Co Ltd
MG Motor UK Ltd
SAIC MAXUS
SAIC Volkswagen

GROWTH PLANS/SPECIAL FEATURES:

SAIC Motor Corporation Limited is a state-owned entity and one of China's largest automotive companies. The group operates manufacturing facilities, mainly near Shanghai, that make passenger cars, trucks, buses and automotive parts. SAIC has branches in Korea, Japan, Hong Kong, the U.S. and Europe. The firm sold nearly 7 million vehicles in 2017, up 6.8% from the previous year. SAIC Motor's business covers the research, production and vehicle sales of both passenger cars and commercial vehicles. The company actively promotes new energy vehicles, the commercialization of internet-connected cars and is exploring intelligent driving technology. SAIC is engaged in the research and development, production and sales of parts for motor drive systems, chassis systems, interior/exterior decoration, battery, electric drive and power electronics, as well as auto-related services such as logistics, eCommerce, travel, energy saving/charging services, finance, insurance and investments. Subsidiaries under SAIC include: General Motors India Private Limited; SAIC USA, Inc.; SAIC Europe GmbH; SAIC Motor-CP Co., Ltd.; SAIC Hong Kong Co., Ltd.; and MG Motor U.K. Ltd. Affiliated vehicle companies include Morris Garages, SAIC MAXUS, SAIC Volkswagen, SAIC-GM, Shanghai General Motors Wuling, NAVECO, SAIC-IVECO Hongyan and Shanghai Sunwin Bus Corporation.

CONTACTS: *Note: Officers with more than one job title may be intentionally listed here more than once.*

Chen Zhixin, Pres.
Wei Yong, Interim CFO
Wang Jianzhang, Sec.
Chen Demei, VP
Chen Zhixin, Exec. VP
Xiao Guopu, Exec. VP
Yu Jianwei, VP-Nanjing Automotive Group
Zhu Genlin, VP
Chen Hong, Chmn.

FINANCIAL DATA:
Note: Data for latest year may not have been available at press time.

In U.S. $	2017	2016	2015	2014	2013	2012
Revenue	132,474,000,000	108,846,000,000	100,370,000,000	101,389,843,328	91,756,700,000	77,921,100,000
R&D Expense						
Operating Income						
Operating Margin %						
SGA Expense						
Net Income	5,283,550,000	46,048,000	4,545,109,272	4,501,862,834	4,039,300,000	3,379,400,000
Operating Cash Flow						
Capital Expenditure						
EBITDA						
Return on Assets %						
Return on Equity %						
Debt to Equity						

CONTACT INFORMATION:

Phone: 86-21-2201-1888   Fax: 86-21-2201-1777
Toll-Free:
Address: 489 WeiHai Rd., Shanghai, Shanghai 200041 China

STOCK TICKER/OTHER:

Stock Ticker: 600104.SS
Employees: 180,749
Parent Company:

Exchange: Shanghai
Fiscal Year Ends: 12/31

SALARIES/BONUSES:

Top Exec. Salary: $ Bonus: $
Second Exec. Salary: $ Bonus: $

OTHER THOUGHTS:

Estimated Female Officers or Directors: 1
Hot Spot for Advancement for Women/Minorities:

Salini Impregilo SpA

NAIC Code: 237000

www.salini-impregilo.com/en/#

TYPES OF BUSINESS:
Heavy Construction
Civil Engineering
Environmental Engineering
Infrastructure Management
Airport Operations

BRANDS/DIVISIONS/AFFILIATES:
Salini Costruttori SpA

CONTACTS:
Note: Officers with more than one job title may be intentionally listed here more than once.

Pietro Salini, CEO
Massimo Ferrari, CFO
Alberto Giovannini, Chmn.

GROWTH PLANS/SPECIAL FEATURES:

Salini Impregilo SpA is a leading Italian civil engineering and construction company, active in over 50 countries. The firm provides design and construction services to all sectors requiring complex, large-scale infrastructures. Infrastructure operations include dams, hydroelectric plants, motorways, roads, bridges, railways, metro systems, civil buildings, industrial buildings and airports. Salini has built 257 dams and hydroelectric plants on five different continents, with an installed capacity of more than 37,500 megawatts (MW) of clean energy. It has constructed over 32,000 miles (51,660 km) of roads and motorways, as well as over 217 miles (350 km) of bridges and viaducts worldwide. Salini has built more than 4,200 miles (6,830 km) of railways, 248 miles (400 km) of metro systems and 900 miles (1,450 km) of underground works. Salini covers an important role in the construction of innovative and iconic buildings worldwide, including the Great Mosque in Abu Dhabi and the Kingdom Centre in Riyadh. The group has also built hospital complexes, university campuses, government buildings as well as buildings which play an important cultural role such as the Nigeria Cultura Centre and Millennium Tower. The firm currently has construction projects in Italy, the U.S., Saudi Arabia, United Arab Emirates and Kuwait. Salini Impregilo operates as a subsidiary of Salini Costruttori SpA.

FINANCIAL DATA:
Note: Data for latest year may not have been available at press time.

In U.S. $	2017	2016	2015	2014	2013	2012
Revenue		7,265,935,000	5,852,054,000	5,179,322,000	2,869,093,000	2,816,803,000
R&D Expense						
Operating Income		340,231,900	336,703,800	319,078,000	194,964,100	-31,462,870
Operating Margin %		4.68%	5.75%	6.16%	6.79%	-1.11%
SGA Expense						
Net Income		73,996,640	74,825,260	115,800,600	231,850,600	744,225,600
Operating Cash Flow		354,952,000	525,924,400	177,029,600	4,538,270	-20,289,460
Capital Expenditure		321,141,600	343,551,300	378,853,500	47,207,880	90,334,420
EBITDA		724,325,100	620,089,400	541,079,100	322,459,200	104,074,000
Return on Assets %		.72%	.87%	1.77%	4.35%	13.11%
Return on Equity %		5.21%	5.49%	7.56%	11.78%	39.43%
Debt to Equity		1.53	1.09	0.85	0.20	0.18

CONTACT INFORMATION:
Phone: 39 244422111 Fax: 39 244422293
Toll-Free:
Address: Via de Missaglia, 97, Milan, 20142 Italy

STOCK TICKER/OTHER:
Stock Ticker: IMPJY   Exchange: PINX
Employees: 34,440   Fiscal Year Ends: 12/31
Parent Company: Salini Costruttori SpA

SALARIES/BONUSES:
Top Exec. Salary: $ Bonus: $
Second Exec. Salary: $ Bonus: $

OTHER THOUGHTS:
Estimated Female Officers or Directors: 1
Hot Spot for Advancement for Women/Minorities:

Samsung Electronics Co Ltd

NAIC Code: 334310

www.samsung.com

TYPES OF BUSINESS:
Consumer Electronics
Semiconductors and Memory Products
Smartphones
Computers & Accessories
Digital Cameras
Fuel-Cell Technology
LCD Displays
Solar Energy Panels

BRANDS/DIVISIONS/AFFILIATES:
Samsung Group
Galaxy
Harman
Harman International Industries Inc

CONTACTS: Note: Officers with more than one job title may be intentionally listed here more than once.
Oh-Hyun Kwon, CEO
Oh-Hyun Kwon, Vice Chmn.
Gregory Lee, CEO

GROWTH PLANS/SPECIAL FEATURES:

Samsung Electronics Co., Ltd., flagship company of the Samsung Group, is a global leader in semiconductor, telecommunications and digital convergence technology. Samsung is comprised of its headquarters in Korea and 276 worldwide subsidiaries. The company is organized into four segments: consumer electronics (CE), information technology and mobile communications (IM), device solutions (DS) and Harman. The CE division includes nine regional headquarters and offers TVs, monitors, printers, air conditioners, refrigerators, washing machines and medical devices. The IM division also has nine regional headquarters, and offers mobile innovation products such as its Galaxy series mobile phones and tablets. It focuses on software technology for enhancing mobile product differentiation. The DS division includes five regional headquarters and offers semiconductor and display systems. Its semiconductor unit is divided into memory and system LSI (large-scale integration) businesses, in which memory manufactures and sells DRAM (dynamic random access memory) and NAND (a logic gate) products, and system LSI manufactures mobile application processors and various sensors. Its display systems unit manufactures and sells displays and panels, including TFT-LCD (thin film transistor liquid crystal display) and OLED (a light-emitting diode containing organic electroluminescent material for visual displays). This division's recent development (2017) of an LED screen for digital cinema was publicly demonstrated at Lotte Cinema World Tower in Seoul. Last, the Harman division develops and engineers connected products and solutions for automakers, consumers and enterprises worldwide, including connected car systems, audio/visual products, enterprise automation solutions and connected services. In March 2017, the firm acquired Harman International Industries, Inc., an automotive technology manufacturer, for $112 a share in cash for a total of $8 billion. That May, Samsung Electronics was given permission from The Ministry of Land, Infrastructure and Transport of Korea to start testing a self-driving car technology.

FINANCIAL DATA: Note: Data for latest year may not have been available at press time.

In U.S. $	2017	2016	2015	2014	2013	2012
Revenue		188,572,400,000	187,439,000,000	192,625,900,000	213,631,600,000	187,859,500,000
R&D Expense		13,818,160,000	12,803,080,000	13,438,120,000	13,376,370,000	10,773,280,000
Operating Income		27,314,970,000	24,673,930,000	23,376,990,000	34,362,460,000	27,136,230,000
Operating Margin %		14.48%	13.16%	12.13%	16.08%	14.44%
SGA Expense		21,345,040,000	21,323,880,000	22,201,260,000	19,906,170,000	17,311,350,000
Net Income		20,939,420,000	17,463,450,000	21,562,350,000	27,857,270,000	21,658,450,000
Operating Cash Flow		44,264,960,000	37,423,410,000	34,540,300,000	43,631,420,000	35,472,030,000
Capital Expenditure		23,531,660,000	25,578,800,000	21,828,350,000	22,505,680,000	22,060,860,000
EBITDA		48,367,700,000	44,333,520,000	43,457,630,000	51,498,400,000	42,797,330,000
Return on Assets %		8.88%	7.91%	10.38%	15.09%	13.77%
Return on Equity %		12.48%	11.16%	15.06%	22.82%	21.63%
Debt to Equity					0.01	0.04

CONTACT INFORMATION:
Phone: 82-31-200-1114　Fax: 82-31-200-7538
Toll-Free:
Address: 129 Samsung-ro, Yeongtong-gu, Suwon-si, 443-742 South Korea

STOCK TICKER/OTHER:
Stock Ticker: SSNLF
Employees: 95,798
Parent Company: Samsung Group

Exchange: GREY
Fiscal Year Ends: 12/31

SALARIES/BONUSES:
Top Exec. Salary: $　　Bonus: $
Second Exec. Salary: $　Bonus: $

OTHER THOUGHTS:
Estimated Female Officers or Directors:
Hot Spot for Advancement for Women/Minorities:

Sales, profits and employees may be estimates. Financial information, benefits and other data can change quickly and may vary from those stated here.

Plunkett Research, Ltd.   515

SanDisk Corporation   www.sandisk.com
NAIC Code: 334112

TYPES OF BUSINESS:
Flash-Based Data Storage Products
Flash Memory Cards

GROWTH PLANS/SPECIAL FEATURES:
SanDisk Corporation designs, manufactures and distributes innovative flash storage products for the electronics industry. The company's state-of-the-art solutions are utilized in many of the world's largest data centers, and embedded in advanced smartphones, tablets and PCs. In the data center or in the cloud, SanDisk's flash technology enables fast, reliable access to mission-critical data. The firm's solid state drives offer low-power, compact and durable alternatives to traditional hard-disk drives for desktops, laptops and ultra-thin PCs. High-performance flash storage is essential in smartphones, tablets and other mobile devices; therefore, SanDisk delivers embedded memory solutions to every major mobile device manufacturer. SanDisk technology is in many consumer electronics, from cameras to USB drives to MP3 players. SanDisk is a wholly-owned subsidiary of Western Digital Corporation.

BRANDS/DIVISIONS/AFFILIATES:
Western Digital Corporation

CONTACTS: Note: Officers with more than one job title may be intentionally listed here more than once.
Michael Charles Ray, Pres.
Judy Bruner, CFO
Siva Sivaram, Executive VP, Divisional
Sumit Sadana, Executive VP
Shuki Nir, General Manager, Divisional
Mark Brazeal, Other Executive Officer

FINANCIAL DATA: Note: Data for latest year may not have been available at press time.

In U.S. $	2017	2016	2015	2014	2013	2012
Revenue	5,500,000,000	5,500,000,000	5,564,872,192	6,627,701,248	6,170,002,944	5,052,509,184
R&D Expense						
Operating Income						
Operating Margin %						
SGA Expense						
Net Income			388,478,016	1,007,446,016	1,042,657,024	417,404,000
Operating Cash Flow						
Capital Expenditure						
EBITDA						
Return on Assets %						
Return on Equity %						
Debt to Equity						

CONTACT INFORMATION:
Phone: 408 801-1000   Fax: 408 542-0503
Toll-Free:
Address: 951 SanDisk Dr., Milpitas, CA 95035 United States

STOCK TICKER/OTHER:
Stock Ticker: Subsidiary   Exchange:
Employees: 8,790   Fiscal Year Ends: 12/31
Parent Company: Western Digital Corporation

SALARIES/BONUSES:
Top Exec. Salary: $ Bonus: $
Second Exec. Salary: $ Bonus: $

OTHER THOUGHTS:
Estimated Female Officers or Directors: 2
Hot Spot for Advancement for Women/Minorities:

Sales, profits and employees may be estimates. Financial information, benefits and other data can change quickly and may vary from those stated here.

Sanmina Corporation

www.sanmina.com

NAIC Code: 334418

TYPES OF BUSINESS:
Printed Circuit Assembly (Electronic Assembly) Manufacturing
Assembly & Testing
Logistics Services
Support Services
Product Design & Engineering
Repair & Maintenance Services

BRANDS/DIVISIONS/AFFILIATES:
Viking Technology
SCI Technology Inc

CONTACTS:
Note: Officers with more than one job title may be intentionally listed here more than once.

David Anderson, CFO
Jure Sola, Chairman of the Board
Brent Billinger, Chief Accounting Officer
Robert Eulau, Director
Alan Reid, Executive VP, Divisional
Gerry Fay, Executive VP

GROWTH PLANS/SPECIAL FEATURES:

Sanmina Corporation is a global provider of customized, integrated electronics manufacturing services (EMS). With production facilities in 23 countries, the firm is one of the largest global EMS providers. The firm has two business segments: integrated manufacturing solutions (IMS) and components, products and services (CPS). The IMS includes printed circuit board assembly and test, which involves attaching electronic components such as integrated circuits, capacitors, microprocessors to printed circuit boards; final system assembly and test, which consists of combining assemblies and modules to form finished products; and direct-order-fulfillment, which involves receiving customer orders, configuring products and delivering the products either to the OEM, a distribution channel. The CPS segment include interconnect systems (printed circuit board fabrication, backplane and cable assemblies) and mechanical systems (enclosures, precision machining and plastic injection molding). This segment also includes the operations of Viking Technology, a manufacturer of flash memory and related storage products and SCI Technology, Inc.'s defense and aerospace products, as well as logistics and repair services. The company caters to defense and aerospace, computing and storage, automotive, multi-media, clean technology, medical systems and communications network industries.

Employee benefits include a 401(k); tuition reimbursement; credit union membership; an employee assistance program; flexible spending accounts; and medical, prescription, dental, vision, life and AD&D insurance.

FINANCIAL DATA:
Note: Data for latest year may not have been available at press time.

In U.S. $	2017	2016	2015	2014	2013	2012
Revenue	6,868,619,000	6,481,181,000	6,374,541,000	6,215,106,000	5,917,124,000	6,093,334,000
R&D Expense	33,716,000	37,746,000	33,083,000	32,495,000	25,571,000	21,899,000
Operating Income	230,955,000	228,486,000	209,431,000	211,702,000	161,278,000	169,953,000
Operating Margin %	3.36%	3.52%	3.28%	3.40%	2.72%	2.78%
SGA Expense	251,568,000	244,604,000	239,288,000	242,288,000	238,072,000	240,863,000
Net Income	138,833,000	187,838,000	377,261,000	197,165,000	79,351,000	180,234,000
Operating Cash Flow	250,961,000	390,116,000	174,896,000	307,382,000	317,889,000	215,413,000
Capital Expenditure	111,833,000	120,400,000	119,097,000	69,507,000	75,950,000	78,631,000
EBITDA	354,165,000	341,438,000	301,771,000	290,220,000	240,431,000	221,164,000
Return on Assets %	3.71%	5.27%	11.08%	6.25%	2.57%	5.52%
Return on Equity %	8.52%	12.00%	27.26%	16.86%	7.72%	20.78%
Debt to Equity	0.23	0.26	0.27	0.31	0.51	0.86

CONTACT INFORMATION:
Phone: 408-964-3500 Fax: 408-964-3636
Toll-Free:
Address: 2700 N. First St., San Jose, CA 95134 United States

SALARIES/BONUSES:
Top Exec. Salary: $1,064,423 Bonus: $
Second Exec. Salary: $586,731 Bonus: $

STOCK TICKER/OTHER:
Stock Ticker: SANM
Employees: 45,397
Parent Company:

Exchange: NAS
Fiscal Year Ends: 09/30

OTHER THOUGHTS:
Estimated Female Officers or Directors:
Hot Spot for Advancement for Women/Minorities:

Sales, profits and employees may be estimates. Financial information, benefits and other data can change quickly and may vary from those stated here.

ative text
Sanofi Genzyme
NAIC Code: 325412

www.sanofigenzyme.com

TYPES OF BUSINESS:
Pharmaceuticals Discovery & Development
Genetic Disease Treatments
Surgical Products
Diagnostic Products
Genetic Testing Services
Oncology Products
Biomaterials
Medical Devices

BRANDS/DIVISIONS/AFFILIATES:
Sanofi SA
Aldurazyme
Caprelsa
Dupixent
Eloxatin
Kevzara
Taxotere
Zaltrap

CONTACTS:
Note: Officers with more than one job title may be intentionally listed here more than once.

Bill Sibold, Managing Dir.
Robin Swartz, Head-Bus. Oper.
David Meeker, Pres.
Philippe Sauvage, CFO
Bo Piela, Dir.-Communications
Deb Shapiro, Head-Human Resources
Richard J. Gregory, Head-R&D
William Aitchison, Head-Global Mfg.
Tracey L. Quarles, General Counsel
Charles Thyne, Head-Global Quality, Industrial Oper.
G. Andre Turenne, Head- Strategy & Bus. Dev.
Caren P. Arnstein, Head-Corp. Comm.
Ron C. Branning, Chief Quality Officer
Nicholas Grund, Sr. VP-Asia Pacific & Canada
Carlo Incerti, Head-Global Medical Affairs
Yoshi Nakamura, Pres., Japan-Asia Pacific
Robin Kenselaar, Head-EMEA

GROWTH PLANS/SPECIAL FEATURES:
Sanofi Genzyme is the specialty care global business unit of Sanofi SA, with a focus on rare diseases, multiple sclerosis, immunology and oncology. The rare diseases segment develops therapeutic products to treat patients suffering from genetic and other chronic debilitating diseases, including lysosomal storage disorders (LSDs) and endocrinology. More than 7,000 different rare disease collectively affect over 350 million people worldwide. The multiple sclerosis (MS) segment works to deliver scientific advances and novel therapeutic options to the more than 2.3 million people affected by MS worldwide. MS is a chronic disease caused when the body's immune system attacks the central nervous system, damaging the myelin sheath, the protective layer covering the nerves that carry signals between the brain and spinal cord and the rest of the body. This division offers both oral and infusion treatment options. The immunology segment researches and develops new therapeutic candidates that may have a significant impact on people affected by immune system disorders, including atopic dermatitis, rheumatoid arthritis, asthma, nasal polyposis and eosinophilic esophagitis. Last, the oncology segment builds on Sanofi Genzyme's established legacy in cancer treatment by researching potential new options to offer in this area of medicine. This division is building a pipeline of future therapies in immune-oncology, in which a patient's immune system is used to fight cancer cells. Sanofi Genzyme's product portfolio includes: Aldurazyme, Aubagio, Caprelsa, Cerdelga, Cerezyme, Clolar, Dupixent, Elitek, Eloxatin, Fabrazyme, Jevtana, Kevzara, Lemtrada, Lumizyme, Mozobil, Taxotere, Thymoglobulin, Thyrogen and Zaltrap.

Employees of the company receive benefits including medical, dental, vision, life and disability coverage; college tuition savings plans; a 401(k); and work and life assistance benefits.

FINANCIAL DATA:
Note: Data for latest year may not have been available at press time.

In U.S. $	2017	2016	2015	2014	2013	2012
Revenue	4,200,000,000	4,150,000,000	4,097,534,726	3,380,000,000		
R&D Expense						
Operating Income						
Operating Margin %						
SGA Expense						
Net Income						
Operating Cash Flow						
Capital Expenditure						
EBITDA						
Return on Assets %						
Return on Equity %						
Debt to Equity						

CONTACT INFORMATION:
Phone: 617-252-7500   Fax: 617-252-7600
Toll-Free:
Address: 500 Kendall St., Cambridge, MA 02142 United States

SALARIES/BONUSES:
Top Exec. Salary: $ Bonus: $
Second Exec. Salary: $ Bonus: $

STOCK TICKER/OTHER:
Stock Ticker: Subsidiary   Exchange:
Employees: 13,500   Fiscal Year Ends: 12/31
Parent Company: Sanofi SA

OTHER THOUGHTS:
Estimated Female Officers or Directors: 4
Hot Spot for Advancement for Women/Minorities: Y

Sales, profits and employees may be estimates. Financial information, benefits and other data can change quickly and may vary from those stated here.

Sanofi SA

NAIC Code: 325412

en.sanofi.com

TYPES OF BUSINESS:
Pharmaceuticals Development & Manufacturing
Over-the-Counter Drugs
Cardiovascular Drugs
CNS Drugs
Oncology Drugs
Diabetes Drugs
Generics
Vaccines

BRANDS/DIVISIONS/AFFILIATES:
Sanofi Pasteur
Cerezyme
Aubagio
Jevtana
Dupixent
Lantus
Praluent
Bioverativ Inc

CONTACTS: Note: Officers with more than one job title may be intentionally listed here more than once.

Olivier Brandicourt, CEO
Elias Zerhouni, Pres., Global R&D
Karen Linehan, General Counsel
David-Alexandre Gros, Chief Strategy Officer
David Meeker, CEO-Genzyme
Olivier Charmeil, Sr. VP-Vaccines
Philippe Luscan, Exec. VP-Global Industrial Affairs
Serge Weinberg, Chmn.
Peter Guenter, Exec. VP-Global Commercial Oper.

GROWTH PLANS/SPECIAL FEATURES:
Sanofi SA is an international pharmaceutical group engaged in the research, development, manufacturing and marketing of healthcare products. It operates in three primary segments: pharmaceuticals, consumer healthcare and vaccines. The most important pharmaceutical products marketed by Sanofi include: rare diseases, comprising a portfolio of enzyme replacement therapies, including Cerezyme for Gaucher disease and Myozyme for Pompe disease, among others; multiple sclerosis, including Aubagio, a once-daily oral immunomodulator and Lemtrada, a monoclonal antibody; oncology, including Jevtana, for patients with prostate cancer and Taxotere, for several types of cancer, among others; immunology, including Dupixent, for adults with moderate-to-severe atopic dermatitis and Kevzara, for adults with severe rheumatoid arthritis; diabetes, including Lantus, a long-acting human insulin analog and Amaryl, an oral once-daily sulfonylurea, among others; and cardiovascular diseases, including Praluent, a cholesterol-lowering drug and Multaq, an anti-arrhythmic drug. The consumer healthcare segment is supported by four strategic categories: allergy cough and cold, pain, digestive, and nutritionals. Last, the vaccines segment operates through Sanofi Pasteur, which sells leading vaccines in five areas: pediatric vaccines, influenza vaccines, adult and adolescent booster vaccines, meningitis vaccines, and travel and endemic vaccines. During early-2018, the firm acquired Bioverativ, Inc., a biotechnology company focused on therapies for hemophilia and other rare blood disorders; agreed to acquire Ablynx NV, a biopharmaceutical company engaged in the discovery and development of Nanobodies.

FINANCIAL DATA:
Note: Data for latest year may not have been available at press time.

In U.S. $	2017	2016	2015	2014	2013	2012
Revenue	44,708,440,000	42,861,030,000	43,049,960,000	42,121,320,000	41,129,690,000	44,403,420,000
R&D Expense	6,757,391,000	6,386,920,000	6,275,779,000	5,957,174,000	5,890,489,000	6,078,194,000
Operating Income	8,892,539,000	8,056,509,000	8,494,900,000	8,031,811,000	7,147,621,000	8,922,177,000
Operating Margin %	19.89%	18.79%	19.73%	19.06%	17.37%	20.09%
SGA Expense	12,420,660,000	12,516,980,000	11,585,860,000	11,246,270,000	10,622,640,000	11,048,680,000
Net Income	10,415,170,000	5,815,160,000	5,294,031,000	5,421,226,000	4,590,136,000	6,133,765,000
Operating Cash Flow	9,112,352,000	10,106,450,000	11,015,340,000	9,496,406,000	8,587,517,000	10,090,390,000
Capital Expenditure	2,415,471,000	2,572,304,000	3,423,152,000	1,922,744,000	1,726,395,000	1,990,664,000
EBITDA	11,494,480,000	11,567,340,000	12,445,360,000	12,488,580,000	13,317,200,000	14,000,100,000
Return on Assets %	8.24%	4.54%	4.29%	4.53%	3.78%	4.95%
Return on Equity %	14.58%	8.14%	7.50%	7.76%	6.50%	8.74%
Debt to Equity	0.24	0.29	0.22	0.23	0.18	0.18

CONTACT INFORMATION:
Phone: 33-1-53-77-40-00   Fax:
Toll-Free:
Address: 54, rue La Boetie, Paris, 75008 France

STOCK TICKER/OTHER:
Stock Ticker: SNY
Employees: 1,068,529
Parent Company:

Exchange: NYS
Fiscal Year Ends: 12/31

SALARIES/BONUSES:
Top Exec. Salary: $1,200,000   Bonus: $
Second Exec. Salary: $700,000   Bonus: $

OTHER THOUGHTS:
Estimated Female Officers or Directors: 6
Hot Spot for Advancement for Women/Minorities: Y

SAP SE

NAIC Code: 0

www.sap.com

TYPES OF BUSINESS:
Computer Software, Business Management & ERP
Consulting & Training Services
Hosting Services
Software Licensing
Software Development

BRANDS/DIVISIONS/AFFILIATES:
SAP HANA
SAP Cloud Platform
Gigya

CONTACTS:
Note: Officers with more than one job title may be intentionally listed here more than once.

Bill McDermott, CEO
Luka Mucic, CFO
Stefan Ries, Chief Human Resources Officer
Luca Mucic, Head-Global Finance
Jim Hagemann Snabe, Co-CEO
Bernd Leukert, Head- Application Innovation

GROWTH PLANS/SPECIAL FEATURES:

SAP SE is a provider of business application, analytics software and enterprise cloud solutions. SAP's products provide what is needed for enterprises to become digital businesses. The firm's products are categorized into eight divisions. The ERP (enterprise resource planning) and digital core division serves small, medium and large companies via the SAP HANA database management system software for data storage, analytics and insights, as well as ERP cloud solutions. The cloud and data platforms division offers the SAP Cloud Platform, HANA management solutions and databases, data warehousing, big data, application integration and infrastructure. The procurement and networks division offers supplier management, strategic sourcing, procurement, external workforce, selling and fulfillment products and solutions. The analytics division offers business intelligence, enterprise performance management and predictive analytics. The customer engagement and commerce division offers products and solutions relating to marketing, sales, service, commerce and revenue. The Internet of Things (IoT) and digital supply chain division offers product and solutions that relate to supply chain, IoT, manufacturing, R&D, engineering and asset management. The human resources division offers products such as core HR, payroll, time and attendance management, recruiting, onboarding, learning and development, performance and compensation, workforce planning and analytics. Last, the finance division offers solutions such as government compliance and risk, financial planning, analysis, accounting, financial close, treasury management, payables/receivables, real estate management and travel and expense. SAP SE serves more than 355,000 customers in over 180 countries through its 245 subsidiaries. Recently, SAP announced plans to invest $2.2 billion, from 2016 through 2021, in connected sensors and smart devices. In September 2017, SAP agreed to acquire Gigya, a customer identity and access management platform.

SAP provides employees with medical, dental, disability, life and vision insurance; flexible spending accounts; employee assistance programs; and retirement savings and employee stock purchase plans.

FINANCIAL DATA:
Note: Data for latest year may not have been available at press time.

In U.S. $	2017	2016	2015	2014	2013	2012
Revenue	28,970,830,000	27,244,440,000	25,677,340,000	21,686,140,000	20,764,900,000	20,033,840,000
R&D Expense	4,139,396,000	3,759,046,000	3,513,300,000	2,878,560,000	2,818,049,000	2,782,237,000
Operating Income	6,248,611,000	6,374,571,000	6,018,919,000	5,884,315,000	5,618,810,000	5,037,171,000
Operating Margin %	21.56%	23.39%	23.44%	27.13%	27.05%	25.14%
SGA Expense	9,877,991,000	8,977,747,000	7,963,892,000	6,416,558,000	6,170,812,000	5,994,221,000
Net Income	4,961,842,000	4,502,458,000	3,783,744,000	4,050,483,000	4,107,289,000	3,486,132,000
Operating Cash Flow	6,230,088,000	5,715,132,000	4,492,578,000	4,320,927,000	4,732,150,000	4,719,801,000
Capital Expenditure	1,574,502,000	1,236,138,000	785,398,500	910,123,800	698,955,300	668,082,700
EBITDA	8,120,724,000	7,902,147,000	6,824,076,000	6,812,962,000	6,826,546,000	6,002,865,000
Return on Assets %	9.26%	8.51%	7.66%	9.99%	12.33%	11.27%
Return on Equity %	15.48%	14.68%	14.32%	18.45%	22.02%	21.01%
Debt to Equity	0.19	0.24	0.37	0.45	0.22	0.30

CONTACT INFORMATION:
Phone: 49 6227747474   Fax: 49 6227757575
Toll-Free: 800-872-1727
Address: Dietmar-Hopp-Allee 16, Walldorf, 69190 Germany

SALARIES/BONUSES:
Top Exec. Salary: $1,420,139   Bonus: $
Second Exec. Salary: $864,432   Bonus: $

STOCK TICKER/OTHER:
Stock Ticker: SAP   Exchange: NYS
Employees: 84,183   Fiscal Year Ends: 12/31
Parent Company:

OTHER THOUGHTS:
Estimated Female Officers or Directors: 4
Hot Spot for Advancement for Women/Minorities: Y

Sales, profits and employees may be estimates. Financial information, benefits and other data can change quickly and may vary from those stated here.

Sargent & Lundy LLC

www.sargentlundy.com

NAIC Code: 541330

TYPES OF BUSINESS:
Engineering Consulting Services
Consulting
Engineering
Design

BRANDS/DIVISIONS/AFFILIATES:

CONTACTS:
Note: Officers with more than one job title may be intentionally listed here more than once.

Thomas White, CEO
Paula Scholl, Sr. VP
Michael Helminski, Exec. VP-Finance
Thomas White, Chmn.

GROWTH PLANS/SPECIAL FEATURES:

Sargent & Lundy, LLC is a consulting, engineering, design, analysis and project provider for electric power generation and power delivery projects worldwide. Its client base consists of investor-owned and government utilities, developers, industrial complexes, rural cooperatives, municipal and public power systems, regional transmission organizations, financial institutions and gas-line and oil companies. Sargent & Lundy operates through eight divisions. The nuclear power division has been Sargent & Lundy's core competency since 1954, with its services addressing emerging issues with solutions for both nuclear unit design and upgrades to operating units. The coal, oil and gas division designs and services fossil-fueled power plants. The environmental services division offers integrated environmental solutions such as compliance planning, permitting, civil/geotechnical, water optimization, modeling, siting and transmission routing, due diligence and decommissioning. The power transmission division provides services necessary to successfully execute all aspects of transmission grid projects. These services range from cross-country bulk power transmission lines to enclosed gas-insulated substations within tightly-constrained urban locations. The renewable energy division provides solutions that tackle all aspects of renewable energy projects, from planning to commissioning, and from evaluating generation technology options to grid interconnection solutions. Projects include wind, solar, biomass, geothermal, hydroelectric, energy storage, hybrid power plants, microgrids and more. The energy business consulting division offers project development/planning, engineering site services, due diligence, asset transaction services, financial modeling, analysis, operational assessments and grid modernization consulting. The construction management and commissioning division provides service for both new and existing power stations, as well as for transmission and distribution systems. Last, the operations and maintenance support services division assists clients with continuous operational improvements in relation to nuclear and fossil power plants, new-generation nuclear and fossil power plants, and transmission and substation facilities.

FINANCIAL DATA:
Note: Data for latest year may not have been available at press time.

In U.S. $	2017	2016	2015	2014	2013	2012
Revenue						
R&D Expense						
Operating Income						
Operating Margin %						
SGA Expense						
Net Income						
Operating Cash Flow						
Capital Expenditure						
EBITDA						
Return on Assets %						
Return on Equity %						
Debt to Equity						

CONTACT INFORMATION:
Phone: 312-269-2000   Fax: 312-269-3680
Toll-Free:
Address: 55 E. Monroe St., Chicago, IL 60603 United States

STOCK TICKER/OTHER:
Stock Ticker: Private
Employees: 2,500
Parent Company:

Exchange:
Fiscal Year Ends:

SALARIES/BONUSES:
Top Exec. Salary: $ Bonus: $
Second Exec. Salary: $ Bonus: $

OTHER THOUGHTS:
Estimated Female Officers or Directors:
Hot Spot for Advancement for Women/Minorities:

Sales, profits and employees may be estimates. Financial information, benefits and other data can change quickly and may vary from those stated here.

Plunkett Research, Ltd.

SAS Institute Inc
www.sas.com
NAIC Code: 0

TYPES OF BUSINESS:
Software-Statistical Analysis
Business Intelligence Software
Data Warehousing
Online Bookstore
Consulting

BRANDS/DIVISIONS/AFFILIATES:

CONTACTS: Note: Officers with more than one job title may be intentionally listed here more than once.
James Goodnight, CEO
Don Parker, VP
Randy Guard, VP
Jenn Mann, VP-Human Resources
Keith Collins, VP
John Boswell, Chief Legal Officer
Carl Farrell, Exec. VP-SAS Americas
John Sall, Exec. VP
Mikael Hagstrom, Exec. VP-EMEA & Asia Pacific

GROWTH PLANS/SPECIAL FEATURES:
SAS Institute, Inc. provides statistical analysis software. The company's products are designed to extract, manage and analyze large volumes of data, often assisting in financial reporting and credit analysis. Individual contracts can be tailored to specific global and local industries, such as banking, manufacturing and government. SAS' advanced analytics software is infused with cutting-edge, innovative algorithms that help its clients solve their most intractable problems, make the best decisions possible and capture new opportunities. The software comprises data mining, statistical analysis, forecasting, text analysis, optimization and stimulation features. Other products that provide enterprise solutions include business intelligence, cloud analytics, customer intelligence, data management, fraud and security intelligence, in-memory analytics, performance management, risk management, solutions for Hadoop and supply chain intelligence. Industries that utilize SAS products and solutions include automotive, banking, capital markets, casinos, communications, consumer goods, defense/security, government, healthcare, high-tech manufacturing, education, hotels, insurance, life science, manufacturing, media, oil and gas, retail, sports, travel, transportation and utilities. SAS serves more than 80,000 business, government and university sites in 148 different countries, including 94 of the top 100 companies on the 2016 Fortune Global 500 list.

SAS offers its employees life, disability, medical, dental, auto, home and vision insurance; flexible spending accounts; onsite health care and fitness centers; an employee assistance program; adoption assistance; scholarship programs; a 401(k); and a pro

FINANCIAL DATA: Note: Data for latest year may not have been available at press time.

In U.S. $	2017	2016	2015	2014	2013	2012
Revenue	3,240,000,000	3,200,000,000	3,160,000,000	3,090,000,000	3,020,000,000	2,870,000,000
R&D Expense						
Operating Income						
Operating Margin %						
SGA Expense						
Net Income						
Operating Cash Flow						
Capital Expenditure						
EBITDA						
Return on Assets %						
Return on Equity %						
Debt to Equity						

CONTACT INFORMATION:
Phone: 919-677-8000   Fax: 919-677-4444
Toll-Free: 800-727-0025
Address: 100 SAS Campus Dr., Cary, NC 27513 United States

STOCK TICKER/OTHER:
Stock Ticker: Private   Exchange:
Employees: 14,051   Fiscal Year Ends: 12/31
Parent Company:

SALARIES/BONUSES:
Top Exec. Salary: $ Bonus: $
Second Exec. Salary: $ Bonus: $

OTHER THOUGHTS:
Estimated Female Officers or Directors: 1
Hot Spot for Advancement for Women/Minorities: Y

Sales, profits and employees may be estimates. Financial information, benefits and other data can change quickly and may vary from those stated here.

Sasol Limited

NAIC Code: 325110

www.sasol.com

TYPES OF BUSINESS:
Synthetic Fuels Manufacturing
Crude Oil Refining
Natural Gas Production
Coal Mining
Polymers
Solvents

BRANDS/DIVISIONS/AFFILIATES:

CONTACTS: Note: Officers with more than one job title may be intentionally listed here more than once.
Bongani Nqwabab, Co-CEO
Stephen Cornell, Co-CEO
Paul Victor, CFO
Jacqui OSullian, Gen. Mgr.- Group Comm.
Samantha Barnfather, Gen. Mgr.-Investors Rel.

GROWTH PLANS/SPECIAL FEATURES:

Sasol Limited, based in South Africa, is an integrated energy and chemicals company. The firm develops and commercializes technologies, and builds and operates world-scale facilities for the production of products such as liquid fuels, chemicals and low-carbon electricity. Sasol operates in two segments: mining, and exploration and production international (E&PI). The mining segment is responsible for securing coal feedstock for the Southern African value chain, mainly for gasification, but also to generate electricity and steam. This division operates six coal mines, and exports some of its coal to international power generation customers. E&PI develops and manages the groups' upstream interests in oil and gas exploration and production in Mozambique, Canada, Gabon South Africa and Australia. This segment produces natural gas and condensate from Mozambique's Pande and Temane fields; shale gas and condensate from Sasol's share in the Farrell Creek and Cypress A assets in Canada; and oil in Gabon, South Africa, through the firm's share in the offshore Etame Marin Permit, which is operated by Houston-based VAALCO Energy. Other strategic business units include energy, which is responsible for the sales and marketing of liquid fuels, natural gas and electricity; new energy, which is engaged in the development and commercialization of new technologies, and implementing and operating facilities based on these technologies in relation to power generation and low-carbon and renewable energy alternatives; and Sasol Financing, which manages the group's treasury and is responsible for meeting funding requirements and expansion objectives while mitigating financial risks. In addition, Sasol has energy businesses in other African countries; chemical businesses in Europe, the U.S., the Middle East, and Asia; a joint venture gas-to-liquids facility in Qatar, the U.S. and Canada.

FINANCIAL DATA: Note: Data for latest year may not have been available at press time.

In U.S. $	2017	2016	2015	2014	2013	2012
Revenue	14,282,390,000	14,326,710,000	15,347,640,000	16,790,490,000	15,016,530,000	14,037,100,000
R&D Expense						
Operating Income	3,196,093,000	3,312,237,000	4,045,298,000	3,661,246,000	3,828,585,000	3,024,944,000
Operating Margin %	22.37%	23.11%	26.35%	21.80%	25.49%	21.54%
SGA Expense	3,068,518,000	3,026,766,000	2,859,344,000	2,844,019,000	2,761,509,000	1,522,040,000
Net Income	1,687,805,000	1,095,574,000	2,461,707,000	2,450,440,000	2,176,899,000	1,953,642,000
Operating Cash Flow	3,650,725,000	4,529,172,000	3,391,184,000	3,642,938,000	3,184,993,000	2,321,540,000
Capital Expenditure	4,998,882,000	5,832,761,000	3,736,632,000	3,212,496,000	2,674,774,000	2,415,647,000
EBITDA	3,955,249,000	3,501,529,000	5,080,563,000	5,016,361,000	4,316,934,000	3,950,196,000
Return on Assets %	5.16%	3.70%	9.84%	7.59%	7.47%	12.35%
Return on Equity %	9.73%	6.63%	16.39%	18.45%	19.12%	20.25%
Debt to Equity	0.35	0.37	0.20	0.13	0.14	0.10

CONTACT INFORMATION:
Phone: 27-11-441-3111 Fax: 27-11-788-5092
Toll-Free:
Address: 50 Katherine St., Sandton, 2196 South Africa

SALARIES/BONUSES:
Top Exec. Salary: $1,876,000 Bonus: $4,502,000
Second Exec. Salary: $1,042,390 Bonus: $1,097,645

STOCK TICKER/OTHER:
Stock Ticker: SSL Exchange: NYS
Employees: 30,900 Fiscal Year Ends: 06/30
Parent Company:

OTHER THOUGHTS:
Estimated Female Officers or Directors: 2
Hot Spot for Advancement for Women/Minorities: Y

Saudi Aramco (Saudi Arabian Oil Co)

NAIC Code: 211111

www.saudiaramco.com

TYPES OF BUSINESS:
Oil & Gas-Exploration & Production
Oil Refining
Crude Oil Distribution
Pipelines
Oil Tankers
Petrochemicals

BRANDS/DIVISIONS/AFFILIATES:

CONTACTS: Note: Officers with more than one job title may be intentionally listed here more than once.
Amin H. Nasser, CEO
Khalid A. Al-Falih, Pres.
Abdallah I. Al-Saadan, Sr. VP-Finance, Strategy & Development
Khalid G. Al-Buainain, Sr. VP-Eng.
David B. Kultgen, General Counsel
Khalid G. Al-Buainain, Sr. VP-Oper. Support & Capital
Mohammad A. Al-Ali, Sr. VP-Finance
Salim S. Al-Aydh, Sr. VP
Amin H. Nasser, Sr. VP-Upstream Oper.
Abdulrahman F. Al-Wuhaib, Sr. VP-Oper. Svcs.
Abdulaziz F. Al-Khayyal, Sr. VP-Industrial Rel.
Khalid A. Al-Falih, Chmn.

GROWTH PLANS/SPECIAL FEATURES:

Saudi Aramco (Saudi Arabian Oil Company) is among the world's largest holders and producers of crude oil and natural gas, with reserves of 260.8 billion barrels of oil and 298.7 trillion cubic feet of gas. The company conducts extensive surveying and exploration activities while harvesting oil from some of the largest oil fields in the world, such as the Manifa, Dhahran, Khurais, Shaybah and Ghawar fields. It also operates an extensive network of pipelines, refineries and oil tankers. Saudi Aramco produced 10.5 million barrels per day in 2016 of crude oil; exported 2.6 billion barrels of crude oil; delivered 8.3 billion standard cubic feet of gas per day; delivered 920 million standard cubic feet of ethane per day; has natural gas liquid (NGL) from hydrocarbon gases comprising 497.5 million barrels of reserves; processed 12 billion standard cubic feet per day of raw gas, as well as 665 million barrels of refined products and 296 million barrels of refined product exports. Exports by region include Northwest Europe, producing 5.9% of Aramco's crude oil and 11.9% of refined products; Asia, producing 66.7% crude oil, 32.5% refined products and 31.1% NGL; the Mediterranean, producing 5.4% crude oil, 9.5% refined products and 5.1% NGL; the U.S., producing 15.8% crude oil; and other regions, accounting for 6.2% crude oil, 46.1% refined products and 63.8% NGL. Worldwide office locations include Saudi Arabia, the U.K., the Netherlands, India, Italy, the U.S., China, Japan, Korea and Singapore. Aramco owns or is a partner in several major refineries and chemicals plants, including Arlanxeo in Europe and Sadara on the U.S. Gulf Coast. Saudi Aramco's goal is to become the world's largest integrated oil company, with a global network of petrochemicals plants. The firm hopes to launch a massive IPO of its stock to raise funds for this expansion.

FINANCIAL DATA: Note: Data for latest year may not have been available at press time.

In U.S. $	2017	2016	2015	2014	2013	2012
Revenue	300,000,000,000	288,000,000,000	262,000,000,000	316,300,000,000	351,500,000,000	336,100,000,000
R&D Expense						
Operating Income						
Operating Margin %						
SGA Expense						
Net Income						
Operating Cash Flow						
Capital Expenditure						
EBITDA						
Return on Assets %						
Return on Equity %						
Debt to Equity						

CONTACT INFORMATION:
Phone: 966-3-872-0115   Fax: 966-3-873-8190
Toll-Free:
Address: North Park 3, Building 3302, Dhahran, 31311 Saudi Arabia

STOCK TICKER/OTHER:
Stock Ticker: Government-Owned
Employees: 65,266
Parent Company:

Exchange:
Fiscal Year Ends: 12/31

SALARIES/BONUSES:
Top Exec. Salary: $ Bonus: $
Second Exec. Salary: $ Bonus: $

OTHER THOUGHTS:
Estimated Female Officers or Directors:
Hot Spot for Advancement for Women/Minorities:

Sales, profits and employees may be estimates. Financial information, benefits and other data can change quickly and may vary from those stated here.

Schlumberger Limited

NAIC Code: 213112

www.slb.com

TYPES OF BUSINESS:

Oil & Gas Field Services
Seismic Services
Reservoir Imaging
Data & IT Consulting Services
Outsourcing
Stimulation Services
Management Consulting
Project Management

BRANDS/DIVISIONS/AFFILIATES:

Cameron
M-I SWACO
WesternGeco

CONTACTS: Note: Officers with more than one job title may be intentionally listed here more than once.

Paal Kibsgaard, CEO
Khaled Mogharbel, President, Divisional
Simon Ayat, CFO
Howard Guild, Chief Accounting Officer
Patrick Schorn, Executive VP, Divisional
Jean-Francois Poupeau, Executive VP, Divisional
Ashok Belani, Executive VP, Divisional
Alexander Juden, General Counsel
Vijay Kasibhatla, Other Corporate Officer
Saul Laureles, Other Corporate Officer
Pierre Chereque, Other Corporate Officer
Olivier Le Peuch, President, Divisional
Abdellah Merad, President, Divisional
Hinda Gharbi, President, Divisional
Aaron Floridia, President, Divisional
Catherine MacGregor, President, Divisional
Stephane Biguet, Vice President

GROWTH PLANS/SPECIAL FEATURES:

Schlumberger Limited (SLB) is a leading oil field service company offering technology, project management and information solutions for customers in the international oil and gas industry. SLB operates in 85 countries throughout North America, Latin America, Europe, Africa, the Middle East and Asia. It also maintains a global network of research and engineering facilities. The SLB oilfield services segment is divided into four groups: reservoir characterization, which is involved in finding and defining hydrocarbon deposits; drilling, which includes the drilling and positioning of gas and oil wells; production, which includes the principal technologies associated with the lifetime production of gas and oil reservoirs; and Cameron, which consists of the technologies involved in pressure and flow control for drilling and intervention rigs, oil and gas wells and production facilities. The overall purpose of the oilfield services sector is to provide proper exploration with production services and technologies throughout the entire life cycle of a reservoir. The company's wholly owned subsidiary M-I SWACO offers drilling and completion fluids to stabilize rock and minimize formation damage. WesternGeco, another subsidiary, offers worldwide marine and seismic reservoir imaging, data processing centers and a multi-client seismic library for monitoring and development services. In October 2017, Schlumberger and Torxen Energy agreed to purchase the Palliser Block located in Alberta, Canada, from Cenovous Energy for approximately $1 billion. The Palliser Block consists of oil and gas wells, surface facilities, a pipeline network and approximately 800,000 acres of oil and gas development rights. The asset has current production of about 54,000 barrels of oil equivalent per day (BOE/d).

FINANCIAL DATA: Note: Data for latest year may not have been available at press time.

In U.S. $	2017	2016	2015	2014	2013	2012
Revenue	30,440,000,000	27,810,000,000	35,475,000,000	48,580,000,000	45,266,000,000	42,149,000,000
R&D Expense	787,000,000	1,012,000,000	1,094,000,000	1,217,000,000	1,174,000,000	1,168,000,000
Operating Income	2,678,000,000	2,285,000,000	5,566,000,000	9,490,000,000	8,345,000,000	7,520,000,000
Operating Margin %	8.79%	8.21%	15.68%	19.53%	18.43%	17.84%
SGA Expense	432,000,000	403,000,000	494,000,000	475,000,000	416,000,000	405,000,000
Net Income	-1,505,000,000	-1,687,000,000	2,072,000,000	5,438,000,000	6,732,000,000	5,490,000,000
Operating Cash Flow	5,663,000,000	6,261,000,000	8,572,000,000	11,219,000,000	9,786,000,000	6,688,000,000
Capital Expenditure	2,107,000,000	2,055,000,000	2,410,000,000	3,976,000,000	3,943,000,000	4,695,000,000
EBITDA	3,220,000,000	2,759,000,000	7,305,000,000	12,102,000,000	12,748,000,000	11,031,000,000
Return on Assets %	-2.00%	-2.31%	3.07%	8.11%	10.46%	9.40%
Return on Equity %	-3.86%	-4.39%	5.63%	14.06%	18.14%	16.63%
Debt to Equity	0.40	0.40	0.40	0.27	0.26	0.27

CONTACT INFORMATION:

Phone: 713 375-3400   Fax:
Toll-Free:
Address: 5599 San Felipe St., 17/Fl, Houston, TX 77056 United States

SALARIES/BONUSES:

Top Exec. Salary: $2,000,000   Bonus: $
Second Exec. Salary: $1,000,000   Bonus: $

STOCK TICKER/OTHER:

Stock Ticker: SLB
Employees: 100,000
Parent Company:

Exchange: NYS
Fiscal Year Ends: 12/31

OTHER THOUGHTS:

Estimated Female Officers or Directors: 3
Hot Spot for Advancement for Women/Minorities: Y

Schneider Electric SE

NAIC Code: 335311

www.schneider-electric.com

TYPES OF BUSINESS:
Electrical Distribution Products
Infrastructure Products
Building Automation & Control Products

BRANDS/DIVISIONS/AFFILIATES:
EcoStruxure
ASCO Power Technologies
AVEVA Group plc

CONTACTS:
Note: Officers with more than one job title may be intentionally listed here more than once.

Jean-Pascal Tricoire, CEO
Chris Leong, CMO
Olivier Blum, Exec. VP-Global Human Resources
Herve Coureil, CIO
Emmanuel Babeau, Deputy CEO-Legal Affairs
Julio Rodriguez, Exec. VP-Global Oper.
Michael Crochon, Exec. VP-Strategy
Emmanuel Babeau, Deputy CEO-Finance
Clemens Blum, Exec. VP-Industry Bus.
Philippe Delorme, Exec. VP-Partner Bus.
Zhu Hai, Exec. VP-China Oper.
Danille Doime, Exec VP-IT
Jean-Pascal Tricoire, Chmn.
Laurent Vernerey, Exec. VP-North America Oper. & End User Bus. Group
Annette Clayton, Exec. VP-Global Supply Chain

GROWTH PLANS/SPECIAL FEATURES:

Schneider Electric SE develops connected technologies and solutions for managing and processing energy in safe, reliable, efficient and sustainable ways. The company's products are divided into eight broad groups. Industrial automation and control products include boxes, cabling, interfaces, relays, enclosures, terminals, industrial computers, measurement/instrumentation, robotics, motor starters, protection components, controllers, transformers, switches, lights, joysticks, sensors/RFID systems, signaling software, telemetry systems and drives. Medium voltage distribution and grid automation products include feeder, grid and substation automation solutions; medium/low voltage switchgears, transformers and prefabricated substations; outdoor equipment; monitoring and control systems; and protection relays by application and by range. Critical power, cooling and racks products include cooling systems and components, data center software, IT power distribution, modules, racks, accessories, security/environmental monitoring, surge protection, power conditioning and uninterruptible power supply (UPS). Low voltage products and systems include boxes, cabling, interfaces, busway/cable management, circuit breakers, switches, protection relays, electrical car charging, emergency lighting, fuses, terminals, sockets, motor starters, protection components, pushbuttons, joysticks and switchboards. Solar and energy storage products include solutions for commercial and industrial sectors, residential solar, off-grid solar and backup. Building automation and control products include building management services, emergency lighting, fire and security solutions, network infrastructure and connectivity solutions, power monitoring, valves, actuators, sensors, speed drives, starters and video management systems. Residential and small business products include electrical car charging, protection, lighting, automation, security, network infrastructure, solar, switchboards, enclosures and UPS. Last, software products include various offerings and options by function or by industry. Schneider Electric's EcoStruxure is an open, interoperable and Internet of Things-enabled system architecture and platform. It leverages advancements in IoT, mobility, sensing, cloud, analytics and cybersecurity, and has been deployed in 450,00+ installations. During 2017, the firm acquired ASCO Power Technologies; and AVEVA Group plc.

FINANCIAL DATA:
Note: Data for latest year may not have been available at press time.

In U.S. $	2017	2016	2015	2014	2013	2012
Revenue		30,493,470,000	32,897,820,000	30,797,250,000	29,083,210,000	29,571,000,000
R&D Expense		660,673,300	697,720,400	700,190,200	660,673,300	626,096,000
Operating Income		4,055,422,000	4,122,107,000	3,983,798,000	4,072,711,000	4,036,899,000
Operating Margin %		13.29%	12.53%	12.93%	14.00%	13.65%
SGA Expense		6,637,605,000	6,963,620,000	6,640,075,000	6,105,362,000	6,217,738,000
Net Income		2,161,081,000	1,737,509,000	2,396,947,000	2,331,497,000	2,272,222,000
Operating Cash Flow		3,667,663,000	3,497,246,000	3,128,010,000	3,582,455,000	3,458,964,000
Capital Expenditure		1,060,782,000	1,117,587,000	1,075,601,000	1,015,091,000	971,868,900
EBITDA		4,499,988,000	3,822,026,000	4,015,906,000	4,687,693,000	4,519,746,000
Return on Assets %		4.14%	3.36%	4.96%	5.16%	5.10%
Return on Equity %		8.46%	6.93%	10.50%	11.15%	11.30%
Debt to Equity		0.28	0.30	0.26	0.35	0.39

CONTACT INFORMATION:
Phone: 33 141297000 Fax: 33 141297100
Toll-Free:
Address: 35 rue Joseph Monier, Rueil Malmaison, 92500 France

STOCK TICKER/OTHER:
Stock Ticker: SU N
Employees: 153,124
Parent Company:

Exchange: MEX
Fiscal Year Ends: 12/31

SALARIES/BONUSES:
Top Exec. Salary: $ Bonus: $
Second Exec. Salary: $ Bonus: $

OTHER THOUGHTS:
Estimated Female Officers or Directors: 2
Hot Spot for Advancement for Women/Minorities:

Science Applications International Corporation (SAIC)

www.saic.com
NAIC Code: 541512

TYPES OF BUSINESS:
IT Consulting
IT Infrastructure Management
Research & Development
Software Development
Engineering

BRANDS/DIVISIONS/AFFILIATES:

CONTACTS: Note: Officers with more than one job title may be intentionally listed here more than once.
Anthony Moraco, CEO
Charles Mathis, CFO
Edward Sanderson, Chairman of the Board
Nazzic Keene, COO
Steven Mahon, General Counsel
Karen Wheeler, Other Executive Officer

GROWTH PLANS/SPECIAL FEATURES:

Science Applications International Corporation (SAIC) provides technical, engineering and enterprise IT services to commercial operations and government agencies. The company's clients include all four branches of the U.S. military (Army, Air Force, Navy and Marines), the U.S. Defense Logistics Agency, the National Aeronautics and Space Administration, the U.S. Department of State and the U.S. Department of Homeland Security. In fiscal 2017, more than 95% of total revenues were derived from contracts with the U.S. government or from subcontracts with other contractors engaged in work for the U.S. government, all of which were entities located in the U.S. The firm's offerings include: engineering; technology and equipment platform integration; maintenance of ground and maritime systems; logistics; training and simulation; operation and program support services; and end-to-end services that span design, development, integration, deployment, management and operations, sustainment and security of customers' entire IT infrastructure. SAIC serves customers through approximately 1,400 active contracts and task orders via 15,500 employees. In December 2017, the firm opened a new technology integration gateway office in Cookeville, Tennessee, where employees serve the federal defense and civilian agencies, state and local governments, and commercial businesses.

FINANCIAL DATA: Note: Data for latest year may not have been available at press time.

In U.S. $	2017	2016	2015	2014	2013	2012
Revenue	4,450,000,000	4,315,000,000	3,885,000,000	4,121,000,000	11,173,000,000	
R&D Expense						
Operating Income	281,000,000	253,000,000	240,000,000	241,000,000	772,000,000	
Operating Margin %	6.31%	5.86%	6.17%	5.84%	6.90%	
SGA Expense	166,000,000	158,000,000	95,000,000	92,000,000	592,000,000	
Net Income	148,000,000	117,000,000	141,000,000	113,000,000	526,000,000	
Operating Cash Flow	273,000,000	226,000,000	277,000,000	183,000,000	345,000,000	
Capital Expenditure	15,000,000	20,000,000	22,000,000	16,000,000	48,000,000	
EBITDA	325,000,000	289,000,000	261,000,000	196,000,000	865,000,000	
Return on Assets %	7.10%	6.64%	9.91%	3.08%	8.38%	
Return on Equity %	40.32%	32.27%	39.05%	7.60%	22.58%	
Debt to Equity	2.88	2.66	1.32	1.29	0.50	

CONTACT INFORMATION:
Phone: 703 676-4300   Fax:
Toll-Free:
Address: 1710 SAIC Dr., McLean, VA 22102 United States

SALARIES/BONUSES:
Top Exec. Salary: $1,038,462   Bonus: $
Second Exec. Salary: $614,039   Bonus: $

STOCK TICKER/OTHER:
Stock Ticker: SAIC
Employees: 15,500
Parent Company:

Exchange: NYS
Fiscal Year Ends: 01/31

OTHER THOUGHTS:
Estimated Female Officers or Directors: 5
Hot Spot for Advancement for Women/Minorities: Y

Plunkett Research, Ltd.

Seagate Technology plc
NAIC Code: 334112

www.seagate.com

TYPES OF BUSINESS:
Computer Storage Equipment-Disk & Tape Drives
Driver Components
Business Intelligence Software

BRANDS/DIVISIONS/AFFILIATES:
Seagate
LaCie
Backup Plus
Expansion
Maxtor

CONTACTS:
Note: Officers with more than one job title may be intentionally listed here more than once.

David Mosley, CEO
David H. Morton Jr., CFO
James Murphy, Sr. VP-Sales & Mktg.
Ravi Naik, CIO
Mark Re, Sr. VP
Ken Massaroni, Chief Admin. Officer
Ken Massaroni, General Counsel
Dave Mosley, Exec. VP-Oper. & Tech.
Terry Cunningham, Pres
John Grieci, Sr. VP-Customer Advocacy

GROWTH PLANS/SPECIAL FEATURES:
Seagate Technology plc manufactures rigid disk drives, often called disk drives or hard drives, used for storing electronic information in desktop and notebook computers, consumer electronic devices and data centers. The company produces disk drive products used in enterprise servers, mainframes, workstations, PCs, digital video recorders, gaming platforms and digital music players. Wireless drives provide tablet and smartphone users with additional storage for media content, and are sold under the Seagate and LaCie brand names. Enterprise storage products are designed for high performance servicers that require high capacity; client compute is the company's family of laptops drivers; and client non-compute products are for use in video streaming and video surveillance applications. Seagate ships external storage devices under the Backup Plus and Expansion lines, as well as under the Maxtor and LaCie brands. The company sells its products primarily to original equipment manufacturers (OEMs), including Hewlett-Packard and Dell, as well as to independent distributors and retailers. OEM customers typically enter into master purchase agreements with the firm, which provide for pricing, volume discounts, product support and other terms. Sales to OEMs accounted for 67% of company revenues in fiscal 2017, with 18% to distributors and 15% to retailers. Seagate maintains sales offices across the U.S., as well as in Asia and Europe. It has manufacturing facilities in China, Malaysia, Northern Ireland, Singapore, Thailand and the U.S. In September 2017, the firm, along with a consortium led by Bain Capital Private Equity, agreed to acquire Toshiba Memory Corporation from Toshiba Corporation.

Seagate offers employees medical coverage, life insurance, a 401(k) plan, disability coverage, a stock purchase plan, flexible spending accounts, degree assistance and an employee assistance program, among other benefits.

FINANCIAL DATA:
Note: Data for latest year may not have been available at press time.

In U.S. $	2017	2016	2015	2014	2013	2012
Revenue	10,771,000,000	11,160,000,000	13,739,000,000	13,724,000,000	14,351,000,000	14,939,000,000
R&D Expense	1,232,000,000	1,237,000,000	1,353,000,000	1,226,000,000	1,133,000,000	1,006,000,000
Operating Income	1,232,000,000	620,000,000	1,470,000,000	1,800,000,000	2,093,000,000	3,112,000,000
Operating Margin %	11.43%	5.55%	10.69%	13.11%	14.58%	20.83%
SGA Expense	606,000,000	635,000,000	857,000,000	722,000,000	635,000,000	528,000,000
Net Income	772,000,000	248,000,000	1,742,000,000	1,570,000,000	1,838,000,000	2,862,000,000
Operating Cash Flow	1,916,000,000	1,680,000,000	2,647,000,000	2,558,000,000	3,047,000,000	3,262,000,000
Capital Expenditure	434,000,000	587,000,000	747,000,000	559,000,000	786,000,000	636,000,000
EBITDA	1,786,000,000	1,282,000,000	3,018,000,000	2,630,000,000	2,918,000,000	3,937,000,000
Return on Assets %	8.81%	2.74%	18.01%	16.76%	18.99%	29.61%
Return on Equity %	52.21%	10.75%	59.55%	49.62%	52.57%	96.04%
Debt to Equity	3.68	2.59	1.37	1.38	0.79	0.81

CONTACT INFORMATION:
Phone: 353 12343136   Fax:
Toll-Free: 800-732-4283
Address: 38/39 Fitzwilliam Square, Dublin, 2 Ireland

SALARIES/BONUSES:
Top Exec. Salary: $353,856   Bonus: $1,500,000
Second Exec. Salary: $1,200,056   Bonus: $

STOCK TICKER/OTHER:
Stock Ticker: STX   Exchange: NAS
Employees: 41,000   Fiscal Year Ends: 06/30
Parent Company:

OTHER THOUGHTS:
Estimated Female Officers or Directors: 3
Hot Spot for Advancement for Women/Minorities: Y

Sales, profits and employees may be estimates. Financial information, benefits and other data can change quickly and may vary from those stated here.

Seiko Epson Corporation

NAIC Code: 334118

www.epson.jp/

TYPES OF BUSINESS:
Printers, Computer, Manufacturing
Computers & Peripherals
Business Machines
Precision Components
Semiconductors
Industrial Robotics
Quartz Devices
Liquid Crystal Display Panels

BRANDS/DIVISIONS/AFFILIATES:
Epson Sales Co Ltd
WorkSense W-01

CONTACTS:
Note: Officers with more than one job title may be intentionally listed here more than once.

Minoru Usui Akihiro Fukaishi, Pres.
Motonori Okumua Motonori Okumura, Mgr.-Gen. Admin.
Hiroshi Komatsu, Gen. Admin. Mgr.-Bus. Infrastructure Dev.
Koichi Endo, Managing Dir.-Epson Singapore Pte. Ltd.
Hiromi Taba, Pres., Epson Europe BV
Kiyofumi Koike, Pres., Epson (China) Co., Ltd.
Takashi Oguchi, Pres., P.T. Indonesia Epson Industry
John Lang, CEO

GROWTH PLANS/SPECIAL FEATURES:
Seiko Epson Corporation, based in Japan, develops, markets, manufactures, sells and services IT-related products, imaging products, electronic devices and precision products. The firm operates through five business segments: printing solutions, visual communications, wearable/industrial products, robotics and microdevices. The printing solutions segment consists of inkjet printers for home and office, commercial printers, industrial printers and scanners. The visual communication segment consists of projectors, smart eyewear, and high-temperature polysilicon thin-film-transistor liquid crystal display panels. The wearable/industrial products segment comprises wearable equipment such as wearable devices for health and sports purposes, and include watches and sensing systems. The robotics segment develops and produces robot systems as well as robotics solutions such as integrated circuit (IC) test handlers. In November 2017, this division commercially launched a seeing, sensing, thinking, working autonomous dual-arm robot that expands the scope of automated production. The new robot's name is WorkSense W-01. The micro devices segment produces crystal devices, semiconductors, powdered metals and surface treatment processing solutions. Seiko Epson comprises 86 companies, of which 16 are domestic and 70 are overseas (as of September 2017). The company's primary subsidiary, Epson Sales Co. Ltd., is headquartered in Tokyo, and sells printers, scanners, color copy servers, computers, projectors, point-of-sale systems, accounting systems, finance/tax/business software and other information equipment made by the Seiko Epson group of companies.

FINANCIAL DATA:
Note: Data for latest year may not have been available at press time.

In U.S. $	2017	2016	2015	2014	2013	2012
Revenue	9,547,756,000	10,177,760,000	10,120,560,000	9,349,786,000	7,930,846,000	8,179,589,000
R&D Expense						
Operating Income	632,504,200	791,429,100	943,516,000	791,587,500	198,025,000	229,429,900
Operating Margin %	6.62%	7.77%	9.32%	8.46%	2.49%	2.80%
SGA Expense	2,796,413,000	2,913,248,000	2,744,997,000			
Net Income	450,158,400	426,420,800	1,048,631,000	779,746,600	-94,009,690	46,879,080
Operating Cash Flow	902,487,400	1,053,233,000	1,013,863,000	1,036,454,000	400,521,700	248,537,400
Capital Expenditure	722,340,300	616,284,700	398,574,600	376,178,500	408,477,800	341,969,500
EBITDA	1,052,795,000	1,320,151,000	1,674,707,000	1,062,102,000	370,346,600	537,721,300
Return on Assets %	5.04%	4.70%	12.02%	10.17%	-1.32%	.65%
Return on Equity %	10.06%	9.51%	26.68%	27.61%	-4.01%	1.95%
Debt to Equity	0.14			0.40	0.55	0.55

CONTACT INFORMATION:
Phone: 81-266-52-3131   Fax:
Toll-Free:
Address: 3-3-5 Owa, Suwa, Nagano, 392-8502 Japan

STOCK TICKER/OTHER:
Stock Ticker: SEKEY
Employees: 73,171
Parent Company:

Exchange: PINX
Fiscal Year Ends: 03/31

SALARIES/BONUSES:
Top Exec. Salary: $ Bonus: $
Second Exec. Salary: $ Bonus: $

OTHER THOUGHTS:
Estimated Female Officers or Directors:
Hot Spot for Advancement for Women/Minorities:

Sales, profits and employees may be estimates. Financial information, benefits and other data can change quickly and may vary from those stated here.

Sembcorp Industries Ltd

NAIC Code: 221112

www.sembcorp.com.sg

TYPES OF BUSINESS:
Electric Utility
Marine Construction & Shipbuilding
Heavy Construction
Environmental Engineering & Waste Management
Industrial Parks and Real Estate Development
Internet Service Provider
Floating Oil Production Platforms
Pipelines

BRANDS/DIVISIONS/AFFILIATES:

CONTACTS:
Note: Officers with more than one job title may be intentionally listed here more than once.

Neil McGregor, CEO
Tang Kin Fei, Pres.
Koh Chiap Khiong, CFO
Tan Cheng Guan, Exec. VP-Bus. Dev., Commercial & Corp. Planning
Wong Weng Sun, Pres.
Ng Meng Poh, Head-Utilities
Ang Kong Hua, Chmn.

GROWTH PLANS/SPECIAL FEATURES:

Sembcorp Industries, Ltd. is one of Singapore's leading utilities and marine groups. The firm's primary business segments include utilities, marine and urban development. The utilities segment develops, owns and operates energy and water assets globally. It supplies power, steam and natural gas, as well as water and wastewater treatment solutions to industries and households. This division's energy portfolio comprises more than 11,000 megawatts, including thermal power plants, renewable wind and solar power assets, as well as biomass and energy-from-waste facilities. The marine segment provides a full spectrum of innovative marine and offshore engineering solutions to the global marine and offshore industries. This division's yards are located in Singapore, Indonesia, India, the U.K. and Brazil, and provide capabilities such as rigs and floaters, repairs and upgrades, offshore platforms and specialized shipbuilding. The urban development segment transforms raw land into sustainable urban developments. This division's portfolio includes 13 private sector-led and government-support projects spanning more than 10,000 acres in these markets. It has more than 800 multi-national and leading local corporations as tenants.

Sembcorp Industries offers employees health and welfare benefits, term life insurance, personal accident insurance and a loan and interest subsidy.

FINANCIAL DATA:
Note: Data for latest year may not have been available at press time.

In U.S. $	2017	2016	2015	2014	2013	2012
Revenue	6,363,890,000	6,029,470,000	7,278,192,000	8,307,655,000	8,233,660,000	7,769,603,000
R&D Expense						
Operating Income	458,691,500	678,179,800	563,701,400	888,975,100	723,060,000	808,206,500
Operating Margin %	7.20%	11.24%	7.74%	10.70%	8.78%	10.40%
SGA Expense	320,336,300	275,146,400	399,857,400	268,786,000	258,534,400	244,303,800
Net Income	175,973,800	301,120,200	418,526,000	610,870,800	625,627,500	574,411,300
Operating Cash Flow	495,909,700	664,994,600	-536,703,500	-43,782,220	1,121,135,000	473,108,100
Capital Expenditure	569,324,400	637,467,500	1,092,085,000	1,020,163,000	913,494,700	861,579,100
EBITDA	1,039,677,000	1,050,117,000	810,911,200	1,242,203,000	1,247,182,000	1,186,213,000
Return on Assets %	1.01%	1.68%	2.95%	5.11%	6.15%	6.11%
Return on Equity %	3.37%	5.41%	9.11%	14.59%	16.85%	17.48%
Debt to Equity	1.18	1.05	0.78	0.64	0.28	0.48

CONTACT INFORMATION:
Phone: 65 6723-3113 Fax: 65 6822-3254
Toll-Free:
Address: 30 Hill St., #05-04, Singapore, 179360 Singapore

STOCK TICKER/OTHER:
Stock Ticker: SCRPF
Employees: 7,000
Parent Company:

Exchange: PINX
Fiscal Year Ends: 12/31

SALARIES/BONUSES:
Top Exec. Salary: $ Bonus: $
Second Exec. Salary: $ Bonus: $

OTHER THOUGHTS:
Estimated Female Officers or Directors: 1
Hot Spot for Advancement for Women/Minorities:

Sembcorp Marine Ltd

www.sembcorpmarine.com.sg

NAIC Code: 541330

TYPES OF BUSINESS:
Marine & Offshore Engineering
Ship Construction & Conversion

BRANDS/DIVISIONS/AFFILIATES:
Estaleiro Jurong Aracruz
Gravifloat AS
LMG Marin AS
Sembmarine SLP Limited
Sembmarine SSP Inc

CONTACTS:
Note: Officers with more than one job title may be intentionally listed here more than once.

Wong Weng Sun, CEO
Ong Poh Kwee, COO
Wong Weng Sun, Pres.
Tan Cheng Tat, CFO
Chua San Lye, Dir.-Human Resources
Chia Chee Hing, Dir.-IT
Jessie Lau, VP-Admin.
Kwong Sook May, Company Sec.
Wee Keng Hwee, Sr. VP-Corp. Dev.
Judy Han, Sr. VP-Comm.
Judy Han, Sr. VP-Investor Rel.
Tan Heng Jack, VP-Internal Audit
Chionh Keat Yee, Sr. VP-Performance Mgmt., Mergers & Acquisitions
Ong Poh Kwee, Deputy Pres.
Ng Thiam Poh, Chief Risk Officer
Chia Chee Hing, Sr. VP-Mgmt. Information Sys.
Tan Sri Mohd Hassan Marican, Chmn.
John Chen, Pres.

GROWTH PLANS/SPECIAL FEATURES:

Sembcorp Marine Ltd. is a marine engineering firm headquartered in Singapore, with international operations in Indonesia, the U.K., the U.S., Norway, Brazil and Indonesia. The company's expertise and capabilities include rigs and floaters, repairs and upgrades, offshore platforms and specialized shipbuilding. The rigs and floaters division designs and executes solutions for complex projects, with product areas including drillships, semi-submersibles (for drilling, accommodation and well-intervention), jack-up rigs, and various tension-leg platforms (TLP) and spar floating platforms. The repairs and upgrades division offers solutions across all types of vessel projects, whether routine or complex. This unit's products and services include repair, refurbishment, retrofitting, life extension and upgrading of vessels, as well as marine and offshore structures; jumboization/dejumboization (ship enlargement/reduction); and ship conversion. Its repair services include afloat, underwater, emergency, engine maintenance, mechanical, steel/pipe work, electrical, motor rewind, navigation, automation, safety/fire protection, cleaning, waste disposal, hydro jetting/vacuum blasting, reconditioning and vessel/crew towage and transport. The offshore division offers products and solutions in relation to offshore platforms, including integrated and process solutions, production, riser, drilling, wellhead, power generation, manifold, accommodation, windfarm stations and liquid natural gas (LNG) modules. Last, the specialized shipbuilding division designs and builds specialized vessels. This division's products and solutions include accommodation, crane barges, offshore support vessels, tugs, dredgers, research/seismic/multi-purpose vessels, heavy-lift pipelay vessels and carriers. Sembcorp overseas subsidiaries include Estaleiro Jurong Aracruz, Gravifloat AS, LMG Marin AS, Sembmarine SLP Limited and Sembmarine SSP, Inc.

FINANCIAL DATA:
Note: Data for latest year may not have been available at press time.

In U.S. $	2017	2016	2015	2014	2013	2012
Revenue	1,820,462,000	2,703,078,000	3,788,418,000	4,447,609,000	4,213,727,000	3,378,163,000
R&D Expense						
Operating Income	15,596,310	171,805,700	-114,374,700	539,137,500	491,274,200	422,615,500
Operating Margin %	.85%	6.35%	-3.01%	12.12%	11.65%	12.51%
SGA Expense	75,291,290	86,920,080	221,446,500	116,223,900	113,193,500	113,820,300
Net Income	10,733,570	60,070,910	-220,887,600	427,122,100	423,781,400	410,594,000
Operating Cash Flow	37,858,010	433,516,100	-754,231,300	-387,580,400	714,629,400	158,255,300
Capital Expenditure	135,650,400	321,326,800	711,322,900	583,644,200	621,456,400	394,094,800
EBITDA	207,431,000	257,828,300	-151,814,800	642,898,400	589,944,300	554,290,800
Return on Assets %	.15%	.84%	-3.32%	7.23%	8.52%	9.93%
Return on Equity %	.55%	3.10%	-10.57%	19.85%	21.72%	22.19%
Debt to Equity	1.31	1.08	0.98	0.44	0.22	0.12

CONTACT INFORMATION:
Phone: 65 6265-1766   Fax: 65 6261-0738
Toll-Free:
Address: 29 Tanjong Kling Rd., Singapore, 628054 Singapore

SALARIES/BONUSES:
Top Exec. Salary: $ Bonus: $
Second Exec. Salary: $ Bonus: $

STOCK TICKER/OTHER:
Stock Ticker: SMBMF   Exchange: PINX
Employees: 11,689   Fiscal Year Ends: 12/31
Parent Company:

OTHER THOUGHTS:
Estimated Female Officers or Directors: 5
Hot Spot for Advancement for Women/Minorities: Y

Sener Ingenieria Y Sistemas SA

NAIC Code: 541330

www.sener.es

TYPES OF BUSINESS:
Engineering Services
Engineering

BRANDS/DIVISIONS/AFFILIATES:
FORAN
Torresol Energy
NTE Healthcare

CONTACTS:
Note: Officers with more than one job title may be intentionally listed here more than once.

Jorge Snedagorta Gomendio, Pres.

GROWTH PLANS/SPECIAL FEATURES:

Sener Ingenieria Y Sistemas SA is an engineering and construction company with more than 50 years' experience. It specializes in aerospace engineering, infrastructure and transport, power and marine engineering. The aerospace engineering division is responsible for projects related to space, defense, security, aeronautics and vehicles, healthcare and solar energy. Infrastructure and transport offers integrated engineering services for projects involving railroads, urban transport systems, airports, roads, ports and marine infrastructures, hydraulic engineering, environmental projects, architecture and urban planning. The power division specializes in renewables, power, oil and gas high technology projects, as well as turnkey projects which encompass engineering, purchasing, and the construction and commissioning of the facility. This division also provides operation and maintenance services. The marine division contributes to the shipbuilding industry by offering marine engineering services related to carrying out conceptual, basic, classification, detail and construction projects of any type of ship or marine artifacts. This division also develops and commercializes FORAN, a worldwide reference program for computer design and marine construction. Sener has offices and representatives located in the U.S., Mexico, South America, the U.K., Spain, Portugal, Morocco, Algeria, Poland, Qatar, United Arab Emirates, South Africa, India, China and South Korea. Subsidiaries of the firm include, but are not limited to: Torresol Energy, which promotes the technological development, construction, operation and maintenance of large concentrated solar power plants worldwide; and NTE Healthcare, which develops high value-added engineering and technological solutions for the healthcare sector.

FINANCIAL DATA:
Note: Data for latest year may not have been available at press time.

In U.S. $	2017	2016	2015	2014	2013	2012
Revenue	1,100,000,000	1,071,623,111	777,015,511	1,548,336,975	1,433,477,417	1,382,995,814
R&D Expense						
Operating Income						
Operating Margin %						
SGA Expense						
Net Income		19,992,285	-84,390,289	103,392,410	39,542,880	107,045,819
Operating Cash Flow						
Capital Expenditure						
EBITDA						
Return on Assets %						
Return on Equity %						
Debt to Equity						

CONTACT INFORMATION:
Phone: 34-944-817-500   Fax: 34-944-817-51
Toll-Free:
Address: Avda. de Zugazarte 56, ENTRANCE Cervantes, 8, Getxo (Biscay), 48930 Spain

STOCK TICKER/OTHER:
Stock Ticker: Private
Employees: 2,500
Parent Company:

Exchange:
Fiscal Year Ends:

SALARIES/BONUSES:
Top Exec. Salary: $ Bonus: $
Second Exec. Salary: $ Bonus: $

OTHER THOUGHTS:
Estimated Female Officers or Directors:
Hot Spot for Advancement for Women/Minorities:

Sales, profits and employees may be estimates. Financial information, benefits and other data can change quickly and may vary from those stated here.

SEPCO Electric Power Construction Corporation

http://en.sepco.net.cn/
NAIC Code: 541330

TYPES OF BUSINESS:
Engineering Services

BRANDS/DIVISIONS/AFFILIATES:
Power Construction Corporation Group Co Ltd
Shandong Electric Power Construction

CONTACTS: Note: Officers with more than one job title may be intentionally listed here more than once.
Liu Chuanming, Pres.

GROWTH PLANS/SPECIAL FEATURES:
SEPCO Electric Power Construction Corporation is a comprehensive engineering company in investment, financing, survey, design, equipment supply, construction, commissioning, and operation of electric power projects and infrastructures. SEPCO stands for Shandong Electric Power Construction, and is a wholly-owned subsidiary of Power Construction Corporation Group Co. Ltd. (also known as POWERCHINA), an engineering company. The firm's main business is engineering, procurement and construction (EPC) of overseas power projects as well as project investment and financing. SEPCO operates primarily in the regions of Asia, Africa and South America, with recent projects in India, Zambia, Saudi Arabia, Sudan, Brazil, Indonesia and Nigeria. SEPCO operates four regional companies in Southeast Asia, the Middle East, Africa and Central Asia; three subsidiaries in India, Zambia and Saudi Arabia; and has five offices in South Africa, Iran, Pakistan, Indonesia and the Russian-speaking region of Central Asia. The firm provides customers with direct investment and China-sourced financing, planning, design, construction, manufacturing, operation, maintenance and other services.

FINANCIAL DATA: Note: Data for latest year may not have been available at press time.

In U.S. $	2017	2016	2015	2014	2013	2012
Revenue						
R&D Expense						
Operating Income						
Operating Margin %						
SGA Expense						
Net Income						
Operating Cash Flow						
Capital Expenditure						
EBITDA						
Return on Assets %						
Return on Equity %						
Debt to Equity						

CONTACT INFORMATION:
Phone: 86-531-55697751 Fax: 86-531-55967777
Toll-Free:
Address: No.10567, Jing Shi Rd., Jinan City, SHG 250 014 China

SALARIES/BONUSES:
Top Exec. Salary: $ Bonus: $
Second Exec. Salary: $ Bonus: $

STOCK TICKER/OTHER:
Stock Ticker: Government-Owned   Exchange:
Employees: 5,000   Fiscal Year Ends:
Parent Company: Power Construction Corporation Group Co Ltd

OTHER THOUGHTS:
Estimated Female Officers or Directors:
Hot Spot for Advancement for Women/Minorities:

Sales, profits and employees may be estimates. Financial information, benefits and other data can change quickly and may vary from those stated here.

Shanghai Construction Group Co Ltd

www.scg.com.cn

NAIC Code: 541330

TYPES OF BUSINESS:
Engineering Services
Construction
Engineering

BRANDS/DIVISIONS/AFFILIATES:
Shanghai Construction (Group) General Corporation
Shanghai Construction No 1 (Group) Co Ltd
Shanghai Installation Engineering Group Co Ltd
Shanghai Foundation Engineering Group Co Ltd
Shanghai Building Decoration Engineering Group Co
SCG Real Estate Co Ltd
Shanghai Garden & Landscape (Group) Co Ltd
SCG Design & Research Institute Co Ltd

GROWTH PLANS/SPECIAL FEATURES:
Shanghai Construction Group Co., Ltd. is a Chinese construction and engineering company serving both domestic and international markets. The firm specializes in the construction of high-rise buildings, large bridges, light railways, public culture facilities, sport facilities, industrial plants, major environment protection projects and more. Shanghai Construction has completed more than 100 landmark projects in over 30 overseas countries and regions. The company not only engages in the construction of urban infrastructure, but invests in and operates several of them as well. Shanghai Construction has more than 15 subsidiaries, including Shanghai Construction No. 1 (Group) Co., Ltd.; Shanghai Installation Engineering Group Co., Ltd.; Shanghai Foundation Engineering Group Co., Ltd.; Shanghai Building Decoration Engineering Group Co., Ltd.; S. C. G. Real Estate Co., Ltd.; Shanghai Garden & Landscape (Group) Co., Ltd.; and S. C. G. Design & Research Institute Co., Ltd. Shanghai Construction Group itself operates as a subsidiary of Shanghai Construction (Group) General Corporation.

CONTACTS: Note: Officers with more than one job title may be intentionally listed here more than once.

Yingwei Hang, Managing Dir.
Zheng Xu, Chmn.

FINANCIAL DATA:
Note: Data for latest year may not have been available at press time.

In U.S. $	2017	2016	2015	2014	2013	2012
Revenue	21,634,900,000	19,800,000,000	18,894,200,000	18,048,100,000	16,303,700,000	
R&D Expense						
Operating Income						
Operating Margin %						
SGA Expense						
Net Income	396,765,000	315,000,000	288,256,000	287,966,000	264,482,000	
Operating Cash Flow						
Capital Expenditure						
EBITDA						
Return on Assets %						
Return on Equity %						
Debt to Equity						

CONTACT INFORMATION:
Phone: 86-21-55885959   Fax: 86-21-5588-6222
Toll-Free:
Address: 666 Daming Rd. E., Shanghai, Shanghai 200080 China

STOCK TICKER/OTHER:
Stock Ticker: 600170   Exchange: Shanghai
Employees: 35,015   Fiscal Year Ends:
Parent Company: Shanghai Construction (Group) General Corporation

SALARIES/BONUSES:
Top Exec. Salary: $ Bonus: $
Second Exec. Salary: $ Bonus: $

OTHER THOUGHTS:
Estimated Female Officers or Directors:
Hot Spot for Advancement for Women/Minorities:

Sales, profits and employees may be estimates. Financial information, benefits and other data can change quickly and may vary from those stated here.

Sharp Corporation

NAIC Code: 334310

www.sharp-world.com

TYPES OF BUSINESS:
Audiovisual & Communications Equipment
Electronic Components
Solar Cells & Advanced Batteries
Home Appliances
Computers & Information Equipment
Consumer Electronics
LCD Flat Panel TVs, Monitors & Displays
Managed Print Services

BRANDS/DIVISIONS/AFFILIATES:
Foxconn Technology Co Ltd
Sharp Marketing Japan Corporation (SMJ)
SMJ Home Solutions Company
SMJ Business Solutions Company
Sharp Energy Solutions Corporation
Sharp Trading Corporation
ScienBiziP Japan Co Ltd

GROWTH PLANS/SPECIAL FEATURES:
Sharp Corporation designs, manufactures and distributes audiovisual and communication equipment, electric and electronic application equipment, as well as electronic components. The company's products include liquid crystal display (LCD) televisions, mobile phones, home appliances, electronic components, solar cells and integrated circuits. Sharp has 63 companies and facilities in 26 countries, which are engaged in sales, manufacturing, R&D, solar power generation or finance. A few of its Japanese subsidiaries include: Sharp Marketing Japan Corporation (SMJ), SMJ Home Solutions Company, SMJ Business Solutions Company, Sharp Energy Solutions Corporation, Sharp Trading Corporation and ScienBiziP Japan Co. Ltd. Foxconn Technology Co. Ltd. owns a 66% stake in Sharp Corporation.

CONTACTS:
Note: Officers with more than one job title may be intentionally listed here more than once.

Jeng-Wu Tai, CEO
Mototaka Taneya, Exec. Gen. Mgr.-Corp. R&D Group
Toshihiko Fujimoto, Exec. Gen. Mgr.-Bus. Dev. Group
Shogo Fukahori, Chief Officer-In-House Comm.
Shinichi Niihara, Exec. Officer
Fujikazu Nakayama, Sr. Exec. Managing Officer-Products Bus. Group
Akihiko Imaya, Exec. Group Gen. Mgr.-Display Device Business
Masahiro Okitsu, Exec. Group Gen. Mgr.-Health & Environment
Paul Molyneux, Exec. Gen. Mgr.-Sales & Mktg., Europe

FINANCIAL DATA:
Note: Data for latest year may not have been available at press time.

In U.S. $	2017	2016	2015	2014	2013	2012
Revenue	19,104,150,000	22,932,640,000	25,957,300,000	27,270,230,000	23,090,980,000	22,879,170,000
R&D Expense						
Operating Income	581,842,800	-1,508,916,000	-447,782,800	1,011,366,000	-1,362,642,000	-349,841,700
Operating Margin %	3.04%	-6.57%	-1.72%	3.70%	-5.90%	-1.52%
SGA Expense						
Net Income	-231,758,900	-2,384,684,000	-2,071,427,000	107,685,900	-5,080,558,000	-3,503,596,000
Operating Cash Flow	1,185,308,000	-175,759,300	161,533,500	1,853,773,000	-755,310,300	-1,335,029,000
Capital Expenditure	721,045,300	431,935,900	463,107,900	425,815,200	572,563,800	1,100,876,000
EBITDA	689,789,500	-1,263,993,000	-524,762,500	1,774,474,000	-2,564,300,000	173,672,400
Return on Assets %	-1.48%	-14.49%	-10.73%	.54%	-23.19%	-13.67%
Return on Equity %	-19.81%		-197.35%	7.22%	-145.31%	-45.53%
Debt to Equity	1.80		3.76	1.48	1.86	0.81

CONTACT INFORMATION:
Phone: 81 666211221   Fax:
Toll-Free:
Address: 1 Takumi-cho Sakai-Ku, Sakai City, Osaka, 590-8522 Japan

STOCK TICKER/OTHER:
Stock Ticker: SHCAF
Employees: 41,898
Parent Company: Foxconn Technology Co Ltd

Exchange: PINX
Fiscal Year Ends: 03/31

SALARIES/BONUSES:
Top Exec. Salary: $ Bonus: $
Second Exec. Salary: $ Bonus: $

OTHER THOUGHTS:
Estimated Female Officers or Directors:
Hot Spot for Advancement for Women/Minorities:

Sheladia Associates Inc

NAIC Code: 541330

www.sheladia.com

TYPES OF BUSINESS:
Engineering Consulting Services
Consulting

BRANDS/DIVISIONS/AFFILIATES:

CONTACTS:
Note: Officers with more than one job title may be intentionally listed here more than once.

Manish Kothari, Chmn.

GROWTH PLANS/SPECIAL FEATURES:

Sheladia Associates, Inc. is a multi-disciplinary international consulting firm serving the transportation, irrigation, agriculture, water supply, sanitation, facilities, vertical structures, energy, wastewater and environment industries. Sheladia provides project development services that include economic and financial analysis, policy design and institutional strengthening, planning and feasibility studies, detailed engineering design, environmental and social studies, procurement assistance and management, maintenance planning and management, construction supervision/management as well as monitoring and evaluation. Sheladia primarily serves the transportation, architecture, water resources, monitoring and evaluation, energy and environment and agriculture sectors. To international clients, the company provides technical assistance to governments, their agencies and private sectors in order to strengthen and support institutional capabilities through organizational development, technology transfer and training. Clients of the firm include U.S. state governments and local agencies such as the Maryland State Highway Administration, U.S. private sectors such as Verizon, educational institutions such as the University of Maryland, international donor agencies such as the World Bank, international governments such as Zambia and U.S. federal agencies such as the Department of State. Headquartered in Rockville, Maryland, the firm services the metropolitan Washington, D.C. area, and has international offices in Afghanistan, Ethiopia, India, Indonesia, Kenya, Pakistan, the Philippines and Zambia. Sheladia has more than 1,000 projects via 300 clients across 70 countries.

FINANCIAL DATA:
Note: Data for latest year may not have been available at press time.

In U.S. $	2017	2016	2015	2014	2013	2012
Revenue						
R&D Expense						
Operating Income						
Operating Margin %						
SGA Expense						
Net Income						
Operating Cash Flow						
Capital Expenditure						
EBITDA						
Return on Assets %						
Return on Equity %						
Debt to Equity						

CONTACT INFORMATION:
Phone: 301-590-3939 Fax: 301-948-7174
Toll-Free:
Address: 15825 Shady Grove Rd., Ste. 100, Rockville, MD 20850 United States

STOCK TICKER/OTHER:
Stock Ticker: Private
Employees: 313
Parent Company:

Exchange:
Fiscal Year Ends:

SALARIES/BONUSES:
Top Exec. Salary: $ Bonus: $
Second Exec. Salary: $ Bonus: $

OTHER THOUGHTS:
Estimated Female Officers or Directors:
Hot Spot for Advancement for Women/Minorities:

Shin-Etsu Chemical Co Ltd

NAIC Code: 325211

www.shinetsu.co.jp

TYPES OF BUSINESS:
Organic & Inorganic Chemicals
PVC
Silicones
Semiconductor Silicon
Rare Earth Magnets & Refined Rare Earth Elements
Synthetic Quartz
Construction & Plant Engineering
Importing & Exporting Goods

BRANDS/DIVISIONS/AFFILIATES:

CONTACTS: Note: Officers with more than one job title may be intentionally listed here more than once.
Yasuhiko Saitoh, Pres.
Fumio Akiya, Exec. VP
Yasuhiko Saitoh, Exec. VP
Toshinobu Ishihara, Sr. Managing Dir.
Kiichi Habata, Managing Dir.

GROWTH PLANS/SPECIAL FEATURES:
Shin-Etsu Chemical Co., Ltd. was founded in 1926, and is a chemical company based in Japan. The firm operates through six business segments: PVC/Chlor-Alkali, silicones, specialty chemicals, semiconductor silicon, electronics and functional materials, and diversified business. PVC/Chlor-Alkali produces polyvinyl chloride (PVC), a general-use resin for a wide application in goods used in daily life, as well as in all kinds of industrial materials; chloromethane, used as a cleaning agent for metals and precision instruments, as well as for molds for plastic parts; methanol, used in antifreeze, solvents and dissolvents, as well as a chemical reagent in the production of many organic chemical compounds; and caustic soda, which is produced by electrolysis of industrial salt, and is widely used in the chemical industry as a basic material in items such as synthetic textiles, paper, pulp, soap and food. The silicones segment includes the manufacturing and marketing of fluids, resins, rubber and grease which feature a number of properties such as resistance to heat, cold, water, weather, as well as adhesive, anti-foaming, anti-sticking and electrical insulation. Specialty chemicals include the firm's development of liquid fluoroelastomers by using silicone addition-related technology; its products help to resist cold, oils, solvents and chemicals for automotive, aircraft, electronics, office equipment and petrochemical industries. Semiconductor silicon produces silicon wafers for integrated circuit products worldwide. Electronics and functional materials comprise the extraction and merchandising of rare earth magnets, oxides, compounds and metals used in cathode ray tubes, fluorescent lamps, electronic parts, automobile sensors and more; the production of photoresists for excimer lasers as a photosensitive material used in inscribing semiconductor circuitry; and the production of photomask blanks, the base material of photomasks used as the patterning templates of circuit during the semiconductor lithography process. The diversified segment comprises the production of cellulose derivatives, synthetic pheromones and aroma chemicals.

FINANCIAL DATA: Note: Data for latest year may not have been available at press time.

In U.S. $	2017	2016	2015	2014	2013	2012
Revenue	11,527,900,000	11,922,930,000	11,696,880,000	10,860,990,000	9,552,907,000	9,760,863,000
R&D Expense						
Operating Income	2,223,011,000	1,942,668,000	1,726,570,000	1,619,247,000	1,463,052,000	1,394,019,000
Operating Margin %	19.28%	16.29%	14.76%	14.90%	15.31%	14.28%
SGA Expense						
Net Income	1,638,830,000	1,386,622,000	1,198,118,000	1,058,478,000	984,851,900	937,609,500
Operating Cash Flow	2,709,819,000	2,623,840,000	2,268,111,000	2,419,732,000	2,195,100,000	899,636,700
Capital Expenditure	1,269,555,000	1,379,216,000	813,937,100	645,220,900	760,751,000	756,698,400
EBITDA	3,127,902,000	2,989,780,000	2,755,106,000	2,542,594,000	2,287,088,000	2,217,775,000
Return on Assets %	6.81%	5.99%	5.53%	5.51%	5.66%	5.60%
Return on Equity %	8.45%	7.46%	6.88%	6.77%	6.96%	6.97%
Debt to Equity						

CONTACT INFORMATION:
Phone: 81 332465091 Fax:
Toll-Free:
Address: 6-1, Ohtemachi 2-chome, Chiyoda-ku, Tokyo, 100-0004 Japan

SALARIES/BONUSES:
Top Exec. Salary: $ Bonus: $
Second Exec. Salary: $ Bonus: $

STOCK TICKER/OTHER:
Stock Ticker: SHECF
Employees: 19,206
Parent Company:

Exchange: PINX
Fiscal Year Ends: 03/31

OTHER THOUGHTS:
Estimated Female Officers or Directors:
Hot Spot for Advancement for Women/Minorities:

Sales, profits and employees may be estimates. Financial information, benefits and other data can change quickly and may vary from those stated here.

Plunkett Research, Ltd.

Showa Denko KK
NAIC Code: 325110

www.sdk.co.jp

TYPES OF BUSINESS:
Petrochemical Manufacturing
Aluminum
Electronic Components
Basic & Specialty Chemicals
Ceramic Materials
Carbon Nanofiber
Graphite

BRANDS/DIVISIONS/AFFILIATES:
Showa Denko Gas Products Co Ltd
Union Showa KK
Showa Denko Kenzai KK
Showa Denko Aluminum Trading KK
Showa Denko Packaging Co Ltd

CONTACTS: Note: Officers with more than one job title may be intentionally listed here more than once.
Kohei Morikawa, CEO
Hideo Ichikawa, Pres.
Toshiharu Kato, CFO
Tetsuo Nakajo, Exec. Officer.-R&D
Shunji Fukada, Dir.-Corp. Strategy
Saburo Muto, Gen. Mgr.-Finance & Acct.
Tatsuharu Arai, Gen. Mgr.-Petrochemicals Div. & Olefins Department
Yoshiharu Mizuno, Corp. Officer-Ceramics & Carbons Div.
Masaru Amano, Chief Risk Mgmt. Officer
Robert C. Whitten, CEO
Hideo Ichikawa, Chmn.
Atushi Mizutani, Dir.-China

GROWTH PLANS/SPECIAL FEATURES:
Showa Denko KK is a leading Japanese chemicals and industrial materials production firm. It operates in six segments: petrochemicals, chemicals, inorganic materials, aluminum, electronics and other. Showa's chief petrochemical products are plastic products; olefins, including propylene and ethylene; and organic chemicals, such as vinyl acetate monomer, acetic acid and ethyl acetate. Chemical products include: oxygen, hydrogen, nitrogen and fluorocarbon gasses; electronic chemicals such as high-purity gases/chemicals and equipment used in the LCP (link control protocol), LED (light-emitting diode) and solar cell manufacturing processes; functional chemicals such as unsaturable polyester resin, vinyl ester resin and synthetic resins; specialty chemicals, such as analytical columns, specialized polymers, amino acids and stabilized vitamin C; and basic chemicals, such as chlorine, ammonia, caustic soda and acrylonitrile. Inorganic products consist of ceramics, such as abrasives, alumina, aluminum hydroxide and refractories; and carbons, such as graphite electrodes, carbon nanofiber and artificial graphite powder. The firms' highly crystalline carbon nanofibers, which are easier to handle than carbon nanotubes, can be used to manufacture batteries, to reinforce resin parts and resin sheets, to make electrically conductive paints and adhesives and to improve thermal conductivity and corrosion resistance of metals. Aluminum products include extruded products, sheets, ingots, high-purity capacitor foils and fabricated products, such as beverage cans, heat exchangers, forged products and aluminum cylinders for laser printers. Electronic products include high-definition (HD) media, compound semiconductors such as ultra-high-bright LEDs rare earth magnetic alloys, and lithium-ion battery materials. Last, the other segment sells chemicals, resins, metals and electronic materials, and provides building materials. Subsidiaries include Showa Denko Gas Products Co. Ltd., Union Showa KK, Showa Denko Kenzai KK, Showa Denko Aluminum Trading KK and Showa Denko Packaging Co. Ltd., among others.

FINANCIAL DATA: Note: Data for latest year may not have been available at press time.

In U.S. $	2017	2016	2015	2014	2013	2012
Revenue	7,270,235,000	6,252,646,000	7,275,554,000	8,166,387,000	7,900,792,000	6,892,221,000
R&D Expense						
Operating Income	724,967,500	391,783,100	313,694,800	194,848,100	241,783,100	261,850,200
Operating Margin %	9.97%	6.26%	4.31%	2.38%	3.06%	3.79%
SGA Expense						
Net Income	311,812,900	114,635,700	9,027,390	32,606,670	84,451,280	87,274,090
Operating Cash Flow	626,830,700	642,342,100	581,498,100	614,831,400	592,183,700	496,646,200
Capital Expenditure	362,139,000	356,968,500	378,656,600	412,502,400	410,974,500	385,373,600
EBITDA	821,296,900	554,406,600	502,040,300	529,895,700	646,404,000	589,892,000
Return on Assets %	3.41%	1.31%	.09%	.35%	.94%	.99%
Return on Equity %	10.37%	4.14%	.32%	1.16%	3.15%	3.57%
Debt to Equity	0.56	0.77	0.76	0.75	0.71	0.79

CONTACT INFORMATION:
Phone: 81-3-5470-3235   Fax: 81-3-3431-6215
Toll-Free:
Address: 13-9 Shiba Daimon 1-chome, Minato-ku, Tokyo, 105-8518 Japan

STOCK TICKER/OTHER:
Stock Ticker: SHWDF
Employees: 11,562
Parent Company:

Exchange: GREY
Fiscal Year Ends: 12/31

SALARIES/BONUSES:
Top Exec. Salary: $ Bonus: $
Second Exec. Salary: $ Bonus: $

OTHER THOUGHTS:
Estimated Female Officers or Directors:
Hot Spot for Advancement for Women/Minorities:

Sales, profits and employees may be estimates. Financial information, benefits and other data can change quickly and may vary from those stated here.

Siemens AG

NAIC Code: 334513

www.siemens.com

TYPES OF BUSINESS:
Industrial Control Manufacturing
Energy & Power Plant Systems & Consulting
Medical & Health Care Services & Equipment
Lighting & Optical Systems
Automation Systems
Transportation & Logistics Systems

BRANDS/DIVISIONS/AFFILIATES:
Siemens Healthineers
Siemens Wind Power

CONTACTS:
Note: Officers with more than one job title may be intentionally listed here more than once.

Joe Kaeser, CEO
Joe Kaeser, Pres.
Klaus Helmrich, CTO
Peter Y. Solmssen, Head-Corp. Legal & Compliance
Joe Kaeser, Head-Controlling
Roland Busch, CEO-Infrastructure & Cities Sector
Hermann Requardt, CEO-Health Care Sector
Michael Suess, CEO-Energy Sector
Siegfried Russwurm, CEO-Industry Sector
Gerhard Cromme, Chmn.
Barbara Kux, Chief Sustainability Officer

GROWTH PLANS/SPECIAL FEATURES:
Siemens AG is engaged in electrification, automation and digitalization. Its businesses are grouped into eight divisions. The building technologies division offers fire protection, security, building automation, heating, ventilation and air conditioning (HVAC) and energy management products and services in relation to environmentally-friendly buildings and infrastructure. The digital factory division offers seamlessly integrated hardware, software and technology-based services that supports manufacturing companies worldwide in enhancing the flexibility and efficiency of their manufacturing processes. The energy management division supplies products, systems, solutions and services for the economical, reliable and intelligent transmission and distribution of electrical power. The financial services division provides business-to-business financial solutions worldwide, and supports customer investments with project and structured financing as well as leasing and equipment finance. The mobility division offers integrated products, solutions and services concerning the transportation of people and goods by rail and road. The power and gas division provides products and solutions for the oil and gas, power and industrial markets. The power generation services division offers products and services for ensuring reliable rotating power equipment within the utility, oil and gas, and industrial processing sectors worldwide. Last, the process industries and drives division provides innovative, integrated technology across the entire lifecycle in relation to products, processes and plants. Siemens Healthineers and Siemens Wind Power recently became separately-managed businesses. Healthineers supplies medical infrastructure, and develops and markets medical imaging, laboratory diagnostics and clinical IT products and solutions. Wind Power supplies environmentally-friendly renewable energy solutions. In March 2017, the firm concluded the merger of its wind power business with Gamesa Corp. Tecnologica SA. That September, Siemens signed an agreement with Alstom SA to merge their rail operations, creating a 50-50 joint venture to be called Siemens Alstom.

FINANCIAL DATA:
Note: Data for latest year may not have been available at press time.

In U.S. $	2017	2016	2015	2014	2013	2012
Revenue	102,557,500,000	98,352,640,000	93,403,140,000	88,814,250,000	93,706,930,000	96,687,990,000
R&D Expense	6,377,041,000	5,843,563,000	5,536,071,000	5,019,882,000	5,298,970,000	5,233,521,000
Operating Income	9,802,663,000	9,345,748,000	7,556,374,000	7,933,019,000	6,825,311,000	8,402,282,000
Operating Margin %	8.68%	8.77%	7.35%	8.44%	6.35%	8.69%
SGA Expense	15,096,690,000	14,410,090,000	14,089,010,000	12,872,630,000	13,937,120,000	13,783,990,000
Net Income	7,466,226,000	6,730,223,000	8,992,566,000	6,635,136,000	5,289,091,000	5,505,199,000
Operating Cash Flow	8,861,666,000	9,398,850,000	8,165,180,000	8,767,814,000	9,064,191,000	8,610,981,000
Capital Expenditure	2,971,177,000	2,636,519,000	2,342,611,000	2,261,108,000	2,308,034,000	2,724,197,000
EBITDA	15,520,270,000	13,777,820,000	13,071,450,000	13,092,450,000	11,756,280,000	14,511,350,000
Return on Assets %	4.65%	4.42%	6.46%	5.19%	4.07%	4.19%
Return on Equity %	15.64%	15.86%	22.25%	18.19%	14.56%	14.31%
Debt to Equity	0.62	0.72	0.77	0.62	0.65	0.54

CONTACT INFORMATION:
Phone: 49 8963633032
Fax: 49 8932825
Toll-Free:
Address: Wittelsbacherplatz 2, Munich, 80333 Germany

STOCK TICKER/OTHER:
Stock Ticker: SIEGY
Employees: 372,000
Parent Company:

Exchange: PINX
Fiscal Year Ends: 09/30

SALARIES/BONUSES:
Top Exec. Salary: $2,469,807   Bonus: $1,679,345
Second Exec. Salary: $1,679,418   Bonus: $680,135

OTHER THOUGHTS:
Estimated Female Officers or Directors: 5
Hot Spot for Advancement for Women/Minorities: Y

Sales, profits and employees may be estimates. Financial information, benefits and other data can change quickly and may vary from those stated here.

Siemens Corporate Technology

www.siemens.com/global/en/home/company/innovation/corporate-technology.html

NAIC Code: 541712

TYPES OF BUSINESS:
Research & Development
Materials
Microsystems
Production Processes
Power & Sensor Systems
Software Products
Communications

BRANDS/DIVISIONS/AFFILIATES:
Siemens AG

CONTACTS:
Note: Officers with more than one job title may be intentionally listed here more than once.

Joe Kaeser, CEO
Joe Kaeser, Pres.

GROWTH PLANS/SPECIAL FEATURES:

Siemens Corporate Technology (CT) is the central research and development division of Siemens AG, and engaged in developing technologies and the business models that stem from them. Working in close collaboration with Siemens' core business units, CT analyzes company data to develop blueprints for future developments while also watching research trends to link scientific advances with potential new business applications. CT also works to safeguard new technologies on behalf of the company through its Corporate Intellectual Property subdivision. Research is organized into seven broad technology divisions: innovation strategy, energy systems and electrification, patent and trademark protection, digitalization and automation, research cooperations, digitalization competence and business excellence. Therefore, CT provides important services along the entire value chain, from R&D to production and quality assurance, as well as optimized business processes. As a partner of Siemens' business units, CT has shapes the technology and innovation strategy of the Group, which together hold more than 59,800 granted patents. The firm maintains research and development locations worldwide. In January 2018, CT joined Princeton E-ffiliates Partnership, an initiative that forges research collaborations between practitioners outside academia and experts across Princeton University to pursue transformational innovations in the fields of energy and the environment. These innovations will have a focus on developing technological solutions that reduce greenhouse gas emissions and energy use by the transportation, building and electricity generation sectors.

FINANCIAL DATA:
Note: Data for latest year may not have been available at press time.

In U.S. $	2017	2016	2015	2014	2013	2012
Revenue						
R&D Expense						
Operating Income						
Operating Margin %						
SGA Expense						
Net Income						
Operating Cash Flow						
Capital Expenditure						
EBITDA						
Return on Assets %						
Return on Equity %						
Debt to Equity						

CONTACT INFORMATION:
Phone: 609-734-6500 Fax:
Toll-Free:
Address: 755 College Rd. E., Princeton, NJ 08540 United States

STOCK TICKER/OTHER:
Stock Ticker: Subsidiary   Exchange:
Employees: 7,400   Fiscal Year Ends: 09/30
Parent Company: Siemens AG

SALARIES/BONUSES:
Top Exec. Salary: $ Bonus: $
Second Exec. Salary: $ Bonus: $

OTHER THOUGHTS:
Estimated Female Officers or Directors:
Hot Spot for Advancement for Women/Minorities:

Sales, profits and employees may be estimates. Financial information, benefits and other data can change quickly and may vary from those stated here.

Siemens Gamesa Renewable Energy SA

www.gamesacorp.com/en/

NAIC Code: 333611

TYPES OF BUSINESS:
Wind Turbine Manufacturing
Wind Farms
Solar Facilities, Development & Maintenance

BRANDS/DIVISIONS/AFFILIATES:
Siemens AG
Siemens Wind HoldCo SL
Gamesa Corporacion Tecnologica SA

CONTACTS:
Note: Officers with more than one job title may be intentionally listed here more than once.

Markus Tacke, CEO
Andrew Hall, CFO
Ricardo Chocarro, Manager-Oper.
Xabier Etxeberria, CEO-Business
Rosa Maria Garcia, Chmn.

GROWTH PLANS/SPECIAL FEATURES:

Siemens Gamesa Renewable Energy SA (formerly Gamesa Corporacion Tecnologica SA), based in Spain, manufactures wind turbines, and supplies products, installations and services in relation to them. Gamesa also develops and markets wind farms. The company's wind turbine division designs and manufactures 2 megawatt (MW), 2.5 MW, 3.3 MW and 5 MW wind turbines. Its wind farm power projects take about three to four years to develop, about six to nine months to install and operate more than 20 years. Services within the wind farm division include site prospection, wind measurements, permits, civil engineering, wind turbine assembly, and operation and maintenance contracts handled by Siemens Gamesa. The company also develops products for the following markets: photovoltaic (PV), wind power, hydroelectric energy, nuclear, marine, power electronics products designed for adapting the behavior of wind farms and PV plants, drives and converters, electric vehicle, permanent magnets and custom-built solutions for rotating electrical machines and power electronics. Siemens Gamesa also provides end-to-end management of the gearbox lifecycle, from design to manufacturing and sale and extension of life via re-engineering. The firm develops off-grid solutions that combine wind and solar energy with diesel. In April 2017, Gamesa Corporacion Tecnologica was acquired by Siemens Wind HoldCo SL, a subsidiary of Siemens AG. Gamesa was then merged with Siemens Wind to form Siemens Gamesa Renewable Energy SA. The new company's shares are listed under the SGRE ticker symbol on Bolsa de Madrid stock market (BME). That October, the firm inaugurated its first rotor blade factory in Africa and the Middle East, located in Tangier, Morocco.

FINANCIAL DATA:
Note: Data for latest year may not have been available at press time.

In U.S. $	2017	2016	2015	2014	2013	2012
Revenue		5,695,353,000	4,326,857,000	3,514,729,000	2,884,262,000	3,290,821,000
R&D Expense						
Operating Income		610,380,600	359,095,100	233,578,300	160,868,400	-265,545,000
Operating Margin %		10.71%	8.29%	6.64%	5.57%	-8.06%
SGA Expense		119,995,600				
Net Income		372,049,200	210,200,300	113,423,400	55,611,400	-814,344,600
Operating Cash Flow		810,490,500	401,422,600	381,691,400	263,439,500	622,543,200
Capital Expenditure		260,667,100	207,288,400	137,166,900	170,779,700	277,513,600
EBITDA		958,187,500	653,770,200	450,116,100	352,525,400	334,909,500
Return on Assets %		5.71%	3.82%	2.03%	.91%	-12.27%
Return on Equity %		18.30%	11.68%	7.66%	4.42%	-48.74%
Debt to Equity		0.24	0.29	0.38	0.51	1.09

CONTACT INFORMATION:
Phone: 34-91-503-1700   Fax:
Toll-Free:
Address: C/ Ramirez de Arellano, 37, Zamudio, 48170 Spain

STOCK TICKER/OTHER:
Stock Ticker: SGREN
Employees: 9,103
Parent Company: Siemens AG

Exchange: MEX
Fiscal Year Ends: 12/31

SALARIES/BONUSES:
Top Exec. Salary: $ Bonus: $
Second Exec. Salary: $ Bonus: $

OTHER THOUGHTS:
Estimated Female Officers or Directors:
Hot Spot for Advancement for Women/Minorities: Y

Sales, profits and employees may be estimates. Financial information, benefits and other data can change quickly and may vary from those stated here.

Plunkett Research, Ltd.   541

Siemens Healthineers
NAIC Code: 339100

www.healthcare.siemens.com

TYPES OF BUSINESS:
Medical Equipment Manufacturing
Information Systems
Management Consulting
Diagnostic Tests
Healthcare Consulting

BRANDS/DIVISIONS/AFFILIATES:
Siemens AG
Medicalis Corporation
Fast Track Diagnostics

GROWTH PLANS/SPECIAL FEATURES:
Siemens Healthineers, a business segment of Siemens AG, is one of the largest suppliers to the healthcare industry. Siemens Healthcare and its subsidiaries offer innovative medical technologies, healthcare information systems, management consulting and support services. The company operates in three business divisions: imaging, diagnostics and advanced therapies. The imaging business comprises computed tomography, magnetic resonance, molecular imaging, X-ray products, syngo software and ultrasound. The diagnostic business comprises clinical chemistry/immunoassay, hemostasis/hematology, blood gas, urinalysis, molecular virology, liquid biopsy, automation and IT. Last, the advanced therapies business comprises angio systems, mobile C-arms, hybrid operating roomss and imaging for radiation oncology. During 2017, the firm acquired Medicalis Corporation, a provider of software solutions for diagnostic imaging; and acquired Fast Track Diagnostics, a Luxembourg-based supplier of molecular diagnostic tests.

CONTACTS: Note: Officers with more than one job title may be intentionally listed here more than once.

Bernd Montag, CEO
Michael Reitermann, COO
Jochen Schmitz, CFO
J. Marc Overhage, Chief Medical Informatics Officer
Michael Long, Sr. VP-Exec. & Customer Rel.
Brenna Quinn, Sr. VP-Solutions Dev.
Carlos Arglebe, VP-Quality Mgmt.
Gail Latimer, VP
Hartmut Schaper, Sr. VP-Health Svcs., Int'l

FINANCIAL DATA: Note: Data for latest year may not have been available at press time.

In U.S. $	2017	2016	2015	2014	2013	2012
Revenue	13,800,000,000	14,259,900,000	14,608,637,250	13,051,160,000	18,865,185,289	17,613,100,000
R&D Expense						
Operating Income						
Operating Margin %						
SGA Expense						
Net Income	2,500,000,000	2,449,530,000	2,468,149,320	2,342,500,000	2,841,292,799	2,343,350,000
Operating Cash Flow						
Capital Expenditure						
EBITDA						
Return on Assets %						
Return on Equity %						
Debt to Equity						

CONTACT INFORMATION:
Phone: 49-69-797-6602   Fax:
Toll-Free:
Address: Henkestrasse 127, Erlangen, D-91052 Germany

STOCK TICKER/OTHER:
Stock Ticker: Subsidiary   Exchange:
Employees: 45,000   Fiscal Year Ends: 09/30
Parent Company: Siemens AG

SALARIES/BONUSES:
Top Exec. Salary: $ Bonus: $
Second Exec. Salary: $ Bonus: $

OTHER THOUGHTS:
Estimated Female Officers or Directors: 3
Hot Spot for Advancement for Women/Minorities: Y

Sales, profits and employees may be estimates. Financial information, benefits and other data can change quickly and may vary from those stated here.

Singapore Technologies Engineering Limited

www.stengg.com

NAIC Code: 336411

TYPES OF BUSINESS:
Aircraft Overhaul
Aircraft Repair & Development
Electronic Systems
Military Equipment & Vehicles
Industrial, Commercial & Construction Vehicles
Shipbuilding

BRANDS/DIVISIONS/AFFILIATES:
Temasek Holdings Private Limited
Singapore Technologies Aeropace Ltd
Singapore Technologies Electronics Ltd
Singapore Technologies Kinetics Ltd
Singapore Technologies Marine Ltd

CONTACTS:
Note: Officers with more than one job title may be intentionally listed here more than once.

Vincent Chong, CEO
Pheng Hock Tan, Pres.
Saik Hay Fong, CTO
Boon Jin Gan, Chief Systems Engineer
Steven Cheong, Sr. VP-Mergers & Acquisitions
Alice Chua, Sr. VP-Risk Mgmt.
Meng Wai Low, Sr. VP-Legal
Robin Thevathasan, Sr. VP-Strategic Plans
Lina Poa, Sr. VP-Corp. Comm.
Augustine Syn, Sr. VP-Europe Oper.
Eve Chan, Group Finance Controller
Grace Kwok, Sr. VP-Internal Audit
Parmesh Singh, Exec. VP-Special Projects
Harnek Singh, VP-Bus. Excellence
Alex Teo, Sr. VP-Defense Bus.
Chong Seng Kwa, Chmn.
John Coburn, CEO-US Oper.

GROWTH PLANS/SPECIAL FEATURES:
Singapore Technologies Engineering Limited is an international aerospace, technology and engineering firm with diversified operations. The company comprises a network of over 100 subsidiaries in 24 countries. Its operations are divided into four segments: aerospace, electronics, land systems and marine technology. Singapore Technologies (ST) Aerospace Ltd. specializes in the repair and overhaul of aircraft owned by air forces, commercial airlines and freight forwarding companies. This division also repairs helicopters and advanced military aircraft; offers engine support; and assists in the design, development and upgrading process. ST Electronics Ltd. provides information communications technologies (ICT) systems to a variety of different sectors, with a focus on the commercial, industrial, government and defense markets. Services include broadband radio frequency and microwave communication; rail and traffic management; military services such as command and control operations and training and simulation systems; and IT security and mobile commerce support. Within the land systems segment, ST Kinetics Ltd., designs and builds land systems and specialty vehicles for military and industrial applications. Products include armored vehicles; emergency vehicles; construction vehicles, such as excavators, dump trucks and asphalt pavers; distribution vehicles, including refrigerated trailers; and other vehicles. Last, the marine technology segment comprises ST Marine Ltd., which provides turnkey and sustainable solutions in the marine, offshore and environmental engineering industries. In shipbuilding, this division offers design, construction, onboard system installation and integration, commissioning and lifecycle support services. It provides sustainable environmental engineering solutions to meet the global demand for innovative green solutions in water, wastewater, solid waste and renewable energy. Singapore Technologies Engineering operates as a subsidiary of Temasek Holdings Private Limited. In December 2017, the firm announced that it had completed the liquidation of ST Marine (Wuhan) Engineering Design Consultancy Co. Ltd.

FINANCIAL DATA:
Note: Data for latest year may not have been available at press time.

In U.S. $	2017	2016	2015	2014	2013	2012
Revenue	5,047,652,000	5,096,642,000	4,830,733,000	4,986,604,000	5,058,069,000	4,864,927,000
R&D Expense						
Operating Income	421,949,800	359,221,400	389,104,000	423,191,200	513,355,900	501,676,800
Operating Margin %	8.35%	7.04%	8.05%	8.48%	10.14%	10.31%
SGA Expense	490,722,100	502,191,500	494,564,600	494,125,300	489,938,900	517,010,000
Net Income	390,332,400	369,463,100	403,415,400	405,636,700	442,911,400	439,361,000
Operating Cash Flow	582,325,800	578,622,000	354,926,000	476,072,900	709,007,900	793,671,600
Capital Expenditure	263,712,000	249,919,900	225,361,400	194,181,000	266,280,300	184,020,900
EBITDA	672,145,000	671,339,800	661,538,800	660,657,300	723,989,600	693,659,400
Return on Assets %	6.07%	5.86%	6.41%	6.24%	6.94%	7.46%
Return on Equity %	23.15%	22.46%	24.81%	25.04%	28.96%	31.47%
Debt to Equity	0.39	0.45	0.47	0.44	0.44	0.56

CONTACT INFORMATION:
Phone: 65 6722-1818   Fax: 65 6720-2293
Toll-Free:
Address: 1 Ang Mo Kio Electronics Park Road, #07-01, Singapore, 567710 Singapore

STOCK TICKER/OTHER:
Stock Ticker: SGGKY   Exchange: PINX
Employees: 22,000   Fiscal Year Ends: 12/31
Parent Company: Temasek Holdings Private Limited

SALARIES/BONUSES:
Top Exec. Salary: $ Bonus: $
Second Exec. Salary: $ Bonus: $

OTHER THOUGHTS:
Estimated Female Officers or Directors: 4
Hot Spot for Advancement for Women/Minorities: Y

Sino-Thai Engineering & Construction PCL

www.stecon.co.th/

NAIC Code: 237310

TYPES OF BUSINESS:
Industrial Engineering Services

BRANDS/DIVISIONS/AFFILIATES:

CONTACTS:
Note: Officers with more than one job title may be intentionally listed here more than once.
Woraphant Chontong, Sr. Exec. VP-Admin.
Woraphant Chontong, Sr. Exec. VP-Finance
Rawat Chamchalerm, Chmn.

GROWTH PLANS/SPECIAL FEATURES:
Sino-Thai Engineering & Construction PCL (STECON) is a construction company serving the public and private sectors in Thailand. The company operates in five segments: infrastructure, industrial works, buildings, energy and environmental works. The infrastructure segment constructs roads, elevated roads, highways, express ways, bridges and other facilities. In its Industrial works segment, the firm provides turnkey construction of refineries, petrochemical plants, steel structures and oil and gas pipelines. The building operations include the construction of office buildings, condominiums, aircraft maintenance centers, sports auditoriums, schools, hospitals, museums, convention buildings and airport terminals. The energy segment constructs power plants, sub-stations, oil refineries and natural gas facilities. The environmental works segment constructs wastewater treatment plants, water supply systems, solid waste management plants and irrigation systems. STECON's facilities include two fabrication plants; a pre-cast concrete plant; a construction equipment center (CEC); a construction assets center (CAC); an inventory control section (ICS); and a warehouse, all of which are located in Chonburi, Thailand. It also has a second warehouse located in the Map-ta-put estate in Thailand.

FINANCIAL DATA:
Note: Data for latest year may not have been available at press time.

In U.S. $	2017	2016	2015	2014	2013	2012
Revenue	645,473,200	577,240,100	589,391,100	696,182,300	716,827,300	638,938,000
R&D Expense						
Operating Income	-60,767,180	33,752,330	41,257,710	52,533,240	51,022,190	35,766,570
Operating Margin %	-9.41%	5.84%	7.00%	7.54%	7.11%	5.59%
SGA Expense	13,472,970	17,807,010	14,406,530	18,749,640	17,336,020	18,052,240
Net Income	-19,640,090	44,395,830	49,082,740	48,889,360	55,728,120	37,468,820
Operating Cash Flow	188,546,000	45,319,920	-75,963,940	-30,233,020	65,387,800	141,528,700
Capital Expenditure	23,236,150	4,779,774	14,733,160	28,408,920	25,355,700	7,347,605
EBITDA	-9,427,672	72,899,980	76,327,960	76,031,420	83,181,660	58,199,220
Return on Assets %	-2.10%	5.79%	6.40%	6.08%	7.65%	6.40%
Return on Equity %	-6.24%	14.05%	17.30%	19.07%	25.23%	19.78%
Debt to Equity	0.04			0.01	0.01	0.02

CONTACT INFORMATION:
Phone: 66 26104900 Fax: 66 22601339
Toll-Free:
Address: 32/59-60, Sukhumvit 21 Rd., Asoke Road, Klongtoey-Nua, Wattana, Bangkok, 10110 Thailand

SALARIES/BONUSES:
Top Exec. Salary: $ Bonus: $
Second Exec. Salary: $ Bonus: $

STOCK TICKER/OTHER:
Stock Ticker: SINOF Exchange: GREY
Employees: 1,030 Fiscal Year Ends: 12/31
Parent Company:

OTHER THOUGHTS:
Estimated Female Officers or Directors: 2
Hot Spot for Advancement for Women/Minorities:

SK Engineering & Construction Co Ltd

NAIC Code: 541330

www.skec.com

TYPES OF BUSINESS:
Engineering Services

BRANDS/DIVISIONS/AFFILIATES:
SK Group

CONTACTS:
Note: Officers with more than one job title may be intentionally listed here more than once.

Ahn G. Hyun, Pres.
Cho Ki Haeng, Chmn.

GROWTH PLANS/SPECIAL FEATURES:

SK Engineering & Construction Co. Ltd. (SK E&C), part of the SK Group, is an engineering, procurement and construction (EPC) company. The firm has management capabilities in various areas of construction, including architecture, infrastructure, plants and specialized technologies. SK E&C's architecture division is a leader of intelligent buildings based on cutting-edge construction methods and state-of-the-art systems, featuring designs that balance function and aesthetics. Architecture projects include educational environments, cultural and commercial facilities, hotels and sports complexes. The infrastructure division provides civil engineering via leading-edge technology, particularly for underground storage, and has introduced state-of-the-art measurement systems that it uses to achieve perfection in design, construction and maintenance in all areas of civil engineering, including SOC projects, high-speed rail and subway construction, mixed-use complexes, reclamation and port construction. The plant division is further divided into three groups: oil and gas plants, with a diverse portfolio such as refineries, petrochemicals, liquid natural gas storage and oil sands; power plants, including coal-fired, combined-cycle, cogeneration, nuclear and renewable; and industrial plants, including semiconductor, electric vehicle batter material, pharmaceutical and more. Last, the special technologies division includes technologies designed and developed for a variety of applications, including compressed air energy storage, underground excavation/tunnel methods, carbon dioxide geological storage, building facades and energy and water resource management systems.

SK E&C offers employees medical benefits, daycare centers and holiday pay.

FINANCIAL DATA:
Note: Data for latest year may not have been available at press time.

In U.S. $	2017	2016	2015	2014	2013	2012
Revenue	6,029,540,000	5,953,240,000	7,418,570,000	7,667,750,000	7,058,690,000	7,059,530,000
R&D Expense						
Operating Income						
Operating Margin %						
SGA Expense						
Net Income	81,842,200	72,445,900	24,239,000	-160,790,000	-463,702,000	9,571,460
Operating Cash Flow						
Capital Expenditure						
EBITDA						
Return on Assets %						
Return on Equity %						
Debt to Equity						

CONTACT INFORMATION:
Phone: 82-2-3700-7114
Fax: 82-23700-8200
Toll-Free:
Address: 32 Insadong 7-gil, Jongno-gu, Seoul, 135-798 South Korea

STOCK TICKER/OTHER:
Stock Ticker: Subsidiary
Employees: 5,400
Parent Company: SK Group
Exchange:
Fiscal Year Ends:

SALARIES/BONUSES:
Top Exec. Salary: $
Bonus: $
Second Exec. Salary: $
Bonus: $

OTHER THOUGHTS:
Estimated Female Officers or Directors:
Hot Spot for Advancement for Women/Minorities:

Skidmore Owings & Merrill LLP

NAIC Code: 541330

www.som.com

TYPES OF BUSINESS:
Architectural & Engineering Services
Urban Design Services
Transportation Planning
Seismic Analysis & Consulting
Environmental Engineering
Digital Design
Graphics
Interior Design

BRANDS/DIVISIONS/AFFILIATES:

CONTACTS: Note: Officers with more than one job title may be intentionally listed here more than once.
Xuan Fu, Managing Partner
William F. Baker, Partner-Civil & Structural Eng.
Gene Schnair, Managing Partner-San Francisco
Thomas Behr, Managing Dir-New York
Rod Garrett, Managing Dir.-Washington, D.C.
Xuan Fu, Managing Partner-Chicago
Silas Chiow, Dir.-China

GROWTH PLANS/SPECIAL FEATURES:
Skidmore, Owings & Merrill, LLP (SOM) is a leading global architecture, urban design, engineering and interior architecture firm. Its services span architectural design, interior design, graphics, branding, structural and civil engineering, sustainable design, tall buildings, urban design and planning, as well as mechanical, electrical and plumbing (MEP) engineering and planning. The firm's projects serve the aviation, civic/government, commercial, office, convention, cultural, education, health/science, hospitality, mixed-use, residential, sports and transportation markets. SOM's digital design service provides virtual modeling for potential projects. The company's sustainable designs include extensive uses of natural light and low-impact environmental building systems designed to reduce waste and energy use. SOM's mechanical and electrical engineering group provides design engineering services for new and existing buildings, such as developing solar heating and cooling for new and existing buildings, modeling energy consumption patterns, forecasting probable operating costs and developing energy recovery systems. Its urban planning services assist city officials in providing plans for efficient commuting, potable water, adequate housing and related problems. Signature projects include Bronzeville Metra Station, Centennial Tower, 7 World Trade Center, Willis Tower (formerly known as the Sears Tower) and John Hancock Tower. Current projects (2018) include: residential and mixed-use developments in London, U.K. (Manhattan Loft Gardens) and Chicago, Illinois (Taylor Street Apartments and Roosevelt Branch Library); urban-scale city projects in Washington, D.C. (Capitol Crossing), San Francisco, California (Moscone Convention Center expansion and improvement) and Singapore (Tanjong Pagar Centre); commercial spaces in Guadalajara, Mexico (Bio-Esfera) and Chicago, Illinois (1515 West Webster Ave. and Optimo Hat Factory; and a tower in Tianjin, China (Tianjin CTF Finance Centre). SOM has completed more than 10,000 projects in over 50 countries, and has earned nearly 2,000 awards, including winning the Architecture Firm Award twice from the American Institute of Architects.

FINANCIAL DATA: Note: Data for latest year may not have been available at press time.

In U.S. $	2017	2016	2015	2014	2013	2012
Revenue	345,000,000	339,900,000	356,070,000	283,000,000	277,000,000	255,000,000
R&D Expense						
Operating Income						
Operating Margin %						
SGA Expense						
Net Income						
Operating Cash Flow						
Capital Expenditure						
EBITDA						
Return on Assets %						
Return on Equity %						
Debt to Equity						

CONTACT INFORMATION:
Phone: 312-554-9090 Fax: 312-360-4545
Toll-Free: 866-269-2688
Address: 224 S. Michigan Ave., Ste. 1000, Chicago, IL 60604 United States

STOCK TICKER/OTHER:
Stock Ticker: Private
Employees: 785
Parent Company:

Exchange:
Fiscal Year Ends: 09/30

SALARIES/BONUSES:
Top Exec. Salary: $ Bonus: $
Second Exec. Salary: $ Bonus: $

OTHER THOUGHTS:
Estimated Female Officers or Directors: 8
Hot Spot for Advancement for Women/Minorities: Y

Sales, profits and employees may be estimates. Financial information, benefits and other data can change quickly and may vary from those stated here.

SMEC Holdings Limited

www.smec.com

NAIC Code: 541330

TYPES OF BUSINESS:
Engineering Consulting Services

BRANDS/DIVISIONS/AFFILIATES:
Temasek Holdings Pte Ltd
Surbana Jurong Private Limited
SMEC Foundation

CONTACTS:
Note: Officers with more than one job title may be intentionally listed here more than once.

Heang Fine Wong, CEO
Thiam Guan Teo, Dir.-Group Finance
Max Findlay, Chmn.

GROWTH PLANS/SPECIAL FEATURES:

SMEC Holdings Limited is a professional services firm that provides high-quality consultancy services on major infrastructure projects. SMEC has an established network of 120 offices in 40 countries throughout Australasia, Asia, the Middle East, Africa and the Americas. The company provides consultancy services to a broad range of industry sectors, including transport, water, environment, built environment, energy, management services, resources/industry, education, governance and government advisory. SMEC's consulting services combine in-house expertise with state-of-the-art systems to deliver innovative solutions to these industry sectors. The firm's services cover the life of a project, from initial concept, feasibility, planning and design to construction, commissioning, operation and maintenance. SMEC has delivered thousands of civil, transport, water, environment and power projects in more than 100 countries. In addition to its consultancy work, SMEC also runs the SMEC Foundation. The SMEC Foundation, established in 2001, provides small-scale grant support to community groups and development projects in Australia and overseas. The principle areas of interest of the foundation include: health, education, environment, community development and emergency relief. SMEC Holdings is owned by Surbana Jurong Private Limited, a consultancy company with a focus on infrastructure and urban development. Surbana Jurong itself operates as a subsidiary of Temasek Holdings Pte. Ltd.

FINANCIAL DATA:
Note: Data for latest year may not have been available at press time.

In U.S. $	2017	2016	2015	2014	2013	2012
Revenue	450,000,000	420,414,000	418,771,637			
R&D Expense						
Operating Income						
Operating Margin %						
SGA Expense						
Net Income						
Operating Cash Flow						
Capital Expenditure						
EBITDA						
Return on Assets %						
Return on Equity %						
Debt to Equity						

CONTACT INFORMATION:
Phone: 61-3-9514-1500   Fax: 61-3-9514-1502
Toll-Free:
Address: 71 Quees Rd., 10/Fl, Melbourne, VIC 3004 Australia

STOCK TICKER/OTHER:
Stock Ticker: Private   Exchange:
Employees: 5,800   Fiscal Year Ends:
Parent Company: Temasek Holdings Pte Ltd

SALARIES/BONUSES:
Top Exec. Salary: $ Bonus: $
Second Exec. Salary: $ Bonus: $

OTHER THOUGHTS:
Estimated Female Officers or Directors:
Hot Spot for Advancement for Women/Minorities:

Smith & Nephew plc

NAIC Code: 339113

www.smith-nephew.com

TYPES OF BUSINESS:
Implants, Surgical, Manufacturing
Reconstructive Joint Implants
Arthroscopic Enabling Technologies
Wound Management Products

BRANDS/DIVISIONS/AFFILIATES:
Rotation Medical Inc

CONTACTS: Note: Officers with more than one job title may be intentionally listed here more than once.
Namal Nawana, CEO
Graham Baker, CFO
Brad Cannon, CMO
Elga Lohler, Chief Human Resources Officer
Ros Rivaz, CTO
Jack Campo, Chief Legal Officer
Gordon Howe, Pres., Global Oper.
Cyrille Petit, Chief Corp. Dev. Officer
Phil Cowdy, Head-Corp. Affairs
Phil Cowdy, Head-Corp. Affairs & Strategic Planning
Mike Frazzette, Pres., Advanced Surgical Devices
Arjun Rajaratnam, Chief Compliance Officer
Roberto Quarta, Chmn.
Francisco Canal Vega, Pres., Latin America

GROWTH PLANS/SPECIAL FEATURES:
Smith & Nephew plc develops and markets advanced medical technology devices for healthcare professionals. The company organizes its business into four business units: orthopedics reconstruction, advanced wound management, sports medicine and trauma & extremities. The orthopedics reconstruction segment is comprised of joint replacement systems for knees, hip and shoulders as well as ancillary products, like bone cement used in reconstructive surgery. The advanced wound management unit supplies products for chronic and acute wounds. Chronic wounds, such as pressure, leg or diabetic foot ulcers, are generally difficult to heal; and acute wounds, such as burns and post-operative wounds, are generally life threatening, with potential scarring and infection. Many products for this segment target wounds associated with older populations. The sports medicine segment offers minimally invasive surgery techniques, with a focus on the surgery of joints, including knee, shoulder and hip; fixation systems and specialized devices for damaged tissue repair; and radiofrequency wands, mechanical blades as well as fluid management equipment for surgical access. The trauma & extremities segment includes internal and external fixation devices and orthobiological materials used in the stabilization of severe fractures and deformity correction procedures. In December 2017, Smith & Nephew acquired tissue regeneration developer Rotation Medical, Inc.

FINANCIAL DATA: Note: Data for latest year may not have been available at press time.

In U.S. $	2017	2016	2015	2014	2013	2012
Revenue	4,765,000,000	4,669,000,000	4,634,000,000	4,617,000,000	4,351,000,000	4,137,000,000
R&D Expense	223,000,000	230,000,000	222,000,000	235,000,000	231,000,000	171,000,000
Operating Income	934,000,000	801,000,000	628,000,000	749,000,000	810,000,000	906,000,000
Operating Margin %	19.60%	17.15%	13.55%	16.22%	18.61%	21.89%
SGA Expense	2,360,000,000	2,366,000,000	2,641,000,000	2,471,000,000	2,210,000,000	2,050,000,000
Net Income	767,000,000	784,000,000	410,000,000	501,000,000	556,000,000	729,000,000
Operating Cash Flow	1,090,000,000	849,000,000	1,030,000,000	683,000,000	867,000,000	902,000,000
Capital Expenditure	376,000,000	392,000,000	358,000,000	375,000,000	340,000,000	265,000,000
EBITDA	1,388,000,000	1,584,000,000	1,112,000,000	1,186,000,000	1,184,000,000	1,484,000,000
Return on Assets %	10.08%	10.80%	5.66%	7.63%	9.70%	14.03%
Return on Equity %	17.83%	19.78%	10.24%	12.39%	14.02%	20.61%
Debt to Equity	0.30	0.39	0.36	0.41	0.08	0.11

CONTACT INFORMATION:
Phone: 44 2074017646 Fax: 44 2079303353
Toll-Free:
Address: 15 Adam St., London, WC2N 6LA United Kingdom

STOCK TICKER/OTHER:
Stock Ticker: SNN
Employees: 16,737
Parent Company:

Exchange: NYS
Fiscal Year Ends: 12/31

SALARIES/BONUSES:
Top Exec. Salary: $1,330,347   Bonus: $1,208,911
Second Exec. Salary: $547,273   Bonus: $683,797

OTHER THOUGHTS:
Estimated Female Officers or Directors: 6
Hot Spot for Advancement for Women/Minorities: Y

Sales, profits and employees may be estimates. Financial information, benefits and other data can change quickly and may vary from those stated here.

Smiths Group plc

www.smiths.com

NAIC Code: 339100

TYPES OF BUSINESS:
Machinery, Manufacturing
Medical Devices, Manufacturing

BRANDS/DIVISIONS/AFFILIATES:
Smiths Detection
Smiths Medical
Smiths Interconnect
John Crane
Flex-Tek
Morpho Detection LLC

CONTACTS: *Note: Officers with more than one job title may be intentionally listed here more than once.*
Andrew Reynolds Smith, CEO
John Francis Shipsey, CFO
Sheena Mackay, Dir.-Human Resources
George Buckley, Chmn.

GROWTH PLANS/SPECIAL FEATURES:
Smiths Group plc is a global technology company with five main divisions: Smiths Detection, Smiths Medical, Smiths Interconnect, John Crane and Flex-Tek. Smiths Detection provides security equipment for the detection and identification of explosives, chemical and biological agents, weapons, narcotics and contraband. This equipment is used by military forces, airport security, customs officers and emergency services. Smiths Medical is a provider of specialist medical devices and equipment, which include airway management, pain management, needle safety, temperature monitoring, infusion systems, vascular access and in-vitro fertilization. Smiths Interconnect manufactures electronic components and sub-systems such as millimeter wave components and antennas, fiber optic and coaxial cables, industrial surge protectors and wireless technology products. John Crane provides products and services to the oil and gas, power generation, chemicals, pharmaceutical, pulp and paper and mining industries. Flex-Tek provides components such as flexible hose and ducting for heating and conveying gas, liquid and airborne solids to the aerospace, medical, industrial, construction and domestic appliance industries. Smiths Group has operations in more than 50 countries, and its products and services reach approximately 200 countries and territories. During 2017, the firm sold Interconnect's microwave telecoms business; completed the acquisition of Morpho Detection, LLC; and sold Morpho's explosive trace detection business to OSI Systems, Inc. for $75.5 million. In early-2018, Smiths Group sold John Crane's bearings business; and agreed to acquire Seebach GmbH, a provider of highly-engineered filtration solutions.

FINANCIAL DATA: *Note: Data for latest year may not have been available at press time.*

In U.S. $	2017	2016	2015	2014	2013	2012
Revenue	4,671,699,000	4,200,256,000	4,126,193,000	4,203,960,000	4,427,574,000	4,315,767,000
R&D Expense						
Operating Income	710,725,000	551,203,500	561,173,600	537,815,100	701,182,100	535,251,400
Operating Margin %	15.21%	13.12%	13.60%	12.79%	15.83%	12.40%
SGA Expense	1,461,330,000	1,392,964,000	1,337,416,000	1,350,947,000	1,313,631,000	1,436,263,000
Net Income	803,304,400	368,893,300	350,377,400	331,576,700	507,904,900	365,475,000
Operating Cash Flow	682,239,000	509,898,900	378,863,400	364,905,300	503,347,100	472,155,000
Capital Expenditure	152,399,900	153,824,200	135,308,400	133,884,100	136,732,700	129,896,000
EBITDA	1,119,499,000	739,210,900	723,543,700	700,612,400	910,839,000	815,838,200
Return on Assets %	11.71%	6.12%	6.52%	6.10%	9.29%	7.09%
Return on Equity %	30.20%	16.90%	18.52%	17.09%	29.00%	21.87%
Debt to Equity	0.76	0.69	0.81	0.79	0.64	0.84

CONTACT INFORMATION:
Phone: 44 2078085500 Fax: 44 2078085544
Toll-Free:
Address: 4/Fl, 11-12 St. Jame's Square, London, SW1Y 4LB United Kingdom

STOCK TICKER/OTHER:
Stock Ticker: SMGKF Exchange: PINX
Employees: 22,000 Fiscal Year Ends: 07/31
Parent Company:

SALARIES/BONUSES:
Top Exec. Salary: $1,110,953 Bonus: $1,914,257
Second Exec. Salary: $576,841 Bonus: $818,972

OTHER THOUGHTS:
Estimated Female Officers or Directors:
Hot Spot for Advancement for Women/Minorities: Y

Plunkett Research, Ltd.

SNC-Lavalin Group Inc
NAIC Code: 541330

www.snclavalin.com

TYPES OF BUSINESS:
Engineering Services
Consulting
Chemicals & Petroleum
Mining & Metallurgy
Operations & Maintenance
Infrastructure Concessions
Nuclear Reactor Design & Development
Pharmaceuticals & Biotechnology Facilities

BRANDS/DIVISIONS/AFFILIATES:
WS Atkins plc

CONTACTS: Note: Officers with more than one job title may be intentionally listed here more than once.
Kevin Lynch, Director
Erik Ryan, Executive VP, Divisional
James Cullens, Executive VP, Divisional
Sylvain Girard, Executive VP
Hartland Paterson, Executive VP
Chantal Sorel, Executive VP
Marie-Claude Dumas, President, Divisional
Ian Edwards, President, Divisional
Jose Suarez, President, Divisional
Alexander Taylor, President, Divisional
Christian Brown, President, Divisional
Nicholas Roberts, President, Divisional
Neil Bruce, President

GROWTH PLANS/SPECIAL FEATURES:
SNC-Lavalin Group, Inc. is a construction, engineering, procurement and technical services company with operations in over 50 countries. The firm serves five primary markets: infrastructure, which includes equity investments, engineering, construction, operations and maintenance services; mining and metallurgy, which includes solutions related to mining of aluminum, gold, copper, iron ore, nickel, as well as fertilizers and sulfur product sectors; oil & gas, which includes upgrading, refining, carbon capture and utilization among others; clean power, covering projects and services in hydro, transmission, distribution, renewables, intelligent networks, cyber security and digital utility transformation; and nuclear, solving challenges across the full nuclear fuel cycle, from major new build programs through operations to later life management and waste management practices. SNC-Lavalin provides its clients with comprehensive end-to-end project solutions, including financing and asset management, consulting and advisory, digital and artificial intelligence, design, engineering, procurement, construction, project management, operations, maintenance and sustaining capital. During 2017, SNC-Lavalin acquired WS Atkins plc, a British multinational engineering, design, planning, architectural design, project management and consulting services company based in London, U.K. That December, SNC-Lavalin agreed to form a joint venture with ABB for the delivery of substation projects globally at 66 kV AC and above, with SNC-Lavalin being the majority shareholder.

FINANCIAL DATA: Note: Data for latest year may not have been available at press time.

In U.S. $	2017	2016	2015	2014	2013	2012
Revenue	7,399,697,000	6,518,498,000	7,422,519,000	5,814,249,000	5,667,309,000	5,965,783,000
R&D Expense						
Operating Income	472,344,000	131,133,600	205,891,400	-349,698,000	-384,153,000	-48,638,130
Operating Margin %	6.38%	2.01%	2.77%	-6.01%	-6.77%	-.81%
SGA Expense	918,492,300	574,011,100	678,266,400	666,995,600	663,169,300	674,765,800
Net Income	302,841,900	202,562,800	320,520,000	1,056,951,000	28,353,550	245,037,700
Operating Cash Flow	-186,964,700	83,728,900	-408,000,000	209,388,000	264,124,400	399,766,900
Capital Expenditure	98,942,530	119,967,500	91,934,210	1,367,947,000	1,304,081,000	749,402,300
EBITDA	653,336,500	366,315,500	582,925,900	1,654,686,000	350,846,600	537,436,400
Return on Assets %	3.31%	2.58%	3.94%	12.24%	.33%	3.44%
Return on Equity %	8.39%	6.60%	11.27%	49.91%	1.73%	15.61%
Debt to Equity	0.53	0.21	0.22	0.26	1.90	1.13

CONTACT INFORMATION:
Phone: 514 393-1000 Fax: 514 866-0795
Toll-Free:
Address: 455 Rene-Levesque Blvd. W., Montreal, QC H2Z 1Z3 Canada

STOCK TICKER/OTHER:
Stock Ticker: SNC   Exchange: TSE
Employees: 36,754   Fiscal Year Ends: 12/31
Parent Company:

SALARIES/BONUSES:
Top Exec. Salary: $ Bonus: $
Second Exec. Salary: $ Bonus: $

OTHER THOUGHTS:
Estimated Female Officers or Directors: 3
Hot Spot for Advancement for Women/Minorities: Y

Sales, profits and employees may be estimates. Financial information, benefits and other data can change quickly and may vary from those stated here.

Solvay SA

NAIC Code: 325180

www.solvay.com

TYPES OF BUSINESS:
Chemicals & Plastics
Pipeline Systems
Detergents
Alternative Energy
Nanotechnology

BRANDS/DIVISIONS/AFFILIATES:
Acetow
Novecare
Fibras
RusVinyl LLC

CONTACTS:
Note: Officers with more than one job title may be intentionally listed here more than once.

Jean-Pierre Clamadieu, CEO
Karim Hajjar, CFO
Cecile Tandeau de Marsac, Dir.-Human Resources
Michel Defourny, Group Corp. Sec.
Jean-Pierre Labroue, Group General Counsel
Michel Defourny, General Mgr.-Communication
Jean-Pierre Clamadieu, Chmn.

GROWTH PLANS/SPECIAL FEATURES:

Solvay SA, headquartered in Brussels, Belgium, is an international specialty chemicals and plastics company. It manages nearly 140 sites in 58 countries. Solvay operates in five segments: advanced materials, performance chemicals, advanced formulations, functional polymers and corporate and business services. Advanced materials include specialty polymers such as aromatic polymers, fluorinated polymers, high-barrier polymers and cross-linkable compounds; silica; special chemical solutions products such as thermal insulation foams, fluorinated intermediates, process chemicals and barium salts; and composite materials such as light-weighting material solutions that enables customers to design, develop and manufacture complex composite structures. Performance chemicals manufactures soda ash and derivatives and peroxides. This division also comprises Acetow, a producer of cellulose acetate for cigarette filter manufacturers, as well as for textiles and plastics production. Advanced formulations comprises Novecare, which designs formulations with specific properties such as cleaning, softening, gelling and texturing, found in shampoos, detergents, stimulation fluids, lubricants, paints, crop protection and mining; technology solutions, which specializes in mining reagents, phosphine-based chemistry, and solutions for stabilization of polymers; and aroma performance, which produces vanillin for food, flavors and fragrances industries, and produces synthetic intermediates used in perfumery, pharmaceuticals, agrochemicals and electronics. Functional polymers is divided into three groups: performance polyamides, for the production of intermediates and polymers for value-added engineering plastics; Fibras, which develops, manufactures and commercializes textile and industrial yarns and staple fibers for use in clothing and industrial applications; and chlorovinyls, which is operated by joint venture, RusVinyl, LLC. Corporate and business services provides energy optimization programs and shared/administrative services for the company and its clients.

FINANCIAL DATA:
Note: Data for latest year may not have been available at press time.

In U.S. $	2017	2016	2015	2014	2013	2012
Revenue	13,449,330,000	14,081,600,000	13,641,980,000	13,125,790,000	12,802,240,000	15,845,040,000
R&D Expense	358,122,000	376,645,500	342,068,200	305,021,100	292,672,100	322,309,800
Operating Income	1,474,475,000	1,115,118,000	1,195,386,000	1,024,970,000	873,076,700	1,290,474,000
Operating Margin %	10.96%	7.91%	8.76%	7.80%	6.81%	8.14%
SGA Expense	1,774,556,000	1,809,133,000	1,638,717,000	1,512,756,000	1,480,649,000	1,396,676,000
Net Income	1,310,232,000	766,874,900	501,370,800	98,792,260	333,423,900	721,183,600
Operating Cash Flow	1,980,785,000	2,208,007,000	1,714,046,000	2,001,778,000	1,578,206,000	1,799,254,000
Capital Expenditure	1,015,091,000	1,211,440,000	1,280,595,000	1,218,850,000	1,000,272,000	969,399,100
EBITDA	2,472,276,000	2,610,586,000	2,093,161,000	2,375,954,000	1,917,805,000	2,326,558,000
Return on Assets %	4.65%	2.51%	1.87%	.44%	1.46%	3.09%
Return on Equity %	10.96%	6.49%	5.07%	1.17%	4.08%	9.48%
Debt to Equity	0.33	0.42	0.59	0.22	0.38	0.53

CONTACT INFORMATION:
Phone: 32 22642111   Fax: 32 22643061
Toll-Free:
Address: Rue De Ransbeek, 310, Brussels, 1120 Belgium

STOCK TICKER/OTHER:
Stock Ticker: SVYSF
Employees: 24,500
Parent Company:

Exchange: PINX
Fiscal Year Ends: 12/31

SALARIES/BONUSES:
Top Exec. Salary: $ Bonus: $
Second Exec. Salary: $ Bonus: $

OTHER THOUGHTS:
Estimated Female Officers or Directors: 1
Hot Spot for Advancement for Women/Minorities:

Sales, profits and employees may be estimates. Financial information, benefits and other data can change quickly and may vary from those stated here.

Plunkett Research, Ltd.

Sony Corporation
NAIC Code: 334310

www.sony.net

TYPES OF BUSINESS:
Consumer Electronics Manufacturer
Film & Television Production
Music Production
Sensors and Cameras for use in Smartphones
Semiconductors
Technology Research
Video Games
Financial Services

BRANDS/DIVISIONS/AFFILIATES:
Sony Mobile Communications Inc
Sony Semiconductor Solutions Corporation
Sony Semiconductor Manufacturing Corporation
Sony Energy Devices Corporation
Sony Storage Media and Devices Corporation
Sony Financial Holdings Inc
Sony Life Insurance Co Ltd
Sony Bank Inc

CONTACTS:
Note: Officers with more than one job title may be intentionally listed here more than once.
Kazuo Hirai, CEO
Kazuo Hirai, Pres.
Kenichiro Yoshida, CFO

GROWTH PLANS/SPECIAL FEATURES:
Sony Corporation develops, designs, produces, manufactures, offers and sells electronic equipment, instruments and devices for consumer, professional and industrial markets. These products and services are divided into nine primary segments, operated through Sony subsidiaries. Sony Mobile Communications, Inc. provides internet broadband network services to subscribers, as well as creates and distributes content through its portal services to various electronics product platforms such as personal computers (PCs) and mobile phones. The Game & Network Services segment provides PlayStation hardware, software, content and network services. Imaging Products & Solutions provides interchangeable lens cameras, compact digital cameras, consumer and professional video cameras, as well as display products such as projectors and medical equipment. Home Entertainment & Sound produces televisions, and video and sound products. Sony Semiconductor Solutions Corporation and its subsidiary, Sony Semiconductor Manufacturing Corporation, deliver products for complementary metal oxide semiconductor (CMOS) image sensors, charge-coupled devices (CCDs), large-scale integration systems (LSIs) and other semiconductors. Sony Energy Devices Corporation delivers products for batteries; and Sony Storage Media and Devices Corporation delivers products for audio/video/data recording media and storage media. The pictures segment is grouped into three categories: motion pictures, which includes worldwide production, acquisition and distribution of live-action and animated motion pictures; television pictures, which does the same but with television programming; and media networks, which operates television and digital networks worldwide. The music segment is grouped into three categories: recorded, comprising the distribution of physical and digital recorded music; publishing, including the management and licensing of the words and music of songs; and visual media and platform, which includes the production and distribution of animation titles, game applications and related service offerings. Last, Sony Financial Holdings, Inc. is a holding company for Sony Life Insurance Co. Ltd., Sony Assurance, Inc. and Sony Bank, Inc., providing insurance, savings and loan products and services.

FINANCIAL DATA:
Note: Data for latest year may not have been available at press time.

In U.S. $	2017	2016	2015	2014	2013	2012
Revenue	70,833,330,000	75,514,370,000	76,540,720,000	72,361,340,000	63,358,030,000	60,492,010,000
R&D Expense						
Operating Income	4,044,531,000	3,159,400,000	2,294,438,000	768,911,900	17,039,310	-48,183,340
Operating Margin %	5.70%	4.18%	2.99%	1.06%	.02%	-.07%
SGA Expense	14,029,770,000	15,762,340,000	16,875,920,000	16,103,220,000	13,579,520,000	12,818,030,000
Net Income	682,774,400	1,376,849,000	-1,173,654,000	-1,195,910,000	400,913,000	-4,254,332,000
Operating Cash Flow	7,539,240,000	6,978,657,000	7,030,371,000	6,187,032,000	4,485,858,000	4,840,125,000
Capital Expenditure	3,107,034,000	3,497,401,000	2,011,515,000	2,640,740,000	3,041,644,000	3,563,900,000
EBITDA	5,526,468,000	6,771,763,000	3,893,730,000	3,967,729,000	5,616,658,000	2,420,719,000
Return on Assets %	.42%	.90%	-.80%	-.86%	.31%	-3.48%
Return on Equity %	2.95%	6.18%	-5.50%	-5.76%	2.03%	-19.95%
Debt to Equity	0.27	0.22	0.30	0.40	0.42	0.37

CONTACT INFORMATION:
Phone: 81 367482111   Fax: 81 367482244
Toll-Free:
Address: 1-7-1 Konan, Minato-Ku, Tokyo, 108-0075 Japan

STOCK TICKER/OTHER:
Stock Ticker: SNE
Employees: 128,400
Parent Company:

Exchange: NYS
Fiscal Year Ends: 03/31

SALARIES/BONUSES:
Top Exec. Salary: $61,000,000   Bonus: $
Second Exec. Salary: $4,788,523   Bonus: $

OTHER THOUGHTS:
Estimated Female Officers or Directors:

Hot Spot for Advancement for Women/Minorities:

Sony Mobile Communications AB

www.sonymobile.com

NAIC Code: 334220

TYPES OF BUSINESS:
Smartphones
Mobile Phone Accessories
PC Cards
Machine-to-Machine Communications Systems
Communications Products

BRANDS/DIVISIONS/AFFILIATES:
Sony Corporation
Xperia
Xperia XZ2
Xperia Ear Duo
Xperia touch

CONTACTS: Note: Officers with more than one job title may be intentionally listed here more than once.
Kunimasa Suzuki, CEO
Hiroki Totoki, Pres.
William Glaser, Jr., CFO
Bob Ishida, Deputy CEO
Tommi Laine-Ylijoki, Exec. VP-Operations

GROWTH PLANS/SPECIAL FEATURES:
Sony Mobile Communications AB, a wholly-owned subsidiary of Sony Corporation, provides mobile multimedia devices and accessories with an emphasis on the development of tablet and smartphone devices through its Xperia brand. Sony Mobile's product portfolio includes phones that support GSM, TDMA, CDMA and satellite technologies; accessories including batteries, micro travel phone chargers, messaging, connectivity, entertainment and hands-free products (Bluetooth devices); and PC cards compatible with CSD, EDGE, GPRS, GSM and WLAN networks. The Xperia line of smartphones and tablets run on Google's Android platform and include access to the Google Play store, Video Unlimited, Music Unlimited, the Sony Entertainment Network and PlayStation Mobile. Sony Mobile's website features downloadable ring tones, picture messaging and applications to create mobile movies. Additionally, software and service packages can be accessed online and added to consumer phones; add-on features include portable photo albums, picture messaging, image editors and navigation systems. Recent products of the firm include the Xperia XZ2 smartphone, featuring a 19MP motion eye camera, 4K high-definition-resolution movie recording and 18.9 full HD+ HDR display on a 5.7-inch screen; the Xperia Ear Duo, an open-style wireless listening device for dual listening capabilities, and comprises a daily assistant to help with communications and reminders throughout the day; and the Xperia touch, a touchscreen projector for games, chat and more.

FINANCIAL DATA: Note: Data for latest year may not have been available at press time.

In U.S. $	2017	2016	2015	2014	2013	2012
Revenue	5,250,000,000	5,500,000,000	6,320,000,000	9,806,026,946	7,163,454,232	7,934,394,074
R&D Expense						
Operating Income						
Operating Margin %						
SGA Expense						
Net Income				103,671,706	-571,981,268	73,375,553
Operating Cash Flow						
Capital Expenditure						
EBITDA						
Return on Assets %						
Return on Equity %						
Debt to Equity						

CONTACT INFORMATION:
Phone: 4420-8762-5858 Fax:
Toll-Free:
Address: 202 Hammersmith Rd., London, W6 7DN United Kingdom

STOCK TICKER/OTHER:
Stock Ticker: Subsidiary
Employees: 8,830
Parent Company: Sony Corporation

Exchange:
Fiscal Year Ends: 12/31

SALARIES/BONUSES:
Top Exec. Salary: $ Bonus: $
Second Exec. Salary: $ Bonus: $

OTHER THOUGHTS:
Estimated Female Officers or Directors: 1
Hot Spot for Advancement for Women/Minorities:

Sales, profits and employees may be estimates. Financial information, benefits and other data can change quickly and may vary from those stated here.

Plunkett Research, Ltd.

SpaceX (Space Exploration Technologies Corporation)
www.spacex.com
NAIC Code: 336414

TYPES OF BUSINESS:
Guided Missile and Space Vehicle Manufacturing
Satellite Launch Services

BRANDS/DIVISIONS/AFFILIATES:
Draper Fisher Jurveston
Founders Fund
Valor Equity Partners
Capricorn
Google
Fidelity
Falcon 9
Dragon

CONTACTS: Note: Officers with more than one job title may be intentionally listed here more than once.
Elon Musk, CEO
Gwynne Shotwell, COO
Gwynne Shotwell, Pres.
Andy Lambert, VP-Prod.
Timothy Hughes, General Counsel
Barry Matsumori, VP-Bus. Dev.
Elon Musk, Chief Designer
Tim Buzza, VP-Launch & Test
James Henderson, VP-Quality Assurance
Hans Koenigsmann, VP-Mission Assurance

GROWTH PLANS/SPECIAL FEATURES:
Space Exploration Technologies Corporation (SpaceX) designs, manufactures and launches rockets and spacecraft. The firm is privately-owned, with minority interests held by Draper Fisher Jurvetson, Founders Fund, Valor Equity Partners, Capricorn, Google and Fidelity. SpaceX is one of the few private companies to return a spacecraft from low-earth orbit and conduct official cargo resupply missions for NASA to the International Space Station (ISS). As of April 2018, SpaceX has flown at least 20 missions to the ISS under a cargo resupply contract, with a recent NASA contract for at least six more missions from 2019 onward. The firm's launch vehicles consist of the Falcon family of rockets, offering medium and heavy lift launch capabilities. The firm's medium rocket, the Falcon 9, is a two-stage rocket powered by the SpaceX Merlin Engine. This model is used for the ISS resupply mission and is capable of carrying other spacecraft. The Falcon Heavy, its heavy lift rocket, has a liftoff thrust of 5million pounds and carries spacecraft or satellites weighing over 64 metric tons, making it one of the most powerful rockets in the world. Falcon Heavy successfully lifted off from Launch Complex 39A at Kennedy Space Center in February 2018. Finally, the firm offers a free-flying reusable spacecraft, the Dragon. Developed by SpaceX under NASA's Commercial Orbital Transportation Services program, Dragon was the craft used in conjunction with the Falcon 9 for the ISS resupply mission. In June 2017, Dragon's resupply mission represented the first re-flight of a commercial spacecraft to and from the ISS. Dragon was scheduled to depart the station in May 2018 and return to Earth with more than 3,500 pounds of research, hardware and crew supplies. A manned version of Dragon is currently in development.

FINANCIAL DATA: Note: Data for latest year may not have been available at press time.

In U.S. $	2017	2016	2015	2014	2013	2012
Revenue	1,500,000,000	1,250,000,000	1,000,000,000	800,000,000	400,000,000	
R&D Expense						
Operating Income						
Operating Margin %						
SGA Expense						
Net Income						
Operating Cash Flow						
Capital Expenditure						
EBITDA						
Return on Assets %						
Return on Equity %						
Debt to Equity						

CONTACT INFORMATION:
Phone: 310-363-6000 Fax:
Toll-Free:
Address: 1 Rocket Rd., Hawthorne, CA 90250 United States

STOCK TICKER/OTHER:
Stock Ticker: Private
Employees: 3,500
Parent Company:

Exchange:
Fiscal Year Ends:

SALARIES/BONUSES:
Top Exec. Salary: $ Bonus: $
Second Exec. Salary: $ Bonus: $

OTHER THOUGHTS:
Estimated Female Officers or Directors: 1
Hot Spot for Advancement for Women/Minorities:

Sales, profits and employees may be estimates. Financial information, benefits and other data can change quickly and may vary from those stated here.

Spirit AeroSystems Holdings Inc

NAIC Code: 336413

www.spiritaero.com

TYPES OF BUSINESS:
Aircraft Fuselage Wing Tail and Similar Assemblies Manufacturing
Aerostructures
Fuselages
Wings & Flight Control Components
Engineering, Design & Materials Testing
Custom Tool Fabrication
Spare Parts & Maintenance Services
Supply Chain Management

BRANDS/DIVISIONS/AFFILIATES:
Onex Corporation

CONTACTS:
Note: Officers with more than one job title may be intentionally listed here more than once.

Sanjay Kapoor, CFO
Robert Johnson, Chairman of the Board
John Gilson, Chief Accounting Officer
Samantha Marnick, Chief Administrative Officer
John Pilla, Chief Technology Officer
Mark Suchinski, Controller
Thomas Gentile, Director
Stacy Cozad, General Counsel
Michelle Lohmeier, General Manager, Divisional
Duane Hawkins, General Manager, Divisional
William Brown, General Manager, Divisional
Ronald Rabe, Senior VP, Divisional
Krisstie Kondrotis, Senior VP, Divisional

GROWTH PLANS/SPECIAL FEATURES:

Spirit AeroSystems Holdings, Inc. is an independent designer and manufacturer of aircraft parts and aerostructures for commercial and military aircraft. With its headquarters in Wichita, Kansas, the firm operates throughout the U.S., Europe and Asia. The firm operates through three principal segments: fuselage systems, propulsion systems and wing systems. The fuselage systems segment includes development, production and marketing of forward, mid and rear fuselage sections and systems, primarily to aircraft OEMs, as well as related spares. Additionally, it offers services that include numerical control programming, materials testing, onsite planning and global supply chain management. The propulsion systems segment offers production, development and marketing of struts, pylons, nacelles, thrust reversers and related engine structural components primarily to aircraft or engine OEMs, as well as related spares. The wing systems segment produces wings, wing components and flight control surfaces. Spirit Aerosystems is also engaged in tooling, the fabrication of custom tools and the manufacturing of structural components for military aircraft. The firm's tooling capabilities include tool design, computer numerical control (CNC) programming, machining, composite, aluminum and invar tooling. The company offers spare parts and components for all items of which it is the original production supplier and provides maintenance, repair and overhaul work for nacelles, fuselage doors, structural components and modification kits. Spirit Aerosystems is the largest independent supplier of aerostructures to Boeing and one of the largest to Airbus. The company is majority-controlled by Onex Corporation. In April 2018, Spirit AeroSystems sold its stake in joint venture Haeco Spirit AeroSystems (JinJiang) Co., Ltd., exiting the maintenance, repair and overhaul business in China.

Employee benefits include a company profit sharing bonus; 401(k); relocation benefits; medical, vision and life insurance; healthcare spending accounts; disability coverage; and tuition assistance.

FINANCIAL DATA:
Note: Data for latest year may not have been available at press time.

In U.S. $	2017	2016	2015	2014	2013	2012
Revenue	6,983,000,000	6,792,900,000	6,643,900,000	6,799,200,000	5,961,000,000	5,397,700,000
R&D Expense	31,200,000	23,800,000	27,800,000	29,300,000	34,700,000	34,100,000
Operating Income	589,000,000	737,200,000	863,000,000	825,100,000	-334,000,000	-62,300,000
Operating Margin %	8.43%	10.85%	12.98%	12.13%	-5.60%	-1.15%
SGA Expense	200,300,000	228,300,000	220,800,000	233,800,000	200,800,000	180,600,000
Net Income	354,900,000	469,700,000	788,700,000	358,800,000	-621,400,000	34,800,000
Operating Cash Flow	573,700,000	716,900,000	1,289,700,000	361,600,000	260,600,000	544,400,000
Capital Expenditure	273,100,000	254,000,000	360,100,000	220,200,000	272,600,000	249,000,000
EBITDA	790,600,000	926,600,000	1,041,900,000	526,500,000	-199,400,000	250,500,000
Return on Assets %	6.64%	8.39%	14.41%	6.98%	-11.81%	.65%
Return on Equity %	19.02%	23.19%	42.16%	23.13%	-35.74%	1.73%
Debt to Equity	0.62	0.54	0.51	0.70	0.77	0.58

CONTACT INFORMATION:
Phone: 316 526-9000 Fax:
Toll-Free: 800-501-7597
Address: 3801 S. Oliver St., Wichita, KS 67210 United States

SALARIES/BONUSES:
Top Exec. Salary: $1,144,223 Bonus: $
Second Exec. Salary: $650,000 Bonus: $

STOCK TICKER/OTHER:
Stock Ticker: SPR
Employees: 14,400
Parent Company: Onex Corporation

Exchange: NYS
Fiscal Year Ends: 12/31

OTHER THOUGHTS:
Estimated Female Officers or Directors: 2
Hot Spot for Advancement for Women/Minorities: Y

Sales, profits and employees may be estimates. Financial information, benefits and other data can change quickly and may vary from those stated here.

SSOE Group

NAIC Code: 541330

www.ssoe.com

TYPES OF BUSINESS:
Engineering Consulting Services
Engineering
Construction
Procurement
Management

BRANDS/DIVISIONS/AFFILIATES:

CONTACTS:
Note: Officers with more than one job title may be intentionally listed here more than once.

Bob Howell, CEO
Vince DiPofi, Jr., COO
Jim Jaros, CFO

GROWTH PLANS/SPECIAL FEATURES:

SSOE Group is a privately-owned firm that provides engineering, procurement and construction (EPC) management services. SSOE has approximately 30 offices worldwide, including the U.S., Mexico, Malaysia, India, Germany and China, with projects in more than 40 countries. The firm's markets include: energy, consisting of alternative energy, petroleum refining, pipeline and terminals and power; life sciences, consisting of education, healthcare, pharmaceutical, science and technology; manufacturing/process, consisting of aerospace and defense, automotive, chemical, consumer products, food, general manufacturing, glass, carbon fiber and advanced composites and semiconductor; and telecommunications, consisting of wireless systems and data centers. SSOE's services include design, engineering, construction management, project and program management, tool install, virtual design, virtual design construction and specialty services.

The company offers employees health, dental and vision insurance; profit sharing and 401(k) plans; bonuses; life insurance; short- and long-term disability; and college savings and tuition reimbursement.

FINANCIAL DATA:
Note: Data for latest year may not have been available at press time.

In U.S. $	2017	2016	2015	2014	2013	2012
Revenue						
R&D Expense						
Operating Income						
Operating Margin %						
SGA Expense						
Net Income						
Operating Cash Flow						
Capital Expenditure						
EBITDA						
Return on Assets %						
Return on Equity %						
Debt to Equity						

CONTACT INFORMATION:
Phone: 419-255-3830 Fax: 419-255-6101
Toll-Free:
Address: 1001 Madison Ave., Toledo, OH 43604 United States

STOCK TICKER/OTHER:
Stock Ticker: Private
Employees: 858
Parent Company:

Exchange:
Fiscal Year Ends:

SALARIES/BONUSES:
Top Exec. Salary: $ Bonus: $
Second Exec. Salary: $ Bonus: $

OTHER THOUGHTS:
Estimated Female Officers or Directors:
Hot Spot for Advancement for Women/Minorities:

Stanley Black & Decker Inc

www.stanleyblackanddecker.com

NAIC Code: 333991

TYPES OF BUSINESS:
Power Tools & Accessories Manufacturer
Security Solutions
Household Appliances
Home Improvement Products
Fastening & Assembly Systems
Plumbing Products
Automotive Machinery

BRANDS/DIVISIONS/AFFILIATES:
Bostitch
Black & Decker
Stanley
FatMax
Porter-Cable
DeWALT
GripCo
Craftsman

CONTACTS: Note: Officers with more than one job title may be intentionally listed here more than once.
James Loree, CEO
Donald Allan, CFO
Jocelyn Belisle, Chief Accounting Officer
George Buckley, Director
Jeffery Ansell, Executive VP
Janet Link, General Counsel
Joseph Voelker, Other Executive Officer
John Wyatt, President, Divisional
Jaime Ramirez, President, Divisional

GROWTH PLANS/SPECIAL FEATURES:

Stanley Black & Decker, Inc. is a global manufacturer and marketer of power tools and accessories, hardware and home improvement products, security solutions and technology-based fastening systems. The firm is also a worldwide supplier of engineered fastening and assembly systems. Stanley Black & Decker products and services are marketed in hardware and home improvement stores around the globe. The firm operates in three business tools & storage, security and industrial. The tools & storage segment includes professional and consumer power tools and accessories, lawn and garden tools, consumer mechanics tools, storage systems and pneumatic tools and fasteners. The security segment provides both mechanical and electric access and security systems primarily for retailers; educational, financial and health care institutions; and commercial, government and industrial customers. The industrial segment manufactures and markets professional industrial and automotive mechanics tools and storage systems; metal and plastic fasteners and engineered fastening systems; hydraulic tools and accessories; plumbing, heating and air conditioning tools; assembly tools and systems; and specialty tools. The company sells these products to industrial clients in the automotive, transportation, aerospace, electronics and machine tool industries primarily through third-party distributors. Brand names include DeWALT, Porter-Cable, Bostitch, FatMax, Powers, Oldham, Guaranteed Tough and Black & Decker as well as Mac Tools, GripCo, CRC, LaBounty, Dubuis and Sargent & Greenleaf. In October 2016, the firm acquired the tools business of Newell Brands, for $1.95 billion. In May 2017, the company completed the acquisition of the Craftsman brand from Sears Holdings Corporation, for approximately $900 million.

Employee benefits include medical, dental, life and disability insurance; and a 401(k).

FINANCIAL DATA: Note: Data for latest year may not have been available at press time.

In U.S. $	2017	2016	2015	2014	2013	2012
Revenue	12,747,200,000	11,406,900,000	11,171,800,000	11,338,600,000	11,001,200,000	10,190,500,000
R&D Expense						
Operating Income	1,785,700,000	1,643,300,000	1,585,600,000	1,506,800,000	1,218,300,000	1,184,200,000
Operating Margin %	14.00%	14.40%	14.19%	13.28%	11.07%	11.62%
SGA Expense	2,977,900,000	2,602,000,000	2,459,100,000	2,575,000,000	2,700,900,000	2,509,100,000
Net Income	1,226,000,000	965,300,000	883,700,000	760,900,000	490,300,000	883,800,000
Operating Cash Flow	1,418,600,000	1,485,200,000	1,182,300,000	1,295,900,000	868,000,000	966,200,000
Capital Expenditure	442,400,000	347,000,000	311,400,000	291,000,000	365,600,000	386,000,000
EBITDA	2,209,400,000	1,828,600,000	1,745,200,000	1,711,800,000	1,188,300,000	1,117,100,000
Return on Assets %	7.06%	6.26%	5.69%	4.69%	3.02%	5.55%
Return on Equity %	17.62%	15.85%	14.43%	11.50%	7.28%	12.92%
Debt to Equity	0.37	0.59	0.66	0.59	0.55	0.52

CONTACT INFORMATION:
Phone: 860 225-5111 Fax: 860 827-3895
Toll-Free:
Address: 1000 Stanley Dr., New Britain, CT 06053 United States

SALARIES/BONUSES:
Top Exec. Salary: $1,204,167 Bonus: $
Second Exec. Salary: $238,667 Bonus: $740,000

STOCK TICKER/OTHER:
Stock Ticker: SWK
Employees: 54,023
Parent Company:

Exchange: NYS
Fiscal Year Ends: 12/31

OTHER THOUGHTS:
Estimated Female Officers or Directors: 5
Hot Spot for Advancement for Women/Minorities: Y

Sales, profits and employees may be estimates. Financial information, benefits and other data can change quickly and may vary from those stated here.

Stanley Consultants Inc

NAIC Code: 541330

www.stanleyconsultants.com

TYPES OF BUSINESS:
Engineering Consulting Services

BRANDS/DIVISIONS/AFFILIATES:

CONTACTS:
Note: Officers with more than one job title may be intentionally listed here more than once.

Kate Harris, CEO
Mike Hunzinger, COO
Gayle Roberts, Chmn.

GROWTH PLANS/SPECIAL FEATURES:

Stanley Consultants, Inc. is a consulting engineering firm with a focus on energy, water, transportation and federal agencies. The company offers services in program management, consulting and planning, engineering and design, design-build, environmental, urban design and construction administration. Stanley's energy division serves electric utilities, project developers, industrial manufacturers, healthcare institutions, university and college utilities as well as the federal government. Stanley Consultants provides power generation via new plant design, upgrades and retrofits, environmental compliance and renewable energy technologies; power delivery via transmission, substations and distribution; and facilities such as central plants, utility distribution, building services and commissioning. The water division offers consulting services covering the full water cycle such as potable water, including water supply and reuse, water treatment and desalination, water transmission, distribution, pumping and water storage facilities; wastewater, including wastewater collection and pumping, peak weather facilities, wastewater treatment and reclamation as well as wastewater disposal and reuse; and water resources, including floodplain management, natural resource enhancement and levee restoration. The transportation division provides planning, engineering and design; traffic engineering and management; and construction management for local, state, federal and international transportation clients. Transportation infrastructures include roads, bridges, freeways, interchanges and multimodal systems. Last, the federal division serves federal agencies such as the Department of Defense, Veterans Administration and the Department of Interior. Services include engineers, planners, scientists and architects that assist with military and air bases, ecosystem restoration, flood control, energy efficiency as well as disaster recovery.

FINANCIAL DATA:
Note: Data for latest year may not have been available at press time.

In U.S. $	2017	2016	2015	2014	2013	2012
Revenue						
R&D Expense						
Operating Income						
Operating Margin %						
SGA Expense						
Net Income						
Operating Cash Flow						
Capital Expenditure						
EBITDA						
Return on Assets %						
Return on Equity %						
Debt to Equity						

CONTACT INFORMATION:
Phone: 563-264-6600   Fax: 563-264-6658
Toll-Free: 800-553-9694
Address: 225 Iowa Ave., Muscatine, IA 52761 United States

SALARIES/BONUSES:
Top Exec. Salary: $ Bonus: $
Second Exec. Salary: $ Bonus: $

STOCK TICKER/OTHER:
Stock Ticker: Private   Exchange:
Employees: 1,000   Fiscal Year Ends:
Parent Company:

OTHER THOUGHTS:
Estimated Female Officers or Directors:
Hot Spot for Advancement for Women/Minorities:

Statoil ASA

NAIC Code: 211111

www.statoil.com

TYPES OF BUSINESS:
Oil & Gas Exploration & Production
Refining
Pipelines
Energy Marketing
Oil Sands Production
Wind Turbine Production

BRANDS/DIVISIONS/AFFILIATES:

CONTACTS:
Note: Officers with more than one job title may be intentionally listed here more than once.

Eldar Saetre, CEO
Jannicke Nilsson, COO
Hans Jakob Hegge, CFO
Jens Okland, Exec. VP-Mktg., Midstream, Processing
Tim Dodson, Exec. VP-Exploration
Margareth Ovrum, Exec. VP-IT
John Knight, Exec. VP-Bus. Dev. & Global Strategy
William Maloney, Exec. VP-Dev. & Prod., North America
Oystein Michelsen, Exec. VP-Dev. & Prod., Norway
Jon Erik Reinhardsen, Chmn.
Lars Christian Bacher, Exec. VP-Intl Dev. & Prod.

GROWTH PLANS/SPECIAL FEATURES:

Statoil ASA is a Norwegian oil and gas company that operates worldwide. The firm is roughly 67%-owned by the Norwegian government. Statoil has exploration licenses in North America, South America, sub-Saharan Africa, North Africa, the Middle East, Europe, Asia and Oceania (Australia and New Zealand). The company has proved reserves of approximately 1,200 million barrels of oil and condensate equivalent per day(mmboe/d), including natural gas liquids (NGL) and condensate from the Norwegian continental shelf. Statoil also produces 2,004 thousand barrels of oil equivalent (mboe), as well as 51.2 billion cubic meters of natural gas. The firm operates through four divisions: development and production Norway (DPN); development and production international (DPI); development and production United States (DPUSA); and marketing, midstream and processing (MMP). DPN is comprised of Statoil's upstream activities on the Norwegian continental shelf. DPI is comprised of the firm's worldwide upstream activities that are not included in the DPN and DPUSA business areas. DPUSA is comprised of upstream activities in the U.S. and Mexico. MMP is comprised of Statoil's marketing and trading of oil products and natural gas, transportation, processing and manufacturing, as well as the development of oil and gas value chains. MMP's focus is to maximize value creation in the firm's midstream, marketing and renewable energy business. Other business activities include new energy solutions, technology, projects and drilling. In October 2017, the firm signed a partnership agreement with Shell and Total to mature the development of carbon storage on the Norwegian continental shelf, with a goal of developing full-scale carbon capture and storage in Norway. Earlier that year, Statoil acquired interests (35% and 90%) in two additional offshore frontier blocks, expanding its exploration licenses and activities in South Africa.

Statoil offers employees benefits such as pension and insurance schemes, sick pay and a share saving scheme.

FINANCIAL DATA:
Note: Data for latest year may not have been available at press time.

In U.S. $	2017	2016	2015	2014	2013	2012
Revenue	60,999,000,000	45,992,000,000	54,957,430,000	83,794,790,000	101,847,900,000	126,398,000,000
R&D Expense						
Operating Income	13,583,000,000	198,000,000	1,717,775,000	14,768,330,000	22,050,050,000	33,296,560,000
Operating Margin %	22.26%	.43%	3.12%	17.62%	21.64%	26.34%
SGA Expense	738,000,000	762,000,000	853,199,600	981,865,100	1,512,755,000	1,988,121,000
Net Income	4,590,000,000	-2,922,000,000	-4,265,998,000	2,945,595,000	6,560,752,000	12,340,680,000
Operating Cash Flow	14,363,000,000	9,034,000,000	12,399,830,000	17,014,510,000	16,656,750,000	22,926,080,000
Capital Expenditure	10,755,000,000	12,191,000,000	14,185,870,000	16,489,950,000	18,629,900,000	20,131,970,000
EBITDA	22,554,000,000	11,995,000,000	16,153,910,000	28,864,140,000	34,760,470,000	48,180,600,000
Return on Assets %	4.25%	-2.72%	-3.51%	2.11%	4.58%	9.16%
Return on Equity %	12.25%	-7.74%	-9.31%	5.37%	11.34%	23.75%
Debt to Equity	0.60	0.79	0.74	0.53	0.46	0.31

CONTACT INFORMATION:
Phone: 47 51990000   Fax: 47 51990050
Toll-Free:
Address: Forusbeen 50, Stavanger, 4035 Norway

STOCK TICKER/OTHER:
Stock Ticker: STO
Employees: 20,500
Parent Company:

Exchange: NYS
Fiscal Year Ends: 12/31

SALARIES/BONUSES:
Top Exec. Salary: $917,594   Bonus: $366,034
Second Exec. Salary: $557,478   Bonus: $278,804

OTHER THOUGHTS:
Estimated Female Officers or Directors: 6
Hot Spot for Advancement for Women/Minorities: Y

Sales, profits and employees may be estimates. Financial information, benefits and other data can change quickly and may vary from those stated here.

Stellar Group Inc (The)

NAIC Code: 541330

www.stellar.net

TYPES OF BUSINESS:
Engineering Consulting Services
Engineering
Design
Construction
Management

BRANDS/DIVISIONS/AFFILIATES:

CONTACTS: Note: Officers with more than one job title may be intentionally listed here more than once.
Ronald H. Foster, Jr., CEO
Michael Santarone, Pres.
Clint Pyle, CFO
Ronald H. Foster Jr., Chmn.

GROWTH PLANS/SPECIAL FEATURES:

The Stellar Group, Inc. provides fully-integrated design build, engineering, construction and mechanical services worldwide. Stellar serves include commercial, food and public sectors. Its services include design, pre-construction, construction, refrigeration, planning, mechanical and utility, building envelope and total operations and maintenance. Design services include architecture, comprehensive engineering, process engineering, automation engineering and sustainability engineering; pre-construction includes site selection, supply chain and logistics services, energy optimization planning, sustainability planning and refrigeration planning. Construction includes design-build, general contracting, construction management and construction risks; refrigeration includes refrigeration design and contracting, mechanical design and contracting, parts and services, compressor services, automation, fabrication and installation services and energy optimization planning. Planning includes feasibility studies, site selection, concept planning, asset optimization, catastrophe response, supply chain and logistics and sustainable solutions. Mechanical and utility consists of chill water systems, domestic piping, process water systems, steam systems, pre-fabrication and modular utility, HVAC installation and commissioning and compressed air. The building envelope includes insulated floors, metal wall, roof and ceiling panels, freezer floor repairs, low-temperature doors and roofing systems. Total operations and maintenance consists of compressor rebuild/repair, 24/7 operations management, parts and service, remote monitoring, inventory management and process safety/regulatory compliance management.

FINANCIAL DATA: Note: Data for latest year may not have been available at press time.

In U.S. $	2017	2016	2015	2014	2013	2012
Revenue	575,000,000	550,000,000	541,200,000	515,000,000	501,100,000	
R&D Expense						
Operating Income						
Operating Margin %						
SGA Expense						
Net Income						
Operating Cash Flow						
Capital Expenditure						
EBITDA						
Return on Assets %						
Return on Equity %						
Debt to Equity						

CONTACT INFORMATION:
Phone: 904-260-2900 Fax:
Toll-Free: 800-488-2900
Address: 2900 Hartley Rd., Jacksonville, FL 32257 United States

SALARIES/BONUSES:
Top Exec. Salary: $ Bonus: $
Second Exec. Salary: $ Bonus: $

STOCK TICKER/OTHER:
Stock Ticker: Private   Exchange:
Employees: 639   Fiscal Year Ends:
Parent Company:

OTHER THOUGHTS:
Estimated Female Officers or Directors:
Hot Spot for Advancement for Women/Minorities:

Sales, profits and employees may be estimates. Financial information, benefits and other data can change quickly and may vary from those stated here.

STMicroelectronics NV

www.st.com

NAIC Code: 334413

TYPES OF BUSINESS:
Semiconductor Manufacturing
Integrated Circuits
Transistors & Diodes

BRANDS/DIVISIONS/AFFILIATES:
Atollic

CONTACTS: Note: Officers with more than one job title may be intentionally listed here more than once.
Carlo Bozotti, CEO
Jean-Marc Chery, Deputy CEO
Carlo Bozotti, Pres.
Carlo Ferro, CFO
Marco Cassis, Global Sales & Mktg.
Georges Penalver, Human Resources
Orio Belleza, Exec. VP-Front-End Mfg. & Tech. R&D
Pierre Ollivier, General Counsel
Mario Arlati, Exec. VP-Strategies & Bus. Dev.
George Penalver, Chief Strategy Officer
Lorenzo Grandi, Financial Controller
Otto Kosgalwies, Exec. VP-Infrastructure & Svcs.
Fabio Gualandris, Corp. VP-Product Quality Excellence
Bob Krysiak, Pres., Americas
Francois Guibert, Pres., Greater China & South Asia
Paul Grimme, Pres., EMEA
Marco Cassis, Pres., Japan & Korea

GROWTH PLANS/SPECIAL FEATURES:
STMicroelectronics NV is one of the world's largest semiconductor companies. Its semiconductors business designs, develops, manufactures and markets a broad range of products, including discrete and standard commodity components, application-specific integrated circuits (ASICs), full- and semi-custom devices and application-specific standard products (ASSPs) for analog, digital and mixed-signal applications. In addition, the firm participates in the manufacturing of smartcard products, which include the production and sale of both silicon chips and smartcards. STM organizes it business along two product line segments: sense & power and automotive products (SP&A), comprising automotive (APG), industrial and power discrete (IPD) and analog & microelectromechanical systems/MEMS (AMS); and embedded processing solutions (EPS), comprising digital convergence group (DCG), imaging, BiCMOS ASIC and silicon photonics (IBP), and microcontrollers, memory and secure microcontroller unit (MMS). SP&A's automotive products include digital and mixed signal devices that enable features like airbag controls, anti-skid braking systems, vehicle stability control, ignition and injection circuits, multiplex wiring, RF and power management for body and chassis electronics, engine management, advanced safety, instrumentation, car radio and infotainment. SP&A's IPD develops a broad range of innovative and competitive products including power, smart power and analog ICs (integrated circuits). SP&A's AMS comprises MEMS, sensors, interfaces, low power RF transceivers and analog front-end. EPS' DCG provides solutions across a broad range of applications for delivering high-definition content and rich services to end users, from complex ASICs for network infrastructure and gaming to ASSP for digital set-top boxes and monitors. EPS' IBP develops innovative and low power solutions and systems for Bi-CMOS ASIC and silicon photonics as well as imaging products. MMS focuses on microcontrollers dedicated to general purpose and secure applications. In December 2017, the firm acquired Atollic, a software development tools specialist.

FINANCIAL DATA: Note: Data for latest year may not have been available at press time.

In U.S. $	2017	2016	2015	2014	2013	2012
Revenue	8,347,000,000	6,973,000,000	6,897,000,000	7,404,000,000	8,082,000,000	8,493,000,000
R&D Expense	1,302,000,000	1,242,000,000	1,281,000,000	1,520,000,000	1,816,000,000	2,413,000,000
Operating Income	1,039,000,000	312,000,000	154,000,000	51,000,000	-268,000,000	-796,000,000
Operating Margin %	12.44%	4.47%	2.23%	.68%	-3.31%	-9.37%
SGA Expense	983,000,000	911,000,000	897,000,000	927,000,000	1,066,000,000	1,166,000,000
Net Income	802,000,000	165,000,000	104,000,000	128,000,000	-500,000,000	-1,158,000,000
Operating Cash Flow	1,707,000,000	1,039,000,000	842,000,000	715,000,000	366,000,000	612,000,000
Capital Expenditure	1,372,000,000	653,000,000	565,000,000	563,000,000	635,000,000	492,000,000
EBITDA	1,655,000,000	937,000,000	865,000,000	947,000,000	341,000,000	-995,000,000
Return on Assets %	9.06%	2.03%	1.20%	1.40%	-5.10%	-10.28%
Return on Equity %	16.13%	3.59%	2.16%	2.40%	-8.42%	-16.74%
Debt to Equity	0.29	0.29	0.30	0.32	0.16	0.10

CONTACT INFORMATION:
Phone: 41 229292929 Fax: 41 229292988
Toll-Free:
Address: 39, Chemin du Champ des FillesPlan-Les-Ouates, Geneva, CH1228 Switzerland

SALARIES/BONUSES:
Top Exec. Salary: $860,468 Bonus: $
Second Exec. Salary: $ Bonus: $

STOCK TICKER/OTHER:
Stock Ticker: STM
Employees: 43,480
Parent Company:

Exchange: NYS
Fiscal Year Ends: 12/31

OTHER THOUGHTS:
Estimated Female Officers or Directors: 1
Hot Spot for Advancement for Women/Minorities: Y

Sales, profits and employees may be estimates. Financial information, benefits and other data can change quickly and may vary from those stated here.

Plunkett Research, Ltd.

Stryker Corporation
NAIC Code: 339100

www.stryker.com

TYPES OF BUSINESS:
Equipment-Orthopedic Implants
Powered Surgical Instruments
Endoscopic Systems
Patient Care & Handling Equipment
Imaging Software
Small Bone Innovations

BRANDS/DIVISIONS/AFFILIATES:
Sage Products LLC
Physio-Control International Inc

CONTACTS: Note: Officers with more than one job title may be intentionally listed here more than once.
Kevin Lobo, CEO
Glenn Boehnlein, CFO
William Berry, Chief Accounting Officer
Bijoy Sagar, Chief Information Officer
Michael Hutchinson, General Counsel
M. Fink, Other Executive Officer
Graham McLean, President, Divisional
David Floyd, President, Divisional
Timothy Scannell, President, Divisional
Lonny Carpenter, President, Divisional
Katherine Owen, Vice President, Divisional
Yin Becker, Vice President, Divisional

GROWTH PLANS/SPECIAL FEATURES:
Stryker Corporation develops, manufactures and markets specialty surgical and medical products for the global market. Products include orthopedic implants, patient care and handling equipment, powered surgical instruments and endoscopic systems. The firm's products are produced by three segments: orthopaedics, MedSurg, and neurotechnology and spine. The orthopaedics segment's products consist primarily of implants for knee and hip joint replacements and trauma surgeries as well as products designed for upper and lower extremity small bone indications, with a focus on small joint replacement. The MedSurg segment includes surgical instruments and surgical navigation systems; endoscopic and communications systems; patient handling and emergency medical equipment; and reprocessed and remanufactured medical devices. The neurotechnology and spine segment's products primarily include neurosurgical and neurovascular devices, including products for traditional brain and open skull base procedures. This segment's offerings also include products used for minimally invasive endovascular techniques; orthobiologic and biosurgery products, including synthetic bone grafts and vertebral augmentation products; minimally invasive products for the treatment of acute ischemic and hemorrhagic stroke; and spinal implant products such as cervical, thoracolumbar and interbody systems. The company's products are sold in over 100 countries worldwide. During 2016, the firm acquired Sage Products, LLC, a developer, manufacturer and distributor of intensive care disposable products; Physio-Control International, Inc., which produces monitors/defibrillators and CPR-assisted devices; and Synergetic's neuro portfolio, including the Malis generator, Spetzler Mails disposable forceps, Sonopet tips and radio frequency generator.

Stryker offers its employees medical, vision, prescription, dental, long- and short-term disability and life insurance; an employee stock purchase plan; a 401(k); flexible spending; an employee assistance program; onsite fitness centers and cafeteria; wel

FINANCIAL DATA: Note: Data for latest year may not have been available at press time.

In U.S. $	2017	2016	2015	2014	2013	2012
Revenue	12,444,000,000	11,325,000,000	9,946,000,000	9,675,000,000	9,021,000,000	8,657,000,000
R&D Expense	787,000,000	715,000,000	625,000,000	614,000,000	536,000,000	471,000,000
Operating Income	2,463,000,000	2,324,000,000	2,157,000,000	2,007,000,000	1,304,000,000	1,816,000,000
Operating Margin %	19.79%	20.52%	21.68%	20.74%	14.45%	20.97%
SGA Expense	4,552,000,000	4,137,000,000	3,610,000,000	3,575,000,000	4,066,000,000	3,466,000,000
Net Income	1,020,000,000	1,647,000,000	1,439,000,000	515,000,000	1,006,000,000	1,298,000,000
Operating Cash Flow	1,559,000,000	1,812,000,000	899,000,000	1,782,000,000	1,886,000,000	1,657,000,000
Capital Expenditure	598,000,000	490,000,000	270,000,000	233,000,000	195,000,000	210,000,000
EBITDA	3,105,000,000	2,870,000,000	2,554,000,000	2,385,000,000	1,611,000,000	2,093,000,000
Return on Assets %	4.78%	8.97%	8.47%	3.07%	6.95%	10.13%
Return on Equity %	10.45%	18.23%	16.82%	5.83%	11.40%	15.94%
Debt to Equity	0.66	0.70	0.38	0.37	0.30	0.20

CONTACT INFORMATION:
Phone: 269 385-2600 Fax: 269 385-1062
Toll-Free:
Address: 2825 Airview Blvd., Kalamazoo, MI 49002 United States

SALARIES/BONUSES:
Top Exec. Salary: $1,163,333 Bonus: $
Second Exec. Salary: $631,667 Bonus: $

STOCK TICKER/OTHER:
Stock Ticker: SYK Exchange: NYS
Employees: 33,000 Fiscal Year Ends: 12/31
Parent Company:

OTHER THOUGHTS:
Estimated Female Officers or Directors: 7
Hot Spot for Advancement for Women/Minorities: Y

Sales, profits and employees may be estimates. Financial information, benefits and other data can change quickly and may vary from those stated here.

STV Group Incorporated

www.stvinc.com

NAIC Code: 541330

TYPES OF BUSINESS:
Architectural & Engineering Services
Construction Management
Infrastructure Design
Defense Systems Engineering
Industrial Process Engineering

BRANDS/DIVISIONS/AFFILIATES:

CONTACTS:
Note: Officers with more than one job title may be intentionally listed here more than once.

Milo E. Riverso, CEO
Milo E. Riverso, Pres.
Thomas Butcher, CFO
Debra B. Trace, Dir.-Corp. Comm.
Michael D. Garz, Sr. VP-Buildings & Facilities Div.
William F. Matts, Exec. VP
Steve Pressler, Exec. VP
Gerald Donnelly, Exec. VP-STV Energy Svcs. Div.
Dominick M. Servedio, Chmn.

GROWTH PLANS/SPECIAL FEATURES:

STV Group, Incorporated is a 100% employee-owned architectural, engineering, planning, environmental and construction management firm. STV specializes in constructing airports, highways, bridges, ports, railroad systems and schools, almost all of which are in the U.S. The firm operates through four divisions: construction management, energy services, buildings/facilities and transportation/infrastructure. Construction management undertakes design and building contracts in nearly every field of industry; the company's personnel oversee construction programs through administrative, inspection and surveillance. STV's energy services division offers services related to engineering design, permitting and the environment, construction support and industry specialty support. The buildings/facilities division works directly with architects, to address the safety, practicality, cost and efficiency of its buildings. Transportation/infrastructure focuses on the management, planning and design of transportation systems and facilities. Specialties of the firm include aviation/transportation architecture, defense systems and sustainable design. Some of STV's representative projects include the MetroLink in St. Louis, Missouri; the Villanova University Center for Engineering Education and Research; Sprint PCS Environmental Site Assessments in seven states; the Metra Inner Circumferential Rail Study in Chicago, Illinois; Shea Stadium in Queens, New York; and engineering and technical services for the U.S. Naval Air Warfare Center in Patuxent River, Maryland.

The company offers employees health and life insurance, short- and long-term disability benefits, an employee assistance program, paid time off and a credit union membership.

FINANCIAL DATA:
Note: Data for latest year may not have been available at press time.

In U.S. $	2017	2016	2015	2014	2013	2012
Revenue	525,000,000	500,000,000	450,000,000	430,000,000	410,000,000	373,538,000
R&D Expense						
Operating Income						
Operating Margin %						
SGA Expense						
Net Income						
Operating Cash Flow						
Capital Expenditure						
EBITDA						
Return on Assets %						
Return on Equity %						
Debt to Equity						

CONTACT INFORMATION:
Phone: 610-385-8200   Fax: 610-385-8500
Toll-Free:
Address: 205 W. Welsh Dr., Douglassville, PA 19518 United States

STOCK TICKER/OTHER:
Stock Ticker: Private
Employees: 1,800
Parent Company:

Exchange:
Fiscal Year Ends: 09/30

SALARIES/BONUSES:
Top Exec. Salary: $ Bonus: $
Second Exec. Salary: $ Bonus: $

OTHER THOUGHTS:
Estimated Female Officers or Directors: 2
Hot Spot for Advancement for Women/Minorities: Y

Sales, profits and employees may be estimates. Financial information, benefits and other data can change quickly and may vary from those stated here.

Subaru Corporation

NAIC Code: 336111

www.subaru.co.jp/en/

TYPES OF BUSINESS:
Automobile Manufacturing
Aircraft Manufacturing & Components
Heavy-Duty Engines & Equipment
Sanitation Vehicles
Specialty Vehicles
Waste Treatment, Recycling & Alternative Energy Technologies
Industrial Robotics

BRANDS/DIVISIONS/AFFILIATES:
Fuji Heavy Industries Ltd
Subaru
Outback
Forester
Impreza
Baja
Legacy
Levor

CONTACTS: Note: Officers with more than one job title may be intentionally listed here more than once.

Yasuyuki Yoshinaga, CEO
Yasuyuki Yoshinaga, Pres.
Jun Kondo, Chmn.

GROWTH PLANS/SPECIAL FEATURES:

Subaru Corporation, formerly Fuji Heavy Industries Ltd., best known for its Subaru cars, is a transportation conglomerate that also manufactures engines, aircraft components and specialty vehicles. It operates in two main divisions: automotive and aerospace products. The automotive division does business as Subaru, producing all-wheel-drive vehicles, such as the Outback and Forester models, which are built on small-car platforms but maintain the look and feel of an SUV. Other models include the Tribeca, Legacy, Levorg, Exiga, Baja, WRX/STI and Impreza. The Subaru engine incorporates an unusual design, called the Horizontally-Opposed Boxer Engine, which the firm claims reduces vibration and is generally more compact than other designs. The aerospace division manufactures, sells and repairs fixed wing aircraft and parts. It also conducts research specifically for the Japan Aerospace Exploration Agency. The company developed the Flying Forward Observation System (FFOS), an unmanned aircraft technology, for its primary contractor, the Japan Military of Defense (MOD). Its branded offerings consist of the T-7 and T-5 defense trainer jets. The firm is also the sole manufacturer of attack helicopters, AH-64D, in Japan. Additionally, FHI's aerospace division is responsible for the design and building of the center wing section of the Boeing 777 and 787. In April 2017, Fuji Heavy Industries Ltd. changed its name to Subaru Corporation.

FINANCIAL DATA: Note: Data for latest year may not have been available at press time.

In U.S. $	2017	2016	2015	2014	2013	2012
Revenue	30,985,580,000	30,112,340,000	26,811,190,000	22,434,590,000	17,821,580,000	14,133,640,000
R&D Expense						
Operating Income	3,827,185,000	5,269,135,000	3,941,168,000	3,041,634,000	1,121,772,000	409,530,500
Operating Margin %	12.35%	17.49%	14.69%	13.55%	6.29%	2.89%
SGA Expense						
Net Income	2,630,464,000	4,067,953,000	2,439,659,000	1,924,874,000	1,114,105,000	358,235,500
Operating Cash Flow	3,218,204,000	5,722,527,000	2,902,394,000	2,916,191,000	1,553,149,000	511,132,900
Capital Expenditure		1,180,660,000	1,072,974,000	678,731,200	607,685,900	486,892,100
EBITDA	4,492,212,000	6,469,536,000	4,350,010,000	3,662,707,000	1,471,604,000	1,073,878,000
Return on Assets %	10.54%	18.22%	12.81%	11.92%	8.16%	3.02%
Return on Equity %	20.15%	36.90%	29.29%	30.36%	22.87%	8.91%
Debt to Equity	0.04	0.06	0.12	0.21	0.33	0.50

CONTACT INFORMATION:
Phone: 81-3 6447-8000   Fax: 81-3 6447-8184
Toll-Free:
Address: 1-20-8, Ebisu, Shibuya-ku, Tokyo, 150-8554 Japan

STOCK TICKER/OTHER:
Stock Ticker: FUJHF   Exchange: PINX
Employees: 31,151   Fiscal Year Ends: 03/31
Parent Company:

SALARIES/BONUSES:
Top Exec. Salary: $ Bonus: $
Second Exec. Salary: $ Bonus: $

OTHER THOUGHTS:
Estimated Female Officers or Directors:
Hot Spot for Advancement for Women/Minorities:

Sales, profits and employees may be estimates. Financial information, benefits and other data can change quickly and may vary from those stated here.

Sumitomo Chemical Co Ltd

www.sumitomo-chem.co.jp

NAIC Code: 325110

TYPES OF BUSINESS:
Chemicals Manufacture
Basic Chemicals
Petrochemicals
Fine Chemicals
Agricultural Chemicals
IT-Related Chemicals
Pharmaceuticals
Sumitomo Group

BRANDS/DIVISIONS/AFFILIATES:
Sumitomo Corporation
Dainippon Sumitomo Pharma
Nihon Medi-Physics Co Ltd

CONTACTS:
Note: Officers with more than one job title may be intentionally listed here more than once.

Masakazu Tojura, Pres.
Ikuzo Ogawa, Exec. VP-R&D
Yoshimasa Takao, Managing Exec. Officer-Legal Dept.
Ikuzo Ogawa, Exec. Officer-Corp. Planning & Coordination
Kunio Nozaki, Managing Exec. Officer-Corp. Comm.
Kunio Nozaki, Managing Exec. Officer-Finance & Acct.
Ray Nishimoto, Managing Exec. Officer-Health & Crops Sciences
Tomohisa Ohno, Exec. Officer-Petrochemicals & Plastics
Yoshihiko Okamoto, Sr. Managing Exec. Officer-Basic Chemicals
Toshihisa Deguchi, Managing Exec. Officer-IT Related Chemicals
Osamu Ishitobi, Chmn.
Masaki Morimoto, Exec. VP-Procurement & Logistics

GROWTH PLANS/SPECIAL FEATURES:

Sumitomo Chemical Co., Ltd., part of Sumitomo Corporation, is a Japanese chemicals manufacturer. The company operates in five segments. The energy and functional materials segment provides chemical products that contribute to reducing the burden on the environment as well as to conserving energy and natural resources. Products in this division include alumina and aluminum used for energy-efficient products, high-performance polymer additives and rubber chemicals, automotive diesel particulate filters enabling better exhaust emission controls and synthetic rubber for fuel-efficient tires. The petrochemicals and plastics segment supplies organic chemicals, plastics, polymer alloys, synthetic resins, synthetic rubber and downstream plastic products. The IT-related chemicals segment is comprised of the optical materials division, the semiconductor process materials division and the electronic materials division. Products include positive-type photoresists, high purity chemicals, super engineering chemicals and composite molding materials. The health and crop sciences segment has products including plant protection chemicals such as insecticides, fungicides and herbicides and new types of products such as amino acid feed additives. Last, the pharmaceutical sector segment produces synthetic medicines. This division consists of Dainippon Sumitomo Pharma, which produces prescription drugs to treat diabetes and the central nervous system, and Nihon Medi-Physics Co., Ltd., which makes diagnostic radio-pharmaceuticals. Sumitomo Chemical includes more than 100 subsidiaries and affiliates, and markets its products worldwide. In February 2018, to accelerate the development of CO_2 separation membranes geared toward a variety of environmental- and energy-related applications, Sumitomo Chemical merged wholly-owned subsidiary CO2 M-Tech Co., Ltd. into itself.

FINANCIAL DATA:
Note: Data for latest year may not have been available at press time.

In U.S. $	2017	2016	2015	2014	2013	2012
Revenue	18,206,480,000	19,580,440,000	22,141,770,000	20,903,620,000	18,189,790,000	18,146,860,000
R&D Expense	1,440,768,000	1,424,334,000	1,351,146,000	1,290,917,000	1,135,103,000	1,103,792,000
Operating Income	2,481,768,000	2,731,750,000	2,367,990,000	2,055,711,000	1,351,835,000	1,516,266,000
Operating Margin %	13.63%	13.95%	10.69%	9.83%	7.43%	8.35%
SGA Expense	783,202,900	838,410,700	896,609,000	836,771,000	743,171,300	788,615,700
Net Income	796,366,700	758,813,200	486,230,700	344,484,800	-475,833,800	52,049,560
Operating Cash Flow	1,746,283,000	2,433,128,000	2,430,166,000	1,810,714,000	1,598,612,000	1,159,782,000
Capital Expenditure						
EBITDA	2,477,837,000	2,665,800,000	2,323,104,000	2,000,848,000	1,311,506,000	1,408,916,000
Return on Assets %	3.09%	2.93%	1.84%	1.40%	-2.12%	.23%
Return on Equity %	10.77%	10.45%	7.27%	6.48%	-10.39%	1.10%
Debt to Equity	0.69	0.78	0.87	1.13	1.42	1.40

CONTACT INFORMATION:
Phone: 81 355435500   Fax: 81 355435901
Toll-Free:
Address: 27-1, Shinkawa 2-chome, Chuo-ku, Tokyo, 104-8260 Japan

STOCK TICKER/OTHER:
Stock Ticker: SOMMF
Employees: 31,094
Parent Company: Sumitomo Corporation

Exchange: GREY
Fiscal Year Ends: 03/31

SALARIES/BONUSES:
Top Exec. Salary: $ Bonus: $
Second Exec. Salary: $ Bonus: $

OTHER THOUGHTS:
Estimated Female Officers or Directors:
Hot Spot for Advancement for Women/Minorities:

Sales, profits and employees may be estimates. Financial information, benefits and other data can change quickly and may vary from those stated here.

Suzuki Motor Corporation

NAIC Code: 336111

www.globalsuzuki.com

TYPES OF BUSINESS:
Automobile Manufacturing
Motorcycles
ATVs
Marine Products
Wheelchairs
Industrial Equipment

BRANDS/DIVISIONS/AFFILIATES:
Suzuki Auto Parts Mfg Co Ltd
Snic Co Ltd
Suzuki Akita Auto Parts Mfg Co Ltd
Suzuki Motor Gujarat Private Limited
Suzuki Toyama Auto Parts Mgf Co Ltd
Suzuki Transportation & Packing Co Ltd
Suzuki Engineering Co Ltd
Suzuki Finance Co Ltd

CONTACTS:
Note: Officers with more than one job title may be intentionally listed here more than once.

Toshihiro Suzuki, CEO
Minoru Tamura, Exec. VP
Osamu Honda, Exec. VP
Toshihiro Suzuki, Exec. VP
Yasuhito Harayama, Exec. VP
Osamu Suzuki, Chmn.

GROWTH PLANS/SPECIAL FEATURES:
Suzuki Motor Corporation designs and manufactures all-terrain vehicles (ATVs), motorcycles, outboard motors, passenger cars, compact and subcompact cars, commercial vehicles and other products. The firm also manufactures boats, electric scooters, motorized wheelchairs and industrial equipment. Suzuki is one of the largest manufacturers of minicars and motorcycles in Japan. Its production facilities are spread throughout 20 countries. Overall, the company's network serves approximately 200 countries and territory areas. The firm's products include the Celerio, Ignis, Swift, Swift Sport, Dzire, Baleno, Jimny, Vitara, SX4 S-Cross, Grand Vitara, Ciaz, Ertiga and APV automobiles; the GSX, Hayabusa, SV650, V-Strom, Suzuki Boulevard, Burgman, Address, Inazuma, DR-Z, TU, VanVan, RMX and RM-Z motorcycles and scooters; the KingQuad, OZARK and QuadSport ATVs; and the 2- and 4-stroke outboard marine engine models. Suzuki has developed an ultra-low-emission, direct-injection turbo engine for the minicar category in Japan as well as a line of motorcycles incorporating an electronically controlled, continuously variable transmission. Manufacturing companies of the firm include Suzuki Auto Parts Mfg. Co. Ltd.; Snic Co. Ltd.; Suzuki Akita Auto Parts Mfg. Co. Ltd.; Suzuki Motor Gujarat Private Limited; and Suzuki Toyama Auto Parts Mfg. Co. Ltd.; non-manufacturing companies include Suzuki Transportation & Packing Co. Ltd.; Suzuki Business Co. Ltd.; Suzuki Engineering Co. Ltd.; Suzuki Support Co. Ltd.; Suzuki Finance Co. Ltd.; and Suzuki Consultant Co. Ltd.; as well as sales company Suzuki Marine Co. Ltd.

FINANCIAL DATA:
Note: Data for latest year may not have been available at press time.

In U.S. $	2017	2016	2015	2014	2013	2012
Revenue	29,528,060,000	29,631,630,000	28,092,610,000	27,373,900,000	24,020,100,000	23,404,010,000
R&D Expense						
Operating Income	2,484,498,000	1,819,536,000	1,671,558,000	1,749,096,000	1,346,795,000	1,111,468,000
Operating Margin %	8.41%	6.14%	5.95%	6.38%	5.60%	4.74%
SGA Expense						
Net Income	1,490,181,000	1,086,827,000	902,385,000	1,001,342,000	748,919,400	502,021,600
Operating Cash Flow	3,412,661,000	2,739,845,000	2,375,974,000	3,008,338,000	1,770,607,000	2,112,148,000
Capital Expenditure	1,789,212,000	1,514,570,000	1,795,174,000	1,907,388,000	1,527,194,000	1,110,583,000
EBITDA	4,316,825,000	3,915,847,000	3,140,079,000	2,985,243,000	2,222,778,000	2,092,584,000
Return on Assets %	5.49%	3.91%	3.16%	4.00%	3.35%	2.38%
Return on Equity %	15.39%	9.56%	6.89%	8.68%	7.53%	5.50%
Debt to Equity	0.37	0.27	0.18	0.15	0.19	0.06

CONTACT INFORMATION:
Phone: 81-53-440-2061   Fax:
Toll-Free:
Address: 300 Takatsuka-cho, Minami-ku, Hamamatsu, 432-8611 Japan

SALARIES/BONUSES:
Top Exec. Salary: $ Bonus: $
Second Exec. Salary: $ Bonus: $

STOCK TICKER/OTHER:
Stock Ticker: SZKMF   Exchange: PINX
Employees: 50,241   Fiscal Year Ends: 03/31
Parent Company:

OTHER THOUGHTS:
Estimated Female Officers or Directors:
Hot Spot for Advancement for Women/Minorities:

Sales, profits and employees may be estimates. Financial information, benefits and other data can change quickly and may vary from those stated here.

Symantec Corporation

www.symantec.com

NAIC Code: 0

TYPES OF BUSINESS:
Computer Software, Security & Anti-Virus
Remote Management Products
Consulting-Cyber Security
Information Protection Products

BRANDS/DIVISIONS/AFFILIATES:
Norton
LifeLock Inc

CONTACTS:
Note: Officers with more than one job title may be intentionally listed here more than once.

Daniel Schulman, Chairman of the Board
Nicholas Noviello, Chief Accounting Officer
Gregory Clark, Director
Francis Rosch, Executive VP, Divisional
Scott Taylor, Executive VP
Roxane Divol, Executive VP
Michael Fey, President
Amy Cappellanti-Wolf, Senior VP

GROWTH PLANS/SPECIAL FEATURES:

Symantec Corporation provides a range of software, appliances and services designed to secure and manage information technology (IT) infrastructure. The company provides customers worldwide with software and services that protect, manage and control information risks related to security, data protection, storage, compliance and systems management. The firm has two operating segments: enterprise security and consumer security. The enterprise security segment protects organizations so they can securely conduct business while leveraging new platforms and data. This segment includes Symantec's threat protection products, information protection products, cyber security services, and website security offerings, previously named trust services. These products and services help secure information in transit and wherever it resides in the network path, from the user's device to the data's resting place. In addition, these products help to prevent the loss of confidential data by insiders, and help customers achieve and maintain compliance with laws and regulations. The consumer security focuses on making it simple for customers to be productive and protected at home and at work. The firm's Norton-branded services provide multi-layer security and identity protection on major desktop and mobile operating systems, to defend against increasingly complex online threats to individuals, families, and small businesses. Norton Security products help customers protect against increasingly complex threats and address the need for identity protection, while also managing the rapid increase in mobile and digital data, such as personal financial records, photos, music and videos. Symantec operates in over 40 countries. During 2017, the firm acquired LifeLock, Inc., a provider of identity theft protection; sold its website security and related public key infrastructure (PKI) solutions to DigiCert, Inc.; and agreed to acquire Fireglass, an agentless, real-time threat isolation solution, and Skycure, a mobile threat defense company.

Symantec offers employees a 401(k) with company match, tuition reimbursement and adoption assistance.

FINANCIAL DATA:
Note: Data for latest year may not have been available at press time.

In U.S. $	2017	2016	2015	2014	2013	2012
Revenue	4,019,000,000	3,600,000,000	6,508,000,000	6,676,000,000	6,906,000,000	6,730,000,000
R&D Expense	823,000,000	748,000,000	1,144,000,000	1,038,000,000	1,012,000,000	969,000,000
Operating Income	173,000,000	593,000,000	1,401,000,000	1,453,000,000	1,248,000,000	1,139,000,000
Operating Margin %	4.30%	16.47%	21.52%	21.76%	18.07%	16.92%
SGA Expense	2,023,000,000	1,587,000,000	2,702,000,000	2,880,000,000	3,185,000,000	3,251,000,000
Net Income	-106,000,000	2,488,000,000	878,000,000	898,000,000	765,000,000	1,172,000,000
Operating Cash Flow	-220,000,000	796,000,000	1,312,000,000	1,281,000,000	1,593,000,000	1,901,000,000
Capital Expenditure	70,000,000	272,000,000	381,000,000	260,000,000	336,000,000	286,000,000
EBITDA	476,000,000	766,000,000	1,611,000,000	1,731,000,000	1,800,000,000	2,241,000,000
Return on Assets %	-.70%	19.90%	6.55%	6.43%	5.58%	9.10%
Return on Equity %	-2.95%	51.77%	14.96%	16.00%	14.55%	24.36%
Debt to Equity	1.97	0.60	0.29	0.36	0.38	0.40

CONTACT INFORMATION:
Phone: 650 527-8000   Fax:
Toll-Free:
Address: 350 Ellis St., Mountain View, CA 94043 United States

SALARIES/BONUSES:
Top Exec. Salary: $720,000   Bonus: $150,000
Second Exec. Salary: $600,000   Bonus: $150,000

STOCK TICKER/OTHER:
Stock Ticker: SYMC
Employees: 13,000
Parent Company:

Exchange: NAS
Fiscal Year Ends: 03/31

OTHER THOUGHTS:
Estimated Female Officers or Directors: 3
Hot Spot for Advancement for Women/Minorities: Y

Sales, profits and employees may be estimates. Financial information, benefits and other data can change quickly and may vary from those stated here.

Syngenta AG

NAIC Code: 325320

www.syngenta.com

TYPES OF BUSINESS:
Pesticide and Other Agricultural Chemical Manufacturing
Crop Protection Products
Seeds

BRANDS/DIVISIONS/AFFILIATES:
China National Chemical Corporation (ChemChina)
Dual Gold
Reglone
Bravo
Amistar
PLENE
CEEDS
Avicta

CONTACTS:
Note: Officers with more than one job title may be intentionally listed here more than once.

J. Erik Fyrwald, CEO
Mark Patrick, CFO
Laure Roberts, Head-Human Resources
Robert Berendes, Interim Head-R&D
Christoph Mader, Head-Legal & Taxes
Mark Peacock, Head-Global Oper.
Davor Pisk, COO
Jonathan Seabrook, Head-Corp. Affairs
Jianxin Ren, Chmn.

GROWTH PLANS/SPECIAL FEATURES:
Syngenta AG is an international agrochemical company and a leading worldwide supplier of conventional and bioengineered crop protection and seeds. The firm's products designed for crop protection include seed treatments to control weeds, insects and diseases; herbicides; fungicides; and insecticides. Syngenta produces seeds for field crops, vegetables and flowers. Its leading marketed products include the following: Dual Gold, Axial and Fusilade selective herbicides; Touchdown, Reglone and Gramoxone non-selective herbicides; Bravo, Score and Amistar fungicides; Proclaim, Match and Actara insecticides; PLENE, a platform of integrated sugar cane solutions; CEEDS, a crop expansion encapsulation and drilling system; and Dividend, Apron, Maxim, Avicta and Cruiser seed care treatments. Syngenta has a seed portfolio of over 200 product lines and more than 5,000 varieties. The seeds that the company markets are for field crops, vegetables, fruits and garden plants. The company spends more than $1 billion annually on research and development at its laboratories in the U.S., Sweden, Chile, China, France, India, Singapore and the Netherlands. Syngenta comprises more than 105 production and supply sites, and 119 research and development sites spread across 90 countries worldwide. During 2017, the firm was acquired by China National Chemical Corporation (ChemChina), and operates as its subsidiary.

FINANCIAL DATA:
Note: Data for latest year may not have been available at press time.

In U.S. $	2017	2016	2015	2014	2013	2012
Revenue	12,649,000,000	12,789,999,616	13,411,000,320	15,134,000,128	14,688,000,000	14,202,000,384
R&D Expense						
Operating Income						
Operating Margin %						
SGA Expense						
Net Income	1,130,000,000	1,178,000,000	1,339,000,064	1,619,000,064	1,644,000,000	1,872,000,000
Operating Cash Flow						
Capital Expenditure						
EBITDA						
Return on Assets %						
Return on Equity %						
Debt to Equity						

CONTACT INFORMATION:
Phone: 41 613231111 Fax: 41 613231212
Toll-Free:
Address: Schwarzwaldallee 215, Basel, 4058 Switzerland

SALARIES/BONUSES:
Top Exec. Salary: $ Bonus: $
Second Exec. Salary: $ Bonus: $

STOCK TICKER/OTHER:
Stock Ticker: Subsidiary   Exchange:
Employees: 27,600   Fiscal Year Ends: 12/31
Parent Company: China National Chemical Corporation (ChemChina)

OTHER THOUGHTS:
Estimated Female Officers or Directors: 3
Hot Spot for Advancement for Women/Minorities: Y

Sales, profits and employees may be estimates. Financial information, benefits and other data can change quickly and may vary from those stated here.

Synopsys Inc

www.synopsys.com

NAIC Code: 0

TYPES OF BUSINESS:
Computer Software-Electronic Design Automation
Consulting & Support Services

BRANDS/DIVISIONS/AFFILIATES:
DesignWare IP
Sentaurus
Proteus
CATS
Yield
QuantumWise
Sidense Corporation
Black Duck Software

CONTACTS: *Note: Officers with more than one job title may be intentionally listed here more than once.*
Trac Pham, CFO
Aart De Geus, Chairman of the Board
Sudhindra Kankanwadi, Chief Accounting Officer
Chi-Foon Chan, Co-CEO
John Runkel, General Counsel
Joseph Logan, Other Corporate Officer

GROWTH PLANS/SPECIAL FEATURES:
Synopsys, Inc. is a supplier of electronic design automation (EDA) software and related services for the design, creation and testing of integrated circuits (ICs). The company's products and services are divided into four groups: core EDA, intellectual property (IP), manufacturing solutions and professional services. Core EDA products and services include the company's digital and custom IC design software, its functional register transfer level verification products, and its field-programmable gate array design software. Designers use these core EDA products to automate the IC design process and to reduce errors. IP products and services include the company's DesignWare IP portfolio, system-level design products, as well as software quality and security testing solutions. Synopsys is a leading provider of high-quality, silicon-proven IP solutions for system-on-chips (SoCs), including wired and wireless interfaces, logic libraries, embedded memories, processor solutions, IP subsystems for audio/sensor/data fusion functionality and analog IP. Manufacturing solutions' software products and technologies enable semiconductor manufacturers to more quickly develop new fabrication processes that produce production-level yields. This group's solutions include Sentaurus technology computer-aided design device and process simulation products; Proteus mask synthesis tools; CATS mask data preparation software; and Yield Explorer Odyssey and Yield Manager management solutions. Last, professional services include consultation and design services that address all phases of the SoC development process. These services assist Synopsys customers with new tool and methodology adoption, chip architecture and specification development, functional and low-power design and verification, and physical implementation and signoff. This division also provides a range of training and workshops on the company's latest tools and methodologies. During 2017, the firm acquired QuantumWise, Sidense Corporation and Black Duck Software.

Employee benefits include medical, dental and vision coverage; life, AD&D and disability insurance; an employee assistance program; educational assistance; adoption benefits; and a wellness program.

FINANCIAL DATA: *Note: Data for latest year may not have been available at press time.*

In U.S. $	2017	2016	2015	2014	2013	2012
Revenue	2,724,880,000	2,422,532,000	2,242,211,000	2,057,472,000	1,962,214,000	1,756,017,000
R&D Expense	908,841,000	856,705,000	776,229,000	718,768,000	669,197,000	581,628,000
Operating Income	384,149,000	327,028,000	281,554,000	248,717,000	246,493,000	190,024,000
Operating Margin %	14.09%	13.49%	12.55%	12.08%	12.56%	10.82%
SGA Expense	746,092,000	668,330,000	639,504,000	608,294,000	569,773,000	573,088,000
Net Income	136,563,000	266,826,000	225,934,000	259,124,000	247,800,000	182,402,000
Operating Cash Flow	634,565,000	586,635,000	495,160,000	550,953,000	496,705,000	486,068,000
Capital Expenditure	73,554,000	71,040,000	90,647,000	106,913,000	69,068,000	57,493,000
EBITDA	579,843,000	540,351,000	496,245,000	466,863,000	464,766,000	359,966,000
Return on Assets %	2.56%	5.18%	4.60%	5.67%	5.82%	4.85%
Return on Equity %	4.22%	8.43%	7.29%	8.86%	9.36%	7.92%
Debt to Equity	0.04			0.01	0.02	0.04

CONTACT INFORMATION:
Phone: 650 584-5000 Fax: 650 965-8637
Toll-Free: 800-541-7737
Address: 690 E. Middlefield Road, Mountain View, CA 94043 United States

STOCK TICKER/OTHER:
Stock Ticker: SNPS
Employees: 10,669
Parent Company:

Exchange: NAS
Fiscal Year Ends: 10/31

SALARIES/BONUSES:
Top Exec. Salary: $525,000   Bonus: $
Second Exec. Salary: $525,000   Bonus: $

OTHER THOUGHTS:
Estimated Female Officers or Directors: 3
Hot Spot for Advancement for Women/Minorities: Y

Sales, profits and employees may be estimates. Financial information, benefits and other data can change quickly and may vary from those stated here.

Plunkett Research, Ltd.

Taisei Corporation

NAIC Code: 541330

www.taisei.co.jp/

TYPES OF BUSINESS:
Civil Engineering Services

BRANDS/DIVISIONS/AFFILIATES:

CONTACTS: *Note: Officers with more than one job title may be intentionally listed here more than once.*
Yoshiyuki Murata, CEO

GROWTH PLANS/SPECIAL FEATURES:
Taisei Corporation is a Japanese corporation founded in 1873, and is primarily engaged in building construction, civil engineering and real estate development. The firm's building construction division builds or renovates buildings such as airports, office buildings, commercial facilities, factories, hospitals and housing. It is also active in research and development as well as engineering technologies that contribute to low-carbon and recycling economies. The civil engineering division constructs infrastructures such as tunnels, bridges, roads and dams, and builds social infrastructure that supports citizens' lives and industries with high technological capabilities. The real estate development division proposes urban renewal by fully utilizing accumulated methods and expertise regarding diverse business schemes such as redevelopment, private finance initiatives (PFI), property management and condominium sales projects. Taisei provides solutions at every phase of its businesses, including contract research, technology provision and environmental measurements. The firm has domestic branches throughout Japan, as well as offices overseas, including the Middle East, India, Asia and Africa.

FINANCIAL DATA: *Note: Data for latest year may not have been available at press time.*

In U.S. $	2017	2016	2015	2014	2013	2012
Revenue	13,855,520,000	14,401,800,000	14,656,890,000	14,286,130,000	13,196,340,000	12,330,010,000
R&D Expense						
Operating Income	1,311,934,000	1,094,364,000	656,018,300	500,968,900	331,712,300	339,910,600
Operating Margin %	9.46%	7.59%	4.47%	3.50%	2.51%	2.75%
SGA Expense	796,171,100	746,394,600	722,545,200	719,694,500	710,005,600	754,648,800
Net Income	843,730,200	717,766,000	355,664,300	298,947,300	186,789,600	11,002,420
Operating Cash Flow	2,032,402,000	888,392,100	224,315,300	1,292,612,000	680,836,700	979,131,800
Capital Expenditure	67,318,800	95,220,790	65,502,150	113,592,300	58,533,630	62,614,120
EBITDA	1,337,917,000	1,179,262,000	739,361,000	550,307,500	428,582,100	299,785,700
Return on Assets %	5.29%	4.53%	2.28%	2.04%	1.31%	.08%
Return on Equity %	16.66%	15.29%	8.75%	8.86%	6.33%	.40%
Debt to Equity	0.20	0.26	0.31	0.49	0.68	0.75

CONTACT INFORMATION:
Phone: 81 333481111   Fax: 81 333450481
Toll-Free:
Address: 1-25-1 Nishi-Shinjuku, Tokyo, 163-0606 Japan

STOCK TICKER/OTHER:
Stock Ticker: TISCY
Employees: 7,945
Parent Company:

Exchange: PINX
Fiscal Year Ends: 03/31

SALARIES/BONUSES:
Top Exec. Salary: $ Bonus: $
Second Exec. Salary: $ Bonus: $

OTHER THOUGHTS:
Estimated Female Officers or Directors:
Hot Spot for Advancement for Women/Minorities:

Sales, profits and employees may be estimates. Financial information, benefits and other data can change quickly and may vary from those stated here.

Taiwan Semiconductor Manufacturing Co Ltd (TSMC)

www.tsmc.com
NAIC Code: 334413

TYPES OF BUSINESS:
Contract Manufacturing-Semiconductors
Assembly & Testing Services
CAD Software Products

BRANDS/DIVISIONS/AFFILIATES:
WaferTech LLC
TSMC China Company Limited
TSMC Nanjing
Motech Industries Inc
Global Unichip Corporation
Xintec Inc
Systems on Silicon Manufacturing Co Pty Ltd
Vanguard International Semiconductor Corp

CONTACTS:
Note: Officers with more than one job title may be intentionally listed here more than once.

Mark Liu, Co-CEO
C.C. Wei, Co-CEO
Lora Ho, CFO
Connie Ma, VP-Human Resources
Wei-Jen Lo, VP-R&D
Stephen T. Tso, CIO
Jack Sun, CTO
Y.P. Chin, VP-Prod. Dev.
Richard Thurston, General Counsel
M.C. Tzeng, VP-Oper.
Irene Sun, VP-Corp. Planning Organization
Rick Tsai, Chmn.
Burn J. Lin, VP-R&D
Y.J. Mii, VP-R&D
N.S. Tsai, VP-Quality & Reliability
Morris Chang, Chmn.
Rick Cassidy, VP

GROWTH PLANS/SPECIAL FEATURES:
Taiwan Semiconductor Manufacturing Co., Ltd. (TSMC) is one of the world's largest dedicated semiconductor foundries. Using a variety of advanced and mainstream manufacturing processes, the company produces semiconductors for customers based on their own designs or based on proprietary third-party integrated circuit (IC) designs. TSMC offers a range of wafer fabrication processes, including processes to manufacture complementary metal oxide silicon (CMOS) logic, mixed-signal, radio frequency, embedded memory, BiCMOS (bipolar CMOS) mixed-signal and other semiconductors. The company also provides design, mask making, probing and assembly services. The firm operates three advanced 12-inch wafer fabs, six 8-inch wafer fabs and one 6-inch wafer fabs. TSMC also manages two 8-inch fabs at wholly-owned subsidiaries: WaferTech, LLC in the U.S. and TSMC China Company Limited. Operations are primarily centralized in Taiwan near the firm's headquarters, with additional production facilities located in Shanghai and in the U.S. Moreover, TSMC Nanjing owns use rights to land in Nanjing, China where the firm plans to open a fab facility. Other products by the company include the Open Innovation Platform, which aids the semiconductor manufacturing process from design to completion; and CyberShuttle, a service that allows a number of customers to share design and prototyping processes, thus reducing production costs. TSMC has a 12% stake in Motech Industries, Inc., a manufacturer of solar cells; 35% stake in Global Unichip Corporation; a 41.1% stake in Xintec, Inc., offering a wafer level chip size package service; a 39% stake in Systems on Silicon Manufacturing Company Pty. Ltd., which fabricates and supplies ICs; and a 28% stake in Vanguard International Semiconductor Corporation, which manufactures, packages, tests and sells memory ICs and related parts. The firm has offices in the U.S., Canada, Japan, China, South Korea and the Netherlands.

TSMC offers employees health, fitness, incentive and employee assistance plans, and tuition reimbursement.

FINANCIAL DATA:
Note: Data for latest year may not have been available at press time.

In U.S. $	2017	2016	2015	2014	2013	2012
Revenue		32,342,910,000	28,779,470,000	26,026,350,000	20,369,990,000	17,272,800,000
R&D Expense		2,429,551,000	2,236,330,000	1,938,954,000	1,636,084,000	1,378,488,000
Operating Income		12,895,030,000	10,976,660,000	10,126,290,000	7,165,635,000	6,178,382,000
Operating Margin %		39.86%	38.14%	38.90%	35.17%	35.76%
SGA Expense		876,740,900	782,077,100	819,570,800	797,946,000	755,249,200
Net Income		11,317,810,000	10,333,030,000	8,676,563,000	6,277,171,000	5,669,207,000
Operating Cash Flow		18,418,730,000	18,079,070,000	14,382,060,000	11,852,450,000	9,862,628,000
Capital Expenditure		11,364,890,000	8,932,434,000	9,976,441,000	9,906,349,000	8,398,014,000
EBITDA		20,916,990,000	19,658,590,000	17,249,350,000	12,787,540,000	10,710,830,000
Return on Assets %		18.72%	19.21%	18.44%	16.59%	19.21%
Return on Equity %		25.98%	27.33%	27.40%	23.63%	24.56%
Debt to Equity		0.11	0.16	0.20	0.25	0.11

CONTACT INFORMATION:
Phone: 886 35636688　　Fax: 866 35637000
Toll-Free:
Address: No. 8, Li-Hsin Rd. 6, Hsinchu Science Park, Hsinchu, 300 Taiwan

STOCK TICKER/OTHER:
Stock Ticker: TSM
Employees: 43,591
Parent Company:

Exchange: NYS
Fiscal Year Ends: 12/31

SALARIES/BONUSES:
Top Exec. Salary: $　　Bonus: $
Second Exec. Salary: $　　Bonus: $

OTHER THOUGHTS:
Estimated Female Officers or Directors: 4
Hot Spot for Advancement for Women/Minorities: Y

Sales, profits and employees may be estimates. Financial information, benefits and other data can change quickly and may vary from those stated here.

Takeda Pharmaceutical Company Limited

NAIC Code: 325412

www.takeda.com

TYPES OF BUSINESS:
Pharmaceuticals Discovery & Development
Over-the-Counter Drugs
Vitamins

BRANDS/DIVISIONS/AFFILIATES:
Lansoprazole
Pantoprazole
Bortezomib
Ixazomib
Vortioxetine
Alogliptin Benzoate
Azilsartan
Febuxostat

CONTACTS:
Note: Officers with more than one job title may be intentionally listed here more than once.

Christophe Weber, CEO
Costa Saroukos, CFO
David Osborne, Global Human Resources Officer
Tadataka Yamada, Chief Medical & Scientific Officer
Nancy Joseph-Ridge, Gen. Mgr.-Pharmaceutical Dev. Div.
Toyoji Yoshida, Managing Dir.-Internal Control & Special Missions
Shinji Honda, Sr. VP-Corp. Strategy
Frank Morich, Chief Commercial Officer
Trevor Smith, CEO-Takeda Pharmaceuticals Europe Ltd.
Masato Iwasaki, Sr. VP-Pharmaceutical Mktg. Div.
Haruhiko Hirate, Sr. VP
Anna Protopapas, Exec. VP-Global Bus. Dev.
Yasuchika Hasegawa, Chmn.
Frank Morich, CEO-Takeda Pharmaceuticals Intl

GROWTH PLANS/SPECIAL FEATURES:
Takeda Pharmaceutical Company Limited, based in Japan, is an international research-based global pharmaceuticals company. It operates research and development facilities in eight countries, and production facilities in 18 countries. Takeda discovers, develops, manufactures and markets pharmaceutical products, which are grouped into five categories: gastrointestinal, oncology, central nervous system (CNS), cardiovascular and metabolic, and others. Gastrointestinal products include Lansoprazole, for peptic ulcers; Dexlansoprazole, for acid reflux disease; Lubiprostone, for chronic idiopathic constipation and opioid-induced constipation; Pantoprazole, for gastric acid-related disorders; Vonoprazan, for acid-related diseases; and Vedolizumab, for ulcerative colitis and Crohn's disease. Oncology products include Bortezomib, for multiple myeloma; Leuprorelin Acetate, for prostate/breast cancer and endometriosis; Brentuximab Vedotin, for malignant lymphoma; and Ixazomib, for multiple myeloma. CNS' Vortioxetine is a treatment for major depressive disorder. Cardiovascular and metabolic products include Alogliptin Benzoate, for Type-2 diabetes; and Azilsartan, for hypertension. Other products include Febuxostat and Colchicine, each for hyperuricemia and gout. In early-2018, Takeda agreed to acquire TiGenix, a European cell therapy company. In May 2018, the firm agreed to acquire Shire Plc, an Irish pharmaceuticals company, for £40 billion ($62.4 billion). The deal, which is expected to close in the first half of 2019, would be one of the biggest deals ever in the pharmaceuticals industry.

FINANCIAL DATA:
Note: Data for latest year may not have been available at press time.

In U.S. $	2017	2016	2015	2014	2013	2012
Revenue	16,136,120,000	16,837,880,000	16,562,550,000	15,760,060,000	14,507,800,000	14,057,500,000
R&D Expense	2,909,475,000	3,222,722,000	3,559,680,000	3,182,039,000		
Operating Income	793,879,300	1,398,668,000	798,611,900	1,494,783,000	1,141,280,000	2,469,042,000
Operating Margin %	4.91%	8.30%	4.82%	9.48%	7.86%	17.56%
SGA Expense	5,767,291,000	6,062,726,000	5,707,220,000	5,181,759,000	9,196,330,000	7,552,739,000
Net Income	1,070,803,000	746,841,900	-1,358,068,000	993,646,400	1,222,694,000	1,156,717,000
Operating Cash Flow	2,434,908,000	237,479,000	1,700,364,000	1,381,917,000	2,866,676,000	3,135,551,000
Capital Expenditure	1,043,665,000	790,544,100	1,012,838,000	731,498,100	892,146,500	576,709,600
EBITDA	3,627,567,000	3,259,279,000	1,382,448,000	3,775,983,000	3,112,875,000	3,768,912,000
Return on Assets %	2.81%	1.97%	-3.28%	2.50%	3.48%	3.90%
Return on Equity %	5.98%	3.92%	-6.32%	4.60%	6.29%	6.05%
Debt to Equity	0.31	0.27	0.29	0.28	0.25	0.15

CONTACT INFORMATION:
Phone: 81 33278-2111   Fax: 81 33278-2880
Toll-Free:
Address: 1-1, Nihonbashi-Honcho 2-Chome, Chuo-ku, Tokyo, 103-0023 Japan

STOCK TICKER/OTHER:
Stock Ticker: TKPYY
Employees: 19,654
Parent Company:

Exchange: PINX
Fiscal Year Ends: 03/31

SALARIES/BONUSES:
Top Exec. Salary: $ Bonus: $
Second Exec. Salary: $ Bonus: $

OTHER THOUGHTS:
Estimated Female Officers or Directors: 3
Hot Spot for Advancement for Women/Minorities: Y

Take-Two Interactive Software Inc

www.take2games.com

NAIC Code: 0

TYPES OF BUSINESS:
Computer Software, Electronic Games, Apps & Entertainment
Software Distribution
Apps

BRANDS/DIVISIONS/AFFILIATES:
Rockstar Games
2K
2K Games
2K Sports
2K Play
Battleborn
Social Point SL
Kerbal Space Program

CONTACTS: Note: Officers with more than one job title may be intentionally listed here more than once.
Strauss Zelnick, CEO
Lainie Goldstein, CFO
Daniel Emerson, Executive VP
Karl Slatoff, President

GROWTH PLANS/SPECIAL FEATURES:
Take-Two Interactive Software, Inc. is a global publisher, developer and distributor of interactive entertainment software. The firm develops, markets and publishes software titles for leading gaming and entertainment hardware platforms, including Sony's PlayStation (PS3 and PS4), Microsoft's Xbox One and Xbox 360, as well as handheld gaming devices, personal computers and mobile devices. The company distributes its software through retail stores and online through digital download stores, online platforms and cloud streaming devices. Its business strategy is to capitalize on the success of popular games by creating sequels and perpetuating its consistently popular franchises while continuing to appeal to a broad range of demographics, from game enthusiasts to casual gamers and families. A majority of Take-Two's leading games are developed internally with intellectual property owned by the company, although it selectively markets and publishes externally developed titles and software based on licensed property, including sports and games based on Nick Jr. titles. The firm wholly-owns the labels Rockstar Games and 2K, and publishes titles under 2K Games, 2K Sports and 2K Play. 2K publishes owned and licensed titles across a range of genres including shooter, action, role-playing, strategy, sports and family/casual. Rockstar Games titles are primarily internally developed and include the Grand Theft Auto series. Other published franchises include Battleborn, BioShock, Borderlands, Carnival Games, Evolve, Mafia, NBA 2K, Sid Meier's Civilization, WWE 2K and XCOM. The company has internal development studios located in Canada, China, Czech Republic, Spain, the U.K. and the U.S. During 2017, the firm acquired Spanish social and mobile game developer, Social Point SL; and acquired Kerbal Space Program, a space flight simulation video game.

FINANCIAL DATA: Note: Data for latest year may not have been available at press time.

In U.S. $	2017	2016	2015	2014	2013	2012
Revenue	1,779,748,000	1,413,698,000	1,082,938,000	2,350,568,000	1,214,483,000	825,823,000
R&D Expense	137,915,000	119,807,000	115,043,000	105,256,000	78,184,000	64,162,000
Operating Income	91,305,000	60,457,000	-258,463,000	415,256,000	5,239,000	-84,266,000
Operating Margin %	5.13%	4.27%	-23.86%	17.66%	.43%	-10.20%
SGA Expense	496,862,000	390,761,000	410,434,000	402,370,000	404,589,000	304,949,000
Net Income	67,303,000	-8,302,000	-279,470,000	361,605,000	-29,491,000	-108,816,000
Operating Cash Flow	331,429,000	261,305,000	212,814,000	700,262,000	-4,567,000	-84,964,000
Capital Expenditure	21,167,000	37,280,000	49,501,000	29,813,000	16,820,000	10,786,000
EBITDA	350,661,000	223,889,000	-103,609,000	697,706,000	253,621,000	79,540,000
Return on Assets %	2.34%	-.34%	-13.86%	23.50%	-2.42%	-10.26%
Return on Equity %	8.49%	-1.45%	-40.95%	52.03%	-4.98%	-17.97%
Debt to Equity	0.25	0.85	0.84	0.56	0.57	0.53

CONTACT INFORMATION:
Phone: 646 536-2842 Fax: 646 536-2926
Toll-Free:
Address: 622 Broadway, New York, NY 10012 United States

SALARIES/BONUSES:
Top Exec. Salary: $676,520   Bonus: $
Second Exec. Salary: $500,000   Bonus: $

STOCK TICKER/OTHER:
Stock Ticker: TTWO
Employees: 3,707
Parent Company:

Exchange: NAS
Fiscal Year Ends: 03/31

OTHER THOUGHTS:
Estimated Female Officers or Directors: 1
Hot Spot for Advancement for Women/Minorities:

Sales, profits and employees may be estimates. Financial information, benefits and other data can change quickly and may vary from those stated here.

Tata Motors Limited

NAIC Code: 336111

www.tatamotors.com

TYPES OF BUSINESS:
Automobile Manufacturing
Light & Medium Commercial Vehicles Manufacturing
Heavy Commercial Vehicles Manufacturing
Passenger Vehicles Manufacturing

BRANDS/DIVISIONS/AFFILIATES:
Tata Group
Jaguar
Land Rover
Nex-Gen ULTRA
NEXON AMT
Tata Hexa

CONTACTS:
Note: Officers with more than one job title may be intentionally listed here more than once.

Guenter Butschek, CEO
Satish Borwankar, COO
P.B. Balaji, CFO
Gajendra Chandel, Chief Human Resources Officer
Tajendra Petkar, CTO
Rajesh Bagga, VP-Legal
Ravindra Pisharody, Pres., Commercial Vehicles
S.B. Borwankar, Exec. Dir.
Ravi Kant, Vice Chmn.
N. Chandrasekaran, Chmn.
Venkatram Mamillapalle, Sr. VP

GROWTH PLANS/SPECIAL FEATURES:

Tata Motors Limited, part of Tata Group, is one of India's largest automobile manufacturers with vehicles sold in over 50 countries. The company manufactures commercial and passenger vehicles and also provides automobile financing services. Tata Motors' products include passenger vehicles; utility vehicles; light commercial vehicles, including pick-up trucks; and medium and heavy commercial vehicles. Through its subsidiaries, the firm is also engaged in areas such as engineering, construction equipment manufacturing, vehicle components manufacturing, supply chain management, factory automation and automotive retailing and servicing. The company employs a significant number of engineers and scientists and maintains R&D centers in India, South Korea, Spain and the U.K. Tata Motors is among the world's leading bus manufacturers, and the company has expanded these activities through strategic partnerships with: Tata Hispano Motors Carrocera SA, a Spanish bus and coach manufacturer; and Marcopolo SA, a Brazil-based company engaged in the manufacture of bodies for buses and coaches. The firm has also expanded its international presence through such activities as the manufacture and marketing of pick-up trucks in Thailand, and the marketing of Fiat-branded cars in India as well as through vehicle sales in several countries in Europe, Africa, the Middle East, Australia and Asia. Tata Motors also owns the Jaguar and Land Rover brands, with an additional 75 subsidiaries in its portfolio. In early-2018, the firm announced the nation-wide launch of Nex-Gen ULTRA range of trucks; opened bookings for the new NEXON AMT with HyprDrive Self-Shift Gears; and celebrated the first anniversary of the Tata Hexa, a crossover lifestyle vehicle.

FINANCIAL DATA:
Note: Data for latest year may not have been available at press time.

In U.S. $	2017	2016	2015	2014	2013	2012
Revenue	40,746,540,000	41,374,290,000	40,267,520,000	35,919,000,000	28,987,540,000	25,536,280,000
R&D Expense	523,589,000	532,055,800	437,380,700	393,449,900	309,731,000	212,584,900
Operating Income	1,607,665,000	2,985,919,000	3,782,777,000	3,204,474,000	2,510,111,000	1,203,003,000
Operating Margin %	3.94%	7.21%	9.39%	8.92%	8.65%	4.71%
SGA Expense	4,413,016,000	4,476,696,000	3,885,138,000	3,324,243,000	2,581,574,000	6,302,672,000
Net Income	938,874,700	1,470,704,000	1,967,789,000	2,004,999,000	1,360,475,000	1,774,032,000
Operating Cash Flow	4,649,199,000	5,747,519,000	5,604,692,000	5,697,189,000	3,419,445,000	3,347,264,000
Capital Expenditure	4,702,734,000	4,779,504,000	4,626,126,000	3,969,805,000	2,847,956,000	2,128,127,000
EBITDA	4,949,345,000	5,220,788,000	5,904,686,000	5,260,514,000	3,731,060,000	3,280,482,000
Return on Assets %	2.31%	3.86%	5.66%	6.78%	5.72%	7.96%
Return on Equity %	9.43%	14.76%	22.07%	26.20%	25.38%	36.50%
Debt to Equity	1.13	0.66	1.02	0.72	0.88	0.87

CONTACT INFORMATION:
Phone: 91-22-66658282   Fax:
Toll-Free:
Address: Homi Mody St., Bombay House, 24, Mumbai, 400 001 India

SALARIES/BONUSES:
Top Exec. Salary: $3,459,053   Bonus: $
Second Exec. Salary: $631,929   Bonus: $

STOCK TICKER/OTHER:
Stock Ticker: TTM
Employees: 79,558
Parent Company: Tata Group
Exchange: NYS
Fiscal Year Ends: 03/31

OTHER THOUGHTS:
Estimated Female Officers or Directors:
Hot Spot for Advancement for Women/Minorities:

Tate & Lyle plc

www.tateandlyle.com

NAIC Code: 311942

TYPES OF BUSINESS:
Synthetic Sweeteners (i.e., sweetening agents) Manufacturing
Animal Feed
Bulk Storage
Starches & Proteins
Sweeteners
Ethanol
Flavors & Ingredients
Cosmetic Ingredients

BRANDS/DIVISIONS/AFFILIATES:
Splenda
Zemea
DuPont Tate & Lyle BioProducts
STA-LITE

CONTACTS:
Note: Officers with more than one job title may be intentionally listed here more than once.

Nick Hampton, CEO
Melissa Law, Pres., Global Oper.
Rob Luijten, Exec. VP-Human Resources
Robert Gibber, General Counsel
Karl Kramer, Pres., Innovation & Commercial Dev.
Olivier Rigaud, Pres., Specialty Food Ingredients
Matthew Wineinger, Pres., Bulk Ingredients
Gerry Murphy, Chmn.

GROWTH PLANS/SPECIAL FEATURES:

Tate & Lyle plc is a global leader in the processing of food and industrial ingredients. The company's ingredients can be found in sugars and syrups, ointments, creams, toothpaste, animal feeds, biofuels and pharmaceuticals. Tate & Lyle operates in two main divisions: specialty ingredients, deriving 30% of sales revenue in 2017; and bulk ingredients, deriving 70%. Both operations are supported by the Innovation and Commercial Development unit. Specialty ingredients are products created technologically or through intellectual property that allow customers to produce unique products. This division mainly includes wellness ingredients and dietary fibers; texturants, such as starch and gums; and sweeteners, including SPLENDA sucralose and crystalline fructose. The sucralose unit manufactures the no-calorie, high-intensity sweetener at its facility in Singapore. Through an alliance with Heartland Food Products Group, Tate & Lyle is the sole manufacturer of Splenda-brand sucralose sweetener, which is used in the sweetening of more than 4,000 food, beverage and pharmaceutical products globally. The specialty ingredients division also includes blended or combination ingredients for small and medium businesses. The firm's remaining products such as high fructose corn syrup, acidulants, corn-base bulk sweeteners and industrial starches, are classified as bulk ingredients. The by-products of specialty and bulk ingredients, most notably the corn gluten meal and corn gluten feed, are sold as animal feed for livestock, fish and pets. The firm operates from more than 30 facilities around the world. In December 2017, Tate & Lyle completed the expansion of capacity at its STA-LITE polydextrose facility in Nantong, China, increasing capacity by more than three times. Food producers use STA-LITE for fiber-enrichment purposes in reduced sugars and calorie products.

FINANCIAL DATA:
Note: Data for latest year may not have been available at press time.

In U.S. $	2017	2016	2015	2014	2013	2012
Revenue	3,921,094,000	3,354,223,000	3,355,647,000	4,482,268,000	4,637,516,000	4,398,234,000
R&D Expense	52,699,040	41,304,660	45,577,550	47,001,850		41,304,660
Operating Income	366,044,700	180,885,900	47,001,850	458,624,100	478,564,300	479,988,600
Operating Margin %	9.33%	5.39%	1.40%	10.23%	10.31%	10.91%
SGA Expense						
Net Income	364,620,400	232,160,700	42,728,960	388,833,500	394,530,700	434,411,000
Operating Cash Flow	424,441,000	267,768,100	254,949,400	546,930,600	357,498,900	329,013,000
Capital Expenditure	217,917,700	282,011,100	220,766,300	226,463,500	190,856,000	185,158,800
EBITDA	588,235,300	384,560,600	273,465,300	633,812,900	636,661,400	732,089,500
Return on Assets %	9.61%	6.55%	1.21%	10.27%	9.73%	10.24%
Return on Equity %	21.69%	16.60%	3.02%	26.18%	26.77%	30.76%
Debt to Equity	0.45	0.53	0.49	0.41	0.79	0.77

CONTACT INFORMATION:
Phone: 44 2072572100   Fax: 44 2072572200
Toll-Free:
Address: 1 Kingsway, London, WC2B 6AT United Kingdom

SALARIES/BONUSES:
Top Exec. Salary: $1,026,919   Bonus: $1,437,117
Second Exec. Salary: $730,665   Bonus: $1,150,833

STOCK TICKER/OTHER:
Stock Ticker: TATYF
Employees: 4,146
Parent Company:

Exchange: PINX
Fiscal Year Ends: 03/31

OTHER THOUGHTS:
Estimated Female Officers or Directors: 3
Hot Spot for Advancement for Women/Minorities: Y

TechnipFMC plc

NAIC Code: 333132

www.technipfmc.com/

TYPES OF BUSINESS:
Oil & Gas Production & Processing Equipment
Airport & Airline Equipment
Food Handling & Processing Systems
Robotics

BRANDS/DIVISIONS/AFFILIATES:

CONTACTS: Note: Officers with more than one job title may be intentionally listed here more than once.
Douglas J. Pferdehirt, CEO
Maryann Mannen, Exec. VP
Arnaud Pieton, Exec. VP-Human Resources
Bradley Beitler, Exec. VP-IT
Douglas Pferdehirt, Director
Bradley Beitler, Executive VP, Divisional
Mark Scott, Executive VP, Divisional
Thierry Parmentier, Executive VP, Divisional
Maryann Mannen, Executive VP
Thierry Pilenko, Chmn.
Richard Alabaster, President, Divisional
Barry Glickman, President, Divisional

GROWTH PLANS/SPECIAL FEATURES:

TechnipFMC plc is an offshore energy services giant. The firm is a global leader in oil and gas projects, technologies, systems and services. TechnipFMC operates across three distinct segments: subsea, onshore/offshore and surface technologies. The subsea segment is further divided into three groups: products, which include trees, manifolds, controls, templates, flowline systems, umbilicals, flexibles and processing; projects, comprising front-end to decommissioning, field architecture, integrated design, engineering, procurement, construction and installation; and services, including drilling, installation, completion, asset management, well intervention and manipulator systems. The onshore/offshore segment provides technical, technological and project management expertise across fixed, floating and onshore facilities. Its offerings are also divided into three groups: onshore, including liquefied natural gas (LNG), gas treatment, petrochemicals/fertilizers, refining/hydrogen and mining/metals; offshore, including fixed facilities such as jackets, self-elevating platforms and artificial islands, and floating facilities such as floating production storage and offloading (FPSO), semi-submersibles, Spar, tension-leg platforms and floating LNG; and services, including project management consultancy and process technologies. Last, the surface technologies segment designs, manufactures and supplies wellhead systems as well as technologically-advanced high-pressure valves, flowlines and pumps used in stimulation activities for oilfield service companies. This division also provides frac systems and services, and production, separation and flow processing systems for exploration/production companies in the oil/gas industry, as well as measurement systems and loading arms solutions for energy customers. TechnipFMC comprises two global headquarter locations: Paris, France and Texas, USA. In October 2017, TechnipFMC agreed to acquire Plexus Holding plc's wellhead exploration equipment and services business for jack up applications, which will integrate into the surface technologies segment when the transaction is completed.

FINANCIAL DATA: Note: Data for latest year may not have been available at press time.

In U.S. $	2017	2016	2015	2014	2013	2012
Revenue	15,056,900,000	9,199,600,000	11,302,450,000	12,249,990,000	12,891,960,000	10,849,710,000
R&D Expense	212,900,000	105,400,000	94,133,340	100,442,600	104,255,800	90,856,190
Operating Income	1,258,500,000	891,600,000	815,603,600	924,047,900	1,166,147,000	1,086,703,000
Operating Margin %	8.35%	9.69%	7.21%	7.54%	9.04%	10.01%
SGA Expense	1,060,900,000	572,600,000	676,098,200	783,963,200	989,809,200	899,965,600
Net Income	113,300,000	393,300,000	49,307,940	530,911,000	777,569,100	713,756,700
Operating Cash Flow	210,700,000	493,800,000	689,873,900	152,001,600	1,820,818,000	588,118,600
Capital Expenditure	255,700,000	312,900,000	320,337,600	456,004,700	860,283,300	686,248,600
EBITDA	1,873,200,000	1,192,300,000	696,980,300	1,268,544,000	1,488,580,000	1,344,460,000
Return on Assets %	.48%	2.33%	.31%	3.06%	4.62%	4.73%
Return on Equity %	1.22%	7.85%	.96%	9.61%	14.09%	14.24%
Debt to Equity	0.28	0.36	0.35	0.54	0.57	0.42

CONTACT INFORMATION:
Phone: 440-203-4293950 Fax:
Toll-Free:
Address: One St. Paul's Churchyard, London, EC4M 8AP United Kingdom

STOCK TICKER/OTHER:
Stock Ticker: FTI
Employees: 38,297
Parent Company:

Exchange: NYS
Fiscal Year Ends: 12/31

SALARIES/BONUSES:
Top Exec. Salary: $ Bonus: $
Second Exec. Salary: $ Bonus: $

OTHER THOUGHTS:
Estimated Female Officers or Directors: 3
Hot Spot for Advancement for Women/Minorities: Y

Tecnica Y Proyectos SA (TYPSA)

NAIC Code: 541330

www.typsa.com/en/

TYPES OF BUSINESS:
Engineering Consulting Services

BRANDS/DIVISIONS/AFFILIATES:

CONTACTS: Note: Officers with more than one job title may be intentionally listed here more than once.
Pablo Bueno Tomas, CEO
Julio Grande Florez, Deputy CEO
Javier Segura Fontcuberta, CFO
Jorge Garcia Perez, COO
Nicolas Rodriguez-Arias Ambrosini, Human Resources
Miguel Mondria Garcia, CTO
Pablo Bueno Sainz, Chmn.

GROWTH PLANS/SPECIAL FEATURES:
Tecnica Y Proyectos SA (TYPSA), along with its subsidiaries, provides consulting services in the fields of civil engineering, architecture, building technology, energy and environment worldwide. It has been involved in the development of all types of infrastructure and facilities across both Spanish and international markets since its 1966 inception. Over 70% of the firm's professionals are engineers, architects or other university graduates who work in highly-skilled multidisciplinary teams. TYPSA is experienced in the fields of transport, water, urban development, renewable energy and the environment. Its professional services include master plans; technical, economic and environmental studies and reports, feasibility studies, preliminary and schematic designs, final designs, construction management and site supervision; construction project management; auditing and due diligence; operation and maintenance management; concession studies, expropriation management; identification, management and evaluation of projects and programs; health and safety; and environmental control laboratory. TYPSA has offices in Africa, Europe, Latin America, the Middle East, Asia and the U.S. The firm allocates more than 1% of its revenue to innovation and technological development. Some of TYPSA's key innovative/technological projects underway include: ROAD-BIM, designing and development BIM technologies for highway design validation and management, as well as highway operation and road safety management; ZEUS-FLUEM, a reservoir management project using terrestrial video systems; ASDECO, an automated system project for desalination dilution control; REALITTECH, a concentrated saline rejection treatment environmental technology using a non-profitable solid waste as an energy source; and URWASTTECH, an innovative urban waste treatment project using a sustainable approach via hydrodynamic and biological technologies.

FINANCIAL DATA: Note: Data for latest year may not have been available at press time.

In U.S. $	2017	2016	2015	2014	2013	2012
Revenue	250,000,000	242,520,000	256,935,000	246,278,960	206,874,326	212,137,000
R&D Expense						
Operating Income						
Operating Margin %						
SGA Expense						
Net Income		12,750,300	12,507,400	13,622,400		
Operating Cash Flow						
Capital Expenditure						
EBITDA						
Return on Assets %						
Return on Equity %						
Debt to Equity						

CONTACT INFORMATION:
Phone: 34-917-227-300 Fax: 34-916-517-588
Toll-Free:
Address: Gomera 9, S.S. de los Reyes, Madrid, 28703 Spain

STOCK TICKER/OTHER:
Stock Ticker: Private
Employees: 2,500
Parent Company:
Exchange:
Fiscal Year Ends:

SALARIES/BONUSES:
Top Exec. Salary: $ Bonus: $
Second Exec. Salary: $ Bonus: $

OTHER THOUGHTS:
Estimated Female Officers or Directors:
Hot Spot for Advancement for Women/Minorities:

Sales, profits and employees may be estimates. Financial information, benefits and other data can change quickly and may vary from those stated here.

Teledyne Technologies Inc

www.teledyne.com

NAIC Code: 334511

TYPES OF BUSINESS:
Defense Electronics and Instrumentation
Systems Engineering Solutions
Aerospace Engines & Components
Energy Systems

BRANDS/DIVISIONS/AFFILIATES:
Bolt Technology Corporation
Teledyne Scientific Company
Optech Incorporated
Teledyne Brown Engineering Inc
e2v technologies plc

CONTACTS:
Note: Officers with more than one job title may be intentionally listed here more than once.

Jason Connell, Assistant General Counsel
Carl Adams, VP, Divisional
Robert Mehrabian, CEO
Susan Main, CFO
Cynthia Belak, Chief Accounting Officer
Scott Hudson, Chief Information Officer
Aldo Pichelli, COO
Melanie Cibik, General Counsel
Michael Read, President, Divisional
Janice Hess, President, Divisional
Thomas Reslewic, President, Divisional
George Bobb, President, Subsidiary
Edwin Roks, President, Subsidiary
Jason VanWees, Senior VP, Divisional
Stephen Blackwood, Treasurer
Glenn Seemann, Vice President, Divisional

GROWTH PLANS/SPECIAL FEATURES:

Teledyne Technologies, Inc., together with its subsidiaries, is a leading manufacturer of electronic components, instruments and communications products. The firm operates in four segments: instrumentation, aerospace and defense electronics, digital imaging and engineered systems. The instrumentation segment provides monitoring and control instruments for marine, environmental, industrial and other applications, as well as electronic test and measurement equipment. This division also provides power and communications connectivity devices for distributed instrumentation systems and sensor networks deployed in mission critical, harsh environments. Segment subsidiaries include Bolt Technology Corporation and Teledyne Scientific Company. The aerospace and defense electronics segment provides sophisticated electronic components and subsystems and communications products, including defense electronics, general aviation batteries, harsh environment interconnects, data acquisition and communications equipment for aircraft, and components and subsystems for wireless and satellite communications. The digital imaging segment includes high-performance sensors, cameras and systems within the visible, infrared, ultraviolet and X-ray spectra for use in industrial, government and medical applications, as well as micro electro-mechanical systems (MEMS). This segment includes wholly-owned subsidiary Optech Incorporated. The engineered systems segment provides innovative systems engineering and integration and advanced technology development, as well as manufacturing solutions for defense, space, environmental and energy applications. This division also designs and manufactures electrochemical energy systems and small turbine engines. Subsidiary Teledyne Brown Engineering, Inc. operates within this business segment, manufacturing components in the nuclear power market, and performing radiological analysis at the firm's laboratory in Knoxville, Tennessee. During 2017, the firm acquired assets of Scientific Systems, Inc., which manufactures precision components and subassemblies used in analytical and diagnostic instrumentation; and acquired e2v technologies plc, which provides high-performance image sensors and customer camera solutions and applications.

FINANCIAL DATA:
Note: Data for latest year may not have been available at press time.

In U.S. $	2017	2016	2015	2014	2013	2012
Revenue	2,603,800,000	2,149,900,000	2,298,100,000	2,394,000,000	2,338,600,000	2,127,300,000
R&D Expense						
Operating Income	335,600,000	253,800,000	281,700,000	294,500,000	240,300,000	243,100,000
Operating Margin %	12.88%	11.80%	12.25%	12.30%	10.27%	11.42%
SGA Expense	656,000,000	578,100,000	588,600,000	612,400,000	598,300,000	505,100,000
Net Income	227,200,000	190,900,000	195,800,000	217,700,000	185,000,000	164,100,000
Operating Cash Flow	374,700,000	317,000,000	210,200,000	287,900,000	204,100,000	189,500,000
Capital Expenditure	58,500,000	87,600,000	47,000,000	43,500,000	72,600,000	65,300,000
EBITDA	448,600,000	341,100,000	372,000,000	388,800,000	331,400,000	324,300,000
Return on Assets %	6.86%	6.95%	7.01%	7.75%	7.17%	7.75%
Return on Equity %	12.97%	13.17%	14.12%	15.01%	14.12%	15.42%
Debt to Equity	0.54	0.33	0.56	0.43	0.37	0.48

CONTACT INFORMATION:
Phone: 805 373-4545   Fax: 310 893-1669
Toll-Free:
Address: 1049 Camino Dos Rios, Thousand Oaks, CA 91360 United States

STOCK TICKER/OTHER:
Stock Ticker: TDY
Employees: 8,970
Parent Company:
Exchange: NYS
Fiscal Year Ends: 12/31

SALARIES/BONUSES:
Top Exec. Salary: $975,385   Bonus: $
Second Exec. Salary: $561,215   Bonus: $

OTHER THOUGHTS:
Estimated Female Officers or Directors: 6
Hot Spot for Advancement for Women/Minorities: Y

Telefon AB LM Ericsson (Ericsson)

NAIC Code: 334220

www.ericsson.com

TYPES OF BUSINESS:
Wireless Telecommunications Equipment
Mobile Phones
Pagers
Networking Equipment
Defense Electronics
Telecommunications Software
Professional Services
Research & Development

BRANDS/DIVISIONS/AFFILIATES:
Red Bee Media

CONTACTS: Note: Officers with more than one job title may be intentionally listed here more than once.
Borje Ekholm, CEO
Hans Vestberg, Pres.
Carl Mellander, Sr. VP
Helena Norrman, Sr. VP-Mktg. & Communications
MajBritt Arfert, Sr. VP-Human Resources
Erik Ekudden, Sr. VP
Nina Macpherson, General Counsel
Douglas L. Gilstrap, Sr. VP-Function Strategy
Helena Norrman, Sr. VP-Comm..
Jan Frykhammar, Head-Group Function Finance
Angel Ruiz, Head-North America
Magnus Mandersson, Head-Global Svcs.
Rima Qureshi, Sr. VP-Strategic Projects
Johan Wibergh, Exec. VP-Networks
Ronnie Leten, Chmn.
Mats H. Olsson, Head-Asia Pacific

GROWTH PLANS/SPECIAL FEATURES:

Telefon AB LM Ericsson (Ericsson) is a leading global supplier of mobile phone handsets and equipment for mobile and fixed-line telecommunications operators. The firm's services include consumer and business applications, communication, fixed broadband and convergence, managed services, mobile broadband, operations and business support systems and TV and media management. The company is structured into three business units: networks, services and managed services. The networks unit is grouped into mobile and fixed access, core transmission networks, microwave transport and next generation IP-networks. The mobile networks division provides radio base stations, base station controllers and radio network controllers, mobile switching centers, service application nodes and other nodes for billing and operations support for GSM (global system for mobile) and CDMA (code-division multiple access) networks. Fixed network operators are moving from single-service networks toward new multi-service networks that have the ability to simultaneously handle multiple services, such as voice, text and images. The services unit maintains network and services centers, which collectively supply customer support services, network rollout, managed services, systems integration and consulting. The managed services business unit offers experience-centric managed services, connected venues, network design, network optimization and 5G physical/virtual network management. In addition, Ericsson's Internet of Things (IoT) solutions include connectivity, an IoT platform and IoT for the automotive sector. Ericsson holds 45,000 patents, including many in wireless communications. The company's focus is to facilitate new business development for its telecom service provider customers, and this via a unified delivery network and security/risk management. In early-2018, Ericsson announced plans to divest 51% of its media business to an external partner, and then focus on developing Red Bee Media as an independent, in-house media and services business.

FINANCIAL DATA: Note: Data for latest year may not have been available at press time.

In U.S. $	2017	2016	2015	2014	2013	2012
Revenue	23,768,830,000	26,284,420,000	29,155,060,000	26,919,070,000	26,847,400,000	26,894,980,000
R&D Expense	4,473,504,000	3,735,299,000	4,114,202,000	4,287,064,000	3,806,263,000	3,876,753,000
Operating Income	-3,072,073,000	692,391,200	2,561,044,000	2,245,667,000	2,109,054,000	1,561,422,000
Operating Margin %	-12.92%	2.63%	8.78%	8.34%	7.85%	5.80%
SGA Expense	3,858,215,000	3,408,350,000	3,457,823,000	3,199,830,000	3,102,182,000	3,072,663,000
Net Income	-4,156,945,000	202,616,500	1,599,797,000	1,365,890,000	1,417,489,000	681,882,600
Operating Cash Flow	1,133,637,000	1,654,229,000	2,431,989,000	2,208,237,000	2,053,204,000	2,601,308,000
Capital Expenditure	457,776,400	723,681,100	1,374,392,000	808,222,700	639,729,800	834,789,600
EBITDA	-3,524,772,000	1,684,575,000	3,722,075,000	3,201,483,000	3,384,617,000	2,563,642,000
Return on Assets %	-12.94%	.60%	4.68%	4.11%	4.41%	2.07%
Return on Equity %	-29.41%	1.19%	9.31%	8.13%	8.66%	4.12%
Debt to Equity	0.30	0.13	0.15	0.15	0.15	0.17

CONTACT INFORMATION:
Phone: 46 87190000
Fax: 46 87191976
Toll-Free:
Address: Torshamnsgatan 23, Kista, Stockholm, 164 83 Sweden

SALARIES/BONUSES:
Top Exec. Salary: $1,555,882   Bonus: $1,350,866
Second Exec. Salary: $ Bonus: $

STOCK TICKER/OTHER:
Stock Ticker: ERIC
Employees: 111,464
Parent Company:

Exchange: NAS
Fiscal Year Ends: 12/31

OTHER THOUGHTS:
Estimated Female Officers or Directors: 10
Hot Spot for Advancement for Women/Minorities: Y

Sales, profits and employees may be estimates. Financial information, benefits and other data can change quickly and may vary from those stated here.

Tellabs Inc

NAIC Code: 334210

www.tellabs.com

TYPES OF BUSINESS:
Wireline & Wireless Products & Services
Consulting

BRANDS/DIVISIONS/AFFILIATES:
Marlin Equity Partners LLC

CONTACTS: Note: Officers with more than one job title may be intentionally listed here more than once.
Jim Norrod, CEO
Daniel P. Kelly, Pres.
David Brown, CFO
James M. Sheehan, Chief Admin. Officer
James M. Sheehan, General Counsel
John M. Brots, Exec. VP-Global Oper.
Kenneth G. Craft, Exec. VP-Product Dev.

GROWTH PLANS/SPECIAL FEATURES:
Tellabs, Inc. provides products and services that enable customers to deliver wireline and wireless voice, data and video services to business and residential customers. It operates in two segments: enterprise and broadband. The enterprise segment offers a passive optical local area network (LAN) infrastructure, which is secure, scalable and sustainable. This division serves the business enterprise, federal government, hospitality, higher education, K-12 education and healthcare industries. The broadband segment offers solutions to service providers that deliver stability and scalability while increasing flexibility. These broadband solutions help telecommunications companies grow HSI (high-speed internet) subscribers, extend service area coverage and offer faster internet service speeds. They also enable Ethernet business services while continuing to support time-division multiplexing (TDM) and automated teller machine (ATM) services. Tellabs is a subsidiary of Marlin Equity Partners, LLC.

The firm offers its employees medical, dental & vision insurance; company-paid life and AD&D insurance; short-and long-term disability; flexible spending accounts; health savings account; and a 401(k) retirement savings plan with company match.

FINANCIAL DATA: Note: Data for latest year may not have been available at press time.

In U.S. $	2017	2016	2015	2014	2013	2012
Revenue	1,391,000,000	1,372,000,000	1,375,000,000	1,325,000,000	1,100,000,000	1,052,600,000
R&D Expense						
Operating Income						
Operating Margin %						
SGA Expense						
Net Income						
Operating Cash Flow						
Capital Expenditure						
EBITDA						
Return on Assets %						
Return on Equity %						
Debt to Equity						

CONTACT INFORMATION:
Phone: 972-588-7000   Fax: 972-588-7070
Toll-Free:
Address: 18583 N. Dallas Pkwy., Ste. 200, Dallas, TX 75287 United States

STOCK TICKER/OTHER:
Stock Ticker: Private
Employees: 2,635
Parent Company: Marlin Equity Partners LLC

Exchange:
Fiscal Year Ends: 12/31

SALARIES/BONUSES:
Top Exec. Salary: $ Bonus: $
Second Exec. Salary: $ Bonus: $

OTHER THOUGHTS:
Estimated Female Officers or Directors: 1
Hot Spot for Advancement for Women/Minorities: Y

Sales, profits and employees may be estimates. Financial information, benefits and other data can change quickly and may vary from those stated here.

Tenneco Inc

NAIC Code: 336300

www.tenneco.com

TYPES OF BUSINESS:
Automotive Parts Manufacturer
Advanced Suspension Technologies
Ride Control Products
Emissions Systems
Performance Mufflers
Noise Control Systems

BRANDS/DIVISIONS/AFFILIATES:
Walker
XNOx
Fonos
DynoMax
Monroe
Rancho
Clevite
Axios

CONTACTS:
Note: Officers with more than one job title may be intentionally listed here more than once.

Brian Kesseler, CEO
Benny Patel, Chief Technology Officer
Gregg Sherrill, Director
Kenneth Trammell, Executive VP
Peng Guo, Executive VP
Martin Hendricks, Executive VP
Brandon Smith, General Counsel
Jason Hollar, Senior VP, Divisional
Gregg Bolt, Senior VP, Divisional
Paul Novas, Vice President, Divisional

GROWTH PLANS/SPECIAL FEATURES:

Tenneco, Inc. designs, manufactures and distributes highly-engineered products for both original equipment vehicle manufacturers (OEMs) and the repair and replacement markets worldwide. The firm is one of the world's largest producers of clean air and ride performance products and systems for light vehicle, commercial, truck, off-highway and other vehicle applications. Tenneco's business is organized in three geographical areas--North America, Europe and South America, and Asia Pacific. Within these geographical areas, each operating segment manufactures and distributes either clean air or ride performance products. Clean air systems consist of vehicle emission control products which play a role in safely conveying noxious exhaust gases away from the passenger compartment and reducing the level of pollutants and engine exhaust noise emitted to acceptable levels. These products include catalytic converters, various types of filters, burner systems, lean NOx traps, hydrocarbon vaporizers/injectors, mufflers, pipes, elastomeric hangers and isolators, and more. Clean air brands include Walker, XNOx, Fonos, DynoMax and Thrush. This division operates 64 clean air manufacturing facilities worldwide, of which 16 are located in North America, 21 in Europe and South America, and 27 in Asia Pacific. Ride performance systems include shock absorbers and struts, as well as vibration control components and suspension technologies and systems. Ride performance brands include Monroe, Rancho, Clevite, Axios, Kinetic and Fric-Rot. This division operates 28 ride performance manufacturing facilities, of which nine are in North America, 10 in Europe and South America, and nine in Asia Pacific. In April 2018, Icahn Enterprises LP agreed to sell Federal-Mogul, its automotive parts manufacturer subsidiary, to Tenneco for $2.5 billion. Tenneco plans to create two independent, public companies from the acquisition: the aftermarket and ride performance company will include Tenneco Ride Performance and Federal-Mogul Motorparts; and the powertrain technology company will include Tenneco Clean Air and Federal-Mogul Powertrain.

FINANCIAL DATA:
Note: Data for latest year may not have been available at press time.

In U.S. $	2017	2016	2015	2014	2013	2012
Revenue	9,274,000,000	8,599,000,000	8,209,000,000	8,420,000,000	7,964,000,000	7,363,000,000
R&D Expense	158,000,000	154,000,000	146,000,000	169,000,000	144,000,000	126,000,000
Operating Income	432,000,000	533,000,000	524,000,000	499,000,000	428,000,000	435,000,000
Operating Margin %	4.65%	6.19%	6.38%	5.92%	5.37%	5.90%
SGA Expense	648,000,000	589,000,000	491,000,000	519,000,000	453,000,000	427,000,000
Net Income	207,000,000	363,000,000	247,000,000	226,000,000	183,000,000	275,000,000
Operating Cash Flow	629,000,000	489,000,000	517,000,000	341,000,000	503,000,000	365,000,000
Capital Expenditure	419,000,000	345,000,000	309,000,000	344,000,000	269,000,000	276,000,000
EBITDA	641,000,000	740,000,000	722,000,000	700,000,000	629,000,000	633,000,000
Return on Assets %	4.50%	8.73%	6.19%	5.76%	4.92%	7.91%
Return on Equity %	32.24%	71.10%	53.11%	48.60%	53.90%	72.55%
Debt to Equity	1.95	2.20	2.59	2.15	2.35	4.33

CONTACT INFORMATION:
Phone: 847 482-5000
Fax: 847 482-5940
Toll-Free:
Address: 500 N. Field Dr., Lake Forest, IL 60045 United States

STOCK TICKER/OTHER:
Stock Ticker: TEN
Employees: 31,000
Parent Company:
Exchange: NYS
Fiscal Year Ends: 12/31

SALARIES/BONUSES:
Top Exec. Salary: $1,200,000
Bonus: $73,125
Second Exec. Salary: $970,479
Bonus: $52,853

OTHER THOUGHTS:
Estimated Female Officers or Directors: 4
Hot Spot for Advancement for Women/Minorities: Y

Sales, profits and employees may be estimates. Financial information, benefits and other data can change quickly and may vary from those stated here.

Terex Corporation

www.terex.com

NAIC Code: 333120

TYPES OF BUSINESS:
Heavy Equipment
Cranes
Mining Equipment
Aerial Work Platforms
Road Building Equipment
Utility Products
Construction Equipment
Materials Handling Equipment

BRANDS/DIVISIONS/AFFILIATES:
Terex
Powerscreen
Fuchs
Evoquip
CBI

CONTACTS:
Note: Officers with more than one job title may be intentionally listed here more than once.

John Garrison, CEO
Mark Clair, Chief Accounting Officer
David Sachs, Director
Stoyan Filipov, President, Divisional
Matthew Fearon, President, Divisional
Kieran Hegarty, President, Divisional
Kevin Barr, Senior VP, Divisional
Brian Henry, Senior VP, Divisional
John Sheehan, Senior VP
Eric Cohen, Senior VP

GROWTH PLANS/SPECIAL FEATURES:

Terex Corporation is a diversified global manufacturer specializing in tools and equipment for the construction, quarrying, mining, refining, transportation and energy industries. It operates in three business segments: aerial work platforms (AWP), cranes and materials processing (MP). The AWP segment designs, manufactures and markets products such as material lifts, portable aerial work platforms, trailer-mounted articulating booms, self-propelled articulating and telescopic booms, scissor lifts, construction trailers and related components and parts. The cranes segment produces mobile telescopic cranes, tower cranes, lattice boom crawler cranes and truck-mounted cranes as well as their related replacement parts and components under the Terex and Demag brand names. It also offers specialized port and rail equipment. The MP segment designs, manufactures and markets materials processing and specialty equipment, including crushers, washing systems, screens, apron feeders, material handlers, wood processing, biomass and recycling equipment, concrete mixer trucks and concrete pavers. These products are utilized in construction, infrastructure and recycling projects, in various quarrying and mining applications, as well as in landscaping and biomass production industries, material handling applications and in building roads and bridges. The MP products are marketed principally under the Terex, Powerscreen, Fuchs, Evoquip and CBI brands. In September 2017, Terex sold its minority shares of Konecranes Plc.

FINANCIAL DATA:
Note: Data for latest year may not have been available at press time.

In U.S. $	2017	2016	2015	2014	2013	2012
Revenue	4,363,400,000	4,443,100,000	6,543,100,000	7,308,900,000	7,084,000,000	7,348,400,000
R&D Expense						
Operating Income	173,600,000	28,200,000	389,900,000	423,100,000	419,100,000	398,600,000
Operating Margin %	3.97%	.63%	5.95%	5.78%	5.91%	5.42%
SGA Expense	642,400,000	684,200,000	918,600,000	1,030,400,000	1,020,400,000	1,047,000,000
Net Income	128,700,000	-176,100,000	145,900,000	319,000,000	226,000,000	105,800,000
Operating Cash Flow	153,000,000	367,000,000	212,900,000	410,700,000	188,500,000	292,300,000
Capital Expenditure	43,500,000	73,000,000	103,800,000	81,500,000	82,800,000	82,500,000
EBITDA	246,000,000	-72,000,000	459,400,000	572,000,000	569,700,000	473,200,000
Return on Assets %	3.03%	-3.30%	2.52%	5.11%	3.40%	1.53%
Return on Equity %	9.50%	-10.47%	7.51%	15.20%	10.76%	5.40%
Debt to Equity	0.80	1.05	0.93	0.81	0.86	1.00

CONTACT INFORMATION:
Phone: 203 222-7170 Fax: 203 222-7976
Toll-Free:
Address: 200 Nyala Farm Rd., Westport, CT 06880 United States

STOCK TICKER/OTHER:
Stock Ticker: TEX Exchange: NYS
Employees: 11,300 Fiscal Year Ends: 12/31
Parent Company:

SALARIES/BONUSES:
Top Exec. Salary: $900,000 Bonus: $900,000
Second Exec. Salary: $580,253 Bonus: $580,253

OTHER THOUGHTS:
Estimated Female Officers or Directors: 1
Hot Spot for Advancement for Women/Minorities:

Tesla Inc

www.teslamotors.com

NAIC Code: 336111

TYPES OF BUSINESS:
Automobile Manufacturing, All-Electric
Battery Manufacturing
Lithium Ion Battery Storage Technologies
Energy Storage Systems

BRANDS/DIVISIONS/AFFILIATES:
Model S
70D
Model X
Model 3
Tesla Powerwall
Gigafactory
SolarCity
Solar Roof

CONTACTS: Note: Officers with more than one job title may be intentionally listed here more than once.

Elon Musk, CEO
Deepak Ahuja, CFO
Jeffrey Straubel, Chief Technology Officer
Douglas Field, Senior VP, Divisional

GROWTH PLANS/SPECIAL FEATURES:

Tesla, Inc. manufactures high-performance all-electric automobiles and energy storage products. Its sales have been impressive, despite the relatively high price of its initial models, and the company is widely admired for its innovation, design, engineering and marketing. The Model S features a lightweight aluminum body. The car can be ordered with either of two battery packs. The 70kWh battery version, called the 70D, offers all-wheel drive at a price of about $75,000. The 85 kWh model features 265-mile range and 0-60 acceleration of 5.4 seconds in the standard edition or 4.2 seconds in the performance model. Batteries come with an 8-year, 125,000-mile warranty. The Model X crossover, featuring gullwing doors, can cost more than $130,000 when fully equipped. Tesla also plans to launch a Model 3 sedan in 2017 with a base price of about $35,000, capable of traveling about 215 miles per charge. Battery-wise, each Tesla car has thousands of small, lithium-ion batteries linked together, similar to the batteries found in consumer electronics. The firm's network of convenient car charger stations, called Tesla Superchargers, can fully-charge a Tesla in 75 minutes and are located in North America, Europe and Asia. The Tesla Powerwall is an easy-to-install home-sized energy storage system intended to store local, solar-generated power for later use. The company's Gigafactory near Reno, Nevada, manufactures battery packs for the company's energy storage products and plans to do the same for its vehicles. The factory is expected to have an annual capacity equal to 35 gigawatt-hours' worth of batteries (the equivalent of generating one billion watts for a single hour). In November 2016, the firm acquired SolarCity, a solar energy provider. Later that month, the firm unveiled Solar Roof, a roofing option that is cheaper than a conventional roof per average square foot, while reducing a home's electricity bill.

FINANCIAL DATA:
Note: Data for latest year may not have been available at press time.

In U.S. $	2017	2016	2015	2014	2013	2012
Revenue	11,758,750,000	7,000,132,000	4,046,025,000	3,198,356,000	2,013,496,000	413,256,000
R&D Expense	1,378,073,000	834,408,000	717,900,000	464,700,000	231,976,000	273,978,000
Operating Income	-1,632,086,000	-667,340,000	-716,629,000	-186,689,000	-61,283,000	-394,283,000
Operating Margin %	-13.87%	-9.53%	-17.71%	-5.83%	-3.04%	-95.40%
SGA Expense	2,476,500,000	1,432,189,000	922,232,000	603,660,000	285,569,000	150,372,000
Net Income	-1,961,400,000	-674,914,000	-888,663,000	-294,040,000	-74,014,000	-396,213,000
Operating Cash Flow	-60,654,000	-123,829,000	-524,499,000	-57,337,000	257,994,000	-266,081,000
Capital Expenditure	4,081,354,000	1,440,471,000	1,634,850,000	969,885,000	264,224,000	239,228,000
EBITDA	-101,770,000	399,561,000	-334,183,000	48,181,000	67,591,000	-366,998,000
Return on Assets %	-7.64%	-4.38%	-12.74%	-7.11%	-4.19%	-43.35%
Return on Equity %	-43.63%	-23.10%	-88.83%	-37.24%	-18.69%	-227.22%
Debt to Equity	2.22	1.25	1.91	2.05	0.89	3.29

CONTACT INFORMATION:
Phone: 650 681-5000 Fax:
Toll-Free:
Address: 3500 Deer Creek, Palo Alto, CA 94304 United States

SALARIES/BONUSES:
Top Exec. Salary: $501,931 Bonus: $
Second Exec. Salary: $501,923 Bonus: $

STOCK TICKER/OTHER:
Stock Ticker: TSLA
Employees: 17,782
Parent Company:

Exchange: NAS
Fiscal Year Ends: 12/31

OTHER THOUGHTS:
Estimated Female Officers or Directors: 1
Hot Spot for Advancement for Women/Minorities:

Sales, profits and employees may be estimates. Financial information, benefits and other data can change quickly and may vary from those stated here.

Plunkett Research, Ltd.

Texas Instruments Inc (TI)
NAIC Code: 334413

www.ti.com

TYPES OF BUSINESS:
Chips-Digital Signal Processors
Semiconductors
Calculators
Educational Software
Power Management Products
Broadband RF/IF & Digital Radio
MEMS
Microcontrollers (MCU)

BRANDS/DIVISIONS/AFFILIATES:

CONTACTS:
Note: Officers with more than one job title may be intentionally listed here more than once.

Richard Templeton, CEO
Cynthia Trochu, Senior VP
Rafael Lizardi, CFO
Brian Crutcher, Executive VP
Stephen Anderson, Senior VP
R. Delagi, Senior VP
Kevin Ritchie, Senior VP
Darla Whitaker, Senior VP
Niels Anderskouv, Senior VP
Bing Xie, Senior VP
Haviv Ilan, Senior VP
Julie Van Haren, Senior VP
Ellen Barker, Senior VP

GROWTH PLANS/SPECIAL FEATURES:

Texas Instruments, Inc. (TI), founded in 1930, is a global designer and manufacturer of semiconductors with operations located in more than 30 countries, serving 90,000 customers worldwide. The firm operates in three segments: analog, embedded processing and other. Analog semiconductors change real-world signals, such as sound, temperature, pressure or images, by conditioning them, amplifying them and often converting them to a stream of digital data that can be processed by other semiconductors, such as embedded processors. Analog semiconductors are also used to manage power in every electronic device, whether plugged into a wall or running off a battery. Product lines include power supply controls, switches, interfaces, protection devices, high-voltage products, mobile lighting, display products, signal chain products, and high volume integrated analog and standard products. Embedded processors are designed to handle specific tasks and can be optimized for various combinations of performance, power and cost, depending on the application. The devices vary from simple, low-cost products used in electric toothbrushes to highly specialized, complex devices used in wireless base station communications infrastructure equipment. Products include processors, microcontrollers and connectivity. Last, the other division includes semiconductors such as the firm's proprietary DLP optical semiconductor products, which enable clear video and microprocessors that serve as the brains of everything from high-end computer servers to high definition televisions (HDTVs). This segment also includes educational products, such as handheld graphing calculators, business calculators and scientific calculators as well as a wide range of advanced classroom tools and professional development resources, including educational software.

TI offers its employees medical, dental, vision and life insurance; an employee assistance program; professional financial services; and product discounts on cars, appliances and software.

FINANCIAL DATA:
Note: Data for latest year may not have been available at press time.

In U.S. $	2017	2016	2015	2014	2013	2012
Revenue	14,961,000,000	13,370,000,000	13,000,000,000	13,045,000,000	12,205,000,000	12,825,000,000
R&D Expense	1,508,000,000	1,370,000,000	1,280,000,000	1,358,000,000	1,522,000,000	1,877,000,000
Operating Income	6,470,000,000	5,103,000,000	4,532,000,000	4,226,000,000	2,984,000,000	2,687,000,000
Operating Margin %	43.24%	38.16%	34.86%	32.39%	24.44%	20.95%
SGA Expense	1,755,000,000	1,767,000,000	1,748,000,000	1,843,000,000	1,858,000,000	1,804,000,000
Net Income	3,682,000,000	3,595,000,000	2,986,000,000	2,821,000,000	2,162,000,000	1,759,000,000
Operating Cash Flow	5,363,000,000	4,614,000,000	4,268,000,000	3,892,000,000	3,384,000,000	3,414,000,000
Capital Expenditure	695,000,000	531,000,000	551,000,000	385,000,000	412,000,000	495,000,000
EBITDA	7,062,000,000	5,965,000,000	5,439,000,000	5,198,000,000	4,146,000,000	3,319,000,000
Return on Assets %	21.41%	21.73%	17.33%	15.15%	10.90%	8.52%
Return on Equity %	35.06%	34.77%	28.94%	26.20%	19.52%	15.77%
Debt to Equity	0.34	0.28	0.31	0.35	0.38	0.38

CONTACT INFORMATION:
Phone: 972 995-3773 Fax: 972 995-4360
Toll-Free: 800-336-5236
Address: 12500 TI Blvd., Dallas, TX 75266-0199 United States

SALARIES/BONUSES:
Top Exec. Salary: $1,188,004 Bonus: $
Second Exec. Salary: $870,833 Bonus: $

STOCK TICKER/OTHER:
Stock Ticker: TXN Exchange: NAS
Employees: 29,865 Fiscal Year Ends: 12/31
Parent Company:

OTHER THOUGHTS:
Estimated Female Officers or Directors: 3
Hot Spot for Advancement for Women/Minorities: Y

Sales, profits and employees may be estimates. Financial information, benefits and other data can change quickly and may vary from those stated here.

Textron Inc

www.textron.com

NAIC Code: 336411

TYPES OF BUSINESS:
Helicopters & General Aviation Aircraft Manufacturing
Aerospace
Electrical Test & Measurement Equipment
Fiber Optic Equipment
Off-Road Vehicles
Financing

BRANDS/DIVISIONS/AFFILIATES:
Bell Helicopter
Textron Systems
Textron Aviation
Textron Financial Corporation
E-Z-GO
Jacobsen
Kautex
Arctic Cat Inc

CONTACTS:
Note: Officers with more than one job title may be intentionally listed here more than once.

Scott Donnelly, CEO
Frank Connor, CFO
Mark Bamford, Chief Accounting Officer
Julie Duffy, Executive VP, Divisional
Robert Lupone, Executive VP

GROWTH PLANS/SPECIAL FEATURES:

Textron, Inc. is a global multi-industry company active in the aircraft, defense, industrial and finance industries. The company divides its operations into five segments: Bell Helicopter, Textron Systems, Textron Aviation, industrial and finance. Bell Helicopter supplies helicopters, tilt rotor aircraft and helicopter-related spare parts and services for military and commercial applications. It also offers commercially-certified helicopters to corporate; offshore petroleum exploration; utility; charter; and police, fire, rescue and emergency medical helicopter operators. Textron Systems manufactures weapons systems and surveillance and intelligence products for the defense, aerospace, homeland security and general aviation markets. It sells most of its products to U.S. government customers, but also to customers outside the U.S. through foreign military sales sponsored by the U.S. government and directly through commercial sales channels. Textron Aviation is home to the Beechcraft, Cessna and Hawker brands, which account for more than half of all general aviation aircraft flying. Its product portfolio includes five business lines: business jets, general aviation and special mission turboprop aircraft, high performance piston aircraft, military trainer and defense aircraft and a customer service organization. The industrial segment includes the business of E-Z-GO, Jacobsen, Kautex and Greenlee. These companies design, manufacture and sell diverse products such as golf carts, off-road utility vehicles, turf maintenance equipment, blow-molded fuel systems, electrical test and measurement instruments and fiber optic connectors. The finance segment consists of Textron Financial Corporation and its subsidiaries, which primarily support the company's other segments. During 2017, the firm acquired Arctic Cat, Inc., a North American manufacturer of snowmobiles and all-terrain vehicles.

Textron offers its employees medical, prescription, dental and vision coverage; flexible spending accounts; life, AD&D, business travel and disability insurance; adoption assistance; discounts on products and auto and home insurance; and educational assis

FINANCIAL DATA:
Note: Data for latest year may not have been available at press time.

In U.S. $	2017	2016	2015	2014	2013	2012
Revenue	14,129,000,000	13,710,000,000	13,340,000,000	13,775,000,000	11,972,000,000	12,022,000,000
R&D Expense						
Operating Income	997,000,000	1,095,000,000	1,057,000,000	993,000,000	715,000,000	838,000,000
Operating Margin %	7.05%	7.98%	7.92%	7.20%	5.97%	6.97%
SGA Expense	1,337,000,000	1,304,000,000	1,304,000,000	1,361,000,000	1,126,000,000	1,168,000,000
Net Income	307,000,000	962,000,000	697,000,000	600,000,000	498,000,000	589,000,000
Operating Cash Flow	953,000,000	1,012,000,000	1,090,000,000	1,208,000,000	810,000,000	927,000,000
Capital Expenditure	423,000,000	446,000,000	420,000,000	429,000,000	444,000,000	480,000,000
EBITDA	1,383,000,000	1,499,000,000	1,601,000,000	1,503,000,000	1,236,000,000	1,436,000,000
Return on Assets %	2.00%	6.39%	4.75%	4.35%	3.83%	4.42%
Return on Equity %	5.47%	18.25%	15.09%	13.86%	13.50%	20.53%
Debt to Equity	0.69	0.59	0.67	0.90	0.72	1.15

CONTACT INFORMATION:
Phone: 401 421-2800 Fax: 401 421-2878
Toll-Free:
Address: 40 Westminster St., Providence, RI 02903 United States

SALARIES/BONUSES:
Top Exec. Salary: $1,191,154 Bonus: $
Second Exec. Salary: $990,385 Bonus: $

STOCK TICKER/OTHER:
Stock Ticker: TXT   Exchange: NYS
Employees: 36,000   Fiscal Year Ends: 12/31
Parent Company:

OTHER THOUGHTS:
Estimated Female Officers or Directors: 10
Hot Spot for Advancement for Women/Minorities: Y

Sales, profits and employees may be estimates. Financial information, benefits and other data can change quickly and may vary from those stated here.

Thornton Tomasetti Inc

NAIC Code: 541330

www.thorntontomasetti.com

TYPES OF BUSINESS:
Engineering Consulting Services
Engineering
Design

BRANDS/DIVISIONS/AFFILIATES:
Weildlinger Transportation
Weildlinger Protective Design
Weildlinger Applied Sciences

CONTACTS:
Note: Officers with more than one job title may be intentionally listed here more than once.

Thomas Z. Scarangello, CEO
Raymond Daddazio, Pres.
Jim Dray, CIO

GROWTH PLANS/SPECIAL FEATURES:
Thornton Tomasetti, Inc. provides engineering design, investigation and analysis services to clients worldwide. It takes on projects of every size and level of complexity, and addresses the full life cycle of structures through its ten integrated practices. The ten services include structural engineering, construction engineering, facade engineering, sustainability, renewal, forensics, property loss consulting, Weildlinger Transportation, Weildlinger Protective Design and Weildlinger Applied Sciences. Structural engineering includes design, exploratory studies, optimization and advanced structural analysis. It seeks the best balance among the demands of form, function, sustainability, constructability, schedule and budget. Construction engineering includes construction support, field engineering, site representation, integrated modeling and structural steel connection design. Facade engineering includes consulting, construction support and specialty faÃ§ade analysis. Sustainability provides sustainable design strategies, energy analysis, building certification (including green building), existing building sustainability as well as sustainability education and training. Renewal designs repairs, renovations and alterations, and oversees those executions. Forensics delivers reports, advanced analytics, architectural forensics, deconstruction engineering, emergency response, litigation support, MEP (mechanical, electrical, plumbing) forensics and structural forensics. Property loss consulting includes investigation of damaged buildings, building code upgrade analysis, pre-loss services and post-loss services. Weildlinger Transportation provides engineering solutions including design, analysis and construction inspection for a range of transportation infrastructure. Weildlinger Protective Design offers of physical security analysis, advice and design to architects, developers and building owners. Last, Weildlinger Applied Sciences includes engineering solutions and technologies in solid and fluid dynamics, materials, acoustics, mechanics, software development and computational simulation. Thornton Tomasetti has more than 40 offices worldwide.

FINANCIAL DATA:
Note: Data for latest year may not have been available at press time.

In U.S. $	2017	2016	2015	2014	2013	2012
Revenue						
R&D Expense						
Operating Income						
Operating Margin %						
SGA Expense						
Net Income						
Operating Cash Flow						
Capital Expenditure						
EBITDA						
Return on Assets %						
Return on Equity %						
Debt to Equity						

CONTACT INFORMATION:
Phone: 917-661-7800   Fax: 917-661-7801
Toll-Free:
Address: 51 Madison Ave., New York, NY 10010 United States

STOCK TICKER/OTHER:
Stock Ticker: Private   Exchange:
Employees: 1,200   Fiscal Year Ends:
Parent Company:

SALARIES/BONUSES:
Top Exec. Salary: $ Bonus: $
Second Exec. Salary: $ Bonus: $

OTHER THOUGHTS:
Estimated Female Officers or Directors:
Hot Spot for Advancement for Women/Minorities:

Sales, profits and employees may be estimates. Financial information, benefits and other data can change quickly and may vary from those stated here.

Toshiba Corporate R&D Center

www.toshiba.co.jp/rdc/index.htm

NAIC Code: 541712

TYPES OF BUSINESS:
Research & Development
Semiconductor Processes
MEMS Applications
Biotechnology Tools
Electronic Devices
Software
Medical Devices
Speech Recognition Technology

BRANDS/DIVISIONS/AFFILIATES:
Toshiba Corporation

CONTACTS:
Note: Officers with more than one job title may be intentionally listed here more than once.
Osamu Hori, Managing Dir.

GROWTH PLANS/SPECIAL FEATURES:
Toshiba Corporate R&D Center (CRDC) manages a global network of research laboratories, test facilities and planning groups that support the ongoing commercialization of products and technologies for Toshiba Corporation, its parent company. Toshiba is a global leader in the manufacture of consumer, industrial, medical and communications electronics. CRDC has focused the bulk of its short-term research and development initiatives on digital products and electronic devices, while its scientists and engineers continue to develop a range of platform technologies, including new nanometric semiconductor processes, innovative microelectromechanical systems (MEMS) applications and chip-based biotech tools. The firm has facilities in Japan, the U.K. and China. Its research and development areas include: information and communication, comprising the development of wireless video transmission technology, transmitting full HD video from multiple surveillance cameras, and quantum key distribution speed beyond 10 megabits per second; artificial intelligence (AI) technology, comprising AI technology that contributes to safety and security in large facilities by tracking multiple people at once; and nano materials and devices, comprising a gate dielectric process technology for improving the reliability of GaN-MOSFET (gallium nitride/metal-oxide semiconductor field-effect transistor), a next-generation lithium-ion battery with new anode material, and a hydrogen sensor with rapid detection and low-power consumption for a safer hydrogen society.

FINANCIAL DATA:
Note: Data for latest year may not have been available at press time.

In U.S. $	2017	2016	2015	2014	2013	2012
Revenue						
R&D Expense						
Operating Income						
Operating Margin %						
SGA Expense						
Net Income						
Operating Cash Flow						
Capital Expenditure						
EBITDA						
Return on Assets %						
Return on Equity %						
Debt to Equity						

CONTACT INFORMATION:
Phone: 81-44-549-2056 Fax:
Toll-Free:
Address: 1 Komukai Toshiba-cho, Saiwai-ku, Kawasaki-shi, 212-8582 Japan

STOCK TICKER/OTHER:
Stock Ticker: Subsidiary
Employees: 49
Parent Company: Toshiba Corporation
Exchange:
Fiscal Year Ends: 03/31

SALARIES/BONUSES:
Top Exec. Salary: $ Bonus: $
Second Exec. Salary: $ Bonus: $

OTHER THOUGHTS:
Estimated Female Officers or Directors:
Hot Spot for Advancement for Women/Minorities:

Sales, profits and employees may be estimates. Financial information, benefits and other data can change quickly and may vary from those stated here.

Toshiba Corporation

NAIC Code: 334413

www.toshiba.co.jp

TYPES OF BUSINESS:
Memory Chip Manufacturing
Industrial Equipment
Telecommunications Equipment
Semiconductors
Nuclear Power Plant Technologies and Services
Elevators
Lighting Systems

BRANDS/DIVISIONS/AFFILIATES:
Toshiba Infrastructure Systems & Solutions Corp
Toshiba Energy Systems & Solutions Corporation
Toshiba Electronic Devices & Storage Corporation
Toshiba Digital Solutions Corporation

CONTACTS:
Note: Officers with more than one job title may be intentionally listed here more than once.

Satoshi Tsunakawa, CEO
Hisao Tanaka, Pres.
Norio Sasaki, Vice Chmn.
Hidejiro Shimomitsu, Sr. Exec. VP
Hideo Kitamura, Sr. Exec. VP
Makoto Kubo, Sr. Exec. VP
Shigenori Shiga, Chmn.

GROWTH PLANS/SPECIAL FEATURES:
Toshiba Corporation is a technology firm with a focus on infrastructure, but also has active operations in energy, electronic devices and digital solutions. These businesses are operated through four wholly-owned subsidiaries. Toshiba Infrastructure Systems & Solutions Corporation is engaged in public infrastructure, including water treatment, power transmission and distribution, disaster prevention, roads, broadcasting, air traffic control, postal services and more. This division is also active in cultivating business growth in the areas of rechargeable batteries, elevators, air conditioning, railway systems and logistics systems. Toshiba Energy Systems & Solutions Corporation offers services associated with thermal and hydro power generation, as well as power transmission and distribution. It promotes the technical development of hydrogen energy, which is seen as a next-generation energy source. Toshiba Electronic Devices & Storage Corporation manufactures and sells industrial semiconductors and hard disk drives (HDDs). It continually seeks to expand its business through enhanced cooperation with customers in the areas of Internet of Things (IoT) and in-vehicle systems. Last, Toshiba Digital Solutions Corporation is focused on system integration for public offices and manufacturing infrastructures, as well as the development digital services in regard to IoT and artificial intelligence (AI). In March 2017, the firm announced a $6.3 billion write down on the value of its nuclear reactor unit, which was encountering significant problems with new power plant installations. That October, the nuclear energy systems division was merged into Toshiba Energy.

FINANCIAL DATA:
Note: Data for latest year may not have been available at press time.

In U.S. $	2017	2016	2015	2014	2013	2012
Revenue	45,377,060,000	52,810,580,000	62,007,590,000	60,459,310,000	54,977,350,000	57,546,170,000
R&D Expense						
Operating Income	2,680,287,000	-3,854,723,000	1,587,842,000	2,395,435,000	2,751,109,000	2,640,144,000
Operating Margin %	5.90%	-7.29%	2.56%	3.96%	5.00%	4.58%
SGA Expense	9,377,223,000	11,819,940,000	13,102,540,000	12,733,270,000	11,380,200,000	11,738,910,000
Net Income	-8,996,302,000	-4,285,570,000	-352,385,000	561,207,400	722,312,300	686,649,900
Operating Cash Flow	1,249,888,000	-11,458,920	3,078,461,000	2,647,028,000	1,232,681,000	3,120,896,000
Capital Expenditure	1,683,762,000	2,715,344,000	2,681,982,000	2,346,739,000	2,759,558,000	2,717,841,000
EBITDA	3,771,977,000	-3,712,717,000	3,275,256,000	3,613,080,000	3,782,346,000	4,017,049,000
Return on Assets %	-19.90%	-7.81%	-.60%	.98%	1.30%	1.32%
Return on Equity %		-65.11%	-3.58%	5.84%	8.15%	8.49%
Debt to Equity		2.52	0.96	1.15	1.00	1.04

CONTACT INFORMATION:
Phone: 81 334572096   Fax: 81 354449202
Toll-Free:
Address: 1-1, Shibaura 1-chome, Minato-ku, Tokyo, 105-8001 Japan

STOCK TICKER/OTHER:
Stock Ticker: TOSBF
Employees: 210,000
Parent Company:

Exchange: PINX
Fiscal Year Ends: 03/31

SALARIES/BONUSES:
Top Exec. Salary: $ Bonus: $
Second Exec. Salary: $ Bonus: $

OTHER THOUGHTS:
Estimated Female Officers or Directors:
Hot Spot for Advancement for Women/Minorities:

Sales, profits and employees may be estimates. Financial information, benefits and other data can change quickly and may vary from those stated here.

Total SA

www.total.com

NAIC Code: 211111

TYPES OF BUSINESS:
Oil & Gas Exploration & Production
Petrochemicals
Specialty Chemicals
Hydrocarbons
Service Stations
Photovoltaic Cells

BRANDS/DIVISIONS/AFFILIATES:
GreenFlex
Maersk Oil

CONTACTS: Note: Officers with more than one job title may be intentionally listed here more than once.
Patrick Pouyanne, CEO
Arnaud Breuillac, Pres.-Exploration & Production
Patrick de la Chevardiere, CFO
Nomar Nguer, Pres., Mktg. & Svcs.
Namita Shah, Pres.-People & Social Responsibility
Yves-Louis Darricarrere, Pres., Exploration & Prod.
Jean-Jacques Guilbaud, Chief Admin. Officer
Patrick Pouyanne, Pres., Refining Chemicals

GROWTH PLANS/SPECIAL FEATURES:

Total SA is one of the world's largest energy companies, with operations in more than 130 countries. The firm's activities are divided into three segments: upstream, refining and chemicals, and marketing and services. The upstream sector handles oil and gas exploration, development and production. Total produces 2.5 million barrels of oil (BOE) per day. The company has exploration and production activities in more than 50 countries. The refining and chemicals division prepares petrochemicals and fertilizers for the industrial/commercial markets; it is also involved in rubber processing, resins, adhesives and electroplating. The company is focusing on high-growth zones (such as Africa, the Mediterranean Basin and Asia) as well as specialty products such as liquefied petroleum gas (LPG), aviation fuel, lubricants, waxes, bitumens and solvents. The marketing and services segment consists of the company's services station, general fuel trade and solar and bio energy businesses. Total's worldwide service stations serve more than 4 million customers every day. During 2017, the firm sold its Martin Linge field interest; acquired Engie's upstream liquefied natural gas (LNG) business; sold its fuel marketing activities in Italy; entered the petroleum product retail sector in Mexico; acquired GreenFlex, expanding its energy efficiency business; sold its remaining 15% interest in Gina Krog Field in Norway; and acquired Maersk Oil, the oil and gas division of AP Moller-Maersk, for $7.45 billion.

FINANCIAL DATA: Note: Data for latest year may not have been available at press time.

In U.S. $	2017	2016	2015	2014	2013	2012
Revenue	149,099,000,000	127,925,000,000	143,421,000,000	212,018,000,000	237,033,600,000	241,091,600,000
R&D Expense						
Operating Income	7,019,000,000	5,115,000,000	26,707,000,000	36,626,000,000	24,210,830,000	28,046,390,000
Operating Margin %	4.70%	3.99%	18.62%	17.27%	10.21%	11.63%
SGA Expense						
Net Income	8,631,000,000	6,196,000,000	5,087,000,000	4,244,000,000	11,654,560,000	14,142,880,000
Operating Cash Flow	22,319,000,000	16,521,000,000	19,946,000,000	25,608,000,000	29,651,470,000	29,706,140,000
Capital Expenditure	13,767,000,000	18,106,000,000	25,132,000,000	26,320,000,000	30,931,540,000	26,324,490,000
EBITDA	28,875,000,000	22,230,000,000	26,740,000,000	34,123,000,000	41,757,570,000	46,037,770,000
Return on Assets %	3.64%	2.72%	2.23%	1.80%	4.99%	6.43%
Return on Equity %	8.21%	6.48%	5.56%	4.45%	11.84%	15.32%
Debt to Equity	0.37	0.43	0.48	0.50	0.34	0.30

CONTACT INFORMATION:
Phone: 33 147444546   Fax: 33 147444944
Toll-Free:
Address: 2 Place Jean Miller, La Defense 6, Paris, 92400 France

STOCK TICKER/OTHER:
Stock Ticker: TOT
Employees: 98,277
Parent Company:

Exchange: NYS
Fiscal Year Ends: 12/31

SALARIES/BONUSES:
Top Exec. Salary: $1,728,865   Bonus: $2,888,933
Second Exec. Salary: $ Bonus: $

OTHER THOUGHTS:
Estimated Female Officers or Directors: 4
Hot Spot for Advancement for Women/Minorities: Y

Sales, profits and employees may be estimates. Financial information, benefits and other data can change quickly and may vary from those stated here.

Toyoda Gosei Co Ltd

NAIC Code: 336300

www.toyoda-gosei.com

TYPES OF BUSINESS:
Automotive Components
LEDs & Optoelectronics
Consumer Products
Airbags

BRANDS/DIVISIONS/AFFILIATES:
Toyota Group

CONTACTS:
Note: Officers with more than one job title may be intentionally listed here more than once.

Naoki Miyazaki, Pres.
Nobuo Fujiwara, Sr. Managing Dir.
Tetsumi Ichioka, Pres., Europe
Kyoji Ikki, Pres., Asia
Toru Koyama, Pres., North America

GROWTH PLANS/SPECIAL FEATURES:

Toyoda Gosei Co., Ltd., a member of the Toyota Group, produces and distributes automotive components. The company has approximately 67 consolidated subsidiaries operating in 18 nations and regions around the world. Toyoda's automotive business operates in four segments: interior and exterior parts, automotive sealing products, functional components and safety system products. The interior and exterior parts division produces instrument panel modules and components, such as integrated center clusters, registers, cup holders, audio covers and glove compartments; interior parts, such as assist grips, front pillar garnishes and lighting illumination scuff plates; exterior parts, such as radiator grilles, side protection molding, roof spoilers, hybrid wheels, mud guards and wheel caps; applied LED products; and automobile accessories, such as console boxes, blue light grilles and front bumper spoilers. The automotive sealing products division primarily makes weather stripping rubber products which are attached to door or window frames to keep out rain, wind and noise. The functional components division develops fuel tanks and components; power train parts (such as water and air hoses), cylinder head covers and insulation plates for hybrid cars; and chassis and drive-train parts, including brake hoses, piston cups, pinion boots and dust covers. The safety system products division makes steering wheels and airbags. Toyoda Gosei also produces optoelectronic products and general industry products. In the optoelectronic products division, the firm offers LED lighting and LED lamps/chips. The company also produces a variety of other consumer products, including communications equipment components, air-conditioning products, home-related components and construction and production machinery components. The firm also engages in partnership agreements with various worldwide companies for the development, manufacturing and distribution of LED products.

FINANCIAL DATA:
Note: Data for latest year may not have been available at press time.

In U.S. $	2017	2016	2015	2014	2013	2012
Revenue	7,039,324,000	7,284,200,000	6,780,753,000	6,423,300,000	5,586,128,000	4,700,187,000
R&D Expense						
Operating Income	630,082,000	666,592,200	631,563,300	646,133,800	545,668,000	370,700,600
Operating Margin %	8.95%	9.15%	9.31%	10.05%	9.76%	7.88%
SGA Expense	54,937,580	57,881,500	44,671,140	42,146,460	38,988,260	33,761,880
Net Income	151,229,700	188,699,500	197,084,000	244,214,700	199,636,700	83,575,560
Operating Cash Flow	562,707,300	724,473,700	477,762,300	516,564,200	488,643,600	476,169,200
Capital Expenditure	512,427,800	524,557,500	558,785,200	416,648,100	358,077,200	372,004,900
EBITDA	687,581,500	774,939,500	753,130,200	803,400,500	709,586,400	578,088,300
Return on Assets %	2.68%	3.38%	3.67%	5.08%	4.53%	2.05%
Return on Equity %	5.24%	6.55%	7.12%	9.82%	9.01%	4.07%
Debt to Equity	0.18	0.14	0.13	0.11	0.09	0.15

CONTACT INFORMATION:
Phone: 81 524005131   Fax:
Toll-Free:
Address: 1 Haruhinagahata Kiyosu, Kiyosu, 452-8564 Japan

STOCK TICKER/OTHER:
Stock Ticker: TGOSY
Employees: 25,792
Parent Company: Toyota Group

Exchange: PINX
Fiscal Year Ends: 03/31

SALARIES/BONUSES:
Top Exec. Salary: $ Bonus: $
Second Exec. Salary: $ Bonus: $

OTHER THOUGHTS:
Estimated Female Officers or Directors:
Hot Spot for Advancement for Women/Minorities:

Sales, profits and employees may be estimates. Financial information, benefits and other data can change quickly and may vary from those stated here.

Toyota Motor Corporation

www.toyota.co.jp

NAIC Code: 336111

TYPES OF BUSINESS:
Automobile Manufacturing
Manufactured Housing
Advertising & e-Commerce Services
Financial Services
Telecommunications Services
Information Technology
Nanotechnology Research

BRANDS/DIVISIONS/AFFILIATES:
Daihatsu Motor Co Ltd
Hino Motors Ltd
Toyota Financial Services Corporation
Toyota Motor Credit Corporation
Toyota Research Institute Inc
Toyota
Lexus
Hino

CONTACTS:
Note: Officers with more than one job title may be intentionally listed here more than once.

Akio Toyoda, Pres.
Satoshi Ozawa, Exec. VP-Gen. Admin.
Mitsuhisa Kato, Exec. VP-Customer Service Oper.
Mamoru Furuhashi, CEO-Govt & Public Affairs
Satoshi Ozawa, Exec. VP-Acct.
Takeshi Uchiyamada, Chmn.
Satoshi Ozawa, Exec VP-European Oper.

GROWTH PLANS/SPECIAL FEATURES:
Toyota Motor Corporation designs, manufactures, assembles and sells passenger cars, minivans, commercial vehicles and related parts and accessories in 190 countries under the Toyota, Lexus, Daihatsu and Hino brands. The firm operates in three segments: automotive, financial and other. Its primary automotive markets are Japan, which generates approximately 25.4% of fiscal 2017 sales; North America, 31.6%; Asia, 17.7%; Europe, 10.3%; and other countries generate the remainder. Toyota produces both conventional engine vehicles and hybrid vehicles, with automobile types including subcompact and compact cars; mini-vehicles; mid-size, luxury, sports and specialty cars; recreational and sport-utility vehicles; pickup trucks; minivans; and buses. Wholly-owned subsidiary Daihatsu Motor Co. Ltd. produces and sells mini-vehicles and compact cars. Hino Motors Ltd. produces and sells commercial vehicles such as trucks and buses. Toyota produces automobiles and related components through over 50 manufacturing companies in 28 countries. Nearly 60% of the firm's vehicles sold in North America are produced in North America, and 76% of its vehicles sold in Europe are produced in Europe. The company offers financial services in 35 countries through subsidiary Toyota Financial Services Corporation, and in the U.S. through subsidiary Toyota Motor Credit Corporation. The company's Toyota Research Institute, Inc. is research and development enterprise with a focus on artificial intelligence technology and robotics. In 2017, the firm announced it will cease manufacturing vehicles and engines in Australia by year's end. In January 2018, Toyota announced its first-ever integration of smartphone control (currently only available for Apple phones with Apple Carplay) and smartwatch controllers with Amazon Alexa in the Avalon model.

FINANCIAL DATA:
Note: Data for latest year may not have been available at press time.

In U.S. $	2017	2016	2015	2014	2013	2012
Revenue	257,100,700,000	264,608,900,000	253,722,000,000	239,350,800,000	205,554,300,000	173,128,900,000
R&D Expense						
Operating Income	18,579,950,000	26,588,140,000	25,624,780,000	21,353,750,000	12,305,650,000	3,313,090,000
Operating Margin %	7.22%	10.04%	10.09%	8.92%	5.98%	1.91%
SGA Expense	26,723,360,000	27,423,910,000	24,616,000,000	24,209,610,000	19,585,520,000	17,136,780,000
Net Income	17,058,960,000	21,545,500,000	20,247,230,000	16,984,530,000	8,963,695,000	2,641,690,000
Operating Cash Flow	31,807,690,000	41,558,200,000	34,337,180,000	33,967,160,000	22,836,930,000	13,531,160,000
Capital Expenditure	32,992,710,000	37,816,430,000	31,279,750,000	24,955,200,000	18,391,580,000	14,273,170,000
EBITDA	35,719,480,000	43,270,180,000	40,290,430,000	34,577,630,000	23,586,040,000	14,194,380,000
Return on Assets %	3.78%	4.84%	4.87%	4.74%	2.90%	.93%
Return on Equity %	10.63%	13.75%	13.90%	13.69%	8.47%	2.71%
Debt to Equity	0.56	0.58	0.59	0.59	0.60	0.57

CONTACT INFORMATION:
Phone: 81 565282121   Fax: 81 565235800
Toll-Free:
Address: 1 Toyota-Cho, Toyota City, Toyota, Aichi Prefecture 471-8571 Japan

STOCK TICKER/OTHER:
Stock Ticker: TM
Employees: 364,445
Parent Company:

Exchange: NYS
Fiscal Year Ends: 03/31

SALARIES/BONUSES:
Top Exec. Salary: $1,993,665   Bonus: $4,359,978
Second Exec. Salary: $931,619   Bonus: $2,058,878

OTHER THOUGHTS:
Estimated Female Officers or Directors:
Hot Spot for Advancement for Women/Minorities:

Sales, profits and employees may be estimates. Financial information, benefits and other data can change quickly and may vary from those stated here.

TPV Technology Limited

NAIC Code: 334118

www.tpvholdings.com

TYPES OF BUSINESS:
Monitors, Computer Peripheral Equipment, Manufacturing
LCD Television Manufacturing

BRANDS/DIVISIONS/AFFILIATES:
Top Victory Investments Ltd
Envision Peripherals Inc
P-Harmony Monitors Hong Kong Holding Ltd
MMD-Monitors & Displays Holding Ltd
TP Vision
Envision
AOC

GROWTH PLANS/SPECIAL FEATURES:
TPV Technology Limited is a leading contract manufacturer of television and computer display monitors. The firm targets both the PC and TV markets on an original design manufacturer (ODM) basis. Products include CRT (cathode ray tube) PC monitors, TFT (thin-film transistor)-LCD monitors and LCD TVs, which generate the vast majority of the firm's revenue. The company also sells its own CRT monitors in over 30 countries worldwide under the Envision brand name as well as both CRT and LCD monitors under the AOC (Admiral Overseas Corporation) brand name. It is incorporated in Bermuda, but conducts its manufacturing operations in China, Brazil, Poland and Russia, and sells its products worldwide. Major subsidiaries include Top Victory Investments, Ltd.; Envision Peripherals, Inc.; P-Harmony Monitors Hong Kong Holding, Ltd.; MMD-Monitors & Displays Holding, Ltd.; and TP Vision.

CONTACTS:
Note: Officers with more than one job title may be intentionally listed here more than once.

Jason Hsuan, CEO
Shane Tyau, CFO
Lu Being-Chang, Sr. VP-R&D
Chen Nai-Yung, CIO
Lee Neng-Sung, CTO
Houng Yu-Te, Sr. VP-Admin.
Houng Yu-Te, Sr. VP-Finance
Jason Hsuan, Chmn.
Hsieh Chi Tsung, Sr. VP-Procurement

FINANCIAL DATA:
Note: Data for latest year may not have been available at press time.

In U.S. $	2017	2016	2015	2014	2013	2012
Revenue	9,600,000,000	9,808,336,896	11,061,525,504	11,681,427,456	11,972,698,112	11,974,836,224
R&D Expense						
Operating Income						
Operating Margin %						
SGA Expense						
Net Income		38,523,000	-31,337,000	41,808,000	-140,588,992	83,384,000
Operating Cash Flow						
Capital Expenditure						
EBITDA						
Return on Assets %						
Return on Equity %						
Debt to Equity						

CONTACT INFORMATION:
Phone: 852-2858-5736   Fax: 852-2546-8884
Toll-Free:
Address: Units 1208-16, 12/Fl, 108 Wai Yip St., Kwun Tong, Kowloon, Hong Kong

STOCK TICKER/OTHER:
Stock Ticker: TPVTF   Exchange: GREY
Employees: 30,129   Fiscal Year Ends: 12/31
Parent Company:

SALARIES/BONUSES:
Top Exec. Salary: $ Bonus: $
Second Exec. Salary: $ Bonus: $

OTHER THOUGHTS:
Estimated Female Officers or Directors: 1
Hot Spot for Advancement for Women/Minorities:

TRC Companies Inc

www.trcsolutions.com

NAIC Code: 541330

TYPES OF BUSINESS:
Engineering Services
Financial Risk Management
Technical Services
Environmental Engineering
Energy Services
Security Services
Hazardous Waste Disposal
Construction

BRANDS/DIVISIONS/AFFILIATES:
American Environmental Consultants Inc

CONTACTS:
Note: Officers with more than one job title may be intentionally listed here more than once.

Christopher Vincze, CEO
Thomas Bennet, CFO
James Mayer, Other Corporate Officer
John Cowdery, Other Corporate Officer
Martin Dodd, Senior VP

GROWTH PLANS/SPECIAL FEATURES:
TRC Companies, Inc. is a national consulting, engineering and construction management firm. TRC's services are focused on four principal market areas: energy, environmental, infrastructure and pipeline. The energy segment serves key areas within the energy market, offering support in the licensing and engineering design of new sources of power generation and electric transmission and distribution system upgrades. This division is also engaged in green building design and the development of codes, standards and policy. The environmental segment is TRC's largest operation, and is a market leader in the areas of air quality modeling, air emissions testing and monitoring, cultural and natural resource management, permitting of energy and energy-related facilities and remediation of contaminated sites. The infrastructure segment offers a variety of services to infrastructure clients related to: rehabilitation of overburdened and deteriorating infrastructure systems; and design, construction engineering inspection and construction management associated with new infrastructure projects. This division offers transportation services, general civil engineering, structural engineering, inspection, hydraulic/hydrological studies, geographic information systems, and surveying and mapping services. Last, the pipeline segment provides engineering, procurement, EPC (engineering, procurement and construction) services, project management, integrity and field services to the oil and gas and electric utility industries. TRC provides services through a network of approximately 130 offices nationwide, including California, Massachusetts, New Jersey, New York, Connecticut, Maine, Wisconsin, South Carolina and Oklahoma. In early-2018, the company acquired American Environmental Consultants, Inc., a hazardous materials assessment company based in Massachusetts.

FINANCIAL DATA:
Note: Data for latest year may not have been available at press time.

In U.S. $	2017	2016	2015	2014	2013	2012
Revenue		481,299,008	414,648,000	372,881,984	325,156,000	302,688,992
R&D Expense						
Operating Income						
Operating Margin %						
SGA Expense						
Net Income		41,000	19,415,000	12,051,000	36,275,000	33,575,000
Operating Cash Flow						
Capital Expenditure						
EBITDA						
Return on Assets %						
Return on Equity %						
Debt to Equity						

CONTACT INFORMATION:
Phone: 860 298-9692   Fax: 860 298-6291
Toll-Free:
Address: 21 Griffin Rd. N., Windsor, CT 06095 United States

STOCK TICKER/OTHER:
Stock Ticker: Private
Employees: 3,700
Parent Company: Mountain Partners IV

Exchange:
Fiscal Year Ends: 06/30

SALARIES/BONUSES:
Top Exec. Salary: $ Bonus: $
Second Exec. Salary: $ Bonus: $

OTHER THOUGHTS:
Estimated Female Officers or Directors: 2
Hot Spot for Advancement for Women/Minorities:

Trevi-Finanziaria Industriale SpA (Trevi Group)

www.trevigroup.com
NAIC Code: 541330

TYPES OF BUSINESS:
Engineering & Construction Services
Underground Construction Services
Foundation & Drilling Machinery & Services
Wind Farms
Geothermal Energy Projects

BRANDS/DIVISIONS/AFFILIATES:
Solimec SpA
Drillmec Inc
Petreven SpA

CONTACTS:
Note: Officers with more than one job title may be intentionally listed here more than once.

Davide Trevisani, Pres.
Franco Cicognani, Head-Corp. Comm. Dept.
Stefano Trevisani, Managing Dir.
Cesare Trevisani, Managing Dir.

GROWTH PLANS/SPECIAL FEATURES:

Trevi-Finanziaria Industriale SpA (Trevi Group) is a global leader in subsoil engineering for special foundations, tunnel excavations, soil consolidation, production and marketing of machinery and specialized equipment. The firm also operates in the drilling sector, both as a plant manufacturer and as a supplier of oil drilling services; and in the construction of automated underground car parks and integrated parking management systems. Trevi Group specializes in dams, maritime works, routes of communication, industrial/civil construction, restoration, research on hydrocarbons and gases, environment, automated parking lots and water search. In business for more than 60, years, Trevi Group comprises more than 40 companies across 55 locations in 32 different countries. Subsidiary Soilmec SpA produces plants and machinery used for the engineering of subsoil; Drillmec, Inc. produces mechanical systems, innovative hydraulic systems and related accessories for oil, geothermal and water drilling; and Petreven SpA is engaged in the development and new technology of hydraulic systems produced by Drillmec. Approximately 28% of the Trevi Group's revenue is derived from Asia; 24% from Latin America; 22% from Africa; 10% from the U.S. and Canada; 5% from Europe; 5% from Italy; and 6% from the rest of the world.

FINANCIAL DATA:
Note: Data for latest year may not have been available at press time.

In U.S. $	2017	2016	2015	2014	2013	2012
Revenue		1,276,194,000	1,600,385,000	1,495,463,000	1,536,164,000	1,339,376,000
R&D Expense						
Operating Income		-49,018,250	-112,589,800	77,277,780	99,175,090	77,891,530
Operating Margin %		-3.84%	-7.03%	5.16%	6.45%	5.81%
SGA Expense						
Net Income		-106,695,600	-142,244,800	30,150,160	16,995,970	13,340,660
Operating Cash Flow		-11,461,140	11,158,590	-35,441,720	107,504,500	82,258,140
Capital Expenditure						
EBITDA		8,781,398	-54,416,020	147,711,700	167,299,800	126,872,700
Return on Assets %		-4.73%	-6.07%	1.42%	.90%	.71%
Return on Equity %		-16.65%	-18.98%	4.63%	3.33%	2.55%
Debt to Equity		0.21	0.68	0.40	0.52	0.57

CONTACT INFORMATION:
Phone: 39 547319111 Fax: 39 547319313
Toll-Free:
Address: 201 Via Larga, Cesena, FO 47522 Italy

STOCK TICKER/OTHER:
Stock Ticker: TVFZF   Exchange: GREY
Employees: 7,237   Fiscal Year Ends: 12/31
Parent Company:

SALARIES/BONUSES:
Top Exec. Salary: $ Bonus: $
Second Exec. Salary: $ Bonus: $

OTHER THOUGHTS:
Estimated Female Officers or Directors: 1
Hot Spot for Advancement for Women/Minorities:

Sales, profits and employees may be estimates. Financial information, benefits and other data can change quickly and may vary from those stated here.

Tutor Perini Corporation

NAIC Code: 237310

www.tutorperini.com

TYPES OF BUSINESS:
Construction Services
Hospitality & Casino Construction
Construction Management Services
Civic & Infrastructure Construction
Design Services

BRANDS/DIVISIONS/AFFILIATES:

CONTACTS: Note: Officers with more than one job title may be intentionally listed here more than once.
Leonard Rejcek, CEO, Divisional
Ronald Tutor, CEO
Gary Smalley, Chief Accounting Officer
James Frost, COO
Michael Klein, Director
John Barrett, Secretary

GROWTH PLANS/SPECIAL FEATURES:

Tutor Perini Corporation and its subsidiaries provide general contracting, construction management and design-build services worldwide. It operates in three segments: building, civil and specialty contractors. The building segment focuses on large, complex projects in the hospitality and gaming, transportation, healthcare, municipal offices, sports and entertainment, education, correctional facilities, biotech, pharmaceutical, industrial and high-tech markets. The civil segment focuses on public works construction, including the new construction, repair, replacement and reconstruction of public infrastructure such as highways, bridges, mass transit systems and wastewater treatment facilities. The company's customers primarily award contracts through the public competitive bid, in which price is the major determining factor; or through a request for proposals, where contracts are awarded based on a combination of technical capability and price. The specialty contractors segment engages in electrical, mechanical, HVAC (heating, ventilation and air conditioning), plumbing and pneumatically paced concrete for construction projects in the commercial, industrial, hospitality, transportation and gaming markets.

The firm offers employees medical, dental, vision and life insurance; a flexible spending account; an employee assistance program; educational assistance; and reimbursement on health club memberships.

FINANCIAL DATA: Note: Data for latest year may not have been available at press time.

In U.S. $	2017	2016	2015	2014	2013	2012
Revenue	4,757,208,000	4,973,076,000	4,920,472,000	4,492,309,000	4,175,672,000	4,111,471,000
R&D Expense						
Operating Income	179,477,000	201,920,000	105,413,000	241,690,000	203,822,000	154,763,000
Operating Margin %	3.77%	4.06%	2.14%	5.38%	4.88%	3.76%
SGA Expense	274,928,000	255,270,000	250,840,000	263,752,000	263,082,000	260,369,000
Net Income	148,382,000	95,822,000	45,292,000	107,936,000	87,296,000	-265,400,000
Operating Cash Flow	163,550,000	113,336,000	14,072,000	-56,678,000	50,728,000	-67,863,000
Capital Expenditure	30,280,000	15,743,000	35,912,000	75,013,000	42,360,000	41,352,000
EBITDA	275,289,000	276,199,000	161,595,000	288,126,000	244,657,000	-162,211,000
Return on Assets %	3.57%	2.37%	1.15%	3.01%	2.60%	-7.68%
Return on Equity %	9.08%	6.44%	3.25%	8.26%	7.30%	-20.86%
Debt to Equity	0.41	0.43	0.51	0.57	0.49	0.58

CONTACT INFORMATION:
Phone: 818 362-8391 Fax:
Toll-Free:
Address: 15901 Olden St., Sylmar, CA 91342 United States

STOCK TICKER/OTHER:
Stock Ticker: TPC
Employees: 11,603
Parent Company:

Exchange: NYS
Fiscal Year Ends: 12/31

SALARIES/BONUSES:
Top Exec. Salary: $1,750,000 Bonus: $
Second Exec. Salary: $1,000,000 Bonus: $250,000

OTHER THOUGHTS:
Estimated Female Officers or Directors:
Hot Spot for Advancement for Women/Minorities:

Sales, profits and employees may be estimates. Financial information, benefits and other data can change quickly and may vary from those stated here.

UCB SA

NAIC Code: 325412

www.ucb-group.com

TYPES OF BUSINESS:
Pharmaceuticals Development
Industrial Chemical Products
Allergy & Respiratory Treatments
Central Nervous System Disorder Treatments

BRANDS/DIVISIONS/AFFILIATES:
Cimzia
Briviact
Keppra
Vimpat
Neupro
Nootropil
Xyrem
Element Genomics

CONTACTS:
Note: Officers with more than one job title may be intentionally listed here more than once.

Jean-Christophe Tellier, CEO
Charl van Zyl, COO
Detlef Thielgen, CFO
Bharat Tewarie, CMO
Jean-Luc Fleurial, Chief Talent Officer
Iris Low-Friedrich, Chief Medical Officer
Dhavalkumar Patel, Chief Scientific Officer
Anna S. Richo, General Counsel
Iris Low-Friedrich, Exec. VP-Dev. & Global Projects
Fabrice Enderlin, Exec. VP-Corp. Comm.
Jean-Christophe Tellier, Exec. VP-Brands & Solutions
Ismail Kola, Exec. VP
Mark McDade, Exec. VP-Supply, Established Brands & Solutions

GROWTH PLANS/SPECIAL FEATURES:

UCB SA is a Belgian biopharmaceutical firm with operations in more than 40 countries. The firm's main products are focused within the fields of immunology and neurology. UCB's immunology product is used to treat rheumatoid arthritis, osteoporosis, axial spondyloarthritis, psoriatic arthritis, Chrohn's disease, Lupus, psoriasis and juvenile idiopathic arthritis. Cimzia is this division's primary biopharmaceutical product. Its neurology products are used to treat epilepsy, Parkinson's disease and Restless Legs Syndrome. This division's biopharmaceutical products include: Briviact, for epilepsy; Keppra, for epilepsy; Vimpat, for epilepsy; and Neupro, for both Parkinson's disease and Restless Legs Syndrom. Other products include Nootropil, for memory; Xyrem, for narcolepsy; Xyzal, for allergies; and Zyrtec, for allergies. UCB has two research centers located in Slough, U.K. and Braine-l'Alleud, Belgium; as well as two biotech plants located in Belgium and Switzerland. Geographical net sales during 2017 include 50% from the U.S., 31% from Europe, and 19% from international markets, with 52% deriving from neurologic therapeutic areas, 34% from immunologic therapeutic areas and 14% from established brands. In April 2018, UCB acquired Element Genomics, a small-size biotech spin-off from Duke University, based in Durham, North Carolina. Element Genomics' platform is a suite of technologies to improve understanding of genome structure and function.

FINANCIAL DATA:
Note: Data for latest year may not have been available at press time.

In U.S. $	2017	2016	2015	2014	2013	2012
Revenue	5,594,112,000	5,159,426,000	4,786,485,000	4,129,517,000	4,212,255,000	4,275,236,000
R&D Expense	1,305,293,000	1,259,601,000	1,280,595,000	1,145,990,000	1,057,077,000	1,099,064,000
Operating Income	1,376,917,000	1,137,346,000	787,868,400	454,444,400	574,230,100	542,122,600
Operating Margin %	24.61%	22.04%	16.46%	11.00%	13.63%	12.68%
SGA Expense	1,397,911,000	1,388,031,000	1,353,454,000	1,210,205,000	1,243,548,000	1,325,051,000
Net Income	929,882,200	642,149,800	769,344,800	258,094,800	255,625,000	316,135,300
Operating Cash Flow	1,144,755,000	527,303,700	302,551,300	632,270,500	368,001,200	438,390,700
Capital Expenditure	258,094,800	170,416,700	180,295,900	198,819,400	435,920,900	272,913,600
EBITDA	1,578,206,000	1,337,400,000	940,996,400	587,814,000	839,734,300	760,700,500
Return on Assets %	7.48%	4.91%	5.90%	2.08%	2.14%	2.76%
Return on Equity %	13.21%	9.23%	11.67%	4.35%	4.50%	5.43%
Debt to Equity	0.26	0.28	0.27	0.34	0.44	0.41

CONTACT INFORMATION:
Phone: 32-2-559-99-99   Fax: 32-2-559-99-00
Toll-Free:
Address: Allee de la Recherche, 60, Brussels, 1070 Belgium

STOCK TICKER/OTHER:
Stock Ticker: UCBJF
Employees: 7,563
Parent Company:

Exchange: PINX
Fiscal Year Ends: 12/31

SALARIES/BONUSES:
Top Exec. Salary: $ Bonus: $
Second Exec. Salary: $ Bonus: $

OTHER THOUGHTS:
Estimated Female Officers or Directors: 5
Hot Spot for Advancement for Women/Minorities: Y

Union Carbide Corporation

www.unioncarbide.com

NAIC Code: 325211

TYPES OF BUSINESS:
Basic Chemicals, Manufacturing
Polymers

BRANDS/DIVISIONS/AFFILIATES:
Dow Chemical Company (The)
Univation Technologies LLC
South Charleston Technology Park

CONTACTS: Note: Officers with more than one job title may be intentionally listed here more than once.
Richard A. Wells, CEO
James A. Varilek, Pres.
Bruce D. Fitzgerald, VP

GROWTH PLANS/SPECIAL FEATURES:
Union Carbide Corporation (UCC), a wholly-owned subsidiary of The Dow Chemical Company (DOW), manufactures basic chemicals and polymers primarily for commercial manufacturers. UCC produces ethylene from crude oil and natural gas and converts it to polyethylene or ethylene oxide, a precursor to many company products. The firm operates seven manufacturing and production sites throughout the southern U.S., where it produces a broad range of chemicals, including ethylene glycol, solvents, alcohols, surfactants, amines, specialty products, polypropylene, polyethylene, biocides, anti-icing fluids and solution vinyl resins for industrial coatings. These chemicals provide vital functions for various businesses, such as deicing airplanes, soil removal, inhibiting bacterial growth in cosmetics and coating pills to make them easier to swallow. In Virginia, the company also manages the South Charleston Technology Park, a center for engineering, research and development and integrated data processing. Customers for UCC's chemicals include companies in the paints and coatings, packaging, wire and cable, household products, personal care, pharmaceuticals, automotive, textiles, agriculture and oil and gas industries. UCC primarily sells its products to its parent company, then markets its products to customers who make everyday items such as food containers, toys, automotive antifreeze, rubbing alcohol, paper towels, cosmetics and cleaning products. Wholly-owned by DOW, Univation Technologies, LLC is a Texas, U.S. firm that develops, markets and licenses polyethylene process technology and related catalysts.

UCC offers its employees a comprehensive medical plan, life insurance, long-term care insurance, personal lines insurance, a pension plan and a 401(k) plan.

FINANCIAL DATA: Note: Data for latest year may not have been available at press time.

In U.S. $	2017	2016	2015	2014	2013	2012
Revenue	5,165,000,000	4,919,000,000	5,842,000,000	6,835,000,000	6,948,000,000	6,247,000,000
R&D Expense						
Operating Income						
Operating Margin %						
SGA Expense						
Net Income	205,000,000	89,000,000	808,000,000	587,000,000	748,000,000	-114,000,000
Operating Cash Flow						
Capital Expenditure						
EBITDA						
Return on Assets %						
Return on Equity %						
Debt to Equity						

CONTACT INFORMATION:
Phone: 281-966-2016 Fax: 281-966-2394
Toll-Free:
Address: 1254 Enclave Pkwy., Houston, TX 77077 United States

STOCK TICKER/OTHER:
Stock Ticker: Subsidiary Exchange:
Employees: 2,300 Fiscal Year Ends: 12/31
Parent Company: Dow Chemical Company (The)

SALARIES/BONUSES:
Top Exec. Salary: $ Bonus: $
Second Exec. Salary: $ Bonus: $

OTHER THOUGHTS:
Estimated Female Officers or Directors:
Hot Spot for Advancement for Women/Minorities:

Sales, profits and employees may be estimates. Financial information, benefits and other data can change quickly and may vary from those stated here.

Plunkett Research, Ltd.

Unisys Corp

NAIC Code: 541512

www.unisys.com

TYPES OF BUSINESS:
IT Consulting
Enterprise Systems & Servers
Outsourcing Services
Infrastructure Services
Security Technology
Server Software & Middleware

BRANDS/DIVISIONS/AFFILIATES:
ClearPath
Unisys Stealth

CONTACTS:
Note: Officers with more than one job title may be intentionally listed here more than once.

Peter Altabef, CEO
Michael Thomson, Chief Accounting Officer
Ann Ruckstuhl, Chief Marketing Officer
Tarek El Sadany, Chief Technology Officer
Paul Weaver, Director
Eric Hutto, President, Divisional
Jeffrey Renzi, President, Divisional
Venkatapathi Puvvada, President, Divisional
David Loeser, Senior VP, Divisional
Inder Singh, Senior VP
Gerald Kenney, Senior VP
Shalabh Gupta, Vice President

GROWTH PLANS/SPECIAL FEATURES:

Unisys Corp. is a worldwide information technology services company. The firm offers services for systems integration, outsourcing, infrastructure, server technology and consulting to commercial businesses and governments. Unisys operates in two business segments: services and technology. The services unit provides end-to-end services designed to help clients improve their competitiveness and efficiency in four main categories: systems integration and consulting, outsourcing, infrastructure services and core maintenance. Systems integration and consulting services include check processing systems, public welfare systems, airline reservations and messaging technology. Outsourcing services provide for the management of a customer's internal information systems and its specific business processes, such as insurance claims processing, mortgage administration and cargo management. Infrastructure services involve the design, warranty and support of customers' IT infrastructure and enterprise-wide network and devices. Core maintenance services include the maintenance of Unisys proprietary products and those of third party technology providers. In the technology segment, the company designs and develops servers and related products. Major technology offerings include enterprise-class servers based on Cellular Multi-Processing architecture, such as the ClearPath family of servers and the Unisys Stealth family of security software. Primary markets served by Unisys include the financial services, communications, transportation, commercial and public sectors. The firm owns over 827 active U.S. patents and over 90 active patents granted outside the U.S. Unisys maintains working partnerships with leading technology companies, including Dell, Intel, Microsoft and Oracle, among others.

The firm offers employees health services, recreational facilities and employee discounts.

FINANCIAL DATA:
Note: Data for latest year may not have been available at press time.

In U.S. $	2017	2016	2015	2014	2013	2012
Revenue	2,741,800,000	2,820,700,000	3,015,100,000	3,356,400,000	3,456,500,000	3,706,400,000
R&D Expense	47,200,000	55,400,000	76,400,000	68,800,000	69,500,000	81,500,000
Operating Income	4,600,000	47,600,000	-55,100,000	154,900,000	219,500,000	319,200,000
Operating Margin %	.16%	1.68%	-1.82%	4.61%	6.35%	8.61%
SGA Expense	426,500,000	455,600,000	519,600,000	554,100,000	559,400,000	572,800,000
Net Income	-65,300,000	-47,700,000	-109,900,000	46,700,000	108,500,000	145,600,000
Operating Cash Flow	166,400,000	218,200,000	1,200,000	121,400,000	187,400,000	261,300,000
Capital Expenditure	176,500,000	147,100,000	213,700,000	212,800,000	151,400,000	132,600,000
EBITDA	137,200,000	203,500,000	133,200,000	323,300,000	388,900,000	456,200,000
Return on Assets %	-2.86%	-2.29%	-4.89%	1.81%	3.74%	5.14%
Return on Equity %						
Debt to Equity						

CONTACT INFORMATION:
Phone: 215 986-4011 Fax: 215 986-6850
Toll-Free: 800-874-8647
Address: Unisys Way, Blue Bell, PA 19424 United States

SALARIES/BONUSES:
Top Exec. Salary: $991,000 Bonus: $
Second Exec. Salary: $575,000 Bonus: $40,000

STOCK TICKER/OTHER:
Stock Ticker: UIS Exchange: NYS
Employees: 21,000 Fiscal Year Ends: 12/31
Parent Company:

OTHER THOUGHTS:
Estimated Female Officers or Directors: 2
Hot Spot for Advancement for Women/Minorities: Y

Sales, profits and employees may be estimates. Financial information, benefits and other data can change quickly and may vary from those stated here.

United Microelectronics Corp

www.umc.com

NAIC Code: 334413

TYPES OF BUSINESS:
Chips/Semiconductors

BRANDS/DIVISIONS/AFFILIATES:

CONTACTS: Note: Officers with more than one job title may be intentionally listed here more than once.
SC Chien, Pres.
Jason Wang, Pres.
Peter Courture, General Counsel
Stan Hung, Chmn.

GROWTH PLANS/SPECIAL FEATURES:

United Microelectronics Corp. (UMC), based in Taiwan, is one of the world's largest semiconductor foundries, providing comprehensive wafer fabrication services and technologies to customers based on their designs. The company has 11 manufacturing facilities in Taiwan and Singapore. It works closely with customers through each of the five steps required to produce viable products: circuit design, mask tooling, wafer fabrication, assembly and testing. At the initial step, circuit design, UMC's engineers work with clients to ensure their designs can be manufactured successfully and cost effectively in the company's facilities. During the mask tooling process, its engineers assist in the design or purchase of masks that work best with UMC's equipment. During the wafer fabrication stage, a photosensitive material is deposited on the wafer and exposed to light through the mask to form a transistor and other circuit elements, then tested, generally on-site to ensure quality. UMC also offers turnkey services, providing subcontracted assembly and testing services at its manufacturing facilities. Its products include a range of advanced processors, such as 28-nanometer (nm), 45/40nm, embedded memories and Mixed Signal/RF CMOS.

UMC offers its employees counseling services and the use of a recreation center at its Hsinchu headquarters, which features sports facilities, an art gallery, a performance venue and meeting spaces.

FINANCIAL DATA: Note: Data for latest year may not have been available at press time.

In U.S. $	2017	2016	2015	2014	2013	2012
Revenue		5,045,212,000	4,941,499,000	4,777,102,000	4,224,355,000	3,946,732,000
R&D Expense		461,713,300	415,395,400	466,200,600	426,253,100	333,918,900
Operating Income		229,192,800	404,100,900	362,185,600	139,430,900	119,575,200
Operating Margin %		4.54%	8.17%	7.58%	3.30%	3.02%
SGA Expense		354,511,300	265,935,800	258,402,100	235,848,100	208,823,200
Net Income		294,146,800	452,218,500	379,028,300	430,205,100	266,793,400
Operating Cash Flow		1,584,854,000	2,048,616,000	1,528,140,000	1,483,246,000	1,383,026,000
Capital Expenditure		3,177,007,000	2,101,486,000	1,514,564,000	1,221,233,000	1,806,569,000
EBITDA		1,977,354,000	2,033,881,000	1,873,719,000	1,820,909,000	1,508,019,000
Return on Assets %		2.39%	4.10%	3.67%	4.38%	2.78%
Return on Equity %		3.95%	6.03%	5.26%	6.18%	3.81%
Debt to Equity		0.28	0.21	0.15	0.13	0.15

CONTACT INFORMATION:
Phone: 886 35782258 Fax: 886 35779392
Toll-Free:
Address: 3 Li-Hsin 2nd Rd., Hsinchu Science Park, Hsinchu, Taiwan

STOCK TICKER/OTHER:
Stock Ticker: UMC
Employees: 18,458
Parent Company:

Exchange: NYS
Fiscal Year Ends: 12/31

SALARIES/BONUSES:
Top Exec. Salary: $ Bonus: $
Second Exec. Salary: $ Bonus: $

OTHER THOUGHTS:
Estimated Female Officers or Directors:
Hot Spot for Advancement for Women/Minorities:

United Technologies Corporation

NAIC Code: 336412

www.utc.com

TYPES OF BUSINESS:
Aircraft Engine and Engine Parts Manufacturing
Elevator & Escalator Systems
HVAC Systems
Aircraft Parts & Maintenance

BRANDS/DIVISIONS/AFFILIATES:
Otis
Pratt & Whitney

CONTACTS:
Note: Officers with more than one job title may be intentionally listed here more than once.

Gregory Hayes, CEO
Akhil Johri, CFO
Robert Bailey, Chief Accounting Officer
Michael Dumais, Executive VP, Divisional
Charles Gill, Executive VP
Elizabeth Amato, Executive VP
David Gitlin, President, Divisional
Robert Mcdonough, President, Divisional
Robert Leduc, President, Divisional
Judith Marks, President, Divisional
David Whitehouse, Vice President

GROWTH PLANS/SPECIAL FEATURES:

United Technologies Corporation (UTC) provides high technology products and services to the building systems and aerospace industries worldwide. The company operates through four principle segments: Otis; UTC climate, controls & security; Pratt & Whitney; and UTC aerospace systems. Otis manufactures, sells, installs and services a wide range of passenger and freight elevators for low-, medium-, and high-speed applications, as well as a broad line of escalators and moving walkways. UTC climate, controls & security is the leading provider of HVAC (heating, ventilation and air conditioning) and refrigeration systems, including controls for residential, commercial, industrial and transportation applications. This segment is also a global provider of security and fire safety products and services such as alarms, access control systems and video surveillance systems. Pratt & Whitney supplies aircraft engines and maintenance services for the commercial, military, business jet and general aviation markets. Pratt & Whitney Canada (P&WC) is a world leader in the production of engines powering general and business aviation, as well as regional airline, utility and military airplanes and helicopters, and provides maintenance, repair and overhaul services, including the sale of spare parts. UTC Aerospace Systems supplies technologically advanced aerospace products and aftermarket solutions for aircraft manufacturers, airlines, regional, business and general aviation markets, military, space and undersea operations. In September 2017, United Technologies agreed to acquire aerospace firm Rockwell Collins for $23 billion.

UTC offers employees benefits including medical and dental insurance, health care reimbursement accounts, long-term disability coverage, an Employee Scholar Program that features paid time off for academic pursuits as well as academic expense reimbursemen

FINANCIAL DATA:
Note: Data for latest year may not have been available at press time.

In U.S. $	2017	2016	2015	2014	2013	2012
Revenue	59,837,000,000	57,244,000,000	56,098,000,000	65,100,000,000	62,626,000,000	57,708,000,000
R&D Expense	2,387,000,000	2,337,000,000	2,279,000,000	2,635,000,000	2,529,000,000	2,371,000,000
Operating Income	8,672,000,000	8,172,000,000	7,291,000,000	9,769,000,000	9,209,000,000	7,684,000,000
Operating Margin %	14.49%	14.27%	12.99%	15.00%	14.70%	13.31%
SGA Expense	6,183,000,000	6,060,000,000	5,886,000,000	6,500,000,000	6,718,000,000	6,452,000,000
Net Income	4,552,000,000	5,055,000,000	7,608,000,000	6,220,000,000	5,721,000,000	5,130,000,000
Operating Cash Flow	5,631,000,000	3,880,000,000	6,326,000,000	7,336,000,000	6,877,000,000	6,646,000,000
Capital Expenditure	2,394,000,000	2,087,000,000	2,089,000,000	2,304,000,000	2,410,000,000	2,932,000,000
EBITDA	10,920,000,000	10,256,000,000	9,275,000,000	11,894,000,000	11,167,000,000	9,328,000,000
Return on Assets %	4.87%	5.70%	8.51%	6.83%	6.35%	6.80%
Return on Equity %	15.91%	18.40%	25.97%	19.72%	19.80%	21.46%
Debt to Equity	0.84	0.78	0.70	0.57	0.61	0.83

CONTACT INFORMATION:
Phone: 860 728-7000　　Fax: 860 728-7028
Toll-Free:
Address: 10 Farm Springs Rd., Farmington, CT 06032 United States

STOCK TICKER/OTHER:
Stock Ticker: UTX　　Exchange: NYS
Employees: 202,000　　Fiscal Year Ends: 12/31
Parent Company:

SALARIES/BONUSES:
Top Exec. Salary: $1,500,000　　Bonus: $3,300,000
Second Exec. Salary: $851,250　　Bonus: $1,100,000

OTHER THOUGHTS:
Estimated Female Officers or Directors: 2
Hot Spot for Advancement for Women/Minorities: Y

UniversalPegasus International Inc

www.universalpegasus.com

NAIC Code: 541330

TYPES OF BUSINESS:
Engineering Consulting Services
Engineering
Management

BRANDS/DIVISIONS/AFFILIATES:
Huntington Ingalls Industries Inc
Mobile Inspection Platform

CONTACTS: Note: Officers with more than one job title may be intentionally listed here more than once.
Tom Davison, CEO
Kevin Kelly, CFO
Valerie Cloke, VP-Human Resources
Mark Zuniga, VP-IT

GROWTH PLANS/SPECIAL FEATURES:

UniversalPegasus International, Inc. provides engineering, project management and construction management for the energy industry. The firm's services are divided into five categories: engineering and design, survey, project and program management, construction management and inspection. Engineering and design offers engineering and consulting services across a variety of upstream, midstream and power-related projects for both onshore and offshore purposes. Its disciplines and specialty areas include process engineering, mechanical, materials, pipeline, structural, civil, electrical, instrumentation, subsea and automation. The survey category offers pipeline survey services, including well and pad location, preliminary survey for pipeline routing, boundary survey, easement survey, lease roads, volumetric, retention ponds, as-built, route maps, plats, permit drawings, alignment sheets, bore drill diagrams, regulatory support, web-based and status reporting and custom data model construction. The project and program management category provides a data-driven approach toward project execution, with services including conception, design, contracting and procurement support, project cost control, construction management and commissioning. The custom management category utilizes state-of-the-art systems, controls and procedures to: help prevent errors and delays, manage scheduling challenges, and manage order change. Last, the inspection category provides inspection services with its proprietary Mobile Inspection Platform (MIP) solution, which ensures Pipeline and Hazardous Materials Safety Administration (PHMSA) compliance for client assets worldwide. UniversalPegasus serves clients in more than 50 nations. It is a subsidiary of Huntington Ingalls Industries, Inc., an American shipbuilding company.

FINANCIAL DATA: Note: Data for latest year may not have been available at press time.

In U.S. $	2017	2016	2015	2014	2013	2012
Revenue						
R&D Expense						
Operating Income						
Operating Margin %						
SGA Expense						
Net Income						
Operating Cash Flow						
Capital Expenditure						
EBITDA						
Return on Assets %						
Return on Equity %						
Debt to Equity						

CONTACT INFORMATION:
Phone: 713-425-6000 Fax:
Toll-Free:
Address: 4848 Loop Central Dr., Ste. 137, Houston, TX 77081 United States

STOCK TICKER/OTHER:
Stock Ticker: Subsidiary   Exchange:
Employees: 900   Fiscal Year Ends:
Parent Company: Huntington Ingalls Industries Inc

OTHER THOUGHTS:
Estimated Female Officers or Directors:
Hot Spot for Advancement for Women/Minorities:

SALARIES/BONUSES:
Top Exec. Salary: $ Bonus: $
Second Exec. Salary: $ Bonus: $

Sales, profits and employees may be estimates. Financial information, benefits and other data can change quickly and may vary from those stated here.

UTStarcom Inc

NAIC Code: 334210

www.utstar.com

TYPES OF BUSINESS:
Telecommunications Equipment
Voice, Data & Broadband Networking Equipment
Network Access Systems
Wireless Network Equipment
Handsets
Telecommunications Software & Hardware
Optical Products

BRANDS/DIVISIONS/AFFILIATES:
Packet Transport Network
NetRing Transport Network
SOO Products

CONTACTS:
Note: Officers with more than one job title may be intentionally listed here more than once.

Tim Ti, CEO
Robert Pu, CFO
Jing Ou-Yang, Contact-Investor Rel.
Himanshu Shah, Chmn.

GROWTH PLANS/SPECIAL FEATURES:
UTStarcom, Inc. provides media operational support services and broadband equipment products and services. Most of its business is based in Japan, China, Taiwan, India and other Asian markets. The company's focus is to deploy a TV over IP services platform, which allows customers to easily integrate its products with other industry standard hardware and software. The firm's core business consists of broadband products, solutions and services. Products include Packet Transport Network (PTN) product line, which converts and translates data video, voice or other traffic into an optical signal; NetRing Transport Network optical transport system, based on the latest Multi-Protocol Label Switch Transport Profile (MPLS-TP) and Carrier Ethernet (CE) technologies; SOO products, based on Software Defined Network (SDN) technology; Carrier Wi-Fi product line, which includes a complete carrier-grade solution for a managed wireless access network; and MSAN (multi-service access node) based products and services. The services segment provides services and support for the company's equipment products as well as operation support. Equipment based services are offered to customers after their purchase of equipment. Operational support services provide integrated multi-screen viewing from a single managed platform, time and location shifting, reliable high definition streaming and support services for the company's video service cloud platform.

FINANCIAL DATA:
Note: Data for latest year may not have been available at press time.

In U.S. $	2017	2016	2015	2014	2013	2012
Revenue		120,000,000	117,103,000	129,420,000	164,439,008	186,728,000
R&D Expense						
Operating Income						
Operating Margin %						
SGA Expense						
Net Income			-20,657,000	-30,264,000	-22,721,000	-34,385,000
Operating Cash Flow						
Capital Expenditure						
EBITDA						
Return on Assets %						
Return on Equity %						
Debt to Equity						

CONTACT INFORMATION:
Phone: 86-852-3951-9757 Fax: 86-852-3951-9898
Toll-Free:
Address: Level 6, 28 Hennessy Rd., Hong Kong, Hong Kong

STOCK TICKER/OTHER:
Stock Ticker: UTSI
Employees: 562
Parent Company:
Exchange: NSA
Fiscal Year Ends: 12/31

SALARIES/BONUSES:
Top Exec. Salary: $ Bonus: $
Second Exec. Salary: $ Bonus: $

OTHER THOUGHTS:
Estimated Female Officers or Directors:
Hot Spot for Advancement for Women/Minorities:

Sales, profits and employees may be estimates. Financial information, benefits and other data can change quickly and may vary from those stated here.

Valeo SA

NAIC Code: 336300

www.valeo.com

TYPES OF BUSINESS:
Automobile Parts Manufacturing
Security Systems
Electrical & Electronic Systems
Lighting Systems
Thermal Systems
Aftermarket Products
Transmission Components

BRANDS/DIVISIONS/AFFILIATES:
Valeo Service

CONTACTS: Note: Officers with more than one job title may be intentionally listed here more than once.

Jacques Aschenbroich, CEO
Jean-Francois Tarabbia, Sr. VP-R&D & Product Mktg.
Geric Lebedoff, General Counsel
Francois Marion, VP-Corp. Strategy & Planning
Axel Joachim Maschka, Sr. VP-Bus. Dev.
Fabienne de Brebisson, VP-Comm.
Antoine Doutriaux, Pres., Visibility Systems
Alain Marmugi, Pres., Thermal Systems
Marc Vrecko, Pres., Comfort & Driving Assistance Systems
Catherine Delhaye, Chief Ethics & Compliance Officer
Sergio-Pancini Sa, National Dir.-South America

GROWTH PLANS/SPECIAL FEATURES:

Valeo SA is an independent industrial group focused on the design, production and sale of components, systems and modules for cars and trucks, both in the original equipment and aftermarket sectors. Valeo is a supplier to all automakers worldwide. It operates in four divisions: powertrain systems, thermal systems, comfort & driving assistance systems and visibility systems. The powertrain division consists of: electrical systems, including stop-start components, motor drives and drive trains; transmission systems such as friction materials and clutch systems; and clean engines systems such as exhaust recirculation, air intake and superchargers. The thermal systems division covers climate control, powertrain thermal systems, compressors and engine cooling implements. The comfort & driving assistance systems segment produces driving assistance products such as sensors, radars and cameras for all-around vehicle detection; interior controls and electronics; and access mechanisms, including smart keys and keyless ignition systems. The visibility systems division is responsible for the production of lighting systems, wiper systems and wiper motors. Through Valeo Service, the firm coordinates its products for the aftermarket sector and provides repair and maintenance services. As of December 2017, the firm had a presence in 33 countries, operating approximately 184 production sites, 55 research and development centers and 15 distribution platforms. In November 2017, Valeo formed a joint venture with PHC Group of South Korea, to develop automatic and continuous variable transmissions. In March 2018, Valeo signed a partnership agreement with startup Ellcie Healthy SAS, to develop smart connected eyeglasses.

FINANCIAL DATA: Note: Data for latest year may not have been available at press time.

In U.S. $	2017	2016	2015	2014	2013	2012
Revenue		20,399,370,000	17,960,430,000	15,714,150,000	14,954,680,000	14,521,230,000
R&D Expense		1,431,253,000	1,164,514,000	1,027,440,000	963,224,600	940,996,400
Operating Income		1,572,032,000	1,308,998,000	1,064,487,000	981,748,200	895,304,900
Operating Margin %		7.70%	7.28%	6.77%	6.56%	6.16%
SGA Expense		976,808,500	884,190,800	810,096,600	784,163,600	771,814,600
Net Income		1,142,286,000	900,244,500	694,015,700	542,122,600	469,263,300
Operating Cash Flow		2,333,967,000	2,135,148,000	1,614,019,000	1,652,301,000	1,158,339,000
Capital Expenditure		1,605,374,000	1,381,857,000	1,183,037,000	1,128,702,000	1,076,836,000
EBITDA		2,690,854,000	2,182,074,000	1,842,476,000	1,585,616,000	1,557,213,000
Return on Assets %		7.16%	6.79%	5.89%	4.88%	4.34%
Return on Equity %		24.37%	23.46%	21.95%	19.81%	19.05%
Debt to Equity		0.50	0.32	0.53	0.63	0.76

CONTACT INFORMATION:
Phone: 33 140552020   Fax: 33 140552171
Toll-Free:
Address: 43 rue Bayen Cedex 17, Paris, 75848 France

STOCK TICKER/OTHER:
Stock Ticker: VLEEF
Employees: 82,800
Parent Company:

Exchange: PINX
Fiscal Year Ends: 12/31

SALARIES/BONUSES:
Top Exec. Salary: $ Bonus: $
Second Exec. Salary: $ Bonus: $

OTHER THOUGHTS:
Estimated Female Officers or Directors: 4
Hot Spot for Advancement for Women/Minorities: Y

VEPICA Grupo Internacional SL

NAIC Code: 541330

www.vepica.com

TYPES OF BUSINESS:
Engineering Consulting Services
Engineering
Procurement
Design

BRANDS/DIVISIONS/AFFILIATES:

CONTACTS: *Note: Officers with more than one job title may be intentionally listed here more than once.*
Derek Blackwood, CEO

GROWTH PLANS/SPECIAL FEATURES:

VEPICA Grupo Internacional SL is a Venezuelan company that supports the industrial sector in the development of engineering, procurement and construction (EPC) management services. The firm has been involved with more than 4,000 projects developed worldwide. VEPICA's services include studies, permitting, engineering, design, projects, EPCs, investments/financing, laser scanning, managing data, reverse engineering, 3D digital assets/data and Internet of Things (IoT). The company can integrate its services as a single provider, fully responsible from project conception to startup, or can offer single discipline support and linked teams. Market primarily served by VEPICA include oil and gas, chemical, petrochemical, power generation and transmission, renewable energy, mining, metallurgy, buildings and infrastructure. The firm's technologies include laser scanning and data management. Its 3D laser scanning services specialize in the collection of geometrical and dimensional data of existing assets using state-of-the-art laser scanners and robotic total stations. Bubble view files and Point Cloud data files can be delivered to the client through its web portal for access from field office or remote locations without compromising control of the data. The data can be accessed without the use of specialized software, and ideal for use in 3D intelligent modeling, 4D virtual facility and asset performance management systems. Based in Baruta, Caracas, Venezuela, the firm has international operations in Canada, the U.S., China and Colombia.

FINANCIAL DATA: *Note: Data for latest year may not have been available at press time.*

In U.S. $	2017	2016	2015	2014	2013	2012
Revenue						
R&D Expense						
Operating Income						
Operating Margin %						
SGA Expense						
Net Income						
Operating Cash Flow						
Capital Expenditure						
EBITDA						
Return on Assets %						
Return on Equity %						
Debt to Equity						

CONTACT INFORMATION:
Phone: 58 212 822-8000   Fax:
Toll-Free:
Address: Edif. Vepica. Calle F, Parcela 2. Urbanización Guaicay, Baruta Caracas, Miranda, 1080 Venezuela

STOCK TICKER/OTHER:
Stock Ticker: Private   Exchange:
Employees: 1,200   Fiscal Year Ends:
Parent Company:

SALARIES/BONUSES:
Top Exec. Salary: $ Bonus: $
Second Exec. Salary: $ Bonus: $

OTHER THOUGHTS:
Estimated Female Officers or Directors:
Hot Spot for Advancement for Women/Minorities:

VeriSign Inc

www.verisigninc.com

NAIC Code: 0

TYPES OF BUSINESS:
Computer Software, Security & Anti-Virus
Domain Name Registration

BRANDS/DIVISIONS/AFFILIATES:
Registry Services
Domain Name System
Security Services
Distributed Denial of Service
Managed Domain Name System Services

CONTACTS:
Note: Officers with more than one job title may be intentionally listed here more than once.

D. Bidzos, CEO
George Kilguss, CFO
Todd Strubbe, Executive VP
Thomas Indelicarto, Executive VP

GROWTH PLANS/SPECIAL FEATURES:
VeriSign, Inc. is a global provider of domain name registry services and internet security, enabling internet navigation for many of the world's most recognized domain names and providing protection for websites and enterprises around the world (Registry Services). VeriSign's Registry Services ensure the security, stability, and resiliency of key internet infrastructure and services, including the .com and .net domains, two of the internet's root servers, and operation of the root-zone maintainer functions for the core of the internet's Domain Name System. Additionally, VeriSign's product suite also includes Security Services consisting of Distributed Denial of Service (DDoS) protection services and Managed Domain Name System (Managed DNS) Services. The sole reportable segment of the firm consists of Registry Services and Security Services. In April 2017, the firm sold its iDefense security intelligence services business.

Employees of VeriSign receive a flexible benefits package that includes health, dental, vision, disability and life insurance; flexible spending accounts; a 401(k); an employee assistance program; a group legal plan; domestic partner coverage; tuition ass

FINANCIAL DATA:
Note: Data for latest year may not have been available at press time.

In U.S. $	2017	2016	2015	2014	2013	2012
Revenue	1,165,095,000	1,142,167,000	1,059,366,000	1,010,117,000	965,087,000	873,592,000
R&D Expense	52,342,000	59,100,000	63,718,000	67,777,000	70,297,000	61,694,000
Operating Income	707,722,000	686,572,000	605,946,000	564,427,000	528,232,000	456,562,000
Operating Margin %	60.74%	60.11%	57.19%	55.87%	54.73%	52.26%
SGA Expense	211,705,000	198,253,000	196,914,000	189,488,000	179,545,000	187,736,000
Net Income	457,248,000	440,645,000	375,236,000	355,260,000	544,450,000	320,032,000
Operating Cash Flow	702,761,000	667,949,000	651,482,000	600,949,000	579,397,000	537,630,000
Capital Expenditure	49,499,000	169,574,000	40,656,000	39,327,000	65,594,000	53,023,000
EBITDA	785,226,000	754,904,000	656,772,000	632,995,000	592,187,000	517,710,000
Return on Assets %	17.33%	18.78%	16.63%	14.75%	23.05%	16.33%
Return on Equity %						
Debt to Equity						

CONTACT INFORMATION:
Phone: 703 948-3200 Fax:
Toll-Free: 800-922-4917
Address: 12061 Bluemont Way, Reston, VA 20190 United States

SALARIES/BONUSES:
Top Exec. Salary: $842,308 Bonus: $
Second Exec. Salary: $550,000 Bonus: $

STOCK TICKER/OTHER:
Stock Ticker: VRSN Exchange: NAS
Employees: 990 Fiscal Year Ends: 12/31
Parent Company:

OTHER THOUGHTS:
Estimated Female Officers or Directors:
Hot Spot for Advancement for Women/Minorities:

Vestas Wind Systems A/S

NAIC Code: 333611   www.vestas.com

TYPES OF BUSINESS:
Wind Turbine Manufacturing
Turbine Installation, Repair & Maintenance Services
Online Turbine Operating Systems

BRANDS/DIVISIONS/AFFILIATES:
Vestas Manufacturing A/S
Vestas Blades Deutschland Gmbh
Vestas Control Systems Spain SLU
Vestas Nacelles Italia Srl
Vestas Towers America Inc
Vestas Blades Italia Srl
Vestas Blades America Inc
Vestas Nacelles Estonia

CONTACTS:
Note: Officers with more than one job title may be intentionally listed here more than once.

Anders Runevad, CEO
Jean-Marc Lechene, COO
Anders Runevad, Pres.
Markia Fredriksson, CFO
Juan Araluce, Chief Sales Officer
Anders Vedel, Chief Turbines Officer
Anders Vedel, Chief Technology Officer

GROWTH PLANS/SPECIAL FEATURES:

Vestas Wind Systems A/S is a leading international manufacturer of wind turbines, having installed turbines in 75 countries worldwide and exceeding 85 gigawatts (GW) in installed wind capacity. The firm offers site and project studies and develops, manufactures, sells, installs and services wind turbines, ranging from the V90-2.0 MW (megawatt) onshore turbine to the V150-4.2 MW onshore/offshore turbine. Vestas offers land and offshore models as well as installation, repair and maintenance services. The firm's Supervisory Control and Data Acquisition System (SCADA), called VestasOnline, offers a range of monitoring and control functions, which allow plants to be operated in a manner similar to conventional power plants. It allows customers to view performance data, monitor and control turbines remotely and receive alarm messages via e-mail through its SCADA web server. The company has a number production units, including blades, with facilities in Denmark, Germany, Spain and the U.S., which is comprised of wholly-owned subsidiaries Vestas Manufacturing A/S, Vestas Blades Deutschland Gmbh, Vestas Blades Italia Srl, Vestas Blades America Inc. and Vestas Blades Spain SLU; control systems, with a facility in Spain via Vestas Control Systems Spain SLU; nacelles (housing for turbine engines and equipment), with facilities in Italy, Germany, Estonia and the U.S. via Vestas Nacelles Italia Srl, Vestas Nacelles Deutschland GMBH, Vestas Nacelles Estonia and Vestas Nacelles America, Inc.; and towers, with a facility in the U.S. via Vestas Towers America Inc.

FINANCIAL DATA:
Note: Data for latest year may not have been available at press time.

In U.S. $	2017	2016	2015	2014	2013	2012
Revenue	12,290,990,000	12,641,700,000	10,401,590,000	8,533,182,000	7,513,151,000	8,911,062,000
R&D Expense	290,202,300	280,323,100	260,564,600	263,034,400	303,786,200	314,900,400
Operating Income	1,518,931,000	1,754,798,000	1,060,782,000	680,431,700	223,517,500	-167,946,800
Operating Margin %	12.35%	13.88%	10.19%	7.97%	2.97%	-1.88%
SGA Expense	614,981,900	590,283,800	535,948,000	502,605,700	548,297,100	676,727,000
Net Income	1,104,004,000	1,191,682,000	845,908,800	484,082,100	-101,262,100	-1,189,212,000
Operating Cash Flow	2,006,718,000	2,693,324,000	1,817,778,000	1,390,501,000	1,541,159,000	-90,147,940
Capital Expenditure	606,337,500	603,867,700	454,444,400	343,303,100	323,544,700	414,927,500
EBITDA	2,010,423,000	2,121,564,000	1,542,394,000	1,154,635,000	556,941,400	422,336,900
Return on Assets %	8.59%	10.42%	8.79%	6.20%	-1.30%	-13.13%
Return on Equity %	28.37%	31.69%	25.95%	20.08%	-5.21%	-45.87%
Debt to Equity	0.15	0.15	0.17		0.39	0.89

CONTACT INFORMATION:
Phone: 45 97300000   Fax: 45 97300001
Toll-Free:
Address: Hedeager 42, Aarhus, 8200 Denmark

STOCK TICKER/OTHER:
Stock Ticker: VWDRY   Exchange: PINX
Employees: 23,303   Fiscal Year Ends: 12/31
Parent Company:

SALARIES/BONUSES:
Top Exec. Salary: $ Bonus: $
Second Exec. Salary: $ Bonus: $

OTHER THOUGHTS:
Estimated Female Officers or Directors: 3
Hot Spot for Advancement for Women/Minorities: Y

Sales, profits and employees may be estimates. Financial information, benefits and other data can change quickly and may vary from those stated here.

VINCI SA

NAIC Code: 237310

TYPES OF BUSINESS:
Highway, Street, and Bridge Construction
Infrastructure Management
Information & Energy Technologies
Commercial Construction
Engineering Services
Highway Construction
Airport Management & Support Services
Power Transmission Services

BRANDS/DIVISIONS/AFFILIATES:
VINCI Concessions SA
VINCI Contracting LLC
VINCI Autoroutes
VINCI Airports
VINCI Energies
Eurovia
VINCI Construction
Seymour Whyte

CONTACTS:
Note: Officers with more than one job title may be intentionally listed here more than once.

Xavier Huillard, CEO
Christian Labeyrie, CFO
Franck Mougin, VP-Human Resources and Corporate Social Responsibility

www.vinci.com

GROWTH PLANS/SPECIAL FEATURES:

VINCI SA is one of the largest companies operating in construction and related services worldwide. The company designs, finances, builds and operates infrastructures and facilities that help improve daily life and mobility for all. It consists of two major subsidiary divisions: VINCI Concessions SA, comprising VINCI Autoroutes, VINCI Airports and other concessions; and VINCI Contracting, LLC, comprising VINCI Energies, Eurovia and VINCI Construction. The concessions division is Europe's leading transport infrastructure concession operator, operating in the motorway, airport, bridge and tunnel, rail, stadium and parking facility sectors. VINCI Autoroutes operates more than 2,700 miles of motorways in France, carrying over 2 million customers each day; VINCI Airports operates 34 airports in Portugal, France, Chile, Japan, Dominican Republic and Cambodia, transporting nearly 100 million passengers each year; and other concessions include motorways, bridges, tunnels, rail and parking facilities. The contracting division is engaged in building contracting, value engineering, interior design, insulation works, metal and steel structures, electrical works, plumbing works and air conditioning (HVAC), having worked on approximately 300,000 projects in some 110 countries. VINCI Energies serves public authorities and business clients by helping them to deploy electrical power & heating, HVAC, mechanical engineering and communication equipment, as well as operating their energy, transport and communication infrastructures; Eurovia is a world leader in transport infrastructure and urban development, building and upgrading roads, motorways, rail systems, airport hard surfaces and industrial facilities; and VINCI Construction brings together nearly 800 consolidated companies in some 100 countries by delivering capabilities in building, civil engineering, hydraulic engineering and contracting-related specialties. In October 2017, the firm acquired the Seymour Whyte company based in Queensland, Australia, operating in the fields of civil engineering, earthworks and utilities.

FINANCIAL DATA:
Note: Data for latest year may not have been available at press time.

In U.S. $	2017	2016	2015	2014	2013	2012
Revenue	50,726,120,000	47,763,590,000	48,557,640,000	48,400,800,000	50,623,630,000	48,676,930,000
R&D Expense						
Operating Income	5,491,615,000	5,059,399,000	4,567,907,000	4,406,135,000	4,423,424,000	4,405,765,000
Operating Margin %	10.82%	10.59%	9.40%	9.10%	8.73%	9.05%
SGA Expense						
Net Income	3,392,280,000	3,093,433,000	2,526,612,000	3,069,970,000	2,422,880,000	2,366,939,000
Operating Cash Flow	5,286,621,000	5,368,124,000	5,582,998,000	4,490,108,000	4,501,222,000	4,772,161,000
Capital Expenditure	2,371,014,000	1,889,402,000	2,019,067,000	1,860,999,000	1,904,221,000	2,462,521,000
EBITDA	8,403,517,000	7,653,931,000	7,201,956,000	7,868,804,000	7,274,815,000	6,985,725,000
Return on Assets %	3.98%	3.85%	3.26%	3.94%	3.14%	3.13%
Return on Equity %	16.02%	15.86%	13.70%	17.21%	14.28%	14.61%
Debt to Equity	0.93	0.98	0.99	1.16	1.24	1.24

CONTACT INFORMATION:
Phone: 33 147163500   Fax: 33 147519102
Toll-Free:
Address: 1 Cours Ferdinand-de-Lesseps, Cedex, 92851 France

STOCK TICKER/OTHER:
Stock Ticker: VCISY   Exchange: PINX
Employees: 38,000   Fiscal Year Ends: 12/31
Parent Company:

SALARIES/BONUSES:
Top Exec. Salary: $ Bonus: $
Second Exec. Salary: $ Bonus: $

OTHER THOUGHTS:
Estimated Female Officers or Directors: 2
Hot Spot for Advancement for Women/Minorities:

Sales, profits and employees may be estimates. Financial information, benefits and other data can change quickly and may vary from those stated here.

Visteon Corporation

NAIC Code: 336300

www.visteon.com

TYPES OF BUSINESS:
Automobile Parts
Climate Control Products
Fuel Storage & Delivery Products
Chassis & Power Train Components
Multimedia Systems

BRANDS/DIVISIONS/AFFILIATES:
SmartCore
DriveCore

CONTACTS:
Note: Officers with more than one job title may be intentionally listed here more than once.

Sachin Lawande, CEO
Stephanie Marianos, Chief Accounting Officer
Markus Schupfner, Chief Technology Officer
Francis Scricco, Director
Christian Garcia, Executive VP
Brett Pynnonen, General Counsel
Robert Vallance, Senior VP, Divisional
Sunil Bilolikar, Senior VP, Divisional
Matthew Cole, Senior VP, Divisional

GROWTH PLANS/SPECIAL FEATURES:

Visteon Corporation is a global automotive supplier that designs, engineers and manufactures innovative electronics products for nearly every original equipment vehicle manufacturer (OEM). The company operates through a single segment, electronics. The electronics division provides vehicle cockpit electronics products to its customers, including instrument clusters, information displays, infotainment systems, audio systems, telematics solutions and head up displays. Instrument clusters include standard analog gauge clusters to high-resolutions, all-digital, fully reconfigurable, 2d and 3D display-based devices. Information displays are utilized alongside various applications within the cockpit and can integrate a range of user interface technologies and graphics management capabilities such as 3D, dual view, cameras, optics, haptic feedback, light effects and dual organic light-emitting diode (OLED) displays. Infotainment and audio systems include the company's Phoenix display audio and embedded infotainment platform, and the Android embedded infotainment open-source system. These systems are designed to allow vehicle occupants to easily connect their mobile devices and safely access phone functions, listen to music, stream media and more. Visteon's telematics solution uses a single hardware and flexible software architecture to support regional telematics service providers and mobile networks. It also offers a hands-free telephone unit that provides Bluetooth and Universal Serial Bus (USB) connectivity. Head up displays provide critical information to the driver in a convenient vehicle location and at a comfortable focal distance through a compact, transparent screen mounted on a panel. In addition, Visteon's SmartCore domain controller can independently operate the infotainment system, instrument cluster, head-up display and other features on a single, multi-core chip; and its DriveCore technology platform consists of the hardware, middleware and frameworks to develop machine learning algorithms for autonomous driving applications of Level 3 and above. The firm's customers include Ford, Mazda, Renault/Nissan, General Motors, Jaguar/Land Rover, Honda, Volkswagen, BMW and Daimler.

FINANCIAL DATA:
Note: Data for latest year may not have been available at press time.

In U.S. $	2017	2016	2015	2014	2013	2012
Revenue	3,146,000,000	3,161,000,000	3,245,000,000	7,509,000,000	7,439,000,000	6,857,000,000
R&D Expense						
Operating Income	277,000,000	245,000,000	185,000,000	421,000,000	317,000,000	220,000,000
Operating Margin %	8.80%	7.75%	5.70%	5.60%	4.26%	3.20%
SGA Expense	222,000,000	220,000,000	245,000,000	377,000,000	367,000,000	369,000,000
Net Income	176,000,000	75,000,000	2,284,000,000	-295,000,000	690,000,000	100,000,000
Operating Cash Flow	217,000,000	120,000,000	338,000,000	284,000,000	312,000,000	239,000,000
Capital Expenditure	99,000,000	75,000,000	187,000,000	340,000,000	269,000,000	229,000,000
EBITDA	331,000,000	263,000,000	257,000,000	568,000,000	1,191,000,000	599,000,000
Return on Assets %	7.52%	2.12%	45.65%	-5.19%	12.34%	1.97%
Return on Equity %	28.78%	9.12%	237.66%	-21.18%	41.75%	7.42%
Debt to Equity	0.54	0.59	0.32	0.96	0.32	0.34

CONTACT INFORMATION:
Phone: 734 710-5800 Fax:
Toll-Free: 800-847-8366
Address: 1 Village Center Dr., Van Buren Township, MI 48111 United States

STOCK TICKER/OTHER:
Stock Ticker: VC
Employees: 10,000
Parent Company:

Exchange: NAS
Fiscal Year Ends: 12/31

SALARIES/BONUSES:
Top Exec. Salary: $1,022,500 Bonus: $
Second Exec. Salary: $147,500 Bonus: $500,000

OTHER THOUGHTS:
Estimated Female Officers or Directors:
Hot Spot for Advancement for Women/Minorities: Y

Volkswagen AG (VW)

NAIC Code: 336111

www.volkswagenag.com

TYPES OF BUSINESS:
- Automobile Manufacturing
- Truck Manufacturing
- Car Rental Services
- Consumer Financing
- Digital Services
- Electric Cars

BRANDS/DIVISIONS/AFFILIATES:
- Volkswagen
- Audi
- Bentley
- Bugatti
- Lamborghini
- SEAT
- Skoda
- Ducati

CONTACTS: *Note: Officers with more than one job title may be intentionally listed here more than once.*

Matthias Muller, CEO
Frank Witter, Dir.-Finance
Karlheinz Blessing, Dir.-Human Resources & Organization
Michael Macht, Dir.-Group Production
Hans Dieter Potsch, Dir.-Finance
Leif Ostling, Dir.-Group Commercial Vehicles
Matthias Mueller, Chmn.
Jochem Heizmann, Dir.-China
Francisco Javier Garcia Sanz, Dir.-Procurement

GROWTH PLANS/SPECIAL FEATURES:

Volkswagen AG (VW) is one of the world's leading automobile manufacturers. The firm's production base consists of 120 plants in more than 30 countries worldwide. The company's automobiles are made up of twelve brands from seven European countries: passenger cars, including Volkswagen, Audi, Bentley, Bugatti, Lamborghini, SEAT, Skoda and Porsche; motorcycles under the Ducati brand; trucks, buses and diesel engines under the Scania and MAN brand names; and Volkswagen commercial vehicles. Each brand operates as an independent entity on the market, with products ranging from low-consumption small cars to luxury class vehicles to motorcycles. Models offered under the Volkswagen brand include the Up!, eco up!, e-up!, up! GTI, load up!, e-load up!, cross up!, Golf, Passat, Touran, Sharan, Tourareg, Ameo (Russia/India), Polo, Voyage (South America), Gol (South America), Fox (South America), Jetta (North America/China), Sagitar (China), The Beetle (North America), and many more. In the commercial vehicle segment, products include pick-ups, busses and heavy trucks. VW is also active in other fields of business, manufacturing large-bore diesel engines for marine and stationary applications, turbochargers and machinery, special gear units, compressors and chemical reactors. In addition, the group offers a wide range of financial services, including dealer and customer financing, leasing, banking and insurance activities, as well as fleet management services. In March 2018, the firm announced plans to produce battery-powered vehicles at nine more plants worldwide within the next two years (it currently produces them at three), and at 16 locations worldwide by the end of 2022.

FINANCIAL DATA: *Note: Data for latest year may not have been available at press time.*

In U.S. $	2017	2016	2015	2014	2013	2012
Revenue	284,870,000,000	268,305,000,000	263,395,000,000	250,016,100,000	243,285,800,000	237,936,200,000
R&D Expense						
Operating Income	16,600,810,000	10,284,270,000	-1,527,575,000	14,979,380,000	14,198,920,000	15,390,600,000
Operating Margin %	5.82%	3.83%	-.57%	5.99%	5.83%	6.46%
SGA Expense	38,237,550,000	37,091,560,000	37,926,350,000	33,506,630,000	32,778,040,000	30,962,730,000
Net Income	14,021,090,000	6,352,343,000	-1,953,617,000	13,395,000,000	11,195,630,000	26,818,400,000
Operating Cash Flow	-1,463,360,000	11,645,140,000	16,892,240,000	13,317,200,000	15,553,610,000	8,902,418,000
Capital Expenditure	22,613,550,000	23,342,140,000	22,517,230,000	20,515,450,000	19,024,920,000	16,187,110,000
EBITDA	45,600,040,000	36,013,490,000	23,613,820,000	40,492,480,000	34,492,080,000	49,099,760,000
Return on Assets %	2.72%	1.29%	-.43%	3.21%	2.85%	7.71%
Return on Equity %	11.26%	5.69%	-1.77%	12.20%	10.97%	32.16%
Debt to Equity	0.73	0.68	0.81	0.74	0.68	0.79

CONTACT INFORMATION:
Phone: 49 536190
Fax:
Toll-Free:
Address: Brieffach 1848-2, Wolfsburg, 38436 Germany

STOCK TICKER/OTHER:
Stock Ticker: VLKAY
Employees: 615,081
Parent Company:

Exchange: PINX
Fiscal Year Ends: 12/31

SALARIES/BONUSES:
Top Exec. Salary: $ Bonus: $
Second Exec. Salary: $ Bonus: $

OTHER THOUGHTS:
Estimated Female Officers or Directors:
Hot Spot for Advancement for Women/Minorities:

Sales, profits and employees may be estimates. Financial information, benefits and other data can change quickly and may vary from those stated here.

Volvo Car Corporation

NAIC Code: 336111

www.volvocars.com

TYPES OF BUSINESS:
Automobile Manufacturing

BRANDS/DIVISIONS/AFFILIATES:
Zhejiang Geely Holding Group Co Ltd
Volvo Cars of North America
Volvo Cars Financial Services US LLC
Zenuity
Sunfleet
S60
V90
XC40

CONTACTS:
Note: Officers with more than one job title may be intentionally listed here more than once.

Hakan Samuelsson, CEO
Hakan Samuelsson, Pres.
Hans Oscarsson, CFO
Hanna Fager, Sr.. VP-Human Resources
Peter Mertens, Sr. VP-R&D
Atif Rafiq, Sr. VP-IT
Lars Wrebo, Sr. VP-Mfg. & Purchasing
Maria Hemberg, General Counsel
Anders Karrberg, Acting Sr. VP-Corp. Comm.
Nils Mosko, Head-Investor Rel.
Thomas Ingenlath, VP-Design
Paul Gustavsson, Sr. VP-Bus. Office Dev.
Lex Kerssemakers, Sr. VP-Prod. Strategy & Vehicle Line Mgmt.
Paul Welander, Sr. VP-Quality & Customer Satisfaction
Li Shufu, Chmn.
Lars Danielson, Sr. VP-China Oper.

GROWTH PLANS/SPECIAL FEATURES:

Volvo Car Corporation, founded in 1927, is a Swedish designer, developer and manufacturer of cars known for safety and reliability. Volvo is owned by Zhejiang Geely Holding Group Co. Ltd, based in Hangzhou, China. Its largest markets are the U.K., Sweden, China and Germany. Volvo cars are manufactured at seven facilities, with the largest facilities in Sweden and Belgium and smaller plants in China. Its current models include the S60 and S90 sedans; the V40, V60 and V90 Estate hatchback models; and the XC40, XC60 and XC90 SUVs. The firm's cars have won numerous awards for safety, design, environmental issues and overall value. It offers environmentally savvy FlexiFuel cars (so named because they can run on either ethanol or gasoline), and hopes to expand its production of those models. Available in California and certain Northeastern states in the U.S., Volvo's PZEV (partial zero emission vehicle) engines produce exhaust which, in heavy city traffic, may be cleaner than the ambient air. Volvo's U.S. companies include Volvo Cars of North America and Volvo Cars Financial Services U.S., LLC (VCFS). Polestar is the performance brand of Volvo cars, where customers can optimize their vehicles for increased engine performance. Volvo has a partnership with Uber to develop fully-autonomous driving cars. The company's joint venture with Autoliv, called Zenuity, develops advanced driver assist systems and autonomous driving technologies. In addition, Volvo plans to establish a shared-mobility business unit primarily through subsidiary Sunfleet, a car-sharing company. Volvo recently (early-2017) launched a Get Away Lodge with hotel curator Tablet Hotels; this package includes lodging in the Swedish mountains and a Volvo V90 cross country rental. Volvo plans to release its first all-electric car by 2019.

FINANCIAL DATA:
Note: Data for latest year may not have been available at press time.

In U.S. $	2017	2016	2015	2014	2013	2012
Revenue	25,664,200,000	21,604,490,000	20,166,314,523	15,361,045,464	18,654,768,151	19,132,800,000
R&D Expense						
Operating Income						
Operating Margin %						
SGA Expense						
Net Income	1,244,200,000	106,675,000	74,648,800	62,453,113	146,497,535	-73,737,200
Operating Cash Flow						
Capital Expenditure						
EBITDA						
Return on Assets %						
Return on Equity %						
Debt to Equity						

CONTACT INFORMATION:
Phone: 46-31-59-00-00   Fax:
Toll-Free:
Address: VAK Bldg., Assar Gabrielssons vag, Goteborg, 405 31 Sweden

STOCK TICKER/OTHER:
Stock Ticker: Subsidiary   Exchange:
Employees: 38,000   Fiscal Year Ends: 12/31
Parent Company: Zhejiang Geely Holding Group Co Ltd

SALARIES/BONUSES:
Top Exec. Salary: $ Bonus: $
Second Exec. Salary: $ Bonus: $

OTHER THOUGHTS:
Estimated Female Officers or Directors: 3
Hot Spot for Advancement for Women/Minorities: Y

Sales, profits and employees may be estimates. Financial information, benefits and other data can change quickly and may vary from those stated here.

VSE Corporation

www.vsecorp.com

NAIC Code: 541330

TYPES OF BUSINESS:
Engineering Consulting Services
Engineering Services
Logistics Services
Technology Research & Development
Equipment Maintenance, Refurbishment & Implementation
Information Technology Support

BRANDS/DIVISIONS/AFFILIATES:

CONTACTS: Note: Officers with more than one job title may be intentionally listed here more than once.
Maurice Gauthier, CEO
Thomas Loftus, CFO
Joseph Brown, President, Divisional
Paul Goffredi, President, Subsidiary
Chad Wheeler, President, Subsidiary
Thomas Kiernan, Secretary

GROWTH PLANS/SPECIAL FEATURES:
VSE Corporation is a supply chain management company that assists its clients in extending their service life and improving the performance of their transportation, equipment and other assets and systems. The firm provides logistics and distribution services for legacy systems and equipment, as well as professional and technical services to the U.S. Government, including the Department of Defense, the U.S. Post Office, federal civilian agencies and commercial and other customers. VSE's businesses are organized into four groups: supply chain management, generating 29.7% of 2016 revenue; aviation, 19.3%; federal services, 44.2%; and IT, energy and management consulting, 6.8%. Supply chain management revenues are derived from the sale of vehicle parts to government and commercial clients; aviation revenues are derived from the sale of aircraft parts and performance of maintenance, repair and overhaul (MRO) services for private and commercial aircraft owners and related equipment manufacturers; and federal services and IT, energy and management consulting revenues result primarily from cost plus fixed fee, cost plus award fee, time and materials, or fixed-price contracts with the government. These business segments offer supply chain and inventory management services; vehicle fleet sustainment programs; vehicle fleet parts supply and distribution; MRO of aircraft engines and engine components; aircraft engine parts supply and distribution; engineering support for military vehicles; military equipment refurbishment and modification; ship MRO and follow-on technical support; logistics management support; machinery condition analysis; specification preparation for ship alterations; ship's force crew training; life cycle support for ships; ship communication systems; energy conservation, energy efficiency, sustainable energy supply and electric power grid modernization projects; technology road-mapping; IT enterprise architecture development, information assurance, security risk management and network services; medical logistics; and medical command and control.

FINANCIAL DATA: Note: Data for latest year may not have been available at press time.

In U.S. $	2017	2016	2015	2014	2013	2012
Revenue	760,113,000	691,790,000	533,982,000	424,071,000	471,638,000	546,755,000
R&D Expense						
Operating Income	54,325,000	51,529,000	50,539,000	36,930,000	44,103,000	52,101,000
Operating Margin %	7.14%	7.44%	9.46%	8.70%	9.35%	9.52%
SGA Expense	2,429,000	6,609,000	3,288,000	4,140,000	3,285,000	3,968,000
Net Income	39,096,000	26,793,000	24,918,000	19,365,000	22,852,000	21,294,000
Operating Cash Flow	50,420,000	47,193,000	37,574,000	49,715,000	56,598,000	59,475,000
Capital Expenditure	3,743,000	6,546,000	10,562,000	3,414,000	4,416,000	20,863,000
EBITDA	80,207,000	77,575,000	76,080,000	55,700,000	64,119,000	73,263,000
Return on Assets %	6.05%	4.17%	5.09%	5.26%	5.77%	4.92%
Return on Equity %	14.26%	11.06%	11.46%	9.87%	13.01%	13.83%
Debt to Equity	0.63	0.84	1.04	0.23	0.48	0.87

CONTACT INFORMATION:
Phone: 703 960-4600　　Fax: 703 960-2688
Toll-Free:
Address: 6348 Walker Ln., Alexandria, VA 22310 United States

STOCK TICKER/OTHER:
Stock Ticker: VSEC
Employees: 2,523
Parent Company:

Exchange: NAS
Fiscal Year Ends: 12/31

SALARIES/BONUSES:
Top Exec. Salary: $780,000　　Bonus: $
Second Exec. Salary: $337,006　　Bonus: $

OTHER THOUGHTS:
Estimated Female Officers or Directors: 6
Hot Spot for Advancement for Women/Minorities: Y

Sales, profits and employees may be estimates. Financial information, benefits and other data can change quickly and may vary from those stated here.

VTech Holdings Limited

NAIC Code: 334210

www.vtech.com

TYPES OF BUSINESS:
Cordless Telephone Sets
Electronic Learning Products
Contract Manufacturing Services
Data Networking Products

BRANDS/DIVISIONS/AFFILIATES:
Vtech

CONTACTS:
Note: Officers with more than one job title may be intentionally listed here more than once.

Allan Chi Yun Wong, CEO
King Fai Pang, Pres.
Andy Leung Hon Kwong, CEO-Contract Mfg. Svcs.
William To, Pres., Vtech Electronics North America
Gordon Chow, Pres., Vtech Technologies Canada
Nicholas Delany, Pres., Vtech Communications, Inc.
Allan Chi Yun Wong, Chmn.

GROWTH PLANS/SPECIAL FEATURES:
VTech Holdings Limited is a global electronic learning products company, as well as a manufacturer of cordless phones. Based in Hong Kong, the firm has manufacturing facilities in China, and various operations across 13 countries and regions worldwide. VTech's products and services are categorized into three business divisions: electronic learning products, telecommunication products and contract manufacturing services. Electronic learning products include learning-based toys for children aged from infancy through toddler/preschool, as well as kid-based smart watches, tablets, laptops, desks and phones. These products are offered in 31 languages. Telecommunications products include cordless phones and handsets for residential and commercial use. Other offerings within this division include a variety of wireless monitoring systems, audio/video baby monitors and conference phone systems. Last, contract manufacturing services include professional audio equipment, hearables, medical/health products and industrial products. All products are marketed under the VTech brand.

FINANCIAL DATA:
Note: Data for latest year may not have been available at press time.

In U.S. $	2017	2016	2015	2014	2013	2012
Revenue	2,079,300,000	1,856,500,000	1,879,800,000	1,898,900,000	1,858,000,000	1,784,500,000
R&D Expense	77,200,000	56,300,000	56,100,000	58,000,000	57,100,000	57,200,000
Operating Income	200,000,000	202,300,000	220,100,000	226,100,000	224,700,000	209,500,000
Operating Margin %	9.61%	10.89%	11.70%	11.90%	12.09%	11.73%
SGA Expense	412,200,000	324,700,000	334,300,000	350,200,000	316,000,000	304,100,000
Net Income	179,000,000	181,400,000	198,100,000	203,300,000	202,300,000	191,900,000
Operating Cash Flow	185,300,000	216,700,000	229,500,000	233,500,000	196,500,000	211,200,000
Capital Expenditure	35,700,000	38,300,000	30,900,000	30,100,000	29,900,000	29,700,000
EBITDA	234,500,000	237,400,000	251,700,000	257,400,000	254,000,000	236,900,000
Return on Assets %	18.16%	19.81%	21.53%	21.83%	21.80%	21.44%
Return on Equity %	32.26%	34.04%	35.48%	35.42%	35.85%	34.88%
Debt to Equity						

CONTACT INFORMATION:
Phone: 852 26801000 Fax: 852 26801300
Toll-Free:
Address: 57 Ting Kok Rd., Tai Ping Ctr., Block 1, 23/Fl, Hong Kong, Hong Kong

STOCK TICKER/OTHER:
Stock Ticker: VTKLF   Exchange: PINX
Employees: 27,000   Fiscal Year Ends: 03/31
Parent Company:

SALARIES/BONUSES:
Top Exec. Salary: $ Bonus: $
Second Exec. Salary: $ Bonus: $

OTHER THOUGHTS:
Estimated Female Officers or Directors:
Hot Spot for Advancement for Women/Minorities:

Sales, profits and employees may be estimates. Financial information, benefits and other data can change quickly and may vary from those stated here.

Waldemar S Nelson and Company Inc

www.wsnelson.com

NAIC Code: 541330

TYPES OF BUSINESS:
Engineering Consulting Services
Engineering
Management
Architecture

BRANDS/DIVISIONS/AFFILIATES:

CONTACTS: Note: Officers with more than one job title may be intentionally listed here more than once.
Kenneth H. Nelson, Pres.
James B. Lane, CFO
Charles W. Nelson, Chmn.

GROWTH PLANS/SPECIAL FEATURES:
Waldemar S. Nelson and Company, Inc. provides engineering and architectural design, project management, procurement, environmental compliance and remediation consulting. The firm has offices in New Orleans, Louisiana and Houston, Texas, and has served multiple clients in a broad range of projects across the U.S., and at selective international sites, since 1945. Nelson's services also comprise chemical and process engineering, civil and structural engineering, control systems engineering, electrical engineer, environmental engineering, LEED (leadership in energy and environmental design) consulting, energy audits, mechanical engineering, project and construction management and more. Industries the company has served include electrical utilities, marine, material handling, mining, oil and gas, petrochemical, public works and renewable energy, among others. Nelson is experienced in all aspects of design and construction management for industrial, manufacturing and power generation facilities such as offshore production platforms, floating production systems, refineries, petrochemical plants, gas processing plants, pipeline facilities, pumping stations, docks and marine terminals, water treating plants, pollution control and abatement systems, machine design for locks and bridges, drainage pump systems, steel manufacturing facilities and shipyard facilities.

FINANCIAL DATA: Note: Data for latest year may not have been available at press time.

In U.S. $	2017	2016	2015	2014	2013	2012
Revenue						
R&D Expense						
Operating Income						
Operating Margin %						
SGA Expense						
Net Income						
Operating Cash Flow						
Capital Expenditure						
EBITDA						
Return on Assets %						
Return on Equity %						
Debt to Equity						

CONTACT INFORMATION:
Phone: 504-523-5281
Fax: 504-523-4587
Toll-Free:
Address: 1200 St. Charles Ave., New Orleans, LA 70130 United States

SALARIES/BONUSES:
Top Exec. Salary: $ Bonus: $
Second Exec. Salary: $ Bonus: $

STOCK TICKER/OTHER:
Stock Ticker: Private
Employees: 300
Parent Company:

Exchange:
Fiscal Year Ends:

OTHER THOUGHTS:
Estimated Female Officers or Directors:
Hot Spot for Advancement for Women/Minorities:

Sales, profits and employees may be estimates. Financial information, benefits and other data can change quickly and may vary from those stated here.

Wanxiang Group Corporation

NAIC Code: 336300

www.wanxiang.com.cn

TYPES OF BUSINESS:
Automotive Parts Manufacturer
Agricultural Engineering
Aquaculture
Restaurant & Hotel Management
Road & Bridge Construction
Power Plant Construction
Leasing & Financial Services
Trade Consulting

BRANDS/DIVISIONS/AFFILIATES:
Wanxiang Innovative Energy Fusion City
Xanxiang Sannong
Zhejiang Ocean Family Co Ltd
Chengde Lolo Co Ltd
Beijing Doneed Seeds Industry Co Ltd

CONTACTS:
Note: Officers with more than one job title may be intentionally listed here more than once.

Weiding Lu, CEO
Gary E. Wetzel, COO
Pin Ni, Pres., Wanxiang America Corp.

GROWTH PLANS/SPECIAL FEATURES:

Wanxiang Group Corporation is one of China's largest auto parts manufacturers, with more than 45 factories supplying automotive components worldwide. Within China, the group has six manufacturing facilities, recognizing more than a 60% market share in the relevant industry. Internationally, the firm owns 30 overseas subsidiaries, and more than 40 factories across the U.S., Great Britain, Germany and other countries. Its automotive parts and accessories include the development, production and selling of drive shafts, brakes, shock absorbers, rolling elements and related components. Wanxiang has supporting partnerships with mainstream automotive manufacturers such as General Motors, Volkswagen, Ford and Chrysler. The group has recently invested billions in new energy, innovation and transformation technologies and solutions for the purpose of becoming a clean energy company. The firm's Wanxiang Innovative Energy Fusion City is a hub that focuses on new energy automobile components, batteries, as well as battery/electric passenger buses and vehicles. Subsidiaries include: Wanxiang Sannong, an agricultural industry group that provides services to agriculture, farmer and rural areas; Zhejiang Ocean Family Co. Ltd., which owns and operates ocean fisheries, and is engaged in seafood processing as well as the import/export of seafood products; Chengde Lolo Co Ltd., a provider of healthy, plant-based food and beverages; and Beijing Doneed Seeds Industry Co. Ltd., a high-tech comprehensive seed enterprise, focusing on the research, production, management and service of seeds for the agricultural industry.

FINANCIAL DATA:
Note: Data for latest year may not have been available at press time.

In U.S. $	2017	2016	2015	2014	2013	2012
Revenue	20,000,000,000	19,000,000,000	18,000,000,000	17,500,000,000	16,000,000,000	14,500,000,000
R&D Expense						
Operating Income						
Operating Margin %						
SGA Expense						
Net Income						
Operating Cash Flow						
Capital Expenditure						
EBITDA						
Return on Assets %						
Return on Equity %						
Debt to Equity						

CONTACT INFORMATION:
Phone: 86-571-8283-2999   Fax: 86-571-8283-3999
Toll-Free:
Address: Wang Xiang Rd., Xiao Shan District, Hangzhou, Zhejiang 311215 China

STOCK TICKER/OTHER:
Stock Ticker: Private
Employees: 48,500
Parent Company:

Exchange:
Fiscal Year Ends: 03/31

SALARIES/BONUSES:
Top Exec. Salary: $ Bonus: $
Second Exec. Salary: $ Bonus: $

OTHER THOUGHTS:
Estimated Female Officers or Directors:
Hot Spot for Advancement for Women/Minorities:

Sales, profits and employees may be estimates. Financial information, benefits and other data can change quickly and may vary from those stated here.

Waymo LLC

NAIC Code: 511210

www.waymo.com

TYPES OF BUSINESS:
Technology for Self-Driving Vehicles
Self-Driving Hardware
Self-Driving Software

BRANDS/DIVISIONS/AFFILIATES:
Alphabet Inc
Google

CONTACTS: Note: Officers with more than one job title may be intentionally listed here more than once.
John Krafcik, CEO

GROWTH PLANS/SPECIAL FEATURES:
Waymo, LLC is an autonomous car development company and subsidiary of Alphabet, Inc., which is also the owner of Google. Waymo was enabled as a separate entity in order to commercialize and distribute the self-driving vehicle technology that was developed by Google. Waymo has an exceptional amount of experience in this regard, as its test vehicles have completed several million miles on the road, as well as 2.7 billion miles in simulation in 2017 alone. Waymo offers both software and hardware for self-driving vehicles, enabling auto makers and truck makers an opportunity to purchase complete technology platforms. In November 2017, Waymo began testing driverless cars without anyone in the driver's seat, and utilized a public trial of its self-driving vehicles. In early-2018, the firm placed separate orders for thousands of hybrid-drive Pacifica minivans and Jaguar I-PACE electric sedans for the purpose of launching a driverless ride-hailing service. How the driverless system works: vehicles have sensors and software designed to detect pedestrians, cyclists, vehicles, road work and more from up to three football fields away in all 360 degrees. The sensors and software detect and predict the behavior of all road users within the range. The sensors can even observe when a cyclist has extended his/her arm as a traffic signal. This signals the Waymo vehicle to slow down and make room for the cyclist to pass safely.

FINANCIAL DATA: Note: Data for latest year may not have been available at press time.

In U.S. $	2017	2016	2015	2014	2013	2012
Revenue						
R&D Expense						
Operating Income						
Operating Margin %						
SGA Expense						
Net Income						
Operating Cash Flow						
Capital Expenditure						
EBITDA						
Return on Assets %						
Return on Equity %						
Debt to Equity						

CONTACT INFORMATION:
Phone: 650-253-0000 Fax:
Toll-Free:
Address: 1600 Amphitheatre Parkway, Mountain View, CA 94043 United States

STOCK TICKER/OTHER:
Stock Ticker: Subsidiary
Employees:
Parent Company: Alphabet Inc

Exchange:
Fiscal Year Ends:

SALARIES/BONUSES:
Top Exec. Salary: $ Bonus: $
Second Exec. Salary: $ Bonus: $

OTHER THOUGHTS:
Estimated Female Officers or Directors:
Hot Spot for Advancement for Women/Minorities:

Sales, profits and employees may be estimates. Financial information, benefits and other data can change quickly and may vary from those stated here.

Western Digital Corporation

www.wdc.com

NAIC Code: 334112

TYPES OF BUSINESS:
Data Storage Hardware
Hard Drives

BRANDS/DIVISIONS/AFFILIATES:
Western Digital
Hitachi Global Storage Technologies
ScanDisk
HGST
WD
Upthere
Tegile Systems

CONTACTS:
Note: Officers with more than one job title may be intentionally listed here more than once.

Mark Long, CFO
Michael Cordano, COO
Stephen Milligan, Director
Matthew Massengill, Director
Srinivasan Sivaram, Executive VP, Divisional
Manish Bhatia, Executive VP, Divisional
Martin Fink, Executive VP
Jacqueline DeMaria, Executive VP
Michael Ray, Executive VP

GROWTH PLANS/SPECIAL FEATURES:

Western Digital Corporation develops, manufactures and sells data storage devices, cloud storage solutions and home entertainment products under the HGST, WD and ScanDisk brands. The company operates under the subsidiaries Western Digital (WD), Hitachi Global Storage Technologies (HGST) and ScanDisk. Western Digital's portfolio of offerings addresses three categories: data center devices and solutions, client devices and client solutions. Data center devices and solutions products include capacity and performance enterprise hard disk drives (HDDs), enterprise solid state drives (SSDs), datacenter software and system solutions. Enterprise HDDs are optimized for performance applications providing a range of capacity and performance levels for use in enterprise servers, supporting high volume on-line transactions, data analysis and other enterprise applications. Enterprise SSDs include high-performance NAND-flash SSDs and software solutions designed to improve the performance in various enterprise workload environments. Client devices products consist of HDDs and SSDs for desktop PCs, notebook PCs, gaming consoles, set top boxes, security surveillance systems and other computing devices, embedded NAND-flash storage for mobile phones, tablets, notebook PCs and other portable and wearable devices, as well as in automotive and connected home applications and NAND-flash wafers. The client solutions segment includes such products as HDDs embedded into WD- and HGST-branded external storage products and SanDisk-branded removable NAND-flash products which include cards, universal serial bus flash drives and wireless drives. During 2017, the firm acquired Upthere, a cloud services company; and Tegile Systems, a manufacturer of flash storage arrays.

The firm offers its employees a 401(k) plan; health, dental and vision coverage; life and AD&D insurance; educational reimbursements; adoption assistance; and an employee assistance program.

FINANCIAL DATA:
Note: Data for latest year may not have been available at press time.

In U.S. $	2017	2016	2015	2014	2013	2012
Revenue	19,093,000,000	12,994,000,000	14,572,000,000	15,130,000,000	15,351,000,000	12,478,000,000
R&D Expense	2,441,000,000	1,627,000,000	1,646,000,000	1,661,000,000	1,572,000,000	1,055,000,000
Operating Income	2,175,000,000	811,000,000	1,802,000,000	1,938,000,000	2,085,000,000	2,065,000,000
Operating Margin %	11.39%	6.24%	12.36%	12.80%	13.58%	16.54%
SGA Expense	1,456,000,000	997,000,000	773,000,000	761,000,000	706,000,000	518,000,000
Net Income	397,000,000	242,000,000	1,465,000,000	1,617,000,000	980,000,000	1,612,000,000
Operating Cash Flow	3,437,000,000	1,983,000,000	2,242,000,000	2,816,000,000	3,119,000,000	3,067,000,000
Capital Expenditure	578,000,000	584,000,000	612,000,000	628,000,000	952,000,000	717,000,000
EBITDA	3,744,000,000	1,573,000,000	2,916,000,000	3,182,000,000	3,318,000,000	2,608,000,000
Return on Assets %	1.26%	1.00%	9.55%	10.94%	6.93%	14.44%
Return on Equity %	3.51%	2.37%	16.22%	19.32%	12.59%	24.50%
Debt to Equity	1.13	1.22	0.23	0.26	0.21	0.25

CONTACT INFORMATION:
Phone: 408-717-6000 Fax:
Toll-Free:
Address: 5601 Great Oaks Pkwy., San Jose, CA 95119 United States

STOCK TICKER/OTHER:
Stock Ticker: WDC
Employees: 67,629
Parent Company:

Exchange: NAS
Fiscal Year Ends: 06/30

SALARIES/BONUSES:
Top Exec. Salary: $1,150,000 Bonus: $
Second Exec. Salary: $800,000 Bonus: $

OTHER THOUGHTS:
Estimated Female Officers or Directors: 1
Hot Spot for Advancement for Women/Minorities:

Sales, profits and employees may be estimates. Financial information, benefits and other data can change quickly and may vary from those stated here.

Westinghouse Electric Company LLC www.westinghousenuclear.com
NAIC Code: 332410

TYPES OF BUSINESS:
Nuclear Power Plant Equipment
Nuclear Power Plant Repair Services
Nuclear Fuel
Nuclear Power Plant Design & Engineering

BRANDS/DIVISIONS/AFFILIATES:
Brookfield Business Partners LP
AP1000 PWR

CONTACTS: Note: Officers with more than one job title may be intentionally listed here more than once.
Jose Emeterio Gutierrez, Interim CEO & Pres.
Danny Roderick, Pres.
Yves Brachet, Pres., EMEA
Jack Allen, Pres., Asia

GROWTH PLANS/SPECIAL FEATURES:
Westinghouse Electric Company, LLC provides plant design, services, fuel, technology and equipment to utility, government and industrial clients in the international commercial nuclear electric power market. The company operates in four segments: nuclear services, nuclear automation, nuclear fuel and nuclear power plants. The nuclear services division provides field services, such as outage support, component services and training; engineering services that improve plant reliability, including plant analyses and management programs; and installation and modification services, including plant engineering, welding and machining, site installation and decommissioning and dismantling services. Westinghouse's nuclear automation segment offers instrumentation and control solutions and related services for new nuclear power plant designs and the operation of existing plants. The nuclear fuel division offers fuel products, materials and components, services and technology for pressurized water reactors (PWRs), boiling water reactors (BWRs) and advanced gas-cooled reactors (AGRs). The nuclear power plants division supplies plant design expertise, equipment and component manufacturing for nuclear power plants. The firm states that its new AP1000 PWR nuclear power plant is the safest and most economical within the global commercial market. Westinghouse's regional operations are categorized into the Americas, Asia and EMEA (Europe, the Middle East and Africa). In April 2018, the firm was acquired out of bankruptcy by Brookfield Business Partners LP.

FINANCIAL DATA: Note: Data for latest year may not have been available at press time.

In U.S. $	2017	2016	2015	2014	2013	2012
Revenue	4,150,000,000	4,000,000,000	4,500,000,000	5,400,000,000	5,150,000,000	5,000,000,000
R&D Expense						
Operating Income						
Operating Margin %						
SGA Expense						
Net Income						
Operating Cash Flow						
Capital Expenditure						
EBITDA						
Return on Assets %						
Return on Equity %						
Debt to Equity						

CONTACT INFORMATION:
Phone: 412-374-4111   Fax: 412-374-3272
Toll-Free: 888-943-8442
Address: 1000 Westinghouse Dr., Ste. 572A, Cranberry Township, PA 16066 United States

STOCK TICKER/OTHER:
Stock Ticker: Subsidiary
Employees: 11,000
Parent Company: Brookfield Business Partners LP
Exchange:
Fiscal Year Ends: 03/31

SALARIES/BONUSES:
Top Exec. Salary: $ Bonus: $
Second Exec. Salary: $ Bonus: $

OTHER THOUGHTS:
Estimated Female Officers or Directors:
Hot Spot for Advancement for Women/Minorities:

Plunkett Research, Ltd.

Whirlpool Corporation

NAIC Code: 335224

www.whirlpoolcorp.com

TYPES OF BUSINESS:
Home Appliance Manufacturer
Laundry Appliances
Refrigerators & Freezers
Air Conditioning Equipment
Kitchen Appliances

BRANDS/DIVISIONS/AFFILIATES:
Whirlpool
Maytag
KitchenAid
Brastemp
Hotpoint
Diqua
Gladiator
Jenn-Air

CONTACTS:
Note: Officers with more than one job title may be intentionally listed here more than once.

Marc Bitzer, CEO
James Peters, CFO
Jeff Fettig, Chairman of the Board
Joseph Lovechio, Chief Accounting Officer
Esther Berrozpe-Galindo, Executive VP
Joseph Liotine, Executive VP
Joao Brega, Executive VP

GROWTH PLANS/SPECIAL FEATURES:
Whirlpool Corporation is a worldwide manufacturer and marketer of major home appliances. It manufactures products in 15 countries under several principal brand names, including Whirlpool, Maytag, KitchenAid, Consul, Brastemp, Amana, Bauknecht, Hotpoint, Affresh, Acros, Diqua, Gladiator, Jenn-Air and Indesit. Operating 43 manufacturing sites internationally, Whirlpool Corporation markets its products in nearly every country around the world. The company's principal products are laundry appliances, refrigerators, freezers, cooking appliances, dishwashers, mixers and other small household appliances. Additionally, the company aims to produce Energy Star grade appliances, with increased overall efficiency than normal grade appliances. In April 2018, the firm agreed to sell its Embraco compressor business to Nidec Corporation for approximately $1.08 billion, subject to regulatory approvals and conditions.

Whirlpool offers its employees health, dental and vision coverage; educational leave; flexible spending accounts; scholarship programs for employees' dependents; and fitness and weight loss rebates.

FINANCIAL DATA:
Note: Data for latest year may not have been available at press time.

In U.S. $	2017	2016	2015	2014	2013	2012
Revenue	21,253,000,000	20,718,000,000	20,891,000,000	19,872,000,000	18,769,000,000	18,143,000,000
R&D Expense						
Operating Income	1,411,000,000	1,527,000,000	1,486,000,000	1,324,000,000	1,445,000,000	1,106,000,000
Operating Margin %	6.63%	7.37%	7.11%	6.66%	7.69%	6.09%
SGA Expense	2,112,000,000	2,084,000,000	2,130,000,000	2,038,000,000	1,828,000,000	1,757,000,000
Net Income	350,000,000	888,000,000	783,000,000	650,000,000	827,000,000	401,000,000
Operating Cash Flow	1,264,000,000	1,203,000,000	1,225,000,000	1,479,000,000	1,262,000,000	696,000,000
Capital Expenditure	684,000,000	660,000,000	689,000,000	720,000,000	578,000,000	476,000,000
EBITDA	1,790,000,000	2,009,000,000	1,953,000,000	1,748,000,000	1,789,000,000	1,420,000,000
Return on Assets %	1.78%	4.65%	4.01%	3.65%	5.34%	2.62%
Return on Equity %	7.80%	18.66%	16.26%	13.25%	18.00%	9.50%
Debt to Equity	1.04	0.81	0.73	0.72	0.37	0.45

CONTACT INFORMATION:
Phone: 269 923-5000   Fax: 269 923-3978
Toll-Free:
Address: 2000 N. M-63, Benton Harbor, MI 49022-2692 United States

STOCK TICKER/OTHER:
Stock Ticker: WHR
Employees: 93,000
Parent Company:

Exchange: NYS
Fiscal Year Ends: 12/31

SALARIES/BONUSES:
Top Exec. Salary: $1,480,000   Bonus: $
Second Exec. Salary: $1,091,667   Bonus: $

OTHER THOUGHTS:
Estimated Female Officers or Directors: 4
Hot Spot for Advancement for Women/Minorities: Y

Sales, profits and employees may be estimates. Financial information, benefits and other data can change quickly and may vary from those stated here.

William Demant Holding Group

NAIC Code: 334510

www.demant.com

TYPES OF BUSINESS:
Human Hearing Assistance Technology
Hearing Aids
Diagnostic Instruments
Personal Communications Technology

BRANDS/DIVISIONS/AFFILIATES:
Oticon
Bernafon
Sonic
Phonic Ear
FrontRow
Interacoustics
Maico
Micromedical

CONTACTS:
Note: Officers with more than one job title may be intentionally listed here more than once.

Soren Nielsen, CEO
Niels Jacobsen, Pres.
Rene Schneider, CFO
Niels B. Christiansen, Chmn.

GROWTH PLANS/SPECIAL FEATURES:

William Demant Holding Group is a Danish holding company that oversees the operations of several subsidiaries engaged in the development and manufacturing of hearing devices, hearing implants and diagnostic instruments in over 130 countries. The hearing devices division derives 87% of the firm's total revenue, and includes the Oticon, Bernafon and Sonic brands of devices. Oticon is a leading manufacturer of hearing care solutions such as hearing aids and fitting systems; Bernafon develops quality hearing systems via Swiss engineering and technology; and Sonic is a U.S.-based manufacturer of hearing instruments renowned for superior sound processing, noise reduction, directional capabilities and award-winning design. Other brands in this division include Phonic Ear and FrontRow. The hearing implants division (4%) is comprised of Oticon Medical, which develops bone anchored hearing systems and implant solutions such as cochlear implants that help overcome several to total bilateral (second degree) hearing loss. The diagnostic instruments division (9%) includes the Maico, Interacoustics, Amplivox, Grason-Stadler, MedRx and Micromedical brands which develop, manufacture and distribute audiometers for hearing measurement, as well as other instruments used by audiologists and ear-nose-and-throat specialists.

FINANCIAL DATA:
Note: Data for latest year may not have been available at press time.

In U.S. $	2017	2016	2015	2014	2013	2012
Revenue	2,183,935,000	1,987,382,000	1,765,992,000	1,547,582,000	1,524,896,000	1,416,602,000
R&D Expense	152,175,000	138,928,000	126,343,300	112,599,600	109,950,200	107,963,100
Operating Income	378,367,600	308,158,500	303,025,300	280,836,500	295,408,300	271,729,200
Operating Margin %	17.32%	15.50%	17.15%	18.14%	19.37%	19.18%
SGA Expense	1,129,639,000	1,048,169,000	877,945,400	734,712,200	699,442,000	634,862,800
Net Income	290,440,600	241,592,300	237,783,800	219,569,100	216,919,700	190,922,500
Operating Cash Flow	309,980,000	278,021,600	263,615,400	247,553,500	218,575,600	210,627,400
Capital Expenditure	72,527,370	77,991,750	73,024,130	74,845,590	68,222,090	56,796,540
EBITDA	447,086,500	381,513,800	359,987,400	335,314,800	341,276,000	312,298,200
Return on Assets %	11.04%	9.74%	11.21%	12.29%	13.69%	14.04%
Return on Equity %	24.38%	21.67%	23.76%	24.86%	28.65%	31.32%
Debt to Equity	0.31	0.28	0.32		0.01	0.01

CONTACT INFORMATION:
Phone: 45 39177300   Fax: 45 39278900
Toll-Free:
Address: Kongebakken 9, Smorum, 2765 Denmark

SALARIES/BONUSES:
Top Exec. Salary: $ Bonus: $
Second Exec. Salary: $ Bonus: $

STOCK TICKER/OTHER:
Stock Ticker: WILYY
Employees: 13,280
Parent Company:

Exchange: PINX
Fiscal Year Ends: 12/31

OTHER THOUGHTS:
Estimated Female Officers or Directors: 1
Hot Spot for Advancement for Women/Minorities:

Wipro Limited

NAIC Code: 541512

www.wipro.com

TYPES OF BUSINESS:
IT Consulting
Computer Hardware & Software Design
Hydraulic Equipment
Medical Electronics
Lighting Equipment
Soaps & Toiletries

BRANDS/DIVISIONS/AFFILIATES:

CONTACTS:
Note: Officers with more than one job title may be intentionally listed here more than once.

Abidali Z. Neemuchwala, CEO
Bhanumurthy B. M., Pres.
Jatin Dalal, CFO
Rishad Premji, Chief Strategy Officer
Saurabh Govil, Chief Human Resources Officer
Sangita Singh, Sr. VP- Health Care & Life Sciences
Anurag Behar, Chief Sustainability Officer
N.S. Bala, Sr. VP-Mfg. & High Tech.
Inderpreet Sawhney, Sr. VP
Rishad Premji, Chief Strategy Officer
Ayan Mukerji, Sr. VP-Media & Telecom
Vineet Agrawal, Pres., Wipro Consumer Care & Lighting
Anurag Behar, Chief Sustainability Officer
Alexis Samuel, Chief Process Officer
Rajat Mathur Rajat Mathur Rajat Mathur, Chief Sales & Oper. Officer-Growth Markets
Azim H. Premji, Chmn.
Ulrich Meister, Sr. VP-Continental Europe

GROWTH PLANS/SPECIAL FEATURES:

Wipro Limited is a leading global information technology (IT), consulting and business process services company. The firm's operations are divided into two segments: IT services and IT products. The IT services segment generates 95% of Wipro's annual revenue, and develops and integrates innovative solutions that enable Wipro clients to leverage IT in order to achieve business objectives at competitive costs. This division advises, designs and executes technology transformation products and solutions as well as support programs for its business and enterprise customers. The IT products segment provides a range of IT and IT-enables services such as digital strategy advisory, customer-centric design, technology consulting, IT consulting, custom applications design, development, re-engineering and maintenance, systems integration, package implementation, global infrastructure services, analytics services, business process services, research and development and hardware/software design to enterprises worldwide. Industries Wipro serves include aerospace and defense, communications, engineering and construction, new age, media, education, network equipment providers, platforms and software products, public sector, semiconductors, automotive, consumer electronics, healthcare, medical device, oil and gas, process and industrial manufacturing, retail, travel and transportation, banking, consumer packaged goods, insurance, natural resources, pharmaceutical and life sciences, professional services, securities and capital markets and utilities. In October 2017, the firm agreed to acquire Cooper, a design and business strategy consultancy.

FINANCIAL DATA:
Note: Data for latest year may not have been available at press time.

In U.S. $	2017	2016	2015	2014	2013	2012
Revenue	8,442,318,000	7,860,040,000	7,202,096,000	6,661,017,000	5,740,510,000	5,705,462,000
R&D Expense						
Operating Income	1,382,026,000	1,428,839,000	1,407,856,000	1,319,031,000	1,032,984,000	931,581,200
Operating Margin %	16.37%	18.17%	19.54%	19.80%	17.99%	16.32%
SGA Expense	984,406,900	928,851,000	850,272,100	809,655,900	709,327,000	737,212,400
Net Income	1,302,158,000	1,363,926,000	1,327,206,000	1,195,894,000	1,017,845,000	854,812,300
Operating Cash Flow	1,422,995,000	1,209,790,000	1,200,418,000	1,041,435,000	1,080,165,000	614,704,100
Capital Expenditure	319,852,900	213,986,800	194,200,200	136,711,700	162,833,100	199,047,200
EBITDA	2,076,505,000	2,010,810,000	1,921,510,000	1,732,924,000	1,384,971,000	1,278,767,000
Return on Assets %	11.18%	13.42%	15.69%	16.55%	15.15%	13.80%
Return on Equity %	17.21%	20.34%	23.02%	24.85%	23.31%	21.23%
Debt to Equity	0.03	0.03	0.03	0.03		0.07

CONTACT INFORMATION:
Phone: 91 8028440055 Fax: 91 8028440256
Toll-Free:
Address: Doddakannelli, Sarjapur Rd., Bangalore, Karnataka 560035 India

STOCK TICKER/OTHER:
Stock Ticker: WIT   Exchange: NYS
Employees: 160,000   Fiscal Year Ends: 03/31
Parent Company:

SALARIES/BONUSES:
Top Exec. Salary: $800,000   Bonus: $150,244
Second Exec. Salary: $468,173   Bonus: $144,403

OTHER THOUGHTS:
Estimated Female Officers or Directors: 3
Hot Spot for Advancement for Women/Minorities: Y

WL Meinhardt Group Pty Ltd

www.meinhardtgroup.com

NAIC Code: 541330

TYPES OF BUSINESS:
Engineering Consulting Services

BRANDS/DIVISIONS/AFFILIATES:

GROWTH PLANS/SPECIAL FEATURES:
WL Meinhardt Group Pty Ltd provides engineering consulting capabilities in infrastructure civil & infrastructure, environment, design, mechanical, electrical & plumbing (MEP), project management and planning & urban development. The firm's specialist capabilities cover facade engineering; environmentally sustainable design (ESD); specialist and architectural lighting; fire performance engineering; integrated design management; and mission critical facility design. The Meinhardt Group has 45 offices across Australia, Greater China, India, Pakistan, Singapore, Malaysia, Indonesia, Thailand, Vietnam, the Philippines, Middle East, North Africa and the U.K. Some of the firm's key projects include Shanghai Peninsula Hotel (China), TAMAR Development (Hong Kong), Victoria Theatre and Concert Hall (Singapore), Grand Hyatt and Plaza (Indonesia), Virgin Atlantic Hangar (U.K.), Victorian County Court (Australia), University Technology Petronas (Malaysia), Phu My Bridge (Vietnam) and Vijayawada Airport (India).

CONTACTS:
Note: Officers with more than one job title may be intentionally listed here more than once.

Omar Shahzad, Group CEO
Shahzad Nasim, Chmn.

FINANCIAL DATA:
Note: Data for latest year may not have been available at press time.

In U.S. $	2017	2016	2015	2014	2013	2012
Revenue						
R&D Expense						
Operating Income						
Operating Margin %						
SGA Expense						
Net Income						
Operating Cash Flow						
Capital Expenditure						
EBITDA						
Return on Assets %						
Return on Equity %						
Debt to Equity						

CONTACT INFORMATION:
Phone: 61-3-8676-1200   Fax: 61-3-8676-1201
Toll-Free:
Address: 501 Swaston St., Fl. 12, Melbourne, VIC 3000 Australia

SALARIES/BONUSES:
Top Exec. Salary: $ Bonus: $
Second Exec. Salary: $ Bonus: $

STOCK TICKER/OTHER:
Stock Ticker: Private   Exchange:
Employees: 4,050   Fiscal Year Ends:
Parent Company:

OTHER THOUGHTS:
Estimated Female Officers or Directors:
Hot Spot for Advancement for Women/Minorities:

Sales, profits and employees may be estimates. Financial information, benefits and other data can change quickly and may vary from those stated here.

WS Atkins plc

www.atkinsglobal.com

NAIC Code: 541330

TYPES OF BUSINESS:
Engineering Consulting Services
Engineering
Design
Consultancy

BRANDS/DIVISIONS/AFFILIATES:
SNC-Lavalin Group Inc

CONTACTS:
Note: Officers with more than one job title may be intentionally listed here more than once.

Nick Roberts, Pres.
Simon Cole, Dir.-Finance
James Culles, Exec. VP-Human Resources

GROWTH PLANS/SPECIAL FEATURES:
WS Atkins plc is a design, engineering and project management consultancy service company. The firm is primarily structured regionally through five divisions: U.K., North America, Middle East, Asia Pacific and Europe and energy. The U.K. business segment delivers engineering and technically integrated design, as well as project and cost management services, to a wide range of clients in the public, regulated and private sectors. Areas of operation for this segment include water, environment, education, aerospace, defense, infrastructure design and transportation. The North America business segment provides infrastructure planning, engineering, construction management, environmental consulting, urban planning, architecture and program management services to state and local government clients, federal agencies and private businesses. The Middle East business segment provides design, engineering and project management services for buildings, transportation and other infrastructure programs from its eight centers. The Asia Pacific and Europe business segment provides engineering, planning, urban design, architectural and rail design services. In mainland China, this division's focus is on urban planning as well as architectural and landscape design. The European portion comprises operations in Denmark, Norway, Sweden, Poland, Portugal and Ireland. The energy business segment operates across multiple geographies with main centers in the U.K. and North America. This division provides engineering and project management services and are engaged in developing the energy market with allied issues of climate change, sustainability and energy security. In mid-2017, WS Atkins was acquired by SNC-Lavalin Group, Inc., and subsequently delisted from public trading. WS Atkins now operates as a wholly-owned subsidiary of SNC-Lavalin.

FINANCIAL DATA:
Note: Data for latest year may not have been available at press time.

In U.S. $	2017	2016	2015	2014	2013	2012
Revenue	2,400,000,000	2,379,424,768	2,244,856,064	2,236,549,376	2,179,169,280	2,186,709,248
R&D Expense						
Operating Income						
Operating Margin %						
SGA Expense						
Net Income		131,884,976	109,520,760	122,683,696	113,354,624	136,357,824
Operating Cash Flow						
Capital Expenditure						
EBITDA						
Return on Assets %						
Return on Equity %						
Debt to Equity						

CONTACT INFORMATION:
Phone: 44-1372-726140   Fax: 44-1372-740055
Toll-Free:
Address: Woodcote Grove, Ashley Rd., Epsom, Surrey KT18 5UZ United Kingdom

STOCK TICKER/OTHER:
Stock Ticker: Subsidiary   Exchange: GREY
Employees: 17,500   Fiscal Year Ends: 03/31
Parent Company: SNC-Lavalin Group Inc

SALARIES/BONUSES:
Top Exec. Salary: $ Bonus: $
Second Exec. Salary: $ Bonus: $

OTHER THOUGHTS:
Estimated Female Officers or Directors:
Hot Spot for Advancement for Women/Minorities:

Sales, profits and employees may be estimates. Financial information, benefits and other data can change quickly and may vary from those stated here.

WSP Global Inc

www.wsp-pb.com

NAIC Code: 541614

TYPES OF BUSINESS:
Distribution and Logistics Consulting Services
Engineering
Infrastructure
Consulting
Asset Management
Project Management

BRANDS/DIVISIONS/AFFILIATES:
Poch
Leggette Brashears and Graham Inc
Concol
ISS Proko Oy
ISS Suunnittelupalvelut Oy
UnionConsult Gruppen AS
Opus International Consultants Limited
WSP Opus

CONTACTS:
Note: Officers with more than one job title may be intentionally listed here more than once.

Hugo Blasutta, CEO, Geographical
David Ackert, CEO, Geographical
Gregory Kelly, CEO, Geographical
Guy Templeton, CEO, Geographical
Bruno Roy, CFO
Christopher Cole, Chairman of the Board
Paul Dollin, COO
Alexandre LHeureux, Director
Pierre Shoiry, Director
Jan Meyer, Managing Director, Geographical
Mark Naysmith, Managing Director, Geographical
Tom Smith, Other Corporate Officer
Isabelle Adjahi, Vice President, Divisional
Barbara Oberleitner, Vice President

GROWTH PLANS/SPECIAL FEATURES:

WSP Global, Inc. develops comprehensive and sustainable engineering solutions, with more than 500 offices in 40 countries. The company provides integrated architecture services including planning and design; engineering services such as mechanical, electrical and structural work; asset management; and project management services. It also offers municipal rehabilitation and development, water distribution and treatment, wastewater collection and treatment, public utilities, storm water management, land development, municipal road networks, lighting and various municipal facility services. The firm's power generation projects include hydroelectric, wind, solar and thermal power generation as well as nuclear safety, cogeneration and related distribution and transmission systems to public suppliers of electricity and private developers. WSP offers planning, modeling, engineering, project management and contract administration services for roads, bridges, civil engineering structures, harbor, railways and airport facilities, mass and urban transit facilities, traffic systems and other transportation-related projects. The company also provides environment services, such as impact and ecosystem studies; environmental assessments; monitoring surveys and characterizations; management systems; permitting, compliance audits and mapping; and economic and risk management services. During 2017, WSP acquired the following companies: Poch, a Latin American engineering, environmental services, project and construction management firm; Leggette, Brashears and Graham, Inc., a groundwater and environmental engineering services company based in the U.S.; Concol, a multi-disciplinary pure play consulting firm based in Colombia; ISS Proko Oy, along with its wholly-owned subsidiary ISS Suunnittelupalvelut Oy, which provide construction and project services in Finland; UnionConsult Gruppen AS, a Norwegian design and technical advisory firm; and Opus International Consultants Limited, which now does business as WSP Opus, an engineering professional services consulting firm operating in New Zealand.

FINANCIAL DATA:
Note: Data for latest year may not have been available at press time.

In U.S. $	2017	2016	2015	2014	2013	2012
Revenue	5,503,131,000	5,057,154,000	4,806,976,000	2,300,753,000	1,598,098,000	996,829,200
R&D Expense						
Operating Income	296,076,100	264,605,600	232,738,800	127,229,500	78,715,820	51,525,960
Operating Margin %	5.38%	5.23%	4.84%	5.52%	4.92%	5.16%
SGA Expense	3,440,904,000	3,116,290,000	2,711,058,000	1,397,384,000	992,945,000	597,304,800
Net Income	169,084,400	157,828,000	149,663,100	49,782,000	56,837,100	36,702,340
Operating Cash Flow	313,436,400	306,619,100	161,553,700	178,121,300	94,807,770	76,099,880
Capital Expenditure	82,520,810	114,466,900	82,996,430	36,305,980	22,592,150	15,537,060
EBITDA	415,774,900	363,694,000	345,937,400	141,656,800	127,388,000	83,392,780
Return on Assets %	3.37%	3.23%	3.39%	1.84%	3.90%	3.64%
Return on Equity %	7.33%	6.89%	7.45%	4.01%	7.58%	6.52%
Debt to Equity	0.29	0.31	0.29	0.36	0.19	0.24

CONTACT INFORMATION:
Phone: 514 340-0046 Fax: 514 340-1337
Toll-Free:
Address: 1600 Rene Levesque W., Montreal, QC H3H 1P9 Canada

STOCK TICKER/OTHER:
Stock Ticker: WSP
Employees: 36,000
Parent Company:

Exchange: TSE
Fiscal Year Ends: 12/31

SALARIES/BONUSES:
Top Exec. Salary: $ Bonus: $
Second Exec. Salary: $ Bonus: $

OTHER THOUGHTS:
Estimated Female Officers or Directors: 2
Hot Spot for Advancement for Women/Minorities:

Sales, profits and employees may be estimates. Financial information, benefits and other data can change quickly and may vary from those stated here.

WSP Opus
NAIC Code: 541330

www.opus.co.nz

TYPES OF BUSINESS:
Engineering Consulting Services
Engineering
Consulting
Building

BRANDS/DIVISIONS/AFFILIATES:
WSP Global Inc

GROWTH PLANS/SPECIAL FEATURES:
WSP Opus (formerly Opus International Consultants Limited) is the New Zealand operation of engineering professional services firm, WSP. The company specializes in infrastructure consultancy, offering end-to-end asset management and development services. WSP Opus' work spans eight key sectors: buildings, transport, water, environmental, energy, resources, research and telecommunications. The firm's technical experts and advisors include engineers, technicians, scientists, planners, surveyors, environmental specialists, as well as other design, program and construction management professionals. In New Zealand, WSP Opus operates from a network of 40 offices. During 2017, Opus International Consultants was acquired by WSP Global, Inc., and renamed WSP Opus.

CONTACTS:
Note: Officers with more than one job title may be intentionally listed here more than once.

David Prentice, CEO
Gordon Davidson, CFO

FINANCIAL DATA:
Note: Data for latest year may not have been available at press time.

In U.S. $	2017	2016	2015	2014	2013	2012
Revenue		346,774,656	371,971,264	397,198,784	338,435,936	300,038,272
R&D Expense						
Operating Income						
Operating Margin %						
SGA Expense						
Net Income		-21,994,844	12,332,842	19,322,532	16,773,932	17,225,330
Operating Cash Flow						
Capital Expenditure						
EBITDA						
Return on Assets %						
Return on Equity %						
Debt to Equity						

CONTACT INFORMATION:
Phone: 64-4-471-7243   Fax: 64-4-473-3017
Toll-Free:
Address: 100 Willis St., Majestic Ctr., 9/Fl, Wellington, 6011 New Zealand

STOCK TICKER/OTHER:
Stock Ticker: Subsidiary
Employees: 2,832
Parent Company: WSP Global Inc

Exchange: GREY
Fiscal Year Ends:

SALARIES/BONUSES:
Top Exec. Salary: $ Bonus: $
Second Exec. Salary: $ Bonus: $

OTHER THOUGHTS:
Estimated Female Officers or Directors:
Hot Spot for Advancement for Women/Minorities:

X Development LLC

NAIC Code: 541712

x.company

TYPES OF BUSINESS:
Research and Development in the Physical, Engineering, and Life Sciences (except Biotechnology)
Robotics
Self-Driving Cars
Machine Learning
Artificial Intelligence

BRANDS/DIVISIONS/AFFILIATES:
Alphabet Inc
Project Loon
Makani
Project Wing

CONTACTS: Note: Officers with more than one job title may be intentionally listed here more than once.
Astro Teller, COO

GROWTH PLANS/SPECIAL FEATURES:

X Development, LLC, a subsidiary of Alphabet, Inc., considers itself as a moonshot factory with a mission to invent and launch moonshot technologies to help make the world a better place. The firm's X moonshot model consists of looking for big problems and deriving solutions and technologies for them. X Development's Project Loon is a network of balloons traveling on the edge of space, designed to connect people in rural and remote areas, help fill coverage gaps and bring people back online after disasters. Since Project Loon's first launch in 2013 in New Zealand, X Development has flown millions of test kilometers around the world trying to learn what it will take to provide this desired form of connectivity. Project Loon balloons float twice as high as airplanes and the weather, shares cellular spectrums with partner telecommunications companies and connectivity signals are then passed across the balloon network and back down to the global internet on Earth. The Makani project involves the creation of kites that harness energy from wind. Coupled with technology, this combination has the potential to advance the global adoption of renewable energy. The Makani energy kite is an aerodynamic wing tethered to a ground station; it climbs to a desired altitude and positions itself downwind; the wing-mounted rotors consume a small amount of power to produce thrust; and the kite transitions into crosswind flight. Wind spins the rotors, driving onboard generators to produce electricity, which is transferred back to the ground via the tether. X Development's latest prototype transfers up to 600 kilowatts to the grid, enough to power about 300 homes. Last, Project Wing is engaged in building delivery drones capable of delivering anything, from consumer goods to emergency medicine. These aircraft will be able to fly pre-planned routes on-demand via sensors and software.

FINANCIAL DATA: Note: Data for latest year may not have been available at press time.

In U.S. $	2017	2016	2015	2014	2013	2012
Revenue						
R&D Expense						
Operating Income						
Operating Margin %						
SGA Expense						
Net Income						
Operating Cash Flow						
Capital Expenditure						
EBITDA						
Return on Assets %						
Return on Equity %						
Debt to Equity						

CONTACT INFORMATION:
Phone:　　　　　　　　Fax:
Toll-Free:
Address: 1600 Amphitheatre Pkwy., Mountain View, CA 94043 United States

STOCK TICKER/OTHER:
Stock Ticker: Subsidiary　　　　Exchange:
Employees: 250　　　　　　　Fiscal Year Ends:
Parent Company: Alphabet Inc

SALARIES/BONUSES:
Top Exec. Salary: $　　Bonus: $
Second Exec. Salary: $　Bonus: $

OTHER THOUGHTS:
Estimated Female Officers or Directors:
Hot Spot for Advancement for Women/Minorities:

Sales, profits and employees may be estimates. Financial information, benefits and other data can change quickly and may vary from those stated here.

Xerox Corporation

www.xerox.com

NAIC Code: 334118

TYPES OF BUSINESS:
Document Processing Technologies
Copiers
Software
Multipurpose Office Machines
Desktop Printers
Equipment Financing

BRANDS/DIVISIONS/AFFILIATES:
Conduent Inc

CONTACTS:
Note: Officers with more than one job title may be intentionally listed here more than once.

William Osbourn, CFO
Robert Keegan, Chairman of the Board
Joseph Mancini, Chief Accounting Officer
Farooq Muzaffar, Chief Marketing Officer
Steve Hoover, Chief Technology Officer
Jeffrey Jacobson, Director
Sarah McConnell, Executive VP
Darrell Ford, Executive VP
Kevin Warren, Executive VP
Herve Tessler, Executive VP
Michael Feldman, Executive VP
Yehia Maaty, Other Executive Officer

GROWTH PLANS/SPECIAL FEATURES:

Xerox Corporation is a document systems company operating in the global market. The company's primary offerings span three main areas: managed document services, workplace solutions and graphic communications. The managed document services division offers products that help Xerox customers in regards to managing their documents, including optimizing their printing and related document workflow and business processes. Its customers include small businesses as well as global enterprises. The workplace solutions and graphic communications divisions offer products and solutions that support the work processes of Xerox customers, by providing them with an efficient, cost-effective printing and communications infrastructure. Xeros applies innovation in digital print technology and services to create value for its customers and shareholders. These investments include areas such as workflow automation, color printing, customized communication and new/novel applications of printing technology for enhanced digital printing, personalization at scale, enterprise agility and usable analytics purposes. In January 2017, the firm spun-off its business process outsourcing business into a new firm, Conduent, Inc. That June, Xerox agreed to sell its European research center in Grenoble, France to NAVER Corporation.

Xerox employees receive health care, life insurance, employee assistance programs, retirement plans and child care/elder care resources.

FINANCIAL DATA:
Note: Data for latest year may not have been available at press time.

In U.S. $	2017	2016	2015	2014	2013	2012
Revenue	9,971,000,000	10,446,000,000	17,699,000,000	19,153,000,000	20,952,000,000	21,793,000,000
R&D Expense	446,000,000	476,000,000	563,000,000	577,000,000	601,000,000	655,000,000
Operating Income	637,000,000	707,000,000	485,000,000	1,179,000,000	1,095,000,000	1,358,000,000
Operating Margin %	6.38%	6.76%	2.74%	6.15%	5.22%	6.23%
SGA Expense	2,631,000,000	2,695,000,000	3,559,000,000	3,788,000,000	4,137,000,000	4,288,000,000
Net Income	195,000,000	-477,000,000	474,000,000	969,000,000	1,159,000,000	1,195,000,000
Operating Cash Flow	34,000,000	1,095,000,000	1,611,000,000	2,063,000,000	2,375,000,000	2,580,000,000
Capital Expenditure	105,000,000	138,000,000	342,000,000	452,000,000	427,000,000	513,000,000
EBITDA	1,216,000,000	1,312,000,000	1,825,000,000	2,869,000,000	2,913,000,000	2,847,000,000
Return on Assets %	1.06%	-2.33%	1.71%	3.33%	3.84%	3.89%
Return on Equity %	3.59%	-7.40%	4.64%	8.36%	9.81%	10.16%
Debt to Equity	0.99	1.10	0.73	0.59	0.57	0.66

CONTACT INFORMATION:
Phone: 203 968-3000 Fax:
Toll-Free: 800-275-9376
Address: 45 Glover Ave., Norwalk, CT 06856 United States

STOCK TICKER/OTHER:
Stock Ticker: XRX
Employees: 37,600
Parent Company:

Exchange: NYS
Fiscal Year Ends: 12/31

SALARIES/BONUSES:
Top Exec. Salary: $503,846   Bonus: $1,750,000
Second Exec. Salary: $1,100,000   Bonus: $

OTHER THOUGHTS:
Estimated Female Officers or Directors: 11
Hot Spot for Advancement for Women/Minorities: Y

ZF Friedrichshafen AG (ZF)

www.zf.com

NAIC Code: 336350

TYPES OF BUSINESS:

Automotive Components
Transmissions & Power Trains
Axles
Steering Systems
Chassis Components
Repair Services
Agricultural & Construction Machinery
Boat & Helicopter Transmissions

BRANDS/DIVISIONS/AFFILIATES:

Zeppelin Foundation
Friction Material Group North America Inc

CONTACTS: Note: Officers with more than one job title may be intentionally listed here more than once.

Wolf-Henning Scheider, CEO
Konstantin Sauer, CFO
Jurgen Holeksa, Human Resources
Stefan Sommer, Dir.-Corp. Dev
Stefan Sommer, Dir.-Corp. Comm.
Konstantin Sauer, Exec. VP-Finance & Controlling
Wilhelm Rehm, Exec. VP-Industrial Tech.
Gerhard Wagner, Exec. VP-Powertrain Tech. Div.
Reinhard Buhl, Exec. VP-Car Chassis Tech. Div.
Rolf Lutz, Exec. VP-Commercial Vehicles, South America
Peter Ottenbruch, Exec. VP-Tech., Asia Pacific

GROWTH PLANS/SPECIAL FEATURES:

ZF Friedrichshafen AG (ZF) designs and manufactures transmissions, steering systems, chassis components and axle systems and modules. Zeppelin Foundation, which is administered by the city of Friedrichsafen, holds a majority interest in the firm. ZF's business units mostly operate as jointly- or wholly-owned subsidiaries. The company operates through seven divisions: car powertrain technology, car chassis technology, commercial vehicle technology, industrial technology, e-mobility, ZF aftermarket and active & passive safety technology. Car powertrain technology includes automatic transmissions, manual transmissions, dual clutch transmissions, axle drives, powertrain modules, electric drive technology and die casting technology. Car chassis technology includes chassis systems, chassis components and suspension technology. Commercial vehicle (CV) technology includes truck and van driveline technology, axle and transmission systems for buses and coaches, CV chassis modules, CV damper technology and CV powertrain modules. Industrial technology includes off-highway systems, test systems, special driveline technology, marine propulsion systems, aviation technology and wind power technology. The e-mobility segment includes electronic systems, system house and electric traction drive systems. The ZF aftermarket segment includes original equipment services, specific original equipment, manufacturing services and Friction Material Group North America, Inc., which specializes in automotive brakes. The active & passive safety technology includes braking systems, steering systems, electronics, occupant safety systems, body control systems and parts and services. ZF's global workforce includes more than 145,000 employees at 230 locations in approximately 40 countries. The firm is one of the largest automotive suppliers in the world. In April 2018, ZF announced that it was building a new production facility in Pancevo, Serbia to produce electric and hybrid drives. Production is scheduled for early-2019.

FINANCIAL DATA: Note: Data for latest year may not have been available at press time.

In U.S. $	2017	2016	2015	2014	2013	2012
Revenue	43,654,900,000	37,230,900,000	32,785,130,700	20,538,000,000	22,108,636,677	20,387,164,759
R&D Expense						
Operating Income						
Operating Margin %						
SGA Expense						
Net Income	1,397,910,000	978,257,000	1,145,916,450	749,412,000	606,598,851	433,284,893
Operating Cash Flow						
Capital Expenditure						
EBITDA						
Return on Assets %						
Return on Equity %						
Debt to Equity						

CONTACT INFORMATION:

Phone: 49-7541-77-0 Fax: 49-7541-77-908000
Toll-Free:
Address: Lowentaler Strasse 20, Friedrichshafen, 88046 Germany

SALARIES/BONUSES:

Top Exec. Salary: $ Bonus: $
Second Exec. Salary: $ Bonus: $

STOCK TICKER/OTHER:

Stock Ticker: Private
Employees: 146,148
Parent Company: Zeppelin Foundation

Exchange:
Fiscal Year Ends: 12/31

OTHER THOUGHTS:

Estimated Female Officers or Directors:
Hot Spot for Advancement for Women/Minorities:

Sales, profits and employees may be estimates. Financial information, benefits and other data can change quickly and may vary from those stated here.

Plunkett Research, Ltd.

ZTE Corporation

NAIC Code: 334210

www.zte.com.cn

TYPES OF BUSINESS:
Telecommunications Equipment Manufacturing
Optical Networking Equipment
Intelligent & Next-Generation Network Systems
Mobile Phones

BRANDS/DIVISIONS/AFFILIATES:

CONTACTS:
Note: Officers with more than one job title may be intentionally listed here more than once.
Zhao Xianming, CEO
Yin Yimin, Chmn.

GROWTH PLANS/SPECIAL FEATURES:

ZTE Corporation is one of China's largest telecommunications equipment providers, specializing in offering customized network solutions for telecom carriers in more than 160 countries. The company develops and manufactures telecommunications equipment for voice, data, multimedia and wireless broadband applications. ZTE's business is organized into seven primary product divisions: device, including smartphones, gateways and mobile hotspot solutions; wireless, including base stations, controllers and network management solutions; bearer, including data communication and optical transmission solutions; cloud computing and IT, including cloud and data center solutions; core network, including convergence user data solutions, intelligent open source solutions and voice communication solutions; fixed access, including optical and copper access equipment and solutions, and customer-premises equipment (CPE) such as telephones, routers, switches, gateways and more; and energy, including telecommunications power, hybrid power, solar power, smart streetlighting, micro-grid energy storage, uninterruptible power sources, micro-modular data center solutions, container data center solutions and data center intelligent management solutions. ZTE's products and solutions include consulting services, customer support, integration services, service tools, learning services, managed services and UniCare service transformation services. The firm has global sales outlets throughout North America, Latin America, Africa, Europe, Commonwealth of Independent States, China and Asia-Pacific.

FINANCIAL DATA:
Note: Data for latest year may not have been available at press time.

In U.S. $	2017	2016	2015	2014	2013	2012
Revenue	17,344,120,000	16,135,610,000	15,968,760,000	12,985,750,000	11,991,540,000	13,423,760,000
R&D Expense						
Operating Income	756,073,300	407,432,500	546,199,200	491,047,200	229,248,000	-534,824,900
Operating Margin %	4.35%	2.52%	3.42%	3.78%	1.91%	-3.98%
SGA Expense	2,416,609,000	2,382,262,000	2,256,176,000	1,959,006,000	1,945,539,000	2,145,732,000
Net Income	728,123,200	-375,750,000	511,306,400	419,766,200	216,397,600	-452,822,300
Operating Cash Flow	1,150,795,000	838,426,800	1,180,233,000	400,490,100	410,363,200	247,057,800
Capital Expenditure	953,793,500	637,954,000	393,552,700	329,556,400	372,483,800	378,975,500
EBITDA	1,670,368,000	449,282,000	1,218,478,000	1,100,578,000	828,869,600	230,128,000
Return on Assets %	3.19%	-1.79%	2.82%	2.55%	1.30%	-2.66%
Return on Equity %	15.73%	-8.41%	11.76%	11.10%	6.16%	-12.42%
Debt to Equity	0.09	0.19	0.20	0.40	0.51	0.33

CONTACT INFORMATION:
Phone: 86 75526770000   Fax: 86 75526770286
Toll-Free:
Address: Hi-tech Rd. S., No. 55, Shenzhen, Guangdong 518057 China

STOCK TICKER/OTHER:
Stock Ticker: ZTCOF   Exchange: PINX
Employees: 75,609   Fiscal Year Ends: 12/31
Parent Company:

SALARIES/BONUSES:
Top Exec. Salary: $ Bonus: $
Second Exec. Salary: $ Bonus: $

OTHER THOUGHTS:
Estimated Female Officers or Directors:
Hot Spot for Advancement for Women/Minorities:

Sales, profits and employees may be estimates. Financial information, benefits and other data can change quickly and may vary from those stated here.

ADDITIONAL INDEXES

CONTENTS:

Index of Firms Noted as "Hot Spots for Advancement" for Women/Minorities	**630**
Index by Subsidiaries, Brand Names and Selected Affiliations	**632**

INDEX OF FIRMS NOTED AS HOT SPOTS FOR ADVANCEMENT FOR WOMEN & MINORITIES

3M Company
AB Volvo
ABB Ltd
Abbott Laboratories
Abengoa SA
Accenture plc
Adobe Systems Inc
Advanced Micro Devices Inc (AMD)
Advanced Semiconductor Engineering Inc
AECOM
Agilent Technologies Inc
Air Products and Chemicals Inc
Albany Molecular Research Inc
Alcon Inc
Allergan plc
Alphabet Inc
Alstom SA
Altana AG
Amdocs Limited
Amgen Inc
Analog Devices Inc
Applied Materials Inc
Arcadis NV
Areva SA
AstraZeneca plc
ATS Automation Tooling Systems Inc
Autodesk Inc
Babcock & Wilcox Enterprises Inc
BAE Systems plc
Baker Huges, A GE Company
BASF SE
Bausch & Lomb Inc
Baxter International Inc
Bechtel Group Inc
Beckman Coulter Inc
Becton Dickinson & Company
Belden Inc
Biogen Inc
BIOS-BIOENERGYSYSTEME GmbH
Black & Veatch Holding Company
BMC Software Inc
BMW (Bayerische Motoren Werke AG)
Boeing Company (The)
Bombardier Inc
Boston Scientific Corporation
Bouygues SA
BP plc
Bristol-Myers Squibb Co
CA Inc (CA Technologies)
Caterpillar Inc
Celanese Corporation
Celestica Inc
CGI Group Inc
CH2M HILL Inc
Chevron Corporation
Chicago Bridge & Iron Company NV (CB&I)
Cisco Systems Inc
ConocoPhillips Company
Corning Inc
Cray Inc
CSL Limited
Cummins Inc
Daimler AG
Dana Incorporated
Dassault Systemes SA
Deere & Company (John Deere)
Dell EMC
Dell Technologies Inc
Diebold Nixdorf Inc
DNV GL Group AS
DowDupont Inc
Downer EDI Limited
Eastman Chemical Company
Eaton Corporation plc
Eli Lilly and Company
Emerson Electric Co
Empresas ICA SAB de CV
ENGlobal Corporation
Eni SpA
Essilor International SA
Exxon Mobil Corporation (ExxonMobil)
FCA US LLC
Flex Ltd
Fluor Corporation
Fomento de Construcciones y Contratas SA (FCC)
Ford Motor Co
GE Aviation
GE Healthcare
Gemalto NV
Genentech Inc
General Dynamics Corporation
General Electric Company (GE)
General Motors Company (GM)
Georg Fischer Ltd
Gilead Sciences Inc
GlaxoSmithKline plc
Globalvia Inversiones SAU
Halliburton Company
Harris Corporation
Harsco Corporation
Hewlett Packard Laboratories (HP Labs)
HGST Inc
Hill-Rom Holdings Inc
Honeywell International Inc
Huawei Technologies Co Ltd
IBM Global Business Services
Illinois Tool Works Inc
IMI plc
Ingersoll-Rand plc

Innolux Corporation
Intel Corporation
Intellectual Ventures Management LLC
International Business Machines Corporation (IBM)
Intertek Group plc
Intuit Inc
IQVIA Holdings Inc
ITT Inc
Jabil Inc
Jacobs Engineering Group Inc
Johnson & Johnson
Johnson Controls International plc
Juniper Networks Inc
KBR Inc
Koninklijke Philips NV (Royal Philips)
Lanxess AG
Lockheed Martin Corporation
LyondellBasell Industries NV
Marathon Oil Corporation
McAfee Inc
McDermott International Inc
Medtronic plc
Merck & Co Inc
Merck Serono SA
Meritor Inc
Microsoft Corporation
Monsanto Company
MWH Global Inc
NCR Corporation
NetApp Inc
Nokia Corporation
Northrop Grumman Corporation
Novartis AG
Novo-Nordisk AS
Novozymes
NVIDIA Corporation
Oracle Corporation
Palo Alto Research Center Incorporated (PARC)
PAREXEL International Corporation
Peugeot SA (Groupe PSA)
Pfizer Inc
Qualcomm Incorporated
Raytheon Company
Renault SA
Robert Bosch GmbH
Roche Holding AG
Rolls-Royce plc
Royal Dutch Shell plc
Saab AB
Safran SA
Sanofi Genzyme
Sanofi SA
SAP SE
SAS Institute Inc
Sasol Limited
Schlumberger Limited
Science Applications International Corporation (SAIC)
Seagate Technology plc

Sembcorp Marine Ltd
Siemens AG
Siemens Gamesa Renewable Energy SA
Siemens Healthineers
Singapore Technologies Engineering Limited
Skidmore Owings & Merrill LLP
Smith & Nephew plc
Smiths Group plc
SNC-Lavalin Group Inc
Spirit AeroSystems Holdings Inc
Stanley Black & Decker Inc
Statoil ASA
STMicroelectronics NV
Stryker Corporation
STV Group Incorporated
Symantec Corporation
Syngenta AG
Synopsys Inc
Taiwan Semiconductor Manufacturing Co Ltd (TSMC)
Takeda Pharmaceutical Company Limited
Tate & Lyle plc
TechnipFMC plc
Teledyne Technologies Inc
Telefon AB LM Ericsson (Ericsson)
Tellabs Inc
Tenneco Inc
Texas Instruments Inc (TI)
Textron Inc
Total SA
UCB SA
Unisys Corp
United Technologies Corporation
Valeo SA
Vestas Wind Systems A/S
Visteon Corporation
Volvo Car Corporation
VSE Corporation
Whirlpool Corporation
Wipro Limited
Xerox Corporation

INDEX OF SUBSIDIARIES, BRAND NAMES AND AFFILIATIONS

1QBit; **Accenture plc**
2K; **Take-Two Interactive Software Inc**
2K Games; **Take-Two Interactive Software Inc**
2K Play; **Take-Two Interactive Software Inc**
2K Sports; **Take-Two Interactive Software Inc**
370Z; **Nissan Motor Co Ltd**
3D Xpoint; **Micron Technology Inc**
3DEXCITE; **Dassault Systemes SA**
3ds Max; **Autodesk Inc**
3DVIA; **Dassault Systemes SA**
3M Purification Inc; **3M Company**
4U60; **HGST Inc**
70D; **Tesla Inc**
737; **Boeing Company (The)**
747; **Boeing Company (The)**
767; **Boeing Company (The)**
777; **Boeing Company (The)**
787; **Boeing Company (The)**
A-20 Super Tucano; **Embraer SA**
A320; **Airbus SE**
A330-200F; **Airbus SE**
A4 Holding SpA; **Abertis Infraestructuras SA**
A8; **Audi AG**
A-B; **Rockwell Automation Inc**
Accent; **Hyundai Motor Company**
Accenture Consulting; **Accenture plc**
Access; **Alphabet Inc**
Acciona Agua; **Acciona SA**
Accord; **Honda Motor Co Ltd**
ACCROPODE; **Artelia**
Acer; **Acer Inc**
Acetow; **Solvay SA**
ACKG Ltd; **Oriental Consultants Global Co Ltd**
AcrySof; **Alcon Inc**
ACT Independent Turbo Services; **Doosan Heavy Industries & Construction Co Ltd**
ACTEGA Coatings & Sealants; **Altana AG**
Actelion Ltd; **Johnson & Johnson**
ACTICA; **Empresas ICA SAB de CV**
ActiveScale; **HGST Inc**
ActiveScale Cloud Management; **HGST Inc**
Activision Publishing Inc; **Activision Blizzard Inc**
Acura; **Honda Motor Co Ltd**
ACX; **Juniper Networks Inc**
Adalat; **Bayer HealthCare Pharmaceuticals Inc**
Adam Opel AG; **Peugeot SA (Groupe PSA)**
Adaptive Methods Inc; **L3 Technologies Inc**
Adobe Acrobat; **Adobe Systems Inc**
Adobe Creative Cloud; **Adobe Systems Inc**
Adobe Creative Suite; **Adobe Systems Inc**
Adobe Dreamweaver; **Adobe Systems Inc**
Adobe InDesign; **Adobe Systems Inc**
Adobe Photoshop; **Adobe Systems Inc**
Adobe PostScript; **Adobe Systems Inc**
Adobe Stock; **Adobe Systems Inc**

Advics South Africa Pty Ltd; **Aisin Seiki Co Ltd**
Aecon Atlantic Industrial Inc; **Aecon Group Inc**
Aecon Concessions; **Aecon Group Inc**
Aecon Constructors; **Aecon Group Inc**
Aecon Industrial; **Aecon Group Inc**
Aecon Mining; **Aecon Group Inc**
Aecon Utilities; **Aecon Group Inc**
Aecon Water Infrastructure; **Aecon Group Inc**
Aerostructures; **Saab AB**
AFF A-Series; **NetApp Inc**
Agfa Graphics; **Agfa-Gevaert NV**
Agfa HealthCare; **Agfa-Gevaert NV**
Agfa Specialty Products; **Agfa-Gevaert NV**
Agilent CrossLab; **Agilent Technologies Inc**
Agilent Technologies Research Laboratories; **Agilent Technologies Inc**
Agricultural Airplane Ipanema; **Embraer SA**
Air Multiplier; **Dyson Limited**
Airbus Group SE; **Airbus SE**
Airbus SAS; **Airbus SE**
AirPower; **Apple Inc**
Aisin AI Brasil Industria Automotiva Ltda; **Aisin Seiki Co Ltd**
Aisin Asia Pte Ltd; **Aisin Seiki Co Ltd**
Aisin Europe Manufacturing (UK) Ltd; **Aisin Seiki Co Ltd**
Aisin Europe SA; **Aisin Seiki Co Ltd**
Aisin Holdings of America Inc; **Aisin Seiki Co Ltd**
Aisin Tianlin Body Parts Co Ltd; **Aisin Seiki Co Ltd**
Akashi-Kikai Industry Co Ltd; **Daihatsu Motor Co Ltd**
Alan Auld Group Ltd; **Golder Associates Corporation**
Alaris; **Becton Dickinson & Company**
Alaway; **Bausch & Lomb Inc**
Alba; **Akzo Nobel NV**
Alcon; **Novartis AG**
Aldo Abela Surveys Limited; **Intertek Group plc**
Aldurazyme; **Sanofi Genzyme**
Alere Inc; **Abbott Laboratories**
Alestra; **ALFA SAB de CV**
Aleve; **Bayer AG**
Aleve; **Bayer Corporation**
Alfa Romeo; **FCA US LLC**
Alimta; **Eli Lilly and Company**
Alka-Seltzer Plus; **Bayer Corporation**
All Flash FAS; **NetApp Inc**
Allen-Bradley; **Rockwell Automation Inc**
Alliance Truck Parts; **Daimler Trucks North America LLC**
Alloderm; **Allergan plc**
Alogliptin Benzoate; **Takeda Pharmaceutical Company Limited**
Alpek; **ALFA SAB de CV**
Alphabet Inc; **Waymo LLC**
Alphabet Inc; **X Development LLC**
Alpine Electronics Inc; **Alps Electric Co Ltd**
Alps Logistics Co Ltd; **Alps Electric Co Ltd**
Alrex; **Bausch & Lomb Inc**
Altima; **Nissan Motor Co Ltd**
Amazon Dash; **Amazon Lab126 Inc**

INDEX OF SUBSIDIARIES, BRAND NAMES AND AFFILIATIONS, CONT.

Amazon Echo; **Amazon Lab126 Inc**
Amazon Fire TV; **Amazon Lab126 Inc**
Amazon.com Inc; **Amazon Lab126 Inc**
AMD Embedded G-Series; **Advanced Micro Devices Inc (AMD)**
AMD Embedded Radeon; **Advanced Micro Devices Inc (AMD)**
AMD Embedded R-Series; **Advanced Micro Devices Inc (AMD)**
AMD EPYC; **Advanced Micro Devices Inc (AMD)**
AMD Opteron; **Advanced Micro Devices Inc (AMD)**
AMD PRO; **Advanced Micro Devices Inc (AMD)**
AMD Ryzen PRO; **Advanced Micro Devices Inc (AMD)**
Amdocs CES; **Amdocs Limited**
Amdocs CES 10; **Amdocs Limited**
Amdocs CES 10.2; **Amdocs Limited**
Amdocs Optima; **Amdocs Limited**
American Civil Constructors Inc; **ACC Companies (The)**
American Environmental Consultants Inc; **TRC Companies Inc**
American Fire Protection LLC; **CHA Consulting Inc**
American Standard; **Ingersoll-Rand plc**
Amistar; **Syngenta AG**
Andes Airport Services; **Acciona SA**
Anyo Pioneer Motor Info Tech Co Ltd; **Pioneer Corporation**
AOC; **TPV Technology Limited**
Aoi Machine Industry Co Ltd; **Daihatsu Motor Co Ltd**
AP1000 PWR; **Westinghouse Electric Company LLC**
Apiary; **Oracle Corporation**
AppDynamics Inc; **Cisco Systems Inc**
Apple TV; **Apple Inc**
Apple Watch; **Apple Inc**
Aptis; **Alstom SA**
Aral; **BP plc**
Aranesp; **Amgen Inc**
Arctic Cat Inc; **Textron Inc**
AREVA Australia Holdings Pty Ltd; **Areva SA**
AREVA Gabon; **Areva SA**
AREVA Mongol; **Areva SA**
AREVA NC; **Areva SA**
AREVA NP; **Areva SA**
AREVA Projects; **Areva SA**
AREVA Resources Namibia; **Areva SA**
AREZ; **ASUSTeK Computer Inc**
Ariane 5; **Safran SA**
ArianeGroup; **Airbus SE**
ArianeGroup; **Safran SA**
ArianeGroup; **Airbus SE**
Aricept; **Eisai Co Ltd**
Arlanxeo; **Lanxess AG**
ARO; **Ingersoll-Rand plc**
Artelia Italia; **Artelia**
Artificial Lift; **Halliburton Company**
ASCO Power Technologies; **Schneider Electric SE**

ASE Electronics Inc; **Advanced Semiconductor Engineering Inc**
Asgrow; **Monsanto Company**
Aspirata; **Aurecon Group Brand (Pte) Ltd**
Aspire Defence; **KBR Inc**
ASSET360; **Black & Veatch Holding Company**
ASUS NovaGo; **ASUSTeK Computer Inc**
AT India Auto Parts Pvt Ltd; **Aisin Seiki Co Ltd**
Atenza; **Mazda Motor Corporation**
Athlon Car Lease International; **Daimler AG**
Atollic; **STMicroelectronics NV**
Atonix Digital; **Black & Veatch Holding Company**
Atrenne Integrated Solutions Inc; **Celestica Inc**
ATS SmartVision; **ATS Automation Tooling Systems Inc**
ATS SuperTrak; **ATS Automation Tooling Systems Inc**
ATS850; **ATS Automation Tooling Systems Inc**
Attrage; **Mitsubishi Motors Corp**
Aubagio; **Sanofi SA**
Audi; **Porsche Automobil Holding SE**
Audi; **Volkswagen AG (VW)**
Audi Aicon; **Audi AG**
Audi Elaine; **Audi AG**
Audi e-tron; **Audi AG**
Audi Sport GmbH; **Audi AG**
AUO Crystal (Malaysia) Sdn Bhd; **AU Optronics Corp**
AUO Crystal Corp; **AU Optronics Corp**
AUO Green Energy America Corp; **AU Optronics Corp**
AUO Green Energy Europe BV; **AU Optronics Corp**
AUO SunPower Sdn Bhd; **AU Optronics Corp**
Aurecon Advisory; **Aurecon Group Brand (Pte) Ltd**
Aurecon Hatch; **Aurecon Group Brand (Pte) Ltd**
Auscom Engineering Inc; **Compal Electronics Inc**
AutoCAD; **Autodesk Inc**
AutoCAD LT; **Autodesk Inc**
Automic Holding GmbH; **CA Inc (CA Technologies)**
Autopista Central; **Abertis Infraestructuras SA**
Auxitec Ingenierie; **Artelia**
Avalox; **Bayer HealthCare Pharmaceuticals Inc**
AVEVA Group plc; **Schneider Electric SE**
Avicta; **Syngenta AG**
Avionics; **GE Aviation**
Avionics Systems; **Saab AB**
AVK; **Cummins Inc**
AVONEX; **Biogen Inc**
AvtoVAZ OAO; **Renault SA**
Axela; **Mazda Motor Corporation**
Axios; **Tenneco Inc**
Axtel; **ALFA SAB de CV**
Azilsartan; **Takeda Pharmaceutical Company Limited**
Azure; **Microsoft Corporation**
Babcock & Wilcox Beijing Company Ltd; **Babcock & Wilcox Enterprises Inc**
Babcock & Wilcox MEGTEC Holdings Inc; **Babcock & Wilcox Enterprises Inc**
Backup Plus; **Seagate Technology plc**
Bactine; **Bayer Corporation**

INDEX OF SUBSIDIARIES, BRAND NAMES AND AFFILIATIONS, CONT.

BAE Systems Applied Intelligence; **BAE Systems plc**
BAE Systems Australia; **BAE Systems plc**
BAE Systems India; **BAE Systems plc**
BAE Systems Saudi Arabia; **BAE Systems plc**
Baja; **Subaru Corporation**
Baker Hughes a GE company; **General Electric Company (GE)**
Baker Hughes Inc; **Baker Huges, A GE Company**
Band-Aid; **Johnson & Johnson**
Banque PSA Finance; **Peugeot SA (Groupe PSA)**
Baraclude; **Bristol-Myers Squibb Co**
Baroid; **Halliburton Company**
Basell AF SCA; **LyondellBasell Industries NV**
BASF 3D Printing Solutions GmbH; **BASF New Business GmbH**
BASF SE; **BASF New Business GmbH**
BASF Venture Capital GmbH; **BASF New Business GmbH**
Battleborn; **Take-Two Interactive Software Inc**
Battlefield; **Electronic Arts Inc (EA)**
Bausch + Lomb; **Bausch & Lomb Inc**
Bavaria Wirtschaftsagentur GmbH; **BMW (Bayerische Motoren Werke AG)**
Bayer; **Bayer Corporation**
Bayer AG; **Bayer HealthCare Pharmaceuticals Inc**
Bayer AG; **Bayer Corporation**
Bayer Aspirin; **Bayer AG**
Bbox Miami; **Bouygues SA**
BD Hypak; **Becton Dickinson & Company**
BD Life Sciences; **Becton Dickinson & Company**
BD Medical; **Becton Dickinson & Company**
BD Vacutainer; **Becton Dickinson & Company**
Beca AMEC; **Beca Group Limited**
Beca Warnes; **Beca Group Limited**
Beijing Doneed Seeds Industry Co Ltd; **Wanxiang Group Corporation**
Belco; **Kaneka Corporation**
Bell Helicopter; **Textron Inc**
Beluga; **Airbus SE**
BELVIQ; **Eisai Co Ltd**
BenQ Solar; **AU Optronics Corp**
Bentley; **Volkswagen AG (VW)**
Bentley; **Porsche Automobil Holding SE**
Bepanthen/Bepanthol; **Bayer AG**
Berger Group Holdings Inc; **Louis Berger Group Inc (The)**
Berkshire Hathaway Inc; **BYD Company Limited**
Bernafon; **William Demant Holding Group**
Betaferon; **Bayer HealthCare Pharmaceuticals Inc**
BharatBenz; **Daimler AG**
Bilfinger arnholdt; **Bilfinger SE**
Bilfinger Chemserv; **Bilfinger SE**
Bilfinger Deutsch Babcock Middle East; **Bilfinger SE**
Bilfinger Industrial Automation Services; **Bilfinger SE**
Bilfinger Maintenance; **Bilfinger SE**
Bilfinger Personalmanagement; **Bilfinger SE**

Bilfinger ROB Group; **Bilfinger SE**
Bilfinger Salamis Inc; **Bilfinger SE**
Bilfinger SE; **Bilfinger Tebodin BV**
BIM 360; **Autodesk Inc**
Bimba Manufacturing Company; **IMI plc**
BioMaxEff; **BIOS-BIOENERGYSYSTEME GmbH**
BIOSTROM Erzeugungs GmbH; **BIOS-BIOENERGYSYSTEME GmbH**
Biotrue; **Bausch & Lomb Inc**
Bioverativ Inc; **Sanofi SA**
BIOVIA; **Dassault Systemes SA**
Bizcom Electronics Inc; **Compal Electronics Inc**
Black & Decker; **Stanley Black & Decker Inc**
Black Duck Software; **Synopsys Inc**
Blizzard Entertainment Inc; **Activision Blizzard Inc**
BMW Motoren; **BMW (Bayerische Motoren Werke AG)**
BMW Technik; **BMW (Bayerische Motoren Werke AG)**
Boeing Capital Corporation; **Boeing Company (The)**
Bollgard II; **Monsanto Company**
Bolon; **Essilor International SA**
Bolt Technology Corporation; **Teledyne Technologies Inc**
Bongo; **Mazda Motor Corporation**
Bortezomib; **Takeda Pharmaceutical Company Limited**
Bosch Battery Systems; **Robert Bosch GmbH**
Bosch Boxberg Proving Ground; **Robert Bosch GmbH**
Bosch Engineering; **Robert Bosch GmbH**
Bosch Mahle TurboSystems; **Robert Bosch GmbH**
Bosch Packaging Technology; **Robert Bosch GmbH**
Bosch Rexroth; **Robert Bosch GmbH**
Bostitch; **Stanley Black & Decker Inc**
Botox; **Allergan plc**
Bouygues Construction; **Bouygues SA**
Bouygues Immobilier; **Bouygues SA**
Boxer Parent Company Inc; **BMC Software Inc**
BP; **BP plc**
Braden; **PACCAR Inc**
Brammo Inc; **Cummins Inc**
Brastemp; **Whirlpool Corporation**
Bravo; **Syngenta AG**
Briviact; **UCB SA**
Brookfield Business Partners LP; **Westinghouse Electric Company LLC**
Brown & Root Industrial Services; **KBR Inc**
Bugatti; **Volkswagen AG (VW)**
Bugatti; **Porsche Automobil Holding SE**
Buick; **General Motors Company (GM)**
Buoygues Telecom; **Bouygues SA**
Butamax; **BP plc**
BYD Auto Company Limited; **BYD Company Limited**
BYK Additives & Instruments; **Altana AG**
BYK-Chemie; **Altana AG**
BYK-Gardner; **Altana AG**
BYOC; **Acer Inc**
C Series; **Bombardier Inc**
CA Technologies; **CA Inc (CA Technologies)**
Cadillac; **General Motors Company (GM)**

INDEX OF SUBSIDIARIES, BRAND NAMES AND AFFILIATIONS, CONT.

Calico; **Alphabet Inc**
Call of Duty; **Activision Blizzard Inc**
CAM Solutions; **Autodesk Inc**
Cameron; **Schlumberger Limited**
Cameron International Corporation; **Ingersoll-Rand plc**
Candy Crush; **Activision Blizzard Inc**
Canesten; **Bayer AG**
Canon Medical Systems Corporation; **Canon Inc**
Capital Group International Inc; **Bayer Corporation**
CapitalG; **Alphabet Inc**
Caprelsa; **Sanofi Genzyme**
Capricorn; **SpaceX (Space Exploration Technologies Corporation)**
Carco; **PACCAR Inc**
Carlyl Group (The); **Albany Molecular Research Inc**
Carlyle Group (The); **Pharmaceutical Product Development LLC**
Casio America Inc; **Casio Computer Co Ltd**
Casio Electronic Manufacturing Co Ltd; **Casio Computer Co Ltd**
Casio Europe GmbH; **Casio Computer Co Ltd**
Casio Middle East FZE; **Casio Computer Co Ltd**
Castrol; **BP plc**
Cat; **Caterpillar Inc**
Caterpillar Financial Services Corporation; **Caterpillar Inc**
Caterpillar Insurance Holdings Inc; **Caterpillar Inc**
CATIA; **Dassault Systemes SA**
CATS; **Synopsys Inc**
CBI; **Terex Corporation**
CBMI Construction Co Ltd; **China National Materials Co Ltd**
CEEDS; **Syngenta AG**
Celebrex; **Pfizer Inc**
Cell Design Labs Inc; **Gilead Sciences Inc**
Cementos Portland Valderrivas; **Fomento de Construcciones y Contratas SA (FCC)**
Central Plastics; **Georg Fischer Ltd**
Cerezyme; **Sanofi SA**
Cetrotide; **Merck Serono SA**
CF34; **GE Aviation**
CGGC-UN Power Co Ltd; **China Power Engineering Consulting Group Corporation**
CH2M Beca; **Beca Group Limited**
CH2M HILL Companies Ltd; **Jacobs Engineering Group Inc**
CHA Tech Services LLC; **CHA Consulting Inc**
Challenger; **Bombardier Inc**
Chemtura Corporation; **Lanxess AG**
Chengde Lolo Co Ltd; **Wanxiang Group Corporation**
Chevrolet; **General Motors Company (GM)**
Chevrolet; **GM Korea**
Chevron; **Chevron Corporation**
Chevron Phillips Chemical Company LLC; **Chevron Corporation**
Chiba Chemicals Manufacturing LLP; **Mitsui Chemicals Inc**
Chiba Phenol Co Ltd; **Mitsui Chemicals Inc**
China Construction American Co; **China State Construction Engineering Corp (CSCEC)**
China Construction Decoration Engineering Co; **China State Construction Engineering Corp (CSCEC)**
China Construction Development Co Ltd; **China State Construction Engineering Corp (CSCEC)**
China Energy Engineering Group Co Ltd; **China Power Engineering Consulting Group Corporation**
China National Automotive Industry International; **China National Machinery Industry Corporation**
China National Chemical Corporation (ChemChina); **Syngenta AG**
China National Erzhong Group Company; **China National Machinery Industry Corporation**
China National Machinery & Equipment I/E Corp; **China National Machinery Industry Corporation**
China National Petroleum Corporation; **China Petroleum Engineering & Construction Corporation**
China National Petroleum Corporation; **China Petroleum Pipeline Engineering Co Ltd**
China Petroleum Engineering & Construction Corp; **China Energy Engineering Corporation Limited**
China Petroleum Pipeline College; **China Petroleum Pipeline Engineering Co Ltd**
China Petroleum Pipeline Inspection Technologies; **China Petroleum Pipeline Engineering Co Ltd**
China Power Engineering Consulting Group Co Ltd; **China Power Engineering Consulting Group Corporation**
China State Construction International Co; **China State Construction Engineering Corp (CSCEC)**
China United Engineering Corporation; **China National Machinery Industry Corporation**
China-Mozambique Oil Engineering Company; **China Petroleum Engineering & Construction Corporation**
Chiyoda Almana Engineering LLC; **Chiyoda Corporation**
Chiyoda Oceania Pty Ltd; **Chiyoda Corporation**
Chiyoda System Technologies Corporation; **Chiyoda Corporation**
Chiyoda U-Tech Co Ltd; **Chiyoda Corporation**
Chromspun; **Eastman Chemical Company**
Chrysler; **FCA US LLC**
Chugai Pharmaceutical Co Ltd; **Roche Holding AG**
Cimic Group; **ACS Actividades de Construccion y Servicios SA**
CIMIC Group Limited; **HOCHTIEF AG**
Cimzia; **UCB SA**
CinemaStar; **HGST Inc**
Cintra; **Ferrovial SA**
Cion/Coulter; **Ingenium Group Inc**
Cisco Umbrella; **Cisco Systems Inc**
Cisco Unified Computing System; **Cisco Systems Inc**
Citrix Receiver; **Citrix Systems Inc**
Citrix Workspace Suite; **Citrix Systems Inc**
Citroen; **Peugeot SA (Groupe PSA)**
Civic; **Honda Motor Co Ltd**

INDEX OF SUBSIDIARIES, BRAND NAMES AND AFFILIATIONS, CONT.

Claritin; **Bayer AG**
ClearCurve; **Corning Inc**
ClearLLab Regeants; **Beckman Coulter Inc**
ClearPath; **Unisys Corp**
Clevite; **Tenneco Inc**
Cloud CPE; **Juniper Networks Inc**
Club Car; **Ingersoll-Rand plc**
Cobalt Light Systems; **Agilent Technologies Inc**
Coban; **Eli Lilly and Company**
Colas; **Bouygues SA**
Combitech; **Saab AB**
Command; **3M Company**
Compal (Vietnam) Co Ltd; **Compal Electronics Inc**
Computer (Hong Kong) Ltd; **Casio Computer Co Ltd**
Concol; **WSP Global Inc**
Conduent Inc; **Xerox Corporation**
Connected Solutions Company of North America; **Panasonic Corporation**
Control Empresarial de Capitales SA de CV; **Fomento de Construcciones y Contratas SA (FCC)**
Coolsculpting; **Allergan plc**
Cooper-Atkins; **Emerson Electric Co**
Coppertone; **Bayer AG**
Coral; **Akzo Nobel NV**
Corpus Christi Polymers LLC; **ALFA SAB de CV**
Cosma International of America Inc; **Magna International Inc**
CPP LONGWAY Engineering Project Management Co; **China Petroleum Pipeline Engineering Co Ltd**
C-Quest; **KEO International Consultants WLL**
CR Bard Inc; **Becton Dickinson & Company**
Craftsman; **Stanley Black & Decker Inc**
Cray CS; **Cray Inc**
Cray DataWarp Applications Accelerator; **Cray Inc**
Cray Sonexion; **Cray Inc**
Cray Urika-GX; **Cray Inc**
Cray XC; **Cray Inc**
Crizal; **Essilor International SA**
CRJ Series; **Bombardier Inc**
CR-V; **Honda Motor Co Ltd**
CSCEC Property Management Co; **China State Construction Engineering Corp (CSCEC)**
CSL Plasma; **CSL Limited**
CSRA Inc; **General Dynamics Corporation**
CSYS; **Dyson Limited**
Cu-Beam; **Dyson Limited**
Cuberg Inc; **Boeing Company (The)**
CX-5; **Mazda Motor Corporation**
Cyramza; **Eli Lilly and Company**
Dacia; **Renault SA**
Daelim Corporation; **Daelim Industrial Co Ltd**
Daelim Educational Foundation; **Daelim Industrial Co Ltd**
Daelim Energy Co Ltd; **Daelim Industrial Co Ltd**
Daelim Motor Co Ltd; **Daelim Industrial Co Ltd**
DAF Trucks; **PACCAR Inc**

Daihatsu Business Support & Engineering Center; **Daihatsu Motor Co Ltd**
Daihatsu Credit Co Ltd; **Daihatsu Motor Co Ltd**
Daihatsu Metal Co Ltd; **Daihatsu Motor Co Ltd**
Daihatsu Motor Co Ltd; **Toyota Motor Corporation**
Daihatsu Motor Kyushu Co Ltd; **Daihatsu Motor Co Ltd**
Daihatsu Transportation Co Ltd; **Daihatsu Motor Co Ltd**
Daimler; **Daimler AG**
Daimler AG; **Daimler Trucks North America LLC**
Daimler AG; **Renault SA**
Daimler Truck Financial; **Daimler Trucks North America LLC**
Dainippon Sumitomo Pharma; **Sumitomo Chemical Co Ltd**
Danaher Corporation; **Beckman Coulter Inc**
Dassalt Falcon Jet Corp; **Dassault Aviation SA**
Dassault Falcon; **Dassault Aviation SA**
Dassault Falcon Service SARL; **Dassault Aviation SA**
Dassault Group; **Dassault Aviation SA**
Dassault Procurement Services inc; **Dassault Aviation SA**
Day & Zimmermann Company; **Mason & Hanger**
DC Capital Partners LLC; **Michael Baker International LLC**
De Ruiter; **Monsanto Company**
DEKALB; **Monsanto Company**
Delft Univeristy of Technology; **QuTech**
Dell; **Dell Technologies Inc**
Dell EMC; **Dell Technologies Inc**
Dell Technologies Inc; **Dell EMC**
DELMIA; **Dassault Systemes SA**
Deltapine; **Monsanto Company**
Demio; **Mazda Motor Corporation**
DENSO; **Denso Corporation**
Denso Pres Tech Inc; **Denso Corporation**
DesignWare IP; **Synopsys Inc**
Det Norske Veritas Holding AS; **DNV GL Group AS**
Detroit Diesel Corporation; **Daimler Trucks North America LLC**
DeWALT; **Stanley Black & Decker Inc**
Diqua; **Whirlpool Corporation**
Direct Connect Architecture; **Advanced Micro Devices Inc (AMD)**
Distributed Denial of Service; **VeriSign Inc**
DLZ Hydrokinetic Company; **DLZ Corporation**
DM NovaFoam Ltd; **Mitsui Chemicals Inc**
Dodge; **FCA US LLC**
Domain Name System; **VeriSign Inc**
Dongfeng; **AB Volvo**
Donkey Kong; **Nintendo Co Ltd**
Doosan Babcock; **Doosan Heavy Industries & Construction Co Ltd**
Doosan Enpure; **Doosan Heavy Industries & Construction Co Ltd**
Doosan IMGB; **Doosan Heavy Industries & Construction Co Ltd**

INDEX OF SUBSIDIARIES, BRAND NAMES AND AFFILIATIONS, CONT.

Doosan Lentjes; **Doosan Heavy Industries & Construction Co Ltd**
Doosan Power Systems; **Doosan Heavy Industries & Construction Co Ltd**
Doosan Skoda Power; **Doosan Heavy Industries & Construction Co Ltd**
Doosan Turbomachinery Services; **Doosan Heavy Industries & Construction Co Ltd**
Dorsch Gruppe BDC; **Dorsch Gruppe**
Dorsch Gruppe DC Asia; **Dorsch Gruppe**
Dorsch Gruppe DC India; **Dorsch Gruppe**
Dorsch Gruppe DC-Abu Dhabi; **Dorsch Gruppe**
Dorsch International Consultants GmbH; **Dorsch Gruppe**
Doss Aviation Inc; **L3 Technologies Inc**
Dow Chemical Company (The); **Union Carbide Corporation**
Dow Corning Corporation; **DowDupont Inc**
Dowty; **GE Aviation**
Dr Straetmans GmbH; **Evonik Industries AG**
Dr. Scholl's; **Bayer AG**
Dragados SA; **ACS Actividades de Construccion y Servicios SA**
Dragon; **SpaceX (Space Exploration Technologies Corporation)**
Draper Fisher Jurveston; **SpaceX (Space Exploration Technologies Corporation)**
Drawbridge Health; **General Electric Company (GE)**
Drillmec Inc; **Trevi-Finanziaria Industriale SpA (Trevi Group)**
DRIVE; **NVIDIA Corporation**
DriveCore; **Visteon Corporation**
DroneSense; **FLIR Systems Inc**
DS Automobiles; **Peugeot SA (Groupe PSA)**
DSME Shandong Co Ltd; **Daewoo Shipbuilding & Marine Engineering Co Ltd**
Dual Gold; **Syngenta AG**
Ducati; **Audi AG**
Ducati; **Volkswagen AG (VW)**
Dulux; **Akzo Nobel NV**
Dupixent; **Sanofi Genzyme**
Dupixent; **Sanofi SA**
DuPont; **DowDupont Inc**
DuPont Tate & Lyle BioProducts; **Tate & Lyle plc**
DX2000; **NEC Corporation**
DxC 700 AU; **Beckman Coulter Inc**
Dynamics; **Microsoft Corporation**
DynoMax; **Tenneco Inc**
Dyson Airblade; **Dyson Limited**
Dyson Supersonic; **Dyson Limited**
E E Cruz and Company; **HOCHTIEF AG**
e2v technologies plc; **Teledyne Technologies Inc**
Eagle XG; **Corning Inc**
EAS; **Abbott Laboratories**
EasyMile; **Alstom SA**
ECC/Quantum Murray LP; **ECC**
ECKART Effect Pigments; **Altana AG**
ECOPODE; **Artelia**
EcoStruxure; **Schneider Electric SE**
Effient; **Eli Lilly and Company**
EF-Series; **NetApp Inc**
Eicher; **AB Volvo**
E-Jets; **Embraer SA**
ELANTAS Electrical Insulation; **Altana AG**
Elantra; **Hyundai Motor Company**
ELC Consulting & Engineering; **Royal HaskoningDHV**
Element Genomics; **UCB SA**
Eliquis; **Bristol-Myers Squibb Co**
Eliquis; **Pfizer Inc**
Elmiron; **Bayer Corporation**
Eloxatin; **Sanofi Genzyme**
Embrel; **Amgen Inc**
Emcision Limited; **Boston Scientific Corporation**
EMD Serono; **Merck KGaA**
EMD Serono Inc; **Merck Serono SA**
Empliciti; **Bristol-Myers Squibb Co**
Enable; **ExxonMobil Chemical Company Inc**
Enbrel; **Pfizer Inc**
Enercom; **BIOS-BIOENERGYSYSTEME GmbH**
ENERCON SCADA; **ENERCON GmbH**
ENERCON Storm Control; **ENERCON GmbH**
Energo; **KBR Inc**
Engie; **Lahmeyer International GmbH**
ENGlobal Emerging Markets Inc; **ENGlobal Corporation**
ENGlobal Government Services Inc; **ENGlobal Corporation**
ENGlobal International Inc; **ENGlobal Corporation**
ENGlobal US Inc; **ENGlobal Corporation**
Envision; **TPV Technology Limited**
Envision Peripherals Inc; **TPV Technology Limited**
Envista; **Downer EDI Limited**
E-Pace; **Jaguar Land Rover Limited**
EPOGEN; **Amgen Inc**
Epson Sales Co Ltd; **Seiko Epson Corporation**
Eptisa Romania SRL; **Eptisa**
Eptisa Servicios de Ingeneieria SL; **Eptisa**
Eptisa Tecnologias de la Informacion SA; **Eptisa**
Erasito Beca; **Beca Group Limited**
Erga Mio; **Isuzu Motors Limited**
ERJ 145; **Embraer SA**
Escola De Aviacao Aerocondor SA; **L3 Technologies Inc**
Essilor; **Essilor International SA**
Esso; **Exxon Mobil Corporation (ExxonMobil)**
Estaleiro Jurong Aracruz; **Sembcorp Marine Ltd**
Estrace; **Allergan plc**
Estrobond; **Eastman Chemical Company**
Estron; **Eastman Chemical Company**
Eurovia; **VINCI SA**
EU-UltraLowDust; **BIOS-BIOENERGYSYSTEME GmbH**
EVENITY; **Amgen Inc**
Evonik Nutrition & Care GmbH; **Evonik Industries AG**

INDEX OF SUBSIDIARIES, BRAND NAMES AND AFFILIATIONS, CONT.

Evonik Performance Materials GmbH; **Evonik Industries AG**
Evonik Resource Efficiency GmbH; **Evonik Industries AG**
Evonik Technology & Infrastructure GmbH; **Evonik Industries AG**
Evoquip; **Terex Corporation**
EXALEAD; **Dassault Systemes SA**
EXO Technologies; **Lear Corporation**
Expancel; **Akzo Nobel NV**
Expansion; **Seagate Technology plc**
Express 5800; **NEC Corporation**
Extech; **FLIR Systems Inc**
Exxcore; **ExxonMobil Chemical Company Inc**
Exxon; **Exxon Mobil Corporation (ExxonMobil)**
Exxon Mobil Corporation; **ExxonMobil Chemical Company Inc**
ExxonMobil; **Exxon Mobil Corporation (ExxonMobil)**
ExxonMobile Chemical Technology Licensing LLC; **ExxonMobil Chemical Company Inc**
Eyezen; **Essilor International SA**
EZ10; **Alstom SA**
E-Z-GO; **Textron Inc**
F Hoffmann-La Roche Ltd; **Roche Holding AG**
F110; **GE Aviation**
FACC Industrial; **Fomento de Construcciones y Contratas SA (FCC)**
FactoryTalk; **Rockwell Automation Inc**
Falcon 9; **SpaceX (Space Exploration Technologies Corporation)**
Fall Line Testing & inspection LLC; **Paul C Rizzo Associates Inc**
Fast Track Diagnostics; **Siemens Healthineers**
FatMax; **Stanley Black & Decker Inc**
FAW Assets Operation and Management Co Ltd; **FAW Group Corporation (First Automotive Works)**
FAW Bus and Coach Co Ltd; **FAW Group Corporation (First Automotive Works)**
FAW Foundry Co Ltd; **FAW Group Corporation (First Automotive Works)**
FAW Group Import and Export Corporation; **FAW Group Corporation (First Automotive Works)**
FAW Jiefang Truck Co Ltd; **FAW Group Corporation (First Automotive Works)**
FAW Jilin Automobile Co Ltd; **FAW Group Corporation (First Automotive Works)**
FAW Tool and Die Co Ltd; **FAW Group Corporation (First Automotive Works)**
FCA Italy SpA; **Magneti Marelli SpA**
FCC Aqualia; **Fomento de Construcciones y Contratas SA (FCC)**
FCC Concessiones; **Fomento de Construcciones y Contratas SA (FCC)**
FCC Construction; **Fomento de Construcciones y Contratas SA (FCC)**
Febuxostat; **Takeda Pharmaceutical Company Limited**

Fiasp; **Novo-Nordisk AS**
Fiat; **FCA US LLC**
Fiat Chrysler Automobiles NV; **FCA US LLC**
Fiat Chrysler Automobiles NV; **Magneti Marelli SpA**
Fibras; **Solvay SA**
Fidelity; **SpaceX (Space Exploration Technologies Corporation)**
Filtrete; **3M Company**
First Automotive Works; **FAW Group Corporation (First Automotive Works)**
First Marine International; **Royal HaskoningDHV**
Fit; **Honda Motor Co Ltd**
Flair; **Mazda Motor Corporation**
Flatiron; **HOCHTIEF AG**
Flatiron Health; **Roche Holding AG**
Fleetguard; **Cummins Inc**
Flexa; **Akzo Nobel NV**
FlexPod; **NetApp Inc**
FlexProcess for Ever Changing Business; **NEC Corporation**
Flex-Tek; **Smiths Group plc**
FLEXX; **Bombardier Inc**
FLIR; **FLIR Systems Inc**
Fonos; **Tenneco Inc**
FORAN; **Sener Ingenieria y Sistemas SA**
Forcepoint; **Raytheon Company**
Ford; **Ford Motor Co**
Ford Escape Hybrid SUV; **Ford Motor Co**
Ford F150; **Ford Motor Co**
Ford Focus; **Ford Motor Co**
Ford Motor Credit Co; **Ford Motor Co**
Ford Mustang; **Ford Motor Co**
Forester; **Subaru Corporation**
Founders Fund; **SpaceX (Space Exploration Technologies Corporation)**
Foxconn Technology Co Ltd; **Sharp Corporation**
Foxconn Technology Group; **Hon Hai Precision Industry Company Ltd**
F-Pace; **Jaguar Land Rover Limited**
Free2 Move; **Peugeot SA (Groupe PSA)**
Freechoice; **Magneti Marelli SpA**
Freightliner; **Daimler AG**
Freightliner Trucks; **Daimler Trucks North America LLC**
Friction Material Group North America Inc; **ZF Friedrichshafen AG (ZF)**
FRIGOBLOCK; **Ingersoll-Rand plc**
FrontRow; **William Demant Holding Group**
F-Type; **Jaguar Land Rover Limited**
Fuchs; **Terex Corporation**
Fuji Heavy Industries Ltd; **Subaru Corporation**
Fuji Xerox Co Ltd; **FUJIFILM Holdings Corporation**
FUJIFILM Business Expert Corporation; **FUJIFILM Holdings Corporation**
FUJIFILM Corporation; **FUJIFILM Holdings Corporation**

INDEX OF SUBSIDIARIES, BRAND NAMES AND AFFILIATIONS, CONT.

Fujitsu Laboratories of America Inc; **Fujitsu Laboratories Ltd**
Fujitsu Laboratories of Europe Limited; **Fujitsu Laboratories Ltd**
Fujitsu Limited; **Fujitsu Laboratories Ltd**
Fujitsu Limited; **Fujitsu Technology Solutions (Holding) BV**
Fujitsu Research and Development Center Co Ltd; **Fujitsu Laboratories Ltd**
Fujitsu Semiconductor Limited; **Fujitsu Limited**
FUMADERM; **Biogen Inc**
Fycompa; **Eisai Co Ltd**
G280; **Gulfstream Aerospace Corporation**
g3baxi partnership; **Hatch Group**
G500; **General Dynamics Corporation**
G500; **Gulfstream Aerospace Corporation**
G550; **Gulfstream Aerospace Corporation**
G600; **General Dynamics Corporation**
G600; **Gulfstream Aerospace Corporation**
G650; **Gulfstream Aerospace Corporation**
G650ER; **Gulfstream Aerospace Corporation**
Gabriel Acquisitions GmbH; **Evonik Industries AG**
Galaxy; **Samsung Electronics Co Ltd**
Gamesa Corporacion Tecnologica SA; **Siemens Gamesa Renewable Energy SA**
GANCOM; **Gannett Fleming Inc**
Gannet Fleming Architects Inc; **Gannett Fleming Inc**
Gannett Fleming IT; **Gannett Fleming Inc**
Gannett Fleming Project Development Corporation; **Gannett Fleming Inc**
Gannett Fleming Valuation and Rate Consultants LLC; **Gannett Fleming Inc**
GAZYVA; **Biogen Inc**
GE Additive; **General Electric Company (GE)**
GE Capital; **General Electric Company (GE)**
GE Digital; **General Electric Company (GE)**
GE Lighting; **General Electric Company (GE)**
GE Power; **General Electric Company (GE)**
GE Renewable Energy; **General Electric Company (GE)**
GE90; **GE Aviation**
Gearmatic; **PACCAR Inc**
GeForce; **NVIDIA Corporation**
Genentech Inc; **Roche Holding AG**
General Dynamics Corporation; **Gulfstream Aerospace Corporation**
General Electric Company; **Baker Huges, A GE Company**
General Electric Company; **GE Aviation**
General Electric Company (GE); **GE Global Research**
General Electric Company (GE); **GE Healthcare**
General Motors Company (GM); **GM Korea**
General Motors India Private Limited; **SAIC Motor Corporation Limited**
GeoDecisions; **Gannett Fleming Inc**
Geostrada Engineering Materials Laboratory; **Aurecon Group Brand (Pte) Ltd**
Geosyntec Australia & New Zealand; **Geosyntec Consultants Inc**
Geosyntec Europe; **Geosyntec Consultants Inc**
Gigafactory; **Tesla Inc**
Gigya; **SAP SE**
GKN Aerospace; **GKN plc**
GKN Driveline; **GKN plc**
GKN Hoeganaes; **GKN plc**
GKN Off-Highway Powertrain; **GKN plc**
GKN Powder Metallurgy; **GKN plc**
GKN Sinter Metals; **GKN plc**
GKN Wheels and Structures; **GKN plc**
Gladiator; **Whirlpool Corporation**
GlidePoint; **Alps Electric Co Ltd**
Global; **Bombardier Inc**
Global Drug Development; **Novartis AG**
Global Unichip Corporation; **Taiwan Semiconductor Manufacturing Co Ltd (TSMC)**
Glucobay; **Bayer HealthCare Pharmaceuticals Inc**
GMC; **General Motors Company (GM)**
GO; **Nissan Motor Co Ltd**
GONAL-f; **Merck Serono SA**
Goodmind Srl; **Pininfarina SpA**
Google; **Waymo LLC**
Google; **SpaceX (Space Exploration Technologies Corporation)**
Google LLC; **Alphabet Inc**
Gorilla; **Corning Inc**
Gottlieb Paludan Architects; **AF AB**
Granherne; **KBR Inc**
Granite Construction Company; **Granite Construction Incorporated**
Granite Construction Northeast Inc; **Granite Construction Incorporated**
Granite Infrastructure Constructors Inc; **Granite Construction Incorporated**
Gravifloat AS; **Sembcorp Marine Ltd**
Green Harbor Energy; **Geosyntec Consultants Inc**
GreenFlex; **Total SA**
GRID; **NVIDIA Corporation**
GripCo; **Stanley Black & Decker Inc**
Grupo Ferrovial SA; **Amey plc**
Gryphon International Engineering Services Inc; **CHA Consulting Inc**
G-SHOCK; **Casio Computer Co Ltd**
GTCR LLC; **Albany Molecular Research Inc**
Guangdong Power Engineering Corporation; **China Energy Engineering Corporation Limited**
Guangxi Water & Power Group Co Ltd; **China Energy Engineering Corporation Limited**
Gulf Interstate Field Services; **Gulf Interstate Engineering Company**
Gulfstream Aerospace Corporation; **General Dynamics Corporation**
GV; **Alphabet Inc**
GVA; **KBR Inc**

INDEX OF SUBSIDIARIES, BRAND NAMES AND AFFILIATIONS, CONT.

G'xEYE; **Casio Computer Co Ltd**
Halaven; **Eisai Co Ltd**
Halley & Mellowes Pty Ltd; **Babcock & Wilcox Enterprises Inc**
Happold LLP; **BuroHappold Ltd**
Harman; **Samsung Electronics Co Ltd**
Harman International Industries Inc; **Samsung Electronics Co Ltd**
Harsco Industrial Air-X-Changers; **Harsco Corporation**
Harsco Industrial IKG; **Harsco Corporation**
Harsco Industrial Patterson-Kelley; **Harsco Corporation**
Harvoni; **Gilead Sciences Inc**
Hawkins; **Downer EDI Limited**
HDR/Archer; **HDR Inc**
Hellman & Friedman; **Pharmaceutical Product Development LLC**
HEMLIBRA; **Genentech Inc**
Hewlet Packard Labs; **Hewlett Packard Enterprise Company**
Hewlett-Packard Enterprise Company; **Hewlett Packard Laboratories (HP Labs)**
Hforce; **Airbus SE**
HGST; **Western Digital Corporation**
Hidro Dizayn Group; **Lahmeyer International GmbH**
Hillstate; **Hyundai Engineering & Construction Company Ltd**
Hino; **Toyota Motor Corporation**
Hino Motors Ltd; **Toyota Motor Corporation**
Hitachi Global Storage Technologies; **Western Digital Corporation**
Hitachi Limited; **Hitachi High Technologies America Inc**
Hochtief AG; **ACS Actividades de Construccion y Servicios SA**
HOCHTIEF Insurance Broking and Risk; **HOCHTIEF AG**
HOCHTIEF Solutions AG; **HOCHTIEF AG**
Holden; **General Motors Company (GM)**
HomePod; **Apple Inc**
Honda; **Honda Motor Co Ltd**
HondaJet; **Honda Motor Co Ltd**
Horlicks; **GlaxoSmithKline plc**
Hotpoint; **Whirlpool Corporation**
Houston Interests LLC; **Matrix Service Company**
HPNow ApS; **Evonik Industries AG**
HQC (Guangdong) Company; **China HuanQiu Contracting & Engineering Corporation**
HTC Bolt; **HTC Corporation**
HTC U Ultra; **HTC Corporation**
HTC U11; **HTC Corporation**
Huaewi Matebook; **Huawei Technologies Co Ltd**
Huanqiu Equipment Manufacture Company; **China HuanQiu Contracting & Engineering Corporation**
Huanqiu Lanzhou Company; **China HuanQiu Contracting & Engineering Corporation**
Huanqiu Liaoning Company; **China HuanQiu Contracting & Engineering Corporation**
Huanqiu North China Institute; **China HuanQiu Contracting & Engineering Corporation**
Huanqiu Project Management Company; **China HuanQiu Contracting & Engineering Corporation**
Huanqiu Shanghai Company; **China HuanQiu Contracting & Engineering Corporation**
Huawei Marine Networks; **Huawei Technologies Co Ltd**
Huawei Watch 2; **Huawei Technologies Co Ltd**
Humira; **Eisai Co Ltd**
Humulin; **Eli Lilly and Company**
Hunan Thermal Power Construction Company; **China Energy Engineering Corporation Limited**
Huntington Ingalls Industries Inc; **UniversalPegasus International Inc**
Huntsman International LLC; **Huntsman Corporation**
Hydranautics; **Nitto Denko Corporation**
Hyperledger Project; **IBM Research**
Hyundai Capital Germany GmbH; **Hyundai Motor Company**
Hyundai Engineering Co Ltd; **Hyundai Engineering & Construction Company Ltd**
Hyundai Motor America; **Hyundai Motor Company**
Hyundai Motor Company; **Kia Motors Corporation**
i3; **BMW (Bayerische Motoren Werke AG)**
i30 N; **Hyundai Motor Company**
IBM Cnnsulting; **IBM Global Business Services**
IBM Cognitive Solutions; **International Business Machines Corporation (IBM)**
IBM Global Business Services; **International Business Machines Corporation (IBM)**
IBM Global Financing; **International Business Machines Corporation (IBM)**
IBM Global Process Services; **IBM Global Business Services**
IBM Quantum Experience; **IBM Research**
IBM Systems; **International Business Machines Corporation (IBM)**
IBM Technology Services & Cloud Platforms; **International Business Machines Corporation (IBM)**
ICA Fluor; **Empresas ICA SAB de CV**
Icahn Enterprises LP; **Federal-Mogul LLC**
ICM-Russia; **Baran Group Ltd**
ideapad; **Lenovo Group Limited**
Idorsia Ltd; **Johnson & Johnson**
Ignyta Inc; **Roche Holding AG**
IM Flash Technologies LLC; **Micron Technology Inc**
IMEG Limited; **Associated Consulting Engineers**
IMI CCI; **IMI plc**
IMI Critical Engineering; **IMI plc**
IMI Flow Design; **IMI plc**
IMI Hydronic Engineering; **IMI plc**
IMI Norgren; **IMI plc**
IMI Presicion Engineering; **IMI plc**
IMI Truflo Marine; **IMI plc**
i-MiEV; **Mitsubishi Motors Corp**
IMIS; **Aurecon Group Brand (Pte) Ltd**

INDEX OF SUBSIDIARIES, BRAND NAMES AND AFFILIATIONS, CONT.

Impreza; **Subaru Corporation**
India Hydropower Development Company LLC; **DLZ Corporation**
INESA Intelligent Technology Co Ltd; **Fujitsu Limited**
Infineon Technologies Asia Pacific Pte Ltd; **Infineon Technologies AG**
Infineon Technologies Japan KK; **Infineon Technologies AG**
Infineon Technologies North America Corp; **Infineon Technologies AG**
InfiniCor; **Corning Inc**
InfiniFlash All-Flash; **HGST Inc**
Ingersoll Rand; **Ingersoll-Rand plc**
Inliner; **Layne Christensen Company**
Innolux Optoelectronics Europe BV; **Innolux Corporation**
Innolux Optoelectronics Germany GmbH; **Innolux Corporation**
Innolux Optoelectronics Japan Co Ltd; **Innolux Corporation**
Innolux Optoelectronics Japan Co Ltd; **Innolux Corporation**
Innolux Optoelectronics USA Inc; **Innolux Corporation**
Innolux Technology Europe BV; **Innolux Corporation**
Innolux Technology Japan Co Ltd; **Innolux Corporation**
Innolux Technology USA Inc; **Innolux Corporation**
InSite; **KEO International Consultants WLL**
Intel Corporation; **McAfee Inc**
Intellectual Ventures Lab; **Intellectual Ventures Management LLC**
Interacoustics; **William Demant Holding Group**
Interceptor Plus; **Eli Lilly and Company**
International Business Machines Corporation (IBM); **IBM Global Business Services**
International Business Machines Corporation (IBM); **IBM Research**
Internet Revolution Inc; **Konami Holdings Corporation**
InterVISTAS Consulting Group; **Royal HaskoningDHV**
InTime Software Systems Ltd; **Baran Group Ltd**
iOS; **Apple Inc**
I-Pace; **Jaguar Land Rover Limited**
iPad; **Apple Inc**
iPhone; **Apple Inc**
IPS International; **IPS - Integrated Project Service LLC**
IPS-Mehtalia Pvt Ltd; **IPS - Integrated Project Service LLC**
IQVIA CORE; **IQVIA Holdings Inc**
Iridium Concesiones de Infraestructuras; **ACS Actividades de Construccion y Servicios SA**
Iris; **Corning Inc**
ISE Labs Inc; **Advanced Semiconductor Engineering Inc**
ISS Proko Oy; **WSP Global Inc**
ISS Suunnittelupalvelut Oy; **WSP Global Inc**
Isuzu (China) Holding Co Ltd; **Isuzu Motors Limited**
Isuzu D-MAX; **Isuzu Motors Limited**
Isuzu Malaysia Sendirian Berhad; **Isuzu Motors Limited**
Isuzu Philippines Corporation; **Isuzu Motors Limited**

Isuzu Remanufactura de Colombia SAS; **Isuzu Motors Limited**
ix5; **Dongfeng Motor Corporation**
Ixazomib; **Takeda Pharmaceutical Company Limited**
Jabil Circuit Inc; **Jabil Inc**
Jacobs Engineering Group Inc; **CH2M HILL Inc**
Jacobsen; **Textron Inc**
Jaguar; **Tata Motors Limited**
Japan Telegraph & Telephone Corporation; **NTT DATA Corporation**
JCG Gulf International Co Ltd; **JGC Corporation**
Jeep; **FCA US LLC**
Jenn-Air; **Whirlpool Corporation**
Jevtana; **Sanofi SA**
JGC Algeria SpA; **JGC Corporation**
JGC America Inc; **JGC Corporation**
JGC Catalysts & Chemicals Ltd; **JGC Corporation**
JGC China Engineering Co Ltd; **JGC Corporation**
JGC Plant Innovation Co Ltd; **JGC Corporation**
JK Aurecon; **Aurecon Group Brand (Pte) Ltd**
JKTech; **Aurecon Group Brand (Pte) Ltd**
John Crane; **Smiths Group plc**
John Deere; **Deere & Company (John Deere)**
JRG Gunzenhauser AG; **Georg Fischer Ltd**
Junos; **Juniper Networks Inc**
Kalray; **Safran SA**
Kaneka; **Kaneka Corporation**
Kaneka Coenzyme Q10; **Kaneka Corporation**
Kaneka Shokuhin Co Ltd; **Kaneka Corporation**
Kanekalon; **Kaneka Corporation**
Kautex; **Textron Inc**
KC-390; **Embraer SA**
Keller Medical Inc; **Allergan plc**
Kenny Construction Company; **Granite Construction Incorporated**
Kenworth Truck Company; **PACCAR Inc**
Keppra; **UCB SA**
Kerbal Space Program; **Take-Two Interactive Software Inc**
Kevzara; **Sanofi Genzyme**
Kia Motors Corporation; **Hyundai Motor Company**
Kia Quoris; **Kia Motors Corporation**
Kia Soul EV; **Kia Motors Corporation**
Kigre Inc; **L3 Technologies Inc**
Kindle; **Amazon Lab126 Inc**
Kindle Oasis; **Amazon Lab126 Inc**
Kindle Touch; **Amazon Lab126 Inc**
Kindle Voyage; **Amazon Lab126 Inc**
King Digital Entertainment; **Activision Blizzard Inc**
KitchenAid; **Whirlpool Corporation**
Kite Pharma Inc; **Gilead Sciences Inc**
Koch Industries Inc; **Molex LLC**
Kockums; **Saab AB**
Koei Research & Consulting Inc; **Nippon Koei Group**
Kogenare; **Bayer HealthCare Pharmaceuticals Inc**

INDEX OF SUBSIDIARIES, BRAND NAMES AND AFFILIATIONS, CONT.

Konami Amusement Co Ltd; **Konami Holdings Corporation**
Konami Australia Pty Ltd; **Konami Holdings Corporation**
Konami Digital Entertainment Co Ltd; **Konami Holdings Corporation**
Konami Gaming Inc; **Konami Holdings Corporation**
Konami Sports Club Co Ltd; **Konami Holdings Corporation**
Konami Sports Life Co Ltd; **Konami Holdings Corporation**
Korea Electric Power Corporation (KEPCO); **KEPCO Engineering & Construction Company Inc**
KPE Inc; **Konami Holdings Corporation**
Kumho Asiana Group; **Kumho Industrial Co Ltd**
L&T Defence; **Larsen & Toubro Limited (L&T)**
L&T Finance Holdings; **Larsen & Toubro Limited (L&T)**
L&T Heavy Engineering; **Larsen & Toubro Limited (L&T)**
L&T Hydrocarbon Engineering; **Larsen & Toubro Limited (L&T)**
L&T Infrastructure Development Projects Ltd; **Larsen & Toubro Limited (L&T)**
L&T Metro Rail; **Larsen & Toubro Limited (L&T)**
L&T Technology Services; **Larsen & Toubro Limited (L&T)**
L&T Valves; **Larsen & Toubro Limited (L&T)**
L&T-Chiyoda Limited; **Chiyoda Corporation**
Lacerte; **Intuit Inc**
Lachente; **Kaneka Corporation**
LaCie; **Seagate Technology plc**
Lahmeyer and Tractebel Engineering Consultancy LLC; **Lahmeyer International GmbH**
Lahmeyer Hydroprojekt GmbH; **Lahmeyer International GmbH**
Lahmeyer IDP Consult Inc; **Lahmeyer International GmbH**
Lahmeyer International Qatar LLC; **Lahmeyer International GmbH**
Lamborghini; **Audi AG**
Lamborghini; **Volkswagen AG (VW)**
Lamborghini; **Porsche Automobil Holding SE**
Land Rover; **Tata Motors Limited**
Landmark; **Halliburton Company**
Langan International; **Langan Engineering and Environmental Services Inc**
Lansoprazole; **Takeda Pharmaceutical Company Limited**
Lantus; **Sanofi SA**
Layne Inliner LLC; **Layne Christensen Company**
LCI; **Bouygues SA**
LDP Group Inc; **Gannett Fleming Inc**
LEAF; **Corning Inc**
Learjet; **Bombardier Inc**
LeddarTech Inc; **Magneti Marelli SpA**
Legacy; **Embraer SA**
Legacy; **Subaru Corporation**
Legend of Zelda (The); **Nintendo Co Ltd**
Leggette Brashears and Graham Inc; **WSP Global Inc**
Leighton Holdings Limited; **HOCHTIEF AG**
Lenovo; **Lenovo Group Limited**
Lenvima; **Eisai Co Ltd**
Levor; **Subaru Corporation**
Lexus; **Toyota Motor Corporation**
LG Display Co Ltd; **LG Electronics Inc**
LG Electronics Institute of Technology; **LG Electronics Inc**
LG Electronics USA Inc; **LG Electronics Inc**
LGB Elettropompe Srl; **Nidec Corporation**
LifeCell Corporation; **Allergan plc**
LifeLock Inc; **Symantec Corporation**
Lightsource BP; **BP plc**
Lincoln; **Ford Motor Co**
Lincoln Navigator SUV; **Ford Motor Co**
Lineage 1000E; **Embraer SA**
Linear Technology Corporation; **Analog Devices Inc**
LinkedIn Corporation; **Microsoft Corporation**
Lipitor; **Pfizer Inc**
Liposorber; **Kaneka Corporation**
LiquiForce; **Granite Construction Incorporated**
Listerine; **Johnson & Johnson**
Lite-On Group Co Ltd; **Lite-On Technology Corporation**
Lite-On Skyla; **Lite-On Technology Corporation**
LM6000; **GE Aviation**
LMG Marin AS; **Sembcorp Marine Ltd**
Lockwood Andrews & Newman Inc; **Leo A Daly Company**
LogMeIn Inc; **Citrix Systems Inc**
Los Portales; **Empresas ICA SAB de CV**
Louis Berger Power KSA; **Louis Berger Group Inc (The)**
LS Power Semitech Co Ltd; **Infineon Technologies AG**
Lucentis; **Genentech Inc**
Lyondell Chemical Co; **LyondellBasell Industries NV**
Lyrica; **Pfizer Inc**
M; **Juniper Networks Inc**
M Setek Co Ltd; **AU Optronics Corp**
M&E Collection; **Autodesk Inc**
M1A2 Abrams Tank; **General Dynamics Corporation**
Mack; **AB Volvo**
Maersk Oil; **Total SA**
Magna Exteriors and Interiors Corp; **Magna International Inc**
Magna Powertrain Inc; **Magna International Inc**
Magna Seating Inc; **Magna International Inc**
Magna Steyr AG & Co KG; **Magna International Inc**
Magna Structural Systems Inc; **Magna International Inc**
Magneti Marelli Checkstar Service Network; **Magneti Marelli SpA**
Mahindra Group; **Pininfarina SpA**
Maico; **William Demant Holding Group**
Makani; **X Development LLC**
Malcolm Pirnie Inc; **Arcadis NV**

INDEX OF SUBSIDIARIES, BRAND NAMES AND AFFILIATIONS, CONT.

Managed Domain Name System Services; **VeriSign Inc**
Mantenimiento Marino de Mexico; **KBR Inc**
Markon; **Cummins Inc**
Marlin Equity Partners LLC; **Tellabs Inc**
Mass Effect; **Electronic Arts Inc (EA)**
Matrix Applied Technologies; **Matrix Service Company**
Matrix NAC; **Matrix Service Company**
Matrix PDM Engineering; **Matrix Service Company**
Matrix Service; **Matrix Service Company**
Maxtor; **Seagate Technology plc**
Maya; **Autodesk Inc**
Maybach; **Daimler AG**
Maytag; **Whirlpool Corporation**
Medicalis Corporation; **Siemens Healthineers**
Melior Innovations Inc; **Altana AG**
Melloy Industrial Services Inc; **PCL Construction Group Inc**
Mercedes-AMG; **Daimler AG**
Mercedes-Benz; **Daimler AG**
Merck KGaA; **Merck Serono SA**
Merck Sharp & Dohme Corp; **Merck & Co Inc**
MG Motor UK Ltd; **SAIC Motor Corporation Limited**
M-I SWACO; **Schlumberger Limited**
Microchip Technology Incorporated; **Atmel Corporation**
Micromedical; **William Demant Holding Group**
mi-DO; **Nissan Motor Co Ltd**
MINI; **BMW (Bayerische Motoren Werke AG)**
Mister Auto; **Peugeot SA (Groupe PSA)**
Mitsubishi Corporation; **Mitsubishi Electric Corporation**
Mitsubishi Corporation; **Mitsubishi Motors Corp**
Mitsui Chemicals America Inc; **Mitsui Chemicals Inc**
Mitsui Chemicals Asia Pacific Ltd; **Mitsui Chemicals Inc**
Mitsui Chemicals Europe GmbH; **Mitsui Chemicals Inc**
MMD-Monitors & Displays Holding Ltd; **TPV Technology Limited**
MMG; **Ramboll Group A/S**
MMI Engineering; **Geosyntec Consultants Inc**
mmWave; **Lite-On Technology Corporation**
Moat; **Oracle Corporation**
Mobil; **Exxon Mobil Corporation (ExxonMobil)**
Mobile Inspection Platform; **UniversalPegasus International Inc**
Mobileye NV; **Intel Corporation**
Model 3; **Tesla Inc**
Model S; **Tesla Inc**
Model X; **Tesla Inc**
Molex; **Molex LLC**
Monroe; **Tenneco Inc**
moovel NA; **Daimler AG**
Morpho Detection LLC; **Smiths Group plc**
Mortara Instrument Inc; **Hill-Rom Holdings Inc**
Motech Industries Inc; **Taiwan Semiconductor Manufacturing Co Ltd (TSMC)**
Motrin; **Johnson & Johnson**
Multi-Chem; **Halliburton Company**
Multiplicom NV; **Agilent Technologies Inc**

mu-X; **Isuzu Motors Limited**
MX; **Juniper Networks Inc**
NB-IoT; **Huawei Technologies Co Ltd**
NEC Corporation; **NEC Laboratories America Inc**
Need for Speed; **Electronic Arts Inc (EA)**
Nemak; **ALFA SAB de CV**
Neosporin; **Johnson & Johnson**
Nest; **Alphabet Inc**
NetApp OnCommand; **NetApp Inc**
Netherlands Airport Consultants B V; **Royal HaskoningDHV**
Netherlands Organization for Applied Scientific; **QuTech**
NetRing Transport Network; **UTStarcom Inc**
NetScaler ADC; **Citrix Systems Inc**
NetScaler SD-WAN; **Citrix Systems Inc**
Neulasta; **Amgen Inc**
Neupro; **UCB SA**
nEUROn Uninhabited Combat Aircraft Vehicle; **Dassault Aviation SA**
Newpek; **ALFA SAB de CV**
Nexavar; **Bayer HealthCare Pharmaceuticals Inc**
Nex-Gen ULTRA; **Tata Motors Limited**
NEXON AMT; **Tata Motors Limited**
Nihon Medi-Physics Co Ltd; **Sumitomo Chemical Co Ltd**
Nikon CeLL innovation Co Ltd; **Nikon Corporation**
Nikon Image Space; **Nikon Corporation**
Ningxia Building Materials Group Co Ltd; **China National Materials Co Ltd**
Nintendo 3DS; **Nintendo Co Ltd**
Nintendo DS; **Nintendo Co Ltd**
Nintendo DSi; **Nintendo Co Ltd**
Nippon Keoi Latin America-Caribbean Co Ltd; **Nippon Koei Group**
Nippon Koei Co Ltd; **Nippon Koei Group**
Nippon Koei India; **Nippon Koei Group**
Niro; **Kia Motors Corporation**
Nissan Motor Co Ltd; **Calsonic Kansei Corporation**
Nissan Motor Co Ltd; **Renault SA**
Nissan Motor Co Ltd; **Mitsubishi Motors Corp**
Nitto Denko America Inc; **Nitto Denko Corporation**
Nitto Denko Automotive Inc; **Nitto Denko Corporation**
Nitto Denko Avecia Inc; **Nitto Denko Corporation**
Nokia Corporation; **Nokia Bell Labs**
Nomad Holdings; **Alstom SA**
Nootropil; **UCB SA**
Nordlys Environmental LP; **ECC**
NORR; **Ingenium Group Inc**
NorthStar; **Juniper Networks Inc**
Northwest Power Construction; **China Energy Engineering Corporation Limited**
Norton; **Symantec Corporation**
Novara GeoSolutions; **CHA Consulting Inc**
Novartis AG; **Alcon Inc**
Novartis Business Services; **Novartis AG**
Novartis Institutes for BioMedical Research; **Novartis AG**
Novartis Technical Operations; **Novartis AG**

INDEX OF SUBSIDIARIES, BRAND NAMES AND AFFILIATIONS, CONT.

Novecare; **Solvay SA**
NTE Healthcare; **Sener Ingenieria y Sistemas SA**
NTT DATA Business Solutions Australia Pty Ltd; **NTT DATA Corporation**
NTT DATA Business Solutions Malaysia Sdn Bhd; **NTT DATA Corporation**
NTT DATA Business Solutions Singapore Pte Ltd; **NTT DATA Corporation**
Nuclear Structural Engineering Pty Ltd; **Paul C Rizzo Associates Inc**
nusemi inc; **Cadence Design Systems Inc**
NV; **Nissan Motor Co Ltd**
nVision Medical Corporation; **Boston Scientific Corporation**
Ocata Therapeutics Inc; **Astellas Pharma Inc**
Ocean Shipping Consultants; **Royal HaskoningDHV**
Ocean-Server Technology; **L3 Technologies Inc**
OCREVUS; **Biogen Inc**
OCX1100; **Juniper Networks Inc**
Odos Imaging; **Rockwell Automation Inc**
Office 365; **Microsoft Corporation**
OMA; **Empresas ICA SAB de CV**
One-A-Day; **Bayer Corporation**
OneTree Microdevices Inc; **Analog Devices Inc**
Onex Corporation; **Spirit AeroSystems Holdings Inc**
ONTAP Cloud; **NetApp Inc**
Opdivo; **Bristol-Myers Squibb Co**
Opel; **General Motors Company (GM)**
Open Water Power; **L3 Technologies Inc**
Optech Incorporated; **Teledyne Technologies Inc**
Optifog; **Essilor International SA**
Opti-Free; **Alcon Inc**
Optima; **Kia Motors Corporation**
Opus International Consultants Limited; **WSP Global Inc**
Orencia; **Bristol-Myers Squibb Co**
Origin; **Electronic Arts Inc (EA)**
Oticon; **William Demant Holding Group**
Otis; **United Technologies Corporation**
Outback; **Subaru Corporation**
Outlander; **Mitsubishi Motors Corp**
Overwatch; **Activision Blizzard Inc**
Overwatch League; **Activision Blizzard Inc**
Ovidrel; **Merck Serono SA**
OZO; **Nokia Corporation**
P Series; **Lenovo Group Limited**
PACCAR Financial Services; **PACCAR Inc**
Packet Transport Network; **UTStarcom Inc**
Pajero Montero; **Mitsubishi Motors Corp**
Pamplona Capital Management LLP; **PAREXEL International Corporation**
Panadol; **GlaxoSmithKline plc**
PanaHome; **Panasonic Corporation**
Panasonic Factory Solutions Company of America; **Panasonic Corporation**
Panasonic Media Entertainment Company; **Panasonic Corporation**
Panasonic System Communications Co North America; **Panasonic Corporation**
Panasonic System Solutions Co North America; **Panasonic Corporation**
Panther; **Isuzu Motors Limited**
Pantoprazole; **Takeda Pharmaceutical Company Limited**
Papre; **Kaneka Corporation**
Paradigm; **Emerson Electric Co**
PAREXEL Access; **PAREXEL International Corporation**
Pariet; **Eisai Co Ltd**
Parks Closure Group LLC; **ECC**
Passport; **GE Aviation**
Pataday; **Alcon Inc**
PCL Civil Constructors Inc; **PCL Construction Group Inc**
PCL Constructors Bahamas Ltd; **PCL Construction Group Inc**
PCL Constructors Pacific Rim Pty Ltd; **PCL Construction Group Inc**
PCL Energy Inc; **PCL Construction Group Inc**
PCL Industrial Services Inc; **PCL Construction Group Inc**
PDT Architects; **CHA Consulting Inc**
Pemex Drilling and Services; **Petroleos Mexicanos (Pemex)**
Pemex Etileno; **Petroleos Mexicanos (Pemex)**
Pemex Fertilizantes; **Petroleos Mexicanos (Pemex)**
Pemex Logistica; **Petroleos Mexicanos (Pemex)**
Pemex Transformacion Industrial; **Petroleos Mexicanos (Pemex)**
Peterbilt Motors; **PACCAR Inc**
Petreven SpA; **Trevi-Finanziaria Industriale SpA (Trevi Group)**
Petrobras; **Petrobras (Petroleo Brasileiro SA)**
Petrobras Distribuidora SA; **Petrobras (Petroleo Brasileiro SA)**
Peugeot; **Peugeot SA (Groupe PSA)**
P-Harmony Monitors Hong Kong Holding Ltd; **TPV Technology Limited**
PhilKoei International Inc; **Nippon Koei Group**
Phonic Ear; **William Demant Holding Group**
Physio-Control International Inc; **Stryker Corporation**
Picanto; **Kia Motors Corporation**
Pininfarina Automotive Engineering Shanghai Co; **Pininfarina SpA**
Pininfarina Deutschland GmbH; **Pininfarina SpA**
Pininfarina Deutschland Holding GmbH; **Pininfarina SpA**
Pininfarina Extra Srl; **Pininfarina SpA**
Pininfarina of America Corp; **Pininfarina SpA**
Pioneer Digital Design and Manufacturing Corp; **Pioneer Corporation**
Pivotal; **Dell Technologies Inc**
PLEGRIDY; **Biogen Inc**
PLENE; **Syngenta AG**
PM Devereux; **PM Group**
Poch; **WSP Global Inc**

INDEX OF SUBSIDIARIES, BRAND NAMES AND AFFILIATIONS, CONT.

Pokemon; **Nintendo Co Ltd**
Porsche; **Porsche Automobil Holding SE**
Porter-Cable; **Stanley Black & Decker Inc**
Post Oak Graphics; **Gulf Interstate Engineering Company**
Power Construction Corporation Group Co Ltd; **SEPCO Electric Power Construction Corporation**
Powerscreen; **Terex Corporation**
Praluent; **Sanofi SA**
Pratt & Whitney; **United Technologies Corporation**
Premarin; **Pfizer Inc**
PreserVision; **Bausch & Lomb Inc**
PRET; **Empresas ICA SAB de CV**
PREVELEAK; **Baxter International Inc**
Prevnar 13; **Pfizer Inc**
Proactiva; **Empresas ICA SAB de CV**
ProConnect; **Intuit Inc**
ProConnect Tax Online; **Intuit Inc**
Product Design Collection; **Autodesk Inc**
ProFile; **Intuit Inc**
Project Loon; **X Development LLC**
Project Wing; **X Development LLC**
Prolia; **Amgen Inc**
ProSeries; **Intuit Inc**
ProSys Inc; **Emerson Electric Co**
Proteus; **Synopsys Inc**
PSA Powertrain; **Peugeot SA (Groupe PSA)**
PT IndoKoei International; **Nippon Koei Group**
PTC Creo; **PTC Inc**
PTC Creo View; **PTC Inc**
PTC Mathcad; **PTC Inc**
PTC Servigistics; **PTC Inc**
PTC Servigistics; **PTC Inc**
PTC Windchill; **PTC Inc**
PTX; **Juniper Networks Inc**
PureVision; **Bausch & Lomb Inc**
Puridify; **GE Healthcare**
Q Series; **Bombardier Inc**
Quadro; **NVIDIA Corporation**
QuantumWise; **Synopsys Inc**
QuickBooks Online; **Intuit Inc**
Quintiles IMS Holdings Inc; **IQVIA Holdings Inc**
QX80; **Nissan Motor Co Ltd**
Rafale; **Dassault Aviation SA**
RAG Foundation; **Evonik Industries AG**
RAG-Stiftung Beteiligungsgesellschaft GmbH; **Dorsch Gruppe**
RAG-Stiftung Investment Company; **Dorsch Gruppe**
Ram; **FCA US LLC**
Ramboll Foundation; **Ramboll Group A/S**
Ramboll Group A/S; **Ramboll Environ Inc**
Rancho; **Tenneco Inc**
Raymarine; **FLIR Systems Inc**
Rebif; **Merck Serono SA**
RECOTHROM; **Baxter International Inc**
Red Bee Media; **Telefon AB LM Ericsson (Ericsson)**
Registry Services; **VeriSign Inc**
Reglone; **Syngenta AG**
Remedy Service Management Suite; **BMC Software Inc**
Remedyforce; **BMC Software Inc**
Renault; **Renault SA**
Renault; **AB Volvo**
Renault Minute; **Renault SA**
Renault Samsung Motors; **Renault SA**
Renault-Nissan; **Mitsubishi Motors Corp**
Renault-Nissan BV; **Renault SA**
ReNu; **Bausch & Lomb Inc**
Respawn Entertainment LLC; **Electronic Arts Inc (EA)**
Rexene; **Akzo Nobel NV**
Reyataz; **Bristol-Myers Squibb Co**
RF360 Holdings Singapore Pte Ltd; **Qualcomm Incorporated**
Rheinmetall Automotive AG; **Rheinmetall AG**
Rheinmetall Defence AG; **Rheinmetall AG**
Ricardo Knowledge; **Ricardo plc**
Ricardo Software; **Ricardo plc**
Ricoh Asia Pacific Pte Ltd; **Ricoh Company Ltd**
Ricoh Europe plc; **Ricoh Company Ltd**
Ricoh USA Inc; **Ricoh Company Ltd**
Rio; **Kia Motors Corporation**
Risperdal Consta; **Johnson & Johnson**
RITUXAN; **Biogen Inc**
Rizzo Associates Czech a s; **Paul C Rizzo Associates Inc**
Roadster; **Mazda Motor Corporation**
Roche Holding AG; **Genentech Inc**
Rockstar Games; **Take-Two Interactive Software Inc**
Rockwell Software; **Rockwell Automation Inc**
ROG; **ASUSTeK Computer Inc**
Rolic AG; **BASF SE**
Rolls-Royce AB; **Rolls-Royce plc**
Rolls-Royce Marine Power Operations Limited; **Rolls-Royce plc**
Rolls-Royce Motor Cars; **BMW (Bayerische Motoren Werke AG)**
Rolls-Royce North America Inc; **Rolls-Royce plc**
Rotation Medical Inc; **Smith & Nephew plc**
Roundup Ready; **Monsanto Company**
RSA; **Dell Technologies Inc**
Rumensin; **Eli Lilly and Company**
RusVinyl LLC; **Solvay SA**
Ryzodeg; **Novo-Nordisk AS**
S60; **Volvo Car Corporation**
Saab Technology Centre; **Saab AB**
Sage Products LLC; **Stryker Corporation**
SAIC Europe GmbH; **SAIC Motor Corporation Limited**
SAIC Hong Kong Co Ltd; **SAIC Motor Corporation Limited**
SAIC MAXUS; **SAIC Motor Corporation Limited**
SAIC Motor-CP Co ltd; **SAIC Motor Corporation Limited**
SAIC USA Inc; **SAIC Motor Corporation Limited**
SAIC Volkswagen; **SAIC Motor Corporation Limited**

INDEX OF SUBSIDIARIES, BRAND NAMES AND AFFILIATIONS, CONT.

Saiia Construction Company LLC; **ACC Companies (The)**
Saizen; **Merck Serono SA**
Salini Costruttori SpA; **Salini Impregilo SpA**
Sallyport Global Holdings; **Michael Baker International LLC**
Samsung Group; **Samsung Electronics Co Ltd**
Samwoo Heavy Industries Co Ltd; **Daewoo Shipbuilding & Marine Engineering Co Ltd**
San Martin; **Empresas ICA SAB de CV**
SANAE; **Artelia**
Sandoz; **Novartis AG**
Sanofi Pasteur; **Sanofi SA**
Sanofi SA; **Sanofi Genzyme**
SAP Cloud Platform; **SAP SE**
SAP HANA; **SAP SE**
Sardegna Matrica; **Eni SpA**
Savron; **Geosyntec Consultants Inc**
ScanDisk; **Western Digital Corporation**
SCG Design & Research Institute Co Ltd; **Shanghai Construction Group Co Ltd**
SCG Real Estate Co Ltd; **Shanghai Construction Group Co Ltd**
SCI Technology Inc; **Sanmina Corporation**
ScienBiziP Japan Co Ltd; **Sharp Corporation**
Scotch; **3M Company**
Scott Safety; **3M Company**
Scrum; **Mazda Motor Corporation**
Seagate; **Seagate Technology plc**
SEAMS; **Arcadis NV**
SEAT; **Porsche Automobil Holding SE**
SEAT; **Volkswagen AG (VW)**
Seattle SpinCo Inc; **Hewlett Packard Enterprise Company**
Secoup Holding GmbH; **Nidec Corporation**
Sector; **BIOS-BIOENERGYSYSTEME GmbH**
Secureworks; **Dell Technologies Inc**
Security Services; **VeriSign Inc**
Securus Medical Group Inc; **Boston Scientific Corporation**
Sega Inc; **POWER Engineers Inc**
SelecTrucks; **Daimler Trucks North America LLC**
Sembmarine SLP Limited; **Sembcorp Marine Ltd**
Sembmarine SSP Inc; **Sembcorp Marine Ltd**
Sensipar; **Amgen Inc**
Sensodyne; **GlaxoSmithKline plc**
Sentaurus; **Synopsys Inc**
Sentra; **Nissan Motor Co Ltd**
Seqirus; **CSL Limited**
Seresto; **Bayer HealthCare Pharmaceuticals Inc**
Serostim; **Merck Serono SA**
Seymour Whyte; **VINCI SA**
Shandong Electric Power Construction; **SEPCO Electric Power Construction Corporation**
Shanghai Building Decoration Engineering Group Co; **Shanghai Construction Group Co Ltd**

Shanghai Construction (Group) General Corporation; **Shanghai Construction Group Co Ltd**
Shanghai Construction No 1 (Group) Co Ltd; **Shanghai Construction Group Co Ltd**
Shanghai Foundation Engineering Group Co Ltd; **Shanghai Construction Group Co Ltd**
Shanghai Garden & Landscape (Group) Co Ltd; **Shanghai Construction Group Co Ltd**
Shanghai Installation Engineering Group Co Ltd; **Shanghai Construction Group Co Ltd**
Sharp Energy Solutions Corporation; **Sharp Corporation**
Sharp Marketing Japan Corporation (SMJ); **Sharp Corporation**
Sharp Trading Corporation; **Sharp Corporation**
Shasta; **Cray Inc**
Shenzhen BYD Automobile Company Limited; **BYD Company Limited**
Shenzhen Huawei Investment & Holding Co; **Huawei Technologies Co Ltd**
SHIELD; **NVIDIA Corporation**
Shinhan Heavy Industries Co Ltd; **Daewoo Shipbuilding & Marine Engineering Co Ltd**
Showa Denko Aluminum Trading KK; **Showa Denko KK**
Showa Denko Gas Products Co Ltd; **Showa Denko KK**
Showa Denko Kenzai KK; **Showa Denko KK**
Showa Denko Packaging Co Ltd; **Showa Denko KK**
Sidense Corporation; **Synopsys Inc**
Siemens AG; **Mentor Graphics Inc**
Siemens AG; **Siemens Corporate Technology**
Siemens AG; **Siemens Gamesa Renewable Energy SA**
Siemens AG; **Siemens Healthineers**
Siemens Healthineers; **Siemens AG**
Siemens Wind HoldCo SL; **Siemens Gamesa Renewable Energy SA**
Siemens Wind Power; **Siemens AG**
Sigma; **ALFA SAB de CV**
Sigma Bravo Pty Ltd; **KBR Inc**
Silver Lake Partners; **Avaya Holdings Corp**
Sims vs Zombies (The); **Electronic Arts Inc (EA)**
SIMULIA; **Dassault Systemes SA**
Singapore Technologies Aeropace Ltd; **Singapore Technologies Engineering Limited**
Singapore Technologies Electronics Ltd; **Singapore Technologies Engineering Limited**
Singapore Technologies Kinetics Ltd; **Singapore Technologies Engineering Limited**
Singapore Technologies Marine Ltd; **Singapore Technologies Engineering Limited**
Sinoma (Handan) Construction Co Ltd; **China National Materials Co Ltd**
Sinoma (Suzhou) Construction Co Ltd; **China National Materials Co Ltd**
Sinoma Cement Co Ltd; **China National Materials Co Ltd**
Sinoma Wind Power Blade Co Ltd; **China National Materials Co Ltd**

INDEX OF SUBSIDIARIES, BRAND NAMES AND AFFILIATIONS, CONT.

SINOMACH; **China National Machinery Industry Corporation**
SINOMACH Finance Co Ltd; **China National Machinery Industry Corporation**
Sir Frederick Snow and Partners Ltd; **Associated Consulting Engineers**
SiREM; **Geosyntec Consultants Inc**
Sixth Construction Company of Huanqiu; **China HuanQiu Contracting & Engineering Corporation**
SK Group; **SK Engineering & Construction Co Ltd**
SKODA; **Porsche Automobil Holding SE**
Skoda; **Volkswagen AG (VW)**
SmartCore; **Visteon Corporation**
SmartStax; **Monsanto Company**
SMEC Foundation; **SMEC Holdings Limited**
Smiths Detection; **Smiths Group plc**
Smiths Interconnect; **Smiths Group plc**
Smiths Medical; **Smiths Group plc**
SMJ Business Solutions Company; **Sharp Corporation**
SMJ Home Solutions Company; **Sharp Corporation**
SnapBridge; **Nikon Corporation**
SNC-Lavalin Group Inc; **WS Atkins plc**
Snic Co Ltd; **Suzuki Motor Corporation**
Social Point SL; **Take-Two Interactive Software Inc**
Sogitec Industries SA; **Dassault Aviation SA**
Solar Roof; **Tesla Inc**
SolarCity; **Tesla Inc**
Solekia Limited; **Fujitsu Limited**
SolidFire All-Flash Arrays; **NetApp Inc**
SOLIDWORKS; **Dassault Systemes SA**
Solimec SpA; **Trevi-Finanziaria Industriale SpA (Trevi Group)**
SOMAIR; **Areva SA**
Sonata; **Hyundai Motor Company**
Sonic; **William Demant Holding Group**
Sony Bank Inc; **Sony Corporation**
Sony Corporation; **Sony Mobile Communications AB**
Sony Energy Devices Corporation; **Sony Corporation**
Sony Financial Holdings Inc; **Sony Corporation**
Sony Life Insurance Co Ltd; **Sony Corporation**
Sony Mobile Communications Inc; **Sony Corporation**
Sony Semiconductor Manufacturing Corporation; **Sony Corporation**
Sony Semiconductor Solutions Corporation; **Sony Corporation**
Sony Storage Media and Devices Corporation; **Sony Corporation**
SOO Products; **UTStarcom Inc**
Sorento; **Kia Motors Corporation**
sortimat Discovery; **ATS Automation Tooling Systems Inc**
sortimat Spaceline; **ATS Automation Tooling Systems Inc**
South Charleston Technology Park; **Union Carbide Corporation**
Sovaldi; **Gilead Sciences Inc**
Sperry; **Halliburton Company**

SPIG SpA; **Babcock & Wilcox Enterprises Inc**
SPINRAZA; **Biogen Inc**
Splenda; **Tate & Lyle plc**
Spotless Group Holdings Limited; **Downer EDI Limited**
Sprycel; **Bristol-Myers Squibb Co**
SQL; **Microsoft Corporation**
STA-LITE; **Tate & Lyle plc**
Stamford; **Cummins Inc**
Stanley; **Stanley Black & Decker Inc**
Stantec Inc; **MWH Global Inc**
Stiefel Laboratories Inc; **GlaxoSmithKline plc**
Stork Holding BV; **Fluor Corporation**
Subaru; **Subaru Corporation**
Sumitomo Corporation; **Sumitomo Chemical Co Ltd**
Summit ESP; **Halliburton Company**
Sun Chemicals Corporation; **DIC Corporation**
Sunfleet; **Volvo Car Corporation**
SUNSTORE 4; **BIOS-BIOENERGYSYSTEME GmbH**
SUNVIEO; **Mitsui Chemicals Inc**
Surbana Jurong Private Limited; **SMEC Holdings Limited**
SureSearch; **Cardno Limited**
SureSource; **FuelCell Energy Inc**
Suzuki Akita Auto Parts Mfg Co Ltd; **Suzuki Motor Corporation**
Suzuki Auto Parts Mfg Co Ltd; **Suzuki Motor Corporation**
Suzuki Engineering Co Ltd; **Suzuki Motor Corporation**
Suzuki Finance Co Ltd; **Suzuki Motor Corporation**
Suzuki Motor Gujarat Private Limited; **Suzuki Motor Corporation**
Suzuki Toyama Auto Parts Mgf Co Ltd; **Suzuki Motor Corporation**
Suzuki Transportation & Packing Co Ltd; **Suzuki Motor Corporation**
SVIA; **ABB Ltd**
synNotch; **Gilead Sciences Inc**
Systane; **Alcon Inc**
Systems on Silicon Manufacturing Co Pty Ltd; **Taiwan Semiconductor Manufacturing Co Ltd (TSMC)**
Taishan Fiberglass Inc; **China National Materials Co Ltd**
Tata Group; **Tata Motors Limited**
Tata Hexa; **Tata Motors Limited**
Tata Motors Limited; **Jaguar Land Rover Limited**
Taxotere; **Sanofi Genzyme**
TECENTRIQ; **Genentech Inc**
TECFIDERA; **Biogen Inc**
Technics; **Panasonic Corporation**
Tegile Systems; **Western Digital Corporation**
Tegra; **NVIDIA Corporation**
Teledyne Brown Engineering Inc; **Teledyne Technologies Inc**
Teledyne Scientific Company; **Teledyne Technologies Inc**
Temasek Holdings Private Limited; **Singapore Technologies Engineering Limited**
Temasek Holdings Pte Ltd; **SMEC Holdings Limited**
Terex; **Terex Corporation**

INDEX OF SUBSIDIARIES, BRAND NAMES AND AFFILIATIONS, CONT.

TerraSure; **Gannett Fleming Inc**
Tesla; **NVIDIA Corporation**
Tesla Powerwall; **Tesla Inc**
Texaco; **Chevron Corporation**
Textron Aviation; **Textron Inc**
Textron Financial Corporation; **Textron Inc**
Textron Systems; **Textron Inc**
TF1; **Bouygues SA**
ThaiKoei International Co Ltd; **Nippon Koei Group**
Thermax Babcock & Wilcox Energy Solutions; **Babcock & Wilcox Enterprises Inc**
Thermo King; **Ingersoll-Rand plc**
ThingWorx; **PTC Inc**
Thinklogical Holdings LLC; **Belden Inc**
ThinkPad; **Lenovo Group Limited**
Thinsulate; **3M Company**
Thoma Bravo LLC; **McAfee Inc**
Thomas Built Buses; **Daimler Trucks North America LLC**
Throttle; **Gilead Sciences Inc**
Titanfall; **Electronic Arts Inc (EA)**
TMC; **Bouygues SA**
Top Victory Investments Ltd; **TPV Technology Limited**
Torresol Energy; **Sener Ingenieria y Sistemas SA**
Toshiba Corporation; **Toshiba Corporate R&D Center**
Toshiba Digital Solutions Corporation; **Toshiba Corporation**
Toshiba Electronic Devices & Storage Corporation; **Toshiba Corporation**
Toshiba Energy Systems & Solutions Corporation; **Toshiba Corporation**
Toshiba Infrastructure Systems & Solutions Corp; **Toshiba Corporation**
Toyama Chemical Co Ltd; **FUJIFILM Holdings Corporation**
Toyota; **Toyota Motor Corporation**
Toyota Financial Services Corporation; **Toyota Motor Corporation**
Toyota Group; **Toyoda Gosei Co Ltd**
Toyota Motor Corporation; **Daihatsu Motor Co Ltd**
Toyota Motor Credit Corporation; **Toyota Motor Corporation**
Toyota Research Institute Inc; **Toyota Motor Corporation**
TP Vision; **TPV Technology Limited**
TPC Capital; **Avaya Holdings Corp**
TPG Capital; **McAfee Inc**
Tractebel Engineering; **Lahmeyer International GmbH**
Trajenta; **Eli Lilly and Company**
Trane; **Ingersoll-Rand plc**
Transitions; **Essilor International SA**
Travelstar; **HGST Inc**
Trent; **Rolls-Royce plc**
Tresiba; **Novo-Nordisk AS**
Trimetal; **Akzo Nobel NV**
Triton; **Mitsubishi Motors Corp**

Truven Health Analytics; **International Business Machines Corporation (IBM)**
TSMC China Company Limited; **Taiwan Semiconductor Manufacturing Co Ltd (TSMC)**
TSMC Nanjing; **Taiwan Semiconductor Manufacturing Co Ltd (TSMC)**
TurboTax; **Intuit Inc**
Turner Construction Company; **HOCHTIEF AG**
Turner Construction Company; **ACS Actividades de Construccion y Servicios SA**
Tylenol; **Johnson & Johnson**
UA Healthbox; **HTC Corporation**
Uconnect; **FCA US LLC**
UD; **AB Volvo**
Ultrastar; **HGST Inc**
Union Showa KK; **Showa Denko KK**
UnionConsult Gruppen AS; **WSP Global Inc**
Unisys Stealth; **Unisys Corp**
Unium; **Nokia Corporation**
Univation Technologies LLC; **Union Carbide Corporation**
Universal Acoustic & Emission Technologies Inc; **Babcock & Wilcox Enterprises Inc**
Universal Scientific Industrial Co Ltd; **Advanced Semiconductor Engineering Inc**
Upthere; **Western Digital Corporation**
V2X; **Lite-On Technology Corporation**
V90; **Volvo Car Corporation**
Valeant Pharmaceuticals International Inc; **Bausch & Lomb Inc**
Valeo Service; **Valeo SA**
Valor Equity Partners; **SpaceX (Space Exploration Technologies Corporation)**
Vamco International Inc; **Nidec Corporation**
Vanguard International Semiconductor Corp; **Taiwan Semiconductor Manufacturing Co Ltd (TSMC)**
Varilux; **Essilor International SA**
Vascade; **Corning Inc**
Vauxhall; **General Motors Company (GM)**
VEC Consultant JSC; **Nippon Koei Group**
Vegetalia Inc; **Mitsubishi Corporation**
Vemlidy; **Gilead Sciences Inc**
Venator Materials PLC; **Huntsman Corporation**
Veoneer Inc; **Autoliv Inc**
Veracode Inc; **CA Inc (CA Technologies)**
Verily; **Alphabet Inc**
Versa; **Nissan Motor Co Ltd**
Vestas Blades America Inc; **Vestas Wind Systems A/S**
Vestas Blades Deutschland Gmbh; **Vestas Wind Systems A/S**
Vestas Blades Italia Srl; **Vestas Wind Systems A/S**
Vestas Control Systems Spain SLU; **Vestas Wind Systems A/S**
Vestas Manufacturing A/S; **Vestas Wind Systems A/S**
Vestas Nacelles Estonia; **Vestas Wind Systems A/S**
Vestas Nacelles Italia Srl; **Vestas Wind Systems A/S**

INDEX OF SUBSIDIARIES, BRAND NAMES AND AFFILIATIONS, CONT.

Vestas Towers America Inc; **Vestas Wind Systems A/S**
Viela Bio Inc; **AstraZeneca plc**
ViiV Healthcare; **GlaxoSmithKline plc**
Viking Technology; **Sanmina Corporation**
Vimpat; **UCB SA**
VINCI Airports; **VINCI SA**
VINCI Autoroutes; **VINCI SA**
VINCI Concessions SA; **VINCI SA**
VINCI Construction; **VINCI SA**
VINCI Contracting LLC; **VINCI SA**
VINCI Energies; **VINCI SA**
VirtuStream; **Dell Technologies Inc**
Visual Studio; **Microsoft Corporation**
VitalHealth; **Koninklijke Philips NV (Royal Philips)**
VIVE; **HTC Corporation**
Vive Ica; **Empresas ICA SAB de CV**
Vmware; **Dell Technologies Inc**
Volkswagen; **Volkswagen AG (VW)**
Volkswagen AG; **Audi AG**
Volkswagen Group; **Porsche Automobil Holding SE**
Volvo; **AB Volvo**
Volvo Cars Financial Services US LLC; **Volvo Car Corporation**
Volvo Cars of North America; **Volvo Car Corporation**
Volvo Group; **AB Volvo**
Vortioxetine; **Takeda Pharmaceutical Company Limited**
Vricon; **Saab AB**
Vtech; **VTech Holdings Limited**
Vuforia; **PTC Inc**
W Lahmeyer & Co; **Lahmeyer International GmbH**
WaferTech LLC; **Taiwan Semiconductor Manufacturing Co Ltd (TSMC)**
Walker; **Tenneco Inc**
Wanxiang Innovative Energy Fusion City; **Wanxiang Group Corporation**
watchOS; **Apple Inc**
Watermark ECC LLC; **ECC**
Watson; **International Business Machines Corporation (IBM)**
Waymo; **Alphabet Inc**
WD; **Western Digital Corporation**
Weildlinger Applied Sciences; **Thornton Tomasetti Inc**
Weildlinger Protective Design; **Thornton Tomasetti Inc**
Weildlinger Transportation; **Thornton Tomasetti Inc**
Wercker; **Oracle Corporation**
Western Digital; **Western Digital Corporation**
Western Digital Corporation; **HGST Inc**
Western Digital Corporation; **SanDisk Corporation**
Western Star Truck Sales Inc; **Daimler Trucks North America LLC**
WesternGeco; **Schlumberger Limited**
Whirlpool; **Whirlpool Corporation**
Wii; **Nintendo Co Ltd**
Wii U; **Nintendo Co Ltd**
Williams Electric Company Inc; **Parsons Corporation**
Windows; **Microsoft Corporation**
Wintershall AG; **BASF SE**
Wintershall DEA; **BASF SE**
Wirtgen Group Holding GmbH; **Deere & Company (John Deere)**
WorkSense W-01; **Seiko Epson Corporation**
World of Warcraft; **Activision Blizzard Inc**
Worldwide Logistics Group; **Compal Electronics Inc**
WS Atkins plc; **SNC-Lavalin Group Inc**
WSP Global Inc; **WSP Opus**
WSP Opus; **WSP Global Inc**
www.gene.com; **Genentech Inc**
X2; **BMW (Bayerische Motoren Werke AG)**
X3; **BMW (Bayerische Motoren Werke AG)**
Xanxiang Sannong; **Wanxiang Group Corporation**
Xbox; **Microsoft Corporation**
XC40; **Volvo Car Corporation**
Xcient; **Hyundai Motor Company**
XE; **Jaguar Land Rover Limited**
Xeljanz; **Pfizer Inc**
XenApp; **Citrix Systems Inc**
XenDesktop; **Citrix Systems Inc**
XenMobile; **Citrix Systems Inc**
Xerox Corporation; **Palo Alto Research Center Incorporated (PARC)**
XF; **Jaguar Land Rover Limited**
XGEVA; **Amgen Inc**
Xinjiang Tianshan Cement Joint-Stock Co; **China National Materials Co Ltd**
Xintec Inc; **Taiwan Semiconductor Manufacturing Co Ltd (TSMC)**
XJ; **Jaguar Land Rover Limited**
XNOx; **Tenneco Inc**
Xodus Group (Holdings) Ltd; **Chiyoda Corporation**
Xperia; **Sony Mobile Communications AB**
Xperia Ear Duo; **Sony Mobile Communications AB**
Xperia touch; **Sony Mobile Communications AB**
Xperia XZ2; **Sony Mobile Communications AB**
Xperio; **Essilor International SA**
XTO; **Exxon Mobil Corporation (ExxonMobil)**
Xultophy; **Novo-Nordisk AS**
Xyrem; **UCB SA**
Yamagata Casio Co Ltd; **Casio Computer Co Ltd**
Yellowline Asphalt Products Ltd; **Aecon Group Inc**
Yervoy; **Bristol-Myers Squibb Co**
Yescarta; **Gilead Sciences Inc**
Yield; **Synopsys Inc**
YieldGard; **Monsanto Company**
YOGA; **Lenovo Group Limited**
Yumi Robot; **ABB Ltd**
Zachry Holdings Inc; **Ambitech Engineering Corporation**
Zaltrap; **Sanofi Genzyme**
Zeltiq Aesthetics Inc; **Allergan plc**
Zemea; **Tate & Lyle plc**
ZenFone 5 Series; **ASUSTeK Computer Inc**
Zenith; **LG Electronics Inc**
Zenpep; **Allergan plc**

INDEX OF SUBSIDIARIES, BRAND NAMES AND AFFILIATIONS, CONT.

Zenuity; **Autoliv Inc**
Zenuity; **Volvo Car Corporation**
Zephyr Environmental Corporation; **POWER Engineers Inc**
Zeppelin Foundation; **ZF Friedrichshafen AG (ZF)**
Zhejiang Geely Holding Group Co Ltd; **Volvo Car Corporation**
Zhejiang Geely Holding Group Co Ltd; **AB Volvo**
Zhejiang Ocean Family Co Ltd; **Wanxiang Group Corporation**
zIT Consulting; **CA Inc (CA Technologies)**
Zone Perfect; **Abbott Laboratories**
Zweihorn; **Akzo Nobel NV**

A Short Engineering & Research Industry Glossary

3-D Printer: See "Additive Manufacturing."

3-D Printing: See "Additive Manufacturing."

510(k): An application filed with the FDA for a new medical device to show that the apparatus is "substantially equivalent" to one that is already marketed.

802.11a (Wi-Fi): A faster wireless network standard than 802.11b ("Wi-Fi"). 802.11a operates in the 5-GHz band at speeds of 54 Mbps. This standard may be affected by weather and is not as suitable for outdoor use. 802.11 standards are set by the IEEE (Institute of Electrical and Electronics Engineers).

802.11ac: An ultra-high-speed Wi-Fi standard. It operates on the 5 Ghz band and is backwards compatible with older 802.11 standards. 802.11 standards are set by the IEEE (Institute of Electrical and Electronics Engineers). This specification is capable of 1 gigabit per second data transfer speeds.

802.11b (Wi-Fi): A Wi-Fi short-range wireless connection standard created by the IEEE (Institute of Electrical and Electronics Engineers). It operates at 11 Mbps and can be used to connect computer devices to each other. 802.11b competes with the Bluetooth standard. Its range is up to 380 feet, but 150 feet or so may be more practical in some installations.

802.11g (Wi-Fi): An addition to the series of 802.11 specifications for Wi-Fi wireless networks, 802.11g provides data transfer at speeds of up to 54 Mbps in the 2.4-GHz band. It can easily exchange data with 802.11b-enabled devices, but at much higher speed. 802.11g equipment, such as wireless access points, will be able to provide simultaneous WLAN connectivity for both 802.11g and 802.11b equipment. The 802.11 standards are set by the IEEE (Institute of Electrical and Electronics Engineers).

802.11n (MIMO): Multiple Input Multiple Output antenna technology. MIMO is a new standard in the series of 802.11 Wi-Fi specifications for wireless networks. It has the potential of providing data transfer speeds of 100 to perhaps as much as 500 Mbps. 802.11n also boasts better operating distances than current networks. MIMO uses spectrum more efficiently without any loss of reliability. The technology is based on several different antennas all tuned to the same channel, each transmitting a different signal.

802.15: See "Ultrawideband (UWB)." For 802.15.1, see "Bluetooth."

802.15.1: See "Bluetooth."

802.16: See "WiMAX."

Abbreviated New Drug Application (ANDA): An application filed with the FDA showing that a substance is the same as an existing, previously approved drug (i.e., a generic version).

Absorption, Distribution, Metabolism and Excretion (ADME): In clinical trials, the bodily processes studied to determine the extent and duration of systemic exposure to a drug.

Access Network: The network that connects a user's telephone equipment to the telephone exchange.

Active Server Page (ASP): A web page that includes one or more embedded programs, usually written in Java or Visual Basic code. See "Java."

Active X: A set of technologies developed by Microsoft Corporation for sharing information across different applications.

Additive Manufacturing: The use of 3-D "printers" that that build up layers of materials such as plastics, ceramic powders or metallic powders in order to create a finished product. Such printers follow instructions from computerized design files. Originally used mainly for creating prototypes of product concepts, this process is growing in popularity as a final manufacturing process.

ADME: See "Absorption, Distribution, Metabolism and Excretion (ADME)."

ADN: See "Advanced Digital Network (ADN)."

ADSL: See "Asymmetrical Digital Subscriber Line (ADSL)."

Advanced Digital Network (ADN): See "Integrated Digital Network (IDN)."

AI: See "Artificial Intelligence (AI)."

Ambient: Refers to any unconfined portion of the air. Also refers to open air.

Analog: A form of transmitting information characterized by continuously variable quantities. Digital transmission, in contrast, is characterized by discrete bits of information in numerical steps. An analog signal responds to changes in light, sound, heat and pressure.

Analog IC (Integrated Circuit): A semiconductor that processes a continuous wave of electrical signals based on real-world analog quantities such as speed, pressure, temperature, light, sound and voltage.

ANDA: See "Abbreviated New Drug Application (ANDA)."

ANSI: American National Standards Institute. Founded in 1918, ANSI is a private, non-profit organization that administers and coordinates the U.S. voluntary standardization and conformity assessment system. Its mission is to enhance both the global competitiveness of U.S. business and the quality of U.S. life by promoting and facilitating voluntary consensus standards and conformity assessment systems, and safeguarding their integrity. See www.ansi.org.

API: See "Application Program Interface (API)."

Application Program Interface (API): A set of protocols, routines and tools used by computer programmers as a way of setting common definitions regarding how one piece of software communicates with another. For example, an API can be used to connect an accounting or customer transaction database to an email service or a CRM (customer relationship management) system.

Application Service Provider (ASP): A web site that enables utilization of software and databases that reside permanently on a service company's remote web server, rather than having to be downloaded to the user's computer. Advantages include the ability for multiple remote users to access the same tools over the Internet and the fact that the ASP provider is responsible for developing and maintaining the software. (ASP is also an acronym for "active server page," which is not related.) For the latest developments in ASP, see "Software as a Service (SaaS)."

Applied Research: The application of compounds, processes, materials or other items discovered during basic research to practical uses. The goal is to move discoveries along to the final development phase.

ARPANet: Advanced Research Projects Agency Network. The forefather of the Internet, ARPANet was developed during the latter part of the 1960s by the United States Department of Defense.

Artificial Intelligence (AI): The use of computer technology to perform functions somewhat like those normally associated with human intelligence, such as reasoning, learning and self-improvement.

ASCII: American Standard Code for Information Exchange. There are 128 standard ASCII codes that represent all Latin letters, numbers and punctuation. Each ASCII code is represented by a seven-digit binary number, such as 0000000 or 0000111. This code is accepted as a standard throughout the world.

Asia Pacific Advisory Committee (APAC): A multi-country committee representing the Asia and Pacific region.

ASP: See "Application Service Provider (ASP)."

Assay: A laboratory test to identify and/or measure the amount of a particular substance in a sample. Types of assays include endpoint assays, in which a single measurement is made at a fixed time; kinetic assays, in which increasing amounts of a product are formed with time and are monitored at multiple points; microbiological assays, which measure the concentration of antimicrobials in biological material; and immunological assays, in which analysis or measurement is based on antigen-antibody reactions.

Association of Southeast Asian Nations (ASEAN): Association of Southeast Asian Nations. A regional economic development association established in 1967 by five original member countries: Indonesia, Malaysia, Philippines, Singapore, and Thailand. Brunei joined on 8 January 1984, Vietnam on 28 July 1995, Laos and Myanmar on 23 July 1997, and Cambodia on 30 April 1999.

Asymmetrical Digital Subscriber Line (ADSL): High-speed technology that enables the transfer of data over existing copper phone lines, allowing more bandwidth downstream than upstream.

Asynchronous Communications: A stream of data routed through a network as generated instead of in organized message blocks. Most personal computers use this format to send data.

Asynchronous Transfer Mode (ATM): A digital switching and transmission technology based on high speed. ATM allows voice, video and data signals to be sent over a single telephone line at speeds from 25 million to 1 billion bits per second (bps). This digital ATM speed is much faster than traditional analog phone lines, which allow no more than 2 million bps. See "Broadband."

Backbone: Traditionally the part of a communications network that carries the heaviest traffic; the high-speed line or series of connections that forms a large pathway within a network or within a region. The combined networks of AT&T, MCI and other large telecommunications companies make up the backbone of the Internet.

Baseline: A set of data used in clinical studies, or other types of research, for control or comparison.

Basic Research: Attempts to discover compounds, materials, processes or other items that may be largely or entirely new and/or unique. Basic research may start with a theoretical concept that has yet to be proven. The goal is to create discoveries that can be moved along to applied research. Basic research is sometimes referred to as "blue sky" research.

Baud: Refers to how many times the carrier signal in a modem switches value per second or how many bits a modem can send and receive in a second.

Beam: The coverage and geographic service area offered by a satellite transponder. A global beam effectively covers one-third of the earth's surface. A spot beam provides a very specific high-powered downlink pattern that is limited to a particular geographical area to which it may be steered or pointed.

Binhex: A means of changing non-ASCII (or non-text) files into text/ASCII files so that they can be used, for example, as e-mail.

Bioavailability: In pharmaceuticals, the rate and extent to which a drug is absorbed or is otherwise available to the treatment site in the body.

Biochemical Engineering: A sector of chemical engineering that deals with biological structures and processes. Biochemical engineers may be found in the pharmaceutical, biotechnology and environmental fields, among others.

Bioengineering: Engineering principles applied when working in biology and pharmaceuticals.

Bioequivalence: In pharmaceuticals, the demonstration that a drug's rate and extent of absorption are not significantly different from those of an existing drug that is already approved by the FDA. This is the basis upon which generic and brand name drugs are compared.

Bioinformatics: Research, development or application of computational tools and approaches for expanding the use of biological, medical, behavioral or health data, including those to acquire, store, organize, archive, analyze or visualize such data. Bioinformatics is often applied to the study of genetic data. It applies principles of information sciences and technologies to make vast, diverse and complex life sciences data more understandable and useful.

Biologics: Drugs that are synthesized from living organisms. That is, drugs created using biotechnology, sometimes referred to as biopharmaceuticals. Specifically, biologics may be any virus, therapeutic serum, toxin, antitoxin, vaccine, blood, blood component or derivative, allergenic or analogous product, or arsphenamine or one of its derivatives used for the prevention, treatment or cure of disease. Also, see "Biologics License Application (BLA)," "Follow-on Biologics," and "Biopharmaceuticals."

Biologics License Application (BLA): An application to be submitted to the FDA when a firm wants to obtain permission to market a novel, new biological drug product. Specifically, these are drugs created through the use of biotechnology. It was formerly known as Product License Application (PLA). Also see "Biologics."

Biopharmaceuticals: That portion of the pharmaceutical industry focused on the use of biotechnology to create new drugs. A biopharmaceutical can be any biological compound that is intended to be used as a therapeutic drug, including recombinant proteins, monoclonal and polyclonal antibodies, antisense oligonucleotides, therapeutic genes, and recombinant and DNA vaccines. Also, see "Biologics."

Biotechnology: A set of powerful tools that employ living organisms (or parts of organisms) to make or modify products, improve plants or animals (including humans) or develop microorganisms for specific uses. Biotechnology is most commonly thought of to include the development of human medical therapies and processes using recombinant DNA, cell fusion, other genetic techniques and bioremediation.

Bit: A single digit number, either a one or a zero, which is the smallest unit of computerized data.

Bits Per Second (Bps): An indicator of the speed of data movement.

BLA: See "Biologics License Application (BLA)."

Bluetooth: An industry standard for a technology that enables wireless, short-distance infrared connections between devices such as cell phone headsets, Palm Pilots or PDAs, laptops, printers and Internet appliances.

BPO: See "Business Process Outsourcing (BPO)."

Bps: See "Bits Per Second (Bps)."

Brand: A marketing strategy that places a focus on the brand name of a product, service or firm in order to increase the brand's market share, increase sales, establish credibility, improve satisfaction, raise the profile of the firm and increase profits. Also, see "Brand."

Branding: A marketing strategy that places a focus on the brand name of a product, service or firm in order to increase the brand's market share, increase sales, establish credibility, improve satisfaction, raise the profile of the firm and increase profits. Also, see "Brand."

Broadband: The high-speed transmission range for telecommunications and computer data. Broadband generally refers to any transmission at 2 million bps (bits per second) or higher (much higher than analog speed). A broadband network can carry voice, video and data all at the same time. Internet users enjoying broadband access typically connect to the Internet via DSL line, cable modem or T1 line. Several wireless methods offer broadband as well.

B-to-B, or B2B: See "Business-to-Business."

B-to-C, or B2C: See "Business-to-Consumer."

B-to-G, or B2G: See "Business-to-Government."

Buffer: A location for temporarily storing data being sent or received. It is usually located between two devices that have different data transmission rates.

Business Process Outsourcing (BPO): The process of hiring another company to handle business activities. BPO is one of the fastest-growing segments in the offshoring sector. Services include human resources management, billing and purchasing and call centers, as well as many types of customer service or marketing activities, depending on the industry involved. Also, see "Knowledge Process Outsourcing (KPO)" and "Business Transformation Outsourcing (BTO)."

Business Transformation Outsourcing (BTO): A segment within outsourcing in which the client company revamps its business processes with the goal of transforming its business by following a collaborative approach with its outsourced services provider.

Business-to-Business: An organization focused on selling products, services or data to commercial customers rather than individual consumers. Also known as B2B.

Business-to-Consumer: An organization focused on selling products, services or data to individual consumers rather than commercial customers. Also known as B2C.

Business-to-Government: An organization focused on selling products, services or data to government units rather than commercial businesses or consumers. Also known as B2G.

Byte: A set of eight bits that represent a single character.

Cable Modem: An interface between a cable television system and a computer or router. Most cable modems are external devices that connect to the PC through a standard 10Base-T Ethernet card and twisted-pair wiring. External Universal Serial Bus (USB) modems and internal PCI modem cards are also available.

Caching: A method of storing data in a temporary location closer to the user so that it can be retrieved quickly when requested.

CAD: See "Computer-Aided Design (CAD)."

CAD/CAM: Refers to the combination of Computer-Aided Design (CAD) and Computer-Aided Manufacturing (CAM). Also, see "Computer Numerical Control," "Computer-Aided Manufacturing (CAM)," and "Computer-Aided Design (CAD)."

CAE: See "Computer-Aided Engineering (CAE)."

CAM: See "Computer Aided Machining or Manufacturing (CAM)."

CANDA: See "Computer-Assisted New Drug Application (CANDA)."

Capability Maturity Model (CMM): A global process management standard for software development established by the Software Engineering Institute at Carnegie Mellon University.

Capacitor: An electronic circuit device for temporary storage of electrical energy.

Carbon Capture and Storage: See "Carbon Sequestration."

Carbon Sequestration: The absorption and storage of CO2 from the atmosphere by the roots and leaves of plants; the carbon builds up as organic matter in the soil. In the energy industry, carbon sequestration refers to the process of isolating and storing carbon dioxide (a so-called greenhouse gas). One use is to avoid releasing carbon dioxide into the air when burning coal at a coal-fired power plant. Instead, the carbon dioxide is stored in the ground or otherwise stored in a permanent or semi-permanent fashion. Other uses include the return to the ground of carbon dioxide that is produced at natural gas wells, and the introduction of carbon dioxide into oil wells in order to increase internal pressure and production. This process is also known as carbon capture and storage (CCS).

Cardiac Catheterization Laboratory: Facilities offering special diagnostic procedures for cardiac patients, including the introduction of a catheter into the interior of the heart by way of a vein or artery or by direct needle puncture. Procedures must be performed in a laboratory or a special procedure room.

Carrier: In communications, the basic radio, television or telephony center of transmit signal. The carrier in an analog signal is modulated by varying volume or shifting frequency up or down in relation to the incoming signal. Satellite carriers operating in the analog mode are usually frequency-modulated.

CASE: See "Computer-Assisted Software Engineering (CASE)."

CAT Scan: See "Computed Tomography (CT)."

Catheter: A tubular instrument used to add or withdraw fluids. Heart or cardiac catheterization involves the passage of flexible catheters into the great vessels and chambers of the heart. IV catheters add intravenous fluids to the veins. Foley catheters withdraw fluid from the bladder. Significant recent advances in technology allow administration of powerful drug and diagnostic therapies via catheters.

CATV: Cable television.

CBER: See "Center for Biologics Evaluation and Research (CBER)."

CCS: See "Carbon Sequestration."

CDER: See "Center for Drug Evaluation and Research (CDER)."

CDMA: See "Code Division Multiple Access (CDMA)."

CDRH: See "Center for Devices and Radiological Health (CDRH)."

CEM: Contract electronic manufacturing. See "Contract Manufacturing."

Center for Biologics Evaluation and Research (CBER): The branch of the FDA responsible for the regulation of biological products, including blood, vaccines, therapeutics and related drugs and devices, to ensure purity, potency, safety, availability and effectiveness. www.fda.gov/cber

Center for Devices and Radiological Health (CDRH): The branch of the FDA responsible for the regulation of medical devices. www.fda.gov/cdrh

Center for Drug Evaluation and Research (CDER): The branch of the FDA responsible for the regulation of drug products. www.fda.gov/cder

Central Processing Unit (CPU): The part of a computer that interprets and executes instructions. It is composed of an arithmetic logic unit, a control unit and a small amount of memory.

Ceramic: Ceramics are nonmetallic materials that have been created under intense heat. Ceramics tend to be extremely hard, heat-resistant and corrosion-resistant. They are generally poor conductors of temperature changes or electricity. Ceramics are used in low-tech and high-tech applications, ranging from the insulators in spark plugs to the heat shield on the Space Shuttle.

CGI: See "Common Gateway Interface (CGI)."

CGI-BIN: The frequently used name of a directory on a web server where CGI programs exist.

Channel Definition Format (CDF): Used in Internet-based broadcasting. With this format, a channel serves as a web site that also sends an information file about that specific site. Users subscribe to a channel by downloading the file.

Chemical Engineering: The sector that deals with technologies, safety issues, refining, production and delivery of chemicals and products that are manufactured partly or largely through the use of chemicals. Chemical engineers are also involved in the design and construction of major industrial plants, as well as the application of chemicals to scientific and industrial needs.

Class I Device: An FDA classification of medical devices for which general controls are sufficient to ensure safety and efficacy.

Class II Device: An FDA classification of medical devices for which performance standards and special controls are sufficient to ensure safety and efficacy.

Class III Device: An FDA classification of medical devices for which pre-market approval is required to ensure safety and efficacy, unless the device is substantially equivalent to a currently marketed device. See "510 K."

CLEC: See "Competitive Local Exchange Carrier (CLEC)."

Client/Server: In networking, a way of running a large computer setup. The server is the host computer that acts as the central holding ground for files, databases and application software. The clients are all of the PCs connected to the network that share data with the server. This represents a vast change from past networks, which were connected to expensive, complicated "mainframe" computers.

Climate Change (Greenhouse Effect): A theory that assumes an increasing mean global surface temperature of the Earth caused by gases (sometimes referred to as greenhouse gases) in the atmosphere (including carbon dioxide, methane, nitrous oxide, ozone and chlorofluorocarbons). The greenhouse effect allows solar radiation to penetrate the Earth's atmosphere but absorbs the infrared radiation returning to space.

Cloning (Reproductive): A method of reproducing an exact copy of an animal or, potentially, an exact copy of a human being. A scientist removes the nucleus from a donor's unfertilized egg, inserts a nucleus from the animal to be copied and then stimulates the nucleus to begin dividing to form an embryo. In the case of a mammal, such as a human, the embryo would then be implanted in the uterus of a host female. Also see "Cloning (Therapeutic)."

Cloning (Therapeutic): A method of reproducing exact copies of cells needed for research or for the development of replacement tissue or organs. A scientist removes the nucleus from a donor's unfertilized egg, inserts a nucleus from the animal whose cells are to be copied and then stimulates the nucleus to begin dividing to form an embryo. However, the embryo is never allowed to grow to any significant stage of development. Instead, it is allowed to grow for a few hours or days, and stem cells are then removed from it for use in regenerating tissue. Also see "Cloning (Reproductive)."

CMM: See "Capability Maturity Model (CMM)."

CMOS: Complementary Metal Oxide Semiconductor; the technology used in making modern silicon-based microchips.

Coaxial Cable: A type of cable widely used to transmit telephone and broadcast traffic. The distinguishing feature is an inner strand of wires surrounded by an insulator that is in turn surrounded by another conductor, which serves as the ground. Cable TV wiring is typically coaxial.

Code Division Multiple Access (CDMA): A cellular telephone multiple-access scheme whereby stations use spread-spectrum modulations and orthogonal codes to avoid interfering with one another. IS-95 (also known as CDMAOne) is the 2G CDMA standard. CDMA2000 is the 3G standard. CDMA in the 1xEV-DO standard offers data transfer speeds up to 2.4 Mbps. CDMA 1xRTT is a slower standard offering speeds of 144 kbps.

Code of Federal Regulations (CFR): A codification of the general and permanent rules published in the Federal Register by the executive departments and agencies of the Federal Government. The code is divided into 50 titles that represent broad areas subject to federal regulation. Title 21 of the CFR covers FDA regulations.

Codec: Hardware or software that converts analog to digital and digital to analog (in both audio and video formats). Codecs can be found in digital telephones, set-top boxes, computers and videoconferencing equipment. The term is also used to refer to the compression of digital information into a smaller format.

Co-Location: Refers to the hosting of computer servers at locations operated by service organizations. Co-location is offered by firms that operate specially designed co-location centers with high levels of security, extremely high-speed telecommunication lines for Internet connectivity and reliable backup electrical power systems in case of power failure, as well as a temperature-controlled environment for optimum operation of computer systems.

Commerce Chain Management (CCM): Refers to Internet-based tools to facilitate sales, distribution, inventory management and content personalization in the e-commerce industry. Also see "Supply Chain."

Committee for Veterinary Medicinal Products (CVMP): A committee that is a veterinary equivalent of the CPMP (see "Committee on Proprietary Medicinal Products (CPMP)") in the EU. See "European Union (EU)."

Committee on Proprietary Medicinal Products (CPMP): A committee, composed of two people from each EU Member State (see "European Union (EU)"), that is responsible for the scientific evaluation and assessment of marketing applications for medicinal products in the EU. The CPMP is the major body involved in the harmonization of pharmaceutical regulations within the EU and receives administrative support from the European Medicines Evaluation Agency. See "European Medicines Evaluation Agency (EMEA)."

Common Gateway Interface (CGI): A set of guidelines that determines the manner in which a web server receives and sends information to and from software on the same machine.

Communications Satellite Corporation (COMSAT): Serves as the U.S. Signatory to INTELSAT and INMARSAT.

Competitive Local Exchange Carrier (CLEC): A newer company providing local telephone service that competes against larger, traditional firms known as ILECs (incumbent local exchange carriers).

Compression: A technology in which a communications signal is squeezed so that it uses less bandwidth (or capacity) than it normally would. This saves storage space and shortens transfer time. The original data is decompressed when read back into memory.

Computed Tomography (CT): An imaging method that uses x-rays to create cross-sectional pictures of the body. The technique is frequently referred to as a "CAT Scan." A patient lies on a narrow platform while the machine's x-ray beam rotates around him or her. Small detectors inside the scanner measure the amount of x-rays that make it through the part of the body being studied. A computer takes this information and uses it to create several individual images, called slices. These images can be stored, viewed on a monitor, or printed on film. Three-dimensional models of organs can be created by stacking the individual slices together. The newest machines are capable of operating at 256 slice levels, creating very high resolution images in a short period of time.

Computer Aided Machining or Manufacturing (CAM): The use of software to facilitate automated machine tools, based on 3D computer model (CAD or Computer Aided Design) data. When the two are used together, this is generally referred to as CAD/CAM. Also see "CAD" and "CNC".

Computer Numerical Control (CNC): A technology used on the factory floor. It converts a design that was originally created in CAD (Computer Aided Design) software into numbers that plot the coordinates of a grid. This grid is then digitally applied to the material about to be cut or shaped into the desired design by tools such as a router.

Computer-Aided Design (CAD): A tool used to provide three-dimensional, on-screen design for everything from buildings to automobiles to clothing. It generally runs on workstations.

Computer-Aided Engineering (CAE): The use of computers to assist with a broad spectrum of engineering design work, including conceptual and analytical design.

Computer-Assisted New Drug Application (CANDA): An electronic submission of a new drug application (NDA) to the FDA.

Computer-Assisted Software Engineering (CASE): The application of computer technology to systems development activities, techniques and methodologies. Sometimes referred to as "computer-aided systems engineering."

COMSAT: See "Communications Satellite Corporation (COMSAT)."

Contract Manufacturing: A business arrangement whereby a company manufactures products that will be sold under the brand names of its client companies. For example, a large number of consumer electronics, such as laptop computers, are manufactured by contract manufacturers for leading brand-name computer companies such as Dell and Apple. Many other types of products, such as shoes and apparel, are made under contract manufacturing. Also see "Original Equipment Manufacturer (OEM)" and "Original Design Manufacturer (ODM)."

Contract Research Organization (CRO): An independent organization that contracts with a client to conduct part of the work on a study or research project. For example, drug and medical device makers frequently outsource clinical trials and other research work to CROs.

Coordinator: In clinical trials, the person at an investigative site who handles the administrative responsibilities of the trial, acts as a liaison between the investigative site and the sponsor, and reviews data and records during a monitoring visit.

Cost Plus Contract: A contract that sets the contractor's compensation as a percentage of the total cost of labor and materials.

COSTART: In medical and drug product development, a dictionary of adverse events and body systems used for coding and classifying adverse events.

CPMP: See "Committee on Proprietary Medicinal Products (CPMP)."

CPU: See "Central Processing Unit (CPU)."

CRO: See "Contract Research Organization (CRO)."

CT: See "Computed Tomography (CT)."

CVMP: See "Committee for Veterinary Medicinal Products (CVMP)."

Data Over Cable Service Interface Specification (DOCSIS): A set of standards for transferring data over cable television. DOCSIS 3.1 will enable very high-speed Internet access that may eventually reach 2 Gigabytes or more (2 Gbps).

Decompression: See "Compression."

Defibrillator: In medicine, an instrument used externally (as electrodes on the chest) or implanted (as a small device similar in size to a pacemaker) that delivers an electric shock to return the heart to its normal rhythm.

Demand Chain: A similar concept to a supply chain, but with an emphasis on the end user.

Dendrimer: A type of molecule that can be used with small molecules to give them certain desirable characteristics. Dendrimers are utilized in technologies for electronic displays. See "Organic LED (OLED)."

Design Patent: A patent that may be granted by the U.S. Patent and Trademark Office to anyone who invents a new, original, and ornamental design for an article of manufacture.

Development: The phase of research and development (R&D) in which researchers attempt to create new products from the results of discoveries and applications created during basic and applied research.

Device: In medical products, an instrument, apparatus, implement, machine, contrivance, implant, in vitro reagent or other similar or related article, including any component, part or accessory, that 1) is recognized in the official National Formulary or United States Pharmacopoeia or any supplement to them, 2) is intended for use in the diagnosis of disease or other conditions, or in the cure, mitigation, treatment or prevention of disease, in man or animals or 3) is intended to affect the structure of the body of man or animals and does not achieve any of its principal intended purposes through chemical action within or on the body of man or animals and is not dependent upon being metabolized for the achievement of any of its principal intended purposes.

DFSS: Design for Six Sigma. See "Six Sigma."

Diagnostic Radioisotope Facility: A medical facility in which radioactive isotopes (radiopharmaceuticals) are used as tracers or indicators to detect an abnormal condition or disease in the body.

Digital Local Telephone Switch: A computer that interprets signals (dialed numbers) from a telephone caller and routes calls to their proper destinations. A digital switch also provides a variety of calling features not available in older analog switches, such as call waiting.

Digital Rights Management (DRM): Restrictions placed on the use of digital content by copyright holders and hardware manufacturers. DRM for Apple, Inc.'s iTunes, for example, allows downloaded music to be played only on Apple's iPod player and iPhones, per agreement with music production companies Universal Music Group, SonyBMG, Warner Music and EMI.

Digital Signal Processor: A chip that converts analog signals such as sound and light into digital signals.

Digital Subscriber Line (DSL): A broadband (high-speed) Internet connection provided via telecommunications systems. These lines are a cost-effective means of providing homes and small businesses with relatively fast Internet access. Common variations include ADSL and SDSL. DSL competes with cable modem access and wireless access.

Disaster Recovery: A set of rules and procedures that allow a computer site to be put back in operation after a disaster has occurred. Moving backups off-site constitutes the minimum basic precaution for disaster recovery. The remote copy is used to recover data if the local storage is inaccessible after a disaster.

Discrete Semiconductor: A chip with one diode or transistor.

Disk Mirroring: A data redundancy technique in which data is recorded identically on multiple separate disk drives at the same time. When the primary disk is off-line, the alternate takes over, providing continuous access to data. Disk mirroring is sometimes referred to as RAID.

Distributor: An individual or business involved in marketing, warehousing and/or shipping of products manufactured by others to a specific group of end users. Distributors do not sell to the general public. In order to develop a competitive advantage, distributors often focus on serving one industry or one set of niche clients. For example, within the medical industry, there are major distributors that focus on providing pharmaceuticals, surgical supplies or dental supplies to clinics and hospitals.

DNA Chip: A revolutionary tool used to identify mutations in genes like BRCA1 and BRCA2. The chip, which consists of a small glass plate encased in plastic, is manufactured using a process similar to the one used to make computer microchips. On the surface, each chip contains synthetic single-stranded DNA sequences identical to a normal gene.

DOCSIS: See "Data Over Cable Service Interface Specification (DOCSIS)."

Drug Utilization Review: A quantitative assessment of patient drug use and physicians' patterns of prescribing drugs in an effort to determine the usefulness of drug therapy.

DS-1: A digital transmission format that transmits and receives information at a rate of 1,544,000 bits per second.

DSL: See "Digital Subscriber Line (DSL)."

Duplicate Host: A single host name that maps to duplicate IP addresses.

Dynamic HTML: Web content that changes with each individual viewing. For example, the same site could appear differently depending on geographic location of the reader, time of day, previous pages viewed or the user's profile.

Ecology: The study of relationships among all living organisms and the environment, especially the totality or pattern of interactions; a view that includes all plant and animal species and their unique contributions to a particular habitat.

ELA: See "Establishment License Application (ELA)."

Electronic Data Interchange (EDI): An accepted standard format for the exchange of data between various companies' networks. EDI allows for the transfer of e-mail as well as orders, invoices and other files from one company to another.

Emission: The release or discharge of a substance into the environment. Generally refers to the release of gases or particulates into the air.

Endpoint: A clinical or laboratory measurement used to assess safety, efficacy or other trial objectives of a test article in a clinical trial.

Engineering Plastics: Plastics that hold up well under stress from such factors as a wide range in temperatures, mechanical or physical stress and exposure to chemicals. Engineering plastics are often used as structural components. Engineered plastics are generating novel ways to reduce weight, reduce costs and increase performance of materials. Performance enhancements may include heat resistance, chemical resistance, compressive strength or stiffness. Such plastics can be very effective replacements for steel, titanium, ceramics or aluminum, particularly in applications like consumer electronics, aircraft or automobiles, where the reduction of overall product weight can be a vital concern. Also, see "Performance Plastics."

Engineering, Procurement and Construction (EPC): A type of contractual agreement often used in large construction projects. All three major phases of a project may be given to one EPC Contractor, including the engineering/design of the project; the specification, bidding and purchasing/procurement of all of the equipment, materials and subcontractors required; and all related construction functions.

Enterprise Resource Planning (ERP): An integrated information system that helps manage all aspects of a business, including accounting, ordering and human resources, typically across all locations of a major corporation or organization. ERP is considered to be a critical tool for management of large organizations. Suppliers of ERP tools include SAP and Oracle.

Environmental Audit: An independent assessment of a facility's compliance procedures, policies and controls. Many pollution prevention initiatives require an audit to determine where wastes may be reduced or eliminated or energy conserved.

EPC: See "Engineering, Procurement and Construction (EPC)."

EPC Contractor: See "Engineering, Procurement and Construction (EPC)."

ERP: See "Enterprise Resource Planning (ERP)."

Establishment License Application (ELA): Required for the approval of a biologic (see "Biologics"). It permits a specific facility to manufacture a biological product for commercial purposes. Compare to "Product License Agreement (PLA)."

ESWL: See "Extracorporeal Shock Wave Lithotripter (ESWL)."

Ethernet: The standard format on which local area network equipment works. Abiding by Ethernet standards allows equipment from various manufacturers to work together.

EU: See "European Union (EU)."

EU Competence: The jurisdiction in which the European Union (EU) can take legal action.

European Community (EC): See "European Union (EU)."

European Medicines Evaluation Agency (EMEA): The European agency responsible for supervising and coordinating applications for marketing medicinal products in the European Union (see "European Union (EU)" and "Committee on Proprietary Medicinal Products (CPMP)"). The EMEA is headquartered in the U.K. www.eudraportal.eudra.org

European Union (EU): A consolidation of European countries (member states) functioning as one body to facilitate trade. Previously known as the European Community (EC). The EU has a unified currency, the Euro. See europa.eu.int.

Expert Systems: A practical development of AI that requires creation of a knowledge base of facts and rules furnished by human experts and uses a defined set of rules to access this information in order to suggest solutions to problems. See "Artificial Intelligence (AI)."

Extensible Markup Language (XML): A programming language that enables designers to add extra functionality to documents that could not otherwise be utilized with standard HTML coding. XML was developed by the World Wide Web Consortium. It can communicate to various software programs the actual meanings contained in HTML documents. For example, it can enable the gathering and use of information from a large number of databases at once and place that information into one web site window. XML is an important protocol to web services. See "Web Services."

Extracorporeal Shock Wave Lithotripter (ESWL): A medical device used for treating stones in the kidney or urethra. The device disintegrates kidney stones noninvasively through the transmission of acoustic shock waves directed at the stones.

Extranet: A computer network that is accessible in part to authorized outside persons, as opposed to an intranet, which uses a firewall to limit accessibility.

Fab Lab: See "3-D Printing."

Fabless: A method of operation used by a product supplier that does not have its own fabrication or manufacturing facilities. This phrase is often used to describe certain semiconductor firms that design chips but rely on outside, contract manufacturers for their actual fabrication.

Failure Modes and Effects Analysis (FMEA): An approach to determining points of possible failure in a design, a process, a service or a product.

FASB: See "Financial Accounting Standards Board (FASB)."

FDA: See "Food and Drug Administration (FDA)."

FDDI: See "Fiber Distributed Data Interface (FDDI)."

FDM: See "Fused Deposition Modeling (FDM)."

Federal Communications Commission (FCC): The U.S. Government agency that regulates broadcast television and radio, as well as satellite transmission, telephony and all uses of radio spectrum.

Femtosecond: One a billionth of one millionth of a second.

Fiber Distributed Data Interface (FDDI): A token ring passing scheme that operates at 100 Mbps over fiber-optic lines with a built-in geographic limitation of 100 kilometers. This type of connection is faster than both Ethernet and T-3 connections. See "Token Ring."

Fiber Optics (Fibre Optics): A type of telephone and data transmission cable that can handle vast amounts of voice, data and video at once by carrying them along on beams of light via glass or plastic threads embedded in a cable. Fiber optics are rapidly replacing older copper wire technologies. Fiber optics offer much higher speeds and the ability to handle extremely large quantities of voice or data transmissions at once.

Fiber to the Home (FTTH): Refers to the extension of a fiber-optic system through the last mile so that it touches the home or office where it will be used. This can provide very high speed Internet access. Another phrase used to describe such installations is FTTP, or Fiber to the Premises.

Field Emission Display (FED): A self-luminescent display that can be extremely thin, draw very low power, and be very bright from all angles and in all types of light. The latest FEDs are based on carbon nanotubes. Samsung is a leader in this field. Early applications include high-end television and computer monitors.

File Server: A computer that is modified to store and transfer large amounts of data to other computers. File servers often receive data from mainframes and store it for transfer to other, smaller computers, or from small computers to mainframes.

File Transfer Protocol (FTP): A widely used method of transferring data and files between two Internet sites.

Financial Accounting Standards Board (FASB): An independent organization that establishes the Generally Accepted Accounting Principles (GAAP).

Finite Element Analysis (FEA): Finite Element Analysis (FEA) is a tool in computerized design that can detect flaws in a computer-generated model. It analyzes how the model would react to extremes in heat, vibration and pressure by breaking it down into small pieces or cells in a three-dimensional grid. The computer applies simulated stimuli to one cell in the model and then tracks the response of that cell and those that surround it.

Firewall: Hardware or software that keeps unauthorized users from accessing a server or network. Firewalls are designed to prevent data theft and unauthorized web site manipulation by "hackers."

Fissure: A long narrow crack or opening.

FMEA: See "Failure Modes and Effects Analysis (FMEA)."

Follow-on Biologics: A term used to describe generic versions of drugs that have been created using biotechnology. Because biotech drugs ("biologics") are made from living cells, a generic version of a drug probably won't be biochemically identical to the original branded version of the drug. Consequently, they are described as "follow-on" biologics to set them apart. Since these drugs won't be exactly the same as the originals, there are concerns that they may not be as safe or effective unless they go through clinical trials for proof of quality. In Europe, these drugs are referred to as "biosimilars." See "Biologics."

Food and Drug Administration (FDA): The U.S. government agency responsible for the enforcement of the Federal Food, Drug and Cosmetic Act, ensuring industry compliance with laws regulating products in commerce. The FDA's mission is to protect the public from harm and encourage technological advances that hold the promise of benefiting society. www.fda.gov

Fracture: A break or rupture in the surface of a laminate due to external or internal forces.

Frame Relay: An accepted standard for sending large amounts of data over phone lines and private datanets. The term refers to the way data is broken down into standard-size "frames" prior to transmission.

Frequency: The number of times that an alternating current goes through its complete cycle in one second. One cycle per second is referred to as one hertz; 1,000 cycles per second, one kilohertz; 1 million cycles per second, one megahertz; and 1 billion cycles per second, one gigahertz.

Frequency Band: A term for designating a range of frequencies in the electromagnetic spectrum.

FTP: See "File Transfer Protocol (FTP)."

FTTH: See "Fiber to the Home (FTTH)."

Fuel Cell: An environmentally friendly electrochemical engine that generates electricity using hydrogen and oxygen as fuel, emitting only heat and water as byproducts.

Fused Deposition Modeling (FDM): A type of 3-D printing, based on the extruding and depositing of thermoplastics.

Fusion: See "Nuclear Fusion."

Fuzzy Logic: Recognizes that some statements are not just "true" or "false," but also "more or less certain" or "very unlikely." Fuzzy logic is used in artificial intelligence. See "Artificial Intelligence (AI)."

GAAP: See "Generally Accepted Accounting Principles (GAAP)."

Gateway: A device connecting two or more networks that may use different protocols and media. Gateways translate between the different networks and can connect locally or over wide area networks.

GCP: See "Good Clinical Practices (GCP)."

GDP: See "Gross Domestic Product (GDP)."

Gene Chip: See "DNA Chip."

Generally Accepted Accounting Principles (GAAP): A set of accounting standards administered by the Financial Accounting Standards Board (FASB) and enforced by the U.S. Security and Exchange Commission (SEC). GAAP is primarily used in the U.S.

Genetically Modified (GM) Foods: Food crops that are bioengineered to resist herbicides, diseases or insects; have higher nutritional value than non-engineered plants; produce a higher yield per acre; and/or last longer on the shelf. Additional traits may include resistance to temperature and moisture extremes. Agricultural animals also may be genetically modified organisms.

Geological Information System (GIS): A computer software system which captures, stores, updates, manipulates, analyzes, and displays all forms of geographically referenced information.

Geostationary: A geosynchronous satellite angle with zero inclination, making a satellite appear to hover over one spot on the earth's equator.

GERD: Gross domestic expenditure on R&D (research & development).

GHG: See "Greenhouse Gas (GHG)."

Gigabyte: 1,024 megabytes.

Gigahertz (GHz): One billion cycles per second. See "Frequency."

Global Positioning System (GPS): A satellite system, originally designed by the U.S. Department of Defense for navigation purposes. Today, GPS is in wide use for consumer and business purposes, such as navigation for drivers, boaters and hikers. It utilizes satellites orbiting the earth at 10,900 miles to enable users to pinpoint precise locations using small, electronic wireless receivers.

Global System for Mobile Communications (GSM): The standard cellular format used throughout Europe, making one type of cellular phone usable in every nation on the continent and in the U.K. In the U.S., Cingular and T-Mobile also run GSM networks. The original GSM, introduced in 1991, has transfer speeds of only 9.6 kbps. GSM EDGE offers 2.75G data transfer speeds of up to 473.6 kbps. GSM GPRS offers slower 2.5G theoretical speeds of 144 kbps.

Global Warming: An increase in the near-surface temperature of the Earth. Global warming has occurred in the distant past as the result of natural influences, but the term is most often used to refer to a theory that warming occurs as a result of increased use of hydrocarbon fuels by man. See "Climate Change (Greenhouse Effect)."

Globalization: The increased mobility of goods, services, labor, technology and capital throughout the world. Although globalization is not a new development, its pace has increased with the advent of new technologies.

GLP: See "Good Laboratory Practices (GLP)."

GMP: See "Good Manufacturing Practices (GMP)."

GNR: The convergence of three of the world's most promising technologies: genetics, nanotechnology and robotics. Some observers believe that synergies between these technologies will enable revolutionary breakthroughs in science, technology, manufacturing and medicine.

Good Clinical Practices (GCP): FDA regulations and guidelines that define the responsibilities of the key figures involved in a clinical trial, including the sponsor, the investigator, the monitor and the Institutional Review Board. See "Institutional Review Board (IRB)."

Good Laboratory Practices (GLP): A collection of regulations and guidelines to be used in laboratories where research is conducted on drugs, biologics or devices that are intended for submission to the FDA.

Good Manufacturing Practices (GMP): A collection of regulations and guidelines to be used in manufacturing drugs, biologics and medical devices.

GPS: See "Global Positioning System (GPS)."

Graphic Interchange Format (GIF): A widely used format for image files.

Greenhouse Gas (GHG): See "Climate Change (Greenhouse Effect)."

Gross Domestic Product (GDP): The total value of a nation's output, income and expenditures produced with a nation's physical borders.

Gross National Product (GNP): A country's total output of goods and services from all forms of economic activity measured at market prices for one calendar year. It differs from Gross Domestic Product (GDP) in that GNP includes income from investments made in foreign nations.

GSM: See "Global System for Mobile Communications (GSM)."

Handheld Devices Markup Language (HDML): A text-based markup language designed for display on a smaller screen (e.g., a cellular phone, PDA or pager). Enables the mobile user to send, receive and redirect e-mail as well as access the Internet (HDML-enabled web sites only).

HD Radio (High Definition Radio): A technology that enables station operators to slice existing radio spectrum into multiple, thin bands. Each band is capable of transmitting additional programming. One existing radio station's spectrum may be sliced into as many as eight channels.

HDML: See "Handheld Devices Markup Language (HDML)."

HDSL: See "High-Data-Rate Digital Subscriber Line (HDSL)."

Hertz: A measure of frequency equal to one cycle per second. Most radio signals operate in ranges of megahertz or gigahertz.

High-Data-Rate Digital Subscriber Line (HDSL): High-data-rate DSL, delivering up to T1 or E1 speeds.

High-Throughput Screening (HTP): Makes use of techniques that allow for a fast and simple test on the presence or absence of a desirable structure, such as a specific DNA sequence. HTP screening often uses DNA chips or microarrays and automated data processing for large-scale screening, for instance, to identify new targets for drug development.

HTML: See "Hypertext Markup Language (HTML)."

HTTP: See "Hypertext Transfer Protocol (HTTP)."

Hypertext Markup Language (HTML): A language for coding text for viewing on the World Wide Web. HTML is unique because it enables the use of hyperlinks from one site to another, creating a web.

Hypertext Transfer Protocol (HTTP): The protocol used most frequently on the World Wide Web to move hypertext files between clients and servers on the Internet.

ICANN: The Internet Corporation for Assigned Names and Numbers. ICANN acts as the central coordinator for the Internet's technical operations.

ICD9: International Classification of Diseases - Version 9. A government coding system used for classifying diseases and diagnoses.

IDE: See "Investigational New Device Exemption (IDE)."

IEEE: See "Institute of Electrical and Electronic Engineers (IEEE)."

IFRS: See "International Financials Reporting Standards (IFRS)."

ILEC: See "Incumbent Local Exchange Carrier (ILEC)."

Imaging: In medicine, the viewing of the body's organs through external, high-tech means. This reduces the need for broad exploratory surgery. These advances, along with new types of surgical instruments, have made minimally invasive surgery possible. Imaging includes MRI (magnetic resonance imaging), CT (computed tomography or CAT scan), MEG (magnetoencephalography), improved x-ray technology, mammography, ultrasound and angiography.

Immunoassay: An immunological assay. Types include agglutination, complement-fixation, precipitation, immunodiffusion and electrophoretic assays. Each type of assay utilizes either a particular type of antibody or a specific support medium (such as a gel) to determine the amount of antigen present.

In Vitro: Laboratory experiments conducted in the test tube, or otherwise, without using live animals and/or humans.

In Vivo: Laboratory experiments conducted with live animals and/or humans.

Incumbent Local Exchange Carrier (ILEC): A traditional telephone company that was providing local service prior to the establishment of the Telecommunications Act of 1996, when upstart companies

(CLECs, or competitive local exchange carriers) were enabled to compete against the ILECS and were granted access to their system wiring.

IND: See "Investigational New Drug Application (IND)."

Industry Code: A descriptive code assigned to any company in order to group it with firms that operate in similar businesses. Common industry codes include the NAICS (North American Industrial Classification System) and the SIC (Standard Industrial Classification), both of which are standards widely used in America, as well as the International Standard Industrial Classification of all Economic Activities (ISIC), the Standard International Trade Classification established by the United Nations (SITC) and the General Industrial Classification of Economic Activities within the European Communities (NACE).

Inert Ingredients: Substances that are not active, such as water, petroleum distillates, talc, corn meal or soaps.

Information Technology (IT): The systems, including hardware and software, that move and store voice, video and data via computers and telecommunications.

Infrastructure: 1) The equipment that comprises a system. 2) Public-use assets such as roads, bridges, water systems, sewers and other assets necessary for public accommodation and utilities. 3) The underlying base of a system or network. 4) Transportation and shipping support systems such as ports, airports and railways.

Infrastructure (Telecommunications): The entity made up of all the cable and equipment installed in the worldwide telecommunications market. Most of today's telecommunications infrastructure is connected by copper and fiber-optic cable, which represents a huge capital investment that telephone companies would like to continue to utilize in as many ways as possible.

Initial Public Offering (IPO): A company's first effort to sell its stock to investors (the public). Investors in an up-trending market eagerly seek stocks offered in many IPOs because the stocks of newly public companies that seem to have great promise may appreciate very rapidly in price, reaping great profits for those who were able to get the stock at the first offering. In the United States, IPOs are regulated by the SEC (U.S. Securities Exchange Commission) and by the state-level regulatory agencies of the states in which the IPO shares are offered.

INMARSAT: The International Maritime Satellite Organization. INMARSAT operates a network of satellites used in transmissions for all types of international mobile services, including maritime, aeronautical and land mobile.

Institute of Electrical and Electronic Engineers (IEEE): An organization that sets global technical standards and acts as an authority in technical areas including computer engineering, biomedical technology, telecommunications, electric power, aerospace and consumer electronics, among others. www.ieee.org.

Institutional Review Board (IRB): A group of individuals usually found in medical institutions that is responsible for reviewing protocols for ethical consideration (to ensure the rights of the patients). An IRB also evaluates the benefit-to-risk ratio of a new drug to see that the risk is acceptable for patient exposure. Responsibilities of an IRB are defined in FDA regulations.

Integrated Circuit (IC): Another name for a semiconductor, an IC is a piece of silicon on which thousands (or millions) of transistors have been combined.

Integrated Services Digital Networks (ISDN): Internet connection services offered at higher speeds than standard "dial-up" service. While ISDN was considered to be an advanced service at one time, it has been eclipsed by much faster DSL, cable modem and T1 line service.

Intellectual Property (IP): The exclusive ownership of original concepts, ideas, designs, engineering plans or other assets that are protected by law. Examples include items covered by trademarks, copyrights and patents. Items such as software, engineering plans, fashion designs and architectural designs, as well as games, books, songs and other entertainment items are among the many things that may be considered to be intellectual property. (Also, see "Patent.")

INTELSAT: The International Telecommunications Satellite Organization. INTELSAT operates a network of 20 satellites, primarily for international transmissions, and provides domestic services to some 40 countries.

Interactive TV (ITV): Allows two-way data flow between a viewer and the cable TV system. A user can exchange information with the cable system—for example, by ordering a product related to a show he/she is watching or by voting in an interactive survey.

Interexchange Carrier (IXC or IEC): Any company providing long-distance phone service between LECs and LATAs. See "Local Exchange Carrier (LEC)" and "Local Access and Transport Area (LATA)."

Interface: Refers to (1) a common boundary between two or more items of equipment or between a terminal and a communication channel, (2) the electronic device that interconnects two or more devices or items of equipment having similar or dissimilar characteristics or (3) the electronic device placed between a terminal and a communication channel to protect the network from the hazard of excess voltage levels.

International Financials Reporting Standards (IFRS): A set of accounting standards established by the International Accounting Standards Board (IASB) for the preparation of public financial statements. IFRS has been adopted by much of the world, including the European Union, Russia and Singapore.

International Telecommunications Union (ITU): The international body responsible for telephone and computer communications standards describing interface techniques and practices. These standards include those that define how a nation's telephone and data systems connect to the worldwide communications network.

Internet: A global computer network that provides an easily accessible way for hundreds of millions of users to send and receive data electronically when appropriately connected via computers or wireless devices. Access is generally through HTML-enabled sites on the World Wide Web. Also known as the Net.

Internet Appliance: A non-PC device that connects users to the Internet for specific or general purposes. A good example is an electronic game machine with a screen and Internet capabilities.

Internet Protocol (IP): A set of tools and/or systems used to communicate across the World Wide Web.

Internet Service Provider (ISP): A company that sells access to the Internet to individual subscribers. Leading examples are MSN and AOL.

Internet Telephony: See "Voice Over Internet Protocol (VOIP)."

Intranet: A network protected by a firewall for sharing data and e-mail within an organization or company. Usually, intranets are used by organizations for internal communication.

Investigational New Device Exemption (IDE): A document that must be filed with the FDA prior to initiating clinical trials of medical devices considered to pose a significant risk to human subjects.

Investigational New Drug Application (IND): A document that must be filed with the FDA prior to initiating clinical trials of drugs or biologics.

Investigator: In clinical trials, a clinician who agrees to supervise the use of an investigational drug, device or biologic in humans. Responsibilities of the investigator, as defined in FDA regulations, include administering the drug, observing and testing the patient, collecting data and monitoring the care and welfare of the patient.

IP: See "Intellectual Property (IP)."

IP Number/IP Address: A number or address with four parts that are separated by dots. Each machine on the Internet has its own IP (Internet protocol) number, which serves as an identifier.

IRB: See "Institutional Review Board (IRB)."

ISDN: See "Integrated Services Digital Networks (ISDN)."

ISO 9000, 9001, 9002, 9003: Standards set by the International Organization for Standardization. ISO 9000, 9001, 9002 and 9003 are the highest quality certifications awarded to organizations that meet exacting standards in their operating practices and procedures.

IT: See "Information Technology (IT)."

IT-Enabled Services (ITES): The portion of the Information Technology industry focused on providing business services, such as call centers, insurance claims processing and medical records transcription, by utilizing the power of IT, especially the Internet. Most ITES functions are considered to be back-office procedures. Also, see "Business Process Outsourcing (BPO)."

ITES: See "IT-Enabled Services (ITES)."

ITU: See "International Telecommunications Union (ITU)."

ITV: See "Interactive TV (ITV)."

Java: A programming language developed by Sun Microsystems that allows web pages to display interactive graphics. Any type of computer or operating systems can read Java.

Joint Photographic Experts Group (JPEG): A widely used format for digital image files.

Just-in-Time (JIT) Delivery: Refers to a supply chain practice whereby manufacturers receive components on or just before the time that they are needed on the assembly line, rather than bearing the cost of maintaining several days' or weeks' supply in a warehouse. This adds greatly to the cost-effectiveness of a manufacturing plant and puts the burden of warehousing and timely delivery on the supplier of the components.

Ka-Band: The frequency range from 18 to 31 GHz. The spectrum allocated for satellite communications is 30 GHz for the up-link and 20 GHz for the downlink.

Kavli Prize: The Kavli Prizes are a partnership between The Norwegian Academy of Science and Letters, The Kavli Foundation (USA) and The Norwegian Ministry of Education and Research. The Kavli Prize recognizes scientists for their seminal advances in three research areas: astrophysics, nanoscience and neuroscience. The Kavli Prize consists of 1,000,000 US Dollars in each of the scientific fields. In addition to the prize money the laureates receive a scroll and a gold medal. The Kavli Prize is awarded every second year by The Norwegian Academy of Science and Letters at a ceremony in Oslo, Norway.

Kbps: One thousand bits per second.

Kilobyte: One thousand (or 1,024) bytes.

Kilohertz (kHz): A measure of frequency equal to 1,000 Hertz.

Knowledge Process Outsourcing (KPO): The use of outsourced and/or offshore workers to perform business tasks that require judgment and analysis. Examples include such professional tasks as patent research, legal research, architecture, design, engineering, market research, scientific research, accounting and tax return preparation. Also, see "Business Process Outsourcing (BPO)."

LAC: Latin America and the Caribbean.

Large-Scale Integration (LSI): The placement of thousands of electronic gates on a single chip. This makes the manufacture of powerful computers possible.

LATA: See "Local Access and Transport Area (LATA)."

LDCs: See "Least Developed Countries (LDCs)."

Leased Line: A phone line that is rented for use in continuous, long-term data connections.

Least Developed Countries (LDCs): Nations determined by the U.N. Economic and Social Council to be the poorest and weakest members of the international community. There are currently 50 LDCs, of which 34 are in Africa, 15 are in Asia Pacific and the remaining one (Haiti) is in Latin America. The top 10 on the LDC list, in descending order from top to 10th, are Afghanistan, Angola, Bangladesh, Benin, Bhutan, Burkina Faso, Burundi, Cambodia, Cape Verde and the Central African Republic. Sixteen of the LDCs are also Landlocked Least Developed Countries (LLDCs) which present them with additional difficulties often due to the high cost of transporting trade goods. Eleven of the LDCs are Small Island Developing States (SIDS), which are often at risk of extreme weather phenomenon (hurricanes, typhoons, Tsunami); have fragile ecosystems; are often dependent on foreign energy sources; can have high disease rates for HIV/AIDS and malaria; and can have poor market access and trade terms.

LEC: See "Local Exchange Carrier (LEC)."

LIDAR: See "Light Detection and Ranging (LIDAR)."

Light Detection and Ranging (LIDAR): A remote sensing method that uses light in the form of a pulsed laser to measure ranges (that is, variable distances) from the LIDAR unit to other objects. In self-driving cars and other vehicles, LIDAR is a primary method for determining distance to nearby vehicles and other objects. LIDAR is also an advanced method for airborne topographic and bathymetric mapping of the Earth.

Light Emitting Diode (LED): A small tube containing material that emits light when exposed to electricity. The color of the light depends upon the type of material. The LED was first developed in 1962 at the University of Illinois at Urbana-Champaign. LEDs are important to a wide variety of industries, from wireless telephone handsets to signage to displays for medical equipment, because they provide a very high quality of light with very low power requirements. They also have a very long useful life and produce very low heat output when. All of these characteristics are great improvements over a conventional incandescent bulb. Several advancements have been made in LED technology. See "Organic LED (OLED)," "Polymer Light Emitting Diode (PLED)," "Small Molecule Organic Light Emitting Diode (SMOLED)" and "Dendrimer."

LINUX: An open, free operating system that is shared readily with millions of users worldwide. These users continuously improve and add to the software's code. It can be used to operate computer networks and Internet appliances as well as servers and PCs.

Lithography: In the manufacture of semiconductors and MEMS (microelectromechanical systems), lithography refers to the transfer of a pattern of photosensitive material by exposing it to light or radiation. The photosensitive material changes physical properties when exposed to a source of radiation. Typically, a mask is employed that creates a desired pattern by blocking out light to some areas. Using this process to deposit materials on a substrate, integrated circuits can be manufactured.

Local Access and Transport Area (LATA): An operational service area established after the breakup of AT&T to distinguish local telephone service from long-distance service. The U.S. is divided into over 160 LATAs.

Local Area Network (LAN): A computer network that is generally within one office or one building. A LAN can be very inexpensive and efficient to set up when small numbers of computers are involved. It may require a network administrator and a serious investment if hundreds of computers are hooked up to the LAN. A LAN enables all computers within the office to share files and printers, to access common databases and to send e-mail to others on the network.

Local Exchange Carrier (LEC): Any local telephone company, i.e., a carrier, that provides ordinary phone service under regulation within a service area. Also see "Incumbent Local Exchange Carrier (ILEC)" and "Competitive Local Exchange Carrier (CLEC)."

LSI: See "Large-Scale Integration (LSI)."

M2M: See "Machine-to-Machine (M2M)."

M3 (Measurement): Cubic meters.

Machine-to-Machine (M2M): Refers to the transmission of data from one device to another, typically through wireless means such as Wi-Fi or cellular. For example, a Wi-Fi network might be employed to control several machines in a household from a central computer. Such machines might include air conditioning and entertainment systems. Wireless sensor networks (WSNs) will be a major growth factor in M2M communications, in everything from factory automation to agriculture and transportation. In logistics and retailing, M2M can refer to the use of RFID tags to transmit information. See "Radio Frequency Identification (RFID)."

MAN: See "Metropolitan Area Network (MAN)."

Managed Service Provider (MSP): An outsourcer that deploys, manages and maintains the back-end software and hardware infrastructure for Internet businesses.

Manufacturing Resource Planning (MRP II): A methodology that supports effective planning with regard to all resources of a manufacturing company, linking MRP with sales and operations planning, production planning and master production scheduling.

Material Safety Data Sheet (MSDS): A document, required by OSHA (U.S. Occupational Safety and Health Administration) regulations, that provides a thorough profile of a potentially hazardous substance or product. The MSDS profile includes recommendations of how to handle the product, as well as how to treat a person who swallows the product, gets the product in the eyes or is otherwise overexposed. Manufacturers of such products, such as cleansers, solvents and coatings, provide these MSDS sheets at no cost to customers and end users. Employers using these substances in the workplace are required to have MSDS sheets on hand.

Materials Science: The study of the structure, properties and performance of such materials as metals, ceramics, polymers and composites.

Mbps (Megabits per second): One million bits transmitted per second.

M-Commerce: Mobile e-commerce over wireless devices.

Medical Device: See "Device."

Megabytes: One million bytes, or 1,024 kilobytes.

Megahertz (MHz): A measure of frequency equal to 1 million Hertz.

Metamaterials: Used to describe a material that has been engineered or modified to have properties that do not occur naturally. Metamaterials are designed to offer unique advantages, and may have unique electromagnetic or light refracting abilities. The basic component of metamaterials is sometimes called a "superatom," which is a cluster of multiple atoms that behave as if they are a single atom.

Metrology: The science of measurement.

Metropolitan Area Network (MAN): A data and communications network that operates over metropolitan areas and recently has been expanded to nationwide and even worldwide connectivity of high-speed data networks. A MAN can carry video and data.

Microprocessor: A computer on a digital semiconductor chip. It performs math and logic operations and executes instructions from memory. (Also known as a central processing unit or CPU.)

Microwave: Line-of sight, point-to-point transmission of signals at high frequency. Microwaves are used in data, voice and all other types of information transmission. The growth of fiber-optic networks has tended to curtail the growth and use of microwave relays.

MIME: See "Multipurpose Internet Mail Extensions (MIME)."

MMS: See "Multimedia Messaging System (MMS)."

Modem: A device that allows a computer to be connected to a phone line, which in turn enables the computer to receive and exchange data with other machines via the Internet.

Modulator: A device that modulates a carrier. Modulators are found in broadcasting transmitters and satellite transponders. The devices are also used by cable TV companies to place a baseband video television signal onto a desired VHF or UHF channel. Home video tape recorders also have built-in modulators that enable the recorded video information to be played back using a television receiver tuned to VHF channel 3 or 4.

MPEG, MPEG-1, MPEG-2, MPEG-3, MPEG-4: Moving Picture Experts Group. It is a digital standard for the compression of motion or still video for transmission or storage. MPEGs are used in digital cameras and for Internet-based viewing.

MSDS: See "Material Safety Data Sheet (MSDS)."

MSP: See "Managed Service Provider (MSP)."

Multimedia Messaging System (MMS): See "Text Messaging."

Multipoint Distribution System (MDS): A common carrier licensed by the FCC to operate a broadcast-like omni-directional microwave transmission facility within a given city. MDS carriers often pick up satellite pay-TV programming and distribute it, via their local MDS transmitter, to specially installed antennas and receivers.

Multipurpose Internet Mail Extensions (MIME): A widely used method for attaching non-text files to e-mails.

NAFTA: See "North American Free Trade Agreement (NAFTA)."

NAND: An advanced type of flash memory chip. It is popular for use in consumer electronics such as MP3 players and digital cameras.

Nanoparticle: A nanoscale spherical or capsule-shaped structure. Most, though not all, nanoparticles are hollow, which provides a central reservoir that can be filled with anticancer drugs, detection agents, or chemicals, known as reporters, that can signal if a drug is having a therapeutic effect. The surface of a nanoparticle can also be adorned with various targeting agents, such as antibodies, drugs, imaging agents, and reporters. Most nanoparticles are constructed to be small enough to pass through blood capillaries and enter cells.

Nanosecond (NS): A billionth of a second. A common unit of measure of computer operating speed.

Nanotechnology: The science of designing, building or utilizing unique structures that are smaller than 100 nanometers (a nanometer is one billionth of a meter). This involves microscopic structures that are no larger than the width of some cell membranes.

Nanowires: A nanometer-scale wire made of metal atoms, silicon, or other materials that conduct electricity. Nanowires are built atom by atom on a solid surface, often as part of a microfluidic device. They can be coated with molecules such as antibodies that will bind to proteins and other substances of interest to researchers and clinicians. By the very nature of their nanoscale size, nanowires are incredibly sensitive to such binding events and respond by altering the electrical current flowing through them, and thus can form the basis of ultra sensitive molecular detectors.

National Institutes of Health (NIH): A branch of the U.S. Public Health Service that conducts biomedical research. www.nih.gov

NDA: See "New Drug Application (NDA)."

Network: In computing, a network is created when two or more computers are connected. Computers may be connected by wireless methods, using such technologies as 802.11b, or by a system of cables, switches and routers.

Network Numbers: The first portion of an IP address, which identifies the network to which hosts in the rest of the address are connected.

New Drug Application (NDA): An application requesting FDA approval, after completion of the all-important Phase III Clinical Trials, to market a new drug for human use in the U.S. The drug may contain chemical compounds that were previously approved by the FDA as distinct molecular entities suitable for use in drug trials (NMEs). See "New Molecular Entity (NME)."

New Molecular Entity (NME): Defined by the FDA as a medication containing chemical compound that has never before been approved for marketing in any form in the U.S. An NME is sometimes referred to as a New Chemical Entity (NCE). Also, see "New Drug Application (NDA)."

New Urbanism: A relatively new term that refers to neighborhood developments that feature shorter blocks, more sidewalks and pedestrian ways, access to convenient mass transit, bicycle paths and conveniently placed open spaces. The intent is to promote walking and social interaction while decreasing automobile traffic. The concept may also include close proximity to stores and offices that may be reached by walking rather than driving.

NIH: See "National Institutes of Health (NIH)."

NME: See "New Molecular Entity (NME)."

Node: Any single computer connected to a network or a junction of communications paths in a network.

Nonclinical Studies: In vitro (laboratory) or in vivo (animal) pharmacology, toxicology and pharmacokinetic studies that support the testing of a product in humans. Usually at least two species are evaluated prior to Phase I clinical trials. Nonclinical studies continue throughout all phases of research to evaluate long-term safety issues.

North American Free Trade Agreement (NAFTA): A trade agreement signed in December 1992 by U.S.

President George H. W. Bush, Canadian Prime Minister Brian Mulroney and Mexican President Carlos Salinas de Gortari. The agreement eliminates tariffs on most goods originating in and traveling between the three member countries. It was approved by the legislatures of the three countries and had entered into force by January 1994. When it was created, NAFTA formed one of the largest free-trade areas of its kind in the world.

North American Industrial Classification System (NAICS): See "Industry Code."

NS: See "Nanosecond (NS)."

Nuclear Fusion: An atomic energy-releasing process in which light weight atomic nuclei, which might be hydrogen or deuterium, combine to form heavier nuclei, such as helium. The result is the release of a tremendous amount of energy in the form of heat. This is potentially an endless supply of energy for mankind, somewhat similar to the power of the Sun. Fusion is undergoing significant research efforts, including a multinational research consortium named ITER. In one approach, magnetic fusion, plasma heated to 100 million-degrees Celsius creates multiple fusion bursts controlled by powerful magnets. Under a different research approach, massive lasers bombard a frozen pellet of fuel creating a brief, intense fusion.

Object Technology: By merging data and software into "objects," a programming system becomes object-oriented. For example, an object called "weekly inventory sold" would have the data and programming needed to construct a flow chart. Some new programming systems–including Java–contain this feature. Object technology is also featured in many Microsoft products. See "Java."

OC3, up to OC768: Very high-speed data lines that run at speeds from 155 to 39,813.12 Mbps.

ODM: See "Original Design Manufacturer (ODM)."

OECD: See "Organisation for Economic Co-operation and Development (OECD)."

OEM: See "Original Equipment Manufacturer (OEM)."

OLED: See "Organic LED (OLED)."

Onshoring: The opposite of "offshoring." Providing or maintaining manufacturing or services within or nearby a company's domestic location. Sometimes referred to as reshoring.

Open Innovation: A collaborative approach to new product design, problem solving and innovation. In an open innovation project, an organization will ask a large number of people to participate, submit their ideas and submit their designs. Ideally, the group will include employees and non-employees, as well as experts and non-experts. The theory is that a broad range of input will deliver the most innovative results.

Open Source (Open Standards): A software program for which the source code is openly available for modification and enhancement as various users and developers see fit. Open software is typically developed as a public collaboration and grows in usefulness over time. See "LINUX."

Optical Character Recognition (OCR): An industry-wide classification system for coding information onto merchandise. It enables retailers to record information on each SKU when it is sold and to transmit that information to a computer. This is accomplished through computerized cash registers that include bar-code scanners (called point-of-sale terminals).

Optical Fiber (Fibre): See "Fiber Optics (Fibre Optics)."

Organic LED (OLED): A type of electronic display based on the use of organic materials that produce light when stimulated by electricity. Also see "Polymer," "Polymer Light Emitting Diode (PLED)," "Small Molecule Organic Light Emitting Diode (SMOLED)" and "Dendrimer."

Organic Polymer: See "Polymer."

Organisation for Economic Co-operation and Development (OECD): A group of more than 30 nations that are strongly committed to the market economy and democracy. Some of the OECD members include Japan, the U.S., Spain, Germany, Australia, Korea, the U.K., Canada and Mexico. Although not members, Estonia, Israel and Russia are invited to member talks; and Brazil, China, India, Indonesia and South Africa have enhanced engagement policies with the OECD. The Organisation provides statistics, as well as social and economic data; and researches social changes, including patterns in evolving fiscal policy, agriculture, technology, trade, the environment and other areas. It publishes over 250 titles annually; publishes a corporate magazine, the OECD Observer; has radio and TV studios; and has centers in Tokyo, Washington, D.C., Berlin and Mexico City that distributed the Organisation's work and organizes events.

Original Design Manufacturer (ODM): A contract manufacturer that offers complete, end-to-end design, engineering and manufacturing services. ODMs design and build products, such as consumer electronics, that client companies can then brand and sell as their own. For example, a large percentage of laptop computers, cell phones and PDAs are made by ODMs. Also see "Original Equipment Manufacturer (OEM)" and "Contract Manufacturing."

Original Equipment Manufacturer (OEM): 1) A company that manufactures a component (or a completed product) for sale to a customer that will integrate the component into a final product. The OEM's customer will put its own brand name on the end product and distribute or resell it to end users. 2) A firm that buys a component and then incorporates it into a final product, or buys a completed product and then resells it under the firm's own brand name. This usage is most often found in the computer industry, where OEM is sometimes used as a verb. Also see "Original Design Manufacturer (ODM)" and "Contract Manufacturing."

Orphan Drug: A drug or biologic designated by the FDA as providing therapeutic benefit for a rare disease affecting less than 200,000 people in the U.S. Companies that market orphan drugs are granted a period of market exclusivity in return for the limited commercial potential of the drug.

OS: See "Operating System (OS)."

OTC: See "Over-the-Counter Drugs (OTC)."

Over-the-Counter Drugs (OTC): FDA-regulated products that do not require a physician's prescription. Some examples are aspirin, sunscreen, nasal spray and sunglasses.

Packet Switching: A higher-speed way to move data through a network, in which files are broken down into smaller "packets" that are reassembled electronically after transmission.

Patent: An intellectual property right granted by a national government to an inventor to exclude others from making, using, offering for sale, or selling the invention throughout that nation or importing the invention into the nation for a limited time in exchange for public disclosure of the invention when the patent is granted. In addition to national patenting agencies, such as the United States Patent and Trademark Office, and regional organizations such as the European Patent Office, there is a cooperative international patent organization, the World Intellectual Property Organization, or WIPO, established by the United Nations.

PCMCIA: Personal Computer Memory Card International Association.

PDE Pulse Detonation Engine: Pulse detonation (PDE) is an advanced technology for jet engines. It does away with the intricate high-pressure compressor and the turbine found in today's jet engines, relying instead on the PDE Combustor. As a result, much higher output per engine may be possible, which may push aircraft to new levels of speed. Commercial models may be between 2015 and 2020.

Peer Review: The process used by the scientific community, whereby review of a paper, project or report is obtained through comments of independent colleagues in the same field.

Petabyte: 1,024 terabytes, or about 1 million gigabytes.

Pharmacodynamics (PD): The study of reactions between drugs and living systems. It can be thought of as the study of what a drug does to the body.

Pharmacoeconomics: The study of the costs and benefits associated with various drug treatments.

Pharmacogenetics: The investigation of the different reactions of human beings to drugs and the underlying genetic predispositions. The differences in reaction are mainly caused by mutations in certain enzymes responsible for drug metabolization. As a result, the degradation of the active substance can lead to harmful by-products, or the drug might have no effect at all.

Pharmacokinetics (PK): The study of the processes of bodily absorption, distribution, metabolism and excretion of compounds and medicines. It can be thought of as the study of what the body does to a drug. See "Absorption, Distribution, Metabolism and Excretion (ADME)."

Phase I Clinical Trials: Studies in this phase include initial introduction of an investigational drug into humans. These studies are closely monitored and are usually conducted in healthy volunteers. Phase I trials are conducted after the completion of extensive nonclinical or pre-clinical trials not involving humans. Phase I studies include the determination of clinical pharmacology, bioavailability, drug interactions and side effects associated with increasing doses of the drug.

Phase II Clinical Trials: Include randomized, masked, controlled clinical studies conducted to evaluate the effectiveness of a drug for a particular indication(s). During Phase II trials, the minimum effective dose and dosing intervals should be determined.

Phase III Clinical Trials: Consist of controlled and uncontrolled trials that are performed after preliminary evidence of effectiveness of a drug has been established. They are conducted to document the safety and efficacy of the drug, as well as to determine adequate directions (labeling) for use by the physician. A specific patient population needs to be clearly identified from the results of these studies. Trials during Phase III are conducted using a large number of patients to determine the frequency of adverse events and to obtain data regarding intolerance.

Phase IV Clinical Trials: Conducted after approval of a drug has been obtained to gather data supporting new or revised labeling, marketing or advertising claims.

Pivotal Studies: In clinical trials, a Phase III trial that is designed specifically to support approval of a product. These studies are well-controlled (usually by placebo) and are generally designed with input from the FDA so that they will provide data that is adequate to support approval of the product. Two pivotal studies are required for drug product approval, but usually only one study is required for biologics.

PLA: See "Product License Agreement (PLA)."

Plant Patent: A plant patent may be granted by the U.S. Patent and Trademark Office to anyone who invents or discovers and asexually reproduces any distinct and new variety of plant.

PLC: See "Programmable Logic Controller (PLC)."

PLED: See "Polymer Light Emitting Diode (PLED)."

PLM: See "Product Lifecyle Management (PLM)."

Plug-In: Any small piece of software that adds extra functions to a larger piece of software.

PMA: See "Pre-Market Approval (PMA)."

Polymer: An organic or inorganic substance of many parts. Most common polymers, such as polyethylene and polypropylene, are organic. Organic polymers consist of molecules from organic sources (carbon compounds). Polymer means many parts. Generally, a polymer is constructed of many structural units (smaller, simpler molecules) that are joined together by a chemical bond. Some polymers are natural. For example, rubber is a natural polymer. Scientists have developed ways to manufacture synthetic polymers from organic materials. Plastic is a synthetic polymer.

Polymer Light Emitting Diode (PLED): An advanced technology that utilizes plastics (polymers) for the creation of electronic displays (screens). It is based on the use of organic polymers which emit light when stimulated with electricity. They are solution processable, which means they can be applied to substrates via ink jet printing. Also referred to as P-OLEDs.

Port: An interface (or connector) between the computer and the outside world. The number of ports on a communications controller or front-end processor determines the number of communications channels that can be connected to it. The number of ports on a computer determines the number of peripheral devices that can be attached to it.

Portal: A comprehensive web site that is designed to be the first site seen when a computer logs on to the web. Portal sites are aimed at broad audiences with common interests and often have links to e-mail usage, a search engine and other features. Yahoo! and msn.com are portals.

Positron Emission Tomography (PET): Positron Emission Tomography (often referred to as a PET scan) is a nuclear medicine imaging technology that uses computers and radioactive (positron emitting) isotopes, which are created in a cyclotron or generator, to produce composite pictures of the brain and heart at work. PET scanning produces sectional images depicting metabolic activity or blood flow rather than anatomy.

Post-Marketing Surveillance: The FDA's ongoing safety monitoring of marketed drugs.

Powerline: A method of networking computers, peripherals and appliances together via the electrical wiring that is built in to a home or office. Powerline competes with 802.11b and other wireless networking methods.

Preclinical Studies: See "Nonclinical Studies."

Pre-Market Approval (PMA): Required for the approval of a new medical device or a device that is to be used for life-sustaining or life-supporting purposes, is implanted in the human body or presents potential risk of illness or injury.

Product License Agreement (PLA): See "Biologics License Application (BLA)."

Product Lifecycle (Product Life Cycle): The prediction of the life of a product or brand. Stages are described as Introduction, Growth, Maturity and finally Sales Decline. These stages track a product from its initial introduction to the market through to the end of its usefulness as a commercially viable product. The goal of Product Lifecycle Management is to maximize production efficiency, consumer acceptance and profits. Consequently, critical processes around the product need to be adjusted during its lifecycle, including pricing, advertising, promotion, distribution and packaging.

Product Lifecycle Management (PLM): See "Product Lifecycle (Product Life Cycle)."

Programmable Logic Controller (PLC): A special computer that controls processes in industrial applications.

Proteomics: The study of gene expression at the protein level, by the identification and characterization of proteins present in a biological sample.

Protocol: A set of rules for communicating between computers. The use of standard protocols allows products from different vendors to communicate on a common network.

PSTN: See "Public Switched Telephone Network (PSTN)."

Public Switched Telephone Network (PSTN): A term that refers to the traditional telephone system.

Public-Private Partnership (PPP, or P3): Partnerships that involve government agencies with private companies in the construction, operation and/or funding of publicly-needed buildings and infrastructure, such as toll roads, airports, waterworks, sewage plants or power plants.

Pugh Analysis: Charts that are a method of evaluating multiple options against each other. The method was invented by Stuart Pugh of the University of Strathclyde, Scotland, as an aide to selecting the correct option from a group of alternatives.

Qdots: See "Quantum Dots (Qdots)."

QFD: See "Quality Function Deployment (QFD)."

QOL: See "Quality of Life (QOL)."

Quality Function Deployment (QFD): A method of determining the level of customer satisfaction with a design and prioritizing customers' needs and expectations.

Quality of Life (QOL): In medicine, an endpoint of therapeutic assessment used to adjust measures of effectiveness for clinical decision-making. Typically, QOL endpoints measure the improvement of a patient's day-to-day living as a result of specific therapy.

Quantum Computing: A technology that uses the unique abilities of quantum systems, to be in multiple states at once. Such superpositions would allow the computer to perform many different computations simultaneously. This is a merger of physics (and its laws of quantum mechanics) with computer science. Quantum computing works quantum bits, also known as qubits. The laws of quantum mechanics differ radically from the laws of traditional physics. Eventually, quantum computers incredible processing speeds may become feasible.

Quantum Dots (Qdots): Nanometer sized semiconductor particles, made of cadmium selenide (CdSe), cadmium sulfide (CdS) or cadmium telluride (CdTe) with an inert polymer coating. The semiconductor material used for the core is chosen based upon the emission wavelength range being targeted: CdS for UV-blue, CdSe for the bulk of the visible spectrum, CdTe for the far red and near-infrared, with the particle's size determining the exact color of a given quantum dot. The polymer coating safeguards cells from cadmium toxicity but also affords the opportunity to attach any variety targeting molecules, including monoclonal antibodies directed to tumor-specific biomarkers. Because of their small size, quantum dots can function as cell- and even molecule-specific markers that will not interfere with the normal workings of a cell. In addition, the availability of quantum dots of different colors provides a powerful tool for following the actions of multiple cells and molecules simultaneously.

Qubit: The basic unit of information in a quantum computer. A qubit can exist not only in a state corresponding to 0 or 1 as in a binary bit, but also in states corresponding to a blend or superposition of these states. See "Quantum Computing."

R&D: Research and development. Also see "Applied Research" and "Basic Research."

R&D-Flex Building: Industrial-type buildings that are designed to satisfy tenants that require an above-average amount of office space as well as an above-average level of finish that presents a more office-like environment, such as more windows and better landscape. From 30% to 100% of the space in such buildings may be devoted to office or laboratory space, with the balance devoted to light assembly or warehouse space.

Radiation Therapy: Radiation therapy is frequently used to destroy cancerous cells. This branch of medicine is concerned with radioactive substances and the usage of various techniques of imaging, for the diagnosis and treatment of disease. Services can include megavoltage radiation therapy, radioactive implants, stereotactic radiosurgery, therapeutic radioisotope services, or the use of x-rays, gamma rays and other radiation sources.

Radio Frequency Identification (RFID): A technology that applies a special microchip-enabled tag to an individual item or piece of merchandise or inventory. RFID technology enables wireless, computerized tracking of that inventory item as it moves through the supply chain from factory to transport to warehouse to retail store or end user. Also known as radio tags.

Radioisotope: An object that has varying properties that allows it to penetrate other objects at different rates. For example, a sheet of paper can stop an alpha particle, a beta particle can penetrate tissues in the body and a gamma ray can penetrate concrete. The varying penetration capabilities allow radioisotopes to be used in different ways. (Also called radioactive isotope or radionuclide.)

RAM: See "Random Access Memory (RAM)."

Random Access Memory (RAM): Computer memory used to hold programs and data temporarily.

Rapid Prototyping: See "3-D Printing."

RBOC: See "Regional Bell Operating Company (RBOC)."

Real Time: A system or software product specially designed to acquire, process, store and display large amounts of rapidly changing information almost instantaneously, with microsecond responses as changes occur.

Regional Bell Operating Company (RBOC): Former Bell system telephone companies (or their successors), created as a result of the breakup of AT&T by a Federal Court decree on December 31, 1983 (e.g., Bell Atlantic, now part of Verizon).

Reinforcement Learning: A type of machine learning (related to artificial intelligence) whereby software learns best practices and solutions through repetitive effort at given tasks. It is somewhat related to theories of behavioral psychology. Reinforcement learning is being used in self-driving vehicles, and was the principle behind a computer's ability to defeat a world champion in the extremely complex board game known as Go.

Request for Bids (RFB): A request for pricing and supporting details, sent by a firm that requires products or services, outlining all the firm's requirements. Proposing companies are asked to place a bid based on the requested goods or services.

Request for Quotation (RFQ): A proposal that asks companies to submit pricing for goods or a described level of services. See "Request for Bids (RFB)."

Reshore: With regard to manufacturing, the return of some of the business to plants based in the country where sales are typically made. An example would be if Nike should shift some of its production from Asia to the U.S.

RFID: See "Radio Frequency Identification (RFID)."

Router: An electronic device that enables networks to communicate with each other. For example, the local area network (LAN) in an office connects to a router to give the LAN access to an Internet connection such as a T1 or DSL. Routers can be bundled with several added features, such as firewalls.

S&R: Science and research.

SaaS: See "Software as a Service (SaaS)."

SACD: See "Super Audio Compact Disc (SACD)."

Safe Medical Devices Act (SMDA): An act that amends the Food, Drug and Cosmetic Act to impose additional regulations on medical devices. The act became law in 1990.

SAN: See "Storage Area Network (SAN)."

SBIR: See "Small Business Innovative Research (SBIR)."

SCADA: Supervisory Control and Data Acquisition.

Scalable: Refers to a network that can grow and adapt as customer needs increase and change. Scalable networks can easily manage increasing numbers of workstations, servers, user workloads and added functionality.

SCSI: See "Small Computer System Interface (SCSI)."

Selective Deposition Lamination (SDL): A paper-based 3D printing technology that lowers operating costs by using regular A4 size paper rather than polymers or metals.

Semiconductor: A generic term for a device that controls electrical signals. It specifically refers to a material (such as silicon, germanium or gallium arsenide) that can be altered either to conduct electrical current or to block its passage. Carbon nanotubes may eventually be used as semiconductors. Semiconductors are partly responsible for the miniaturization of modern electronic devices, as they are vital components in computer memory and processor chips. The manufacture of semiconductors is carried out by small firms, and by industry giants such as Intel and Advanced Micro Devices.

Serial Line Internet Protocol (SLIP): The connection of a traditional telephone line, or serial line, and modem to connect a computer to an Internet site.

Server: A computer that performs and manages specific duties for a central network such as a LAN. It may include storage devices and other peripherals. Competition within the server manufacturing industry is intense among leaders Dell, IBM, HP and others.

Short Messaging System (SMS): See "Text Messaging."

Simple Mail Transfer Protocol (SMTP): The primary form of protocol used in the transference of e-mail.

Simple Network Management Protocol (SNMP): A set of communication standards for use between computers connected to TCP/IP networks.

Six Sigma: A quality enhancement strategy designed to reduce the number of products coming from a manufacturing plant that do not conform to specifications. Six Sigma states that no more than 3.4 defects per million parts is the goal of high-quality output. Motorola invented the system in the 1980s in order to enhance its competitive position against Japanese electronics manufacturers.

SLIP: See "Serial Line Internet Protocol (SLIP)."

Small Business Innovative Research (SBIR): A three-phase program developed by the U.S. Department of

Defense that allocates early-stage research and development funding to small technology companies.

Small Computer System Interface (SCSI): A dominant, international standard interface used by UNIX servers and many desktop computers to connect to storage devices; a physical connection between devices.

Small Molecule Organic Light Emitting Diode (SMOLED): A type of organic LED that relies on expensive manufacturing methods. Newer technologies are more promising. See "Polymer" and "Polymer Light Emitting Diode (PLED)."

Smart Buildings: Buildings or homes that have been designed with interconnected electronic sensors and electrical systems which can be controlled by computers. Advantages include the ability to turn appliances and systems on or off remotely or on a set schedule, leading to greatly enhanced energy efficiency.

SMDA: See "Safe Medical Devices Act (SMDA)."

SMDS: See "Switched Multimegabit Data Service (SMDS)."

SMOLED: See "Small Molecule Organic Light Emitting Diode (SMOLED)."

SMS: See "Short Messaging System (SMS)."

SMTP: See "Simple Mail Transfer Protocol (SMTP)."

SNMP: See "Simple Network Management Protocol (SNMP)."

Software as a Service (SaaS): Refers to the practice of providing users with software applications that are hosted on remote servers and accessed via the Internet. Excellent examples include the CRM (Customer Relationship Management) software provided in SaaS format by Salesforce. An earlier technology that operated in a similar, but less sophisticated, manner was called ASP or Application Service Provider.

SONET: See "Synchronous Optical Network Technology (SONET)."

SPECT: Single Photon Emission Computerized Tomography. A nuclear medicine imaging technology that combines existing technology of gamma camera imaging with computed tomographic (CT) imaging technology to provide a more precise and clear image.

Sponsor: The individual or company that assumes responsibility for the investigation of a new drug, including compliance with the FD&C Act and regulations. The sponsor may be an individual, partnership, corporation or governmental agency and may be a manufacturer, scientific institution or investigator regularly and lawfully engaged in the investigation of new drugs. The sponsor assumes most of the legal and financial responsibility of the clinical trial.

SRDF: See "Symmetrix Remote Data Facility (SRDF)."

Standard Industrial Classification (SIC): See "Industry Code."

Stem Cells: Cells found in human bone marrow, the blood stream and the umbilical cord that can be replicated indefinitely and can turn into any type of mature blood cell, including platelets, white blood cells or red blood cells. Also referred to as pluripotent cells.

Storage Area Network (SAN): Links host computers to advanced data storage systems.

Study Coordinator: See "Coordinator."

Subsidiary, Wholly-Owned: A company that is wholly controlled by another company through stock ownership.

Super Audio Compact Disc (SACD): A technology that offers high-resolution digital audio.

Superatom: See "Metamaterials."

Superconductivity: The ability of a material to act as a conductor for electricity without the gradual loss of electricity over distance (due to resistance) that is normally associated with electric transmission. There are two types of superconductivity. "Low-temperature" superconductivity (LTS) requires that transmission cable be cooled to -418 degrees Fahrenheit. Newer technologies are creating a so-called "high-temperature" superconductivity (HTS) that requires cooling to a much warmer -351 degrees Fahrenheit.

Supervisory Control and Data Acquisition (SCADA): A process in which data is gathered from remote sensors, analyzed and necessary corrective actions taken in M2M communications networks.

Supply Chain: The complete set of suppliers of goods and services required for a company to operate its business. For example, a manufacturer's supply chain may include providers of raw materials, components, custom-made parts and packaging materials.

Sustainable Development: Development that ensures that the use of resources and the environment today does not impair their availability to be used by future generations.

Switch: A network device that directs packets of data between multiple ports, often filtering the data so that it travels more quickly.

Switched Multimegabit Data Service (SMDS): A method of extremely high-speed transference of data.

Symmetrix Remote Data Facility (SRDF): A high-performance, host-independent business solution that enables users to maintain a duplicate copy of all or some of their data at a remote site.

Synchronous Optical Network Technology (SONET): A mode of high-speed transmission meant to take full advantage of the wide bandwidth in fiber-optic cables.

T1: A standard for broadband digital transmission over phone lines. Generally, it can transmit at least 24 voice channels at once over copper wires, at a high speed of 1.5 Mbps. Higher speed versions include T3 and OC3 lines.

T3: Transmission over phone lines that supports data rates of 45 Mbps. T3 lines consist of 672 channels, and such lines are generally used by Internet service providers. They are also referred to as DS3 lines.

Taste Masking: The creation of a barrier between a drug molecule and taste receptors so the drug is easier to take. It masks bitter or unpleasant tastes.

TCP/IP: See "Transmission Control Protocol/Internet Protocol (TCP/IP)."

TDMA: See "Time Division Multiple Access (TDMA)."

Technical Barriers to Trade (TBT): Instances when technical regulations and industrial standards differ from country to country, making free trade of goods difficult if not impossible.

Telecommunications: Systems and networks of hardware and software used to carry voice, video and/or data within buildings and between locations around the world. This includes telephone wires, satellite signals, wireless networks, fiber networks, Internet networks and related devices.

Telnet: A terminal emulation program for TCP/IP networks like the Internet, which runs on a computer and connects to a particular network. Directions entered on a computer that is connected using Telnet will be read and followed just as if they had been entered on the server itself. Through Telnet, users are able to control a server and communicate with other servers on the same network at the same time. Telnet is commonly used to control web servers remotely.

Terabyte: A measure of data equal to 1,024 gigabytes, or about 1 trillion bytes of data.

TESS: See "Adverse Event (AE)."

Text Messaging: The transmission of very short, text messages in a format similar to e-mail. Generally, text messaging is used as an additional service on cell phones. The format has typically been SMS (Short Messaging System), but a newer standard is evolving: MMS (Multimedia Messaging System). MMS can transmit pictures, sound and video as well as text.

Time Division Multiple Access (TDMA): A 2G digital service for relatively large users of international public-switched telephony, data, facsimile and telex. TDMA also refers to a method of multiplexing digital signals that combines a number of signals passing through a common point by transmitting them sequentially, with each signal sent in bursts at different times. TDMA is sometimes referred to as IS-136 or D-AMPS.

Tokamak: A reactor used in nuclear fusion in which a spiral magnetic field inside doughnut-shaped tube is used to confine high temperature plasma produced during fusion. See "Nuclear Fusion."

Token Ring: A local area network architecture in which a token, or continuously repeating frame, is passed sequentially from station to station. Only the station possessing the token can communicate on the network.

Transistor: A device used for amplification or switching of electrical current.

Transmission Control Protocol/Internet Protocol (TCP/IP): The combination of a network and transport protocol developed by ARPANet for internetworking IP-based networks.

Trial Coordinator: See "Coordinator."

UDDI: See "Universal Description, Discovery and Integration (UDDI)."

Ultrashort Pulse Laser (USP): A technology that utilizes ultrafast lasers that pulse on and off at almost immeasurable speed. Scientists estimate that USP flashes once every femtosecond, which is a billionth of a millionth of a second. USP destroys atoms by knocking out electrons, which causes no rise in temperature in surrounding atoms as is associated with traditional lasers. Potential applications include vastly improved laser surgery, scanning for explosives, gemstone verification and processing donated human tissue for transplantation.

Ultrasound: The use of acoustic waves above the range of 20,000 cycles per second to visualize internal body structures. Frequently used to observe a fetus.

Ultrawideband (UWB): A means of low-power, limited-range wireless data transmission that takes advantage of bandwidth set aside by the FCC in 2002. UWB encodes signals in a dramatically different way, sending digital pulses in a relatively secure manner that will not interfere with other wireless systems that may be operating nearby. It has the potential to deliver very large amounts of data to a distance of about 230 feet, even through doors and other obstacles, and requires very little power. Speeds are scalable from approximately 100 Mbps to 2Gbps. UWB works on the 802.15.3 IEEE specification.

Uniform Resource Locator (URL): The address that allows an Internet browser to locate a homepage or web site.

Universal Description, Discovery and Integration (UDDI): A vital protocol used in web services. UDDI enables businesses to create a standard description of their activities so that they can be searched for appropriately by automatic software tools.

Universal Design: An approach to residential as well as commercial building design that attempts to accommodate as many people as possible, regardless of physical or mental limitations. For example, design elements may include wider doorways and stepless entries that are easy for the physically challenged to navigate.

Universal Memory: Future-generation digital memory storage systems that would be ultradense and run on extremely low power needs. Potentially, universal memory could replace today's flash memory, RAM and many other types of memory. The technology may be based on the use of vast numbers of tiny carbon nanotubes resulting in the storage of trillions of bits of data per square centimeter.

UNIX: A multi-user, multitasking operating system that runs on a wide variety of computer systems, from PCs to mainframes.

URL: See "Uniform Resource Locator (URL)."

Utility Patent: A utility patent may be granted by the U.S. Patent and Trademark Office to anyone who invents or discovers any new, useful, and non-obvious process, machine, article of manufacture, or composition of matter, or any new and useful improvement thereof.

UWB: See "Ultrawideband (UWB)."

Validation of Data: The procedure carried out to ensure that the data contained in a final clinical trial report match the original observations.

Value Added Tax (VAT): A tax that imposes a levy on businesses at every stage of manufacturing based on the value it adds to a product. Each business in the supply chain pays its own VAT and is subsequently repaid by the next link down the chain; hence, a VAT is ultimately paid by the consumer, being the last link in the supply chain, making it comparable to a sales tax. Generally, VAT only applies to goods bought for consumption within a given country; export goods are exempt from VAT, and purchasers from other countries taking goods back home may apply for a VAT refund.

VDSL: Very high-data-rate digital subscriber line, operating at data rates from 55 to 100 Mbps.

Vertical Integration: A business model in which one company owns many (or all) of the means of production of the many goods that comprise its product line. For example, founder Henry Ford designed Ford Motor Company's early River Rogue plant so that coal, iron ore and other needed raw materials arrived at one end of the plant and were processed into steel, which was then converted on-site into finished components. At the final stage of the plant, completed automobiles were assembled.

Very Small Aperture Terminal (VSAT): A small Earth station terminal, generally 0.6 to 2.4 meters in size, that is often portable and primarily designed to handle data transmission and private-line voice and video communications.

Voice Over Internet Protocol (VOIP): The ability to make telephone calls and send faxes over IP-based data networks, i.e., real-time voice between computers via the Internet. Leading providers of VOIP service include independent firms Skype and Vonage. However, all major telecom companies, such as SBC are planning or offering VOIP service. VOIP can offer greatly reduced telephone bills to users, since toll charges, certain taxes and other fees can be bypassed. Long-distance calls can pass to anywhere in the world using VOIP. Over the mid-term, many telephone handsets, including cellular phones, will have the ability to detect wireless networks offering VOIP connections and will switch seamlessly between landline and VOIP or cellular and VOIP as needed.

VOIP: See "Voice Over Internet Protocol (VOIP)."

WAN: See "Wide Area Network (WAN)."

WAP: See "Wireless Access Protocol (WAP)."

Web Services: Self-contained modular applications that can be described, published, located and invoked over the World Wide Web or another network. Web services architecture evolved from object-oriented design and is geared toward e-business solutions. Microsoft Corporation is focusing on web services with its .NET initiative. Also see "Extensible Markup Language (XML)."

Web Services Description Language (WSDL): An important protocol to web services that describes the web service being offered.

Wide Area Network (WAN): A regional or global network that provides links between all local area networks within a company. For example, Ford Motor Company might use a WAN to enable its factory in Detroit to talk to its sales offices in New York and Chicago, its plants in England and its buying offices in Taiwan. Also see "Local Area Network (LAN)."

WiFi: See "Wi-Fi."

Wi-Fi: A popular phrase that refers to 802.11 specifications. See "802.11g (Wi-Fi)."

WiMAX: An advanced wireless standard with significant speed and distance capabilities, WiMAX is officially known as the 802.16 standard. Using microwave technologies, it has the theoretical potential to broadcast at distances up to 30 miles and speeds of up to 70 Mbps. The mid-term goal of the WiMAX industry is to offer 15 Mbps speed for mobile WiMAX (802.16e) users and 40 Mbps for fixed WiMAX (802.16d) users. (The 802.XX standards are set by the IEEE (Institute of Electrical and Electronics Engineers). WiMax2, or 802.16m, will offer mobile access speeds of 170 to 300 Mbps.

Wireless Access Protocol (WAP): A technology that enables the delivery of World Wide Web pages in a smaller format readable by screens on cellular phones.

Wireless LAN (WLAN): A wireless local area network. WLANs frequently operate on 802.11-enabled equipment (Wi-Fi).

WLAN: See "Wireless LAN (WLAN)."

Workstation: A high-powered desktop computer, usually used by engineers.

World Health Organization (WHO): A United Nations agency that assists governments in strengthening health services, furnishing technical assistance and aid in emergencies, working on the prevention and control of epidemics and promoting cooperation among different countries to improve nutrition, housing, sanitation, recreation and other aspects of environmental hygiene. Any country that is a member of the United Nations may become a member of the WHO by accepting its constitution. The WHO currently has 191 member states.

World Trade Organization (WTO): One of the only globally active international organizations dealing with the trade rules between nations. Its goal is to assist the free flow of trade goods, ensuring a smooth, predictable supply of goods to help raise the quality of life of member citizens. Members form consensus decisions that are then ratified by their respective parliaments. The WTO's conflict resolution process generally emphasizes interpreting existing commitments and agreements, and discovers how to ensure trade policies to conform to those agreements, with the ultimate aim of avoiding military or political conflict.

WSDL: See "Web Services Description Language (WSDL)."

WTO: See "World Trade Organization (WTO)."

Zettabyte: A unit of measure, used in describing data, a zettabyte is roughly 1,000 exabytes or 1 million terabytes.

ZigBee: May become the ultimate wireless control system for home and office lighting and entertainment systems. The ZigBee Alliance is an association of companies working together to enable reliable, cost-effective, low-power, wirelessly networked monitoring and control products based on an open global standard, 802.15.4 entertainment systems.

CPSIA information can be obtained
at www.ICGtesting.com
Printed in the USA
FHW01n0211260918
48556136-52467FF